IFRS® Standards

**required for accounting periods
beginning on or after 1 January 2022,
excluding changes not yet required**

This edition is issued in three parts

PART A

contains the text of IFRS Standards including IAS® Standards,
IFRIC® Interpretations and SIC® Interpretations, together with
the *Conceptual Framework for Financial Reporting*
(Glossary included)

See also Parts B and C of this edition:

Part B

*contains the illustrative examples and implementation guidance
that accompany the Standards, together with
IFRS practice statements*

Part C

*contains the bases for conclusions that accompany the
Standards, the* Conceptual Framework for Financial
Reporting *and IFRS practice statements, together with
the* Constitution *and* Due Process Handbook *of the IFRS
Foundation*

Contents

continued...

IFRIC Interpretations

continued...

SIC Interpretations

Introduction to this edition

The International Accounting Standards Board

The International Accounting Standards Board (IASB) is an independent standard-setting body of the IFRS® Foundation (Foundation). Appointed, overseen and funded by the Foundation, the IASB is responsible for preparing and issuing IFRS Standards. The Trustees of the IFRS Foundation (Trustees) are responsible for governance and oversight. The IFRS Foundation Monitoring Board provides a formal link between the Trustees and public authorities to enhance the Foundation's public accountability.

IFRS Standards

IFRS Standards (Standards) are mandatory pronouncements and comprise:

(a)   IFRS Standards;

(b)   IAS® Standards; and

(c)   Interpretations developed by the IFRS Interpretations Committee (IFRIC® Interpretations) or its predecessor body, the Standing Interpretations Committee (SIC® Interpretations).

Standards are issued after formal due process. An entity is permitted to state that its financial statements comply with IFRS Standards only if the financial statements comply with all applicable requirements in the Standards.

The requirements of a Standard, including any appendices setting out mandatory application guidance, are usually accompanied by non-mandatory material, including:

(a)   a basis for conclusions, which summarises the IASB's considerations when it was developing the Standard;

(b)   dissenting opinions, if any, by individual IASB members who voted against the publication of the Standard or amendment to the Standard;

(c)   implementation guidance; and

(d)   illustrative examples.

The rubric after the contents page of each Standard sets out the authority of the information contained in or accompanying that Standard.

The title page of each Standard details its history.

Each new Standard and amendment to a Standard sets out its effective date and may contain transition provisions. The IASB generally allows an entity to apply a newly issued Standard or amendment before its effective date.

What does this edition contain?

This edition contains only Standards issued by the IASB as at 31 December 2021 that are required for accounting periods beginning on or after 1 January 2022 (that is, all Standards with an effective date on or before 1 January 2022).

Standards and amendments to Standards issued by 31 December 2021 with an effective date after 1 January 2022 are excluded from this edition and will be included in *IFRS® Standards — Issued at 1 January 2022* and in *The Annotated IFRS® Standards — Standards issued at 1 January 2022*.

Publications and translations

The Foundation holds the copyright for IFRS Standards, IAS Standards, IFRIC Interpretations, SIC Interpretations, exposure drafts, discussion papers and other IASB publications in all countries, except where the Foundation has expressly waived the right to enforce copyright on portions of that material. For more information regarding the Foundation's copyrights, please refer to the copyright notice with this edition or on the website at www.ifrs.org.

IFRS Standards have been translated into a number of languages. The Foundation considers additional translations as needs arise. For more information, contact the Translation, Adoption and Copyright team on tac@ifrs.org.

More information

The Foundation's website, www.ifrs.org, provides news, updates and other resources related to the Boards and the Foundation. The latest publications and subscription services can be ordered from shop.ifrs.org.

For more information about the Foundation, or to obtain copies of its publications and details of the Foundation's subscription services, visit the website or write to:

IFRS Foundation
Customer Services Department
Columbus Building
7 Westferry Circus
Canary Wharf
London E14 4HD
United Kingdom

Telephone: +44 (0)20 7332 2730
Email: customerservices@ifrs.org
Website: www.ifrs.org

Changes in this edition

This section is a brief guide to the changes incorporated in this 2022 edition since the publication of IFRS® Standards – Required at 1 January 2021.

Basis of preparation

This edition contains only IFRS Standards issued by the International Accounting Standards Board (IASB) as at 31 December 2021 that are required for accounting periods beginning on or after 1 January 2022 (that is, all Standards with an effective date on or before 1 January 2022).

Standards and amendments to Standards issued by 31 December 2021 with an effective date after 1 January 2022 are excluded from this edition; they will be reproduced in IFRS® Standards – Issued at 1 January 2022 and in The Annotated IFRS® Standards – Standards issued at 1 January 2022.

New in this edition

The documents and amendments in this edition are effective from 1 January 2022 and include:

- a revised version of the IFRS Foundation Constitution;

- amendments to four Standards, issued in Property, Plant and Equipment: Proceeds before Intended Use, Onerous Contracts – Cost of Fulfilling a Contract, References to the Conceptual Framework and Covid-19-Related Rent Concessions beyond 30 June 2021; and

- amendments to three Standards issued in Annual Improvements to IFRS Standards 2018-2020.

The table and subsequent summaries provide further details about the documents and amendments.

Standard/ amendment	When issued	Effective date (early application is possible unless otherwise noted)	Standards/ Interpretations amended	Standard withdrawn
Annual Improvements to IFRS Standards 2018–2020 Amendments to IFRS 1, IFRS 9 and IAS 41	May 2020	1 January 2022	IFRS 1, IFRS 9, IAS 41	
Property, Plant and Equipment: Proceeds before Intended Use Amendment to IAS 16	May 2020	1 January 2022	IAS 16	

continued...

...continued

Table—New requirements effective from 1 January 2022				
Standard/ amendment	When issued	Effective date (early application is possible unless otherwise noted)	Standards/ Interpretations amended	Standard withdrawn
Onerous Contracts— Cost of Fulfilling a Contract Amendments to IAS 37	May 2020	1 January 2022	IAS 37	
Reference to the Conceptual Framework Amendments to IFRS 3	May 2020	1 January 2022	IFRS 3	
Covid-19-Related Rent Concessions beyond 30 June 2021 Amendments to IFRS 16	March 2021	1 January 2022	IFRS 16	

The Glossary has been revised. Minor editorial corrections to Standards (including necessary updating) have also been made; a list of all such corrections is available at www.ifrs.org/issued-standards/editorial-corrections/.

New and revised Standards, IFRIC Interpretations and Practice Statements are available to IFRS Digital subscribers at www.ifrs.org.

This section summarises changes and amendments in this edition.

IFRS Foundation *Constitution*

To create the necessary institutional arrangements to establish the International Sustainability Standards Board (ISSB), the IFRS Foundation Trustees revised the IFRS Foundation *Constitution* in October 2021.

Amendments to Standards

Annual Improvements to IFRS Standards 2018–2020

Annual Improvements to IFRS Standards 2018–2020 contains these amendments.

Standard	Subject of amendment
IFRS 1 *First-time Adoption of International Financial Reporting Standards*	Subsidiary as a First-time Adopter
IFRS 9 *Financial Instruments*	Fees in the '10 per cent' Test for Derecognition of Financial Liabilities
IAS 41 *Agriculture*	Taxation in Fair Value Measurements

Property, Plant and Equipment: Proceeds before Intended Use

Property, Plant and Equipment: Proceeds before Intended Use amends IAS 16 *Property, Plant and Equipment*. The amendments prohibit an entity from deducting from the cost of property, plant and equipment amounts received from selling items produced while the entity is preparing the asset for its intended use. Instead, an entity will recognise such sales proceeds and related cost in profit or loss.

Onerous Contracts—Cost of Fulfilling a Contract

Onerous Contracts—Cost of Fulfilling a Contract amends IAS 37 *Provisions, Contingent Liabilities and Contingent Assets*. The amendments clarify that for the purpose of assessing whether a contract is onerous, the cost of fulfilling the contract includes both the incremental costs of fulfilling that contract and an allocation of other costs that relate directly to fulfilling contracts.

Reference to the Conceptual Framework

Reference to the Conceptual Framework updates a reference to the *Conceptual Framework* in IFRS 3 *Business Combinations* and makes further amendments to IFRS 3 to prevent unintended consequences of updating the reference.

Covid-19-Related Rent Concessions beyond 30 June 2021

Covid-19-Related Rent Concessions beyond 30 June 2021 amended IFRS 16 to extend by one year the application period of the practical expedient in paragraph 46A to help lessees accounting for Covid-19-related rent concessions.

Disclosure of the possible effect of issued Standards that are not yet required

This edition does not include Standards that have an effective date later than 1 January 2022.

These Standards are relevant, however, even if an entity does not intend to adopt a requirement early. Paragraph 30 of IAS 8 *Accounting Policies, Changes in Accounting Estimates and Errors* requires an entity to disclose 'information relevant to assessing the possible impact that application of the new IFRS [Standard] will have on the entity's financial statements in the period of initial application'.

The table shows amendments and Standards that have an effective date after 1 January 2022.

Table–Standards and amendments issued, but not effective, as at 1 January 2022				
Standard/ amendment	When issued	Effective date (early application is possible unless otherwise noted)	Standards/ Interpretations amended	Standard withdrawn
Sale or Contribution of Assets Amendments to IFRS 10 and IAS 28	September 2014	Postponed indefinitely	IFRS 10; IAS 28	
IFRS 17 *Insurance Contracts*[a]	May 2017	1 January 2023	IFRS 1, IFRS 3, IFRS 3 (as amended by IFRS 16), IFRS 5, IFRS 7, IFRS 7 (as amended by IFRS 16), IFRS 9, IFRS 15; IAS 1, IAS 7, IAS 16, IAS 19, IAS 28, IAS 32, IAS 36, IAS 37, IAS 38, IAS 40; SIC 27	IFRS 4
Classification of Liabilities as Current or Non-current[b] Amendments to IAS 1	January 2020	1 January 2023	IAS 1	
Amendments to IFRS 17	June 2020	1 January 2023	IFRS 3, IFRS 7, IFRS 9, IFRS 17; IAS 1, IAS 32, IAS 36, IAS 38	
Classification of Liabilities as Current or Non-current—Deferral of Effective Date Amendment to IAS 1	July 2020	1 January 2023	IAS 1	
Disclosure of Accounting Policies Amendments to IAS 1 and IFRS Practice Statement 2	February 2021	1 January 2023	IAS 1	
Definition of Accounting Estimates Amendments to IAS 8	February 2021	1 January 2023	IAS 8	

continued...

...continued

Table—Standards and amendments issued, but not effective, as at 1 January 2022				
Standard/ amendment	When issued	Effective date (early application is possible unless otherwise noted)	Standards/ Interpretations amended	Standard withdrawn
Deferred Tax relating to Assets and Liabilities arising from a Single Transaction Amendments to IAS 12	May 2021	1 January 2023	IAS 12, IFRS 1	

(a) Amendments to this Standard were issued in June 2020.
(b) In July 2020, the effective date of this amendment was deferred to 1 January 2023.

This section summarises changes to be introduced by the documents listed in the table 'Standards issued, but not effective, as at 1 January 2022'.

Sale or Contribution of Assets between an Investor and its Associate or Joint Venture

Sale or Contribution of Assets between an Investor and its Associate or Joint Venture, which amends IFRS 10 and IAS 28, was issued in September 2014. The amendments address the conflict between the requirements in IFRS 10 *Consolidated Financial Statements* and IAS 28 *Investments in Associates and Joint Ventures* when accounting for the sale or contribution of a subsidiary to a joint venture or associate (resulting in the loss of control of the subsidiary). In December 2015 the IASB deferred the effective date of this amendment indefinitely.

IFRS 17 *Insurance Contracts* and *Amendments to IFRS 17*

IFRS 17 *Insurance Contracts* applies to: insurance contracts, including reinsurance contracts, issued by an entity with specified exceptions; reinsurance contracts held by an entity; and investment contracts with discretionary participation features issued by an entity that issues insurance contracts. An insurance contract is defined as 'a contract under which one party (the issuer) accepts significant insurance risk from another party (the policyholder) by agreeing to compensate the policyholder if a specified uncertain future event (the insured event) adversely affects the policyholder'.

In the statement of financial position, an entity is required to measure profitable insurance contracts at the risk-adjusted present value of the future cash flows plus unearned profit for services to be provided under the contract.

IFRS 17 requires an entity to recognise profit from a group of insurance contracts over the period the entity provides services, and as the entity is released from risk. If a group of contracts is or becomes loss-making, the entity is required to recognise the loss immediately.

The Standard also requires insurance revenue, insurance service expenses, and insurance finance income or expenses to be presented separately.

Since the IASB issued IFRS 17 in May 2017, it has been carrying out activities to support entities and monitor their progress in implementing the Standard. These activities helped the IASB to understand the concerns and challenges that some entities identified while implementing the Standard. The IASB considered these concerns and challenges and decided to amend IFRS 17. The objective of the amendments is to assist entities implementing the Standard, while not unduly disrupting implementation or diminishing the usefulness of the information provided by applying IFRS 17.

IFRS 17, as amended in June 2020, is effective for annual reporting periods beginning on or after 1 January 2023.

Classification of Liabilities as Current and Non-current and Classification of Liabilities as Current and Non-current—Deferral of Effective Date

Classification of Liabilities as Current or Non-current clarifies a criterion in IAS 1 *Presentation of Financial Statements* for classifying a liability as non-current: the requirement for an entity to have the right to defer settlement of the liability for at least 12 months after the reporting period.

Classification of Liabilities as Current or Non-current — Deferral of Effective Date was issued in July 2020 and deferred the mandatory effective date of amendments to IAS 1 *Classification of Liabilities as Current or Non-current* to annual reporting periods beginning on or after 1 January 2023.

Definition of Accounting Estimates

Definition of Accounting Estimates amends IAS 8 *Accounting Policies, Changes in Accounting Estimates and Errors*. The amendments introduced the definition of accounting estimates and included other amendments to help entities distinguish changes in accounting estimates from changes in accounting policies.

Disclosure of Accounting Policies

Disclosure of Accounting Policies amends IAS 1 *Presentation of Financial Statements* and IFRS Practice Statement 2 *Making Materiality Judgements*. The amendments replace the requirement for entities to disclose their significant accounting policies with the requirement to disclose their material accounting policy information. The amendments also include guidance to help entities apply the definition of material in making decisions about accounting policy disclosures.

Deferred Tax related to Assets and Liabilities arising from a Single Transaction

Deferred Tax related to Assets and Liabilities arising from a Single Transaction amends IAS 12 *Income Taxes*. The amendments narrowed the scope of the recognition exemption in paragraphs 15 and 24 of IAS 12 so that it no longer applies to transactions that, on initial recognition, give rise to equal taxable and deductible temporary differences. The amendments apply to transactions such as leases and decommissioning obligations.

15   The approved text of any discussion document, exposure draft or Standard is that approved by the Board in the English language. The Board may approve translations in other languages, provided that the translation is prepared in accordance with a process that provides assurance of the quality of the translation, and the Board may license other translations.

Conceptual Framework for Financial Reporting

Conceptual Framework for Financial Reporting was issued by the International Accounting Standards Board in September 2010. It was revised in March 2018.

CONTENTS

continued...

© IFRS Foundation

...continued

continued...

FOR THE BASIS FOR CONCLUSIONS, SEE PART C OF THIS EDITION

BASIS FOR CONCLUSIONS

STATUS AND PURPOSE OF THE *CONCEPTUAL FRAMEWORK*

SP1.1 The *Conceptual Framework for Financial Reporting* (*Conceptual Framework*) describes the objective of, and the concepts for, general purpose financial reporting. The purpose of the *Conceptual Framework* is to:

(a) assist the International Accounting Standards Board (Board) to develop IFRS Standards (Standards) that are based on consistent concepts;

(b) assist preparers to develop consistent accounting policies when no Standard applies to a particular transaction or other event, or when a Standard allows a choice of accounting policy; and

(c) assist all parties to understand and interpret the Standards.

SP1.2 The *Conceptual Framework* is not a Standard. Nothing in the *Conceptual Framework* overrides any Standard or any requirement in a Standard.

SP1.3 To meet the objective of general purpose financial reporting, the Board may sometimes specify requirements that depart from aspects of the *Conceptual Framework*. If the Board does so, it will explain the departure in the Basis for Conclusions on that Standard.

SP1.4 The *Conceptual Framework* may be revised from time to time on the basis of the Board's experience of working with it. Revisions of the *Conceptual Framework* will not automatically lead to changes to the Standards. Any decision to amend a Standard would require the Board to go through its due process for adding a project to its agenda and developing an amendment to that Standard.

SP1.5 The *Conceptual Framework* contributes to the stated mission of the IFRS Foundation and of the Board, which is part of the IFRS Foundation. That mission is to develop Standards that bring transparency, accountability and efficiency to financial markets around the world. The Board's work serves the public interest by fostering trust, growth and long-term financial stability in the global economy. The *Conceptual Framework* provides the foundation for Standards that:

(a) contribute to transparency by enhancing the international comparability and quality of financial information, enabling investors and other market participants to make informed economic decisions.

(b) strengthen accountability by reducing the information gap between the providers of capital and the people to whom they have entrusted their money. Standards based on the *Conceptual Framework* provide information needed to hold management to account. As a source of globally comparable information, those Standards are also of vital importance to regulators around the world.

(c) contribute to economic efficiency by helping investors to identify opportunities and risks across the world, thus improving capital allocation. For businesses, the use of a single, trusted accounting language derived from Standards based on the *Conceptual Framework* lowers the cost of capital and reduces international reporting costs.

CONTENTS

Introduction

1.1   The objective of general purpose financial reporting forms the foundation of the *Conceptual Framework*. Other aspects of the *Conceptual Framework*—the qualitative characteristics of, and the cost constraint on, useful financial information, a reporting entity concept, elements of financial statements, recognition and derecognition, measurement, presentation and disclosure — flow logically from the objective.

Objective, usefulness and limitations of general purpose financial reporting

1.2   The objective of general purpose financial reporting[1] is to provide financial information about the reporting entity that is useful to existing and potential investors, lenders and other creditors in making decisions relating to providing resources to the entity.[2] Those decisions involve decisions about:

(a)   buying, selling or holding equity and debt instruments;

(b)   providing or settling loans and other forms of credit; or

(c)   exercising rights to vote on, or otherwise influence, management's actions that affect the use of the entity's economic resources.

1.3   The decisions described in paragraph 1.2 depend on the returns that existing and potential investors, lenders and other creditors expect, for example, dividends, principal and interest payments or market price increases. Investors', lenders' and other creditors' expectations about returns depend on their assessment of the amount, timing and uncertainty of (the prospects for) future net cash inflows to the entity and on their assessment of management's stewardship of the entity's economic resources. Existing and potential investors, lenders and other creditors need information to help them make those assessments.

1.4   To make the assessments described in paragraph 1.3, existing and potential investors, lenders and other creditors need information about:

(a)   the economic resources of the entity, claims against the entity and changes in those resources and claims (see paragraphs 1.12–1.21); and

(b)   how efficiently and effectively the entity's management and governing board[3] have discharged their responsibilities to use the entity's economic resources (see paragraphs 1.22–1.23).

---

1   Throughout the *Conceptual Framework*, the terms 'financial reports' and 'financial reporting' refer to general purpose financial reports and general purpose financial reporting unless specifically indicated otherwise.

2   Throughout the *Conceptual Framework*, the term 'entity' refers to the reporting entity unless specifically indicated otherwise.

3   Throughout the *Conceptual Framework*, the term 'management' refers to management and the governing board of an entity unless specifically indicated otherwise.

1.5 Many existing and potential investors, lenders and other creditors cannot require reporting entities to provide information directly to them and must rely on general purpose financial reports for much of the financial information they need. Consequently, they are the primary users to whom general purpose financial reports are directed.[4]

1.6 However, general purpose financial reports do not and cannot provide all of the information that existing and potential investors, lenders and other creditors need. Those users need to consider pertinent information from other sources, for example, general economic conditions and expectations, political events and political climate, and industry and company outlooks.

1.7 General purpose financial reports are not designed to show the value of a reporting entity; but they provide information to help existing and potential investors, lenders and other creditors to estimate the value of the reporting entity.

1.8 Individual primary users have different, and possibly conflicting, information needs and desires. The Board, in developing Standards, will seek to provide the information set that will meet the needs of the maximum number of primary users. However, focusing on common information needs does not prevent the reporting entity from including additional information that is most useful to a particular subset of primary users.

1.9 The management of a reporting entity is also interested in financial information about the entity. However, management need not rely on general purpose financial reports because it is able to obtain the financial information it needs internally.

1.10 Other parties, such as regulators and members of the public other than investors, lenders and other creditors, may also find general purpose financial reports useful. However, those reports are not primarily directed to these other groups.

1.11 To a large extent, financial reports are based on estimates, judgements and models rather than exact depictions. The *Conceptual Framework* establishes the concepts that underlie those estimates, judgements and models. The concepts are the goal towards which the Board and preparers of financial reports strive. As with most goals, the *Conceptual Framework*'s vision of ideal financial reporting is unlikely to be achieved in full, at least not in the short term, because it takes time to understand, accept and implement new ways of analysing transactions and other events. Nevertheless, establishing a goal towards which to strive is essential if financial reporting is to evolve so as to improve its usefulness.

---

4 Throughout the *Conceptual Framework*, the terms 'primary users' and 'users' refer to those existing and potential investors, lenders and other creditors who must rely on general purpose financial reports for much of the financial information they need.

Information about a reporting entity's economic resources, claims against the entity and changes in resources and claims

1.12   General purpose financial reports provide information about the financial position of a reporting entity, which is information about the entity's economic resources and the claims against the reporting entity. Financial reports also provide information about the effects of transactions and other events that change a reporting entity's economic resources and claims. Both types of information provide useful input for decisions relating to providing resources to an entity.

Economic resources and claims

1.13   Information about the nature and amounts of a reporting entity's economic resources and claims can help users to identify the reporting entity's financial strengths and weaknesses. That information can help users to assess the reporting entity's liquidity and solvency, its needs for additional financing and how successful it is likely to be in obtaining that financing. That information can also help users to assess management's stewardship of the entity's economic resources. Information about priorities and payment requirements of existing claims helps users to predict how future cash flows will be distributed among those with a claim against the reporting entity.

1.14   Different types of economic resources affect a user's assessment of the reporting entity's prospects for future cash flows differently. Some future cash flows result directly from existing economic resources, such as accounts receivable. Other cash flows result from using several resources in combination to produce and market goods or services to customers. Although those cash flows cannot be identified with individual economic resources (or claims), users of financial reports need to know the nature and amount of the resources available for use in a reporting entity's operations.

Changes in economic resources and claims

1.15   Changes in a reporting entity's economic resources and claims result from that entity's financial performance (see paragraphs 1.17–1.20) and from other events or transactions such as issuing debt or equity instruments (see paragraph 1.21). To properly assess both the prospects for future net cash inflows to the reporting entity and management's stewardship of the entity's economic resources, users need to be able to identify those two types of changes.

1.16   Information about a reporting entity's financial performance helps users to understand the return that the entity has produced on its economic resources. Information about the return the entity has produced can help users to assess management's stewardship of the entity's economic resources. Information about the variability and components of that return is also important, especially in assessing the uncertainty of future cash flows. Information about a reporting entity's past financial performance and how its management discharged its stewardship responsibilities is usually helpful in predicting the entity's future returns on its economic resources.

Financial performance reflected by accrual accounting

1.17   Accrual accounting depicts the effects of transactions and other events and circumstances on a reporting entity's economic resources and claims in the periods in which those effects occur, even if the resulting cash receipts and payments occur in a different period. This is important because information about a reporting entity's economic resources and claims and changes in its economic resources and claims during a period provides a better basis for assessing the entity's past and future performance than information solely about cash receipts and payments during that period.

1.18   Information about a reporting entity's financial performance during a period, reflected by changes in its economic resources and claims other than by obtaining additional resources directly from investors and creditors (see paragraph 1.21), is useful in assessing the entity's past and future ability to generate net cash inflows. That information indicates the extent to which the reporting entity has increased its available economic resources, and thus its capacity for generating net cash inflows through its operations rather than by obtaining additional resources directly from investors and creditors. Information about a reporting entity's financial performance during a period can also help users to assess management's stewardship of the entity's economic resources.

1.19   Information about a reporting entity's financial performance during a period may also indicate the extent to which events such as changes in market prices or interest rates have increased or decreased the entity's economic resources and claims, thereby affecting the entity's ability to generate net cash inflows.

Financial performance reflected by past cash flows

1.20   Information about a reporting entity's cash flows during a period also helps users to assess the entity's ability to generate future net cash inflows and to assess management's stewardship of the entity's economic resources. That information indicates how the reporting entity obtains and spends cash, including information about its borrowing and repayment of debt, cash dividends or other cash distributions to investors, and other factors that may affect the entity's liquidity or solvency. Information about cash flows helps users understand a reporting entity's operations, evaluate its financing and investing activities, assess its liquidity or solvency and interpret other information about financial performance.

Changes in economic resources and claims not resulting from financial performance

1.21   A reporting entity's economic resources and claims may also change for reasons other than financial performance, such as issuing debt or equity instruments. Information about this type of change is necessary to give users a complete understanding of why the reporting entity's economic resources and claims changed and the implications of those changes for its future financial performance.

Information about use of the entity's economic resources

1.22 Information about how efficiently and effectively the reporting entity's management has discharged its responsibilities to use the entity's economic resources helps users to assess management's stewardship of those resources. Such information is also useful for predicting how efficiently and effectively management will use the entity's economic resources in future periods. Hence, it can be useful for assessing the entity's prospects for future net cash inflows.

1.23 Examples of management's responsibilities to use the entity's economic resources include protecting those resources from unfavourable effects of economic factors, such as price and technological changes, and ensuring that the entity complies with applicable laws, regulations and contractual provisions.

CONTENTS

Introduction

2.1   The qualitative characteristics of useful financial information discussed in this chapter identify the types of information that are likely to be most useful to the existing and potential investors, lenders and other creditors for making decisions about the reporting entity on the basis of information in its financial report (financial information).

2.2   Financial reports provide information about the reporting entity's economic resources, claims against the reporting entity and the effects of transactions and other events and conditions that change those resources and claims. (This information is referred to in the *Conceptual Framework* as information about the economic phenomena.) Some financial reports also include explanatory material about management's expectations and strategies for the reporting entity, and other types of forward-looking information.

2.3   The qualitative characteristics of useful financial information[5] apply to financial information provided in financial statements, as well as to financial information provided in other ways. Cost, which is a pervasive constraint on the reporting entity's ability to provide useful financial information, applies similarly. However, the considerations in applying the qualitative characteristics and the cost constraint may be different for different types of information. For example, applying them to forward-looking information may be different from applying them to information about existing economic resources and claims and to changes in those resources and claims.

Qualitative characteristics of useful financial information

2.4   If financial information is to be useful, it must be relevant and faithfully represent what it purports to represent. The usefulness of financial information is enhanced if it is comparable, verifiable, timely and understandable.

Fundamental qualitative characteristics

2.5   The fundamental qualitative characteristics are relevance and faithful representation.

Relevance

2.6   Relevant financial information is capable of making a difference in the decisions made by users. Information may be capable of making a difference in a decision even if some users choose not to take advantage of it or are already aware of it from other sources.

2.7   Financial information is capable of making a difference in decisions if it has predictive value, confirmatory value or both.

---

5   Throughout the *Conceptual Framework*, the terms 'qualitative characteristics' and 'cost constraint' refer to the qualitative characteristics of, and the cost constraint on, useful financial information.

2.8 Financial information has predictive value if it can be used as an input to processes employed by users to predict future outcomes. Financial information need not be a prediction or forecast to have predictive value. Financial information with predictive value is employed by users in making their own predictions.

2.9 Financial information has confirmatory value if it provides feedback about (confirms or changes) previous evaluations.

2.10 The predictive value and confirmatory value of financial information are interrelated. Information that has predictive value often also has confirmatory value. For example, revenue information for the current year, which can be used as the basis for predicting revenues in future years, can also be compared with revenue predictions for the current year that were made in past years. The results of those comparisons can help a user to correct and improve the processes that were used to make those previous predictions.

Materiality

2.11 Information is material if omitting, misstating or obscuring it could reasonably be expected to influence decisions that the primary users of general purpose financial reports (see paragraph 1.5) make on the basis of those reports, which provide financial information about a specific reporting entity. In other words, materiality is an entity-specific aspect of relevance based on the nature or magnitude, or both, of the items to which the information relates in the context of an individual entity's financial report. Consequently, the Board cannot specify a uniform quantitative threshold for materiality or predetermine what could be material in a particular situation.

Faithful representation

2.12 Financial reports represent economic phenomena in words and numbers. To be useful, financial information must not only represent relevant phenomena, but it must also faithfully represent the substance of the phenomena that it purports to represent. In many circumstances, the substance of an economic phenomenon and its legal form are the same. If they are not the same, providing information only about the legal form would not faithfully represent the economic phenomenon (see paragraphs 4.59–4.62).

2.13 To be a perfectly faithful representation, a depiction would have three characteristics. It would be complete, neutral and free from error. Of course, perfection is seldom, if ever, achievable. The Board's objective is to maximise those qualities to the extent possible.

2.14 A complete depiction includes all information necessary for a user to understand the phenomenon being depicted, including all necessary descriptions and explanations. For example, a complete depiction of a group of assets would include, at a minimum, a description of the nature of the assets in the group, a numerical depiction of all of the assets in the group, and a description of what the numerical depiction represents (for example, historical cost or fair value). For some items, a complete depiction may also entail explanations of significant facts about the quality and nature of the items, factors and circumstances that might affect their quality and nature, and the process used to determine the numerical depiction.

2.15   A neutral depiction is without bias in the selection or presentation of financial information. A neutral depiction is not slanted, weighted, emphasised, de-emphasised or otherwise manipulated to increase the probability that financial information will be received favourably or unfavourably by users. Neutral information does not mean information with no purpose or no influence on behaviour. On the contrary, relevant financial information is, by definition, capable of making a difference in users' decisions.

2.16   Neutrality is supported by the exercise of prudence. Prudence is the exercise of caution when making judgements under conditions of uncertainty. The exercise of prudence means that assets and income are not overstated and liabilities and expenses are not understated.[6] Equally, the exercise of prudence does not allow for the understatement of assets or income or the overstatement of liabilities or expenses. Such misstatements can lead to the overstatement or understatement of income or expenses in future periods.

2.17   The exercise of prudence does not imply a need for asymmetry, for example, a systematic need for more persuasive evidence to support the recognition of assets or income than the recognition of liabilities or expenses. Such asymmetry is not a qualitative characteristic of useful financial information. Nevertheless, particular Standards may contain asymmetric requirements if this is a consequence of decisions intended to select the most relevant information that faithfully represents what it purports to represent.

2.18   Faithful representation does not mean accurate in all respects. Free from error means there are no errors or omissions in the description of the phenomenon, and the process used to produce the reported information has been selected and applied with no errors in the process. In this context, free from error does not mean perfectly accurate in all respects. For example, an estimate of an unobservable price or value cannot be determined to be accurate or inaccurate. However, a representation of that estimate can be faithful if the amount is described clearly and accurately as being an estimate, the nature and limitations of the estimating process are explained, and no errors have been made in selecting and applying an appropriate process for developing the estimate.

2.19   When monetary amounts in financial reports cannot be observed directly and must instead be estimated, measurement uncertainty arises. The use of reasonable estimates is an essential part of the preparation of financial information and does not undermine the usefulness of the information if the estimates are clearly and accurately described and explained. Even a high level of measurement uncertainty does not necessarily prevent such an estimate from providing useful information (see paragraph 2.22).

---

6   Assets, liabilities, income and expenses are defined in Table 4.1. They are the elements of financial statements.

Applying the fundamental qualitative characteristics

2.20   Information must both be relevant and provide a faithful representation of what it purports to represent if it is to be useful. Neither a faithful representation of an irrelevant phenomenon nor an unfaithful representation of a relevant phenomenon helps users make good decisions.

2.21   The most efficient and effective process for applying the fundamental qualitative characteristics would usually be as follows (subject to the effects of enhancing characteristics and the cost constraint, which are not considered in this example). First, identify an economic phenomenon, information about which is capable of being useful to users of the reporting entity's financial information. Second, identify the type of information about that phenomenon that would be most relevant. Third, determine whether that information is available and whether it can provide a faithful representation of the economic phenomenon. If so, the process of satisfying the fundamental qualitative characteristics ends at that point. If not, the process is repeated with the next most relevant type of information.

2.22   In some cases, a trade-off between the fundamental qualitative characteristics may need to be made in order to meet the objective of financial reporting, which is to provide useful information about economic phenomena. For example, the most relevant information about a phenomenon may be a highly uncertain estimate. In some cases, the level of measurement uncertainty involved in making that estimate may be so high that it may be questionable whether the estimate would provide a sufficiently faithful representation of that phenomenon. In some such cases, the most useful information may be the highly uncertain estimate, accompanied by a description of the estimate and an explanation of the uncertainties that affect it. In other such cases, if that information would not provide a sufficiently faithful representation of that phenomenon, the most useful information may include an estimate of another type that is slightly less relevant but is subject to lower measurement uncertainty. In limited circumstances, there may be no estimate that provides useful information. In those limited circumstances, it may be necessary to provide information that does not rely on an estimate.

Enhancing qualitative characteristics

2.23   Comparability, verifiability, timeliness and understandability are qualitative characteristics that enhance the usefulness of information that both is relevant and provides a faithful representation of what it purports to represent. The enhancing qualitative characteristics may also help determine which of two ways should be used to depict a phenomenon if both are considered to provide equally relevant information and an equally faithful representation of that phenomenon.

Comparability

2.24   Users' decisions involve choosing between alternatives, for example, selling or holding an investment, or investing in one reporting entity or another. Consequently, information about a reporting entity is more useful if it can be compared with similar information about other entities and with similar information about the same entity for another period or another date.

2.25   Comparability is the qualitative characteristic that enables users to identify and understand similarities in, and differences among, items. Unlike the other qualitative characteristics, comparability does not relate to a single item. A comparison requires at least two items.

2.26   Consistency, although related to comparability, is not the same. Consistency refers to the use of the same methods for the same items, either from period to period within a reporting entity or in a single period across entities. Comparability is the goal; consistency helps to achieve that goal.

2.27   Comparability is not uniformity. For information to be comparable, like things must look alike and different things must look different. Comparability of financial information is not enhanced by making unlike things look alike any more than it is enhanced by making like things look different.

2.28   Some degree of comparability is likely to be attained by satisfying the fundamental qualitative characteristics. A faithful representation of a relevant economic phenomenon should naturally possess some degree of comparability with a faithful representation of a similar relevant economic phenomenon by another reporting entity.

2.29   Although a single economic phenomenon can be faithfully represented in multiple ways, permitting alternative accounting methods for the same economic phenomenon diminishes comparability.

Verifiability

2.30   Verifiability helps assure users that information faithfully represents the economic phenomena it purports to represent. Verifiability means that different knowledgeable and independent observers could reach consensus, although not necessarily complete agreement, that a particular depiction is a faithful representation. Quantified information need not be a single point estimate to be verifiable. A range of possible amounts and the related probabilities can also be verified.

2.31   Verification can be direct or indirect. Direct verification means verifying an amount or other representation through direct observation, for example, by counting cash. Indirect verification means checking the inputs to a model, formula or other technique and recalculating the outputs using the same methodology. An example is verifying the carrying amount of inventory by checking the inputs (quantities and costs) and recalculating the ending inventory using the same cost flow assumption (for example, using the first-in, first-out method).

2.32   It may not be possible to verify some explanations and forward-looking financial information until a future period, if at all. To help users decide whether they want to use that information, it would normally be necessary to disclose the underlying assumptions, the methods of compiling the information and other factors and circumstances that support the information.

Timeliness

2.33   Timeliness means having information available to decision-makers in time to be capable of influencing their decisions. Generally, the older the information is the less useful it is. However, some information may continue to be timely long after the end of a reporting period because, for example, some users may need to identify and assess trends.

Understandability

2.34   Classifying, characterising and presenting information clearly and concisely makes it understandable.

2.35   Some phenomena are inherently complex and cannot be made easy to understand. Excluding information about those phenomena from financial reports might make the information in those financial reports easier to understand. However, those reports would be incomplete and therefore possibly misleading.

2.36   Financial reports are prepared for users who have a reasonable knowledge of business and economic activities and who review and analyse the information diligently. At times, even well-informed and diligent users may need to seek the aid of an adviser to understand information about complex economic phenomena.

Applying the enhancing qualitative characteristics

2.37   Enhancing qualitative characteristics should be maximised to the extent possible. However, the enhancing qualitative characteristics, either individually or as a group, cannot make information useful if that information is irrelevant or does not provide a faithful representation of what it purports to represent.

2.38   Applying the enhancing qualitative characteristics is an iterative process that does not follow a prescribed order. Sometimes, one enhancing qualitative characteristic may have to be diminished to maximise another qualitative characteristic. For example, a temporary reduction in comparability as a result of prospectively applying a new Standard may be worthwhile to improve relevance or faithful representation in the longer term. Appropriate disclosures may partially compensate for non-comparability.

The cost constraint on useful financial reporting

2.39   Cost is a pervasive constraint on the information that can be provided by financial reporting. Reporting financial information imposes costs, and it is important that those costs are justified by the benefits of reporting that information. There are several types of costs and benefits to consider.

2.40   Providers of financial information expend most of the effort involved in collecting, processing, verifying and disseminating financial information, but users ultimately bear those costs in the form of reduced returns. Users of financial information also incur costs of analysing and interpreting the information provided. If needed information is not provided, users incur additional costs to obtain that information elsewhere or to estimate it.

2.41   Reporting financial information that is relevant and faithfully represents what it purports to represent helps users to make decisions with more confidence. This results in more efficient functioning of capital markets and a lower cost of capital for the economy as a whole. An individual investor, lender or other creditor also receives benefits by making more informed decisions. However, it is not possible for general purpose financial reports to provide all the information that every user finds relevant.

2.42   In applying the cost constraint, the Board assesses whether the benefits of reporting particular information are likely to justify the costs incurred to provide and use that information. When applying the cost constraint in developing a proposed Standard, the Board seeks information from providers of financial information, users, auditors, academics and others about the expected nature and quantity of the benefits and costs of that Standard. In most situations, assessments are based on a combination of quantitative and qualitative information.

2.43   Because of the inherent subjectivity, different individuals' assessments of the costs and benefits of reporting particular items of financial information will vary. Therefore, the Board seeks to consider costs and benefits in relation to financial reporting generally, and not just in relation to individual reporting entities. That does not mean that assessments of costs and benefits always justify the same reporting requirements for all entities. Differences may be appropriate because of different sizes of entities, different ways of raising capital (publicly or privately), different users' needs or other factors.

CONTENTS

Financial statements

3.1   Chapters 1 and 2 discuss information provided in general purpose financial reports and Chapters 3–8 discuss information provided in general purpose financial statements, which are a particular form of general purpose financial reports. Financial statements[7] provide information about economic resources of the reporting entity, claims against the entity, and changes in those resources and claims, that meet the definitions of the elements of financial statements (see Table 4.1).

Objective and scope of financial statements

3.2   The objective of financial statements is to provide financial information about the reporting entity's assets, liabilities, equity, income and expenses[8] that is useful to users of financial statements in assessing the prospects for future net cash inflows to the reporting entity and in assessing management's stewardship of the entity's economic resources (see paragraph 1.3).

3.3   That information is provided:

(a)   in the statement of financial position, by recognising assets, liabilities and equity;

(b)   in the statement(s) of financial performance,[9] by recognising income and expenses; and

(c)   in other statements and notes, by presenting and disclosing information about:

(i)   recognised assets, liabilities, equity, income and expenses (see paragraph 5.1), including information about their nature and about the risks arising from those recognised assets and liabilities;

(ii)   assets and liabilities that have not been recognised (see paragraph 5.6), including information about their nature and about the risks arising from them;

(iii)   cash flows;

(iv)   contributions from holders of equity claims and distributions to them; and

(v)   the methods, assumptions and judgements used in estimating the amounts presented or disclosed, and changes in those methods, assumptions and judgements.

---

7   Throughout the *Conceptual Framework*, the term 'financial statements' refers to general purpose financial statements.

8   Assets, liabilities, equity, income and expenses are defined in Table 4.1. They are the elements of financial statements.

9   The *Conceptual Framework* does not specify whether the statement(s) of financial performance comprise(s) a single statement or two statements.

Reporting period

3.4   Financial statements are prepared for a specified period of time (reporting period) and provide information about:

(a)   assets and liabilities—including unrecognised assets and liabilities—and equity that existed at the end of the reporting period, or during the reporting period; and

(b)   income and expenses for the reporting period.

3.5   To help users of financial statements to identify and assess changes and trends, financial statements also provide comparative information for at least one preceding reporting period.

3.6   Information about possible future transactions and other possible future events (forward-looking information) is included in financial statements if it:

(a)   relates to the entity's assets or liabilities—including unrecognised assets or liabilities—or equity that existed at the end of the reporting period, or during the reporting period, or to income or expenses for the reporting period; and

(b)   is useful to users of financial statements.

For example, if an asset or liability is measured by estimating future cash flows, information about those estimated future cash flows may help users of financial statements to understand the reported measures. Financial statements do not typically provide other types of forward-looking information, for example, explanatory material about management's expectations and strategies for the reporting entity.

3.7   Financial statements include information about transactions and other events that have occurred after the end of the reporting period if providing that information is necessary to meet the objective of financial statements (see paragraph 3.2).

Perspective adopted in financial statements

3.8   Financial statements provide information about transactions and other events viewed from the perspective of the reporting entity as a whole, not from the perspective of any particular group of the entity's existing or potential investors, lenders or other creditors.

Going concern assumption

3.9   Financial statements are normally prepared on the assumption that the reporting entity is a going concern and will continue in operation for the foreseeable future. Hence, it is assumed that the entity has neither the intention nor the need to enter liquidation or to cease trading. If such an intention or need exists, the financial statements may have to be prepared on a different basis. If so, the financial statements describe the basis used.

The reporting entity

3.10 A reporting entity is an entity that is required, or chooses, to prepare financial statements. A reporting entity can be a single entity or a portion of an entity or can comprise more than one entity. A reporting entity is not necessarily a legal entity.

3.11 Sometimes one entity (parent) has control over another entity (subsidiary). If a reporting entity comprises both the parent and its subsidiaries, the reporting entity's financial statements are referred to as 'consolidated financial statements' (see paragraphs 3.15–3.16). If a reporting entity is the parent alone, the reporting entity's financial statements are referred to as 'unconsolidated financial statements' (see paragraphs 3.17–3.18).

3.12 If a reporting entity comprises two or more entities that are not all linked by a parent-subsidiary relationship, the reporting entity's financial statements are referred to as 'combined financial statements'.

3.13 Determining the appropriate boundary of a reporting entity can be difficult if the reporting entity:

(a) is not a legal entity; and

(b) does not comprise only legal entities linked by a parent-subsidiary relationship.

3.14 In such cases, determining the boundary of the reporting entity is driven by the information needs of the primary users of the reporting entity's financial statements. Those users need relevant information that faithfully represents what it purports to represent. Faithful representation requires that:

(a) the boundary of the reporting entity does not contain an arbitrary or incomplete set of economic activities;

(b) including that set of economic activities within the boundary of the reporting entity results in neutral information; and

(c) a description is provided of how the boundary of the reporting entity was determined and of what constitutes the reporting entity.

Consolidated and unconsolidated financial statements

3.15 Consolidated financial statements provide information about the assets, liabilities, equity, income and expenses of both the parent and its subsidiaries as a single reporting entity. That information is useful for existing and potential investors, lenders and other creditors of the parent in their assessment of the prospects for future net cash inflows to the parent. This is because net cash inflows to the parent include distributions to the parent from its subsidiaries, and those distributions depend on net cash inflows to the subsidiaries.

3.16 Consolidated financial statements are not designed to provide separate information about the assets, liabilities, equity, income and expenses of any particular subsidiary. A subsidiary's own financial statements are designed to provide that information.

3.17 Unconsolidated financial statements are designed to provide information about the parent's assets, liabilities, equity, income and expenses, and not about those of its subsidiaries. That information can be useful to existing and potential investors, lenders and other creditors of the parent because:

(a) a claim against the parent typically does not give the holder of that claim a claim against subsidiaries; and

(b) in some jurisdictions, the amounts that can be legally distributed to holders of equity claims against the parent depend on the distributable reserves of the parent.

Another way to provide information about some or all assets, liabilities, equity, income and expenses of the parent alone is in consolidated financial statements, in the notes.

3.18 Information provided in unconsolidated financial statements is typically not sufficient to meet the information needs of existing and potential investors, lenders and other creditors of the parent. Accordingly, when consolidated financial statements are required, unconsolidated financial statements cannot serve as a substitute for consolidated financial statements. Nevertheless, a parent may be required, or choose, to prepare unconsolidated financial statements in addition to consolidated financial statements.

CONTENTS

Introduction

4.1   The elements of financial statements defined in the *Conceptual Framework* are:

(a)   assets, liabilities and equity, which relate to a reporting entity's financial position; and

(b)   income and expenses, which relate to a reporting entity's financial performance.

4.2   Those elements are linked to the economic resources, claims and changes in economic resources and claims discussed in Chapter 1, and are defined in Table 4.1.

Table 4.1 — The elements of financial statements

Item discussed in Chapter 1	Element	Definition or description
Economic resource	Asset	A present economic resource controlled by the entity as a result of past events. An economic resource is a right that has the potential to produce economic benefits.
Claim	Liability	A present obligation of the entity to transfer an economic resource as a result of past events.
	Equity	The residual interest in the assets of the entity after deducting all its liabilities.
Changes in economic resources and claims, reflecting financial performance	Income	Increases in assets, or decreases in liabilities, that result in increases in equity, other than those relating to contributions from holders of equity claims.
	Expenses	Decreases in assets, or increases in liabilities, that result in decreases in equity, other than those relating to distributions to holders of equity claims.
Other changes in economic resources and claims	–	Contributions from holders of equity claims, and distributions to them.
	–	Exchanges of assets or liabilities that do not result in increases or decreases in equity.

Definition of an asset

4.3   An asset is a present economic resource controlled by the entity as a result of past events.

4.4   An economic resource is a right that has the potential to produce economic benefits.

4.5   This section discusses three aspects of those definitions:

(a)   right (see paragraphs 4.6–4.13);

(b)   potential to produce economic benefits (see paragraphs 4.14–4.18); and

(c)   control (see paragraphs 4.19–4.25).

Right

4.6   Rights that have the potential to produce economic benefits take many forms, including:

(a)   rights that correspond to an obligation of another party (see paragraph 4.39), for example:

(i)   rights to receive cash.

(ii)   rights to receive goods or services.

(iii)   rights to exchange economic resources with another party on favourable terms. Such rights include, for example, a forward contract to buy an economic resource on terms that are currently favourable or an option to buy an economic resource.

(iv)   rights to benefit from an obligation of another party to transfer an economic resource if a specified uncertain future event occurs (see paragraph 4.37).

(b)   rights that do not correspond to an obligation of another party, for example:

(i)   rights over physical objects, such as property, plant and equipment or inventories. Examples of such rights are a right to use a physical object or a right to benefit from the residual value of a leased object.

(ii)   rights to use intellectual property.

4.7   Many rights are established by contract, legislation or similar means. For example, an entity might obtain rights from owning or leasing a physical object, from owning a debt instrument or an equity instrument, or from owning a registered patent. However, an entity might also obtain rights in other ways, for example:

(a)   by acquiring or creating know-how that is not in the public domain (see paragraph 4.22); or

(b)   through an obligation of another party that arises because that other party has no practical ability to act in a manner inconsistent with its customary practices, published policies or specific statements (see paragraph 4.31).

4.8   Some goods or services—for example, employee services—are received and immediately consumed. An entity's right to obtain the economic benefits produced by such goods or services exists momentarily until the entity consumes the goods or services.

4.9   Not all of an entity's rights are assets of that entity—to be assets of the entity, the rights must both have the potential to produce for the entity economic benefits beyond the economic benefits available to all other parties (see paragraphs 4.14–4.18) and be controlled by the entity (see paragraphs

4.19–4.25). For example, rights available to all parties without significant cost — for instance, rights of access to public goods, such as public rights of way over land, or know-how that is in the public domain — are typically not assets for the entities that hold them.

4.10   An entity cannot have a right to obtain economic benefits from itself. Hence:

(a)   debt instruments or equity instruments issued by the entity and repurchased and held by it — for example, treasury shares — are not economic resources of that entity; and

(b)   if a reporting entity comprises more than one legal entity, debt instruments or equity instruments issued by one of those legal entities and held by another of those legal entities are not economic resources of the reporting entity.

4.11   In principle, each of an entity's rights is a separate asset. However, for accounting purposes, related rights are often treated as a single unit of account that is a single asset (see paragraphs 4.48–4.55). For example, legal ownership of a physical object may give rise to several rights, including:

(a)   the right to use the object;

(b)   the right to sell rights over the object;

(c)   the right to pledge rights over the object; and

(d)   other rights not listed in (a)–(c).

4.12   In many cases, the set of rights arising from legal ownership of a physical object is accounted for as a single asset. Conceptually, the economic resource is the set of rights, not the physical object. Nevertheless, describing the set of rights as the physical object will often provide a faithful representation of those rights in the most concise and understandable way.

4.13   In some cases, it is uncertain whether a right exists. For example, an entity and another party might dispute whether the entity has a right to receive an economic resource from that other party. Until that existence uncertainty is resolved — for example, by a court ruling — it is uncertain whether the entity has a right and, consequently, whether an asset exists. (Paragraph 5.14 discusses recognition of assets whose existence is uncertain.)

Potential to produce economic benefits

4.14   An economic resource is a right that has the potential to produce economic benefits. For that potential to exist, it does not need to be certain, or even likely, that the right will produce economic benefits. It is only necessary that the right already exists and that, in at least one circumstance, it would produce for the entity economic benefits beyond those available to all other parties.

4.15   A right can meet the definition of an economic resource, and hence can be an asset, even if the probability that it will produce economic benefits is low. Nevertheless, that low probability might affect decisions about what information to provide about the asset and how to provide that information, including decisions about whether the asset is recognised (see paragraphs 5.15–5.17) and how it is measured.

4.16 An economic resource could produce economic benefits for an entity by entitling or enabling it to do, for example, one or more of the following:

(a) receive contractual cash flows or another economic resource;

(b) exchange economic resources with another party on favourable terms;

(c) produce cash inflows or avoid cash outflows by, for example:

(i) using the economic resource either individually or in combination with other economic resources to produce goods or provide services;

(ii) using the economic resource to enhance the value of other economic resources; or

(iii) leasing the economic resource to another party;

(d) receive cash or other economic resources by selling the economic resource; or

(e) extinguish liabilities by transferring the economic resource.

4.17 Although an economic resource derives its value from its present potential to produce future economic benefits, the economic resource is the present right that contains that potential, not the future economic benefits that the right may produce. For example, a purchased option derives its value from its potential to produce economic benefits through exercise of the option at a future date. However, the economic resource is the present right—the right to exercise the option at a future date. The economic resource is not the future economic benefits that the holder will receive if the option is exercised.

4.18 There is a close association between incurring expenditure and acquiring assets, but the two do not necessarily coincide. Hence, when an entity incurs expenditure, this may provide evidence that the entity has sought future economic benefits, but does not provide conclusive proof that the entity has obtained an asset. Similarly, the absence of related expenditure does not preclude an item from meeting the definition of an asset. Assets can include, for example, rights that a government has granted to the entity free of charge or that another party has donated to the entity.

Control

4.19 Control links an economic resource to an entity. Assessing whether control exists helps to identify the economic resource for which the entity accounts. For example, an entity may control a proportionate share in a property without controlling the rights arising from ownership of the entire property. In such cases, the entity's asset is the share in the property, which it controls, not the rights arising from ownership of the entire property, which it does not control.

4.20   An entity controls an economic resource if it has the present ability to direct the use of the economic resource and obtain the economic benefits that may flow from it. Control includes the present ability to prevent other parties from directing the use of the economic resource and from obtaining the economic benefits that may flow from it. It follows that, if one party controls an economic resource, no other party controls that resource.

4.21   An entity has the present ability to direct the use of an economic resource if it has the right to deploy that economic resource in its activities, or to allow another party to deploy the economic resource in that other party's activities.

4.22   Control of an economic resource usually arises from an ability to enforce legal rights. However, control can also arise if an entity has other means of ensuring that it, and no other party, has the present ability to direct the use of the economic resource and obtain the benefits that may flow from it. For example, an entity could control a right to use know-how that is not in the public domain if the entity has access to the know-how and the present ability to keep the know-how secret, even if that know-how is not protected by a registered patent.

4.23   For an entity to control an economic resource, the future economic benefits from that resource must flow to the entity either directly or indirectly rather than to another party. This aspect of control does not imply that the entity can ensure that the resource will produce economic benefits in all circumstances. Instead, it means that if the resource produces economic benefits, the entity is the party that will obtain them either directly or indirectly.

4.24   Having exposure to significant variations in the amount of the economic benefits produced by an economic resource may indicate that the entity controls the resource. However, it is only one factor to consider in the overall assessment of whether control exists.

4.25   Sometimes one party (a principal) engages another party (an agent) to act on behalf of, and for the benefit of, the principal. For example, a principal may engage an agent to arrange sales of goods controlled by the principal. If an agent has custody of an economic resource controlled by the principal, that economic resource is not an asset of the agent. Furthermore, if the agent has an obligation to transfer to a third party an economic resource controlled by the principal, that obligation is not a liability of the agent, because the economic resource that would be transferred is the principal's economic resource, not the agent's.

Definition of a liability

4.26   A liability is a present obligation of the entity to transfer an economic resource as a result of past events.

4.27   For a liability to exist, three criteria must all be satisfied:

        (a)   the entity has an obligation (see paragraphs 4.28–4.35);

(b)   the obligation is to transfer an economic resource (see paragraphs 4.36–4.41); and

(c)   the obligation is a present obligation that exists as a result of past events (see paragraphs 4.42–4.47).

Obligation

4.28   The first criterion for a liability is that the entity has an obligation.

4.29   An obligation is a duty or responsibility that an entity has no practical ability to avoid. An obligation is always owed to another party (or parties). The other party (or parties) could be a person or another entity, a group of people or other entities, or society at large. It is not necessary to know the identity of the party (or parties) to whom the obligation is owed.

4.30   If one party has an obligation to transfer an economic resource, it follows that another party (or parties) has a right to receive that economic resource. However, a requirement for one party to recognise a liability and measure it at a specified amount does not imply that the other party (or parties) must recognise an asset or measure it at the same amount. For example, particular Standards may contain different recognition criteria or measurement requirements for the liability of one party and the corresponding asset of the other party (or parties) if those different criteria or requirements are a consequence of decisions intended to select the most relevant information that faithfully represents what it purports to represent.

4.31   Many obligations are established by contract, legislation or similar means and are legally enforceable by the party (or parties) to whom they are owed. Obligations can also arise, however, from an entity's customary practices, published policies or specific statements if the entity has no practical ability to act in a manner inconsistent with those practices, policies or statements. The obligation that arises in such situations is sometimes referred to as a 'constructive obligation'.

4.32   In some situations, an entity's duty or responsibility to transfer an economic resource is conditional on a particular future action that the entity itself may take. Such actions could include operating a particular business or operating in a particular market on a specified future date, or exercising particular options within a contract. In such situations, the entity has an obligation if it has no practical ability to avoid taking that action.

4.33   A conclusion that it is appropriate to prepare an entity's financial statements on a going concern basis also implies a conclusion that the entity has no practical ability to avoid a transfer that could be avoided only by liquidating the entity or by ceasing to trade.

4.34   The factors used to assess whether an entity has the practical ability to avoid transferring an economic resource may depend on the nature of the entity's duty or responsibility. For example, in some cases, an entity may have no practical ability to avoid a transfer if any action that it could take to avoid the transfer would have economic consequences significantly more adverse than the transfer itself. However, neither an intention to make a transfer, nor a high likelihood of a transfer, is sufficient reason for concluding that the entity has no practical ability to avoid a transfer.

4.35   In some cases, it is uncertain whether an obligation exists. For example, if another party is seeking compensation for an entity's alleged act of wrongdoing, it might be uncertain whether the act occurred, whether the entity committed it or how the law applies. Until that existence uncertainty is resolved—for example, by a court ruling—it is uncertain whether the entity has an obligation to the party seeking compensation and, consequently, whether a liability exists. (Paragraph 5.14 discusses recognition of liabilities whose existence is uncertain.)

Transfer of an economic resource

4.36   The second criterion for a liability is that the obligation is to transfer an economic resource.

4.37   To satisfy this criterion, the obligation must have the potential to require the entity to transfer an economic resource to another party (or parties). For that potential to exist, it does not need to be certain, or even likely, that the entity will be required to transfer an economic resource—the transfer may, for example, be required only if a specified uncertain future event occurs. It is only necessary that the obligation already exists and that, in at least one circumstance, it would require the entity to transfer an economic resource.

4.38   An obligation can meet the definition of a liability even if the probability of a transfer of an economic resource is low. Nevertheless, that low probability might affect decisions about what information to provide about the liability and how to provide that information, including decisions about whether the liability is recognised (see paragraphs 5.15–5.17) and how it is measured.

4.39   Obligations to transfer an economic resource include, for example:

   (a)   obligations to pay cash.

   (b)   obligations to deliver goods or provide services.

   (c)   obligations to exchange economic resources with another party on unfavourable terms. Such obligations include, for example, a forward contract to sell an economic resource on terms that are currently unfavourable or an option that entitles another party to buy an economic resource from the entity.

   (d)   obligations to transfer an economic resource if a specified uncertain future event occurs.

   (e)   obligations to issue a financial instrument if that financial instrument will oblige the entity to transfer an economic resource.

4.40   Instead of fulfilling an obligation to transfer an economic resource to the party that has a right to receive that resource, entities sometimes decide to, for example:

   (a)   settle the obligation by negotiating a release from the obligation;

(b)   transfer the obligation to a third party; or

(c)   replace that obligation to transfer an economic resource with another obligation by entering into a new transaction.

4.41   In the situations described in paragraph 4.40, an entity has the obligation to transfer an economic resource until it has settled, transferred or replaced that obligation.

Present obligation as a result of past events

4.42   The third criterion for a liability is that the obligation is a present obligation that exists as a result of past events.

4.43   A present obligation exists as a result of past events only if:

(a)   the entity has already obtained economic benefits or taken an action; and

(b)   as a consequence, the entity will or may have to transfer an economic resource that it would not otherwise have had to transfer.

4.44   The economic benefits obtained could include, for example, goods or services. The action taken could include, for example, operating a particular business or operating in a particular market. If economic benefits are obtained, or an action is taken, over time, the resulting present obligation may accumulate over that time.

4.45   If new legislation is enacted, a present obligation arises only when, as a consequence of obtaining economic benefits or taking an action to which that legislation applies, an entity will or may have to transfer an economic resource that it would not otherwise have had to transfer. The enactment of legislation is not in itself sufficient to give an entity a present obligation. Similarly, an entity's customary practice, published policy or specific statement of the type mentioned in paragraph 4.31 gives rise to a present obligation only when, as a consequence of obtaining economic benefits, or taking an action, to which that practice, policy or statement applies, the entity will or may have to transfer an economic resource that it would not otherwise have had to transfer.

4.46   A present obligation can exist even if a transfer of economic resources cannot be enforced until some point in the future. For example, a contractual liability to pay cash may exist now even if the contract does not require a payment until a future date. Similarly, a contractual obligation for an entity to perform work at a future date may exist now even if the counterparty cannot require the entity to perform the work until that future date.

4.47   An entity does not yet have a present obligation to transfer an economic resource if it has not yet satisfied the criteria in paragraph 4.43, that is, if it has not yet obtained economic benefits, or taken an action, that would or could require the entity to transfer an economic resource that it would not otherwise have had to transfer. For example, if an entity has entered into a contract to pay an employee a salary in exchange for receiving the employee's services, the entity does not have a present obligation to pay the salary until it has received the employee's services. Before then the contract is executory—the entity has a combined right and obligation to exchange future salary for future employee services (see paragraphs 4.56–4.58).

Assets and liabilities

Unit of account

4.48   The unit of account is the right or the group of rights, the obligation or the group of obligations, or the group of rights and obligations, to which recognition criteria and measurement concepts are applied.

4.49   A unit of account is selected for an asset or liability when considering how recognition criteria and measurement concepts will apply to that asset or liability and to the related income and expenses. In some circumstances, it may be appropriate to select one unit of account for recognition and a different unit of account for measurement. For example, contracts may sometimes be recognised individually but measured as part of a portfolio of contracts. For presentation and disclosure, assets, liabilities, income and expenses may need to be aggregated or separated into components.

4.50   If an entity transfers part of an asset or part of a liability, the unit of account may change at that time, so that the transferred component and the retained component become separate units of account (see paragraphs 5.26–5.33).

4.51   A unit of account is selected to provide useful information, which implies that:

(a)   the information provided about the asset or liability and about any related income and expenses must be relevant. Treating a group of rights and obligations as a single unit of account may provide more relevant information than treating each right or obligation as a separate unit of account if, for example, those rights and obligations:

(i)   cannot be or are unlikely to be the subject of separate transactions;

(ii)   cannot or are unlikely to expire in different patterns;

(iii)   have similar economic characteristics and risks and hence are likely to have similar implications for the prospects for future net cash inflows to the entity or net cash outflows from the entity; or

(iv)   are used together in the business activities conducted by an entity to produce cash flows and are measured by reference to estimates of their interdependent future cash flows.

(b)   the information provided about the asset or liability and about any related income and expenses must faithfully represent the substance of the transaction or other event from which they have arisen. Therefore, it may be necessary to treat rights or obligations arising from different sources as a single unit of account, or to separate the rights or obligations arising from a single source (see paragraph 4.62). Equally, to provide a faithful representation of unrelated rights and obligations, it may be necessary to recognise and measure them separately.

4.52   Just as cost constrains other financial reporting decisions, it also constrains the selection of a unit of account. Hence, in selecting a unit of account, it is important to consider whether the benefits of the information provided to users of financial statements by selecting that unit of account are likely to justify the costs of providing and using that information. In general, the costs associated with recognising and measuring assets, liabilities, income and expenses increase as the size of the unit of account decreases. Hence, in general, rights or obligations arising from the same source are separated only if the resulting information is more useful and the benefits outweigh the costs.

4.53   Sometimes, both rights and obligations arise from the same source. For example, some contracts establish both rights and obligations for each of the parties. If those rights and obligations are interdependent and cannot be separated, they constitute a single inseparable asset or liability and hence form a single unit of account. For example, this is the case with executory contracts (see paragraph 4.57). Conversely, if rights are separable from obligations, it may sometimes be appropriate to group the rights separately from the obligations, resulting in the identification of one or more separate assets and liabilities. In other cases, it may be more appropriate to group separable rights and obligations in a single unit of account treating them as a single asset or a single liability.

4.54   Treating a set of rights and obligations as a single unit of account differs from offsetting assets and liabilities (see paragraph 7.10).

4.55   Possible units of account include:

(a)   an individual right or individual obligation;

(b)   all rights, all obligations, or all rights and all obligations, arising from a single source, for example, a contract;

(c)   a subgroup of those rights and/or obligations—for example, a subgroup of rights over an item of property, plant and equipment for which the useful life and pattern of consumption differ from those of the other rights over that item;

(d)   a group of rights and/or obligations arising from a portfolio of similar items;

(e)   a group of rights and/or obligations arising from a portfolio of dissimilar items—for example, a portfolio of assets and liabilities to be disposed of in a single transaction; and

(f)   a risk exposure within a portfolio of items—if a portfolio of items is subject to a common risk, some aspects of the accounting for that portfolio could focus on the aggregate exposure to that risk within the portfolio.

Executory contracts

4.56 An executory contract is a contract, or a portion of a contract, that is equally unperformed—neither party has fulfilled any of its obligations, or both parties have partially fulfilled their obligations to an equal extent.

4.57 An executory contract establishes a combined right and obligation to exchange economic resources. The right and obligation are interdependent and cannot be separated. Hence, the combined right and obligation constitute a single asset or liability. The entity has an asset if the terms of the exchange are currently favourable; it has a liability if the terms of the exchange are currently unfavourable. Whether such an asset or liability is included in the financial statements depends on both the recognition criteria (see Chapter 5) and the measurement basis (see Chapter 6) selected for the asset or liability, including, if applicable, any test for whether the contract is onerous.

4.58 To the extent that either party fulfils its obligations under the contract, the contract is no longer executory. If the reporting entity performs first under the contract, that performance is the event that changes the reporting entity's right and obligation to exchange economic resources into a right to receive an economic resource. That right is an asset. If the other party performs first, that performance is the event that changes the reporting entity's right and obligation to exchange economic resources into an obligation to transfer an economic resource. That obligation is a liability.

Substance of contractual rights and contractual obligations

4.59 The terms of a contract create rights and obligations for an entity that is a party to that contract. To represent those rights and obligations faithfully, financial statements report their substance (see paragraph 2.12). In some cases, the substance of the rights and obligations is clear from the legal form of the contract. In other cases, the terms of the contract or a group or series of contracts require analysis to identify the substance of the rights and obligations.

4.60 All terms in a contract—whether explicit or implicit—are considered unless they have no substance. Implicit terms could include, for example, obligations imposed by statute, such as statutory warranty obligations imposed on entities that enter into contracts to sell goods to customers.

4.61 Terms that have no substance are disregarded. A term has no substance if it has no discernible effect on the economics of the contract. Terms that have no substance could include, for example:

(a) terms that bind neither party; or

(b) rights, including options, that the holder will not have the practical ability to exercise in any circumstances.

4.62   A group or series of contracts may achieve or be designed to achieve an overall commercial effect. To report the substance of such contracts, it may be necessary to treat rights and obligations arising from that group or series of contracts as a single unit of account. For example, if the rights or obligations in one contract merely nullify all the rights or obligations in another contract entered into at the same time with the same counterparty, the combined effect is that the two contracts create no rights or obligations. Conversely, if a single contract creates two or more sets of rights or obligations that could have been created through two or more separate contracts, an entity may need to account for each set as if it arose from separate contracts in order to faithfully represent the rights and obligations (see paragraphs 4.48–4.55).

Definition of equity

4.63   Equity is the residual interest in the assets of the entity after deducting all its liabilities.

4.64   Equity claims are claims on the residual interest in the assets of the entity after deducting all its liabilities. In other words, they are claims against the entity that do not meet the definition of a liability. Such claims may be established by contract, legislation or similar means, and include, to the extent that they do not meet the definition of a liability:

(a)   shares of various types, issued by the entity; and

(b)   some obligations of the entity to issue another equity claim.

4.65   Different classes of equity claims, such as ordinary shares and preference shares, may confer on their holders different rights, for example, rights to receive some or all of the following from the entity:

(a)   dividends, if the entity decides to pay dividends to eligible holders;

(b)   the proceeds from satisfying the equity claims, either in full on liquidation, or in part at other times; or

(c)   other equity claims.

4.66   Sometimes, legal, regulatory or other requirements affect particular components of equity, such as share capital or retained earnings. For example, some such requirements permit an entity to make distributions to holders of equity claims only if the entity has sufficient reserves that those requirements specify as being distributable.

4.67   Business activities are often undertaken by entities such as sole proprietorships, partnerships, trusts or various types of government business undertakings. The legal and regulatory frameworks for such entities are often different from frameworks that apply to corporate entities. For example, there may be few, if any, restrictions on the distribution to holders of equity claims against such entities. Nevertheless, the definition of equity in paragraph 4.63 of the *Conceptual Framework* applies to all reporting entities.

Definitions of income and expenses

4.68   Income is increases in assets, or decreases in liabilities, that result in increases in equity, other than those relating to contributions from holders of equity claims.

4.69   Expenses are decreases in assets, or increases in liabilities, that result in decreases in equity, other than those relating to distributions to holders of equity claims.

4.70   It follows from these definitions of income and expenses that contributions from holders of equity claims are not income, and distributions to holders of equity claims are not expenses.

4.71   Income and expenses are the elements of financial statements that relate to an entity's financial performance. Users of financial statements need information about both an entity's financial position and its financial performance. Hence, although income and expenses are defined in terms of changes in assets and liabilities, information about income and expenses is just as important as information about assets and liabilities.

4.72   Different transactions and other events generate income and expenses with different characteristics. Providing information separately about income and expenses with different characteristics can help users of financial statements to understand the entity's financial performance (see paragraphs 7.14–7.19).

CONTENTS

The recognition process

5.1   Recognition is the process of capturing for inclusion in the statement of financial position or the statement(s) of financial performance an item that meets the definition of one of the elements of financial statements—an asset, a liability, equity, income or expenses. Recognition involves depicting the item in one of those statements—either alone or in aggregation with other items—in words and by a monetary amount, and including that amount in one or more totals in that statement. The amount at which an asset, a liability or equity is recognised in the statement of financial position is referred to as its 'carrying amount'.

5.2   The statement of financial position and statement(s) of financial performance depict an entity's recognised assets, liabilities, equity, income and expenses in structured summaries that are designed to make financial information comparable and understandable. An important feature of the structures of those summaries is that the amounts recognised in a statement are included in the totals and, if applicable, subtotals that link the items recognised in the statement.

5.3   Recognition links the elements, the statement of financial position and the statement(s) of financial performance as follows (see Diagram 5.1):

(a)   in the statement of financial position at the beginning and end of the reporting period, total assets minus total liabilities equal total equity; and

(b)   recognised changes in equity during the reporting period comprise:

(i)   income minus expenses recognised in the statement(s) of financial performance; plus

(ii)   contributions from holders of equity claims, minus distributions to holders of equity claims.

5.4   The statements are linked because the recognition of one item (or a change in its carrying amount) requires the recognition or derecognition of one or more other items (or changes in the carrying amount of one or more other items). For example:

(a)   the recognition of income occurs at the same time as:

(i)   the initial recognition of an asset, or an increase in the carrying amount of an asset; or

(ii)   the derecognition of a liability, or a decrease in the carrying amount of a liability.

(b)   the recognition of expenses occurs at the same time as:

(i)   the initial recognition of a liability, or an increase in the carrying amount of a liability; or

(ii)   the derecognition of an asset, or a decrease in the carrying amount of an asset.

Diagram 5.1: How recognition links the elements of financial statements

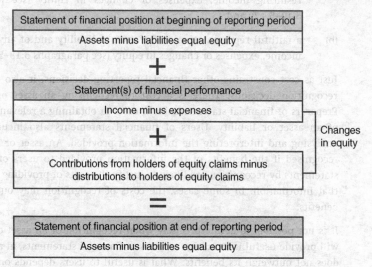

Statement of financial position at beginning of reporting period
Assets minus liabilities equal equity

$+$

Statement(s) of financial performance
Income minus expenses

$+$

Contributions from holders of equity claims minus distributions to holders of equity claims

Changes in equity

$=$

Statement of financial position at end of reporting period
Assets minus liabilities equal equity

5.5 The initial recognition of assets or liabilities arising from transactions or other events may result in the simultaneous recognition of both income and related expenses. For example, the sale of goods for cash results in the recognition of both income (from the recognition of one asset — the cash) and an expense (from the derecognition of another asset — the goods sold). The simultaneous recognition of income and related expenses is sometimes referred to as the matching of costs with income. Application of the concepts in the *Conceptual Framework* leads to such matching when it arises from the recognition of changes in assets and liabilities. However, matching of costs with income is not an objective of the *Conceptual Framework*. The *Conceptual Framework* does not allow the recognition in the statement of financial position of items that do not meet the definition of an asset, a liability or equity.

Recognition criteria

5.6 Only items that meet the definition of an asset, a liability or equity are recognised in the statement of financial position. Similarly, only items that meet the definition of income or expenses are recognised in the statement(s) of financial performance. However, not all items that meet the definition of one of those elements are recognised.

5.7 Not recognising an item that meets the definition of one of the elements makes the statement of financial position and the statement(s) of financial performance less complete and can exclude useful information from financial statements. On the other hand, in some circumstances, recognising some items that meet the definition of one of the elements would not provide useful information. An asset or liability is recognised only if recognition of that asset or liability and of any resulting income, expenses or changes in equity provides users of financial statements with information that is useful, ie with:

(a)   relevant information about the asset or liability and about any resulting income, expenses or changes in equity (see paragraphs 5.12–5.17); and

(b)   a faithful representation of the asset or liability and of any resulting income, expenses or changes in equity (see paragraphs 5.18–5.25).

5.8   Just as cost constrains other financial reporting decisions, it also constrains recognition decisions. There is a cost to recognising an asset or liability. Preparers of financial statements incur costs in obtaining a relevant measure of an asset or liability. Users of financial statements also incur costs in analysing and interpreting the information provided. An asset or liability is recognised if the benefits of the information provided to users of financial statements by recognition are likely to justify the costs of providing and using that information. In some cases, the costs of recognition may outweigh its benefits.

5.9   It is not possible to define precisely when recognition of an asset or liability will provide useful information to users of financial statements, at a cost that does not outweigh its benefits. What is useful to users depends on the item and the facts and circumstances. Consequently, judgement is required when deciding whether to recognise an item, and thus recognition requirements may need to vary between and within Standards.

5.10   It is important when making decisions about recognition to consider the information that would be given if an asset or liability were not recognised. For example, if no asset is recognised when expenditure is incurred, an expense is recognised. Over time, recognising the expense may, in some cases, provide useful information, for example, information that enables users of financial statements to identify trends.

5.11   Even if an item meeting the definition of an asset or liability is not recognised, an entity may need to provide information about that item in the notes. It is important to consider how to make such information sufficiently visible to compensate for the item's absence from the structured summary provided by the statement of financial position and, if applicable, the statement(s) of financial performance.

Relevance

5.12   Information about assets, liabilities, equity, income and expenses is relevant to users of financial statements. However, recognition of a particular asset or liability and any resulting income, expenses or changes in equity may not always provide relevant information. That may be the case if, for example:

(a)   it is uncertain whether an asset or liability exists (see paragraph 5.14); or

(b)   an asset or liability exists, but the probability of an inflow or outflow of economic benefits is low (see paragraphs 5.15–5.17).

5.13   The presence of one or both of the factors described in paragraph 5.12 does not lead automatically to a conclusion that the information provided by recognition lacks relevance. Moreover, factors other than those described in paragraph 5.12 may also affect the conclusion. It may be a combination of factors and not any single factor that determines whether recognition provides relevant information.

Existence uncertainty

5.14   Paragraphs 4.13 and 4.35 discuss cases in which it is uncertain whether an asset or liability exists. In some cases, that uncertainty, possibly combined with a low probability of inflows or outflows of economic benefits and an exceptionally wide range of possible outcomes, may mean that the recognition of an asset or liability, necessarily measured at a single amount, would not provide relevant information. Whether or not the asset or liability is recognised, explanatory information about the uncertainties associated with it may need to be provided in the financial statements.

Low probability of an inflow or outflow of economic benefits

5.15   An asset or liability can exist even if the probability of an inflow or outflow of economic benefits is low (see paragraphs 4.15 and 4.38).

5.16   If the probability of an inflow or outflow of economic benefits is low, the most relevant information about the asset or liability may be information about the magnitude of the possible inflows or outflows, their possible timing and the factors affecting the probability of their occurrence. The typical location for such information is in the notes.

5.17   Even if the probability of an inflow or outflow of economic benefits is low, recognition of the asset or liability may provide relevant information beyond the information described in paragraph 5.16. Whether that is the case may depend on a variety of factors. For example:

    (a)   if an asset is acquired or a liability is incurred in an exchange transaction on market terms, its cost generally reflects the probability of an inflow or outflow of economic benefits. Thus, that cost may be relevant information, and is generally readily available. Furthermore, not recognising the asset or liability would result in the recognition of expenses or income at the time of the exchange, which might not be a faithful representation of the transaction (see paragraph 5.25(a)).

    (b)   if an asset or liability arises from an event that is not an exchange transaction, recognition of the asset or liability typically results in recognition of income or expenses. If there is only a low probability that the asset or liability will result in an inflow or outflow of economic benefits, users of financial statements might not regard the recognition of the asset and income, or the liability and expenses, as providing relevant information.

Faithful representation

5.18   Recognition of a particular asset or liability is appropriate if it provides not only relevant information, but also a faithful representation of that asset or liability and of any resulting income, expenses or changes in equity. Whether a faithful representation can be provided may be affected by the level of measurement uncertainty associated with the asset or liability or by other factors.

Measurement uncertainty

5.19   For an asset or liability to be recognised, it must be measured. In many cases, such measures must be estimated and are therefore subject to measurement uncertainty. As noted in paragraph 2.19, the use of reasonable estimates is an essential part of the preparation of financial information and does not undermine the usefulness of the information if the estimates are clearly and accurately described and explained. Even a high level of measurement uncertainty does not necessarily prevent such an estimate from providing useful information.

5.20   In some cases, the level of uncertainty involved in estimating a measure of an asset or liability may be so high that it may be questionable whether the estimate would provide a sufficiently faithful representation of that asset or liability and of any resulting income, expenses or changes in equity. The level of measurement uncertainty may be so high if, for example, the only way of estimating that measure of the asset or liability is by using cash-flow-based measurement techniques and, in addition, one or more of the following circumstances exists:

(a)   the range of possible outcomes is exceptionally wide and the probability of each outcome is exceptionally difficult to estimate.

(b)   the measure is exceptionally sensitive to small changes in estimates of the probability of different outcomes—for example, if the probability of future cash inflows or outflows occurring is exceptionally low, but the magnitude of those cash inflows or outflows will be exceptionally high if they occur.

(c)   measuring the asset or liability requires exceptionally difficult or exceptionally subjective allocations of cash flows that do not relate solely to the asset or liability being measured.

5.21   In some of the cases described in paragraph 5.20, the most useful information may be the measure that relies on the highly uncertain estimate, accompanied by a description of the estimate and an explanation of the uncertainties that affect it. This is especially likely to be the case if that measure is the most relevant measure of the asset or liability. In other cases, if that information would not provide a sufficiently faithful representation of the asset or liability and of any resulting income, expenses or changes in equity, the most useful information may be a different measure (accompanied by any necessary descriptions and explanations) that is slightly less relevant but is subject to lower measurement uncertainty.

5.22   In limited circumstances, all relevant measures of an asset or liability that are available (or can be obtained) may be subject to such high measurement uncertainty that none would provide useful information about the asset or liability (and any resulting income, expenses or changes in equity), even if the measure were accompanied by a description of the estimates made in producing it and an explanation of the uncertainties that affect those estimates. In those limited circumstances, the asset or liability would not be recognised.

5.23   Whether or not an asset or liability is recognised, a faithful representation of the asset or liability may need to include explanatory information about the uncertainties associated with the asset or liability's existence or measurement, or with its outcome—the amount or timing of any inflow or outflow of economic benefits that will ultimately result from it (see paragraphs 6.60–6.62).

Other factors

5.24   Faithful representation of a recognised asset, liability, equity, income or expenses involves not only recognition of that item, but also its measurement as well as presentation and disclosure of information about it (see Chapters 6–7).

5.25   Hence, when assessing whether the recognition of an asset or liability can provide a faithful representation of the asset or liability, it is necessary to consider not merely its description and measurement in the statement of financial position, but also:

(a)   the depiction of resulting income, expenses and changes in equity. For example, if an entity acquires an asset in exchange for consideration, not recognising the asset would result in recognising expenses and would reduce the entity's profit and equity. In some cases, for example, if the entity does not consume the asset immediately, that result could provide a misleading representation that the entity's financial position has deteriorated.

(b)   whether related assets and liabilities are recognised. If they are not recognised, recognition may create a recognition inconsistency (accounting mismatch). That may not provide an understandable or faithful representation of the overall effect of the transaction or other event giving rise to the asset or liability, even if explanatory information is provided in the notes.

(c)   presentation and disclosure of information about the asset or liability, and resulting income, expenses or changes in equity. A complete depiction includes all information necessary for a user of financial statements to understand the economic phenomenon depicted, including all necessary descriptions and explanations. Hence, presentation and disclosure of related information can enable a recognised amount to form part of a faithful representation of an asset, a liability, equity, income or expenses.

Derecognition

5.26 Derecognition is the removal of all or part of a recognised asset or liability from an entity's statement of financial position. Derecognition normally occurs when that item no longer meets the definition of an asset or of a liability:

(a) for an asset, derecognition normally occurs when the entity loses control of all or part of the recognised asset; and

(b) for a liability, derecognition normally occurs when the entity no longer has a present obligation for all or part of the recognised liability.

5.27 Accounting requirements for derecognition aim to faithfully represent both:

(a) any assets and liabilities retained after the transaction or other event that led to the derecognition (including any asset or liability acquired, incurred or created as part of the transaction or other event); and

(b) the change in the entity's assets and liabilities as a result of that transaction or other event.

5.28 The aims described in paragraph 5.27 are normally achieved by:

(a) derecognising any assets or liabilities that have expired or have been consumed, collected, fulfilled or transferred, and recognising any resulting income and expenses. In the rest of this chapter, the term 'transferred component' refers to all those assets and liabilities;

(b) continuing to recognise the assets or liabilities retained, referred to as the 'retained component', if any. That retained component becomes a unit of account separate from the transferred component. Accordingly, no income or expenses are recognised on the retained component as a result of the derecognition of the transferred component, unless the derecognition results in a change in the measurement requirements applicable to the retained component; and

(c) applying one or more of the following procedures, if that is necessary to achieve one or both of the aims described in paragraph 5.27:

(i) presenting any retained component separately in the statement of financial position;

(ii) presenting separately in the statement(s) of financial performance any income and expenses recognised as a result of the derecognition of the transferred component; or

(iii) providing explanatory information.

5.29 In some cases, an entity might appear to transfer an asset or liability, but that asset or liability might nevertheless remain an asset or liability of the entity. For example:

(a)   if an entity has apparently transferred an asset but retains exposure to significant positive or negative variations in the amount of economic benefits that may be produced by the asset, this sometimes indicates that the entity might continue to control that asset (see paragraph 4.24); or

(b)   if an entity has transferred an asset to another party that holds the asset as an agent for the entity, the transferor still controls the asset (see paragraph 4.25).

5.30   In the cases described in paragraph 5.29, derecognition of that asset or liability is not appropriate because it would not achieve either of the two aims described in paragraph 5.27.

5.31   When an entity no longer has a transferred component, derecognition of the transferred component faithfully represents that fact. However, in some of those cases, derecognition may not faithfully represent how much a transaction or other event changed the entity's assets or liabilities, even when supported by one or more of the procedures described in paragraph 5.28(c). In those cases, derecognition of the transferred component might imply that the entity's financial position has changed more significantly than it has. This might occur, for example:

(a)   if an entity has transferred an asset and, at the same time, entered into another transaction that results in a present right or present obligation to reacquire the asset. Such present rights or present obligations may arise from, for example, a forward contract, a written put option, or a purchased call option.

(b)   if an entity has retained exposure to significant positive or negative variations in the amount of economic benefits that may be produced by a transferred component that the entity no longer controls.

5.32   If derecognition is not sufficient to achieve both aims described in paragraph 5.27, even when supported by one or more of the procedures described in paragraph 5.28(c), those two aims might sometimes be achieved by continuing to recognise the transferred component. This has the following consequences:

(a)   no income or expenses are recognised on either the retained component or the transferred component as a result of the transaction or other event;

(b)   the proceeds received (or paid) upon transfer of the asset (or liability) are treated as a loan received (or given); and

(c)   separate presentation of the transferred component in the statement of financial position, or provision of explanatory information, is needed to depict the fact that the entity no longer has any rights or obligations arising from the transferred component. Similarly, it may be necessary to provide information about income or expenses arising from the transferred component after the transfer.

5.33 One case in which questions about derecognition arise is when a contract is modified in a way that reduces or eliminates existing rights or obligations. In deciding how to account for contract modifications, it is necessary to consider which unit of account provides users of financial statements with the most useful information about the assets and liabilities retained after the modification, and about how the modification changed the entity's assets and liabilities:

(a) if a contract modification only eliminates existing rights or obligations, the discussion in paragraphs 5.26–5.32 is considered in deciding whether to derecognise those rights or obligations;

(b) if a contract modification only adds new rights or obligations, it is necessary to decide whether to treat the added rights or obligations as a separate asset or liability, or as part of the same unit of account as the existing rights and obligations (see paragraphs 4.48–4.55); and

(c) if a contract modification both eliminates existing rights or obligations and adds new rights or obligations, it is necessary to consider both the separate and the combined effect of those modifications. In some such cases, the contract has been modified to such an extent that, in substance, the modification replaces the old asset or liability with a new asset or liability. In cases of such extensive modification, the entity may need to derecognise the original asset or liability, and recognise the new asset or liability.

Contents

Introduction

6.1   Elements recognised in financial statements are quantified in monetary terms. This requires the selection of a measurement basis. A measurement basis is an identified feature—for example, historical cost, fair value or fulfilment value —of an item being measured. Applying a measurement basis to an asset or liability creates a measure for that asset or liability and for related income and expenses.

6.2   Consideration of the qualitative characteristics of useful financial information and of the cost constraint is likely to result in the selection of different measurement bases for different assets, liabilities, income and expenses.

6.3   A Standard may need to describe how to implement the measurement basis selected in that Standard. That description could include:

   (a)   specifying techniques that may or must be used to estimate a measure applying a particular measurement basis;

   (b)   specifying a simplified measurement approach that is likely to provide information similar to that provided by a preferred measurement basis; or

   (c)   explaining how to modify a measurement basis, for example, by excluding from the fulfilment value of a liability the effect of the possibility that the entity may fail to fulfil that liability (own credit risk).

Measurement bases

Historical cost

6.4   Historical cost measures provide monetary information about assets, liabilities and related income and expenses, using information derived, at least in part, from the price of the transaction or other event that gave rise to them. Unlike current value, historical cost does not reflect changes in values, except to the extent that those changes relate to impairment of an asset or a liability becoming onerous (see paragraphs 6.7(c) and 6.8(b)).

6.5   The historical cost of an asset when it is acquired or created is the value of the costs incurred in acquiring or creating the asset, comprising the consideration paid to acquire or create the asset plus transaction costs. The historical cost of a liability when it is incurred or taken on is the value of the consideration received to incur or take on the liability minus transaction costs.

6.6   When an asset is acquired or created, or a liability is incurred or taken on, as a result of an event that is not a transaction on market terms (see paragraph 6.80), it may not be possible to identify a cost, or the cost may not provide relevant information about the asset or liability. In some such cases, a current value of the asset or liability is used as a deemed cost on initial recognition and that deemed cost is then used as a starting point for subsequent measurement at historical cost.

6.7   The historical cost of an asset is updated over time to depict, if applicable:

(a)   the consumption of part or all of the economic resource that constitutes the asset (depreciation or amortisation);

(b)   payments received that extinguish part or all of the asset;

(c)   the effect of events that cause part or all of the historical cost of the asset to be no longer recoverable (impairment); and

(d)   accrual of interest to reflect any financing component of the asset.

6.8   The historical cost of a liability is updated over time to depict, if applicable:

(a)   fulfilment of part or all of the liability, for example, by making payments that extinguish part or all of the liability or by satisfying an obligation to deliver goods;

(b)   the effect of events that increase the value of the obligation to transfer the economic resources needed to fulfil the liability to such an extent that the liability becomes onerous. A liability is onerous if the historical cost is no longer sufficient to depict the obligation to fulfil the liability; and

(c)   accrual of interest to reflect any financing component of the liability.

6.9   One way to apply a historical cost measurement basis to financial assets and financial liabilities is to measure them at amortised cost. The amortised cost of a financial asset or financial liability reflects estimates of future cash flows, discounted at a rate determined at initial recognition. For variable rate instruments, the discount rate is updated to reflect changes in the variable rate. The amortised cost of a financial asset or financial liability is updated over time to depict subsequent changes, such as the accrual of interest, the impairment of a financial asset and receipts or payments.

Current value

6.10   Current value measures provide monetary information about assets, liabilities and related income and expenses, using information updated to reflect conditions at the measurement date. Because of the updating, current values of assets and liabilities reflect changes, since the previous measurement date, in estimates of cash flows and other factors reflected in those current values (see paragraphs 6.14–6.15 and 6.20). Unlike historical cost, the current value of an asset or liability is not derived, even in part, from the price of the transaction or other event that gave rise to the asset or liability.

6.11   Current value measurement bases include:

(a)   fair value (see paragraphs 6.12–6.16);

(b)   value in use for assets and fulfilment value for liabilities (see paragraphs 6.17–6.20); and

(c)   current cost (see paragraphs 6.21–6.22).

Fair value

6.12   Fair value is the price that would be received to sell an asset, or paid to transfer a liability, in an orderly transaction between market participants at the measurement date.

6.13   Fair value reflects the perspective of market participants—participants in a market to which the entity has access. The asset or liability is measured using the same assumptions that market participants would use when pricing the asset or liability if those market participants act in their economic best interest.

6.14   In some cases, fair value can be determined directly by observing prices in an active market. In other cases, it is determined indirectly using measurement techniques, for example, cash-flow-based measurement techniques (see paragraphs 6.91–6.95), reflecting all the following factors:

(a)   estimates of future cash flows.

(b)   possible variations in the estimated amount or timing of future cash flows for the asset or liability being measured, caused by the uncertainty inherent in the cash flows.

(c)   the time value of money.

(d)   the price for bearing the uncertainty inherent in the cash flows (a risk premium or risk discount). The price for bearing that uncertainty depends on the extent of that uncertainty. It also reflects the fact that investors would generally pay less for an asset (and generally require more for taking on a liability) that has uncertain cash flows than for an asset (or liability) whose cash flows are certain.

(e)   other factors, for example, liquidity, if market participants would take those factors into account in the circumstances.

6.15   The factors mentioned in paragraphs 6.14(b) and 6.14(d) include the possibility that a counterparty may fail to fulfil its liability to the entity (credit risk), or that the entity may fail to fulfil its liability (own credit risk).

6.16   Because fair value is not derived, even in part, from the price of the transaction or other event that gave rise to the asset or liability, fair value is not increased by the transaction costs incurred when acquiring the asset and is not decreased by the transaction costs incurred when the liability is incurred or taken on. In addition, fair value does not reflect the transaction costs that would be incurred on the ultimate disposal of the asset or on transferring or settling the liability.

Value in use and fulfilment value

6.17   Value in use is the present value of the cash flows, or other economic benefits, that an entity expects to derive from the use of an asset and from its ultimate disposal. Fulfilment value is the present value of the cash, or other economic resources, that an entity expects to be obliged to transfer as it fulfils a liability. Those amounts of cash or other economic resources include not only the amounts to be transferred to the liability counterparty, but also the amounts that the entity expects to be obliged to transfer to other parties to enable it to fulfil the liability.

6.18   Because value in use and fulfilment value are based on future cash flows, they do not include transaction costs incurred on acquiring an asset or taking on a liability. However, value in use and fulfilment value include the present value of any transaction costs an entity expects to incur on the ultimate disposal of the asset or on fulfilling the liability.

6.19   Value in use and fulfilment value reflect entity-specific assumptions rather than assumptions by market participants. In practice, there may sometimes be little difference between the assumptions that market participants would use and those that an entity itself uses.

6.20   Value in use and fulfilment value cannot be observed directly and are determined using cash-flow-based measurement techniques (see paragraphs 6.91–6.95). Value in use and fulfilment value reflect the same factors described for fair value in paragraph 6.14, but from an entity-specific perspective rather than from a market-participant perspective.

Current cost

6.21   The current cost of an asset is the cost of an equivalent asset at the measurement date, comprising the consideration that would be paid at the measurement date plus the transaction costs that would be incurred at that date. The current cost of a liability is the consideration that would be received for an equivalent liability at the measurement date minus the transaction costs that would be incurred at that date. Current cost, like historical cost, is an entry value: it reflects prices in the market in which the entity would acquire the asset or would incur the liability. Hence, it is different from fair value, value in use and fulfilment value, which are exit values. However, unlike historical cost, current cost reflects conditions at the measurement date.

6.22   In some cases, current cost cannot be determined directly by observing prices in an active market and must be determined indirectly by other means. For example, if prices are available only for new assets, the current cost of a used asset might need to be estimated by adjusting the current price of a new asset to reflect the current age and condition of the asset held by the entity.

Information provided by particular measurement bases

6.23   When selecting a measurement basis, it is important to consider the nature of the information that the measurement basis will produce in both the statement of financial position and the statement(s) of financial performance. Table 6.1 summarises that information and paragraphs 6.24–6.42 provide additional discussion.

Historical cost

6.24 Information provided by measuring an asset or liability at historical cost may be relevant to users of financial statements, because historical cost uses information derived, at least in part, from the price of the transaction or other event that gave rise to the asset or liability.

6.25 Normally, if an entity acquired an asset in a recent transaction on market terms, the entity expects that the asset will provide sufficient economic benefits that the entity will at least recover the cost of the asset. Similarly, if a liability was incurred or taken on as a result of a recent transaction on market terms, the entity expects that the value of the obligation to transfer economic resources to fulfil the liability will normally be no more than the value of the consideration received minus transaction costs. Hence, measuring an asset or liability at historical cost in such cases provides relevant information about both the asset or liability and the price of the transaction that gave rise to that asset or liability.

6.26 Because historical cost is reduced to reflect consumption of an asset and its impairment, the amount expected to be recovered from an asset measured at historical cost is at least as great as its carrying amount. Similarly, because the historical cost of a liability is increased when it becomes onerous, the value of the obligation to transfer the economic resources needed to fulfil the liability is no more than the carrying amount of the liability.

6.27 If an asset other than a financial asset is measured at historical cost, consumption or sale of the asset, or of part of the asset, gives rise to an expense measured at the historical cost of the asset, or of part of the asset, consumed or sold.

6.28 The expense arising from the sale of an asset is recognised at the same time as the consideration for that sale is recognised as income. The difference between the income and the expense is the margin resulting from the sale. Expenses arising from consumption of an asset can be compared to related income to provide information about margins.

6.29 Similarly, if a liability other than a financial liability was incurred or taken on in exchange for consideration and is measured at historical cost, the fulfilment of all or part of the liability gives rise to income measured at the value of the consideration received for the part fulfilled. The difference between that income and the expenses incurred in fulfilling the liability is the margin resulting from the fulfilment.

6.30 Information about the cost of assets sold or consumed, including goods and services consumed immediately (see paragraph 4.8), and about the consideration received, may have predictive value. That information can be used as an input in predicting future margins from the future sale of goods (including goods not currently held by the entity) and services and hence to assess the entity's prospects for future net cash inflows. To assess an entity's prospects for future cash flows, users of financial statements often focus on the entity's prospects for generating future margins over many periods, not just on its prospects for generating margins from goods already held. Income and expenses measured at historical cost may also have confirmatory value because they may provide feedback to users of financial statements about their previous predictions of cash flows or of margins. Information about the cost of assets sold or consumed may also help in an assessment of how efficiently and effectively the entity's management has discharged its responsibilities to use the entity's economic resources.

6.31   For similar reasons, information about interest earned on assets, and interest incurred on liabilities, measured at amortised cost may have predictive and confirmatory value.

Current value

Fair value

6.32   Information provided by measuring assets and liabilities at fair value may have predictive value because fair value reflects market participants' current expectations about the amount, timing and uncertainty of future cash flows. These expectations are priced in a manner that reflects the current risk preferences of market participants. That information may also have confirmatory value by providing feedback about previous expectations.

6.33   Income and expenses reflecting market participants' current expectations may have some predictive value, because such income and expenses can be used as an input in predicting future income and expenses. Such income and expenses may also help in an assessment of how efficiently and effectively the entity's management has discharged its responsibilities to use the entity's economic resources.

6.34   A change in the fair value of an asset or liability can result from various factors identified in paragraph 6.14. When those factors have different characteristics, identifying separately income and expenses that result from those factors can provide useful information to users of financial statements (see paragraph 7.14(b)).

6.35   If an entity acquired an asset in one market and determines fair value using prices in a different market (the market in which the entity would sell the asset), any difference between the prices in those two markets is recognised as income when that fair value is first determined.

6.36   Sale of an asset or transfer of a liability would normally be for consideration of an amount similar to its fair value, if the transaction were to occur in the market that was the source for the prices used when measuring that fair value. In those cases, if the asset or liability is measured at fair value, the net income or net expenses arising at the time of the sale or transfer would usually be small, unless the effect of transaction costs is significant.

Value in use and fulfilment value

6.37   Value in use provides information about the present value of the estimated cash flows from the use of an asset and from its ultimate disposal. This information may have predictive value because it can be used in assessing the prospects for future net cash inflows.

6.38   Fulfilment value provides information about the present value of the estimated cash flows needed to fulfil a liability. Hence, fulfilment value may have predictive value, particularly if the liability will be fulfilled, rather than transferred or settled by negotiation.

6.39   Updated estimates of value in use or fulfilment value, combined with information about estimates of the amount, timing and uncertainty of future cash flows, may also have confirmatory value because they provide feedback about previous estimates of value in use or fulfilment value.

Current cost

6.40   Information about assets and liabilities measured at current cost may be relevant because current cost reflects the cost at which an equivalent asset could be acquired or created at the measurement date or the consideration that would be received for incurring or taking on an equivalent liability.

6.41   Like historical cost, current cost provides information about the cost of an asset consumed or about income from the fulfilment of liabilities. That information can be used to derive current margins and can be used as an input in predicting future margins. Unlike historical cost, current cost reflects prices prevailing at the time of consumption or fulfilment. When price changes are significant, margins based on current cost may be more useful for predicting future margins than margins based on historical cost.

6.42   To report the current cost of consumption (or current income from fulfilment), it is necessary to split the change in the carrying amount in the reporting period into the current cost of consumption (or current income from fulfilment), and the effect of changes in prices. The effect of a change in prices is sometimes referred to as a 'holding gain' or a 'holding loss'.

Table 6.1 – Summary of information provided by particular measurement bases

Assets

Statement of financial position				
	Historical cost	**Fair value (market-participant assumptions)**	**Value in use (entity-specific assumptions)**[a]	**Current cost**
Carrying amount	Historical cost (including transaction costs), to the extent unconsumed or uncollected, and recoverable. (Includes interest accrued on any financing component.)	Price that would be received to sell the asset (without deducting transaction costs on disposal).	Present value of future cash flows from the use of the asset and from its ultimate disposal (after deducting present value of transaction costs on disposal).	Current cost (including transaction costs), to the extent unconsumed or uncollected, and recoverable.

Statement(s) of financial performance				
Event	**Historical cost**	**Fair value (market-participant assumptions)**	**Value in use (entity-specific assumptions)**	**Current cost**
Initial recognition[b]	—	Difference between consideration paid and fair value of the asset acquired.[c] Transaction costs on acquiring the asset.	Difference between consideration paid and value in use of the asset acquired. Transaction costs on acquiring the asset.	—
Sale or consumption of the asset[d],[e]	Expenses equal to historical cost of the asset sold or consumed. Income received. (Could be presented gross or net.) Expenses for transaction costs on selling the asset.	Expenses equal to fair value of the asset sold or consumed. Income received. (Could be presented gross or net.) Expenses for transaction costs on selling the asset.	Expenses equal to value in use of the asset sold or consumed. Income received. (Could be presented gross or net.)	Expenses equal to current cost of the asset sold or consumed. Income received. (Could be presented gross or net.) Expenses for transaction costs on selling the asset.

continued...

...continued

	Statement(s) of financial performance			
Event	Historical cost	Fair value (market-participant assumptions)	Value in use (entity-specific assumptions)	Current cost
Interest income	Interest income, at historical rates, updated if the asset bears variable interest.	Reflected in income and expenses from changes in fair value. (Could be identified separately.)	Reflected in income and expenses from changes in value in use. (Could be identified separately.)	Interest income, at current rates.
Impairment	Expenses arising because historical cost is no longer recoverable.	Reflected in income and expenses from changes in fair value. (Could be identified separately.)	Reflected in income and expenses from changes in value in use. (Could be identified separately.)	Expenses arising because current cost is no longer recover-able.
Value changes	Not recognised, except to reflect an impairment.	Reflected in income and expenses from changes in fair value.	Reflected in income and expenses from changes in value in use.	Income and expenses reflecting the effect of changes in prices (holding gains and holding losses).
	For financial assets—income and expenses from changes in estimated cash flows.			

(a) This column summarises the information provided if value in use is used as a measurement basis. However, as noted in paragraph 6.75, value in use may not be a practical measurement basis for regular remeasurements.

(b) Income or expenses may arise on the initial recognition of an asset not acquired on market terms.

(c) Income or expenses may arise if the market in which an asset is acquired is different from the market that is the source of the prices used when measuring the fair value of the asset.

(d) Consumption of the asset is typically reported through cost of sales, depreciation or amortisation.

(e) Income received is often equal to the consideration received but will depend on the measurement basis used for any related liability.

Liabilities

Statement of financial position				
	Historical cost	**Fair value (market-participant assumptions)**	**Fulfilment value (entity-specific assumptions)**	**Current cost**
Carrying amount	Consideration received (net of transaction costs) for taking on the unfulfilled part of the liability, increased by excess of estimated cash outflows over consideration received. (Includes interest accrued on any financing component.)	Price that would be paid to transfer the unfulfilled part of the liability (not including transaction costs that would be incurred on transfer).	Present value of future cash flows that will arise in fulfilling the unfulfilled part of the liability (including present value of transaction costs to be incurred in fulfilment or transfer).	Consideration (net of transaction costs) that would be currently received for taking on the unfulfilled part of the liability, increased by excess of estimated cash outflows over that consideration.

Statement(s) of financial performance				
Event	**Historical cost**	**Fair value (market-participant assumptions)**	**Fulfilment value (entity-specific assumptions)**	**Current cost**
Initial recognition[a]	—	Difference between consideration received and the fair value of the liability.[b] Transaction costs on incurring or taking on the liability.	Difference between consideration received and the fulfilment value of the liability. Transaction costs on incurring or taking on the liability.	—

continued...

...continued

Statement(s) of financial performance				
Event	Historical cost	Fair value (market-participant assumptions)	Fulfilment value (entity-specific assumptions)	Current cost
Fulfilment of the liability	Income equal to historical cost of the liability fulfilled (reflects historical consideration). Expenses for costs incurred in fulfilling the liability. (Could be presented net or gross.)	Income equal to fair value of the liability fulfilled. Expenses for costs incurred in fulfilling the liability. (Could be presented net or gross. If gross, historical consideration could be presented separately.)	Income equal to fulfilment value of the liability fulfilled. Expenses for costs incurred in fulfilling the liability. (Could be presented net or gross. If gross, historical consideration could be presented separately.)	Income equal to current cost of the liability fulfilled (reflects current consideration). Expenses for costs incurred in fulfilling the liability. (Could be presented net or gross. If gross, historical consideration could be presented separately.)
Transfer of the liability	Income equal to historical cost of the liability transferred (reflects historical consideration). Expenses for costs paid (including transaction costs) to transfer the liability. (Could be presented net or gross.)	Income equal to fair value of the liability transferred. Expenses for costs paid (including transaction costs) to transfer the liability. (Could be presented net or gross.)	Income equal to fulfilment value of the liability transferred. Expenses for costs paid (including transaction costs) to transfer the liability. (Could be presented net or gross.)	Income equal to current cost of the liability transferred (reflects current consideration). Expenses for costs paid (including transaction costs) to transfer the liability. (Could be presented net or gross.)
Interest expenses	Interest expenses, at historical rates, updated if the liability bears variable interest.	Reflected in income and expenses from changes in fair value. (Could be identified separately.)	Reflected in income and expenses from changes in fulfilment value. (Could be identified separately.)	Interest expenses, at current rates.

continued...

...continued

Statement(s) of financial performance				
Event	Historical cost	Fair value (market-participant assumptions)	Fulfilment value (entity-specific assumptions)	Current cost
Effect of events that cause a liability to become onerous	Expenses equal to the excess of the estimated cash outflows over the historical cost of the liability, or a subsequent change in that excess.	Reflected in income and expenses from changes in fair value. (Could be identified separately.)	Reflected in income and expenses from changes in fulfilment value. (Could be identified separately.)	Expenses equal to the excess of the estimated cash outflows over the current cost of the liability, or a subsequent change in that excess.
Value changes	Not recognised except to the extent that the liability is onerous. For financial liabilities—income and expenses from changes in estimated cash flows.	Reflected in income and expenses from changes in fair value.	Reflected in income and expenses from changes in fulfilment value.	Income and expenses reflecting the effect of changes in prices (holding gains and holding losses).

(a) Income or expenses may arise on the initial recognition of a liability incurred or taken on not on market terms.

(b) Income or expenses may arise if the market in which a liability is incurred or taken on is different from the market that is the source of the prices used when measuring the fair value of the liability.

Factors to consider when selecting a measurement basis

6.43   In selecting a measurement basis for an asset or liability and for the related income and expenses, it is necessary to consider the nature of the information that the measurement basis will produce in both the statement of financial position and the statement(s) of financial performance (see paragraphs 6.23–6.42 and Table 6.1), as well as other factors (see paragraphs 6.44–6.86).

6.44   In most cases, no single factor will determine which measurement basis should be selected. The relative importance of each factor will depend on facts and circumstances.

6.45   The information provided by a measurement basis must be useful to users of financial statements. To achieve this, the information must be relevant and it must faithfully represent what it purports to represent. In addition, the information provided should be, as far as possible, comparable, verifiable, timely and understandable.

6.46   As explained in paragraph 2.21, the most efficient and effective process for applying the fundamental qualitative characteristics would usually be to identify the most relevant information about an economic phenomenon. If that information is not available or cannot be provided in a way that faithfully represents the economic phenomenon, the next most relevant type of information is considered. Paragraphs 6.49–6.76 provide further discussion of the role played by the qualitative characteristics in the selection of a measurement basis.

6.47   The discussion in paragraphs 6.49–6.76 focuses on the factors to be considered in selecting a measurement basis for recognised assets and recognised liabilities. Some of that discussion may also apply in selecting a measurement basis for information provided in the notes, for recognised or unrecognised items.

6.48   Paragraphs 6.77–6.82 discuss additional factors to consider in selecting a measurement basis on initial recognition. If the initial measurement basis is inconsistent with the subsequent measurement basis, income and expenses might be recognised at the time of the first subsequent measurement solely because of the change in measurement basis. Recognising such income and expenses might appear to depict a transaction or other event when, in fact, no such transaction or event has occurred. Hence, the choice of measurement basis for an asset or liability, and for the related income and expenses, is determined by considering both initial measurement and subsequent measurement.

Relevance

6.49   The relevance of information provided by a measurement basis for an asset or liability and for the related income and expenses is affected by:

    (a)   the characteristics of the asset or liability (see paragraphs 6.50–6.53); and

    (b)   how that asset or liability contributes to future cash flows (see paragraphs 6.54–6.57).

Characteristics of the asset or liability

6.50   The relevance of information provided by a measurement basis depends partly on the characteristics of the asset or liability, in particular, on the variability of cash flows and on whether the value of the asset or liability is sensitive to market factors or other risks.

6.51   If the value of an asset or liability is sensitive to market factors or other risks, its historical cost might differ significantly from its current value. Consequently, historical cost may not provide relevant information if information about changes in value is important to users of financial statements. For example, amortised cost cannot provide relevant information about a financial asset or financial liability that is a derivative.

6.52   Furthermore, if historical cost is used, changes in value are reported not when that value changes, but when an event such as disposal, impairment or fulfilment occurs. This could be incorrectly interpreted as implying that all the income and expenses recognised at the time of that event arose then, rather than over the periods during which the asset or liability was held. Moreover, because measurement at historical cost does not provide timely information about changes in value, income and expenses reported on that basis may lack predictive value and confirmatory value by not depicting the full effect of the entity's exposure to risk arising from holding the asset or liability during the reporting period.

6.53   Changes in the fair value of an asset or liability reflect changes in expectations of market participants and changes in their risk preferences. Depending on the characteristics of the asset or liability being measured and on the nature of the entity's business activities, information reflecting those changes may not always provide predictive value or confirmatory value to users of financial statements. This may be the case when the entity's business activities do not involve selling the asset or transferring the liability, for example, if the entity holds assets solely for use or solely for collecting contractual cash flows or if the entity is to fulfil liabilities itself.

Contribution to future cash flows

6.54   As noted in paragraph 1.14, some economic resources produce cash flows directly; in other cases, economic resources are used in combination to produce cash flows indirectly. How economic resources are used, and hence how assets and liabilities produce cash flows, depends in part on the nature of the business activities conducted by the entity.

6.55   When a business activity of an entity involves the use of several economic resources that produce cash flows indirectly, by being used in combination to produce and market goods or services to customers, historical cost or current cost is likely to provide relevant information about that activity. For example, property, plant and equipment is typically used in combination with an entity's other economic resources. Similarly, inventory typically cannot be sold to a customer, except by making extensive use of the entity's other economic resources (for example, in production and marketing activities). Paragraphs 6.24–6.31 and 6.40–6.42 explain how measuring such assets at historical cost or current cost can provide relevant information that can be used to derive margins achieved during the period.

6.56   For assets and liabilities that produce cash flows directly, such as assets that can be sold independently and without a significant economic penalty (for example, without significant business disruption), the measurement basis that provides the most relevant information is likely to be a current value that incorporates current estimates of the amount, timing and uncertainty of the future cash flows.

6.57   When a business activity of an entity involves managing financial assets and financial liabilities with the objective of collecting contractual cash flows, amortised cost may provide relevant information that can be used to derive the margin between the interest earned on the assets and the interest incurred on the liabilities. However, in assessing whether amortised cost will provide useful information, it is also necessary to consider the characteristics of the financial asset or financial liability. Amortised cost is unlikely to provide relevant information about cash flows that depend on factors other than principal and interest.

Faithful representation

6.58   When assets and liabilities are related in some way, using different measurement bases for those assets and liabilities can create a measurement inconsistency (accounting mismatch). If financial statements contain measurement inconsistencies, those financial statements may not faithfully represent some aspects of the entity's financial position and financial performance. Consequently, in some circumstances, using the same measurement basis for related assets and liabilities may provide users of financial statements with information that is more useful than the information that would result from using different measurement bases. This may be particularly likely when the cash flows from one asset or liability are directly linked to the cash flows from another asset or liability.

6.59   As noted in paragraphs 2.13 and 2.18, although a perfectly faithful representation is free from error, this does not mean that measures must be perfectly accurate in all respects.

6.60   When a measure cannot be determined directly by observing prices in an active market and must instead be estimated, measurement uncertainty arises. The level of measurement uncertainty associated with a particular measurement basis may affect whether information provided by that measurement basis provides a faithful representation of an entity's financial position and financial performance. A high level of measurement uncertainty does not necessarily prevent the use of a measurement basis that provides relevant information. However, in some cases the level of measurement uncertainty is so high that information provided by a measurement basis might not provide a sufficiently faithful representation (see paragraph 2.22). In such cases, it is appropriate to consider selecting a different measurement basis that would also result in relevant information.

6.61   Measurement uncertainty is different from both outcome uncertainty and existence uncertainty:

(a)   outcome uncertainty arises when there is uncertainty about the amount or timing of any inflow or outflow of economic benefits that will result from an asset or liability.

(b)   existence uncertainty arises when it is uncertain whether an asset or a liability exists. Paragraphs 5.12–5.14 discuss how existence uncertainty may affect decisions about whether an entity recognises an asset or liability when it is uncertain whether that asset or liability exists.

6.62 The presence of outcome uncertainty or existence uncertainty may sometimes contribute to measurement uncertainty. However, outcome uncertainty or existence uncertainty does not necessarily result in measurement uncertainty. For example, if the fair value of an asset can be determined directly by observing prices in an active market, no measurement uncertainty is associated with the measurement of that fair value, even if it is uncertain how much cash the asset will ultimately produce and hence there is outcome uncertainty.

Enhancing qualitative characteristics and the cost constraint

6.63 The enhancing qualitative characteristics of comparability, understandability and verifiability, and the cost constraint, have implications for the selection of a measurement basis. The following paragraphs discuss those implications. Paragraphs 6.69–6.76 discuss further implications specific to particular measurement bases. The enhancing qualitative characteristic of timeliness has no specific implications for measurement.

6.64 Just as cost constrains other financial reporting decisions, it also constrains the selection of a measurement basis. Hence, in selecting a measurement basis, it is important to consider whether the benefits of the information provided to users of financial statements by that measurement basis are likely to justify the costs of providing and using that information.

6.65 Consistently using the same measurement bases for the same items, either from period to period within a reporting entity or in a single period across entities, can help make financial statements more comparable.

6.66 A change in measurement basis can make financial statements less understandable. However, a change may be justified if other factors outweigh the reduction in understandability, for example, if the change results in more relevant information. If a change is made, users of financial statements may need explanatory information to enable them to understand the effect of that change.

6.67 Understandability depends partly on how many different measurement bases are used and on whether they change over time. In general, if more measurement bases are used in a set of financial statements, the resulting information becomes more complex and, hence, less understandable and the totals or subtotals in the statement of financial position and the statement(s) of financial performance become less informative. However, it could be appropriate to use more measurement bases if that is necessary to provide useful information.

6.68 Verifiability is enhanced by using measurement bases that result in measures that can be independently corroborated either directly, for example, by observing prices, or indirectly, for example, by checking inputs to a model. If a measure cannot be verified, users of financial statements may need explanatory information to enable them to understand how the measure was determined. In some such cases, it may be necessary to specify the use of a different measurement basis.

Historical cost

6.69　In many situations, it is simpler, and hence less costly, to measure historical cost than it is to measure a current value. In addition, measures determined applying a historical cost measurement basis are generally well understood and, in many cases, verifiable.

6.70　However, estimating consumption and identifying and measuring impairment losses or onerous liabilities can be subjective. Hence, the historical cost of an asset or liability can sometimes be as difficult to measure or verify as a current value.

6.71　Using a historical cost measurement basis, identical assets acquired, or liabilities incurred, at different times can be reported in the financial statements at different amounts. This can reduce comparability, both from period to period for a reporting entity and in a single period across entities.

Current value

6.72　Because fair value is determined from the perspective of market participants, not from an entity-specific perspective, and is independent of when the asset was acquired or the liability was incurred, identical assets or liabilities measured at fair value will, in principle, be measured at the same amount by entities that have access to the same markets. This can enhance comparability both from period to period for a reporting entity and in a single period across entities. In contrast, because value in use and fulfilment value reflect an entity-specific perspective, those measures could differ for identical assets or liabilities in different entities. Those differences may reduce comparability, particularly if the assets or liabilities contribute to cash flows in a similar manner.

6.73　If the fair value of an asset or liability can be determined directly by observing prices in an active market, the process of fair value measurement is low-cost, simple and easy to understand; and the fair value can be verified through direct observation.

6.74　Valuation techniques, sometimes including the use of cash-flow-based measurement techniques, may be needed to estimate fair value when it cannot be observed directly in an active market and are generally needed when determining value in use and fulfilment value. Depending on the techniques used:

(a)　estimating inputs to the valuation and applying the valuation technique may be costly and complex.

(b)　the inputs into the process may be subjective and it may be difficult to verify both the inputs and the validity of the process itself. Consequently, the measures of identical assets or liabilities may differ. That would reduce comparability.

6.75　In many cases, value in use cannot be determined meaningfully for an individual asset used in combination with other assets. Instead, the value in use is determined for a group of assets and the result may then need to be allocated to individual assets. This process can be subjective and arbitrary. In addition, estimates of value in use for an asset may inadvertently reflect the effect of synergies with other assets in the group. Hence, determining the value in use of an asset used in combination with other assets can be a costly process and its complexity and subjectivity reduces verifiability. For these reasons, value in use may not be a practical measurement basis for regular remeasurements of such assets. However, it may be useful for occasional remeasurements of assets, for example, when it is used in an impairment test to determine whether historical cost is fully recoverable.

6.76 Using a current cost measurement basis, identical assets acquired or liabilities incurred at different times are reported in the financial statements at the same amount. This can enhance comparability, both from period to period for a reporting entity and in a single period across entities. However, determining current cost can be complex, subjective and costly. For example, as noted in paragraph 6.22, it may be necessary to estimate the current cost of an asset by adjusting the current price of a new asset to reflect the current age and condition of the asset held by the entity. In addition, because of changes in technology and changes in business practices, many assets would not be replaced with identical assets. Thus, a further subjective adjustment to the current price of a new asset would be required in order to estimate the current cost of an asset equivalent to the existing asset. Also, splitting changes in current cost carrying amounts between the current cost of consumption and the effect of changes in prices (see paragraph 6.42) may be complex and require arbitrary assumptions. Because of these difficulties, current cost measures may lack verifiability and understandability.

Factors specific to initial measurement

6.77 Paragraphs 6.43–6.76 discuss factors to consider when selecting a measurement basis, whether for initial recognition or subsequent measurement. Paragraphs 6.78–6.82 discuss some additional factors to consider at initial recognition.

6.78 At initial recognition, the cost of an asset acquired, or of a liability incurred, as a result of an event that is a transaction on market terms is normally similar to its fair value at that date, unless transaction costs are significant. Nevertheless, even if those two amounts are similar, it is necessary to describe what measurement basis is used at initial recognition. If historical cost will be used subsequently, that measurement basis is also normally appropriate at initial recognition. Similarly, if a current value will be used subsequently, it is also normally appropriate at initial recognition. Using the same measurement basis for initial recognition and subsequent measurement avoids recognising income or expenses at the time of the first subsequent measurement solely because of a change in measurement basis (see paragraph 6.48).

6.79 When an entity acquires an asset, or incurs a liability, in exchange for transferring another asset or liability as a result of a transaction on market terms, the initial measure of the asset acquired, or the liability incurred, determines whether any income or expenses arise from the transaction. When an asset or liability is measured at cost, no income or expenses arise at initial recognition, unless income or expenses arise from the derecognition of the transferred asset or liability, or unless the asset is impaired or the liability is onerous.

6.80   Assets may be acquired, or liabilities may be incurred, as a result of an event that is not a transaction on market terms. For example:

(a)   the transaction price may be affected by relationships between the parties, or by financial distress or other duress of one of the parties;

(b)   an asset may be granted to the entity free of charge by a government or donated to the entity by another party;

(c)   a liability may be imposed by legislation or regulation; or

(d)   a liability to pay compensation or a penalty may arise from an act of wrongdoing.

6.81   In such cases, measuring the asset acquired, or the liability incurred, at its historical cost may not provide a faithful representation of the entity's assets and liabilities and of any income or expenses arising from the transaction or other event. Hence, it may be appropriate to measure the asset acquired, or the liability incurred, at deemed cost, as described in paragraph 6.6. Any difference between that deemed cost and any consideration given or received would be recognised as income or expenses at initial recognition.

6.82   When assets are acquired, or liabilities incurred, as a result of an event that is not a transaction on market terms, all relevant aspects of the transaction or other event need to be identified and considered. For example, it may be necessary to recognise other assets, other liabilities, contributions from holders of equity claims or distributions to holders of equity claims to faithfully represent the substance of the effect of the transaction or other event on the entity's financial position (see paragraphs 4.59–4.62) and any related effect on the entity's financial performance.

More than one measurement basis

6.83   Sometimes, consideration of the factors described in paragraphs 6.43–6.76 may lead to the conclusion that more than one measurement basis is needed for an asset or liability and for related income and expenses in order to provide relevant information that faithfully represents both the entity's financial position and its financial performance.

6.84   In most cases, the most understandable way to provide that information is:

(a)   to use a single measurement basis both for the asset or liability in the statement of financial position and for related income and expenses in the statement(s) of financial performance; and

(b)   to provide in the notes additional information applying a different measurement basis.

6.85   However, in some cases, that information is more relevant, or results in a more faithful representation of both the entity's financial position and its financial performance, through the use of:

(a) a current value measurement basis for the asset or liability in the statement of financial position; and

(b) a different measurement basis for the related income and expenses in the statement of profit or loss[10] (see paragraphs 7.17–7.18).

In selecting those measurement bases, it is necessary to consider the factors discussed in paragraphs 6.43–6.76.

6.86 In such cases, the total income or total expenses arising in the period from the change in the current value of the asset or liability is separated and classified (see paragraphs 7.14–7.19) so that:

(a) the statement of profit or loss includes the income or expenses measured applying the measurement basis selected for that statement; and

(b) other comprehensive income includes all the remaining income or expenses. As a result, the accumulated other comprehensive income related to that asset or liability equals the difference between:

(i) the carrying amount of the asset or liability in the statement of financial position; and

(ii) the carrying amount that would have been determined applying the measurement basis selected for the statement of profit or loss.

Measurement of equity

6.87 The total carrying amount of equity (total equity) is not measured directly. It equals the total of the carrying amounts of all recognised assets less the total of the carrying amounts of all recognised liabilities.

6.88 Because general purpose financial statements are not designed to show an entity's value, the total carrying amount of equity will not generally equal:

(a) the aggregate market value of equity claims on the entity;

(b) the amount that could be raised by selling the entity as a whole on a going concern basis; or

(c) the amount that could be raised by selling all of the entity's assets and settling all of its liabilities.

6.89 Although total equity is not measured directly, it may be appropriate to measure directly the carrying amount of some individual classes of equity (see paragraph 4.65) and some components of equity (see paragraph 4.66). Nevertheless, because total equity is measured as a residual, at least one class of equity cannot be measured directly. Similarly, at least one component of equity cannot be measured directly.

---

10 The *Conceptual Framework* does not specify whether the statement(s) of financial performance comprise(s) a single statement or two statements. The *Conceptual Framework* uses the term 'statement of profit or loss' to refer both to a separate statement and to a separate section within a single statement of financial performance.

6.90　　The total carrying amount of an individual class of equity or component of equity is normally positive, but can be negative in some circumstances. Similarly, total equity is generally positive, but it can be negative, depending on which assets and liabilities are recognised and on how they are measured.

Cash-flow-based measurement techniques

6.91　　Sometimes, a measure cannot be observed directly. In some such cases, one way to estimate the measure is by using cash-flow-based measurement techniques. Such techniques are not measurement bases. They are techniques used in applying a measurement basis. Hence, when using such a technique, it is necessary to identify which measurement basis is used and the extent to which the technique reflects the factors applicable to that measurement basis. For example, if the measurement basis is fair value, the applicable factors are those described in paragraph 6.14.

6.92　　Cash-flow-based measurement techniques can be used in applying a modified measurement basis, for example, fulfilment value modified to exclude the effect of the possibility that the entity may fail to fulfil a liability (own credit risk). Modifying measurement bases may sometimes result in information that is more relevant to the users of financial statements or that may be less costly to produce or to understand. However, modified measurement bases may also be more difficult for users of financial statements to understand.

6.93　　Outcome uncertainty (see paragraph 6.61(a)) arises from uncertainties about the amount or timing of future cash flows. Those uncertainties are important characteristics of assets and liabilities. When measuring an asset or liability by reference to estimates of uncertain future cash flows, one factor to consider is possible variations in the estimated amount or timing of those cash flows (see paragraph 6.14(b)). Those variations are considered in selecting a single amount from within the range of possible cash flows. The amount selected is itself sometimes the amount of a possible outcome, but this is not always the case. The amount that provides the most relevant information is usually one from within the central part of the range (a central estimate). Different central estimates provide different information. For example:

　　(a)　　the expected value (the probability-weighted average, also known as the statistical mean) reflects the entire range of outcomes and gives more weight to the outcomes that are more likely. The expected value is not intended to predict the ultimate inflow or outflow of cash or other economic benefits arising from that asset or liability.

　　(b)　　the maximum amount that is more likely than not to occur (similar to the statistical median) indicates that the probability of a subsequent loss is no more than 50% and that the probability of a subsequent gain is no more than 50%.

　　(c)　　the most likely outcome (the statistical mode) is the single most likely ultimate inflow or outflow arising from an asset or liability.

6.94   A central estimate depends on estimates of future cash flows and possible variations in their amounts or timing. It does not capture the price for bearing the uncertainty that the ultimate outcome may differ from that central estimate (that is, the factor described in paragraph 6.14(d)).

6.95   No central estimate gives complete information about the range of possible outcomes. Hence users may need information about the range of possible outcomes.

CONTENTS

Presentation and disclosure as communication tools

7.1   A reporting entity communicates information about its assets, liabilities, equity, income and expenses by presenting and disclosing information in its financial statements.

7.2   Effective communication of information in financial statements makes that information more relevant and contributes to a faithful representation of an entity's assets, liabilities, equity, income and expenses. It also enhances the understandability and comparability of information in financial statements. Effective communication of information in financial statements requires:

(a)   focusing on presentation and disclosure objectives and principles rather than focusing on rules;

(b)   classifying information in a manner that groups similar items and separates dissimilar items; and

(c)   aggregating information in such a way that it is not obscured either by unnecessary detail or by excessive aggregation.

7.3   Just as cost constrains other financial reporting decisions, it also constrains decisions about presentation and disclosure. Hence, in making decisions about presentation and disclosure, it is important to consider whether the benefits provided to users of financial statements by presenting or disclosing particular information are likely to justify the costs of providing and using that information.

Presentation and disclosure objectives and principles

7.4   To facilitate effective communication of information in financial statements, when developing presentation and disclosure requirements in Standards a balance is needed between:

(a)   giving entities the flexibility to provide relevant information that faithfully represents the entity's assets, liabilities, equity, income and expenses; and

(b)   requiring information that is comparable, both from period to period for a reporting entity and in a single reporting period across entities.

7.5   Including presentation and disclosure objectives in Standards supports effective communication in financial statements because such objectives help entities to identify useful information and to decide how to communicate that information in the most effective manner.

7.6   Effective communication in financial statements is also supported by considering the following principles:

(a)   entity-specific information is more useful than standardised descriptions, sometimes referred to as 'boilerplate'; and

(b)   duplication of information in different parts of the financial statements is usually unnecessary and can make financial statements less understandable.

Classification

7.7   Classification is the sorting of assets, liabilities, equity, income or expenses on the basis of shared characteristics for presentation and disclosure purposes. Such characteristics include—but are not limited to—the nature of the item, its role (or function) within the business activities conducted by the entity, and how it is measured.

7.8   Classifying dissimilar assets, liabilities, equity, income or expenses together can obscure relevant information, reduce understandability and comparability and may not provide a faithful representation of what it purports to represent.

Classification of assets and liabilities

7.9   Classification is applied to the unit of account selected for an asset or liability (see paragraphs 4.48–4.55). However, it may sometimes be appropriate to separate an asset or liability into components that have different characteristics and to classify those components separately. That would be appropriate when classifying those components separately would enhance the usefulness of the resulting financial information. For example, it could be appropriate to separate an asset or liability into current and non-current components and to classify those components separately.

Offsetting

7.10   Offsetting occurs when an entity recognises and measures both an asset and liability as separate units of account, but groups them into a single net amount in the statement of financial position. Offsetting classifies dissimilar items together and therefore is generally not appropriate.

7.11   Offsetting assets and liabilities differs from treating a set of rights and obligations as a single unit of account (see paragraphs 4.48–4.55).

Classification of equity

7.12   To provide useful information, it may be necessary to classify equity claims separately if those equity claims have different characteristics (see paragraph 4.65).

7.13   Similarly, to provide useful information, it may be necessary to classify components of equity separately if some of those components are subject to particular legal, regulatory or other requirements. For example, in some jurisdictions, an entity is permitted to make distributions to holders of equity claims only if the entity has sufficient reserves specified as distributable (see paragraph 4.66). Separate presentation or disclosure of those reserves may provide useful information.

Classification of income and expenses

7.14   Classification is applied to:

(a)   income and expenses resulting from the unit of account selected for an asset or liability; or

(b)   components of such income and expenses if those components have different characteristics and are identified separately. For example, a change in the current value of an asset can include the effects of value changes and the accrual of interest (see Table 6.1). It would be appropriate to classify those components separately if doing so would enhance the usefulness of the resulting financial information.

Profit or loss and other comprehensive income

7.15   Income and expenses are classified and included either:

(a)   in the statement of profit or loss;[11] or

(b)   outside the statement of profit or loss, in other comprehensive income.

7.16   The statement of profit or loss is the primary source of information about an entity's financial performance for the reporting period. That statement contains a total for profit or loss that provides a highly summarised depiction of the entity's financial performance for the period. Many users of financial statements incorporate that total in their analysis either as a starting point for that analysis or as the main indicator of the entity's financial performance for the period. Nevertheless, understanding an entity's financial performance for the period requires an analysis of all recognised income and expenses — including income and expenses included in other comprehensive income — as well as an analysis of other information included in the financial statements.

7.17   Because the statement of profit or loss is the primary source of information about an entity's financial performance for the period, all income and expenses are, in principle, included in that statement. However, in developing Standards, the Board may decide in exceptional circumstances that income or expenses arising from a change in the current value of an asset or liability are to be included in other comprehensive income when doing so would result in the statement of profit or loss providing more relevant information, or providing a more faithful representation of the entity's financial performance for that period.

7.18   Income and expenses that arise on a historical cost measurement basis (see Table 6.1) are included in the statement of profit or loss. That is also the case when income and expenses of that type are separately identified as a component of a change in the current value of an asset or liability. For example, if a financial asset is measured at current value and if interest

---

11 The *Conceptual Framework* does not specify whether the statement(s) of financial performance comprise(s) a single statement or two statements. The *Conceptual Framework* uses the term 'statement of profit or loss' to refer to a separate statement and to a separate section within a single statement of financial performance. Likewise, it uses the term 'total for profit or loss' to refer both to a total for a separate statement and to a subtotal for a section within a single statement of financial performance.

income is identified separately from other changes in value, that interest income is included in the statement of profit or loss.

7.19 In principle, income and expenses included in other comprehensive income in one period are reclassified from other comprehensive income into the statement of profit or loss in a future period when doing so results in the statement of profit or loss providing more relevant information, or providing a more faithful representation of the entity's financial performance for that future period. However, if, for example, there is no clear basis for identifying the period in which reclassification would have that result, or the amount that should be reclassified, the Board may, in developing Standards, decide that income and expenses included in other comprehensive income are not to be subsequently reclassified.

Aggregation

7.20 Aggregation is the adding together of assets, liabilities, equity, income or expenses that have shared characteristics and are included in the same classification.

7.21 Aggregation makes information more useful by summarising a large volume of detail. However, aggregation conceals some of that detail. Hence, a balance needs to be found so that relevant information is not obscured either by a large amount of insignificant detail or by excessive aggregation.

7.22 Different levels of aggregation may be needed in different parts of the financial statements. For example, typically, the statement of financial position and the statement(s) of financial performance provide summarised information and more detailed information is provided in the notes.

CONTENTS

> *The material included in Chapter 8 has been carried forward unchanged from the* Conceptual Framework for Financial Reporting *issued in 2010. That material originally appeared in the* Framework for the Preparation and Presentation of Financial Statements *issued in 1989.*

Concepts of capital

8.1 A financial concept of capital is adopted by most entities in preparing their financial statements. Under a financial concept of capital, such as invested money or invested purchasing power, capital is synonymous with the net assets or equity of the entity. Under a physical concept of capital, such as operating capability, capital is regarded as the productive capacity of the entity based on, for example, units of output per day.

8.2 The selection of the appropriate concept of capital by an entity should be based on the needs of the users of its financial statements. Thus, a financial concept of capital should be adopted if the users of financial statements are primarily concerned with the maintenance of nominal invested capital or the purchasing power of invested capital. If, however, the main concern of users is with the operating capability of the entity, a physical concept of capital should be used. The concept chosen indicates the goal to be attained in determining profit, even though there may be some measurement difficulties in making the concept operational.

Concepts of capital maintenance and the determination of profit

8.3 The concepts of capital in paragraph 8.1 give rise to the following concepts of capital maintenance:

(a) *Financial capital maintenance*. Under this concept a profit is earned only if the financial (or money) amount of the net assets at the end of the period exceeds the financial (or money) amount of net assets at the beginning of the period, after excluding any distributions to, and contributions from, owners during the period. Financial capital maintenance can be measured in either nominal monetary units or units of constant purchasing power.

(b) *Physical capital maintenance*. Under this concept a profit is earned only if the physical productive capacity (or operating capability) of the entity (or the resources or funds needed to achieve that capacity) at the end of the period exceeds the physical productive capacity at the beginning of the period, after excluding any distributions to, and contributions from, owners during the period.

8.4 The concept of capital maintenance is concerned with how an entity defines the capital that it seeks to maintain. It provides the linkage between the concepts of capital and the concepts of profit because it provides the point of reference by which profit is measured; it is a prerequisite for distinguishing between an entity's return on capital and its return of capital; only inflows of assets in excess of amounts needed to maintain capital may be regarded as profit and therefore as a return on capital. Hence, profit is the residual amount that remains after expenses (including capital maintenance adjustments, where appropriate) have been deducted from income. If expenses exceed income the residual amount is a loss.

8.5   The physical capital maintenance concept requires the adoption of the current cost basis of measurement. The financial capital maintenance concept, however, does not require the use of a particular basis of measurement. Selection of the basis under this concept is dependent on the type of financial capital that the entity is seeking to maintain.

8.6   The principal difference between the two concepts of capital maintenance is the treatment of the effects of changes in the prices of assets and liabilities of the entity. In general terms, an entity has maintained its capital if it has as much capital at the end of the period as it had at the beginning of the period. Any amount over and above that required to maintain the capital at the beginning of the period is profit.

8.7   Under the concept of financial capital maintenance where capital is defined in terms of nominal monetary units, profit represents the increase in nominal money capital over the period. Thus, increases in the prices of assets held over the period, conventionally referred to as holding gains, are, conceptually, profits. They may not be recognised as such, however, until the assets are disposed of in an exchange transaction. When the concept of financial capital maintenance is defined in terms of constant purchasing power units, profit represents the increase in invested purchasing power over the period. Thus, only that part of the increase in the prices of assets that exceeds the increase in the general level of prices is regarded as profit. The rest of the increase is treated as a capital maintenance adjustment and, hence, as part of equity.

8.8   Under the concept of physical capital maintenance when capital is defined in terms of the physical productive capacity, profit represents the increase in that capital over the period. All price changes affecting the assets and liabilities of the entity are viewed as changes in the measurement of the physical productive capacity of the entity; hence, they are treated as capital maintenance adjustments that are part of equity and not as profit.

8.9   The selection of the measurement bases and concept of capital maintenance will determine the accounting model used in the preparation of the financial statements. Different accounting models exhibit different degrees of relevance and reliability and, as in other areas, management must seek a balance between relevance and reliability. This *Conceptual Framework* is applicable to a range of accounting models and provides guidance on preparing and presenting the financial statements constructed under the chosen model. At the present time, it is not the intention of the Board to prescribe a particular model other than in exceptional circumstances, such as for those entities reporting in the currency of a hyperinflationary economy. This intention will, however, be reviewed in the light of world developments.

Capital maintenance adjustments

8.10   The revaluation or restatement of assets and liabilities gives rise to increases or decreases in equity. While these increases or decreases meet the definition of income and expenses, they are not included in the income statement under certain concepts of capital maintenance. Instead these items are included in equity as capital maintenance adjustments or revaluation reserves.

Appendix
Defined terms

The following defined terms are extracted or derived from the relevant paragraphs of the Conceptual Framework for Financial Reporting.

aggregation	The adding together of assets, liabilities, equity, income or expenses that have shared characteristics and are included in the same classification.	CF.7.20
asset	A present economic resource controlled by the entity as a result of past events.	CF.4.3
carrying amount	The amount at which an asset, a liability or equity is recognised in the statement of financial position.	CF.5.1
classification	The sorting of assets, liabilities, equity, income or expenses on the basis of shared characteristics for presentation and disclosure purposes.	CF.7.7
combined financial statements	Financial statements of a reporting entity that comprises two or more entities that are not all linked by a parent-subsidiary relationship.	CF.3.12
consolidated financial statements	Financial statements of a reporting entity that comprises both the parent and its subsidiaries.	CF.3.11
control of an economic resource	The present ability to direct the use of the economic resource and obtain the economic benefits that may flow from it.	CF.4.20
derecognition	The removal of all or part of a recognised asset or liability from an entity's statement of financial position.	CF.5.26
economic resource	A right that has the potential to produce economic benefits.	CF.4.4
enhancing qualitative characteristic	A qualitative characteristic that makes useful information more useful. The enhancing qualitative characteristics are comparability, verifiability, timeliness and understandability.	CF.2.4, CF.2.23
equity	The residual interest in the assets of the entity after deducting all its liabilities.	CF.4.63
equity claim	A claim on the residual interest in the assets of the entity after deducting all its liabilities.	CF.4.64
executory contract	A contract, or a portion of a contract, that is equally unperformed — neither party has fulfilled any of its obligations, or both parties have partially fulfilled their obligations to an equal extent.	CF.4.56
existence uncertainty	Uncertainty about whether an asset or liability exists.	CF.4.13, CF.4.35

continued...

...continued

expenses	Decreases in assets, or increases in liabilities, that result in decreases in equity, other than those relating to distributions to holders of equity claims.	CF.4.69
fundamental qualitative characteristic	A qualitative characteristic that financial information must possess to be useful to the primary users of general purpose financial reports. The fundamental qualitative characteristics are relevance and faithful representation.	CF.2.4, CF.2.5
general purpose financial report	A report that provides financial information about the reporting entity's economic resources, claims against the entity and changes in those economic resources and claims that is useful to primary users in making decisions relating to providing resources to the entity.	CF.1.2, CF.1.12
general purpose financial statements	A particular form of general purpose financial reports that provide information about the reporting entity's assets, liabilities, equity, income and expenses.	CF.3.2
income	Increases in assets, or decreases in liabilities, that result in increases in equity, other than those relating to contributions from holders of equity claims.	CF.4.68
liability	A present obligation of the entity to transfer an economic resource as a result of past events.	CF.4.26
material information	Information is material if omitting, misstating, or obscuring it could reasonably be expected to influence decisions that the primary users of general purpose financial reports make on the basis of those reports, which provide financial information about a specific reporting entity.	CF.2.11
measure	The result of applying a measurement basis to an asset or liability and related income and expenses.	CF.6.1
measurement basis	An identified feature—for example, historical cost, fair value or fulfilment value—of an item being measured.	CF.6.1
measurement uncertainty	Uncertainty that arises when monetary amounts in financial reports cannot be observed directly and must instead be estimated.	CF.2.19
offsetting	Grouping an asset and liability that are recognised and measured as separate units of account into a single net amount in the statement of financial position.	CF.7.10

continued...

...continued

outcome uncertainty	Uncertainty about the amount or timing of any inflow or outflow of economic benefits that will result from an asset or liability.	CF.6.61
potential to produce economic benefits	Within an economic resource, a feature that already exists and that, in at least one circumstance, would produce for the entity economic benefits beyond those available to all other parties.	CF.4.14
primary users (of general purpose financial reports)	Existing and potential investors, lenders and other creditors.	CF.1.2
prudence	The exercise of caution when making judgements under conditions of uncertainty. The exercise of prudence means that assets and income are not overstated and liabilities and expenses are not understated. Equally, the exercise of prudence does not allow for the understatement of assets or income or the overstatement of liabilities or expenses.	CF.2.16
recognition	The process of capturing for inclusion in the statement of financial position or the statement(s) of financial performance an item that meets the definition of one of the elements of financial statements — an asset, a liability, equity, income or expenses. Recognition involves depicting the item in one of those statements — either alone or in aggregation with other items — in words and by a monetary amount, and including that amount in one or more totals in that statement.	CF.5.1
reporting entity	An entity that is required, or chooses, to prepare general purpose financial statements.	CF.3.10
unconsolidated financial statements	Financial statements of a reporting entity that is the parent alone.	CF.3.11
unit of account	The right or the group of rights, the obligation or the group of obligations, or the group of rights and obligations, to which recognition criteria and measurement concepts are applied.	CF.4.48
useful financial information	Financial information that is useful to primary users of general purpose financial reports in making decisions relating to providing resources to the reporting entity. To be useful, financial information must be relevant and faithfully represent what it purports to represent.	CF.1.2, CF.2.4

continued...

...continued

| **users (of general purpose financial reports)** | See primary users (of general purpose financial reports). | – |

Approval by the Board of the *Conceptual Framework for Financial Reporting* issued in March 2018

The *Conceptual Framework for Financial Reporting* was approved for issue by 13 of the 14 members of the International Accounting Standards Board. Ms Tarca abstained in view of her recent appointment to the Board.

Hans Hoogervorst	Chairman
Suzanne Lloyd	Vice-Chair
Nick Anderson	
Martin Edelmann	
Françoise Flores	
Amaro Luiz De Oliveira Gomes	
Gary Kabureck	
Jianqiao Lu	
Takatsugu Ochi	
Darrel Scott	
Thomas Scott	
Chungwoo Suh	
Ann Tarca	
Mary Tokar	

First-time Adoption of International Financial Reporting Standards

In April 2001 the International Accounting Standards Board (Board) adopted SIC-8 *First-time Application of IASs as the Primary Basis of Accounting*, which had been issued by the Standing Interpretations Committee of the International Accounting Standards Committee in July 1998.

In June 2003 the Board issued IFRS 1 *First-time Adoption of International Financial Reporting Standards* to replace SIC-8. IAS 1 *Presentation of Financial Statements* (as revised in 2007) amended the terminology used throughout IFRS Standards, including IFRS 1.

The Board restructured IFRS 1 in November 2008. In December 2010 the Board amended IFRS 1 to reflect that a first-time adopter would restate past transactions from the date of transition to IFRS Standards instead of at 1 January 2004.

Since it was issued in 2003, IFRS 1 was amended to accommodate first-time adoption requirements resulting from new or amended Standards. IFRS 1 was amended by *Government Loans* (issued March 2012), which added an exception to the retrospective application of IFRS to require that first time adopters apply the requirements in IFRS 9 *Financial Instruments* and IAS 20 *Accounting for Government Grants and Disclosure of Government Assistance* prospectively to government loans existing at the date of transition to IFRS.

Other Standards have made minor amendments to IFRS 1. They include *Improvements to IFRSs* (issued May 2010), Revised IFRS 3 *Business Combinations* (issued January 2008), *Severe Hyperinflation and Removal of Fixed Dates for First-time Adopters* (Amendments to IFRS 1) (issued December 2010), IFRS 10 *Consolidated Financial Statements* (issued May 2011), IFRS 11 *Joint Arrangements* (issued May 2011), IFRS 13 *Fair Value Measurement* (issued May 2011), IAS 19 *Employee Benefits* (issued June 2011), *Presentation of Items of Other Comprehensive Income* (Amendments to IAS 1) (issued June 2011), IFRIC 20 *Stripping Costs in the Production Phase of a Surface Mine* (issued October 2011), *Government Loans* (issued March 2012), *Annual Improvements to IFRSs 2009–2011 Cycle* (issued May 2012), *Consolidated Financial Statements, Joint Arrangements and Disclosure of Interests in Other Entities: Transition Guidance* (Amendments to IFRS 10, IFRS 11 and IFRS 12) (issued June 2012), *Investment Entities* (Amendments to IFRS 10, IFRS 12 and IAS 27) (issued October 2012), IFRS 9 *Financial Instruments* (Hedge Accounting and amendments to IFRS 9, IFRS 7 and IAS 39) (issued November 2013), IFRS 14 *Regulatory Deferral Accounts* (issued January 2014), *Accounting for Acquisitions of Interests in Joint Operations* (Amendments to IFRS 11) (issued May 2014), IFRS 15 *Revenue from Contracts with Customers* (issued May 2014), IFRS 9 *Financial Instruments* (issued July 2014), *Equity Method in Separate Financial Statements* (Amendments to IAS 27) (issued August 2014), IFRS 16 *Leases* (issued January 2016), *Annual Improvements to IFRS Standards 2014–2016 Cycle* (issued December 2016), which deleted several lapsed short-term exemptions, IFRIC 22 *Foreign Currency Transactions and Advance Consideration* (issued December 2016), IFRIC 23 *Uncertainty over Income Tax Treatments* (issued June 2017), *Amendments to References to the Conceptual Framework in IFRS Standards* (issued March 2018) and *Annual Improvements to IFRS Standards 2018–2020* (issued May 2020).

CONTENTS

FOR THE ACCOMPANYING GUIDANCE LISTED BELOW, SEE PART B OF THIS EDITION

FOR THE BASIS FOR CONCLUSIONS, SEE PART C OF THIS EDITION

© IFRS Foundation

International Financial Reporting Standard 1 *First-time Adoption of International Financial Reporting Standards* (IFRS 1) is set out in paragraphs 1–40 and Appendices A–E. All the paragraphs have equal authority. Paragraphs in **bold type** state the main principles. Terms defined in Appendix A are in *italics* the first time they appear in the IFRS. Definitions of other terms are given in the Glossary for International Financial Reporting Standards. IFRS 1 should be read in the context of its objective and the Basis for Conclusions, the *Preface to IFRS Standards* and the *Conceptual Framework for Financial Reporting.* IAS 8 *Accounting Policies, Changes in Accounting Estimates and Errors* provides a basis for selecting and applying accounting policies in the absence of explicit guidance.

International Financial Reporting Standard 1
First-time Adoption of International Financial Reporting Standards

Objective

1   The objective of this IFRS is to ensure that an entity's *first IFRS financial statements*, and its interim financial reports for part of the period covered by those financial statements, contain high quality information that:

(a)   is transparent for users and comparable over all periods presented;

(b)   provides a suitable starting point for accounting in accordance with *International Financial Reporting Standards (IFRSs)*; and

(c)   can be generated at a cost that does not exceed the benefits.

Scope

2   An entity shall apply this IFRS in:

(a)   its first IFRS financial statements; and

(b)   each interim financial report, if any, that it presents in accordance with IAS 34 *Interim Financial Reporting* for part of the period covered by its first IFRS financial statements.

3   An entity's first IFRS financial statements are the first annual financial statements in which the entity adopts IFRSs, by an explicit and unreserved statement in those financial statements of compliance with IFRSs. Financial statements in accordance with IFRSs are an entity's first IFRS financial statements if, for example, the entity:

(a)   presented its most recent previous financial statements:

(i)   in accordance with national requirements that are not consistent with IFRSs in all respects;

(ii)   in conformity with IFRSs in all respects, except that the financial statements did not contain an explicit and unreserved statement that they complied with IFRSs;

(iii)   containing an explicit statement of compliance with some, but not all, IFRSs;

(iv)   in accordance with national requirements inconsistent with IFRSs, using some individual IFRSs to account for items for which national requirements did not exist; or

(v)   in accordance with national requirements, with a reconciliation of some amounts to the amounts determined in accordance with IFRSs;

(b)   prepared financial statements in accordance with IFRSs for internal use only, without making them available to the entity's owners or any other external users;

(c)   prepared a reporting package in accordance with IFRSs for consolidation purposes without preparing a complete set of financial statements as defined in IAS 1 *Presentation of Financial Statements* (as revised in 2007); or

(d)   did not present financial statements for previous periods.

4   This IFRS applies when an entity first adopts IFRSs. It does not apply when, for example, an entity:

(a)   stops presenting financial statements in accordance with national requirements, having previously presented them as well as another set of financial statements that contained an explicit and unreserved statement of compliance with IFRSs;

(b)   presented financial statements in the previous year in accordance with national requirements and those financial statements contained an explicit and unreserved statement of compliance with IFRSs; or

(c)   presented financial statements in the previous year that contained an explicit and unreserved statement of compliance with IFRSs, even if the auditors qualified their audit report on those financial statements.

4A   Notwithstanding the requirements in paragraphs 2 and 3, an entity that has applied IFRSs in a previous reporting period, but whose most recent previous annual financial statements did not contain an explicit and unreserved statement of compliance with IFRSs, must either apply this IFRS or else apply IFRSs retrospectively in accordance with IAS 8 *Accounting Policies, Changes in Accounting Estimates and Errors* as if the entity had never stopped applying IFRSs.

4B   When an entity does not elect to apply this IFRS in accordance with paragraph 4A, the entity shall nevertheless apply the disclosure requirements in paragraphs 23A–23B of IFRS 1, in addition to the disclosure requirements in IAS 8.

5   This IFRS does not apply to changes in accounting policies made by an entity that already applies IFRSs. Such changes are the subject of:

(a)   requirements on changes in accounting policies in IAS 8 *Accounting Policies, Changes in Accounting Estimates and Errors*; and

(b)   specific transitional requirements in other IFRSs.

Recognition and measurement

Opening IFRS statement of financial position

6   An entity shall prepare and present an *opening IFRS statement of financial position* at the *date of transition to IFRSs*. This is the starting point for its accounting in accordance with IFRSs.

Accounting policies

7   An entity shall use the same accounting policies in its opening IFRS statement of financial position and throughout all periods presented in its first IFRS financial statements. Those accounting policies shall comply with each IFRS effective at the end of its *first IFRS reporting period*, except as specified in paragraphs 13–19 and Appendices B–E.

8   An entity shall not apply different versions of IFRSs that were effective at earlier dates. An entity may apply a new IFRS that is not yet mandatory if that IFRS permits early application.

Example: Consistent application of latest version of IFRSs

Background

The end of entity A's first IFRS reporting period is 31 December 20X5. Entity A decides to present comparative information in those financial statements for one year only (see paragraph 21). Therefore, its date of transition to IFRSs is the beginning of business on 1 January 20X4 (or, equivalently, close of business on 31 December 20X3). Entity A presented financial statements in accordance with its *previous GAAP* annually to 31 December each year up to, and including, 31 December 20X4.

Application of requirements

Entity A is required to apply the IFRSs effective for periods ending on 31 December 20X5 in:

(a)   preparing and presenting its opening IFRS statement of financial position at 1 January 20X4; and

(b)   preparing and presenting its statement of financial position for 31 December 20X5 (including comparative amounts for 20X4), statement of comprehensive income, statement of changes in equity and statement of cash flows for the year to 31 December 20X5 (including comparative amounts for 20X4) and disclosures (including comparative information for 20X4).

If a new IFRS is not yet mandatory but permits early application, entity A is permitted, but not required, to apply that IFRS in its first IFRS financial statements.

---

9   The transitional provisions in other IFRSs apply to changes in accounting policies made by an entity that already uses IFRSs; they do not apply to a *first-time adopter*'s transition to IFRSs, except as specified in Appendices B–E.

10   Except as described in paragraphs 13–19 and Appendices B–E, an entity shall, in its opening IFRS statement of financial position:

(a)   recognise all assets and liabilities whose recognition is required by IFRSs;

(b)   not recognise items as assets or liabilities if IFRSs do not permit such recognition;

(c) reclassify items that it recognised in accordance with previous GAAP as one type of asset, liability or component of equity, but are a different type of asset, liability or component of equity in accordance with IFRSs; and

(d) apply IFRSs in measuring all recognised assets and liabilities.

11 The accounting policies that an entity uses in its opening IFRS statement of financial position may differ from those that it used for the same date using its previous GAAP. The resulting adjustments arise from events and transactions before the date of transition to IFRSs. Therefore, an entity shall recognise those adjustments directly in retained earnings (or, if appropriate, another category of equity) at the date of transition to IFRSs.

12 This IFRS establishes two categories of exceptions to the principle that an entity's opening IFRS statement of financial position shall comply with each IFRS:

(a) paragraphs 14–17 and Appendix B prohibit retrospective application of some aspects of other IFRSs.

(b) Appendices C–E grant exemptions from some requirements of other IFRSs.

Exceptions to the retrospective application of other IFRSs

13 This IFRS prohibits retrospective application of some aspects of other IFRSs. These exceptions are set out in paragraphs 14–17 and Appendix B.

Estimates

14 An entity's estimates in accordance with IFRSs at the date of transition to IFRSs shall be consistent with estimates made for the same date in accordance with previous GAAP (after adjustments to reflect any difference in accounting policies), unless there is objective evidence that those estimates were in error.

15 An entity may receive information after the date of transition to IFRSs about estimates that it had made under previous GAAP. In accordance with paragraph 14, an entity shall treat the receipt of that information in the same way as non-adjusting events after the reporting period in accordance with IAS 10 *Events after the Reporting Period*. For example, assume that an entity's date of transition to IFRSs is 1 January 20X4 and new information on 15 July 20X4 requires the revision of an estimate made in accordance with previous GAAP at 31 December 20X3. The entity shall not reflect that new information in its opening IFRS statement of financial position (unless the estimates need adjustment for any differences in accounting policies or there is objective evidence that the estimates were in error). Instead, the entity shall reflect that new information in profit or loss (or, if appropriate, other comprehensive income) for the year ended 31 December 20X4.

16   An entity may need to make estimates in accordance with IFRSs at the date of transition to IFRSs that were not required at that date under previous GAAP. To achieve consistency with IAS 10, those estimates in accordance with IFRSs shall reflect conditions that existed at the date of transition to IFRSs. In particular, estimates at the date of transition to IFRSs of market prices, interest rates or foreign exchange rates shall reflect market conditions at that date.

17   Paragraphs 14–16 apply to the opening IFRS statement of financial position. They also apply to a comparative period presented in an entity's first IFRS financial statements, in which case the references to the date of transition to IFRSs are replaced by references to the end of that comparative period.

Exemptions from other IFRSs

18   An entity may elect to use one or more of the exemptions contained in Appendices C–E. An entity shall not apply these exemptions by analogy to other items.

19   [Deleted]

Presentation and disclosure

20   This IFRS does not provide exemptions from the presentation and disclosure requirements in other IFRSs.

Comparative information

21   An entity's first IFRS financial statements shall include at least three statements of financial position, two statements of profit or loss and other comprehensive income, two separate statements of profit or loss (if presented), two statements of cash flows and two statements of changes in equity and related notes, including comparative information for all statements presented.

Non-IFRS comparative information and historical summaries

22   Some entities present historical summaries of selected data for periods before the first period for which they present full comparative information in accordance with IFRSs. This IFRS does not require such summaries to comply with the recognition and measurement requirements of IFRSs. Furthermore, some entities present comparative information in accordance with previous GAAP as well as the comparative information required by IAS 1. In any financial statements containing historical summaries or comparative information in accordance with previous GAAP, an entity shall:

(a)   label the previous GAAP information prominently as not being prepared in accordance with IFRSs; and

(b)   disclose the nature of the main adjustments that would make it comply with IFRSs. An entity need not quantify those adjustments.

Explanation of transition to IFRSs

23   An entity shall explain how the transition from previous GAAP to IFRSs affected its reported financial position, financial performance and cash flows.

23A   An entity that has applied IFRSs in a previous period, as described in paragraph 4A, shall disclose:

      (a)   the reason it stopped applying IFRSs; and

      (b)   the reason it is resuming the application of IFRSs.

23B   When an entity, in accordance with paragraph 4A, does not elect to apply IFRS 1, the entity shall explain the reasons for electing to apply IFRSs as if it had never stopped applying IFRSs.

Reconciliations

24   To comply with paragraph 23, an entity's first IFRS financial statements shall include:

      (a)   reconciliations of its equity reported in accordance with previous GAAP to its equity in accordance with IFRSs for both of the following dates:

           (i)   the date of transition to IFRSs; and

           (ii)   the end of the latest period presented in the entity's most recent annual financial statements in accordance with previous GAAP.

      (b)   a reconciliation to its total comprehensive income in accordance with IFRSs for the latest period in the entity's most recent annual financial statements. The starting point for that reconciliation shall be total comprehensive income in accordance with previous GAAP for the same period or, if an entity did not report such a total, profit or loss under previous GAAP.

      (c)   if the entity recognised or reversed any impairment losses for the first time in preparing its opening IFRS statement of financial position, the disclosures that IAS 36 *Impairment of Assets* would have required if the entity had recognised those impairment losses or reversals in the period beginning with the date of transition to IFRSs.

25   The reconciliations required by paragraph 24(a) and (b) shall give sufficient detail to enable users to understand the material adjustments to the statement of financial position and statement of comprehensive income. If an entity presented a statement of cash flows under its previous GAAP, it shall also explain the material adjustments to the statement of cash flows.

26   If an entity becomes aware of errors made under previous GAAP, the reconciliations required by paragraph 24(a) and (b) shall distinguish the correction of those errors from changes in accounting policies.

27 IAS 8 does not apply to the changes in accounting policies an entity makes when it adopts IFRSs or to changes in those policies until after it presents its first IFRS financial statements. Therefore, IAS 8's requirements about changes in accounting policies do not apply in an entity's first IFRS financial statements.

27A If during the period covered by its first IFRS financial statements an entity changes its accounting policies or its use of the exemptions contained in this IFRS, it shall explain the changes between its first IFRS interim financial report and its first IFRS financial statements, in accordance with paragraph 23, and it shall update the reconciliations required by paragraph 24(a) and (b).

28 If an entity did not present financial statements for previous periods, its first IFRS financial statements shall disclose that fact.

Designation of financial assets or financial liabilities

29 An entity is permitted to designate a previously recognised financial asset as a financial asset measured at fair value through profit or loss in accordance with paragraph D19A. The entity shall disclose the fair value of financial assets so designated at the date of designation and their classification and carrying amount in the previous financial statements.

29A An entity is permitted to designate a previously recognised financial liability as a financial liability at fair value through profit or loss in accordance with paragraph D19. The entity shall disclose the fair value of financial liabilities so designated at the date of designation and their classification and carrying amount in the previous financial statements.

Use of fair value as deemed cost

30 If an entity uses fair value in its opening IFRS statement of financial position as *deemed cost* for an item of property, plant and equipment, an investment property, an intangible asset or a right-of-use asset (see paragraphs D5 and D7), the entity's first IFRS financial statements shall disclose, for each line item in the opening IFRS statement of financial position:

  (a) the aggregate of those fair values; and

  (b) the aggregate adjustment to the carrying amounts reported under previous GAAP.

Use of deemed cost for investments in subsidiaries, joint ventures and associates

31 Similarly, if an entity uses a deemed cost in its opening IFRS statement of financial position for an investment in a subsidiary, joint venture or associate in its separate financial statements (see paragraph D15), the entity's first IFRS separate financial statements shall disclose:

  (a) the aggregate deemed cost of those investments for which deemed cost is their previous GAAP carrying amount;

(b)   the aggregate deemed cost of those investments for which deemed cost is fair value; and

(c)   the aggregate adjustment to the carrying amounts reported under previous GAAP.

Use of deemed cost for oil and gas assets

31A   If an entity uses the exemption in paragraph D8A(b) for oil and gas assets, it shall disclose that fact and the basis on which carrying amounts determined under previous GAAP were allocated.

Use of deemed cost for operations subject to rate regulation

31B   If an entity uses the exemption in paragraph D8B for operations subject to rate regulation, it shall disclose that fact and the basis on which carrying amounts were determined under previous GAAP.

Use of deemed cost after severe hyperinflation

31C   If an entity elects to measure assets and liabilities at fair value and to use that fair value as the deemed cost in its opening IFRS statement of financial position because of severe hyperinflation (see paragraphs D26–D30), the entity's first IFRS financial statements shall disclose an explanation of how, and why, the entity had, and then ceased to have, a functional currency that has both of the following characteristics:

(a)   a reliable general price index is not available to all entities with transactions and balances in the currency.

(b)   exchangeability between the currency and a relatively stable foreign currency does not exist.

Interim financial reports

32   To comply with paragraph 23, if an entity presents an interim financial report in accordance with IAS 34 for part of the period covered by its first IFRS financial statements, the entity shall satisfy the following requirements in addition to the requirements of IAS 34:

(a)   Each such interim financial report shall, if the entity presented an interim financial report for the comparable interim period of the immediately preceding financial year, include:

(i)   a reconciliation of its equity in accordance with previous GAAP at the end of that comparable interim period to its equity under IFRSs at that date; and

(ii)   a reconciliation to its total comprehensive income in accordance with IFRSs for that comparable interim period (current and year to date). The starting point for that reconciliation shall be total comprehensive income in accordance with previous GAAP for that period or, if an entity did not report such a total, profit or loss in accordance with previous GAAP.

(b) In addition to the reconciliations required by (a), an entity's first interim financial report in accordance with IAS 34 for part of the period covered by its first IFRS financial statements shall include the reconciliations described in paragraph 24(a) and (b) (supplemented by the details required by paragraphs 25 and 26) or a cross-reference to another published document that includes these reconciliations.

(c) If an entity changes its accounting policies or its use of the exemptions contained in this IFRS, it shall explain the changes in each such interim financial report in accordance with paragraph 23 and update the reconciliations required by (a) and (b).

33 IAS 34 requires minimum disclosures, which are based on the assumption that users of the interim financial report also have access to the most recent annual financial statements. However, IAS 34 also requires an entity to disclose 'any events or transactions that are material to an understanding of the current interim period'. Therefore, if a first-time adopter did not, in its most recent annual financial statements in accordance with previous GAAP, disclose information material to an understanding of the current interim period, its interim financial report shall disclose that information or include a cross-reference to another published document that includes it.

Effective date

34 An entity shall apply this IFRS if its first IFRS financial statements are for a period beginning on or after 1 July 2009. Earlier application is permitted.

35 An entity shall apply the amendments in paragraphs D1(n) and D23 for annual periods beginning on or after 1 July 2009. If an entity applies IAS 23 *Borrowing Costs* (as revised in 2007) for an earlier period, those amendments shall be applied for that earlier period.

36 IFRS 3 *Business Combinations* (as revised in 2008) amended paragraphs 19, C1 and C4(f) and (g). If an entity applies IFRS 3 (revised 2008) for an earlier period, the amendments shall also be applied for that earlier period.

37 IAS 27 *Consolidated and Separate Financial Statements* (as amended in 2008) amended paragraphs B1 and B7. If an entity applies IAS 27 (amended 2008) for an earlier period, the amendments shall be applied for that earlier period.

38 *Cost of an Investment in a Subsidiary, Jointly Controlled Entity or Associate* (Amendments to IFRS 1 and IAS 27), issued in May 2008, added paragraphs 31, D1(g), D14 and D15. An entity shall apply those paragraphs for annual periods beginning on or after 1 July 2009. Earlier application is permitted. If an entity applies the paragraphs for an earlier period, it shall disclose that fact.

39 Paragraph B7 was amended by *Improvements to IFRSs* issued in May 2008. An entity shall apply those amendments for annual periods beginning on or after 1 July 2009. If an entity applies IAS 27 (amended 2008) for an earlier period, the amendments shall be applied for that earlier period.

39A   *Additional Exemptions for First-time Adopters* (Amendments to IFRS 1), issued in July 2009, added paragraphs 31A, D8A, D9A and D21A and amended paragraph D1(c), (d) and (l). An entity shall apply those amendments for annual periods beginning on or after 1 January 2010. Earlier application is permitted. If an entity applies the amendments for an earlier period it shall disclose that fact.

39B   [Deleted]

39C   IFRIC 19 *Extinguishing Financial Liabilities with Equity Instruments* added paragraph D25. An entity shall apply that amendment when it applies IFRIC 19.

39D   [Deleted]

39E   *Improvements to IFRSs* issued in May 2010 added paragraphs 27A, 31B and D8B and amended paragraphs 27, 32, D1(c) and D8. An entity shall apply those amendments for annual periods beginning on or after 1 January 2011. Earlier application is permitted. If an entity applies the amendments for an earlier period it shall disclose that fact. Entities that adopted IFRSs in periods before the effective date of IFRS 1 or applied IFRS 1 in a previous period are permitted to apply the amendment to paragraph D8 retrospectively in the first annual period after the amendment is effective. An entity applying paragraph D8 retrospectively shall disclose that fact.

39F   [Deleted]

39G   [Deleted]

39H   *Severe Hyperinflation and Removal of Fixed Dates for First-time Adopters* (Amendments to IFRS 1), issued in December 2010, amended paragraphs B2, D1 and D20 and added paragraphs 31C and D26–D30. An entity shall apply those amendments for annual periods beginning on or after 1 July 2011. Earlier application is permitted.

39I   IFRS 10 *Consolidated Financial Statements* and IFRS 11 *Joint Arrangements*, issued in May 2011, amended paragraphs 31, B7, C1, D1, D14 and D15 and added paragraph D31. An entity shall apply those amendments when it applies IFRS 10 and IFRS 11.

39J   IFRS 13 *Fair Value Measurement*, issued in May 2011, deleted paragraph 19, amended the definition of fair value in Appendix A and amended paragraphs D15 and D20. An entity shall apply those amendments when it applies IFRS 13.

39K   *Presentation of Items of Other Comprehensive Income* (Amendments to IAS 1), issued in June 2011, amended paragraph 21. An entity shall apply that amendment when it applies IAS 1 as amended in June 2011.

39L   IAS 19 *Employee Benefits* (as amended in June 2011) amended paragraph D1 and deleted paragraphs D10 and D11. An entity shall apply those amendments when it applies IAS 19 (as amended in June 2011).

39M IFRIC 20 *Stripping Costs in the Production Phase of a Surface Mine* added paragraph D32 and amended paragraph D1. An entity shall apply that amendment when it applies IFRIC 20.

39N *Government Loans* (Amendments to IFRS 1), issued in March 2012, added paragraphs B1(f) and B10–B12. An entity shall apply those paragraphs for annual periods beginning on or after 1 January 2013. Earlier application is permitted.

39O Paragraphs B10 and B11 refer to IFRS 9. If an entity applies this IFRS but does not yet apply IFRS 9, the references in paragraphs B10 and B11 to IFRS 9 shall be read as references to IAS 39 *Financial Instruments: Recognition and Measurement*.

39P *Annual Improvements 2009–2011 Cycle*, issued in May 2012, added paragraphs 4A–4B and 23A–23B. An entity shall apply that amendment retrospectively in accordance with IAS 8 *Accounting Policies, Changes in Accounting Estimates and Errors* for annual periods beginning on or after 1 January 2013. Earlier application is permitted. If an entity applies that amendment for an earlier period it shall disclose that fact.

39Q *Annual Improvements 2009–2011 Cycle*, issued in May 2012, amended paragraph D23. An entity shall apply that amendment retrospectively in accordance with IAS 8 *Accounting Policies, Changes in Accounting Estimates and Errors* for annual periods beginning on or after 1 January 2013. Earlier application is permitted. If an entity applies that amendment for an earlier period it shall disclose that fact.

39R *Annual Improvements 2009–2011 Cycle*, issued in May 2012, amended paragraph 21. An entity shall apply that amendment retrospectively in accordance with IAS 8 *Accounting Policies, Changes in Accounting Estimates and Errors* for annual periods beginning on or after 1 January 2013. Earlier application is permitted. If an entity applies that amendment for an earlier period it shall disclose that fact.

39S *Consolidated Financial Statements, Joint Arrangements and Disclosure of Interests in Other Entities: Transition Guidance* (Amendments to IFRS 10, IFRS 11 and IFRS 12), issued in June 2012, amended paragraph D31. An entity shall apply that amendment when it applies IFRS 11 (as amended in June 2012).

39T *Investment Entities* (Amendments to IFRS 10, IFRS 12 and IAS 27), issued in October 2012, amended paragraphs D16, D17 and Appendix C. An entity shall apply those amendments for annual periods beginning on or after 1 January 2014. Earlier application of *Investment Entities* is permitted. If an entity applies those amendments earlier it shall also apply all amendments included in *Investment Entities* at the same time.

39U [Deleted]

39V IFRS 14 *Regulatory Deferral Accounts*, issued in January 2014, amended paragraph D8B. An entity shall apply that amendment for annual periods beginning on or after 1 January 2016. Earlier application is permitted. If an entity applies IFRS 14 for an earlier period, the amendment shall be applied for that earlier period.

39W *Accounting for Acquisitions of Interests in Joint Operations* (Amendments to IFRS 11), issued in May 2014, amended paragraph C5. An entity shall apply that amendment in annual periods beginning on or after 1 January 2016. If an entity applies related amendments to IFRS 11 from *Accounting for Acquisitions of Interests in Joint Operations* (Amendments to IFRS 11) in an earlier period, the amendment to paragraph C5 shall be applied in that earlier period.

39X IFRS 15 *Revenue from Contracts with Customers*, issued in May 2014, amended paragraph D1, deleted paragraph D24 and its related heading and added paragraphs D34–D35 and their related heading. An entity shall apply those amendments when it applies IFRS 15.

39Y IFRS 9 *Financial Instruments*, as issued in July 2014, amended paragraphs 29, B1–B6, D1, D14, D15, D19 and D20, deleted paragraphs 39B, 39G and 39U and added paragraphs 29A, B8–B8G, B9, D19A–D19C, D33, E1 and E2. An entity shall apply those amendments when it applies IFRS 9.

39Z *Equity Method in Separate Financial Statements* (Amendments to IAS 27), issued in August 2014, amended paragraph D14 and added paragraph D15A. An entity shall apply those amendments for annual periods beginning on or after 1 January 2016. Earlier application is permitted. If an entity applies those amendments for an earlier period, it shall disclose that fact.

39AA [Deleted]

39AB IFRS 16 *Leases*, issued in January 2016, amended paragraphs 30, C4, D1, D7, D8B and D9, deleted paragraph D9A and added paragraphs D9B–D9E. An entity shall apply those amendments when it applies IFRS 16.

39AC IFRIC 22 *Foreign Currency Transactions and Advance Consideration* added paragraph D36 and amended paragraph D1. An entity shall apply that amendment when it applies IFRIC 22.

39AD *Annual Improvements to IFRS Standards 2014–2016 Cycle*, issued in December 2016, amended paragraphs 39L and 39T and deleted paragraphs 39D, 39F, 39AA and E3–E7. An entity shall apply those amendments for annual periods beginning on or after 1 January 2018.

39AE *[This paragraph refers to amendments that are not yet effective, and is therefore not included in this edition.]*

39AF IFRIC 23 *Uncertainty over Income Tax Treatments* added paragraph E8. An entity shall apply that amendment when it applies IFRIC 23.

39AG   *Annual Improvements to IFRS Standards 2018–2020*, issued in May 2020, amended paragraph D1(f) and added paragraph D13A. An entity shall apply that amendment for annual reporting periods beginning on or after 1 January 2022. Earlier application is permitted. If an entity applies the amendment for an earlier period, it shall disclose that fact.

39AH   *[This paragraph refers to amendments that are not yet effective, and is therefore not included in this edition.]*

Withdrawal of IFRS 1 (issued 2003)

40   This IFRS supersedes IFRS 1 (issued 2003 and amended at May 2008).

than foreign currency risk). However, if an entity designated a net position as a hedged item in accordance with previous GAAP, it may designate as a hedged item in accordance with IFRSs an individual item within that net position, or a net position if that meets the requirements in paragraph 6.6.1 of IFRS 9, provided that it does so no later than the date of transition to IFRSs.

B6   If, before the date of transition to IFRSs, an entity had designated a transaction as a hedge but the hedge does not meet the conditions for hedge accounting in IFRS 9, the entity shall apply paragraphs 6.5.6 and 6.5.7 of IFRS 9 to discontinue hedge accounting. Transactions entered into before the date of transition to IFRSs shall not be retrospectively designated as hedges.

Non-controlling interests

B7   A first-time adopter shall apply the following requirements of IFRS 10 prospectively from the date of transition to IFRSs:

(a)   the requirement in paragraph B94 that total comprehensive income is attributed to the owners of the parent and to the non-controlling interests even if this results in the non-controlling interests having a deficit balance;

(b)   the requirements in paragraphs 23 and B96 for accounting for changes in the parent's ownership interest in a subsidiary that do not result in a loss of control; and

(c)   the requirements in paragraphs B97–B99 for accounting for a loss of control over a subsidiary, and the related requirements of paragraph 8A of IFRS 5 *Non-current Assets Held for Sale and Discontinued Operations*.

However, if a first-time adopter elects to apply IFRS 3 retrospectively to past business combinations, it shall also apply IFRS 10 in accordance with paragraph C1 of this IFRS.

Classification and measurement of financial instruments

B8   An entity shall assess whether a financial asset meets the conditions in paragraph 4.1.2 of IFRS 9 or the conditions in paragraph 4.1.2A of IFRS 9 on the basis of the facts and circumstances that exist at the date of transition to IFRSs.

B8A   If it is impracticable to assess a modified time value of money element in accordance with paragraphs B4.1.9B–B4.1.9D of IFRS 9 on the basis of the facts and circumstances that exist at the date of transition to IFRSs, an entity shall assess the contractual cash flow characteristics of that financial asset on the basis of the facts and circumstances that existed at the date of transition to IFRSs without taking into account the requirements related to the modification of the time value of money element in paragraphs B4.1.9B–B4.1.9D of IFRS 9. (In this case, the entity shall also apply paragraph 42R of IFRS 7 but references to 'paragraph 7.2.4 of IFRS 9' shall be read to mean this paragraph and references to 'initial recognition of the financial asset' shall be read to mean 'at the date of transition to IFRSs'.)

B8B   If it is impracticable to assess whether the fair value of a prepayment feature is insignificant in accordance with paragraph B4.1.12(c) of IFRS 9 on the basis of the facts and circumstances that exist at the date of transition to IFRSs, an entity shall assess the contractual cash flow characteristics of that financial asset on the basis of the facts and circumstances that existed at the date of transition to IFRSs without taking into account the exception for prepayment features in paragraph B4.1.12 of IFRS 9. (In this case, the entity shall also apply paragraph 42S of IFRS 7 but references to 'paragraph 7.2.5 of IFRS 9' shall be read to mean this paragraph and references to 'initial recognition of the financial asset' shall be read to mean 'at the date of transition to IFRSs'.)

B8C   If it is impracticable (as defined in IAS 8) for an entity to apply retrospectively the effective interest method in IFRS 9, the fair value of the financial asset or the financial liability at the date of transition to IFRSs shall be the new gross carrying amount of that financial asset or the new amortised cost of that financial liability at the date of transition to IFRSs.

Impairment of financial assets

B8D   An entity shall apply the impairment requirements in Section 5.5 of IFRS 9 retrospectively subject to paragraphs B8E–B8G and E1–E2.

B8E   At the date of transition to IFRSs, an entity shall use reasonable and supportable information that is available without undue cost or effort to determine the credit risk at the date that financial instruments were initially recognised (or for loan commitments and financial guarantee contracts the date that the entity became a party to the irrevocable commitment in accordance with paragraph 5.5.6 of IFRS 9) and compare that to the credit risk at the date of transition to IFRSs (also see paragraphs B7.2.2–B7.2.3 of IFRS 9).

B8F   When determining whether there has been a significant increase in credit risk since initial recognition, an entity may apply:

      (a)   the requirements in paragraph 5.5.10 and B5.5.22–B5.5.24 of IFRS 9; and

      (b)   the rebuttable presumption in paragraph 5.5.11 of IFRS 9 for contractual payments that are more than 30 days past due if an entity will apply the impairment requirements by identifying significant increases in credit risk since initial recognition for those financial instruments on the basis of past due information.

B8G   If, at the date of transition to IFRSs, determining whether there has been a significant increase in credit risk since the initial recognition of a financial instrument would require undue cost or effort, an entity shall recognise a loss allowance at an amount equal to lifetime expected credit losses at each reporting date until that financial instrument is derecognised (unless that financial instrument is low credit risk at a reporting date, in which case paragraph B8F(a) applies).

(ii)   assets, including goodwill, and liabilities that were not recognised in the acquirer's consolidated statement of financial position in accordance with previous GAAP and also would not qualify for recognition in accordance with IFRSs in the separate statement of financial position of the acquiree (see (f)–(i) below).

The first-time adopter shall recognise any resulting change by adjusting retained earnings (or, if appropriate, another category of equity), unless the change results from the recognition of an intangible asset that was previously subsumed within goodwill (see (g)(i) below).

(c)   The first-time adopter shall exclude from its opening IFRS statement of financial position any item recognised in accordance with previous GAAP that does not qualify for recognition as an asset or liability under IFRSs. The first-time adopter shall account for the resulting change as follows:

(i)   the first-time adopter may have classified a past business combination as an acquisition and recognised as an intangible asset an item that does not qualify for recognition as an asset in accordance with IAS 38 *Intangible Assets*. It shall reclassify that item (and, if any, the related deferred tax and non-controlling interests) as part of goodwill (unless it deducted goodwill directly from equity in accordance with previous GAAP, see (g) (i) and (i) below).

(ii)   the first-time adopter shall recognise all other resulting changes in retained earnings.[2]

(d)   IFRSs require subsequent measurement of some assets and liabilities on a basis that is not based on original cost, such as fair value. The first-time adopter shall measure these assets and liabilities on that basis in its opening IFRS statement of financial position, even if they were acquired or assumed in a past business combination. It shall recognise any resulting change in the carrying amount by adjusting retained earnings (or, if appropriate, another category of equity), rather than goodwill.

(e)   Immediately after the business combination, the carrying amount in accordance with previous GAAP of assets acquired and liabilities assumed in that business combination shall be their deemed cost in accordance with IFRSs at that date. If IFRSs require a cost-based measurement of those assets and liabilities at a later date, that deemed cost shall be the basis for cost-based depreciation or amortisation from the date of the business combination.

---

2   Such changes include reclassifications from or to intangible assets if goodwill was not recognised in accordance with previous GAAP as an asset. This arises if, in accordance with previous GAAP, the entity (a) deducted goodwill directly from equity or (b) did not treat the business combination as an acquisition.

(f)   If an asset acquired, or liability assumed, in a past business combination was not recognised in accordance with previous GAAP, it does not have a deemed cost of zero in the opening IFRS statement of financial position. Instead, the acquirer shall recognise and measure it in its consolidated statement of financial position on the basis that IFRSs would require in the statement of financial position of the acquiree. To illustrate: if the acquirer had not, in accordance with its previous GAAP, capitalised leases acquired in a past business combination in which the acquiree was a lessee, it shall capitalise those leases in its consolidated financial statements, as IFRS 16 *Leases* would require the acquiree to do in its IFRS statement of financial position. Similarly, if the acquirer had not, in accordance with its previous GAAP, recognised a contingent liability that still exists at the date of transition to IFRSs, the acquirer shall recognise that contingent liability at that date unless IAS 37 *Provisions, Contingent Liabilities and Contingent Assets* would prohibit its recognition in the financial statements of the acquiree. Conversely, if an asset or liability was subsumed in goodwill in accordance with previous GAAP but would have been recognised separately under IFRS 3, that asset or liability remains in goodwill unless IFRSs would require its recognition in the financial statements of the acquiree.

(g)   The carrying amount of goodwill in the opening IFRS statement of financial position shall be its carrying amount in accordance with previous GAAP at the date of transition to IFRSs, after the following two adjustments:

   (i)   If required by (c)(i) above, the first-time adopter shall increase the carrying amount of goodwill when it reclassifies an item that it recognised as an intangible asset in accordance with previous GAAP. Similarly, if (f) above requires the first-time adopter to recognise an intangible asset that was subsumed in recognised goodwill in accordance with previous GAAP, the first-time adopter shall decrease the carrying amount of goodwill accordingly (and, if applicable, adjust deferred tax and non-controlling interests).

   (ii)   Regardless of whether there is any indication that the goodwill may be impaired, the first-time adopter shall apply IAS 36 in testing the goodwill for impairment at the date of transition to IFRSs and in recognising any resulting impairment loss in retained earnings (or, if so required by IAS 36, in revaluation surplus). The impairment test shall be based on conditions at the date of transition to IFRSs.

(h)   No other adjustments shall be made to the carrying amount of goodwill at the date of transition to IFRSs. For example, the first-time adopter shall not restate the carrying amount of goodwill:

(i)   to exclude in-process research and development acquired in that business combination (unless the related intangible asset would qualify for recognition in accordance with IAS 38 in the statement of financial position of the acquiree);

(ii)   to adjust previous amortisation of goodwill;

(iii)   to reverse adjustments to goodwill that IFRS 3 would not permit, but were made in accordance with previous GAAP because of adjustments to assets and liabilities between the date of the business combination and the date of transition to IFRSs.

(i)   If the first-time adopter recognised goodwill in accordance with previous GAAP as a deduction from equity:

      (i)   it shall not recognise that goodwill in its opening IFRS statement of financial position. Furthermore, it shall not reclassify that goodwill to profit or loss if it disposes of the subsidiary or if the investment in the subsidiary becomes impaired.

      (ii)   adjustments resulting from the subsequent resolution of a contingency affecting the purchase consideration shall be recognised in retained earnings.

(j)   In accordance with its previous GAAP, the first-time adopter may not have consolidated a subsidiary acquired in a past business combination (for example, because the parent did not regard it as a subsidiary in accordance with previous GAAP or did not prepare consolidated financial statements). The first-time adopter shall adjust the carrying amounts of the subsidiary's assets and liabilities to the amounts that IFRSs would require in the subsidiary's statement of financial position. The deemed cost of goodwill equals the difference at the date of transition to IFRSs between:

      (i)   the parent's interest in those adjusted carrying amounts; and

      (ii)   the cost in the parent's separate financial statements of its investment in the subsidiary.

(k)   The measurement of non-controlling interests and deferred tax follows from the measurement of other assets and liabilities. Therefore, the above adjustments to recognised assets and liabilities affect non-controlling interests and deferred tax.

C5   The exemption for past business combinations also applies to past acquisitions of investments in associates, interests in joint ventures and interests in joint operations in which the activity of the joint operation constitutes a business, as defined in IFRS 3. Furthermore, the date selected for paragraph C1 applies equally for all such acquisitions.

Appendix D
Exemptions from other IFRSs

This appendix is an integral part of the IFRS.

D1   An entity may elect to use one or more of the following exemptions:

(a)   share-based payment transactions (paragraphs D2 and D3);

(b)   insurance contracts (paragraph D4);

(c)   deemed cost (paragraphs D5–D8B);

(d)   leases (paragraphs D9 and D9B–D9E);

(e)   [deleted]

(f)   cumulative translation differences (paragraphs D12–D13A);

(g)   investments in subsidiaries, joint ventures and associates (paragraphs D14–D15A);

(h)   assets and liabilities of subsidiaries, associates and joint ventures (paragraphs D16 and D17);

(i)   compound financial instruments (paragraph D18);

(j)   designation of previously recognised financial instruments (paragraphs D19–D19C);

(k)   fair value measurement of financial assets or financial liabilities at initial recognition (paragraph D20);

(l)   decommissioning liabilities included in the cost of property, plant and equipment (paragraphs D21 and D21A);

(m)   financial assets or intangible assets accounted for in accordance with IFRIC 12 *Service Concession Arrangements* (paragraph D22);

(n)   borrowing costs (paragraph D23);

(o)   [deleted]

(p)   extinguishing financial liabilities with equity instruments (paragraph D25);

(q)   severe hyperinflation (paragraphs D26–D30);

(r)   joint arrangements (paragraph D31);

(s)   stripping costs in the production phase of a surface mine (paragraph D32);

(t)   designation of contracts to buy or sell a non-financial item (paragraph D33);

(u)   revenue (paragraphs D34 and D35); and

(v)   foreign currency transactions and advance consideration (paragraph D36).

An entity shall not apply these exemptions by analogy to other items.

Share-based payment transactions

D2   A first-time adopter is encouraged, but not required, to apply IFRS 2 *Share-based Payment* to equity instruments that were granted on or before 7 November 2002. A first-time adopter is also encouraged, but not required, to apply IFRS 2 to equity instruments that were granted after 7 November 2002 and vested before the later of (a) the date of transition to IFRSs and (b) 1 January 2005. However, if a first-time adopter elects to apply IFRS 2 to such equity instruments, it may do so only if the entity has disclosed publicly the fair value of those equity instruments, determined at the measurement date, as defined in IFRS 2. For all grants of equity instruments to which IFRS 2 has not been applied (eg equity instruments granted on or before 7 November 2002), a first-time adopter shall nevertheless disclose the information required by paragraphs 44 and 45 of IFRS 2. If a first-time adopter modifies the terms or conditions of a grant of equity instruments to which IFRS 2 has not been applied, the entity is not required to apply paragraphs 26–29 of IFRS 2 if the modification occurred before the date of transition to IFRSs.

D3   A first-time adopter is encouraged, but not required, to apply IFRS 2 to liabilities arising from share-based payment transactions that were settled before the date of transition to IFRSs. A first-time adopter is also encouraged, but not required, to apply IFRS 2 to liabilities that were settled before 1 January 2005. For liabilities to which IFRS 2 is applied, a first-time adopter is not required to restate comparative information to the extent that the information relates to a period or date that is earlier than 7 November 2002.

Insurance contracts

D4   A first-time adopter may apply the transitional provisions in IFRS 4 *Insurance Contracts*. IFRS 4 restricts changes in accounting policies for insurance contracts, including changes made by a first-time adopter.

Deemed cost

D5   An entity may elect to measure an item of property, plant and equipment at the date of transition to IFRSs at its fair value and use that fair value as its deemed cost at that date.

D6   A first-time adopter may elect to use a previous GAAP revaluation of an item of property, plant and equipment at, or before, the date of transition to IFRSs as deemed cost at the date of the revaluation, if the revaluation was, at the date of the revaluation, broadly comparable to:

(a)   fair value; or

(b)   cost or depreciated cost in accordance with IFRSs, adjusted to reflect, for example, changes in a general or specific price index.

D7 The elections in paragraphs D5 and D6 are also available for:

(a) investment property, if an entity elects to use the cost model in IAS 40 *Investment Property*;

(aa) right-of-use assets (IFRS 16 *Leases*); and

(b) intangible assets that meet:

(i) the recognition criteria in IAS 38 (including reliable measurement of original cost); and

(ii) the criteria in IAS 38 for revaluation (including the existence of an active market).

An entity shall not use these elections for other assets or for liabilities.

D8 A first-time adopter may have established a deemed cost in accordance with previous GAAP for some or all of its assets and liabilities by measuring them at their fair value at one particular date because of an event such as a privatisation or initial public offering.

(a) If the measurement date is *at or before* the date of transition to IFRSs, the entity may use such event-driven fair value measurements as deemed cost for IFRSs at the date of that measurement.

(b) If the measurement date is *after* the date of transition to IFRSs, but during the period covered by the first IFRS financial statements, the event-driven fair value measurements may be used as deemed cost when the event occurs. An entity shall recognise the resulting adjustments directly in retained earnings (or if appropriate, another category of equity) at the measurement date. At the date of transition to IFRSs, the entity shall either establish the deemed cost by applying the criteria in paragraphs D5–D7 or measure assets and liabilities in accordance with the other requirements in this IFRS.

D8A Under some national accounting requirements exploration and development costs for oil and gas properties in the development or production phases are accounted for in cost centres that include all properties in a large geographical area. A first-time adopter using such accounting under previous GAAP may elect to measure oil and gas assets at the date of transition to IFRSs on the following basis:

(a) exploration and evaluation assets at the amount determined under the entity's previous GAAP; and

(b) assets in the development or production phases at the amount determined for the cost centre under the entity's previous GAAP. The entity shall allocate this amount to the cost centre's underlying assets pro rata using reserve volumes or reserve values as of that date.

The entity shall test exploration and evaluation assets and assets in the development and production phases for impairment at the date of transition to IFRSs in accordance with IFRS 6 *Exploration for and Evaluation of Mineral Resources* or IAS 36 respectively and, if necessary, reduce the amount determined in accordance with (a) or (b) above. For the purposes of this paragraph, oil and gas assets comprise only those assets used in the exploration, evaluation, development or production of oil and gas.

D8B   Some entities hold items of property, plant and equipment, right-of-use assets or intangible assets that are used, or were previously used, in operations subject to rate regulation. The carrying amount of such items might include amounts that were determined under previous GAAP but do not qualify for capitalisation in accordance with IFRSs. If this is the case, a first-time adopter may elect to use the previous GAAP carrying amount of such an item at the date of transition to IFRSs as deemed cost. If an entity applies this exemption to an item, it need not apply it to all items. At the date of transition to IFRSs, an entity shall test for impairment in accordance with IAS 36 each item for which this exemption is used. For the purposes of this paragraph, operations are subject to rate regulation if they are governed by a framework for establishing the prices that can be charged to customers for goods or services and that framework is subject to oversight and/or approval by a rate regulator (as defined in IFRS 14 *Regulatory Deferral Accounts*).

Leases

D9   A first-time adopter may assess whether a contract existing at the date of transition to IFRSs contains a lease by applying paragraphs 9–11 of IFRS 16 to those contracts on the basis of facts and circumstances existing at that date.

D9A   [Deleted]

D9B   When a first-time adopter that is a lessee recognises lease liabilities and right-of-use assets, it may apply the following approach to all of its leases (subject to the practical expedients described in paragraph D9D):

(a)   measure a lease liability at the date of transition to IFRSs. A lessee following this approach shall measure that lease liability at the present value of the remaining lease payments (see paragraph D9E), discounted using the lessee's incremental borrowing rate (see paragraph D9E) at the date of transition to IFRSs.

(b)   measure a right-of-use asset at the date of transition to IFRSs. The lessee shall choose, on a lease-by-lease basis, to measure that right-of-use asset at either:

(i)   its carrying amount as if IFRS 16 had been applied since the commencement date of the lease (see paragraph D9E), but discounted using the lessee's incremental borrowing rate at the date of transition to IFRSs; or

(ii)   an amount equal to the lease liability, adjusted by the amount of any prepaid or accrued lease payments relating to that lease recognised in the statement of financial position immediately before the date of transition to IFRSs.

(c)   apply IAS 36 to right-of-use assets at the date of transition to IFRSs.

D9C   Notwithstanding the requirements in paragraph D9B, a first-time adopter that is a lessee shall measure the right-of-use asset at fair value at the date of transition to IFRSs for leases that meet the definition of investment property in IAS 40 and are measured using the fair value model in IAS 40 from the date of transition to IFRSs.

D9D   A first-time adopter that is a lessee may do one or more of the following at the date of transition to IFRSs, applied on a lease-by-lease basis:

(a)   apply a single discount rate to a portfolio of leases with reasonably similar characteristics (for example, a similar remaining lease term for a similar class of underlying asset in a similar economic environment).

(b)   elect not to apply the requirements in paragraph D9B to leases for which the lease term (see paragraph D9E) ends within 12 months of the date of transition to IFRSs. Instead, the entity shall account for (including disclosure of information about) these leases as if they were short-term leases accounted for in accordance with paragraph 6 of IFRS 16.

(c)   elect not to apply the requirements in paragraph D9B to leases for which the underlying asset is of low value (as described in paragraphs B3–B8 of IFRS 16). Instead, the entity shall account for (including disclosure of information about) these leases in accordance with paragraph 6 of IFRS 16.

(d)   exclude initial direct costs (see paragraph D9E) from the measurement of the right-of-use asset at the date of transition to IFRSs.

(e)   use hindsight, such as in determining the lease term if the contract contains options to extend or terminate the lease.

D9E   Lease payments, lessee, lessee's incremental borrowing rate, commencement date of the lease, initial direct costs and lease term are defined terms in IFRS 16 and are used in this Standard with the same meaning.

D10–D11   [Deleted]

Cumulative translation differences

D12   IAS 21 requires an entity:

(a)   to recognise some translation differences in other comprehensive income and accumulate these in a separate component of equity; and

(b)   on disposal of a foreign operation, to reclassify the cumulative translation difference for that foreign operation (including, if applicable, gains and losses on related hedges) from equity to profit or loss as part of the gain or loss on disposal.

D13   However, a first-time adopter need not comply with these requirements for cumulative translation differences that existed at the date of transition to IFRSs. If a first-time adopter uses this exemption:

(a)   the cumulative translation differences for all foreign operations are deemed to be zero at the date of transition to IFRSs; and

(b)   the gain or loss on a subsequent disposal of any foreign operation shall exclude translation differences that arose before the date of transition to IFRSs and shall include later translation differences.

D13A   Instead of applying paragraph D12 or paragraph D13, a subsidiary that uses the exemption in paragraph D16(a) may elect, in its financial statements, to measure cumulative translation differences for all foreign operations at the carrying amount that would be included in the parent's consolidated financial statements, based on the parent's date of transition to IFRSs, if no adjustments were made for consolidation procedures and for the effects of the business combination in which the parent acquired the subsidiary. A similar election is available to an associate or joint venture that uses the exemption in paragraph D16(a).

Investments in subsidiaries, joint ventures and associates

D14   When an entity prepares separate financial statements, IAS 27 requires it to account for its investments in subsidiaries, joint ventures and associates either:

(a)   at cost;

(b)   in accordance with IFRS 9; or

(c)   using the equity method as described in IAS 28.

D15   If a first-time adopter measures such an investment at cost in accordance with IAS 27, it shall measure that investment at one of the following amounts in its separate opening IFRS statement of financial position:

(a)   cost determined in accordance with IAS 27; or

(b)   deemed cost. The deemed cost of such an investment shall be its:

(i)   fair value at the entity's date of transition to IFRSs in its separate financial statements; or

(ii)   previous GAAP carrying amount at that date.

A first-time adopter may choose either (i) or (ii) above to measure its investment in each subsidiary, joint venture or associate that it elects to measure using a deemed cost.

D15A   If a first-time adopter accounts for such an investment using the equity method procedures as described in IAS 28:

(a)   the first-time adopter applies the exemption for past business combinations (Appendix C) to the acquisition of the investment.

(b)   if the entity becomes a first-time adopter for its separate financial statements earlier than for its consolidated financial statements, and

     (i)   later than its parent, the entity shall apply paragraph D16 in its separate financial statements.

     (ii)   later than its subsidiary, the entity shall apply paragraph D17 in its separate financial statements.

Assets and liabilities of subsidiaries, associates and joint ventures

D16   If a subsidiary becomes a first-time adopter later than its parent, the subsidiary shall, in its financial statements, measure its assets and liabilities at either:

    (a)   the carrying amounts that would be included in the parent's consolidated financial statements, based on the parent's date of transition to IFRSs, if no adjustments were made for consolidation procedures and for the effects of the business combination in which the parent acquired the subsidiary (this election is not available to a subsidiary of an investment entity, as defined in IFRS 10, that is required to be measured at fair value through profit or loss); or

    (b)   the carrying amounts required by the rest of this IFRS, based on the subsidiary's date of transition to IFRSs. These carrying amounts could differ from those described in (a):

        (i)   when the exemptions in this IFRS result in measurements that depend on the date of transition to IFRSs.

        (ii)   when the accounting policies used in the subsidiary's financial statements differ from those in the consolidated financial statements. For example, the subsidiary may use as its accounting policy the cost model in IAS 16 *Property, Plant and Equipment*, whereas the group may use the revaluation model.

A similar election is available to an associate or joint venture that becomes a first-time adopter later than an entity that has significant influence or joint control over it.

D17   However, if an entity becomes a first-time adopter later than its subsidiary (or associate or joint venture) the entity shall, in its consolidated financial statements, measure the assets and liabilities of the subsidiary (or associate or joint venture) at the same carrying amounts as in the financial statements of the subsidiary (or associate or joint venture), after adjusting for consolidation and equity accounting adjustments and for the effects of the business combination in which the entity acquired the subsidiary. Notwithstanding this requirement, a non-investment entity parent shall not apply the exception to consolidation that is used by any investment entity subsidiaries. Similarly, if a parent becomes a first-time adopter for its separate financial statements earlier or later than for its consolidated financial statements, it shall measure its assets and liabilities at the same amounts in both financial statements, except for consolidation adjustments.

Compound financial instruments

D18   IAS 32 *Financial Instruments: Presentation* requires an entity to split a compound financial instrument at inception into separate liability and equity components. If the liability component is no longer outstanding, retrospective application of IAS 32 involves separating two portions of equity. The first portion is in retained earnings and represents the cumulative interest accreted on the liability component. The other portion represents the original equity component. However, in accordance with this IFRS, a first-time adopter need not separate these two portions if the liability component is no longer outstanding at the date of transition to IFRSs.

Designation of previously recognised financial instruments

D19   IFRS 9 permits a financial liability (provided it meets certain criteria) to be designated as a financial liability at fair value through profit or loss. Despite this requirement an entity is permitted to designate, at the date of transition to IFRSs, any financial liability as at fair value through profit or loss provided the liability meets the criteria in paragraph 4.2.2 of IFRS 9 at that date.

D19A   An entity may designate a financial asset as measured at fair value through profit or loss in accordance with paragraph 4.1.5 of IFRS 9 on the basis of the facts and circumstances that exist at the date of transition to IFRSs.

D19B   An entity may designate an investment in an equity instrument as at fair value through other comprehensive income in accordance with paragraph 5.7.5 of IFRS 9 on the basis of the facts and circumstances that exist at the date of transition to IFRSs.

D19C   For a financial liability that is designated as a financial liability at fair value through profit or loss, an entity shall determine whether the treatment in paragraph 5.7.7 of IFRS 9 would create an accounting mismatch in profit or loss on the basis of the facts and circumstances that exist at the date of transition to IFRSs.

Fair value measurement of financial assets or financial liabilities at initial recognition

D20   Despite the requirements of paragraphs 7 and 9, an entity may apply the requirements in paragraph B5.1.2A(b) of IFRS 9 prospectively to transactions entered into on or after the date of transition to IFRSs.

Decommissioning liabilities included in the cost of property, plant and equipment

D21   IFRIC 1 *Changes in Existing Decommissioning, Restoration and Similar Liabilities* requires specified changes in a decommissioning, restoration or similar liability to be added to or deducted from the cost of the asset to which it relates; the adjusted depreciable amount of the asset is then depreciated prospectively over its remaining useful life. A first-time adopter need not comply with these requirements for changes in such liabilities that occurred before the date of transition to IFRSs. If a first-time adopter uses this exemption, it shall:

(a)   measure the liability as at the date of transition to IFRSs in accordance with IAS 37;

(b)   to the extent that the liability is within the scope of IFRIC 1, estimate the amount that would have been included in the cost of the related asset when the liability first arose, by discounting the liability to that date using its best estimate of the historical risk-adjusted discount rate(s) that would have applied for that liability over the intervening period; and

(c)   calculate the accumulated depreciation on that amount, as at the date of transition to IFRSs, on the basis of the current estimate of the useful life of the asset, using the depreciation policy adopted by the entity in accordance with IFRSs.

D21A   An entity that uses the exemption in paragraph D8A(b) (for oil and gas assets in the development or production phases accounted for in cost centres that include all properties in a large geographical area under previous GAAP) shall, instead of applying paragraph D21 or IFRIC 1:

(a)   measure decommissioning, restoration and similar liabilities as at the date of transition to IFRSs in accordance with IAS 37; and

(b)   recognise directly in retained earnings any difference between that amount and the carrying amount of those liabilities at the date of transition to IFRSs determined under the entity's previous GAAP.

Financial assets or intangible assets accounted for in accordance with IFRIC 12

D22   A first-time adopter may apply the transitional provisions in IFRIC 12.

Borrowing costs

D23   A first-time adopter can elect to apply the requirements of IAS 23 from the date of transition or from an earlier date as permitted by paragraph 28 of IAS 23. From the date on which an entity that applies this exemption begins to apply IAS 23, the entity:

(a)   shall not restate the borrowing cost component that was capitalised under previous GAAP and that was included in the carrying amount of assets at that date; and

(b)   shall account for borrowing costs incurred on or after that date in accordance with IAS 23, including those borrowing costs incurred on or after that date on qualifying assets already under construction.

D24   [Deleted]

Extinguishing financial liabilities with equity instruments

D25 A first-time adopter may apply the transitional provisions in IFRIC 19 *Extinguishing Financial Liabilities with Equity Instruments*.

Severe hyperinflation

D26 If an entity has a functional currency that was, or is, the currency of a hyperinflationary economy, it shall determine whether it was subject to severe hyperinflation before the date of transition to IFRSs. This applies to entities that are adopting IFRSs for the first time, as well as entities that have previously applied IFRSs.

D27 The currency of a hyperinflationary economy is subject to severe hyperinflation if it has both of the following characteristics:

(a) a reliable general price index is not available to all entities with transactions and balances in the currency.

(b) exchangeability between the currency and a relatively stable foreign currency does not exist.

D28 The functional currency of an entity ceases to be subject to severe hyperinflation on the functional currency normalisation date. That is the date when the functional currency no longer has either, or both, of the characteristics in paragraph D27, or when there is a change in the entity's functional currency to a currency that is not subject to severe hyperinflation.

D29 When an entity's date of transition to IFRSs is on, or after, the functional currency normalisation date, the entity may elect to measure all assets and liabilities held before the functional currency normalisation date at fair value on the date of transition to IFRSs. The entity may use that fair value as the deemed cost of those assets and liabilities in the opening IFRS statement of financial position.

D30 When the functional currency normalisation date falls within a 12-month comparative period, the comparative period may be less than 12 months, provided that a complete set of financial statements (as required by paragraph 10 of IAS 1) is provided for that shorter period.

Joint arrangements

D31 A first-time adopter may apply the transition provisions in IFRS 11 with the following exceptions:

(a) When applying the transition provisions in IFRS 11, a first-time adopter shall apply these provisions at the date of transition to IFRS.

(b) When changing from proportionate consolidation to the equity method, a first-time adopter shall test for impairment the investment in accordance with IAS 36 as at the date of transition to IFRS, regardless of whether there is any indication that the investment may be impaired. Any resulting impairment shall be recognised as an adjustment to retained earnings at the date of transition to IFRS.

Stripping costs in the production phase of a surface mine

D32 A first-time adopter may apply the transitional provisions set out in paragraphs A1 to A4 of IFRIC 20 *Stripping Costs in the Production Phase of a Surface Mine*. In that paragraph, reference to the effective date shall be interpreted as 1 January 2013 or the beginning of the first IFRS reporting period, whichever is later.

Designation of contracts to buy or sell a non-financial item

D33 IFRS 9 permits some contracts to buy or sell a non-financial item to be designated at inception as measured at fair value through profit or loss (see paragraph 2.5 of IFRS 9). Despite this requirement an entity is permitted to designate, at the date of transition to IFRSs, contracts that already exist on that date as measured at fair value through profit or loss but only if they meet the requirements of paragraph 2.5 of IFRS 9 at that date and the entity designates all similar contracts.

Revenue

D34 A first-time adopter may apply the transition provisions in paragraph C5 of IFRS 15. In those paragraphs references to the 'date of initial application' shall be interpreted as the beginning of the first IFRS reporting period. If a first-time adopter decides to apply those transition provisions, it shall also apply paragraph C6 of IFRS 15.

D35 A first-time adopter is not required to restate contracts that were completed before the earliest period presented. A completed contract is a contract for which the entity has transferred all of the goods or services identified in accordance with previous GAAP.

Foreign currency transactions and advance consideration

D36 A first-time adopter need not apply IFRIC 22 *Foreign Currency Transactions and Advance Consideration* to assets, expenses and income in the scope of that Interpretation initially recognised before the date of transition to IFRS Standards.

Appendix E
Short-term exemptions from IFRSs

This appendix is an integral part of the IFRS.

Exemption from the requirement to restate comparative information for IFRS 9

E1 If an entity's first IFRS reporting period begins before 1 January 2019 and the entity applies the completed version of IFRS 9 (issued in 2014), the comparative information in the entity's first IFRS financial statements need not comply with IFRS 7 *Financial Instruments: Disclosure* or the completed version of IFRS 9 (issued in 2014), to the extent that the disclosures required by IFRS 7 relate to items within the scope of IFRS 9. For such entities, references to the 'date of transition to IFRSs' shall mean, in the case of IFRS 7 and IFRS 9 (2014) only, the beginning of the first IFRS reporting period.

E2 An entity that chooses to present comparative information that does not comply with IFRS 7 and the completed version of IFRS 9 (issued in 2014) in its first year of transition shall:

(a) apply the requirements of its previous GAAP in place of the requirements of IFRS 9 to comparative information about items within the scope of IFRS 9.

(b) disclose this fact together with the basis used to prepare this information.

(c) treat any adjustment between the statement of financial position at the comparative period's reporting date (ie the statement of financial position that includes comparative information under previous GAAP) and the statement of financial position at the start of the *first IFRS reporting period* (ie the first period that includes information that complies with IFRS 7 and the completed version of IFRS 9 (issued in 2014)) as arising from a change in accounting policy and give the disclosures required by paragraph 28(a)–(e) and (f)(i) of IAS 8. Paragraph 28(f)(i) applies only to amounts presented in the statement of financial position at the comparative period's reporting date.

(d) apply paragraph 17(c) of IAS 1 to provide additional disclosures when compliance with the specific requirements in IFRSs is insufficient to enable users to understand the impact of particular transactions, other events and conditions on the entity's financial position and financial performance.

E3–E7 [Deleted]

Uncertainty over income tax treatments

E8   A first-time adopter whose date of transition to IFRSs is before 1 July 2017 may elect not to reflect the application of IFRIC 23 *Uncertainty over Income Tax Treatments* in comparative information in its first IFRS financial statements. An entity that makes that election shall recognise the cumulative effect of applying IFRIC 23 as an adjustment to the opening balance of retained earnings (or other component of equity, as appropriate) at the beginning of its first IFRS reporting period.

Approval by the Board of IFRS 1 issued in November 2008

International Financial Reporting Standard 1 *First-time Adoption of International Financial Reporting Standards* (as revised in 2008) was approved for issue by the thirteen members of the International Accounting Standards Board.[3]

Sir David Tweedie	Chairman
Thomas E Jones	Vice-Chairman
Mary E Barth	
Stephen Cooper	
Philippe Danjou	
Jan Engström	
Robert P Garnett	
Gilbert Gélard	
James J Leisenring	
Warren J McGregor	
John T Smith	
Tatsumi Yamada	
Wei-Guo Zhang	

---

3 Professor Barth and Mr Danjou dissented from *Cost of an Investment in a Subsidiary, Jointly Controlled Entity or Associate* (Amendments to IFRS 1 and IAS 27) issued in May 2008. Their dissenting opinions are set out after the Basis for Conclusions on IAS 27.

Approval by the Board of *Additional Exemptions for First-time Adopters* (Amendments to IFRS 1) issued in July 2009

Additional Exemptions for First-time Adopters (Amendments to IFRS 1) was approved for issue by the fourteen members of the International Accounting Standards Board.

Sir David Tweedie	Chairman
Thomas E Jones	Vice-Chairman
Mary E Barth	
Stephen Cooper	
Philippe Danjou	
Jan Engström	
Robert P Garnett	
Gilbert Gélard	
Prabhakar Kalavacherla	
James J Leisenring	
Warren J McGregor	
John T Smith	
Tatsumi Yamada	
Wei-Guo Zhang	

Approval by the Board of *Limited Exemption from Comparative IFRS 7 Disclosures for First-time Adopters* (Amendment to IFRS 1) issued in January 2010

Limited Exemption from Comparative IFRS 7 Disclosures for First-time Adopters (Amendment to IFRS 1) was approved for issue by the fifteen members of the International Accounting Standards Board.

Sir David Tweedie   Chairman

Stephen Cooper

Philippe Danjou

Jan Engström

Patrick Finnegan

Robert P Garnett

Gilbert Gélard

Amaro Luiz de Oliveira Gomes

Prabhakar Kalavacherla

James J Leisenring

Patricia McConnell

Warren J McGregor

John T Smith

Tatsumi Yamada

Wei-Guo Zhang

Approval by the Board of *Severe Hyperinflation and Removal of Fixed Dates for First-time Adopters* (Amendments to IFRS 1) issued in December 2010

Severe Hyperinflation and Removal of Fixed Dates for First-time Adopters was approved for issue by the fifteen members of the International Accounting Standards Board.

Sir David Tweedie	Chairman
Stephen Cooper	
Philippe Danjou	
Jan Engström	
Patrick Finnegan	
Amaro Luiz de Oliveira Gomes	
Prabhakar Kalavacherla	
Elke König	
Patricia McConnell	
Warren J McGregor	
Paul Pacter	
Darrel Scott	
John T Smith	
Tatsumi Yamada	
Wei-Guo Zhang	

Approval by the Board of *Government Loans* (Amendments to IFRS 1) issued in March 2012

Government Loans (Amendments to IFRS 1) was approved for issue by the fourteen members of the International Accounting Standards Board.

Hans Hoogervorst	Chairman
Ian Mackintosh	Vice-Chairman
Stephen Cooper	
Philippe Danjou	
Jan Engström	
Patrick Finnegan	
Amaro Luiz de Oliveira Gomes	
Prabhakar Kalavacherla	
Patricia McConnell	
Takatsugu Ochi	
Paul Pacter	
Darrel Scott	
John T Smith	
Wei-Guo Zhang	

IFRS 2

Share-based Payment

In February 2004 the International Accounting Standards Board (Board) issued IFRS 2 *Share-based Payment*. The Board amended IFRS 2 to clarify its scope in January 2008 and to incorporate the guidance contained in two related Interpretations (IFRIC 8 *Scope of IFRS 2* and IFRIC 11 *IFRS 2 – Group and Treasury Share Transactions*) in June 2009.

In June 2016 the Board issued *Classification and Measurement of Share-based Payment Transactions* (Amendments to IFRS 2). This amended IFRS 2 to clarify the accounting for (a) the effects of vesting and non-vesting conditions on the measurement of cash-settled share-based payments; (b) share-based payment transactions with a net settlement feature for withholding tax obligations; and (c) a modification to the terms and conditions of a share-based payment that changes the classification of the transaction from cash-settled to equity-settled.

Other Standards have made minor consequential amendments to IFRS 2. They include IFRS 10 *Consolidated Financial Statements* (issued May 2011), IFRS 11 *Joint Arrangements* (issued May 2011), IFRS 13 *Fair Value Measurement* (issued May 2011), *Annual Improvements to IFRSs 2010–2012 Cycle* (issued December 2013), IFRS 9 *Financial Instruments* (issued July 2014), *Amendments to References to the Conceptual Framework in IFRS Standards* (issued March 2018) and *Definition of Material* (Amendments to IAS 1 and IAS 8) (issued October 2018).

CONTENTS

continued...

...continued

FOR THE ACCOMPANYING GUIDANCE LISTED BELOW, SEE PART B OF THIS EDITION

IMPLEMENTATION GUIDANCE

TABLE OF CONCORDANCE

FOR THE BASIS FOR CONCLUSIONS, SEE PART C OF THIS EDITION

BASIS FOR CONCLUSIONS

International Financial Reporting Standard 2 *Share-based Payment* (IFRS 2) is set out in paragraphs 1–64 and Appendices A–C. All the paragraphs have equal authority. Paragraphs in **bold type** state the main principles. Terms defined in Appendix A are in *italics* the first time they appear in the Standard. Definitions of other terms are given in the Glossary for International Financial Reporting Standards. IFRS 2 should be read in the context of its objective and the Basis for Conclusions, the *Preface to IFRS Standards* and the *Conceptual Framework for Financial Reporting*. IAS 8 *Accounting Policies, Changes in Accounting Estimates and Errors* provides a basis for selecting and applying accounting policies in the absence of explicit guidance.

International Financial Reporting Standard 2
Share-based Payment

Objective

1   The objective of this IFRS is to specify the financial reporting by an entity when it undertakes a *share-based payment transaction*. In particular, it requires an entity to reflect in its profit or loss and financial position the effects of share-based payment transactions, including expenses associated with transactions in which *share options* are granted to employees.

Scope

2   An entity shall apply this IFRS in accounting for all share-based payment transactions, whether or not the entity can identify specifically some or all of the goods or services received, including:

(a)   *equity-settled share-based payment transactions,*

(b)   *cash-settled share-based payment transactions,* and

(c)   transactions in which the entity receives or acquires goods or services and the terms of the arrangement provide either the entity or the supplier of those goods or services with a choice of whether the entity settles the transaction in cash (or other assets) or by issuing equity instruments,

except as noted in paragraphs 3A–6. In the absence of specifically identifiable goods or services, other circumstances may indicate that goods or services have been (or will be) received, in which case this IFRS applies.

3   [Deleted]

3A   A share-based payment transaction may be settled by another group entity (or a shareholder of any group entity) on behalf of the entity receiving or acquiring the goods or services. Paragraph 2 also applies to an entity that

(a)   receives goods or services when another entity in the same group (or a shareholder of any group entity) has the obligation to settle the share-based payment transaction, or

(b)   has an obligation to settle a share-based payment transaction when another entity in the same group receives the goods or services

unless the transaction is clearly for a purpose other than payment for goods or services supplied to the entity receiving them.

4   For the purposes of this IFRS, a transaction with an employee (or other party) in his/her capacity as a holder of equity instruments of the entity is not a share-based payment transaction. For example, if an entity grants all holders of a particular class of its equity instruments the right to acquire additional equity instruments of the entity at a price that is less than the fair value of those equity instruments, and an employee receives such a right because

he/she is a holder of equity instruments of that particular class, the granting or exercise of that right is not subject to the requirements of this IFRS.

5   As noted in paragraph 2, this IFRS applies to share-based payment transactions in which an entity acquires or receives goods or services. Goods includes inventories, consumables, property, plant and equipment, intangible assets and other non-financial assets. However, an entity shall not apply this IFRS to transactions in which the entity acquires goods as part of the net assets acquired in a business combination as defined by IFRS 3 *Business Combinations* (as revised in 2008), in a combination of entities or businesses under common control as described in paragraphs B1–B4 of IFRS 3, or the contribution of a business on the formation of a joint venture as defined by IFRS 11 *Joint Arrangements*. Hence, equity instruments issued in a business combination in exchange for control of the acquiree are not within the scope of this IFRS. However, equity instruments granted to employees of the acquiree in their capacity as employees (eg in return for continued service) are within the scope of this IFRS. Similarly, the cancellation, replacement or other modification of *share-based payment arrangements* because of a business combination or other equity restructuring shall be accounted for in accordance with this IFRS. IFRS 3 provides guidance on determining whether equity instruments issued in a business combination are part of the consideration transferred in exchange for control of the acquiree (and therefore within the scope of IFRS 3) or are in return for continued service to be recognised in the post-combination period (and therefore within the scope of this IFRS).

6   This IFRS does not apply to share-based payment transactions in which the entity receives or acquires goods or services under a contract within the scope of paragraphs 8–10 of IAS 32 *Financial Instruments: Presentation* (as revised in 2003)[1] or paragraphs 2.4–2.7 of IFRS 9 *Financial Instruments*.

6A   This IFRS uses the term 'fair value' in a way that differs in some respects from the definition of fair value in IFRS 13 *Fair Value Measurement*. Therefore, when applying IFRS 2 an entity measures fair value in accordance with this IFRS, not IFRS 13.

Recognition

7   An entity shall recognise the goods or services received or acquired in a share-based payment transaction when it obtains the goods or as the services are received. The entity shall recognise a corresponding increase in equity if the goods or services were received in an equity-settled share-based payment transaction, or a liability if the goods or services were acquired in a cash-settled share-based payment transaction.

8   When the goods or services received or acquired in a share-based payment transaction do not qualify for recognition as assets, they shall be recognised as expenses.

---

1   The title of IAS 32 was amended in 2005.

9   Typically, an expense arises from the consumption of goods or services. For example, services are typically consumed immediately, in which case an expense is recognised as the counterparty renders service. Goods might be consumed over a period of time or, in the case of inventories, sold at a later date, in which case an expense is recognised when the goods are consumed or sold. However, sometimes it is necessary to recognise an expense before the goods or services are consumed or sold, because they do not qualify for recognition as assets. For example, an entity might acquire goods as part of the research phase of a project to develop a new product. Although those goods have not been consumed, they might not qualify for recognition as assets under the applicable IFRS.

Equity-settled share-based payment transactions

Overview

10   **For equity-settled share-based payment transactions, the entity shall measure the goods or services received, and the corresponding increase in equity, directly, at the fair value of the goods or services received, unless that fair value cannot be estimated reliably. If the entity cannot estimate reliably the fair value of the goods or services received, the entity shall measure their value, and the corresponding increase in equity, indirectly, by reference to[2] the fair value of the equity instruments granted.**

11   To apply the requirements of paragraph 10 to transactions with *employees and others providing similar services*,[3] the entity shall measure the fair value of the services received by reference to the fair value of the equity instruments granted, because typically it is not possible to estimate reliably the fair value of the services received, as explained in paragraph 12. The fair value of those equity instruments shall be measured at *grant date*.

12   Typically, shares, share options or other equity instruments are granted to employees as part of their remuneration package, in addition to a cash salary and other employment benefits. Usually, it is not possible to measure directly the services received for particular components of the employee's remuneration package. It might also not be possible to measure the fair value of the total remuneration package independently, without measuring directly the fair value of the equity instruments granted. Furthermore, shares or share options are sometimes granted as part of a bonus arrangement, rather than as a part of basic remuneration, eg as an incentive to the employees to remain in the entity's employ or to reward them for their efforts in improving the entity's performance. By granting shares or share options, in addition to other remuneration, the entity is paying additional remuneration to obtain additional benefits. Estimating the fair value of those additional benefits is

---

2   This IFRS uses the phrase 'by reference to' rather than 'at', because the transaction is ultimately measured by multiplying the fair value of the equity instruments granted, measured at the date specified in paragraph 11 or 13 (whichever is applicable), by the number of equity instruments that vest, as explained in paragraph 19.

3   In the remainder of this IFRS, all references to employees also include others providing similar services.

likely to be difficult. Because of the difficulty of measuring directly the fair value of the services received, the entity shall measure the fair value of the employee services received by reference to the fair value of the equity instruments granted.

13   To apply the requirements of paragraph 10 to transactions with parties other than employees, there shall be a rebuttable presumption that the fair value of the goods or services received can be estimated reliably. That fair value shall be measured at the date the entity obtains the goods or the counterparty renders service. In rare cases, if the entity rebuts this presumption because it cannot estimate reliably the fair value of the goods or services received, the entity shall measure the goods or services received, and the corresponding increase in equity, indirectly, by reference to the fair value of the equity instruments granted, measured at the date the entity obtains the goods or the counterparty renders service.

13A   In particular, if the identifiable consideration received (if any) by the entity appears to be less than the fair value of the equity instruments granted or liability incurred, typically this situation indicates that other consideration (ie unidentifiable goods or services) has been (or will be) received by the entity. The entity shall measure the identifiable goods or services received in accordance with this IFRS. The entity shall measure the unidentifiable goods or services received (or to be received) as the difference between the fair value of the share-based payment and the fair value of any identifiable goods or services received (or to be received). The entity shall measure the unidentifiable goods or services received at the grant date. However, for cash-settled transactions, the liability shall be remeasured at the end of each reporting period until it is settled in accordance with paragraphs 30–33.

Transactions in which services are received

14   If the equity instruments granted *vest* immediately, the counterparty is not required to complete a specified period of service before becoming unconditionally entitled to those equity instruments. In the absence of evidence to the contrary, the entity shall presume that services rendered by the counterparty as consideration for the equity instruments have been received. In this case, on grant date the entity shall recognise the services received in full, with a corresponding increase in equity.

15   If the equity instruments granted do not vest until the counterparty completes a specified period of service, the entity shall presume that the services to be rendered by the counterparty as consideration for those equity instruments will be received in the future, during the *vesting period*. The entity shall account for those services as they are rendered by the counterparty during the vesting period, with a corresponding increase in equity. For example:

(a)   if an employee is granted share options conditional upon completing three years' service, then the entity shall presume that the services to be rendered by the employee as consideration for the share options will be received in the future, over that three-year vesting period.

(b) if an employee is granted share options conditional upon the achievement of a *performance condition* and remaining in the entity's employ until that performance condition is satisfied, and the length of the vesting period varies depending on when that performance condition is satisfied, the entity shall presume that the services to be rendered by the employee as consideration for the share options will be received in the future, over the expected vesting period. The entity shall estimate the length of the expected vesting period at grant date, based on the most likely outcome of the performance condition. If the performance condition is a *market condition*, the estimate of the length of the expected vesting period shall be consistent with the assumptions used in estimating the fair value of the options granted, and shall not be subsequently revised. If the performance condition is not a market condition, the entity shall revise its estimate of the length of the vesting period, if necessary, if subsequent information indicates that the length of the vesting period differs from previous estimates.

Transactions measured by reference to the fair value of the equity instruments granted

Determining the fair value of equity instruments granted

16   For transactions measured by reference to the fair value of the equity instruments granted, an entity shall measure the fair value of equity instruments granted at the *measurement date*, based on market prices if available, taking into account the terms and conditions upon which those equity instruments were granted (subject to the requirements of paragraphs 19–22).

17   If market prices are not available, the entity shall estimate the fair value of the equity instruments granted using a valuation technique to estimate what the price of those equity instruments would have been on the measurement date in an arm's length transaction between knowledgeable, willing parties. The valuation technique shall be consistent with generally accepted valuation methodologies for pricing financial instruments, and shall incorporate all factors and assumptions that knowledgeable, willing market participants would consider in setting the price (subject to the requirements of paragraphs 19–22).

18   Appendix B contains further guidance on the measurement of the fair value of shares and share options, focusing on the specific terms and conditions that are common features of a grant of shares or share options to employees.

Treatment of vesting conditions

19   A grant of equity instruments might be conditional upon satisfying specified vesting conditions. For example, a grant of shares or share options to an employee is typically conditional on the employee remaining in the entity's employ for a specified period of time. There might be performance conditions that must be satisfied, such as the entity achieving a specified growth in profit or a specified increase in the entity's share price. Vesting

conditions, other than market conditions, shall not be taken into account when estimating the fair value of the shares or share options at the measurement date. Instead, vesting conditions, other than market conditions, shall be taken into account by adjusting the number of equity instruments included in the measurement of the transaction amount so that, ultimately, the amount recognised for goods or services received as consideration for the equity instruments granted shall be based on the number of equity instruments that eventually vest. Hence, on a cumulative basis, no amount is recognised for goods or services received if the equity instruments granted do not vest because of failure to satisfy a *vesting condition*, other than a market condition, for example, the counterparty fails to complete a specified service period, or a performance condition is not satisfied, subject to the requirements of paragraph 21.

20   To apply the requirements of paragraph 19, the entity shall recognise an amount for the goods or services received during the vesting period based on the best available estimate of the number of equity instruments expected to vest and shall revise that estimate, if necessary, if subsequent information indicates that the number of equity instruments expected to vest differs from previous estimates. On vesting date, the entity shall revise the estimate to equal the number of equity instruments that ultimately vested, subject to the requirements of paragraph 21.

21   Market conditions, such as a target share price upon which vesting (or exercisability) is conditioned, shall be taken into account when estimating the fair value of the equity instruments granted. Therefore, for grants of equity instruments with market conditions, the entity shall recognise the goods or services received from a counterparty who satisfies all other vesting conditions (eg services received from an employee who remains in service for the specified period of service), irrespective of whether that market condition is satisfied.

Treatment of non-vesting conditions

21A   Similarly, an entity shall take into account all non-vesting conditions when estimating the fair value of the equity instruments granted. Therefore, for grants of equity instruments with non-vesting conditions, the entity shall recognise the goods or services received from a counterparty that satisfies all vesting conditions that are not market conditions (eg services received from an employee who remains in service for the specified period of service), irrespective of whether those non-vesting conditions are satisfied.

Treatment of a reload feature

22   For options with a *reload feature*, the reload feature shall not be taken into account when estimating the fair value of options granted at the measurement date. Instead, a *reload option* shall be accounted for as a new option grant, if and when a reload option is subsequently granted.

After vesting date

23   Having recognised the goods or services received in accordance with paragraphs 10–22, and a corresponding increase in equity, the entity shall make no subsequent adjustment to total equity after vesting date. For example, the entity shall not subsequently reverse the amount recognised for services received from an employee if the vested equity instruments are later forfeited or, in the case of share options, the options are not exercised. However, this requirement does not preclude the entity from recognising a transfer within equity, ie a transfer from one component of equity to another.

If the fair value of the equity instruments cannot be estimated reliably

24   The requirements in paragraphs 16–23 apply when the entity is required to measure a share-based payment transaction by reference to the fair value of the equity instruments granted. In rare cases, the entity may be unable to estimate reliably the fair value of the equity instruments granted at the measurement date, in accordance with the requirements in paragraphs 16–22. In these rare cases only, the entity shall instead:

(a)   measure the equity instruments at their *intrinsic value*, initially at the date the entity obtains the goods or the counterparty renders service and subsequently at the end of each reporting period and at the date of final settlement, with any change in intrinsic value recognised in profit or loss. For a grant of share options, the share-based payment arrangement is finally settled when the options are exercised, are forfeited (eg upon cessation of employment) or lapse (eg at the end of the option's life).

(b)   recognise the goods or services received based on the number of equity instruments that ultimately vest or (where applicable) are ultimately exercised. To apply this requirement to share options, for example, the entity shall recognise the goods or services received during the vesting period, if any, in accordance with paragraphs 14 and 15, except that the requirements in paragraph 15(b) concerning a market condition do not apply. The amount recognised for goods or services received during the vesting period shall be based on the number of share options expected to vest. The entity shall revise that estimate, if necessary, if subsequent information indicates that the number of share options expected to vest differs from previous estimates. On vesting date, the entity shall revise the estimate to equal the number of equity instruments that ultimately vested. After vesting date, the entity shall reverse the amount recognised for goods or services received if the share options are later forfeited, or lapse at the end of the share option's life.

25   If an entity applies paragraph 24, it is not necessary to apply paragraphs 26–29, because any modifications to the terms and conditions on which the equity instruments were granted will be taken into account when applying the intrinsic value method set out in paragraph 24. However, if an entity settles a grant of equity instruments to which paragraph 24 has been applied:

(a)   if the settlement occurs during the vesting period, the entity shall account for the settlement as an acceleration of vesting, and shall therefore recognise immediately the amount that would otherwise have been recognised for services received over the remainder of the vesting period.

(b)   any payment made on settlement shall be accounted for as the repurchase of equity instruments, ie as a deduction from equity, except to the extent that the payment exceeds the intrinsic value of the equity instruments, measured at the repurchase date. Any such excess shall be recognised as an expense.

Modifications to the terms and conditions on which equity instruments were granted, including cancellations and settlements

26   An entity might modify the terms and conditions on which the equity instruments were granted. For example, it might reduce the exercise price of options granted to employees (ie reprice the options), which increases the fair value of those options. The requirements in paragraphs 27–29 to account for the effects of modifications are expressed in the context of share-based payment transactions with employees. However, the requirements shall also be applied to share-based payment transactions with parties other than employees that are measured by reference to the fair value of the equity instruments granted. In the latter case, any references in paragraphs 27–29 to grant date shall instead refer to the date the entity obtains the goods or the counterparty renders service.

27   The entity shall recognise, as a minimum, the services received measured at the grant date fair value of the equity instruments granted, unless those equity instruments do not vest because of failure to satisfy a vesting condition (other than a market condition) that was specified at grant date. This applies irrespective of any modifications to the terms and conditions on which the equity instruments were granted, or a cancellation or settlement of that grant of equity instruments. In addition, the entity shall recognise the effects of modifications that increase the total fair value of the share-based payment arrangement or are otherwise beneficial to the employee. Guidance on applying this requirement is given in Appendix B.

28   If a grant of equity instruments is cancelled or settled during the vesting period (other than a grant cancelled by forfeiture when the vesting conditions are not satisfied):

(a)   the entity shall account for the cancellation or settlement as an acceleration of vesting, and shall therefore recognise immediately the amount that otherwise would have been recognised for services received over the remainder of the vesting period.

(b)   any payment made to the employee on the cancellation or settlement of the grant shall be accounted for as the repurchase of an equity interest, ie as a deduction from equity, except to the extent that the payment exceeds the fair value of the equity instruments granted, measured at the repurchase date. Any such excess shall be recognised as an expense. However, if the share-based payment arrangement included liability components, the entity shall remeasure the fair value of the liability at the date of cancellation or settlement. Any payment made to settle the liability component shall be accounted for as an extinguishment of the liability.

(c)   if new equity instruments are granted to the employee and, on the date when those new equity instruments are granted, the entity identifies the new equity instruments granted as replacement equity instruments for the cancelled equity instruments, the entity shall account for the granting of replacement equity instruments in the same way as a modification of the original grant of equity instruments, in accordance with paragraph 27 and the guidance in Appendix B. The incremental fair value granted is the difference between the fair value of the replacement equity instruments and the net fair value of the cancelled equity instruments, at the date the replacement equity instruments are granted. The net fair value of the cancelled equity instruments is their fair value, immediately before the cancellation, less the amount of any payment made to the employee on cancellation of the equity instruments that is accounted for as a deduction from equity in accordance with (b) above. If the entity does not identify new equity instruments granted as replacement equity instruments for the cancelled equity instruments, the entity shall account for those new equity instruments as a new grant of equity instruments.

28A   If an entity or counterparty can choose whether to meet a non-vesting condition, the entity shall treat the entity's or counterparty's failure to meet that non-vesting condition during the vesting period as a cancellation.

29   If an entity repurchases vested equity instruments, the payment made to the employee shall be accounted for as a deduction from equity, except to the extent that the payment exceeds the fair value of the equity instruments repurchased, measured at the repurchase date. Any such excess shall be recognised as an expense.

Cash-settled share-based payment transactions

30   For cash-settled share-based payment transactions, the entity shall measure the goods or services acquired and the liability incurred at the fair value of the liability, subject to the requirements of paragraphs 31–33D. Until the liability is settled, the entity shall remeasure the fair value of the liability at the end of each reporting period and at the date of settlement, with any changes in fair value recognised in profit or loss for the period.

31   For example, an entity might grant share appreciation rights to employees as part of their remuneration package, whereby the employees will become entitled to a future cash payment (rather than an equity instrument), based on the increase in the entity's share price from a specified level over a specified period of time. Alternatively, an entity might grant to its employees a right to receive a future cash payment by granting to them a right to shares (including

shares to be issued upon the exercise of share options) that are redeemable, either mandatorily (for example, upon cessation of employment) or at the employee's option. These arrangements are examples of cash-settled share-based payment transactions. Share appreciation rights are used to illustrate some of the requirements in paragraphs 32–33D; however, the requirements in those paragraphs apply to all cash-settled share-based payment transactions.

32   The entity shall recognise the services received, and a liability to pay for those services, as the employees render service. For example, some share appreciation rights vest immediately, and the employees are therefore not required to complete a specified period of service to become entitled to the cash payment. In the absence of evidence to the contrary, the entity shall presume that the services rendered by the employees in exchange for the share appreciation rights have been received. Thus, the entity shall recognise immediately the services received and a liability to pay for them. If the share appreciation rights do not vest until the employees have completed a specified period of service, the entity shall recognise the services received, and a liability to pay for them, as the employees render service during that period.

33   The liability shall be measured, initially and at the end of each reporting period until settled, at the fair value of the share appreciation rights, by applying an option pricing model, taking into account the terms and conditions on which the share appreciation rights were granted, and the extent to which the employees have rendered service to date—subject to the requirements of paragraphs 33A–33D. An entity might modify the terms and conditions on which a cash-settled share-based payment is granted. Guidance for a modification of a share-based payment transaction that changes its classification from cash-settled to equity-settled is given in paragraphs B44A–B44C in Appendix B.

Treatment of vesting and non-vesting conditions

33A   A cash-settled share-based payment transaction might be conditional upon satisfying specified vesting conditions. There might be performance conditions that must be satisfied, such as the entity achieving a specified growth in profit or a specified increase in the entity's share price. Vesting conditions, other than market conditions, shall not be taken into account when estimating the fair value of the cash-settled share-based payment at the measurement date. Instead, vesting conditions, other than market conditions, shall be taken into account by adjusting the number of awards included in the measurement of the liability arising from the transaction.

33B   To apply the requirements in paragraph 33A, the entity shall recognise an amount for the goods or services received during the vesting period. That amount shall be based on the best available estimate of the number of awards that are expected to vest. The entity shall revise that estimate, if necessary, if subsequent information indicates that the number of awards that are expected to vest differs from previous estimates. On the vesting date, the entity shall revise the estimate to equal the number of awards that ultimately vested.

33C   Market conditions, such as a target share price upon which vesting (or exercisability) is conditioned, as well as non-vesting conditions, shall be taken into account when estimating the fair value of the cash-settled share-based payment granted and when remeasuring the fair value at the end of each reporting period and at the date of settlement.

33D   As a result of applying paragraphs 30–33C, the cumulative amount ultimately recognised for goods or services received as consideration for the cash-settled share-based payment is equal to the cash that is paid.

Share-based payment transactions with a net settlement feature for withholding tax obligations

33E   Tax laws or regulations may oblige an entity to withhold an amount for an employee's tax obligation associated with a share-based payment and transfer that amount, normally in cash, to the tax authority on the employee's behalf. To fulfil this obligation, the terms of the share-based payment arrangement may permit or require the entity to withhold the number of equity instruments equal to the monetary value of the employee's tax obligation from the total number of equity instruments that otherwise would have been issued to the employee upon exercise (or vesting) of the share-based payment (ie the share-based payment arrangement has a 'net settlement feature').

33F   As an exception to the requirements in paragraph 34, the transaction described in paragraph 33E shall be classified in its entirety as an equity-settled share-based payment transaction if it would have been so classified in the absence of the net settlement feature.

33G   The entity applies paragraph 29 of this Standard to account for the withholding of shares to fund the payment to the tax authority in respect of the employee's tax obligation associated with the share-based payment. Therefore, the payment made shall be accounted for as a deduction from equity for the shares withheld, except to the extent that the payment exceeds the fair value at the net settlement date of the equity instruments withheld.

33H   The exception in paragraph 33F does not apply to:

       (a)   a share-based payment arrangement with a net settlement feature for which there is no obligation on the entity under tax laws or regulations to withhold an amount for an employee's tax obligation associated with that share-based payment; or

       (b)   any equity instruments that the entity withholds in excess of the employee's tax obligation associated with the share-based payment (ie the entity withheld an amount of shares that exceeds the monetary value of the employee's tax obligation). Such excess shares withheld shall be accounted for as a cash-settled share-based payment when this amount is paid in cash (or other assets) to the employee.

Share-based payment transactions with cash alternatives

34   For share-based payment transactions in which the terms of the arrangement provide either the entity or the counterparty with the choice of whether the entity settles the transaction in cash (or other assets) or by issuing equity instruments, the entity shall account for that transaction, or the components of that transaction, as a cash-settled share-based payment transaction if, and to the extent that, the entity has incurred a liability to settle in cash or other assets, or as an equity-settled share-based payment transaction if, and to the extent that, no such liability has been incurred.

Share-based payment transactions in which the terms of the arrangement provide the counterparty with a choice of settlement

35   If an entity has granted the counterparty the right to choose whether a share-based payment transaction is settled in cash[4] or by issuing equity instruments, the entity has granted a compound financial instrument, which includes a debt component (ie the counterparty's right to demand payment in cash) and an equity component (ie the counterparty's right to demand settlement in equity instruments rather than in cash). For transactions with parties other than employees, in which the fair value of the goods or services received is measured directly, the entity shall measure the equity component of the compound financial instrument as the difference between the fair value of the goods or services received and the fair value of the debt component, at the date when the goods or services are received.

36   For other transactions, including transactions with employees, the entity shall measure the fair value of the compound financial instrument at the measurement date, taking into account the terms and conditions on which the rights to cash or equity instruments were granted.

37   To apply paragraph 36, the entity shall first measure the fair value of the debt component, and then measure the fair value of the equity component — taking into account that the counterparty must forfeit the right to receive cash in order to receive the equity instrument. The fair value of the compound financial instrument is the sum of the fair values of the two components. However, share-based payment transactions in which the counterparty has the choice of settlement are often structured so that the fair value of one settlement alternative is the same as the other. For example, the counterparty might have the choice of receiving share options or cash-settled share appreciation rights. In such cases, the fair value of the equity component is zero, and hence the fair value of the compound financial instrument is the same as the fair value of the debt component. Conversely, if the fair values of the settlement alternatives differ, the fair value of the equity component usually will be greater than zero, in which case the fair value of the compound financial instrument will be greater than the fair value of the debt component.

---

4   In paragraphs 35–43, all references to cash also include other assets of the entity.

38   The entity shall account separately for the goods or services received or acquired in respect of each component of the compound financial instrument. For the debt component, the entity shall recognise the goods or services acquired, and a liability to pay for those goods or services, as the counterparty supplies goods or renders service, in accordance with the requirements applying to cash-settled share-based payment transactions (paragraphs 30–33). For the equity component (if any), the entity shall recognise the goods or services received, and an increase in equity, as the counterparty supplies goods or renders service, in accordance with the requirements applying to equity-settled share-based payment transactions (paragraphs 10–29).

39   At the date of settlement, the entity shall remeasure the liability to its fair value. If the entity issues equity instruments on settlement rather than paying cash, the liability shall be transferred direct to equity, as the consideration for the equity instruments issued.

40   If the entity pays in cash on settlement rather than issuing equity instruments, that payment shall be applied to settle the liability in full. Any equity component previously recognised shall remain within equity. By electing to receive cash on settlement, the counterparty forfeited the right to receive equity instruments. However, this requirement does not preclude the entity from recognising a transfer within equity, ie a transfer from one component of equity to another.

Share-based payment transactions in which the terms of the arrangement provide the entity with a choice of settlement

41   For a share-based payment transaction in which the terms of the arrangement provide an entity with the choice of whether to settle in cash or by issuing equity instruments, the entity shall determine whether it has a present obligation to settle in cash and account for the share-based payment transaction accordingly. The entity has a present obligation to settle in cash if the choice of settlement in equity instruments has no commercial substance (eg because the entity is legally prohibited from issuing shares), or the entity has a past practice or a stated policy of settling in cash, or generally settles in cash whenever the counterparty asks for cash settlement.

42   If the entity has a present obligation to settle in cash, it shall account for the transaction in accordance with the requirements applying to cash-settled share-based payment transactions, in paragraphs 30–33.

43   If no such obligation exists, the entity shall account for the transaction in accordance with the requirements applying to equity-settled share-based payment transactions, in paragraphs 10–29. Upon settlement:

    (a)   if the entity elects to settle in cash, the cash payment shall be accounted for as the repurchase of an equity interest, ie as a deduction from equity, except as noted in (c) below.

(b)   if the entity elects to settle by issuing equity instruments, no further accounting is required (other than a transfer from one component of equity to another, if necessary), except as noted in (c) below.

(c)   if the entity elects the settlement alternative with the higher fair value, as at the date of settlement, the entity shall recognise an additional expense for the excess value given, ie the difference between the cash paid and the fair value of the equity instruments that would otherwise have been issued, or the difference between the fair value of the equity instruments issued and the amount of cash that would otherwise have been paid, whichever is applicable.

Share-based payment transactions among group entities (2009 amendments)

43A   For share-based payment transactions among group entities, in its separate or individual financial statements, the entity receiving the goods or services shall measure the goods or services received as either an equity-settled or a cash-settled share-based payment transaction by assessing:

(a)   the nature of the awards granted, and

(b)   its own rights and obligations.

The amount recognised by the entity receiving the goods or services may differ from the amount recognised by the consolidated group or by another group entity settling the share-based payment transaction.

43B   The entity receiving the goods or services shall measure the goods or services received as an equity-settled share-based payment transaction when:

(a)   the awards granted are its own equity instruments, or

(b)   the entity has no obligation to settle the share-based payment transaction.

The entity shall subsequently remeasure such an equity-settled share-based payment transaction only for changes in non-market vesting conditions in accordance with paragraphs 19–21. In all other circumstances, the entity receiving the goods or services shall measure the goods or services received as a cash-settled share-based payment transaction.

43C   The entity settling a share-based payment transaction when another entity in the group receives the goods or services shall recognise the transaction as an equity-settled share-based payment transaction only if it is settled in the entity's own equity instruments. Otherwise, the transaction shall be recognised as a cash-settled share-based payment transaction.

43D   Some group transactions involve repayment arrangements that require one group entity to pay another group entity for the provision of the share-based payments to the suppliers of goods or services. In such cases, the entity that receives the goods or services shall account for the share-based payment transaction in accordance with paragraph 43B regardless of intragroup repayment arrangements.

Disclosures

44   An entity shall disclose information that enables users of the financial statements to understand the nature and extent of share-based payment arrangements that existed during the period.

45   To give effect to the principle in paragraph 44, the entity shall disclose at least the following:

(a)   a description of each type of share-based payment arrangement that existed at any time during the period, including the general terms and conditions of each arrangement, such as vesting requirements, the maximum term of options granted, and the method of settlement (eg whether in cash or equity). An entity with substantially similar types of share-based payment arrangements may aggregate this information, unless separate disclosure of each arrangement is necessary to satisfy the principle in paragraph 44.

(b)   the number and weighted average exercise prices of share options for each of the following groups of options:

(i)   outstanding at the beginning of the period;

(ii)   granted during the period;

(iii)   forfeited during the period;

(iv)   exercised during the period;

(v)   expired during the period;

(vi)   outstanding at the end of the period; and

(vii)   exercisable at the end of the period.

(c)   for share options exercised during the period, the weighted average share price at the date of exercise. If options were exercised on a regular basis throughout the period, the entity may instead disclose the weighted average share price during the period.

(d)   for share options outstanding at the end of the period, the range of exercise prices and weighted average remaining contractual life. If the range of exercise prices is wide, the outstanding options shall be divided into ranges that are meaningful for assessing the number and timing of additional shares that may be issued and the cash that may be received upon exercise of those options.

46   An entity shall disclose information that enables users of the financial statements to understand how the fair value of the goods or services received, or the fair value of the equity instruments granted, during the period was determined.

47   If the entity has measured the fair value of goods or services received as consideration for equity instruments of the entity indirectly, by reference to the fair value of the equity instruments granted, to give effect to the principle in paragraph 46, the entity shall disclose at least the following:

(a)   for share options granted during the period, the weighted average fair value of those options at the measurement date and information on how that fair value was measured, including:

   (i)   the option pricing model used and the inputs to that model, including the weighted average share price, exercise price, expected volatility, option life, expected dividends, the risk-free interest rate and any other inputs to the model, including the method used and the assumptions made to incorporate the effects of expected early exercise;

   (ii)   how expected volatility was determined, including an explanation of the extent to which expected volatility was based on historical volatility; and

   (iii)   whether and how any other features of the option grant were incorporated into the measurement of fair value, such as a market condition.

(b)   for other equity instruments granted during the period (ie other than share options), the number and weighted average fair value of those equity instruments at the measurement date, and information on how that fair value was measured, including:

   (i)   if fair value was not measured on the basis of an observable market price, how it was determined;

   (ii)   whether and how expected dividends were incorporated into the measurement of fair value; and

   (iii)   whether and how any other features of the equity instruments granted were incorporated into the measurement of fair value.

(c)   for share-based payment arrangements that were modified during the period:

   (i)   an explanation of those modifications;

   (ii)   the incremental fair value granted (as a result of those modifications); and

   (iii)   information on how the incremental fair value granted was measured, consistently with the requirements set out in (a) and (b) above, where applicable.

48   If the entity has measured directly the fair value of goods or services received during the period, the entity shall disclose how that fair value was determined, eg whether fair value was measured at a market price for those goods or services.

49   If the entity has rebutted the presumption in paragraph 13, it shall disclose that fact, and give an explanation of why the presumption was rebutted.

provided the specified **vesting conditions**, if any, are met. If that agreement is subject to an approval process (for example, by shareholders), grant date is the date when that approval is obtained.

intrinsic value The difference between the **fair value** of the shares to which the counterparty has the (conditional or unconditional) right to subscribe or which it has the right to receive, and the price (if any) the counterparty is (or will be) required to pay for those shares. For example, a **share option** with an exercise price of CU15,[6] on a share with a fair value of CU20, has an intrinsic value of CU5.

market condition A **performance condition** upon which the exercise price, vesting or exercisability of an **equity instrument** depends that is related to the market price (or value) of the entity's **equity instruments** (or the equity instruments of another entity in the same group), such as:

(a) attaining a specified share price or a specified amount of **intrinsic value** of a **share option**; or

(b) achieving a specified target that is based on the market price (or value) of the entity's **equity instruments** (or the equity instruments of another entity in the same group) relative to an index of market prices of **equity instruments** of other entities.

A market condition requires the counterparty to complete a specified period of service (ie a **service condition**); the service requirement can be explicit or implicit.

measurement date The date at which the **fair value** of the **equity instruments granted** is measured for the purposes of this IFRS. For transactions with **employees and others providing similar services**, the measurement date is **grant date**. For transactions with parties other than employees (and those providing similar services), the measurement date is the date the entity obtains the goods or the counterparty renders service.

performance condition A **vesting condition** that requires:

(a) the counterparty to complete a specified period of service (ie a **service condition**); the service requirement can be explicit or implicit; and

(b) specified performance target(s) to be met while the counterparty is rendering the service required in (a).

---

6 In this appendix, monetary amounts are denominated in 'currency units (CU)'.

The period of achieving the performance target(s):

(a)   shall not extend beyond the end of the service period; and

(b)   may start before the service period on the condition that the commencement date of the performance target is not substantially before the commencement of the service period.

A performance target is defined by reference to:

(a)   the entity's own operations (or activities) or the operations or activities of another entity in the same group (ie a non-market condition); or

(b)   the price (or value) of the entity's **equity instruments** or the equity instruments of another entity in the same group (including shares and **share options**) (ie a **market condition**).

A performance target might relate either to the performance of the entity as a whole or to some part of the entity (or part of the group), such as a division or an individual employee.

reload feature   A feature that provides for an automatic grant of additional **share options** whenever the option holder exercises previously granted options using the entity's shares, rather than cash, to satisfy the exercise price.

reload option   A new **share option** granted when a share is used to satisfy the exercise price of a previous share option.

service condition   A **vesting condition** that requires the counterparty to complete a specified period of service during which services are provided to the entity. If the counterparty, regardless of the reason, ceases to provide service during the **vesting period**, it has failed to satisfy the condition. A service condition does not require a performance target to be met.

share-based payment arrangement   An agreement between the entity (or another group[7] entity or any shareholder of any group entity) and another party (including an employee) that entitles the other party to receive

(a)   cash or other assets of the entity for amounts that are based on the price (or value) of **equity instruments** (including shares or **share options**) of the entity or another group entity, or

(b)   **equity instruments** (including shares or **share options**) of the entity or another group entity,

provided the specified **vesting conditions**, if any, are met.

---

7   A 'group' is defined in Appendix A of IFRS 10 *Consolidated Financial Statements* as 'a parent and its subsidiaries' from the perspective of the reporting entity's ultimate parent.

share-based payment transaction	A transaction in which the entity

    (a)   receives goods or services from the supplier of those goods or services (including an employee) in a **share-based payment arrangement**, or

    (b)   incurs an obligation to settle the transaction with the supplier in a **share-based payment arrangement** when another group entity receives those goods or services.

share option	A contract that gives the holder the right, but not the obligation, to subscribe to the entity's shares at a fixed or determinable price for a specified period of time.
vest	To become an entitlement. Under a **share-based payment arrangement**, a counterparty's right to receive cash, other assets or **equity instruments** of the entity vests when the counterparty's entitlement is no longer conditional on the satisfaction of any **vesting conditions**.
vesting condition	A condition that determines whether the entity receives the services that entitle the counterparty to receive cash, other assets or **equity instruments** of the entity, under a **share-based payment arrangement**. A vesting condition is either a **service condition** or a **performance condition**.
vesting period	The period during which all the specified **vesting conditions** of a **share-based payment arrangement** are to be satisfied.

Appendix B
Application guidance

This appendix is an integral part of the IFRS.

Estimating the fair value of equity instruments granted

B1   Paragraphs B2–B41 of this appendix discuss measurement of the fair value of shares and share options granted, focusing on the specific terms and conditions that are common features of a grant of shares or share options to employees. Therefore, it is not exhaustive. Furthermore, because the valuation issues discussed below focus on shares and share options granted to employees, it is assumed that the fair value of the shares or share options is measured at grant date. However, many of the valuation issues discussed below (eg determining expected volatility) also apply in the context of estimating the fair value of shares or share options granted to parties other than employees at the date the entity obtains the goods or the counterparty renders service.

Shares

B2   For shares granted to employees, the fair value of the shares shall be measured at the market price of the entity's shares (or an estimated market price, if the entity's shares are not publicly traded), adjusted to take into account the terms and conditions upon which the shares were granted (except for vesting conditions that are excluded from the measurement of fair value in accordance with paragraphs 19–21).

B3   For example, if the employee is not entitled to receive dividends during the vesting period, this factor shall be taken into account when estimating the fair value of the shares granted. Similarly, if the shares are subject to restrictions on transfer after vesting date, that factor shall be taken into account, but only to the extent that the post-vesting restrictions affect the price that a knowledgeable, willing market participant would pay for that share. For example, if the shares are actively traded in a deep and liquid market, post-vesting transfer restrictions may have little, if any, effect on the price that a knowledgeable, willing market participant would pay for those shares. Restrictions on transfer or other restrictions that exist during the vesting period shall not be taken into account when estimating the grant date fair value of the shares granted, because those restrictions stem from the existence of vesting conditions, which are accounted for in accordance with paragraphs 19–21.

Share options

B4   For share options granted to employees, in many cases market prices are not available, because the options granted are subject to terms and conditions that do not apply to traded options. If traded options with similar terms and conditions do not exist, the fair value of the options granted shall be estimated by applying an option pricing model.

B5   The entity shall consider factors that knowledgeable, willing market participants would consider in selecting the option pricing model to apply. For example, many employee options have long lives, are usually exercisable during the period between vesting date and the end of the options' life, and are often exercised early. These factors should be considered when estimating the grant date fair value of the options. For many entities, this might preclude the use of the Black-Scholes-Merton formula, which does not allow for the possibility of exercise before the end of the option's life and may not adequately reflect the effects of expected early exercise. It also does not allow for the possibility that expected volatility and other model inputs might vary over the option's life. However, for share options with relatively short contractual lives, or that must be exercised within a short period of time after vesting date, the factors identified above may not apply. In these instances, the Black-Scholes-Merton formula may produce a value that is substantially the same as a more flexible option pricing model.

B6   All option pricing models take into account, as a minimum, the following factors:

(a)   the exercise price of the option;

(b)   the life of the option;

(c)   the current price of the underlying shares;

(d)   the expected volatility of the share price;

(e)   the dividends expected on the shares (if appropriate); and

(f)   the risk-free interest rate for the life of the option.

B7   Other factors that knowledgeable, willing market participants would consider in setting the price shall also be taken into account (except for vesting conditions and reload features that are excluded from the measurement of fair value in accordance with paragraphs 19–22).

B8   For example, a share option granted to an employee typically cannot be exercised during specified periods (eg during the vesting period or during periods specified by securities regulators). This factor shall be taken into account if the option pricing model applied would otherwise assume that the option could be exercised at any time during its life. However, if an entity uses an option pricing model that values options that can be exercised only at the end of the options' life, no adjustment is required for the inability to exercise them during the vesting period (or other periods during the options' life), because the model assumes that the options cannot be exercised during those periods.

B9   Similarly, another factor common to employee share options is the possibility of early exercise of the option, for example, because the option is not freely transferable, or because the employee must exercise all vested options upon cessation of employment. The effects of expected early exercise shall be taken into account, as discussed in paragraphs B16–B21.

B10   Factors that a knowledgeable, willing market participant would not consider in setting the price of a share option (or other equity instrument) shall not be taken into account when estimating the fair value of share options (or other equity instruments) granted. For example, for share options granted to employees, factors that affect the value of the option from the individual employee's perspective only are not relevant to estimating the price that would be set by a knowledgeable, willing market participant.

Inputs to option pricing models

B11   In estimating the expected volatility of and dividends on the underlying shares, the objective is to approximate the expectations that would be reflected in a current market or negotiated exchange price for the option. Similarly, when estimating the effects of early exercise of employee share options, the objective is to approximate the expectations that an outside party with access to detailed information about employees' exercise behaviour would develop based on information available at the grant date.

B12   Often, there is likely to be a range of reasonable expectations about future volatility, dividends and exercise behaviour. If so, an expected value should be calculated, by weighting each amount within the range by its associated probability of occurrence.

B13   Expectations about the future are generally based on experience, modified if the future is reasonably expected to differ from the past. In some circumstances, identifiable factors may indicate that unadjusted historical experience is a relatively poor predictor of future experience. For example, if an entity with two distinctly different lines of business disposes of the one that was significantly less risky than the other, historical volatility may not be the best information on which to base reasonable expectations for the future.

B14   In other circumstances, historical information may not be available. For example, a newly listed entity will have little, if any, historical data on the volatility of its share price. Unlisted and newly listed entities are discussed further below.

B15   In summary, an entity should not simply base estimates of volatility, exercise behaviour and dividends on historical information without considering the extent to which the past experience is expected to be reasonably predictive of future experience.

Expected early exercise

B16   Employees often exercise share options early, for a variety of reasons. For example, employee share options are typically non-transferable. This often causes employees to exercise their share options early, because that is the only way for the employees to liquidate their position. Also, employees who cease employment are usually required to exercise any vested options within a short period of time, otherwise the share options are forfeited. This factor also causes the early exercise of employee share options. Other factors causing early exercise are risk aversion and lack of wealth diversification.

B17   The means by which the effects of expected early exercise are taken into account depends upon the type of option pricing model applied. For example, expected early exercise could be taken into account by using an estimate of the option's expected life (which, for an employee share option, is the period of time from grant date to the date on which the option is expected to be exercised) as an input into an option pricing model (eg the Black-Scholes-Merton formula). Alternatively, expected early exercise could be modelled in a binomial or similar option pricing model that uses contractual life as an input.

B18   Factors to consider in estimating early exercise include:

(a)   the length of the vesting period, because the share option typically cannot be exercised until the end of the vesting period. Hence, determining the valuation implications of expected early exercise is based on the assumption that the options will vest. The implications of vesting conditions are discussed in paragraphs 19–21.

(b)   the average length of time similar options have remained outstanding in the past.

(c)   the price of the underlying shares. Experience may indicate that the employees tend to exercise options when the share price reaches a specified level above the exercise price.

(d)   the employee's level within the organisation. For example, experience might indicate that higher-level employees tend to exercise options later than lower-level employees (discussed further in paragraph B21).

(e)   expected volatility of the underlying shares. On average, employees might tend to exercise options on highly volatile shares earlier than on shares with low volatility.

B19   As noted in paragraph B17, the effects of early exercise could be taken into account by using an estimate of the option's expected life as an input into an option pricing model. When estimating the expected life of share options granted to a group of employees, the entity could base that estimate on an appropriately weighted average expected life for the entire employee group or on appropriately weighted average lives for subgroups of employees within the group, based on more detailed data about employees' exercise behaviour (discussed further below).

B20   Separating an option grant into groups for employees with relatively homogeneous exercise behaviour is likely to be important. Option value is not a linear function of option term; value increases at a decreasing rate as the term lengthens. For example, if all other assumptions are equal, although a two-year option is worth more than a one-year option, it is not worth twice as much. That means that calculating estimated option value on the basis of a single weighted average life that includes widely differing individual lives would overstate the total fair value of the share options granted. Separating options granted into several groups, each of which has a relatively narrow range of lives included in its weighted average life, reduces that overstatement.

B21   Similar considerations apply when using a binomial or similar model. For example, the experience of an entity that grants options broadly to all levels of employees might indicate that top-level executives tend to hold their options longer than middle-management employees hold theirs and that lower-level employees tend to exercise their options earlier than any other group. In addition, employees who are encouraged or required to hold a minimum amount of their employer's equity instruments, including options, might on average exercise options later than employees not subject to that provision. In those situations, separating options by groups of recipients with relatively homogeneous exercise behaviour will result in a more accurate estimate of the total fair value of the share options granted.

Expected volatility

B22   Expected volatility is a measure of the amount by which a price is expected to fluctuate during a period. The measure of volatility used in option pricing models is the annualised standard deviation of the continuously compounded rates of return on the share over a period of time. Volatility is typically expressed in annualised terms that are comparable regardless of the time period used in the calculation, for example, daily, weekly or monthly price observations.

B23   The rate of return (which may be positive or negative) on a share for a period measures how much a shareholder has benefited from dividends and appreciation (or depreciation) of the share price.

B24   The expected annualised volatility of a share is the range within which the continuously compounded annual rate of return is expected to fall approximately two-thirds of the time. For example, to say that a share with an expected continuously compounded rate of return of 12 per cent has a volatility of 30 per cent means that the probability that the rate of return on the share for one year will be between −18 per cent (12% − 30%) and 42 per cent (12% + 30%) is approximately two-thirds. If the share price is CU100 at the beginning of the year and no dividends are paid, the year-end share price would be expected to be between CU83.53 (CU100 × $e^{-0.18}$) and CU152.20 (CU100 × $e^{0.42}$) approximately two-thirds of the time.

B25   Factors to consider in estimating expected volatility include:

   (a)   implied volatility from traded share options on the entity's shares, or other traded instruments of the entity that include option features (such as convertible debt), if any.

   (b)   the historical volatility of the share price over the most recent period that is generally commensurate with the expected term of the option (taking into account the remaining contractual life of the option and the effects of expected early exercise).

   (c)   the length of time an entity's shares have been publicly traded. A newly listed entity might have a high historical volatility, compared with similar entities that have been listed longer. Further guidance for newly listed entities is given below.

(d) the tendency of volatility to revert to its mean, ie its long-term average level, and other factors indicating that expected future volatility might differ from past volatility. For example, if an entity's share price was extraordinarily volatile for some identifiable period of time because of a failed takeover bid or a major restructuring, that period could be disregarded in computing historical average annual volatility.

(e) appropriate and regular intervals for price observations. The price observations should be consistent from period to period. For example, an entity might use the closing price for each week or the highest price for the week, but it should not use the closing price for some weeks and the highest price for other weeks. Also, the price observations should be expressed in the same currency as the exercise price.

Newly listed entities

B26 As noted in paragraph B25, an entity should consider historical volatility of the share price over the most recent period that is generally commensurate with the expected option term. If a newly listed entity does not have sufficient information on historical volatility, it should nevertheless compute historical volatility for the longest period for which trading activity is available. It could also consider the historical volatility of similar entities following a comparable period in their lives. For example, an entity that has been listed for only one year and grants options with an average expected life of five years might consider the pattern and level of historical volatility of entities in the same industry for the first six years in which the shares of those entities were publicly traded.

Unlisted entities

B27 An unlisted entity will not have historical information to consider when estimating expected volatility. Some factors to consider instead are set out below.

B28 In some cases, an unlisted entity that regularly issues options or shares to employees (or other parties) might have set up an internal market for its shares. The volatility of those share prices could be considered when estimating expected volatility.

B29 Alternatively, the entity could consider the historical or implied volatility of similar listed entities, for which share price or option price information is available, to use when estimating expected volatility. This would be appropriate if the entity has based the value of its shares on the share prices of similar listed entities.

B30 If the entity has not based its estimate of the value of its shares on the share prices of similar listed entities, and has instead used another valuation methodology to value its shares, the entity could derive an estimate of expected volatility consistent with that valuation methodology. For example, the entity might value its shares on a net asset or earnings basis. It could consider the expected volatility of those net asset values or earnings.

Expected dividends

B31   Whether expected dividends should be taken into account when measuring the fair value of shares or options granted depends on whether the counterparty is entitled to dividends or dividend equivalents.

B32   For example, if employees were granted options and are entitled to dividends on the underlying shares or dividend equivalents (which might be paid in cash or applied to reduce the exercise price) between grant date and exercise date, the options granted should be valued as if no dividends will be paid on the underlying shares, ie the input for expected dividends should be zero.

B33   Similarly, when the grant date fair value of shares granted to employees is estimated, no adjustment is required for expected dividends if the employee is entitled to receive dividends paid during the vesting period.

B34   Conversely, if the employees are not entitled to dividends or dividend equivalents during the vesting period (or before exercise, in the case of an option), the grant date valuation of the rights to shares or options should take expected dividends into account. That is to say, when the fair value of an option grant is estimated, expected dividends should be included in the application of an option pricing model. When the fair value of a share grant is estimated, that valuation should be reduced by the present value of dividends expected to be paid during the vesting period.

B35   Option pricing models generally call for expected dividend yield. However, the models may be modified to use an expected dividend amount rather than a yield. An entity may use either its expected yield or its expected payments. If the entity uses the latter, it should consider its historical pattern of increases in dividends. For example, if an entity's policy has generally been to increase dividends by approximately 3 per cent per year, its estimated option value should not assume a fixed dividend amount throughout the option's life unless there is evidence that supports that assumption.

B36   Generally, the assumption about expected dividends should be based on publicly available information. An entity that does not pay dividends and has no plans to do so should assume an expected dividend yield of zero. However, an emerging entity with no history of paying dividends might expect to begin paying dividends during the expected lives of its employee share options. Those entities could use an average of their past dividend yield (zero) and the mean dividend yield of an appropriately comparable peer group.

Risk-free interest rate

B37   Typically, the risk-free interest rate is the implied yield currently available on zero-coupon government issues of the country in whose currency the exercise price is expressed, with a remaining term equal to the expected term of the option being valued (based on the option's remaining contractual life and taking into account the effects of expected early exercise). It may be necessary to use an appropriate substitute, if no such government issues exist or circumstances indicate that the implied yield on zero-coupon government issues is not representative of the risk-free interest rate (for example, in high inflation economies). Also, an appropriate substitute should be used if market participants would typically determine the risk-free interest rate by using that substitute, rather than the implied yield of zero-coupon government issues, when estimating the fair value of an option with a life equal to the expected term of the option being valued.

Capital structure effects

B38 Typically, third parties, not the entity, write traded share options. When these share options are exercised, the writer delivers shares to the option holder. Those shares are acquired from existing shareholders. Hence the exercise of traded share options has no dilutive effect.

B39 In contrast, if share options are written by the entity, new shares are issued when those share options are exercised (either actually issued or issued in substance, if shares previously repurchased and held in treasury are used). Given that the shares will be issued at the exercise price rather than the current market price at the date of exercise, this actual or potential dilution might reduce the share price, so that the option holder does not make as large a gain on exercise as on exercising an otherwise similar traded option that does not dilute the share price.

B40 Whether this has a significant effect on the value of the share options granted depends on various factors, such as the number of new shares that will be issued on exercise of the options compared with the number of shares already issued. Also, if the market already expects that the option grant will take place, the market may have already factored the potential dilution into the share price at the date of grant.

B41 However, the entity should consider whether the possible dilutive effect of the future exercise of the share options granted might have an impact on their estimated fair value at grant date. Option pricing models can be adapted to take into account this potential dilutive effect.

Modifications to equity-settled share-based payment arrangements

B42 Paragraph 27 requires that, irrespective of any modifications to the terms and conditions on which the equity instruments were granted, or a cancellation or settlement of that grant of equity instruments, the entity should recognise, as a minimum, the services received measured at the grant date fair value of the equity instruments granted, unless those equity instruments do not vest because of failure to satisfy a vesting condition (other than a market condition) that was specified at grant date. In addition, the entity should recognise the effects of modifications that increase the total fair value of the share-based payment arrangement or are otherwise beneficial to the employee.

B43 To apply the requirements of paragraph 27:

(a) if the modification increases the fair value of the equity instruments granted (eg by reducing the exercise price), measured immediately before and after the modification, the entity shall include the incremental fair value granted in the measurement of the amount recognised for services received as consideration for the equity instruments granted. The incremental fair value granted is the difference between the fair value of the modified equity instrument and that of the original equity instrument, both estimated as at the date of the modification. If the modification occurs during the vesting period, the incremental fair value granted is included in the measurement of the amount recognised for services received over the period from the modification date until the date when the modified equity instruments vest, in addition to the amount based on the grant date fair value of the original equity instruments, which is recognised over the remainder of the original vesting period. If the modification occurs after vesting date, the incremental fair value granted is recognised immediately, or over the vesting period if the employee is required to complete an additional period of service before becoming unconditionally entitled to those modified equity instruments.

(b)   similarly, if the modification increases the number of equity instruments granted, the entity shall include the fair value of the additional equity instruments granted, measured at the date of the modification, in the measurement of the amount recognised for services received as consideration for the equity instruments granted, consistently with the requirements in (a) above. For example, if the modification occurs during the vesting period, the fair value of the additional equity instruments granted is included in the measurement of the amount recognised for services received over the period from the modification date until the date when the additional equity instruments vest, in addition to the amount based on the grant date fair value of the equity instruments originally granted, which is recognised over the remainder of the original vesting period.

(c)   if the entity modifies the vesting conditions in a manner that is beneficial to the employee, for example, by reducing the vesting period or by modifying or eliminating a performance condition (other than a market condition, changes to which are accounted for in accordance with (a) above), the entity shall take the modified vesting conditions into account when applying the requirements of paragraphs 19–21.

B44   Furthermore, if the entity modifies the terms or conditions of the equity instruments granted in a manner that reduces the total fair value of the share-based payment arrangement, or is not otherwise beneficial to the employee, the entity shall nevertheless continue to account for the services received as consideration for the equity instruments granted as if that modification had not occurred (other than a cancellation of some or all the equity instruments granted, which shall be accounted for in accordance with paragraph 28). For example:

(a)   if the modification reduces the fair value of the equity instruments granted, measured immediately before and after the modification, the entity shall not take into account that decrease in fair value and shall continue to measure the amount recognised for services received as consideration for the equity instruments based on the grant date fair value of the equity instruments granted.

(b)   if the modification reduces the number of equity instruments granted to an employee, that reduction shall be accounted for as a cancellation of that portion of the grant, in accordance with the requirements of paragraph 28.

(c)   if the entity modifies the vesting conditions in a manner that is not beneficial to the employee, for example, by increasing the vesting period or by modifying or adding a performance condition (other than a market condition, changes to which are accounted for in accordance with (a) above), the entity shall not take the modified vesting conditions into account when applying the requirements of paragraphs 19–21.

Accounting for a modification of a share-based payment transaction that changes its classification from cash-settled to equity-settled

B44A   If the terms and conditions of a cash-settled share-based payment transaction are modified with the result that it becomes an equity-settled share-based payment transaction, the transaction is accounted for as such from the date of the modification. Specifically:

(a)   The equity-settled share-based payment transaction is measured by reference to the fair value of the equity instruments granted at the modification date. The equity-settled share-based payment transaction is recognised in equity on the modification date to the extent to which goods or services have been received.

(b)   The liability for the cash-settled share-based payment transaction as at the modification date is derecognised on that date.

(c)   Any difference between the carrying amount of the liability derecognised and the amount of equity recognised on the modification date is recognised immediately in profit or loss.

B44B   If, as a result of the modification, the vesting period is extended or shortened, the application of the requirements in paragraph B44A reflect the modified vesting period. The requirements in paragraph B44A apply even if the modification occurs after the vesting period.

B44C   A cash-settled share-based payment transaction may be cancelled or settled (other than a transaction cancelled by forfeiture when the vesting conditions are not satisfied). If equity instruments are granted and, on that grant date, the entity identifies them as a replacement for the cancelled cash-settled share-based payment, the entity shall apply paragraphs B44A and B44B.

Share-based payment transactions among group entities (2009 amendments)

B45 Paragraphs 43A–43C address the accounting for share-based payment transactions among group entities in each entity's separate or individual financial statements. Paragraphs B46–B61 discuss how to apply the requirements in paragraphs 43A–43C. As noted in paragraph 43D, share-based payment transactions among group entities may take place for a variety of reasons depending on facts and circumstances. Therefore, this discussion is not exhaustive and assumes that when the entity receiving the goods or services has no obligation to settle the transaction, the transaction is a parent's equity contribution to the subsidiary, regardless of any intragroup repayment arrangements.

B46 Although the discussion below focuses on transactions with employees, it also applies to similar share-based payment transactions with suppliers of goods or services other than employees. An arrangement between a parent and its subsidiary may require the subsidiary to pay the parent for the provision of the equity instruments to the employees. The discussion below does not address how to account for such an intragroup payment arrangement.

B47 Four issues are commonly encountered in share-based payment transactions among group entities. For convenience, the examples below discuss the issues in terms of a parent and its subsidiary.

Share-based payment arrangements involving an entity's own equity instruments

B48 The first issue is whether the following transactions involving an entity's own equity instruments should be accounted for as equity-settled or as cash-settled in accordance with the requirements of this IFRS:

(a) an entity grants to its employees rights to equity instruments of the entity (eg share options), and either chooses or is required to buy equity instruments (ie treasury shares) from another party, to satisfy its obligations to its employees; and

(b) an entity's employees are granted rights to equity instruments of the entity (eg share options), either by the entity itself or by its shareholders, and the shareholders of the entity provide the equity instruments needed.

B49 The entity shall account for share-based payment transactions in which it receives services as consideration for its own equity instruments as equity-settled. This applies regardless of whether the entity chooses or is required to buy those equity instruments from another party to satisfy its obligations to its employees under the share-based payment arrangement. It also applies regardless of whether:

(a) the employee's rights to the entity's equity instruments were granted by the entity itself or by its shareholder(s); or

(b) the share-based payment arrangement was settled by the entity itself or by its shareholder(s).

B50   If the shareholder has an obligation to settle the transaction with its investee's employees, it provides equity instruments of its investee rather than its own. Therefore, if its investee is in the same group as the shareholder, in accordance with paragraph 43C, the shareholder shall measure its obligation in accordance with the requirements applicable to cash-settled share-based payment transactions in the shareholder's separate financial statements and those applicable to equity-settled share-based payment transactions in the shareholder's consolidated financial statements.

Share-based payment arrangements involving equity instruments of the parent

B51   The second issue concerns share-based payment transactions between two or more entities within the same group involving an equity instrument of another group entity. For example, employees of a subsidiary are granted rights to equity instruments of its parent as consideration for the services provided to the subsidiary.

B52   Therefore, the second issue concerns the following share-based payment arrangements:

(a)   a parent grants rights to its equity instruments directly to the employees of its subsidiary: the parent (not the subsidiary) has the obligation to provide the employees of the subsidiary with the equity instruments; and

(b)   a subsidiary grants rights to equity instruments of its parent to its employees: the subsidiary has the obligation to provide its employees with the equity instruments.

A parent grants rights to its equity instruments to the employees of its subsidiary (paragraph B52(a))

B53   The subsidiary does not have an obligation to provide its parent's equity instruments to the subsidiary's employees. Therefore, in accordance with paragraph 43B, the subsidiary shall measure the services received from its employees in accordance with the requirements applicable to equity-settled share-based payment transactions, and recognise a corresponding increase in equity as a contribution from the parent.

B54   The parent has an obligation to settle the transaction with the subsidiary's employees by providing the parent's own equity instruments. Therefore, in accordance with paragraph 43C, the parent shall measure its obligation in accordance with the requirements applicable to equity-settled share-based payment transactions.

A subsidiary grants rights to equity instruments of its parent to its employees (paragraph B52(b))

B55   Because the subsidiary does not meet either of the conditions in paragraph 43B, it shall account for the transaction with its employees as cash-settled. This requirement applies irrespective of how the subsidiary obtains the equity instruments to satisfy its obligations to its employees.

Share-based payment arrangements involving cash-settled payments to employees

B56 The third issue is how an entity that receives goods or services from its suppliers (including employees) should account for share-based arrangements that are cash-settled when the entity itself does not have any obligation to make the required payments to its suppliers. For example, consider the following arrangements in which the parent (not the entity itself) has an obligation to make the required cash payments to the employees of the entity:

(a) the employees of the entity will receive cash payments that are linked to the price of its equity instruments.

(b) the employees of the entity will receive cash payments that are linked to the price of its parent's equity instruments.

B57 The subsidiary does not have an obligation to settle the transaction with its employees. Therefore, the subsidiary shall account for the transaction with its employees as equity-settled, and recognise a corresponding increase in equity as a contribution from its parent. The subsidiary shall remeasure the cost of the transaction subsequently for any changes resulting from non-market vesting conditions not being met in accordance with paragraphs 19–21. This differs from the measurement of the transaction as cash-settled in the consolidated financial statements of the group.

B58 Because the parent has an obligation to settle the transaction with the employees, and the consideration is cash, the parent (and the consolidated group) shall measure its obligation in accordance with the requirements applicable to cash-settled share-based payment transactions in paragraph 43C.

Transfer of employees between group entities

B59 The fourth issue relates to group share-based payment arrangements that involve employees of more than one group entity. For example, a parent might grant rights to its equity instruments to the employees of its subsidiaries, conditional upon the completion of continuing service with the group for a specified period. An employee of one subsidiary might transfer employment to another subsidiary during the specified vesting period without the employee's rights to equity instruments of the parent under the original share-based payment arrangement being affected. If the subsidiaries have no obligation to settle the share-based payment transaction with their employees, they account for it as an equity-settled transaction. Each subsidiary shall measure the services received from the employee by reference to the fair value of the equity instruments at the date the rights to those equity instruments were originally granted by the parent as defined in Appendix A, and the proportion of the vesting period the employee served with each subsidiary.

B60 If the subsidiary has an obligation to settle the transaction with its employees in its parent's equity instruments, it accounts for the transaction as cash-settled. Each subsidiary shall measure the services received on the basis of grant date fair value of the equity instruments for the proportion of the vesting period the employee served with each subsidiary. In addition, each subsidiary shall recognise any change in the fair value of the equity instruments during the employee's service period with each subsidiary.

B61   Such an employee, after transferring between group entities, may fail to satisfy a vesting condition other than a market condition as defined in Appendix A, eg the employee leaves the group before completing the service period. In this case, because the vesting condition is service to the group, each subsidiary shall adjust the amount previously recognised in respect of the services received from the employee in accordance with the principles in paragraph 19. Hence, if the rights to the equity instruments granted by the parent do not vest because of an employee's failure to meet a vesting condition other than a market condition, no amount is recognised on a cumulative basis for the services received from that employee in the financial statements of any group entity.

Appendix C
Amendments to other IFRSs

The amendments in this appendix become effective for annual financial statements covering periods beginning on or after 1 January 2005. If an entity applies this Standard for an earlier period, these amendments become effective for that earlier period.

* * * * *

The amendments contained in this appendix when this Standard was issued in 2004 have been incorporated into the relevant Standards published in this volume.

Approval by the Board of IFRS 2 issued in February 2004

International Financial Reporting Standard 2 *Share-based Payment* was approved for issue by the fourteen members of the International Accounting Standards Board.

Sir David Tweedie	Chairman
Thomas E Jones	Vice-Chairman
Mary E Barth	
Hans-Georg Bruns	
Anthony T Cope	
Robert P Garnett	
Gilbert Gélard	
James J Leisenring	
Warren J McGregor	
Patricia L O'Malley	
Harry K Schmid	
John T Smith	
Geoffrey Whittington	
Tatsumi Yamada	

Approval by the Board of *Vesting Conditions and Cancellations* (Amendments to IFRS 2) issued in January 2008

Vesting Conditions and Cancellations (Amendments to IFRS 2) was approved for issue by the thirteen members of the International Accounting Standards Board.

Sir David Tweedie	Chairman
Thomas E Jones	Vice-Chairman
Mary E Barth	
Stephen Cooper	
Philippe Danjou	
Jan Engström	
Robert P Garnett	
Gilbert Gélard	
James J Leisenring	
Warren J McGregor	
John T Smith	
Tatsumi Yamada	
Wei-Guo Zhang	

Approval by the Board of *Group Cash-settled Share-based Payment Transactions* (Amendments to IFRS 2) issued in June 2009

Group Cash-settled Share-based Payment Transactions (Amendments to IFRS 2) was approved for issue by thirteen of the fourteen members of the International Accounting Standards Board. Mr Kalavacherla abstained in view of his recent appointment to the Board.

Sir David Tweedie	Chairman
Thomas E Jones	Vice-Chairman
Mary E Barth	
Stephen Cooper	
Philippe Danjou	
Jan Engström	
Robert P Garnett	
Gilbert Gélard	
Prabhakar Kalavacherla	
James J Leisenring	
Warren J McGregor	
John T Smith	
Tatsumi Yamada	
Wei-Guo Zhang	

Approval by the Board of *Classification and Measurement of Share-based Payment Transactions* (Amendments to IFRS 2) issued in June 2016

Classification and Measurement of Share-based Payment Transactions was approved for issue by the fourteen members of the International Accounting Standards Board.

Hans Hoogervorst	Chairman
Ian Mackintosh	Vice-Chairman
Stephen Cooper	
Philippe Danjou	
Martin Edelmann	
Patrick Finnegan	
Amaro Gomes	
Gary Kabureck	
Suzanne Lloyd	
Takatsugu Ochi	
Darrel Scott	
Chungwoo Suh	
Mary Tokar	
Wei-Guo Zhang	

IFRS 3

Business Combinations

In April 2001 the International Accounting Standards Board (Board) adopted IAS 22 *Business Combinations*, which had originally been issued by the International Accounting Standards Committee in October 1998. IAS 22 was itself a revised version of IAS 22 *Business Combinations* that was issued in November 1983.

In March 2004 the Board replaced IAS 22 and three related Interpretations (SIC-9 *Business Combinations—Classification either as Acquisitions or Unitings of Interests*, SIC-22 *Business Combinations—Subsequent Adjustment of Fair Values and Goodwill Initially Reported* and SIC-28 *Business Combinations—'Date of Exchange' and Fair Value of Equity Instruments*) when it issued IFRS 3 *Business Combinations*.

Minor amendments were made to IFRS 3 in March 2004 by IFRS 5 *Non-current Assets Held for Sale and Discontinued Operations* and IAS 1 *Presentation of Financial Statements* (as revised in September 2007), which amended the terminology used throughout the Standards, including IFRS 3.

In January 2008 the Board issued a revised IFRS 3. Please refer to *Background Information* in the Basis for Conclusions on IFRS 3 for a fuller description of those revisions.

In October 2018, the Board amended IFRS 3 by issuing *Definition of a Business* (Amendments to IFRS 3). This amended IFRS 3 to narrow and clarify the definition of a business, and to permit a simplified assessment of whether an acquired set of activities and assets is a group of assets rather than a business.

In May 2020, the Board amended IFRS 3 by issuing *Reference to the Conceptual Framework*. This updated a reference in IFRS 3 and made further amendments to avoid unintended consequences of updating the reference.

Other Standards have made minor consequential amendments to IFRS 3. They include *Improvements to IFRSs* (issued in May 2010), IFRS 10 *Consolidated Financial Statements* (issued May 2011), IFRS 13 *Fair Value Measurement* (issued May 2011), *Investment Entities* (Amendments to IFRS 10, IFRS 12 and IAS 27) (issued October 2012), IFRS 9 *Financial Instruments* (Hedge Accounting and amendments to IFRS 9, IFRS 7 and IAS 39) (issued November 2013), *Annual Improvements to IFRSs 2010–2012 Cycle* (issued December 2013), *Annual Improvements to IFRSs 2011–2013 Cycle* (issued December 2013), IFRS 15 *Revenue from Contracts with Customers* (issued May 2014), IFRS 9 *Financial Instruments* (issued July 2014), IFRS 16 *Leases* (issued January 2016), *Annual Improvements to IFRS Standards 2015–2017 Cycle* (issued December 2017) and *Amendments to References to the Conceptual Framework in IFRS Standards* (issued March 2018).

Contents

FOR THE ACCOMPANYING GUIDANCE LISTED BELOW, SEE PART B OF THIS EDITION

ILLUSTRATIVE EXAMPLES

continued...

International Financial Reporting Standard 3 *Business Combinations* (IFRS 3) is set out in paragraphs 1–68 and Appendices A–C. All the paragraphs have equal authority. Paragraphs in **bold type** state the main principles. Terms defined in Appendix A are in *italics* the first time they appear in the IFRS. Definitions of other terms are given in the Glossary for International Financial Reporting Standards. IFRS 3 should be read in the context of its objective and the Basis for Conclusions, the *Preface to IFRS Standards* and the *Conceptual Framework for Financial Reporting*. IAS 8 *Accounting Policies, Changes in Accounting Estimates and Errors* provides a basis for selecting and applying accounting policies in the absence of explicit guidance.

International Financial Reporting Standard 3
Business Combinations

Objective

1   The objective of this IFRS is to improve the relevance, reliability and comparability of the information that a reporting entity provides in its financial statements about a *business combination* and its effects. To accomplish that, this IFRS establishes principles and requirements for how the *acquirer*:

   (a)   recognises and measures in its financial statements the *identifiable* assets acquired, the liabilities assumed and any *non-controlling interest* in the *acquiree*;

   (b)   recognises and measures the *goodwill* acquired in the business combination or a gain from a bargain purchase; and

   (c)   determines what information to disclose to enable users of the financial statements to evaluate the nature and financial effects of the business combination.

Scope

2   This IFRS applies to a transaction or other event that meets the definition of a business combination. This IFRS does not apply to:

   (a)   the accounting for the formation of a joint arrangement in the financial statements of the joint arrangement itself.

   (b)   the acquisition of an asset or a group of assets that does not constitute a *business*. In such cases the acquirer shall identify and recognise the individual identifiable assets acquired (including those assets that meet the definition of, and recognition criteria for, *intangible assets* in IAS 38 *Intangible Assets*) and liabilities assumed. The cost of the group shall be allocated to the individual identifiable assets and liabilities on the basis of their relative *fair values* at the date of purchase. Such a transaction or event does not give rise to goodwill.

   (c)   a combination of entities or businesses under common control (paragraphs B1–B4 provide related application guidance).

2A   The requirements of this Standard do not apply to the acquisition by an investment entity, as defined in IFRS 10 *Consolidated Financial Statements*, of an investment in a subsidiary that is required to be measured at fair value through profit or loss.

Identifying a business combination

3   An entity shall determine whether a transaction or other event is a business combination by applying the definition in this IFRS, which requires that the assets acquired and liabilities assumed constitute a business. If the assets acquired are not a business, the reporting entity

shall account for the transaction or other event as an asset acquisition. Paragraphs B5–B12D provide guidance on identifying a business combination and the definition of a business.

The acquisition method

4   An entity shall account for each business combination by applying the acquisition method.

5   Applying the acquisition method requires:

     (a)   identifying the acquirer;

     (b)   determining the *acquisition date*;

     (c)   recognising and measuring the identifiable assets acquired, the liabilities assumed and any non-controlling interest in the acquiree; and

     (d)   recognising and measuring goodwill or a gain from a bargain purchase.

Identifying the acquirer

6   **For each business combination, one of the combining entities shall be identified as the acquirer.**

7   The guidance in IFRS 10 shall be used to identify the acquirer—the entity that obtains *control* of another entity, ie the acquiree. If a business combination has occurred but applying the guidance in IFRS 10 does not clearly indicate which of the combining entities is the acquirer, the factors in paragraphs B14–B18 shall be considered in making that determination.

Determining the acquisition date

8   **The acquirer shall identify the acquisition date, which is the date on which it obtains control of the acquiree.**

9   The date on which the acquirer obtains control of the acquiree is generally the date on which the acquirer legally transfers the consideration, acquires the assets and assumes the liabilities of the acquiree—the closing date. However, the acquirer might obtain control on a date that is either earlier or later than the closing date. For example, the acquisition date precedes the closing date if a written agreement provides that the acquirer obtains control of the acquiree on a date before the closing date. An acquirer shall consider all pertinent facts and circumstances in identifying the acquisition date.

Recognising and measuring the identifiable assets acquired, the liabilities assumed and any non-controlling interest in the acquiree

Recognition principle

10   As of the acquisition date, the acquirer shall recognise, separately from goodwill, the identifiable assets acquired, the liabilities assumed and any non-controlling interest in the acquiree. Recognition of identifiable assets acquired and liabilities assumed is subject to the conditions specified in paragraphs 11 and 12.

Recognition conditions

11   To qualify for recognition as part of applying the acquisition method, the identifiable assets acquired and liabilities assumed must meet the definitions of assets and liabilities in the *Conceptual Framework for Financial Reporting* at the acquisition date. For example, costs the acquirer expects but is not obliged to incur in the future to effect its plan to exit an activity of an acquiree or to terminate the employment of or relocate an acquiree's employees are not liabilities at the acquisition date. Therefore, the acquirer does not recognise those costs as part of applying the acquisition method. Instead, the acquirer recognises those costs in its post-combination financial statements in accordance with other IFRSs.

12   In addition, to qualify for recognition as part of applying the acquisition method, the identifiable assets acquired and liabilities assumed must be part of what the acquirer and the acquiree (or its former *owners*) exchanged in the business combination transaction rather than the result of separate transactions. The acquirer shall apply the guidance in paragraphs 51–53 to determine which assets acquired or liabilities assumed are part of the exchange for the acquiree and which, if any, are the result of separate transactions to be accounted for in accordance with their nature and the applicable IFRSs.

13   The acquirer's application of the recognition principle and conditions may result in recognising some assets and liabilities that the acquiree had not previously recognised as assets and liabilities in its financial statements. For example, the acquirer recognises the acquired identifiable intangible assets, such as a brand name, a patent or a customer relationship, that the acquiree did not recognise as assets in its financial statements because it developed them internally and charged the related costs to expense.

14   Paragraphs B31–B40 provide guidance on recognising intangible assets. Paragraphs 21A–28B specify the types of identifiable assets and liabilities that include items for which this IFRS provides limited exceptions to the recognition principle and conditions.

Classifying or designating identifiable assets acquired and liabilities assumed in a business combination

15   At the acquisition date, the acquirer shall classify or designate the identifiable assets acquired and liabilities assumed as necessary to apply other IFRSs subsequently. The acquirer shall make those classifications or designations on the basis of the contractual terms, economic conditions, its operating or accounting policies and other pertinent conditions as they exist at the acquisition date.

16   In some situations, IFRSs provide for different accounting depending on how an entity classifies or designates a particular asset or liability. Examples of classifications or designations that the acquirer shall make on the basis of the pertinent conditions as they exist at the acquisition date include but are not limited to:

(a)   classification of particular financial assets and liabilities as measured at fair value through profit or loss or at amortised cost, or as a financial asset measured at fair value through other comprehensive income in accordance with IFRS 9 *Financial Instruments*;

(b)   designation of a derivative instrument as a hedging instrument in accordance with IFRS 9; and

(c)   assessment of whether an embedded derivative should be separated from a host contract in accordance with IFRS 9 (which is a matter of 'classification' as this IFRS uses that term).

17   This IFRS provides two exceptions to the principle in paragraph 15:

(a)   classification of a lease contract in which the acquiree is the lessor as either an operating lease or a finance lease in accordance with IFRS 16 *Leases*; and

(b)   classification of a contract as an insurance contract in accordance with IFRS 4 *Insurance Contracts*.

The acquirer shall classify those contracts on the basis of the contractual terms and other factors at the inception of the contract (or, if the terms of the contract have been modified in a manner that would change its classification, at the date of that modification, which might be the acquisition date).

Measurement principle

18   The acquirer shall measure the identifiable assets acquired and the liabilities assumed at their acquisition-date fair values.

19   For each business combination, the acquirer shall measure at the acquisition date components of non-controlling interests in the acquiree that are present ownership interests and entitle their holders to a proportionate share of the entity's net assets in the event of liquidation at either:

(a)   fair value; or

(b)   the present ownership instruments' proportionate share in the recognised amounts of the acquiree's identifiable net assets.

All other components of non-controlling interests shall be measured at their acquisition-date fair values, unless another measurement basis is required by IFRSs.

20   Paragraphs 24–31 specify the types of identifiable assets and liabilities that include items for which this IFRS provides limited exceptions to the measurement principle.

Exceptions to the recognition or measurement principles

21   This IFRS provides limited exceptions to its recognition and measurement principles. Paragraphs 21A–31 specify both the particular items for which exceptions are provided and the nature of those exceptions. The acquirer shall account for those items by applying the requirements in paragraphs 21A–31, which will result in some items being:

(a)   recognised either by applying recognition conditions in addition to those in paragraphs 11 and 12 or by applying the requirements of other IFRSs, with results that differ from applying the recognition principle and conditions.

(b)   measured at an amount other than their acquisition-date fair values.

Exceptions to the recognition principle

Liabilities and contingent liabilities within the scope of IAS 37 or IFRIC 21

21A   Paragraph 21B applies to liabilities and contingent liabilities that would be within the scope of IAS 37 *Provisions, Contingent Liabilities and Contingent Assets* or IFRIC 21 *Levies* if they were incurred separately rather than assumed in a business combination.

21B   The *Conceptual Framework for Financial Reporting* defines a liability as 'a present obligation of the entity to transfer an economic resource as a result of past events'. For a provision or contingent liability that would be within the scope of IAS 37, the acquirer shall apply paragraphs 15–22 of IAS 37 to determine whether at the acquisition date a present obligation exists as a result of past events. For a levy that would be within the scope of IFRIC 21, the acquirer shall apply IFRIC 21 to determine whether the obligating event that gives rise to a liability to pay the levy has occurred by the acquisition date.

21C   A present obligation identified in accordance with paragraph 21B might meet the definition of a contingent liability set out in paragraph 22(b). If so, paragraph 23 applies to that contingent liability.

Contingent liabilities and contingent assets

22   IAS 37 defines a contingent liability as:

(a)   a possible obligation that arises from past events and whose existence will be confirmed only by the occurrence or non-occurrence of one or more uncertain future events not wholly within the control of the entity; or

(b)   a present obligation that arises from past events but is not recognised because:

      (i)   it is not probable that an outflow of resources embodying economic benefits will be required to settle the obligation; or

      (ii)   the amount of the obligation cannot be measured with sufficient reliability.

23   The acquirer shall recognise as of the acquisition date a contingent liability assumed in a business combination if it is a present obligation that arises from past events and its fair value can be measured reliably. Therefore, contrary to paragraphs 14(b), 23, 27, 29 and 30 of IAS 37, the acquirer recognises a contingent liability assumed in a business combination at the acquisition date even if it is not probable that an outflow of resources embodying economic benefits will be required to settle the obligation. Paragraph 56 of this IFRS provides guidance on the subsequent accounting for contingent liabilities.

23A   IAS 37 defines a contingent asset as 'a possible asset that arises from past events and whose existence will be confirmed only by the occurrence or non-occurrence of one or more uncertain future events not wholly within the control of the entity'. The acquirer shall not recognise a contingent asset at the acquisition date.

Exceptions to both the recognition and measurement principles

Income taxes

24   The acquirer shall recognise and measure a deferred tax asset or liability arising from the assets acquired and liabilities assumed in a business combination in accordance with IAS 12 *Income Taxes*.

25   The acquirer shall account for the potential tax effects of temporary differences and carryforwards of an acquiree that exist at the acquisition date or arise as a result of the acquisition in accordance with IAS 12.

Employee benefits

26   The acquirer shall recognise and measure a liability (or asset, if any) related to the acquiree's employee benefit arrangements in accordance with IAS 19 *Employee Benefits*.

Indemnification assets

27   The seller in a business combination may contractually indemnify the acquirer for the outcome of a contingency or uncertainty related to all or part of a specific asset or liability. For example, the seller may indemnify the acquirer against losses above a specified amount on a liability arising from a particular contingency; in other words, the seller will guarantee that the acquirer's liability will not exceed a specified amount. As a result, the acquirer obtains an indemnification asset. The acquirer shall recognise an indemnification asset at the same time that it recognises the indemnified item measured on the same basis as the indemnified item, subject to the need for a valuation allowance for uncollectible amounts. Therefore, if the

indemnification relates to an asset or a liability that is recognised at the acquisition date and measured at its acquisition-date fair value, the acquirer shall recognise the indemnification asset at the acquisition date measured at its acquisition-date fair value. For an indemnification asset measured at fair value, the effects of uncertainty about future cash flows because of collectibility considerations are included in the fair value measure and a separate valuation allowance is not necessary (paragraph B41 provides related application guidance).

28   In some circumstances, the indemnification may relate to an asset or a liability that is an exception to the recognition or measurement principles. For example, an indemnification may relate to a contingent liability that is not recognised at the acquisition date because its fair value is not reliably measurable at that date. Alternatively, an indemnification may relate to an asset or a liability, for example, one that results from an employee benefit, that is measured on a basis other than acquisition-date fair value. In those circumstances, the indemnification asset shall be recognised and measured using assumptions consistent with those used to measure the indemnified item, subject to management's assessment of the collectibility of the indemnification asset and any contractual limitations on the indemnified amount. Paragraph 57 provides guidance on the subsequent accounting for an indemnification asset.

Leases in which the acquiree is the lessee

28A   The acquirer shall recognise right-of-use assets and lease liabilities for leases identified in accordance with IFRS 16 in which the acquiree is the lessee. The acquirer is not required to recognise right-of-use assets and lease liabilities for:

(a)   leases for which the lease term (as defined in IFRS 16) ends within 12 months of the acquisition date; or

(b)   leases for which the underlying asset is of low value (as described in paragraphs B3–B8 of IFRS 16).

28B   The acquirer shall measure the lease liability at the present value of the remaining lease payments (as defined in IFRS 16) as if the acquired lease were a new lease at the acquisition date. The acquirer shall measure the right-of-use asset at the same amount as the lease liability, adjusted to reflect favourable or unfavourable terms of the lease when compared with market terms.

Exceptions to the measurement principle

Reacquired rights

29   The acquirer shall measure the value of a reacquired right recognised as an intangible asset on the basis of the remaining contractual term of the related contract regardless of whether market participants would consider potential contractual renewals when measuring its fair value. Paragraphs B35 and B36 provide related application guidance.

Share-based payment transactions

30   The acquirer shall measure a liability or an equity instrument related to share-based payment transactions of the acquiree or the replacement of an acquiree's share-based payment transactions with share-based payment transactions of the acquirer in accordance with the method in IFRS 2 *Share-based Payment* at the acquisition date. (This IFRS refers to the result of that method as the 'market-based measure' of the share-based payment transaction.)

Assets held for sale

31   The acquirer shall measure an acquired non-current asset (or disposal group) that is classified as held for sale at the acquisition date in accordance with IFRS 5 *Non-current Assets Held for Sale and Discontinued Operations* at fair value less costs to sell in accordance with paragraphs 15–18 of that IFRS.

31A   *[This paragraph refers to amendments that are not yet effective, and is therefore not included in this edition.]*

Recognising and measuring goodwill or a gain from a bargain purchase

32   The acquirer shall recognise goodwill as of the acquisition date measured as the excess of (a) over (b) below:

(a)   the aggregate of:

(i)   the consideration transferred measured in accordance with this IFRS, which generally requires acquisition-date fair value (see paragraph 37);

(ii)   the amount of any non-controlling interest in the acquiree measured in accordance with this IFRS; and

(iii) in a business combination achieved in stages (see paragraphs 41 and 42), the acquisition-date fair value of the acquirer's previously held equity interest in the acquiree.

(b)   the net of the acquisition-date amounts of the identifiable assets acquired and the liabilities assumed measured in accordance with this IFRS.

33   In a business combination in which the acquirer and the acquiree (or its former owners) exchange only equity interests, the acquisition-date fair value of the acquiree's equity interests may be more reliably measurable than the acquisition-date fair value of the acquirer's equity interests. If so, the acquirer shall determine the amount of goodwill by using the acquisition-date fair value of the acquiree's equity interests instead of the acquisition-date fair value of the equity interests transferred. To determine the amount of goodwill in a business combination in which no consideration is transferred, the acquirer shall use the acquisition-date fair value of the acquirer's interest in the acquiree in place of the acquisition-date fair value of the consideration

transferred (paragraph 32(a)(i)). Paragraphs B46–B49 provide related application guidance.

Bargain purchases

34   Occasionally, an acquirer will make a bargain purchase, which is a business combination in which the amount in paragraph 32(b) exceeds the aggregate of the amounts specified in paragraph 32(a). If that excess remains after applying the requirements in paragraph 36, the acquirer shall recognise the resulting gain in profit or loss on the acquisition date. The gain shall be attributed to the acquirer.

35   A bargain purchase might happen, for example, in a business combination that is a forced sale in which the seller is acting under compulsion. However, the recognition or measurement exceptions for particular items discussed in paragraphs 22–31 may also result in recognising a gain (or change the amount of a recognised gain) on a bargain purchase.

36   Before recognising a gain on a bargain purchase, the acquirer shall reassess whether it has correctly identified all of the assets acquired and all of the liabilities assumed and shall recognise any additional assets or liabilities that are identified in that review. The acquirer shall then review the procedures used to measure the amounts this IFRS requires to be recognised at the acquisition date for all of the following:

(a)   the identifiable assets acquired and liabilities assumed;

(b)   the non-controlling interest in the acquiree, if any;

(c)   for a business combination achieved in stages, the acquirer's previously held equity interest in the acquiree; and

(d)   the consideration transferred.

The objective of the review is to ensure that the measurements appropriately reflect consideration of all available information as of the acquisition date.

Consideration transferred

37   The consideration transferred in a business combination shall be measured at fair value, which shall be calculated as the sum of the acquisition-date fair values of the assets transferred by the acquirer, the liabilities incurred by the acquirer to former owners of the acquiree and the equity interests issued by the acquirer. (However, any portion of the acquirer's share-based payment awards exchanged for awards held by the acquiree's employees that is included in consideration transferred in the business combination shall be measured in accordance with paragraph 30 rather than at fair value.) Examples of potential forms of consideration include cash, other assets, a business or a subsidiary of the acquirer, *contingent consideration*, ordinary or preference equity instruments, options, warrants and member interests of *mutual entities*.

38   The consideration transferred may include assets or liabilities of the acquirer that have carrying amounts that differ from their fair values at the acquisition date (for example, non-monetary assets or a business of the acquirer). If so, the acquirer shall remeasure the transferred assets or liabilities to their fair values as of the acquisition date and recognise the resulting gains or losses, if any, in profit or loss. However, sometimes the transferred assets or liabilities remain within the combined entity after the business combination (for example, because the assets or liabilities were transferred to the acquiree rather than to its former owners), and the acquirer therefore retains control of them. In that situation, the acquirer shall measure those assets and liabilities at their carrying amounts immediately before the acquisition date and shall not recognise a gain or loss in profit or loss on assets or liabilities it controls both before and after the business combination.

Contingent consideration

39   The consideration the acquirer transfers in exchange for the acquiree includes any asset or liability resulting from a contingent consideration arrangement (see paragraph 37). The acquirer shall recognise the acquisition-date fair value of contingent consideration as part of the consideration transferred in exchange for the acquiree.

40   The acquirer shall classify an obligation to pay contingent consideration that meets the definition of a financial instrument as a financial liability or as equity on the basis of the definitions of an equity instrument and a financial liability in paragraph 11 of IAS 32 *Financial Instruments: Presentation*. The acquirer shall classify as an asset a right to the return of previously transferred consideration if specified conditions are met. Paragraph 58 provides guidance on the subsequent accounting for contingent consideration.

Additional guidance for applying the acquisition method to particular types of business combinations

A business combination achieved in stages

41   An acquirer sometimes obtains control of an acquiree in which it held an equity interest immediately before the acquisition date. For example, on 31 December 20X1, Entity A holds a 35 per cent non-controlling equity interest in Entity B. On that date, Entity A purchases an additional 40 per cent interest in Entity B, which gives it control of Entity B. This IFRS refers to such a transaction as a business combination achieved in stages, sometimes also referred to as a step acquisition.

42   In a business combination achieved in stages, the acquirer shall remeasure its previously held equity interest in the acquiree at its acquisition-date fair value and recognise the resulting gain or loss, if any, in profit or loss or other comprehensive income, as appropriate. In prior reporting periods, the acquirer may have recognised changes in the value of its equity interest in the acquiree in other comprehensive income. If so, the amount that was recognised in other comprehensive income shall be recognised on the same

basis as would be required if the acquirer had disposed directly of the previously held equity interest.

42A   When a party to a joint arrangement (as defined in IFRS 11 *Joint Arrangements*) obtains control of a business that is a joint operation (as defined in IFRS 11), and had rights to the assets and obligations for the liabilities relating to that joint operation immediately before the acquisition date, the transaction is a business combination achieved in stages. The acquirer shall therefore apply the requirements for a business combination achieved in stages, including remeasuring its previously held interest in the joint operation in the manner described in paragraph 42. In doing so, the acquirer shall remeasure its entire previously held interest in the joint operation.

A business combination achieved without the transfer of consideration

43   An acquirer sometimes obtains control of an acquiree without transferring consideration. The acquisition method of accounting for a business combination applies to those combinations. Such circumstances include:

(a)   The acquiree repurchases a sufficient number of its own shares for an existing investor (the acquirer) to obtain control.

(b)   Minority veto rights lapse that previously kept the acquirer from controlling an acquiree in which the acquirer held the majority voting rights.

(c)   The acquirer and acquiree agree to combine their businesses by contract alone. The acquirer transfers no consideration in exchange for control of an acquiree and holds no equity interests in the acquiree, either on the acquisition date or previously. Examples of business combinations achieved by contract alone include bringing two businesses together in a stapling arrangement or forming a dual listed corporation.

44   In a business combination achieved by contract alone, the acquirer shall attribute to the owners of the acquiree the amount of the acquiree's net assets recognised in accordance with this IFRS. In other words, the equity interests in the acquiree held by parties other than the acquirer are a non-controlling interest in the acquirer's post-combination financial statements even if the result is that all of the equity interests in the acquiree are attributed to the non-controlling interest.

Measurement period

45   If the initial accounting for a business combination is incomplete by the end of the reporting period in which the combination occurs, the acquirer shall report in its financial statements provisional amounts for the items for which the accounting is incomplete. During the measurement period, the acquirer shall retrospectively adjust the provisional amounts recognised at the acquisition date to reflect new information obtained about facts and circumstances that existed as of the acquisition date and, if known, would have affected the measurement of the amounts recognised

as of that date. During the measurement period, the acquirer shall also recognise additional assets or liabilities if new information is obtained about facts and circumstances that existed as of the acquisition date and, if known, would have resulted in the recognition of those assets and liabilities as of that date. The measurement period ends as soon as the acquirer receives the information it was seeking about facts and circumstances that existed as of the acquisition date or learns that more information is not obtainable. However, the measurement period shall not exceed one year from the acquisition date.

46   The measurement period is the period after the acquisition date during which the acquirer may adjust the provisional amounts recognised for a business combination. The measurement period provides the acquirer with a reasonable time to obtain the information necessary to identify and measure the following as of the acquisition date in accordance with the requirements of this IFRS:

(a)   the identifiable assets acquired, liabilities assumed and any non-controlling interest in the acquiree;

(b)   the consideration transferred for the acquiree (or the other amount used in measuring goodwill);

(c)   in a business combination achieved in stages, the equity interest in the acquiree previously held by the acquirer; and

(d)   the resulting goodwill or gain on a bargain purchase.

47   The acquirer shall consider all pertinent factors in determining whether information obtained after the acquisition date should result in an adjustment to the provisional amounts recognised or whether that information results from events that occurred after the acquisition date. Pertinent factors include the date when additional information is obtained and whether the acquirer can identify a reason for a change to provisional amounts. Information that is obtained shortly after the acquisition date is more likely to reflect circumstances that existed at the acquisition date than is information obtained several months later. For example, unless an intervening event that changed its fair value can be identified, the sale of an asset to a third party shortly after the acquisition date for an amount that differs significantly from its provisional fair value measured at that date is likely to indicate an error in the provisional amount.

48   The acquirer recognises an increase (decrease) in the provisional amount recognised for an identifiable asset (liability) by means of a decrease (increase) in goodwill. However, new information obtained during the measurement period may sometimes result in an adjustment to the provisional amount of more than one asset or liability. For example, the acquirer might have assumed a liability to pay damages related to an accident in one of the acquiree's facilities, part or all of which are covered by the acquiree's liability insurance policy. If the acquirer obtains new information during the measurement period about the acquisition-date fair value of that liability, the adjustment to goodwill resulting from a change to the provisional amount

recognised for the liability would be offset (in whole or in part) by a corresponding adjustment to goodwill resulting from a change to the provisional amount recognised for the claim receivable from the insurer.

49   During the measurement period, the acquirer shall recognise adjustments to the provisional amounts as if the accounting for the business combination had been completed at the acquisition date. Thus, the acquirer shall revise comparative information for prior periods presented in financial statements as needed, including making any change in depreciation, amortisation or other income effects recognised in completing the initial accounting.

50   After the measurement period ends, the acquirer shall revise the accounting for a business combination only to correct an error in accordance with IAS 8 *Accounting Policies, Changes in Accounting Estimates and Errors*.

Determining what is part of the business combination transaction

51   **The acquirer and the acquiree may have a pre-existing relationship or other arrangement before negotiations for the business combination began, or they may enter into an arrangement during the negotiations that is separate from the business combination. In either situation, the acquirer shall identify any amounts that are not part of what the acquirer and the acquiree (or its former owners) exchanged in the business combination, ie amounts that are not part of the exchange for the acquiree. The acquirer shall recognise as part of applying the acquisition method only the consideration transferred for the acquiree and the assets acquired and liabilities assumed in the exchange for the acquiree. Separate transactions shall be accounted for in accordance with the relevant IFRSs.**

52   A transaction entered into by or on behalf of the acquirer or primarily for the benefit of the acquirer or the combined entity, rather than primarily for the benefit of the acquiree (or its former owners) before the combination, is likely to be a separate transaction. The following are examples of separate transactions that are not to be included in applying the acquisition method:

(a)   a transaction that in effect settles pre-existing relationships between the acquirer and acquiree;

(b)   a transaction that remunerates employees or former owners of the acquiree for future services; and

(c)   a transaction that reimburses the acquiree or its former owners for paying the acquirer's acquisition-related costs.

Paragraphs B50–B62 provide related application guidance.

Acquisition-related costs

53   Acquisition-related costs are costs the acquirer incurs to effect a business combination. Those costs include finder's fees; advisory, legal, accounting, valuation and other professional or consulting fees; general administrative costs, including the costs of maintaining an internal acquisitions department; and costs of registering and issuing debt and equity securities. The acquirer

shall account for acquisition-related costs as expenses in the periods in which the costs are incurred and the services are received, with one exception. The costs to issue debt or equity securities shall be recognised in accordance with IAS 32 and IFRS 9.

Subsequent measurement and accounting

54   In general, an acquirer shall subsequently measure and account for assets acquired, liabilities assumed or incurred and equity instruments issued in a business combination in accordance with other applicable IFRSs for those items, depending on their nature. However, this IFRS provides guidance on subsequently measuring and accounting for the following assets acquired, liabilities assumed or incurred and equity instruments issued in a business combination:

     (a)   reacquired rights;

     (b)   contingent liabilities recognised as of the acquisition date;

     (c)   indemnification assets; and

     (d)   contingent consideration.

     Paragraph B63 provides related application guidance.

Reacquired rights

55   A reacquired right recognised as an intangible asset shall be amortised over the remaining contractual period of the contract in which the right was granted. An acquirer that subsequently sells a reacquired right to a third party shall include the carrying amount of the intangible asset in determining the gain or loss on the sale.

Contingent liabilities

56   After initial recognition and until the liability is settled, cancelled or expires, the acquirer shall measure a contingent liability recognised in a business combination at the higher of:

     (a)   the amount that would be recognised in accordance with IAS 37; and

     (b)   the amount initially recognised less, if appropriate, the cumulative amount of income recognised in accordance with the principles of IFRS 15 *Revenue from Contracts with Customers*.

     This requirement does not apply to contracts accounted for in accordance with IFRS 9.

Indemnification assets

57   At the end of each subsequent reporting period, the acquirer shall measure an indemnification asset that was recognised at the acquisition date on the same basis as the indemnified liability or asset, subject to any contractual limitations on its amount and, for an indemnification asset that is not

subsequently measured at its fair value, management's assessment of the collectibility of the indemnification asset. The acquirer shall derecognise the indemnification asset only when it collects the asset, sells it or otherwise loses the right to it.

Contingent consideration

58   Some changes in the fair value of contingent consideration that the acquirer recognises after the acquisition date may be the result of additional information that the acquirer obtained after that date about facts and circumstances that existed at the acquisition date. Such changes are measurement period adjustments in accordance with paragraphs 45–49. However, changes resulting from events after the acquisition date, such as meeting an earnings target, reaching a specified share price or reaching a milestone on a research and development project, are not measurement period adjustments. The acquirer shall account for changes in the fair value of contingent consideration that are not measurement period adjustments as follows:

(a)   Contingent consideration classified as equity shall not be remeasured and its subsequent settlement shall be accounted for within equity.

(b)   Other contingent consideration that:

(i)   is within the scope of IFRS 9 shall be measured at fair value at each reporting date and changes in fair value shall be recognised in profit or loss in accordance with IFRS 9.

(ii)   is not within the scope of IFRS 9 shall be measured at fair value at each reporting date and changes in fair value shall be recognised in profit or loss.

Disclosures

59   The acquirer shall disclose information that enables users of its financial statements to evaluate the nature and financial effect of a business combination that occurs either:

(a)   during the current reporting period; or

(b)   after the end of the reporting period but before the financial statements are authorised for issue.

60   To meet the objective in paragraph 59, the acquirer shall disclose the information specified in paragraphs B64 – B66.

61   The acquirer shall disclose information that enables users of its financial statements to evaluate the financial effects of adjustments recognised in the current reporting period that relate to business combinations that occurred in the period or previous reporting periods.

62   To meet the objective in paragraph 61, the acquirer shall disclose the information specified in paragraph B67.

63   If the specific disclosures required by this and other IFRSs do not meet the objectives set out in paragraphs 59 and 61, the acquirer shall disclose whatever additional information is necessary to meet those objectives.

Effective date and transition

Effective date

64   This IFRS shall be applied prospectively to business combinations for which the acquisition date is on or after the beginning of the first annual reporting period beginning on or after 1 July 2009. Earlier application is permitted. However, this IFRS shall be applied only at the beginning of an annual reporting period that begins on or after 30 June 2007. If an entity applies this IFRS before 1 July 2009, it shall disclose that fact and apply IAS 27 (as amended in 2008) at the same time.

64A   [Deleted]

64B   *Improvements to IFRSs* issued in May 2010 amended paragraphs 19, 30 and B56 and added paragraphs B62A and B62B. An entity shall apply those amendments for annual periods beginning on or after 1 July 2010. Earlier application is permitted. If an entity applies the amendments for an earlier period it shall disclose that fact. Application should be prospective from the date when the entity first applied this IFRS.

64C   Paragraphs 65A–65E were added by *Improvements to IFRSs* issued in May 2010. An entity shall apply those amendments for annual periods beginning on or after 1 July 2010. Earlier application is permitted. If an entity applies the amendments for an earlier period it shall disclose that fact. The amendments shall be applied to contingent consideration balances arising from business combinations with an acquisition date prior to the application of this IFRS, as issued in 2008.

64D   [Deleted]

64E   IFRS 10, issued in May 2011, amended paragraphs 7, B13, B63(e) and Appendix A. An entity shall apply those amendments when it applies IFRS 10.

64F   IFRS 13 *Fair Value Measurement*, issued in May 2011, amended paragraphs 20, 29, 33, 47, amended the definition of fair value in Appendix A and amended paragraphs B22, B40, B43–B46, B49 and B64. An entity shall apply those amendments when it applies IFRS 13.

64G   *Investment Entities* (Amendments to IFRS 10, IFRS 12 and IAS 27), issued in October 2012, amended paragraph 7 and added paragraph 2A. An entity shall apply those amendments for annual periods beginning on or after 1 January 2014. Earlier application of *Investment Entities* is permitted. If an entity applies these amendments earlier it shall also apply all amendments included in *Investment Entities* at the same time.

64H   [Deleted]

64I   *Annual Improvements to IFRSs 2010–2012 Cycle*, issued in December 2013, amended paragraphs 40 and 58 and added paragraph 67A and its related heading. An entity shall apply that amendment prospectively to business combinations for which the acquisition date is on or after 1 July 2014. Earlier application is permitted. An entity may apply the amendment earlier provided that IFRS 9 and IAS 37 (both as amended by *Annual Improvements to IFRSs 2010–2012 Cycle*) have also been applied. If an entity applies that amendment earlier it shall disclose that fact.

64J   *Annual Improvements Cycle 2011–2013* issued in December 2013 amended paragraph 2(a). An entity shall apply that amendment prospectively for annual periods beginning on or after 1 July 2014. Earlier application is permitted. If an entity applies that amendment for an earlier period it shall disclose that fact.

64K   IFRS 15 *Revenue from Contracts with Customers*, issued in May 2014, amended paragraph 56. An entity shall apply that amendment when it applies IFRS 15.

64L   IFRS 9, as issued in July 2014, amended paragraphs 16, 42, 53, 56, 58 and B41 and deleted paragraphs 64A, 64D and 64H. An entity shall apply those amendments when it applies IFRS 9.

64M   IFRS 16, issued in January 2016, amended paragraphs 14, 17, B32 and B42, deleted paragraphs B28–B30 and their related heading and added paragraphs 28A–28B and their related heading. An entity shall apply those amendments when it applies IFRS 16.

64N   *[This paragraph refers to amendments that are not yet effective, and is therefore not included in this edition.]*

64O   *Annual Improvements to IFRS Standards 2015–2017 Cycle*, issued in December 2017, added paragraph 42A. An entity shall apply those amendments to business combinations for which the acquisition date is on or after the beginning of the first annual reporting period beginning on or after 1 January 2019. Earlier application is permitted. If an entity applies those amendments earlier, it shall disclose that fact.

64P   *Definition of a Business*, issued in October 2018, added paragraphs B7A–B7C, B8A and B12A–B12D, amended the definition of the term 'business' in Appendix A, amended paragraphs 3, B7–B9, B11 and B12 and deleted paragraph B10. An entity shall apply these amendments to business combinations for which the acquisition date is on or after the beginning of the first annual reporting period beginning on or after 1 January 2020 and to asset acquisitions that occur on or after the beginning of that period. Earlier application of these amendments is permitted. If an entity applies these amendments for an earlier period, it shall disclose that fact.

64Q   *Reference to the Conceptual Framework*, issued in May 2020, amended paragraphs 11, 14, 21, 22 and 23 and added paragraphs 21A, 21B, 21C and 23A. An entity shall apply those amendments to business combinations for which the acquisition date is on or after the beginning of the first annual reporting period beginning on or after 1 January 2022. Earlier application is permitted if at the same time or earlier an entity also applies all the amendments made by

Amendments to References to the Conceptual Framework in IFRS Standards, issued in March 2018.

Transition

65 Assets and liabilities that arose from business combinations whose acquisition dates preceded the application of this IFRS shall not be adjusted upon application of this IFRS.

65A Contingent consideration balances arising from business combinations whose acquisition dates preceded the date when an entity first applied this IFRS as issued in 2008 shall not be adjusted upon first application of this IFRS. Paragraphs 65B–65E shall be applied in the subsequent accounting for those balances. Paragraphs 65B–65E shall not apply to the accounting for contingent consideration balances arising from business combinations with acquisition dates on or after the date when the entity first applied this IFRS as issued in 2008. In paragraphs 65B–65E business combination refers exclusively to business combinations whose acquisition date preceded the application of this IFRS as issued in 2008.

65B If a business combination agreement provides for an adjustment to the cost of the combination contingent on future events, the acquirer shall include the amount of that adjustment in the cost of the combination at the acquisition date if the adjustment is probable and can be measured reliably.

65C A business combination agreement may allow for adjustments to the cost of the combination that are contingent on one or more future events. The adjustment might, for example, be contingent on a specified level of profit being maintained or achieved in future periods, or on the market price of the instruments issued being maintained. It is usually possible to estimate the amount of any such adjustment at the time of initially accounting for the combination without impairing the reliability of the information, even though some uncertainty exists. If the future events do not occur or the estimate needs to be revised, the cost of the business combination shall be adjusted accordingly.

65D However, when a business combination agreement provides for such an adjustment, that adjustment is not included in the cost of the combination at the time of initially accounting for the combination if it either is not probable or cannot be measured reliably. If that adjustment subsequently becomes probable and can be measured reliably, the additional consideration shall be treated as an adjustment to the cost of the combination.

65E In some circumstances, the acquirer may be required to make a subsequent payment to the seller as compensation for a reduction in the value of the assets given, equity instruments issued or liabilities incurred or assumed by the acquirer in exchange for control of the acquiree. This is the case, for example, when the acquirer guarantees the market price of equity or debt instruments issued as part of the cost of the business combination and is required to issue additional equity or debt instruments to restore the originally determined cost. In such cases, no increase in the cost of the business combination is recognised. In the case of equity instruments, the fair value of the additional payment is offset by an equal reduction in the value attributed to the instruments initially issued. In the case of debt instruments, the additional payment is regarded as a reduction in the premium or an increase in the discount on the initial issue.

66   An entity, such as a mutual entity, that has not yet applied IFRS 3 and had one or more business combinations that were accounted for using the purchase method shall apply the transition provisions in paragraphs B68 and B69.

Income taxes

67   For business combinations in which the acquisition date was before this IFRS is applied, the acquirer shall apply the requirements of paragraph 68 of IAS 12, as amended by this IFRS, prospectively. That is to say, the acquirer shall not adjust the accounting for prior business combinations for previously recognised changes in recognised deferred tax assets. However, from the date when this IFRS is applied, the acquirer shall recognise, as an adjustment to profit or loss (or, if IAS 12 requires, outside profit or loss), changes in recognised deferred tax assets.

Reference to IFRS 9

67A   If an entity applies this Standard but does not yet apply IFRS 9, any reference to IFRS 9 should be read as a reference to IAS 39.

Withdrawal of IFRS 3 (2004)

68   This IFRS supersedes IFRS 3 *Business Combinations* (as issued in 2004).

Appendix A
Defined terms

This appendix is an integral part of the IFRS.

acquiree	The business or businesses that the **acquirer** obtains control of in a **business combination**.
acquirer	The entity that obtains control of the **acquiree**.
acquisition date	The date on which the **acquirer** obtains control of the **acquiree**.
business	An integrated set of activities and assets that is capable of being conducted and managed for the purpose of providing goods or services to customers, generating investment income (such as dividends or interest) or generating other income from ordinary activities.
business combination	A transaction or other event in which an **acquirer** obtains control of one or more **businesses**. Transactions sometimes referred to as 'true mergers' or 'mergers of equals' are also **business combinations** as that term is used in this IFRS.
contingent consideration	Usually, an obligation of the **acquirer** to transfer additional assets or **equity interests** to the former owners of an **acquiree** as part of the exchange for control of the acquiree if specified future events occur or conditions are met. However, *contingent consideration* also may give the acquirer the right to the return of previously transferred consideration if specified conditions are met.
equity interests	For the purposes of this IFRS, *equity interests* is used broadly to mean ownership interests of investor-owned entities and owner, member or participant interests of **mutual entities**.
fair value	*Fair value* is the price that would be received to sell an asset or paid to transfer a liability in an orderly transaction between market participants at the measurement date. (See IFRS 13.)
goodwill	An asset representing the future economic benefits arising from other assets acquired in a **business combination** that are not individually identified and separately recognised.
identifiable	An asset is *identifiable* if it either:

(a) is separable, ie capable of being separated or divided from the entity and sold, transferred, licensed, rented or exchanged, either individually or together with a related contract, identifiable asset or liability, regardless of whether the entity intends to do so; or

(b) arises from contractual or other legal rights, regardless of whether those rights are transferable or separable from the entity or from other rights and obligations.

intangible asset	An **identifiable** non-monetary asset without physical substance.
mutual entity	An entity, other than an investor-owned entity, that provides dividends, lower costs or other economic benefits directly to its **owners**, members or participants. For example, a mutual insurance company, a credit union and a co-operative entity are all mutual entities.
non-controlling interest	The equity in a subsidiary not attributable, directly or indirectly, to a parent.
owners	For the purposes of this IFRS, *owners* is used broadly to include holders of **equity interests** of investor-owned entities and owners or members of, or participants in, **mutual entities**.

Appendix B
Application guidance

This appendix is an integral part of the IFRS.

Business combinations of entities under common control (application of paragraph 2(c))

B1   This IFRS does not apply to a business combination of entities or businesses under common control. A business combination involving entities or businesses under common control is a business combination in which all of the combining entities or businesses are ultimately controlled by the same party or parties both before and after the business combination, and that control is not transitory.

B2   A group of individuals shall be regarded as controlling an entity when, as a result of contractual arrangements, they collectively have the power to govern its financial and operating policies so as to obtain benefits from its activities. Therefore, a business combination is outside the scope of this IFRS when the same group of individuals has, as a result of contractual arrangements, ultimate collective power to govern the financial and operating policies of each of the combining entities so as to obtain benefits from their activities, and that ultimate collective power is not transitory.

B3   An entity may be controlled by an individual or by a group of individuals acting together under a contractual arrangement, and that individual or group of individuals may not be subject to the financial reporting requirements of IFRSs. Therefore, it is not necessary for combining entities to be included as part of the same consolidated financial statements for a business combination to be regarded as one involving entities under common control.

B4   The extent of non-controlling interests in each of the combining entities before and after the business combination is not relevant to determining whether the combination involves entities under common control. Similarly, the fact that one of the combining entities is a subsidiary that has been excluded from the consolidated financial statements is not relevant to determining whether a combination involves entities under common control.

Identifying a business combination (application of paragraph 3)

B5   This IFRS defines a business combination as a transaction or other event in which an acquirer obtains control of one or more businesses. An acquirer might obtain control of an acquiree in a variety of ways, for example:

    (a)   by transferring cash, cash equivalents or other assets (including net assets that constitute a business);

    (b)   by incurring liabilities;

    (c)   by issuing equity interests;

(d) by providing more than one type of consideration; or

(e) without transferring consideration, including by contract alone (see paragraph 43).

B6 A business combination may be structured in a variety of ways for legal, taxation or other reasons, which include but are not limited to:

(a) one or more businesses become subsidiaries of an acquirer or the net assets of one or more businesses are legally merged into the acquirer;

(b) one combining entity transfers its net assets, or its owners transfer their equity interests, to another combining entity or its owners;

(c) all of the combining entities transfer their net assets, or the owners of those entities transfer their equity interests, to a newly formed entity (sometimes referred to as a roll-up or put-together transaction); or

(d) a group of former owners of one of the combining entities obtains control of the combined entity.

Definition of a business (application of paragraph 3)

B7 A business consists of inputs and processes applied to those inputs that have the ability to contribute to the creation of outputs. The three elements of a business are defined as follows (see paragraphs B8–B12D for guidance on the elements of a business):

(a) **Input:** Any economic resource that creates outputs, or has the ability to contribute to the creation of outputs when one or more processes are applied to it. Examples include non-current assets (including intangible assets or rights to use non-current assets), intellectual property, the ability to obtain access to necessary materials or rights and employees.

(b) **Process:** Any system, standard, protocol, convention or rule that when applied to an input or inputs, creates outputs or has the ability to contribute to the creation of outputs. Examples include strategic management processes, operational processes and resource management processes. These processes typically are documented, but the intellectual capacity of an organised workforce having the necessary skills and experience following rules and conventions may provide the necessary processes that are capable of being applied to inputs to create outputs. (Accounting, billing, payroll and other administrative systems typically are not processes used to create outputs.)

(c) **Output:** The result of inputs and processes applied to those inputs that provide goods or services to customers, generate investment income (such as dividends or interest) or generate other income from ordinary activities.

Optional test to identify concentration of fair value

B7A   Paragraph B7B sets out an optional test (the concentration test) to permit a simplified assessment of whether an acquired set of activities and assets is not a business. An entity may elect to apply, or not apply, the test. An entity may make such an election separately for each transaction or other event. The concentration test has the following consequences:

(a)   if the concentration test is met, the set of activities and assets is determined not to be a business and no further assessment is needed.

(b)   if the concentration test is not met, or if the entity elects not to apply the test, the entity shall then perform the assessment set out in paragraphs B8–B12D.

B7B   The concentration test is met if substantially all of the fair value of the gross assets acquired is concentrated in a single identifiable asset or group of similar identifiable assets. For the concentration test:

(a)   gross assets acquired shall exclude cash and cash equivalents, deferred tax assets, and goodwill resulting from the effects of deferred tax liabilities.

(b)   the fair value of the gross assets acquired shall include any consideration transferred (plus the fair value of any non-controlling interest and the fair value of any previously held interest) in excess of the fair value of net identifiable assets acquired. The fair value of the gross assets acquired may normally be determined as the total obtained by adding the fair value of the consideration transferred (plus the fair value of any non-controlling interest and the fair value of any previously held interest) to the fair value of the liabilities assumed (other than deferred tax liabilities), and then excluding the items identified in subparagraph (a). However, if the fair value of the gross assets acquired is more than that total, a more precise calculation may sometimes be needed.

(c)   a single identifiable asset shall include any asset or group of assets that would be recognised and measured as a single identifiable asset in a business combination.

(d)   if a tangible asset is attached to, and cannot be physically removed and used separately from, another tangible asset (or from an underlying asset subject to a lease, as defined in IFRS 16 *Leases*), without incurring significant cost, or significant diminution in utility or fair value to either asset (for example, land and buildings), those assets shall be considered a single identifiable asset.

(e)   when assessing whether assets are similar, an entity shall consider the nature of each single identifiable asset and the risks associated with managing and creating outputs from the assets (that is, the risk characteristics).

(f) the following shall not be considered similar assets:

(i) a tangible asset and an intangible asset;

(ii) tangible assets in different classes (for example, inventory, manufacturing equipment and automobiles) unless they are considered a single identifiable asset in accordance with the criterion in subparagraph (d);

(iii) identifiable intangible assets in different classes (for example, brand names, licences and intangible assets under development);

(iv) a financial asset and a non-financial asset;

(v) financial assets in different classes (for example, accounts receivable and investments in equity instruments); and

(vi) identifiable assets that are within the same class of asset but have significantly different risk characteristics.

B7C The requirements in paragraph B7B do not modify the guidance on similar assets in IAS 38 *Intangible Assets*; nor do they modify the meaning of the term 'class' in IAS 16 *Property, Plant and Equipment*, IAS 38 and IFRS 7 *Financial Instruments: Disclosures*.

Elements of a business

B8 Although businesses usually have outputs, outputs are not required for an integrated set of activities and assets to qualify as a business. To be capable of being conducted and managed for the purpose identified in the definition of a business, an integrated set of activities and assets requires two essential elements—inputs and processes applied to those inputs. A business need not include all of the inputs or processes that the seller used in operating that business. However, to be considered a business, an integrated set of activities and assets must include, at a minimum, an input and a substantive process that together significantly contribute to the ability to create output. Paragraphs B12–B12D specify how to assess whether a process is substantive.

B8A If an acquired set of activities and assets has outputs, continuation of revenue does not on its own indicate that both an input and a substantive process have been acquired.

B9 The nature of the elements of a business varies by industry and by the structure of an entity's operations (activities), including the entity's stage of development. Established businesses often have many different types of inputs, processes and outputs, whereas new businesses often have few inputs and processes and sometimes only a single output (product). Nearly all businesses also have liabilities, but a business need not have liabilities. Furthermore, an acquired set of activities and assets that is not a business might have liabilities.

B10 [Deleted]

B11   Determining whether a particular set of activities and assets is a business shall be based on whether the integrated set is capable of being conducted and managed as a business by a market participant. Thus, in evaluating whether a particular set is a business, it is not relevant whether a seller operated the set as a business or whether the acquirer intends to operate the set as a business.

Assessing whether an acquired process is substantive

B12   Paragraphs B12A–B12D explain how to assess whether an acquired process is substantive if the acquired set of activities and assets does not have outputs (paragraph B12B) and if it does have outputs (paragraph B12C).

B12A   An example of an acquired set of activities and assets that does not have outputs at the acquisition date is an early-stage entity that has not started generating revenue. Moreover, if an acquired set of activities and assets was generating revenue at the acquisition date, it is considered to have outputs at that date, even if subsequently it will no longer generate revenue from external customers, for example because it will be integrated by the acquirer.

B12B   If a set of activities and assets does not have outputs at the acquisition date, an acquired process (or group of processes) shall be considered substantive only if:

(a)   it is critical to the ability to develop or convert an acquired input or inputs into outputs; and

(b)   the inputs acquired include both an organised workforce that has the necessary skills, knowledge, or experience to perform that process (or group of processes) and other inputs that the organised workforce could develop or convert into outputs. Those other inputs could include:

(i)   intellectual property that could be used to develop a good or service;

(ii)   other economic resources that could be developed to create outputs; or

(iii)   rights to obtain access to necessary materials or rights that enable the creation of future outputs.

Examples of the inputs mentioned in subparagraphs (b)(i)–(iii) include technology, in-process research and development projects, real estate and mineral interests.

B12C   If a set of activities and assets has outputs at the acquisition date, an acquired process (or group of processes) shall be considered substantive if, when applied to an acquired input or inputs, it:

(a)   is critical to the ability to continue producing outputs, and the inputs acquired include an organised workforce with the necessary skills, knowledge, or experience to perform that process (or group of processes); or

(b)   significantly contributes to the ability to continue producing outputs and:

    (i)   is considered unique or scarce; or

    (ii)   cannot be replaced without significant cost, effort, or delay in the ability to continue producing outputs.

B12D   The following additional discussion supports both paragraphs B12B and B12C:

    (a)   an acquired contract is an input and not a substantive process. Nevertheless, an acquired contract, for example, a contract for outsourced property management or outsourced asset management, may give access to an organised workforce. An entity shall assess whether an organised workforce accessed through such a contract performs a substantive process that the entity controls, and thus has acquired. Factors to be considered in making that assessment include the duration of the contract and its renewal terms.

    (b)   difficulties in replacing an acquired organised workforce may indicate that the acquired organised workforce performs a process that is critical to the ability to create outputs.

    (c)   a process (or group of processes) is not critical if, for example, it is ancillary or minor within the context of all the processes required to create outputs.

Identifying the acquirer (application of paragraphs 6 and 7)

B13   The guidance in IFRS 10 *Consolidated Financial Statements* shall be used to identify the acquirer—the entity that obtains control of the acquiree. If a business combination has occurred but applying the guidance in IFRS 10 does not clearly indicate which of the combining entities is the acquirer, the factors in paragraphs B14–B18 shall be considered in making that determination.

B14   In a business combination effected primarily by transferring cash or other assets or by incurring liabilities, the acquirer is usually the entity that transfers the cash or other assets or incurs the liabilities.

B15   In a business combination effected primarily by exchanging equity interests, the acquirer is usually the entity that issues its equity interests. However, in some business combinations, commonly called 'reverse acquisitions', the issuing entity is the acquiree. Paragraphs B19–B27 provide guidance on accounting for reverse acquisitions. Other pertinent facts and circumstances shall also be considered in identifying the acquirer in a business combination effected by exchanging equity interests, including:

    (a)   *the relative voting rights in the combined entity after the business combination*— The acquirer is usually the combining entity whose owners as a group retain or receive the largest portion of the voting rights in the combined entity. In determining which group of owners retains or receives the largest portion of the voting rights, an entity shall consider the existence of any unusual or special voting arrangements and options, warrants or convertible securities.

(b) *the existence of a large minority voting interest in the combined entity if no other owner or organised group of owners has a significant voting interest* — The acquirer is usually the combining entity whose single owner or organised group of owners holds the largest minority voting interest in the combined entity.

(c) *the composition of the governing body of the combined entity* — The acquirer is usually the combining entity whose owners have the ability to elect or appoint or to remove a majority of the members of the governing body of the combined entity.

(d) *the composition of the senior management of the combined entity* — The acquirer is usually the combining entity whose (former) management dominates the management of the combined entity.

(e) *the terms of the exchange of equity interests* — The acquirer is usually the combining entity that pays a premium over the pre-combination fair value of the equity interests of the other combining entity or entities.

B16 The acquirer is usually the combining entity whose relative size (measured in, for example, assets, revenues or profit) is significantly greater than that of the other combining entity or entities.

B17 In a business combination involving more than two entities, determining the acquirer shall include a consideration of, among other things, which of the combining entities initiated the combination, as well as the relative size of the combining entities.

B18 A new entity formed to effect a business combination is not necessarily the acquirer. If a new entity is formed to issue equity interests to effect a business combination, one of the combining entities that existed before the business combination shall be identified as the acquirer by applying the guidance in paragraphs B13–B17. In contrast, a new entity that transfers cash or other assets or incurs liabilities as consideration may be the acquirer.

Reverse acquisitions

B19 A reverse acquisition occurs when the entity that issues securities (the legal acquirer) is identified as the acquiree for accounting purposes on the basis of the guidance in paragraphs B13–B18. The entity whose equity interests are acquired (the legal acquiree) must be the acquirer for accounting purposes for the transaction to be considered a reverse acquisition. For example, reverse acquisitions sometimes occur when a private operating entity wants to become a public entity but does not want to register its equity shares. To accomplish that, the private entity will arrange for a public entity to acquire its equity interests in exchange for the equity interests of the public entity. In this example, the public entity is the **legal acquirer** because it issued its equity interests, and the private entity is the **legal acquiree** because its equity interests were acquired. However, application of the guidance in paragraphs B13–B18 results in identifying:

(a)   the public entity as the **acquiree** for accounting purposes (the accounting acquiree); and

(b)   the private entity as the **acquirer** for accounting purposes (the accounting acquirer).

The accounting acquiree must meet the definition of a business for the transaction to be accounted for as a reverse acquisition, and all of the recognition and measurement principles in this IFRS, including the requirement to recognise goodwill, apply.

Measuring the consideration transferred

B20   In a reverse acquisition, the accounting acquirer usually issues no consideration for the acquiree. Instead, the accounting acquiree usually issues its equity shares to the owners of the accounting acquirer. Accordingly, the acquisition-date fair value of the consideration transferred by the accounting acquirer for its interest in the accounting acquiree is based on the number of equity interests the legal subsidiary would have had to issue to give the owners of the legal parent the same percentage equity interest in the combined entity that results from the reverse acquisition. The fair value of the number of equity interests calculated in that way can be used as the fair value of consideration transferred in exchange for the acquiree.

Preparation and presentation of consolidated financial statements

B21   Consolidated financial statements prepared following a reverse acquisition are issued under the name of the legal parent (accounting acquiree) but described in the notes as a continuation of the financial statements of the legal subsidiary (accounting acquirer), with one adjustment, which is to adjust retroactively the accounting acquirer's legal capital to reflect the legal capital of the accounting acquiree. That adjustment is required to reflect the capital of the legal parent (the accounting acquiree). Comparative information presented in those consolidated financial statements also is retroactively adjusted to reflect the legal capital of the legal parent (accounting acquiree).

B22   Because the consolidated financial statements represent the continuation of the financial statements of the legal subsidiary except for its capital structure, the consolidated financial statements reflect:

(a)   the assets and liabilities of the legal subsidiary (the accounting acquirer) recognised and measured at their pre-combination carrying amounts.

(b)   the assets and liabilities of the legal parent (the accounting acquiree) recognised and measured in accordance with this IFRS.

(c)   the retained earnings and other equity balances of the legal subsidiary (accounting acquirer) **before** the business combination.

(d)   the amount recognised as issued equity interests in the consolidated financial statements determined by adding the issued equity interest of the legal subsidiary (the accounting acquirer) outstanding immediately before the business combination to the fair value of the legal parent (accounting acquiree). However, the equity structure (ie the number and type of equity interests issued) reflects the equity structure of the legal parent (the accounting acquiree), including the equity interests the legal parent issued to effect the combination. Accordingly, the equity structure of the legal subsidiary (the accounting acquirer) is restated using the exchange ratio established in the acquisition agreement to reflect the number of shares of the legal parent (the accounting acquiree) issued in the reverse acquisition.

(e)   the non-controlling interest's proportionate share of the legal subsidiary's (accounting acquirer's) pre-combination carrying amounts of retained earnings and other equity interests as discussed in paragraphs B23 and B24.

Non-controlling interest

B23   In a reverse acquisition, some of the owners of the legal acquiree (the accounting acquirer) might not exchange their equity interests for equity interests of the legal parent (the accounting acquiree). Those owners are treated as a non-controlling interest in the consolidated financial statements after the reverse acquisition. That is because the owners of the legal acquiree that do not exchange their equity interests for equity interests of the legal acquirer have an interest in only the results and net assets of the legal acquiree—not in the results and net assets of the combined entity. Conversely, even though the legal acquirer is the acquiree for accounting purposes, the owners of the legal acquirer have an interest in the results and net assets of the combined entity.

B24   The assets and liabilities of the legal acquiree are measured and recognised in the consolidated financial statements at their pre-combination carrying amounts (see paragraph B22(a)). Therefore, in a reverse acquisition the non-controlling interest reflects the non-controlling shareholders' proportionate interest in the pre-combination carrying amounts of the legal acquiree's net assets even if the non-controlling interests in other acquisitions are measured at their fair value at the acquisition date.

Earnings per share

B25   As noted in paragraph B22(d), the equity structure in the consolidated financial statements following a reverse acquisition reflects the equity structure of the legal acquirer (the accounting acquiree), including the equity interests issued by the legal acquirer to effect the business combination.

B26   In calculating the weighted average number of ordinary shares outstanding (the denominator of the earnings per share calculation) during the period in which the reverse acquisition occurs:

(a)   the number of ordinary shares outstanding from the beginning of that period to the acquisition date shall be computed on the basis of the weighted average number of ordinary shares of the legal acquiree (accounting acquirer) outstanding during the period multiplied by the exchange ratio established in the merger agreement; and

(b)   the number of ordinary shares outstanding from the acquisition date to the end of that period shall be the actual number of ordinary shares of the legal acquirer (the accounting acquiree) outstanding during that period.

B27   The basic earnings per share for each comparative period before the acquisition date presented in the consolidated financial statements following a reverse acquisition shall be calculated by dividing:

(a)   the profit or loss of the legal acquiree attributable to ordinary shareholders in each of those periods by

(b)   the legal acquiree's historical weighted average number of ordinary shares outstanding multiplied by the exchange ratio established in the acquisition agreement.

Recognising particular assets acquired and liabilities assumed (application of paragraphs 10–13)

B28–B30   [Deleted]

Intangible assets

B31   The acquirer shall recognise, separately from goodwill, the identifiable intangible assets acquired in a business combination. An intangible asset is identifiable if it meets either the separability criterion or the contractual-legal criterion.

B32   An intangible asset that meets the contractual-legal criterion is identifiable even if the asset is not transferable or separable from the acquiree or from other rights and obligations. For example:

(a)   [deleted]

(b)   an acquiree owns and operates a nuclear power plant. The licence to operate that power plant is an intangible asset that meets the contractual-legal criterion for recognition separately from goodwill, even if the acquirer cannot sell or transfer it separately from the acquired power plant. An acquirer may recognise the fair value of the operating licence and the fair value of the power plant as a single asset for financial reporting purposes if the useful lives of those assets are similar.

(c)   an acquiree owns a technology patent. It has licensed that patent to others for their exclusive use outside the domestic market, receiving a specified percentage of future foreign revenue in exchange. Both the technology patent and the related licence agreement meet the contractual-legal criterion for recognition separately from goodwill even if selling or exchanging the patent and the related licence agreement separately from one another would not be practical.

B33   The separability criterion means that an acquired intangible asset is capable of being separated or divided from the acquiree and sold, transferred, licensed, rented or exchanged, either individually or together with a related contract, identifiable asset or liability. An intangible asset that the acquirer would be able to sell, license or otherwise exchange for something else of value meets the separability criterion even if the acquirer does not intend to sell, license or otherwise exchange it. An acquired intangible asset meets the separability criterion if there is evidence of exchange transactions for that type of asset or an asset of a similar type, even if those transactions are infrequent and regardless of whether the acquirer is involved in them. For example, customer and subscriber lists are frequently licensed and thus meet the separability criterion. Even if an acquiree believes its customer lists have characteristics different from other customer lists, the fact that customer lists are frequently licensed generally means that the acquired customer list meets the separability criterion. However, a customer list acquired in a business combination would not meet the separability criterion if the terms of confidentiality or other agreements prohibit an entity from selling, leasing or otherwise exchanging information about its customers.

B34   An intangible asset that is not individually separable from the acquiree or combined entity meets the separability criterion if it is separable in combination with a related contract, identifiable asset or liability. For example:

(a)   market participants exchange deposit liabilities and related depositor relationship intangible assets in observable exchange transactions. Therefore, the acquirer should recognise the depositor relationship intangible asset separately from goodwill.

(b)   an acquiree owns a registered trademark and documented but unpatented technical expertise used to manufacture the trademarked product. To transfer ownership of a trademark, the owner is also required to transfer everything else necessary for the new owner to produce a product or service indistinguishable from that produced by the former owner. Because the unpatented technical expertise must be separated from the acquiree or combined entity and sold if the related trademark is sold, it meets the separability criterion.

Reacquired rights

B35   As part of a business combination, an acquirer may reacquire a right that it had previously granted to the acquiree to use one or more of the acquirer's recognised or unrecognised assets. Examples of such rights include a right to use the acquirer's trade name under a franchise agreement or a right to use the acquirer's technology under a technology licensing agreement. A reacquired right is an identifiable intangible asset that the acquirer recognises separately from goodwill. Paragraph 29 provides guidance on measuring a reacquired right and paragraph 55 provides guidance on the subsequent accounting for a reacquired right.

B36 If the terms of the contract giving rise to a reacquired right are favourable or unfavourable relative to the terms of current market transactions for the same or similar items, the acquirer shall recognise a settlement gain or loss. Paragraph B52 provides guidance for measuring that settlement gain or loss.

Assembled workforce and other items that are not identifiable

B37 The acquirer subsumes into goodwill the value of an acquired intangible asset that is not identifiable as of the acquisition date. For example, an acquirer may attribute value to the existence of an assembled workforce, which is an existing collection of employees that permits the acquirer to continue to operate an acquired business from the acquisition date. An assembled workforce does not represent the intellectual capital of the skilled workforce — the (often specialised) knowledge and experience that employees of an acquiree bring to their jobs. Because the assembled workforce is not an identifiable asset to be recognised separately from goodwill, any value attributed to it is subsumed into goodwill.

B38 The acquirer also subsumes into goodwill any value attributed to items that do not qualify as assets at the acquisition date. For example, the acquirer might attribute value to potential contracts the acquiree is negotiating with prospective new customers at the acquisition date. Because those potential contracts are not themselves assets at the acquisition date, the acquirer does not recognise them separately from goodwill. The acquirer should not subsequently reclassify the value of those contracts from goodwill for events that occur after the acquisition date. However, the acquirer should assess the facts and circumstances surrounding events occurring shortly after the acquisition to determine whether a separately recognisable intangible asset existed at the acquisition date.

B39 After initial recognition, an acquirer accounts for intangible assets acquired in a business combination in accordance with the provisions of IAS 38 *Intangible Assets*. However, as described in paragraph 3 of IAS 38, the accounting for some acquired intangible assets after initial recognition is prescribed by other IFRSs.

B40 The identifiability criteria determine whether an intangible asset is recognised separately from goodwill. However, the criteria neither provide guidance for measuring the fair value of an intangible asset nor restrict the assumptions used in measuring the fair value of an intangible asset. For example, the acquirer would take into account the assumptions that market participants would use when pricing the intangible asset, such as expectations of future contract renewals, in measuring fair value. It is not necessary for the renewals themselves to meet the identifiability criteria. (However, see paragraph 29, which establishes an exception to the fair value measurement principle for reacquired rights recognised in a business combination.) Paragraphs 36 and 37 of IAS 38 provide guidance for determining whether intangible assets should be combined into a single unit of account with other intangible or tangible assets.

Measuring the fair value of particular identifiable assets and a non-controlling interest in an acquiree (application of paragraphs 18 and 19)

Assets with uncertain cash flows (valuation allowances)

B41   The acquirer shall not recognise a separate valuation allowance as of the acquisition date for assets acquired in a business combination that are measured at their acquisition-date fair values because the effects of uncertainty about future cash flows are included in the fair value measure. For example, because this IFRS requires the acquirer to measure acquired receivables, including loans, at their acquisition-date fair values in accounting for a business combination, the acquirer does not recognise a separate valuation allowance for the contractual cash flows that are deemed to be uncollectible at that date or a loss allowance for expected credit losses.

Assets subject to operating leases in which the acquiree is the lessor

B42   In measuring the acquisition-date fair value of an asset such as a building or a patent that is subject to an operating lease in which the acquiree is the lessor, the acquirer shall take into account the terms of the lease. The acquirer does not recognise a separate asset or liability if the terms of an operating lease are either favourable or unfavourable when compared with market terms.

Assets that the acquirer intends not to use or to use in a way that is different from the way other market participants would use them

B43   To protect its competitive position, or for other reasons, the acquirer may intend not to use an acquired non-financial asset actively, or it may not intend to use the asset according to its highest and best use. For example, that might be the case for an acquired research and development intangible asset that the acquirer plans to use defensively by preventing others from using it. Nevertheless, the acquirer shall measure the fair value of the non-financial asset assuming its highest and best use by market participants in accordance with the appropriate valuation premise, both initially and when measuring fair value less costs of disposal for subsequent impairment testing.

Non-controlling interest in an acquiree

B44   This IFRS allows the acquirer to measure a non-controlling interest in the acquiree at its fair value at the acquisition date. Sometimes an acquirer will be able to measure the acquisition-date fair value of a non-controlling interest on the basis of a quoted price in an active market for the equity shares (ie those not held by the acquirer). In other situations, however, a quoted price in an active market for the equity shares will not be available. In those situations, the acquirer would measure the fair value of the non-controlling interest using other valuation techniques.

B45   The fair values of the acquirer's interest in the acquiree and the non-controlling interest on a per-share basis might differ. The main difference is likely to be the inclusion of a control premium in the per-share fair value of the acquirer's interest in the acquiree or, conversely, the inclusion of a discount for lack of control (also referred to as a non-controlling interest discount) in the per-share fair value of the non-controlling interest if market participants would take into account such a premium or discount when pricing the non-controlling interest.

Measuring goodwill or a gain from a bargain purchase

Measuring the acquisition-date fair value of the acquirer's interest in the acquiree using valuation techniques (application of paragraph 33)

B46   In a business combination achieved without the transfer of consideration, the acquirer must substitute the acquisition-date fair value of its interest in the acquiree for the acquisition-date fair value of the consideration transferred to measure goodwill or a gain on a bargain purchase (see paragraphs 32–34).

Special considerations in applying the acquisition method to combinations of mutual entities (application of paragraph 33)

B47   When two mutual entities combine, the fair value of the equity or member interests in the acquiree (or the fair value of the acquiree) may be more reliably measurable than the fair value of the member interests transferred by the acquirer. In that situation, paragraph 33 requires the acquirer to determine the amount of goodwill by using the acquisition-date fair value of the acquiree's equity interests instead of the acquisition-date fair value of the acquirer's equity interests transferred as consideration. In addition, the acquirer in a combination of mutual entities shall recognise the acquiree's net assets as a direct addition to capital or equity in its statement of financial position, not as an addition to retained earnings, which is consistent with the way in which other types of entities apply the acquisition method.

B48   Although they are similar in many ways to other businesses, mutual entities have distinct characteristics that arise primarily because their members are both customers and owners. Members of mutual entities generally expect to receive benefits for their membership, often in the form of reduced fees charged for goods and services or patronage dividends. The portion of patronage dividends allocated to each member is often based on the amount of business the member did with the mutual entity during the year.

B49   A fair value measurement of a mutual entity should include the assumptions that market participants would make about future member benefits as well as any other relevant assumptions market participants would make about the mutual entity. For example, a present value technique may be used to measure the fair value of a mutual entity. The cash flows used as inputs to the model should be based on the expected cash flows of the mutual entity, which are likely to reflect reductions for member benefits, such as reduced fees charged for goods and services.

Determining what is part of the business combination transaction (application of paragraphs 51 and 52)

B50   The acquirer should consider the following factors, which are neither mutually exclusive nor individually conclusive, to determine whether a transaction is part of the exchange for the acquiree or whether the transaction is separate from the business combination:

(a)   **the reasons for the transaction** – Understanding the reasons why the parties to the combination (the acquirer and the acquiree and their owners, directors and managers – and their agents) entered into a particular transaction or arrangement may provide insight into whether it is part of the consideration transferred and the assets acquired or liabilities assumed. For example, if a transaction is arranged primarily for the benefit of the acquirer or the combined entity rather than primarily for the benefit of the acquiree or its former owners before the combination, that portion of the transaction price paid (and any related assets or liabilities) is less likely to be part of the exchange for the acquiree. Accordingly, the acquirer would account for that portion separately from the business combination.

(b)   **who initiated the transaction** – Understanding who initiated the transaction may also provide insight into whether it is part of the exchange for the acquiree. For example, a transaction or other event that is initiated by the acquirer may be entered into for the purpose of providing future economic benefits to the acquirer or combined entity with little or no benefit received by the acquiree or its former owners before the combination. On the other hand, a transaction or arrangement initiated by the acquiree or its former owners is less likely to be for the benefit of the acquirer or the combined entity and more likely to be part of the business combination transaction.

(c)   **the timing of the transaction** – The timing of the transaction may also provide insight into whether it is part of the exchange for the acquiree. For example, a transaction between the acquirer and the acquiree that takes place during the negotiations of the terms of a business combination may have been entered into in contemplation of the business combination to provide future economic benefits to the acquirer or the combined entity. If so, the acquiree or its former owners before the business combination are likely to receive little or no benefit from the transaction except for benefits they receive as part of the combined entity.

Effective settlement of a pre-existing relationship between the acquirer and acquiree in a business combination (application of paragraph 52(a))

B51 The acquirer and acquiree may have a relationship that existed before they contemplated the business combination, referred to here as a 'pre-existing relationship'. A pre-existing relationship between the acquirer and acquiree may be contractual (for example, vendor and customer or licensor and licensee) or non-contractual (for example, plaintiff and defendant).

B52 If the business combination in effect settles a pre-existing relationship, the acquirer recognises a gain or loss, measured as follows:

(a) for a pre-existing non-contractual relationship (such as a lawsuit), fair value.

(b) for a pre-existing contractual relationship, the lesser of (i) and (ii):

(i) the amount by which the contract is favourable or unfavourable from the perspective of the acquirer when compared with terms for current market transactions for the same or similar items. (An unfavourable contract is a contract that is unfavourable in terms of current market terms. It is not necessarily an onerous contract in which the unavoidable costs of meeting the obligations under the contract exceed the economic benefits expected to be received under it.)

(ii) the amount of any stated settlement provisions in the contract available to the counterparty to whom the contract is unfavourable.

If (ii) is less than (i), the difference is included as part of the business combination accounting.

The amount of gain or loss recognised may depend in part on whether the acquirer had previously recognised a related asset or liability, and the reported gain or loss therefore may differ from the amount calculated by applying the above requirements.

B53 A pre-existing relationship may be a contract that the acquirer recognises as a reacquired right. If the contract includes terms that are favourable or unfavourable when compared with pricing for current market transactions for the same or similar items, the acquirer recognises, separately from the business combination, a gain or loss for the effective settlement of the contract, measured in accordance with paragraph B52.

Arrangements for contingent payments to employees or selling shareholders (application of paragraph 52(b))

B54 Whether arrangements for contingent payments to employees or selling shareholders are contingent consideration in the business combination or are separate transactions depends on the nature of the arrangements. Understanding the reasons why the acquisition agreement includes a provision for contingent payments, who initiated the arrangement and when the parties entered into the arrangement may be helpful in assessing the nature of the arrangement.

B55 If it is not clear whether an arrangement for payments to employees or selling shareholders is part of the exchange for the acquiree or is a transaction separate from the business combination, the acquirer should consider the following indicators:

(a) *Continuing employment*—The terms of continuing employment by the selling shareholders who become key employees may be an indicator of the substance of a contingent consideration arrangement. The relevant terms of continuing employment may be included in an employment agreement, acquisition agreement or some other document. A contingent consideration arrangement in which the payments are automatically forfeited if employment terminates is remuneration for post-combination services. Arrangements in which the contingent payments are not affected by employment termination may indicate that the contingent payments are additional consideration rather than remuneration.

(b) *Duration of continuing employment*—If the period of required employment coincides with or is longer than the contingent payment period, that fact may indicate that the contingent payments are, in substance, remuneration.

(c) *Level of remuneration*—Situations in which employee remuneration other than the contingent payments is at a reasonable level in comparison with that of other key employees in the combined entity may indicate that the contingent payments are additional consideration rather than remuneration.

(d) *Incremental payments to employees*—If selling shareholders who do not become employees receive lower contingent payments on a per-share basis than the selling shareholders who become employees of the combined entity, that fact may indicate that the incremental amount of contingent payments to the selling shareholders who become employees is remuneration.

(e) *Number of shares owned*—The relative number of shares owned by the selling shareholders who remain as key employees may be an indicator of the substance of the contingent consideration arrangement. For example, if the selling shareholders who owned substantially all of the shares in the acquiree continue as key employees, that fact may indicate that the arrangement is, in substance, a profit-sharing arrangement intended to provide remuneration for post-combination services. Alternatively, if selling shareholders who continue as key employees owned only a small number of shares of the acquiree and all selling shareholders receive the same amount of contingent consideration on a per-share basis, that fact may indicate that the contingent payments are additional consideration. The pre-acquisition ownership interests held by parties related to selling shareholders who continue as key employees, such as family members, should also be considered.

(f) *Linkage to the valuation* — If the initial consideration transferred at the acquisition date is based on the low end of a range established in the valuation of the acquiree and the contingent formula relates to that valuation approach, that fact may suggest that the contingent payments are additional consideration. Alternatively, if the contingent payment formula is consistent with prior profit-sharing arrangements, that fact may suggest that the substance of the arrangement is to provide remuneration.

(g) *Formula for determining consideration* — The formula used to determine the contingent payment may be helpful in assessing the substance of the arrangement. For example, if a contingent payment is determined on the basis of a multiple of earnings, that might suggest that the obligation is contingent consideration in the business combination and that the formula is intended to establish or verify the fair value of the acquiree. In contrast, a contingent payment that is a specified percentage of earnings might suggest that the obligation to employees is a profit-sharing arrangement to remunerate employees for services rendered.

(h) *Other agreements and issues* — The terms of other arrangements with selling shareholders (such as agreements not to compete, executory contracts, consulting contracts and property lease agreements) and the income tax treatment of contingent payments may indicate that contingent payments are attributable to something other than consideration for the acquiree. For example, in connection with the acquisition, the acquirer might enter into a property lease arrangement with a significant selling shareholder. If the lease payments specified in the lease contract are significantly below market, some or all of the contingent payments to the lessor (the selling shareholder) required by a separate arrangement for contingent payments might be, in substance, payments for the use of the leased property that the acquirer should recognise separately in its post-combination financial statements. In contrast, if the lease contract specifies lease payments that are consistent with market terms for the leased property, the arrangement for contingent payments to the selling shareholder may be contingent consideration in the business combination.

Acquirer share-based payment awards exchanged for awards held by the acquiree's employees (application of paragraph 52(b))

B56　　An acquirer may exchange its share-based payment awards[1] (replacement awards) for awards held by employees of the acquiree. Exchanges of share options or other share-based payment awards in conjunction with a business combination are accounted for as modifications of share-based payment awards in accordance with IFRS 2 *Share-based Payment*. If the acquirer replaces the acquiree awards, either all or a portion of the market-based measure of the acquirer's replacement awards shall be included in measuring the consideration transferred in the business combination. Paragraphs B57–B62 provide guidance on how to allocate the market-based measure. However, in situations in which acquiree awards would expire as a consequence of a business combination and if the acquirer replaces those awards when it is not obliged to do so, all of the market-based measure of the replacement awards shall be recognised as remuneration cost in the post-combination financial statements in accordance with IFRS 2. That is to say, none of the market-based measure of those awards shall be included in measuring the consideration transferred in the business combination. The acquirer is obliged to replace the acquiree awards if the acquiree or its employees have the ability to enforce replacement. For example, for the purposes of applying this guidance, the acquirer is obliged to replace the acquiree's awards if replacement is required by:

(a)　　the terms of the acquisition agreement;

(b)　　the terms of the acquiree's awards; or

(c)　　applicable laws or regulations.

B57　　To determine the portion of a replacement award that is part of the consideration transferred for the acquiree and the portion that is remuneration for post-combination service, the acquirer shall measure both the replacement awards granted by the acquirer and the acquiree awards as of the acquisition date in accordance with IFRS 2. The portion of the market-based measure of the replacement award that is part of the consideration transferred in exchange for the acquiree equals the portion of the acquiree award that is attributable to pre-combination service.

B58　　The portion of the replacement award attributable to pre-combination service is the market-based measure of the acquiree award multiplied by the ratio of the portion of the vesting period completed to the greater of the total vesting period or the original vesting period of the acquiree award. The vesting period is the period during which all the specified vesting conditions are to be satisfied. Vesting conditions are defined in IFRS 2.

1　　In paragraphs B56–B62 the term 'share-based payment awards' refers to vested or unvested share-based payment transactions.

B59   The portion of a non-vested replacement award attributable to post-combination service, and therefore recognised as remuneration cost in the post-combination financial statements, equals the total market-based measure of the replacement award less the amount attributed to pre-combination service. Therefore, the acquirer attributes any excess of the market-based measure of the replacement award over the market-based measure of the acquiree award to post-combination service and recognises that excess as remuneration cost in the post-combination financial statements. The acquirer shall attribute a portion of a replacement award to post-combination service if it requires post-combination service, regardless of whether employees had rendered all of the service required for their acquiree awards to vest before the acquisition date.

B60   The portion of a non-vested replacement award attributable to pre-combination service, as well as the portion attributable to post-combination service, shall reflect the best available estimate of the number of replacement awards expected to vest. For example, if the market-based measure of the portion of a replacement award attributed to pre-combination service is CU100 and the acquirer expects that only 95 per cent of the award will vest, the amount included in consideration transferred in the business combination is CU95. Changes in the estimated number of replacement awards expected to vest are reflected in remuneration cost for the periods in which the changes or forfeitures occur not as adjustments to the consideration transferred in the business combination. Similarly, the effects of other events, such as modifications or the ultimate outcome of awards with performance conditions, that occur after the acquisition date are accounted for in accordance with IFRS 2 in determining remuneration cost for the period in which an event occurs.

B61   The same requirements for determining the portions of a replacement award attributable to pre-combination and post-combination service apply regardless of whether a replacement award is classified as a liability or as an equity instrument in accordance with the provisions of IFRS 2. All changes in the market-based measure of awards classified as liabilities after the acquisition date and the related income tax effects are recognised in the acquirer's post-combination financial statements in the period(s) in which the changes occur.

B62   The income tax effects of replacement awards of share-based payments shall be recognised in accordance with the provisions of IAS 12 *Income Taxes*.

Equity-settled share-based payment transactions of the acquiree

B62A   The acquiree may have outstanding share-based payment transactions that the acquirer does not exchange for its share-based payment transactions. If vested, those acquiree share-based payment transactions are part of the non-controlling interest in the acquiree and are measured at their market-based measure. If unvested, they are measured at their market-based measure as if the acquisition date were the grant date in accordance with paragraphs 19 and 30.

B62B   The market-based measure of unvested share-based payment transactions is allocated to the non-controlling interest on the basis of the ratio of the portion of the vesting period completed to the greater of the total vesting period and the original vesting period of the share-based payment transaction. The balance is allocated to post-combination service.

Other IFRSs that provide guidance on subsequent measurement and accounting (application of paragraph 54)

B63   Examples of other IFRSs that provide guidance on subsequently measuring and accounting for assets acquired and liabilities assumed or incurred in a business combination include:

(a)   IAS 38 prescribes the accounting for identifiable intangible assets acquired in a business combination. The acquirer measures goodwill at the amount recognised at the acquisition date less any accumulated impairment losses. IAS 36 *Impairment of Assets* prescribes the accounting for impairment losses.

(b)   IFRS 4 *Insurance Contracts* provides guidance on the subsequent accounting for an insurance contract acquired in a business combination.

(c)   IAS 12 prescribes the subsequent accounting for deferred tax assets (including unrecognised deferred tax assets) and liabilities acquired in a business combination.

(d)   IFRS 2 provides guidance on subsequent measurement and accounting for the portion of replacement share-based payment awards issued by an acquirer that is attributable to employees' future services.

(e)   IFRS 10 provides guidance on accounting for changes in a parent's ownership interest in a subsidiary after control is obtained.

Disclosures (application of paragraphs 59 and 61)

B64   To meet the objective in paragraph 59, the acquirer shall disclose the following information for each business combination that occurs during the reporting period:

(a)   the name and a description of the acquiree.

(b)   the acquisition date.

(c)   the percentage of voting equity interests acquired.

(d)   the primary reasons for the business combination and a description of how the acquirer obtained control of the acquiree.

(e)   a qualitative description of the factors that make up the goodwill recognised, such as expected synergies from combining operations of the acquiree and the acquirer, intangible assets that do not qualify for separate recognition or other factors.

(f) the acquisition-date fair value of the total consideration transferred and the acquisition-date fair value of each major class of consideration, such as:

  (i) cash;

  (ii) other tangible or intangible assets, including a business or subsidiary of the acquirer;

  (iii) liabilities incurred, for example, a liability for contingent consideration; and

  (iv) equity interests of the acquirer, including the number of instruments or interests issued or issuable and the method of measuring the fair value of those instruments or interests.

(g) for contingent consideration arrangements and indemnification assets:

  (i) the amount recognised as of the acquisition date;

  (ii) a description of the arrangement and the basis for determining the amount of the payment; and

  (iii) an estimate of the range of outcomes (undiscounted) or, if a range cannot be estimated, that fact and the reasons why a range cannot be estimated. If the maximum amount of the payment is unlimited, the acquirer shall disclose that fact.

(h) for acquired receivables:

  (i) the fair value of the receivables;

  (ii) the gross contractual amounts receivable; and

  (iii) the best estimate at the acquisition date of the contractual cash flows not expected to be collected.

The disclosures shall be provided by major class of receivable, such as loans, direct finance leases and any other class of receivables.

(i) the amounts recognised as of the acquisition date for each major class of assets acquired and liabilities assumed.

(j) for each contingent liability recognised in accordance with paragraph 23, the information required in paragraph 85 of IAS 37 *Provisions, Contingent Liabilities and Contingent Assets*. If a contingent liability is not recognised because its fair value cannot be measured reliably, the acquirer shall disclose:

  (i) the information required by paragraph 86 of IAS 37; and

  (ii) the reasons why the liability cannot be measured reliably.

(k) the total amount of goodwill that is expected to be deductible for tax purposes.

(l)   for transactions that are recognised separately from the acquisition of assets and assumption of liabilities in the business combination in accordance with paragraph 51:

    (i)   a description of each transaction;

    (ii)   how the acquirer accounted for each transaction;

    (iii)   the amounts recognised for each transaction and the line item in the financial statements in which each amount is recognised; and

    (iv)   if the transaction is the effective settlement of a pre-existing relationship, the method used to determine the settlement amount.

(m)   the disclosure of separately recognised transactions required by (l) shall include the amount of acquisition-related costs and, separately, the amount of those costs recognised as an expense and the line item or items in the statement of comprehensive income in which those expenses are recognised. The amount of any issue costs not recognised as an expense and how they were recognised shall also be disclosed.

(n)   in a bargain purchase (see paragraphs 34–36):

    (i)   the amount of any gain recognised in accordance with paragraph 34 and the line item in the statement of comprehensive income in which the gain is recognised; and

    (ii)   a description of the reasons why the transaction resulted in a gain.

(o)   for each business combination in which the acquirer holds less than 100 per cent of the equity interests in the acquiree at the acquisition date:

    (i)   the amount of the non-controlling interest in the acquiree recognised at the acquisition date and the measurement basis for that amount; and

    (ii)   for each non-controlling interest in an acquiree measured at fair value, the valuation technique(s) and significant inputs used to measure that value.

(p)   in a business combination achieved in stages:

    (i)   the acquisition-date fair value of the equity interest in the acquiree held by the acquirer immediately before the acquisition date; and

    (ii)   the amount of any gain or loss recognised as a result of remeasuring to fair value the equity interest in the acquiree held by the acquirer before the business combination (see paragraph 42) and the line item in the statement of comprehensive income in which that gain or loss is recognised.

(q)   the following information:

    (i)   the amounts of revenue and profit or loss of the acquiree since the acquisition date included in the consolidated statement of comprehensive income for the reporting period; and

    (ii)   the revenue and profit or loss of the combined entity for the current reporting period as though the acquisition date for all business combinations that occurred during the year had been as of the beginning of the annual reporting period.

If disclosure of any of the information required by this subparagraph is impracticable, the acquirer shall disclose that fact and explain why the disclosure is impracticable. This IFRS uses the term 'impracticable' with the same meaning as in IAS 8 *Accounting Policies, Changes in Accounting Estimates and Errors*.

B65   For individually immaterial business combinations occurring during the reporting period that are material collectively, the acquirer shall disclose in aggregate the information required by paragraph B64(e)–(q).

B66   If the acquisition date of a business combination is after the end of the reporting period but before the financial statements are authorised for issue, the acquirer shall disclose the information required by paragraph B64 unless the initial accounting for the business combination is incomplete at the time the financial statements are authorised for issue. In that situation, the acquirer shall describe which disclosures could not be made and the reasons why they cannot be made.

B67   To meet the objective in paragraph 61, the acquirer shall disclose the following information for each material business combination or in the aggregate for individually immaterial business combinations that are material collectively:

    (a)   if the initial accounting for a business combination is incomplete (see paragraph 45) for particular assets, liabilities, non-controlling interests or items of consideration and the amounts recognised in the financial statements for the business combination thus have been determined only provisionally:

    (i)   the reasons why the initial accounting for the business combination is incomplete;

    (ii)   the assets, liabilities, equity interests or items of consideration for which the initial accounting is incomplete; and

    (iii)   the nature and amount of any measurement period adjustments recognised during the reporting period in accordance with paragraph 49.

    (b)   for each reporting period after the acquisition date until the entity collects, sells or otherwise loses the right to a contingent consideration asset, or until the entity settles a contingent consideration liability or the liability is cancelled or expires:

(i)   any changes in the recognised amounts, including any differences arising upon settlement;

(ii)   any changes in the range of outcomes (undiscounted) and the reasons for those changes; and

(iii)   the valuation techniques and key model inputs used to measure contingent consideration.

(c)   for contingent liabilities recognised in a business combination, the acquirer shall disclose the information required by paragraphs 84 and 85 of IAS 37 for each class of provision.

(d)   a reconciliation of the carrying amount of goodwill at the beginning and end of the reporting period showing separately:

(i)   the gross amount and accumulated impairment losses at the beginning of the reporting period.

(ii)   additional goodwill recognised during the reporting period, except goodwill included in a disposal group that, on acquisition, meets the criteria to be classified as held for sale in accordance with IFRS 5 *Non-current Assets Held for Sale and Discontinued Operations*.

(iii)   adjustments resulting from the subsequent recognition of deferred tax assets during the reporting period in accordance with paragraph 67.

(iv)   goodwill included in a disposal group classified as held for sale in accordance with IFRS 5 and goodwill derecognised during the reporting period without having previously been included in a disposal group classified as held for sale.

(v)   impairment losses recognised during the reporting period in accordance with IAS 36. (IAS 36 requires disclosure of information about the recoverable amount and impairment of goodwill in addition to this requirement.)

(vi)   net exchange rate differences arising during the reporting period in accordance with IAS 21 *The Effects of Changes in Foreign Exchange Rates*.

(vii)   any other changes in the carrying amount during the reporting period.

(viii)   the gross amount and accumulated impairment losses at the end of the reporting period.

(e)   the amount and an explanation of any gain or loss recognised in the current reporting period that both:

(i)   relates to the identifiable assets acquired or liabilities assumed in a business combination that was effected in the current or previous reporting period; and

(ii) is of such a size, nature or incidence that disclosure is relevant to understanding the combined entity's financial statements.

Transitional provisions for business combinations involving only mutual entities or by contract alone (application of paragraph 66)

B68 Paragraph 64 provides that this IFRS applies prospectively to business combinations for which the acquisition date is on or after the beginning of the first annual reporting period beginning on or after 1 July 2009. Earlier application is permitted. However, an entity shall apply this IFRS only at the beginning of an annual reporting period that begins on or after 30 June 2007. If an entity applies this IFRS before its effective date, the entity shall disclose that fact and shall apply IAS 27 (as amended in 2008) at the same time.

B69 The requirement to apply this IFRS prospectively has the following effect for a business combination involving only mutual entities or by contract alone if the acquisition date for that business combination is before the application of this IFRS:

(a) *Classification*—An entity shall continue to classify the prior business combination in accordance with the entity's previous accounting policies for such combinations.

(b) *Previously recognised goodwill*—At the beginning of the first annual period in which this IFRS is applied, the carrying amount of goodwill arising from the prior business combination shall be its carrying amount at that date in accordance with the entity's previous accounting policies. In determining that amount, the entity shall eliminate the carrying amount of any accumulated amortisation of that goodwill and the corresponding decrease in goodwill. No other adjustments shall be made to the carrying amount of goodwill.

(c) *Goodwill previously recognised as a deduction from equity*—The entity's previous accounting policies may have resulted in goodwill arising from the prior business combination being recognised as a deduction from equity. In that situation the entity shall not recognise that goodwill as an asset at the beginning of the first annual period in which this IFRS is applied. Furthermore, the entity shall not recognise in profit or loss any part of that goodwill when it disposes of all or part of the business to which that goodwill relates or when a cash-generating unit to which the goodwill relates becomes impaired.

(d) *Subsequent accounting for goodwill*—From the beginning of the first annual period in which this IFRS is applied, an entity shall discontinue amortising goodwill arising from the prior business combination and shall test goodwill for impairment in accordance with IAS 36.

(e) *Previously recognised negative goodwill*—An entity that accounted for the prior business combination by applying the purchase method may have recognised a deferred credit for an excess of its interest in the net fair value of the acquiree's identifiable assets and liabilities over the cost of that interest (sometimes called negative goodwill). If so, the entity shall derecognise the carrying amount of that deferred credit at the beginning of the first annual period in which this IFRS is applied with a corresponding adjustment to the opening balance of retained earnings at that date.

Appendix C
Amendments to other IFRSs

The amendments in this appendix shall be applied for annual reporting periods beginning on or after 1 July 2009. If an entity applies this IFRS for an earlier period, these amendments shall be applied for that earlier period. Amended paragraphs are shown with new text underlined and deleted text struck through.

* * * * *

The amendments contained in this appendix when this revised IFRS was issued in 2008 have been incorporated into the relevant IFRSs published in this volume.

Approval by the Board of IFRS 3 issued in January 2008

International Financial Reporting Standard 3 *Business Combinations* (as revised in 2008) was approved for issue by eleven of the fourteen members of the International Accounting Standards Board. Professor Barth and Messrs Garnett and Smith dissented. Their dissenting opinions are set out after the Basis for Conclusions.

Sir David Tweedie	Chairman
Thomas E Jones	Vice-Chairman
Mary E Barth	
Hans-Georg Bruns	
Anthony T Cope	
Philippe Danjou	
Jan Engström	
Robert P Garnett	
Gilbert Gélard	
James J Leisenring	
Warren J McGregor	
Patricia L O'Malley	
John T Smith	
Tatsumi Yamada	

Approval by the Board of *Definition of a Business* issued in October 2018

Definition of a Business was approved for issue by all of the 14 members of the International Accounting Standards Board.

Hans Hoogervorst   Chairman

Suzanne Lloyd   Vice-Chair

Nick Anderson

Martin Edelmann

Françoise Flores

Amaro Luiz de Oliveira Gomes

Gary Kabureck

Jianqiao Lu

Takatsugu Ochi

Darrel Scott

Thomas Scott

Chungwoo Suh

Ann Tarca

Mary Tokar

Approval by the Board of *Reference to the Conceptual Framework* issued in May 2020

Reference to the Conceptual Framework, which amended IFRS 3, was approved for issue by all 14 members of the International Accounting Standards Board.

Hans Hoogervorst	Chairman
Suzanne Lloyd	Vice-Chair
Nick Anderson	
Tadeu Cendon	
Martin Edelmann	
Françoise Flores	
Gary Kabureck	
Jianqiao Lu	
Darrel Scott	
Thomas Scott	
Chungwoo Suh	
Rika Suzuki	
Ann Tarca	
Mary Tokar	

IFRS 4

Insurance Contracts

In March 2004 the International Accounting Standards Board (the Board) issued IFRS 4 *Insurance Contracts*. In August 2005 the Board amended the scope of IFRS 4 to clarify that most financial guarantee contracts would be accounted for by applying the financial instruments requirements. In December 2005 the Board issued revised guidance on implementing IFRS 4.

In September 2016 IFRS 4 was amended by *Applying IFRS 9* Financial Instruments *with IFRS 4* Insurance Contracts. These amendments address concerns arising from the different effective dates of IFRS 9 and the forthcoming insurance contracts Standard. Accordingly, these amendments introduce two optional approaches: a temporary exemption from applying IFRS 9; and an overlay approach.

In June 2020 IFRS 4 was amended by *Extension of the Temporary Exemption from Applying IFRS 9* which extended the temporary exemption from applying IFRS 9 by two years.

In August 2020 the Board issued *Interest Rate Benchmark Reform—Phase 2* which amended requirements in IFRS 9, IAS 39, IFRS 7, IFRS 4 and IFRS 16 relating to:

- changes in the basis for determining contractual cash flows of financial assets, financial liabilities and lease liabilities;

- hedge accounting; and

- disclosures.

The Phase 2 amendments apply only to changes required by the interest rate benchmark reform to financial instruments and hedging relationships.

Other Standards have made minor consequential amendments to IFRS 4. They include IFRS 13 *Fair Value Measurement* (issued May 2011), IFRS 9 *Financial Instruments* (Hedge Accounting and amendments to IFRS 9, IFRS 7 and IAS 39) (issued November 2013), IFRS 15 *Revenue from Contracts with Customers* (issued May 2014), IFRS 9 *Financial Instruments* (issued July 2014), IFRS 16 *Leases* (issued January 2016), *Amendments to References to the Conceptual Framework in IFRS Standards* (issued March 2018) and *Definition of Material* (Amendments to IAS 1 and IAS 8) (issued October 2018).

Contents

continued...

...*continued*

FOR THE ACCOMPANYING GUIDANCE LISTED BELOW, SEE PART B OF THIS EDITION

IMPLEMENTATION GUIDANCE

FOR THE BASIS FOR CONCLUSIONS, SEE PART C OF THIS EDITION

BASIS FOR CONCLUSIONS

DISSENTING OPINIONS

International Financial Reporting Standard 4 *Insurance Contracts* (IFRS 4) is set out in paragraphs 1–51 and Appendices A–C. All the paragraphs have equal authority. Paragraphs in **bold type** state the main principles. Terms defined in Appendix A are in *italics* the first time they appear in the Standard. Definitions of other terms are given in the Glossary for International Financial Reporting Standards. IFRS 4 should be read in the context of its objective and the Basis for Conclusions, the *Preface to IFRS Standards* and the *Conceptual Framework for Financial Reporting*. IAS 8 *Accounting Policies, Changes in Accounting Estimates and Errors* provides a basis for selecting and applying accounting policies in the absence of explicit guidance.

> (b) the percentage of the total carrying amount of its liabilities connected with insurance (see paragraph 20E) relative to the total carrying amount of all its liabilities is:
>
> > (i) greater than 90 per cent; or
> >
> > (ii) less than or equal to 90 per cent but greater than 80 per cent, and the insurer does not engage in a significant activity unconnected with insurance (see paragraph 20F).

20E   For the purposes of applying paragraph 20D(b), liabilities connected with insurance comprise:

> (a) liabilities arising from contracts within the scope of this IFRS, as described in paragraph 20D(a);
>
> (b) non-derivative investment contract liabilities measured at fair value through profit or loss applying IAS 39 (including those designated as at fair value through profit or loss to which the insurer has applied the requirements in IFRS 9 for the presentation of gains and losses (see paragraphs 20B(a) and 20C)); and
>
> (c) liabilities that arise because the insurer issues, or fulfils obligations arising from, the contracts in (a) and (b). Examples of such liabilities include derivatives used to mitigate risks arising from those contracts and from the assets backing those contracts, relevant tax liabilities such as the deferred tax liabilities for taxable temporary differences on liabilities arising from those contracts, and debt instruments issued that are included in the insurer's regulatory capital.

20F   In assessing whether it engages in a significant activity unconnected with insurance for the purposes of applying paragraph 20D(b)(ii), an insurer shall consider:

> (a) only those activities from which it may earn income and incur expenses; and
>
> (b) quantitative or qualitative factors (or both), including publicly available information such as the industry classification that users of financial statements apply to the insurer.

20G   Paragraph 20B(b) requires an entity to assess whether it qualifies for the temporary exemption from IFRS 9 at its annual reporting date that immediately precedes 1 April 2016. After that date:

> (a) an entity that previously qualified for the temporary exemption from IFRS 9 shall reassess whether its activities are predominantly connected with insurance at a subsequent annual reporting date if, and only if, there was a change in the entity's activities, as described in paragraphs 20H–20I, during the annual period that ended on that date.
>
> (b) an entity that previously did not qualify for the temporary exemption from IFRS 9 is permitted to reassess whether its activities are predominantly connected with insurance at a subsequent annual reporting date before 31 December 2018 if, and only if, there was a

change in the entity's activities, as described in paragraphs 20H–20I, during the annual period that ended on that date.

20H   For the purposes of applying paragraph 20G, a change in an entity's activities is a change that:

(a)   is determined by the entity's senior management as a result of external or internal changes;

(b)   is significant to the entity's operations; and

(c)   is demonstrable to external parties.

Accordingly, such a change occurs only when the entity begins or ceases to perform an activity that is significant to its operations or significantly changes the magnitude of one of its activities; for example, when the entity has acquired, disposed of or terminated a business line.

20I   A change in an entity's activities, as described in paragraph 20H, is expected to be very infrequent. The following are not changes in an entity's activities for the purposes of applying paragraph 20G:

(a)   a change in the entity's funding structure that in itself does not affect the activities from which the entity earns income and incurs expenses.

(b)   the entity's plan to sell a business line, even if the assets and liabilities are classified as held for sale applying IFRS 5 *Non-current Assets Held for Sale and Discontinued Operations*. A plan to sell a business line could change the entity's activities and give rise to a reassessment in the future but has yet to affect the liabilities recognised on its statement of financial position.

20J   If an entity no longer qualifies for the temporary exemption from IFRS 9 as a result of a reassessment (see paragraph 20G(a)), then the entity is permitted to continue to apply the temporary exemption from IFRS 9 only until the end of the annual period that began immediately after that reassessment. Nevertheless, the entity must apply IFRS 9 for annual periods beginning on or after 1 January 2023. For example, if an entity determines that it no longer qualifies for the temporary exemption from IFRS 9 applying paragraph 20G(a) on 31 December 2018 (the end of its annual period), then the entity is permitted to continue to apply the temporary exemption from IFRS 9 only until 31 December 2019.

20K   An insurer that previously elected to apply the temporary exemption from IFRS 9 may at the beginning of any subsequent annual period irrevocably elect to apply IFRS 9.

First-time adopter

20L   A first-time adopter, as defined in IFRS 1 *First-time Adoption of International Financial Reporting Standards*, may apply the temporary exemption from IFRS 9 described in paragraph 20A if, and only if, it meets the criteria described in paragraph 20B. In applying paragraph 20B(b), the first-time adopter shall use the carrying amounts determined applying IFRSs at the date specified in that paragraph.

20M   IFRS 1 contains requirements and exemptions applicable to a first-time adopter. Those requirements and exemptions (for example, paragraphs D16–D17 of IFRS 1) do not override the requirements in paragraphs 20A–20Q and 39B–39J of this IFRS. For example, the requirements and exemptions in IFRS 1 do not override the requirement that a first-time adopter must meet the criteria specified in paragraph 20L to apply the temporary exemption from IFRS 9.

20N   A first-time adopter that discloses the information required by paragraphs 39B–39J shall use the requirements and exemptions in IFRS 1 that are relevant to making the assessments required for those disclosures.

Temporary exemption from specific requirements in IAS 28

20O   Paragraphs 35–36 of IAS 28 *Investments in Associates and Joint Ventures* require an entity to apply uniform accounting policies when using the equity method. Nevertheless, for annual periods beginning before 1 January 2023, an entity is permitted, but not required, to retain the relevant accounting policies applied by the associate or joint venture as follows:

(a)   the entity applies IFRS 9 but the associate or joint venture applies the temporary exemption from IFRS 9; or

(b)   the entity applies the temporary exemption from IFRS 9 but the associate or joint venture applies IFRS 9.

20P   When an entity uses the equity method to account for its investment in an associate or joint venture:

(a)   if IFRS 9 was previously applied in the financial statements used to apply the equity method to that associate or joint venture (after reflecting any adjustments made by the entity), then IFRS 9 shall continue to be applied.

(b)   if the temporary exemption from IFRS 9 was previously applied in the financial statements used to apply the equity method to that associate or joint venture (after reflecting any adjustments made by the entity), then IFRS 9 may be subsequently applied.

20Q   An entity may apply paragraphs 20O and 20P(b) separately for each associate or joint venture.

Changes in the basis for determining the contractual cash flows as a result of interest rate benchmark reform

20R   An insurer applying the temporary exemption from IFRS 9 shall apply the requirements in paragraphs 5.4.6–5.4.9 of IFRS 9 to a financial asset or financial liability if, and only if, the basis for determining the contractual cash flows of that financial asset or financial liability changes as a result of interest rate benchmark reform. For this purpose, the term 'interest rate benchmark reform' refers to the market-wide reform of an interest rate benchmark as described in paragraph 102B of IAS 39.

20S   For the purpose of applying paragraphs 5.4.6–5.4.9 of the amendments to IFRS 9, the references to paragraph B5.4.5 of IFRS 9 shall be read as referring to paragraph AG7 of IAS 39. References to paragraphs 5.4.3 and B5.4.6 of IFRS 9 shall be read as referring to paragraph AG8 of IAS 39.

Changes in accounting policies

21   Paragraphs 22–30 apply both to changes made by an insurer that already applies IFRSs and to changes made by an insurer adopting IFRSs for the first time.

22   **An insurer may change its accounting policies for insurance contracts if, and only if, the change makes the financial statements more relevant to the economic decision-making needs of users and no less reliable, or more reliable and no less relevant to those needs. An insurer shall judge relevance and reliability by the criteria in IAS 8.**

23   To justify changing its accounting policies for insurance contracts, an insurer shall show that the change brings its financial statements closer to meeting the criteria in IAS 8, but the change need not achieve full compliance with those criteria. The following specific issues are discussed below:

   (a)   current interest rates (paragraph 24);

   (b)   continuation of existing practices (paragraph 25);

   (c)   prudence (paragraph 26);

   (d)   future investment margins (paragraphs 27–29); and

   (e)   shadow accounting (paragraph 30).

Current market interest rates

24   An insurer is permitted, but not required, to change its accounting policies so that it remeasures designated insurance liabilities[3] to reflect current market interest rates and recognises changes in those liabilities in profit or loss. At that time, it may also introduce accounting policies that require other current estimates and assumptions for the designated liabilities. The election in this paragraph permits an insurer to change its accounting policies for designated liabilities, without applying those policies consistently to all similar liabilities as IAS 8 would otherwise require. If an insurer designates liabilities for this election, it shall continue to apply current market interest rates (and, if applicable, the other current estimates and assumptions) consistently in all periods to all these liabilities until they are extinguished.

Continuation of existing practices

25   An insurer may continue the following practices, but the introduction of any of them does not satisfy paragraph 22:

   (a)   measuring insurance liabilities on an undiscounted basis.

---

3   In this paragraph, insurance liabilities include related deferred acquisition costs and related intangible assets, such as those discussed in paragraphs 31 and 32.

(b) measuring contractual rights to future investment management fees at an amount that exceeds their fair value as implied by a comparison with current fees charged by other market participants for similar services. It is likely that the fair value at inception of those contractual rights equals the origination costs paid, unless future investment management fees and related costs are out of line with market comparables.

(c) using non-uniform accounting policies for the insurance contracts (and related deferred acquisition costs and related intangible assets, if any) of subsidiaries, except as permitted by paragraph 24. If those accounting policies are not uniform, an insurer may change them if the change does not make the accounting policies more diverse and also satisfies the other requirements in this IFRS.

Prudence

26 An insurer need not change its accounting policies for insurance contracts to eliminate excessive prudence. However, if an insurer already measures its insurance contracts with sufficient prudence, it shall not introduce additional prudence.

Future investment margins

27 An insurer need not change its accounting policies for insurance contracts to eliminate future investment margins. However, there is a rebuttable presumption that an insurer's financial statements will become less relevant and reliable if it introduces an accounting policy that reflects future investment margins in the measurement of insurance contracts, unless those margins affect the contractual payments. Two examples of accounting policies that reflect those margins are:

(a) using a discount rate that reflects the estimated return on the insurer's assets; or

(b) projecting the returns on those assets at an estimated rate of return, discounting those projected returns at a different rate and including the result in the measurement of the liability.

28 An insurer may overcome the rebuttable presumption described in paragraph 27 if, and only if, the other components of a change in accounting policies increase the relevance and reliability of its financial statements sufficiently to outweigh the decrease in relevance and reliability caused by the inclusion of future investment margins. For example, suppose that an insurer's existing accounting policies for insurance contracts involve excessively prudent assumptions set at inception and a discount rate prescribed by a regulator without direct reference to market conditions, and ignore some embedded options and guarantees. The insurer might make its financial statements more relevant and no less reliable by switching to a comprehensive investor-oriented basis of accounting that is widely used and involves:

(a) current estimates and assumptions;

(b)   a reasonable (but not excessively prudent) adjustment to reflect risk and uncertainty;

(c)   measurements that reflect both the intrinsic value and time value of embedded options and guarantees; and

(d)   a current market discount rate, even if that discount rate reflects the estimated return on the insurer's assets.

29   In some measurement approaches, the discount rate is used to determine the present value of a future profit margin. That profit margin is then attributed to different periods using a formula. In those approaches, the discount rate affects the measurement of the liability only indirectly. In particular, the use of a less appropriate discount rate has a limited or no effect on the measurement of the liability at inception. However, in other approaches, the discount rate determines the measurement of the liability directly. In the latter case, because the introduction of an asset-based discount rate has a more significant effect, it is highly unlikely that an insurer could overcome the rebuttable presumption described in paragraph 27.

Shadow accounting

30   In some accounting models, realised gains or losses on an insurer's assets have a direct effect on the measurement of some or all of (a) its insurance liabilities, (b) related deferred acquisition costs and (c) related intangible assets, such as those described in paragraphs 31 and 32. An insurer is permitted, but not required, to change its accounting policies so that a recognised but unrealised gain or loss on an asset affects those measurements in the same way that a realised gain or loss does. The related adjustment to the insurance liability (or deferred acquisition costs or intangible assets) shall be recognised in other comprehensive income if, and only if, the unrealised gains or losses are recognised in other comprehensive income. This practice is sometimes described as 'shadow accounting'.

Insurance contracts acquired in a business combination or portfolio transfer

31   To comply with IFRS 3, an insurer shall, at the acquisition date, measure at fair value the insurance liabilities assumed and *insurance assets* acquired in a business combination. However, an insurer is permitted, but not required, to use an expanded presentation that splits the fair value of acquired insurance contracts into two components:

(a)   a liability measured in accordance with the insurer's accounting policies for insurance contracts that it issues; and

(b)   an intangible asset, representing the difference between (i) the fair value of the contractual insurance rights acquired and insurance obligations assumed and (ii) the amount described in (a). The subsequent measurement of this asset shall be consistent with the measurement of the related insurance liability.

32   An insurer acquiring a portfolio of insurance contracts may use the expanded presentation described in paragraph 31.

33   The intangible assets described in paragraphs 31 and 32 are excluded from the scope of IAS 36 *Impairment of Assets* and IAS 38. However, IAS 36 and IAS 38 apply to customer lists and customer relationships reflecting the expectation of future contracts that are not part of the contractual insurance rights and contractual insurance obligations that existed at the date of a business combination or portfolio transfer.

Discretionary participation features

Discretionary participation features in insurance contracts

34   Some insurance contracts contain a discretionary participation feature as well as a *guaranteed element*. The issuer of such a contract:

(a)   may, but need not, recognise the guaranteed element separately from the discretionary participation feature. If the issuer does not recognise them separately, it shall classify the whole contract as a liability. If the issuer classifies them separately, it shall classify the guaranteed element as a liability.

(b)   shall, if it recognises the discretionary participation feature separately from the guaranteed element, classify that feature as either a liability or a separate component of equity. This IFRS does not specify how the issuer determines whether that feature is a liability or equity. The issuer may split that feature into liability and equity components and shall use a consistent accounting policy for that split. The issuer shall not classify that feature as an intermediate category that is neither liability nor equity.

(c)   may recognise all premiums received as revenue without separating any portion that relates to the equity component. The resulting changes in the guaranteed element and in the portion of the discretionary participation feature classified as a liability shall be recognised in profit or loss. If part or all of the discretionary participation feature is classified in equity, a portion of profit or loss may be attributable to that feature (in the same way that a portion may be attributable to non-controlling interests). The issuer shall recognise the portion of profit or loss attributable to any equity component of a discretionary participation feature as an allocation of profit or loss, not as expense or income (see IAS 1 *Presentation of Financial Statements*).

(d)   shall, if the contract contains an embedded derivative within the scope of IFRS 9, apply IFRS 9 to that embedded derivative.

(e)   shall, in all respects not described in paragraphs 14–20 and 34(a)–(d), continue its existing accounting policies for such contracts, unless it changes those accounting policies in a way that complies with paragraphs 21–30.

Discretionary participation features in financial instruments

35   The requirements in paragraph 34 also apply to a financial instrument that contains a discretionary participation feature. In addition:

(a)   if the issuer classifies the entire discretionary participation feature as a liability, it shall apply the liability adequacy test in paragraphs 15–19 to the whole contract (ie both the guaranteed element and the discretionary participation feature). The issuer need not determine the amount that would result from applying IFRS 9 to the guaranteed element.

(b)   if the issuer classifies part or all of that feature as a separate component of equity, the liability recognised for the whole contract shall not be less than the amount that would result from applying IFRS 9 to the guaranteed element. That amount shall include the intrinsic value of an option to surrender the contract, but need not include its time value if paragraph 9 exempts that option from measurement at fair value. The issuer need not disclose the amount that would result from applying IFRS 9 to the guaranteed element, nor need it present that amount separately. Furthermore, the issuer need not determine that amount if the total liability recognised is clearly higher.

(c)   although these contracts are financial instruments, the issuer may continue to recognise the premiums for those contracts as revenue and recognise as an expense the resulting increase in the carrying amount of the liability.

(d)   although these contracts are financial instruments, an issuer applying paragraph 20(b) of IFRS 7 to contracts with a discretionary participation feature shall disclose the total interest expense recognised in profit or loss, but need not calculate such interest expense using the effective interest method.

35A   The temporary exemptions in paragraphs 20A, 20L and 20O and the overlay approach in paragraph 35B are also available to an issuer of a financial instrument that contains a discretionary participation feature. Accordingly, all references in paragraphs 3(a)–3(b), 20A–20Q, 35B–35N, 39B–39M and 46–49 to an insurer shall be read as also referring to an issuer of a financial instrument that contains a discretionary participation feature.

Presentation

The overlay approach

35B   An insurer is permitted, but not required, to apply the overlay approach to designated financial assets. An insurer that applies the overlay approach shall:

(a) reclassify between profit or loss and other comprehensive income an amount that results in the profit or loss at the end of the reporting period for the designated financial assets being the same as if the insurer had applied IAS 39 to the designated financial assets. Accordingly, the amount reclassified is equal to the difference between:

  (i) the amount reported in profit or loss for the designated financial assets applying IFRS 9; and

  (ii) the amount that would have been reported in profit or loss for the designated financial assets if the insurer had applied IAS 39.

(b) apply all other applicable IFRSs to its financial instruments, except as described in paragraphs 35B–35N, 39K–39M and 48–49 of this IFRS.

35C An insurer may elect to apply the overlay approach described in paragraph 35B only when it first applies IFRS 9, including when it first applies IFRS 9 after previously applying:

(a) the temporary exemption from IFRS 9 described in paragraph 20A; or

(b) only the requirements for the presentation of gains and losses on financial liabilities designated as at fair value through profit or loss in paragraphs 5.7.1(c), 5.7.7–5.7.9, 7.2.14 and B5.7.5–B5.7.20 of IFRS 9.

35D An insurer shall present the amount reclassified between profit or loss and other comprehensive income applying the overlay approach:

(a) in profit or loss as a separate line item; and

(b) in other comprehensive income as a separate component of other comprehensive income.

35E A financial asset is eligible for designation for the overlay approach if, and only if, the following criteria are met:

(a) it is measured at fair value through profit or loss applying IFRS 9 but would not have been measured at fair value through profit or loss in its entirety applying IAS 39; and

(b) it is not held in respect of an activity that is unconnected with contracts within the scope of this IFRS. Examples of financial assets that would not be eligible for the overlay approach are those assets held in respect of banking activities or financial assets held in funds relating to investment contracts that are outside the scope of this IFRS.

35F An insurer may designate an eligible financial asset for the overlay approach when it elects to apply the overlay approach (see paragraph 35C). Subsequently, it may designate an eligible financial asset for the overlay approach when, and only when:

(a)   that asset is initially recognised; or

(b)   that asset newly meets the criterion in paragraph 35E(b) having previously not met that criterion.

35G   An insurer is permitted to designate eligible financial assets for the overlay approach applying paragraph 35F on an instrument-by-instrument basis.

35H   When relevant, for the purposes of applying the overlay approach to a newly designated financial asset applying paragraph 35F(b):

(a)   its fair value at the date of designation shall be its new amortised cost carrying amount; and

(b)   the effective interest rate shall be determined based on its fair value at the date of designation.

35I   An entity shall continue to apply the overlay approach to a designated financial asset until that financial asset is derecognised. However, an entity:

(a)   shall de-designate a financial asset when the financial asset no longer meets the criterion in paragraph 35E(b). For example, a financial asset will no longer meet that criterion when an entity transfers that asset so that it is held in respect of its banking activities or when an entity ceases to be an insurer.

(b)   may, at the beginning of any annual period, stop applying the overlay approach to all designated financial assets. An entity that elects to stop applying the overlay approach shall apply IAS 8 to account for the change in accounting policy.

35J   When an entity de-designates a financial asset applying paragraph 35I(a), it shall reclassify from accumulated other comprehensive income to profit or loss as a reclassification adjustment (see IAS 1) any balance relating to that financial asset.

35K   If an entity stops using the overlay approach applying the election in paragraph 35I(b) or because it is no longer an insurer, it shall not subsequently apply the overlay approach. An insurer that has elected to apply the overlay approach (see paragraph 35C) but has no eligible financial assets (see paragraph 35E) may subsequently apply the overlay approach when it has eligible financial assets.

Interaction with other requirements

35L   Paragraph 30 of this IFRS permits a practice that is sometimes described as 'shadow accounting'. If an insurer applies the overlay approach, shadow accounting may be applicable.

35M   Reclassifying an amount between profit or loss and other comprehensive income applying paragraph 35B may have consequential effects for including other amounts in other comprehensive income, such as income taxes. An insurer shall apply the relevant IFRS, such as IAS 12 *Income Taxes*, to determine any such consequential effects.

First-time adopter

35N   If a first-time adopter elects to apply the overlay approach, it shall restate comparative information to reflect the overlay approach if, and only if, it restates comparative information to comply with IFRS 9 (see paragraphs E1–E2 of IFRS 1).

Disclosure

Explanation of recognised amounts

36   An insurer shall disclose information that identifies and explains the amounts in its financial statements arising from insurance contracts.

37   To comply with paragraph 36, an insurer shall disclose:

(a)   its accounting policies for insurance contracts and related assets, liabilities, income and expense.

(b)   the recognised assets, liabilities, income and expense (and, if it presents its statement of cash flows using the direct method, cash flows) arising from insurance contracts. Furthermore, if the insurer is a cedant, it shall disclose:

(i)   gains and losses recognised in profit or loss on buying reinsurance; and

(ii)   if the cedant defers and amortises gains and losses arising on buying reinsurance, the amortisation for the period and the amounts remaining unamortised at the beginning and end of the period.

(c)   the process used to determine the assumptions that have the greatest effect on the measurement of the recognised amounts described in (b). When practicable, an insurer shall also give quantified disclosure of those assumptions.

(d)   the effect of changes in assumptions used to measure insurance assets and insurance liabilities, showing separately the effect of each change that has a material effect on the financial statements.

(e)   reconciliations of changes in insurance liabilities, reinsurance assets and, if any, related deferred acquisition costs.

Nature and extent of risks arising from insurance contracts

38   An insurer shall disclose information that enables users of its financial statements to evaluate the nature and extent of risks arising from insurance contracts.

39   To comply with paragraph 38, an insurer shall disclose:

(a)   its objectives, policies and processes for managing risks arising from insurance contracts and the methods used to manage those risks.

(b)   [deleted]

(c)   information about *insurance risk* (both before and after risk mitigation by reinsurance), including information about:

    (i)   sensitivity to insurance risk (see paragraph 39A).

    (ii)   concentrations of insurance risk, including a description of how management determines concentrations and a description of the shared characteristic that identifies each concentration (eg type of insured event, geographical area, or currency).

    (iii)   actual claims compared with previous estimates (ie claims development). The disclosure about claims development shall go back to the period when the earliest material claim arose for which there is still uncertainty about the amount and timing of the claims payments, but need not go back more than ten years. An insurer need not disclose this information for claims for which uncertainty about the amount and timing of claims payments is typically resolved within one year.

(d)   information about credit risk, liquidity risk and market risk that paragraphs 31–42 of IFRS 7 would require if the insurance contracts were within the scope of IFRS 7. However:

    (i)   an insurer need not provide the maturity analyses required by paragraph 39(a) and (b) of IFRS 7 if it discloses information about the estimated timing of the net cash outflows resulting from recognised insurance liabilities instead. This may take the form of an analysis, by estimated timing, of the amounts recognised in the statement of financial position.

    (ii)   if an insurer uses an alternative method to manage sensitivity to market conditions, such as an embedded value analysis, it may use that sensitivity analysis to meet the requirement in paragraph 40(a) of IFRS 7. Such an insurer shall also provide the disclosures required by paragraph 41 of IFRS 7.

(e)   information about exposures to market risk arising from embedded derivatives contained in a host insurance contract if the insurer is not required to, and does not, measure the embedded derivatives at fair value.

39A   To comply with paragraph 39(c)(i), an insurer shall disclose either (a) or (b) as follows:

(a)   a sensitivity analysis that shows how profit or loss and equity would have been affected if changes in the relevant risk variable that were reasonably possible at the end of the reporting period had occurred; the methods and assumptions used in preparing the sensitivity analysis; and any changes from the previous period in the methods and assumptions used. However, if an insurer uses an alternative method to manage sensitivity to market conditions, such as an embedded value analysis, it may meet this requirement by disclosing that alternative sensitivity analysis and the disclosures required by paragraph 41 of IFRS 7.

(b)   qualitative information about sensitivity, and information about those terms and conditions of insurance contracts that have a material effect on the amount, timing and uncertainty of the insurer's future cash flows.

Disclosures about the temporary exemption from IFRS 9

39B   An insurer that elects to apply the temporary exemption from IFRS 9 shall disclose information to enable users of financial statements:

(a)   to understand how the insurer qualified for the temporary exemption; and

(b)   to compare insurers applying the temporary exemption with entities applying IFRS 9.

39C   To comply with paragraph 39B(a), an insurer shall disclose the fact that it is applying the temporary exemption from IFRS 9 and how the insurer concluded on the date specified in paragraph 20B(b) that it qualifies for the temporary exemption from IFRS 9, including:

(a)   if the carrying amount of its liabilities arising from contracts within the scope of this IFRS (ie those liabilities described in paragraph 20E(a)) was less than or equal to 90 per cent of the total carrying amount of all its liabilities, the nature and carrying amounts of the liabilities connected with insurance that are not liabilities arising from contracts within the scope of this IFRS (ie those liabilities described in paragraphs 20E(b) and 20E(c));

(b)   if the percentage of the total carrying amount of its liabilities connected with insurance relative to the total carrying amount of all its liabilities was less than or equal to 90 per cent but greater than 80 per cent, how the insurer determined that it did not engage in a significant activity unconnected with insurance, including what information it considered; and

(c)   if the insurer qualified for the temporary exemption from IFRS 9 on the basis of a reassessment applying paragraph 20G(b):

(i)   the reason for the reassessment;

(ii)   the date on which the relevant change in its activities occurred; and

(iii)   a detailed explanation of the change in its activities and a qualitative description of the effect of that change on the insurer's financial statements.

39D   If, applying paragraph 20G(a), an entity concludes that its activities are no longer predominantly connected with insurance, it shall disclose the following information in each reporting period before it begins to apply IFRS 9:

(a) the fact that it no longer qualifies for the temporary exemption from IFRS 9;

(b) the date on which the relevant change in its activities occurred; and

(c) a detailed explanation of the change in its activities and a qualitative description of the effect of that change on the entity's financial statements.

39E To comply with paragraph 39B(b), an insurer shall disclose the fair value at the end of the reporting period and the amount of change in the fair value during that period for the following two groups of financial assets separately:

(a) financial assets with contractual terms that give rise on specified dates to cash flows that are solely payments of principal and interest on the principal amount outstanding (ie financial assets that meet the condition in paragraphs 4.1.2(b) and 4.1.2A(b) of IFRS 9), excluding any financial asset that meets the definition of held for trading in IFRS 9, or that is managed and whose performance is evaluated on a fair value basis (see paragraph B4.1.6 of IFRS 9).

(b) all financial assets other than those specified in paragraph 39E(a); that is, any financial asset:

(i) with contractual terms that do not give rise on specified dates to cash flows that are solely payments of principal and interest on the principal amount outstanding;

(ii) that meets the definition of held for trading in IFRS 9; or

(iii) that is managed and whose performance is evaluated on a fair value basis.

39F When disclosing the information in paragraph 39E, the insurer:

(a) may deem the carrying amount of the financial asset measured applying IAS 39 to be a reasonable approximation of its fair value if the insurer is not required to disclose its fair value applying paragraph 29(a) of IFRS 7 (eg short-term trade receivables); and

(b) shall consider the level of detail necessary to enable users of financial statements to understand the characteristics of the financial assets.

39G To comply with paragraph 39B(b), an insurer shall disclose information about the credit risk exposure, including significant credit risk concentrations, inherent in the financial assets described in paragraph 39E(a). At a minimum, an insurer shall disclose the following information for those financial assets at the end of the reporting period:

(a) by credit risk rating grades as defined in IFRS 7, the carrying amounts applying IAS 39 (in the case of financial assets measured at amortised cost, before adjusting for any impairment allowances).

(b)   for the financial assets described in paragraph 39E(a) that do not have low credit risk at the end of the reporting period, the fair value and the carrying amount applying IAS 39 (in the case of financial assets measured at amortised cost, before adjusting for any impairment allowances). For the purposes of this disclosure, paragraph B5.5.22 of IFRS 9 provides the relevant requirements for assessing whether the credit risk on a financial instrument is considered low.

39H   To comply with paragraph 39B(b), an insurer shall disclose information about where a user of financial statements can obtain any publicly available IFRS 9 information that relates to an entity within the group that is not provided in the group's consolidated financial statements for the relevant reporting period. For example, such IFRS 9 information could be obtained from the publicly available individual or separate financial statements of an entity within the group that has applied IFRS 9.

39I   If an entity elected to apply the exemption in paragraph 20O from particular requirements in IAS 28, it shall disclose that fact.

39J   If an entity applied the temporary exemption from IFRS 9 when accounting for its investment in an associate or joint venture using the equity method (for example, see paragraph 20O(a)), the entity shall disclose the following, in addition to the information required by IFRS 12 *Disclosure of Interests in Other Entities*:

    (a)   the information described by paragraphs 39B–39H for each associate or joint venture that is material to the entity. The amounts disclosed shall be those included in the IFRS financial statements of the associate or joint venture after reflecting any adjustments made by the entity when using the equity method (see paragraph B14(a) of IFRS 12), rather than the entity's share of those amounts.

    (b)   the quantitative information described by paragraphs 39B–39H in aggregate for all individually immaterial associates or joint ventures. The aggregate amounts:

        (i)   disclosed shall be the entity's share of those amounts; and

        (ii)   for associates shall be disclosed separately from the aggregate amounts disclosed for joint ventures.

Disclosures about the overlay approach

39K   An insurer that applies the overlay approach shall disclose information to enable users of financial statements to understand:

    (a)   how the total amount reclassified between profit or loss and other comprehensive income in the reporting period is calculated; and

    (b)   the effect of that reclassification on the financial statements.

39L   To comply with paragraph 39K, an insurer shall disclose:

    (a)   the fact that it is applying the overlay approach;

(b) the carrying amount at the end of the reporting period of financial assets to which the insurer applies the overlay approach by class of financial asset;

(c) the basis for designating financial assets for the overlay approach, including an explanation of any designated financial assets that are held outside the legal entity that issues contracts within the scope of this IFRS;

(d) an explanation of the total amount reclassified between profit or loss and other comprehensive income in the reporting period in a way that enables users of financial statements to understand how that amount is derived, including:

    (i) the amount reported in profit or loss for the designated financial assets applying IFRS 9; and

    (ii) the amount that would have been reported in profit or loss for the designated financial assets if the insurer had applied IAS 39.

(e) the effect of the reclassification described in paragraphs 35B and 35M on each affected line item in profit or loss; and

(f) if during the reporting period the insurer has changed the designation of financial assets:

    (i) the amount reclassified between profit or loss and other comprehensive income in the reporting period relating to newly designated financial assets applying the overlay approach (see paragraph 35F(b));

    (ii) the amount that would have been reclassified between profit or loss and other comprehensive income in the reporting period if the financial assets had not been de-designated (see paragraph 35I(a)); and

    (iii) the amount reclassified in the reporting period to profit or loss from accumulated other comprehensive income for financial assets that have been de-designated (see paragraph 35J).

39M If an entity applied the overlay approach when accounting for its investment in an associate or joint venture using the equity method, the entity shall disclose the following, in addition to the information required by IFRS 12:

(a) the information described by paragraphs 39K–39L for each associate or joint venture that is material to the entity. The amounts disclosed shall be those included in the IFRS financial statements of the associate or joint venture after reflecting any adjustments made by the entity when using the equity method (see paragraph B14(a) of IFRS 12), rather than the entity's share of those amounts.

(b)   the quantitative information described by paragraphs 39K–39L(d) and 39L(f), and the effect of the reclassification described in paragraph 35B on profit or loss and other comprehensive income in aggregate for all individually immaterial associates or joint ventures. The aggregate amounts:

(i)   disclosed shall be the entity's share of those amounts; and

(ii)   for associates shall be disclosed separately from the aggregate amounts disclosed for joint ventures.

Effective date and transition

40   The transitional provisions in paragraphs 41–45 apply both to an entity that is already applying IFRSs when it first applies this IFRS and to an entity that applies IFRSs for the first time (a first-time adopter).

41   An entity shall apply this IFRS for annual periods beginning on or after 1 January 2005. Earlier application is encouraged. If an entity applies this IFRS for an earlier period, it shall disclose that fact.

41A   *Financial Guarantee Contracts* (Amendments to IAS 39 and IFRS 4), issued in August 2005, amended paragraphs 4(d), B18(g) and B19(f). An entity shall apply those amendments for annual periods beginning on or after 1 January 2006. Earlier application is encouraged. If an entity applies those amendments for an earlier period, it shall disclose that fact and apply the related amendments to IAS 39 and IAS 32[4] at the same time.

41B   IAS 1 (as revised in 2007) amended the terminology used throughout IFRSs. In addition it amended paragraph 30. An entity shall apply those amendments for annual periods beginning on or after 1 January 2009. If an entity applies IAS 1 (revised 2007) for an earlier period, the amendments shall be applied for that earlier period.

41C   [Deleted]

41D   [Deleted]

41E   IFRS 13 *Fair Value Measurement*, issued in May 2011, amended the definition of fair value in Appendix A. An entity shall apply that amendment when it applies IFRS 13.

41F   [Deleted]

41G   IFRS 15 *Revenue from Contracts with Customers*, issued in May 2014, amended paragraphs 4(a) and (c), B7, B18(h) and B21. An entity shall apply those amendments when it applies IFRS 15.

41H   IFRS 9, as issued in July 2014, amended paragraphs 3, 4, 7, 8, 12, 34, 35, 45, Appendix A and paragraphs B18–B20 and deleted paragraphs 41C, 41D and 41F. An entity shall apply those amendments when it applies IFRS 9.

---

4   When an entity applies IFRS 7, the reference to IAS 32 is replaced by a reference to IFRS 7.

41I   IFRS 16, issued in January 2016, amended paragraph 4. An entity shall apply that amendment when it applies IFRS 16.

Disclosure

42   An entity need not apply the disclosure requirements in this IFRS to comparative information that relates to annual periods beginning before 1 January 2005, except for the disclosures required by paragraph 37(a) and (b) about accounting policies, and recognised assets, liabilities, income and expense (and cash flows if the direct method is used).

43   If it is impracticable to apply a particular requirement of paragraphs 10–35 to comparative information that relates to annual periods beginning before 1 January 2005, an entity shall disclose that fact. Applying the liability adequacy test (paragraphs 15–19) to such comparative information might sometimes be impracticable, but it is highly unlikely to be impracticable to apply other requirements of paragraphs 10–35 to such comparative information. IAS 8 explains the term 'impracticable'.

44   In applying paragraph 39(c)(iii), an entity need not disclose information about claims development that occurred earlier than five years before the end of the first financial year in which it applies this IFRS. Furthermore, if it is impracticable, when an entity first applies this IFRS, to prepare information about claims development that occurred before the beginning of the earliest period for which an entity presents full comparative information that complies with this IFRS, the entity shall disclose that fact.

Redesignation of financial assets

45   Notwithstanding paragraph 4.4.1 of IFRS 9, when an insurer changes its accounting policies for insurance liabilities, it is permitted, but not required, to reclassify some or all of its financial assets so that they are measured at fair value through profit or loss. This reclassification is permitted if an insurer changes accounting policies when it first applies this IFRS and if it makes a subsequent policy change permitted by paragraph 22. The reclassification is a change in accounting policy and IAS 8 applies.

Applying IFRS 4 with IFRS 9

Temporary exemption from IFRS 9

46   *Applying IFRS 9* Financial Instruments *with IFRS 4* Insurance Contracts *(Amendments to IFRS 4)*, issued in September 2016, amended paragraphs 3 and 5, and added paragraphs 20A–20Q, 35A and 39B–39J and headings after paragraphs 20, 20K, 20N and 39A. An entity shall apply those amendments, which permit insurers that meet specified criteria to apply a temporary exemption from IFRS 9, for annual periods beginning on or after 1 January 2018.

47   An entity that discloses the information required by paragraphs 39B–39J shall use the transitional provisions in IFRS 9 that are relevant to making the assessments required for those disclosures. The date of initial application for that purpose shall be deemed to be the beginning of the first annual period beginning on or after 1 January 2018.

The overlay approach

48   *Applying IFRS 9* Financial Instruments *with IFRS 4* Insurance Contracts (Amendments to IFRS 4), issued in September 2016, amended paragraphs 3 and 5, and added paragraphs 35A–35N and 39K–39M and headings after paragraphs 35A, 35K, 35M and 39J. An entity shall apply those amendments, which permit insurers to apply the overlay approach to designated financial assets, when it first applies IFRS 9 (see paragraph 35C).

49   An entity that elects to apply the overlay approach shall:

(a)   apply that approach retrospectively to designated financial assets on transition to IFRS 9. Accordingly, for example, the entity shall recognise as an adjustment to the opening balance of accumulated other comprehensive income an amount equal to the difference between the fair value of the designated financial assets determined applying IFRS 9 and their carrying amount determined applying IAS 39.

(b)   restate comparative information to reflect the overlay approach if, and only if, the entity restates comparative information applying IFRS 9.

50   *Interest Rate Benchmark Reform—Phase 2*, which amended IFRS 9, IAS 39, IFRS 7, IFRS 4 and IFRS 16, issued in August 2020, added paragraphs 20R–20S and paragraph 51. An entity shall apply these amendments for annual periods beginning on or after 1 January 2021. Earlier application is permitted. If an entity applies these amendments for an earlier period, it shall disclose that fact. An entity shall apply these amendments retrospectively in accordance with IAS 8, except as specified in paragraph 51.

51   An entity is not required to restate prior periods to reflect the application of these amendments. The entity may restate prior periods if, and only if, it is possible without the use of hindsight. If an entity does not restate prior periods, the entity shall recognise any difference between the previous carrying amount and the carrying amount at the beginning of the annual reporting period that includes the date of initial application of these amendments in the opening retained earnings (or other component of equity, as appropriate) of the annual reporting period that includes the date of initial application of these amendments.

Appendix A
Defined terms

This appendix is an integral part of the IFRS.

cedant	The **policyholder** under a **reinsurance contract**.
deposit component	A contractual component that is not accounted for as a derivative under IFRS 9 and would be within the scope of IFRS 9 if it were a separate instrument.
direct insurance contract	An **insurance contract** that is not a **reinsurance contract**.

discretionary participation feature

A contractual right to receive, as a supplement to **guaranteed benefits**, additional benefits:

(a) that are likely to be a significant portion of the total contractual benefits;

(b) whose amount or timing is contractually at the discretion of the issuer; and

(c) that are contractually based on:

    (i) the performance of a specified pool of contracts or a specified type of contract;

    (ii) realised and/or unrealised investment returns on a specified pool of assets held by the issuer; or

    (iii) the profit or loss of the company, fund or other entity that issues the contract.

fair value	*Fair value* is the price that would be received to sell an asset or paid to transfer a liability in an orderly transaction between market participants at the measurement date. (See IFRS 13.)
financial guarantee contract	A contract that requires the issuer to make specified payments to reimburse the holder for a loss it incurs because a specified debtor fails to make payment when due in accordance with the original or modified terms of a debt instrument.
financial risk	The risk of a possible future change in one or more of a specified interest rate, financial instrument price, commodity price, foreign exchange rate, index of prices or rates, credit rating or credit index or other variable, provided in the case of a non-financial variable that the variable is not specific to a party to the contract.
guaranteed benefits	Payments or other benefits to which a particular **policyholder** or investor has an unconditional right that is not subject to the contractual discretion of the issuer.
guaranteed element	An obligation to pay **guaranteed benefits**, included in a contract that contains a **discretionary participation feature**.

insurance asset	An **insurer's** net contractual rights under an **insurance contract**.
insurance contract	A contract under which one party (the **insurer**) accepts significant **insurance risk** from another party (the **policyholder**) by agreeing to compensate the policyholder if a specified uncertain future event (the **insured event**) adversely affects the policyholder. (See Appendix B for guidance on this definition.)
insurance liability	An **insurer's** net contractual obligations under an **insurance contract**.
insurance risk	Risk, other than **financial risk**, transferred from the holder of a contract to the issuer.
insured event	An uncertain future event that is covered by an **insurance contract** and creates **insurance risk**.
insurer	The party that has an obligation under an **insurance contract** to compensate a **policyholder** if an **insured event** occurs.
liability adequacy test	An assessment of whether the carrying amount of an **insurance liability** needs to be increased (or the carrying amount of related deferred acquisition costs or related intangible assets decreased), based on a review of future cash flows.
policyholder	A party that has a right to compensation under an **insurance contract** if an **insured event** occurs.
reinsurance assets	A **cedant's** net contractual rights under a **reinsurance contract**.
reinsurance contract	An **insurance contract** issued by one insurer (the **reinsurer**) to compensate another insurer (the **cedant**) for losses on one or more contracts issued by the cedant.
reinsurer	The party that has an obligation under a **reinsurance contract** to compensate a **cedant** if an **insured event** occurs.
unbundle	Account for the components of a contract as if they were separate contracts.

Appendix B
Definition of an insurance contract

This appendix is an integral part of the IFRS.

B1   This appendix gives guidance on the definition of an insurance contract in
        Appendix A. It addresses the following issues:

        (a)   the term 'uncertain future event' (paragraphs B2–B4);

        (b)   payments in kind (paragraphs B5–B7);

        (c)   insurance risk and other risks (paragraphs B8–B17);

        (d)   examples of insurance contracts (paragraphs B18–B21);

        (e)   significant insurance risk (paragraphs B22–B28); and

        (f)   changes in the level of insurance risk (paragraphs B29 and B30).

Uncertain future event

B2   Uncertainty (or risk) is the essence of an insurance contract. Accordingly, at
        least one of the following is uncertain at the inception of an insurance
        contract:

        (a)   whether an *insured event* will occur;

        (b)   when it will occur; or

        (c)   how much the insurer will need to pay if it occurs.

B3   In some insurance contracts, the insured event is the discovery of a loss
        during the term of the contract, even if the loss arises from an event that
        occurred before the inception of the contract. In other insurance contracts,
        the insured event is an event that occurs during the term of the contract, even
        if the resulting loss is discovered after the end of the contract term.

B4   Some insurance contracts cover events that have already occurred, but whose
        financial effect is still uncertain. An example is a reinsurance contract that
        covers the direct insurer against adverse development of claims already
        reported by policyholders. In such contracts, the insured event is the discovery
        of the ultimate cost of those claims.

Payments in kind

B5   Some insurance contracts require or permit payments to be made in kind.
        An example is when the insurer replaces a stolen article directly, instead of
        reimbursing the policyholder. Another example is when an insurer uses its
        own hospitals and medical staff to provide medical services covered by the
        contracts.

B6   Some fixed-fee service contracts in which the level of service depends on an uncertain event meet the definition of an insurance contract in this IFRS but are not regulated as insurance contracts in some countries. One example is a maintenance contract in which the service provider agrees to repair specified equipment after a malfunction. The fixed service fee is based on the expected number of malfunctions, but it is uncertain whether a particular machine will break down. The malfunction of the equipment adversely affects its owner and the contract compensates the owner (in kind, rather than cash). Another example is a contract for car breakdown services in which the provider agrees, for a fixed annual fee, to provide roadside assistance or tow the car to a nearby garage. The latter contract could meet the definition of an insurance contract even if the provider does not agree to carry out repairs or replace parts.

B7   Applying the IFRS to the contracts described in paragraph B6 is likely to be no more burdensome than applying the IFRSs that would be applicable if such contracts were outside the scope of this IFRS:

   (a)   There are unlikely to be material liabilities for malfunctions and breakdowns that have already occurred.

   (b)   If IFRS 15 applied, the service provider would recognise revenue when (or as) it transfers services to the customer (subject to other specified criteria). That approach is also acceptable under this IFRS, which permits the service provider (i) to continue its existing accounting policies for these contracts unless they involve practices prohibited by paragraph 14 and (ii) to improve its accounting policies if so permitted by paragraphs 22–30.

   (c)   The service provider considers whether the cost of meeting its contractual obligation to provide services exceeds the revenue received in advance. To do this, it applies the liability adequacy test described in paragraphs 15–19 of this IFRS. If this IFRS did not apply to these contracts, the service provider would apply IAS 37 to determine whether the contracts are onerous.

   (d)   For these contracts, the disclosure requirements in this IFRS are unlikely to add significantly to disclosures required by other IFRSs.

Distinction between insurance risk and other risks

B8   The definition of an insurance contract refers to insurance risk, which this IFRS defines as risk, other than *financial risk*, transferred from the holder of a contract to the issuer. A contract that exposes the issuer to financial risk without significant insurance risk is not an insurance contract.

B9   The definition of financial risk in Appendix A includes a list of financial and non-financial variables. That list includes non-financial variables that are not specific to a party to the contract, such as an index of earthquake losses in a particular region or an index of temperatures in a particular city. It excludes non-financial variables that are specific to a party to the contract, such as the occurrence or non-occurrence of a fire that damages or destroys an asset of that party. Furthermore, the risk of changes in the fair value of a non-financial asset is not a financial risk if the fair value reflects not only changes in market prices for such assets (a financial variable) but also the condition of a specific non-financial asset held by a party to a contract (a non-financial variable). For example, if a guarantee of the residual value of a specific car exposes the guarantor to the risk of changes in the car's physical condition, that risk is insurance risk, not financial risk.

B10 Some contracts expose the issuer to financial risk, in addition to significant insurance risk. For example, many life insurance contracts both guarantee a minimum rate of return to policyholders (creating financial risk) and promise death benefits that at some times significantly exceed the policyholder's account balance (creating insurance risk in the form of mortality risk). Such contracts are insurance contracts.

B11 Under some contracts, an insured event triggers the payment of an amount linked to a price index. Such contracts are insurance contracts, provided the payment that is contingent on the insured event can be significant. For example, a life-contingent annuity linked to a cost-of-living index transfers insurance risk because payment is triggered by an uncertain event—the survival of the annuitant. The link to the price index is an embedded derivative, but it also transfers insurance risk. If the resulting transfer of insurance risk is significant, the embedded derivative meets the definition of an insurance contract, in which case it need not be separated and measured at fair value (see paragraph 7 of this IFRS).

B12 The definition of insurance risk refers to risk that the insurer accepts from the policyholder. In other words, insurance risk is a pre-existing risk transferred from the policyholder to the insurer. Thus, a new risk created by the contract is not insurance risk.

B13 The definition of an insurance contract refers to an adverse effect on the policyholder. The definition does not limit the payment by the insurer to an amount equal to the financial impact of the adverse event. For example, the definition does not exclude 'new-for-old' coverage that pays the policyholder sufficient to permit replacement of a damaged old asset by a new asset. Similarly, the definition does not limit payment under a term life insurance contract to the financial loss suffered by the deceased's dependants, nor does it preclude the payment of predetermined amounts to quantify the loss caused by death or an accident.

B14 Some contracts require a payment if a specified uncertain event occurs, but do not require an adverse effect on the policyholder as a precondition for payment. Such a contract is not an insurance contract even if the holder uses the contract to mitigate an underlying risk exposure. For example, if the holder uses a derivative to hedge an underlying non-financial variable that is correlated with cash flows from an asset of the entity, the derivative is not an insurance contract because payment is not conditional on whether the holder is adversely affected by a reduction in the cash flows from the asset. Conversely, the definition of an insurance contract refers to an uncertain event for which an adverse effect on the policyholder is a contractual precondition for payment. This contractual precondition does not require the insurer to investigate whether the event actually caused an adverse effect, but permits the insurer to deny payment if it is not satisfied that the event caused an adverse effect.

B15　Lapse or persistency risk (ie the risk that the counterparty will cancel the contract earlier or later than the issuer had expected in pricing the contract) is not insurance risk because the payment to the counterparty is not contingent on an uncertain future event that adversely affects the counterparty. Similarly, expense risk (ie the risk of unexpected increases in the administrative costs associated with the servicing of a contract, rather than in costs associated with insured events) is not insurance risk because an unexpected increase in expenses does not adversely affect the counterparty.

B16　Therefore, a contract that exposes the issuer to lapse risk, persistency risk or expense risk is not an insurance contract unless it also exposes the issuer to insurance risk. However, if the issuer of that contract mitigates that risk by using a second contract to transfer part of that risk to another party, the second contract exposes that other party to insurance risk.

B17　An insurer can accept significant insurance risk from the policyholder only if the insurer is an entity separate from the policyholder. In the case of a mutual insurer, the mutual accepts risk from each policyholder and pools that risk. Although policyholders bear that pooled risk collectively in their capacity as owners, the mutual has still accepted the risk that is the essence of an insurance contract.

Examples of insurance contracts

B18　The following are examples of contracts that are insurance contracts, if the transfer of insurance risk is significant:

(a)　insurance against theft or damage to property.

(b)　insurance against product liability, professional liability, civil liability or legal expenses.

(c)　life insurance and prepaid funeral plans (although death is certain, it is uncertain when death will occur or, for some types of life insurance, whether death will occur within the period covered by the insurance).

(d)　life-contingent annuities and pensions (ie contracts that provide compensation for the uncertain future event — the survival of the annuitant or pensioner — to assist the annuitant or pensioner in maintaining a given standard of living, which would otherwise be adversely affected by his or her survival).

(e)　disability and medical cover.

(f)　surety bonds, fidelity bonds, performance bonds and bid bonds (ie contracts that provide compensation if another party fails to perform a contractual obligation, for example an obligation to construct a building).

(g)   credit insurance that provides for specified payments to be made to reimburse the holder for a loss it incurs because a specified debtor fails to make payment when due under the original or modified terms of a debt instrument. These contracts could have various legal forms, such as that of a guarantee, some types of letter of credit, a credit derivative default contract or an insurance contract. However, although these contracts meet the definition of an insurance contract, they also meet the definition of a financial guarantee contract in IFRS 9 and are within the scope of IAS 32[5] and IFRS 9, not this IFRS (see paragraph 4(d)). Nevertheless, if an issuer of financial guarantee contracts has previously asserted explicitly that it regards such contracts as insurance contracts and has used accounting applicable to insurance contracts, the issuer may elect to apply either IAS 32[6] and IFRS 9 or this IFRS to such financial guarantee contracts.

(h)   product warranties. Product warranties issued by another party for goods sold by a manufacturer, dealer or retailer are within the scope of this IFRS. However, product warranties issued directly by a manufacturer, dealer or retailer are outside its scope, because they are within the scope of IFRS 15 and IAS 37.

(i)   title insurance (ie insurance against the discovery of defects in title to land that were not apparent when the insurance contract was written). In this case, the insured event is the discovery of a defect in the title, not the defect itself.

(j)   travel assistance (ie compensation in cash or in kind to policyholders for losses suffered while they are travelling). Paragraphs B6 and B7 discuss some contracts of this kind.

(k)   catastrophe bonds that provide for reduced payments of principal, interest or both if a specified event adversely affects the issuer of the bond (unless the specified event does not create significant insurance risk, for example if the event is a change in an interest rate or foreign exchange rate).

(l)   insurance swaps and other contracts that require a payment based on changes in climatic, geological or other physical variables that are specific to a party to the contract.

(m)   reinsurance contracts.

B19   The following are examples of items that are not insurance contracts:

(a)   investment contracts that have the legal form of an insurance contract but do not expose the insurer to significant insurance risk, for example life insurance contracts in which the insurer bears no significant mortality risk (such contracts are non-insurance financial instruments or service contracts, see paragraphs B20 and B21).

---

5   When an entity applies IFRS 7, the reference to IAS 32 is replaced by a reference to IFRS 7.

6   When an entity applies IFRS 7, the reference to IAS 32 is replaced by a reference to IFRS 7.

(b)   contracts that have the legal form of insurance, but pass all significant insurance risk back to the policyholder through non-cancellable and enforceable mechanisms that adjust future payments by the policyholder as a direct result of insured losses, for example some financial reinsurance contracts or some group contracts (such contracts are normally non-insurance financial instruments or service contracts, see paragraphs B20 and B21).

(c)   self-insurance, in other words retaining a risk that could have been covered by insurance (there is no insurance contract because there is no agreement with another party).

(d)   contracts (such as gambling contracts) that require a payment if a specified uncertain future event occurs, but do not require, as a contractual precondition for payment, that the event adversely affects the policyholder. However, this does not preclude the specification of a predetermined payout to quantify the loss caused by a specified event such as death or an accident (see also paragraph B13).

(e)   derivatives that expose one party to financial risk but not insurance risk, because they require that party to make payment based solely on changes in one or more of a specified interest rate, financial instrument price, commodity price, foreign exchange rate, index of prices or rates, credit rating or credit index or other variable, provided in the case of a non-financial variable that the variable is not specific to a party to the contract (see IFRS 9).

(f)   a credit-related guarantee (or letter of credit, credit derivative default contract or credit insurance contract) that requires payments even if the holder has not incurred a loss on the failure of the debtor to make payments when due (see IFRS 9).

(g)   contracts that require a payment based on a climatic, geological or other physical variable that is not specific to a party to the contract (commonly described as weather derivatives).

(h)   catastrophe bonds that provide for reduced payments of principal, interest or both, based on a climatic, geological or other physical variable that is not specific to a party to the contract.

B20   If the contracts described in paragraph B19 create financial assets or financial liabilities, they are within the scope of IFRS 9. Among other things, this means that the parties to the contract use what is sometimes called deposit accounting, which involves the following:

(a)   one party recognises the consideration received as a financial liability, rather than as revenue.

(b)   the other party recognises the consideration paid as a financial asset, rather than as an expense.

B21   If the contracts described in paragraph B19 do not create financial assets or financial liabilities, IFRS 15 applies. Under IFRS 15, revenue is recognised when (or as) an entity satisfies a performance obligation by transferring a promised good or service to a customer in an amount that reflects the consideration to which the entity expects to be entitled.

Significant insurance risk

B22   A contract is an insurance contract only if it transfers significant insurance risk. Paragraphs B8–B21 discuss insurance risk. The following paragraphs discuss the assessment of whether insurance risk is significant.

B23   Insurance risk is significant if, and only if, an insured event could cause an insurer to pay significant additional benefits in any scenario, excluding scenarios that lack commercial substance (ie have no discernible effect on the economics of the transaction). If significant additional benefits would be payable in scenarios that have commercial substance, the condition in the previous sentence may be met even if the insured event is extremely unlikely or even if the expected (ie probability-weighted) present value of contingent cash flows is a small proportion of the expected present value of all the remaining contractual cash flows.

B24   The additional benefits described in paragraph B23 refer to amounts that exceed those that would be payable if no insured event occurred (excluding scenarios that lack commercial substance). Those additional amounts include claims handling and claims assessment costs, but exclude:

(a)   the loss of the ability to charge the policyholder for future services. For example, in an investment-linked life insurance contract, the death of the policyholder means that the insurer can no longer perform investment management services and collect a fee for doing so. However, this economic loss for the insurer does not reflect insurance risk, just as a mutual fund manager does not take on insurance risk in relation to the possible death of the client. Therefore, the potential loss of future investment management fees is not relevant in assessing how much insurance risk is transferred by a contract.

(b)   waiver on death of charges that would be made on cancellation or surrender. Because the contract brought those charges into existence, the waiver of these charges does not compensate the policyholder for a pre-existing risk. Hence, they are not relevant in assessing how much insurance risk is transferred by a contract.

(c)   a payment conditional on an event that does not cause a significant loss to the holder of the contract. For example, consider a contract that requires the issuer to pay one million currency units if an asset suffers physical damage causing an insignificant economic loss of one currency unit to the holder. In this contract, the holder transfers to the insurer the insignificant risk of losing one currency unit. At the same time, the contract creates non-insurance risk that the issuer will need to pay 999,999 currency units if the specified event occurs.

Because the issuer does not accept significant insurance risk from the holder, this contract is not an insurance contract.

(d)   possible reinsurance recoveries. The insurer accounts for these separately.

B25   An insurer shall assess the significance of insurance risk contract by contract, rather than by reference to materiality to the financial statements.[7] Thus, insurance risk may be significant even if there is a minimal probability of material losses for a whole book of contracts. This contract-by-contract assessment makes it easier to classify a contract as an insurance contract. However, if a relatively homogeneous book of small contracts is known to consist of contracts that all transfer insurance risk, an insurer need not examine each contract within that book to identify a few non-derivative contracts that transfer insignificant insurance risk.

B26   It follows from paragraphs B23–B25 that if a contract pays a death benefit exceeding the amount payable on survival, the contract is an insurance contract unless the additional death benefit is insignificant (judged by reference to the contract rather than to an entire book of contracts). As noted in paragraph B24(b), the waiver on death of cancellation or surrender charges is not included in this assessment if this waiver does not compensate the policyholder for a pre-existing risk. Similarly, an annuity contract that pays out regular sums for the rest of a policyholder's life is an insurance contract, unless the aggregate life-contingent payments are insignificant.

B27   Paragraph B23 refers to additional benefits. These additional benefits could include a requirement to pay benefits earlier if the insured event occurs earlier and the payment is not adjusted for the time value of money. An example is whole life insurance for a fixed amount (in other words, insurance that provides a fixed death benefit whenever the policyholder dies, with no expiry date for the cover). It is certain that the policyholder will die, but the date of death is uncertain. The insurer will suffer a loss on those individual contracts for which policyholders die early, even if there is no overall loss on the whole book of contracts.

B28   If an insurance contract is unbundled into a deposit component and an insurance component, the significance of insurance risk transfer is assessed by reference to the insurance component. The significance of insurance risk transferred by an embedded derivative is assessed by reference to the embedded derivative.

Changes in the level of insurance risk

B29   Some contracts do not transfer any insurance risk to the issuer at inception, although they do transfer insurance risk at a later time. For example, consider a contract that provides a specified investment return and includes an option for the policyholder to use the proceeds of the investment on maturity to buy a life-contingent annuity at the current annuity rates charged by the insurer

---

7   For this purpose, contracts entered into simultaneously with a single counterparty (or contracts that are otherwise interdependent) form a single contract.

to other new annuitants when the policyholder exercises the option. The contract transfers no insurance risk to the issuer until the option is exercised, because the insurer remains free to price the annuity on a basis that reflects the insurance risk transferred to the insurer at that time. However, if the contract specifies the annuity rates (or a basis for setting the annuity rates), the contract transfers insurance risk to the issuer at inception.

B30   A contract that qualifies as an insurance contract remains an insurance contract until all rights and obligations are extinguished or expire.

Appendix C
Amendments to other IFRSs

The amendments in this appendix shall be applied for annual periods beginning on or after 1 January 2005. If an entity adopts this IFRS for an earlier period, these amendments shall be applied for that earlier period.

* * * * *

The amendments contained in this appendix when this IFRS was issued in 2004 have been incorporated into the relevant IFRSs published in this volume.

Approval by the Board of IFRS 4 issued in March 2004

International Financial Reporting Standard 4 *Insurance Contracts* was approved for issue by eight of the fourteen members of the International Accounting Standards Board. Professor Barth and Messrs Garnett, Gélard, Leisenring, Smith and Yamada dissented. Their dissenting opinions are set out after the Basis for Conclusions on IFRS 4.

Sir David Tweedie	Chairman
Thomas E Jones	Vice-Chairman
Mary E Barth	
Hans-Georg Bruns	
Anthony T Cope	
Robert P Garnett	
Gilbert Gélard	
James J Leisenring	
Warren J McGregor	
Patricia L O'Malley	
Harry K Schmid	
John T Smith	
Geoffrey Whittington	
Tatsumi Yamada	

Approval by the Board of *Financial Guarantee Contracts* (Amendments to IAS 39 and IFRS 4) issued in August 2005

Financial Guarantee Contracts (Amendments to IAS 39 *Financial Instruments: Recognition and Measurement* and to IFRS 4 *Insurance Contracts*) was approved for issue by the fourteen members of the International Accounting Standards Board.

Sir David Tweedie	Chairman
Thomas E Jones	Vice-Chairman
Mary E Barth	
Hans-Georg Bruns	
Anthony T Cope	
Jan Engström	
Robert P Garnett	
Gilbert Gélard	
James J Leisenring	
Warren J McGregor	
Patricia L O'Malley	
John T Smith	
Geoffrey Whittington	
Tatsumi Yamada	

Approval by the Board of *Applying IFRS 9 Financial Instruments with IFRS 4 Insurance Contracts* (Amendments to IFRS 4) issued in September 2016

Applying IFRS 9 Financial Instruments with IFRS 4 Insurance Contracts (Amendments to IFRS 4) was approved for issue by eleven of the twelve members of the International Accounting Standards Board. Ms Tokar dissented. Her dissenting opinion is set out after the Basis for Conclusions.

Hans Hoogervorst	Chairman
Stephen Cooper	
Philippe Danjou	
Amaro Luiz de Oliveira Gomes	
Martin Edelmann	
Gary Kabureck	
Suzanne Lloyd	
Takatsugu Ochi	
Darrel Scott	
Chungwoo Suh	
Mary Tokar	
Wei-Guo Zhang	

Approval by the Board of *Extension of the Temporary Exemption from Applying IFRS 9* issued in June 2020

Extension of the Temporary Exemption from Applying IFRS 9, which amends IFRS 4, was approved for issue by all 14 members of the International Accounting Standards Board.

Hans Hoogervorst	Chairman
Suzanne Lloyd	Vice-Chair
Nick Anderson	
Tadeu Cendon	
Martin Edelmann	
Françoise Flores	
Gary Kabureck	
Jianqiao Lu	
Darrel Scott	
Thomas Scott	
Chungwoo Suh	
Rika Suzuki	
Ann Tarca	
Mary Tokar	

Approval by the Board of *Interest Rate Benchmark Reform—Phase 2* issued in August 2020

Interest Rate Benchmark Reform—Phase 2, which amended IFRS 9, IAS 39, IFRS 7, IFRS 4 and IFRS 16, was approved for issue by 12 of 13 members of the International Accounting Standards Board (Board). Mr Gast abstained in view of his recent appointment to the Board.

Hans Hoogervorst	Chairman
Suzanne Lloyd	Vice-Chair
Nick Anderson	
Tadeu Cendon	
Martin Edelmann	
Françoise Flores	
Zach Gast	
Jianqiao Lu	
Darrel Scott	
Thomas Scott	
Rika Suzuki	
Ann Tarca	
Mary Tokar	

IFRS 5

Non-current Assets Held for Sale and Discontinued Operations

In April 2001 the International Accounting Standards Board (Board) adopted IAS 35 *Discontinuing Operations*, which had originally been issued by the International Accounting Standards Committee in June 1998.

In March 2004 the Board issued IFRS 5 *Non-current Assets Held for Sale and Discontinued Operations* to replace IAS 35.

Other Standards have made minor consequential amendments to IFRS 5. They include *Improvement to IFRSs* (issued April 2009), IFRS 11 *Joint Arrangements* (issued May 2011), IFRS 13 *Fair Value Measurement* (issued May 2011), *Presentation of Items of Other Comprehensive Income* (Amendments to IAS 1) (issued June 2011), IFRS 9 *Financial Instruments* (Hedge Accounting and amendments to IFRS 9, IFRS 7 and IAS 39) (issued November 2013), IFRS 9 *Financial Instruments* (issued July 2014), *Annual Improvements to IFRSs 2012–2014 Cycle* (issued September 2014), IFRS 16 *Leases* (issued January 2016) and *Amendments to References to the Conceptual Framework in IFRS Standards* (issued March 2018).

Contents

FOR THE ACCOMPANYING GUIDANCE LISTED BELOW, SEE PART B OF THIS EDITION

IMPLEMENTATION GUIDANCE

FOR THE BASIS FOR CONCLUSIONS, SEE PART C OF THIS EDITION

BASIS FOR CONCLUSIONS
DISSENTING OPINIONS

© IFRS Foundation

International Financial Reporting Standard 5 *Non-current Assets Held for Sale and Discontinued Operations* (IFRS 5) is set out in paragraphs 1–45 and Appendices A–C. All the paragraphs have equal authority. Paragraphs in **bold type** state the main principles. Terms defined in Appendix A are in *italics* the first time they appear in the Standard. Definitions of other terms are given in the Glossary for International Financial Reporting Standards. IFRS 5 should be read in the context of its objective and the Basis for Conclusions, the *Preface to IFRS Standards* and the *Conceptual Framework for Financial Reporting*. IAS 8 *Accounting Policies, Changes in Accounting Estimates and Errors* provides a basis for selecting and applying accounting policies in the absence of explicit guidance.

International Financial Reporting Standard 5
Non-current Assets Held for Sale and Discontinued Operations

Objective

1   The objective of this IFRS is to specify the accounting for assets held for sale, and the presentation and disclosure of *discontinued operations*. In particular, the IFRS requires:

   (a)   assets that meet the criteria to be classified as held for sale to be measured at the lower of carrying amount and *fair value* less *costs to sell*, and depreciation on such assets to cease; and

   (b)   assets that meet the criteria to be classified as held for sale to be presented separately in the statement of financial position and the results of discontinued operations to be presented separately in the statement of comprehensive income.

Scope

2   The classification and presentation requirements of this IFRS apply to all recognised *non-current assets*[1] and to all *disposal groups* of an entity. The measurement requirements of this IFRS apply to all recognised non-current assets and disposal groups (as set out in paragraph 4), except for those assets listed in paragraph 5 which shall continue to be measured in accordance with the Standard noted.

3   Assets classified as non-current in accordance with IAS 1 *Presentation of Financial Statements* shall not be reclassified as *current assets* until they meet the criteria to be classified as held for sale in accordance with this IFRS. Assets of a class that an entity would normally regard as non-current that are acquired exclusively with a view to resale shall not be classified as current unless they meet the criteria to be classified as held for sale in accordance with this IFRS.

4   Sometimes an entity disposes of a group of assets, possibly with some directly associated liabilities, together in a single transaction. Such a disposal group may be a group of *cash-generating units*, a single cash-generating unit, or part of a cash-generating unit.[2] The group may include any assets and any liabilities of the entity, including current assets, current liabilities and assets excluded by paragraph 5 from the measurement requirements of this IFRS. If a non-current asset within the scope of the measurement requirements of this IFRS is part of a disposal group, the measurement requirements of this IFRS apply to the group as a whole, so that the group is measured at the lower of its

---

1   For assets classified according to a liquidity presentation, non-current assets are assets that include amounts expected to be recovered more than twelve months after the reporting period. Paragraph 3 applies to the classification of such assets.

2   However, once the cash flows from an asset or group of assets are expected to arise principally from sale rather than continuing use, they become less dependent on cash flows arising from other assets, and a disposal group that was part of a cash-generating unit becomes a separate cash-generating unit.

carrying amount and fair value less costs to sell. The requirements for measuring the individual assets and liabilities within the disposal group are set out in paragraphs 18, 19 and 23.

5 The measurement provisions of this IFRS[3] do not apply to the following assets, which are covered by the IFRSs listed, either as individual assets or as part of a disposal group:

(a) deferred tax assets (IAS 12 *Income Taxes*).

(b) assets arising from employee benefits (IAS 19 *Employee Benefits*).

(c) financial assets within the scope of IFRS 9 *Financial Instruments*.

(d) non-current assets that are accounted for in accordance with the fair value model in IAS 40 *Investment Property*.

(e) non-current assets that are measured at fair value less costs to sell in accordance with IAS 41 *Agriculture*.

(f) contractual rights under insurance contracts as defined in IFRS 4 *Insurance Contracts*.

5A The classification, presentation and measurement requirements in this IFRS applicable to a non-current asset (or disposal group) that is classified as held for sale apply also to a non-current asset (or disposal group) that is classified as held for distribution to owners acting in their capacity as owners (held for distribution to owners).

5B This IFRS specifies the disclosures required in respect of non-current assets (or disposal groups) classified as held for sale or discontinued operations. Disclosures in other IFRSs do not apply to such assets (or disposal groups) unless those IFRSs require:

(a) specific disclosures in respect of non-current assets (or disposal groups) classified as held for sale or discontinued operations; or

(b) disclosures about measurement of assets and liabilities within a disposal group that are not within the scope of the measurement requirement of IFRS 5 and such disclosures are not already provided in the other notes to the financial statements.

Additional disclosures about non-current assets (or disposal groups) classified as held for sale or discontinued operations may be necessary to comply with the general requirements of IAS 1, in particular paragraphs 15 and 125 of that Standard.

---

3 Other than paragraphs 18 and 19, which require the assets in question to be measured in accordance with other applicable IFRSs.

Classification of non-current assets (or disposal groups) as held for sale or as held for distribution to owners

6   An entity shall classify a non-current asset (or disposal group) as held for sale if its carrying amount will be recovered principally through a sale transaction rather than through continuing use.

7   For this to be the case, the asset (or disposal group) must be available for immediate sale in its present condition subject only to terms that are usual and customary for sales of such assets (or disposal groups) and its sale must be *highly probable*.

8   For the sale to be highly probable, the appropriate level of management must be committed to a plan to sell the asset (or disposal group), and an active programme to locate a buyer and complete the plan must have been initiated. Further, the asset (or disposal group) must be actively marketed for sale at a price that is reasonable in relation to its current fair value. In addition, the sale should be expected to qualify for recognition as a completed sale within one year from the date of classification, except as permitted by paragraph 9, and actions required to complete the plan should indicate that it is unlikely that significant changes to the plan will be made or that the plan will be withdrawn. The probability of shareholders' approval (if required in the jurisdiction) should be considered as part of the assessment of whether the sale is highly probable.

8A   An entity that is committed to a sale plan involving loss of control of a subsidiary shall classify all the assets and liabilities of that subsidiary as held for sale when the criteria set out in paragraphs 6–8 are met, regardless of whether the entity will retain a non-controlling interest in its former subsidiary after the sale.

9   Events or circumstances may extend the period to complete the sale beyond one year. An extension of the period required to complete a sale does not preclude an asset (or disposal group) from being classified as held for sale if the delay is caused by events or circumstances beyond the entity's control and there is sufficient evidence that the entity remains committed to its plan to sell the asset (or disposal group). This will be the case when the criteria in Appendix B are met.

10   Sale transactions include exchanges of non-current assets for other non-current assets when the exchange has commercial substance in accordance with IAS 16 *Property, Plant and Equipment*.

11   When an entity acquires a non-current asset (or disposal group) exclusively with a view to its subsequent disposal, it shall classify the non-current asset (or disposal group) as held for sale at the acquisition date only if the one-year requirement in paragraph 8 is met (except as permitted by paragraph 9) and it is highly probable that any other criteria in paragraphs 7 and 8 that are not met at that date will be met within a short period following the acquisition (usually within three months).

12   If the criteria in paragraphs 7 and 8 are met after the reporting period, an entity shall not classify a non-current asset (or disposal group) as held for sale in those financial statements when issued. However, when those criteria are met after the reporting period but before the authorisation of the financial statements for issue, the entity shall disclose the information specified in paragraph 41(a), (b) and (d) in the notes.

12A   A non-current asset (or disposal group) is classified as held for distribution to owners when the entity is committed to distribute the asset (or disposal group) to the owners. For this to be the case, the assets must be available for immediate distribution in their present condition and the distribution must be highly probable. For the distribution to be highly probable, actions to complete the distribution must have been initiated and should be expected to be completed within one year from the date of classification. Actions required to complete the distribution should indicate that it is unlikely that significant changes to the distribution will be made or that the distribution will be withdrawn. The probability of shareholders' approval (if required in the jurisdiction) should be considered as part of the assessment of whether the distribution is highly probable.

Non-current assets that are to be abandoned

13   An entity shall not classify as held for sale a non-current asset (or disposal group) that is to be abandoned. This is because its carrying amount will be recovered principally through continuing use. However, if the disposal group to be abandoned meets the criteria in paragraph 32(a)–(c), the entity shall present the results and cash flows of the disposal group as discontinued operations in accordance with paragraphs 33 and 34 at the date on which it ceases to be used. Non-current assets (or disposal groups) to be abandoned include non-current assets (or disposal groups) that are to be used to the end of their economic life and non-current assets (or disposal groups) that are to be closed rather than sold.

14   An entity shall not account for a non-current asset that has been temporarily taken out of use as if it had been abandoned.

Measurement of non-current assets (or disposal groups) classified as held for sale

Measurement of a non-current asset (or disposal group)

15   An entity shall measure a non-current asset (or disposal group) classified as held for sale at the lower of its carrying amount and fair value less costs to sell.

15A   An entity shall measure a non-current asset (or disposal group) classified as held for distribution to owners at the lower of its carrying amount and fair value less costs to distribute.[4]

---

4   Costs to distribute are the incremental costs directly attributable to the distribution, excluding finance costs and income tax expense.

16   If a newly acquired asset (or disposal group) meets the criteria to be classified as held for sale (see paragraph 11), applying paragraph 15 will result in the asset (or disposal group) being measured on initial recognition at the lower of its carrying amount had it not been so classified (for example, cost) and fair value less costs to sell. Hence, if the asset (or disposal group) is acquired as part of a business combination, it shall be measured at fair value less costs to sell.

17   When the sale is expected to occur beyond one year, the entity shall measure the costs to sell at their present value. Any increase in the present value of the costs to sell that arises from the passage of time shall be presented in profit or loss as a financing cost.

18   Immediately before the initial classification of the asset (or disposal group) as held for sale, the carrying amounts of the asset (or all the assets and liabilities in the group) shall be measured in accordance with applicable IFRSs.

19   On subsequent remeasurement of a disposal group, the carrying amounts of any assets and liabilities that are not within the scope of the measurement requirements of this IFRS, but are included in a disposal group classified as held for sale, shall be remeasured in accordance with applicable IFRSs before the fair value less costs to sell of the disposal group is remeasured.

Recognition of impairment losses and reversals

20   An entity shall recognise an impairment loss for any initial or subsequent write-down of the asset (or disposal group) to fair value less costs to sell, to the extent that it has not been recognised in accordance with paragraph 19.

21   An entity shall recognise a gain for any subsequent increase in fair value less costs to sell of an asset, but not in excess of the cumulative impairment loss that has been recognised either in accordance with this IFRS or previously in accordance with IAS 36 *Impairment of Assets*.

22   An entity shall recognise a gain for any subsequent increase in fair value less costs to sell of a disposal group:

(a)   to the extent that it has not been recognised in accordance with paragraph 19; but

(b)   not in excess of the cumulative impairment loss that has been recognised, either in accordance with this IFRS or previously in accordance with IAS 36, on the non-current assets that are within the scope of the measurement requirements of this IFRS.

23   The impairment loss (or any subsequent gain) recognised for a disposal group shall reduce (or increase) the carrying amount of the non-current assets in the group that are within the scope of the measurement requirements of this IFRS, in the order of allocation set out in paragraphs 104(a) and (b) and 122 of IAS 36 (as revised in 2004).

24   A gain or loss not previously recognised by the date of the sale of a non-current asset (or disposal group) shall be recognised at the date of derecognition. Requirements relating to derecognition are set out in:

(a) paragraphs 67–72 of IAS 16 (as revised in 2003) for property, plant and equipment, and

(b) paragraphs 112–117 of IAS 38 *Intangible Assets* (as revised in 2004) for intangible assets.

25 An entity shall not depreciate (or amortise) a non-current asset while it is classified as held for sale or while it is part of a disposal group classified as held for sale. Interest and other expenses attributable to the liabilities of a disposal group classified as held for sale shall continue to be recognised.

Changes to a plan of sale or to a plan of distribution to owners

26 If an entity has classified an asset (or disposal group) as held for sale or as held for distribution to owners, but the criteria in paragraphs 7–9 (for held for sale) or in paragraph 12A (for held for distribution to owners) are no longer met, the entity shall cease to classify the asset (or disposal group) as held for sale or held for distribution to owners (respectively). In such cases an entity shall follow the guidance in paragraphs 27–29 to account for this change except when paragraph 26A applies.

26A If an entity reclassifies an asset (or disposal group) directly from being held for sale to being held for distribution to owners, or directly from being held for distribution to owners to being held for sale, then the change in classification is considered a continuation of the original plan of disposal. The entity:

(a) shall not follow the guidance in paragraphs 27–29 to account for this change. The entity shall apply the classification, presentation and measurement requirements in this IFRS that are applicable to the new method of disposal.

(b) shall measure the non-current asset (or disposal group) by following the requirements in paragraph 15 (if reclassified as held for sale) or 15A (if reclassified as held for distribution to owners) and recognise any reduction or increase in the fair value less costs to sell/costs to distribute of the non-current asset (or disposal group) by following the requirements in paragraphs 20–25.

(c) shall not change the date of classification in accordance with paragraphs 8 and 12A. This does not preclude an extension of the period required to complete a sale or a distribution to owners if the conditions in paragraph 9 are met.

27 The entity shall measure a non-current asset (or disposal group) that ceases to be classified as held for sale or as held for distribution to owners (or ceases to be included in a disposal group classified as held for sale or as held for distribution to owners) at the lower of:

(a)   its carrying amount before the asset (or disposal group) was classified as held for sale or as held for distribution to owners, adjusted for any depreciation, amortisation or revaluations that would have been recognised had the asset (or disposal group) not been classified as held for sale or as held for distribution to owners, and

(b)   its *recoverable amount* at the date of the subsequent decision not to sell or distribute.[5]

28   The entity shall include any required adjustment to the carrying amount of a non-current asset that ceases to be classified as held for sale or as held for distribution to owners in profit or loss[6] from continuing operations in the period in which the criteria in paragraphs 7–9 or 12A, respectively, are no longer met. Financial statements for the periods since classification as held for sale or as held for distribution to owners shall be amended accordingly if the disposal group or non-current asset that ceases to be classified as held for sale or as held for distribution to owners is a subsidiary, joint operation, joint venture, associate, or a portion of an interest in a joint venture or an associate. The entity shall present that adjustment in the same caption in the statement of comprehensive income used to present a gain or loss, if any, recognised in accordance with paragraph 37.

29   If an entity removes an individual asset or liability from a disposal group classified as held for sale, the remaining assets and liabilities of the disposal group to be sold shall continue to be measured as a group only if the group meets the criteria in paragraphs 7–9. If an entity removes an individual asset or liability from a disposal group classified as held for distribution to owners, the remaining assets and liabilities of the disposal group to be distributed shall continue to be measured as a group only if the group meets the criteria in paragraph 12A. Otherwise, the remaining non-current assets of the group that individually meet the criteria to be classified as held for sale (or as held for distribution to owners) shall be measured individually at the lower of their carrying amounts and fair values less costs to sell (or costs to distribute) at that date. Any non-current assets that do not meet the criteria for held for sale shall cease to be classified as held for sale in accordance with paragraph 26. Any non-current assets that do not meet the criteria for held for distribution to owners shall cease to be classified as held for distribution to owners in accordance with paragraph 26.

Presentation and disclosure

30   **An entity shall present and disclose information that enables users of the financial statements to evaluate the financial effects of discontinued operations and disposals of non-current assets (or disposal groups).**

---

5   If the non-current asset is part of a cash-generating unit, its recoverable amount is the carrying amount that would have been recognised after the allocation of any impairment loss arising on that cash-generating unit in accordance with IAS 36.

6   Unless the asset is property, plant and equipment or an intangible asset that had been revalued in accordance with IAS 16 or IAS 38 before classification as held for sale, in which case the adjustment shall be treated as a revaluation increase or decrease.

Presenting discontinued operations

31 A *component of an entity* comprises operations and cash flows that can be clearly distinguished, operationally and for financial reporting purposes, from the rest of the entity. In other words, a component of an entity will have been a cash-generating unit or a group of cash-generating units while being held for use.

32 A discontinued operation is a component of an entity that either has been disposed of, or is classified as held for sale, and

 (a) represents a separate major line of business or geographical area of operations,

 (b) is part of a single co-ordinated plan to dispose of a separate major line of business or geographical area of operations or

 (c) is a subsidiary acquired exclusively with a view to resale.

33 An entity shall disclose:

 (a) a single amount in the statement of comprehensive income comprising the total of:

  (i) the post-tax profit or loss of discontinued operations and

  (ii) the post-tax gain or loss recognised on the measurement to fair value less costs to sell or on the disposal of the assets or disposal group(s) constituting the discontinued operation.

 (b) an analysis of the single amount in (a) into:

  (i) the revenue, expenses and pre-tax profit or loss of discontinued operations;

  (ii) the related income tax expense as required by paragraph 81(h) of IAS 12.

  (iii) the gain or loss recognised on the measurement to fair value less costs to sell or on the disposal of the assets or disposal group(s) constituting the discontinued operation; and

  (iv) the related income tax expense as required by paragraph 81(h) of IAS 12.

  The analysis may be presented in the notes or in the statement of comprehensive income. If it is presented in the statement of comprehensive income it shall be presented in a section identified as relating to discontinued operations, ie separately from continuing operations. The analysis is not required for disposal groups that are newly acquired subsidiaries that meet the criteria to be classified as held for sale on acquisition (see paragraph 11).

 (c) the net cash flows attributable to the operating, investing and financing activities of discontinued operations. These disclosures may be presented either in the notes or in the financial statements. These disclosures are not required for disposal groups that are newly acquired subsidiaries that meet the criteria to be classified as held for sale on acquisition (see paragraph 11).

(d)   the amount of income from continuing operations and from discontinued operations attributable to owners of the parent. These disclosures may be presented either in the notes or in the statement of comprehensive income.

33A   If an entity presents the items of profit or loss in a separate statement as described in paragraph 10A of IAS 1 (as amended in 2011), a section identified as relating to discontinued operations is presented in that statement.

34   An entity shall re-present the disclosures in paragraph 33 for prior periods presented in the financial statements so that the disclosures relate to all operations that have been discontinued by the end of the reporting period for the latest period presented.

35   Adjustments in the current period to amounts previously presented in discontinued operations that are directly related to the disposal of a discontinued operation in a prior period shall be classified separately in discontinued operations. The nature and amount of such adjustments shall be disclosed. Examples of circumstances in which these adjustments may arise include the following:

(a)   the resolution of uncertainties that arise from the terms of the disposal transaction, such as the resolution of purchase price adjustments and indemnification issues with the purchaser.

(b)   the resolution of uncertainties that arise from and are directly related to the operations of the component before its disposal, such as environmental and product warranty obligations retained by the seller.

(c)   the settlement of employee benefit plan obligations, provided that the settlement is directly related to the disposal transaction.

36   If an entity ceases to classify a component of an entity as held for sale, the results of operations of the component previously presented in discontinued operations in accordance with paragraphs 33–35 shall be reclassified and included in income from continuing operations for all periods presented. The amounts for prior periods shall be described as having been re-presented.

36A   An entity that is committed to a sale plan involving loss of control of a subsidiary shall disclose the information required in paragraphs 33–36 when the subsidiary is a disposal group that meets the definition of a discontinued operation in accordance with paragraph 32.

Gains or losses relating to continuing operations

37   Any gain or loss on the remeasurement of a non-current asset (or disposal group) classified as held for sale that does not meet the definition of a discontinued operation shall be included in profit or loss from continuing operations.

Presentation of a non-current asset or disposal group classified as held for sale

38   An entity shall present a non-current asset classified as held for sale and the assets of a disposal group classified as held for sale separately from other assets in the statement of financial position. The liabilities of a disposal group classified as held for sale shall be presented separately from other liabilities in the statement of financial position. Those assets and liabilities shall not be offset and presented as a single amount. The major classes of assets and liabilities classified as held for sale shall be separately disclosed either in the statement of financial position or in the notes, except as permitted by paragraph 39. An entity shall present separately any cumulative income or expense recognised in other comprehensive income relating to a non-current asset (or disposal group) classified as held for sale.

39   If the disposal group is a newly acquired subsidiary that meets the criteria to be classified as held for sale on acquisition (see paragraph 11), disclosure of the major classes of assets and liabilities is not required.

40   An entity shall not reclassify or re-present amounts presented for non-current assets or for the assets and liabilities of disposal groups classified as held for sale in the statements of financial position for prior periods to reflect the classification in the statement of financial position for the latest period presented.

Additional disclosures

41   An entity shall disclose the following information in the notes in the period in which a non-current asset (or disposal group) has been either classified as held for sale or sold:

(a)   a description of the non-current asset (or disposal group);

(b)   a description of the facts and circumstances of the sale, or leading to the expected disposal, and the expected manner and timing of that disposal;

(c)   the gain or loss recognised in accordance with paragraphs 20–22 and, if not separately presented in the statement of comprehensive income, the caption in the statement of comprehensive income that includes that gain or loss;

(d)   if applicable, the reportable segment in which the non-current asset (or disposal group) is presented in accordance with IFRS 8 *Operating Segments*.

42   If either paragraph 26 or paragraph 29 applies, an entity shall disclose, in the period of the decision to change the plan to sell the non-current asset (or disposal group), a description of the facts and circumstances leading to the decision and the effect of the decision on the results of operations for the period and any prior periods presented.

Transitional provisions

43   The IFRS shall be applied prospectively to non-current assets (or disposal groups) that meet the criteria to be classified as held for sale and operations that meet the criteria to be classified as discontinued after the effective date of the IFRS. An entity may apply the requirements of the IFRS to all non-current assets (or disposal groups) that meet the criteria to be classified as held for sale and operations that meet the criteria to be classified as discontinued after any date before the effective date of the IFRS, provided the valuations and other information needed to apply the IFRS were obtained at the time those criteria were originally met.

Effective date

44   An entity shall apply this IFRS for annual periods beginning on or after 1 January 2005. Earlier application is encouraged. If an entity applies the IFRS for a period beginning before 1 January 2005, it shall disclose that fact.

44A   IAS 1 (as revised in 2007) amended the terminology used throughout IFRSs. In addition it amended paragraphs 3 and 38, and added paragraph 33A. An entity shall apply those amendments for annual periods beginning on or after 1 January 2009. If an entity applies IAS 1 (revised 2007) for an earlier period, the amendments shall be applied for that earlier period.

44B   IAS 27 *Consolidated and Separate Financial Statements* (as amended in 2008) added paragraph 33(d). An entity shall apply that amendment for annual periods beginning on or after 1 July 2009. If an entity applies IAS 27 (amended 2008) for an earlier period, the amendment shall be applied for that earlier period. The amendment shall be applied retrospectively.

44C   Paragraphs 8A and 36A were added by *Improvements to IFRSs* issued in May 2008. An entity shall apply those amendments for annual periods beginning on or after 1 July 2009. Earlier application is permitted. However, an entity shall not apply the amendments for annual periods beginning before 1 July 2009 unless it also applies IAS 27 (as amended in January 2008). If an entity applies the amendments before 1 July 2009 it shall disclose that fact. An entity shall apply the amendments prospectively from the date at which it first applied IFRS 5, subject to the transitional provisions in paragraph 45 of IAS 27 (amended January 2008).

44D   Paragraphs 5A, 12A and 15A were added and paragraph 8 was amended by IFRIC 17 *Distributions of Non-cash Assets to Owners* in November 2008. Those amendments shall be applied prospectively to non-current assets (or disposal groups) that are classified as held for distribution to owners in annual periods beginning on or after 1 July 2009. Retrospective application is not permitted. Earlier application is permitted. If an entity applies the amendments for a period beginning before 1 July 2009 it shall disclose that fact and also apply IFRS 3 *Business Combinations* (as revised in 2008), IAS 27 (as amended in January 2008) and IFRIC 17.

44E   Paragraph 5B was added by *Improvements to IFRSs* issued in April 2009. An entity shall apply that amendment prospectively for annual periods beginning on or after 1 January 2010. Earlier application is permitted. If an entity applies the amendment for an earlier period it shall disclose that fact.

44F   [Deleted]

44G   IFRS 11 *Joint Arrangements*, issued in May 2011, amended paragraph 28. An entity shall apply that amendment when it applies IFRS 11.

44H   IFRS 13 *Fair Value Measurement*, issued in May 2011, amended the definition of fair value and the definition of recoverable amount in Appendix A. An entity shall apply those amendments when it applies IFRS 13.

44I   *Presentation of Items of Other Comprehensive Income* (Amendments to IAS 1), issued in June 2011, amended paragraph 33A. An entity shall apply that amendment when it applies IAS 1 as amended in June 2011.

44J   [Deleted]

44K   IFRS 9, as issued in July 2014, amended paragraph 5 and deleted paragraphs 44F and 44J. An entity shall apply those amendments when it applies IFRS 9.

44L   *Annual Improvements to IFRSs 2012–2014 Cycle*, issued in September 2014, amended paragraphs 26–29 and added paragraph 26A. An entity shall apply those amendments prospectively in accordance with IAS 8 *Accounting Policies, Changes in Accounting Estimates and Errors* to changes in a method of disposal that occur in annual periods beginning on or after 1 January 2016. Earlier application is permitted. If an entity applies those amendments for an earlier period it shall disclose that fact.

44M   *[This paragraph refers to amendments that are not yet effective, and is therefore not included in this edition.]*

Withdrawal of IAS 35

45   This IFRS supersedes IAS 35 *Discontinuing Operations*.

Appendix A
Defined terms

This appendix is an integral part of the IFRS.

cash-generating unit	The smallest identifiable group of assets that generates cash inflows that are largely independent of the cash inflows from other assets or groups of assets.
component of an entity	Operations and cash flows that can be clearly distinguished, operationally and for financial reporting purposes, from the rest of the entity.
costs to sell	The incremental costs directly attributable to the disposal of an asset (or **disposal group**), excluding finance costs and income tax expense.
current asset	An entity shall classify an asset as current when:

(a)   it expects to realise the asset, or intends to sell or consume it, in its normal operating cycle;

(b)   it holds the asset primarily for the purpose of trading;

(c)   it expects to realise the asset within twelve months after the reporting period; or

(d)   the asset is cash or a cash equivalent (as defined in IAS 7) unless the asset is restricted from being exchanged or used to settle a liability for at least twelve months after the reporting period.

discontinued operation	A **component of an entity** that either has been disposed of or is classified as held for sale and:

(a)   represents a separate major line of business or geographical area of operations,

(b)   is part of a single co-ordinated plan to dispose of a separate major line of business or geographical area of operations or

(c)   is a subsidiary acquired exclusively with a view to resale.

disposal group	A group of assets to be disposed of, by sale or otherwise, together as a group in a single transaction, and liabilities directly associated with those assets that will be transferred in the transaction. The group includes goodwill acquired in a business combination if the group is a **cash-generating unit** to which goodwill has been allocated in accordance with the requirements of paragraphs 80–87 of IAS 36 *Impairment of Assets* (as revised in 2004) or if it is an operation within such a cash-generating unit.

fair value	*Fair value* is the price that would be received to sell an asset or paid to transfer a liability in an orderly transaction between market participants at the measurement date. (See IFRS 13.)
firm purchase commitment	An agreement with an unrelated party, binding on both parties and usually legally enforceable, that (a) specifies all significant terms, including the price and timing of the transactions, and (b) includes a disincentive for non-performance that is sufficiently large to make performance **highly probable**.
highly probable	Significantly more likely than **probable**.
non-current asset	An asset that does not meet the definition of a **current asset**.
probable	More likely than not.
recoverable amount	The higher of an asset's **fair value** less **costs of disposal** and its **value in use**.
value in use	The present value of estimated future cash flows expected to arise from the continuing use of an asset and from its disposal at the end of its useful life.

Appendix B
Application supplement

This appendix is an integral part of the IFRS.

Extension of the period required to complete a sale

B1 As noted in paragraph 9, an extension of the period required to complete a sale does not preclude an asset (or disposal group) from being classified as held for sale if the delay is caused by events or circumstances beyond the entity's control and there is sufficient evidence that the entity remains committed to its plan to sell the asset (or disposal group). An exception to the one-year requirement in paragraph 8 shall therefore apply in the following situations in which such events or circumstances arise:

(a) at the date an entity commits itself to a plan to sell a non-current asset (or disposal group) it reasonably expects that others (not a buyer) will impose conditions on the transfer of the asset (or disposal group) that will extend the period required to complete the sale, and:

(i) actions necessary to respond to those conditions cannot be initiated until after a *firm purchase commitment* is obtained, and

(ii) a firm purchase commitment is highly probable within one year.

(b) an entity obtains a firm purchase commitment and, as a result, a buyer or others unexpectedly impose conditions on the transfer of a non-current asset (or disposal group) previously classified as held for sale that will extend the period required to complete the sale, and:

(i) timely actions necessary to respond to the conditions have been taken, and

(ii) a favourable resolution of the delaying factors is expected.

(c) during the initial one-year period, circumstances arise that were previously considered unlikely and, as a result, a non-current asset (or disposal group) previously classified as held for sale is not sold by the end of that period, and:

(i) during the initial one-year period the entity took action necessary to respond to the change in circumstances,

(ii) the non-current asset (or disposal group) is being actively marketed at a price that is reasonable, given the change in circumstances, and

(iii) the criteria in paragraphs 7 and 8 are met.

Appendix C
Amendments to other IFRSs

The amendments in this appendix shall be applied for annual periods beginning on or after 1 January 2005. If an entity adopts this IFRS for an earlier period, these amendments shall be applied for that earlier period.

* * * * *

The amendments contained in this appendix when this IFRS was issued in 2004 have been incorporated into the relevant IFRSs published in this volume.

Approval by the Board of IFRS 5 issued in March 2004

International Financial Reporting Standard 5 *Non-current Assets Held for Sale and Discontinued Operations* was approved for issue by twelve of the fourteen members of the International Accounting Standards Board. Messrs Cope and Schmid dissented. Their dissenting opinions are set out after the Basis for Conclusions on IFRS 5.

Sir David Tweedie	Chairman
Thomas E Jones	Vice-Chairman
Mary E Barth	
Hans-Georg Bruns	
Anthony T Cope	
Robert P Garnett	
Gilbert Gélard	
James J Leisenring	
Warren J McGregor	
Patricia L O'Malley	
Harry K Schmid	
John T Smith	
Geoffrey Whittington	
Tatsumi Yamada	

IFRS 6

Exploration for and Evaluation of Mineral Resources

In December 2004 the International Accounting Standards Board issued IFRS 6 *Exploration for and Evaluation of Mineral Resources*.

Other Standards have made minor consequential amendments to IFRS 6, including *Amendments to References to the Conceptual Framework in IFRS Standards* (issued March 2018).

Contents

FOR THE BASIS FOR CONCLUSIONS, SEE PART C OF THIS EDITION

BASIS FOR CONCLUSIONS

DISSENTING OPINIONS

International Financial Reporting Standard 6 *Exploration for and Evaluation of Mineral Resources* (IFRS 6) is set out in paragraphs 1–27 and Appendices A and B. All the paragraphs have equal authority. Paragraphs in **bold type** state the main principles. Terms defined in Appendix A are in *italics* the first time they appear in the Standard. Definitions of other terms are given in the Glossary for International Financial Reporting Standards. IFRS 6 should be read in the context of its objective and the Basis for Conclusions, the *Preface to IFRS Standards* and the *Conceptual Framework for Financial Reporting*. IAS 8 *Accounting Policies, Changes in Accounting Estimates and Errors* provides a basis for selecting and applying accounting policies in the absence of explicit guidance.

International Financial Reporting Standard 6
Exploration for and Evaluation of Mineral Resources

Objective

1   The objective of this IFRS is to specify the financial reporting for the *exploration for and evaluation of mineral resources*.

2   In particular, the IFRS requires:

(a)   limited improvements to existing accounting practices for *exploration and evaluation expenditures*.

(b)   entities that recognise *exploration and evaluation assets* to assess such assets for impairment in accordance with this IFRS and measure any impairment in accordance with IAS 36 *Impairment of Assets*.

(c)   disclosures that identify and explain the amounts in the entity's financial statements arising from the exploration for and evaluation of mineral resources and help users of those financial statements understand the amount, timing and certainty of future cash flows from any exploration and evaluation assets recognised.

Scope

3   An entity shall apply the IFRS to exploration and evaluation expenditures that it incurs.

4   The IFRS does not address other aspects of accounting by entities engaged in the exploration for and evaluation of mineral resources.

5   An entity shall not apply the IFRS to expenditures incurred:

(a)   before the exploration for and evaluation of mineral resources, such as expenditures incurred before the entity has obtained the legal rights to explore a specific area.

(b)   after the technical feasibility and commercial viability of extracting a mineral resource are demonstrable.

Recognition of exploration and evaluation assets

Temporary exemption from IAS 8 paragraphs 11 and 12

6   When developing its accounting policies, an entity recognising exploration and evaluation assets shall apply paragraph 10 of IAS 8 *Accounting Policies, Changes in Accounting Estimates and Errors*.

7   Paragraphs 11 and 12 of IAS 8 specify sources of authoritative requirements and guidance that management is required to consider in developing an accounting policy for an item if no IFRS applies specifically to that item. Subject to paragraphs 9 and 10 below, this IFRS exempts an entity from

applying those paragraphs to its accounting policies for the recognition and measurement of exploration and evaluation assets.

Measurement of exploration and evaluation assets

Measurement at recognition

8   Exploration and evaluation assets shall be measured at cost.

Elements of cost of exploration and evaluation assets

9   An entity shall determine an accounting policy specifying which expenditures are recognised as exploration and evaluation assets and apply the policy consistently. In making this determination, an entity considers the degree to which the expenditure can be associated with finding specific mineral resources. The following are examples of expenditures that might be included in the initial measurement of exploration and evaluation assets (the list is not exhaustive):

    (a)   acquisition of rights to explore;

    (b)   topographical, geological, geochemical and geophysical studies;

    (c)   exploratory drilling;

    (d)   trenching;

    (e)   sampling; and

    (f)   activities in relation to evaluating the technical feasibility and commercial viability of extracting a mineral resource.

10   Expenditures related to the development of mineral resources shall not be recognised as exploration and evaluation assets. The *Conceptual Framework for Financial Reporting* and IAS 38 *Intangible Assets* provide guidance on the recognition of assets arising from development.

11   In accordance with IAS 37 *Provisions, Contingent Liabilities and Contingent Assets* an entity recognises any obligations for removal and restoration that are incurred during a particular period as a consequence of having undertaken the exploration for and evaluation of mineral resources.

Measurement after recognition

12   After recognition, an entity shall apply either the cost model or the revaluation model to the exploration and evaluation assets. If the revaluation model is applied (either the model in IAS 16 *Property, Plant and Equipment* or the model in IAS 38) it shall be consistent with the classification of the assets (see paragraph 15).

Changes in accounting policies

13   An entity may change its accounting policies for exploration and evaluation expenditures if the change makes the financial statements more relevant to the economic decision-making needs of users and no less reliable, or more reliable and no less relevant to those needs. An entity shall judge relevance and reliability using the criteria in IAS 8.

14   To justify changing its accounting policies for exploration and evaluation expenditures, an entity shall demonstrate that the change brings its financial statements closer to meeting the criteria in IAS 8, but the change need not achieve full compliance with those criteria.

Presentation

Classification of exploration and evaluation assets

15   An entity shall classify exploration and evaluation assets as tangible or intangible according to the nature of the assets acquired and apply the classification consistently.

16   Some exploration and evaluation assets are treated as intangible (eg drilling rights), whereas others are tangible (eg vehicles and drilling rigs). To the extent that a tangible asset is consumed in developing an intangible asset, the amount reflecting that consumption is part of the cost of the intangible asset. However, using a tangible asset to develop an intangible asset does not change a tangible asset into an intangible asset.

Reclassification of exploration and evaluation assets

17   An exploration and evaluation asset shall no longer be classified as such when the technical feasibility and commercial viability of extracting a mineral resource are demonstrable. Exploration and evaluation assets shall be assessed for impairment, and any impairment loss recognised, before reclassification.

Impairment

Recognition and measurement

18   Exploration and evaluation assets shall be assessed for impairment when facts and circumstances suggest that the carrying amount of an exploration and evaluation asset may exceed its recoverable amount. When facts and circumstances suggest that the carrying amount exceeds the recoverable amount, an entity shall measure, present and disclose any resulting impairment loss in accordance with IAS 36, except as provided by paragraph 21 below.

19   For the purposes of exploration and evaluation assets only, paragraph 20 of this IFRS shall be applied rather than paragraphs 8–17 of IAS 36 when identifying an exploration and evaluation asset that may be impaired. Paragraph 20 uses the term 'assets' but applies equally to separate exploration and evaluation assets or a cash-generating unit.

Appendix A
Defined terms

This appendix is an integral part of the IFRS.

exploration and evaluation assets	**Exploration and evaluation expenditures** recognised as assets in accordance with the entity's accounting policy.
exploration and evaluation expenditures	Expenditures incurred by an entity in connection with the **exploration for and evaluation of mineral resources** before the technical feasibility and commercial viability of extracting a mineral resource are demonstrable.
exploration for and evaluation of mineral resources	The search for mineral resources, including minerals, oil, natural gas and similar non-regenerative resources after the entity has obtained legal rights to explore in a specific area, as well as the determination of the technical feasibility and commercial viability of extracting the mineral resource.

Appendix B
Amendments to other IFRSs

The amendments in this appendix shall be applied for annual periods beginning on or after 1 January 2006. If an entity applies this IFRS for an earlier period, these amendments shall be applied for that earlier period.

* * * * *

The amendments contained in this appendix when this IFRS was issued in 2004 have been incorporated into the relevant IFRSs published in this volume.

Approval by the Board of IFRS 6 issued in December 2004

International Financial Reporting Standard 6 *Exploration for and Evaluation of Mineral Resources* was approved for issue by ten of the fourteen members of the International Accounting Standards Board. Messrs Garnett, Leisenring, McGregor and Smith dissented. Their dissenting opinions are set out after the Basis for Conclusions.

Sir David Tweedie	Chairman
Thomas E Jones	Vice-Chairman
Mary E Barth	
Hans-Georg Bruns	
Anthony T Cope	
Jan Engström	
Robert P Garnett	
Gilbert Gélard	
James J Leisenring	
Warren J McGregor	
Patricia L O'Malley	
John T Smith	
Geoffrey Whittington	
Tatsumi Yamada	

Approval by the Board of Amendments to IFRS 1 and IFRS 6 issued in June 2005

These Amendments to International Financial Reporting Standard 1 *First-time Adoption of International Financial Reporting Standards* and International Financial Reporting Standard 6 *Exploration for and Evaluation of Mineral Resources* were approved for issue by the fourteen members of the International Accounting Standards Board.

Sir David Tweedie	Chairman
Thomas E Jones	Vice-Chairman
Mary E Barth	
Hans-Georg Bruns	
Anthony T Cope	
Jan Engström	
Robert P Garnett	
Gilbert Gélard	
James J Leisenring	
Warren J McGregor	
Patricia L O'Malley	
John T Smith	
Geoffrey Whittington	
Tatsumi Yamada	

Financial Instruments: Disclosures

In April 2001 the International Accounting Standards Board (Board) adopted IAS 30 *Disclosures in the Financial Statements of Banks and Similar Financial Institutions*, which had originally been issued by the International Accounting Standards Committee in August 1990.

In August 2005 the Board issued IFRS 7 *Financial Instruments*, which replaced IAS 30 and carried forward the disclosure requirements in IAS 32 *Financial Instruments: Disclosure and Presentation*. IAS 32 was subsequently renamed as IAS 32 *Financial Instruments: Presentation*. IAS 1 *Presentation of Financial Statements* (as revised in 2007) amended the terminology used throughout IFRS, including IFRS 7. In March 2009 the IASB enhanced the disclosures about fair value and liquidity risks in IFRS 7.

The Board also amended IFRS 7 to reflect that a new financial instruments Standard was issued—IFRS 9 *Financial Instruments*, which related to the classification of financial assets and financial liabilities.

IFRS 7 was also amended in October 2010 to require entities to supplement disclosures for all transferred financial assets that are not derecognised where there has been some continuing involvement in a transferred asset. The Board amended IFRS 7 in December 2011 to improve disclosures in netting arrangements associated with financial assets and financial liabilities.

In September 2019 the Board amended IFRS 9 and IAS 39 by issuing *Interest Rate Benchmark Reform* to provide specific exceptions to hedge accounting requirements in IFRS 9 and IAS 39 for (a) highly probable requirement; (b) prospective assessments; (c) retrospective assessment (IAS 39 only); and (d) separately identifiable risk components. *Interest Rate Benchmark Reform* also amended IFRS 7 to add specific disclosure requirements for hedging relationships to which an entity applies the exceptions in IFRS 9 or IAS 39.

In August 2020 the Board issued *Interest Rate Benchmark Reform—Phase 2* which amended requirements in IFRS 9, IAS 39, IFRS 7, IFRS 4 and IFRS 16 relating to:

* changes in the basis for determining contractual cash flows of financial assets, financial liabilities and lease liabilities;

* hedge accounting; and

* disclosures.

The Phase 2 amendments apply only to changes required by the interest rate benchmark reform to financial instruments and hedging relationships.

Other Standards have made minor amendments to IFRS 7. They include *Limited Exemption from Comparative IFRS 7 Disclosures for First-time Adopters* (Amendments to IFRS 1) (issued January 2010), *Improvements to IFRSs* (issued May 2010), IFRS 10 *Consolidated Financial Statements* (issued May 2011), IFRS 11 *Joint Arrangements* (issued May 2011), IFRS 13 *Fair Value Measurement* (issued May 2011), *Presentation of Items of Other Comprehensive Income* (Amendments to IAS 1) (issued June 2011), *Mandatory Effective Date and Transition Disclosures* (Amendments to IFRS 9 (2009), IFRS 9 (2010) and IFRS 7) (issued December

2011), *Investment Entities* (Amendments to IFRS 10, IFRS 12 and IAS 27) (issued October 2012), IFRS 9 *Financial Instruments* (Hedge Accounting and amendments to IFRS 9, IFRS 7 and IAS 39) (issued November 2013), *Annual Improvements to IFRSs 2012–2014 Cycle* (issued September 2014), *Disclosure Initiative* (Amendments to IAS 1) (issued December 2014), IFRS 16 *Leases* (issued January 2016) and *Annual Improvements to IFRS Standards 2014–2016 Cycle* (issued December 2016).

Contents

continued...

...continued

FOR THE ACCOMPANYING GUIDANCE LISTED BELOW, SEE PART B OF THIS EDITION

IMPLEMENTATION GUIDANCE

APPENDIX

Amendments to guidance on other IFRSs

FOR THE BASIS FOR CONCLUSIONS, SEE PART C OF THIS EDITION

BASIS FOR CONCLUSIONS

APPENDIX TO THE BASIS FOR CONCLUSIONS

Amendments to Basis for Conclusions on other IFRSs

International Financial Reporting Standard 7 *Financial Instruments: Disclosures* (IFRS 7) is set out in paragraphs 1–45 and Appendices A–C. All the paragraphs have equal authority. Paragraphs in **bold type** state the main principles. Terms defined in Appendix A are in *italics* the first time they appear in the Standard. Definitions of other terms are given in the Glossary for International Financial Reporting Standards. IFRS 7 should be read in the context of its objective and the Basis for Conclusions, the *Preface to IFRS Standards* and the *Conceptual Framework for Financial Reporting*. IAS 8 *Accounting Policies, Changes in Accounting Estimates and Errors* provides a basis for selecting and applying accounting policies in the absence of explicit guidance.

International Financial Reporting Standard 7
Financial Instruments: Disclosures

Objective

1   The objective of this IFRS is to require entities to provide disclosures in their financial statements that enable users to evaluate:

    (a)   the significance of financial instruments for the entity's financial position and performance; and

    (b)   the nature and extent of risks arising from financial instruments to which the entity is exposed during the period and at the end of the reporting period, and how the entity manages those risks.

2   The principles in this IFRS complement the principles for recognising, measuring and presenting financial assets and financial liabilities in IAS 32 *Financial Instruments: Presentation* and IFRS 9 *Financial Instruments*.

Scope

3   This IFRS shall be applied by all entities to all types of financial instruments, except:

    (a)   those interests in subsidiaries, associates or joint ventures that are accounted for in accordance with IFRS 10 *Consolidated Financial Statements*, IAS 27 *Separate Financial Statements* or IAS 28 *Investments in Associates and Joint Ventures*. However, in some cases, IFRS 10, IAS 27 or IAS 28 require or permit an entity to account for an interest in a subsidiary, associate or joint venture using IFRS 9; in those cases, entities shall apply the requirements of this IFRS and, for those measured at fair value, the requirements of IFRS 13 *Fair Value Measurement*. Entities shall also apply this IFRS to all derivatives linked to interests in subsidiaries, associates or joint ventures unless the derivative meets the definition of an equity instrument in IAS 32.

    (b)   employers' rights and obligations arising from employee benefit plans, to which IAS 19 *Employee Benefits* applies.

    (c)   [deleted]

    (d)   insurance contracts as defined in IFRS 4 *Insurance Contracts*. However, this IFRS applies to derivatives that are embedded in insurance contracts if IFRS 9 requires the entity to account for them separately. Moreover, an issuer shall apply this IFRS to *financial guarantee contracts* if the issuer applies IFRS 9 in recognising and measuring the contracts, but shall apply IFRS 4 if the issuer elects, in accordance with paragraph 4(d) of IFRS 4, to apply IFRS 4 in recognising and measuring them.

(e) financial instruments, contracts and obligations under share-based payment transactions to which IFRS 2 *Share-based Payment* applies, except that this IFRS applies to contracts within the scope of IFRS 9.

(f) instruments that are required to be classified as equity instruments in accordance with paragraphs 16A and 16B or paragraphs 16C and 16D of IAS 32.

4 This IFRS applies to recognised and unrecognised financial instruments. Recognised financial instruments include financial assets and financial liabilities that are within the scope of IFRS 9. Unrecognised financial instruments include some financial instruments that, although outside the scope of IFRS 9, are within the scope of this IFRS.

5 This IFRS applies to contracts to buy or sell a non-financial item that are within the scope of IFRS 9.

5A The credit risk disclosure requirements in paragraphs 35A–35N apply to those rights that IFRS 15 *Revenue from Contracts with Customers* specifies are accounted for in accordance with IFRS 9 for the purposes of recognising impairment gains or losses. Any reference to financial assets or financial instruments in these paragraphs shall include those rights unless otherwise specified.

Classes of financial instruments and level of disclosure

6 When this IFRS requires disclosures by class of financial instrument, an entity shall group financial instruments into classes that are appropriate to the nature of the information disclosed and that take into account the characteristics of those financial instruments. An entity shall provide sufficient information to permit reconciliation to the line items presented in the statement of financial position.

Significance of financial instruments for financial position and performance

7 An entity shall disclose information that enables users of its financial statements to evaluate the significance of financial instruments for its financial position and performance.

Statement of financial position

Categories of financial assets and financial liabilities

8 The carrying amounts of each of the following categories, as specified in IFRS 9, shall be disclosed either in the statement of financial position or in the notes:

(a) financial assets measured at fair value through profit or loss, showing separately (i) those designated as such upon initial recognition or subsequently in accordance with paragraph 6.7.1 of IFRS 9 and (ii) those mandatorily measured at fair value through profit or loss in accordance with IFRS 9.

(b)–(d)   [deleted]

(e)   financial liabilities at fair value through profit or loss, showing separately (i) those designated as such upon initial recognition or subsequently in accordance with paragraph 6.7.1 of IFRS 9 and (ii) those that meet the definition of held for trading in IFRS 9.

(f)   financial assets measured at amortised cost.

(g)   financial liabilities measured at amortised cost.

(h)   financial assets measured at fair value through other comprehensive income, showing separately (i) financial assets that are measured at fair value through other comprehensive income in accordance with paragraph 4.1.2A of IFRS 9; and (ii) investments in equity instruments designated as such upon initial recognition in accordance with paragraph 5.7.5 of IFRS 9.

Financial assets or financial liabilities at fair value through profit or loss

9   If the entity has designated as measured at fair value through profit or loss a financial asset (or group of financial assets) that would otherwise be measured at fair value through other comprehensive income or amortised cost, it shall disclose:

(a)   the maximum exposure to *credit risk* (see paragraph 36(a)) of the financial asset (or group of financial assets) at the end of the reporting period.

(b)   the amount by which any related credit derivatives or similar instruments mitigate that maximum exposure to credit risk (see paragraph 36(b)).

(c)   the amount of change, during the period and cumulatively, in the fair value of the financial asset (or group of financial assets) that is attributable to changes in the credit risk of the financial asset determined either:

(i)   as the amount of change in its fair value that is not attributable to changes in market conditions that give rise to *market risk*; or

(ii)   using an alternative method the entity believes more faithfully represents the amount of change in its fair value that is attributable to changes in the credit risk of the asset.

Changes in market conditions that give rise to market risk include changes in an observed (benchmark) interest rate, commodity price, foreign exchange rate or index of prices or rates.

(d)   the amount of the change in the fair value of any related credit derivatives or similar instruments that has occurred during the period and cumulatively since the financial asset was designated.

10 If the entity has designated a financial liability as at fair value through profit or loss in accordance with paragraph 4.2.2 of IFRS 9 and is required to present the effects of changes in that liability's credit risk in other comprehensive income (see paragraph 5.7.7 of IFRS 9), it shall disclose:

 (a) the amount of change, cumulatively, in the fair value of the financial liability that is attributable to changes in the credit risk of that liability (see paragraphs B5.7.13–B5.7.20 of IFRS 9 for guidance on determining the effects of changes in a liability's credit risk).

 (b) the difference between the financial liability's carrying amount and the amount the entity would be contractually required to pay at maturity to the holder of the obligation.

 (c) any transfers of the cumulative gain or loss within equity during the period including the reason for such transfers.

 (d) if a liability is derecognised during the period, the amount (if any) presented in other comprehensive income that was realised at derecognition.

10A If an entity has designated a financial liability as at fair value through profit or loss in accordance with paragraph 4.2.2 of IFRS 9 and is required to present all changes in the fair value of that liability (including the effects of changes in the credit risk of the liability) in profit or loss (see paragraphs 5.7.7 and 5.7.8 of IFRS 9), it shall disclose:

 (a) the amount of change, during the period and cumulatively, in the fair value of the financial liability that is attributable to changes in the credit risk of that liability (see paragraphs B5.7.13–B5.7.20 of IFRS 9 for guidance on determining the effects of changes in a liability's credit risk); and

 (b) the difference between the financial liability's carrying amount and the amount the entity would be contractually required to pay at maturity to the holder of the obligation.

11 The entity shall also disclose:

 (a) a detailed description of the methods used to comply with the requirements in paragraphs 9(c), 10(a) and 10A(a) and paragraph 5.7.7(a) of IFRS 9, including an explanation of why the method is appropriate.

 (b) if the entity believes that the disclosure it has given, either in the statement of financial position or in the notes, to comply with the requirements in paragraph 9(c), 10(a) or 10A(a) or paragraph 5.7.7(a) of IFRS 9 does not faithfully represent the change in the fair value of the financial asset or financial liability attributable to changes in its credit risk, the reasons for reaching this conclusion and the factors it believes are relevant.

(c)   a detailed description of the methodology or methodologies used to determine whether presenting the effects of changes in a liability's credit risk in other comprehensive income would create or enlarge an accounting mismatch in profit or loss (see paragraphs 5.7.7 and 5.7.8 of IFRS 9). If an entity is required to present the effects of changes in a liability's credit risk in profit or loss (see paragraph 5.7.8 of IFRS 9), the disclosure must include a detailed description of the economic relationship described in paragraph B5.7.6 of IFRS 9.

Investments in equity instruments designated at fair value through other comprehensive income

11A   If an entity has designated investments in equity instruments to be measured at fair value through other comprehensive income, as permitted by paragraph 5.7.5 of IFRS 9, it shall disclose:

(a)   which investments in equity instruments have been designated to be measured at fair value through other comprehensive income.

(b)   the reasons for using this presentation alternative.

(c)   the fair value of each such investment at the end of the reporting period.

(d)   dividends recognised during the period, showing separately those related to investments derecognised during the reporting period and those related to investments held at the end of the reporting period.

(e)   any transfers of the cumulative gain or loss within equity during the period including the reason for such transfers.

11B   If an entity derecognised investments in equity instruments measured at fair value through other comprehensive income during the reporting period, it shall disclose:

(a)   the reasons for disposing of the investments.

(b)   the fair value of the investments at the date of derecognition.

(c)   the cumulative gain or loss on disposal.

Reclassification

12–12A   [Deleted]

12B   An entity shall disclose if, in the current or previous reporting periods, it has reclassified any financial assets in accordance with paragraph 4.4.1 of IFRS 9. For each such event, an entity shall disclose:

(a)   the date of reclassification.

(b)   a detailed explanation of the change in business model and a qualitative description of its effect on the entity's financial statements.

(c)   the amount reclassified into and out of each category.

12C   For each reporting period following reclassification until derecognition, an entity shall disclose for assets reclassified out of the fair value through profit or loss category so that they are measured at amortised cost or fair value through other comprehensive income in accordance with paragraph 4.4.1 of IFRS 9:

(a)   the effective interest rate determined on the date of reclassification; and

(b)   the interest revenue recognised.

12D   If, since its last annual reporting date, an entity has reclassified financial assets out of the fair value through other comprehensive income category so that they are measured at amortised cost or out of the fair value through profit or loss category so that they are measured at amortised cost or fair value through other comprehensive income it shall disclose:

(a)   the fair value of the financial assets at the end of the reporting period; and

(b)   the fair value gain or loss that would have been recognised in profit or loss or other comprehensive income during the reporting period if the financial assets had not been reclassified.

13   [Deleted]

Offsetting financial assets and financial liabilities

13A   The disclosures in paragraphs 13B–13E supplement the other disclosure requirements of this IFRS and are required for all recognised financial instruments that are set off in accordance with paragraph 42 of IAS 32. These disclosures also apply to recognised financial instruments that are subject to an enforceable master netting arrangement or similar agreement, irrespective of whether they are set off in accordance with paragraph 42 of IAS 32.

13B   An entity shall disclose information to enable users of its financial statements to evaluate the effect or potential effect of netting arrangements on the entity's financial position. This includes the effect or potential effect of rights of set-off associated with the entity's recognised financial assets and recognised financial liabilities that are within the scope of paragraph 13A.

13C   To meet the objective in paragraph 13B, an entity shall disclose, at the end of the reporting period, the following quantitative information separately for recognised financial assets and recognised financial liabilities that are within the scope of paragraph 13A:

(a)   the gross amounts of those recognised financial assets and recognised financial liabilities;

(b)   the amounts that are set off in accordance with the criteria in paragraph 42 of IAS 32 when determining the net amounts presented in the statement of financial position;

(c)   the net amounts presented in the statement of financial position;

(d)   the amounts subject to an enforceable master netting arrangement or similar agreement that are not otherwise included in paragraph 13C(b), including:

    (i)   amounts related to recognised financial instruments that do not meet some or all of the offsetting criteria in paragraph 42 of IAS 32; and

    (ii)   amounts related to financial collateral (including cash collateral); and

(e)   the net amount after deducting the amounts in (d) from the amounts in (c) above.

The information required by this paragraph shall be presented in a tabular format, separately for financial assets and financial liabilities, unless another format is more appropriate.

13D   The total amount disclosed in accordance with paragraph 13C(d) for an instrument shall be limited to the amount in paragraph 13C(c) for that instrument.

13E   An entity shall include a description in the disclosures of the rights of set-off associated with the entity's recognised financial assets and recognised financial liabilities subject to enforceable master netting arrangements and similar agreements that are disclosed in accordance with paragraph 13C(d), including the nature of those rights.

13F   If the information required by paragraphs 13B–13E is disclosed in more than one note to the financial statements, an entity shall cross-refer between those notes.

Collateral

14   An entity shall disclose:

(a)   the carrying amount of financial assets it has pledged as collateral for liabilities or contingent liabilities, including amounts that have been reclassified in accordance with paragraph 3.2.23(a) of IFRS 9; and

(b)   the terms and conditions relating to its pledge.

15   When an entity holds collateral (of financial or non-financial assets) and is permitted to sell or repledge the collateral in the absence of default by the owner of the collateral, it shall disclose:

(a)   the fair value of the collateral held;

(b)   the fair value of any such collateral sold or repledged, and whether the entity has an obligation to return it; and

(c)   the terms and conditions associated with its use of the collateral.

Allowance account for credit losses

16   [Deleted]

16A   The carrying amount of financial assets measured at fair value through other comprehensive income in accordance with paragraph 4.1.2A of IFRS 9 is not reduced by a loss allowance and an entity shall not present the loss allowance separately in the statement of financial position as a reduction of the carrying amount of the financial asset. However, an entity shall disclose the loss allowance in the notes to the financial statements.

Compound financial instruments with multiple embedded derivatives

17   If an entity has issued an instrument that contains both a liability and an equity component (see paragraph 28 of IAS 32) and the instrument has multiple embedded derivatives whose values are interdependent (such as a callable convertible debt instrument), it shall disclose the existence of those features.

Defaults and breaches

18   For *loans payable* recognised at the end of the reporting period, an entity shall disclose:

(a)   details of any defaults during the period of principal, interest, sinking fund, or redemption terms of those loans payable;

(b)   the carrying amount of the loans payable in default at the end of the reporting period; and

(c)   whether the default was remedied, or the terms of the loans payable were renegotiated, before the financial statements were authorised for issue.

19   If, during the period, there were breaches of loan agreement terms other than those described in paragraph 18, an entity shall disclose the same information as required by paragraph 18 if those breaches permitted the lender to demand accelerated repayment (unless the breaches were remedied, or the terms of the loan were renegotiated, on or before the end of the reporting period).

Statement of comprehensive income

Items of income, expense, gains or losses

20   An entity shall disclose the following items of income, expense, gains or losses either in the statement of comprehensive income or in the notes:

(a)   net gains or net losses on:

(i)   financial assets or financial liabilities measured at fair value through profit or loss, showing separately those on financial assets or financial liabilities designated as such upon initial recognition or subsequently in accordance with paragraph 6.7.1 of IFRS 9, and those on financial assets or financial liabilities that are mandatorily measured at fair value through profit or loss in accordance with IFRS 9 (eg financial liabilities that meet the definition of held for trading in IFRS 9). For financial liabilities designated as at fair value through profit or loss, an entity shall show separately the amount of gain or loss recognised in other comprehensive income and the amount recognised in profit or loss.

    (ii)–(iv) [deleted]

    (v)   financial liabilities measured at amortised cost.

    (vi)   financial assets measured at amortised cost.

    (vii)   investments in equity instruments designated at fair value through other comprehensive income in accordance with paragraph 5.7.5 of IFRS 9.

    (viii)   financial assets measured at fair value through other comprehensive income in accordance with paragraph 4.1.2A of IFRS 9, showing separately the amount of gain or loss recognised in other comprehensive income during the period and the amount reclassified upon derecognition from accumulated other comprehensive income to profit or loss for the period.

    (b)   total interest revenue and total interest expense (calculated using the effective interest method) for financial assets that are measured at amortised cost or that are measured at fair value through other comprehensive income in accordance with paragraph 4.1.2A of IFRS 9 (showing these amounts separately); or financial liabilities that are not measured at fair value through profit or loss.

    (c)   fee income and expense (other than amounts included in determining the effective interest rate) arising from:

    (i)   financial assets and financial liabilities that are not at fair value through profit or loss; and

    (ii)   trust and other fiduciary activities that result in the holding or investing of assets on behalf of individuals, trusts, retirement benefit plans, and other institutions.

    (d)   [deleted]

    (e)   [deleted]

20A   An entity shall disclose an analysis of the gain or loss recognised in the statement of comprehensive income arising from the derecognition of financial assets measured at amortised cost, showing separately gains and losses arising from derecognition of those financial assets. This disclosure shall include the reasons for derecognising those financial assets.

Other disclosures

Accounting policies

21 In accordance with paragraph 117 of IAS 1 *Presentation of Financial Statements* (as revised in 2007), an entity discloses its significant accounting policies comprising the measurement basis (or bases) used in preparing the financial statements and the other accounting policies used that are relevant to an understanding of the financial statements.

Hedge accounting

21A An entity shall apply the disclosure requirements in paragraphs 21B–24F for those risk exposures that an entity hedges and for which it elects to apply hedge accounting. Hedge accounting disclosures shall provide information about:

(a) an entity's risk management strategy and how it is applied to manage risk;

(b) how the entity's hedging activities may affect the amount, timing and uncertainty of its future cash flows; and

(c) the effect that hedge accounting has had on the entity's statement of financial position, statement of comprehensive income and statement of changes in equity.

21B An entity shall present the required disclosures in a single note or separate section in its financial statements. However, an entity need not duplicate information that is already presented elsewhere, provided that the information is incorporated by cross-reference from the financial statements to some other statement, such as a management commentary or risk report, that is available to users of the financial statements on the same terms as the financial statements and at the same time. Without the information incorporated by cross-reference, the financial statements are incomplete.

21C When paragraphs 22A–24F require the entity to separate by risk category the information disclosed, the entity shall determine each risk category on the basis of the risk exposures an entity decides to hedge and for which hedge accounting is applied. An entity shall determine risk categories consistently for all hedge accounting disclosures.

21D To meet the objectives in paragraph 21A, an entity shall (except as otherwise specified below) determine how much detail to disclose, how much emphasis to place on different aspects of the disclosure requirements, the appropriate level of aggregation or disaggregation, and whether users of financial statements need additional explanations to evaluate the quantitative information disclosed. However, an entity shall use the same level of aggregation or disaggregation it uses for disclosure requirements of related information in this IFRS and IFRS 13 *Fair Value Measurement*.

The risk management strategy

22 [Deleted]

22A An entity shall explain its risk management strategy for each risk category of risk exposures that it decides to hedge and for which hedge accounting is applied. This explanation should enable users of financial statements to evaluate (for example):

(a) how each risk arises.

(b) how the entity manages each risk; this includes whether the entity hedges an item in its entirety for all risks or hedges a risk component (or components) of an item and why.

(c) the extent of risk exposures that the entity manages.

22B To meet the requirements in paragraph 22A, the information should include (but is not limited to) a description of:

(a) the hedging instruments that are used (and how they are used) to hedge risk exposures;

(b) how the entity determines the economic relationship between the hedged item and the hedging instrument for the purpose of assessing hedge effectiveness; and

(c) how the entity establishes the hedge ratio and what the sources of hedge ineffectiveness are.

22C When an entity designates a specific risk component as a hedged item (see paragraph 6.3.7 of IFRS 9) it shall provide, in addition to the disclosures required by paragraphs 22A and 22B, qualitative or quantitative information about:

(a) how the entity determined the risk component that is designated as the hedged item (including a description of the nature of the relationship between the risk component and the item as a whole); and

(b) how the risk component relates to the item in its entirety (for example, the designated risk component historically covered on average 80 per cent of the changes in fair value of the item as a whole).

The amount, timing and uncertainty of future cash flows

23 [Deleted]

23A Unless exempted by paragraph 23C, an entity shall disclose by risk category quantitative information to allow users of its financial statements to evaluate the terms and conditions of hedging instruments and how they affect the amount, timing and uncertainty of future cash flows of the entity.

23B To meet the requirement in paragraph 23A, an entity shall provide a breakdown that discloses:

(a) a profile of the timing of the nominal amount of the hedging instrument; and

(b)   if applicable, the average price or rate (for example strike or forward prices etc) of the hedging instrument.

23C   In situations in which an entity frequently resets (ie discontinues and restarts) hedging relationships because both the hedging instrument and the hedged item frequently change (ie the entity uses a dynamic process in which both the exposure and the hedging instruments used to manage that exposure do not remain the same for long—such as in the example in paragraph B6.5.24(b) of IFRS 9) the entity:

     (a)   is exempt from providing the disclosures required by paragraphs 23A and 23B.

     (b)   shall disclose:

          (i)   information about what the ultimate risk management strategy is in relation to those hedging relationships;

          (ii)   a description of how it reflects its risk management strategy by using hedge accounting and designating those particular hedging relationships; and

          (iii)   an indication of how frequently the hedging relationships are discontinued and restarted as part of the entity's process in relation to those hedging relationships.

23D   An entity shall disclose by risk category a description of the sources of hedge ineffectiveness that are expected to affect the hedging relationship during its term.

23E   If other sources of hedge ineffectiveness emerge in a hedging relationship, an entity shall disclose those sources by risk category and explain the resulting hedge ineffectiveness.

23F   For cash flow hedges, an entity shall disclose a description of any forecast transaction for which hedge accounting had been used in the previous period, but which is no longer expected to occur.

The effects of hedge accounting on financial position and performance

24   [Deleted]

24A   An entity shall disclose, in a tabular format, the following amounts related to items designated as hedging instruments separately by risk category for each type of hedge (fair value hedge, cash flow hedge or hedge of a net investment in a foreign operation):

     (a)   the carrying amount of the hedging instruments (financial assets separately from financial liabilities);

     (b)   the line item in the statement of financial position that includes the hedging instrument;

     (c)   the change in fair value of the hedging instrument used as the basis for recognising hedge ineffectiveness for the period; and

(d)   the nominal amounts (including quantities such as tonnes or cubic metres) of the hedging instruments.

24B   An entity shall disclose, in a tabular format, the following amounts related to hedged items separately by risk category for the types of hedges as follows:

     (a)   for fair value hedges:

         (i)   the carrying amount of the hedged item recognised in the statement of financial position (presenting assets separately from liabilities);

         (ii)   the accumulated amount of fair value hedge adjustments on the hedged item included in the carrying amount of the hedged item recognised in the statement of financial position (presenting assets separately from liabilities);

         (iii)   the line item in the statement of financial position that includes the hedged item;

         (iv)   the change in value of the hedged item used as the basis for recognising hedge ineffectiveness for the period; and

         (v)   the accumulated amount of fair value hedge adjustments remaining in the statement of financial position for any hedged items that have ceased to be adjusted for hedging gains and losses in accordance with paragraph 6.5.10 of IFRS 9.

     (b)   for cash flow hedges and hedges of a net investment in a foreign operation:

         (i)   the change in value of the hedged item used as the basis for recognising hedge ineffectiveness for the period (ie for cash flow hedges the change in value used to determine the recognised hedge ineffectiveness in accordance with paragraph 6.5.11(c) of IFRS 9);

         (ii)   the balances in the cash flow hedge reserve and the foreign currency translation reserve for continuing hedges that are accounted for in accordance with paragraphs 6.5.11 and 6.5.13(a) of IFRS 9; and

         (iii)   the balances remaining in the cash flow hedge reserve and the foreign currency translation reserve from any hedging relationships for which hedge accounting is no longer applied.

24C   An entity shall disclose, in a tabular format, the following amounts separately by risk category for the types of hedges as follows:

     (a)   for fair value hedges:

         (i)   hedge ineffectiveness—ie the difference between the hedging gains or losses of the hedging instrument and the hedged item —recognised in profit or loss (or other comprehensive income for hedges of an equity instrument for which an entity has elected to present changes in fair value in other comprehensive income in accordance with paragraph 5.7.5 of IFRS 9); and

    (ii)   the line item in the statement of comprehensive income that includes the recognised hedge ineffectiveness.

(b)   for cash flow hedges and hedges of a net investment in a foreign operation:

    (i)   hedging gains or losses of the reporting period that were recognised in other comprehensive income;

    (ii)   hedge ineffectiveness recognised in profit or loss;

    (iii)   the line item in the statement of comprehensive income that includes the recognised hedge ineffectiveness;

    (iv)   the amount reclassified from the cash flow hedge reserve or the foreign currency translation reserve into profit or loss as a reclassification adjustment (see IAS 1) (differentiating between amounts for which hedge accounting had previously been used, but for which the hedged future cash flows are no longer expected to occur, and amounts that have been transferred because the hedged item has affected profit or loss);

    (v)   the line item in the statement of comprehensive income that includes the reclassification adjustment (see IAS 1); and

    (vi)   for hedges of net positions, the hedging gains or losses recognised in a separate line item in the statement of comprehensive income (see paragraph 6.6.4 of IFRS 9).

24D   When the volume of hedging relationships to which the exemption in paragraph 23C applies is unrepresentative of normal volumes during the period (ie the volume at the reporting date does not reflect the volumes during the period) an entity shall disclose that fact and the reason it believes the volumes are unrepresentative.

24E   An entity shall provide a reconciliation of each component of equity and an analysis of other comprehensive income in accordance with IAS 1 that, taken together:

(a)   differentiates, at a minimum, between the amounts that relate to the disclosures in paragraph 24C(b)(i) and (b)(iv) as well as the amounts accounted for in accordance with paragraph 6.5.11(d)(i) and (d)(iii) of IFRS 9;

(b)   differentiates between the amounts associated with the time value of options that hedge transaction related hedged items and the amounts associated with the time value of options that hedge time-period related hedged items when an entity accounts for the time value of an option in accordance with paragraph 6.5.15 of IFRS 9; and

(c)   differentiates between the amounts associated with forward elements of forward contracts and the foreign currency basis spreads of financial instruments that hedge transaction related hedged items, and the amounts associated with forward elements of forward contracts and the foreign currency basis spreads of financial instruments that hedge time-period related hedged items when an entity accounts for those amounts in accordance with paragraph 6.5.16 of IFRS 9.

24F   An entity shall disclose the information required in paragraph 24E separately by risk category. This disaggregation by risk may be provided in the notes to the financial statements.

Option to designate a credit exposure as measured at fair value through profit or loss

24G   If an entity designated a financial instrument, or a proportion of it, as measured at fair value through profit or loss because it uses a credit derivative to manage the credit risk of that financial instrument it shall disclose:

(a)   for credit derivatives that have been used to manage the credit risk of financial instruments designated as measured at fair value through profit or loss in accordance with paragraph 6.7.1 of IFRS 9, a reconciliation of each of the nominal amount and the fair value at the beginning and at the end of the period;

(b)   the gain or loss recognised in profit or loss on designation of a financial instrument, or a proportion of it, as measured at fair value through profit or loss in accordance with paragraph 6.7.1 of IFRS 9; and

(c)   on discontinuation of measuring a financial instrument, or a proportion of it, at fair value through profit or loss, that financial instrument's fair value that has become the new carrying amount in accordance with paragraph 6.7.4 of IFRS 9 and the related nominal or principal amount (except for providing comparative information in accordance with IAS 1, an entity does not need to continue this disclosure in subsequent periods).

Uncertainty arising from interest rate benchmark reform

24H   For hedging relationships to which an entity applies the exceptions set out in paragraphs 6.8.4–6.8.12 of IFRS 9 or paragraphs 102D–102N of IAS 39, an entity shall disclose:

(a)   the significant interest rate benchmarks to which the entity's hedging relationships are exposed;

(b)   the extent of the risk exposure the entity manages that is directly affected by the interest rate benchmark reform;

(c)   how the entity is managing the process to transition to alternative benchmark rates;

(d) a description of significant assumptions or judgements the entity made in applying these paragraphs (for example, assumptions or judgements about when the uncertainty arising from interest rate benchmark reform is no longer present with respect to the timing and the amount of the interest rate benchmark-based cash flows); and

(e) the nominal amount of the hedging instruments in those hedging relationships.

Additional disclosures related to interest rate benchmark reform

24I To enable users of financial statements to understand the effect of interest rate benchmark reform on an entity's financial instruments and risk management strategy, an entity shall disclose information about:

(a) the nature and extent of risks to which the entity is exposed arising from financial instruments subject to interest rate benchmark reform, and how the entity manages these risks; and

(b) the entity's progress in completing the transition to alternative benchmark rates, and how the entity is managing the transition.

24J To meet the objectives in paragraph 24I, an entity shall disclose:

(a) how the entity is managing the transition to alternative benchmark rates, its progress at the reporting date and the risks to which it is exposed arising from financial instruments because of the transition;

(b) disaggregated by significant interest rate benchmark subject to interest rate benchmark reform, quantitative information about financial instruments that have yet to transition to an alternative benchmark rate as at the end of the reporting period, showing separately:

(i) non-derivative financial assets;

(ii) non-derivative financial liabilities; and

(iii) derivatives; and

(c) if the risks identified in paragraph 24J(a) have resulted in changes to an entity's risk management strategy (see paragraph 22A), a description of these changes.

Fair value

25 Except as set out in paragraph 29, for each class of financial assets and financial liabilities (see paragraph 6), an entity shall disclose the fair value of that class of assets and liabilities in a way that permits it to be compared with its carrying amount.

26 In disclosing fair values, an entity shall group financial assets and financial liabilities into classes, but shall offset them only to the extent that their carrying amounts are offset in the statement of financial position.

27–27B [Deleted]

28   In some cases, an entity does not recognise a gain or loss on initial recognition of a financial asset or financial liability because the fair value is neither evidenced by a quoted price in an active market for an identical asset or liability (ie a Level 1 input) nor based on a valuation technique that uses only data from observable markets (see paragraph B5.1.2A of IFRS 9). In such cases, the entity shall disclose by class of financial asset or financial liability:

(a)   its accounting policy for recognising in profit or loss the difference between the fair value at initial recognition and the transaction price to reflect a change in factors (including time) that market participants would take into account when pricing the asset or liability (see paragraph B5.1.2A(b) of IFRS 9).

(b)   the aggregate difference yet to be recognised in profit or loss at the beginning and end of the period and a reconciliation of changes in the balance of this difference.

(c)   why the entity concluded that the transaction price was not the best evidence of fair value, including a description of the evidence that supports the fair value.

29   Disclosures of fair value are not required:

(a)   when the carrying amount is a reasonable approximation of fair value, for example, for financial instruments such as short-term trade receivables and payables;

(b)   [deleted]

(c)   for a contract containing a discretionary participation feature (as described in IFRS 4) if the fair value of that feature cannot be measured reliably; or

(d)   for lease liabilities.

30   In the case described in paragraph 29(c), an entity shall disclose information to help users of the financial statements make their own judgements about the extent of possible differences between the carrying amount of those contracts and their fair value, including:

(a)   the fact that fair value information has not been disclosed for these instruments because their fair value cannot be measured reliably;

(b)   a description of the financial instruments, their carrying amount, and an explanation of why fair value cannot be measured reliably;

(c)   information about the market for the instruments;

(d)   information about whether and how the entity intends to dispose of the financial instruments; and

(e)   if financial instruments whose fair value previously could not be reliably measured are derecognised, that fact, their carrying amount at the time of derecognition, and the amount of gain or loss recognised.

Nature and extent of risks arising from financial instruments

31 An entity shall disclose information that enables users of its financial statements to evaluate the nature and extent of risks arising from financial instruments to which the entity is exposed at the end of the reporting period.

32 The disclosures required by paragraphs 33–42 focus on the risks that arise from financial instruments and how they have been managed. These risks typically include, but are not limited to, credit risk, *liquidity risk* and market risk.

32A Providing qualitative disclosures in the context of quantitative disclosures enables users to link related disclosures and hence form an overall picture of the nature and extent of risks arising from financial instruments. The interaction between qualitative and quantitative disclosures contributes to disclosure of information in a way that better enables users to evaluate an entity's exposure to risks.

Qualitative disclosures

33 For each type of risk arising from financial instruments, an entity shall disclose:

(a) the exposures to risk and how they arise;

(b) its objectives, policies and processes for managing the risk and the methods used to measure the risk; and

(c) any changes in (a) or (b) from the previous period.

Quantitative disclosures

34 For each type of risk arising from financial instruments, an entity shall disclose:

(a) summary quantitative data about its exposure to that risk at the end of the reporting period. This disclosure shall be based on the information provided internally to key management personnel of the entity (as defined in IAS 24 *Related Party Disclosures*), for example the entity's board of directors or chief executive officer.

(b) the disclosures required by paragraphs 35A–42, to the extent not provided in accordance with (a).

(c) concentrations of risk if not apparent from the disclosures made in accordance with (a) and (b).

35 If the quantitative data disclosed as at the end of the reporting period are unrepresentative of an entity's exposure to risk during the period, an entity shall provide further information that is representative.

Credit risk

Scope and objectives

35A   An entity shall apply the disclosure requirements in paragraphs 35F–35N to financial instruments to which the impairment requirements in IFRS 9 are applied. However:

   (a)   for trade receivables, contract assets and lease receivables, paragraph 35J(a) applies to those trade receivables, contract assets or lease receivables on which lifetime expected credit losses are recognised in accordance with paragraph 5.5.15 of IFRS 9, if those financial assets are modified while more than 30 days past due; and

   (b)   paragraph 35K(b) does not apply to lease receivables.

35B   The credit risk disclosures made in accordance with paragraphs 35F–35N shall enable users of financial statements to understand the effect of credit risk on the amount, timing and uncertainty of future cash flows. To achieve this objective, credit risk disclosures shall provide:

   (a)   information about an entity's credit risk management practices and how they relate to the recognition and measurement of expected credit losses, including the methods, assumptions and information used to measure expected credit losses;

   (b)   quantitative and qualitative information that allows users of financial statements to evaluate the amounts in the financial statements arising from expected credit losses, including changes in the amount of expected credit losses and the reasons for those changes; and

   (c)   information about an entity's credit risk exposure (ie the credit risk inherent in an entity's financial assets and commitments to extend credit) including significant credit risk concentrations.

35C   An entity need not duplicate information that is already presented elsewhere, provided that the information is incorporated by cross-reference from the financial statements to other statements, such as a management commentary or risk report that is available to users of the financial statements on the same terms as the financial statements and at the same time. Without the information incorporated by cross-reference, the financial statements are incomplete.

35D   To meet the objectives in paragraph 35B, an entity shall (except as otherwise specified) consider how much detail to disclose, how much emphasis to place on different aspects of the disclosure requirements, the appropriate level of aggregation or disaggregation, and whether users of financial statements need additional explanations to evaluate the quantitative information disclosed.

35E   If the disclosures provided in accordance with paragraphs 35F–35N are insufficient to meet the objectives in paragraph 35B, an entity shall disclose additional information that is necessary to meet those objectives.

The credit risk management practices

35F   An entity shall explain its credit risk management practices and how they relate to the recognition and measurement of expected credit losses. To meet this objective an entity shall disclose information that enables users of financial statements to understand and evaluate:

(a)   how an entity determined whether the credit risk of financial instruments has increased significantly since initial recognition, including, if and how:

(i)   financial instruments are considered to have low credit risk in accordance with paragraph 5.5.10 of IFRS 9, including the classes of financial instruments to which it applies; and

(ii)   the presumption in paragraph 5.5.11 of IFRS 9, that there have been significant increases in credit risk since initial recognition when financial assets are more than 30 days past due, has been rebutted;

(b)   an entity's definitions of default, including the reasons for selecting those definitions;

(c)   how the instruments were grouped if expected credit losses were measured on a collective basis;

(d)   how an entity determined that financial assets are credit-impaired financial assets;

(e)   an entity's write-off policy, including the indicators that there is no reasonable expectation of recovery and information about the policy for financial assets that are written-off but are still subject to enforcement activity; and

(f)   how the requirements in paragraph 5.5.12 of IFRS 9 for the modification of contractual cash flows of financial assets have been applied, including how an entity:

(i)   determines whether the credit risk on a financial asset that has been modified while the loss allowance was measured at an amount equal to lifetime expected credit losses, has improved to the extent that the loss allowance reverts to being measured at an amount equal to 12-month expected credit losses in accordance with paragraph 5.5.5 of IFRS 9; and

(ii)   monitors the extent to which the loss allowance on financial assets meeting the criteria in (i) is subsequently remeasured at an amount equal to lifetime expected credit losses in accordance with paragraph 5.5.3 of IFRS 9.

35G   An entity shall explain the inputs, assumptions and estimation techniques used to apply the requirements in Section 5.5 of IFRS 9. For this purpose an entity shall disclose:

(a)   the basis of inputs and assumptions and the estimation techniques used to:

    (i)   measure the 12-month and lifetime expected credit losses;

    (ii)   determine whether the credit risk of financial instruments has increased significantly since initial recognition; and

    (iii)   determine whether a financial asset is a credit-impaired financial asset.

(b)   how forward-looking information has been incorporated into the determination of expected credit losses, including the use of macroeconomic information; and

(c)   changes in the estimation techniques or significant assumptions made during the reporting period and the reasons for those changes.

Quantitative and qualitative information about amounts arising from expected credit losses

35H   To explain the changes in the loss allowance and the reasons for those changes, an entity shall provide, by class of financial instrument, a reconciliation from the opening balance to the closing balance of the loss allowance, in a table, showing separately the changes during the period for:

(a)   the loss allowance measured at an amount equal to 12-month expected credit losses;

(b)   the loss allowance measured at an amount equal to lifetime expected credit losses for:

    (i)   financial instruments for which credit risk has increased significantly since initial recognition but that are not credit-impaired financial assets;

    (ii)   financial assets that are credit-impaired at the reporting date (but that are not purchased or originated credit-impaired); and

    (iii)   trade receivables, contract assets or lease receivables for which the loss allowances are measured in accordance with paragraph 5.5.15 of IFRS 9.

(c)   financial assets that are purchased or originated credit-impaired. In addition to the reconciliation, an entity shall disclose the total amount of undiscounted expected credit losses at initial recognition on financial assets initially recognised during the reporting period.

35I   To enable users of financial statements to understand the changes in the loss allowance disclosed in accordance with paragraph 35H, an entity shall provide an explanation of how significant changes in the gross carrying amount of financial instruments during the period contributed to changes in the loss allowance. The information shall be provided separately for financial instruments that represent the loss allowance as listed in paragraph 35H(a)–(c) and shall include relevant qualitative and quantitative information. Examples of changes in the gross carrying amount of financial instruments that contributed to the changes in the loss allowance may include:

(a) changes because of financial instruments originated or acquired during the reporting period;

(b) the modification of contractual cash flows on financial assets that do not result in a derecognition of those financial assets in accordance with IFRS 9;

(c) changes because of financial instruments that were derecognised (including those that were written-off) during the reporting period; and

(d) changes arising from whether the loss allowance is measured at an amount equal to 12-month or lifetime expected credit losses.

35J To enable users of financial statements to understand the nature and effect of modifications of contractual cash flows on financial assets that have not resulted in derecognition and the effect of such modifications on the measurement of expected credit losses, an entity shall disclose:

(a) the amortised cost before the modification and the net modification gain or loss recognised for financial assets for which the contractual cash flows have been modified during the reporting period while they had a loss allowance measured at an amount equal to lifetime expected credit losses; and

(b) the gross carrying amount at the end of the reporting period of financial assets that have been modified since initial recognition at a time when the loss allowance was measured at an amount equal to lifetime expected credit losses and for which the loss allowance has changed during the reporting period to an amount equal to 12-month expected credit losses.

35K To enable users of financial statements to understand the effect of collateral and other credit enhancements on the amounts arising from expected credit losses, an entity shall disclose by class of financial instrument:

(a) the amount that best represents its maximum exposure to credit risk at the end of the reporting period without taking account of any collateral held or other credit enhancements (eg netting agreements that do not qualify for offset in accordance with IAS 32).

(b) a narrative description of collateral held as security and other credit enhancements, including:

(i) a description of the nature and quality of the collateral held;

(ii) an explanation of any significant changes in the quality of that collateral or credit enhancements as a result of deterioration or changes in the collateral policies of the entity during the reporting period; and

(iii) information about financial instruments for which an entity has not recognised a loss allowance because of the collateral.

(c) quantitative information about the collateral held as security and other credit enhancements (for example, quantification of the extent to which collateral and other credit enhancements mitigate credit risk) for financial assets that are credit-impaired at the reporting date.

35L An entity shall disclose the contractual amount outstanding on financial assets that were written off during the reporting period and are still subject to enforcement activity.

Credit risk exposure

35M To enable users of financial statements to assess an entity's credit risk exposure and understand its significant credit risk concentrations, an entity shall disclose, by *credit risk rating grades*, the gross carrying amount of financial assets and the exposure to credit risk on loan commitments and financial guarantee contracts. This information shall be provided separately for financial instruments:

(a) for which the loss allowance is measured at an amount equal to 12-month expected credit losses;

(b) for which the loss allowance is measured at an amount equal to lifetime expected credit losses and that are:

(i) financial instruments for which credit risk has increased significantly since initial recognition but that are not credit-impaired financial assets;

(ii) financial assets that are credit-impaired at the reporting date (but that are not purchased or originated credit-impaired); and

(iii) trade receivables, contract assets or lease receivables for which the loss allowances are measured in accordance with paragraph 5.5.15 of IFRS 9.

(c) that are purchased or originated credit-impaired financial assets.

35N For trade receivables, contract assets and lease receivables to which an entity applies paragraph 5.5.15 of IFRS 9, the information provided in accordance with paragraph 35M may be based on a provision matrix (see paragraph B5.5.35 of IFRS 9).

36 For all financial instruments within the scope of this IFRS, but to which the impairment requirements in IFRS 9 are not applied, an entity shall disclose by class of financial instrument:

(a) the amount that best represents its maximum exposure to credit risk at the end of the reporting period without taking account of any collateral held or other credit enhancements (eg netting agreements that do not quality for offset in accordance with IAS 32); this disclosure is not required for financial instruments whose carrying amount best represents the maximum exposure to credit risk.

(b)   a description of collateral held as security and other credit enhancements, and their financial effect (eg quantification of the extent to which collateral and other credit enhancements mitigate credit risk) in respect of the amount that best represents the maximum exposure to credit risk (whether disclosed in accordance with (a) or represented by the carrying amount of a financial instrument).

(c)   [deleted]

(d)   [deleted]

37   [Deleted]

Collateral and other credit enhancements obtained

38   When an entity obtains financial or non-financial assets during the period by taking possession of collateral it holds as security or calling on other credit enhancements (eg guarantees), and such assets meet the recognition criteria in other IFRSs, an entity shall disclose for such assets held at the reporting date:

(a)   the nature and carrying amount of the assets; and

(b)   when the assets are not readily convertible into cash, its policies for disposing of such assets or for using them in its operations.

Liquidity risk

39   An entity shall disclose:

(a)   a maturity analysis for non-derivative financial liabilities (including issued financial guarantee contracts) that shows the remaining contractual maturities.

(b)   a maturity analysis for derivative financial liabilities. The maturity analysis shall include the remaining contractual maturities for those derivative financial liabilities for which contractual maturities are essential for an understanding of the timing of the cash flows (see paragraph B11B).

(c)   a description of how it manages the liquidity risk inherent in (a) and (b).

Market risk

Sensitivity analysis

40   Unless an entity complies with paragraph 41, it shall disclose:

(a)   a sensitivity analysis for each type of market risk to which the entity is exposed at the end of the reporting period, showing how profit or loss and equity would have been affected by changes in the relevant risk variable that were reasonably possible at that date;

(b)   the methods and assumptions used in preparing the sensitivity analysis; and

(c)   changes from the previous period in the methods and assumptions used, and the reasons for such changes.

41   If an entity prepares a sensitivity analysis, such as value-at-risk, that reflects interdependencies between risk variables (eg interest rates and exchange rates) and uses it to manage financial risks, it may use that sensitivity analysis in place of the analysis specified in paragraph 40. The entity shall also disclose:

(a)   an explanation of the method used in preparing such a sensitivity analysis, and of the main parameters and assumptions underlying the data provided; and

(b)   an explanation of the objective of the method used and of limitations that may result in the information not fully reflecting the fair value of the assets and liabilities involved.

Other market risk disclosures

42   When the sensitivity analyses disclosed in accordance with paragraph 40 or 41 are unrepresentative of a risk inherent in a financial instrument (for example because the year-end exposure does not reflect the exposure during the year), the entity shall disclose that fact and the reason it believes the sensitivity analyses are unrepresentative.

Transfers of financial assets

42A   The disclosure requirements in paragraphs 42B–42H relating to transfers of financial assets supplement the other disclosure requirements of this IFRS. An entity shall present the disclosures required by paragraphs 42B–42H in a single note in its financial statements. An entity shall provide the required disclosures for all transferred financial assets that are not derecognised and for any continuing involvement in a transferred asset, existing at the reporting date, irrespective of when the related transfer transaction occurred. For the purposes of applying the disclosure requirements in those paragraphs, an entity transfers all or a part of a financial asset (the transferred financial asset) if, and only if, it either:

(a)   transfers the contractual rights to receive the cash flows of that financial asset; or

(b)   retains the contractual rights to receive the cash flows of that financial asset, but assumes a contractual obligation to pay the cash flows to one or more recipients in an arrangement.

42B   An entity shall disclose information that enables users of its financial statements:

(a)   to understand the relationship between transferred financial assets that are not derecognised in their entirety and the associated liabilities; and

(b)   to evaluate the nature of, and risks associated with, the entity's continuing involvement in derecognised financial assets.

42C For the purposes of applying the disclosure requirements in paragraphs 42E–42H, an entity has continuing involvement in a transferred financial asset if, as part of the transfer, the entity retains any of the contractual rights or obligations inherent in the transferred financial asset or obtains any new contractual rights or obligations relating to the transferred financial asset. For the purposes of applying the disclosure requirements in paragraphs 42E–42H, the following do not constitute continuing involvement:

(a) normal representations and warranties relating to fraudulent transfer and concepts of reasonableness, good faith and fair dealings that could invalidate a transfer as a result of legal action;

(b) forward, option and other contracts to reacquire the transferred financial asset for which the contract price (or exercise price) is the fair value of the transferred financial asset; or

(c) an arrangement whereby an entity retains the contractual rights to receive the cash flows of a financial asset but assumes a contractual obligation to pay the cash flows to one or more entities and the conditions in paragraph 3.2.5(a)–(c) of IFRS 9 are met.

Transferred financial assets that are not derecognised in their entirety

42D An entity may have transferred financial assets in such a way that part or all of the transferred financial assets do not qualify for derecognition. To meet the objectives set out in paragraph 42B(a), the entity shall disclose at each reporting date for each class of transferred financial assets that are not derecognised in their entirety:

(a) the nature of the transferred assets.

(b) the nature of the risks and rewards of ownership to which the entity is exposed.

(c) a description of the nature of the relationship between the transferred assets and the associated liabilities, including restrictions arising from the transfer on the reporting entity's use of the transferred assets.

(d) when the counterparty (counterparties) to the associated liabilities has (have) recourse only to the transferred assets, a schedule that sets out the fair value of the transferred assets, the fair value of the associated liabilities and the net position (the difference between the fair value of the transferred assets and the associated liabilities).

(e) when the entity continues to recognise all of the transferred assets, the carrying amounts of the transferred assets and the associated liabilities.

(f) when the entity continues to recognise the assets to the extent of its continuing involvement (see paragraphs 3.2.6(c)(ii) and 3.2.16 of IFRS 9), the total carrying amount of the original assets before the transfer, the carrying amount of the assets that the entity continues to recognise, and the carrying amount of the associated liabilities.

Transferred financial assets that are derecognised in their entirety

42E   To meet the objectives set out in paragraph 42B(b), when an entity derecognises transferred financial assets in their entirety (see paragraph 3.2.6(a) and (c)(i) of IFRS 9) but has continuing involvement in them, the entity shall disclose, as a minimum, for each type of continuing involvement at each reporting date:

    (a)   the carrying amount of the assets and liabilities that are recognised in the entity's statement of financial position and represent the entity's continuing involvement in the derecognised financial assets, and the line items in which the carrying amount of those assets and liabilities are recognised.

    (b)   the fair value of the assets and liabilities that represent the entity's continuing involvement in the derecognised financial assets.

    (c)   the amount that best represents the entity's maximum exposure to loss from its continuing involvement in the derecognised financial assets, and information showing how the maximum exposure to loss is determined.

    (d)   the undiscounted cash outflows that would or may be required to repurchase derecognised financial assets (eg the strike price in an option agreement) or other amounts payable to the transferee in respect of the transferred assets. If the cash outflow is variable then the amount disclosed should be based on the conditions that exist at each reporting date.

    (e)   a maturity analysis of the undiscounted cash outflows that would or may be required to repurchase the derecognised financial assets or other amounts payable to the transferee in respect of the transferred assets, showing the remaining contractual maturities of the entity's continuing involvement.

    (f)   qualitative information that explains and supports the quantitative disclosures required in (a)–(e).

42F   An entity may aggregate the information required by paragraph 42E in respect of a particular asset if the entity has more than one type of continuing involvement in that derecognised financial asset, and report it under one type of continuing involvement.

42G   In addition, an entity shall disclose for each type of continuing involvement:

    (a)   the gain or loss recognised at the date of transfer of the assets.

    (b)   income and expenses recognised, both in the reporting period and cumulatively, from the entity's continuing involvement in the derecognised financial assets (eg fair value changes in derivative instruments).

(c) if the total amount of proceeds from transfer activity (that qualifies for derecognition) in a reporting period is not evenly distributed throughout the reporting period (eg if a substantial proportion of the total amount of transfer activity takes place in the closing days of a reporting period):

    (i) when the greatest transfer activity took place within that reporting period (eg the last five days before the end of the reporting period),

    (ii) the amount (eg related gains or losses) recognised from transfer activity in that part of the reporting period, and

    (iii) the total amount of proceeds from transfer activity in that part of the reporting period.

An entity shall provide this information for each period for which a statement of comprehensive income is presented.

Supplementary information

42H An entity shall disclose any additional information that it considers necessary to meet the disclosure objectives in paragraph 42B.

Initial application of IFRS 9

42I In the reporting period that includes the date of initial application of IFRS 9, the entity shall disclose the following information for each class of financial assets and financial liabilities as at the date of initial application:

(a) the original measurement category and carrying amount determined in accordance with IAS 39 or in accordance with a previous version of IFRS 9 (if the entity's chosen approach to applying IFRS 9 involves more than one date of initial application for different requirements);

(b) the new measurement category and carrying amount determined in accordance with IFRS 9;

(c) the amount of any financial assets and financial liabilities in the statement of financial position that were previously designated as measured at fair value through profit or loss but are no longer so designated, distinguishing between those that IFRS 9 requires an entity to reclassify and those that an entity elects to reclassify at the date of initial application.

In accordance with paragraph 7.2.2 of IFRS 9, depending on the entity's chosen approach to applying IFRS 9, the transition can involve more than one date of initial application. Therefore this paragraph may result in disclosure on more than one date of initial application. An entity shall present these quantitative disclosures in a table unless another format is more appropriate.

42J In the reporting period that includes the date of initial application of IFRS 9, an entity shall disclose qualitative information to enable users to understand:

(a) how it applied the classification requirements in IFRS 9 to those financial assets whose classification has changed as a result of applying IFRS 9.

(b) the reasons for any designation or de-designation of financial assets or financial liabilities as measured at fair value through profit or loss at the date of initial application.

In accordance with paragraph 7.2.2 of IFRS 9, depending on the entity's chosen approach to applying IFRS 9, the transition can involve more than one date of initial application. Therefore this paragraph may result in disclosure on more than one date of initial application.

42K In the reporting period that an entity first applies the classification and measurement requirements for financial assets in IFRS 9 (ie when the entity transitions from IAS 39 to IFRS 9 for financial assets), it shall present the disclosures set out in paragraphs 42L–42O of this IFRS as required by paragraph 7.2.15 of IFRS 9.

42L When required by paragraph 42K, an entity shall disclose the changes in the classifications of financial assets and financial liabilities as at the date of initial application of IFRS 9, showing separately:

(a) the changes in the carrying amounts on the basis of their measurement categories in accordance with IAS 39 (ie not resulting from a change in measurement attribute on transition to IFRS 9); and

(b) the changes in the carrying amounts arising from a change in measurement attribute on transition to IFRS 9.

The disclosures in this paragraph need not be made after the annual reporting period in which the entity initially applies the classification and measurement requirements for financial assets in IFRS 9.

42M When required by paragraph 42K, an entity shall disclose the following for financial assets and financial liabilities that have been reclassified so that they are measured at amortised cost and, in the case of financial assets, that have been reclassified out of fair value through profit or loss so that they are measured at fair value through other comprehensive income, as a result of the transition to IFRS 9:

(a) the fair value of the financial assets or financial liabilities at the end of the reporting period; and

(b) the fair value gain or loss that would have been recognised in profit or loss or other comprehensive income during the reporting period if the financial assets or financial liabilities had not been reclassified.

The disclosures in this paragraph need not be made after the annual reporting period in which the entity initially applies the classification and measurement requirements for financial assets in IFRS 9.

42N When required by paragraph 42K, an entity shall disclose the following for financial assets and financial liabilities that have been reclassified out of the fair value through profit or loss category as a result of the transition to IFRS 9:

(a)   the effective interest rate determined on the date of initial application; and

(b)   the interest revenue or expense recognised.

If an entity treats the fair value of a financial asset or a financial liability as the new gross carrying amount at the date of initial application (see paragraph 7.2.11 of IFRS 9), the disclosures in this paragraph shall be made for each reporting period until derecognition. Otherwise, the disclosures in this paragraph need not be made after the annual reporting period in which the entity initially applies the classification and measurement requirements for financial assets in IFRS 9.

42O   When an entity presents the disclosures set out in paragraphs 42K–42N, those disclosures, and the disclosures in paragraph 25 of this IFRS, must permit reconciliation between:

(a)   the measurement categories presented in accordance with IAS 39 and IFRS 9; and

(b)   the class of financial instrument

as at the date of initial application.

42P   On the date of initial application of Section 5.5 of IFRS 9, an entity is required to disclose information that would permit the reconciliation of the ending impairment allowances in accordance with IAS 39 and the provisions in accordance with IAS 37 to the opening loss allowances determined in accordance with IFRS 9. For financial assets, this disclosure shall be provided by the related financial assets' measurement categories in accordance with IAS 39 and IFRS 9, and shall show separately the effect of the changes in the measurement category on the loss allowance at that date.

42Q   In the reporting period that includes the date of initial application of IFRS 9, an entity is not required to disclose the line item amounts that would have been reported in accordance with the classification and measurement requirements (which includes the requirements related to amortised cost measurement of financial assets and impairment in Sections 5.4 and 5.5 of IFRS 9) of:

(a)   IFRS 9 for prior periods; and

(b)   IAS 39 for the current period.

42R   In accordance with paragraph 7.2.4 of IFRS 9, if it is impracticable (as defined in IAS 8) at the date of initial application of IFRS 9 for an entity to assess a modified time value of money element in accordance with paragraphs B4.1.9B–B4.1.9D of IFRS 9 based on the facts and circumstances that existed at the initial recognition of the financial asset, an entity shall assess the contractual cash flow characteristics of that financial asset based on the facts and circumstances that existed at the initial recognition of the financial asset without taking into account the requirements related to the modification of the time value of money element in paragraphs B4.1.9B–B4.1.9D of IFRS 9. An entity shall disclose the carrying amount at the reporting date of the financial assets whose contractual cash flow characteristics have been assessed based on the facts and circumstances that existed at the initial recognition of the financial asset without taking into account the requirements related to the modification of the time value of money element in paragraphs B4.1.9B–B4.1.9D of IFRS 9 until those financial assets are derecognised.

42S In accordance with paragraph 7.2.5 of IFRS 9, if it is impracticable (as defined in IAS 8) at the date of initial application for an entity to assess whether the fair value of a prepayment feature was insignificant in accordance with paragraphs B4.1.12(c) of IFRS 9 based on the facts and circumstances that existed at the initial recognition of the financial asset, an entity shall assess the contractual cash flow characteristics of that financial asset based on the facts and circumstances that existed at the initial recognition of the financial asset without taking into account the exception for prepayment features in paragraph B4.1.12 of IFRS 9. An entity shall disclose the carrying amount at the reporting date of the financial assets whose contractual cash flow characteristics have been assessed based on the facts and circumstances that existed at the initial recognition of the financial asset without taking into account the exception for prepayment features in paragraph B4.1.12 of IFRS 9 until those financial assets are derecognised.

Effective date and transition

43 An entity shall apply this IFRS for annual periods beginning on or after 1 January 2007. Earlier application is encouraged. If an entity applies this IFRS for an earlier period, it shall disclose that fact.

44 If an entity applies this IFRS for annual periods beginning before 1 January 2006, it need not present comparative information for the disclosures required by paragraphs 31–42 about the nature and extent of risks arising from financial instruments.

44A IAS 1 (as revised in 2007) amended the terminology used throughout IFRSs. In addition it amended paragraphs 20, 21, 23(c) and (d), 27(c) and B5 of Appendix B. An entity shall apply those amendments for annual periods beginning on or after 1 January 2009. If an entity applies IAS 1 (revised 2007) for an earlier period, the amendments shall be applied for that earlier period.

44B IFRS 3 (as revised in 2008) deleted paragraph 3(c). An entity shall apply that amendment for annual periods beginning on or after 1 July 2009. If an entity applies IFRS 3 (revised 2008) for an earlier period, the amendment shall also be applied for that earlier period. However, the amendment does not apply to contingent consideration that arose from a business combination for which the acquisition date preceded the application of IFRS 3 (revised 2008). Instead, an entity shall account for such consideration in accordance with paragraphs 65A–65E of IFRS 3 (as amended in 2010).

44C   An entity shall apply the amendment in paragraph 3 for annual periods beginning on or after 1 January 2009. If an entity applies *Puttable Financial Instruments and Obligations Arising on Liquidation* (Amendments to IAS 32 and IAS 1), issued in February 2008, for an earlier period, the amendment in paragraph 3 shall be applied for that earlier period.

44D   Paragraph 3(a) was amended by *Improvements to IFRSs* issued in May 2008. An entity shall apply that amendment for annual periods beginning on or after 1 January 2009. Earlier application is permitted. If an entity applies the amendment for an earlier period it shall disclose that fact and apply for that earlier period the amendments to paragraph 1 of IAS 28, paragraph 1 of IAS 31 and paragraph 4 of IAS 32 issued in May 2008. An entity is permitted to apply the amendment prospectively.

44E   [Deleted]

44F   [Deleted]

44G   *Improving Disclosures about Financial Instruments* (Amendments to IFRS 7), issued in March 2009, amended paragraphs 27, 39 and B11 and added paragraphs 27A, 27B, B10A and B11A–B11F. An entity shall apply those amendments for annual periods beginning on or after 1 January 2009. An entity need not provide the disclosures required by the amendments for:

(a)   any annual or interim period, including any statement of financial position, presented within an annual comparative period ending before 31 December 2009, or

(b)   any statement of financial position as at the beginning of the earliest comparative period as at a date before 31 December 2009.

Earlier application is permitted. If an entity applies the amendments for an earlier period, it shall disclose that fact.[1]

44H–44J   [Deleted]

44K   Paragraph 44B was amended by *Improvements to IFRSs* issued in May 2010. An entity shall apply that amendment for annual periods beginning on or after 1 July 2010. Earlier application is permitted.

44L   *Improvements to IFRSs* issued in May 2010 added paragraph 32A and amended paragraphs 34 and 36–38. An entity shall apply those amendments for annual periods beginning on or after 1 January 2011. Earlier application is permitted. If an entity applies the amendments for an earlier period it shall disclose that fact.

44M   *Disclosures — Transfers of Financial Assets* (Amendments to IFRS 7), issued in October 2010, deleted paragraph 13 and added paragraphs 42A–42H and B29–B39. An entity shall apply those amendments for annual periods beginning on or after 1 July 2011. Earlier application is permitted. If an entity

---

1   Paragraph 44G was amended as a consequence of *Limited Exemption from Comparative IFRS 7 Disclosures for First-time Adopters* (Amendment to IFRS 1) issued in January 2010. The Board amended paragraph 44G to clarify its conclusions and intended transition for *Improving Disclosures about Financial Instruments* (Amendments to IFRS 7).

applies the amendments from an earlier date, it shall disclose that fact. An entity need not provide the disclosures required by those amendments for any period presented that begins before the date of initial application of the amendments.

44N   [Deleted]

44O   IFRS 10 and IFRS 11 *Joint Arrangements*, issued in May 2011, amended paragraph 3. An entity shall apply that amendment when it applies IFRS 10 and IFRS 11.

44P   IFRS 13, issued in May 2011, amended paragraphs 3, 28 and 29 and Appendix A and deleted paragraphs 27–27B. An entity shall apply those amendments when it applies IFRS 13.

44Q   *Presentation of Items of Other Comprehensive Income* (Amendments to IAS 1), issued in June 2011, amended paragraph 27B. An entity shall apply that amendment when it applies IAS 1 as amended in June 2011.

44R   *Disclosures — Offsetting Financial Assets and Financial Liabilities* (Amendments to IFRS 7), issued in December 2011, added paragraphs 13A–13F and B40–B53. An entity shall apply those amendments for annual periods beginning on or after 1 January 2013. An entity shall provide the disclosures required by those amendments retrospectively.

44S–44W [Deleted]

44X   *Investment Entities* (Amendments to IFRS 10, IFRS 12 and IAS 27), issued in October 2012, amended paragraph 3. An entity shall apply that amendment for annual periods beginning on or after 1 January 2014. Earlier application of *Investment Entities* is permitted. If an entity applies that amendment earlier it shall also apply all amendments included in *Investment Entities* at the same time.

44Y   [Deleted]

44Z   IFRS 9, as issued in July 2014, amended paragraphs 2–5, 8–11, 14, 20, 28–30, 36, 42C–42E, Appendix A and paragraphs B1, B5, B9, B10, B22 and B27, deleted paragraphs 12, 12A, 16, 22–24, 37, 44E, 44F, 44H–44J, 44N, 44S–44W, 44Y, B4 and Appendix D and added paragraphs 5A, 10A, 11A, 11B, 12B–12D, 16A, 20A, 21A–21D, 22A–22C, 23A–23F, 24A–24G, 35A–35N, 42I–42S, 44ZA and B8A–B8J. An entity shall apply those amendments when it applies IFRS 9. Those amendments need not be applied to comparative information provided for periods before the date of initial application of IFRS 9.

44ZA   In accordance with paragraph 7.1.2 of IFRS 9, for annual reporting periods prior to 1 January 2018, an entity may elect to early apply only the requirements for the presentation of gains and losses on financial liabilities designated as at fair value through profit or loss in paragraphs 5.7.1(c), 5.7.7–5.7.9, 7.2.14 and B5.7.5–B5.7.20 of IFRS 9 without applying the other requirements in IFRS 9. If an entity elects to apply only those paragraphs of IFRS 9, it shall disclose that fact and provide on an ongoing basis the related disclosures set out in paragraphs 10–11 of this IFRS (as amended by IFRS 9 (2010)).

44AA   *Annual Improvements to IFRSs 2012–2014 Cycle*, issued in September 2014, amended paragraphs 44R and B30 and added paragraph B30A. An entity shall apply those amendments retrospectively in accordance with IAS 8 *Accounting Policies, Changes in Accounting Estimates and Errors* for annual periods beginning on or after 1 January 2016, except that an entity need not apply the amendments to paragraphs B30 and B30A for any period presented that begins before the annual period for which the entity first applies those amendments. Earlier application of the amendments to paragraphs 44R, B30 and B30A is permitted. If an entity applies those amendments for an earlier period it shall disclose that fact.

44BB   *Disclosure Initiative* (Amendments to IAS 1), issued in December 2014, amended paragraphs 21 and B5. An entity shall apply those amendments for annual periods beginning on or after 1 January 2016. Earlier application of those amendments is permitted.

44CC   IFRS 16 *Leases*, issued in January 2016, amended paragraphs 29 and B11D. An entity shall apply those amendments when it applies IFRS 16.

44DD   *[This paragraph refers to amendments that are not yet effective, and is therefore not included in this edition.]*

44EE   *Interest Rate Benchmark Reform*, which amended IFRS 9, IAS 39 and IFRS 7, issued in September 2019, added paragraphs 24H and 44FF. An entity shall apply these amendments when it applies the amendments to IFRS 9 or IAS 39.

44FF   In the reporting period in which an entity first applies *Interest Rate Benchmark Reform*, issued in September 2019, an entity is not required to present the quantitative information required by paragraph 28(f) of IAS 8 *Accounting Policies, Changes in Accounting Estimates and Errors.*

44GG   *Interest Rate Benchmark Reform—Phase 2*, which amended IFRS 9, IAS 39, IFRS 7, IFRS 4 and IFRS 16, issued in August 2020, added paragraphs 24I–24J and 44HH. An entity shall apply these amendments when it applies the amendments to IFRS 9, IAS 39, IFRS 4 or IFRS 16.

44HH   In the reporting period in which an entity first applies *Interest Rate Benchmark Reform—Phase 2*, an entity is not required to disclose the information that would otherwise be required by paragraph 28(f) of IAS 8.

44II   *[This paragraph refers to amendments that are not yet effective, and is therefore not included in this edition.]*

Withdrawal of IAS 30

45   This IFRS supersedes IAS 30 *Disclosures in the Financial Statements of Banks and Similar Financial Institutions.*

Appendix A
Defined terms

This appendix is an integral part of the IFRS.

credit risk	The risk that one party to a financial instrument will cause a financial loss for the other party by failing to discharge an obligation.
credit risk rating grades	Rating of credit risk based on the risk of a default occurring on the financial instrument.
currency risk	The risk that the fair value or future cash flows of a financial instrument will fluctuate because of changes in foreign exchange rates.
interest rate risk	The risk that the fair value or future cash flows of a financial instrument will fluctuate because of changes in market interest rates.
liquidity risk	The risk that an entity will encounter difficulty in meeting obligations associated with financial liabilities that are settled by delivering cash or another financial asset.
loans payable	Loans payable are financial liabilities, other than short-term trade payables on normal credit terms.
market risk	The risk that the fair value or future cash flows of a financial instrument will fluctuate because of changes in market prices. Market risk comprises three types of risk: **currency risk**, **interest rate risk** and **other price risk**.
other price risk	The risk that the fair value or future cash flows of a financial instrument will fluctuate because of changes in market prices (other than those arising from **interest rate risk** or **currency risk**), whether those changes are caused by factors specific to the individual financial instrument or its issuer or by factors affecting all similar financial instruments traded in the market.

The following terms are defined in paragraph 11 of IAS 32, paragraph 9 of IAS 39, Appendix A of IFRS 9 or Appendix A of IFRS 13 and are used in this IFRS with the meaning specified in IAS 32, IAS 39, IFRS 9 and IFRS 13.

- amortised cost of a financial asset or financial liability

- contract asset

- credit-impaired financial assets

- derecognition

- derivative

- dividends

- effective interest method

- equity instrument
- expected credit losses
- fair value
- financial asset
- financial guarantee contract
- financial instrument
- financial liability
- financial liability at fair value through profit or loss
- forecast transaction
- gross carrying amount of a financial asset
- hedging instrument
- held for trading
- impairment gains or losses
- loss allowance
- past due
- purchased or originated credit-impaired financial assets
- reclassification date
- regular way purchase or sale.

Appendix B
Application guidance

This appendix is an integral part of the IFRS.

Classes of financial instruments and level of disclosure (paragraph 6)

B1   Paragraph 6 requires an entity to group financial instruments into classes that are appropriate to the nature of the information disclosed and that take into account the characteristics of those financial instruments. The classes described in paragraph 6 are determined by the entity and are, thus, distinct from the categories of financial instruments specified in IFRS 9 (which determine how financial instruments are measured and where changes in fair value are recognised).

B2   In determining classes of financial instrument, an entity shall, at a minimum:

    (a)   distinguish instruments measured at amortised cost from those measured at fair value.

    (b)   treat as a separate class or classes those financial instruments outside the scope of this IFRS.

B3   An entity decides, in the light of its circumstances, how much detail it provides to satisfy the requirements of this IFRS, how much emphasis it places on different aspects of the requirements and how it aggregates information to display the overall picture without combining information with different characteristics. It is necessary to strike a balance between overburdening financial statements with excessive detail that may not assist users of financial statements and obscuring important information as a result of too much aggregation. For example, an entity shall not obscure important information by including it among a large amount of insignificant detail. Similarly, an entity shall not disclose information that is so aggregated that it obscures important differences between individual transactions or associated risks.

B4   [Deleted]

Other disclosure – accounting policies (paragraph 21)

B5   Paragraph 21 requires disclosure of the measurement basis (or bases) used in preparing the financial statements and the other accounting policies used that are relevant to an understanding of the financial statements. For financial instruments, such disclosure may include:

    (a)   for financial liabilities designated as at fair value through profit or loss:

        (i)   the nature of the financial liabilities the entity has designated as at fair value through profit or loss;

(ii)   the criteria for so designating such financial liabilities on initial recognition; and

(iii)   how the entity has satisfied the conditions in paragraph 4.2.2 of IFRS 9 for such designation.

(aa) for financial assets designated as measured at fair value through profit or loss:

(i)   the nature of the financial assets the entity has designated as measured at fair value through profit or loss; and

(ii)   how the entity has satisfied the criteria in paragraph 4.1.5 of IFRS 9 for such designation.

(b)   [deleted]

(c)   whether regular way purchases and sales of financial assets are accounted for at trade date or at settlement date (see paragraph 3.1.2 of IFRS 9).

(d)   [deleted]

(e)   how net gains or net losses on each category of financial instrument are determined (see paragraph 20(a)), for example, whether the net gains or net losses on items at fair value through profit or loss include interest or dividend income.

(f)   [deleted]

(g)   [deleted]

Paragraph 122 of IAS 1 (as revised in 2007) also requires entities to disclose, along with its significant accounting policies or other notes, the judgements, apart from those involving estimations, that management has made in the process of applying the entity's accounting policies and that have the most significant effect on the amounts recognised in the financial statements.

Nature and extent of risks arising from financial instruments (paragraphs 31–42)

B6   The disclosures required by paragraphs 31–42 shall be either given in the financial statements or incorporated by cross-reference from the financial statements to some other statement, such as a management commentary or risk report, that is available to users of the financial statements on the same terms as the financial statements and at the same time. Without the information incorporated by cross-reference, the financial statements are incomplete.

Quantitative disclosures (paragraph 34)

B7   Paragraph 34(a) requires disclosures of summary quantitative data about an entity's exposure to risks based on the information provided internally to key management personnel of the entity. When an entity uses several methods to manage a risk exposure, the entity shall disclose information using the method or methods that provide the most relevant and reliable information. IAS 8 *Accounting Policies, Changes in Accounting Estimates and Errors* discusses relevance and reliability.

B8   Paragraph 34(c) requires disclosures about concentrations of risk. Concentrations of risk arise from financial instruments that have similar characteristics and are affected similarly by changes in economic or other conditions. The identification of concentrations of risk requires judgement taking into account the circumstances of the entity. Disclosure of concentrations of risk shall include:

(a)   a description of how management determines concentrations;

(b)   a description of the shared characteristic that identifies each concentration (eg counterparty, geographical area, currency or market); and

(c)   the amount of the risk exposure associated with all financial instruments sharing that characteristic.

Credit risk management practices (paragraphs 35F–35G)

B8A   Paragraph 35F(b) requires the disclosure of information about how an entity has defined default for different financial instruments and the reasons for selecting those definitions. In accordance with paragraph 5.5.9 of IFRS 9, the determination of whether lifetime expected credit losses should be recognised is based on the increase in the risk of a default occurring since initial recognition. Information about an entity's definitions of default that will assist users of financial statements in understanding how an entity has applied the expected credit loss requirements in IFRS 9 may include:

(a)   the qualitative and quantitative factors considered in defining default;

(b)   whether different definitions have been applied to different types of financial instruments; and

(c)   assumptions about the cure rate (ie the number of financial assets that return to a performing status) after a default occurred on the financial asset.

B8B   To assist users of financial statements in evaluating an entity's restructuring and modification policies, paragraph 35F(f)(ii) requires the disclosure of information about how an entity monitors the extent to which the loss allowance on financial assets previously disclosed in accordance with paragraph 35F(f)(i) are subsequently measured at an amount equal to lifetime expected credit losses in accordance with paragraph 5.5.3 of IFRS 9. Quantitative information that will assist users in understanding the subsequent increase in credit risk of modified financial assets may include information about modified financial assets meeting the criteria in paragraph 35F(f)(i) for which the loss allowance has reverted to being measured at an amount equal to lifetime expected credit losses (ie a deterioration rate).

B8C   Paragraph 35G(a) requires the disclosure of information about the basis of inputs and assumptions and the estimation techniques used to apply the impairment requirements in IFRS 9. An entity's assumptions and inputs used to measure expected credit losses or determine the extent of increases in credit risk since initial recognition may include information obtained from internal historical information or rating reports and assumptions about the expected life of financial instruments and the timing of the sale of collateral.

Changes in the loss allowance (paragraph 35H)

B8D   In accordance with paragraph 35H, an entity is required to explain the reasons for the changes in the loss allowance during the period. In addition to the reconciliation from the opening balance to the closing balance of the loss allowance, it may be necessary to provide a narrative explanation of the changes. This narrative explanation may include an analysis of the reasons for changes in the loss allowance during the period, including:

     (a)   the portfolio composition;

     (b)   the volume of financial instruments purchased or originated; and

     (c)   the severity of the expected credit losses.

B8E   For loan commitments and financial guarantee contracts the loss allowance is recognised as a provision. An entity should disclose information about the changes in the loss allowance for financial assets separately from those for loan commitments and financial guarantee contracts. However, if a financial instrument includes both a loan (ie financial asset) and an undrawn commitment (ie loan commitment) component and the entity cannot separately identify the expected credit losses on the loan commitment component from those on the financial asset component, the expected credit losses on the loan commitment should be recognised together with the loss allowance for the financial asset. To the extent that the combined expected credit losses exceed the gross carrying amount of the financial asset, the expected credit losses should be recognised as a provision.

Collateral (paragraph 35K)

B8F   Paragraph 35K requires the disclosure of information that will enable users of financial statements to understand the effect of collateral and other credit enhancements on the amount of expected credit losses. An entity is neither required to disclose information about the fair value of collateral and other credit enhancements nor is it required to quantify the exact value of the collateral that was included in the calculation of expected credit losses (ie the loss given default).

B8G   A narrative description of collateral and its effect on amounts of expected credit losses might include information about:

     (a)   the main types of collateral held as security and other credit enhancements (examples of the latter being guarantees, credit derivatives and netting agreements that do not qualify for offset in accordance with IAS 32);

(b)   the volume of collateral held and other credit enhancements and its significance in terms of the loss allowance;

(c)   the policies and processes for valuing and managing collateral and other credit enhancements;

(d)   the main types of counterparties to collateral and other credit enhancements and their creditworthiness; and

(e)   information about risk concentrations within the collateral and other credit enhancements.

Credit risk exposure (paragraphs 35M–35N)

B8H   Paragraph 35M requires the disclosure of information about an entity's credit risk exposure and significant concentrations of credit risk at the reporting date. A concentration of credit risk exists when a number of counterparties are located in a geographical region or are engaged in similar activities and have similar economic characteristics that would cause their ability to meet contractual obligations to be similarly affected by changes in economic or other conditions. An entity should provide information that enables users of financial statements to understand whether there are groups or portfolios of financial instruments with particular features that could affect a large portion of that group of financial instruments such as concentration to particular risks. This could include, for example, loan-to-value groupings, geographical, industry or issuer-type concentrations.

B8I   The number of credit risk rating grades used to disclose the information in accordance with paragraph 35M shall be consistent with the number that the entity reports to key management personnel for credit risk management purposes. If past due information is the only borrower-specific information available and an entity uses past due information to assess whether credit risk has increased significantly since initial recognition in accordance with paragraph 5.5.11 of IFRS 9, an entity shall provide an analysis by past due status for those financial assets.

B8J   When an entity has measured expected credit losses on a collective basis, the entity may not be able to allocate the gross carrying amount of individual financial assets or the exposure to credit risk on loan commitments and financial guarantee contracts to the credit risk rating grades for which lifetime expected credit losses are recognised. In that case, an entity should apply the requirement in paragraph 35M to those financial instruments that can be directly allocated to a credit risk rating grade and disclose separately the gross carrying amount of financial instruments for which lifetime expected credit losses have been measured on a collective basis.

Maximum credit risk exposure (paragraph 36(a))

B9   Paragraphs 35K(a) and 36(a) require disclosure of the amount that best represents the entity's maximum exposure to credit risk. For a financial asset, this is typically the gross carrying amount, net of:

(a)   any amounts offset in accordance with IAS 32; and

(b)   any loss allowance recognised in accordance with IFRS 9.

B10   Activities that give rise to credit risk and the associated maximum exposure to credit risk include, but are not limited to:

(a)   granting loans to customers and placing deposits with other entities. In these cases, the maximum exposure to credit risk is the carrying amount of the related financial assets.

(b)   entering into derivative contracts, eg foreign exchange contracts, interest rate swaps and credit derivatives. When the resulting asset is measured at fair value, the maximum exposure to credit risk at the end of the reporting period will equal the carrying amount.

(c)   granting financial guarantees. In this case, the maximum exposure to credit risk is the maximum amount the entity could have to pay if the guarantee is called on, which may be significantly greater than the amount recognised as a liability.

(d)   making a loan commitment that is irrevocable over the life of the facility or is revocable only in response to a material adverse change. If the issuer cannot settle the loan commitment net in cash or another financial instrument, the maximum credit exposure is the full amount of the commitment. This is because it is uncertain whether the amount of any undrawn portion may be drawn upon in the future. This may be significantly greater than the amount recognised as a liability.

Quantitative liquidity risk disclosures (paragraphs 34(a) and 39(a) and (b))

B10A   In accordance with paragraph 34(a) an entity discloses summary quantitative data about its exposure to liquidity risk on the basis of the information provided internally to key management personnel. An entity shall explain how those data are determined. If the outflows of cash (or another financial asset) included in those data could either:

(a)   occur significantly earlier than indicated in the data, or

(b)   be for significantly different amounts from those indicated in the data (eg for a derivative that is included in the data on a net settlement basis but for which the counterparty has the option to require gross settlement),

the entity shall state that fact and provide quantitative information that enables users of its financial statements to evaluate the extent of this risk unless that information is included in the contractual maturity analyses required by paragraph 39(a) or (b).

B11   In preparing the maturity analyses required by paragraph 39(a) and (b), an entity uses its judgement to determine an appropriate number of time bands. For example, an entity might determine that the following time bands are appropriate:

    (a)   not later than one month;

    (b)   later than one month and not later than three months;

    (c)   later than three months and not later than one year; and

    (d)   later than one year and not later than five years.

B11A In complying with paragraph 39(a) and (b), an entity shall not separate an embedded derivative from a hybrid (combined) financial instrument. For such an instrument, an entity shall apply paragraph 39(a).

B11B Paragraph 39(b) requires an entity to disclose a quantitative maturity analysis for derivative financial liabilities that shows remaining contractual maturities if the contractual maturities are essential for an understanding of the timing of the cash flows. For example, this would be the case for:

    (a)   an interest rate swap with a remaining maturity of five years in a cash flow hedge of a variable rate financial asset or liability.

    (b)   all loan commitments.

B11C Paragraph 39(a) and (b) requires an entity to disclose maturity analyses for financial liabilities that show the remaining contractual maturities for some financial liabilities. In this disclosure:

    (a)   when a counterparty has a choice of when an amount is paid, the liability is allocated to the earliest period in which the entity can be required to pay. For example, financial liabilities that an entity can be required to repay on demand (eg demand deposits) are included in the earliest time band.

    (b)   when an entity is committed to make amounts available in instalments, each instalment is allocated to the earliest period in which the entity can be required to pay. For example, an undrawn loan commitment is included in the time band containing the earliest date it can be drawn down.

    (c)   for issued financial guarantee contracts the maximum amount of the guarantee is allocated to the earliest period in which the guarantee could be called.

B11D The contractual amounts disclosed in the maturity analyses as required by paragraph 39(a) and (b) are the contractual undiscounted cash flows, for example:

    (a)   gross lease liabilities (before deducting finance charges);

    (b)   prices specified in forward agreements to purchase financial assets for cash;

    (c)   net amounts for pay-floating/receive-fixed interest rate swaps for which net cash flows are exchanged;

    (d)   contractual amounts to be exchanged in a derivative financial instrument (eg a currency swap) for which gross cash flows are exchanged; and

(e)   gross loan commitments.

Such undiscounted cash flows differ from the amount included in the statement of financial position because the amount in that statement is based on discounted cash flows. When the amount payable is not fixed, the amount disclosed is determined by reference to the conditions existing at the end of the reporting period. For example, when the amount payable varies with changes in an index, the amount disclosed may be based on the level of the index at the end of the period.

B11E   Paragraph 39(c) requires an entity to describe how it manages the liquidity risk inherent in the items disclosed in the quantitative disclosures required in paragraph 39(a) and (b). An entity shall disclose a maturity analysis of financial assets it holds for managing liquidity risk (eg financial assets that are readily saleable or expected to generate cash inflows to meet cash outflows on financial liabilities), if that information is necessary to enable users of its financial statements to evaluate the nature and extent of liquidity risk.

B11F   Other factors that an entity might consider in providing the disclosure required in paragraph 39(c) include, but are not limited to, whether the entity:

(a)   has committed borrowing facilities (eg commercial paper facilities) or other lines of credit (eg stand-by credit facilities) that it can access to meet liquidity needs;

(b)   holds deposits at central banks to meet liquidity needs;

(c)   has very diverse funding sources;

(d)   has significant concentrations of liquidity risk in either its assets or its funding sources;

(e)   has internal control processes and contingency plans for managing liquidity risk;

(f)   has instruments that include accelerated repayment terms (eg on the downgrade of the entity's credit rating);

(g)   has instruments that could require the posting of collateral (eg margin calls for derivatives);

(h)   has instruments that allow the entity to choose whether it settles its financial liabilities by delivering cash (or another financial asset) or by delivering its own shares; or

(i)   has instruments that are subject to master netting agreements.

B12–B16   [Deleted]

Market risk – sensitivity analysis (paragraphs 40 and 41)

B17   Paragraph 40(a) requires a sensitivity analysis for each type of market risk to which the entity is exposed. In accordance with paragraph B3, an entity decides how it aggregates information to display the overall picture without combining information with different characteristics about exposures to risks from significantly different economic environments. For example:

(a)   an entity that trades financial instruments might disclose this information separately for financial instruments held for trading and those not held for trading.

(b)   an entity would not aggregate its exposure to market risks from areas of hyperinflation with its exposure to the same market risks from areas of very low inflation.

If an entity has exposure to only one type of market risk in only one economic environment, it would not show disaggregated information.

B18   Paragraph 40(a) requires the sensitivity analysis to show the effect on profit or loss and equity of reasonably possible changes in the relevant risk variable (eg prevailing market interest rates, currency rates, equity prices or commodity prices). For this purpose:

(a)   entities are not required to determine what the profit or loss for the period would have been if relevant risk variables had been different. Instead, entities disclose the effect on profit or loss and equity at the end of the reporting period assuming that a reasonably possible change in the relevant risk variable had occurred at the end of the reporting period and had been applied to the risk exposures in existence at that date. For example, if an entity has a floating rate liability at the end of the year, the entity would disclose the effect on profit or loss (ie interest expense) for the current year if interest rates had varied by reasonably possible amounts.

(b)   entities are not required to disclose the effect on profit or loss and equity for each change within a range of reasonably possible changes of the relevant risk variable. Disclosure of the effects of the changes at the limits of the reasonably possible range would be sufficient.

B19   In determining what a reasonably possible change in the relevant risk variable is, an entity should consider:

(a)   the economic environments in which it operates. A reasonably possible change should not include remote or 'worst case' scenarios or 'stress tests'. Moreover, if the rate of change in the underlying risk variable is stable, the entity need not alter the chosen reasonably possible change in the risk variable. For example, assume that interest rates are 5 per cent and an entity determines that a fluctuation in interest rates of ±50 basis points is reasonably possible. It would disclose the effect on profit or loss and equity if interest rates were to change to 4.5 per cent or 5.5 per cent. In the next period, interest rates have increased to 5.5 per cent. The entity continues to believe that interest rates may fluctuate by ±50 basis points (ie that the rate of change in interest rates is stable). The entity would disclose the effect on profit or loss and equity if interest rates were to change to 5 per cent or 6 per cent. The entity would not be required to revise its assessment that interest rates might reasonably fluctuate by ±50 basis points, unless there is evidence that interest rates have become significantly more volatile.

(b)   the time frame over which it is making the assessment. The sensitivity analysis shall show the effects of changes that are considered to be reasonably possible over the period until the entity will next present these disclosures, which is usually its next annual reporting period.

B20   Paragraph 41 permits an entity to use a sensitivity analysis that reflects interdependencies between risk variables, such as a value-at-risk methodology, if it uses this analysis to manage its exposure to financial risks. This applies even if such a methodology measures only the potential for loss and does not measure the potential for gain. Such an entity might comply with paragraph 41(a) by disclosing the type of value-at-risk model used (eg whether the model relies on Monte Carlo simulations), an explanation about how the model works and the main assumptions (eg the holding period and confidence level). Entities might also disclose the historical observation period and weightings applied to observations within that period, an explanation of how options are dealt with in the calculations, and which volatilities and correlations (or, alternatively, Monte Carlo probability distribution simulations) are used.

B21   An entity shall provide sensitivity analyses for the whole of its business, but may provide different types of sensitivity analysis for different classes of financial instruments.

Interest rate risk

B22   *Interest rate risk* arises on interest-bearing financial instruments recognised in the statement of financial position (eg debt instruments acquired or issued) and on some financial instruments not recognised in the statement of financial position (eg some loan commitments).

Currency risk

B23   *Currency risk* (or foreign exchange risk) arises on financial instruments that are denominated in a foreign currency, ie in a currency other than the functional currency in which they are measured. For the purpose of this IFRS, currency risk does not arise from financial instruments that are non-monetary items or from financial instruments denominated in the functional currency.

B24   A sensitivity analysis is disclosed for each currency to which an entity has significant exposure.

Other price risk

B25   *Other price risk* arises on financial instruments because of changes in, for example, commodity prices or equity prices. To comply with paragraph 40, an entity might disclose the effect of a decrease in a specified stock market index, commodity price, or other risk variable. For example, if an entity gives residual value guarantees that are financial instruments, the entity discloses an increase or decrease in the value of the assets to which the guarantee applies.

B26   Two examples of financial instruments that give rise to equity price risk are (a) a holding of equities in another entity and (b) an investment in a trust that in turn holds investments in equity instruments. Other examples include forward contracts and options to buy or sell specified quantities of an equity instrument and swaps that are indexed to equity prices. The fair values of such financial instruments are affected by changes in the market price of the underlying equity instruments.

B27   In accordance with paragraph 40(a), the sensitivity of profit or loss (that arises, for example, from instruments measured at fair value through profit or loss) is disclosed separately from the sensitivity of other comprehensive income (that arises, for example, from investments in equity instruments whose changes in fair value are presented in other comprehensive income).

B28   Financial instruments that an entity classifies as equity instruments are not remeasured. Neither profit or loss nor equity will be affected by the equity price risk of those instruments. Accordingly, no sensitivity analysis is required.

Derecognition (paragraphs 42C–42H)

Continuing involvement (paragraph 42C)

B29   The assessment of continuing involvement in a transferred financial asset for the purposes of the disclosure requirements in paragraphs 42E–42H is made at the level of the reporting entity. For example, if a subsidiary transfers to an unrelated third party a financial asset in which the parent of the subsidiary has continuing involvement, the subsidiary does not include the parent's involvement in the assessment of whether it has continuing involvement in the transferred asset in its separate or individual financial statements (ie when the subsidiary is the reporting entity). However, a parent would include its continuing involvement (or that of another member of the group) in a financial asset transferred by its subsidiary in determining whether it has continuing involvement in the transferred asset in its consolidated financial statements (ie when the reporting entity is the group).

B30   An entity does not have a continuing involvement in a transferred financial asset if, as part of the transfer, it neither retains any of the contractual rights or obligations inherent in the transferred financial asset nor acquires any new contractual rights or obligations relating to the transferred financial asset. An entity does not have continuing involvement in a transferred financial asset if it has neither an interest in the future performance of the transferred financial asset nor a responsibility under any circumstances to make payments in respect of the transferred financial asset in the future. The term 'payment' in this context does not include cash flows of the transferred financial asset that an entity collects and is required to remit to the transferee.

B30A When an entity transfers a financial asset, the entity may retain the right to service that financial asset for a fee that is included in, for example, a servicing contract. The entity assesses the servicing contract in accordance with the guidance in paragraphs 42C and B30 to decide whether the entity has continuing involvement as a result of the servicing contract for the purposes of the disclosure requirements. For example, a servicer will have continuing involvement in the transferred financial asset for the purposes of the disclosure requirements if the servicing fee is dependent on the amount or timing of the cash flows collected from the transferred financial asset. Similarly, a servicer has continuing involvement for the purposes of the disclosure requirements if a fixed fee would not be paid in full because of non-performance of the transferred financial asset. In these examples, the servicer has an interest in the future performance of the transferred financial asset. This assessment is independent of whether the fee to be received is expected to compensate the entity adequately for performing the servicing.

B31 Continuing involvement in a transferred financial asset may result from contractual provisions in the transfer agreement or in a separate agreement with the transferee or a third party entered into in connection with the transfer.

Transferred financial assets that are not derecognised in their entirety (paragraph 42D)

B32 Paragraph 42D requires disclosures when part or all of the transferred financial assets do not qualify for derecognition. Those disclosures are required at each reporting date at which the entity continues to recognise the transferred financial assets, regardless of when the transfers occurred.

Types of continuing involvement (paragraphs 42E–42H)

B33 Paragraphs 42E–42H require qualitative and quantitative disclosures for each type of continuing involvement in derecognised financial assets. An entity shall aggregate its continuing involvement into types that are representative of the entity's exposure to risks. For example, an entity may aggregate its continuing involvement by type of financial instrument (eg guarantees or call options) or by type of transfer (eg factoring of receivables, securitisations and securities lending).

Maturity analysis for undiscounted cash outflows to repurchase transferred assets (paragraph 42E(e))

B34 Paragraph 42E(e) requires an entity to disclose a maturity analysis of the undiscounted cash outflows to repurchase derecognised financial assets or other amounts payable to the transferee in respect of the derecognised financial assets, showing the remaining contractual maturities of the entity's continuing involvement. This analysis distinguishes cash flows that are required to be paid (eg forward contracts), cash flows that the entity may be required to pay (eg written put options) and cash flows that the entity might choose to pay (eg purchased call options).

B35   An entity shall use its judgement to determine an appropriate number of time bands in preparing the maturity analysis required by paragraph 42E(e). For example, an entity might determine that the following maturity time bands are appropriate:

     (a)   not later than one month;

     (b)   later than one month and not later than three months;

     (c)   later than three months and not later than six months;

     (d)   later than six months and not later than one year;

     (e)   later than one year and not later than three years;

     (f)   later than three years and not later than five years; and

     (g)   more than five years.

B36   If there is a range of possible maturities, the cash flows are included on the basis of the earliest date on which the entity can be required or is permitted to pay.

Qualitative information (paragraph 42E(f))

B37   The qualitative information required by paragraph 42E(f) includes a description of the derecognised financial assets and the nature and purpose of the continuing involvement retained after transferring those assets. It also includes a description of the risks to which an entity is exposed, including:

     (a)   a description of how the entity manages the risk inherent in its continuing involvement in the derecognised financial assets.

     (b)   whether the entity is required to bear losses before other parties, and the ranking and amounts of losses borne by parties whose interests rank lower than the entity's interest in the asset (ie its continuing involvement in the asset).

     (c)   a description of any triggers associated with obligations to provide financial support or to repurchase a transferred financial asset.

Gain or loss on derecognition (paragraph 42G(a))

B38   Paragraph 42G(a) requires an entity to disclose the gain or loss on derecognition relating to financial assets in which the entity has continuing involvement. The entity shall disclose if a gain or loss on derecognition arose because the fair values of the components of the previously recognised asset (ie the interest in the asset derecognised and the interest retained by the entity) were different from the fair value of the previously recognised asset as a whole. In that situation, the entity shall also disclose whether the fair value measurements included significant inputs that were not based on observable market data, as described in paragraph 27A.

Supplementary information (paragraph 42H)

B39   The disclosures required in paragraphs 42D–42G may not be sufficient to meet the disclosure objectives in paragraph 42B. If this is the case, the entity shall disclose whatever additional information is necessary to meet the disclosure objectives. The entity shall decide, in the light of its circumstances, how much additional information it needs to provide to satisfy the information needs of users and how much emphasis it places on different aspects of the additional information. It is necessary to strike a balance between burdening financial statements with excessive detail that may not assist users of financial statements and obscuring information as a result of too much aggregation.

Offsetting financial assets and financial liabilities (paragraphs 13A–13F)

Scope (paragraph 13A)

B40   The disclosures in paragraphs 13B–13E are required for all recognised financial instruments that are set off in accordance with paragraph 42 of IAS 32. In addition, financial instruments are within the scope of the disclosure requirements in paragraphs 13B–13E if they are subject to an enforceable master netting arrangement or similar agreement that covers similar financial instruments and transactions, irrespective of whether the financial instruments are set off in accordance with paragraph 42 of IAS 32.

B41   The similar agreements referred to in paragraphs 13A and B40 include derivative clearing agreements, global master repurchase agreements, global master securities lending agreements, and any related rights to financial collateral. The similar financial instruments and transactions referred to in paragraph B40 include derivatives, sale and repurchase agreements, reverse sale and repurchase agreements, securities borrowing, and securities lending agreements. Examples of financial instruments that are not within the scope of paragraph 13A are loans and customer deposits at the same institution (unless they are set off in the statement of financial position), and financial instruments that are subject only to a collateral agreement.

Disclosure of quantitative information for recognised financial assets and recognised financial liabilities within the scope of paragraph 13A (paragraph 13C)

B42   Financial instruments disclosed in accordance with paragraph 13C may be subject to different measurement requirements (for example, a payable related to a repurchase agreement may be measured at amortised cost, while a derivative will be measured at fair value). An entity shall include instruments at their recognised amounts and describe any resulting measurement differences in the related disclosures.

Disclosure of the gross amounts of recognised financial assets and recognised financial liabilities within the scope of paragraph 13A (paragraph 13C(a))

B43 The amounts required by paragraph 13C(a) relate to recognised financial instruments that are set off in accordance with paragraph 42 of IAS 32. The amounts required by paragraph 13C(a) also relate to recognised financial instruments that are subject to an enforceable master netting arrangement or similar agreement irrespective of whether they meet the offsetting criteria. However, the disclosures required by paragraph 13C(a) do not relate to any amounts recognised as a result of collateral agreements that do not meet the offsetting criteria in paragraph 42 of IAS 32. Instead, such amounts are required to be disclosed in accordance with paragraph 13C(d).

Disclosure of the amounts that are set off in accordance with the criteria in paragraph 42 of IAS 32 (paragraph 13C(b))

B44 Paragraph 13C(b) requires that entities disclose the amounts set off in accordance with paragraph 42 of IAS 32 when determining the net amounts presented in the statement of financial position. The amounts of both the recognised financial assets and the recognised financial liabilities that are subject to set-off under the same arrangement will be disclosed in both the financial asset and financial liability disclosures. However, the amounts disclosed (in, for example, a table) are limited to the amounts that are subject to set-off. For example, an entity may have a recognised derivative asset and a recognised derivative liability that meet the offsetting criteria in paragraph 42 of IAS 32. If the gross amount of the derivative asset is larger than the gross amount of the derivative liability, the financial asset disclosure table will include the entire amount of the derivative asset (in accordance with paragraph 13C(a)) and the entire amount of the derivative liability (in accordance with paragraph 13C(b)). However, while the financial liability disclosure table will include the entire amount of the derivative liability (in accordance with paragraph 13C(a)), it will only include the amount of the derivative asset (in accordance with paragraph 13C(b)) that is equal to the amount of the derivative liability.

Disclosure of the net amounts presented in the statement of financial position (paragraph 13C(c))

B45 If an entity has instruments that meet the scope of these disclosures (as specified in paragraph 13A), but that do not meet the offsetting criteria in paragraph 42 of IAS 32, the amounts required to be disclosed by paragraph 13C(c) would equal the amounts required to be disclosed by paragraph 13C(a).

B46 The amounts required to be disclosed by paragraph 13C(c) must be reconciled to the individual line item amounts presented in the statement of financial position. For example, if an entity determines that the aggregation or disaggregation of individual financial statement line item amounts provides more relevant information, it must reconcile the aggregated or disaggregated amounts disclosed in paragraph 13C(c) back to the individual line item amounts presented in the statement of financial position.

Disclosure of the amounts subject to an enforceable master netting arrangement or similar agreement that are not otherwise included in paragraph 13C(b) (paragraph 13C(d))

B47 Paragraph 13C(d) requires that entities disclose amounts that are subject to an enforceable master netting arrangement or similar agreement that are not otherwise included in paragraph 13C(b). Paragraph 13C(d)(i) refers to amounts related to recognised financial instruments that do not meet some or all of the offsetting criteria in paragraph 42 of IAS 32 (for example, current rights of set-off that do not meet the criterion in paragraph 42(b) of IAS 32, or conditional rights of set-off that are enforceable and exercisable only in the event of default, or only in the event of insolvency or bankruptcy of any of the counterparties).

B48 Paragraph 13C(d)(ii) refers to amounts related to financial collateral, including cash collateral, both received and pledged. An entity shall disclose the fair value of those financial instruments that have been pledged or received as collateral. The amounts disclosed in accordance with paragraph 13C(d)(ii) should relate to the actual collateral received or pledged and not to any resulting payables or receivables recognised to return or receive back such collateral.

Limits on the amounts disclosed in paragraph 13C(d) (paragraph 13D)

B49 When disclosing amounts in accordance with paragraph 13C(d), an entity must take into account the effects of over-collateralisation by financial instrument. To do so, the entity must first deduct the amounts disclosed in accordance with paragraph 13C(d)(i) from the amount disclosed in accordance with paragraph 13C(c). The entity shall then limit the amounts disclosed in accordance with paragraph 13C(d)(ii) to the remaining amount in paragraph 13C(c) for the related financial instrument. However, if rights to collateral can be enforced across financial instruments, such rights can be included in the disclosure provided in accordance with paragraph 13D.

Description of the rights of set-off subject to enforceable master netting arrangements and similar agreements (paragraph 13E)

B50 An entity shall describe the types of rights of set-off and similar arrangements disclosed in accordance with paragraph 13C(d), including the nature of those rights. For example, an entity shall describe its conditional rights. For instruments subject to rights of set-off that are not contingent on a future event but that do not meet the remaining criteria in paragraph 42 of IAS 32, the entity shall describe the reason(s) why the criteria are not met. For any financial collateral received or pledged, the entity shall describe the terms of the collateral agreement (for example, when the collateral is restricted).

Disclosure by type of financial instrument or by counterparty

B51 The quantitative disclosures required by paragraph 13C(a)–(e) may be grouped by type of financial instrument or transaction (for example, derivatives, repurchase and reverse repurchase agreements or securities borrowing and securities lending agreements).

B52   Alternatively, an entity may group the quantitative disclosures required by paragraph 13C(a)–(c) by type of financial instrument, and the quantitative disclosures required by paragraph 13C(c)–(e) by counterparty. If an entity provides the required information by counterparty, the entity is not required to identify the counterparties by name. However, designation of counterparties (Counterparty A, Counterparty B, Counterparty C, etc) shall remain consistent from year to year for the years presented to maintain comparability. Qualitative disclosures shall be considered so that further information can be given about the types of counterparties. When disclosure of the amounts in paragraph 13C(c)–(e) is provided by counterparty, amounts that are individually significant in terms of total counterparty amounts shall be separately disclosed and the remaining individually insignificant counterparty amounts shall be aggregated into one line item.

Other

B53   The specific disclosures required by paragraphs 13C–13E are minimum requirements. To meet the objective in paragraph 13B an entity may need to supplement them with additional (qualitative) disclosures, depending on the terms of the enforceable master netting arrangements and related agreements, including the nature of the rights of set-off, and their effect or potential effect on the entity's financial position.

Appendix C
Amendments to other IFRSs

The amendments in this appendix shall be applied for annual periods beginning on or after 1 January 2007. If an entity applies this IFRS for an earlier period, these amendments shall be applied for that earlier period.

* * * * *

The amendments contained in this appendix when this IFRS was issued in 2005 have been incorporated into the text of the relevant IFRSs included in this volume.

Approval by the Board of IFRS 7 issued in August 2005

International Financial Reporting Standard 7 *Financial Instruments: Disclosures* was approved for issue by the fourteen members of the International Accounting Standards Board.

Sir David Tweedie	Chairman
Thomas E Jones	Vice-Chairman
Mary E Barth	
Hans-Georg Bruns	
Anthony T Cope	
Jan Engström	
Robert P Garnett	
Gilbert Gélard	
James J Leisenring	
Warren J McGregor	
Patricia L O'Malley	
John T Smith	
Geoffrey Whittington	
Tatsumi Yamada	

Approval by the Board of *Improving Disclosures about Financial Instruments* (Amendments to IFRS 7) issued in March 2009

Improving Disclosures about Financial Instruments (Amendments to IFRS 7) was approved for issue by the fourteen members of the International Accounting Standards Board.

Sir David Tweedie	Chairman
Thomas E Jones	Vice-Chairman
Mary E Barth	
Stephen Cooper	
Philippe Danjou	
Jan Engström	
Robert P Garnett	
Gilbert Gélard	
Prabhakar Kalavacherla	
James J Leisenring	
Warren J McGregor	
John T Smith	
Tatsumi Yamada	
Wei-Guo Zhang	

Approval by the Board of *Disclosures—Transfers of Financial Assets* (Amendments to IFRS 7) issued in October 2010

Disclosures—Transfers of Financial Assets (Amendments to IFRS 7) was approved for issue by the fourteen members of the International Accounting Standards Board.

Sir David Tweedie	Chairman

Stephen Cooper

Philippe Danjou

Jan Engström

Patrick Finnegan

Amaro Luiz de Oliveira Gomes

Prabhakar Kalavacherla

Elke König

Patricia McConnell

Warren J McGregor

Paul Pacter

John T Smith

Tatsumi Yamada

Wei-Guo Zhang

Approval by the Board of *Mandatory Effective Date of IFRS 9 and Transition Disclosures* (Amendments to IFRS 9 (2009), IFRS 9 (2010) and IFRS 7) issued in December 2011

Mandatory Effective Date of IFRS 9 and Transition Disclosures (Amendments to IFRS 9 (2009), IFRS 9 (2010) and IFRS 7) was approved for publication by fourteen of the fifteen members of the International Accounting Standards Board. Ms McConnell dissented from the issue of the amendments. Her dissenting opinion is set out after the Basis for Conclusions.

Hans Hoogervorst	Chairman
Ian Mackintosh	Vice-Chairman
Stephen Cooper	
Philippe Danjou	
Jan Engström	
Patrick Finnegan	
Amaro Luiz de Oliveira Gomes	
Prabhakar Kalavacherla	
Elke König	
Patricia McConnell	
Takatsugu Ochi	
Paul Pacter	
Darrel Scott	
John T Smith	
Wei-Guo Zhang	

Approval by the Board of *Disclosures—Offsetting Financial Assets and Financial Liabilities* (Amendments to IFRS 7) issued in December 2011

Disclosures—Offsetting Financial Assets and Financial Liabilities (Amendments to IFRS 7) was approved for issue by the fifteen members of the International Accounting Standards Board.

Hans Hoogervorst	Chairman
Ian Mackintosh	Vice-Chairman
Stephen Cooper	
Philippe Danjou	
Jan Engström	
Patrick Finnegan	
Amaro Luiz de Oliveira Gomes	
Prabhakar Kalavacherla	
Elke König	
Patricia McConnell	
Takatsugu Ochi	
Paul Pacter	
Darrel Scott	
John T Smith	
Wei-Guo Zhang	

Approval by the Board of IFRS 9 *Financial Instruments* (Hedge Accounting and amendments to IFRS 9, IFRS 7 and IAS 39) issued in November 2013

IFRS 9 *Financial Instruments* (Hedge Accounting and amendments to IFRS 9, IFRS 7 and IAS 39) was approved for issue by fifteen of the sixteen members of the International Accounting Standards Board. Mr Finnegan dissented. His dissenting opinion is set out after the Basis for Conclusions.

Hans Hoogervorst	Chairman
Ian Mackintosh	Vice-Chairman
Stephen Cooper	
Philippe Danjou	
Martin Edelmann	
Jan Engström	
Patrick Finnegan	
Amaro Luiz de Oliveira Gomes	
Gary Kabureck	
Prabhakar Kalavacherla	
Patricia McConnell	
Takatsugu Ochi	
Darrel Scott	
Chungwoo Suh	
Mary Tokar	
Wei-Guo Zhang	

Approval by the Board of *Interest Rate Benchmark Reform* issued in September 2019

Interest Rate Benchmark Reform, which amended IFRS 9, IAS 39 and IFRS 7, was approved for issue by all 14 members of the International Accounting Standards Board (Board).

Hans Hoogervorst	Chairman
Suzanne Lloyd	Vice-Chair
Nick Anderson	
Tadeu Cendon	
Martin Edelmann	
Françoise Flores	
Gary Kabureck	
Jianqiao Lu	
Darrel Scott	
Thomas Scott	
Chungwoo Suh	
Rika Suzuki	
Ann Tarca	
Mary Tokar	

Approval by the Board of *Interest Rate Benchmark Reform—Phase 2* issued in August 2020

Interest Rate Benchmark Reform—Phase 2, which amended IFRS 9, IAS 39, IFRS 7, IFRS 4 and IFRS 16, was approved for issue by 12 of 13 members of the International Accounting Standards Board (Board). Mr Gast abstained in view of his recent appointment to the Board.

Hans Hoogervorst	Chairman
Suzanne Lloyd	Vice-Chair
Nick Anderson	
Tadeu Cendon	
Martin Edelmann	
Françoise Flores	
Zach Gast	
Jianqiao Lu	
Darrel Scott	
Thomas Scott	
Rika Suzuki	
Ann Tarca	
Mary Tokar	

Approval by the Board of Interest Rate Benchmark Reform—Phase 2 issued in August 2020

Interest Rate Benchmark Reform—Phase 2, which amended IFRS 9, IAS 39, IFRS 7, IFRS 4 and IFRS 16, was approved for issue by 12 of 13 members of the International Accounting Standards Board (Board). Mr Uhl abstained in view of his recent appointment to the Board.

Hans Hoogervorst	Chairman
Suzanne Lloyd	Vice-Chair
Nick Anderson	
Tadeu Cendon	
Martin Edelmann	
Françoise Flores	
Zach Gast	
Jianqiao Lu	
Darrel Scott	
Thomas Scott	
Rika Suzuki	
Ann Tarca	
Mary Tokar	

IFRS 8

Operating Segments

In April 2001 the International Accounting Standards Board (Board) adopted IAS 14 *Segment Reporting*, which had originally been issued by the International Accounting Standards Committee in August 1997. IAS 14 *Segment Reporting* replaced IAS 14 *Reporting Financial Information by Segment*, issued in August 1981.

In November 2006 the Board issued IFRS 8 *Operating Segments* to replace IAS 14. IAS 1 *Presentation of Financial Statements* (as revised in 2007) amended the terminology used throughout the Standards, including IFRS 8.

Other Standards have made minor consequential amendments to IFRS 8. They include IAS 19 *Employee Benefits* (issued June 2011), *Annual Improvements to IFRSs 2010–2012 Cycle* (issued December 2013) and *Amendments to References to the Conceptual Framework in IFRS Standards* (issued March 2018).

Contents

FOR THE ACCOMPANYING GUIDANCE LISTED BELOW, SEE PART B OF THIS EDITION

FOR THE BASIS FOR CONCLUSIONS, SEE PART C OF THIS EDITION

International Financial Reporting Standard 8 *Operating Segments* (IFRS 8) is set out in paragraphs 1–37 and Appendices A and B. All the paragraphs have equal authority. Paragraphs in **bold type** state the main principles. Definitions of terms are given in the Glossary for International Financial Reporting Standards. IFRS 8 should be read in the context of its core principle and the Basis for Conclusions, the *Preface to IFRS Standards* and the *Conceptual Framework for Financial Reporting*. IAS 8 *Accounting Policies, Changes in Accounting Estimates and Errors* provides a basis for selecting and applying accounting policies in the absence of explicit guidance.

International Financial Reporting Standard 8
Operating Segments

Core principle

1   An entity shall disclose information to enable users of its financial statements to evaluate the nature and financial effects of the business activities in which it engages and the economic environments in which it operates.

Scope

2   This IFRS shall apply to:

(a)   the separate or individual financial statements of an entity:

(i)   whose debt or equity instruments are traded in a public market (a domestic or foreign stock exchange or an over-the-counter market, including local and regional markets), or

(ii)   that files, or is in the process of filing, its financial statements with a securities commission or other regulatory organisation for the purpose of issuing any class of instruments in a public market; and

(b)   the consolidated financial statements of a group with a parent:

(i)   whose debt or equity instruments are traded in a public market (a domestic or foreign stock exchange or an over-the-counter market, including local and regional markets), or

(ii)   that files, or is in the process of filing, the consolidated financial statements with a securities commission or other regulatory organisation for the purpose of issuing any class of instruments in a public market.

3   If an entity that is not required to apply this IFRS chooses to disclose information about segments that does not comply with this IFRS, it shall not describe the information as segment information.

4   If a financial report contains both the consolidated financial statements of a parent that is within the scope of this IFRS as well as the parent's separate financial statements, segment information is required only in the consolidated financial statements.

Operating segments

5   An operating segment is a component of an entity:

(a)   that engages in business activities from which it may earn revenues and incur expenses (including revenues and expenses relating to transactions with other components of the same entity),

(b)   whose operating results are regularly reviewed by the entity's chief operating decision maker to make decisions about resources to be allocated to the segment and assess its performance, and

(c)   for which discrete financial information is available.

An operating segment may engage in business activities for which it has yet to earn revenues, for example, start-up operations may be operating segments before earning revenues.

6   Not every part of an entity is necessarily an operating segment or part of an operating segment. For example, a corporate headquarters or some functional departments may not earn revenues or may earn revenues that are only incidental to the activities of the entity and would not be operating segments. For the purposes of this IFRS, an entity's post-employment benefit plans are not operating segments.

7   The term 'chief operating decision maker' identifies a function, not necessarily a manager with a specific title. That function is to allocate resources to and assess the performance of the operating segments of an entity. Often the chief operating decision maker of an entity is its chief executive officer or chief operating officer but, for example, it may be a group of executive directors or others.

8   For many entities, the three characteristics of operating segments described in paragraph 5 clearly identify its operating segments. However, an entity may produce reports in which its business activities are presented in a variety of ways. If the chief operating decision maker uses more than one set of segment information, other factors may identify a single set of components as constituting an entity's operating segments, including the nature of the business activities of each component, the existence of managers responsible for them, and information presented to the board of directors.

9   Generally, an operating segment has a segment manager who is directly accountable to and maintains regular contact with the chief operating decision maker to discuss operating activities, financial results, forecasts, or plans for the segment. The term 'segment manager' identifies a function, not necessarily a manager with a specific title. The chief operating decision maker also may be the segment manager for some operating segments. A single manager may be the segment manager for more than one operating segment. If the characteristics in paragraph 5 apply to more than one set of components of an organisation but there is only one set for which segment managers are held responsible, that set of components constitutes the operating segments.

10   The characteristics in paragraph 5 may apply to two or more overlapping sets of components for which managers are held responsible. That structure is sometimes referred to as a matrix form of organisation. For example, in some entities, some managers are responsible for different product and service lines worldwide, whereas other managers are responsible for specific geographical areas. The chief operating decision maker regularly reviews the operating results of both sets of components, and financial information is available for

both. In that situation, the entity shall determine which set of components constitutes the operating segments by reference to the core principle.

Reportable segments

11 An entity shall report separately information about each operating segment that:

(a) has been identified in accordance with paragraphs 5–10 or results from aggregating two or more of those segments in accordance with paragraph 12, and

(b) exceeds the quantitative thresholds in paragraph 13.

Paragraphs 14–19 specify other situations in which separate information about an operating segment shall be reported.

Aggregation criteria

12 Operating segments often exhibit similar long-term financial performance if they have similar economic characteristics. For example, similar long-term average gross margins for two operating segments would be expected if their economic characteristics were similar. Two or more operating segments may be aggregated into a single operating segment if aggregation is consistent with the core principle of this IFRS, the segments have similar economic characteristics, and the segments are similar in each of the following respects:

(a) the nature of the products and services;

(b) the nature of the production processes;

(c) the type or class of customer for their products and services;

(d) the methods used to distribute their products or provide their services; and

(e) if applicable, the nature of the regulatory environment, for example, banking, insurance or public utilities.

Quantitative thresholds

13 An entity shall report separately information about an operating segment that meets any of the following quantitative thresholds:

(a) Its reported revenue, including both sales to external customers and intersegment sales or transfers, is 10 per cent or more of the combined revenue, internal and external, of all operating segments.

(b) The absolute amount of its reported profit or loss is 10 per cent or more of the greater, in absolute amount, of (i) the combined reported profit of all operating segments that did not report a loss and (ii) the combined reported loss of all operating segments that reported a loss.

(c) Its assets are 10 per cent or more of the combined assets of all operating segments.

Operating segments that do not meet any of the quantitative thresholds may be considered reportable, and separately disclosed, if management believes that information about the segment would be useful to users of the financial statements.

14   An entity may combine information about operating segments that do not meet the quantitative thresholds with information about other operating segments that do not meet the quantitative thresholds to produce a reportable segment only if the operating segments have similar economic characteristics and share a majority of the aggregation criteria listed in paragraph 12.

15   If the total external revenue reported by operating segments constitutes less than 75 per cent of the entity's revenue, additional operating segments shall be identified as reportable segments (even if they do not meet the criteria in paragraph 13) until at least 75 per cent of the entity's revenue is included in reportable segments.

16   Information about other business activities and operating segments that are not reportable shall be combined and disclosed in an 'all other segments' category separately from other reconciling items in the reconciliations required by paragraph 28. The sources of the revenue included in the 'all other segments' category shall be described.

17   If management judges that an operating segment identified as a reportable segment in the immediately preceding period is of continuing significance, information about that segment shall continue to be reported separately in the current period even if it no longer meets the criteria for reportability in paragraph 13.

18   If an operating segment is identified as a reportable segment in the current period in accordance with the quantitative thresholds, segment data for a prior period presented for comparative purposes shall be restated to reflect the newly reportable segment as a separate segment, even if that segment did not satisfy the criteria for reportability in paragraph 13 in the prior period, unless the necessary information is not available and the cost to develop it would be excessive.

19   There may be a practical limit to the number of reportable segments that an entity separately discloses beyond which segment information may become too detailed. Although no precise limit has been determined, as the number of segments that are reportable in accordance with paragraphs 13–18 increases above ten, the entity should consider whether a practical limit has been reached.

Disclosure

20   **An entity shall disclose information to enable users of its financial statements to evaluate the nature and financial effects of the business activities in which it engages and the economic environments in which it operates.**

21   To give effect to the principle in paragraph 20, an entity shall disclose the following for each period for which a statement of comprehensive income is presented:

(a)   general information as described in paragraph 22;

(b)   information about reported segment profit or loss, including specified revenues and expenses included in reported segment profit or loss, segment assets, segment liabilities and the basis of measurement, as described in paragraphs 23–27; and

(c)   reconciliations of the totals of segment revenues, reported segment profit or loss, segment assets, segment liabilities and other material segment items to corresponding entity amounts as described in paragraph 28.

Reconciliations of the amounts in the statement of financial position for reportable segments to the amounts in the entity's statement of financial position are required for each date at which a statement of financial position is presented. Information for prior periods shall be restated as described in paragraphs 29 and 30.

General information

22   An entity shall disclose the following general information:

(a)   factors used to identify the entity's reportable segments, including the basis of organisation (for example, whether management has chosen to organise the entity around differences in products and services, geographical areas, regulatory environments, or a combination of factors and whether operating segments have been aggregated);

(aa)   the judgements made by management in applying the aggregation criteria in paragraph 12. This includes a brief description of the operating segments that have been aggregated in this way and the economic indicators that have been assessed in determining that the aggregated operating segments share similar economic characteristics; and

(b)   types of products and services from which each reportable segment derives its revenues.

Information about profit or loss, assets and liabilities

23   An entity shall report a measure of profit or loss for each reportable segment. An entity shall report a measure of total assets and liabilities for each reportable segment if such amounts are regularly provided to the chief operating decision maker. An entity shall also disclose the following about each reportable segment if the specified amounts are included in the measure of segment profit or loss reviewed by the chief operating decision maker, or are otherwise regularly provided to the chief operating decision maker, even if not included in that measure of segment profit or loss:

(a)   revenues from external customers;

(b)   revenues from transactions with other operating segments of the same entity;

(c)   interest revenue;

(d)   interest expense;

(e)   depreciation and amortisation;

(f)   material items of income and expense disclosed in accordance with paragraph 97 of IAS 1 *Presentation of Financial Statements* (as revised in 2007);

(g)   the entity's interest in the profit or loss of associates and joint ventures accounted for by the equity method;

(h)   income tax expense or income; and

(i)   material non-cash items other than depreciation and amortisation.

An entity shall report interest revenue separately from interest expense for each reportable segment unless a majority of the segment's revenues are from interest and the chief operating decision maker relies primarily on net interest revenue to assess the performance of the segment and make decisions about resources to be allocated to the segment. In that situation, an entity may report that segment's interest revenue net of its interest expense and disclose that it has done so.

24   An entity shall disclose the following about each reportable segment if the specified amounts are included in the measure of segment assets reviewed by the chief operating decision maker or are otherwise regularly provided to the chief operating decision maker, even if not included in the measure of segment assets:

(a)   the amount of investment in associates and joint ventures accounted for by the equity method, and

(b)   the amounts of additions to non-current assets[1] other than financial instruments, deferred tax assets, net defined benefit assets (see IAS 19 *Employee Benefits*) and rights arising under insurance contracts.

Measurement

25   The amount of each segment item reported shall be the measure reported to the chief operating decision maker for the purposes of making decisions about allocating resources to the segment and assessing its performance. Adjustments and eliminations made in preparing an entity's financial statements and allocations of revenues, expenses, and gains or losses shall be included in determining reported segment profit or loss only if they are included in the measure of the segment's profit or loss that is used by the chief operating decision maker. Similarly, only those assets and liabilities that

---

1   For assets classified according to a liquidity presentation, non-current assets are assets that include amounts expected to be recovered more than twelve months after the reporting period.

are included in the measures of the segment's assets and segment's liabilities that are used by the chief operating decision maker shall be reported for that segment. If amounts are allocated to reported segment profit or loss, assets or liabilities, those amounts shall be allocated on a reasonable basis.

26   If the chief operating decision maker uses only one measure of an operating segment's profit or loss, the segment's assets or the segment's liabilities in assessing segment performance and deciding how to allocate resources, segment profit or loss, assets and liabilities shall be reported at those measures. If the chief operating decision maker uses more than one measure of an operating segment's profit or loss, the segment's assets or the segment's liabilities, the reported measures shall be those that management believes are determined in accordance with the measurement principles most consistent with those used in measuring the corresponding amounts in the entity's financial statements.

27   An entity shall provide an explanation of the measurements of segment profit or loss, segment assets and segment liabilities for each reportable segment. At a minimum, an entity shall disclose the following:

(a)   the basis of accounting for any transactions between reportable segments.

(b)   the nature of any differences between the measurements of the reportable segments' profits or losses and the entity's profit or loss before income tax expense or income and discontinued operations (if not apparent from the reconciliations described in paragraph 28). Those differences could include accounting policies and policies for allocation of centrally incurred costs that are necessary for an understanding of the reported segment information.

(c)   the nature of any differences between the measurements of the reportable segments' assets and the entity's assets (if not apparent from the reconciliations described in paragraph 28). Those differences could include accounting policies and policies for allocation of jointly used assets that are necessary for an understanding of the reported segment information.

(d)   the nature of any differences between the measurements of the reportable segments' liabilities and the entity's liabilities (if not apparent from the reconciliations described in paragraph 28). Those differences could include accounting policies and policies for allocation of jointly utilised liabilities that are necessary for an understanding of the reported segment information.

(e)   the nature of any changes from prior periods in the measurement methods used to determine reported segment profit or loss and the effect, if any, of those changes on the measure of segment profit or loss.

(f)   the nature and effect of any asymmetrical allocations to reportable segments. For example, an entity might allocate depreciation expense to a segment without allocating the related depreciable assets to that segment.

Reconciliations

28   An entity shall provide reconciliations of all of the following:

(a)   the total of the reportable segments' revenues to the entity's revenue.

(b)   the total of the reportable segments' measures of profit or loss to the entity's profit or loss before tax expense (tax income) and discontinued operations. However, if an entity allocates to reportable segments items such as tax expense (tax income), the entity may reconcile the total of the segments' measures of profit or loss to the entity's profit or loss after those items.

(c)   the total of the reportable segments' assets to the entity's assets if the segment assets are reported in accordance with paragraph 23.

(d)   the total of the reportable segments' liabilities to the entity's liabilities if segment liabilities are reported in accordance with paragraph 23.

(e)   the total of the reportable segments' amounts for every other material item of information disclosed to the corresponding amount for the entity.

All material reconciling items shall be separately identified and described. For example, the amount of each material adjustment needed to reconcile reportable segment profit or loss to the entity's profit or loss arising from different accounting policies shall be separately identified and described.

Restatement of previously reported information

29   If an entity changes the structure of its internal organisation in a manner that causes the composition of its reportable segments to change, the corresponding information for earlier periods, including interim periods, shall be restated unless the information is not available and the cost to develop it would be excessive. The determination of whether the information is not available and the cost to develop it would be excessive shall be made for each individual item of disclosure. Following a change in the composition of its reportable segments, an entity shall disclose whether it has restated the corresponding items of segment information for earlier periods.

30   If an entity has changed the structure of its internal organisation in a manner that causes the composition of its reportable segments to change and if segment information for earlier periods, including interim periods, is not restated to reflect the change, the entity shall disclose in the year in which the change occurs segment information for the current period on both the old basis and the new basis of segmentation, unless the necessary information is not available and the cost to develop it would be excessive.

Entity-wide disclosures

31 Paragraphs 32–34 apply to all entities subject to this IFRS including those entities that have a single reportable segment. Some entities' business activities are not organised on the basis of differences in related products and services or differences in geographical areas of operations. Such an entity's reportable segments may report revenues from a broad range of essentially different products and services, or more than one of its reportable segments may provide essentially the same products and services. Similarly, an entity's reportable segments may hold assets in different geographical areas and report revenues from customers in different geographical areas, or more than one of its reportable segments may operate in the same geographical area. Information required by paragraphs 32–34 shall be provided only if it is not provided as part of the reportable segment information required by this IFRS.

Information about products and services

32 An entity shall report the revenues from external customers for each product and service, or each group of similar products and services, unless the necessary information is not available and the cost to develop it would be excessive, in which case that fact shall be disclosed. The amounts of revenues reported shall be based on the financial information used to produce the entity's financial statements.

Information about geographical areas

33 An entity shall report the following geographical information, unless the necessary information is not available and the cost to develop it would be excessive:

(a) revenues from external customers (i) attributed to the entity's country of domicile and (ii) attributed to all foreign countries in total from which the entity derives revenues. If revenues from external customers attributed to an individual foreign country are material, those revenues shall be disclosed separately. An entity shall disclose the basis for attributing revenues from external customers to individual countries.

(b) non-current assets[2] other than financial instruments, deferred tax assets, post-employment benefit assets, and rights arising under insurance contracts (i) located in the entity's country of domicile and (ii) located in all foreign countries in total in which the entity holds assets. If assets in an individual foreign country are material, those assets shall be disclosed separately.

The amounts reported shall be based on the financial information that is used to produce the entity's financial statements. If the necessary information is not available and the cost to develop it would be excessive, that fact shall be disclosed. An entity may provide, in addition to the information required by

---

2 For assets classified according to a liquidity presentation, non-current assets are assets that include amounts expected to be recovered more than twelve months after the reporting period.

this paragraph, subtotals of geographical information about groups of countries.

Information about major customers

34   An entity shall provide information about the extent of its reliance on its major customers. If revenues from transactions with a single external customer amount to 10 per cent or more of an entity's revenues, the entity shall disclose that fact, the total amount of revenues from each such customer, and the identity of the segment or segments reporting the revenues. The entity need not disclose the identity of a major customer or the amount of revenues that each segment reports from that customer. For the purposes of this IFRS, a group of entities known to a reporting entity to be under common control shall be considered a single customer. However, judgement is required to assess whether a government (including government agencies and similar bodies whether local, national or international) and entities known to the reporting entity to be under the control of that government are considered a single customer. In assessing this, the reporting entity shall consider the extent of economic integration between those entities.

Transition and effective date

35   An entity shall apply this IFRS in its annual financial statements for periods beginning on or after 1 January 2009. Earlier application is permitted. If an entity applies this IFRS in its financial statements for a period before 1 January 2009, it shall disclose that fact.

35A   Paragraph 23 was amended by *Improvements to IFRSs* issued in April 2009. An entity shall apply that amendment for annual periods beginning on or after 1 January 2010. Earlier application is permitted. If an entity applies the amendment for an earlier period it shall disclose that fact.

36   Segment information for prior years that is reported as comparative information for the initial year of application (including application of the amendment to paragraph 23 made in April 2009) shall be restated to conform to the requirements of this IFRS, unless the necessary information is not available and the cost to develop it would be excessive.

36A   IAS 1 (as revised in 2007) amended the terminology used throughout IFRSs. In addition it amended paragraph 23(f). An entity shall apply those amendments for annual periods beginning on or after 1 January 2009. If an entity applies IAS 1 (revised 2007) for an earlier period, the amendments shall be applied for that earlier period.

36B   IAS 24 *Related Party Disclosures* (as revised in 2009) amended paragraph 34 for annual periods beginning on or after 1 January 2011. If an entity applies IAS 24 (revised 2009) for an earlier period, it shall apply the amendment to paragraph 34 for that earlier period.

36C   *Annual Improvements to IFRSs 2010–2012 Cycle*, issued in December 2013, amended paragraphs 22 and 28. An entity shall apply those amendments for annual periods beginning on or after 1 July 2014. Earlier application is permitted. If an entity applies those amendments for an earlier period it shall disclose that fact.

Withdrawal of IAS 14

37   This IFRS supersedes IAS 14 *Segment Reporting*.

Appendix A
Defined term

This appendix is an integral part of the IFRS.

operating segment	An operating segment is a component of an entity:

(a)   that engages in business activities from which it may earn revenues and incur expenses (including revenues and expenses relating to transactions with other components of the same entity),

(b)   whose operating results are regularly reviewed by the entity's chief operating decision maker to make decisions about resources to be allocated to the segment and assess its performance, and

(c)   for which discrete financial information is available.

Appendix B
Amendments to other IFRSs

The amendments in this appendix shall be applied for annual periods beginning on or after 1 January 2009. If an entity applies this IFRS for an earlier period, these amendments shall be applied for that earlier period. In the amended paragraphs, new text is underlined and deleted text is struck through.

* * * * *

The amendments contained in this appendix when this IFRS was issued in 2006 have been incorporated into the text of the relevant IFRSs in this volume.

Approval by the Board of IFRS 8 issued in November 2006

International Financial Reporting Standard 8 *Operating Segments* was approved for issue by eleven of the thirteen members of the International Accounting Standards Board. Messrs Gélard and Leisenring dissented. Their dissenting opinions are set out after the Basis for Conclusions.

Sir David Tweedie	Chairman
Thomas E Jones	Vice-Chairman
Mary E Barth	
Hans-Georg Bruns	
Anthony T Cope	
Jan Engström	
Robert P Garnett	
Gilbert Gélard	
James J Leisenring	
Warren J McGregor	
Patricia L O'Malley	
John T Smith	
Tatsumi Yamada	

IFRS 9

Financial Instruments

In April 2001 the International Accounting Standards Board (Board) adopted IAS 39 *Financial Instruments: Recognition and Measurement*, which had originally been issued by the International Accounting Standards Committee in March 1999.

The Board had always intended that IFRS 9 *Financial Instruments* would replace IAS 39 in its entirety. However, in response to requests from interested parties that the accounting for financial instruments should be improved quickly, the Board divided its project to replace IAS 39 into three main phases. As the Board completed each phase, it issued chapters in IFRS 9 that replaced the corresponding requirements in IAS 39.

In November 2009 the Board issued the chapters of IFRS 9 relating to the classification and measurement of financial assets. In October 2010 the Board added the requirements related to the classification and measurement of financial liabilities to IFRS 9. This includes requirements on embedded derivatives and how to account for changes in own credit risk on financial liabilities designated under the fair value option.

In October 2010 the Board also decided to carry forward unchanged from IAS 39 the requirements related to the derecognition of financial assets and financial liabilities. Because of these changes, in October 2010 the Board restructured IFRS 9 and its Basis for Conclusions. In December 2011 the Board deferred the mandatory effective date of IFRS 9.

In November 2013 the Board added a Hedge Accounting chapter. IFRS 9 permits an entity to choose as its accounting policy either to apply the hedge accounting requirements of IFRS 9 or to continue to apply the hedge accounting requirements in IAS 39. Consequently, although IFRS 9 is effective (with limited exceptions for entities that issue insurance contracts and entities applying the *IFRS for SMEs* Standard), IAS 39, which now contains only its requirements for hedge accounting, also remains effective.

In July 2014 the Board issued the completed version of IFRS 9. The Board made limited amendments to the classification and measurement requirements for financial assets by addressing a narrow range of application questions and by introducing a 'fair value through other comprehensive income' measurement category for particular simple debt instruments. The Board also added the impairment requirements relating to the accounting for an entity's expected credit losses on its financial assets and commitments to extend credit. A new mandatory effective date was also set.

In October 2017 IFRS 9 was amended by *Prepayment Features with Negative Compensation* (Amendments to IFRS 9). The amendments specify that particular financial assets with prepayment features that may result in reasonable negative compensation for the early termination of such contracts are eligible to be measured at amortised cost or at fair value through other comprehensive income.

In September 2019 the Board amended IFRS 9 and IAS 39 by issuing *Interest Rate Benchmark Reform* to provide specific exceptions to hedge accounting requirements in IFRS 9 and IAS 39 for (a) highly probable requirement; (b) prospective assessments; (c) retrospective assessment (IAS 39 only); and (d) separately identifiable risk components. *Interest Rate*

Benchmark Reform also amended IFRS 7 to add specific disclosure requirements for hedging relationships to which an entity applies the exceptions in IFRS 9 or IAS 39.

In August 2020 the Board issued *Interest Rate Benchmark Reform—Phase 2* which amended requirements in IFRS 9, IAS 39, IFRS 7, IFRS 4 and IFRS 16 relating to:

- changes in the basis for determining contractual cash flows of financial assets, financial liabilities and lease liabilities;

- hedge accounting; and

- disclosures.

The Phase 2 amendments apply only to changes required by the interest rate benchmark reform to financial instruments and hedging relationships.

Other Standards have made minor consequential amendments to IFRS 9. They include *Severe Hyperinflation and Removal of Fixed Dates for First-time Adopters* (Amendments to IFRS 1) (issued December 2010), IFRS 10 *Consolidated Financial Statements* (issued May 2011), IFRS 11 *Joint Arrangements* (issued May 2011), IFRS 13 *Fair Value Measurement* (issued May 2011), IAS 19 *Employee Benefits* (issued June 2011), *Annual Improvements to IFRSs 2010–2012 Cycle* (issued December 2013), IFRS 15 *Revenue from Contracts with Customers* (issued May 2014), IFRS 16 *Leases* (issued January 2016), *Amendments to References to the Conceptual Framework in IFRS Standards* (issued March 2018) and *Annual Improvements to IFRS Standards 2018–2020* (issued May 2020).

Contents

...continued

FOR THE ACCOMPANYING GUIDANCE LISTED BELOW, SEE PART B OF THIS EDITION

ILLUSTRATIVE EXAMPLES

GUIDANCE ON IMPLEMENTING IFRS 9 *FINANCIAL INSTRUMENTS*

APPENDIX

Amendments to the guidance on other Standards

FOR THE BASIS FOR CONCLUSIONS, SEE PART C OF THIS EDITION

BASIS FOR CONCLUSIONS

DISSENTING OPINIONS

APPENDICES TO THE BASIS FOR CONCLUSIONS

A Previous dissenting opinions

B Amendments to the Basis for Conclusions on other Standards

International Financial Reporting Standard 9 *Financial Instruments* (IFRS 9) is set out in paragraphs 1.1–7.3.2 and Appendices A–C. All the paragraphs have equal authority. Paragraphs in **bold type** state the main principles. Terms defined in Appendix A are in *italics* the first time they appear in the IFRS. Definitions of other terms are given in the Glossary for International Financial Reporting Standards. IFRS 9 should be read in the context of its objective and the Basis for Conclusions, the *Preface to IFRS Standards* and the *Conceptual Framework for Financial Reporting*. IAS 8 *Accounting Policies, Changes in Accounting Estimates and Errors* provides a basis for selecting and applying accounting policies in the absence of explicit guidance.

International Financial Reporting Standard 9
Financial Instruments

Chapter 1 Objective

1.1   The objective of this Standard is to establish principles for the financial reporting of *financial assets* and *financial liabilities* that will present relevant and useful information to users of financial statements for their assessment of the amounts, timing and uncertainty of an entity's future cash flows.

Chapter 2 Scope

2.1   This Standard shall be applied by all entities to all types of financial instruments except:

(a)   those interests in subsidiaries, associates and joint ventures that are accounted for in accordance with IFRS 10 *Consolidated Financial Statements*, IAS 27 *Separate Financial Statements* or IAS 28 *Investments in Associates and Joint Ventures*. However, in some cases, IFRS 10, IAS 27 or IAS 28 require or permit an entity to account for an interest in a subsidiary, associate or joint venture in accordance with some or all of the requirements of this Standard. Entities shall also apply this Standard to derivatives on an interest in a subsidiary, associate or joint venture unless the derivative meets the definition of an equity instrument of the entity in IAS 32 *Financial Instruments: Presentation*.

(b)   rights and obligations under leases to which IFRS 16 *Leases* applies. However:

(i)   finance lease receivables (ie net investments in finance leases) and operating lease receivables recognised by a lessor are subject to the derecognition and impairment requirements of this Standard;

(ii)   lease liabilities recognised by a lessee are subject to the derecognition requirements in paragraph 3.3.1 of this Standard; and

(iii)   derivatives that are embedded in leases are subject to the embedded derivatives requirements of this Standard.

(c)   employers' rights and obligations under employee benefit plans, to which IAS 19 *Employee Benefits* applies.

(d)   financial instruments issued by the entity that meet the definition of an equity instrument in IAS 32 (including options and warrants) or that are required to be classified as an equity instrument in accordance with paragraphs 16A and 16B or paragraphs 16C and 16D of IAS 32. However, the holder of such equity instruments shall apply this Standard to those instruments, unless they meet the exception in (a).

(e) rights and obligations arising under (i) an insurance contract as defined in IFRS 4 *Insurance Contracts*, other than an issuer's rights and obligations arising under an insurance contract that meets the definition of a financial guarantee contract, or (ii) a contract that is within the scope of IFRS 4 because it contains a discretionary participation feature. However, this Standard applies to a derivative that is embedded in a contract within the scope of IFRS 4 if the derivative is not itself a contract within the scope of IFRS 4. Moreover, if an issuer of financial guarantee contracts has previously asserted explicitly that it regards such contracts as insurance contracts and has used accounting that is applicable to insurance contracts, the issuer may elect to apply either this Standard or IFRS 4 to such financial guarantee contracts (see paragraphs B2.5–B2.6). The issuer may make that election contract by contract, but the election for each contract is irrevocable.

(f) any forward contract between an acquirer and a selling shareholder to buy or sell an acquiree that will result in a business combination within the scope of IFRS 3 *Business Combinations* at a future acquisition date. The term of the forward contract should not exceed a reasonable period normally necessary to obtain any required approvals and to complete the transaction.

(g) loan commitments other than those loan commitments described in paragraph 2.3. However, an issuer of loan commitments shall apply the impairment requirements of this Standard to loan commitments that are not otherwise within the scope of this Standard. Also, all loan commitments are subject to the derecognition requirements of this Standard.

(h) financial instruments, contracts and obligations under share-based payment transactions to which IFRS 2 *Share-based Payment* applies, except for contracts within the scope of paragraphs 2.4–2.7 of this Standard to which this Standard applies.

(i) rights to payments to reimburse the entity for expenditure that it is required to make to settle a liability that it recognises as a provision in accordance with IAS 37 *Provisions, Contingent Liabilities and Contingent Assets*, or for which, in an earlier period, it recognised a provision in accordance with IAS 37.

(j) rights and obligations within the scope of IFRS 15 *Revenue from Contracts with Customers* that are financial instruments, except for those that IFRS 15 specifies are accounted for in accordance with this Standard.

2.2 The impairment requirements of this Standard shall be applied to those rights that IFRS 15 specifies are accounted for in accordance with this Standard for the purposes of recognising impairment gains or losses.

2.3   The following loan commitments are within the scope of this Standard:

    (a)   loan commitments that the entity designates as financial liabilities at fair value through profit or loss (see paragraph 4.2.2). An entity that has a past practice of selling the assets resulting from its loan commitments shortly after origination shall apply this Standard to all its loan commitments in the same class.

    (b)   loan commitments that can be settled net in cash or by delivering or issuing another financial instrument. These loan commitments are derivatives. A loan commitment is not regarded as settled net merely because the loan is paid out in instalments (for example, a mortgage construction loan that is paid out in instalments in line with the progress of construction).

    (c)   commitments to provide a loan at a below-market interest rate (see paragraph 4.2.1(d)).

2.4   This Standard shall be applied to those contracts to buy or sell a non-financial item that can be settled net in cash or another financial instrument, or by exchanging financial instruments, as if the contracts were financial instruments, with the exception of contracts that were entered into and continue to be held for the purpose of the receipt or delivery of a non-financial item in accordance with the entity's expected purchase, sale or usage requirements. However, this Standard shall be applied to those contracts that an entity designates as measured at fair value through profit or loss in accordance with paragraph 2.5.

2.5   A contract to buy or sell a non-financial item that can be settled net in cash or another financial instrument, or by exchanging financial instruments, as if the contract was a financial instrument, may be irrevocably designated as measured at fair value through profit or loss even if it was entered into for the purpose of the receipt or delivery of a non-financial item in accordance with the entity's expected purchase, sale or usage requirements. This designation is available only at inception of the contract and only if it eliminates or significantly reduces a recognition inconsistency (sometimes referred to as an 'accounting mismatch') that would otherwise arise from not recognising that contract because it is excluded from the scope of this Standard (see paragraph 2.4).

2.6   There are various ways in which a contract to buy or sell a non-financial item can be settled net in cash or another financial instrument or by exchanging financial instruments. These include:

    (a)   when the terms of the contract permit either party to settle it net in cash or another financial instrument or by exchanging financial instruments;

    (b)   when the ability to settle net in cash or another financial instrument, or by exchanging financial instruments, is not explicit in the terms of the contract, but the entity has a practice of settling similar contracts net in cash or another financial instrument or by exchanging financial instruments (whether with the counterparty, by entering into offsetting contracts or by selling the contract before its exercise or lapse);

(c)   when, for similar contracts, the entity has a practice of taking delivery of the underlying and selling it within a short period after delivery for the purpose of generating a profit from short-term fluctuations in price or dealer's margin; and

(d)   when the non-financial item that is the subject of the contract is readily convertible to cash.

A contract to which (b) or (c) applies is not entered into for the purpose of the receipt or delivery of the non-financial item in accordance with the entity's expected purchase, sale or usage requirements and, accordingly, is within the scope of this Standard. Other contracts to which paragraph 2.4 applies are evaluated to determine whether they were entered into and continue to be held for the purpose of the receipt or delivery of the non-financial item in accordance with the entity's expected purchase, sale or usage requirements and, accordingly, whether they are within the scope of this Standard.

2.7   A written option to buy or sell a non-financial item that can be settled net in cash or another financial instrument, or by exchanging financial instruments, in accordance with paragraph 2.6(a) or 2.6(d) is within the scope of this Standard. Such a contract cannot be entered into for the purpose of the receipt or delivery of the non-financial item in accordance with the entity's expected purchase, sale or usage requirements.

Chapter 3 Recognition and derecognition

3.1 Initial recognition

3.1.1   An entity shall recognise a financial asset or a financial liability in its statement of financial position when, and only when, the entity becomes party to the contractual provisions of the instrument (see paragraphs B3.1.1 and B3.1.2). When an entity first recognises a financial asset, it shall classify it in accordance with paragraphs 4.1.1–4.1.5 and measure it in accordance with paragraphs 5.1.1–5.1.3. When an entity first recognises a financial liability, it shall classify it in accordance with paragraphs 4.2.1 and 4.2.2 and measure it in accordance with paragraph 5.1.1.

Regular way purchase or sale of financial assets

3.1.2   A *regular way purchase or sale* of financial assets shall be recognised and derecognised, as applicable, using trade date accounting or settlement date accounting (see paragraphs B3.1.3–B3.1.6).

3.2 Derecognition of financial assets

3.2.1   In consolidated financial statements, paragraphs 3.2.2–3.2.9, B3.1.1, B3.1.2 and B3.2.1–B3.2.17 are applied at a consolidated level. Hence, an entity first consolidates all subsidiaries in accordance with IFRS 10 and then applies those paragraphs to the resulting group.

3.2.2   Before evaluating whether, and to what extent, *derecognition* is appropriate under paragraphs 3.2.3–3.2.9, an entity determines whether those paragraphs should be applied to a part of a financial asset (or a part of a group of similar financial assets) or a financial asset (or a group of similar financial assets) in its entirety, as follows.

(a)   Paragraphs 3.2.3–3.2.9 are applied to a part of a financial asset (or a part of a group of similar financial assets) if, and only if, the part being considered for derecognition meets one of the following three conditions.

(i)   The part comprises only specifically identified cash flows from a financial asset (or a group of similar financial assets). For example, when an entity enters into an interest rate strip whereby the counterparty obtains the right to the interest cash flows, but not the principal cash flows from a debt instrument, paragraphs 3.2.3–3.2.9 are applied to the interest cash flows.

(ii)   The part comprises only a fully proportionate (pro rata) share of the cash flows from a financial asset (or a group of similar financial assets). For example, when an entity enters into an arrangement whereby the counterparty obtains the rights to a 90 per cent share of all cash flows of a debt instrument, paragraphs 3.2.3–3.2.9 are applied to 90 per cent of those cash flows. If there is more than one counterparty, each counterparty is not required to have a proportionate share of the cash flows provided that the transferring entity has a fully proportionate share.

(iii)   The part comprises only a fully proportionate (pro rata) share of specifically identified cash flows from a financial asset (or a group of similar financial assets). For example, when an entity enters into an arrangement whereby the counterparty obtains the rights to a 90 per cent share of interest cash flows from a financial asset, paragraphs 3.2.3–3.2.9 are applied to 90 per cent of those interest cash flows. If there is more than one counterparty, each counterparty is not required to have a proportionate share of the specifically identified cash flows provided that the transferring entity has a fully proportionate share.

(b)   In all other cases, paragraphs 3.2.3–3.2.9 are applied to the financial asset in its entirety (or to the group of similar financial assets in their entirety). For example, when an entity transfers (i) the rights to the first or the last 90 per cent of cash collections from a financial asset (or a group of financial assets), or (ii) the rights to 90 per cent of the cash flows from a group of receivables, but provides a guarantee to compensate the buyer for any credit losses up to 8 per cent of the principal amount of the receivables, paragraphs 3.2.3–3.2.9 are applied to the financial asset (or a group of similar financial assets) in its entirety.

In paragraphs 3.2.3–3.2.12, the term 'financial asset' refers to either a part of a financial asset (or a part of a group of similar financial assets) as identified in (a) above or, otherwise, a financial asset (or a group of similar financial assets) in its entirety.

3.2.3   An entity shall derecognise a financial asset when, and only when:

(a)   the contractual rights to the cash flows from the financial asset expire, or

(b)   it transfers the financial asset as set out in paragraphs 3.2.4 and 3.2.5 and the transfer qualifies for derecognition in accordance with paragraph 3.2.6.

(See paragraph 3.1.2 for regular way sales of financial assets.)

3.2.4   An entity transfers a financial asset if, and only if, it either:

(a)   transfers the contractual rights to receive the cash flows of the financial asset, or

(b)   retains the contractual rights to receive the cash flows of the financial asset, but assumes a contractual obligation to pay the cash flows to one or more recipients in an arrangement that meets the conditions in paragraph 3.2.5.

3.2.5   When an entity retains the contractual rights to receive the cash flows of a financial asset (the 'original asset'), but assumes a contractual obligation to pay those cash flows to one or more entities (the 'eventual recipients'), the entity treats the transaction as a transfer of a financial asset if, and only if, all of the following three conditions are met.

(a)   The entity has no obligation to pay amounts to the eventual recipients unless it collects equivalent amounts from the original asset. Short-term advances by the entity with the right of full recovery of the amount lent plus accrued interest at market rates do not violate this condition.

(b)   The entity is prohibited by the terms of the transfer contract from selling or pledging the original asset other than as security to the eventual recipients for the obligation to pay them cash flows.

(c) The entity has an obligation to remit any cash flows it collects on behalf of the eventual recipients without material delay. In addition, the entity is not entitled to reinvest such cash flows, except for investments in cash or cash equivalents (as defined in IAS 7 *Statement of Cash Flows*) during the short settlement period from the collection date to the date of required remittance to the eventual recipients, and interest earned on such investments is passed to the eventual recipients.

3.2.6 When an entity transfers a financial asset (see paragraph 3.2.4), it shall evaluate the extent to which it retains the risks and rewards of ownership of the financial asset. In this case:

(a) if the entity transfers substantially all the risks and rewards of ownership of the financial asset, the entity shall derecognise the financial asset and recognise separately as assets or liabilities any rights and obligations created or retained in the transfer.

(b) if the entity retains substantially all the risks and rewards of ownership of the financial asset, the entity shall continue to recognise the financial asset.

(c) if the entity neither transfers nor retains substantially all the risks and rewards of ownership of the financial asset, the entity shall determine whether it has retained control of the financial asset. In this case:

(i) if the entity has not retained control, it shall derecognise the financial asset and recognise separately as assets or liabilities any rights and obligations created or retained in the transfer.

(ii) if the entity has retained control, it shall continue to recognise the financial asset to the extent of its continuing involvement in the financial asset (see paragraph 3.2.16).

3.2.7 The transfer of risks and rewards (see paragraph 3.2.6) is evaluated by comparing the entity's exposure, before and after the transfer, with the variability in the amounts and timing of the net cash flows of the transferred asset. An entity has retained substantially all the risks and rewards of ownership of a financial asset if its exposure to the variability in the present value of the future net cash flows from the financial asset does not change significantly as a result of the transfer (eg because the entity has sold a financial asset subject to an agreement to buy it back at a fixed price or the sale price plus a lender's return). An entity has transferred substantially all the risks and rewards of ownership of a financial asset if its exposure to such variability is no longer significant in relation to the total variability in the present value of the future net cash flows associated with the financial asset (eg because the entity has sold a financial asset subject only to an option to buy it back at its *fair value* at the time of repurchase or has transferred a fully proportionate share of the cash flows from a larger financial asset in an arrangement, such as a loan sub-participation, that meets the conditions in paragraph 3.2.5).

3.2.8   Often it will be obvious whether the entity has transferred or retained substantially all risks and rewards of ownership and there will be no need to perform any computations. In other cases, it will be necessary to compute and compare the entity's exposure to the variability in the present value of the future net cash flows before and after the transfer. The computation and comparison are made using as the discount rate an appropriate current market interest rate. All reasonably possible variability in net cash flows is considered, with greater weight being given to those outcomes that are more likely to occur.

3.2.9   Whether the entity has retained control (see paragraph 3.2.6(c)) of the transferred asset depends on the transferee's ability to sell the asset. If the transferee has the practical ability to sell the asset in its entirety to an unrelated third party and is able to exercise that ability unilaterally and without needing to impose additional restrictions on the transfer, the entity has not retained control. In all other cases, the entity has retained control.

Transfers that qualify for derecognition

3.2.10   If an entity transfers a financial asset in a transfer that qualifies for derecognition in its entirety and retains the right to service the financial asset for a fee, it shall recognise either a servicing asset or a servicing liability for that servicing contract. If the fee to be received is not expected to compensate the entity adequately for performing the servicing, a servicing liability for the servicing obligation shall be recognised at its fair value. If the fee to be received is expected to be more than adequate compensation for the servicing, a servicing asset shall be recognised for the servicing right at an amount determined on the basis of an allocation of the carrying amount of the larger financial asset in accordance with paragraph 3.2.13.

3.2.11   If, as a result of a transfer, a financial asset is derecognised in its entirety but the transfer results in the entity obtaining a new financial asset or assuming a new financial liability, or a servicing liability, the entity shall recognise the new financial asset, financial liability or servicing liability at fair value.

3.2.12   On derecognition of a financial asset in its entirety, the difference between:

(a)   the carrying amount (measured at the date of derecognition) and

(b)   the consideration received (including any new asset obtained less any new liability assumed)

shall be recognised in profit or loss.

3.2.13   If the transferred asset is part of a larger financial asset (eg when an entity transfers interest cash flows that are part of a debt instrument, see paragraph 3.2.2(a)) and the part transferred qualifies for derecognition in its entirety, the previous carrying amount of the larger financial asset shall be allocated between the part that continues to be recognised and the part that is derecognised, on the basis of the relative fair values of those parts on the date of the transfer. For this purpose, a retained servicing asset shall be treated as a part that continues to be recognised. The difference between:

(a)   the carrying amount (measured at the date of derecognition) allocated to the part derecognised and

(b)   the consideration received for the part derecognised (including any new asset obtained less any new liability assumed)

shall be recognised in profit or loss.

3.2.14   When an entity allocates the previous carrying amount of a larger financial asset between the part that continues to be recognised and the part that is derecognised, the fair value of the part that continues to be recognised needs to be measured. When the entity has a history of selling parts similar to the part that continues to be recognised or other market transactions exist for such parts, recent prices of actual transactions provide the best estimate of its fair value. When there are no price quotes or recent market transactions to support the fair value of the part that continues to be recognised, the best estimate of the fair value is the difference between the fair value of the larger financial asset as a whole and the consideration received from the transferee for the part that is derecognised.

Transfers that do not qualify for derecognition

3.2.15   If a transfer does not result in derecognition because the entity has retained substantially all the risks and rewards of ownership of the transferred asset, the entity shall continue to recognise the transferred asset in its entirety and shall recognise a financial liability for the consideration received. In subsequent periods, the entity shall recognise any income on the transferred asset and any expense incurred on the financial liability.

Continuing involvement in transferred assets

3.2.16   If an entity neither transfers nor retains substantially all the risks and rewards of ownership of a transferred asset, and retains control of the transferred asset, the entity continues to recognise the transferred asset to the extent of its continuing involvement. The extent of the entity's continuing involvement in the transferred asset is the extent to which it is exposed to changes in the value of the transferred asset. For example:

(a)   When the entity's continuing involvement takes the form of guaranteeing the transferred asset, the extent of the entity's continuing involvement is the lower of (i) the amount of the asset and (ii) the maximum amount of the consideration received that the entity could be required to repay ('the guarantee amount').

(b)   When the entity's continuing involvement takes the form of a written or purchased option (or both) on the transferred asset, the extent of the entity's continuing involvement is the amount of the transferred asset that the entity may repurchase. However, in the case of a written put option on an asset that is measured at fair value, the extent of the entity's continuing involvement is limited to the lower of the fair value of the transferred asset and the option exercise price (see paragraph B3.2.13).

(c)   When the entity's continuing involvement takes the form of a cash-settled option or similar provision on the transferred asset, the extent of the entity's continuing involvement is measured in the same way as that which results from non-cash settled options as set out in (b) above.

3.2.17   When an entity continues to recognise an asset to the extent of its continuing involvement, the entity also recognises an associated liability. Despite the other measurement requirements in this Standard, the transferred asset and the associated liability are measured on a basis that reflects the rights and obligations that the entity has retained. The associated liability is measured in such a way that the net carrying amount of the transferred asset and the associated liability is:

(a)   the amortised cost of the rights and obligations retained by the entity, if the transferred asset is measured at amortised cost, or

(b)   equal to the fair value of the rights and obligations retained by the entity when measured on a stand-alone basis, if the transferred asset is measured at fair value.

3.2.18   The entity shall continue to recognise any income arising on the transferred asset to the extent of its continuing involvement and shall recognise any expense incurred on the associated liability.

3.2.19   For the purpose of subsequent measurement, recognised changes in the fair value of the transferred asset and the associated liability are accounted for consistently with each other in accordance with paragraph 5.7.1, and shall not be offset.

3.2.20   If an entity's continuing involvement is in only a part of a financial asset (eg when an entity retains an option to repurchase part of a transferred asset, or retains a residual interest that does not result in the retention of substantially all the risks and rewards of ownership and the entity retains control), the entity allocates the previous carrying amount of the financial asset between the part it continues to recognise under continuing involvement, and the part it no longer recognises on the basis of the relative fair values of those parts on the date of the transfer. For this purpose, the requirements of paragraph 3.2.14 apply. The difference between:

(a)   the carrying amount (measured at the date of derecognition) allocated to the part that is no longer recognised and

(b)   the consideration received for the part no longer recognised

shall be recognised in profit or loss.

3.2.21   If the transferred asset is measured at amortised cost, the option in this Standard to designate a financial liability as at fair value through profit or loss is not applicable to the associated liability.

All transfers

3.2.22   If a transferred asset continues to be recognised, the asset and the associated liability shall not be offset. Similarly, the entity shall not offset any income arising from the transferred asset with any expense incurred on the associated liability (see paragraph 42 of IAS 32).

3.2.23   If a transferor provides non-cash collateral (such as debt or equity instruments) to the transferee, the accounting for the collateral by the transferor and the transferee depends on whether the transferee has the right to sell or repledge the collateral and on whether the transferor has defaulted. The transferor and transferee shall account for the collateral as follows:

(a)   If the transferee has the right by contract or custom to sell or repledge the collateral, then the transferor shall reclassify that asset in its statement of financial position (eg as a loaned asset, pledged equity instruments or repurchase receivable) separately from other assets.

(b)   If the transferee sells collateral pledged to it, it shall recognise the proceeds from the sale and a liability measured at fair value for its obligation to return the collateral.

(c)   If the transferor defaults under the terms of the contract and is no longer entitled to redeem the collateral, it shall derecognise the collateral, and the transferee shall recognise the collateral as its asset initially measured at fair value or, if it has already sold the collateral, derecognise its obligation to return the collateral.

(d)   Except as provided in (c), the transferor shall continue to carry the collateral as its asset, and the transferee shall not recognise the collateral as an asset.

3.3 Derecognition of financial liabilities

3.3.1   An entity shall remove a financial liability (or a part of a financial liability) from its statement of financial position when, and only when, it is extinguished—ie when the obligation specified in the contract is discharged or cancelled or expires.

3.3.2   An exchange between an existing borrower and lender of debt instruments with substantially different terms shall be accounted for as an extinguishment of the original financial liability and the recognition of a new financial liability. Similarly, a substantial modification of the terms of an existing financial liability or a part of it (whether or not attributable to the financial difficulty of the debtor) shall be accounted for as an extinguishment of the original financial liability and the recognition of a new financial liability.

3.3.3 The difference between the carrying amount of a financial liability (or part of a financial liability) extinguished or transferred to another party and the consideration paid, including any non-cash assets transferred or liabilities assumed, shall be recognised in profit or loss.

3.3.4 If an entity repurchases a part of a financial liability, the entity shall allocate the previous carrying amount of the financial liability between the part that continues to be recognised and the part that is derecognised based on the relative fair values of those parts on the date of the repurchase. The difference between (a) the carrying amount allocated to the part derecognised and (b) the consideration paid, including any non-cash assets transferred or liabilities assumed, for the part derecognised shall be recognised in profit or loss.

3.3.5 *[This paragraph refers to amendments that are not yet effective, and is therefore not included in this edition.]*

Chapter 4 Classification

4.1 Classification of financial assets

4.1.1 Unless paragraph 4.1.5 applies, an entity shall classify financial assets as subsequently measured at amortised cost, fair value through other comprehensive income or fair value through profit or loss on the basis of both:

    (a) the entity's business model for managing the financial assets and

    (b) the contractual cash flow characteristics of the financial asset.

4.1.2 A financial asset shall be measured at amortised cost if both of the following conditions are met:

    (a) the financial asset is held within a business model whose objective is to hold financial assets in order to collect contractual cash flows and

    (b) the contractual terms of the financial asset give rise on specified dates to cash flows that are solely payments of principal and interest on the principal amount outstanding.

    Paragraphs B4.1.1–B4.1.26 provide guidance on how to apply these conditions.

4.1.2A A financial asset shall be measured at fair value through other comprehensive income if both of the following conditions are met:

    (a) the financial asset is held within a business model whose objective is achieved by both collecting contractual cash flows and selling financial assets and

(b)   the contractual terms of the financial asset give rise on specified dates to cash flows that are solely payments of principal and interest on the principal amount outstanding.

Paragraphs B4.1.1–B4.1.26 provide guidance on how to apply these conditions.

4.1.3   For the purpose of applying paragraphs 4.1.2(b) and 4.1.2A(b):

(a)   principal is the fair value of the financial asset at initial recognition. Paragraph B4.1.7B provides additional guidance on the meaning of principal.

(b)   interest consists of consideration for the time value of money, for the credit risk associated with the principal amount outstanding during a particular period of time and for other basic lending risks and costs, as well as a profit margin. Paragraphs B4.1.7A and B4.1.9A–B4.1.9E provide additional guidance on the meaning of interest, including the meaning of the time value of money.

4.1.4   A financial asset shall be measured at fair value through profit or loss unless it is measured at amortised cost in accordance with paragraph 4.1.2 or at fair value through other comprehensive income in accordance with paragraph 4.1.2A. However an entity may make an irrevocable election at initial recognition for particular investments in *equity instruments* that would otherwise be measured at fair value through profit or loss to present subsequent changes in fair value in other comprehensive income (see paragraphs 5.7.5–5.7.6).

Option to designate a financial asset at fair value through profit or loss

4.1.5   Despite paragraphs 4.1.1–4.1.4, an entity may, at initial recognition, irrevocably designate a financial asset as measured at fair value through profit or loss if doing so eliminates or significantly reduces a measurement or recognition inconsistency (sometimes referred to as an 'accounting mismatch') that would otherwise arise from measuring assets or liabilities or recognising the gains and losses on them on different bases (see paragraphs B4.1.29–B4.1.32).

4.2 Classification of financial liabilities

4.2.1   An entity shall classify all financial liabilities as subsequently measured at amortised cost, except for:

(a)   *financial liabilities at fair value through profit or loss.* Such liabilities, including *derivatives* that are liabilities, shall be subsequently measured at fair value.

(b)   financial liabilities that arise when a transfer of a financial asset does not qualify for derecognition or when the continuing involvement approach applies. Paragraphs 3.2.15 and 3.2.17 apply to the measurement of such financial liabilities.

(c) *financial guarantee contracts.* After initial recognition, an issuer of such a contract shall (unless paragraph 4.2.1(a) or (b) applies) subsequently measure it at the higher of:

    (i) the amount of the *loss allowance* determined in accordance with Section 5.5 and

    (ii) the amount initially recognised (see paragraph 5.1.1) less, when appropriate, the cumulative amount of income recognised in accordance with the principles of IFRS 15.

(d) commitments to provide a loan at a below-market interest rate. An issuer of such a commitment shall (unless paragraph 4.2.1(a) applies) subsequently measure it at the higher of:

    (i) the amount of the loss allowance determined in accordance with Section 5.5 and

    (ii) the amount initially recognised (see paragraph 5.1.1) less, when appropriate, the cumulative amount of income recognised in accordance with the principles of IFRS 15.

(e) contingent consideration recognised by an acquirer in a business combination to which IFRS 3 applies. Such contingent consideration shall subsequently be measured at fair value with changes recognised in profit or loss.

Option to designate a financial liability at fair value through profit or loss

4.2.2 An entity may, at initial recognition, irrevocably designate a financial liability as measured at fair value through profit or loss when permitted by paragraph 4.3.5, or when doing so results in more relevant information, because either:

(a) it eliminates or significantly reduces a measurement or recognition inconsistency (sometimes referred to as 'an accounting mismatch') that would otherwise arise from measuring assets or liabilities or recognising the gains and losses on them on different bases (see paragraphs B4.1.29–B4.1.32); or

(b) a group of financial liabilities or financial assets and financial liabilities is managed and its performance is evaluated on a fair value basis, in accordance with a documented risk management or investment strategy, and information about the group is provided internally on that basis to the entity's key management personnel (as defined in IAS 24 *Related Party Disclosures*), for example, the entity's board of directors and chief executive officer (see paragraphs B4.1.33–B4.1.36).

4.3 Embedded derivatives

4.3.1 An embedded derivative is a component of a hybrid contract that also includes a non-derivative host—with the effect that some of the cash flows of the combined instrument vary in a way similar to a stand-alone derivative. An embedded derivative causes some or all of the cash flows that otherwise would be required by the contract to be modified according to a specified interest rate, financial instrument price, commodity price, foreign exchange rate, index of prices or rates, credit rating or credit index, or other variable, provided in the case of a non-financial variable that the variable is not specific to a party to the contract. A derivative that is attached to a *financial instrument* but is contractually transferable independently of that instrument, or has a different counterparty, is not an embedded derivative, but a separate financial instrument.

Hybrid contracts with financial asset hosts

4.3.2 If a hybrid contract contains a host that is an asset within the scope of this Standard, an entity shall apply the requirements in paragraphs 4.1.1–4.1.5 to the entire hybrid contract.

Other hybrid contracts

4.3.3 If a hybrid contract contains a host that is not an asset within the scope of this Standard, an embedded derivative shall be separated from the host and accounted for as a derivative under this Standard if, and only if:

(a) the economic characteristics and risks of the embedded derivative are not closely related to the economic characteristics and risks of the host (see paragraphs B4.3.5 and B4.3.8);

(b) a separate instrument with the same terms as the embedded derivative would meet the definition of a derivative; and

(c) the hybrid contract is not measured at fair value with changes in fair value recognised in profit or loss (ie a derivative that is embedded in a financial liability at fair value through profit or loss is not separated).

4.3.4 If an embedded derivative is separated, the host contract shall be accounted for in accordance with the appropriate Standards. This Standard does not address whether an embedded derivative shall be presented separately in the statement of financial position.

4.3.5 Despite paragraphs 4.3.3 and 4.3.4, if a contract contains one or more embedded derivatives and the host is not an asset within the scope of this Standard, an entity may designate the entire hybrid contract as at fair value through profit or loss unless:

(a) the embedded derivative(s) do(es) not significantly modify the cash flows that otherwise would be required by the contract; or

(b)   it is clear with little or no analysis when a similar hybrid instrument is first considered that separation of the embedded derivative(s) is prohibited, such as a prepayment option embedded in a loan that permits the holder to prepay the loan for approximately its amortised cost.

4.3.6   If an entity is required by this Standard to separate an embedded derivative from its host, but is unable to measure the embedded derivative separately either at acquisition or at the end of a subsequent financial reporting period, it shall designate the entire hybrid contract as at fair value through profit or loss.

4.3.7   If an entity is unable to measure reliably the fair value of an embedded derivative on the basis of its terms and conditions, the fair value of the embedded derivative is the difference between the fair value of the hybrid contract and the fair value of the host. If the entity is unable to measure the fair value of the embedded derivative using this method, paragraph 4.3.6 applies and the hybrid contract is designated as at fair value through profit or loss.

4.4 Reclassification

4.4.1   When, and only when, an entity changes its business model for managing financial assets it shall reclassify all affected financial assets in accordance with paragraphs 4.1.1–4.1.4. See paragraphs 5.6.1–5.6.7, B4.4.1–B4.4.3 and B5.6.1–B5.6.2 for additional guidance on reclassifying financial assets.

4.4.2   An entity shall not reclassify any financial liability.

4.4.3   The following changes in circumstances are not reclassifications for the purposes of paragraphs 4.4.1–4.4.2:

(a)   an item that was previously a designated and effective hedging instrument in a cash flow hedge or net investment hedge no longer qualifies as such;

(b)   an item becomes a designated and effective hedging instrument in a cash flow hedge or net investment hedge; and

(c)   changes in measurement in accordance with Section 6.7.

Chapter 5 Measurement

5.1 Initial measurement

5.1.1   Except for trade receivables within the scope of paragraph 5.1.3, at initial recognition, an entity shall measure a financial asset or financial liability at its fair value plus or minus, in the case of a financial asset or financial liability not at fair value through profit or loss, *transaction costs* that are directly attributable to the acquisition or issue of the financial asset or financial liability.

5.1.1A However, if the fair value of the financial asset or financial liability at initial recognition differs from the transaction price, an entity shall apply paragraph B5.1.2A.

5.1.2 When an entity uses settlement date accounting for an asset that is subsequently measured at amortised cost, the asset is recognised initially at its fair value on the trade date (see paragraphs B3.1.3–B3.1.6).

5.1.3 Despite the requirement in paragraph 5.1.1, at initial recognition, an entity shall measure trade receivables at their transaction price (as defined in IFRS 15) if the trade receivables do not contain a significant financing component in accordance with IFRS 15 (or when the entity applies the practical expedient in accordance with paragraph 63 of IFRS 15).

5.2 Subsequent measurement of financial assets

5.2.1 After initial recognition, an entity shall measure a financial asset in accordance with paragraphs 4.1.1–4.1.5 at:

(a) amortised cost;

(b) fair value through other comprehensive income; or

(c) fair value through profit or loss.

5.2.2 An entity shall apply the impairment requirements in Section 5.5 to financial assets that are measured at amortised cost in accordance with paragraph 4.1.2 and to financial assets that are measured at fair value through other comprehensive income in accordance with paragraph 4.1.2A.

5.2.3 An entity shall apply the hedge accounting requirements in paragraphs 6.5.8–6.5.14 (and, if applicable, paragraphs 89–94 of IAS 39 *Financial Instruments: Recognition and Measurement* for the fair value hedge accounting for a portfolio hedge of interest rate risk) to a financial asset that is designated as a hedged item.[1]

5.3 Subsequent measurement of financial liabilities

5.3.1 After initial recognition, an entity shall measure a financial liability in accordance with paragraphs 4.2.1–4.2.2.

5.3.2 An entity shall apply the hedge accounting requirements in paragraphs 6.5.8–6.5.14 (and, if applicable, paragraphs 89–94 of IAS 39 for the fair value hedge accounting for a portfolio hedge of interest rate risk) to a financial liability that is designated as a hedged item.

---

1 In accordance with paragraph 7.2.21, an entity may choose as its accounting policy to continue to apply the hedge accounting requirements in IAS 39 instead of the requirements in Chapter 6 of this Standard. If an entity has made this election, the references in this Standard to particular hedge accounting requirements in Chapter 6 are not relevant. Instead the entity applies the relevant hedge accounting requirements in IAS 39.

5.4 Amortised cost measurement

Financial assets

Effective interest method

5.4.1 Interest revenue shall be calculated by using the *effective interest method* (see Appendix A and paragraphs B5.4.1–B5.4.7). This shall be calculated by applying the *effective interest rate* to the *gross carrying amount of a financial asset* except for:

    (a) *purchased or originated credit-impaired financial assets*. For those financial assets, the entity shall apply the *credit-adjusted effective interest rate* to the *amortised cost of the financial asset* from initial recognition.

    (b) financial assets that are not purchased or originated credit-impaired financial assets but subsequently have become *credit-impaired financial assets*. For those financial assets, the entity shall apply the effective interest rate to the amortised cost of the financial asset in subsequent reporting periods.

5.4.2 An entity that, in a reporting period, calculates interest revenue by applying the effective interest method to the amortised cost of a financial asset in accordance with paragraph 5.4.1(b), shall, in subsequent reporting periods, calculate the interest revenue by applying the effective interest rate to the gross carrying amount if the credit risk on the financial instrument improves so that the financial asset is no longer credit-impaired and the improvement can be related objectively to an event occurring after the requirements in paragraph 5.4.1(b) were applied (such as an improvement in the borrower's credit rating).

Modification of contractual cash flows

5.4.3 When the contractual cash flows of a financial asset are renegotiated or otherwise modified and the renegotiation or modification does not result in the derecognition of that financial asset in accordance with this Standard, an entity shall recalculate the gross carrying amount of the financial asset and shall recognise a *modification gain or loss* in profit or loss. The gross carrying amount of the financial asset shall be recalculated as the present value of the renegotiated or modified contractual cash flows that are discounted at the financial asset's original effective interest rate (or credit-adjusted effective interest rate for purchased or originated credit-impaired financial assets) or, when applicable, the revised effective interest rate calculated in accordance with paragraph 6.5.10. Any costs or fees incurred adjust the carrying amount of the modified financial asset and are amortised over the remaining term of the modified financial asset.

Write-off

5.4.4   An entity shall directly reduce the gross carrying amount of a financial asset when the entity has no reasonable expectations of recovering a financial asset in its entirety or a portion thereof. A write-off constitutes a derecognition event (see paragraph B3.2.16(r)).

Changes in the basis for determining the contractual cash flows as a result of interest rate benchmark reform

5.4.5   An entity shall apply paragraphs 5.4.6–5.4.9 to a financial asset or financial liability if, and only if, the basis for determining the contractual cash flows of that financial asset or financial liability changes as a result of interest rate benchmark reform. For this purpose, the term 'interest rate benchmark reform' refers to the market-wide reform of an interest rate benchmark as described in paragraph 6.8.2.

5.4.6   The basis for determining the contractual cash flows of a financial asset or financial liability can change:

(a)   by amending the contractual terms specified at the initial recognition of the financial instrument (for example, the contractual terms are amended to replace the referenced interest rate benchmark with an alternative benchmark rate);

(b)   in a way that was not considered by—or contemplated in—the contractual terms at the initial recognition of the financial instrument, without amending the contractual terms (for example, the method for calculating the interest rate benchmark is altered without amending the contractual terms); and/or

(c)   because of the activation of an existing contractual term (for example, an existing fallback clause is triggered).

5.4.7   As a practical expedient, an entity shall apply paragraph B5.4.5 to account for a change in the basis for determining the contractual cash flows of a financial asset or financial liability that is required by interest rate benchmark reform. This practical expedient applies only to such changes and only to the extent the change is required by interest rate benchmark reform (see also paragraph 5.4.9). For this purpose, a change in the basis for determining the contractual cash flows is required by interest rate benchmark reform if, and only if, both these conditions are met:

(a)   the change is necessary as a direct consequence of interest rate benchmark reform; and

(b)   the new basis for determining the contractual cash flows is economically equivalent to the previous basis (ie the basis immediately preceding the change).

5.4.8   Examples of changes that give rise to a new basis for determining the contractual cash flows that is economically equivalent to the previous basis (ie the basis immediately preceding the change) are:

(a)   the replacement of an existing interest rate benchmark used to determine the contractual cash flows of a financial asset or financial liability with an alternative benchmark rate—or the implementation of such a reform of an interest rate benchmark by altering the method used to calculate the interest rate benchmark—with the addition of a fixed spread necessary to compensate for the basis difference between the existing interest rate benchmark and the alternative benchmark rate;

(b)   changes to the reset period, reset dates or the number of days between coupon payment dates in order to implement the reform of an interest rate benchmark; and

(c)   the addition of a fallback provision to the contractual terms of a financial asset or financial liability to enable any change described in (a) and (b) above to be implemented.

5.4.9   If changes are made to a financial asset or financial liability in addition to changes to the basis for determining the contractual cash flows required by interest rate benchmark reform, an entity shall first apply the practical expedient in paragraph 5.4.7 to the changes required by interest rate benchmark reform. The entity shall then apply the applicable requirements in this Standard to any additional changes to which the practical expedient does not apply. If the additional change does not result in the derecognition of the financial asset or financial liability, the entity shall apply paragraph 5.4.3 or paragraph B5.4.6, as applicable, to account for that additional change. If the additional change results in the derecognition of the financial asset or financial liability, the entity shall apply the derecognition requirements.

5.5 Impairment

Recognition of expected credit losses

General approach

5.5.1   An entity shall recognise a loss allowance for *expected credit losses* on a financial asset that is measured in accordance with paragraphs 4.1.2 or 4.1.2A, a lease receivable, a *contract asset* or a loan commitment and a financial guarantee contract to which the impairment requirements apply in accordance with paragraphs 2.1(g), 4.2.1(c) or 4.2.1(d).

5.5.2   An entity shall apply the impairment requirements for the recognition and measurement of a loss allowance for financial assets that are measured at fair value through other comprehensive income in accordance with paragraph 4.1.2A. However, the loss allowance shall be recognised in other comprehensive income and shall not reduce the carrying amount of the financial asset in the statement of financial position.

5.5.3   Subject to paragraphs 5.5.13–5.5.16, at each reporting date, an entity shall measure the loss allowance for a financial instrument at an amount equal to the *lifetime expected credit losses* if the credit risk on that financial instrument has increased significantly since initial recognition.

5.5.4   The objective of the impairment requirements is to recognise lifetime expected credit losses for all financial instruments for which there have been significant increases in credit risk since initial recognition — whether assessed on an individual or collective basis — considering all reasonable and supportable information, including that which is forward-looking.

5.5.5   **Subject to paragraphs 5.5.13–5.5.16, if, at the reporting date, the credit risk on a financial instrument has not increased significantly since initial recognition, an entity shall measure the loss allowance for that financial instrument at an amount equal to *12-month expected credit losses*.**

5.5.6   For loan commitments and financial guarantee contracts, the date that the entity becomes a party to the irrevocable commitment shall be considered to be the date of initial recognition for the purposes of applying the impairment requirements.

5.5.7   If an entity has measured the loss allowance for a financial instrument at an amount equal to lifetime expected credit losses in the previous reporting period, but determines at the current reporting date that paragraph 5.5.3 is no longer met, the entity shall measure the loss allowance at an amount equal to 12-month expected credit losses at the current reporting date.

5.5.8   An entity shall recognise in profit or loss, as an *impairment gain or loss*, the amount of expected credit losses (or reversal) that is required to adjust the loss allowance at the reporting date to the amount that is required to be recognised in accordance with this Standard.

Determining significant increases in credit risk

5.5.9   At each reporting date, an entity shall assess whether the credit risk on a financial instrument has increased significantly since initial recognition. When making the assessment, an entity shall use the change in the risk of a default occurring over the expected life of the financial instrument instead of the change in the amount of expected credit losses. To make that assessment, an entity shall compare the risk of a default occurring on the financial instrument as at the reporting date with the risk of a default occurring on the financial instrument as at the date of initial recognition and consider reasonable and supportable information, that is available without undue cost or effort, that is indicative of significant increases in credit risk since initial recognition.

5.5.10   An entity may assume that the credit risk on a financial instrument has not increased significantly since initial recognition if the financial instrument is determined to have low credit risk at the reporting date (see paragraphs B5.5.22–B5.5.24).

5.5.11   If reasonable and supportable forward-looking information is available without undue cost or effort, an entity cannot rely solely on *past due* information when determining whether credit risk has increased significantly since initial recognition. However, when information that is more forward-looking than past due status (either on an individual or a collective basis) is not available without undue cost or effort, an entity may use past due information to determine whether there have been significant increases in credit risk since initial recognition. Regardless of the way in which an entity assesses significant increases in credit risk, there is a rebuttable presumption that the credit risk on a financial asset has increased significantly since initial recognition when contractual payments are more than 30 days past due. An entity can rebut this presumption if the entity has reasonable and supportable information that is available without undue cost or effort, that demonstrates that the credit risk has not increased significantly since initial recognition even though the contractual payments are more than 30 days past due. When an entity determines that there have been significant increases in credit risk before contractual payments are more than 30 days past due, the rebuttable presumption does not apply.

Modified financial assets

5.5.12   If the contractual cash flows on a financial asset have been renegotiated or modified and the financial asset was not derecognised, an entity shall assess whether there has been a significant increase in the credit risk of the financial instrument in accordance with paragraph 5.5.3 by comparing:

(a)   the risk of a default occurring at the reporting date (based on the modified contractual terms); and

(b)   the risk of a default occurring at initial recognition (based on the original, unmodified contractual terms).

Purchased or originated credit-impaired financial assets

5.5.13   Despite paragraphs 5.5.3 and 5.5.5, at the reporting date, an entity shall only recognise the cumulative changes in lifetime expected credit losses since initial recognition as a loss allowance for purchased or originated credit-impaired financial assets.

5.5.14   At each reporting date, an entity shall recognise in profit or loss the amount of the change in lifetime expected credit losses as an impairment gain or loss. An entity shall recognise favourable changes in lifetime expected credit losses as an impairment gain, even if the lifetime expected credit losses are less than the amount of expected credit losses that were included in the estimated cash flows on initial recognition.

Simplified approach for trade receivables, contract assets and lease receivables

5.5.15   Despite paragraphs 5.5.3 and 5.5.5, an entity shall always measure the loss allowance at an amount equal to lifetime expected credit losses for:

(a)   trade receivables or contract assets that result from transactions that are within the scope of IFRS 15, and that:

(i)   do not contain a significant financing component in accordance with IFRS 15 (or when the entity applies the practical expedient in accordance with paragraph 63 of IFRS 15); or

          (ii)   contain a significant financing component in accordance with IFRS 15, if the entity chooses as its accounting policy to measure the loss allowance at an amount equal to lifetime expected credit losses. That accounting policy shall be applied to all such trade receivables or contract assets but may be applied separately to trade receivables and contract assets.

    (b)   lease receivables that result from transactions that are within the scope of IFRS 16, if the entity chooses as its accounting policy to measure the loss allowance at an amount equal to lifetime expected credit losses. That accounting policy shall be applied to all lease receivables but may be applied separately to finance and operating lease receivables.

5.5.16   An entity may select its accounting policy for trade receivables, lease receivables and contract assets independently of each other.

Measurement of expected credit losses

5.5.17   An entity shall measure expected credit losses of a financial instrument in a way that reflects:

    (a)   an unbiased and probability-weighted amount that is determined by evaluating a range of possible outcomes;

    (b)   the time value of money; and

    (c)   reasonable and supportable information that is available without undue cost or effort at the reporting date about past events, current conditions and forecasts of future economic conditions.

5.5.18   When measuring expected credit losses, an entity need not necessarily identify every possible scenario. However, it shall consider the risk or probability that a credit loss occurs by reflecting the possibility that a credit loss occurs and the possibility that no credit loss occurs, even if the possibility of a credit loss occurring is very low.

5.5.19   The maximum period to consider when measuring expected credit losses is the maximum contractual period (including extension options) over which the entity is exposed to credit risk and not a longer period, even if that longer period is consistent with business practice.

5.5.20   However, some financial instruments include both a loan and an undrawn commitment component and the entity's contractual ability to demand repayment and cancel the undrawn commitment does not limit the entity's exposure to credit losses to the contractual notice period. For such financial instruments, and only those financial instruments, the entity shall measure expected credit losses over the period that the entity is exposed to credit risk and expected credit losses would not be mitigated by credit risk management actions, even if that period extends beyond the maximum contractual period.

5.6 Reclassification of financial assets

5.6.1   If an entity reclassifies financial assets in accordance with paragraph 4.4.1, it shall apply the reclassification prospectively from the *reclassification date*. The entity shall not restate any previously recognised gains, losses (including impairment gains or losses) or interest. Paragraphs 5.6.2–5.6.7 set out the requirements for reclassifications.

5.6.2   If an entity reclassifies a financial asset out of the amortised cost measurement category and into the fair value through profit or loss measurement category, its fair value is measured at the reclassification date. Any gain or loss arising from a difference between the previous amortised cost of the financial asset and fair value is recognised in profit or loss.

5.6.3   If an entity reclassifies a financial asset out of the fair value through profit or loss measurement category and into the amortised cost measurement category, its fair value at the reclassification date becomes its new gross carrying amount. (See paragraph B5.6.2 for guidance on determining an effective interest rate and a loss allowance at the reclassification date.)

5.6.4   If an entity reclassifies a financial asset out of the amortised cost measurement category and into the fair value through other comprehensive income measurement category, its fair value is measured at the reclassification date. Any gain or loss arising from a difference between the previous amortised cost of the financial asset and fair value is recognised in other comprehensive income. The effective interest rate and the measurement of expected credit losses are not adjusted as a result of the reclassification. (See paragraph B5.6.1.)

5.6.5   If an entity reclassifies a financial asset out of the fair value through other comprehensive income measurement category and into the amortised cost measurement category, the financial asset is reclassified at its fair value at the reclassification date. However, the cumulative gain or loss previously recognised in other comprehensive income is removed from equity and adjusted against the fair value of the financial asset at the reclassification date. As a result, the financial asset is measured at the reclassification date as if it had always been measured at amortised cost. This adjustment affects other comprehensive income but does not affect profit or loss and therefore is not a reclassification adjustment (see IAS 1 *Presentation of Financial Statements*). The effective interest rate and the measurement of expected credit losses are not adjusted as a result of the reclassification. (See paragraph B5.6.1.)

5.6.6   If an entity reclassifies a financial asset out of the fair value through profit or loss measurement category and into the fair value through other comprehensive income measurement category, the financial asset continues to be measured at fair value. (See paragraph B5.6.2 for guidance on determining an effective interest rate and a loss allowance at the reclassification date.)

5.6.7   If an entity reclassifies a financial asset out of the fair value through other comprehensive income measurement category and into the fair value through profit or loss measurement category, the financial asset continues to be measured at fair value. The cumulative gain or loss previously recognised in other comprehensive income is reclassified from equity to profit or loss as a reclassification adjustment (see IAS 1) at the reclassification date.

5.7 Gains and losses

5.7.1   A gain or loss on a financial asset or financial liability that is measured at fair value shall be recognised in profit or loss unless:

(a)   it is part of a hedging relationship (see paragraphs 6.5.8–6.5.14 and, if applicable, paragraphs 89–94 of IAS 39 for the fair value hedge accounting for a portfolio hedge of interest rate risk);

(b)   it is an investment in an equity instrument and the entity has elected to present gains and losses on that investment in other comprehensive income in accordance with paragraph 5.7.5;

(c)   it is a financial liability designated as at fair value through profit or loss and the entity is required to present the effects of changes in the liability's *credit risk* in other comprehensive income in accordance with paragraph 5.7.7; or

(d)   it is a financial asset measured at fair value through other comprehensive income in accordance with paragraph 4.1.2A and the entity is required to recognise some changes in fair value in other comprehensive income in accordance with paragraph 5.7.10.

5.7.1A   *Dividends* are recognised in profit or loss only when:

(a)   the entity's right to receive payment of the dividend is established;

(b)   it is probable that the economic benefits associated with the dividend will flow to the entity; and

(c)   the amount of the dividend can be measured reliably.

5.7.2   A gain or loss on a financial asset that is measured at amortised cost and is not part of a hedging relationship (see paragraphs 6.5.8–6.5.14 and, if applicable, paragraphs 89–94 of IAS 39 for the fair value hedge accounting for a portfolio hedge of interest rate risk) shall be recognised in profit or loss when the financial asset is derecognised, reclassified in accordance with paragraph 5.6.2, through the amortisation process or in order to recognise impairment gains or losses. An entity shall apply paragraphs 5.6.2 and 5.6.4 if it reclassifies financial assets out of the amortised cost measurement category. A gain or loss on a financial liability that is measured at amortised cost and is not part of a hedging relationship (see paragraphs 6.5.8–6.5.14 and, if applicable, paragraphs 89–94 of IAS 39 for the fair value hedge accounting for a portfolio hedge of interest rate risk) shall be recognised in profit or loss when the financial liability is derecognised and through the amortisation process. (See paragraph B5.7.2 for guidance on foreign exchange gains or losses.)

5.7.3   A gain or loss on financial assets or financial liabilities that are hedged items in a hedging relationship shall be recognised in accordance with paragraphs 6.5.8–6.5.14 and, if applicable, paragraphs 89–94 of IAS 39 for the fair value hedge accounting for a portfolio hedge of interest rate risk.

5.7.4   If an entity recognises financial assets using settlement date accounting (see paragraphs 3.1.2, B3.1.3 and B3.1.6), any change in the fair value of the asset to be received during the period between the trade date and the settlement date is not recognised for assets measured at amortised cost. For assets measured at fair value, however, the change in fair value shall be recognised in profit or loss or in other comprehensive income, as appropriate in accordance with paragraph 5.7.1. The trade date shall be considered the date of initial recognition for the purposes of applying the impairment requirements.

Investments in equity instruments

5.7.5   At initial recognition, an entity may make an irrevocable election to present in other comprehensive income subsequent changes in the fair value of an investment in an equity instrument within the scope of this Standard that is neither *held for trading* nor contingent consideration recognised by an acquirer in a business combination to which IFRS 3 applies. (See paragraph B5.7.3 for guidance on foreign exchange gains or losses.)

5.7.6   If an entity makes the election in paragraph 5.7.5, it shall recognise in profit or loss dividends from that investment in accordance with paragraph 5.7.1A.

Liabilities designated as at fair value through profit or loss

5.7.7   An entity shall present a gain or loss on a financial liability that is designated as at fair value through profit or loss in accordance with paragraph 4.2.2 or paragraph 4.3.5 as follows:

(a)   The amount of change in the fair value of the financial liability that is attributable to changes in the credit risk of that liability shall be presented in other comprehensive income (see paragraphs B5.7.13–B5.7.20), and

(b)   the remaining amount of change in the fair value of the liability shall be presented in profit or loss

unless the treatment of the effects of changes in the liability's credit risk described in (a) would create or enlarge an accounting mismatch in profit or loss (in which case paragraph 5.7.8 applies). Paragraphs B5.7.5–B5.7.7 and B5.7.10–B5.7.12 provide guidance on determining whether an accounting mismatch would be created or enlarged.

5.7.8   If the requirements in paragraph 5.7.7 would create or enlarge an accounting mismatch in profit or loss, an entity shall present all gains or losses on that liability (including the effects of changes in the credit risk of that liability) in profit or loss.

5.7.9   Despite the requirements in paragraphs 5.7.7 and 5.7.8, an entity shall present in profit or loss all gains and losses on loan commitments and financial guarantee contracts that are designated as at fair value through profit or loss.

Assets measured at fair value through other comprehensive income

5.7.10 A gain or loss on a financial asset measured at fair value through other comprehensive income in accordance with paragraph 4.1.2A shall be recognised in other comprehensive income, except for impairment gains or losses (see Section 5.5) and foreign exchange gains and losses (see paragraphs B5.7.2–B5.7.2A), until the financial asset is derecognised or reclassified. When the financial asset is derecognised the cumulative gain or loss previously recognised in other comprehensive income is reclassified from equity to profit or loss as a reclassification adjustment (see IAS 1). If the financial asset is reclassified out of the fair value through other comprehensive income measurement category, the entity shall account for the cumulative gain or loss that was previously recognised in other comprehensive income in accordance with paragraphs 5.6.5 and 5.6.7. Interest calculated using the effective interest method is recognised in profit or loss.

5.7.11 As described in paragraph 5.7.10, if a financial asset is measured at fair value through other comprehensive income in accordance with paragraph 4.1.2A, the amounts that are recognised in profit or loss are the same as the amounts that would have been recognised in profit or loss if the financial asset had been measured at amortised cost.

Chapter 6 Hedge accounting

6.1 Objective and scope of hedge accounting

6.1.1   The objective of hedge accounting is to represent, in the financial statements, the effect of an entity's risk management activities that use financial instruments to manage exposures arising from particular risks that could affect profit or loss (or other comprehensive income, in the case of investments in equity instruments for which an entity has elected to present changes in fair value in other comprehensive income in accordance with paragraph 5.7.5). This approach aims to convey the context of hedging instruments for which hedge accounting is applied in order to allow insight into their purpose and effect.

6.1.2   An entity may choose to designate a hedging relationship between a hedging instrument and a hedged item in accordance with paragraphs 6.2.1–6.3.7 and B6.2.1–B6.3.25. For hedging relationships that meet the qualifying criteria, an entity shall account for the gain or loss on the hedging instrument and the hedged item in accordance with paragraphs 6.5.1–6.5.14 and B6.5.1–B6.5.28. When the hedged item is a group of items, an entity shall comply with the additional requirements in paragraphs 6.6.1–6.6.6 and B6.6.1–B6.6.16.

6.1.3   For a fair value hedge of the interest rate exposure of a portfolio of financial assets or financial liabilities (and only for such a hedge), an entity may apply the hedge accounting requirements in IAS 39 instead of those in this Standard. In that case, the entity must also apply the specific requirements for the fair value hedge accounting for a portfolio hedge of interest rate risk and designate as the hedged item a portion that is a currency amount (see paragraphs 81A, 89A and AG114–AG132 of IAS 39).

6.2 Hedging instruments

Qualifying instruments

6.2.1   A derivative measured at fair value through profit or loss may be designated as a hedging instrument, except for some written options (see paragraph B6.2.4).

6.2.2   A non-derivative financial asset or a non-derivative financial liability measured at fair value through profit or loss may be designated as a hedging instrument unless it is a financial liability designated as at fair value through profit or loss for which the amount of its change in fair value that is attributable to changes in the credit risk of that liability is presented in other comprehensive income in accordance with paragraph 5.7.7. For a hedge of foreign currency risk, the foreign currency risk component of a non-derivative financial asset or a non-derivative financial liability may be designated as a hedging instrument provided that it is not an investment in an equity instrument for which an entity has elected to present changes in fair value in other comprehensive income in accordance with paragraph 5.7.5.

6.2.3   For hedge accounting purposes, only contracts with a party external to the reporting entity (ie external to the group or individual entity that is being reported on) can be designated as hedging instruments.

Designation of hedging instruments

6.2.4   A qualifying instrument must be designated in its entirety as a hedging instrument. The only exceptions permitted are:

(a)   separating the intrinsic value and time value of an option contract and designating as the hedging instrument only the change in intrinsic value of an option and not the change in its time value (see paragraphs 6.5.15 and B6.5.29–B6.5.33);

(b)   separating the forward element and the spot element of a forward contract and designating as the hedging instrument only the change in the value of the spot element of a forward contract and not the forward element; similarly, the foreign currency basis spread may be separated and excluded from the designation of a financial instrument as the hedging instrument (see paragraphs 6.5.16 and B6.5.34–B6.5.39); and

(c)   a proportion of the entire hedging instrument, such as 50 per cent of the nominal amount, may be designated as the hedging instrument in a hedging relationship. However, a hedging instrument may not be designated for a part of its change in fair value that results from only a portion of the time period during which the hedging instrument remains outstanding.

6.2.5   An entity may view in combination, and jointly designate as the hedging instrument, any combination of the following (including those circumstances in which the risk or risks arising from some hedging instruments offset those arising from others):

(a)   derivatives or a proportion of them; and

(b)   non-derivatives or a proportion of them.

6.2.6   However, a derivative instrument that combines a written option and a purchased option (for example, an interest rate collar) does not qualify as a hedging instrument if it is, in effect, a net written option at the date of designation (unless it qualifies in accordance with paragraph B6.2.4). Similarly, two or more instruments (or proportions of them) may be jointly designated as the hedging instrument only if, in combination, they are not, in effect, a net written option at the date of designation (unless it qualifies in accordance with paragraph B6.2.4).

6.3 Hedged items

Qualifying items

6.3.1   A hedged item can be a recognised asset or liability, an unrecognised *firm commitment*, a *forecast transaction* or a net investment in a foreign operation. The hedged item can be:

(a)   a single item; or

(b)   a group of items (subject to paragraphs 6.6.1–6.6.6 and B6.6.1–B6.6.16).

A hedged item can also be a component of such an item or group of items (see paragraphs 6.3.7 and B6.3.7–B6.3.25).

6.3.2   The hedged item must be reliably measurable.

6.3.3   If a hedged item is a forecast transaction (or a component thereof), that transaction must be highly probable.

6.3.4   An aggregated exposure that is a combination of an exposure that could qualify as a hedged item in accordance with paragraph 6.3.1 and a derivative may be designated as a hedged item (see paragraphs B6.3.3–B6.3.4). This includes a forecast transaction of an aggregated exposure (ie uncommitted but anticipated future transactions that would give rise to an exposure and a derivative) if that aggregated exposure is highly probable and, once it has occurred and is therefore no longer forecast, is eligible as a hedged item.

6.3.5 For hedge accounting purposes, only assets, liabilities, firm commitments or highly probable forecast transactions with a party external to the reporting entity can be designated as hedged items. Hedge accounting can be applied to transactions between entities in the same group only in the individual or separate financial statements of those entities and not in the consolidated financial statements of the group, except for the consolidated financial statements of an investment entity, as defined in IFRS 10, where transactions between an investment entity and its subsidiaries measured at fair value through profit or loss will not be eliminated in the consolidated financial statements.

6.3.6 However, as an exception to paragraph 6.3.5, the foreign currency risk of an intragroup monetary item (for example, a payable/receivable between two subsidiaries) may qualify as a hedged item in the consolidated financial statements if it results in an exposure to foreign exchange rate gains or losses that are not fully eliminated on consolidation in accordance with IAS 21 *The Effects of Changes in Foreign Exchange Rates*. In accordance with IAS 21, foreign exchange rate gains and losses on intragroup monetary items are not fully eliminated on consolidation when the intragroup monetary item is transacted between two group entities that have different functional currencies. In addition, the foreign currency risk of a highly probable forecast intragroup transaction may qualify as a hedged item in consolidated financial statements provided that the transaction is denominated in a currency other than the functional currency of the entity entering into that transaction and the foreign currency risk will affect consolidated profit or loss.

Designation of hedged items

6.3.7 An entity may designate an item in its entirety or a component of an item as the hedged item in a hedging relationship. An entire item comprises all changes in the cash flows or fair value of an item. A component comprises less than the entire fair value change or cash flow variability of an item. In that case, an entity may designate only the following types of components (including combinations) as hedged items:

(a) only changes in the cash flows or fair value of an item attributable to a specific risk or risks (risk component), provided that, based on an assessment within the context of the particular market structure, the risk component is separately identifiable and reliably measurable (see paragraphs B6.3.8–B6.3.15). Risk components include a designation of only changes in the cash flows or the fair value of a hedged item above or below a specified price or other variable (a one-sided risk).

(b) one or more selected contractual cash flows.

(c) components of a nominal amount, ie a specified part of the amount of an item (see paragraphs B6.3.16–B6.3.20).

6.4 Qualifying criteria for hedge accounting

6.4.1   A hedging relationship qualifies for hedge accounting only if all of the following criteria are met:

(a)   the hedging relationship consists only of eligible hedging instruments and eligible hedged items.

(b)   at the inception of the hedging relationship there is formal designation and documentation of the hedging relationship and the entity's risk management objective and strategy for undertaking the hedge. That documentation shall include identification of the hedging instrument, the hedged item, the nature of the risk being hedged and how the entity will assess whether the hedging relationship meets the hedge effectiveness requirements (including its analysis of the sources of hedge ineffectiveness and how it determines the *hedge ratio*).

(c)   the hedging relationship meets all of the following hedge effectiveness requirements:

(i)   there is an economic relationship between the hedged item and the hedging instrument (see paragraphs B6.4.4–B6.4.6);

(ii)   the effect of credit risk does not dominate the value changes that result from that economic relationship (see paragraphs B6.4.7–B6.4.8); and

(iii)   the hedge ratio of the hedging relationship is the same as that resulting from the quantity of the hedged item that the entity actually hedges and the quantity of the hedging instrument that the entity actually uses to hedge that quantity of hedged item. However, that designation shall not reflect an imbalance between the weightings of the hedged item and the hedging instrument that would create hedge ineffectiveness (irrespective of whether recognised or not) that could result in an accounting outcome that would be inconsistent with the purpose of hedge accounting (see paragraphs B6.4.9–B6.4.11).

6.5 Accounting for qualifying hedging relationships

6.5.1   An entity applies hedge accounting to hedging relationships that meet the qualifying criteria in paragraph 6.4.1 (which include the entity's decision to designate the hedging relationship).

6.5.2   There are three types of hedging relationships:

(a)   fair value hedge: a hedge of the exposure to changes in fair value of a recognised asset or liability or an unrecognised firm commitment, or a component of any such item, that is attributable to a particular risk and could affect profit or loss.

(b)   cash flow hedge: a hedge of the exposure to variability in cash flows that is attributable to a particular risk associated with all, or a component of, a recognised asset or liability (such as all or some future interest payments on variable-rate debt) or a highly probable forecast transaction, and could affect profit or loss.

(c)   hedge of a net investment in a foreign operation as defined in IAS 21.

6.5.3   If the hedged item is an equity instrument for which an entity has elected to present changes in fair value in other comprehensive income in accordance with paragraph 5.7.5, the hedged exposure referred to in paragraph 6.5.2(a) must be one that could affect other comprehensive income. In that case, and only in that case, the recognised hedge ineffectiveness is presented in other comprehensive income.

6.5.4   A hedge of the foreign currency risk of a firm commitment may be accounted for as a fair value hedge or a cash flow hedge.

6.5.5   If a hedging relationship ceases to meet the hedge effectiveness requirement relating to the hedge ratio (see paragraph 6.4.1(c)(iii)) but the risk management objective for that designated hedging relationship remains the same, an entity shall adjust the hedge ratio of the hedging relationship so that it meets the qualifying criteria again (this is referred to in this Standard as 'rebalancing' — see paragraphs B6.5.7–B6.5.21).

6.5.6   An entity shall discontinue hedge accounting prospectively only when the hedging relationship (or a part of a hedging relationship) ceases to meet the qualifying criteria (after taking into account any rebalancing of the hedging relationship, if applicable). This includes instances when the hedging instrument expires or is sold, terminated or exercised. For this purpose, the replacement or rollover of a hedging instrument into another hedging instrument is not an expiration or termination if such a replacement or rollover is part of, and consistent with, the entity's documented risk management objective. Additionally, for this purpose there is not an expiration or termination of the hedging instrument if:

(a)   as a consequence of laws or regulations or the introduction of laws or regulations, the parties to the hedging instrument agree that one or more clearing counterparties replace their original counterparty to become the new counterparty to each of the parties. For this purpose, a clearing counterparty is a central counterparty (sometimes called a 'clearing organisation' or 'clearing agency') or an entity or entities, for example, a clearing member of a clearing organisation or a client of a clearing member of a clearing organisation, that are acting as a counterparty in order to effect clearing by a central counterparty. However, when the parties to the hedging instrument replace their original counterparties with different counterparties the requirement in this subparagraph is met only if each of those parties effects clearing with the same central counterparty.

(b)   other changes, if any, to the hedging instrument are limited to those that are necessary to effect such a replacement of the counterparty. Such changes are limited to those that are consistent with the terms that would be expected if the hedging instrument were originally cleared with the clearing counterparty. These changes include changes in the collateral requirements, rights to offset receivables and payables balances, and charges levied.

Discontinuing hedge accounting can either affect a hedging relationship in its entirety or only a part of it (in which case hedge accounting continues for the remainder of the hedging relationship).

6.5.7   An entity shall apply:

(a)   paragraph 6.5.10 when it discontinues hedge accounting for a fair value hedge for which the hedged item is (or is a component of) a financial instrument measured at amortised cost; and

(b)   paragraph 6.5.12 when it discontinues hedge accounting for cash flow hedges.

Fair value hedges

6.5.8   As long as a fair value hedge meets the qualifying criteria in paragraph 6.4.1, the hedging relationship shall be accounted for as follows:

(a)   the gain or loss on the hedging instrument shall be recognised in profit or loss (or other comprehensive income, if the hedging instrument hedges an equity instrument for which an entity has elected to present changes in fair value in other comprehensive income in accordance with paragraph 5.7.5).

(b)   the hedging gain or loss on the hedged item shall adjust the carrying amount of the hedged item (if applicable) and be recognised in profit or loss. If the hedged item is a financial asset (or a component thereof) that is measured at fair value through other comprehensive income in accordance with paragraph 4.1.2A, the hedging gain or loss on the hedged item shall be recognised in profit or loss. However, if the hedged item is an equity instrument for which an entity has elected to present changes in fair value in other comprehensive income in accordance with paragraph 5.7.5, those amounts shall remain in other comprehensive income. When a hedged item is an unrecognised firm commitment (or a component thereof), the cumulative change in the fair value of the hedged item subsequent to its designation is recognised as an asset or a liability with a corresponding gain or loss recognised in profit or loss.

6.5.9   When a hedged item in a fair value hedge is a firm commitment (or a component thereof) to acquire an asset or assume a liability, the initial carrying amount of the asset or the liability that results from the entity meeting the firm commitment is adjusted to include the cumulative change in the fair value of the hedged item that was recognised in the statement of financial position.

6.5.10   Any adjustment arising from paragraph 6.5.8(b) shall be amortised to profit or loss if the hedged item is a financial instrument (or a component thereof) measured at amortised cost. Amortisation may begin as soon as an adjustment exists and shall begin no later than when the hedged item ceases to be adjusted for hedging gains and losses. The amortisation is based on a recalculated effective interest rate at the date that amortisation begins. In the case of a financial asset (or a component thereof) that is a hedged item and that is measured at fair value through other comprehensive income in accordance with paragraph 4.1.2A, amortisation applies in the same manner but to the amount that represents the cumulative gain or loss previously recognised in accordance with paragraph 6.5.8(b) instead of by adjusting the carrying amount.

Cash flow hedges

6.5.11   As long as a cash flow hedge meets the qualifying criteria in paragraph 6.4.1, the hedging relationship shall be accounted for as follows:

(a)   the separate component of equity associated with the hedged item (cash flow hedge reserve) is adjusted to the lower of the following (in absolute amounts):

(i)   the cumulative gain or loss on the hedging instrument from inception of the hedge; and

(ii)   the cumulative change in fair value (present value) of the hedged item (ie the present value of the cumulative change in the hedged expected future cash flows) from inception of the hedge.

(b)   the portion of the gain or loss on the hedging instrument that is determined to be an effective hedge (ie the portion that is offset by the change in the cash flow hedge reserve calculated in accordance with (a)) shall be recognised in other comprehensive income.

(c)   any remaining gain or loss on the hedging instrument (or any gain or loss required to balance the change in the cash flow hedge reserve calculated in accordance with (a)) is hedge ineffectiveness that shall be recognised in profit or loss.

(d)   the amount that has been accumulated in the cash flow hedge reserve in accordance with (a) shall be accounted for as follows:

(i)   if a hedged forecast transaction subsequently results in the recognition of a non-financial asset or non-financial liability, or a hedged forecast transaction for a non-financial asset or a non-financial liability becomes a firm commitment for which fair value hedge accounting is applied, the entity shall remove that amount from the cash flow hedge reserve and include it directly in the initial cost or other carrying amount of the asset or the liability. This is not a reclassification adjustment (see IAS 1) and hence it does not affect other comprehensive income.

(ii) for cash flow hedges other than those covered by (i), that amount shall be reclassified from the cash flow hedge reserve to profit or loss as a reclassification adjustment (see IAS 1) in the same period or periods during which the hedged expected future cash flows affect profit or loss (for example, in the periods that interest income or interest expense is recognised or when a forecast sale occurs).

(iii) however, if that amount is a loss and an entity expects that all or a portion of that loss will not be recovered in one or more future periods, it shall immediately reclassify the amount that is not expected to be recovered into profit or loss as a reclassification adjustment (see IAS 1).

6.5.12 When an entity discontinues hedge accounting for a cash flow hedge (see paragraphs 6.5.6 and 6.5.7(b)) it shall account for the amount that has been accumulated in the cash flow hedge reserve in accordance with paragraph 6.5.11(a) as follows:

(a) if the hedged future cash flows are still expected to occur, that amount shall remain in the cash flow hedge reserve until the future cash flows occur or until paragraph 6.5.11(d)(iii) applies. When the future cash flows occur, paragraph 6.5.11(d) applies.

(b) if the hedged future cash flows are no longer expected to occur, that amount shall be immediately reclassified from the cash flow hedge reserve to profit or loss as a reclassification adjustment (see IAS 1). A hedged future cash flow that is no longer highly probable to occur may still be expected to occur.

Hedges of a net investment in a foreign operation

6.5.13 Hedges of a net investment in a foreign operation, including a hedge of a monetary item that is accounted for as part of the net investment (see IAS 21), shall be accounted for similarly to cash flow hedges:

(a) the portion of the gain or loss on the hedging instrument that is determined to be an effective hedge shall be recognised in other comprehensive income (see paragraph 6.5.11); and

(b) the ineffective portion shall be recognised in profit or loss.

6.5.14 The cumulative gain or loss on the hedging instrument relating to the effective portion of the hedge that has been accumulated in the foreign currency translation reserve shall be reclassified from equity to profit or loss as a reclassification adjustment (see IAS 1) in accordance with paragraphs 48–49 of IAS 21 on the disposal or partial disposal of the foreign operation.

Accounting for the time value of options

6.5.15   When an entity separates the intrinsic value and time value of an option contract and designates as the hedging instrument only the change in intrinsic value of the option (see paragraph 6.2.4(a)), it shall account for the time value of the option as follows (see paragraphs B6.5.29–B6.5.33):

(a)   an entity shall distinguish the time value of options by the type of hedged item that the option hedges (see paragraph B6.5.29):

(i)   a transaction related hedged item; or

(ii)   a time-period related hedged item.

(b)   the change in fair value of the time value of an option that hedges a transaction related hedged item shall be recognised in other comprehensive income to the extent that it relates to the hedged item and shall be accumulated in a separate component of equity. The cumulative change in fair value arising from the time value of the option that has been accumulated in a separate component of equity (the 'amount') shall be accounted for as follows:

(i)   if the hedged item subsequently results in the recognition of a non-financial asset or a non-financial liability, or a firm commitment for a non-financial asset or a non-financial liability for which fair value hedge accounting is applied, the entity shall remove the amount from the separate component of equity and include it directly in the initial cost or other carrying amount of the asset or the liability. This is not a reclassification adjustment (see IAS 1) and hence does not affect other comprehensive income.

(ii)   for hedging relationships other than those covered by (i), the amount shall be reclassified from the separate component of equity to profit or loss as a reclassification adjustment (see IAS 1) in the same period or periods during which the hedged expected future cash flows affect profit or loss (for example, when a forecast sale occurs).

(iii)   however, if all or a portion of that amount is not expected to be recovered in one or more future periods, the amount that is not expected to be recovered shall be immediately reclassified into profit or loss as a reclassification adjustment (see IAS 1).

(c)   the change in fair value of the time value of an option that hedges a time-period related hedged item shall be recognised in other comprehensive income to the extent that it relates to the hedged item and shall be accumulated in a separate component of equity. The time value at the date of designation of the option as a hedging instrument, to the extent that it relates to the hedged item, shall be amortised on a systematic and rational basis over the period during which the hedge adjustment for the option's intrinsic value could affect profit or loss (or other comprehensive income, if the hedged item is an equity instrument for which an entity has elected to present changes in fair value in other comprehensive income in accordance with paragraph 5.7.5). Hence, in each reporting period, the amortisation amount shall be reclassified from the separate component of equity to profit or loss as a reclassification adjustment (see IAS 1). However, if hedge accounting is discontinued for the hedging relationship that includes the change in intrinsic value of the option as the hedging instrument, the net amount (ie including cumulative amortisation) that has been accumulated in the separate component of equity shall be immediately reclassified into profit or loss as a reclassification adjustment (see IAS 1).

Accounting for the forward element of forward contracts and foreign currency basis spreads of financial instruments

6.5.16   When an entity separates the forward element and the spot element of a forward contract and designates as the hedging instrument only the change in the value of the spot element of the forward contract, or when an entity separates the foreign currency basis spread from a financial instrument and excludes it from the designation of that financial instrument as the hedging instrument (see paragraph 6.2.4(b)), the entity may apply paragraph 6.5.15 to the forward element of the forward contract or to the foreign currency basis spread in the same manner as it is applied to the time value of an option. In that case, the entity shall apply the application guidance in paragraphs B6.5.34–B6.5.39.

6.6 Hedges of a group of items

Eligibility of a group of items as the hedged item

6.6.1   A group of items (including a group of items that constitute a net position; see paragraphs B6.6.1–B6.6.8) is an eligible hedged item only if:

(a)   it consists of items (including components of items) that are, individually, eligible hedged items;

(b)   the items in the group are managed together on a group basis for risk management purposes; and

(c)   in the case of a cash flow hedge of a group of items whose variabilities in cash flows are not expected to be approximately proportional to the overall variability in cash flows of the group so that offsetting risk positions arise:

(i)   it is a hedge of foreign currency risk; and

(ii)   the designation of that net position specifies the reporting period in which the forecast transactions are expected to affect profit or loss, as well as their nature and volume (see paragraphs B6.6.7–B6.6.8).

Designation of a component of a nominal amount

6.6.2   A component that is a proportion of an eligible group of items is an eligible hedged item provided that designation is consistent with the entity's risk management objective.

6.6.3   A layer component of an overall group of items (for example, a bottom layer) is eligible for hedge accounting only if:

(a)   it is separately identifiable and reliably measurable;

(b)   the risk management objective is to hedge a layer component;

(c)   the items in the overall group from which the layer is identified are exposed to the same hedged risk (so that the measurement of the hedged layer is not significantly affected by which particular items from the overall group form part of the hedged layer);

(d)   for a hedge of existing items (for example, an unrecognised firm commitment or a recognised asset) an entity can identify and track the overall group of items from which the hedged layer is defined (so that the entity is able to comply with the requirements for the accounting for qualifying hedging relationships); and

(e)   any items in the group that contain prepayment options meet the requirements for components of a nominal amount (see paragraph B6.3.20).

Presentation

6.6.4   For a hedge of a group of items with offsetting risk positions (ie in a hedge of a net position) whose hedged risk affects different line items in the statement of profit or loss and other comprehensive income, any hedging gains or losses in that statement shall be presented in a separate line from those affected by the hedged items. Hence, in that statement the amount in the line item that relates to the hedged item itself (for example, revenue or cost of sales) remains unaffected.

6.6.5   For assets and liabilities that are hedged together as a group in a fair value hedge, the gain or loss in the statement of financial position on the individual assets and liabilities shall be recognised as an adjustment of the carrying amount of the respective individual items comprising the group in accordance with paragraph 6.5.8(b).

Nil net positions

6.6.6   When the hedged item is a group that is a nil net position (ie the hedged items among themselves fully offset the risk that is managed on a group basis), an entity is permitted to designate it in a hedging relationship that does not include a hedging instrument, provided that:

(a)   the hedge is part of a rolling net risk hedging strategy, whereby the entity routinely hedges new positions of the same type as time moves on (for example, when transactions move into the time horizon for which the entity hedges);

(b)   the hedged net position changes in size over the life of the rolling net risk hedging strategy and the entity uses eligible hedging instruments to hedge the net risk (ie when the net position is not nil);

(c)   hedge accounting is normally applied to such net positions when the net position is not nil and it is hedged with eligible hedging instruments; and

(d)   not applying hedge accounting to the nil net position would give rise to inconsistent accounting outcomes, because the accounting would not recognise the offsetting risk positions that would otherwise be recognised in a hedge of a net position.

6.7 Option to designate a credit exposure as measured at fair value through profit or loss

Eligibility of credit exposures for designation at fair value through profit or loss

6.7.1   If an entity uses a credit derivative that is measured at fair value through profit or loss to manage the credit risk of all, or a part of, a financial instrument (credit exposure) it may designate that financial instrument to the extent that it is so managed (ie all or a proportion of it) as measured at fair value through profit or loss if:

(a)   the name of the credit exposure (for example, the borrower, or the holder of a loan commitment) matches the reference entity of the credit derivative ('name matching'); and

(b)   the seniority of the financial instrument matches that of the instruments that can be delivered in accordance with the credit derivative.

An entity may make this designation irrespective of whether the financial instrument that is managed for credit risk is within the scope of this Standard (for example, an entity may designate loan commitments that are outside the scope of this Standard). The entity may designate that financial instrument at, or subsequent to, initial recognition, or while it is unrecognised. The entity shall document the designation concurrently.

Accounting for credit exposures designated at fair value through profit or loss

6.7.2   If a financial instrument is designated in accordance with paragraph 6.7.1 as measured at fair value through profit or loss after its initial recognition, or was previously not recognised, the difference at the time of designation between the carrying amount, if any, and the fair value shall immediately be recognised in profit or loss. For financial assets measured at fair value through other comprehensive income in accordance with paragraph 4.1.2A, the cumulative gain or loss previously recognised in other comprehensive income shall immediately be reclassified from equity to profit or loss as a reclassification adjustment (see IAS 1).

6.7.3 An entity shall discontinue measuring the financial instrument that gave rise to the credit risk, or a proportion of that financial instrument, at fair value through profit or loss if:

(a) the qualifying criteria in paragraph 6.7.1 are no longer met, for example:

(i) the credit derivative or the related financial instrument that gives rise to the credit risk expires or is sold, terminated or settled; or

(ii) the credit risk of the financial instrument is no longer managed using credit derivatives. For example, this could occur because of improvements in the credit quality of the borrower or the loan commitment holder or changes to capital requirements imposed on an entity; and

(b) the financial instrument that gives rise to the credit risk is not otherwise required to be measured at fair value through profit or loss (ie the entity's business model has not changed in the meantime so that a reclassification in accordance with paragraph 4.4.1 was required).

6.7.4 When an entity discontinues measuring the financial instrument that gives rise to the credit risk, or a proportion of that financial instrument, at fair value through profit or loss, that financial instrument's fair value at the date of discontinuation becomes its new carrying amount. Subsequently, the same measurement that was used before designating the financial instrument at fair value through profit or loss shall be applied (including amortisation that results from the new carrying amount). For example, a financial asset that had originally been classified as measured at amortised cost would revert to that measurement and its effective interest rate would be recalculated based on its new gross carrying amount on the date of discontinuing measurement at fair value through profit or loss.

6.8 Temporary exceptions from applying specific hedge accounting requirements

6.8.1 An entity shall apply paragraphs 6.8.4–6.8.12 and paragraphs 7.1.8 and 7.2.26(d) to all hedging relationships directly affected by interest rate benchmark reform. These paragraphs apply only to such hedging relationships. A hedging relationship is directly affected by interest rate benchmark reform only if the reform gives rise to uncertainties about:

(a) the interest rate benchmark (contractually or non-contractually specified) designated as a hedged risk; and/or

(b) the timing or the amount of interest rate benchmark-based cash flows of the hedged item or of the hedging instrument.

6.8.2 For the purpose of applying paragraphs 6.8.4–6.8.12, the term 'interest rate benchmark reform' refers to the market-wide reform of an interest rate benchmark, including the replacement of an interest rate benchmark with an alternative benchmark rate such as that resulting from the recommendations set out in the Financial Stability Board's July 2014 report 'Reforming Major Interest Rate Benchmarks'.[2]

6.8.3 Paragraphs 6.8.4–6.8.12 provide exceptions only to the requirements specified in these paragraphs. An entity shall continue to apply all other hedge accounting requirements to hedging relationships directly affected by interest rate benchmark reform.

Highly probable requirement for cash flow hedges

6.8.4 For the purpose of determining whether a forecast transaction (or a component thereof) is highly probable as required by paragraph 6.3.3, an entity shall assume that the interest rate benchmark on which the hedged cash flows (contractually or non-contractually specified) are based is not altered as a result of interest rate benchmark reform.

Reclassifying the amount accumulated in the cash flow hedge reserve

6.8.5 For the purpose of applying the requirement in paragraph 6.5.12 in order to determine whether the hedged future cash flows are expected to occur, an entity shall assume that the interest rate benchmark on which the hedged cash flows (contractually or non-contractually specified) are based is not altered as a result of interest rate benchmark reform.

Assessing the economic relationship between the hedged item and the hedging instrument

6.8.6 For the purpose of applying the requirements in paragraphs 6.4.1(c)(i) and B6.4.4–B6.4.6, an entity shall assume that the interest rate benchmark on which the hedged cash flows and/or the hedged risk (contractually or non-contractually specified) are based, or the interest rate benchmark on which the cash flows of the hedging instrument are based, is not altered as a result of interest rate benchmark reform.

Designating a component of an item as a hedged item

6.8.7 Unless paragraph 6.8.8 applies, for a hedge of a non-contractually specified benchmark component of interest rate risk, an entity shall apply the requirement in paragraphs 6.3.7(a) and B6.3.8—that the risk component shall be separately identifiable—only at the inception of the hedging relationship.

---

2 The report, 'Reforming Major Interest Rate Benchmarks', is available at http://www.fsb.org/wp-content/uploads/r_140722.pdf.

6.8.8   When an entity, consistent with its hedge documentation, frequently resets (ie discontinues and restarts) a hedging relationship because both the hedging instrument and the hedged item frequently change (ie the entity uses a dynamic process in which both the hedged items and the hedging instruments used to manage that exposure do not remain the same for long), the entity shall apply the requirement in paragraphs 6.3.7(a) and B6.3.8 — that the risk component is separately identifiable — only when it initially designates a hedged item in that hedging relationship. A hedged item that has been assessed at the time of its initial designation in the hedging relationship, whether it was at the time of the hedge inception or subsequently, is not reassessed at any subsequent redesignation in the same hedging relationship.

End of application

6.8.9   An entity shall prospectively cease applying paragraph 6.8.4 to a hedged item at the earlier of:

(a)   when the uncertainty arising from interest rate benchmark reform is no longer present with respect to the timing and the amount of the interest rate benchmark-based cash flows of the hedged item; and

(b)   when the hedging relationship that the hedged item is part of is discontinued.

6.8.10 An entity shall prospectively cease applying paragraph 6.8.5 at the earlier of:

(a)   when the uncertainty arising from interest rate benchmark reform is no longer present with respect to the timing and the amount of the interest rate benchmark-based future cash flows of the hedged item; and

(b)   when the entire amount accumulated in the cash flow hedge reserve with respect to that discontinued hedging relationship has been reclassified to profit or loss.

6.8.11 An entity shall prospectively cease applying paragraph 6.8.6:

(a)   to a hedged item, when the uncertainty arising from interest rate benchmark reform is no longer present with respect to the hedged risk or the timing and the amount of the interest rate benchmark-based cash flows of the hedged item; and

(b)   to a hedging instrument, when the uncertainty arising from interest rate benchmark reform is no longer present with respect to the timing and the amount of the interest rate benchmark-based cash flows of the hedging instrument.

If the hedging relationship that the hedged item and the hedging instrument are part of is discontinued earlier than the date specified in paragraph 6.8.11(a) or the date specified in paragraph 6.8.11(b), the entity shall prospectively cease applying paragraph 6.8.6 to that hedging relationship at the date of discontinuation.

6.8.12   When designating a group of items as the hedged item, or a combination of financial instruments as the hedging instrument, an entity shall prospectively cease applying paragraphs 6.8.4–6.8.6 to an individual item or financial instrument in accordance with paragraphs 6.8.9, 6.8.10, or 6.8.11, as relevant, when the uncertainty arising from interest rate benchmark reform is no longer present with respect to the hedged risk and/or the timing and the amount of the interest rate benchmark-based cash flows of that item or financial instrument.

6.8.13   An entity shall prospectively cease applying paragraphs 6.8.7 and 6.8.8 at the earlier of:

    (a)   when changes required by interest rate benchmark reform are made to the non-contractually specified risk component applying paragraph 6.9.1; or

    (b)   when the hedging relationship in which the non-contractually specified risk component is designated is discontinued.

6.9 Additional temporary exceptions arising from interest rate benchmark reform

6.9.1   As and when the requirements in paragraphs 6.8.4–6.8.8 cease to apply to a hedging relationship (see paragraphs 6.8.9–6.8.13), an entity shall amend the formal designation of that hedging relationship as previously documented to reflect the changes required by interest rate benchmark reform, ie the changes are consistent with the requirements in paragraphs 5.4.6–5.4.8. In this context, the hedge designation shall be amended only to make one or more of these changes:

    (a)   designating an alternative benchmark rate (contractually or non-contractually specified) as a hedged risk;

    (b)   amending the description of the hedged item, including the description of the designated portion of the cash flows or fair value being hedged; or

    (c)   amending the description of the hedging instrument.

6.9.2   An entity also shall apply the requirement in paragraph 6.9.1(c) if these three conditions are met:

    (a)   the entity makes a change required by interest rate benchmark reform using an approach other than changing the basis for determining the contractual cash flows of the hedging instrument (as described in paragraph 5.4.6);

    (b)   the original hedging instrument is not derecognised; and

    (c)   the chosen approach is economically equivalent to changing the basis for determining the contractual cash flows of the original hedging instrument (as described in paragraphs 5.4.7 and 5.4.8).

6.9.3 The requirements in paragraphs 6.8.4–6.8.8 may cease to apply at different times. Therefore, in applying paragraph 6.9.1, an entity may be required to amend the formal designation of its hedging relationships at different times, or may be required to amend the formal designation of a hedging relationship more than once. When, and only when, such a change is made to the hedge designation, an entity shall apply paragraphs 6.9.7–6.9.12 as applicable. An entity also shall apply paragraph 6.5.8 (for a fair value hedge) or paragraph 6.5.11 (for a cash flow hedge) to account for any changes in the fair value of the hedged item or the hedging instrument.

6.9.4 An entity shall amend a hedging relationship as required in paragraph 6.9.1 by the end of the reporting period during which a change required by interest rate benchmark reform is made to the hedged risk, hedged item or hedging instrument. For the avoidance of doubt, such an amendment to the formal designation of a hedging relationship constitutes neither the discontinuation of the hedging relationship nor the designation of a new hedging relationship.

6.9.5 If changes are made in addition to those changes required by interest rate benchmark reform to the financial asset or financial liability designated in a hedging relationship (as described in paragraphs 5.4.6–5.4.8) or to the designation of the hedging relationship (as required by paragraph 6.9.1), an entity shall first apply the applicable requirements in this Standard to determine if those additional changes result in the discontinuation of hedge accounting. If the additional changes do not result in the discontinuation of hedge accounting, an entity shall amend the formal designation of the hedging relationship as specified in paragraph 6.9.1.

6.9.6 Paragraphs 6.9.7–6.9.13 provide exceptions to the requirements specified in those paragraphs only. An entity shall apply all other hedge accounting requirements in this Standard, including the qualifying criteria in paragraph 6.4.1, to hedging relationships that were directly affected by interest rate benchmark reform.

Accounting for qualifying hedging relationships
Cash flow hedges

6.9.7 For the purpose of applying paragraph 6.5.11, at the point when an entity amends the description of a hedged item as required in paragraph 6.9.1(b), the amount accumulated in the cash flow hedge reserve shall be deemed to be based on the alternative benchmark rate on which the hedged future cash flows are determined.

6.9.8 For a discontinued hedging relationship, when the interest rate benchmark on which the hedged future cash flows had been based is changed as required by interest rate benchmark reform, for the purpose of applying paragraph 6.5.12 in order to determine whether the hedged future cash flows are expected to occur, the amount accumulated in the cash flow hedge reserve for that hedging relationship shall be deemed to be based on the alternative benchmark rate on which the hedged future cash flows will be based.

Groups of items

6.9.9   When an entity applies paragraph 6.9.1 to groups of items designated as hedged items in a fair value or cash flow hedge, the entity shall allocate the hedged items to subgroups based on the benchmark rate being hedged and designate the benchmark rate as the hedged risk for each subgroup. For example, in a hedging relationship in which a group of items is hedged for changes in an interest rate benchmark subject to interest rate benchmark reform, the hedged cash flows or fair value of some items in the group could be changed to reference an alternative benchmark rate before other items in the group are changed. In this example, in applying paragraph 6.9.1, the entity would designate the alternative benchmark rate as the hedged risk for that relevant subgroup of hedged items. The entity would continue to designate the existing interest rate benchmark as the hedged risk for the other subgroup of hedged items until the hedged cash flows or fair value of those items are changed to reference the alternative benchmark rate or the items expire and are replaced with hedged items that reference the alternative benchmark rate.

6.9.10   An entity shall assess separately whether each subgroup meets the requirements in paragraph 6.6.1 to be an eligible hedged item. If any subgroup fails to meet the requirements in paragraph 6.6.1, the entity shall discontinue hedge accounting prospectively for the hedging relationship in its entirety. An entity also shall apply the requirements in paragraphs 6.5.8 and 6.5.11 to account for ineffectiveness related to the hedging relationship in its entirety.

Designation of risk components

6.9.11   An alternative benchmark rate designated as a non-contractually specified risk component that is not separately identifiable (see paragraphs 6.3.7(a) and B6.3.8) at the date it is designated shall be deemed to have met that requirement at that date, if, and only if, the entity reasonably expects the alternative benchmark rate will be separately identifiable within 24 months. The 24-month period applies to each alternative benchmark rate separately and starts from the date the entity designates the alternative benchmark rate as a non-contractually specified risk component for the first time (ie the 24-month period applies on a rate-by-rate basis).

6.9.12   If subsequently an entity reasonably expects that the alternative benchmark rate will not be separately identifiable within 24 months from the date the entity designated it as a non-contractually specified risk component for the first time, the entity shall cease applying the requirement in paragraph 6.9.11 to that alternative benchmark rate and discontinue hedge accounting prospectively from the date of that reassessment for all hedging relationships in which the alternative benchmark rate was designated as a non-contractually specified risk component.

6.9.13　In addition to those hedging relationships specified in paragraph 6.9.1, an entity shall apply the requirements in paragraphs 6.9.11 and 6.9.12 to new hedging relationships in which an alternative benchmark rate is designated as a non-contractually specified risk component (see paragraphs 6.3.7(a) and B6.3.8) when, because of interest rate benchmark reform, that risk component is not separately identifiable at the date it is designated.

Chapter 7 Effective date and transition

7.1 Effective date

7.1.1　An entity shall apply this Standard for annual periods beginning on or after 1 January 2018. Earlier application is permitted. If an entity elects to apply this Standard early, it must disclose that fact and apply all of the requirements in this Standard at the same time (but see also paragraphs 7.1.2, 7.2.21 and 7.3.2). It shall also, at the same time, apply the amendments in Appendix C.

7.1.2　Despite the requirements in paragraph 7.1.1, for annual periods beginning before 1 January 2018, an entity may elect to early apply only the requirements for the presentation of gains and losses on financial liabilities designated as at fair value through profit or loss in paragraphs 5.7.1(c), 5.7.7–5.7.9, 7.2.14 and B5.7.5–B5.7.20 without applying the other requirements in this Standard. If an entity elects to apply only those paragraphs, it shall disclose that fact and provide on an ongoing basis the related disclosures set out in paragraphs 10–11 of IFRS 7 *Financial Instruments: Disclosures* (as amended by IFRS 9 (2010)). (See also paragraphs 7.2.2 and 7.2.15.)

7.1.3　*Annual Improvements to IFRSs 2010–2012 Cycle*, issued in December 2013, amended paragraphs 4.2.1 and 5.7.5 as a consequential amendment derived from the amendment to IFRS 3. An entity shall apply that amendment prospectively to business combinations to which the amendment to IFRS 3 applies.

7.1.4　IFRS 15, issued in May 2014, amended paragraphs 3.1.1, 4.2.1, 5.1.1, 5.2.1, 5.7.6, B3.2.13, B5.7.1, C5 and C42 and deleted paragraph C16 and its related heading. Paragraphs 5.1.3 and 5.7.1A, and a definition to Appendix A, were added. An entity shall apply those amendments when it applies IFRS 15.

7.1.5　IFRS 16, issued in January 2016, amended paragraphs 2.1, 5.5.15, B4.3.8, B5.5.34 and B5.5.46. An entity shall apply those amendments when it applies IFRS 16.

7.1.6　*[This paragraph refers to amendments that are not yet effective, and is therefore not included in this edition.]*

7.1.7　*Prepayment Features with Negative Compensation* (Amendments to IFRS 9), issued in October 2017, added paragraphs 7.2.29–7.2.34 and B4.1.12A and amended paragraphs B4.1.11(b) and B4.1.12(b). An entity shall apply these amendments for annual periods beginning on or after 1 January 2019. Earlier application is permitted. If an entity applies these amendments for an earlier period, it shall disclose that fact.

7.1.8   *Interest Rate Benchmark Reform*, which amended IFRS 9, IAS 39 and IFRS 7, issued in September 2019, added Section 6.8 and amended paragraph 7.2.26. An entity shall apply these amendments for annual periods beginning on or after 1 January 2020. Earlier application is permitted. If an entity applies these amendments for an earlier period, it shall disclose that fact.

7.1.9   *Annual Improvements to IFRS Standards 2018–2020*, issued in May 2020, added paragraphs 7.2.35 and B3.3.6A and amended paragraph B3.3.6. An entity shall apply that amendment for annual reporting periods beginning on or after 1 January 2022. Earlier application is permitted. If an entity applies the amendment for an earlier period, it shall disclose that fact.

7.1.10   *Interest Rate Benchmark Reform—Phase 2*, which amended IFRS 9, IAS 39, IFRS 7, IFRS 4 and IFRS 16, issued in August 2020, added paragraphs 5.4.5–5.4.9, 6.8.13, Section 6.9 and paragraphs 7.2.43–7.2.46. An entity shall apply these amendments for annual periods beginning on or after 1 January 2021. Earlier application is permitted. If an entity applies these amendments for an earlier period, it shall disclose that fact.

7.2 Transition

7.2.1   An entity shall apply this Standard retrospectively, in accordance with IAS 8 *Accounting Policies, Changes in Accounting Estimates and Errors*, except as specified in paragraphs 7.2.4–7.2.26 and 7.2.28. This Standard shall not be applied to items that have already been derecognised at the date of initial application.

7.2.2   For the purposes of the transition provisions in paragraphs 7.2.1, 7.2.3–7.2.28 and 7.3.2, the date of initial application is the date when an entity first applies those requirements of this Standard and must be the beginning of a reporting period after the issue of this Standard. Depending on the entity's chosen approach to applying IFRS 9, the transition can involve one or more than one date of initial application for different requirements.

Transition for classification and measurement (Chapters 4 and 5)

7.2.3   At the date of initial application, an entity shall assess whether a financial asset meets the condition in paragraphs 4.1.2(a) or 4.1.2A(a) on the basis of the facts and circumstances that exist at that date. The resulting classification shall be applied retrospectively irrespective of the entity's business model in prior reporting periods.

7.2.4   If, at the date of initial application, it is impracticable (as defined in IAS 8) for an entity to assess a modified time value of money element in accordance with paragraphs B4.1.9B–B4.1.9D on the basis of the facts and circumstances that existed at the initial recognition of the financial asset, an entity shall assess the contractual cash flow characteristics of that financial asset on the basis of the facts and circumstances that existed at the initial recognition of the financial asset without taking into account the requirements related to the modification of the time value of money element in paragraphs B4.1.9B–B4.1.9D. (See also paragraph 42R of IFRS 7.)

7.2.5   If, at the date of initial application, it is impracticable (as defined in IAS 8) for an entity to assess whether the fair value of a prepayment feature was insignificant in accordance with paragraph B4.1.12(c) on the basis of the facts and circumstances that existed at the initial recognition of the financial asset, an entity shall assess the contractual cash flow characteristics of that financial asset on the basis of the facts and circumstances that existed at the initial recognition of the financial asset without taking into account the exception for prepayment features in paragraph B4.1.12. (See also paragraph 42S of IFRS 7.)

7.2.6   If an entity measures a hybrid contract at fair value in accordance with paragraphs 4.1.2A, 4.1.4 or 4.1.5 but the fair value of the hybrid contract had not been measured in comparative reporting periods, the fair value of the hybrid contract in the comparative reporting periods shall be the sum of the fair values of the components (ie the non-derivative host and the embedded derivative) at the end of each comparative reporting period if the entity restates prior periods (see paragraph 7.2.15).

7.2.7   If an entity has applied paragraph 7.2.6 then at the date of initial application the entity shall recognise any difference between the fair value of the entire hybrid contract at the date of initial application and the sum of the fair values of the components of the hybrid contract at the date of initial application in the opening retained earnings (or other component of equity, as appropriate) of the reporting period that includes the date of initial application.

7.2.8   At the date of initial application an entity may designate:

(a)   a financial asset as measured at fair value through profit or loss in accordance with paragraph 4.1.5; or

(b)   an investment in an equity instrument as at fair value through other comprehensive income in accordance with paragraph 5.7.5.

Such a designation shall be made on the basis of the facts and circumstances that exist at the date of initial application. That classification shall be applied retrospectively.

7.2.9   At the date of initial application an entity:

(a)   shall revoke its previous designation of a financial asset as measured at fair value through profit or loss if that financial asset does not meet the condition in paragraph 4.1.5.

(b)   may revoke its previous designation of a financial asset as measured at fair value through profit or loss if that financial asset meets the condition in paragraph 4.1.5.

Such a revocation shall be made on the basis of the facts and circumstances that exist at the date of initial application. That classification shall be applied retrospectively.

7.2.10   At the date of initial application, an entity:

(a)   may designate a financial liability as measured at fair value through profit or loss in accordance with paragraph 4.2.2(a).

(b) shall revoke its previous designation of a financial liability as measured at fair value through profit or loss if such designation was made at initial recognition in accordance with the condition now in paragraph 4.2.2(a) and such designation does not satisfy that condition at the date of initial application.

(c) may revoke its previous designation of a financial liability as measured at fair value through profit or loss if such designation was made at initial recognition in accordance with the condition now in paragraph 4.2.2(a) and such designation satisfies that condition at the date of initial application.

Such a designation and revocation shall be made on the basis of the facts and circumstances that exist at the date of initial application. That classification shall be applied retrospectively.

7.2.11 If it is impracticable (as defined in IAS 8) for an entity to apply retrospectively the effective interest method, the entity shall treat:

(a) the fair value of the financial asset or the financial liability at the end of each comparative period presented as the gross carrying amount of that financial asset or the amortised cost of that financial liability if the entity restates prior periods; and

(b) the fair value of the financial asset or the financial liability at the date of initial application as the new gross carrying amount of that financial asset or the new amortised cost of that financial liability at the date of initial application of this Standard.

7.2.12 If an entity previously accounted at cost (in accordance with IAS 39), for an investment in an equity instrument that does not have a quoted price in an active market for an identical instrument (ie a Level 1 input) (or for a derivative asset that is linked to and must be settled by delivery of such an equity instrument) it shall measure that instrument at fair value at the date of initial application. Any difference between the previous carrying amount and the fair value shall be recognised in the opening retained earnings (or other component of equity, as appropriate) of the reporting period that includes the date of initial application.

7.2.13 If an entity previously accounted for a derivative liability that is linked to, and must be settled by, delivery of an equity instrument that does not have a quoted price in an active market for an identical instrument (ie a Level 1 input) at cost in accordance with IAS 39, it shall measure that derivative liability at fair value at the date of initial application. Any difference between the previous carrying amount and the fair value shall be recognised in the opening retained earnings of the reporting period that includes the date of initial application.

7.2.14 At the date of initial application, an entity shall determine whether the treatment in paragraph 5.7.7 would create or enlarge an accounting mismatch in profit or loss on the basis of the facts and circumstances that exist at the date of initial application. This Standard shall be applied retrospectively on the basis of that determination.

7.2.14A   At the date of initial application, an entity is permitted to make the designation in paragraph 2.5 for contracts that already exist on the date but only if it designates all similar contracts. The change in the net assets resulting from such designations shall be recognised in retained earnings at the date of initial application.

7.2.15   Despite the requirement in paragraph 7.2.1, an entity that adopts the classification and measurement requirements of this Standard (which include the requirements related to amortised cost measurement for financial assets and impairment in Sections 5.4 and 5.5) shall provide the disclosures set out in paragraphs 42L–42O of IFRS 7 but need not restate prior periods. The entity may restate prior periods if, and only if, it is possible without the use of hindsight. If an entity does not restate prior periods, the entity shall recognise any difference between the previous carrying amount and the carrying amount at the beginning of the annual reporting period that includes the date of initial application in the opening retained earnings (or other component of equity, as appropriate) of the annual reporting period that includes the date of initial application. However, if an entity restates prior periods, the restated financial statements must reflect all of the requirements in this Standard. If an entity's chosen approach to applying IFRS 9 results in more than one date of initial application for different requirements, this paragraph applies at each date of initial application (see paragraph 7.2.2). This would be the case, for example, if an entity elects to early apply only the requirements for the presentation of gains and losses on financial liabilities designated as at fair value through profit or loss in accordance with paragraph 7.1.2 before applying the other requirements in this Standard.

7.2.16   If an entity prepares interim financial reports in accordance with IAS 34 *Interim Financial Reporting* the entity need not apply the requirements in this Standard to interim periods prior to the date of initial application if it is impracticable (as defined in IAS 8).

Impairment (Section 5.5)

7.2.17   An entity shall apply the impairment requirements in Section 5.5 retrospectively in accordance with IAS 8 subject to paragraphs 7.2.15 and 7.2.18–7.2.20.

7.2.18   At the date of initial application, an entity shall use reasonable and supportable information that is available without undue cost or effort to determine the credit risk at the date that a financial instrument was initially recognised (or for loan commitments and financial guarantee contracts at the date that the entity became a party to the irrevocable commitment in accordance with paragraph 5.5.6) and compare that to the credit risk at the date of initial application of this Standard.

7.2.19   When determining whether there has been a significant increase in credit risk since initial recognition, an entity may apply:

(a)   the requirements in paragraphs 5.5.10 and B5.5.22–B5.5.24; and

(b)   the rebuttable presumption in paragraph 5.5.11 for contractual payments that are more than 30 days past due if an entity will apply the impairment requirements by identifying significant increases in credit risk since initial recognition for those financial instruments on the basis of past due information.

7.2.20   If, at the date of initial application, determining whether there has been a significant increase in credit risk since initial recognition would require undue cost or effort, an entity shall recognise a loss allowance at an amount equal to lifetime expected credit losses at each reporting date until that financial instrument is derecognised (unless that financial instrument is low credit risk at a reporting date, in which case paragraph 7.2.19(a) applies).

Transition for hedge accounting (Chapter 6)

7.2.21   When an entity first applies this Standard, it may choose as its accounting policy to continue to apply the hedge accounting requirements of IAS 39 instead of the requirements in Chapter 6 of this Standard. An entity shall apply that policy to all of its hedging relationships. An entity that chooses that policy shall also apply IFRIC 16 *Hedges of a Net Investment in a Foreign Operation* without the amendments that conform that Interpretation to the requirements in Chapter 6 of this Standard.

7.2.22   Except as provided in paragraph 7.2.26, an entity shall apply the hedge accounting requirements of this Standard prospectively.

7.2.23   To apply hedge accounting from the date of initial application of the hedge accounting requirements of this Standard, all qualifying criteria must be met as at that date.

7.2.24   Hedging relationships that qualified for hedge accounting in accordance with IAS 39 that also qualify for hedge accounting in accordance with the criteria of this Standard (see paragraph 6.4.1), after taking into account any rebalancing of the hedging relationship on transition (see paragraph 7.2.25(b)), shall be regarded as continuing hedging relationships.

7.2.25   On initial application of the hedge accounting requirements of this Standard, an entity:

(a)   may start to apply those requirements from the same point in time as it ceases to apply the hedge accounting requirements of IAS 39; and

(b)   shall consider the hedge ratio in accordance with IAS 39 as the starting point for rebalancing the hedge ratio of a continuing hedging relationship, if applicable. Any gain or loss from such a rebalancing shall be recognised in profit or loss.

7.2.26   As an exception to prospective application of the hedge accounting requirements of this Standard, an entity:

(a)   shall apply the accounting for the time value of options in accordance with paragraph 6.5.15 retrospectively if, in accordance with IAS 39, only the change in an option's intrinsic value was designated as a hedging instrument in a hedging relationship. This retrospective application applies only to those hedging relationships that existed at the beginning of the earliest comparative period or were designated thereafter.

(b)   may apply the accounting for the forward element of forward contracts in accordance with paragraph 6.5.16 retrospectively if, in accordance with IAS 39, only the change in the spot element of a forward contract was designated as a hedging instrument in a hedging relationship. This retrospective application applies only to those hedging relationships that existed at the beginning of the earliest comparative period or were designated thereafter. In addition, if an entity elects retrospective application of this accounting, it shall be applied to all hedging relationships that qualify for this election (ie on transition this election is not available on a hedging-relationship-by-hedging-relationship basis). The accounting for foreign currency basis spreads (see paragraph 6.5.16) may be applied retrospectively for those hedging relationships that existed at the beginning of the earliest comparative period or were designated thereafter.

(c)   shall apply retrospectively the requirement of paragraph 6.5.6 that there is not an expiration or termination of the hedging instrument if:

(i)   as a consequence of laws or regulations, or the introduction of laws or regulations, the parties to the hedging instrument agree that one or more clearing counterparties replace their original counterparty to become the new counterparty to each of the parties; and

(ii)   other changes, if any, to the hedging instrument are limited to those that are necessary to effect such a replacement of the counterparty.

(d)   shall apply the requirements in Section 6.8 retrospectively. This retrospective application applies only to those hedging relationships that existed at the beginning of the reporting period in which an entity first applies those requirements or were designated thereafter, and to the amount accumulated in the cash flow hedge reserve that existed at the beginning of the reporting period in which an entity first applies those requirements.

Entities that have applied IFRS 9 (2009), IFRS 9 (2010) or IFRS 9 (2013) early

7.2.27   An entity shall apply the transition requirements in paragraphs 7.2.1–7.2.26 at the relevant date of initial application. An entity shall apply each of the transition provisions in paragraphs 7.2.3–7.2.14A and 7.2.17–7.2.26 only once (ie if an entity chooses an approach of applying IFRS 9 that involves more than one date of initial application, it cannot apply any of those provisions again if they were already applied at an earlier date). (See paragraphs 7.2.2 and 7.3.2.)

7.2.28 An entity that applied IFRS 9 (2009), IFRS 9 (2010) or IFRS 9 (2013) and subsequently applies this Standard:

(a) shall revoke its previous designation of a financial asset as measured at fair value through profit or loss if that designation was previously made in accordance with the condition in paragraph 4.1.5 but that condition is no longer satisfied as a result of the application of this Standard;

(b) may designate a financial asset as measured at fair value through profit or loss if that designation would not have previously satisfied the condition in paragraph 4.1.5 but that condition is now satisfied as a result of the application of this Standard;

(c) shall revoke its previous designation of a financial liability as measured at fair value through profit or loss if that designation was previously made in accordance with the condition in paragraph 4.2.2(a) but that condition is no longer satisfied as a result of the application of this Standard; and

(d) may designate a financial liability as measured at fair value through profit or loss if that designation would not have previously satisfied the condition in paragraph 4.2.2(a) but that condition is now satisfied as a result of the application of this Standard.

Such a designation and revocation shall be made on the basis of the facts and circumstances that exist at the date of initial application of this Standard. That classification shall be applied retrospectively.

Transition for *Prepayment Features with Negative Compensation*

7.2.29 An entity shall apply *Prepayment Features with Negative Compensation* (Amendments to IFRS 9) retrospectively in accordance with IAS 8, except as specified in paragraphs 7.2.30–7.2.34.

7.2.30 An entity that first applies these amendments at the same time it first applies this Standard shall apply paragraphs 7.2.1–7.2.28 instead of paragraphs 7.2.31–7.2.34.

7.2.31 An entity that first applies these amendments after it first applies this Standard shall apply paragraphs 7.2.32–7.2.34. The entity shall also apply the other transition requirements in this Standard necessary for applying these amendments. For that purpose, references to the date of initial application shall be read as referring to the beginning of the reporting period in which an entity first applies these amendments (date of initial application of these amendments).

7.2.32   With regard to designating a financial asset or financial liability as measured at fair value through profit or loss, an entity:

(a)   shall revoke its previous designation of a financial asset as measured at fair value through profit or loss if that designation was previously made in accordance with the condition in paragraph 4.1.5 but that condition is no longer satisfied as a result of the application of these amendments;

(b)   may designate a financial asset as measured at fair value through profit or loss if that designation would not have previously satisfied the condition in paragraph 4.1.5 but that condition is now satisfied as a result of the application of these amendments;

(c)   shall revoke its previous designation of a financial liability as measured at fair value through profit or loss if that designation was previously made in accordance with the condition in paragraph 4.2.2(a) but that condition is no longer satisfied as a result of the application of these amendments; and

(d)   may designate a financial liability as measured at fair value through profit or loss if that designation would not have previously satisfied the condition in paragraph 4.2.2(a) but that condition is now satisfied as a result of the application of these amendments.

Such a designation and revocation shall be made on the basis of the facts and circumstances that exist at the date of initial application of these amendments. That classification shall be applied retrospectively.

7.2.33   An entity is not required to restate prior periods to reflect the application of these amendments. The entity may restate prior periods if, and only if, it is possible without the use of hindsight and the restated financial statements reflect all the requirements in this Standard. If an entity does not restate prior periods, the entity shall recognise any difference between the previous carrying amount and the carrying amount at the beginning of the annual reporting period that includes the date of initial application of these amendments in the opening retained earnings (or other component of equity, as appropriate) of the annual reporting period that includes the date of initial application of these amendments.

7.2.34   In the reporting period that includes the date of initial application of these amendments, the entity shall disclose the following information as at that date of initial application for each class of financial assets and financial liabilities that were affected by these amendments:

(a)   the previous measurement category and carrying amount determined immediately before applying these amendments;

(b)   the new measurement category and carrying amount determined after applying these amendments;

(c) the carrying amount of any financial assets and financial liabilities in the statement of financial position that were previously designated as measured at fair value through profit or loss but are no longer so designated; and

(d) the reasons for any designation or de-designation of financial assets or financial liabilities as measured at fair value through profit or loss.

Transition for Annual Improvements to IFRS Standards

7.2.35 An entity shall apply *Annual Improvements to IFRS Standards 2018–2020* to financial liabilities that are modified or exchanged on or after the beginning of the annual reporting period in which the entity first applies the amendment.

7.2.36– *[These paragraphs refer to amendments that are not yet effective, and are therefore not*
7.2.42 *included in this edition.]*

Transition for *Interest Rate Benchmark Reform—Phase 2*

7.2.43 An entity shall apply *Interest Rate Benchmark Reform – Phase 2* retrospectively in accordance with IAS 8, except as specified in paragraphs 7.2.44–7.2.46.

7.2.44 An entity shall designate a new hedging relationship (for example, as described in paragraph 6.9.13) only prospectively (ie an entity is prohibited from designating a new hedge accounting relationship in prior periods). However, an entity shall reinstate a discontinued hedging relationship if, and only if, these conditions are met:

(a) the entity had discontinued that hedging relationship solely due to changes required by interest rate benchmark reform and the entity would not have been required to discontinue that hedging relationship if these amendments had been applied at that time; and

(b) at the beginning of the reporting period in which an entity first applies these amendments (date of initial application of these amendments), that discontinued hedging relationship meets the qualifying criteria for hedge accounting (after taking into account these amendments).

7.2.45 If, in applying paragraph 7.2.44, an entity reinstates a discontinued hedging relationship, the entity shall read references in paragraphs 6.9.11 and 6.9.12 to the date the alternative benchmark rate is designated as a non-contractually specified risk component for the first time as referring to the date of initial application of these amendments (ie the 24-month period for that alternative benchmark rate designated as a non-contractually specified risk component begins from the date of initial application of these amendments).

7.2.46 An entity is not required to restate prior periods to reflect the application of these amendments. The entity may restate prior periods if, and only if, it is possible without the use of hindsight. If an entity does not restate prior periods, the entity shall recognise any difference between the previous carrying amount and the carrying amount at the beginning of the annual reporting period that includes the date of initial application of these amendments in the opening retained earnings (or other component of equity, as appropriate) of the annual reporting period that includes the date of initial application of these amendments.

7.3 Withdrawal of IFRIC 9, IFRS 9 (2009), IFRS 9 (2010) and IFRS 9 (2013)

7.3.1   This Standard supersedes IFRIC 9 *Reassessment of Embedded Derivatives*. The requirements added to IFRS 9 in October 2010 incorporated the requirements previously set out in paragraphs 5 and 7 of IFRIC 9. As a consequential amendment, IFRS 1 *First-time Adoption of International Financial Reporting Standards* incorporated the requirements previously set out in paragraph 8 of IFRIC 9.

7.3.2   This Standard supersedes IFRS 9 (2009), IFRS 9 (2010) and IFRS 9 (2013). However, for annual periods beginning before 1 January 2018, an entity may elect to apply those earlier versions of IFRS 9 instead of applying this Standard if, and only if, the entity's relevant date of initial application is before 1 February 2015.

Appendix A
Defined terms

This appendix is an integral part of the Standard.

12-month expected credit losses	The portion of **lifetime expected credit losses** that represent the **expected credit losses** that result from default events on a financial instrument that are possible within the 12 months after the reporting date.
amortised cost of a financial asset or financial liability	The amount at which the financial asset or financial liability is measured at initial recognition minus the principal repayments, plus or minus the cumulative amortisation using the **effective interest method** of any difference between that initial amount and the maturity amount and, for financial assets, adjusted for any **loss allowance**.
contract assets	Those rights that IFRS 15 *Revenue from Contracts with Customers* specifies are accounted for in accordance with this Standard for the purposes of recognising and measuring impairment gains or losses.
credit-impaired financial asset	A financial asset is credit-impaired when one or more events that have a detrimental impact on the estimated future cash flows of that financial asset have occurred. Evidence that a financial asset is credit-impaired include observable data about the following events:

(a) significant financial difficulty of the issuer or the borrower;

(b) a breach of contract, such as a default or **past due** event;

(c) the lender(s) of the borrower, for economic or contractual reasons relating to the borrower's financial difficulty, having granted to the borrower a concession(s) that the lender(s) would not otherwise consider;

(d) it is becoming probable that the borrower will enter bankruptcy or other financial reorganisation;

(e) the disappearance of an active market for that financial asset because of financial difficulties; or

(f) the purchase or origination of a financial asset at a deep discount that reflects the incurred **credit losses**.

It may not be possible to identify a single discrete event—instead, the combined effect of several events may have caused financial assets to become credit-impaired.

credit loss	The difference between all contractual cash flows that are due to an entity in accordance with the contract and all the cash flows that the entity expects to receive (ie all cash shortfalls), discounted at the original **effective interest rate** (or **credit-adjusted effective interest rate** for **purchased or originated credit-impaired financial assets**). An entity shall estimate cash flows by considering all contractual terms of the financial instrument (for example, prepayment, extension, call and similar options) through the expected life of that financial instrument. The cash flows that are considered shall include cash flows from the sale of collateral held or other credit enhancements that are integral to the contractual terms. There is a presumption that the expected life of a financial instrument can be estimated reliably. However, in those rare cases when it is not possible to reliably estimate the expected life of a financial instrument, the entity shall use the remaining contractual term of the financial instrument.
credit-adjusted effective interest rate	The rate that exactly discounts the estimated future cash payments or receipts through the expected life of the financial asset to the **amortised cost of a financial asset** that is a **purchased or originated credit-impaired financial asset**. When calculating the credit-adjusted effective interest rate, an entity shall estimate the expected cash flows by considering all contractual terms of the financial asset (for example, prepayment, extension, call and similar options) and **expected credit losses**. The calculation includes all fees and points paid or received between parties to the contract that are an integral part of the effective interest rate (see paragraphs B5.4.1–B5.4.3), **transaction costs**, and all other premiums or discounts. There is a presumption that the cash flows and the expected life of a group of similar financial instruments can be estimated reliably. However, in those rare cases when it is not possible to reliably estimate the cash flows or the remaining life of a financial instrument (or group of financial instruments), the entity shall use the contractual cash flows over the full contractual term of the financial instrument (or group of financial instruments).
derecognition	The removal of a previously recognised financial asset or financial liability from an entity's statement of financial position.
derivative	A financial instrument or other contract within the scope of this Standard with all three of the following characteristics.

	(a)	its value changes in response to the change in a specified interest rate, financial instrument price, commodity price, foreign exchange rate, index of prices or rates, credit rating or credit index, or other variable, provided in the case of a non-financial variable that the variable is not specific to a party to the contract (sometimes called the 'underlying').
	(b)	it requires no initial net investment or an initial net investment that is smaller than would be required for other types of contracts that would be expected to have a similar response to changes in market factors.
	(c)	it is settled at a future date.
dividends		Distributions of profits to holders of equity instruments in proportion to their holdings of a particular class of capital.
effective interest method		The method that is used in the calculation of the **amortised cost of a financial asset or a financial liability** and in the allocation and recognition of the interest revenue or interest expense in profit or loss over the relevant period.
effective interest rate		The rate that exactly discounts estimated future cash payments or receipts through the expected life of the financial asset or financial liability to the **gross carrying amount of a financial asset** or to the **amortised cost of a financial liability**. When calculating the effective interest rate, an entity shall estimate the expected cash flows by considering all the contractual terms of the financial instrument (for example, prepayment, extension, call and similar options) but shall not consider the **expected credit losses**. The calculation includes all fees and points paid or received between parties to the contract that are an integral part of the effective interest rate (see paragraphs B5.4.1–B5.4.3), **transaction costs**, and all other premiums or discounts. There is a presumption that the cash flows and the expected life of a group of similar financial instruments can be estimated reliably. However, in those rare cases when it is not possible to reliably estimate the cash flows or the expected life of a financial instrument (or group of financial instruments), the entity shall use the contractual cash flows over the full contractual term of the financial instrument (or group of financial instruments).
expected credit losses		The weighted average of **credit losses** with the respective risks of a default occurring as the weights.
financial guarantee contract		A contract that requires the issuer to make specified payments to reimburse the holder for a loss it incurs because a specified debtor fails to make payment when due in accordance with the original or modified terms of a debt instrument.

financial liability at fair value through profit or loss	A financial liability that meets one of the following conditions: (a) it meets the definition of **held for trading**. (b) upon initial recognition it is designated by the entity as at fair value through profit or loss in accordance with paragraph 4.2.2 or 4.3.5. (c) it is designated either upon initial recognition or subsequently as at fair value through profit or loss in accordance with paragraph 6.7.1.
firm commitment	A binding agreement for the exchange of a specified quantity of resources at a specified price on a specified future date or dates.
forecast transaction	An uncommitted but anticipated future transaction.
gross carrying amount of a financial asset	The **amortised cost of a financial asset**, before adjusting for any **loss allowance**.
hedge ratio	The relationship between the quantity of the hedging instrument and the quantity of the hedged item in terms of their relative weighting.
held for trading	A financial asset or financial liability that: (a) is acquired or incurred principally for the purpose of selling or repurchasing it in the near term; (b) on initial recognition is part of a portfolio of identified financial instruments that are managed together and for which there is evidence of a recent actual pattern of short-term profit-taking; or (c) is a **derivative** (except for a derivative that is a financial guarantee contract or a designated and effective hedging instrument).
impairment gain or loss	Gains or losses that are recognised in profit or loss in accordance with paragraph 5.5.8 and that arise from applying the impairment requirements in Section 5.5.
lifetime expected credit losses	The **expected credit losses** that result from all possible default events over the expected life of a financial instrument.
loss allowance	The allowance for **expected credit losses** on financial assets measured in accordance with paragraph 4.1.2, lease receivables and **contract assets**, the accumulated impairment amount for financial assets measured in accordance with paragraph 4.1.2A and the provision for expected credit losses on loan commitments and **financial guarantee contracts**.
modification gain or loss	The amount arising from adjusting the **gross carrying amount of a financial asset** to reflect the renegotiated or modified contractual cash flows. The entity recalculates the gross carrying amount of a financial asset as the present value of the estimated future cash payments or receipts through the

expected life of the renegotiated or modified financial asset that are discounted at the financial asset's original **effective interest rate** (or the original **credit-adjusted effective interest rate** for **purchased or originated credit-impaired financial assets**) or, when applicable, the revised **effective interest rate** calculated in accordance with paragraph 6.5.10. When estimating the expected cash flows of a financial asset, an entity shall consider all contractual terms of the financial asset (for example, prepayment, call and similar options) but shall not consider the **expected credit losses**, unless the financial asset is a **purchased or originated credit-impaired financial asset**, in which case an entity shall also consider the initial expected credit losses that were considered when calculating the original **credit-adjusted effective interest rate**.

past due	A financial asset is past due when a counterparty has failed to make a payment when that payment was contractually due.
purchased or originated credit-impaired financial asset	Purchased or originated financial asset(s) that are **credit-impaired** on initial recognition.
reclassification date	The first day of the first reporting period following the change in business model that results in an entity reclassifying financial assets.
regular way purchase or sale	A purchase or sale of a financial asset under a contract whose terms require delivery of the asset within the time frame established generally by regulation or convention in the marketplace concerned.
transaction costs	Incremental costs that are directly attributable to the acquisition, issue or disposal of a financial asset or financial liability (see paragraph B5.4.8). An incremental cost is one that would not have been incurred if the entity had not acquired, issued or disposed of the financial instrument.

The following terms are defined in paragraph 11 of IAS 32, Appendix A of IFRS 7, Appendix A of IFRS 13 or Appendix A of IFRS 15 and are used in this Standard with the meanings specified in IAS 32, IFRS 7, IFRS 13 or IFRS 15:

(a)   credit risk;[3]

(b)   equity instrument;

(c)   fair value;

(d)   financial asset;

(e)   financial instrument;

(f)   financial liability;

---

3   This term (as defined in IFRS 7) is used in the requirements for presenting the effects of changes in credit risk on liabilities designated as at fair value through profit or loss (see paragraph 5.7.7).

(g)   transaction price.

Appendix B
Application guidance

This appendix is an integral part of the Standard.

Scope (Chapter 2)

B2.1 Some contracts require a payment based on climatic, geological or other physical variables. (Those based on climatic variables are sometimes referred to as 'weather derivatives'.) If those contracts are not within the scope of IFRS 4 *Insurance Contracts*, they are within the scope of this Standard.

B2.2 This Standard does not change the requirements relating to employee benefit plans that comply with IAS 26 *Accounting and Reporting by Retirement Benefit Plans* and royalty agreements based on the volume of sales or service revenues that are accounted for under IFRS 15 *Revenue from Contracts with Customers*.

B2.3 Sometimes, an entity makes what it views as a 'strategic investment' in equity instruments issued by another entity, with the intention of establishing or maintaining a long-term operating relationship with the entity in which the investment is made. The investor or joint venturer entity uses IAS 28 *Investments in Associates and Joint Ventures* to determine whether the equity method of accounting shall be applied to such an investment.

B2.4 This Standard applies to the financial assets and financial liabilities of insurers, other than rights and obligations that paragraph 2.1(e) excludes because they arise under contracts within the scope of IFRS 4.

B2.5 Financial guarantee contracts may have various legal forms, such as a guarantee, some types of letter of credit, a credit default contract or an insurance contract. Their accounting treatment does not depend on their legal form. The following are examples of the appropriate treatment (see paragraph 2.1(e)):

   (a) Although a financial guarantee contract meets the definition of an insurance contract in IFRS 4 if the risk transferred is significant, the issuer applies this Standard. Nevertheless, if the issuer has previously asserted explicitly that it regards such contracts as insurance contracts and has used accounting that is applicable to insurance contracts, the issuer may elect to apply either this Standard or IFRS 4 to such financial guarantee contracts. If this Standard applies, paragraph 5.1.1 requires the issuer to recognise a financial guarantee contract initially at fair value. If the financial guarantee contract was issued to an unrelated party in a stand-alone arm's length transaction, its fair value at inception is likely to equal the premium received, unless there is evidence to the contrary. Subsequently, unless the financial guarantee contract was designated at inception as at fair value through profit or loss or unless paragraphs 3.2.15–3.2.23 and B3.2.12–B3.2.17 apply (when a transfer of a financial asset does not qualify for derecognition or the continuing involvement approach applies), the issuer measures it at the higher of:

(i)   the amount determined in accordance with Section 5.5; and

(ii)   the amount initially recognised less, when appropriate, the cumulative amount of income recognised in accordance with the principles of IFRS 15 (see paragraph 4.2.1(c)).

(b)   Some credit-related guarantees do not, as a precondition for payment, require that the holder is exposed to, and has incurred a loss on, the failure of the debtor to make payments on the guaranteed asset when due. An example of such a guarantee is one that requires payments in response to changes in a specified credit rating or credit index. Such guarantees are not financial guarantee contracts as defined in this Standard, and are not insurance contracts as defined in IFRS 4. Such guarantees are derivatives and the issuer applies this Standard to them.

(c)   If a financial guarantee contract was issued in connection with the sale of goods, the issuer applies IFRS 15 in determining when it recognises the revenue from the guarantee and from the sale of goods.

B2.6   Assertions that an issuer regards contracts as insurance contracts are typically found throughout the issuer's communications with customers and regulators, contracts, business documentation and financial statements. Furthermore, insurance contracts are often subject to accounting requirements that are distinct from the requirements for other types of transaction, such as contracts issued by banks or commercial companies. In such cases, an issuer's financial statements typically include a statement that the issuer has used those accounting requirements.

Recognition and derecognition (Chapter 3)

Initial recognition (Section 3.1)

B3.1.1   As a consequence of the principle in paragraph 3.1.1, an entity recognises all of its contractual rights and obligations under derivatives in its statement of financial position as assets and liabilities, respectively, except for derivatives that prevent a transfer of financial assets from being accounted for as a sale (see paragraph B3.2.14). If a transfer of a financial asset does not qualify for derecognition, the transferee does not recognise the transferred asset as its asset (see paragraph B3.2.15).

B3.1.2   The following are examples of applying the principle in paragraph 3.1.1:

(a)   Unconditional receivables and payables are recognised as assets or liabilities when the entity becomes a party to the contract and, as a consequence, has a legal right to receive or a legal obligation to pay cash.

(b)   Assets to be acquired and liabilities to be incurred as a result of a firm commitment to purchase or sell goods or services are generally not recognised until at least one of the parties has performed under the agreement. For example, an entity that receives a firm order does not generally recognise an asset (and the entity that places the order does not recognise a liability) at the time of the commitment but, instead, delays recognition until the ordered goods or services have been shipped, delivered or rendered. If a firm commitment to buy or sell non-financial items is within the scope of this Standard in accordance with paragraphs 2.4–2.7, its net fair value is recognised as an asset or a liability on the commitment date (see paragraph B4.1.30(c)). In addition, if a previously unrecognised firm commitment is designated as a hedged item in a fair value hedge, any change in the net fair value attributable to the hedged risk is recognised as an asset or a liability after the inception of the hedge (see paragraphs 6.5.8(b) and 6.5.9).

(c) A forward contract that is within the scope of this Standard (see paragraph 2.1) is recognised as an asset or a liability on the commitment date, instead of on the date on which settlement takes place. When an entity becomes a party to a forward contract, the fair values of the right and obligation are often equal, so that the net fair value of the forward is zero. If the net fair value of the right and obligation is not zero, the contract is recognised as an asset or liability.

(d) Option contracts that are within the scope of this Standard (see paragraph 2.1) are recognised as assets or liabilities when the holder or writer becomes a party to the contract.

(e) Planned future transactions, no matter how likely, are not assets and liabilities because the entity has not become a party to a contract.

Regular way purchase or sale of financial assets

B3.1.3 A regular way purchase or sale of financial assets is recognised using either trade date accounting or settlement date accounting as described in paragraphs B3.1.5 and B3.1.6. An entity shall apply the same method consistently for all purchases and sales of financial assets that are classified in the same way in accordance with this Standard. For this purpose assets that are mandatorily measured at fair value through profit or loss form a separate classification from assets designated as measured at fair value through profit or loss. In addition, investments in equity instruments accounted for using the option provided in paragraph 5.7.5 form a separate classification.

B3.1.4 A contract that requires or permits net settlement of the change in the value of the contract is not a regular way contract. Instead, such a contract is accounted for as a derivative in the period between the trade date and the settlement date.

B3.1.5 The trade date is the date that an entity commits itself to purchase or sell an asset. Trade date accounting refers to (a) the recognition of an asset to be received and the liability to pay for it on the trade date, and (b) derecognition of an asset that is sold, recognition of any gain or loss on disposal and the recognition of a receivable from the buyer for payment on the trade date.

Generally, interest does not start to accrue on the asset and corresponding liability until the settlement date when title passes.

B3.1.6 The settlement date is the date that an asset is delivered to or by an entity. Settlement date accounting refers to (a) the recognition of an asset on the day it is received by the entity, and (b) the derecognition of an asset and recognition of any gain or loss on disposal on the day that it is delivered by the entity. When settlement date accounting is applied an entity accounts for any change in the fair value of the asset to be received during the period between the trade date and the settlement date in the same way as it accounts for the acquired asset. In other words, the change in value is not recognised for assets measured at amortised cost; it is recognised in profit or loss for assets classified as financial assets measured at fair value through profit or loss; and it is recognised in other comprehensive income for financial assets measured at fair value through other comprehensive income in accordance with paragraph 4.1.2A and for investments in equity instruments accounted for in accordance with paragraph 5.7.5.

Derecognition of financial assets (Section 3.2)

B3.2.1   The following flow chart illustrates the evaluation of whether and to what extent a financial asset is derecognised.

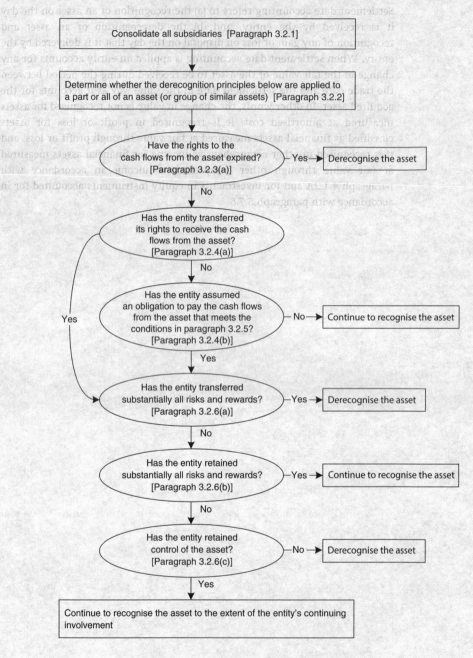

Arrangements under which an entity retains the contractual rights to receive the cash flows of a financial asset, but assumes a contractual obligation to pay the cash flows to one or more recipients (paragraph 3.2.4(b))

B3.2.2 The situation described in paragraph 3.2.4(b) (when an entity retains the contractual rights to receive the cash flows of the financial asset, but assumes a contractual obligation to pay the cash flows to one or more recipients) occurs, for example, if the entity is a trust, and issues to investors beneficial interests in the underlying financial assets that it owns and provides servicing of those financial assets. In that case, the financial assets qualify for derecognition if the conditions in paragraphs 3.2.5 and 3.2.6 are met.

B3.2.3 In applying paragraph 3.2.5, the entity could be, for example, the originator of the financial asset, or it could be a group that includes a subsidiary that has acquired the financial asset and passes on cash flows to unrelated third party investors.

Evaluation of the transfer of risks and rewards of ownership (paragraph 3.2.6)

B3.2.4 Examples of when an entity has transferred substantially all the risks and rewards of ownership are:

(a) an unconditional sale of a financial asset;

(b) a sale of a financial asset together with an option to repurchase the financial asset at its fair value at the time of repurchase; and

(c) a sale of a financial asset together with a put or call option that is deeply out of the money (ie an option that is so far out of the money it is highly unlikely to go into the money before expiry).

B3.2.5 Examples of when an entity has retained substantially all the risks and rewards of ownership are:

(a) a sale and repurchase transaction where the repurchase price is a fixed price or the sale price plus a lender's return;

(b) a securities lending agreement;

(c) a sale of a financial asset together with a total return swap that transfers the market risk exposure back to the entity;

(d) a sale of a financial asset together with a deep in-the-money put or call option (ie an option that is so far in the money that it is highly unlikely to go out of the money before expiry); and

(e) a sale of short-term receivables in which the entity guarantees to compensate the transferee for credit losses that are likely to occur.

B3.2.6 If an entity determines that as a result of the transfer, it has transferred substantially all the risks and rewards of ownership of the transferred asset, it does not recognise the transferred asset again in a future period, unless it reacquires the transferred asset in a new transaction.

Evaluation of the transfer of control

B3.2.7 An entity has not retained control of a transferred asset if the transferee has the practical ability to sell the transferred asset. An entity has retained control of a transferred asset if the transferee does not have the practical ability to sell the transferred asset. A transferee has the practical ability to sell the transferred asset if it is traded in an active market because the transferee could repurchase the transferred asset in the market if it needs to return the asset to the entity. For example, a transferee may have the practical ability to sell a transferred asset if the transferred asset is subject to an option that allows the entity to repurchase it, but the transferee can readily obtain the transferred asset in the market if the option is exercised. A transferee does not have the practical ability to sell the transferred asset if the entity retains such an option and the transferee cannot readily obtain the transferred asset in the market if the entity exercises its option.

B3.2.8 The transferee has the practical ability to sell the transferred asset only if the transferee can sell the transferred asset in its entirety to an unrelated third party and is able to exercise that ability unilaterally and without imposing additional restrictions on the transfer. The critical question is what the transferee is able to do in practice, not what contractual rights the transferee has concerning what it can do with the transferred asset or what contractual prohibitions exist. In particular:

(a) a contractual right to dispose of the transferred asset has little practical effect if there is no market for the transferred asset, and

(b) an ability to dispose of the transferred asset has little practical effect if it cannot be exercised freely. For that reason:

(i) the transferee's ability to dispose of the transferred asset must be independent of the actions of others (ie it must be a unilateral ability), and

(ii) the transferee must be able to dispose of the transferred asset without needing to attach restrictive conditions or 'strings' to the transfer (eg conditions about how a loan asset is serviced or an option giving the transferee the right to repurchase the asset).

B3.2.9 That the transferee is unlikely to sell the transferred asset does not, of itself, mean that the transferor has retained control of the transferred asset. However, if a put option or guarantee constrains the transferee from selling the transferred asset, then the transferor has retained control of the transferred asset. For example, if a put option or guarantee is sufficiently valuable it constrains the transferee from selling the transferred asset because the transferee would, in practice, not sell the transferred asset to a third party without attaching a similar option or other restrictive conditions. Instead, the transferee would hold the transferred asset so as to obtain payments under the guarantee or put option. Under these circumstances the transferor has retained control of the transferred asset.

Transfers that qualify for derecognition

B3.2.10 An entity may retain the right to a part of the interest payments on transferred assets as compensation for servicing those assets. The part of the interest payments that the entity would give up upon termination or transfer of the servicing contract is allocated to the servicing asset or servicing liability. The part of the interest payments that the entity would not give up is an interest-only strip receivable. For example, if the entity would not give up any interest upon termination or transfer of the servicing contract, the entire interest spread is an interest-only strip receivable. For the purposes of applying paragraph 3.2.13, the fair values of the servicing asset and interest-only strip receivable are used to allocate the carrying amount of the receivable between the part of the asset that is derecognised and the part that continues to be recognised. If there is no servicing fee specified or the fee to be received is not expected to compensate the entity adequately for performing the servicing, a liability for the servicing obligation is recognised at fair value.

B3.2.11 When measuring the fair values of the part that continues to be recognised and the part that is derecognised for the purposes of applying paragraph 3.2.13, an entity applies the fair value measurement requirements in IFRS 13 *Fair Value Measurement* in addition to paragraph 3.2.14.

Transfers that do not qualify for derecognition

B3.2.12 The following is an application of the principle outlined in paragraph 3.2.15. If a guarantee provided by the entity for default losses on the transferred asset prevents a transferred asset from being derecognised because the entity has retained substantially all the risks and rewards of ownership of the transferred asset, the transferred asset continues to be recognised in its entirety and the consideration received is recognised as a liability.

Continuing involvement in transferred assets

B3.2.13 The following are examples of how an entity measures a transferred asset and the associated liability under paragraph 3.2.16.

All assets

(a) If a guarantee provided by an entity to pay for default losses on a transferred asset prevents the transferred asset from being derecognised to the extent of the continuing involvement, the transferred asset at the date of the transfer is measured at the lower of (i) the carrying amount of the asset and (ii) the maximum amount of the consideration received in the transfer that the entity could be required to repay ('the guarantee amount'). The associated liability is initially measured at the guarantee amount plus the fair value of the guarantee (which is normally the consideration received for the guarantee). Subsequently, the initial fair value of the guarantee is recognised in profit or loss when (or as) the obligation is satisfied (in accordance with the principles of IFRS 15) and the carrying value of the asset is reduced by any loss allowance.

Assets measured at amortised cost

(b)   If a put option obligation written by an entity or call option right held by an entity prevents a transferred asset from being derecognised and the entity measures the transferred asset at amortised cost, the associated liability is measured at its cost (ie the consideration received) adjusted for the amortisation of any difference between that cost and the gross carrying amount of the transferred asset at the expiration date of the option. For example, assume that the gross carrying amount of the asset on the date of the transfer is CU98 and that the consideration received is CU95. The gross carrying amount of the asset on the option exercise date will be CU100. The initial carrying amount of the associated liability is CU95 and the difference between CU95 and CU100 is recognised in profit or loss using the effective interest method. If the option is exercised, any difference between the carrying amount of the associated liability and the exercise price is recognised in profit or loss.

Assets measured at fair value

(c)   If a call option right retained by an entity prevents a transferred asset from being derecognised and the entity measures the transferred asset at fair value, the asset continues to be measured at its fair value. The associated liability is measured at (i) the option exercise price less the time value of the option if the option is in or at the money, or (ii) the fair value of the transferred asset less the time value of the option if the option is out of the money. The adjustment to the measurement of the associated liability ensures that the net carrying amount of the asset and the associated liability is the fair value of the call option right. For example, if the fair value of the underlying asset is CU80, the option exercise price is CU95 and the time value of the option is CU5, the carrying amount of the associated liability is CU75 (CU80 − CU5) and the carrying amount of the transferred asset is CU80 (ie its fair value).

(d)   If a put option written by an entity prevents a transferred asset from being derecognised and the entity measures the transferred asset at fair value, the associated liability is measured at the option exercise price plus the time value of the option. The measurement of the asset at fair value is limited to the lower of the fair value and the option exercise price because the entity has no right to increases in the fair value of the transferred asset above the exercise price of the option. This ensures that the net carrying amount of the asset and the associated liability is the fair value of the put option obligation. For example, if the fair value of the underlying asset is CU120, the option exercise price is CU100 and the time value of the option is CU5, the carrying amount of the associated liability is CU105 (CU100 + CU5) and the carrying amount of the asset is CU100 (in this case the option exercise price).

(e) If a collar, in the form of a purchased call and written put, prevents a transferred asset from being derecognised and the entity measures the asset at fair value, it continues to measure the asset at fair value. The associated liability is measured at (i) the sum of the call exercise price and fair value of the put option less the time value of the call option, if the call option is in or at the money, or (ii) the sum of the fair value of the asset and the fair value of the put option less the time value of the call option if the call option is out of the money. The adjustment to the associated liability ensures that the net carrying amount of the asset and the associated liability is the fair value of the options held and written by the entity. For example, assume an entity transfers a financial asset that is measured at fair value while simultaneously purchasing a call with an exercise price of CU120 and writing a put with an exercise price of CU80. Assume also that the fair value of the asset is CU100 at the date of the transfer. The time value of the put and call are CU1 and CU5 respectively. In this case, the entity recognises an asset of CU100 (the fair value of the asset) and a liability of CU96 [(CU100 + CU1) − CU5]. This gives a net asset value of CU4, which is the fair value of the options held and written by the entity.

All transfers

B3.2.14 To the extent that a transfer of a financial asset does not qualify for derecognition, the transferor's contractual rights or obligations related to the transfer are not accounted for separately as derivatives if recognising both the derivative and either the transferred asset or the liability arising from the transfer would result in recognising the same rights or obligations twice. For example, a call option retained by the transferor may prevent a transfer of financial assets from being accounted for as a sale. In that case, the call option is not separately recognised as a derivative asset.

B3.2.15 To the extent that a transfer of a financial asset does not qualify for derecognition, the transferee does not recognise the transferred asset as its asset. The transferee derecognises the cash or other consideration paid and recognises a receivable from the transferor. If the transferor has both a right and an obligation to reacquire control of the entire transferred asset for a fixed amount (such as under a repurchase agreement), the transferee may measure its receivable at amortised cost if it meets the criteria in paragraph 4.1.2.

Examples

B3.2.16 The following examples illustrate the application of the derecognition principles of this Standard.

(a) *Repurchase agreements and securities lending.* If a financial asset is sold under an agreement to repurchase it at a fixed price or at the sale price plus a lender's return or if it is loaned under an agreement to return it to the transferor, it is not derecognised because the transferor retains substantially all the risks and rewards of ownership. If the transferee obtains the right to sell or pledge the asset, the transferor reclassifies the asset in its statement of financial position, for example, as a loaned asset or repurchase receivable.

(b) *Repurchase agreements and securities lending — assets that are substantially the same*. If a financial asset is sold under an agreement to repurchase the same or substantially the same asset at a fixed price or at the sale price plus a lender's return or if a financial asset is borrowed or loaned under an agreement to return the same or substantially the same asset to the transferor, it is not derecognised because the transferor retains substantially all the risks and rewards of ownership.

(c) *Repurchase agreements and securities lending — right of substitution*. If a repurchase agreement at a fixed repurchase price or a price equal to the sale price plus a lender's return, or a similar securities lending transaction, provides the transferee with a right to substitute assets that are similar and of equal fair value to the transferred asset at the repurchase date, the asset sold or lent under a repurchase or securities lending transaction is not derecognised because the transferor retains substantially all the risks and rewards of ownership.

(d) *Repurchase right of first refusal at fair value*. If an entity sells a financial asset and retains only a right of first refusal to repurchase the transferred asset at fair value if the transferee subsequently sells it, the entity derecognises the asset because it has transferred substantially all the risks and rewards of ownership.

(e) *Wash sale transaction*. The repurchase of a financial asset shortly after it has been sold is sometimes referred to as a wash sale. Such a repurchase does not preclude derecognition provided that the original transaction met the derecognition requirements. However, if an agreement to sell a financial asset is entered into concurrently with an agreement to repurchase the same asset at a fixed price or the sale price plus a lender's return, then the asset is not derecognised.

(f) *Put options and call options that are deeply in the money*. If a transferred financial asset can be called back by the transferor and the call option is deeply in the money, the transfer does not qualify for derecognition because the transferor has retained substantially all the risks and rewards of ownership. Similarly, if the financial asset can be put back by the transferee and the put option is deeply in the money, the transfer does not qualify for derecognition because the transferor has retained substantially all the risks and rewards of ownership.

(g) *Put options and call options that are deeply out of the money*. A financial asset that is transferred subject only to a deep out-of-the-money put option held by the transferee or a deep out-of-the-money call option held by the transferor is derecognised. This is because the transferor has transferred substantially all the risks and rewards of ownership.

(h) *Readily obtainable assets subject to a call option that is neither deeply in the money nor deeply out of the money.* If an entity holds a call option on an asset that is readily obtainable in the market and the option is neither deeply in the money nor deeply out of the money, the asset is derecognised. This is because the entity (i) has neither retained nor transferred substantially all the risks and rewards of ownership, and (ii) has not retained control. However, if the asset is not readily obtainable in the market, derecognition is precluded to the extent of the amount of the asset that is subject to the call option because the entity has retained control of the asset.

(i) *A not readily obtainable asset subject to a put option written by an entity that is neither deeply in the money nor deeply out of the money.* If an entity transfers a financial asset that is not readily obtainable in the market, and writes a put option that is not deeply out of the money, the entity neither retains nor transfers substantially all the risks and rewards of ownership because of the written put option. The entity retains control of the asset if the put option is sufficiently valuable to prevent the transferee from selling the asset, in which case the asset continues to be recognised to the extent of the transferor's continuing involvement (see paragraph B3.2.9). The entity transfers control of the asset if the put option is not sufficiently valuable to prevent the transferee from selling the asset, in which case the asset is derecognised.

(j) *Assets subject to a fair value put or call option or a forward repurchase agreement.* A transfer of a financial asset that is subject only to a put or call option or a forward repurchase agreement that has an exercise or repurchase price equal to the fair value of the financial asset at the time of repurchase results in derecognition because of the transfer of substantially all the risks and rewards of ownership.

(k) *Cash-settled call or put options.* An entity evaluates the transfer of a financial asset that is subject to a put or call option or a forward repurchase agreement that will be settled net in cash to determine whether it has retained or transferred substantially all the risks and rewards of ownership. If the entity has not retained substantially all the risks and rewards of ownership of the transferred asset, it determines whether it has retained control of the transferred asset. That the put or the call or the forward repurchase agreement is settled net in cash does not automatically mean that the entity has transferred control (see paragraphs B3.2.9 and (g), (h) and (i) above).

(l) *Removal of accounts provision.* A removal of accounts provision is an unconditional repurchase (call) option that gives an entity the right to reclaim assets transferred subject to some restrictions. Provided that such an option results in the entity neither retaining nor transferring substantially all the risks and rewards of ownership, it precludes derecognition only to the extent of the amount subject to repurchase (assuming that the transferee cannot sell the assets). For example, if the carrying amount and proceeds from the transfer of loan assets are CU100,000 and any individual loan could be called back but the aggregate amount of loans that could be repurchased could not exceed CU10,000, CU90,000 of the loans would qualify for derecognition.

(m) *Clean-up calls.* An entity, which may be a transferor, that services transferred assets may hold a clean-up call to purchase remaining transferred assets when the amount of outstanding assets falls to a specified level at which the cost of servicing those assets becomes burdensome in relation to the benefits of servicing. Provided that such a clean-up call results in the entity neither retaining nor transferring substantially all the risks and rewards of ownership and the transferee cannot sell the assets, it precludes derecognition only to the extent of the amount of the assets that is subject to the call option.

(n) *Subordinated retained interests and credit guarantees.* An entity may provide the transferee with credit enhancement by subordinating some or all of its interest retained in the transferred asset. Alternatively, an entity may provide the transferee with credit enhancement in the form of a credit guarantee that could be unlimited or limited to a specified amount. If the entity retains substantially all the risks and rewards of ownership of the transferred asset, the asset continues to be recognised in its entirety. If the entity retains some, but not substantially all, of the risks and rewards of ownership and has retained control, derecognition is precluded to the extent of the amount of cash or other assets that the entity could be required to pay.

(o) *Total return swaps.* An entity may sell a financial asset to a transferee and enter into a total return swap with the transferee, whereby all of the interest payment cash flows from the underlying asset are remitted to the entity in exchange for a fixed payment or variable rate payment and any increases or declines in the fair value of the underlying asset are absorbed by the entity. In such a case, derecognition of all of the asset is prohibited.

(p) *Interest rate swaps.* An entity may transfer to a transferee a fixed rate financial asset and enter into an interest rate swap with the transferee to receive a fixed interest rate and pay a variable interest rate based on a notional amount that is equal to the principal amount of the transferred financial asset. The interest rate swap does not preclude derecognition of the transferred asset provided the payments on the swap are not conditional on payments being made on the transferred asset.

(q) *Amortising interest rate swaps.* An entity may transfer to a transferee a fixed rate financial asset that is paid off over time, and enter into an amortising interest rate swap with the transferee to receive a fixed interest rate and pay a variable interest rate based on a notional amount. If the notional amount of the swap amortises so that it equals the principal amount of the transferred financial asset outstanding at any point in time, the swap would generally result in the entity retaining substantial prepayment risk, in which case the entity either continues to recognise all of the transferred asset or continues to recognise the transferred asset to the extent of its continuing involvement. Conversely, if the amortisation of the notional amount of the swap is not linked to the principal amount outstanding of the transferred asset, such a swap would not result in the entity retaining prepayment risk on the asset. Hence, it would not preclude derecognition of the transferred asset provided the payments on the swap are not conditional on interest payments being made on the transferred asset and the swap does not result in the entity retaining any other significant risks and rewards of ownership on the transferred asset.

(r)   *Write-off*. An entity has no reasonable expectations of recovering the contractual cash flows on a financial asset in its entirety or a portion thereof.

B3.2.17   This paragraph illustrates the application of the continuing involvement approach when the entity's continuing involvement is in a part of a financial asset.

> Assume an entity has a portfolio of prepayable loans whose coupon and effective interest rate is 10 per cent and whose principal amount and amortised cost is CU10,000. It enters into a transaction in which, in return for a payment of CU9,115, the transferee obtains the right to CU9,000 of any collections of principal plus interest thereon at 9.5 per cent. The entity retains rights to CU1,000 of any collections of principal plus interest thereon at 10 per cent, plus the excess spread of 0.5 per cent on the remaining CU9,000 of principal. Collections from prepayments are allocated between the entity and the transferee proportionately in the ratio of 1:9, but any defaults are deducted from the entity's interest of CU1,000 until that interest is exhausted. The fair value of the loans at the date of the transaction is CU10,100 and the fair value of the excess spread of 0.5 per cent is CU40.
>
> The entity determines that it has transferred some significant risks and rewards of ownership (for example, significant prepayment risk) but has also retained some significant risks and rewards of ownership (because of its subordinated retained interest) and has retained control. It therefore applies the continuing involvement approach.
>
> To apply this Standard, the entity analyses the transaction as (a) a retention of a fully proportionate retained interest of CU1,000, plus (b) the subordination of that retained interest to provide credit enhancement to the transferee for credit losses.

continued...

...*continued*

The entity calculates that CU9,090 (90% × CU10,100) of the consideration received of CU9,115 represents the consideration for a fully proportionate 90 per cent share. The remainder of the consideration received (CU25) represents consideration received for subordinating its retained interest to provide credit enhancement to the transferee for credit losses. In addition, the excess spread of 0.5 per cent represents consideration received for the credit enhancement. Accordingly, the total consideration received for the credit enhancement is CU65 (CU25 + CU40).

The entity calculates the gain or loss on the sale of the 90 per cent share of cash flows. Assuming that separate fair values of the 90 per cent part transferred and the 10 per cent part retained are not available at the date of the transfer, the entity allocates the carrying amount of the asset in accordance with paragraph 3.2.14 of IFRS 9 as follows:

	Fair value	Percentage	Allocated carrying amount
Portion transferred	9,090	90%	9,000
Portion retained	1,010	10%	1,000
Total	**10,100**		**10,000**

The entity computes its gain or loss on the sale of the 90 per cent share of the cash flows by deducting the allocated carrying amount of the portion transferred from the consideration received, ie CU90 (CU9,090 – CU9,000). The carrying amount of the portion retained by the entity is CU1,000.

In addition, the entity recognises the continuing involvement that results from the subordination of its retained interest for credit losses. Accordingly, it recognises an asset of CU1,000 (the maximum amount of the cash flows it would not receive under the subordination), and an associated liability of CU1,065 (which is the maximum amount of the cash flows it would not receive under the subordination, ie CU1,000 plus the fair value of the subordination of CU65).

continued...

Classification (Chapter 4)

Classification of financial assets (Section 4.1)

The entity's business model for managing financial assets

B4.1.1   Paragraph 4.1.1(a) requires an entity to classify financial assets on the basis of the entity's business model for managing the financial assets, unless paragraph 4.1.5 applies. An entity assesses whether its financial assets meet the condition in paragraph 4.1.2(a) or the condition in paragraph 4.1.2A(a) on the basis of the business model as determined by the entity's key management personnel (as defined in IAS 24 *Related Party Disclosures*).

B4.1.2   An entity's business model is determined at a level that reflects how groups of financial assets are managed together to achieve a particular business objective. The entity's business model does not depend on management's intentions for an individual instrument. Accordingly, this condition is not an instrument-by-instrument approach to classification and should be determined on a higher level of aggregation. However, a single entity may have more than one business model for managing its financial instruments. Consequently, classification need not be determined at the reporting entity level. For example, an entity may hold a portfolio of investments that it manages in order to collect contractual cash flows and another portfolio of investments that it manages in order to trade to realise fair value changes. Similarly, in some circumstances, it may be appropriate to separate a portfolio of financial assets into subportfolios in order to reflect the level at which an entity manages those financial assets. For example, that may be the case if an entity originates or purchases a portfolio of mortgage loans and manages some of the loans with an objective of collecting contractual cash flows and manages the other loans with an objective of selling them.

B4.1.2A   An entity's business model refers to how an entity manages its financial assets in order to generate cash flows. That is, the entity's business model determines whether cash flows will result from collecting contractual cash flows, selling financial assets or both. Consequently, this assessment is not performed on the basis of scenarios that the entity does not reasonably expect to occur, such as so-called 'worst case' or 'stress case' scenarios. For example, if an entity expects that it will sell a particular portfolio of financial assets only in a stress case scenario, that scenario would not affect the entity's assessment of the business model for those assets if the entity reasonably expects that such a scenario will not occur. If cash flows are realised in a way that is different from the entity's expectations at the date that the entity assessed the business model (for example, if the entity sells more or fewer financial assets than it expected when it classified the assets), that does not give rise to a prior period error in the entity's financial statements (see IAS 8 *Accounting Policies, Changes in Accounting Estimates and Errors*) nor does it change the classification of the remaining financial assets held in that business model (ie those assets that the entity recognised in prior periods and still holds) as long as the entity considered all relevant information that was available at the time that it made the business model assessment. However, when an entity assesses the business model for newly originated or newly purchased financial assets, it must consider information about how cash flows were realised in the past, along with all other relevant information.

B4.1.2B   An entity's business model for managing financial assets is a matter of fact and not merely an assertion. It is typically observable through the activities that the entity undertakes to achieve the objective of the business model. An entity will need to use judgement when it assesses its business model for managing financial assets and that assessment is not determined by a single factor or activity. Instead, the entity must consider all relevant evidence that is available at the date of the assessment. Such relevant evidence includes, but is not limited to:

(a)   how the performance of the business model and the financial assets held within that business model are evaluated and reported to the entity's key management personnel;

(b)   the risks that affect the performance of the business model (and the financial assets held within that business model) and, in particular, the way in which those risks are managed; and

(c)   how managers of the business are compensated (for example, whether the compensation is based on the fair value of the assets managed or on the contractual cash flows collected).

A business model whose objective is to hold assets in order to collect contractual cash flows

B4.1.2C   Financial assets that are held within a business model whose objective is to hold assets in order to collect contractual cash flows are managed to realise cash flows by collecting contractual payments over the life of the instrument. That is, the entity manages the assets held within the portfolio to collect those particular contractual cash flows (instead of managing the overall return on the portfolio by both holding and selling assets). In determining whether cash flows are going to be realised by collecting the financial assets' contractual cash flows, it is necessary to consider the frequency, value and timing of sales in prior periods, the reasons for those sales and expectations about future sales activity. However sales in themselves do not determine the business model and therefore cannot be considered in isolation. Instead, information about past sales and expectations about future sales provide evidence related to how the entity's stated objective for managing the financial assets is achieved and, specifically, how cash flows are realised. An entity must consider information about past sales within the context of the reasons for those sales and the conditions that existed at that time as compared to current conditions.

B4.1.3   Although the objective of an entity's business model may be to hold financial assets in order to collect contractual cash flows, the entity need not hold all of those instruments until maturity. Thus an entity's business model can be to hold financial assets to collect contractual cash flows even when sales of financial assets occur or are expected to occur in the future.

B4.1.3A   The business model may be to hold assets to collect contractual cash flows even if the entity sells financial assets when there is an increase in the assets' credit risk. To determine whether there has been an increase in the assets' credit risk, the entity considers reasonable and supportable information, including forward looking information. Irrespective of their frequency and value, sales due to an increase in the assets' credit risk are not inconsistent with a business model whose objective is to hold financial assets to collect contractual cash flows because the credit quality of financial assets is relevant to the entity's ability to collect contractual cash flows. Credit risk management activities that are aimed at minimising potential credit losses due to credit deterioration are integral to such a business model. Selling a financial asset because it no longer meets the credit criteria specified in the entity's documented investment policy is an example of a sale that has occurred due to an increase in credit risk. However, in the absence of such a policy, the entity may demonstrate in other ways that the sale occurred due to an increase in credit risk.

B4.1.3B   Sales that occur for other reasons, such as sales made to manage credit concentration risk (without an increase in the assets' credit risk), may also be consistent with a business model whose objective is to hold financial assets in order to collect contractual cash flows. In particular, such sales may be consistent with a business model whose objective is to hold financial assets in order to collect contractual cash flows if those sales are infrequent (even if significant in value) or insignificant in value both individually and in aggregate (even if frequent). If more than an infrequent number of such sales are made out of a portfolio and those sales are more than insignificant in value (either individually or in aggregate), the entity needs to assess whether and how such sales are consistent with an objective of collecting contractual cash flows. Whether a third party imposes the requirement to sell the financial assets, or that activity is at the entity's discretion, is not relevant to this assessment. An increase in the frequency or value of sales in a particular period is not necessarily inconsistent with an objective to hold financial assets in order to collect contractual cash flows, if an entity can explain the reasons for those sales and demonstrate why those sales do not reflect a change in the entity's business model. In addition, sales may be consistent with the objective of holding financial assets in order to collect contractual cash flows if the sales are made close to the maturity of the financial assets and the proceeds from the sales approximate the collection of the remaining contractual cash flows.

B4.1.4   The following are examples of when the objective of an entity's business model may be to hold financial assets to collect the contractual cash flows. This list of examples is not exhaustive. Furthermore, the examples are not intended to discuss all factors that may be relevant to the assessment of the entity's business model nor specify the relative importance of the factors.

Example	Analysis
Example 1 An entity holds investments to collect their contractual cash flows. The funding needs of the entity are predictable and the maturity of its financial assets is matched to the entity's estimated funding needs. The entity performs credit risk management activities with the objective of minimising credit losses. In the past, sales have typically occurred when the financial assets' credit risk has increased such that the assets no longer meet the credit criteria specified in the entity's documented investment policy. In addition, infrequent sales have occurred as a result of unanticipated funding needs. Reports to key management personnel focus on the credit quality of the financial assets and the contractual return. The entity also monitors fair values of the financial assets, among other information.	Although the entity considers, among other information, the financial assets' fair values from a liquidity perspective (ie the cash amount that would be realised if the entity needs to sell assets), the entity's objective is to hold the financial assets in order to collect the contractual cash flows. Sales would not contradict that objective if they were in response to an increase in the assets' credit risk, for example if the assets no longer meet the credit criteria specified in the entity's documented investment policy. Infrequent sales resulting from unanticipated funding needs (eg in a stress case scenario) also would not contradict that objective, even if such sales are significant in value.

continued...

...continued

Example	Analysis
Example 2 An entity's business model is to purchase portfolios of financial assets, such as loans. Those portfolios may or may not include financial assets that are credit impaired. If payment on the loans is not made on a timely basis, the entity attempts to realise the contractual cash flows through various means—for example, by contacting the debtor by mail, telephone or other methods. The entity's objective is to collect the contractual cash flows and the entity does not manage any of the loans in this portfolio with an objective of realising cash flows by selling them. In some cases, the entity enters into interest rate swaps to change the interest rate on particular financial assets in a portfolio from a floating interest rate to a fixed interest rate.	The objective of the entity's business model is to hold the financial assets in order to collect the contractual cash flows. The same analysis would apply even if the entity does not expect to receive all of the contractual cash flows (eg some of the financial assets are credit impaired at initial recognition). Moreover, the fact that the entity enters into derivatives to modify the cash flows of the portfolio does not in itself change the entity's business model.

continued...

...*continued*

Example	Analysis
Example 3 An entity has a business model with the objective of originating loans to customers and subsequently selling those loans to a securitisation vehicle. The securitisation vehicle issues instruments to investors. The originating entity controls the securitisation vehicle and thus consolidates it. The securitisation vehicle collects the contractual cash flows from the loans and passes them on to its investors. It is assumed for the purposes of this example that the loans continue to be recognised in the consolidated statement of financial position because they are not derecognised by the securitisation vehicle.	The consolidated group originated the loans with the objective of holding them to collect the contractual cash flows. However, the originating entity has an objective of realising cash flows on the loan portfolio by selling the loans to the securitisation vehicle, so for the purposes of its separate financial statements it would not be considered to be managing this portfolio in order to collect the contractual cash flows.

continued...

...*continued*

Example	Analysis
Example 4 A financial institution holds financial assets to meet liquidity needs in a 'stress case' scenario (eg, a run on the bank's deposits). The entity does not anticipate selling these assets except in such scenarios. The entity monitors the credit quality of the financial assets and its objective in managing the financial assets is to collect the contractual cash flows. The entity evaluates the performance of the assets on the basis of interest revenue earned and credit losses realised. However, the entity also monitors the fair value of the financial assets from a liquidity perspective to ensure that the cash amount that would be realised if the entity needed to sell the assets in a stress case scenario would be sufficient to meet the entity's liquidity needs. Periodically, the entity makes sales that are insignificant in value to demonstrate liquidity.	The objective of the entity's business model is to hold the financial assets to collect contractual cash flows. The analysis would not change even if during a previous stress case scenario the entity had sales that were significant in value in order to meet its liquidity needs. Similarly, recurring sales activity that is insignificant in value is not inconsistent with holding financial assets to collect contractual cash flows. In contrast, if an entity holds financial assets to meet its everyday liquidity needs and meeting that objective involves frequent sales that are significant in value, the objective of the entity's business model is not to hold the financial assets to collect contractual cash flows. Similarly, if the entity is required by its regulator to routinely sell financial assets to demonstrate that the assets are liquid, and the value of the assets sold is significant, the entity's business model is not to hold financial assets to collect contractual cash flows. Whether a third party imposes the requirement to sell the financial assets, or that activity is at the entity's discretion, is not relevant to the analysis.

A business model whose objective is achieved by both collecting contractual cash flows and selling financial assets

B4.1.4A   An entity may hold financial assets in a business model whose objective is achieved by both collecting contractual cash flows and selling financial assets. In this type of business model, the entity's key management personnel have made a decision that both collecting contractual cash flows and selling financial assets are integral to achieving the objective of the business model. There are various objectives that may be consistent with this type of business model. For example, the objective of the business model may be to manage everyday liquidity needs, to maintain a particular interest yield profile or to match the duration of the financial assets to the duration of the liabilities that those assets are funding. To achieve such an objective, the entity will both collect contractual cash flows and sell financial assets.

B4.1.4B   Compared to a business model whose objective is to hold financial assets to collect contractual cash flows, this business model will typically involve greater frequency and value of sales. This is because selling financial assets is integral to achieving the business model's objective instead of being only incidental to it. However, there is no threshold for the frequency or value of sales that must occur in this business model because both collecting contractual cash flows and selling financial assets are integral to achieving its objective.

B4.1.4C   The following are examples of when the objective of the entity's business model may be achieved by both collecting contractual cash flows and selling financial assets. This list of examples is not exhaustive. Furthermore, the examples are not intended to describe all the factors that may be relevant to the assessment of the entity's business model nor specify the relative importance of the factors.

Example	Analysis
Example 5 An entity anticipates capital expenditure in a few years. The entity invests its excess cash in short and long-term financial assets so that it can fund the expenditure when the need arises. Many of the financial assets have contractual lives that exceed the entity's anticipated investment period. The entity will hold financial assets to collect the contractual cash flows and, when an opportunity arises, it will sell financial assets to re-invest the cash in financial assets with a higher return. The managers responsible for the portfolio are remunerated based on the overall return generated by the portfolio.	The objective of the business model is achieved by both collecting contractual cash flows and selling financial assets. The entity will make decisions on an ongoing basis about whether collecting contractual cash flows or selling financial assets will maximise the return on the portfolio until the need arises for the invested cash. In contrast, consider an entity that anticipates a cash outflow in five years to fund capital expenditure and invests excess cash in short-term financial assets. When the investments mature, the entity reinvests the cash in new short-term financial assets. The entity maintains this strategy until the funds are needed, at which time the entity uses the proceeds from the maturing financial assets to fund the capital expenditure. Only sales that are insignificant in value occur before maturity (unless there is an increase in credit risk). The objective of this contrasting business model is to hold financial assets to collect contractual cash flows.

continued...

...*continued*

Example	Analysis
Example 6 A financial institution holds financial assets to meet its everyday liquidity needs. The entity seeks to minimise the costs of managing those liquidity needs and therefore actively manages the return on the portfolio. That return consists of collecting contractual payments as well as gains and losses from the sale of financial assets. As a result, the entity holds financial assets to collect contractual cash flows and sells financial assets to reinvest in higher yielding financial assets or to better match the duration of its liabilities. In the past, this strategy has resulted in frequent sales activity and such sales have been significant in value. This activity is expected to continue in the future.	The objective of the business model is to maximise the return on the portfolio to meet everyday liquidity needs and the entity achieves that objective by both collecting contractual cash flows and selling financial assets. In other words, both collecting contractual cash flows and selling financial assets are integral to achieving the business model's objective.
Example 7 An insurer holds financial assets in order to fund insurance contract liabilities. The insurer uses the proceeds from the contractual cash flows on the financial assets to settle insurance contract liabilities as they come due. To ensure that the contractual cash flows from the financial assets are sufficient to settle those liabilities, the insurer undertakes significant buying and selling activity on a regular basis to rebalance its portfolio of assets and to meet cash flow needs as they arise.	The objective of the business model is to fund the insurance contract liabilities. To achieve this objective, the entity collects contractual cash flows as they come due and sells financial assets to maintain the desired profile of the asset portfolio. Thus both collecting contractual cash flows and selling financial assets are integral to achieving the business model's objective.

Other business models

B4.1.5 Financial assets are measured at fair value through profit or loss if they are not held within a business model whose objective is to hold assets to collect contractual cash flows or within a business model whose objective is achieved by both collecting contractual cash flows and selling financial assets (but see also paragraph 5.7.5). One business model that results in measurement at fair value through profit or loss is one in which an entity manages the financial assets with the objective of realising cash flows through the sale of the assets. The entity makes decisions based on the assets' fair values and manages the assets to realise those fair values. In this case, the entity's objective will typically result in active buying and selling. Even though the entity will collect contractual cash flows while it holds the financial assets, the objective of such a business model is not achieved by both collecting contractual cash flows and selling financial assets. This is because the collection of contractual cash flows is not integral to achieving the business model's objective; instead, it is incidental to it.

B4.1.6 A portfolio of financial assets that is managed and whose performance is evaluated on a fair value basis (as described in paragraph 4.2.2(b)) is neither held to collect contractual cash flows nor held both to collect contractual cash flows and to sell financial assets. The entity is primarily focused on fair value information and uses that information to assess the assets' performance and to make decisions. In addition, a portfolio of financial assets that meets the definition of held for trading is not held to collect contractual cash flows or held both to collect contractual cash flows and to sell financial assets. For such portfolios, the collection of contractual cash flows is only incidental to achieving the business model's objective. Consequently, such portfolios of financial assets must be measured at fair value through profit or loss.

Contractual cash flows that are solely payments of principal and interest on the principal amount outstanding

B4.1.7 Paragraph 4.1.1(b) requires an entity to classify a financial asset on the basis of its contractual cash flow characteristics if the financial asset is held within a business model whose objective is to hold assets to collect contractual cash flows or within a business model whose objective is achieved by both collecting contractual cash flows and selling financial assets, unless paragraph 4.1.5 applies. To do so, the condition in paragraphs 4.1.2(b) and 4.1.2A(b) requires an entity to determine whether the asset's contractual cash flows are solely payments of principal and interest on the principal amount outstanding.

B4.1.7A Contractual cash flows that are solely payments of principal and interest on the principal amount outstanding are consistent with a basic lending arrangement. In a basic lending arrangement, consideration for the time value of money (see paragraphs B4.1.9A–B4.1.9E) and credit risk are typically the most significant elements of interest. However, in such an arrangement, interest can also include consideration for other basic lending risks (for example, liquidity risk) and costs (for example, administrative costs) associated with holding the financial asset for a particular period of time. In addition, interest can include a profit margin that is consistent with a basic lending arrangement. In extreme economic circumstances, interest can be negative if, for example, the holder of a financial asset either explicitly or implicitly pays for the deposit of its money for a particular period of time (and that fee exceeds the consideration that the holder receives for the time value of money, credit risk and other basic lending risks and costs). However, contractual terms that introduce exposure to risks or volatility in the contractual cash flows that is unrelated to a basic lending arrangement, such as exposure to changes in equity prices or commodity prices, do not give rise to contractual cash flows that are solely payments of principal and interest on the principal amount outstanding. An originated or a purchased financial asset can be a basic lending arrangement irrespective of whether it is a loan in its legal form.

B4.1.7B   In accordance with paragraph 4.1.3(a), principal is the fair value of the financial asset at initial recognition. However that principal amount may change over the life of the financial asset (for example, if there are repayments of principal).

B4.1.8   An entity shall assess whether contractual cash flows are solely payments of principal and interest on the principal amount outstanding for the currency in which the financial asset is denominated.

B4.1.9   Leverage is a contractual cash flow characteristic of some financial assets. Leverage increases the variability of the contractual cash flows with the result that they do not have the economic characteristics of interest. Stand-alone option, forward and swap contracts are examples of financial assets that include such leverage. Thus, such contracts do not meet the condition in paragraphs 4.1.2(b) and 4.1.2A(b) and cannot be subsequently measured at amortised cost or fair value through other comprehensive income.

Consideration for the time value of money

B4.1.9A   Time value of money is the element of interest that provides consideration for only the passage of time. That is, the time value of money element does not provide consideration for other risks or costs associated with holding the financial asset. In order to assess whether the element provides consideration for only the passage of time, an entity applies judgement and considers relevant factors such as the currency in which the financial asset is denominated and the period for which the interest rate is set.

B4.1.9B   However, in some cases, the time value of money element may be modified (ie imperfect). That would be the case, for example, if a financial asset's interest rate is periodically reset but the frequency of that reset does not match the tenor of the interest rate (for example, the interest rate resets every month to a one-year rate) or if a financial asset's interest rate is periodically reset to an average of particular short- and long-term interest rates. In such cases, an entity must assess the modification to determine whether the contractual cash flows represent solely payments of principal and interest on the principal amount outstanding. In some circumstances, the entity may be able to make that determination by performing a qualitative assessment of the time value of money element whereas, in other circumstances, it may be necessary to perform a quantitative assessment.

B4.1.9C   When assessing a modified time value of money element, the objective is to determine how different the contractual (undiscounted) cash flows could be from the (undiscounted) cash flows that would arise if the time value of money element was not modified (the benchmark cash flows). For example, if the financial asset under assessment contains a variable interest rate that is reset every month to a one-year interest rate, the entity would compare that financial asset to a financial instrument with identical contractual terms and the identical credit risk except the variable interest rate is reset monthly to a one-month interest rate. If the modified time value of money element could result in contractual (undiscounted) cash flows that are significantly different from the (undiscounted) benchmark cash flows, the financial asset does not meet the condition in paragraphs 4.1.2(b) and 4.1.2A(b). To make this determination, the entity must consider the effect of the modified time value of money element in each reporting period and cumulatively over the life of the financial instrument. The reason for the interest rate being set in this way is not relevant to the analysis. If it is clear, with little or no analysis, whether the contractual (undiscounted) cash flows on the financial asset under the assessment could (or could not) be significantly different from the (undiscounted) benchmark cash flows, an entity need not perform a detailed assessment.

B4.1.9D   When assessing a modified time value of money element, an entity must consider factors that could affect future contractual cash flows. For example, if an entity is assessing a bond with a five-year term and the variable interest rate is reset every six months to a five-year rate, the entity cannot conclude that the contractual cash flows are solely payments of principal and interest on the principal amount outstanding simply because the interest rate curve at the time of the assessment is such that the difference between a five-year interest rate and a six-month interest rate is not significant. Instead, the entity must also consider whether the relationship between the five-year interest rate and the six-month interest rate could change over the life of the instrument such that the contractual (undiscounted) cash flows over the life of the instrument could be significantly different from the (undiscounted) benchmark cash flows. However, an entity must consider only reasonably possible scenarios instead of every possible scenario. If an entity concludes that the contractual (undiscounted) cash flows could be significantly different from the (undiscounted) benchmark cash flows, the financial asset does not meet the condition in paragraphs 4.1.2(b) and 4.1.2A(b) and therefore cannot be measured at amortised cost or fair value through other comprehensive income.

B4.1.9E   In some jurisdictions, the government or a regulatory authority sets interest rates. For example, such government regulation of interest rates may be part of a broad macroeconomic policy or it may be introduced to encourage entities to invest in a particular sector of the economy. In some of these cases, the objective of the time value of money element is not to provide consideration for only the passage of time. However, despite paragraphs B4.1.9A–B4.1.9D, a regulated interest rate shall be considered a proxy for the time value of money element for the purpose of applying the condition in paragraphs 4.1.2(b) and 4.1.2A(b) if that regulated interest rate provides consideration that is broadly consistent with the passage of time and does not provide exposure to risks or volatility in the contractual cash flows that are inconsistent with a basic lending arrangement.

Contractual terms that change the timing or amount of contractual cash flows

B4.1.10 If a financial asset contains a contractual term that could change the timing or amount of contractual cash flows (for example, if the asset can be prepaid before maturity or its term can be extended), the entity must determine whether the contractual cash flows that could arise over the life of the instrument due to that contractual term are solely payments of principal and interest on the principal amount outstanding. To make this determination, the entity must assess the contractual cash flows that could arise both before, and after, the change in contractual cash flows. The entity may also need to assess the nature of any contingent event (ie the trigger) that would change the timing or amount of the contractual cash flows. While the nature of the contingent event in itself is not a determinative factor in assessing whether the contractual cash flows are solely payments of principal and interest, it may be an indicator. For example, compare a financial instrument with an interest rate that is reset to a higher rate if the debtor misses a particular number of payments to a financial instrument with an interest rate that is reset to a higher rate if a specified equity index reaches a particular level. It is more likely in the former case that the contractual cash flows over the life of the instrument will be solely payments of principal and interest on the principal amount outstanding because of the relationship between missed payments and an increase in credit risk. (See also paragraph B4.1.18.)

B4.1.11 The following are examples of contractual terms that result in contractual cash flows that are solely payments of principal and interest on the principal amount outstanding:

(a) a variable interest rate that consists of consideration for the time value of money, the credit risk associated with the principal amount outstanding during a particular period of time (the consideration for credit risk may be determined at initial recognition only, and so may be fixed) and other basic lending risks and costs, as well as a profit margin;

(b) a contractual term that permits the issuer (ie the debtor) to prepay a debt instrument or permits the holder (ie the creditor) to put a debt instrument back to the issuer before maturity and the prepayment amount substantially represents unpaid amounts of principal and interest on the principal amount outstanding, which may include reasonable compensation for the early termination of the contract; and

(c) a contractual term that permits the issuer or the holder to extend the contractual term of a debt instrument (ie an extension option) and the terms of the extension option result in contractual cash flows during the extension period that are solely payments of principal and interest on the principal amount outstanding, which may include reasonable additional compensation for the extension of the contract.

B4.1.12   Despite paragraph B4.1.10, a financial asset that would otherwise meet the condition in paragraphs 4.1.2(b) and 4.1.2A(b) but does not do so only as a result of a contractual term that permits (or requires) the issuer to prepay a debt instrument or permits (or requires) the holder to put a debt instrument back to the issuer before maturity is eligible to be measured at amortised cost or fair value through other comprehensive income (subject to meeting the condition in paragraph 4.1.2(a) or the condition in paragraph 4.1.2A(a)) if:

    (a)   the entity acquires or originates the financial asset at a premium or discount to the contractual par amount;

    (b)   the prepayment amount substantially represents the contractual par amount and accrued (but unpaid) contractual interest, which may include reasonable compensation for the early termination of the contract; and

    (c)   when the entity initially recognises the financial asset, the fair value of the prepayment feature is insignificant.

B4.1.12A   For the purpose of applying paragraphs B4.1.11(b) and B4.1.12(b), irrespective of the event or circumstance that causes the early termination of the contract, a party may pay **or** receive reasonable compensation for that early termination. For example, a party may pay or receive reasonable compensation when it chooses to terminate the contract early (or otherwise causes the early termination to occur).

B4.1.13   The following examples illustrate contractual cash flows that are solely payments of principal and interest on the principal amount outstanding. This list of examples is not exhaustive.

Instrument	Analysis
Instrument A Instrument A is a bond with a stated maturity date. Payments of principal and interest on the principal amount outstanding are linked to an inflation index of the currency in which the instrument is issued. The inflation link is not leveraged and the principal is protected.	The contractual cash flows are solely payments of principal and interest on the principal amount outstanding. Linking payments of principal and interest on the principal amount outstanding to an unleveraged inflation index resets the time value of money to a current level. In other words, the interest rate on the instrument reflects 'real' interest. Thus, the interest amounts are consideration for the time value of money on the principal amount outstanding. However, if the interest payments were indexed to another variable such as the debtor's performance (eg the debtor's net income) or an equity index, the contractual cash flows are not payments of principal and interest on the principal amount outstanding (unless the indexing to the debtor's performance results in an adjustment that only compensates the holder for changes in the credit risk of the instrument, such that contractual cash flows are solely payments of principal and interest). That is because the contractual cash flows reflect a return that is inconsistent with a basic lending arrangement (see paragraph B4.1.7A).

continued...

...continued

Instrument	Analysis
Instrument B Instrument B is a variable interest rate instrument with a stated maturity date that permits the borrower to choose the market interest rate on an ongoing basis. For example, at each interest rate reset date, the borrower can choose to pay three-month LIBOR for a three-month term or one-month LIBOR for a one-month term.	The contractual cash flows are solely payments of principal and interest on the principal amount outstanding as long as the interest paid over the life of the instrument reflects consideration for the time value of money, for the credit risk associated with the instrument and for other basic lending risks and costs, as well as a profit margin (see paragraph B4.1.7A). The fact that the LIBOR interest rate is reset during the life of the instrument does not in itself disqualify the instrument. However, if the borrower is able to choose to pay a one-month interest rate that is reset every three months, the interest rate is reset with a frequency that does not match the tenor of the interest rate. Consequently, the time value of money element is modified. Similarly, if an instrument has a contractual interest rate that is based on a term that can exceed the instrument's remaining life (for example, if an instrument with a five-year maturity pays a variable rate that is reset periodically but always reflects a five-year maturity), the time value of money element is modified. That is because the interest payable in each period is disconnected from the interest period.

continued...

...continued

Instrument	Analysis
	In such cases, the entity must qualitatively or quantitatively assess the contractual cash flows against those on an instrument that is identical in all respects except the tenor of the interest rate matches the interest period to determine if the cash flows are solely payments of principal and interest on the principal amount outstanding. (But see paragraph B4.1.9E for guidance on regulated interest rates.)
	For example, in assessing a bond with a five-year term that pays a variable rate that is reset every six months but always reflects a five-year maturity, an entity considers the contractual cash flows on an instrument that resets every six months to a six-month interest rate but is otherwise identical.
	The same analysis would apply if the borrower is able to choose between the lender's various published interest rates (eg the borrower can choose between the lender's published one-month variable interest rate and the lender's published three-month variable interest rate).

continued...

...continued

Instrument	Analysis
Instrument C Instrument C is a bond with a stated maturity date and pays a variable market interest rate. That variable interest rate is capped.	The contractual cash flows of both: (a) an instrument that has a fixed interest rate and (b) an instrument that has a variable interest rate are payments of principal and interest on the principal amount outstanding as long as the interest reflects consideration for the time value of money, for the credit risk associated with the instrument during the term of the instrument and for other basic lending risks and costs, as well as a profit margin. (See paragraph B4.1.7A) Consequently, an instrument that is a combination of (a) and (b) (eg a bond with an interest rate cap) can have cash flows that are solely payments of principal and interest on the principal amount outstanding. Such a contractual term may reduce cash flow variability by setting a limit on a variable interest rate (eg an interest rate cap or floor) or increase the cash flow variability because a fixed rate becomes variable.
Instrument D Instrument D is a full recourse loan and is secured by collateral.	The fact that a full recourse loan is collateralised does not in itself affect the analysis of whether the contractual cash flows are solely payments of principal and interest on the principal amount outstanding.

continued...

...continued

Instrument	Analysis
Instrument E Instrument E is issued by a regulated bank and has a stated maturity date. The instrument pays a fixed interest rate and all contractual cash flows are non-discretionary. However, the issuer is subject to legislation that permits or requires a national resolving authority to impose losses on holders of particular instruments, including Instrument E, in particular circumstances. For example, the national resolving authority has the power to write down the par amount of Instrument E or to convert it into a fixed number of the issuer's ordinary shares if the national resolving authority determines that the issuer is having severe financial difficulties, needs additional regulatory capital or is 'failing'.	The holder would analyse the **contractual terms** of the financial instrument to determine whether they give rise to cash flows that are solely payments of principal and interest on the principal amount outstanding and thus are consistent with a basic lending arrangement. That analysis would not consider the payments that arise only as a result of the national resolving authority's power to impose losses on the holders of Instrument E. That is because that power, and the resulting payments, are not **contractual terms** of the financial instrument. In contrast, the contractual cash flows would not be solely payments of principal and interest on the principal amount outstanding if the **contractual terms** of the financial instrument permit or require the issuer or another entity to impose losses on the holder (eg by writing down the par amount or by converting the instrument into a fixed number of the issuer's ordinary shares) as long as those contractual terms are genuine, even if the probability is remote that such a loss will be imposed.

B4.1.14 The following examples illustrate contractual cash flows that are not solely payments of principal and interest on the principal amount outstanding. This list of examples is not exhaustive.

Instrument	Analysis
Instrument F Instrument F is a bond that is convertible into a fixed number of equity instruments of the issuer.	The holder would analyse the convertible bond in its entirety. The contractual cash flows are not payments of principal and interest on the principal amount outstanding because they reflect a return that is inconsistent with a basic lending arrangement (see paragraph B4.1.7A); ie the return is linked to the value of the equity of the issuer.
Instrument G Instrument G is a loan that pays an inverse floating interest rate (ie the interest rate has an inverse relationship to market interest rates).	The contractual cash flows are not solely payments of principal and interest on the principal amount outstanding. The interest amounts are not consideration for the time value of money on the principal amount outstanding.
Instrument H Instrument H is a perpetual instrument but the issuer may call the instrument at any point and pay the holder the par amount plus accrued interest due. Instrument H pays a market interest rate but payment of interest cannot be made unless the issuer is able to remain solvent immediately afterwards. Deferred interest does not accrue additional interest.	The contractual cash flows are not payments of principal and interest on the principal amount outstanding. That is because the issuer may be required to defer interest payments and additional interest does not accrue on those deferred interest amounts. As a result, interest amounts are not consideration for the time value of money on the principal amount outstanding. If interest accrued on the deferred amounts, the contractual cash flows could be payments of principal and interest on the principal amount outstanding.

continued...

...continued

Instrument	Analysis
	The fact that Instrument H is perpetual does not in itself mean that the contractual cash flows are not payments of principal and interest on the principal amount outstanding. In effect, a perpetual instrument has continuous (multiple) extension options. Such options may result in contractual cash flows that are payments of principal and interest on the principal amount outstanding if interest payments are mandatory and must be paid in perpetuity.
	Also, the fact that Instrument H is callable does not mean that the contractual cash flows are not payments of principal and interest on the principal amount outstanding unless it is callable at an amount that does not substantially reflect payment of outstanding principal and interest on that principal amount outstanding. Even if the callable amount includes an amount that reasonably compensates the holder for the early termination of the instrument, the contractual cash flows could be payments of principal and interest on the principal amount outstanding. (See also paragraph B4.1.12.)

B4.1.15   In some cases a financial asset may have contractual cash flows that are described as principal and interest but those cash flows do not represent the payment of principal and interest on the principal amount outstanding as described in paragraphs 4.1.2(b), 4.1.2A(b) and 4.1.3 of this Standard.

B4.1.16   This may be the case if the financial asset represents an investment in particular assets or cash flows and hence the contractual cash flows are not solely payments of principal and interest on the principal amount outstanding. For example, if the contractual terms stipulate that the financial asset's cash flows increase as more automobiles use a particular toll road, those contractual cash flows are inconsistent with a basic lending arrangement. As a result, the instrument would not satisfy the condition in paragraphs 4.1.2(b) and 4.1.2A(b). This could be the case when a creditor's claim is limited to specified assets of the debtor or the cash flows from specified assets (for example, a 'non-recourse' financial asset).

B4.1.17   However, the fact that a financial asset is non-recourse does not in itself necessarily preclude the financial asset from meeting the condition in paragraphs 4.1.2(b) and 4.1.2A(b). In such situations, the creditor is required to assess ('look through to') the particular underlying assets or cash flows to determine whether the contractual cash flows of the financial asset being classified are payments of principal and interest on the principal amount outstanding. If the terms of the financial asset give rise to any other cash flows or limit the cash flows in a manner inconsistent with payments representing principal and interest, the financial asset does not meet the condition in paragraphs 4.1.2(b) and 4.1.2A(b). Whether the underlying assets are financial assets or non-financial assets does not in itself affect this assessment.

B4.1.18   A contractual cash flow characteristic does not affect the classification of the financial asset if it could have only a de minimis effect on the contractual cash flows of the financial asset. To make this determination, an entity must consider the possible effect of the contractual cash flow characteristic in each reporting period and cumulatively over the life of the financial instrument. In addition, if a contractual cash flow characteristic could have an effect on the contractual cash flows that is more than de minimis (either in a single reporting period or cumulatively) but that cash flow characteristic is not genuine, it does not affect the classification of a financial asset. A cash flow characteristic is not genuine if it affects the instrument's contractual cash flows only on the occurrence of an event that is extremely rare, highly abnormal and very unlikely to occur.

B4.1.19   In almost every lending transaction the creditor's instrument is ranked relative to the instruments of the debtor's other creditors. An instrument that is subordinated to other instruments may have contractual cash flows that are payments of principal and interest on the principal amount outstanding if the debtor's non-payment is a breach of contract and the holder has a contractual right to unpaid amounts of principal and interest on the principal amount outstanding even in the event of the debtor's bankruptcy. For example, a trade receivable that ranks its creditor as a general creditor would qualify as having payments of principal and interest on the principal amount outstanding. This is the case even if the debtor issued loans that are collateralised, which in the event of bankruptcy would give that loan holder priority over the claims of the general creditor in respect of the collateral but does not affect the contractual right of the general creditor to unpaid principal and other amounts due.

Contractually linked instruments

B4.1.20   In some types of transactions, an issuer may prioritise payments to the holders of financial assets using multiple contractually linked instruments that create concentrations of credit risk (tranches). Each tranche has a subordination ranking that specifies the order in which any cash flows generated by the issuer are allocated to the tranche. In such situations, the holders of a tranche have the right to payments of principal and interest on the principal amount outstanding only if the issuer generates sufficient cash flows to satisfy higher-ranking tranches.

B4.1.21   In such transactions, a tranche has cash flow characteristics that are payments of principal and interest on the principal amount outstanding only if:

(a)   the contractual terms of the tranche being assessed for classification (without looking through to the underlying pool of financial instruments) give rise to cash flows that are solely payments of principal and interest on the principal amount outstanding (eg the interest rate on the tranche is not linked to a commodity index);

(b)   the underlying pool of financial instruments has the cash flow characteristics set out in paragraphs B4.1.23 and B4.1.24; and

(c)   the exposure to credit risk in the underlying pool of financial instruments inherent in the tranche is equal to or lower than the exposure to credit risk of the underlying pool of financial instruments (for example, the credit rating of the tranche being assessed for classification is equal to or higher than the credit rating that would apply to a single tranche that funded the underlying pool of financial instruments).

B4.1.22   An entity must look through until it can identify the underlying pool of instruments that are creating (instead of passing through) the cash flows. This is the underlying pool of financial instruments.

B4.1.23   The underlying pool must contain one or more instruments that have contractual cash flows that are solely payments of principal and interest on the principal amount outstanding.

B4.1.24   The underlying pool of instruments may also include instruments that:

(a)   reduce the cash flow variability of the instruments in paragraph B4.1.23 and, when combined with the instruments in paragraph B4.1.23, result in cash flows that are solely payments of principal and interest on the principal amount outstanding (eg an interest rate cap or floor or a contract that reduces the credit risk on some or all of the instruments in paragraph B4.1.23); or

(b)   align the cash flows of the tranches with the cash flows of the pool of underlying instruments in paragraph B4.1.23 to address differences in and only in:

(i)   whether the interest rate is fixed or floating;

(ii)   the currency in which the cash flows are denominated, including inflation in that currency; or

(iii)   the timing of the cash flows.

B4.1.25 If any instrument in the pool does not meet the conditions in either paragraph B4.1.23 or paragraph B4.1.24, the condition in paragraph B4.1.21(b) is not met. In performing this assessment, a detailed instrument-by-instrument analysis of the pool may not be necessary. However, an entity must use judgement and perform sufficient analysis to determine whether the instruments in the pool meet the conditions in paragraphs B4.1.23–B4.1.24. (See also paragraph B4.1.18 for guidance on contractual cash flow characteristics that have only a de minimis effect.)

B4.1.26 If the holder cannot assess the conditions in paragraph B4.1.21 at initial recognition, the tranche must be measured at fair value through profit or loss. If the underlying pool of instruments can change after initial recognition in such a way that the pool may not meet the conditions in paragraphs B4.1.23–B4.1.24, the tranche does not meet the conditions in paragraph B4.1.21 and must be measured at fair value through profit or loss. However, if the underlying pool includes instruments that are collateralised by assets that do not meet the conditions in paragraphs B4.1.23–B4.1.24, the ability to take possession of such assets shall be disregarded for the purposes of applying this paragraph unless the entity acquired the tranche with the intention of controlling the collateral.

Option to designate a financial asset or financial liability as at fair value through profit or loss (Sections 4.1 and 4.2)

B4.1.27 Subject to the conditions in paragraphs 4.1.5 and 4.2.2, this Standard allows an entity to designate a financial asset, a financial liability, or a group of financial instruments (financial assets, financial liabilities or both) as at fair value through profit or loss provided that doing so results in more relevant information.

B4.1.28 The decision of an entity to designate a financial asset or financial liability as at fair value through profit or loss is similar to an accounting policy choice (although, unlike an accounting policy choice, it is not required to be applied consistently to all similar transactions). When an entity has such a choice, paragraph 14(b) of IAS 8 requires the chosen policy to result in the financial statements providing reliable and more relevant information about the effects of transactions, other events and conditions on the entity's financial position, financial performance or cash flows. For example, in the case of designation of a financial liability as at fair value through profit or loss, paragraph 4.2.2 sets out the two circumstances when the requirement for more relevant information will be met. Accordingly, to choose such designation in accordance with paragraph 4.2.2, the entity needs to demonstrate that it falls within one (or both) of these two circumstances.

Designation eliminates or significantly reduces an accounting mismatch

B4.1.29   Measurement of a financial asset or financial liability and classification of recognised changes in its value are determined by the item's classification and whether the item is part of a designated hedging relationship. Those requirements can create a measurement or recognition inconsistency (sometimes referred to as an 'accounting mismatch') when, for example, in the absence of designation as at fair value through profit or loss, a financial asset would be classified as subsequently measured at fair value through profit or loss and a liability the entity considers related would be subsequently measured at amortised cost (with changes in fair value not recognised). In such circumstances, an entity may conclude that its financial statements would provide more relevant information if both the asset and the liability were measured as at fair value through profit or loss.

B4.1.30   The following examples show when this condition could be met. In all cases, an entity may use this condition to designate financial assets or financial liabilities as at fair value through profit or loss only if it meets the principle in paragraph 4.1.5 or 4.2.2(a):

(a)   an entity has liabilities under insurance contracts whose measurement incorporates current information (as permitted by paragraph 24 of IFRS 4) and financial assets that it considers to be related and that would otherwise be measured at either fair value through other comprehensive income or amortised cost.

(b)   an entity has financial assets, financial liabilities or both that share a risk, such as interest rate risk, and that gives rise to opposite changes in fair value that tend to offset each other. However, only some of the instruments would be measured at fair value through profit or loss (for example, those that are derivatives, or are classified as held for trading). It may also be the case that the requirements for hedge accounting are not met because, for example, the requirements for hedge effectiveness in paragraph 6.4.1 are not met.

(c)   an entity has financial assets, financial liabilities or both that share a risk, such as interest rate risk, that gives rise to opposite changes in fair value that tend to offset each other and none of the financial assets or financial liabilities qualifies for designation as a hedging instrument because they are not measured at fair value through profit or loss. Furthermore, in the absence of hedge accounting there is a significant inconsistency in the recognition of gains and losses. For example, the entity has financed a specified group of loans by issuing traded bonds whose changes in fair value tend to offset each other. If, in addition, the entity regularly buys and sells the bonds but rarely, if ever, buys and sells the loans, reporting both the loans and the bonds at fair value through profit or loss eliminates the inconsistency in the timing of the recognition of the gains and losses that would otherwise result from measuring them both at amortised cost and recognising a gain or loss each time a bond is repurchased.

B4.1.31　In cases such as those described in the preceding paragraph, to designate, at initial recognition, the financial assets and financial liabilities not otherwise so measured as at fair value through profit or loss may eliminate or significantly reduce the measurement or recognition inconsistency and produce more relevant information. For practical purposes, the entity need not enter into all of the assets and liabilities giving rise to the measurement or recognition inconsistency at exactly the same time. A reasonable delay is permitted provided that each transaction is designated as at fair value through profit or loss at its initial recognition and, at that time, any remaining transactions are expected to occur.

B4.1.32　It would not be acceptable to designate only some of the financial assets and financial liabilities giving rise to the inconsistency as at fair value through profit or loss if to do so would not eliminate or significantly reduce the inconsistency and would therefore not result in more relevant information. However, it would be acceptable to designate only some of a number of similar financial assets or similar financial liabilities if doing so achieves a significant reduction (and possibly a greater reduction than other allowable designations) in the inconsistency. For example, assume an entity has a number of similar financial liabilities that sum to CU100 and a number of similar financial assets that sum to CU50 but are measured on a different basis. The entity may significantly reduce the measurement inconsistency by designating at initial recognition all of the assets but only some of the liabilities (for example, individual liabilities with a combined total of CU45) as at fair value through profit or loss. However, because designation as at fair value through profit or loss can be applied only to the whole of a financial instrument, the entity in this example must designate one or more liabilities in their entirety. It could not designate either a component of a liability (eg changes in value attributable to only one risk, such as changes in a benchmark interest rate) or a proportion (ie percentage) of a liability.

A group of financial liabilities or financial assets and financial liabilities is managed and its performance is evaluated on a fair value basis

B4.1.33　An entity may manage and evaluate the performance of a group of financial liabilities or financial assets and financial liabilities in such a way that measuring that group at fair value through profit or loss results in more relevant information. The focus in this instance is on the way the entity manages and evaluates performance, instead of on the nature of its financial instruments.

B4.1.34　For example, an entity may use this condition to designate financial liabilities as at fair value through profit or loss if it meets the principle in paragraph 4.2.2(b) and the entity has financial assets and financial liabilities that share one or more risks and those risks are managed and evaluated on a fair value basis in accordance with a documented policy of asset and liability management. An example could be an entity that has issued 'structured products' containing multiple embedded derivatives and manages the resulting risks on a fair value basis using a mix of derivative and non-derivative financial instruments.

B4.1.35   As noted above, this condition relies on the way the entity manages and evaluates performance of the group of financial instruments under consideration. Accordingly, (subject to the requirement of designation at initial recognition) an entity that designates financial liabilities as at fair value through profit or loss on the basis of this condition shall so designate all eligible financial liabilities that are managed and evaluated together.

B4.1.36   Documentation of the entity's strategy need not be extensive but should be sufficient to demonstrate compliance with paragraph 4.2.2(b). Such documentation is not required for each individual item, but may be on a portfolio basis. For example, if the performance management system for a department—as approved by the entity's key management personnel—clearly demonstrates that its performance is evaluated on this basis, no further documentation is required to demonstrate compliance with paragraph 4.2.2(b).

Embedded derivatives (Section 4.3)

B4.3.1   When an entity becomes a party to a hybrid contract with a host that is not an asset within the scope of this Standard, paragraph 4.3.3 requires the entity to identify any embedded derivative, assess whether it is required to be separated from the host contract and, for those that are required to be separated, measure the derivatives at fair value at initial recognition and subsequently at fair value through profit or loss.

B4.3.2   If a host contract has no stated or predetermined maturity and represents a residual interest in the net assets of an entity, then its economic characteristics and risks are those of an equity instrument, and an embedded derivative would need to possess equity characteristics related to the same entity to be regarded as closely related. If the host contract is not an equity instrument and meets the definition of a financial instrument, then its economic characteristics and risks are those of a debt instrument.

B4.3.3   An embedded non-option derivative (such as an embedded forward or swap) is separated from its host contract on the basis of its stated or implied substantive terms, so as to result in it having a fair value of zero at initial recognition. An embedded option-based derivative (such as an embedded put, call, cap, floor or swaption) is separated from its host contract on the basis of the stated terms of the option feature. The initial carrying amount of the host instrument is the residual amount after separating the embedded derivative.

B4.3.4   Generally, multiple embedded derivatives in a single hybrid contract are treated as a single compound embedded derivative. However, embedded derivatives that are classified as equity (see IAS 32 *Financial Instruments: Presentation*) are accounted for separately from those classified as assets or liabilities. In addition, if a hybrid contract has more than one embedded derivative and those derivatives relate to different risk exposures and are readily separable and independent of each other, they are accounted for separately from each other.

B4.3.5   The economic characteristics and risks of an embedded derivative are not closely related to the host contract (paragraph 4.3.3(a)) in the following examples. In these examples, assuming the conditions in paragraph 4.3.3(b) and (c) are met, an entity accounts for the embedded derivative separately from the host contract.

(a)   A put option embedded in an instrument that enables the holder to require the issuer to reacquire the instrument for an amount of cash or other assets that varies on the basis of the change in an equity or commodity price or index is not closely related to a host debt instrument.

(b)   An option or automatic provision to extend the remaining term to maturity of a debt instrument is not closely related to the host debt instrument unless there is a concurrent adjustment to the approximate current market rate of interest at the time of the extension. If an entity issues a debt instrument and the holder of that debt instrument writes a call option on the debt instrument to a third party, the issuer regards the call option as extending the term to maturity of the debt instrument provided the issuer can be required to participate in or facilitate the remarketing of the debt instrument as a result of the call option being exercised.

(c)   Equity-indexed interest or principal payments embedded in a host debt instrument or insurance contract — by which the amount of interest or principal is indexed to the value of equity instruments — are not closely related to the host instrument because the risks inherent in the host and the embedded derivative are dissimilar.

(d)   Commodity-indexed interest or principal payments embedded in a host debt instrument or insurance contract — by which the amount of interest or principal is indexed to the price of a commodity (such as gold) — are not closely related to the host instrument because the risks inherent in the host and the embedded derivative are dissimilar.

(e)   A call, put, or prepayment option embedded in a host debt contract or host insurance contract is not closely related to the host contract unless:

(i)   the option's exercise price is approximately equal on each exercise date to the amortised cost of the host debt instrument or the carrying amount of the host insurance contract; or

(ii)   the exercise price of a prepayment option reimburses the lender for an amount up to the approximate present value of lost interest for the remaining term of the host contract. Lost interest is the product of the principal amount prepaid multiplied by the interest rate differential. The interest rate differential is the excess of the effective interest rate of the host contract over the effective interest rate the entity would receive at the prepayment date if it reinvested the principal amount prepaid in a similar contract for the remaining term of the host contract.

The assessment of whether the call or put option is closely related to the host debt contract is made before separating the equity element of a convertible debt instrument in accordance with IAS 32.

(f) Credit derivatives that are embedded in a host debt instrument and allow one party (the 'beneficiary') to transfer the credit risk of a particular reference asset, which it may not own, to another party (the 'guarantor') are not closely related to the host debt instrument. Such credit derivatives allow the guarantor to assume the credit risk associated with the reference asset without directly owning it.

B4.3.6   An example of a hybrid contract is a financial instrument that gives the holder a right to put the financial instrument back to the issuer in exchange for an amount of cash or other financial assets that varies on the basis of the change in an equity or commodity index that may increase or decrease (a 'puttable instrument'). Unless the issuer on initial recognition designates the puttable instrument as a financial liability at fair value through profit or loss, it is required to separate an embedded derivative (ie the indexed principal payment) under paragraph 4.3.3 because the host contract is a debt instrument under paragraph B4.3.2 and the indexed principal payment is not closely related to a host debt instrument under paragraph B4.3.5(a). Because the principal payment can increase and decrease, the embedded derivative is a non-option derivative whose value is indexed to the underlying variable.

B4.3.7   In the case of a puttable instrument that can be put back at any time for cash equal to a proportionate share of the net asset value of an entity (such as units of an open-ended mutual fund or some unit-linked investment products), the effect of separating an embedded derivative and accounting for each component is to measure the hybrid contract at the redemption amount that is payable at the end of the reporting period if the holder exercised its right to put the instrument back to the issuer.

B4.3.8   The economic characteristics and risks of an embedded derivative are closely related to the economic characteristics and risks of the host contract in the following examples. In these examples, an entity does not account for the embedded derivative separately from the host contract.

(a) An embedded derivative in which the underlying is an interest rate or interest rate index that can change the amount of interest that would otherwise be paid or received on an interest-bearing host debt contract or insurance contract is closely related to the host contract unless the hybrid contract can be settled in such a way that the holder would not recover substantially all of its recognised investment or the embedded derivative could at least double the holder's initial rate of return on the host contract and could result in a rate of return that is at least twice what the market return would be for a contract with the same terms as the host contract.

(b)   An embedded floor or cap on the interest rate on a debt contract or insurance contract is closely related to the host contract, provided the cap is at or above the market rate of interest and the floor is at or below the market rate of interest when the contract is issued, and the cap or floor is not leveraged in relation to the host contract. Similarly, provisions included in a contract to purchase or sell an asset (eg a commodity) that establish a cap and a floor on the price to be paid or received for the asset are closely related to the host contract if both the cap and floor were out of the money at inception and are not leveraged.

(c)   An embedded foreign currency derivative that provides a stream of principal or interest payments that are denominated in a foreign currency and is embedded in a host debt instrument (for example, a dual currency bond) is closely related to the host debt instrument. Such a derivative is not separated from the host instrument because IAS 21 *The Effects of Changes in Foreign Exchange Rates* requires foreign currency gains and losses on monetary items to be recognised in profit or loss.

(d)   An embedded foreign currency derivative in a host contract that is an insurance contract or not a financial instrument (such as a contract for the purchase or sale of a non-financial item where the price is denominated in a foreign currency) is closely related to the host contract provided it is not leveraged, does not contain an option feature, and requires payments denominated in one of the following currencies:

(i)   the functional currency of any substantial party to that contract;

(ii)   the currency in which the price of the related good or service that is acquired or delivered is routinely denominated in commercial transactions around the world (such as the US dollar for crude oil transactions); or

(iii)   a currency that is commonly used in contracts to purchase or sell non-financial items in the economic environment in which the transaction takes place (eg a relatively stable and liquid currency that is commonly used in local business transactions or external trade).

(e)   An embedded prepayment option in an interest-only or principal-only strip is closely related to the host contract provided the host contract (i) initially resulted from separating the right to receive contractual cash flows of a financial instrument that, in and of itself, did not contain an embedded derivative, and (ii) does not contain any terms not present in the original host debt contract.

(f)   An embedded derivative in a host lease contract is closely related to the host contract if the embedded derivative is (i) an inflation-related index such as an index of lease payments to a consumer price index (provided that the lease is not leveraged and the index relates to inflation in the entity's own economic environment), (ii) variable lease payments based on related sales or (iii) variable lease payments based on variable interest rates.

(g)   A unit-linking feature embedded in a host financial instrument or host insurance contract is closely related to the host instrument or host contract if the unit-denominated payments are measured at current unit values that reflect the fair values of the assets of the fund. A unit-linking feature is a contractual term that requires payments denominated in units of an internal or external investment fund.

(h)   A derivative embedded in an insurance contract is closely related to the host insurance contract if the embedded derivative and host insurance contract are so interdependent that an entity cannot measure the embedded derivative separately (ie without considering the host contract).

Instruments containing embedded derivatives

B4.3.9   As noted in paragraph B4.3.1, when an entity becomes a party to a hybrid contract with a host that is not an asset within the scope of this Standard and with one or more embedded derivatives, paragraph 4.3.3 requires the entity to identify any such embedded derivative, assess whether it is required to be separated from the host contract and, for those that are required to be separated, measure the derivatives at fair value at initial recognition and subsequently. These requirements can be more complex, or result in less reliable measures, than measuring the entire instrument at fair value through profit or loss. For that reason this Standard permits the entire hybrid contract to be designated as at fair value through profit or loss.

B4.3.10   Such designation may be used whether paragraph 4.3.3 requires the embedded derivatives to be separated from the host contract or prohibits such separation. However, paragraph 4.3.5 would not justify designating the hybrid contract as at fair value through profit or loss in the cases set out in paragraph 4.3.5(a) and (b) because doing so would not reduce complexity or increase reliability.

Reassessment of embedded derivatives

B4.3.11   In accordance with paragraph 4.3.3, an entity shall assess whether an embedded derivative is required to be separated from the host contract and accounted for as a derivative when the entity first becomes a party to the contract. Subsequent reassessment is prohibited unless there is a change in the terms of the contract that significantly modifies the cash flows that otherwise would be required under the contract, in which case reassessment is required. An entity determines whether a modification to cash flows is significant by considering the extent to which the expected future cash flows associated with the embedded derivative, the host contract or both have changed and whether the change is significant relative to the previously expected cash flows on the contract.

B4.3.12 Paragraph B4.3.11 does not apply to embedded derivatives in contracts acquired in:

(a) a business combination (as defined in IFRS 3 *Business Combinations*);

(b) a combination of entities or businesses under common control as described in paragraphs B1–B4 of IFRS 3; or

(c) the formation of a joint venture as defined in IFRS 11 *Joint Arrangements*

or their possible reassessment at the date of acquisition.[4]

Reclassification of financial assets (Section 4.4)

Reclassification of financial assets

B4.4.1 Paragraph 4.4.1 requires an entity to reclassify financial assets if the entity changes its business model for managing those financial assets. Such changes are expected to be very infrequent. Such changes are determined by the entity's senior management as a result of external or internal changes and must be significant to the entity's operations and demonstrable to external parties. Accordingly, a change in an entity's business model will occur only when an entity either begins or ceases to perform an activity that is significant to its operations; for example, when the entity has acquired, disposed of or terminated a business line. Examples of a change in business model include the following:

(a) An entity has a portfolio of commercial loans that it holds to sell in the short term. The entity acquires a company that manages commercial loans and has a business model that holds the loans in order to collect the contractual cash flows. The portfolio of commercial loans is no longer for sale, and the portfolio is now managed together with the acquired commercial loans and all are held to collect the contractual cash flows.

(b) A financial services firm decides to shut down its retail mortgage business. That business no longer accepts new business and the financial services firm is actively marketing its mortgage loan portfolio for sale.

B4.4.2 A change in the objective of the entity's business model must be effected before the reclassification date. For example, if a financial services firm decides on 15 February to shut down its retail mortgage business and hence must reclassify all affected financial assets on 1 April (ie the first day of the entity's next reporting period), the entity must not accept new retail mortgage business or otherwise engage in activities consistent with its former business model after 15 February.

---

4 IFRS 3 addresses the acquisition of contracts with embedded derivatives in a business combination.

B4.4.3   The following are not changes in business model:

(a)   a change in intention related to particular financial assets (even in circumstances of significant changes in market conditions).

(b)   the temporary disappearance of a particular market for financial assets.

(c)   a transfer of financial assets between parts of the entity with different business models.

Measurement (Chapter 5)

Initial measurement (Section 5.1)

B5.1.1   The fair value of a financial instrument at initial recognition is normally the transaction price (ie the fair value of the consideration given or received, see also paragraph B5.1.2A and IFRS 13). However, if part of the consideration given or received is for something other than the financial instrument, an entity shall measure the fair value of the financial instrument. For example, the fair value of a long-term loan or receivable that carries no interest can be measured as the present value of all future cash receipts discounted using the prevailing market rate(s) of interest for a similar instrument (similar as to currency, term, type of interest rate and other factors) with a similar credit rating. Any additional amount lent is an expense or a reduction of income unless it qualifies for recognition as some other type of asset.

B5.1.2   If an entity originates a loan that bears an off-market interest rate (eg 5 per cent when the market rate for similar loans is 8 per cent), and receives an upfront fee as compensation, the entity recognises the loan at its fair value, ie net of the fee it receives.

B5.1.2A   The best evidence of the fair value of a financial instrument at initial recognition is normally the transaction price (ie the fair value of the consideration given or received, see also IFRS 13). If an entity determines that the fair value at initial recognition differs from the transaction price as mentioned in paragraph 5.1.1A, the entity shall account for that instrument at that date as follows:

(a)   at the measurement required by paragraph 5.1.1 if that fair value is evidenced by a quoted price in an active market for an identical asset or liability (ie a Level 1 input) or based on a valuation technique that uses only data from observable markets. An entity shall recognise the difference between the fair value at initial recognition and the transaction price as a gain or loss.

(b)   in all other cases, at the measurement required by paragraph 5.1.1, adjusted to defer the difference between the fair value at initial recognition and the transaction price. After initial recognition, the entity shall recognise that deferred difference as a gain or loss only to the extent that it arises from a change in a factor (including time) that market participants would take into account when pricing the asset or liability.

Subsequent measurement (Sections 5.2 and 5.3)

B5.2.1　If a financial instrument that was previously recognised as a financial asset is measured at fair value through profit or loss and its fair value decreases below zero, it is a financial liability measured in accordance with paragraph 4.2.1. However, hybrid contracts with hosts that are assets within the scope of this Standard are always measured in accordance with paragraph 4.3.2.

B5.2.2　The following example illustrates the accounting for transaction costs on the initial and subsequent measurement of a financial asset measured at fair value with changes through other comprehensive income in accordance with either paragraph 5.7.5 or 4.1.2A. An entity acquires a financial asset for CU100 plus a purchase commission of CU2. Initially, the entity recognises the asset at CU102. The reporting period ends one day later, when the quoted market price of the asset is CU100. If the asset were sold, a commission of CU3 would be paid. On that date, the entity measures the asset at CU100 (without regard to the possible commission on sale) and recognises a loss of CU2 in other comprehensive income. If the financial asset is measured at fair value through other comprehensive income in accordance with paragraph 4.1.2A, the transaction costs are amortised to profit or loss using the effective interest method.

B5.2.2A　The subsequent measurement of a financial asset or financial liability and the subsequent recognition of gains and losses described in paragraph B5.1.2A shall be consistent with the requirements of this Standard.

Investments in equity instruments and contracts on those investments

B5.2.3　All investments in equity instruments and contracts on those instruments must be measured at fair value. However, in limited circumstances, cost may be an appropriate estimate of fair value. That may be the case if insufficient more recent information is available to measure fair value, or if there is a wide range of possible fair value measurements and cost represents the best estimate of fair value within that range.

B5.2.4　Indicators that cost might not be representative of fair value include:

(a)　a significant change in the performance of the investee compared with budgets, plans or milestones.

(b)　changes in expectation that the investee's technical product milestones will be achieved.

(c)　a significant change in the market for the investee's equity or its products or potential products.

(d)　a significant change in the global economy or the economic environment in which the investee operates.

(e)   a significant change in the performance of comparable entities, or in the valuations implied by the overall market.

(f)   internal matters of the investee such as fraud, commercial disputes, litigation, changes in management or strategy.

(g)   evidence from external transactions in the investee's equity, either by the investee (such as a fresh issue of equity), or by transfers of equity instruments between third parties.

B5.2.5   The list in paragraph B5.2.4 is not exhaustive. An entity shall use all information about the performance and operations of the investee that becomes available after the date of initial recognition. To the extent that any such relevant factors exist, they may indicate that cost might not be representative of fair value. In such cases, the entity must measure fair value.

B5.2.6   Cost is never the best estimate of fair value for investments in quoted equity instruments (or contracts on quoted equity instruments).

Amortised cost measurement (Section 5.4)

Effective interest method

B5.4.1   In applying the effective interest method, an entity identifies fees that are an integral part of the effective interest rate of a financial instrument. The description of fees for financial services may not be indicative of the nature and substance of the services provided. Fees that are an integral part of the effective interest rate of a financial instrument are treated as an adjustment to the effective interest rate, unless the financial instrument is measured at fair value, with the change in fair value being recognised in profit or loss. In those cases, the fees are recognised as revenue or expense when the instrument is initially recognised.

B5.4.2   Fees that are an integral part of the effective interest rate of a financial instrument include:

(a)   origination fees received by the entity relating to the creation or acquisition of a financial asset. Such fees may include compensation for activities such as evaluating the borrower's financial condition, evaluating and recording guarantees, collateral and other security arrangements, negotiating the terms of the instrument, preparing and processing documents and closing the transaction. These fees are an integral part of generating an involvement with the resulting financial instrument.

(b)   commitment fees received by the entity to originate a loan when the loan commitment is not measured in accordance with paragraph 4.2.1(a) and it is probable that the entity will enter into a specific lending arrangement. These fees are regarded as compensation for an ongoing involvement with the acquisition of a financial instrument. If the commitment expires without the entity making the loan, the fee is recognised as revenue on expiry.

(c)   origination fees paid on issuing financial liabilities measured at amortised cost. These fees are an integral part of generating an involvement with a financial liability. An entity distinguishes fees and costs that are an integral part of the effective interest rate for the financial liability from origination fees and transaction costs relating to the right to provide services, such as investment management services.

B5.4.3   Fees that are not an integral part of the effective interest rate of a financial instrument and are accounted for in accordance with IFRS 15 include:

(a)   fees charged for servicing a loan;

(b)   commitment fees to originate a loan when the loan commitment is not measured in accordance with paragraph 4.2.1(a) and it is unlikely that a specific lending arrangement will be entered into; and

(c)   loan syndication fees received by an entity that arranges a loan and retains no part of the loan package for itself (or retains a part at the same effective interest rate for comparable risk as other participants).

B5.4.4   When applying the effective interest method, an entity generally amortises any fees, points paid or received, transaction costs and other premiums or discounts that are included in the calculation of the effective interest rate over the expected life of the financial instrument. However, a shorter period is used if this is the period to which the fees, points paid or received, transaction costs, premiums or discounts relate. This will be the case when the variable to which the fees, points paid or received, transaction costs, premiums or discounts relate is repriced to market rates before the expected maturity of the financial instrument. In such a case, the appropriate amortisation period is the period to the next such repricing date. For example, if a premium or discount on a floating-rate financial instrument reflects the interest that has accrued on that financial instrument since the interest was last paid, or changes in the market rates since the floating interest rate was reset to the market rates, it will be amortised to the next date when the floating interest is reset to market rates. This is because the premium or discount relates to the period to the next interest reset date because, at that date, the variable to which the premium or discount relates (ie interest rates) is reset to the market rates. If, however, the premium or discount results from a change in the credit spread over the floating rate specified in the financial instrument, or other variables that are not reset to the market rates, it is amortised over the expected life of the financial instrument.

B5.4.5   For floating-rate financial assets and floating-rate financial liabilities, periodic re-estimation of cash flows to reflect the movements in the market rates of interest alters the effective interest rate. If a floating-rate financial asset or a floating-rate financial liability is recognised initially at an amount equal to the principal receivable or payable on maturity, re-estimating the future interest payments normally has no significant effect on the carrying amount of the asset or the liability.

B5.4.6   If an entity revises its estimates of payments or receipts (excluding modifications in accordance with paragraph 5.4.3 and changes in estimates of expected credit losses), it shall adjust the gross carrying amount of the financial asset or amortised cost of a financial liability (or group of financial instruments) to reflect actual and revised estimated contractual cash flows. The entity recalculates the gross carrying amount of the financial asset or amortised cost of the financial liability as the present value of the estimated future contractual cash flows that are discounted at the financial instrument's original effective interest rate (or credit-adjusted effective interest rate for purchased or originated credit-impaired financial assets) or, when applicable, the revised effective interest rate calculated in accordance with paragraph 6.5.10. The adjustment is recognised in profit or loss as income or expense.

B5.4.7   In some cases a financial asset is considered credit-impaired at initial recognition because the credit risk is very high, and in the case of a purchase it is acquired at a deep discount. An entity is required to include the initial expected credit losses in the estimated cash flows when calculating the credit-adjusted effective interest rate for financial assets that are considered to be purchased or originated credit-impaired at initial recognition. However, this does not mean that a credit-adjusted effective interest rate should be applied solely because the financial asset has high credit risk at initial recognition.

Transaction costs

B5.4.8   Transaction costs include fees and commission paid to agents (including employees acting as selling agents), advisers, brokers and dealers, levies by regulatory agencies and security exchanges, and transfer taxes and duties. Transaction costs do not include debt premiums or discounts, financing costs or internal administrative or holding costs.

Write-off

B5.4.9   Write-offs can relate to a financial asset in its entirety or to a portion of it. For example, an entity plans to enforce the collateral on a financial asset and expects to recover no more than 30 per cent of the financial asset from the collateral. If the entity has no reasonable prospects of recovering any further cash flows from the financial asset, it should write off the remaining 70 per cent of the financial asset.

Impairment (Section 5.5)

Collective and individual assessment basis

B5.5.1   In order to meet the objective of recognising lifetime expected credit losses for significant increases in credit risk since initial recognition, it may be necessary to perform the assessment of significant increases in credit risk on a collective basis by considering information that is indicative of significant increases in credit risk on, for example, a group or sub-group of financial instruments. This is to ensure that an entity meets the objective of recognising lifetime expected credit losses when there are significant increases in credit risk, even

life of 10 years at initial recognition is identical to the risk of a default occurring on that financial instrument when its expected life in a subsequent period is only five years, that may indicate an increase in credit risk. This is because the risk of a default occurring over the expected life usually decreases as time passes if the credit risk is unchanged and the financial instrument is closer to maturity. However, for financial instruments that only have significant payment obligations close to the maturity of the financial instrument the risk of a default occurring may not necessarily decrease as time passes. In such a case, an entity should also consider other qualitative factors that would demonstrate whether credit risk has increased significantly since initial recognition.

B5.5.12 An entity may apply various approaches when assessing whether the credit risk on a financial instrument has increased significantly since initial recognition or when measuring expected credit losses. An entity may apply different approaches for different financial instruments. An approach that does not include an explicit probability of default as an input per se, such as a credit loss rate approach, can be consistent with the requirements in this Standard, provided that an entity is able to separate the changes in the risk of a default occurring from changes in other drivers of expected credit losses, such as collateral, and considers the following when making the assessment:

(a) the change in the risk of a default occurring since initial recognition;

(b) the expected life of the financial instrument; and

(c) reasonable and supportable information that is available without undue cost or effort that may affect credit risk.

B5.5.13 The methods used to determine whether credit risk has increased significantly on a financial instrument since initial recognition should consider the characteristics of the financial instrument (or group of financial instruments) and the default patterns in the past for comparable financial instruments. Despite the requirement in paragraph 5.5.9, for financial instruments for which default patterns are not concentrated at a specific point during the expected life of the financial instrument, changes in the risk of a default occurring over the next 12 months may be a reasonable approximation of the changes in the lifetime risk of a default occurring. In such cases, an entity may use changes in the risk of a default occurring over the next 12 months to determine whether credit risk has increased significantly since initial recognition, unless circumstances indicate that a lifetime assessment is necessary.

B5.5.14 However, for some financial instruments, or in some circumstances, it may not be appropriate to use changes in the risk of a default occurring over the next 12 months to determine whether lifetime expected credit losses should be recognised. For example, the change in the risk of a default occurring in the next 12 months may not be a suitable basis for determining whether credit risk has increased on a financial instrument with a maturity of more than 12 months when:

(a) the financial instrument only has significant payment obligations beyond the next 12 months;

(b) changes in relevant macroeconomic or other credit-related factors occur that are not adequately reflected in the risk of a default occurring in the next 12 months; or

(c) changes in credit-related factors only have an impact on the credit risk of the financial instrument (or have a more pronounced effect) beyond 12 months.

Determining whether credit risk has increased significantly since initial recognition

B5.5.15 When determining whether the recognition of lifetime expected credit losses is required, an entity shall consider reasonable and supportable information that is available without undue cost or effort and that may affect the credit risk on a financial instrument in accordance with paragraph 5.5.17(c). An entity need not undertake an exhaustive search for information when determining whether credit risk has increased significantly since initial recognition.

B5.5.16 Credit risk analysis is a multifactor and holistic analysis; whether a specific factor is relevant, and its weight compared to other factors, will depend on the type of product, characteristics of the financial instruments and the borrower as well as the geographical region. An entity shall consider reasonable and supportable information that is available without undue cost or effort and that is relevant for the particular financial instrument being assessed. However, some factors or indicators may not be identifiable on an individual financial instrument level. In such a case, the factors or indicators should be assessed for appropriate portfolios, groups of portfolios or portions of a portfolio of financial instruments to determine whether the requirement in paragraph 5.5.3 for the recognition of lifetime expected credit losses has been met.

B5.5.17 The following non-exhaustive list of information may be relevant in assessing changes in credit risk:

(a) significant changes in internal price indicators of credit risk as a result of a change in credit risk since inception, including, but not limited to, the credit spread that would result if a particular financial instrument or similar financial instrument with the same terms and the same counterparty were newly originated or issued at the reporting date.

(b) other changes in the rates or terms of an existing financial instrument that would be significantly different if the instrument was newly originated or issued at the reporting date (such as more stringent covenants, increased amounts of collateral or guarantees, or higher income coverage) because of changes in the credit risk of the financial instrument since initial recognition.

(c)   significant changes in external market indicators of credit risk for a particular financial instrument or similar financial instruments with the same expected life. Changes in market indicators of credit risk include, but are not limited to:

    (i)   the credit spread;

    (ii)   the credit default swap prices for the borrower;

    (iii)   the length of time or the extent to which the fair value of a financial asset has been less than its amortised cost; and

    (iv)   other market information related to the borrower, such as changes in the price of a borrower's debt and equity instruments.

(d)   an actual or expected significant change in the financial instrument's external credit rating.

(e)   an actual or expected internal credit rating downgrade for the borrower or decrease in behavioural scoring used to assess credit risk internally. Internal credit ratings and internal behavioural scoring are more reliable when they are mapped to external ratings or supported by default studies.

(f)   existing or forecast adverse changes in business, financial or economic conditions that are expected to cause a significant change in the borrower's ability to meet its debt obligations, such as an actual or expected increase in interest rates or an actual or expected significant increase in unemployment rates.

(g)   an actual or expected significant change in the operating results of the borrower. Examples include actual or expected declining revenues or margins, increasing operating risks, working capital deficiencies, decreasing asset quality, increased balance sheet leverage, liquidity, management problems or changes in the scope of business or organisational structure (such as the discontinuance of a segment of the business) that results in a significant change in the borrower's ability to meet its debt obligations.

(h)   significant increases in credit risk on other financial instruments of the same borrower.

(i)   an actual or expected significant adverse change in the regulatory, economic, or technological environment of the borrower that results in a significant change in the borrower's ability to meet its debt obligations, such as a decline in the demand for the borrower's sales product because of a shift in technology.

(j)   significant changes in the value of the collateral supporting the obligation or in the quality of third-party guarantees or credit enhancements, which are expected to reduce the borrower's economic incentive to make scheduled contractual payments or to otherwise have an effect on the probability of a default occurring. For example, if the value of collateral declines because house prices decline, borrowers in some jurisdictions have a greater incentive to default on their mortgages.

(k) a significant change in the quality of the guarantee provided by a shareholder (or an individual's parents) if the shareholder (or parents) have an incentive and financial ability to prevent default by capital or cash infusion.

(l) significant changes, such as reductions in financial support from a parent entity or other affiliate or an actual or expected significant change in the quality of credit enhancement, that are expected to reduce the borrower's economic incentive to make scheduled contractual payments. Credit quality enhancements or support include the consideration of the financial condition of the guarantor and/or, for interests issued in securitisations, whether subordinated interests are expected to be capable of absorbing expected credit losses (for example, on the loans underlying the security).

(m) expected changes in the loan documentation including an expected breach of contract that may lead to covenant waivers or amendments, interest payment holidays, interest rate step-ups, requiring additional collateral or guarantees, or other changes to the contractual framework of the instrument.

(n) significant changes in the expected performance and behaviour of the borrower, including changes in the payment status of borrowers in the group (for example, an increase in the expected number or extent of delayed contractual payments or significant increases in the expected number of credit card borrowers who are expected to approach or exceed their credit limit or who are expected to be paying the minimum monthly amount).

(o) changes in the entity's credit management approach in relation to the financial instrument; ie based on emerging indicators of changes in the credit risk of the financial instrument, the entity's credit risk management practice is expected to become more active or to be focused on managing the instrument, including the instrument becoming more closely monitored or controlled, or the entity specifically intervening with the borrower.

(p) past due information, including the rebuttable presumption as set out in paragraph 5.5.11.

B5.5.18 In some cases, the qualitative and non-statistical quantitative information available may be sufficient to determine that a financial instrument has met the criterion for the recognition of a loss allowance at an amount equal to lifetime expected credit losses. That is, the information does not need to flow through a statistical model or credit ratings process in order to determine whether there has been a significant increase in the credit risk of the financial instrument. In other cases, an entity may need to consider other information, including information from its statistical models or credit ratings processes.

Alternatively, the entity may base the assessment on both types of information, ie qualitative factors that are not captured through the internal ratings process and a specific internal rating category at the reporting date, taking into consideration the credit risk characteristics at initial recognition, if both types of information are relevant.

More than 30 days past due rebuttable presumption

B5.5.19   The rebuttable presumption in paragraph 5.5.11 is not an absolute indicator that lifetime expected credit losses should be recognised, but is presumed to be the latest point at which lifetime expected credit losses should be recognised even when using forward-looking information (including macroeconomic factors on a portfolio level).

B5.5.20   An entity can rebut this presumption. However, it can do so only when it has reasonable and supportable information available that demonstrates that even if contractual payments become more than 30 days past due, this does not represent a significant increase in the credit risk of a financial instrument. For example when non-payment was an administrative oversight, instead of resulting from financial difficulty of the borrower, or the entity has access to historical evidence that demonstrates that there is no correlation between significant increases in the risk of a default occurring and financial assets on which payments are more than 30 days past due, but that evidence does identify such a correlation when payments are more than 60 days past due.

B5.5.21   An entity cannot align the timing of significant increases in credit risk and the recognition of lifetime expected credit losses to when a financial asset is regarded as credit-impaired or an entity's internal definition of default.

Financial instruments that have low credit risk at the reporting date

B5.5.22   The credit risk on a financial instrument is considered low for the purposes of paragraph 5.5.10, if the financial instrument has a low risk of default, the borrower has a strong capacity to meet its contractual cash flow obligations in the near term and adverse changes in economic and business conditions in the longer term may, but will not necessarily, reduce the ability of the borrower to fulfil its contractual cash flow obligations. Financial instruments are not considered to have low credit risk when they are regarded as having a low risk of loss simply because of the value of collateral and the financial instrument without that collateral would not be considered low credit risk. Financial instruments are also not considered to have low credit risk simply because they have a lower risk of default than the entity's other financial instruments or relative to the credit risk of the jurisdiction within which an entity operates.

B5.5.23   To determine whether a financial instrument has low credit risk, an entity may use its internal credit risk ratings or other methodologies that are consistent with a globally understood definition of low credit risk and that consider the risks and the type of financial instruments that are being assessed. An external rating of 'investment grade' is an example of a financial instrument that may be considered as having low credit risk. However, financial instruments are not required to be externally rated to be considered to have low credit risk. They should, however, be considered to have low credit risk from a market participant perspective taking into account all of the terms and conditions of the financial instrument.

B5.5.24 Lifetime expected credit losses are not recognised on a financial instrument simply because it was considered to have low credit risk in the previous reporting period and is not considered to have low credit risk at the reporting date. In such a case, an entity shall determine whether there has been a significant increase in credit risk since initial recognition and thus whether lifetime expected credit losses are required to be recognised in accordance with paragraph 5.5.3.

Modifications

B5.5.25 In some circumstances, the renegotiation or modification of the contractual cash flows of a financial asset can lead to the derecognition of the existing financial asset in accordance with this Standard. When the modification of a financial asset results in the derecognition of the existing financial asset and the subsequent recognition of the modified financial asset, the modified asset is considered a 'new' financial asset for the purposes of this Standard.

B5.5.26 Accordingly the date of the modification shall be treated as the date of initial recognition of that financial asset when applying the impairment requirements to the modified financial asset. This typically means measuring the loss allowance at an amount equal to 12-month expected credit losses until the requirements for the recognition of lifetime expected credit losses in paragraph 5.5.3 are met. However, in some unusual circumstances following a modification that results in derecognition of the original financial asset, there may be evidence that the modified financial asset is credit-impaired at initial recognition, and thus, the financial asset should be recognised as an originated credit-impaired financial asset. This might occur, for example, in a situation in which there was a substantial modification of a distressed asset that resulted in the derecognition of the original financial asset. In such a case, it may be possible for the modification to result in a new financial asset which is credit-impaired at initial recognition.

B5.5.27 If the contractual cash flows on a financial asset have been renegotiated or otherwise modified, but the financial asset is not derecognised, that financial asset is not automatically considered to have lower credit risk. An entity shall assess whether there has been a significant increase in credit risk since initial recognition on the basis of all reasonable and supportable information that is available without undue cost or effort. This includes historical and forward-looking information and an assessment of the credit risk over the expected life of the financial asset, which includes information about the circumstances that led to the modification. Evidence that the criteria for the recognition of lifetime expected credit losses are no longer met may include a history of up-to-date and timely payment performance against the modified contractual terms. Typically a customer would need to demonstrate consistently good payment behaviour over a period of time before the credit risk is considered to have decreased. For example, a history of missed or incomplete payments would not typically be erased by simply making one payment on time following a modification of the contractual terms.

Measurement of expected credit losses

Expected credit losses

B5.5.28   Expected credit losses are a probability-weighted estimate of credit losses (ie the present value of all cash shortfalls) over the expected life of the financial instrument. A cash shortfall is the difference between the cash flows that are due to an entity in accordance with the contract and the cash flows that the entity expects to receive. Because expected credit losses consider the amount and timing of payments, a credit loss arises even if the entity expects to be paid in full but later than when contractually due.

B5.5.29   For financial assets, a credit loss is the present value of the difference between:

(a)   the contractual cash flows that are due to an entity under the contract; and

(b)   the cash flows that the entity expects to receive.

B5.5.30   For undrawn loan commitments, a credit loss is the present value of the difference between:

(a)   the contractual cash flows that are due to the entity if the holder of the loan commitment draws down the loan; and

(b)   the cash flows that the entity expects to receive if the loan is drawn down.

B5.5.31   An entity's estimate of expected credit losses on loan commitments shall be consistent with its expectations of drawdowns on that loan commitment, ie it shall consider the expected portion of the loan commitment that will be drawn down within 12 months of the reporting date when estimating 12-month expected credit losses, and the expected portion of the loan commitment that will be drawn down over the expected life of the loan commitment when estimating lifetime expected credit losses.

B5.5.32   For a financial guarantee contract, the entity is required to make payments only in the event of a default by the debtor in accordance with the terms of the instrument that is guaranteed. Accordingly, cash shortfalls are the expected payments to reimburse the holder for a credit loss that it incurs less any amounts that the entity expects to receive from the holder, the debtor or any other party. If the asset is fully guaranteed, the estimation of cash shortfalls for a financial guarantee contract would be consistent with the estimations of cash shortfalls for the asset subject to the guarantee.

B5.5.33   For a financial asset that is credit-impaired at the reporting date, but that is not a purchased or originated credit-impaired financial asset, an entity shall measure the expected credit losses as the difference between the asset's gross carrying amount and the present value of estimated future cash flows discounted at the financial asset's original effective interest rate. Any adjustment is recognised in profit or loss as an impairment gain or loss.

B5.5.34 When measuring a loss allowance for a lease receivable, the cash flows used for determining the expected credit losses should be consistent with the cash flows used in measuring the lease receivable in accordance with IFRS 16 *Leases*.

B5.5.35 An entity may use practical expedients when measuring expected credit losses if they are consistent with the principles in paragraph 5.5.17. An example of a practical expedient is the calculation of the expected credit losses on trade receivables using a provision matrix. The entity would use its historical credit loss experience (adjusted as appropriate in accordance with paragraphs B5.5.51–B5.5.52) for trade receivables to estimate the 12-month expected credit losses or the lifetime expected credit losses on the financial assets as relevant. A provision matrix might, for example, specify fixed provision rates depending on the number of days that a trade receivable is past due (for example, 1 per cent if not past due, 2 per cent if less than 30 days past due, 3 per cent if more than 30 days but less than 90 days past due, 20 per cent if 90–180 days past due etc). Depending on the diversity of its customer base, the entity would use appropriate groupings if its historical credit loss experience shows significantly different loss patterns for different customer segments. Examples of criteria that might be used to group assets include geographical region, product type, customer rating, collateral or trade credit insurance and type of customer (such as wholesale or retail).

Definition of default

B5.5.36 Paragraph 5.5.9 requires that when determining whether the credit risk on a financial instrument has increased significantly, an entity shall consider the change in the risk of a default occurring since initial recognition.

B5.5.37 When defining default for the purposes of determining the risk of a default occurring, an entity shall apply a default definition that is consistent with the definition used for internal credit risk management purposes for the relevant financial instrument and consider qualitative indicators (for example, financial covenants) when appropriate. However, there is a rebuttable presumption that default does not occur later than when a financial asset is 90 days past due unless an entity has reasonable and supportable information to demonstrate that a more lagging default criterion is more appropriate. The definition of default used for these purposes shall be applied consistently to all financial instruments unless information becomes available that demonstrates that another default definition is more appropriate for a particular financial instrument.

Period over which to estimate expected credit losses

B5.5.38 In accordance with paragraph 5.5.19, the maximum period over which expected credit losses shall be measured is the maximum contractual period over which the entity is exposed to credit risk. For loan commitments and financial guarantee contracts, this is the maximum contractual period over which an entity has a present contractual obligation to extend credit.

B5.5.39 However, in accordance with paragraph 5.5.20, some financial instruments include both a loan and an undrawn commitment component and the entity's contractual ability to demand repayment and cancel the undrawn commitment does not limit the entity's exposure to credit losses to the contractual notice period. For example, revolving credit facilities, such as credit cards and overdraft facilities, can be contractually withdrawn by the lender with as little as one day's notice. However, in practice lenders continue to extend credit for a longer period and may only withdraw the facility after the credit risk of the borrower increases, which could be too late to prevent some or all of the expected credit losses. These financial instruments generally have the following characteristics as a result of the nature of the financial instrument, the way in which the financial instruments are managed, and the nature of the available information about significant increases in credit risk:

(a) the financial instruments do not have a fixed term or repayment structure and usually have a short contractual cancellation period (for example, one day);

(b) the contractual ability to cancel the contract is not enforced in the normal day-to-day management of the financial instrument and the contract may only be cancelled when the entity becomes aware of an increase in credit risk at the facility level; and

(c) the financial instruments are managed on a collective basis.

B5.5.40 When determining the period over which the entity is expected to be exposed to credit risk, but for which expected credit losses would not be mitigated by the entity's normal credit risk management actions, an entity should consider factors such as historical information and experience about:

(a) the period over which the entity was exposed to credit risk on similar financial instruments;

(b) the length of time for related defaults to occur on similar financial instruments following a significant increase in credit risk; and

(c) the credit risk management actions that an entity expects to take once the credit risk on the financial instrument has increased, such as the reduction or removal of undrawn limits.

Probability-weighted outcome

B5.5.41 The purpose of estimating expected credit losses is neither to estimate a worst-case scenario nor to estimate the best-case scenario. Instead, an estimate of expected credit losses shall always reflect the possibility that a credit loss occurs and the possibility that no credit loss occurs even if the most likely outcome is no credit loss.

B5.5.42 Paragraph 5.5.17(a) requires the estimate of expected credit losses to reflect an unbiased and probability-weighted amount that is determined by evaluating a range of possible outcomes. In practice, this may not need to be a complex analysis. In some cases, relatively simple modelling may be sufficient, without the need for a large number of detailed simulations of scenarios. For example, the average credit losses of a large group of financial instruments with shared risk characteristics may be a reasonable estimate of the probability-weighted amount. In other situations, the identification of scenarios that specify the amount and timing of the cash flows for particular outcomes and the estimated probability of those outcomes will probably be needed. In those situations, the expected credit losses shall reflect at least two outcomes in accordance with paragraph 5.5.18.

B5.5.43   For lifetime expected credit losses, an entity shall estimate the risk of a default occurring on the financial instrument during its expected life. 12-month expected credit losses are a portion of the lifetime expected credit losses and represent the lifetime cash shortfalls that will result if a default occurs in the 12 months after the reporting date (or a shorter period if the expected life of a financial instrument is less than 12 months), weighted by the probability of that default occurring. Thus, 12-month expected credit losses are neither the lifetime expected credit losses that an entity will incur on financial instruments that it predicts will default in the next 12 months nor the cash shortfalls that are predicted over the next 12 months.

Time value of money

B5.5.44   Expected credit losses shall be discounted to the reporting date, not to the expected default or some other date, using the effective interest rate determined at initial recognition or an approximation thereof. If a financial instrument has a variable interest rate, expected credit losses shall be discounted using the current effective interest rate determined in accordance with paragraph B5.4.5.

B5.5.45   For purchased or originated credit-impaired financial assets, expected credit losses shall be discounted using the credit-adjusted effective interest rate determined at initial recognition.

B5.5.46   Expected credit losses on lease receivables shall be discounted using the same discount rate used in the measurement of the lease receivable in accordance with IFRS 16.

B5.5.47   The expected credit losses on a loan commitment shall be discounted using the effective interest rate, or an approximation thereof, that will be applied when recognising the financial asset resulting from the loan commitment. This is because for the purpose of applying the impairment requirements, a financial asset that is recognised following a draw down on a loan commitment shall be treated as a continuation of that commitment instead of as a new financial instrument. The expected credit losses on the financial asset shall therefore be measured considering the initial credit risk of the loan commitment from the date that the entity became a party to the irrevocable commitment.

B5.5.48   Expected credit losses on financial guarantee contracts or on loan commitments for which the effective interest rate cannot be determined shall be discounted by applying a discount rate that reflects the current market assessment of the time value of money and the risks that are specific to the cash flows but only if, and to the extent that, the risks are taken into account by adjusting the discount rate instead of adjusting the cash shortfalls being discounted.

Reasonable and supportable information

B5.5.49   For the purpose of this Standard, reasonable and supportable information is that which is reasonably available at the reporting date without undue cost or effort, including information about past events, current conditions and forecasts of future economic conditions. Information that is available for financial reporting purposes is considered to be available without undue cost or effort.

B5.5.50   An entity is not required to incorporate forecasts of future conditions over the entire expected life of a financial instrument. The degree of judgement that is required to estimate expected credit losses depends on the availability of detailed information. As the forecast horizon increases, the availability of detailed information decreases and the degree of judgement required to estimate expected credit losses increases. The estimate of expected credit losses does not require a detailed estimate for periods that are far in the future—for such periods, an entity may extrapolate projections from available, detailed information.

B5.5.51   An entity need not undertake an exhaustive search for information but shall consider all reasonable and supportable information that is available without undue cost or effort and that is relevant to the estimate of expected credit losses, including the effect of expected prepayments. The information used shall include factors that are specific to the borrower, general economic conditions and an assessment of both the current as well as the forecast direction of conditions at the reporting date. An entity may use various sources of data, that may be both internal (entity-specific) and external. Possible data sources include internal historical credit loss experience, internal ratings, credit loss experience of other entities and external ratings, reports and statistics. Entities that have no, or insufficient, sources of entity-specific data may use peer group experience for the comparable financial instrument (or groups of financial instruments).

B5.5.52   Historical information is an important anchor or base from which to measure expected credit losses. However, an entity shall adjust historical data, such as credit loss experience, on the basis of current observable data to reflect the effects of the current conditions and its forecasts of future conditions that did not affect the period on which the historical data is based, and to remove the effects of the conditions in the historical period that are not relevant to the future contractual cash flows. In some cases, the best reasonable and supportable information could be the unadjusted historical information, depending on the nature of the historical information and when it was calculated, compared to circumstances at the reporting date and the characteristics of the financial instrument being considered. Estimates of changes in expected credit losses should reflect, and be directionally consistent with, changes in related observable data from period to period (such as changes in unemployment rates, property prices, commodity prices, payment status or other factors that are indicative of credit losses on the financial instrument or in the group of financial instruments and in the magnitude of those changes). An entity shall regularly review the methodology and assumptions used for estimating expected credit losses to reduce any differences between estimates and actual credit loss experience.

B5.5.53 When using historical credit loss experience in estimating expected credit losses, it is important that information about historical credit loss rates is applied to groups that are defined in a manner that is consistent with the groups for which the historical credit loss rates were observed. Consequently, the method used shall enable each group of financial assets to be associated with information about past credit loss experience in groups of financial assets with similar risk characteristics and with relevant observable data that reflects current conditions.

B5.5.54 Expected credit losses reflect an entity's own expectations of credit losses. However, when considering all reasonable and supportable information that is available without undue cost or effort in estimating expected credit losses, an entity should also consider observable market information about the credit risk of the particular financial instrument or similar financial instruments.

Collateral

B5.5.55 For the purposes of measuring expected credit losses, the estimate of expected cash shortfalls shall reflect the cash flows expected from collateral and other credit enhancements that are part of the contractual terms and are not recognised separately by the entity. The estimate of expected cash shortfalls on a collateralised financial instrument reflects the amount and timing of cash flows that are expected from foreclosure on the collateral less the costs of obtaining and selling the collateral, irrespective of whether foreclosure is probable (ie the estimate of expected cash flows considers the probability of a foreclosure and the cash flows that would result from it). Consequently, any cash flows that are expected from the realisation of the collateral beyond the contractual maturity of the contract should be included in this analysis. Any collateral obtained as a result of foreclosure is not recognised as an asset that is separate from the collateralised financial instrument unless it meets the relevant recognition criteria for an asset in this or other Standards.

Reclassification of financial assets (Section 5.6)

B5.6.1 If an entity reclassifies financial assets in accordance with paragraph 4.4.1, paragraph 5.6.1 requires that the reclassification is applied prospectively from the reclassification date. Both the amortised cost measurement category and the fair value through other comprehensive income measurement category require that the effective interest rate is determined at initial recognition. Both of those measurement categories also require that the impairment requirements are applied in the same way. Consequently, when an entity reclassifies a financial asset between the amortised cost measurement category and the fair value through other comprehensive income measurement category:

(a)   the recognition of interest revenue will not change and therefore the entity continues to use the same effective interest rate.

(b) the measurement of expected credit losses will not change because both measurement categories apply the same impairment approach. However if a financial asset is reclassified out of the fair value through other comprehensive income measurement category and into the amortised cost measurement category, a loss allowance would be recognised as an adjustment to the gross carrying amount of the financial asset from the reclassification date. If a financial asset is reclassified out of the amortised cost measurement category and into the fair value through other comprehensive income measurement category, the loss allowance would be derecognised (and thus would no longer be recognised as an adjustment to the gross carrying amount) but instead would be recognised as an accumulated impairment amount (of an equal amount) in other comprehensive income and would be disclosed from the reclassification date.

B5.6.2 However, an entity is not required to separately recognise interest revenue or impairment gains or losses for a financial asset measured at fair value through profit or loss. Consequently, when an entity reclassifies a financial asset out of the fair value through profit or loss measurement category, the effective interest rate is determined on the basis of the fair value of the asset at the reclassification date. In addition, for the purposes of applying Section 5.5 to the financial asset from the reclassification date, the date of the reclassification is treated as the date of initial recognition.

Gains and losses (Section 5.7)

B5.7.1 Paragraph 5.7.5 permits an entity to make an irrevocable election to present in other comprehensive income changes in the fair value of an investment in an equity instrument that is not held for trading. This election is made on an instrument-by-instrument (ie share-by-share) basis. Amounts presented in other comprehensive income shall not be subsequently transferred to profit or loss. However, the entity may transfer the cumulative gain or loss within equity. Dividends on such investments are recognised in profit or loss in accordance with paragraph 5.7.6 unless the dividend clearly represents a recovery of part of the cost of the investment.

B5.7.1A Unless paragraph 4.1.5 applies, paragraph 4.1.2A requires that a financial asset is measured at fair value through other comprehensive income if the contractual terms of the financial asset give rise to cash flows that are solely payments of principal and interest on the principal amount outstanding and the asset is held in a business model whose objective is achieved by both collecting contractual cash flows and selling financial assets. This measurement category recognises information in profit or loss as if the financial asset is measured at amortised cost, while the financial asset is measured in the statement of financial position at fair value. Gains or losses, other than those that are recognised in profit or loss in accordance with paragraphs 5.7.10–5.7.11, are recognised in other comprehensive income. When these financial assets are derecognised, cumulative gains or losses previously recognised in other comprehensive income are reclassified to profit or loss. This reflects the gain or loss that would have been recognised in profit or loss upon derecognition if the financial asset had been measured at amortised cost.

B5.7.2   An entity applies IAS 21 to financial assets and financial liabilities that are monetary items in accordance with IAS 21 and denominated in a foreign currency. IAS 21 requires any foreign exchange gains and losses on monetary assets and monetary liabilities to be recognised in profit or loss. An exception is a monetary item that is designated as a hedging instrument in a cash flow hedge (see paragraph 6.5.11), a hedge of a net investment (see paragraph 6.5.13) or a fair value hedge of an equity instrument for which an entity has elected to present changes in fair value in other comprehensive income in accordance with paragraph 5.7.5 (see paragraph 6.5.8).

B5.7.2A For the purpose of recognising foreign exchange gains and losses under IAS 21, a financial asset measured at fair value through other comprehensive income in accordance with paragraph 4.1.2A is treated as a monetary item. Accordingly, such a financial asset is treated as an asset measured at amortised cost in the foreign currency. Exchange differences on the amortised cost are recognised in profit or loss and other changes in the carrying amount are recognised in accordance with paragraph 5.7.10.

B5.7.3   Paragraph 5.7.5 permits an entity to make an irrevocable election to present in other comprehensive income subsequent changes in the fair value of particular investments in equity instruments. Such an investment is not a monetary item. Accordingly, the gain or loss that is presented in other comprehensive income in accordance with paragraph 5.7.5 includes any related foreign exchange component.

B5.7.4   If there is a hedging relationship between a non-derivative monetary asset and a non-derivative monetary liability, changes in the foreign currency component of those financial instruments are presented in profit or loss.

Liabilities designated as at fair value through profit or loss

B5.7.5   When an entity designates a financial liability as at fair value through profit or loss, it must determine whether presenting in other comprehensive income the effects of changes in the liability's credit risk would create or enlarge an accounting mismatch in profit or loss. An accounting mismatch would be created or enlarged if presenting the effects of changes in the liability's credit risk in other comprehensive income would result in a greater mismatch in profit or loss than if those amounts were presented in profit or loss.

B5.7.6   To make that determination, an entity must assess whether it expects that the effects of changes in the liability's credit risk will be offset in profit or loss by a change in the fair value of another financial instrument measured at fair value through profit or loss. Such an expectation must be based on an economic relationship between the characteristics of the liability and the characteristics of the other financial instrument.

B5.7.7   That determination is made at initial recognition and is not reassessed. For practical purposes the entity need not enter into all of the assets and liabilities giving rise to an accounting mismatch at exactly the same time. A reasonable delay is permitted provided that any remaining transactions are expected to occur. An entity must apply consistently its methodology for determining whether presenting in other comprehensive income the effects of changes in the liability's credit risk would create or enlarge an accounting mismatch in profit or loss. However, an entity may use different methodologies when there are different economic relationships between the characteristics of the liabilities designated as at fair value through profit or loss and the characteristics of the other financial instruments. IFRS 7 requires an entity to provide qualitative disclosures in the notes to the financial statements about its methodology for making that determination.

B5.7.8   If such a mismatch would be created or enlarged, the entity is required to present all changes in fair value (including the effects of changes in the credit risk of the liability) in profit or loss. If such a mismatch would not be created or enlarged, the entity is required to present the effects of changes in the liability's credit risk in other comprehensive income.

B5.7.9   Amounts presented in other comprehensive income shall not be subsequently transferred to profit or loss. However, the entity may transfer the cumulative gain or loss within equity.

B5.7.10   The following example describes a situation in which an accounting mismatch would be created in profit or loss if the effects of changes in the credit risk of the liability were presented in other comprehensive income. A mortgage bank provides loans to customers and funds those loans by selling bonds with matching characteristics (eg amount outstanding, repayment profile, term and currency) in the market. The contractual terms of the loan permit the mortgage customer to prepay its loan (ie satisfy its obligation to the bank) by buying the corresponding bond at fair value in the market and delivering that bond to the mortgage bank. As a result of that contractual prepayment right, if the credit quality of the bond worsens (and, thus, the fair value of the mortgage bank's liability decreases), the fair value of the mortgage bank's loan asset also decreases. The change in the fair value of the asset reflects the mortgage customer's contractual right to prepay the mortgage loan by buying the underlying bond at fair value (which, in this example, has decreased) and delivering the bond to the mortgage bank. Consequently, the effects of changes in the credit risk of the liability (the bond) will be offset in profit or loss by a corresponding change in the fair value of a financial asset (the loan). If the effects of changes in the liability's credit risk were presented in other comprehensive income there would be an accounting mismatch in profit or loss. Consequently, the mortgage bank is required to present all changes in fair value of the liability (including the effects of changes in the liability's credit risk) in profit or loss.

B5.7.11   In the example in paragraph B5.7.10, there is a contractual linkage between the effects of changes in the credit risk of the liability and changes in the fair value of the financial asset (ie as a result of the mortgage customer's contractual right to prepay the loan by buying the bond at fair value and delivering the bond to the mortgage bank). However, an accounting mismatch may also occur in the absence of a contractual linkage.

B5.7.12   For the purposes of applying the requirements in paragraphs 5.7.7 and 5.7.8, an accounting mismatch is not caused solely by the measurement method that an entity uses to determine the effects of changes in a liability's credit risk. An accounting mismatch in profit or loss would arise only when the effects of changes in the liability's credit risk (as defined in IFRS 7) are expected to be offset by changes in the fair value of another financial instrument. A mismatch that arises solely as a result of the measurement method (ie because an entity does not isolate changes in a liability's credit risk from some other changes in its fair value) does not affect the determination required by paragraphs 5.7.7 and 5.7.8. For example, an entity may not isolate changes in a liability's credit risk from changes in liquidity risk. If the entity presents the combined effect of both factors in other comprehensive income, a mismatch may occur because changes in liquidity risk may be included in the fair value measurement of the entity's financial assets and the entire fair value change of those assets is presented in profit or loss. However, such a mismatch is caused by measurement imprecision, not the offsetting relationship described in paragraph B5.7.6 and, therefore, does not affect the determination required by paragraphs 5.7.7 and 5.7.8.

The meaning of 'credit risk' (paragraphs 5.7.7 and 5.7.8)

B5.7.13   IFRS 7 defines credit risk as 'the risk that one party to a financial instrument will cause a financial loss for the other party by failing to discharge an obligation'. The requirement in paragraph 5.7.7(a) relates to the risk that the issuer will fail to perform on that particular liability. It does not necessarily relate to the creditworthiness of the issuer. For example, if an entity issues a collateralised liability and a non-collateralised liability that are otherwise identical, the credit risk of those two liabilities will be different, even though they are issued by the same entity. The credit risk on the collateralised liability will be less than the credit risk of the non-collateralised liability. The credit risk for a collateralised liability may be close to zero.

B5.7.14   For the purposes of applying the requirement in paragraph 5.7.7(a), credit risk is different from asset-specific performance risk. Asset-specific performance risk is not related to the risk that an entity will fail to discharge a particular obligation but instead it is related to the risk that a single asset or a group of assets will perform poorly (or not at all).

B5.7.15   The following are examples of asset-specific performance risk:

(a)   a liability with a unit-linking feature whereby the amount due to investors is contractually determined on the basis of the performance of specified assets. The effect of that unit-linking feature on the fair value of the liability is asset-specific performance risk, not credit risk.

(b)   a liability issued by a structured entity with the following characteristics. The entity is legally isolated so the assets in the entity are ring-fenced solely for the benefit of its investors, even in the event of bankruptcy. The entity enters into no other transactions and the assets in the entity cannot be hypothecated. Amounts are due to the entity's investors only if the ring-fenced assets generate cash flows. Thus, changes in the fair value of the liability primarily reflect changes in the fair value of the assets. The effect of the performance of the assets on the fair value of the liability is asset-specific performance risk, not credit risk.

Determining the effects of changes in credit risk

B5.7.16   For the purposes of applying the requirement in paragraph 5.7.7(a), an entity shall determine the amount of change in the fair value of the financial liability that is attributable to changes in the credit risk of that liability either:

(a)   as the amount of change in its fair value that is not attributable to changes in market conditions that give rise to market risk (see paragraphs B5.7.17 and B5.7.18); or

(b)   using an alternative method the entity believes more faithfully represents the amount of change in the liability's fair value that is attributable to changes in its credit risk.

B5.7.17   Changes in market conditions that give rise to market risk include changes in a benchmark interest rate, the price of another entity's financial instrument, a commodity price, a foreign exchange rate or an index of prices or rates.

B5.7.18   If the only significant relevant changes in market conditions for a liability are changes in an observed (benchmark) interest rate, the amount in paragraph B5.7.16(a) can be estimated as follows:

(a)   First, the entity computes the liability's internal rate of return at the start of the period using the fair value of the liability and the liability's contractual cash flows at the start of the period. It deducts from this rate of return the observed (benchmark) interest rate at the start of the period, to arrive at an instrument-specific component of the internal rate of return.

(b)   Next, the entity calculates the present value of the cash flows associated with the liability using the liability's contractual cash flows at the end of the period and a discount rate equal to the sum of (i) the observed (benchmark) interest rate at the end of the period and (ii) the instrument-specific component of the internal rate of return as determined in (a).

(c)   The difference between the fair value of the liability at the end of the period and the amount determined in (b) is the change in fair value that is not attributable to changes in the observed (benchmark) interest rate. This is the amount to be presented in other comprehensive income in accordance with paragraph 5.7.7(a).

B5.7.19   The example in paragraph B5.7.18 assumes that changes in fair value arising from factors other than changes in the instrument's credit risk or changes in observed (benchmark) interest rates are not significant. This method would not be appropriate if changes in fair value arising from other factors are significant. In those cases, an entity is required to use an alternative method that more faithfully measures the effects of changes in the liability's credit risk (see paragraph B5.7.16(b)). For example, if the instrument in the example contains an embedded derivative, the change in fair value of the embedded derivative is excluded in determining the amount to be presented in other comprehensive income in accordance with paragraph 5.7.7(a).

B5.7.20 As with all fair value measurements, an entity's measurement method for determining the portion of the change in the liability's fair value that is attributable to changes in its credit risk must make maximum use of relevant observable inputs and minimum use of unobservable inputs.

Hedge accounting (Chapter 6)

Hedging instruments (Section 6.2)

Qualifying instruments

B6.2.1 Derivatives that are embedded in hybrid contracts, but that are not separately accounted for, cannot be designated as separate hedging instruments.

B6.2.2 An entity's own equity instruments are not financial assets or financial liabilities of the entity and therefore cannot be designated as hedging instruments.

B6.2.3 For hedges of foreign currency risk, the foreign currency risk component of a non-derivative financial instrument is determined in accordance with IAS 21.

Written options

B6.2.4 This Standard does not restrict the circumstances in which a derivative that is measured at fair value through profit or loss may be designated as a hedging instrument, except for some written options. A written option does not qualify as a hedging instrument unless it is designated as an offset to a purchased option, including one that is embedded in another financial instrument (for example, a written call option used to hedge a callable liability).

Designation of hedging instruments

B6.2.5 For hedges other than hedges of foreign currency risk, when an entity designates a non-derivative financial asset or a non-derivative financial liability measured at fair value through profit or loss as a hedging instrument, it may only designate the non-derivative financial instrument in its entirety or a proportion of it.

B6.2.6 A single hedging instrument may be designated as a hedging instrument of more than one type of risk, provided that there is a specific designation of the hedging instrument and of the different risk positions as hedged items. Those hedged items can be in different hedging relationships.

Hedged items (Section 6.3)

Qualifying items

B6.3.1 A firm commitment to acquire a business in a business combination cannot be a hedged item, except for foreign currency risk, because the other risks being hedged cannot be specifically identified and measured. Those other risks are general business risks.

B6.3.2 An equity method investment cannot be a hedged item in a fair value hedge. This is because the equity method recognises in profit or loss the investor's share of the investee's profit or loss, instead of changes in the investment's fair value. For a similar reason, an investment in a consolidated subsidiary cannot be a hedged item in a fair value hedge. This is because consolidation recognises in profit or loss the subsidiary's profit or loss, instead of changes in the investment's fair value. A hedge of a net investment in a foreign operation is different because it is a hedge of the foreign currency exposure, not a fair value hedge of the change in the value of the investment.

B6.3.3 Paragraph 6.3.4 permits an entity to designate as hedged items aggregated exposures that are a combination of an exposure and a derivative. When designating such a hedged item, an entity assesses whether the aggregated exposure combines an exposure with a derivative so that it creates a different aggregated exposure that is managed as one exposure for a particular risk (or risks). In that case, the entity may designate the hedged item on the basis of the aggregated exposure. For example:

(a) an entity may hedge a given quantity of highly probable coffee purchases in 15 months' time against price risk (based on US dollars) using a 15-month futures contract for coffee. The highly probable coffee purchases and the futures contract for coffee in combination can be viewed as a 15-month fixed-amount US dollar foreign currency risk exposure for risk management purposes (ie like any fixed-amount US dollar cash outflow in 15 months' time).

(b) an entity may hedge the foreign currency risk for the entire term of a 10-year fixed-rate debt denominated in a foreign currency. However, the entity requires fixed-rate exposure in its functional currency only for a short to medium term (say two years) and floating rate exposure in its functional currency for the remaining term to maturity. At the end of each of the two-year intervals (ie on a two-year rolling basis) the entity fixes the next two years' interest rate exposure (if the interest level is such that the entity wants to fix interest rates). In such a situation an entity may enter into a 10-year fixed-to-floating cross-currency interest rate swap that swaps the fixed-rate foreign currency debt into a variable-rate functional currency exposure. This is overlaid with a two-year interest rate swap that — on the basis of the functional currency — swaps variable-rate debt into fixed-rate debt. In effect, the fixed-rate foreign currency debt and the 10-year fixed-to-floating cross-currency interest rate swap in combination are viewed as a 10-year variable-rate debt functional currency exposure for risk management purposes.

B6.3.4   When designating the hedged item on the basis of the aggregated exposure, an entity considers the combined effect of the items that constitute the aggregated exposure for the purpose of assessing hedge effectiveness and measuring hedge ineffectiveness. However, the items that constitute the aggregated exposure remain accounted for separately. This means that, for example:

(a)   derivatives that are part of an aggregated exposure are recognised as separate assets or liabilities measured at fair value; and

(b)   if a hedging relationship is designated between the items that constitute the aggregated exposure, the way in which a derivative is included as part of an aggregated exposure must be consistent with the designation of that derivative as the hedging instrument at the level of the aggregated exposure. For example, if an entity excludes the forward element of a derivative from its designation as the hedging instrument for the hedging relationship between the items that constitute the aggregated exposure, it must also exclude the forward element when including that derivative as a hedged item as part of the aggregated exposure. Otherwise, the aggregated exposure shall include a derivative, either in its entirety or a proportion of it.

B6.3.5   Paragraph 6.3.6 states that in consolidated financial statements the foreign currency risk of a highly probable forecast intragroup transaction may qualify as a hedged item in a cash flow hedge, provided that the transaction is denominated in a currency other than the functional currency of the entity entering into that transaction and that the foreign currency risk will affect consolidated profit or loss. For this purpose an entity can be a parent, subsidiary, associate, joint arrangement or branch. If the foreign currency risk of a forecast intragroup transaction does not affect consolidated profit or loss, the intragroup transaction cannot qualify as a hedged item. This is usually the case for royalty payments, interest payments or management charges between members of the same group, unless there is a related external transaction. However, when the foreign currency risk of a forecast intragroup transaction will affect consolidated profit or loss, the intragroup transaction can qualify as a hedged item. An example is forecast sales or purchases of inventories between members of the same group if there is an onward sale of the inventory to a party external to the group. Similarly, a forecast intragroup sale of plant and equipment from the group entity that manufactured it to a group entity that will use the plant and equipment in its operations may affect consolidated profit or loss. This could occur, for example, because the plant and equipment will be depreciated by the purchasing entity and the amount initially recognised for the plant and equipment may change if the forecast intragroup transaction is denominated in a currency other than the functional currency of the purchasing entity.

B6.3.6   If a hedge of a forecast intragroup transaction qualifies for hedge accounting, any gain or loss is recognised in, and taken out of, other comprehensive income in accordance with paragraph 6.5.11. The relevant period or periods during which the foreign currency risk of the hedged transaction affects profit or loss is when it affects consolidated profit or loss.

Designation of hedged items

B6.3.7 A component is a hedged item that is less than the entire item. Consequently, a component reflects only some of the risks of the item of which it is a part or reflects the risks only to some extent (for example, when designating a proportion of an item).

Risk components

B6.3.8 To be eligible for designation as a hedged item, a risk component must be a separately identifiable component of the financial or the non-financial item, and the changes in the cash flows or the fair value of the item attributable to changes in that risk component must be reliably measurable.

B6.3.9 When identifying what risk components qualify for designation as a hedged item, an entity assesses such risk components within the context of the particular market structure to which the risk or risks relate and in which the hedging activity takes place. Such a determination requires an evaluation of the relevant facts and circumstances, which differ by risk and market.

B6.3.10 When designating risk components as hedged items, an entity considers whether the risk components are explicitly specified in a contract (contractually specified risk components) or whether they are implicit in the fair value or the cash flows of an item of which they are a part (non-contractually specified risk components). Non-contractually specified risk components can relate to items that are not a contract (for example, forecast transactions) or contracts that do not explicitly specify the component (for example, a firm commitment that includes only one single price instead of a pricing formula that references different underlyings). For example:

    (a) Entity A has a long-term supply contract for natural gas that is priced using a contractually specified formula that references commodities and other factors (for example, gas oil, fuel oil and other components such as transport charges). Entity A hedges the gas oil component in that supply contract using a gas oil forward contract. Because the gas oil component is specified by the terms and conditions of the supply contract it is a contractually specified risk component. Hence, because of the pricing formula, Entity A concludes that the gas oil price exposure is separately identifiable. At the same time, there is a market for gas oil forward contracts. Hence, Entity A concludes that the gas oil price exposure is reliably measurable. Consequently, the gas oil price exposure in the supply contract is a risk component that is eligible for designation as a hedged item.

    (b) Entity B hedges its future coffee purchases based on its production forecast. Hedging starts up to 15 months before delivery for part of the forecast purchase volume. Entity B increases the hedged volume over time (as the delivery date approaches). Entity B uses two different types of contracts to manage its coffee price risk:

        (i) exchange-traded coffee futures contracts; and

(ii) coffee supply contracts for Arabica coffee from Colombia delivered to a specific manufacturing site. These contracts price a tonne of coffee based on the exchange-traded coffee futures contract price plus a fixed price differential plus a variable logistics services charge using a pricing formula. The coffee supply contract is an executory contract in accordance with which Entity B takes actual delivery of coffee.

For deliveries that relate to the current harvest, entering into the coffee supply contracts allows Entity B to fix the price differential between the actual coffee quality purchased (Arabica coffee from Colombia) and the benchmark quality that is the underlying of the exchange-traded futures contract. However, for deliveries that relate to the next harvest, the coffee supply contracts are not yet available, so the price differential cannot be fixed. Entity B uses exchange-traded coffee futures contracts to hedge the benchmark quality component of its coffee price risk for deliveries that relate to the current harvest as well as the next harvest. Entity B determines that it is exposed to three different risks: coffee price risk reflecting the benchmark quality, coffee price risk reflecting the difference (spread) between the price for the benchmark quality coffee and the particular Arabica coffee from Colombia that it actually receives, and the variable logistics costs. For deliveries related to the current harvest, after Entity B enters into a coffee supply contract, the coffee price risk reflecting the benchmark quality is a contractually specified risk component because the pricing formula includes an indexation to the exchange-traded coffee futures contract price. Entity B concludes that this risk component is separately identifiable and reliably measurable. For deliveries related to the next harvest, Entity B has not yet entered into any coffee supply contracts (ie those deliveries are forecast transactions). Hence, the coffee price risk reflecting the benchmark quality is a non-contractually specified risk component. Entity B's analysis of the market structure takes into account how eventual deliveries of the particular coffee that it receives are priced. Hence, on the basis of this analysis of the market structure, Entity B concludes that the forecast transactions also involve the coffee price risk that reflects the benchmark quality as a risk component that is separately identifiable and reliably measurable even though it is not contractually specified. Consequently, Entity B may designate hedging relationships on a risk components basis (for the coffee price risk that reflects the benchmark quality) for coffee supply contracts as well as forecast transactions.

(c) Entity C hedges part of its future jet fuel purchases on the basis of its consumption forecast up to 24 months before delivery and increases the volume that it hedges over time. Entity C hedges this exposure using different types of contracts depending on the time horizon of the hedge, which affects the market liquidity of the derivatives. For the longer time horizons (12–24 months) Entity C uses crude oil contracts because only these have sufficient market liquidity. For time horizons of 6–12 months Entity C uses gas oil derivatives because they are sufficiently liquid. For time horizons up to six months Entity C uses jet fuel contracts. Entity C's analysis of the market structure for oil and oil products and its evaluation of the relevant facts and circumstances is as follows:

(i)   Entity C operates in a geographical area in which Brent is the crude oil benchmark. Crude oil is a raw material benchmark that affects the price of various refined oil products as their most basic input. Gas oil is a benchmark for refined oil products, which is used as a pricing reference for oil distillates more generally. This is also reflected in the types of derivative financial instruments for the crude oil and refined oil products markets of the environment in which Entity C operates, such as:

- the benchmark crude oil futures contract, which is for Brent crude oil;

- the benchmark gas oil futures contract, which is used as the pricing reference for distillates—for example, jet fuel spread derivatives cover the price differential between jet fuel and that benchmark gas oil; and

- the benchmark gas oil crack spread derivative (ie the derivative for the price differential between crude oil and gas oil—a refining margin), which is indexed to Brent crude oil.

(ii)   the pricing of refined oil products does not depend on which particular crude oil is processed by a particular refinery because those refined oil products (such as gas oil or jet fuel) are standardised products.

Hence, Entity C concludes that the price risk of its jet fuel purchases includes a crude oil price risk component based on Brent crude oil and a gas oil price risk component, even though crude oil and gas oil are not specified in any contractual arrangement. Entity C concludes that these two risk components are separately identifiable and reliably measurable even though they are not contractually specified. Consequently, Entity C may designate hedging relationships for forecast jet fuel purchases on a risk components basis (for crude oil or gas oil). This analysis also means that if, for example, Entity C used crude oil derivatives based on West Texas Intermediate (WTI) crude oil, changes in the price differential between Brent crude oil and WTI crude oil would cause hedge ineffectiveness.

(d)   Entity D holds a fixed-rate debt instrument. This instrument is issued in an environment with a market in which a large variety of similar debt instruments are compared by their spreads to a benchmark rate (for example, LIBOR) and variable-rate instruments in that environment are typically indexed to that benchmark rate. Interest rate swaps are frequently used to manage interest rate risk on the basis of that benchmark rate, irrespective of the spread of debt instruments to that benchmark rate. The price of fixed-rate debt instruments varies directly in response to changes in the benchmark rate as they happen. Entity D concludes that the benchmark rate is a component that can be separately identified and reliably measured. Consequently, Entity D may designate hedging relationships for the fixed-rate debt instrument on a risk component basis for the benchmark interest rate risk.

B6.3.11 When designating a risk component as a hedged item, the hedge accounting requirements apply to that risk component in the same way as they apply to other hedged items that are not risk components. For example, the qualifying criteria apply, including that the hedging relationship must meet the hedge effectiveness requirements, and any hedge ineffectiveness must be measured and recognised.

B6.3.12 An entity can also designate only changes in the cash flows or fair value of a hedged item above or below a specified price or other variable (a 'one-sided risk'). The intrinsic value of a purchased option hedging instrument (assuming that it has the same principal terms as the designated risk), but not its time value, reflects a one-sided risk in a hedged item. For example, an entity can designate the variability of future cash flow outcomes resulting from a price increase of a forecast commodity purchase. In such a situation, the entity designates only cash flow losses that result from an increase in the price above the specified level. The hedged risk does not include the time value of a purchased option, because the time value is not a component of the forecast transaction that affects profit or loss.

B6.3.13 There is a rebuttable presumption that unless inflation risk is contractually specified, it is not separately identifiable and reliably measurable and hence cannot be designated as a risk component of a financial instrument. However, in limited cases, it is possible to identify a risk component for inflation risk that is separately identifiable and reliably measurable because of the particular circumstances of the inflation environment and the relevant debt market.

B6.3.14 For example, an entity issues debt in an environment in which inflation-linked bonds have a volume and term structure that results in a sufficiently liquid market that allows constructing a term structure of zero-coupon real interest rates. This means that for the respective currency, inflation is a relevant factor that is separately considered by the debt markets. In those circumstances the inflation risk component could be determined by discounting the cash flows of the hedged debt instrument using the term structure of zero-coupon real interest rates (ie in a manner similar to how a risk-free (nominal) interest rate component can be determined). Conversely, in many cases an inflation risk component is not separately identifiable and reliably measurable. For example, an entity issues only nominal interest rate debt in an environment with a market for inflation-linked bonds that is not sufficiently liquid to allow a term structure of zero-coupon real interest rates to be constructed. In this case the analysis of the market structure and of the facts and circumstances does not support the entity concluding that inflation is a relevant factor that is separately considered by the debt markets. Hence, the entity cannot overcome the rebuttable presumption that inflation risk that is not contractually specified is not separately identifiable and reliably measurable. Consequently, an inflation risk component would not be eligible for designation as the hedged item. This applies irrespective of any inflation hedging instrument that the entity has actually entered into. In particular, the entity cannot simply impute the terms and conditions of the actual inflation hedging instrument by projecting its terms and conditions onto the nominal interest rate debt.

B6.3.15 A contractually specified inflation risk component of the cash flows of a recognised inflation-linked bond (assuming that there is no requirement to account for an embedded derivative separately) is separately identifiable and reliably measurable, as long as other cash flows of the instrument are not affected by the inflation risk component.

Components of a nominal amount

B6.3.16 There are two types of components of nominal amounts that can be designated as the hedged item in a hedging relationship: a component that is a proportion of an entire item or a layer component. The type of component changes the accounting outcome. An entity shall designate the component for accounting purposes consistently with its risk management objective.

B6.3.17 An example of a component that is a proportion is 50 per cent of the contractual cash flows of a loan.

B6.3.18 A layer component may be specified from a defined, but open, population, or from a defined nominal amount. Examples include:

(a) part of a monetary transaction volume, for example, the next FC10 cash flows from sales denominated in a foreign currency after the first FC20 in March 201X;[5]

(b) a part of a physical volume, for example, the bottom layer, measuring 5 million cubic metres, of the natural gas stored in location XYZ;

(c) a part of a physical or other transaction volume, for example, the first 100 barrels of the oil purchases in June 201X or the first 100 MWh of electricity sales in June 201X; or

(d) a layer from the nominal amount of the hedged item, for example, the last CU80 million of a CU100 million firm commitment, the bottom layer of CU20 million of a CU100 million fixed-rate bond or the top layer of CU30 million from a total amount of CU100 million of fixed-rate debt that can be prepaid at fair value (the defined nominal amount is CU100 million).

B6.3.19 If a layer component is designated in a fair value hedge, an entity shall specify it from a defined nominal amount. To comply with the requirements for qualifying fair value hedges, an entity shall remeasure the hedged item for fair value changes (ie remeasure the item for fair value changes attributable to

---

5   In this Standard monetary amounts are denominated in 'currency units' (CU) and 'foreign currency units' (FC).

the hedged risk). The fair value hedge adjustment must be recognised in profit or loss no later than when the item is derecognised. Consequently, it is necessary to track the item to which the fair value hedge adjustment relates. For a layer component in a fair value hedge, this requires an entity to track the nominal amount from which it is defined. For example, in paragraph B6.3.18(d), the total defined nominal amount of CU100 million must be tracked in order to track the bottom layer of CU20 million or the top layer of CU30 million.

B6.3.20 A layer component that includes a prepayment option is not eligible to be designated as a hedged item in a fair value hedge if the prepayment option's fair value is affected by changes in the hedged risk, unless the designated layer includes the effect of the related prepayment option when determining the change in the fair value of the hedged item.

Relationship between components and the total cash flows of an item

B6.3.21 If a component of the cash flows of a financial or a non-financial item is designated as the hedged item, that component must be less than or equal to the total cash flows of the entire item. However, all of the cash flows of the entire item may be designated as the hedged item and hedged for only one particular risk (for example, only for those changes that are attributable to changes in LIBOR or a benchmark commodity price).

B6.3.22 For example, in the case of a financial liability whose effective interest rate is below LIBOR, an entity cannot designate:

(a)   a component of the liability equal to interest at LIBOR (plus the principal amount in case of a fair value hedge); and

(b)   a negative residual component.

B6.3.23 However, in the case of a fixed-rate financial liability whose effective interest rate is (for example) 100 basis points below LIBOR, an entity can designate as the hedged item the change in the value of that entire liability (ie principal plus interest at LIBOR minus 100 basis points) that is attributable to changes in LIBOR. If a fixed-rate financial instrument is hedged some time after its origination and interest rates have changed in the meantime, the entity can designate a risk component equal to a benchmark rate that is higher than the contractual rate paid on the item. The entity can do so provided that the benchmark rate is less than the effective interest rate calculated on the assumption that the entity had purchased the instrument on the day when it first designates the hedged item. For example, assume that an entity originates a fixed-rate financial asset of CU100 that has an effective interest rate of 6 per cent at a time when LIBOR is 4 per cent. It begins to hedge that asset some time later when LIBOR has increased to 8 per cent and the fair value of the asset has decreased to CU90. The entity calculates that if it had purchased the asset on the date it first designates the related LIBOR interest rate risk as the hedged item, the effective yield of the asset based on its then fair value of CU90 would have been 9.5 per cent. Because LIBOR is less than this effective yield, the entity can designate a LIBOR component of 8 per cent that consists partly of the contractual interest cash flows and partly of the difference between the current fair value (ie CU90) and the amount repayable on maturity (ie CU100).

B6.3.24 If a variable-rate financial liability bears interest of (for example) three-month LIBOR minus 20 basis points (with a floor at zero basis points), an entity can designate as the hedged item the change in the cash flows of that entire liability (ie three-month LIBOR minus 20 basis points – including the floor) that is attributable to changes in LIBOR. Hence, as long as the three-month LIBOR forward curve for the remaining life of that liability does not fall below 20 basis points, the hedged item has the same cash flow variability as a liability that bears interest at three-month LIBOR with a zero or positive spread. However, if the three-month LIBOR forward curve for the remaining life of that liability (or a part of it) falls below 20 basis points, the hedged item has a lower cash flow variability than a liability that bears interest at three-month LIBOR with a zero or positive spread.

B6.3.25 A similar example of a non-financial item is a specific type of crude oil from a particular oil field that is priced off the relevant benchmark crude oil. If an entity sells that crude oil under a contract using a contractual pricing formula that sets the price per barrel at the benchmark crude oil price minus CU10 with a floor of CU15, the entity can designate as the hedged item the entire cash flow variability under the sales contract that is attributable to the change in the benchmark crude oil price. However, the entity cannot designate a component that is equal to the full change in the benchmark crude oil price. Hence, as long as the forward price (for each delivery) does not fall below CU25, the hedged item has the same cash flow variability as a crude oil sale at the benchmark crude oil price (or with a positive spread). However, if the forward price for any delivery falls below CU25, the hedged item has a lower cash flow variability than a crude oil sale at the benchmark crude oil price (or with a positive spread).

Qualifying criteria for hedge accounting (Section 6.4)

Hedge effectiveness

B6.4.1 Hedge effectiveness is the extent to which changes in the fair value or the cash flows of the hedging instrument offset changes in the fair value or the cash flows of the hedged item (for example, when the hedged item is a risk component, the relevant change in fair value or cash flows of an item is the one that is attributable to the hedged risk). Hedge ineffectiveness is the extent to which the changes in the fair value or the cash flows of the hedging instrument are greater or less than those on the hedged item.

B6.4.2 When designating a hedging relationship and on an ongoing basis, an entity shall analyse the sources of hedge ineffectiveness that are expected to affect the hedging relationship during its term. This analysis (including any updates in accordance with paragraph B6.5.21 arising from rebalancing a hedging relationship) is the basis for the entity's assessment of meeting the hedge effectiveness requirements.

B6.4.3   For the avoidance of doubt, the effects of replacing the original counterparty with a clearing counterparty and making the associated changes as described in paragraph 6.5.6 shall be reflected in the measurement of the hedging instrument and therefore in the assessment of hedge effectiveness and the measurement of hedge effectiveness.

Economic relationship between the hedged item and the hedging instrument

B6.4.4   The requirement that an economic relationship exists means that the hedging instrument and the hedged item have values that generally move in the opposite direction because of the same risk, which is the hedged risk. Hence, there must be an expectation that the value of the hedging instrument and the value of the hedged item will systematically change in response to movements in either the same underlying or underlyings that are economically related in such a way that they respond in a similar way to the risk that is being hedged (for example, Brent and WTI crude oil).

B6.4.5   If the underlyings are not the same but are economically related, there can be situations in which the values of the hedging instrument and the hedged item move in the same direction, for example, because the price differential between the two related underlyings changes while the underlyings themselves do not move significantly. That is still consistent with an economic relationship between the hedging instrument and the hedged item if the values of the hedging instrument and the hedged item are still expected to typically move in the opposite direction when the underlyings move.

B6.4.6   The assessment of whether an economic relationship exists includes an analysis of the possible behaviour of the hedging relationship during its term to ascertain whether it can be expected to meet the risk management objective. The mere existence of a statistical correlation between two variables does not, by itself, support a valid conclusion that an economic relationship exists.

The effect of credit risk

B6.4.7   Because the hedge accounting model is based on a general notion of offset between gains and losses on the hedging instrument and the hedged item, hedge effectiveness is determined not only by the economic relationship between those items (ie the changes in their underlyings) but also by the effect of credit risk on the value of both the hedging instrument and the hedged item. The effect of credit risk means that even if there is an economic relationship between the hedging instrument and the hedged item, the level of offset might become erratic. This can result from a change in the credit risk of either the hedging instrument or the hedged item that is of such a magnitude that the credit risk dominates the value changes that result from the economic relationship (ie the effect of the changes in the underlyings). A level of magnitude that gives rise to dominance is one that would result in the loss (or gain) from credit risk frustrating the effect of changes in the underlyings on the value of the hedging instrument or the hedged item, even if those changes were significant. Conversely, if during a particular period there is little change in the underlyings, the fact that even small credit risk-related changes in the value of the hedging instrument or the hedged item might affect the value more than the underlyings does not create dominance.

B6.4.8 An example of credit risk dominating a hedging relationship is when an entity hedges an exposure to commodity price risk using an uncollateralised derivative. If the counterparty to that derivative experiences a severe deterioration in its credit standing, the effect of the changes in the counterparty's credit standing might outweigh the effect of changes in the commodity price on the fair value of the hedging instrument, whereas changes in the value of the hedged item depend largely on the commodity price changes.

Hedge ratio

B6.4.9 In accordance with the hedge effectiveness requirements, the hedge ratio of the hedging relationship must be the same as that resulting from the quantity of the hedged item that the entity actually hedges and the quantity of the hedging instrument that the entity actually uses to hedge that quantity of hedged item. Hence, if an entity hedges less than 100 per cent of the exposure on an item, such as 85 per cent, it shall designate the hedging relationship using a hedge ratio that is the same as that resulting from 85 per cent of the exposure and the quantity of the hedging instrument that the entity actually uses to hedge those 85 per cent. Similarly, if, for example, an entity hedges an exposure using a nominal amount of 40 units of a financial instrument, it shall designate the hedging relationship using a hedge ratio that is the same as that resulting from that quantity of 40 units (ie the entity must not use a hedge ratio based on a higher quantity of units that it might hold in total or a lower quantity of units) and the quantity of the hedged item that it actually hedges with those 40 units.

B6.4.10 However, the designation of the hedging relationship using the same hedge ratio as that resulting from the quantities of the hedged item and the hedging instrument that the entity actually uses shall not reflect an imbalance between the weightings of the hedged item and the hedging instrument that would in turn create hedge ineffectiveness (irrespective of whether recognised or not) that could result in an accounting outcome that would be inconsistent with the purpose of hedge accounting. Hence, for the purpose of designating a hedging relationship, an entity must adjust the hedge ratio that results from the quantities of the hedged item and the hedging instrument that the entity actually uses if that is needed to avoid such an imbalance.

B6.4.11 Examples of relevant considerations in assessing whether an accounting outcome is inconsistent with the purpose of hedge accounting are:

(a) whether the intended hedge ratio is established to avoid recognising hedge ineffectiveness for cash flow hedges, or to achieve fair value hedge adjustments for more hedged items with the aim of increasing the use of fair value accounting, but without offsetting fair value changes of the hedging instrument; and

(b)   whether there is a commercial reason for the particular weightings of the hedged item and the hedging instrument, even though that creates hedge ineffectiveness. For example, an entity enters into and designates a quantity of the hedging instrument that is not the quantity that it determined as the best hedge of the hedged item because the standard volume of the hedging instruments does not allow it to enter into that exact quantity of hedging instrument (a 'lot size issue'). An example is an entity that hedges 100 tonnes of coffee purchases with standard coffee futures contracts that have a contract size of 37,500 lbs (pounds). The entity could only use either five or six contracts (equivalent to 85.0 and 102.1 tonnes respectively) to hedge the purchase volume of 100 tonnes. In that case, the entity designates the hedging relationship using the hedge ratio that results from the number of coffee futures contracts that it actually uses, because the hedge ineffectiveness resulting from the mismatch in the weightings of the hedged item and the hedging instrument would not result in an accounting outcome that is inconsistent with the purpose of hedge accounting.

Frequency of assessing whether the hedge effectiveness requirements are met

B6.4.12   An entity shall assess at the inception of the hedging relationship, and on an ongoing basis, whether a hedging relationship meets the hedge effectiveness requirements. At a minimum, an entity shall perform the ongoing assessment at each reporting date or upon a significant change in the circumstances affecting the hedge effectiveness requirements, whichever comes first. The assessment relates to expectations about hedge effectiveness and is therefore only forward-looking.

Methods for assessing whether the hedge effectiveness requirements are met

B6.4.13   This Standard does not specify a method for assessing whether a hedging relationship meets the hedge effectiveness requirements. However, an entity shall use a method that captures the relevant characteristics of the hedging relationship including the sources of hedge ineffectiveness. Depending on those factors, the method can be a qualitative or a quantitative assessment.

B6.4.14   For example, when the critical terms (such as the nominal amount, maturity and underlying) of the hedging instrument and the hedged item match or are closely aligned, it might be possible for an entity to conclude on the basis of a qualitative assessment of those critical terms that the hedging instrument and the hedged item have values that will generally move in the opposite direction because of the same risk and hence that an economic relationship exists between the hedged item and the hedging instrument (see paragraphs B6.4.4–B6.4.6).

B6.4.15   The fact that a derivative is in or out of the money when it is designated as a hedging instrument does not in itself mean that a qualitative assessment is inappropriate. It depends on the circumstances whether hedge ineffectiveness arising from that fact could have a magnitude that a qualitative assessment would not adequately capture.

B6.4.16   Conversely, if the critical terms of the hedging instrument and the hedged item are not closely aligned, there is an increased level of uncertainty about the extent of offset. Consequently, the hedge effectiveness during the term of the hedging relationship is more difficult to predict. In such a situation it might only be possible for an entity to conclude on the basis of a quantitative assessment that an economic relationship exists between the hedged item and the hedging instrument (see paragraphs B6.4.4–B6.4.6). In some situations a quantitative assessment might also be needed to assess whether the hedge ratio used for designating the hedging relationship meets the hedge effectiveness requirements (see paragraphs B6.4.9–B6.4.11). An entity can use the same or different methods for those two different purposes.

B6.4.17   If there are changes in circumstances that affect hedge effectiveness, an entity may have to change the method for assessing whether a hedging relationship meets the hedge effectiveness requirements in order to ensure that the relevant characteristics of the hedging relationship, including the sources of hedge ineffectiveness, are still captured.

B6.4.18   An entity's risk management is the main source of information to perform the assessment of whether a hedging relationship meets the hedge effectiveness requirements. This means that the management information (or analysis) used for decision-making purposes can be used as a basis for assessing whether a hedging relationship meets the hedge effectiveness requirements.

B6.4.19   An entity's documentation of the hedging relationship includes how it will assess the hedge effectiveness requirements, including the method or methods used. The documentation of the hedging relationship shall be updated for any changes to the methods (see paragraph B6.4.17).

Accounting for qualifying hedging relationships (Section 6.5)

B6.5.1   An example of a fair value hedge is a hedge of exposure to changes in the fair value of a fixed-rate debt instrument arising from changes in interest rates. Such a hedge could be entered into by the issuer or by the holder.

B6.5.2   The purpose of a cash flow hedge is to defer the gain or loss on the hedging instrument to a period or periods in which the hedged expected future cash flows affect profit or loss. An example of a cash flow hedge is the use of a swap to change floating rate debt (whether measured at amortised cost or fair value) to fixed-rate debt (ie a hedge of a future transaction in which the future cash flows being hedged are the future interest payments). Conversely, a forecast purchase of an equity instrument that, once acquired, will be accounted for at fair value through profit or loss, is an example of an item that cannot be the hedged item in a cash flow hedge, because any gain or loss on the hedging instrument that would be deferred could not be appropriately reclassified to profit or loss during a period in which it would achieve offset. For the same reason, a forecast purchase of an equity instrument that, once acquired, will be accounted for at fair value with changes in fair value presented in other comprehensive income also cannot be the hedged item in a cash flow hedge.

B6.5.3 A hedge of a firm commitment (for example, a hedge of the change in fuel price relating to an unrecognised contractual commitment by an electric utility to purchase fuel at a fixed price) is a hedge of an exposure to a change in fair value. Accordingly, such a hedge is a fair value hedge. However, in accordance with paragraph 6.5.4, a hedge of the foreign currency risk of a firm commitment could alternatively be accounted for as a cash flow hedge.

Measurement of hedge ineffectiveness

B6.5.4 When measuring hedge ineffectiveness, an entity shall consider the time value of money. Consequently, the entity determines the value of the hedged item on a present value basis and therefore the change in the value of the hedged item also includes the effect of the time value of money.

B6.5.5 To calculate the change in the value of the hedged item for the purpose of measuring hedge ineffectiveness, an entity may use a derivative that would have terms that match the critical terms of the hedged item (this is commonly referred to as a 'hypothetical derivative'), and, for example for a hedge of a forecast transaction, would be calibrated using the hedged price (or rate) level. For example, if the hedge was for a two-sided risk at the current market level, the hypothetical derivative would represent a hypothetical forward contract that is calibrated to a value of nil at the time of designation of the hedging relationship. If the hedge was for example for a one-sided risk, the hypothetical derivative would represent the intrinsic value of a hypothetical option that at the time of designation of the hedging relationship is at the money if the hedged price level is the current market level, or out of the money if the hedged price level is above (or, for a hedge of a long position, below) the current market level. Using a hypothetical derivative is one possible way of calculating the change in the value of the hedged item. The hypothetical derivative replicates the hedged item and hence results in the same outcome as if that change in value was determined by a different approach. Hence, using a 'hypothetical derivative' is not a method in its own right but a mathematical expedient that can only be used to calculate the value of the hedged item. Consequently, a 'hypothetical derivative' cannot be used to include features in the value of the hedged item that only exist in the hedging instrument (but not in the hedged item). An example is debt denominated in a foreign currency (irrespective of whether it is fixed-rate or variable-rate debt). When using a hypothetical derivative to calculate the change in the value of such debt or the present value of the cumulative change in its cash flows, the hypothetical derivative cannot simply impute a charge for exchanging different currencies even though actual derivatives under which different currencies are exchanged might include such a charge (for example, cross-currency interest rate swaps).

B6.5.6   The change in the value of the hedged item determined using a hypothetical derivative may also be used for the purpose of assessing whether a hedging relationship meets the hedge effectiveness requirements.

Rebalancing the hedging relationship and changes to the hedge ratio

B6.5.7   Rebalancing refers to the adjustments made to the designated quantities of the hedged item or the hedging instrument of an already existing hedging relationship for the purpose of maintaining a hedge ratio that complies with the hedge effectiveness requirements. Changes to designated quantities of a hedged item or of a hedging instrument for a different purpose do not constitute rebalancing for the purpose of this Standard.

B6.5.8   Rebalancing is accounted for as a continuation of the hedging relationship in accordance with paragraphs B6.5.9–B6.5.21. On rebalancing, the hedge ineffectiveness of the hedging relationship is determined and recognised immediately before adjusting the hedging relationship.

B6.5.9   Adjusting the hedge ratio allows an entity to respond to changes in the relationship between the hedging instrument and the hedged item that arise from their underlyings or risk variables. For example, a hedging relationship in which the hedging instrument and the hedged item have different but related underlyings changes in response to a change in the relationship between those two underlyings (for example, different but related reference indices, rates or prices). Hence, rebalancing allows the continuation of a hedging relationship in situations in which the relationship between the hedging instrument and the hedged item changes in a way that can be compensated for by adjusting the hedge ratio.

B6.5.10   For example, an entity hedges an exposure to Foreign Currency A using a currency derivative that references Foreign Currency B and Foreign Currencies A and B are pegged (ie their exchange rate is maintained within a band or at an exchange rate set by a central bank or other authority). If the exchange rate between Foreign Currency A and Foreign Currency B were changed (ie a new band or rate was set), rebalancing the hedging relationship to reflect the new exchange rate would ensure that the hedging relationship would continue to meet the hedge effectiveness requirement for the hedge ratio in the new circumstances. In contrast, if there was a default on the currency derivative, changing the hedge ratio could not ensure that the hedging relationship would continue to meet that hedge effectiveness requirement. Hence, rebalancing does not facilitate the continuation of a hedging relationship in situations in which the relationship between the hedging instrument and the hedged item changes in a way that cannot be compensated for by adjusting the hedge ratio.

B6.5.11   Not every change in the extent of offset between the changes in the fair value of the hedging instrument and the hedged item's fair value or cash flows constitutes a change in the relationship between the hedging instrument and the hedged item. An entity analyses the sources of hedge ineffectiveness that it expected to affect the hedging relationship during its term and evaluates whether changes in the extent of offset are:

(a)   fluctuations around the hedge ratio, which remains valid (ie continues to appropriately reflect the relationship between the hedging instrument and the hedged item); or

(b)   an indication that the hedge ratio no longer appropriately reflects the relationship between the hedging instrument and the hedged item.

An entity performs this evaluation against the hedge effectiveness requirement for the hedge ratio, ie to ensure that the hedging relationship does not reflect an imbalance between the weightings of the hedged item and the hedging instrument that would create hedge ineffectiveness (irrespective of whether recognised or not) that could result in an accounting outcome that would be inconsistent with the purpose of hedge accounting. Hence, this evaluation requires judgement.

B6.5.12   Fluctuation around a constant hedge ratio (and hence the related hedge ineffectiveness) cannot be reduced by adjusting the hedge ratio in response to each particular outcome. Hence, in such circumstances, the change in the extent of offset is a matter of measuring and recognising hedge ineffectiveness but does not require rebalancing.

B6.5.13   Conversely, if changes in the extent of offset indicate that the fluctuation is around a hedge ratio that is different from the hedge ratio that is currently used for that hedging relationship, or that there is a trend leading away from that hedge ratio, hedge ineffectiveness can be reduced by adjusting the hedge ratio, whereas retaining the hedge ratio would increasingly produce hedge ineffectiveness. Hence, in such circumstances, an entity must evaluate whether the hedging relationship reflects an imbalance between the weightings of the hedged item and the hedging instrument that would create hedge ineffectiveness (irrespective of whether recognised or not) that could result in an accounting outcome that would be inconsistent with the purpose of hedge accounting. If the hedge ratio is adjusted, it also affects the measurement and recognition of hedge ineffectiveness because, on rebalancing, the hedge ineffectiveness of the hedging relationship must be determined and recognised immediately before adjusting the hedging relationship in accordance with paragraph B6.5.8.

B6.5.14   Rebalancing means that, for hedge accounting purposes, after the start of a hedging relationship an entity adjusts the quantities of the hedging instrument or the hedged item in response to changes in circumstances that affect the hedge ratio of that hedging relationship. Typically, that adjustment should reflect adjustments in the quantities of the hedging instrument and the hedged item that it actually uses. However, an entity must adjust the hedge ratio that results from the quantities of the hedged item or the hedging instrument that it actually uses if:

(a)   the hedge ratio that results from changes to the quantities of the hedging instrument or the hedged item that the entity actually uses would reflect an imbalance that would create hedge ineffectiveness that could result in an accounting outcome that would be inconsistent with the purpose of hedge accounting; or

(b)   an entity would retain quantities of the hedging instrument and the hedged item that it actually uses, resulting in a hedge ratio that, in new circumstances, would reflect an imbalance that would create hedge ineffectiveness that could result in an accounting outcome that would be inconsistent with the purpose of hedge accounting (ie an entity must not create an imbalance by omitting to adjust the hedge ratio).

B6.5.15   Rebalancing does not apply if the risk management objective for a hedging relationship has changed. Instead, hedge accounting for that hedging relationship shall be discontinued (despite that an entity might designate a new hedging relationship that involves the hedging instrument or hedged item of the previous hedging relationship as described in paragraph B6.5.28).

B6.5.16   If a hedging relationship is rebalanced, the adjustment to the hedge ratio can be effected in different ways:

(a)   the weighting of the hedged item can be increased (which at the same time reduces the weighting of the hedging instrument) by:

(i)   increasing the volume of the hedged item; or

(ii)   decreasing the volume of the hedging instrument.

(b)   the weighting of the hedging instrument can be increased (which at the same time reduces the weighting of the hedged item) by:

(i)   increasing the volume of the hedging instrument; or

(ii)   decreasing the volume of the hedged item.

Changes in volume refer to the quantities that are part of the hedging relationship. Hence, decreases in volumes do not necessarily mean that the items or transactions no longer exist, or are no longer expected to occur, but that they are not part of the hedging relationship. For example, decreasing the volume of the hedging instrument can result in the entity retaining a derivative, but only part of it might remain a hedging instrument of the hedging relationship. This could occur if the rebalancing could be effected only by reducing the volume of the hedging instrument in the hedging relationship, but with the entity retaining the volume that is no longer needed. In that case, the undesignated part of the derivative would be accounted for at fair value through profit or loss (unless it was designated as a hedging instrument in a different hedging relationship).

B6.5.17   Adjusting the hedge ratio by increasing the volume of the hedged item does not affect how the changes in the fair value of the hedging instrument are measured. The measurement of the changes in the value of the hedged item related to the previously designated volume also remains unaffected. However, from the date of rebalancing, the changes in the value of the hedged item also include the change in the value of the additional volume of the hedged item. These changes are measured starting from, and by reference to, the date of rebalancing instead of the date on which the hedging relationship was designated. For example, if an entity originally hedged a volume of 100 tonnes of a commodity at a forward price of CU80 (the forward price at inception of the hedging relationship) and added a volume of 10 tonnes on rebalancing when the forward price was CU90, the hedged item after rebalancing would comprise two layers: 100 tonnes hedged at CU80 and 10 tonnes hedged at CU90.

B6.5.18   Adjusting the hedge ratio by decreasing the volume of the hedging instrument does not affect how the changes in the value of the hedged item are measured. The measurement of the changes in the fair value of the hedging instrument related to the volume that continues to be designated also remains unaffected. However, from the date of rebalancing, the volume by which the hedging instrument was decreased is no longer part of the hedging relationship. For example, if an entity originally hedged the price risk of a commodity using a derivative volume of 100 tonnes as the hedging instrument and reduces that volume by 10 tonnes on rebalancing, a nominal amount of 90 tonnes of the hedging instrument volume would remain (see paragraph B6.5.16 for the consequences for the derivative volume (ie the 10 tonnes) that is no longer a part of the hedging relationship).

B6.5.19   Adjusting the hedge ratio by increasing the volume of the hedging instrument does not affect how the changes in the value of the hedged item are measured. The measurement of the changes in the fair value of the hedging instrument related to the previously designated volume also remains unaffected. However, from the date of rebalancing, the changes in the fair value of the hedging instrument also include the changes in the value of the additional volume of the hedging instrument. The changes are measured starting from, and by reference to, the date of rebalancing instead of the date on which the hedging relationship was designated. For example, if an entity originally hedged the price risk of a commodity using a derivative volume of 100 tonnes as the hedging instrument and added a volume of 10 tonnes on rebalancing, the hedging instrument after rebalancing would comprise a total derivative volume of 110 tonnes. The change in the fair value of the hedging instrument is the total change in the fair value of the derivatives that make up the total volume of 110 tonnes. These derivatives could (and probably would) have different critical terms, such as their forward rates, because they were entered into at different points in time (including the possibility of designating derivatives into hedging relationships after their initial recognition).

B6.5.20   Adjusting the hedge ratio by decreasing the volume of the hedged item does not affect how the changes in the fair value of the hedging instrument are measured. The measurement of the changes in the value of the hedged item related to the volume that continues to be designated also remains unaffected. However, from the date of rebalancing, the volume by which the hedged item was decreased is no longer part of the hedging relationship. For example, if an entity originally hedged a volume of 100 tonnes of a commodity at a forward price of CU80 and reduces that volume by 10 tonnes on rebalancing, the hedged item after rebalancing would be 90 tonnes hedged at CU80. The 10 tonnes of the hedged item that are no longer part of the hedging relationship would be accounted for in accordance with the requirements for the discontinuation of hedge accounting (see paragraphs 6.5.6–6.5.7 and B6.5.22–B6.5.28).

B6.5.21   When rebalancing a hedging relationship, an entity shall update its analysis of the sources of hedge ineffectiveness that are expected to affect the hedging relationship during its (remaining) term (see paragraph B6.4.2). The documentation of the hedging relationship shall be updated accordingly.

Discontinuation of hedge accounting

B6.5.22   Discontinuation of hedge accounting applies prospectively from the date on which the qualifying criteria are no longer met.

B6.5.23   An entity shall not de-designate and thereby discontinue a hedging relationship that:

(a)   still meets the risk management objective on the basis of which it qualified for hedge accounting (ie the entity still pursues that risk management objective); and

(b)   continues to meet all other qualifying criteria (after taking into account any rebalancing of the hedging relationship, if applicable).

B6.5.24   For the purposes of this Standard, an entity's risk management strategy is distinguished from its risk management objectives. The risk management strategy is established at the highest level at which an entity determines how it manages its risk. Risk management strategies typically identify the risks to which the entity is exposed and set out how the entity responds to them. A risk management strategy is typically in place for a longer period and may include some flexibility to react to changes in circumstances that occur while that strategy is in place (for example, different interest rate or commodity price levels that result in a different extent of hedging). This is normally set out in a general document that is cascaded down through an entity through policies containing more specific guidelines. In contrast, the risk management objective for a hedging relationship applies at the level of a particular hedging relationship. It relates to how the particular hedging instrument that has been designated is used to hedge the particular exposure that has been designated as the hedged item. Hence, a risk management strategy can involve many different hedging relationships whose risk management objectives relate to executing that overall risk management strategy. For example:

(a)   an entity has a strategy of managing its interest rate exposure on debt funding that sets ranges for the overall entity for the mix between variable-rate and fixed-rate funding. The strategy is to maintain between 20 per cent and 40 per cent of the debt at fixed rates. The entity decides from time to time how to execute this strategy (ie where it positions itself within the 20 per cent to 40 per cent range for fixed-rate interest exposure) depending on the level of interest rates. If interest rates are low the entity fixes the interest for more debt than when interest rates are high. The entity's debt is CU100 of variable-rate debt of which CU30 is swapped into a fixed-rate exposure. The entity takes advantage of low interest rates to issue an additional CU50 of debt to finance a major investment, which the entity does by issuing a fixed-rate bond. In the light of the low interest rates, the entity decides to set its fixed interest-rate exposure to 40 per cent of the total debt by reducing by CU20 the extent to which it previously hedged its variable-rate exposure, resulting in CU60 of fixed-rate exposure. In this situation the risk management strategy itself remains unchanged. However, in contrast the entity's execution of that strategy has changed and this means that, for CU20 of variable-rate exposure that was previously hedged, the risk management objective has changed (ie at the hedging relationship level). Consequently, in this situation hedge accounting must be discontinued for CU20 of the previously hedged variable-rate exposure. This could involve reducing the swap position by a CU20 nominal amount but, depending on the circumstances, an entity might retain that swap volume and, for example, use it for hedging a different exposure or it might become part of a trading book. Conversely, if an entity instead swapped a part of its new fixed-rate debt into a variable-rate exposure, hedge accounting would have to be continued for its previously hedged variable-rate exposure.

(b) some exposures result from positions that frequently change, for example, the interest rate risk of an open portfolio of debt instruments. The addition of new debt instruments and the derecognition of debt instruments continuously change that exposure (ie it is different from simply running off a position that matures). This is a dynamic process in which both the exposure and the hedging instruments used to manage it do not remain the same for long. Consequently, an entity with such an exposure frequently adjusts the hedging instruments used to manage the interest rate risk as the exposure changes. For example, debt instruments with 24 months' remaining maturity are designated as the hedged item for interest rate risk for 24 months. The same procedure is applied to other time buckets or maturity periods. After a short period of time, the entity discontinues all, some or a part of the previously designated hedging relationships for maturity periods and designates new hedging relationships for maturity periods on the basis of their size and the hedging instruments that exist at that time. The discontinuation of hedge accounting in this situation reflects that those hedging relationships are established in such a way that the entity looks at a new hedging instrument and a new hedged item instead of the hedging instrument and the hedged item that were designated previously. The risk management strategy remains the same, but there is no risk management objective that continues for those previously designated hedging relationships, which as such no longer exist. In such a situation, the discontinuation of hedge accounting applies to the extent to which the risk management objective has changed. This depends on the situation of an entity and could, for example, affect all or only some hedging relationships of a maturity period, or only part of a hedging relationship.

(c)   an entity has a risk management strategy whereby it manages the foreign currency risk of forecast sales and the resulting receivables. Within that strategy the entity manages the foreign currency risk as a particular hedging relationship only up to the point of the recognition of the receivable. Thereafter, the entity no longer manages the foreign currency risk on the basis of that particular hedging relationship. Instead, it manages together the foreign currency risk from receivables, payables and derivatives (that do not relate to forecast transactions that are still pending) denominated in the same foreign currency. For accounting purposes, this works as a 'natural' hedge because the gains and losses from the foreign currency risk on all of those items are immediately recognised in profit or loss. Consequently, for accounting purposes, if the hedging relationship is designated for the period up to the payment date, it must be discontinued when the receivable is recognised, because the risk management objective of the original hedging relationship no longer applies. The foreign currency risk is now managed within the same strategy but on a different basis. Conversely, if an entity had a different risk management objective and managed the foreign currency risk as one continuous hedging relationship specifically for that forecast sales amount and the resulting receivable until the settlement date, hedge accounting would continue until that date.

B6.5.25   The discontinuation of hedge accounting can affect:

(a)   a hedging relationship in its entirety; or

(b)   a part of a hedging relationship (which means that hedge accounting continues for the remainder of the hedging relationship).

B6.5.26   A hedging relationship is discontinued in its entirety when, as a whole, it ceases to meet the qualifying criteria. For example:

(a)   the hedging relationship no longer meets the risk management objective on the basis of which it qualified for hedge accounting (ie the entity no longer pursues that risk management objective);

(b)   the hedging instrument or instruments have been sold or terminated (in relation to the entire volume that was part of the hedging relationship); or

(c)   there is no longer an economic relationship between the hedged item and the hedging instrument or the effect of credit risk starts to dominate the value changes that result from that economic relationship.

B6.5.27   A part of a hedging relationship is discontinued (and hedge accounting continues for its remainder) when only a part of the hedging relationship ceases to meet the qualifying criteria. For example:

(a)   on rebalancing of the hedging relationship, the hedge ratio might be adjusted in such a way that some of the volume of the hedged item is no longer part of the hedging relationship (see paragraph B6.5.20); hence, hedge accounting is discontinued only for the volume of the hedged item that is no longer part of the hedging relationship; or

(b)   when the occurrence of some of the volume of the hedged item that is (or is a component of) a forecast transaction is no longer highly probable, hedge accounting is discontinued only for the volume of the hedged item whose occurrence is no longer highly probable. However, if an entity has a history of having designated hedges of forecast transactions and having subsequently determined that the forecast transactions are no longer expected to occur, the entity's ability to predict forecast transactions accurately is called into question when predicting similar forecast transactions. This affects the assessment of whether similar forecast transactions are highly probable (see paragraph 6.3.3) and hence whether they are eligible as hedged items.

B6.5.28   An entity can designate a new hedging relationship that involves the hedging instrument or hedged item of a previous hedging relationship for which hedge accounting was (in part or in its entirety) discontinued. This does not constitute a continuation of a hedging relationship but is a restart. For example:

(a)   a hedging instrument experiences such a severe credit deterioration that the entity replaces it with a new hedging instrument. This means that the original hedging relationship failed to achieve the risk management objective and is hence discontinued in its entirety. The new hedging instrument is designated as the hedge of the same exposure that was hedged previously and forms a new hedging relationship. Hence, the changes in the fair value or the cash flows of the hedged item are measured starting from, and by reference to, the date of designation of the new hedging relationship instead of the date on which the original hedging relationship was designated.

(b)   a hedging relationship is discontinued before the end of its term. The hedging instrument in that hedging relationship can be designated as the hedging instrument in another hedging relationship (for example, when adjusting the hedge ratio on rebalancing by increasing the volume of the hedging instrument or when designating a whole new hedging relationship).

Accounting for the time value of options

B6.5.29   An option can be considered as being related to a time period because its time value represents a charge for providing protection for the option holder over a period of time. However, the relevant aspect for the purpose of assessing whether an option hedges a transaction or time-period related hedged item are the characteristics of that hedged item, including how and when it affects profit or loss. Hence, an entity shall assess the type of hedged item (see paragraph 6.5.15(a)) on the basis of the nature of the hedged item (regardless of whether the hedging relationship is a cash flow hedge or a fair value hedge):

    (a)   the time value of an option relates to a transaction related hedged item if the nature of the hedged item is a transaction for which the time value has the character of costs of that transaction. An example is when the time value of an option relates to a hedged item that results in the recognition of an item whose initial measurement includes transaction costs (for example, an entity hedges a commodity purchase, whether it is a forecast transaction or a firm commitment, against the commodity price risk and includes the transaction costs in the initial measurement of the inventory). As a consequence of including the time value of the option in the initial measurement of the particular hedged item, the time value affects profit or loss at the same time as that hedged item. Similarly, an entity that hedges a sale of a commodity, whether it is a forecast transaction or a firm commitment, would include the time value of the option as part of the cost related to that sale (hence, the time value would be recognised in profit or loss in the same period as the revenue from the hedged sale).

    (b)   the time value of an option relates to a time-period related hedged item if the nature of the hedged item is such that the time value has the character of a cost for obtaining protection against a risk over a particular period of time (but the hedged item does not result in a transaction that involves the notion of a transaction cost in accordance with (a)). For example, if commodity inventory is hedged against a fair value decrease for six months using a commodity option with a corresponding life, the time value of the option would be allocated to profit or loss (ie amortised on a systematic and rational basis) over that six-month period. Another example is a hedge of a net investment in a foreign operation that is hedged for 18 months using a foreign-exchange option, which would result in allocating the time value of the option over that 18-month period.

B6.5.30   The characteristics of the hedged item, including how and when the hedged item affects profit or loss, also affect the period over which the time value of an option that hedges a time-period related hedged item is amortised, which is consistent with the period over which the option's intrinsic value can affect profit or loss in accordance with hedge accounting. For example, if an interest rate option (a cap) is used to provide protection against increases in the interest expense on a floating rate bond, the time value of that cap is amortised to profit or loss over the same period over which any intrinsic value of the cap would affect profit or loss:

    (a)   if the cap hedges increases in interest rates for the first three years out of a total life of the floating rate bond of five years, the time value of that cap is amortised over the first three years; or

(b) if the cap is a forward start option that hedges increases in interest rates for years two and three out of a total life of the floating rate bond of five years, the time value of that cap is amortised during years two and three.

B6.5.31 The accounting for the time value of options in accordance with paragraph 6.5.15 also applies to a combination of a purchased and a written option (one being a put option and one being a call option) that at the date of designation as a hedging instrument has a net nil time value (commonly referred to as a 'zero-cost collar'). In that case, an entity shall recognise any changes in time value in other comprehensive income, even though the cumulative change in time value over the total period of the hedging relationship is nil. Hence, if the time value of the option relates to:

(a) a transaction related hedged item, the amount of time value at the end of the hedging relationship that adjusts the hedged item or that is reclassified to profit or loss (see paragraph 6.5.15(b)) would be nil.

(b) a time-period related hedged item, the amortisation expense related to the time value is nil.

B6.5.32 The accounting for the time value of options in accordance with paragraph 6.5.15 applies only to the extent that the time value relates to the hedged item (aligned time value). The time value of an option relates to the hedged item if the critical terms of the option (such as the nominal amount, life and underlying) are aligned with the hedged item. Hence, if the critical terms of the option and the hedged item are not fully aligned, an entity shall determine the aligned time value, ie how much of the time value included in the premium (actual time value) relates to the hedged item (and therefore should be treated in accordance with paragraph 6.5.15). An entity determines the aligned time value using the valuation of the option that would have critical terms that perfectly match the hedged item.

B6.5.33 If the actual time value and the aligned time value differ, an entity shall determine the amount that is accumulated in a separate component of equity in accordance with paragraph 6.5.15 as follows:

(a) if, at inception of the hedging relationship, the actual time value is higher than the aligned time value, the entity shall:

(i) determine the amount that is accumulated in a separate component of equity on the basis of the aligned time value; and

(ii) account for the differences in the fair value changes between the two time values in profit or loss.

(b) if, at inception of the hedging relationship, the actual time value is lower than the aligned time value, the entity shall determine the amount that is accumulated in a separate component of equity by reference to the lower of the cumulative change in fair value of:

(i) the actual time value; and

(ii) the aligned time value.

Any remainder of the change in fair value of the actual time value shall be recognised in profit or loss.

Accounting for the forward element of forward contracts and foreign currency basis spreads of financial instruments

B6.5.34   A forward contract can be considered as being related to a time period because its forward element represents charges for a period of time (which is the tenor for which it is determined). However, the relevant aspect for the purpose of assessing whether a hedging instrument hedges a transaction or time-period related hedged item are the characteristics of that hedged item, including how and when it affects profit or loss. Hence, an entity shall assess the type of hedged item (see paragraphs 6.5.16 and 6.5.15(a)) on the basis of the nature of the hedged item (regardless of whether the hedging relationship is a cash flow hedge or a fair value hedge):

(a)   the forward element of a forward contract relates to a transaction related hedged item if the nature of the hedged item is a transaction for which the forward element has the character of costs of that transaction. An example is when the forward element relates to a hedged item that results in the recognition of an item whose initial measurement includes transaction costs (for example, an entity hedges an inventory purchase denominated in a foreign currency, whether it is a forecast transaction or a firm commitment, against foreign currency risk and includes the transaction costs in the initial measurement of the inventory). As a consequence of including the forward element in the initial measurement of the particular hedged item, the forward element affects profit or loss at the same time as that hedged item. Similarly, an entity that hedges a sale of a commodity denominated in a foreign currency against foreign currency risk, whether it is a forecast transaction or a firm commitment, would include the forward element as part of the cost that is related to that sale (hence, the forward element would be recognised in profit or loss in the same period as the revenue from the hedged sale).

(b)   the forward element of a forward contract relates to a time-period related hedged item if the nature of the hedged item is such that the forward element has the character of a cost for obtaining protection against a risk over a particular period of time (but the hedged item does not result in a transaction that involves the notion of a transaction cost in accordance with (a)). For example, if commodity inventory is hedged against changes in fair value for six months using a commodity forward contract with a corresponding life, the forward element of the forward contract would be allocated to profit or loss (ie amortised on a systematic and rational basis) over that six-month period. Another example is a hedge of a net investment in a foreign operation that is hedged for 18 months using a foreign-exchange forward contract, which would result in allocating the forward element of the forward contract over that 18-month period.

B6.5.35　The characteristics of the hedged item, including how and when the hedged item affects profit or loss, also affect the period over which the forward element of a forward contract that hedges a time-period related hedged item is amortised, which is over the period to which the forward element relates. For example, if a forward contract hedges the exposure to variability in three-month interest rates for a three-month period that starts in six months' time, the forward element is amortised during the period that spans months seven to nine.

B6.5.36　The accounting for the forward element of a forward contract in accordance with paragraph 6.5.16 also applies if, at the date on which the forward contract is designated as a hedging instrument, the forward element is nil. In that case, an entity shall recognise any fair value changes attributable to the forward element in other comprehensive income, even though the cumulative fair value change attributable to the forward element over the total period of the hedging relationship is nil. Hence, if the forward element of a forward contract relates to:

(a)　a transaction related hedged item, the amount in respect of the forward element at the end of the hedging relationship that adjusts the hedged item or that is reclassified to profit or loss (see paragraphs 6.5.15(b) and 6.5.16) would be nil.

(b)　a time-period related hedged item, the amortisation amount related to the forward element is nil.

B6.5.37　The accounting for the forward element of forward contracts in accordance with paragraph 6.5.16 applies only to the extent that the forward element relates to the hedged item (aligned forward element). The forward element of a forward contract relates to the hedged item if the critical terms of the forward contract (such as the nominal amount, life and underlying) are aligned with the hedged item. Hence, if the critical terms of the forward contract and the hedged item are not fully aligned, an entity shall determine the aligned forward element, ie how much of the forward element included in the forward contract (actual forward element) relates to the hedged item (and therefore should be treated in accordance with paragraph 6.5.16). An entity determines the aligned forward element using the valuation of the forward contract that would have critical terms that perfectly match the hedged item.

B6.5.38　If the actual forward element and the aligned forward element differ, an entity shall determine the amount that is accumulated in a separate component of equity in accordance with paragraph 6.5.16 as follows:

(a)　if, at inception of the hedging relationship, the absolute amount of the actual forward element is higher than that of the aligned forward element the entity shall:

(i)　determine the amount that is accumulated in a separate component of equity on the basis of the aligned forward element; and

(ii)　account for the differences in the fair value changes between the two forward elements in profit or loss.

(b)   if, at inception of the hedging relationship, the absolute amount of the actual forward element is lower than that of the aligned forward element, the entity shall determine the amount that is accumulated in a separate component of equity by reference to the lower of the cumulative change in fair value of:

    (i)   the absolute amount of the actual forward element; and

    (ii)   the absolute amount of the aligned forward element.

Any remainder of the change in fair value of the actual forward element shall be recognised in profit or loss.

B6.5.39   When an entity separates the foreign currency basis spread from a financial instrument and excludes it from the designation of that financial instrument as the hedging instrument (see paragraph 6.2.4(b)), the application guidance in paragraphs B6.5.34–B6.5.38 applies to the foreign currency basis spread in the same manner as it is applied to the forward element of a forward contract.

Hedge of a group of items (Section 6.6)

Hedge of a net position

Eligibility for hedge accounting and designation of a net position

B6.6.1   A net position is eligible for hedge accounting only if an entity hedges on a net basis for risk management purposes. Whether an entity hedges in this way is a matter of fact (not merely of assertion or documentation). Hence, an entity cannot apply hedge accounting on a net basis solely to achieve a particular accounting outcome if that would not reflect its risk management approach. Net position hedging must form part of an established risk management strategy. Normally this would be approved by key management personnel as defined in IAS 24.

B6.6.2   For example, Entity A, whose functional currency is its local currency, has a firm commitment to pay FC150,000 for advertising expenses in nine months' time and a firm commitment to sell finished goods for FC150,000 in 15 months' time. Entity A enters into a foreign currency derivative that settles in nine months' time under which it receives FC100 and pays CU70. Entity A has no other exposures to FC. Entity A does not manage foreign currency risk on a net basis. Hence, Entity A cannot apply hedge accounting for a hedging relationship between the foreign currency derivative and a net position of FC100 (consisting of FC150,000 of the firm purchase commitment—ie advertising services—and FC149,900 (of the FC150,000) of the firm sale commitment) for a nine-month period.

B6.6.3   If Entity A did manage foreign currency risk on a net basis and did not enter into the foreign currency derivative (because it increases its foreign currency risk exposure instead of reducing it), then the entity would be in a natural hedged position for nine months. Normally, this hedged position would not be reflected in the financial statements because the transactions are recognised in different reporting periods in the future. The nil net position would be eligible for hedge accounting only if the conditions in paragraph 6.6.6 are met.

B6.6.4 When a group of items that constitute a net position is designated as a hedged item, an entity shall designate the overall group of items that includes the items that can make up the net position. An entity is not permitted to designate a non-specific abstract amount of a net position. For example, an entity has a group of firm sale commitments in nine months' time for FC100 and a group of firm purchase commitments in 18 months' time for FC120. The entity cannot designate an abstract amount of a net position up to FC20. Instead, it must designate a gross amount of purchases and a gross amount of sales that together give rise to the hedged net position. An entity shall designate gross positions that give rise to the net position so that the entity is able to comply with the requirements for the accounting for qualifying hedging relationships.

Application of the hedge effectiveness requirements to a hedge of a net position

B6.6.5 When an entity determines whether the hedge effectiveness requirements of paragraph 6.4.1(c) are met when it hedges a net position, it shall consider the changes in the value of the items in the net position that have a similar effect as the hedging instrument in conjunction with the fair value change on the hedging instrument. For example, an entity has a group of firm sale commitments in nine months' time for FC100 and a group of firm purchase commitments in 18 months' time for FC120. It hedges the foreign currency risk of the net position of FC20 using a forward exchange contract for FC20. When determining whether the hedge effectiveness requirements of paragraph 6.4.1(c) are met, the entity shall consider the relationship between:

(a) the fair value change on the forward exchange contract together with the foreign currency risk related changes in the value of the firm sale commitments; and

(b) the foreign currency risk related changes in the value of the firm purchase commitments.

B6.6.6 Similarly, if in the example in paragraph B6.6.5 the entity had a nil net position it would consider the relationship between the foreign currency risk related changes in the value of the firm sale commitments and the foreign currency risk related changes in the value of the firm purchase commitments when determining whether the hedge effectiveness requirements of paragraph 6.4.1(c) are met.

Cash flow hedges that constitute a net position

B6.6.7 When an entity hedges a group of items with offsetting risk positions (ie a net position), the eligibility for hedge accounting depends on the type of hedge. If the hedge is a fair value hedge, then the net position may be eligible as a hedged item. If, however, the hedge is a cash flow hedge, then the net position can only be eligible as a hedged item if it is a hedge of foreign currency risk and the designation of that net position specifies the reporting period in which the forecast transactions are expected to affect profit or loss and also specifies their nature and volume.

B6.6.8   For example, an entity has a net position that consists of a bottom layer of FC100 of sales and a bottom layer of FC150 of purchases. Both sales and purchases are denominated in the same foreign currency. In order to sufficiently specify the designation of the hedged net position, the entity specifies in the original documentation of the hedging relationship that sales can be of Product A or Product B and purchases can be of Machinery Type A, Machinery Type B and Raw Material A. The entity also specifies the volumes of the transactions by each nature. The entity documents that the bottom layer of sales (FC100) is made up of a forecast sales volume of the first FC70 of Product A and the first FC30 of Product B. If those sales volumes are expected to affect profit or loss in different reporting periods, the entity would include that in the documentation, for example, the first FC70 from sales of Product A that are expected to affect profit or loss in the first reporting period and the first FC30 from sales of Product B that are expected to affect profit or loss in the second reporting period. The entity also documents that the bottom layer of the purchases (FC150) is made up of purchases of the first FC60 of Machinery Type A, the first FC40 of Machinery Type B and the first FC50 of Raw Material A. If those purchase volumes are expected to affect profit or loss in different reporting periods, the entity would include in the documentation a disaggregation of the purchase volumes by the reporting periods in which they are expected to affect profit or loss (similarly to how it documents the sales volumes). For example, the forecast transaction would be specified as:

(a)   the first FC60 of purchases of Machinery Type A that are expected to affect profit or loss from the third reporting period over the next ten reporting periods;

(b)   the first FC40 of purchases of Machinery Type B that are expected to affect profit or loss from the fourth reporting period over the next 20 reporting periods; and

(c)   the first FC50 of purchases of Raw Material A that are expected to be received in the third reporting period and sold, ie affect profit or loss, in that and the next reporting period.

Specifying the nature of the forecast transaction volumes would include aspects such as the depreciation pattern for items of property, plant and equipment of the same kind, if the nature of those items is such that the depreciation pattern could vary depending on how the entity uses those items. For example, if the entity uses items of Machinery Type A in two different production processes that result in straight-line depreciation over ten reporting periods and the units of production method respectively, its documentation of the forecast purchase volume for Machinery Type A would disaggregate that volume by which of those depreciation patterns will apply.

B6.6.9   For a cash flow hedge of a net position, the amounts determined in accordance with paragraph 6.5.11 shall include the changes in the value of the items in the net position that have a similar effect as the hedging instrument in conjunction with the fair value change on the hedging instrument.

However, the changes in the value of the items in the net position that have a similar effect as the hedging instrument are recognised only once the transactions that they relate to are recognised, such as when a forecast sale is recognised as revenue. For example, an entity has a group of highly probable forecast sales in nine months' time for FC100 and a group of highly probable forecast purchases in 18 months' time for FC120. It hedges the foreign currency risk of the net position of FC20 using a forward exchange contract for FC20. When determining the amounts that are recognised in the cash flow hedge reserve in accordance with paragraph 6.5.11(a)–6.5.11(b), the entity compares:

(a) the fair value change on the forward exchange contract together with the foreign currency risk related changes in the value of the highly probable forecast sales; with

(b) the foreign currency risk related changes in the value of the highly probable forecast purchases.

However, the entity recognises only amounts related to the forward exchange contract until the highly probable forecast sales transactions are recognised in the financial statements, at which time the gains or losses on those forecast transactions are recognised (ie the change in the value attributable to the change in the foreign exchange rate between the designation of the hedging relationship and the recognition of revenue).

B6.6.10 Similarly, if in the example the entity had a nil net position it would compare the foreign currency risk related changes in the value of the highly probable forecast sales with the foreign currency risk related changes in the value of the highly probable forecast purchases. However, those amounts are recognised only once the related forecast transactions are recognised in the financial statements.

Layers of groups of items designated as the hedged item

B6.6.11 For the same reasons noted in paragraph B6.3.19, designating layer components of groups of existing items requires the specific identification of the nominal amount of the group of items from which the hedged layer component is defined.

B6.6.12 A hedging relationship can include layers from several different groups of items. For example, in a hedge of a net position of a group of assets and a group of liabilities, the hedging relationship can comprise, in combination, a layer component of the group of assets and a layer component of the group of liabilities.

Presentation of hedging instrument gains or losses

B6.6.13 If items are hedged together as a group in a cash flow hedge, they might affect different line items in the statement of profit or loss and other comprehensive income. The presentation of hedging gains or losses in that statement depends on the group of items.

B6.6.14   If the group of items does not have any offsetting risk positions (for example, a group of foreign currency expenses that affect different line items in the statement of profit or loss and other comprehensive income that are hedged for foreign currency risk) then the reclassified hedging instrument gains or losses shall be apportioned to the line items affected by the hedged items. This apportionment shall be done on a systematic and rational basis and shall not result in the grossing up of the net gains or losses arising from a single hedging instrument.

B6.6.15   If the group of items does have offsetting risk positions (for example, a group of sales and expenses denominated in a foreign currency hedged together for foreign currency risk) then an entity shall present the hedging gains or losses in a separate line item in the statement of profit or loss and other comprehensive income. Consider, for example, a hedge of the foreign currency risk of a net position of foreign currency sales of FC100 and foreign currency expenses of FC80 using a forward exchange contract for FC20. The gain or loss on the forward exchange contract that is reclassified from the cash flow hedge reserve to profit or loss (when the net position affects profit or loss) shall be presented in a separate line item from the hedged sales and expenses. Moreover, if the sales occur in an earlier period than the expenses, the sales revenue is still measured at the spot exchange rate in accordance with IAS 21. The related hedging gain or loss is presented in a separate line item, so that profit or loss reflects the effect of hedging the net position, with a corresponding adjustment to the cash flow hedge reserve. When the hedged expenses affect profit or loss in a later period, the hedging gain or loss previously recognised in the cash flow hedge reserve on the sales is reclassified to profit or loss and presented as a separate line item from those that include the hedged expenses, which are measured at the spot exchange rate in accordance with IAS 21.

B6.6.16   For some types of fair value hedges, the objective of the hedge is not primarily to offset the fair value change of the hedged item but instead to transform the cash flows of the hedged item. For example, an entity hedges the fair value interest rate risk of a fixed-rate debt instrument using an interest rate swap. The entity's hedge objective is to transform the fixed-interest cash flows into floating interest cash flows. This objective is reflected in the accounting for the hedging relationship by accruing the net interest accrual on the interest rate swap in profit or loss. In the case of a hedge of a net position (for example, a net position of a fixed-rate asset and a fixed-rate liability), this net interest accrual must be presented in a separate line item in the statement of profit or loss and other comprehensive income. This is to avoid the grossing up of a single instrument's net gains or losses into offsetting gross amounts and recognising them in different line items (for example, this avoids grossing up a net interest receipt on a single interest rate swap into gross interest revenue and gross interest expense).

Effective date and transition (Chapter 7)

Transition (Section 7.2)

Financial assets held for trading

B7.2.1   At the date of initial application of this Standard, an entity must determine whether the objective of the entity's business model for managing any of its financial assets meets the condition in paragraph 4.1.2(a) or the condition in paragraph 4.1.2A(a) or if a financial asset is eligible for the election in paragraph 5.7.5. For that purpose, an entity shall determine whether financial assets meet the definition of held for trading as if the entity had purchased the assets at the date of initial application.

Impairment

B7.2.2   On transition, an entity should seek to approximate the credit risk on initial recognition by considering all reasonable and supportable information that is available without undue cost or effort. An entity is not required to undertake an exhaustive search for information when determining, at the date of transition, whether there have been significant increases in credit risk since initial recognition. If an entity is unable to make this determination without undue cost or effort paragraph 7.2.20 applies.

B7.2.3   In order to determine the loss allowance on financial instruments initially recognised (or loan commitments or financial guarantee contracts to which the entity became a party to the contract) prior to the date of initial application, both on transition and until the derecognition of those items an entity shall consider information that is relevant in determining or approximating the credit risk at initial recognition. In order to determine or approximate the initial credit risk, an entity may consider internal and external information, including portfolio information, in accordance with paragraphs B5.5.1–B5.5.6.

B7.2.4   An entity with little historical information may use information from internal reports and statistics (that may have been generated when deciding whether to launch a new product), information about similar products or peer group experience for comparable financial instruments, if relevant.

Definitions (Appendix A)

Derivatives

BA.1   Typical examples of derivatives are futures and forward, swap and option contracts. A derivative usually has a notional amount, which is an amount of currency, a number of shares, a number of units of weight or volume or other units specified in the contract. However, a derivative instrument does not require the holder or writer to invest or receive the notional amount at the inception of the contract. Alternatively, a derivative could require a fixed payment or payment of an amount that can change (but not proportionally with a change in the underlying) as a result of some future event that is unrelated to a notional amount. For example, a contract may require a fixed payment of CU1,000 if six-month LIBOR increases by 100 basis points. Such a contract is a derivative even though a notional amount is not specified.

BA.2 The definition of a derivative in this Standard includes contracts that are settled gross by delivery of the underlying item (eg a forward contract to purchase a fixed rate debt instrument). An entity may have a contract to buy or sell a non-financial item that can be settled net in cash or another financial instrument or by exchanging financial instruments (eg a contract to buy or sell a commodity at a fixed price at a future date). Such a contract is within the scope of this Standard unless it was entered into and continues to be held for the purpose of delivery of a non-financial item in accordance with the entity's expected purchase, sale or usage requirements. However, this Standard applies to such contracts for an entity's expected purchase, sale or usage requirements if the entity makes a designation in accordance with paragraph 2.5 (see paragraphs 2.4–2.7).

BA.3 One of the defining characteristics of a derivative is that it has an initial net investment that is smaller than would be required for other types of contracts that would be expected to have a similar response to changes in market factors. An option contract meets that definition because the premium is less than the investment that would be required to obtain the underlying financial instrument to which the option is linked. A currency swap that requires an initial exchange of different currencies of equal fair values meets the definition because it has a zero initial net investment.

BA.4 A regular way purchase or sale gives rise to a fixed price commitment between trade date and settlement date that meets the definition of a derivative. However, because of the short duration of the commitment it is not recognised as a derivative financial instrument. Instead, this Standard provides for special accounting for such regular way contracts (see paragraphs 3.1.2 and B3.1.3–B3.1.6).

BA.5 The definition of a derivative refers to non-financial variables that are not specific to a party to the contract. These include an index of earthquake losses in a particular region and an index of temperatures in a particular city. Non-financial variables specific to a party to the contract include the occurrence or non-occurrence of a fire that damages or destroys an asset of a party to the contract. A change in the fair value of a non-financial asset is specific to the owner if the fair value reflects not only changes in market prices for such assets (a financial variable) but also the condition of the specific non-financial asset held (a non-financial variable). For example, if a guarantee of the residual value of a specific car exposes the guarantor to the risk of changes in the car's physical condition, the change in that residual value is specific to the owner of the car.

Financial assets and liabilities held for trading

BA.6 Trading generally reflects active and frequent buying and selling, and financial instruments held for trading generally are used with the objective of generating a profit from short-term fluctuations in price or dealer's margin.

BA.7   Financial liabilities held for trading include:

    (a)   derivative liabilities that are not accounted for as hedging instruments;

    (b)   obligations to deliver financial assets borrowed by a short seller (ie an entity that sells financial assets it has borrowed and does not yet own);

    (c)   financial liabilities that are incurred with an intention to repurchase them in the near term (eg a quoted debt instrument that the issuer may buy back in the near term depending on changes in its fair value); and

    (d)   financial liabilities that are part of a portfolio of identified financial instruments that are managed together and for which there is evidence of a recent pattern of short-term profit-taking.

BA.8   The fact that a liability is used to fund trading activities does not in itself make that liability one that is held for trading.

Appendix C
Amendments to other Standards

This appendix describes the amendments to other Standards that the IASB made when it finalised IFRS 9 (2014). An entity shall apply the amendments for annual periods beginning on or after 1 January 2018. If an entity applies IFRS 9 for an earlier period, these amendments shall be applied for that earlier period.

* * * * *

The amendments contained in this appendix when this Standard was issued in 2014 have been incorporated into the text of the relevant Standards included in this volume.

Approval by the Board of IFRS 9 issued in November 2009

International Financial Reporting Standard 9 *Financial Instruments* was approved for issue by thirteen of the fifteen members of the International Accounting Standards Board. Mr Leisenring and Ms McConnell dissented from the issue of the Standard. Their dissenting opinions are set out after the Basis for Conclusions.

Sir David Tweedie   Chairman

Stephen Cooper

Philippe Danjou

Jan Engström

Patrick Finnegan

Robert P Garnett

Gilbert Gélard

Amaro Luiz de Oliveira Gomes

Prabhakar Kalavacherla

James J Leisenring

Patricia McConnell

Warren J McGregor

John T Smith

Tatsumi Yamada

Wei-Guo Zhang

Approval by the Board of the requirements added to IFRS 9 in October 2010

The requirements added to International Financial Reporting Standard 9 *Financial Instruments* in October 2010 were approved for issue by fourteen of the fifteen members of the International Accounting Standards Board (IASB). Mr Scott abstained in view of his recent appointment to the IASB.

Sir David Tweedie	Chairman

Stephen Cooper

Philippe Danjou

Jan Engström

Patrick Finnegan

Amaro Luiz de Oliveira Gomes

Prabhakar Kalavacherla

Elke König

Patricia McConnell

Warren J McGregor

Paul Pacter

Darrel Scott

John T Smith

Tatsumi Yamada

Wei-Guo Zhang

Approval by the Board of *Mandatory Effective Date* of IFRS 9 and *Transition Disclosures* (Amendments to IFRS 9 (2009), IFRS 9 (2010) and IFRS 7) issued in December 2011

Mandatory Effective Date of IFRS 9 and Transition Disclosures (Amendments to IFRS 9 (2009), IFRS 9 (2010) and IFRS 7) was approved for publication by fourteen of the fifteen members of the International Accounting Standards Board. Ms McConnell dissented from the issue of the amendments. Her dissenting opinion is set out after the Basis for Conclusions.

Hans Hoogervorst	Chairman
Ian Mackintosh	Vice-Chairman
Stephen Cooper	
Philippe Danjou	
Jan Engström	
Patrick Finnegan	
Amaro Luiz de Oliveira Gomes	
Prabhakar Kalavacherla	
Elke König	
Patricia McConnell	
Takatsugu Ochi	
Paul Pacter	
Darrel Scott	
John T Smith	
Wei-Guo Zhang	

Approval by the Board of IFRS 9 *Financial Instruments* (Hedge Accounting and amendments to IFRS 9, IFRS 7 and IAS 39) issued in November 2013

IFRS 9 *Financial Instruments* (Hedge Accounting and amendments to IFRS 9, IFRS 7 and IAS 39) was approved for issue by fifteen of the sixteen members of the International Accounting Standards Board. Mr Finnegan dissented. His dissenting opinion is set out after the Basis for Conclusions.

Hans Hoogervorst	Chairman
Ian Mackintosh	Vice-Chairman
Stephen Cooper	
Philippe Danjou	
Martin Edelmann	
Jan Engström	
Patrick Finnegan	
Amaro Luiz de Oliveira Gomes	
Gary Kabureck	
Prabhakar Kalavacherla	
Patricia McConnell	
Takatsugu Ochi	
Darrel Scott	
Chungwoo Suh	
Mary Tokar	
Wei-Guo Zhang	

Approval by the Board of IFRS 9 *Financial Instruments* issued in July 2014

IFRS 9 *Financial Instruments* (as issued in July 2014) was approved for issue by fourteen of the sixteen members of the International Accounting Standards Board. Messrs Cooper and Engström dissented. Their dissenting opinion is set out after the Basis for Conclusions.

Hans Hoogervorst	Chairman
Ian Mackintosh	Vice-Chairman
Stephen Cooper	
Philippe Danjou	
Martin Edelmann	
Jan Engström	
Patrick Finnegan	
Amaro Luiz de Oliveira Gomes	
Gary Kabureck	
Suzanne Lloyd	
Patricia McConnell	
Takatsugu Ochi	
Darrel Scott	
Chungwoo Suh	
Mary Tokar	
Wei-Guo Zhang	

Approval by the Board of *Prepayment Features with Negative Compensation* (Amendments to IFRS 9) issued in October 2017

Prepayment Features with Negative Compensation (Amendments to IFRS 9) was approved for issue by 11 of 14 members of the International Accounting Standards Board (Board). Messrs Anderson and Lu and Ms Tarca abstained in view of their recent appointments to the Board.

Hans Hoogervorst	Chairman
Suzanne Lloyd	Vice-Chair
Nick Anderson	
Martin Edelmann	
Françoise Flores	
Amaro Luiz de Oliveira Gomes	
Gary Kabureck	
Jianqiao Lu	
Takatsugu Ochi	
Darrel Scott	
Thomas Scott	
Chungwoo Suh	
Ann Tarca	
Mary Tokar	

Approval by the Board of *Interest Rate Benchmark Reform* issued in September 2019

Interest Rate Benchmark Reform, which amended IFRS 9, IAS 39 and IFRS 7, was approved for issue by all 14 members of the International Accounting Standards Board (Board).

Hans Hoogervorst	Chairman
Suzanne Lloyd	Vice-Chair
Nick Anderson	
Tadeu Cendon	
Martin Edelmann	
Françoise Flores	
Gary Kabureck	
Jianqiao Lu	
Darrel Scott	
Thomas Scott	
Chungwoo Suh	
Rika Suzuki	
Ann Tarca	
Mary Tokar	

Approval by the Board of *Interest Rate Benchmark Reform—Phase 2* issued in August 2020

Interest Rate Benchmark Reform—Phase 2, which amended IFRS 9, IAS 39, IFRS 7, IFRS 4 and IFRS 16, was approved for issue by 12 of 13 members of the International Accounting Standards Board (Board). Mr Gast abstained in view of his recent appointment to the Board.

Hans Hoogervorst	Chairman
Suzanne Lloyd	Vice-Chair
Nick Anderson	
Tadeu Cendon	
Martin Edelmann	
Françoise Flores	
Zach Gast	
Jianqiao Lu	
Darrel Scott	
Thomas Scott	
Rika Suzuki	
Ann Tarca	
Mary Tokar	

IFRS 10

Consolidated Financial Statements

In April 2001 the International Accounting Standards Board (Board) adopted IAS 27 *Consolidated Financial Statements and Accounting for Investments in Subsidiaries*, which had originally been issued by the International Accounting Standards Committee in April 1989. IAS 27 replaced most of IAS 3 *Consolidated Financial Statements* (issued in June 1976).

In December 2003, the Board amended and renamed IAS 27 with a new title — *Consolidated and Separate Financial Statements*. The amended IAS 27 also incorporated the guidance contained in two related Interpretations (SIC-12 *Consolidation-Special Purpose Entities* and SIC-33 *Consolidation and Equity Method — Potential Voting Rights and Allocation of Ownership Interests*).

In May 2011 the Board issued IFRS 10 *Consolidated Financial Statements* to supersede IAS 27. IFRS 12 *Disclosure of Interests in Other Entities*, also issued in May 2011, replaced the disclosure requirements in IAS 27. IFRS 10 incorporates the guidance contained in two related Interpretations (SIC-12 *Consolidation-Special Purpose Entities* and SIC-33 *Consolidation*).

In June 2012 IFRS 10 was amended by *Consolidated Financial Statements, Joint Arrangements and Disclosure of Interests in Other Entities: Transition Guidance* (Amendments to IFRS 10, IFRS 11 and IFRS 12). These amendments clarified the transition guidance in IFRS 10. Furthermore, these amendments provided additional transition relief in IFRS 10, limiting the requirement to present adjusted comparative information to only the annual period immediately preceding the first annual period for which IFRS 10 is applied.

In October 2012 IFRS 10 was amended by *Investment Entities* (Amendments to IFRS 10, IFRS 12 and IAS 27), which defined an investment entity and introduced an exception to consolidating particular subsidiaries for investment entities. It also introduced the requirement that an investment entity measures those subsidiaries at fair value through profit or loss in accordance with IFRS 9 *Financial Instruments* in its consolidated and separate financial statements. In addition, the amendments introduced new disclosure requirements for investment entities in IFRS 12 and IAS 27.

In December 2014 IFRS 10 was amended by *Investment Entities: Applying the Consolidation Exception* (Amendments to IFRS 10, IFRS 12 and IAS 28). These amendments clarified which subsidiaries of an investment entity should be consolidated instead of being measured at fair value through profit or loss. The amendments also clarified that the exemption from presenting consolidated financial statements continues to apply to subsidiaries of an investment entity that are themselves parent entities. This is so even if that subsidiary is measured at fair value through profit or loss by the higher level investment entity parent.

Other Standards have made minor consequential amendments to IFRS 10, including *Annual Improvements to IFRS Standards 2014–2016 Cycle* (issued December 2016) and *Amendments to References to the Conceptual Framework in IFRS Standards* (issued March 2018).

CONTENTS

Consolidated Financial Statements, Joint Arrangements and Disclosure of Interests in other Entities: Transition Guidance (Amendments to IFRS 10, IFRS 11 and IFRS 12) issued in June 2012

Investment Entities (Amendments to IFRS 10, IFRS 12 and IAS 27) issued in October 2012

Investment Entities: Applying the Consolidation Exception (Amendments to IFRS 10, IFRS 12 and IAS 28) issued in December 2014

FOR THE ACCOMPANYING GUIDANCE LISTED BELOW, SEE PART B OF THIS EDITION

ILLUSTRATIVE EXAMPLES

AMENDMENTS TO THE GUIDANCE ON OTHER IFRSS

FOR THE BASIS FOR CONCLUSIONS, SEE PART C OF THIS EDITION

BASIS FOR CONCLUSIONS

APPENDICES TO THE BASIS FOR CONCLUSIONS

Previous Board approvals and dissenting opinions

Amendments to the Basis for Conclusions on other IFRSs

International Financial Reporting Standard 10 *Consolidated Financial Statements* (IFRS 10) is set out in paragraphs 1–33 and Appendices A–D. All the paragraphs have equal authority. Paragraphs in **bold type** state the main principles. Terms defined in Appendix A are in *italics* the first time they appear in the Standard. Definitions of other terms are given in the Glossary for International Financial Reporting Standards. IFRS 10 should be read in the context of its objective and the Basis for Conclusions, the *Preface to IFRS Standards* and the *Conceptual Framework for Financial Reporting*. IAS 8 *Accounting Policies, Changes in Accounting Estimates and Errors* provides a basis for selecting and applying accounting policies in the absence of explicit guidance.

International Financial Reporting Standard 10
Consolidated Financial Statements

Objective

1   The objective of this IFRS is to establish principles for the presentation and preparation of consolidated financial statements when an entity controls one or more other entities.

Meeting the objective

2   To meet the objective in paragraph 1, this IFRS:

(a)   requires an entity (the *parent*) that controls one or more other entities (*subsidiaries*) to present consolidated financial statements;

(b)   defines the principle of *control*, and establishes control as the basis for consolidation;

(c)   sets out how to apply the principle of control to identify whether an investor controls an investee and therefore must consolidate the investee;

(d)   sets out the accounting requirements for the preparation of consolidated financial statements; and

(e)   defines an investment entity and sets out an exception to consolidating particular subsidiaries of an investment entity.

3   This IFRS does not deal with the accounting requirements for business combinations and their effect on consolidation, including goodwill arising on a business combination (see IFRS 3 *Business Combinations*).

Scope

4   An entity that is a parent shall present consolidated financial statements. This IFRS applies to all entities, except as follows:

(a)   a parent need not present consolidated financial statements if it meets all the following conditions:

(i)   it is a wholly-owned subsidiary or is a partially-owned subsidiary of another entity and all its other owners, including those not otherwise entitled to vote, have been informed about, and do not object to, the parent not presenting consolidated financial statements;

(ii)   its debt or equity instruments are not traded in a public market (a domestic or foreign stock exchange or an over-the-counter market, including local and regional markets);

(iii) it did not file, nor is it in the process of filing, its financial statements with a securities commission or other regulatory organisation for the purpose of issuing any class of instruments in a public market; and

(iv) its ultimate or any intermediate parent produces financial statements that are available for public use and comply with IFRSs, in which subsidiaries are consolidated or are measured at fair value through profit or loss in accordance with this IFRS.

(b) [deleted]

(c) [deleted]

4A This IFRS does not apply to post-employment benefit plans or other long-term employee benefit plans to which IAS 19 *Employee Benefits* applies.

4B A parent that is an investment entity shall not present consolidated financial statements if it is required, in accordance with paragraph 31 of this IFRS, to measure all of its subsidiaries at fair value through profit or loss.

Control

5 An investor, regardless of the nature of its involvement with an entity (the investee), shall determine whether it is a parent by assessing whether it controls the investee.

6 An investor controls an investee when it is exposed, or has rights, to variable returns from its involvement with the investee and has the ability to affect those returns through its power over the investee.

7 Thus, an investor controls an investee if and only if the investor has all the following:

(a) power over the investee (see paragraphs 10–14);

(b) exposure, or rights, to variable returns from its involvement with the investee (see paragraphs 15 and 16); and

(c) the ability to use its power over the investee to affect the amount of the investor's returns (see paragraphs 17 and 18).

8 An investor shall consider all facts and circumstances when assessing whether it controls an investee. The investor shall reassess whether it controls an investee if facts and circumstances indicate that there are changes to one or more of the three elements of control listed in paragraph 7 (see paragraphs B80–B85).

9 Two or more investors collectively control an investee when they must act together to direct the relevant activities. In such cases, because no investor can direct the activities without the co-operation of the others, no investor individually controls the investee. Each investor would account for its interest in the investee in accordance with the relevant IFRSs, such as IFRS 11 *Joint Arrangements*, IAS 28 *Investments in Associates and Joint Ventures* or IFRS 9 *Financial Instruments*.

Power

10   An investor has power over an investee when the investor has existing rights that give it the current ability to direct the *relevant activities*, ie the activities that significantly affect the investee's returns.

11   Power arises from rights. Sometimes assessing power is straightforward, such as when power over an investee is obtained directly and solely from the voting rights granted by equity instruments such as shares, and can be assessed by considering the voting rights from those shareholdings. In other cases, the assessment will be more complex and require more than one factor to be considered, for example when power results from one or more contractual arrangements.

12   An investor with the current ability to direct the relevant activities has power even if its rights to direct have yet to be exercised. Evidence that the investor has been directing relevant activities can help determine whether the investor has power, but such evidence is not, in itself, conclusive in determining whether the investor has power over an investee.

13   If two or more investors each have existing rights that give them the unilateral ability to direct different relevant activities, the investor that has the current ability to direct the activities that most significantly affect the returns of the investee has power over the investee.

14   An investor can have power over an investee even if other entities have existing rights that give them the current ability to participate in the direction of the relevant activities, for example when another entity has *significant influence*. However, an investor that holds only protective rights does not have power over an investee (see paragraphs B26–B28), and consequently does not control the investee.

Returns

15   An investor is exposed, or has rights, to variable returns from its involvement with the investee when the investor's returns from its involvement have the potential to vary as a result of the investee's performance. The investor's returns can be only positive, only negative or both positive and negative.

16   Although only one investor can control an investee, more than one party can share in the returns of an investee. For example, holders of non-controlling interests can share in the profits or distributions of an investee.

Link between power and returns

17   An investor controls an investee if the investor not only has power over the investee and exposure or rights to variable returns from its involvement with the investee, but also has the ability to use its power to affect the investor's returns from its involvement with the investee.

18   Thus, an investor with decision-making rights shall determine whether it is a principal or an agent. An investor that is an agent in accordance with paragraphs B58–B72 does not control an investee when it exercises decision-making rights delegated to it.

Accounting requirements

19   A parent shall prepare consolidated financial statements using uniform accounting policies for like transactions and other events in similar circumstances.

20   Consolidation of an investee shall begin from the date the investor obtains control of the investee and cease when the investor loses control of the investee.

21   Paragraphs B86–B93 set out guidance for the preparation of consolidated financial statements.

Non-controlling interests

22   A parent shall present non-controlling interests in the consolidated statement of financial position within equity, separately from the equity of the owners of the parent.

23   Changes in a parent's ownership interest in a subsidiary that do not result in the parent losing control of the subsidiary are equity transactions (ie transactions with owners in their capacity as owners).

24   Paragraphs B94–B96 set out guidance for the accounting for non-controlling interests in consolidated financial statements.

Loss of control

25   If a parent loses control of a subsidiary, the parent:

(a)   derecognises the assets and liabilities of the former subsidiary from the consolidated statement of financial position.

(b)   recognises any investment retained in the former subsidiary at its fair value when control is lost and subsequently accounts for it and for any amounts owed by or to the former subsidiary in accordance with relevant IFRSs. That fair value shall be regarded as the fair value on initial recognition of a financial asset in accordance with IFRS 9 or, when appropriate, the cost on initial recognition of an investment in an associate or joint venture.

(c)   recognises the gain or loss associated with the loss of control attributable to the former controlling interest.

26   Paragraphs B97–B99 set out guidance for the accounting for the loss of control.

Determining whether an entity is an investment entity

27   A parent shall determine whether it is an investment entity. An investment entity is an entity that:

(a)   obtains funds from one or more investors for the purpose of providing those investor(s) with investment management services;

(b)   commits to its investor(s) that its business purpose is to invest funds solely for returns from capital appreciation, investment income, or both; and

(c)   measures and evaluates the performance of substantially all of its investments on a fair value basis.

Paragraphs B85A–B85M provide related application guidance.

28   In assessing whether it meets the definition described in paragraph 27, an entity shall consider whether it has the following typical characteristics of an investment entity:

(a)   it has more than one investment (see paragraphs B85O–B85P);

(b)   it has more than one investor (see paragraphs B85Q–B85S);

(c)   it has investors that are not related parties of the entity (see paragraphs B85T–B85U); and

(d)   it has ownership interests in the form of equity or similar interests (see paragraphs B85V–B85W).

The absence of any of these typical characteristics does not necessarily disqualify an entity from being classified as an investment entity. An investment entity that does not have all of these typical characteristics provides additional disclosure required by paragraph 9A of IFRS 12 *Disclosure of Interests in Other Entities*.

29   If facts and circumstances indicate that there are changes to one or more of the three elements that make up the definition of an investment entity, as described in paragraph 27, or the typical characteristics of an investment entity, as described in paragraph 28, a parent shall reassess whether it is an investment entity.

30   A parent that either ceases to be an investment entity or becomes an investment entity shall account for the change in its status prospectively from the date at which the change in status occurred (see paragraphs B100–B101).

Investment entities: exception to consolidation

31   Except as described in paragraph 32, an investment entity shall not consolidate its subsidiaries or apply IFRS 3 when it obtains control of another entity. Instead, an investment entity shall measure an investment in a subsidiary at fair value through profit or loss in accordance with IFRS 9.[1]

32   Notwithstanding the requirement in paragraph 31, if an investment entity has a subsidiary that is not itself an investment entity and whose main purpose and activities are providing services that relate to the investment entity's investment activities (see paragraphs B85C–B85E), it shall consolidate that subsidiary in accordance with paragraphs 19–26 of this IFRS and apply the requirements of IFRS 3 to the acquisition of any such subsidiary.

33   A parent of an investment entity shall consolidate all entities that it controls, including those controlled through an investment entity subsidiary, unless the parent itself is an investment entity.

---

1   Paragraph C7 of IFRS 10 *Consolidated Financial Statements* states "If an entity applies this IFRS but does not yet apply IFRS 9, any reference in this IFRS to IFRS 9 shall be read as a reference to IAS 39 *Financial Instruments: Recognition and Measurement*."

Appendix A
Defined terms

This appendix is an integral part of the IFRS.

consolidated financial statements	The financial statements of a **group** in which the assets, liabilities, equity, income, expenses and cash flows of the **parent** and its **subsidiaries** are presented as those of a single economic entity.
control of an investee	An investor controls an investee when the investor is exposed, or has rights, to variable returns from its involvement with the investee and has the ability to affect those returns through its power over the investee.
decision maker	An entity with decision-making rights that is either a principal or an agent for other parties.
group	A **parent** and its **subsidiaries**.
investment entity	An entity that:

(a) obtains funds from one or more investors for the purpose of providing those investor(s) with investment management services;

(b) commits to its investor(s) that its business purpose is to invest funds solely for returns from capital appreciation, investment income, or both; and

(c) measures and evaluates the performance of substantially all of its investments on a fair value basis.

non-controlling interest	Equity in a **subsidiary** not attributable, directly or indirectly, to a **parent**.
parent	An entity that **controls** one or more entities.
power	Existing rights that give the current ability to direct the **relevant activities**.
protective rights	Rights designed to protect the interest of the party holding those rights without giving that party power over the entity to which those rights relate.
relevant activities	For the purpose of this IFRS, relevant activities are activities of the investee that significantly affect the investee's returns.
removal rights	Rights to deprive the decision maker of its decision-making authority.
subsidiary	An entity that is controlled by another entity.

The following terms are defined in IFRS 11, IFRS 12 *Disclosure of Interests in Other Entities*, IAS 28 (as amended in 2011) or IAS 24 *Related Party Disclosures* and are used in this IFRS with the meanings specified in those IFRSs:

- associate
- interest in another entity
- joint venture
- key management personnel
- related party
- significant influence.

Appendix B
Application guidance

This appendix is an integral part of the IFRS. It describes the application of paragraphs 1–33 and has the same authority as the other parts of the IFRS.

B1   The examples in this appendix portray hypothetical situations. Although some aspects of the examples may be present in actual fact patterns, all facts and circumstances of a particular fact pattern would need to be evaluated when applying IFRS 10.

Assessing control

B2   To determine whether it controls an investee an investor shall assess whether it has all the following:

    (a)   power over the investee;

    (b)   exposure, or rights, to variable returns from its involvement with the investee; and

    (c)   the ability to use its power over the investee to affect the amount of the investor's returns.

B3   Consideration of the following factors may assist in making that determination:

    (a)   the purpose and design of the investee (see paragraphs B5–B8);

    (b)   what the relevant activities are and how decisions about those activities are made (see paragraphs B11–B13);

    (c)   whether the rights of the investor give it the current ability to direct the relevant activities (see paragraphs B14–B54);

    (d)   whether the investor is exposed, or has rights, to variable returns from its involvement with the investee (see paragraphs B55–B57); and

    (e)   whether the investor has the ability to use its power over the investee to affect the amount of the investor's returns (see paragraphs B58–B72).

B4   When assessing control of an investee, an investor shall consider the nature of its relationship with other parties (see paragraphs B73–B75).

Purpose and design of an investee

B5   When assessing control of an investee, an investor shall consider the purpose and design of the investee in order to identify the relevant activities, how decisions about the relevant activities are made, who has the current ability to direct those activities and who receives returns from those activities.

B6   When an investee's purpose and design are considered, it may be clear that an investee is controlled by means of equity instruments that give the holder proportionate voting rights, such as ordinary shares in the investee. In this case, in the absence of any additional arrangements that alter decision-making, the assessment of control focuses on which party, if any, is able to exercise voting rights sufficient to determine the investee's operating and financing policies (see paragraphs B34–B50). In the most straightforward case, the investor that holds a majority of those voting rights, in the absence of any other factors, controls the investee.

B7   To determine whether an investor controls an investee in more complex cases, it may be necessary to consider some or all of the other factors in paragraph B3.

B8   An investee may be designed so that voting rights are not the dominant factor in deciding who controls the investee, such as when any voting rights relate to administrative tasks only and the relevant activities are directed by means of contractual arrangements. In such cases, an investor's consideration of the purpose and design of the investee shall also include consideration of the risks to which the investee was designed to be exposed, the risks it was designed to pass on to the parties involved with the investee and whether the investor is exposed to some or all of those risks. Consideration of the risks includes not only the downside risk, but also the potential for upside.

Power

B9   To have power over an investee, an investor must have existing rights that give it the current ability to direct the relevant activities. For the purpose of assessing power, only substantive rights and rights that are not protective shall be considered (see paragraphs B22–B28).

B10   The determination about whether an investor has power depends on the relevant activities, the way decisions about the relevant activities are made and the rights the investor and other parties have in relation to the investee.

Relevant activities and direction of relevant activities

B11   For many investees, a range of operating and financing activities significantly affect their returns. Examples of activities that, depending on the circumstances, can be relevant activities include, but are not limited to:

      (a)   selling and purchasing of goods or services;

      (b)   managing financial assets during their life (including upon default);

      (c)   selecting, acquiring or disposing of assets;

      (d)   researching and developing new products or processes; and

      (e)   determining a funding structure or obtaining funding.

B12   Examples of decisions about relevant activities include but are not limited to:

      (a)   establishing operating and capital decisions of the investee, including budgets; and

(b)   appointing and remunerating an investee's key management personnel or service providers and terminating their services or employment.

B13   In some situations, activities both before and after a particular set of circumstances arises or event occurs may be relevant activities. When two or more investors have the current ability to direct relevant activities and those activities occur at different times, the investors shall determine which investor is able to direct the activities that most significantly affect those returns consistently with the treatment of concurrent decision-making rights (see paragraph 13). The investors shall reconsider this assessment over time if relevant facts or circumstances change.

Application examples

Example 1

Two investors form an investee to develop and market a medical product. One investor is responsible for developing and obtaining regulatory approval of the medical product – that responsibility includes having the unilateral ability to make all decisions relating to the development of the product and to obtaining regulatory approval. Once the regulator has approved the product, the other investor will manufacture and market it – this investor has the unilateral ability to make all decisions about the manufacture and marketing of the product. If all the activities – developing and obtaining regulatory approval as well as manufacturing and marketing of the medical product – are relevant activities, each investor needs to determine whether it is able to direct the activities that *most* significantly affect the investee's returns. Accordingly, each investor needs to consider whether developing and obtaining regulatory approval or the manufacturing and marketing of the medical product is the activity that most significantly affects the investee's returns and whether it is able to direct that activity. In determining which investor has power, the investors would consider:

(a)   the purpose and design of the investee;

(b)   the factors that determine the profit margin, revenue and value of the investee as well as the value of the medical product;

(c)   the effect on the investee's returns resulting from each investor's decision-making authority with respect to the factors in (b); and

(d)   the investors' exposure to variability of returns.

In this particular example, the investors would also consider:

(e)   the uncertainty of, and effort required in, obtaining regulatory approval (considering the investor's record of successfully developing and obtaining regulatory approval of medical products); and

(f)   which investor controls the medical product once the development phase is successful.

continued...

...continued

Application examples

Example 2

An investment vehicle (the investee) is created and financed with a debt instrument held by an investor (the debt investor) and equity instruments held by a number of other investors. The equity tranche is designed to absorb the first losses and to receive any residual return from the investee. One of the equity investors who holds 30 per cent of the equity is also the asset manager. The investee uses its proceeds to purchase a portfolio of financial assets, exposing the investee to the credit risk associated with the possible default of principal and interest payments of the assets. The transaction is marketed to the debt investor as an investment with minimal exposure to the credit risk associated with the possible default of the assets in the portfolio because of the nature of these assets and because the equity tranche is designed to absorb the first losses of the investee. The returns of the investee are significantly affected by the management of the investee's asset portfolio, which includes decisions about the selection, acquisition and disposal of the assets within portfolio guidelines and the management upon default of any portfolio assets. All those activities are managed by the asset manager until defaults reach a specified proportion of the portfolio value (ie when the value of the portfolio is such that the equity tranche of the investee has been consumed). From that time, a third-party trustee manages the assets according to the instructions of the debt investor. Managing the investee's asset portfolio is the relevant activity of the investee. The asset manager has the ability to direct the relevant activities until defaulted assets reach the specified proportion of the portfolio value; the debt investor has the ability to direct the relevant activities when the value of defaulted assets surpasses that specified proportion of the portfolio value. The asset manager and the debt investor each need to determine whether they are able to direct the activities that *most* significantly affect the investee's returns, including considering the purpose and design of the investee as well as each party's exposure to variability of returns.

Rights that give an investor power over an investee

B14 Power arises from rights. To have power over an investee, an investor must have existing rights that give the investor the current ability to direct the relevant activities. The rights that may give an investor power can differ between investees.

B15 Examples of rights that, either individually or in combination, can give an investor power include but are not limited to:

(a) rights in the form of voting rights (or potential voting rights) of an investee (see paragraphs B34–B50);

(b) rights to appoint, reassign or remove members of an investee's key management personnel who have the ability to direct the relevant activities;

(c)   rights to appoint or remove another entity that directs the relevant activities;

(d)   rights to direct the investee to enter into, or veto any changes to, transactions for the benefit of the investor; and

(e)   other rights (such as decision-making rights specified in a management contract) that give the holder the ability to direct the relevant activities.

B16   Generally, when an investee has a range of operating and financing activities that significantly affect the investee's returns and when substantive decision-making with respect to these activities is required continuously, it will be voting or similar rights that give an investor power, either individually or in combination with other arrangements.

B17   When voting rights cannot have a significant effect on an investee's returns, such as when voting rights relate to administrative tasks only and contractual arrangements determine the direction of the relevant activities, the investor needs to assess those contractual arrangements in order to determine whether it has rights sufficient to give it power over the investee. To determine whether an investor has rights sufficient to give it power, the investor shall consider the purpose and design of the investee (see paragraphs B5–B8) and the requirements in paragraphs B51–B54 together with paragraphs B18–B20.

B18   In some circumstances it may be difficult to determine whether an investor's rights are sufficient to give it power over an investee. In such cases, to enable the assessment of power to be made, the investor shall consider evidence of whether it has the practical ability to direct the relevant activities unilaterally. Consideration is given, but is not limited, to the following, which, when considered together with its rights and the indicators in paragraphs B19 and B20, may provide evidence that the investor's rights are sufficient to give it power over the investee:

(a)   The investor can, without having the contractual right to do so, appoint or approve the investee's key management personnel who have the ability to direct the relevant activities.

(b)   The investor can, without having the contractual right to do so, direct the investee to enter into, or can veto any changes to, significant transactions for the benefit of the investor.

(c)   The investor can dominate either the nominations process for electing members of the investee's governing body or the obtaining of proxies from other holders of voting rights.

(d)   The investee's key management personnel are related parties of the investor (for example, the chief executive officer of the investee and the chief executive officer of the investor are the same person).

(e)   The majority of the members of the investee's governing body are related parties of the investor.

B19   Sometimes there will be indications that the investor has a special relationship with the investee, which suggests that the investor has more than a passive interest in the investee. The existence of any individual indicator, or a particular combination of indicators, does not necessarily mean that the power criterion is met. However, having more than a passive interest in the investee may indicate that the investor has other related rights sufficient to give it power or provide evidence of existing power over an investee. For example, the following suggests that the investor has more than a passive interest in the investee and, in combination with other rights, may indicate power:

(a)   The investee's key management personnel who have the ability to direct the relevant activities are current or previous employees of the investor.

(b)   The investee's operations are dependent on the investor, such as in the following situations:

     (i)   The investee depends on the investor to fund a significant portion of its operations.

     (ii)   The investor guarantees a significant portion of the investee's obligations.

     (iii)   The investee depends on the investor for critical services, technology, supplies or raw materials.

     (iv)   The investor controls assets such as licences or trademarks that are critical to the investee's operations.

     (v)   The investee depends on the investor for key management personnel, such as when the investor's personnel have specialised knowledge of the investee's operations.

(c)   A significant portion of the investee's activities either involve or are conducted on behalf of the investor.

(d)   The investor's exposure, or rights, to returns from its involvement with the investee is disproportionately greater than its voting or other similar rights. For example, there may be a situation in which an investor is entitled, or exposed, to more than half of the returns of the investee but holds less than half of the voting rights of the investee.

B20   The greater an investor's exposure, or rights, to variability of returns from its involvement with an investee, the greater is the incentive for the investor to obtain rights sufficient to give it power. Therefore, having a large exposure to variability of returns is an indicator that the investor may have power. However, the extent of the investor's exposure does not, in itself, determine whether an investor has power over the investee.

B21   When the factors set out in paragraph B18 and the indicators set out in paragraphs B19 and B20 are considered together with an investor's rights, greater weight shall be given to the evidence of power described in paragraph B18.

Substantive rights

B22 An investor, in assessing whether it has power, considers only substantive rights relating to an investee (held by the investor and others). For a right to be substantive, the holder must have the practical ability to exercise that right.

B23 Determining whether rights are substantive requires judgement, taking into account all facts and circumstances. Factors to consider in making that determination include but are not limited to:

(a) Whether there are any barriers (economic or otherwise) that prevent the holder (or holders) from exercising the rights. Examples of such barriers include but are not limited to:

(i) financial penalties and incentives that would prevent (or deter) the holder from exercising its rights.

(ii) an exercise or conversion price that creates a financial barrier that would prevent (or deter) the holder from exercising its rights.

(iii) terms and conditions that make it unlikely that the rights would be exercised, for example, conditions that narrowly limit the timing of their exercise.

(iv) the absence of an explicit, reasonable mechanism in the founding documents of an investee or in applicable laws or regulations that would allow the holder to exercise its rights.

(v) the inability of the holder of the rights to obtain the information necessary to exercise its rights.

(vi) operational barriers or incentives that would prevent (or deter) the holder from exercising its rights (eg the absence of other managers willing or able to provide specialised services or provide the services and take on other interests held by the incumbent manager).

(vii) legal or regulatory requirements that prevent the holder from exercising its rights (eg where a foreign investor is prohibited from exercising its rights).

(b) When the exercise of rights requires the agreement of more than one party, or when the rights are held by more than one party, whether a mechanism is in place that provides those parties with the practical ability to exercise their rights collectively if they choose to do so. The lack of such a mechanism is an indicator that the rights may not be substantive. The more parties that are required to agree to exercise the rights, the less likely it is that those rights are substantive. However, a board of directors whose members are independent of the decision maker may serve as a mechanism for numerous investors to act collectively in exercising their rights. Therefore, removal rights exercisable by an independent board of directors are more likely to be substantive than if the same rights were exercisable individually by a large number of investors.

(c)   Whether the party or parties that hold the rights would benefit from the exercise of those rights. For example, the holder of potential voting rights in an investee (see paragraphs B47–B50) shall consider the exercise or conversion price of the instrument. The terms and conditions of potential voting rights are more likely to be substantive when the instrument is in the money or the investor would benefit for other reasons (eg by realising synergies between the investor and the investee) from the exercise or conversion of the instrument.

B24   To be substantive, rights also need to be exercisable when decisions about the direction of the relevant activities need to be made. Usually, to be substantive, the rights need to be currently exercisable. However, sometimes rights can be substantive, even though the rights are not currently exercisable.

Application examples

Example 3

The investee has annual shareholder meetings at which decisions to direct the relevant activities are made. The next scheduled shareholders' meeting is in eight months. However, shareholders that individually or collectively hold at least 5 per cent of the voting rights can call a special meeting to change the existing policies over the relevant activities, but a requirement to give notice to the other shareholders means that such a meeting cannot be held for at least 30 days. Policies over the relevant activities can be changed only at special or scheduled shareholders' meetings. This includes the approval of material sales of assets as well as the making or disposing of significant investments.

The above fact pattern applies to examples 3A–3D described below. Each example is considered in isolation.

Example 3A

An investor holds a majority of the voting rights in the investee. The investor's voting rights are substantive because the investor is able to make decisions about the direction of the relevant activities when they need to be made. The fact that it takes 30 days before the investor can exercise its voting rights does not stop the investor from having the current ability to direct the relevant activities from the moment the investor acquires the shareholding.

continued...

...continued

Application examples
Example 3B
An investor is party to a forward contract to acquire the majority of shares in the investee. The forward contract's settlement date is in 25 days. The existing shareholders are unable to change the existing policies over the relevant activities because a special meeting cannot be held for at least 30 days, at which point the forward contract will have been settled. Thus, the investor has rights that are essentially equivalent to the majority shareholder in example 3A above (ie the investor holding the forward contract can make decisions about the direction of the relevant activities when they need to be made). The investor's forward contract is a substantive right that gives the investor the current ability to direct the relevant activities even before the forward contract is settled.
Example 3C
An investor holds a substantive option to acquire the majority of shares in the investee that is exercisable in 25 days and is deeply in the money. The same conclusion would be reached as in example 3B.
Example 3D
An investor is party to a forward contract to acquire the majority of shares in the investee, with no other related rights over the investee. The forward contract's settlement date is in six months. In contrast to the examples above, the investor does not have the current ability to direct the relevant activities. The existing shareholders have the current ability to direct the relevant activities because they can change the existing policies over the relevant activities before the forward contract is settled.

B25 Substantive rights exercisable by other parties can prevent an investor from controlling the investee to which those rights relate. Such substantive rights do not require the holders to have the ability to initiate decisions. As long as the rights are not merely protective (see paragraphs B26–B28), substantive rights held by other parties may prevent the investor from controlling the investee even if the rights give the holders only the current ability to approve or block decisions that relate to the relevant activities.

Protective rights

B26 In evaluating whether rights give an investor power over an investee, the investor shall assess whether its rights, and rights held by others, are protective rights. Protective rights relate to fundamental changes to the activities of an investee or apply in exceptional circumstances. However, not all rights that apply in exceptional circumstances or are contingent on events are protective (see paragraphs B13 and B53).

B27 Because protective rights are designed to protect the interests of their holder without giving that party power over the investee to which those rights relate, an investor that holds only protective rights cannot have power or prevent another party from having power over an investee (see paragraph 14).

B28 Examples of protective rights include but are not limited to:

(a) a lender's right to restrict a borrower from undertaking activities that could significantly change the credit risk of the borrower to the detriment of the lender.

(b) the right of a party holding a non-controlling interest in an investee to approve capital expenditure greater than that required in the ordinary course of business, or to approve the issue of equity or debt instruments.

(c) the right of a lender to seize the assets of a borrower if the borrower fails to meet specified loan repayment conditions.

Franchises

B29 A franchise agreement for which the investee is the franchisee often gives the franchisor rights that are designed to protect the franchise brand. Franchise agreements typically give franchisors some decision-making rights with respect to the operations of the franchisee.

B30 Generally, franchisors' rights do not restrict the ability of parties other than the franchisor to make decisions that have a significant effect on the franchisee's returns. Nor do the rights of the franchisor in franchise agreements necessarily give the franchisor the current ability to direct the activities that significantly affect the franchisee's returns.

B31 It is necessary to distinguish between having the current ability to make decisions that significantly affect the franchisee's returns and having the ability to make decisions that protect the franchise brand. The franchisor does not have power over the franchisee if other parties have existing rights that give them the current ability to direct the relevant activities of the franchisee.

B32 By entering into the franchise agreement the franchisee has made a unilateral decision to operate its business in accordance with the terms of the franchise agreement, but for its own account.

B33 Control over such fundamental decisions as the legal form of the franchisee and its funding structure may be determined by parties other than the franchisor and may significantly affect the returns of the franchisee. The lower the level of financial support provided by the franchisor and the lower the franchisor's exposure to variability of returns from the franchisee the more likely it is that the franchisor has only protective rights.

Voting rights

B34 Often an investor has the current ability, through voting or similar rights, to direct the relevant activities. An investor considers the requirements in this section (paragraphs B35–B50) if the relevant activities of an investee are directed through voting rights.

Power with a majority of the voting rights

B35 An investor that holds more than half of the voting rights of an investee has power in the following situations, unless paragraph B36 or paragraph B37 applies:

(a) the relevant activities are directed by a vote of the holder of the majority of the voting rights, or

(b) a majority of the members of the governing body that directs the relevant activities are appointed by a vote of the holder of the majority of the voting rights.

Majority of the voting rights but no power

B36 For an investor that holds more than half of the voting rights of an investee, to have power over an investee, the investor's voting rights must be substantive, in accordance with paragraphs B22–B25, and must provide the investor with the current ability to direct the relevant activities, which often will be through determining operating and financing policies. If another entity has existing rights that provide that entity with the right to direct the relevant activities and that entity is not an agent of the investor, the investor does not have power over the investee.

B37 An investor does not have power over an investee, even though the investor holds the majority of the voting rights in the investee, when those voting rights are not substantive. For example, an investor that has more than half of the voting rights in an investee cannot have power if the relevant activities are subject to direction by a government, court, administrator, receiver, liquidator or regulator.

Power without a majority of the voting rights

B38 An investor can have power even if it holds less than a majority of the voting rights of an investee. An investor can have power with less than a majority of the voting rights of an investee, for example, through:

(a) a contractual arrangement between the investor and other vote holders (see paragraph B39);

(b) rights arising from other contractual arrangements (see paragraph B40);

(c) the investor's voting rights (see paragraphs B41–B45);

(d) potential voting rights (see paragraphs B47–B50); or

(e) a combination of (a)–(d).

Contractual arrangement with other vote holders

B39 A contractual arrangement between an investor and other vote holders can give the investor the right to exercise voting rights sufficient to give the investor power, even if the investor does not have voting rights sufficient to give it power without the contractual arrangement. However, a contractual arrangement might ensure that the investor can direct enough other vote holders on how to vote to enable the investor to make decisions about the relevant activities.

Rights from other contractual arrangements

B40 Other decision-making rights, in combination with voting rights, can give an investor the current ability to direct the relevant activities. For example, the rights specified in a contractual arrangement in combination with voting rights may be sufficient to give an investor the current ability to direct the manufacturing processes of an investee or to direct other operating or financing activities of an investee that significantly affect the investee's returns. However, in the absence of any other rights, economic dependence of an investee on the investor (such as relations of a supplier with its main customer) does not lead to the investor having power over the investee.

The investor's voting rights

B41 An investor with less than a majority of the voting rights has rights that are sufficient to give it power when the investor has the practical ability to direct the relevant activities unilaterally.

B42 When assessing whether an investor's voting rights are sufficient to give it power, an investor considers all facts and circumstances, including:

(a) the size of the investor's holding of voting rights relative to the size and dispersion of holdings of the other vote holders, noting that:

(i) the more voting rights an investor holds, the more likely the investor is to have existing rights that give it the current ability to direct the relevant activities;

(ii) the more voting rights an investor holds relative to other vote holders, the more likely the investor is to have existing rights that give it the current ability to direct the relevant activities;

(iii) the more parties that would need to act together to outvote the investor, the more likely the investor is to have existing rights that give it the current ability to direct the relevant activities;

(b) potential voting rights held by the investor, other vote holders or other parties (see paragraphs B47–B50);

(c) rights arising from other contractual arrangements (see paragraph B40); and

(d)   any additional facts and circumstances that indicate the investor has, or does not have, the current ability to direct the relevant activities at the time that decisions need to be made, including voting patterns at previous shareholders' meetings.

B43   When the direction of relevant activities is determined by majority vote and an investor holds significantly more voting rights than any other vote holder or organised group of vote holders, and the other shareholdings are widely dispersed, it may be clear, after considering the factors listed in paragraph B42(a)–(c) alone, that the investor has power over the investee.

Application examples

Example 4

An investor acquires 48 per cent of the voting rights of an investee. The remaining voting rights are held by thousands of shareholders, none individually holding more than 1 per cent of the voting rights. None of the shareholders has any arrangements to consult any of the others or make collective decisions. When assessing the proportion of voting rights to acquire, on the basis of the relative size of the other shareholdings, the investor determined that a 48 per cent interest would be sufficient to give it control. In this case, on the basis of the absolute size of its holding and the relative size of the other shareholdings, the investor concludes that it has a sufficiently dominant voting interest to meet the power criterion without the need to consider any other evidence of power.

Example 5

Investor A holds 40 per cent of the voting rights of an investee and twelve other investors each hold 5 per cent of the voting rights of the investee. A shareholder agreement grants investor A the right to appoint, remove and set the remuneration of management responsible for directing the relevant activities. To change the agreement, a two-thirds majority vote of the shareholders is required. In this case, investor A concludes that the absolute size of the investor's holding and the relative size of the other shareholdings alone are not conclusive in determining whether the investor has rights sufficient to give it power. However, investor A determines that its contractual right to appoint, remove and set the remuneration of management is sufficient to conclude that it has power over the investee. The fact that investor A might not have exercised this right or the likelihood of investor A exercising its right to select, appoint or remove management shall not be considered when assessing whether investor A has power.

B44   In other situations, it may be clear after considering the factors listed in paragraph B42(a)–(c) alone that an investor does not have power.

Application example

Example 6

Investor A holds 45 per cent of the voting rights of an investee. Two other investors each hold 26 per cent of the voting rights of the investee. The remaining voting rights are held by three other shareholders, each holding 1 per cent. There are no other arrangements that affect decision-making. In this case, the size of investor A's voting interest and its size relative to the other shareholdings are sufficient to conclude that investor A does not have power. Only two other investors would need to co-operate to be able to prevent investor A from directing the relevant activities of the investee.

B45 However, the factors listed in paragraph B42(a)–(c) alone may not be conclusive. If an investor, having considered those factors, is unclear whether it has power, it shall consider additional facts and circumstances, such as whether other shareholders are passive in nature as demonstrated by voting patterns at previous shareholders' meetings. This includes the assessment of the factors set out in paragraph B18 and the indicators in paragraphs B19 and B20. The fewer voting rights the investor holds, and the fewer parties that would need to act together to outvote the investor, the more reliance would be placed on the additional facts and circumstances to assess whether the investor's rights are sufficient to give it power. When the facts and circumstances in paragraphs B18–B20 are considered together with the investor's rights, greater weight shall be given to the evidence of power in paragraph B18 than to the indicators of power in paragraphs B19 and B20.

Application examples

Example 7

An investor holds 45 per cent of the voting rights of an investee. Eleven other shareholders each hold 5 per cent of the voting rights of the investee. None of the shareholders has contractual arrangements to consult any of the others or make collective decisions. In this case, the absolute size of the investor's holding and the relative size of the other shareholdings alone are not conclusive in determining whether the investor has rights sufficient to give it power over the investee. Additional facts and circumstances that may provide evidence that the investor has, or does not have, power shall be considered.

continued...

...*continued*

Application examples

Example 8

An investor holds 35 per cent of the voting rights of an investee. Three other shareholders each hold 5 per cent of the voting rights of the investee. The remaining voting rights are held by numerous other shareholders, none individually holding more than 1 per cent of the voting rights. None of the shareholders has arrangements to consult any of the others or make collective decisions. Decisions about the relevant activities of the investee require the approval of a majority of votes cast at relevant shareholders' meetings—75 per cent of the voting rights of the investee have been cast at recent relevant shareholders' meetings. In this case, the active participation of the other shareholders at recent shareholders' meetings indicates that the investor would not have the practical ability to direct the relevant activities unilaterally, regardless of whether the investor has directed the relevant activities because a sufficient number of other shareholders voted in the same way as the investor.

B46   If it is not clear, having considered the factors listed in paragraph B42(a)–(d), that the investor has power, the investor does not control the investee.

Potential voting rights

B47   When assessing control, an investor considers its potential voting rights as well as potential voting rights held by other parties, to determine whether it has power. Potential voting rights are rights to obtain voting rights of an investee, such as those arising from convertible instruments or options, including forward contracts. Those potential voting rights are considered only if the rights are substantive (see paragraphs B22–B25).

B48   When considering potential voting rights, an investor shall consider the purpose and design of the instrument, as well as the purpose and design of any other involvement the investor has with the investee. This includes an assessment of the various terms and conditions of the instrument as well as the investor's apparent expectations, motives and reasons for agreeing to those terms and conditions.

B49   If the investor also has voting or other decision-making rights relating to the investee's activities, the investor assesses whether those rights, in combination with potential voting rights, give the investor power.

B50   Substantive potential voting rights alone, or in combination with other rights, can give an investor the current ability to direct the relevant activities. For example, this is likely to be the case when an investor holds 40 per cent of the voting rights of an investee and, in accordance with paragraph B23, holds substantive rights arising from options to acquire a further 20 per cent of the voting rights.

Application examples

Example 9

Investor A holds 70 per cent of the voting rights of an investee. Investor B has 30 per cent of the voting rights of the investee as well as an option to acquire half of investor A's voting rights. The option is exercisable for the next two years at a fixed price that is deeply out of the money (and is expected to remain so for that two-year period). Investor A has been exercising its votes and is actively directing the relevant activities of the investee. In such a case, investor A is likely to meet the power criterion because it appears to have the current ability to direct the relevant activities. Although investor B has currently exercisable options to purchase additional voting rights (that, if exercised, would give it a majority of the voting rights in the investee), the terms and conditions associated with those options are such that the options are not considered substantive.

Example 10

Investor A and two other investors each hold a third of the voting rights of an investee. The investee's business activity is closely related to investor A. In addition to its equity instruments, investor A also holds debt instruments that are convertible into ordinary shares of the investee at any time for a fixed price that is out of the money (but not deeply out of the money). If the debt were converted, investor A would hold 60 per cent of the voting rights of the investee. Investor A would benefit from realising synergies if the debt instruments were converted into ordinary shares. Investor A has power over the investee because it holds voting rights of the investee together with substantive potential voting rights that give it the current ability to direct the relevant activities.

Power when voting or similar rights do not have a significant effect on the investee's returns

B51   In assessing the purpose and design of an investee (see paragraphs B5–B8), an investor shall consider the involvement and decisions made at the investee's inception as part of its design and evaluate whether the transaction terms and features of the involvement provide the investor with rights that are sufficient to give it power. Being involved in the design of an investee alone is not sufficient to give an investor control. However, involvement in the design may indicate that the investor had the opportunity to obtain rights that are sufficient to give it power over the investee.

B52   In addition, an investor shall consider contractual arrangements such as call rights, put rights and liquidation rights established at the investee's inception. When these contractual arrangements involve activities that are closely related to the investee, then these activities are, in substance, an integral part of the investee's overall activities, even though they may occur outside the legal boundaries of the investee. Therefore, explicit or implicit decision-making rights embedded in contractual arrangements that are closely related to the investee need to be considered as relevant activities when determining power over the investee.

B53   For some investees, relevant activities occur only when particular circumstances arise or events occur. The investee may be designed so that the direction of its activities and its returns are predetermined unless and until those particular circumstances arise or events occur. In this case, only the decisions about the investee's activities when those circumstances or events occur can significantly affect its returns and thus be relevant activities. The circumstances or events need not have occurred for an investor with the ability to make those decisions to have power. The fact that the right to make decisions is contingent on circumstances arising or an event occurring does not, in itself, make those rights protective.

Application examples

Example 11

An investee's only business activity, as specified in its founding documents, is to purchase receivables and service them on a day-to-day basis for its investors. The servicing on a day-to-day basis includes the collection and passing on of principal and interest payments as they fall due. Upon default of a receivable the investee automatically puts the receivable to an investor as agreed separately in a put agreement between the investor and the investee. The only relevant activity is managing the receivables upon default because it is the only activity that can significantly affect the investee's returns. Managing the receivables before default is not a relevant activity because it does not require substantive decisions to be made that could significantly affect the investee's returns—the activities before default are predetermined and amount only to collecting cash flows as they fall due and passing them on to investors. Therefore, only the investor's right to manage the assets upon default should be considered when assessing the overall activities of the investee that significantly affect the investee's returns.

In this example, the design of the investee ensures that the investor has decision-making authority over the activities that significantly affect the returns at the only time that such decision-making authority is required. The terms of the put agreement are integral to the overall transaction and the establishment of the investee. Therefore, the terms of the put agreement together with the founding documents of the investee lead to the conclusion that the investor has power over the investee even though the investor takes ownership of the receivables only upon default and manages the defaulted receivables outside the legal boundaries of the investee.

Example 12

The only assets of an investee are receivables. When the purpose and design of the investee are considered, it is determined that the only relevant activity is managing the receivables upon default. The party that has the ability to manage the defaulting receivables has power over the investee, irrespective of whether any of the borrowers have defaulted.

B54 An investor may have an explicit or implicit commitment to ensure that an investee continues to operate as designed. Such a commitment may increase the investor's exposure to variability of returns and thus increase the incentive for the investor to obtain rights sufficient to give it power. Therefore a commitment to ensure that an investee operates as designed may be an indicator that the investor has power, but does not, by itself, give an investor power, nor does it prevent another party from having power.

Exposure, or rights, to variable returns from an investee

B55 When assessing whether an investor has control of an investee, the investor determines whether it is exposed, or has rights, to variable returns from its involvement with the investee.

B56 Variable returns are returns that are not fixed and have the potential to vary as a result of the performance of an investee. Variable returns can be only positive, only negative or both positive and negative (see paragraph 15). An investor assesses whether returns from an investee are variable and how variable those returns are on the basis of the substance of the arrangement and regardless of the legal form of the returns. For example, an investor can hold a bond with fixed interest payments. The fixed interest payments are variable returns for the purpose of this IFRS because they are subject to default risk and they expose the investor to the credit risk of the issuer of the bond. The amount of variability (ie how variable those returns are) depends on the credit risk of the bond. Similarly, fixed performance fees for managing an investee's assets are variable returns because they expose the investor to the performance risk of the investee. The amount of variability depends on the investee's ability to generate sufficient income to pay the fee.

B57 Examples of returns include:

(a) dividends, other distributions of economic benefits from an investee (eg interest from debt securities issued by the investee) and changes in the value of the investor's investment in that investee.

(b) remuneration for servicing an investee's assets or liabilities, fees and exposure to loss from providing credit or liquidity support, residual interests in the investee's assets and liabilities on liquidation of that investee, tax benefits, and access to future liquidity that an investor has from its involvement with an investee.

(c) returns that are not available to other interest holders. For example, an investor might use its assets in combination with the assets of the investee, such as combining operating functions to achieve economies of scale, cost savings, sourcing scarce products, gaining access to proprietary knowledge or limiting some operations or assets, to enhance the value of the investor's other assets.

Link between power and returns

Delegated power

B58   When an investor with decision-making rights (a decision maker) assesses whether it controls an investee, it shall determine whether it is a principal or an agent. An investor shall also determine whether another entity with decision-making rights is acting as an agent for the investor. An agent is a party primarily engaged to act on behalf and for the benefit of another party or parties (the principal(s)) and therefore does not control the investee when it exercises its decision-making authority (see paragraphs 17 and 18). Thus, sometimes a principal's power may be held and exercisable by an agent, but on behalf of the principal. A decision maker is not an agent simply because other parties can benefit from the decisions that it makes.

B59   An investor may delegate its decision-making authority to an agent on some specific issues or on all relevant activities. When assessing whether it controls an investee, the investor shall treat the decision-making rights delegated to its agent as held by the investor directly. In situations where there is more than one principal, each of the principals shall assess whether it has power over the investee by considering the requirements in paragraphs B5–B54. Paragraphs B60–B72 provide guidance on determining whether a decision maker is an agent or a principal.

B60   A decision maker shall consider the overall relationship between itself, the investee being managed and other parties involved with the investee, in particular all the factors below, in determining whether it is an agent:

(a)   the scope of its decision-making authority over the investee (paragraphs B62 and B63).

(b)   the rights held by other parties (paragraphs B64–B67).

(c)   the remuneration to which it is entitled in accordance with the remuneration agreement(s) (paragraphs B68–B70).

(d)   the decision maker's exposure to variability of returns from other interests that it holds in the investee (paragraphs B71 and B72).

Different weightings shall be applied to each of the factors on the basis of particular facts and circumstances.

B61   Determining whether a decision maker is an agent requires an evaluation of all the factors listed in paragraph B60 unless a single party holds substantive rights to remove the decision maker (removal rights) and can remove the decision maker without cause (see paragraph B65).

The scope of the decision-making authority

B62   The scope of a decision maker's decision-making authority is evaluated by considering:

(a)   the activities that are permitted according to the decision-making agreement(s) and specified by law, and

(b)   the discretion that the decision maker has when making decisions about those activities.

B63   A decision maker shall consider the purpose and design of the investee, the risks to which the investee was designed to be exposed, the risks it was designed to pass on to the parties involved and the level of involvement the decision maker had in the design of an investee. For example, if a decision maker is significantly involved in the design of the investee (including in determining the scope of decision-making authority), that involvement may indicate that the decision maker had the opportunity and incentive to obtain rights that result in the decision maker having the ability to direct the relevant activities.

Rights held by other parties

B64   Substantive rights held by other parties may affect the decision maker's ability to direct the relevant activities of an investee. Substantive removal or other rights may indicate that the decision maker is an agent.

B65   When a single party holds substantive removal rights and can remove the decision maker without cause, this, in isolation, is sufficient to conclude that the decision maker is an agent. If more than one party holds such rights (and no individual party can remove the decision maker without the agreement of other parties) those rights are not, in isolation, conclusive in determining that a decision maker acts primarily on behalf and for the benefit of others. In addition, the greater the number of parties required to act together to exercise rights to remove a decision maker and the greater the magnitude of, and variability associated with, the decision maker's other economic interests (ie remuneration and other interests), the less the weighting that shall be placed on this factor.

B66   Substantive rights held by other parties that restrict a decision maker's discretion shall be considered in a similar manner to removal rights when evaluating whether the decision maker is an agent. For example, a decision maker that is required to obtain approval from a small number of other parties for its actions is generally an agent. (See paragraphs B22–B25 for additional guidance on rights and whether they are substantive.)

B67   Consideration of the rights held by other parties shall include an assessment of any rights exercisable by an investee's board of directors (or other governing body) and their effect on the decision-making authority (see paragraph B23(b)).

Remuneration

B68   The greater the magnitude of, and variability associated with, the decision maker's remuneration relative to the returns expected from the activities of the investee, the more likely the decision maker is a principal.

B69   In determining whether it is a principal or an agent the decision maker shall also consider whether the following conditions exist:

(a)   The remuneration of the decision maker is commensurate with the services provided.

(b) The remuneration agreement includes only terms, conditions or amounts that are customarily present in arrangements for similar services and level of skills negotiated on an arm's length basis.

B70 A decision maker cannot be an agent unless the conditions set out in paragraph B69(a) and (b) are present. However, meeting those conditions in isolation is not sufficient to conclude that a decision maker is an agent.

Exposure to variability of returns from other interests

B71 A decision maker that holds other interests in an investee (eg investments in the investee or provides guarantees with respect to the performance of the investee), shall consider its exposure to variability of returns from those interests in assessing whether it is an agent. Holding other interests in an investee indicates that the decision maker may be a principal.

B72 In evaluating its exposure to variability of returns from other interests in the investee a decision maker shall consider the following:

(a) the greater the magnitude of, and variability associated with, its economic interests, considering its remuneration and other interests in aggregate, the more likely the decision maker is a principal.

(b) whether its exposure to variability of returns is different from that of the other investors and, if so, whether this might influence its actions. For example, this might be the case when a decision maker holds subordinated interests in, or provides other forms of credit enhancement to, an investee.

The decision maker shall evaluate its exposure relative to the total variability of returns of the investee. This evaluation is made primarily on the basis of returns expected from the activities of the investee but shall not ignore the decision maker's maximum exposure to variability of returns of the investee through other interests that the decision maker holds.

Application examples

Example 13

A decision maker (fund manager) establishes, markets and manages a publicly traded, regulated fund according to narrowly defined parameters set out in the investment mandate as required by its local laws and regulations. The fund was marketed to investors as an investment in a diversified portfolio of equity securities of publicly traded entities. Within the defined parameters, the fund manager has discretion about the assets in which to invest. The fund manager has made a 10 per cent pro rata investment in the fund and receives a market-based fee for its services equal to 1 per cent of the net asset value of the fund. The fees are commensurate with the services provided. The fund manager does not have any obligation to fund losses beyond its 10 per cent investment. The fund is not required to establish, and has not established, an independent board of directors. The investors do not hold any substantive rights that would affect the decision-making authority of the fund manager, but can redeem their interests within particular limits set by the fund.

Although operating within the parameters set out in the investment mandate and in accordance with the regulatory requirements, the fund manager has decision-making rights that give it the current ability to direct the relevant activities of the fund – the investors do not hold substantive rights that could affect the fund manager's decision-making authority. The fund manager receives a market-based fee for its services that is commensurate with the services provided and has also made a pro rata investment in the fund. The remuneration and its investment expose the fund manager to variability of returns from the activities of the fund without creating exposure that is of such significance that it indicates that the fund manager is a principal.

In this example, consideration of the fund manager's exposure to variability of returns from the fund together with its decision-making authority within restricted parameters indicates that the fund manager is an agent. Thus, the fund manager concludes that it does not control the fund.

Example 14

A decision maker establishes, markets and manages a fund that provides investment opportunities to a number of investors. The decision maker (fund manager) must make decisions in the best interests of all investors and in accordance with the fund's governing agreements. Nonetheless, the fund manager has wide decision-making discretion. The fund manager receives a market-based fee for its services equal to 1 per cent of assets under management and 20 per cent of all the fund's profits if a specified profit level is achieved. The fees are commensurate with the services provided.

continued...

...continued

Application examples

Although it must make decisions in the best interests of all investors, the fund manager has extensive decision-making authority to direct the relevant activities of the fund. The fund manager is paid fixed and performance-related fees that are commensurate with the services provided. In addition, the remuneration aligns the interests of the fund manager with those of the other investors to increase the value of the fund, without creating exposure to variability of returns from the activities of the fund that is of such significance that the remuneration, when considered in isolation, indicates that the fund manager is a principal.

The above fact pattern and analysis applies to examples 14A–14C described below. Each example is considered in isolation.

Example 14A

The fund manager also has a 2 per cent investment in the fund that aligns its interests with those of the other investors. The fund manager does not have any obligation to fund losses beyond its 2 per cent investment. The investors can remove the fund manager by a simple majority vote, but only for breach of contract.

The fund manager's 2 per cent investment increases its exposure to variability of returns from the activities of the fund without creating exposure that is of such significance that it indicates that the fund manager is a principal. The other investors' rights to remove the fund manager are considered to be protective rights because they are exercisable only for breach of contract. In this example, although the fund manager has extensive decision-making authority and is exposed to variability of returns from its interest and remuneration, the fund manager's exposure indicates that the fund manager is an agent. Thus, the fund manager concludes that it does not control the fund.

Example 14B

The fund manager has a more substantial pro rata investment in the fund, but does not have any obligation to fund losses beyond that investment. The investors can remove the fund manager by a simple majority vote, but only for breach of contract.

continued...

...continued

Application examples

In this example, the other investors' rights to remove the fund manager are considered to be protective rights because they are exercisable only for breach of contract. Although the fund manager is paid fixed and performance-related fees that are commensurate with the services provided, the combination of the fund manager's investment together with its remuneration could create exposure to variability of returns from the activities of the fund that is of such significance that it indicates that the fund manager is a principal. The greater the magnitude of, and variability associated with, the fund manager's economic interests (considering its remuneration and other interests in aggregate), the more emphasis the fund manager would place on those economic interests in the analysis, and the more likely the fund manager is a principal.

For example, having considered its remuneration and the other factors, the fund manager might consider a 20 per cent investment to be sufficient to conclude that it controls the fund. However, in different circumstances (ie if the remuneration or other factors are different), control may arise when the level of investment is different.

Example 14C

The fund manager has a 20 per cent pro rata investment in the fund, but does not have any obligation to fund losses beyond its 20 per cent investment. The fund has a board of directors, all of whose members are independent of the fund manager and are appointed by the other investors. The board appoints the fund manager annually. If the board decided not to renew the fund manager's contract, the services performed by the fund manager could be performed by other managers in the industry.

Although the fund manager is paid fixed and performance-related fees that are commensurate with the services provided, the combination of the fund manager's 20 per cent investment together with its remuneration creates exposure to variability of returns from the activities of the fund that is of such significance that it indicates that the fund manager is a principal. However, the investors have substantive rights to remove the fund manager —the board of directors provides a mechanism to ensure that the investors can remove the fund manager if they decide to do so.

In this example, the fund manager places greater emphasis on the substantive removal rights in the analysis. Thus, although the fund manager has extensive decision-making authority and is exposed to variability of returns of the fund from its remuneration and investment, the substantive rights held by the other investors indicate that the fund manager is an agent. Thus, the fund manager concludes that it does not control the fund.

continued...

...continued

Application examples

Example 15

An investee is created to purchase a portfolio of fixed rate asset-backed securities, funded by fixed rate debt instruments and equity instruments. The equity instruments are designed to provide first loss protection to the debt investors and receive any residual returns of the investee. The transaction was marketed to potential debt investors as an investment in a portfolio of asset-backed securities with exposure to the credit risk associated with the possible default of the issuers of the asset-backed securities in the portfolio and to the interest rate risk associated with the management of the portfolio. On formation, the equity instruments represent 10 per cent of the value of the assets purchased. A decision maker (the asset manager) manages the active asset portfolio by making investment decisions within the parameters set out in the investee's prospectus. For those services, the asset manager receives a market-based fixed fee (ie 1 per cent of assets under management) and performance-related fees (ie 10 per cent of profits) if the investee's profits exceed a specified level. The fees are commensurate with the services provided. The asset manager holds 35 per cent of the equity in the investee. The remaining 65 per cent of the equity, and all the debt instruments, are held by a large number of widely dispersed unrelated third party investors. The asset manager can be removed, without cause, by a simple majority decision of the other investors.

The asset manager is paid fixed and performance-related fees that are commensurate with the services provided. The remuneration aligns the interests of the fund manager with those of the other investors to increase the value of the fund. The asset manager has exposure to variability of returns from the activities of the fund because it holds 35 per cent of the equity and from its remuneration.

Although operating within the parameters set out in the investee's prospectus, the asset manager has the current ability to make investment decisions that significantly affect the investee's returns—the removal rights held by the other investors receive little weighting in the analysis because those rights are held by a large number of widely dispersed investors. In this example, the asset manager places greater emphasis on its exposure to variability of returns of the fund from its equity interest, which is subordinate to the debt instruments. Holding 35 per cent of the equity creates subordinated exposure to losses and rights to returns of the investee, which are of such significance that it indicates that the asset manager is a principal. Thus, the asset manager concludes that it controls the investee.

continued...

...continued

Application examples

Example 16

A decision maker (the sponsor) sponsors a multi-seller conduit, which issues short-term debt instruments to unrelated third party investors. The transaction was marketed to potential investors as an investment in a portfolio of highly rated medium-term assets with minimal exposure to the credit risk associated with the possible default by the issuers of the assets in the portfolio. Various transferors sell high quality medium-term asset portfolios to the conduit. Each transferor services the portfolio of assets that it sells to the conduit and manages receivables on default for a market-based servicing fee. Each transferor also provides first loss protection against credit losses from its asset portfolio through over-collateralisation of the assets transferred to the conduit. The sponsor establishes the terms of the conduit and manages the operations of the conduit for a market-based fee. The fee is commensurate with the services provided. The sponsor approves the sellers permitted to sell to the conduit, approves the assets to be purchased by the conduit and makes decisions about the funding of the conduit. The sponsor must act in the best interests of all investors.

The sponsor is entitled to any residual return of the conduit and also provides credit enhancement and liquidity facilities to the conduit. The credit enhancement provided by the sponsor absorbs losses of up to 5 per cent of all of the conduit's assets, after losses are absorbed by the transferors. The liquidity facilities are not advanced against defaulted assets. The investors do not hold substantive rights that could affect the decision-making authority of the sponsor.

Even though the sponsor is paid a market-based fee for its services that is commensurate with the services provided, the sponsor has exposure to variability of returns from the activities of the conduit because of its rights to any residual returns of the conduit and the provision of credit enhancement and liquidity facilities (ie the conduit is exposed to liquidity risk by using short-term debt instruments to fund medium-term assets). Even though each of the transferors has decision-making rights that affect the value of the assets of the conduit, the sponsor has extensive decision-making authority that gives it the current ability to direct the activities that most significantly affect the conduit's returns (ie the sponsor established the terms of the conduit, has the right to make decisions about the assets (approving the assets purchased and the transferors of those assets) and the funding of the conduit (for which new investment must be found on a regular basis)). The right to residual returns of the conduit and the provision of credit enhancement and liquidity facilities expose the sponsor to variability of returns from the activities of the conduit that is different from that of the other investors. Accordingly, that exposure indicates that the sponsor is a principal and thus the sponsor concludes that it controls the conduit. The sponsor's obligation to act in the best interest of all investors does not prevent the sponsor from being a principal.

Relationship with other parties

B73   When assessing control, an investor shall consider the nature of its relationship with other parties and whether those other parties are acting on the investor's behalf (ie they are 'de facto agents'). The determination of whether other parties are acting as de facto agents requires judgement, considering not only the nature of the relationship but also how those parties interact with each other and the investor.

B74   Such a relationship need not involve a contractual arrangement. A party is a de facto agent when the investor has, or those that direct the activities of the investor have, the ability to direct that party to act on the investor's behalf. In these circumstances, the investor shall consider its de facto agent's decision-making rights and its indirect exposure, or rights, to variable returns through the de facto agent together with its own when assessing control of an investee.

B75   The following are examples of such other parties that, by the nature of their relationship, might act as de facto agents for the investor:

     (a)   the investor's related parties.

     (b)   a party that received its interest in the investee as a contribution or loan from the investor.

     (c)   a party that has agreed not to sell, transfer or encumber its interests in the investee without the investor's prior approval (except for situations in which the investor and the other party have the right of prior approval and the rights are based on mutually agreed terms by willing independent parties).

     (d)   a party that cannot finance its operations without subordinated financial support from the investor.

     (e)   an investee for which the majority of the members of its governing body or for which its key management personnel are the same as those of the investor.

     (f)   a party that has a close business relationship with the investor, such as the relationship between a professional service provider and one of its significant clients.

Control of specified assets

B76   An investor shall consider whether it treats a portion of an investee as a deemed separate entity and, if so, whether it controls the deemed separate entity.

B77   An investor shall treat a portion of an investee as a deemed separate entity if and only if the following condition is satisfied:

     Specified assets of the investee (and related credit enhancements, if any) are the only source of payment for specified liabilities of, or specified other interests in, the investee. Parties other than those with the specified liability do not have rights or obligations related to the specified assets or to residual cash flows from those assets. In substance, none of the returns from the specified assets can be used by the remaining investee and none of the liabilities of the deemed separate entity are payable from the assets of the remaining investee. Thus, in substance, all the assets, liabilities and equity of that deemed separate entity are ring-fenced from the overall investee. Such a deemed separate entity is often called a 'silo'.

B78　When the condition in paragraph B77 is satisfied, an investor shall identify the activities that significantly affect the returns of the deemed separate entity and how those activities are directed in order to assess whether it has power over that portion of the investee. When assessing control of the deemed separate entity, the investor shall also consider whether it has exposure or rights to variable returns from its involvement with that deemed separate entity and the ability to use its power over that portion of the investee to affect the amount of the investor's returns.

B79　If the investor controls the deemed separate entity, the investor shall consolidate that portion of the investee. In that case, other parties exclude that portion of the investee when assessing control of, and in consolidating, the investee.

Continuous assessment

B80　An investor shall reassess whether it controls an investee if facts and circumstances indicate that there are changes to one or more of the three elements of control listed in paragraph 7.

B81　If there is a change in how power over an investee can be exercised, that change must be reflected in how an investor assesses its power over an investee. For example, changes to decision-making rights can mean that the relevant activities are no longer directed through voting rights, but instead other agreements, such as contracts, give another party or parties the current ability to direct the relevant activities.

B82　An event can cause an investor to gain or lose power over an investee without the investor being involved in that event. For example, an investor can gain power over an investee because decision-making rights held by another party or parties that previously prevented the investor from controlling an investee have lapsed.

B83　An investor also considers changes affecting its exposure, or rights, to variable returns from its involvement with an investee. For example, an investor that has power over an investee can lose control of an investee if the investor ceases to be entitled to receive returns or to be exposed to obligations, because the investor would fail to satisfy paragraph 7(b) (eg if a contract to receive performance-related fees is terminated).

B84　An investor shall consider whether its assessment that it acts as an agent or a principal has changed. Changes in the overall relationship between the investor and other parties can mean that an investor no longer acts as an agent, even though it has previously acted as an agent, and vice versa. For example, if changes to the rights of the investor, or of other parties, occur, the investor shall reconsider its status as a principal or an agent.

B85 An investor's initial assessment of control or its status as a principal or an agent would not change simply because of a change in market conditions (eg a change in the investee's returns driven by market conditions), unless the change in market conditions changes one or more of the three elements of control listed in paragraph 7 or changes the overall relationship between a principal and an agent.

Determining whether an entity is an investment entity

B85A An entity shall consider all facts and circumstances when assessing whether it is an investment entity, including its purpose and design. An entity that possesses the three elements of the definition of an investment entity set out in paragraph 27 is an investment entity. Paragraphs B85B–B85M describe the elements of the definition in more detail.

Business purpose

B85B The definition of an investment entity requires that the purpose of the entity is to invest solely for capital appreciation, investment income (such as dividends, interest or rental income), or both. Documents that indicate what the entity's investment objectives are, such as the entity's offering memorandum, publications distributed by the entity and other corporate or partnership documents, will typically provide evidence of an investment entity's business purpose. Further evidence may include the manner in which the entity presents itself to other parties (such as potential investors or potential investees); for example, an entity may present its business as providing medium-term investment for capital appreciation. In contrast, an entity that presents itself as an investor whose objective is to jointly develop, produce or market products with its investees has a business purpose that is inconsistent with the business purpose of an investment entity, because the entity will earn returns from the development, production or marketing activity as well as from its investments (see paragraph B85I).

B85C An investment entity may provide investment-related services (eg investment advisory services, investment management, investment support and administrative services), either directly or through a subsidiary, to third parties as well as to its investors, even if those activities are substantial to the entity, subject to the entity continuing to meet the definition of an investment entity.

B85D An investment entity may also participate in the following investment-related activities, either directly or through a subsidiary, if these activities are undertaken to maximise the investment return (capital appreciation or investment income) from its investees and do not represent a separate substantial business activity or a separate substantial source of income to the investment entity:

(a) providing management services and strategic advice to an investee; and

(b) providing financial support to an investee, such as a loan, capital commitment or guarantee.

B85E If an investment entity has a subsidiary that is not itself an investment entity and whose main purpose and activities are providing investment-related services or activities that relate to the investment entity's investment activities, such as those described in paragraphs B85C–B85D, to the entity or other parties, it shall consolidate that subsidiary in accordance with paragraph 32. If the subsidiary that provides the investment-related services or activities is itself an investment entity, the investment entity parent shall measure that subsidiary at fair value through profit or loss in accordance with paragraph 31.

Exit strategies

B85F An entity's investment plans also provide evidence of its business purpose. One feature that differentiates an investment entity from other entities is that an investment entity does not plan to hold its investments indefinitely; it holds them for a limited period. Because equity investments and non-financial asset investments have the potential to be held indefinitely, an investment entity shall have an exit strategy documenting how the entity plans to realise capital appreciation from substantially all of its equity investments and non-financial asset investments. An investment entity shall also have an exit strategy for any debt instruments that have the potential to be held indefinitely, for example perpetual debt investments. The entity need not document specific exit strategies for each individual investment but shall identify different potential strategies for different types or portfolios of investments, including a substantive time frame for exiting the investments. Exit mechanisms that are only put in place for default events, such as a breach of contract or non-performance, are not considered exit strategies for the purpose of this assessment.

B85G Exit strategies can vary by type of investment. For investments in private equity securities, examples of exit strategies include an initial public offering, a private placement, a trade sale of a business, distributions (to investors) of ownership interests in investees and sales of assets (including the sale of an investee's assets followed by a liquidation of the investee). For equity investments that are traded in a public market, examples of exit strategies include selling the investment in a private placement or in a public market. For real estate investments, an example of an exit strategy includes the sale of the real estate through specialised property dealers or the open market.

B85H An investment entity may have an investment in another investment entity that is formed in connection with the entity for legal, regulatory, tax or similar business reasons. In this case, the investment entity investor need not have an exit strategy for that investment, provided that the investment entity investee has appropriate exit strategies for its investments.

Earnings from investments

B85I An entity is not investing solely for capital appreciation, investment income, or both, if the entity or another member of the group containing the entity (ie the group that is controlled by the investment entity's ultimate parent) obtains, or has the objective of obtaining, other benefits from the entity's investments that are not available to other parties that are not related to the investee. Such benefits include:

(a) the acquisition, use, exchange or exploitation of the processes, assets or technology of an investee. This would include the entity or another group member having disproportionate, or exclusive, rights to acquire assets, technology, products or services of any investee; for example, by holding an option to purchase an asset from an investee if the asset's development is deemed successful;

(b) joint arrangements (as defined in IFRS 11) or other agreements between the entity or another group member and an investee to develop, produce, market or provide products or services;

(c) financial guarantees or assets provided by an investee to serve as collateral for borrowing arrangements of the entity or another group member (however, an investment entity would still be able to use an investment in an investee as collateral for any of its borrowings);

(d) an option held by a related party of the entity to purchase, from that entity or another group member, an ownership interest in an investee of the entity;

(e) except as described in paragraph B85J, transactions between the entity or another group member and an investee that:

(i) are on terms that are unavailable to entities that are not related parties of either the entity, another group member or the investee;

(ii) are not at fair value; or

(iii) represent a substantial portion of the investee's or the entity's business activity, including business activities of other group entities.

B85J An investment entity may have a strategy to invest in more than one investee in the same industry, market or geographical area in order to benefit from synergies that increase the capital appreciation and investment income from those investees. Notwithstanding paragraph B85I(e), an entity is not disqualified from being classified as an investment entity merely because such investees trade with each other.

Fair value measurement

B85K   An essential element of the definition of an investment entity is that it measures and evaluates the performance of substantially all of its investments on a fair value basis, because using fair value results in more relevant information than, for example, consolidating its subsidiaries or using the equity method for its interests in associates or joint ventures. In order to demonstrate that it meets this element of the definition, an investment entity:

(a)   provides investors with fair value information and measures substantially all of its investments at fair value in its financial statements whenever fair value is required or permitted in accordance with IFRSs; and

(b)   reports fair value information internally to the entity's key management personnel (as defined in IAS 24), who use fair value as the primary measurement attribute to evaluate the performance of substantially all of its investments and to make investment decisions.

B85L   In order to meet the requirement in B85K(a), an investment entity would:

(a)   elect to account for any investment property using the fair value model in IAS 40 *Investment Property*;

(b)   elect the exemption from applying the equity method in IAS 28 for its investments in associates and joint ventures; and

(c)   measure its financial assets at fair value using the requirements in IFRS 9.

B85M   An investment entity may have some non-investment assets, such as a head office property and related equipment, and may also have financial liabilities. The fair value measurement element of the definition of an investment entity in paragraph 27(c) applies to an investment entity's investments. Accordingly, an investment entity need not measure its non-investment assets or its liabilities at fair value.

Typical characteristics of an investment entity

B85N   In determining whether it meets the definition of an investment entity, an entity shall consider whether it displays the typical characteristics of one (see paragraph 28). The absence of one or more of these typical characteristics does not necessarily disqualify an entity from being classified as an investment entity but indicates that additional judgement is required in determining whether the entity is an investment entity.

More than one investment

B85O   An investment entity typically holds several investments to diversify its risk and maximise its returns. An entity may hold a portfolio of investments directly or indirectly, for example by holding a single investment in another investment entity that itself holds several investments.

B85P　　There may be times when the entity holds a single investment. However, holding a single investment does not necessarily prevent an entity from meeting the definition of an investment entity. For example, an investment entity may hold only a single investment when the entity:

(a)　　is in its start-up period and has not yet identified suitable investments and, therefore, has not yet executed its investment plan to acquire several investments;

(b)　　has not yet made other investments to replace those it has disposed of;

(c)　　is established to pool investors' funds to invest in a single investment when that investment is unobtainable by individual investors (eg when the required minimum investment is too high for an individual investor); or

(d)　　is in the process of liquidation.

More than one investor

B85Q　　Typically, an investment entity would have several investors who pool their funds to gain access to investment management services and investment opportunities that they might not have had access to individually. Having several investors would make it less likely that the entity, or other members of the group containing the entity, would obtain benefits other than capital appreciation or investment income (see paragraph B85I).

B85R　　Alternatively, an investment entity may be formed by, or for, a single investor that represents or supports the interests of a wider group of investors (eg a pension fund, government investment fund or family trust).

B85S　　There may also be times when the entity temporarily has a single investor. For example, an investment entity may have only a single investor when the entity:

(a)　　is within its initial offering period, which has not expired and the entity is actively identifying suitable investors;

(b)　　has not yet identified suitable investors to replace ownership interests that have been redeemed; or

(c)　　is in the process of liquidation.

Unrelated investors

B85T　　Typically, an investment entity has several investors that are not related parties (as defined in IAS 24) of the entity or other members of the group containing the entity. Having unrelated investors would make it less likely that the entity, or other members of the group containing the entity, would obtain benefits other than capital appreciation or investment income (see paragraph B85I).

B85U However, an entity may still qualify as an investment entity even though its investors are related to the entity. For example, an investment entity may set up a separate 'parallel' fund for a group of its employees (such as key management personnel) or other related party investor(s), which mirrors the investments of the entity's main investment fund. This 'parallel' fund may qualify as an investment entity even though all of its investors are related parties.

Ownership interests

B85V An investment entity is typically, but is not required to be, a separate legal entity. Ownership interests in an investment entity are typically in the form of equity or similar interests (eg partnership interests), to which proportionate shares of the net assets of the investment entity are attributed. However, having different classes of investors, some of which have rights only to a specific investment or groups of investments or which have different proportionate shares of the net assets, does not preclude an entity from being an investment entity.

B85W In addition, an entity that has significant ownership interests in the form of debt that, in accordance with other applicable IFRSs, does not meet the definition of equity, may still qualify as an investment entity, provided that the debt holders are exposed to variable returns from changes in the fair value of the entity's net assets.

Accounting requirements

Consolidation procedures

B86 Consolidated financial statements:

(a) combine like items of assets, liabilities, equity, income, expenses and cash flows of the parent with those of its subsidiaries.

(b) offset (eliminate) the carrying amount of the parent's investment in each subsidiary and the parent's portion of equity of each subsidiary (IFRS 3 explains how to account for any related goodwill).

(c) eliminate in full intragroup assets and liabilities, equity, income, expenses and cash flows relating to transactions between entities of the group (profits or losses resulting from intragroup transactions that are recognised in assets, such as inventory and fixed assets, are eliminated in full). Intragroup losses may indicate an impairment that requires recognition in the consolidated financial statements. IAS 12 *Income Taxes* applies to temporary differences that arise from the elimination of profits and losses resulting from intragroup transactions.

Uniform accounting policies

B87   If a member of the group uses accounting policies other than those adopted in the consolidated financial statements for like transactions and events in similar circumstances, appropriate adjustments are made to that group member's financial statements in preparing the consolidated financial statements to ensure conformity with the group's accounting policies.

Measurement

B88   An entity includes the income and expenses of a subsidiary in the consolidated financial statements from the date it gains control until the date when the entity ceases to control the subsidiary. Income and expenses of the subsidiary are based on the amounts of the assets and liabilities recognised in the consolidated financial statements at the acquisition date. For example, depreciation expense recognised in the consolidated statement of comprehensive income after the acquisition date is based on the fair values of the related depreciable assets recognised in the consolidated financial statements at the acquisition date.

Potential voting rights

B89   When potential voting rights, or other derivatives containing potential voting rights, exist, the proportion of profit or loss and changes in equity allocated to the parent and non-controlling interests in preparing consolidated financial statements is determined solely on the basis of existing ownership interests and does not reflect the possible exercise or conversion of potential voting rights and other derivatives, unless paragraph B90 applies.

B90   In some circumstances an entity has, in substance, an existing ownership interest as a result of a transaction that currently gives the entity access to the returns associated with an ownership interest. In such circumstances, the proportion allocated to the parent and non-controlling interests in preparing consolidated financial statements is determined by taking into account the eventual exercise of those potential voting rights and other derivatives that currently give the entity access to the returns.

B91   IFRS 9 does not apply to interests in subsidiaries that are consolidated. When instruments containing potential voting rights in substance currently give access to the returns associated with an ownership interest in a subsidiary, the instruments are not subject to the requirements of IFRS 9. In all other cases, instruments containing potential voting rights in a subsidiary are accounted for in accordance with IFRS 9.

Reporting date

B92   The financial statements of the parent and its subsidiaries used in the preparation of the consolidated financial statements shall have the same reporting date. When the end of the reporting period of the parent is different from that of a subsidiary, the subsidiary prepares, for consolidation purposes, additional financial information as of the same date as the financial statements of the parent to enable the parent to consolidate the financial information of the subsidiary, unless it is impracticable to do so.

B93 If it is impracticable to do so, the parent shall consolidate the financial information of the subsidiary using the most recent financial statements of the subsidiary adjusted for the effects of significant transactions or events that occur between the date of those financial statements and the date of the consolidated financial statements. In any case, the difference between the date of the subsidiary's financial statements and that of the consolidated financial statements shall be no more than three months, and the length of the reporting periods and any difference between the dates of the financial statements shall be the same from period to period.

Non-controlling interests

B94 An entity shall attribute the profit or loss and each component of other comprehensive income to the owners of the parent and to the non-controlling interests. The entity shall also attribute total comprehensive income to the owners of the parent and to the non-controlling interests even if this results in the non-controlling interests having a deficit balance.

B95 If a subsidiary has outstanding cumulative preference shares that are classified as equity and are held by non-controlling interests, the entity shall compute its share of profit or loss after adjusting for the dividends on such shares, whether or not such dividends have been declared.

Changes in the proportion held by non-controlling interests

B96 When the proportion of the equity held by non-controlling interests changes, an entity shall adjust the carrying amounts of the controlling and non-controlling interests to reflect the changes in their relative interests in the subsidiary. The entity shall recognise directly in equity any difference between the amount by which the non-controlling interests are adjusted and the fair value of the consideration paid or received, and attribute it to the owners of the parent.

Loss of control

B97 A parent might lose control of a subsidiary in two or more arrangements (transactions). However, sometimes circumstances indicate that the multiple arrangements should be accounted for as a single transaction. In determining whether to account for the arrangements as a single transaction, a parent shall consider all the terms and conditions of the arrangements and their economic effects. One or more of the following indicate that the parent should account for the multiple arrangements as a single transaction:

(a) They are entered into at the same time or in contemplation of each other.

(b) They form a single transaction designed to achieve an overall commercial effect.

(c)   The occurrence of one arrangement is dependent on the occurrence of at least one other arrangement.

(d)   One arrangement considered on its own is not economically justified, but it is economically justified when considered together with other arrangements. An example is when a disposal of shares is priced below market and is compensated for by a subsequent disposal priced above market.

B98   If a parent loses control of a subsidiary, it shall:

(a)   derecognise:

    (i)   the assets (including any goodwill) and liabilities of the subsidiary at their carrying amounts at the date when control is lost; and

    (ii)   the carrying amount of any non-controlling interests in the former subsidiary at the date when control is lost (including any components of other comprehensive income attributable to them).

(b)   recognise:

    (i)   the fair value of the consideration received, if any, from the transaction, event or circumstances that resulted in the loss of control;

    (ii)   if the transaction, event or circumstances that resulted in the loss of control involves a distribution of shares of the subsidiary to owners in their capacity as owners, that distribution; and

    (iii)   any investment retained in the former subsidiary at its fair value at the date when control is lost.

(c)   reclassify to profit or loss, or transfer directly to retained earnings if required by other IFRSs, the amounts recognised in other comprehensive income in relation to the subsidiary on the basis described in paragraph B99.

(d)   recognise any resulting difference as a gain or loss in profit or loss attributable to the parent.

B99   If a parent loses control of a subsidiary, the parent shall account for all amounts previously recognised in other comprehensive income in relation to that subsidiary on the same basis as would be required if the parent had directly disposed of the related assets or liabilities. Therefore, if a gain or loss previously recognised in other comprehensive income would be reclassified to profit or loss on the disposal of the related assets or liabilities, the parent shall reclassify the gain or loss from equity to profit or loss (as a reclassification adjustment) when it loses control of the subsidiary. If a revaluation surplus previously recognised in other comprehensive income would be transferred directly to retained earnings on the disposal of the asset, the parent shall transfer the revaluation surplus directly to retained earnings when it loses control of the subsidiary.

B99A   *[This paragraph refers to amendments that are not yet effective, and is therefore not included in this edition.]*

Accounting for a change in investment entity status

B100   When an entity ceases to be an investment entity, it shall apply IFRS 3 to any subsidiary that was previously measured at fair value through profit or loss in accordance with paragraph 31. The date of the change of status shall be the deemed acquisition date. The fair value of the subsidiary at the deemed acquisition date shall represent the transferred deemed consideration when measuring any goodwill or gain from a bargain purchase that arises from the deemed acquisition. All subsidiaries shall be consolidated in accordance with paragraphs 19–24 of this IFRS from the date of change of status.

B101   When an entity becomes an investment entity, it shall cease to consolidate its subsidiaries at the date of the change in status, except for any subsidiary that shall continue to be consolidated in accordance with paragraph 32. The investment entity shall apply the requirements of paragraphs 25 and 26 to those subsidiaries that it ceases to consolidate as though the investment entity had lost control of those subsidiaries at that date.

Appendix C
Effective date and transition

This appendix is an integral part of the IFRS and has the same authority as the other parts of the IFRS.

Effective date

C1 An entity shall apply this IFRS for annual periods beginning on or after 1 January 2013. Earlier application is permitted. If an entity applies this IFRS earlier, it shall disclose that fact and apply IFRS 11, IFRS 12, IAS 27 *Separate Financial Statements* and IAS 28 (as amended in 2011) at the same time.

C1A *Consolidated Financial Statements, Joint Arrangements and Disclosure of Interests in Other Entities: Transition Guidance* (Amendments to IFRS 10, IFRS 11 and IFRS 12), issued in June 2012, amended paragraphs C2–C6 and added paragraphs C2A–C2B, C4A–C4C, C5A and C6A–C6B. An entity shall apply those amendments for annual periods beginning on or after 1 January 2013. If an entity applies IFRS 10 for an earlier period, it shall apply those amendments for that earlier period.

C1B *Investment Entities* (Amendments to IFRS 10, IFRS 12 and IAS 27), issued in October 2012, amended paragraphs 2, 4, C2A, C6A and Appendix A and added paragraphs 27–33, B85A–B85W, B100–B101 and C3A–C3F. An entity shall apply those amendments for annual periods beginning on or after 1 January 2014. Early application is permitted. If an entity applies those amendments earlier, it shall disclose that fact and apply all amendments included in *Investment Entities* at the same time.

C1C *[This paragraph refers to amendments that are not yet effective, and is therefore not included in this edition.]*

C1D *Investment Entities: Applying the Consolidation Exception* (Amendments to IFRS 10, IFRS 12 and IAS 28), issued in December 2014, amended paragraphs 4, 32, B85C, B85E and C2A and added paragraphs 4A–4B. An entity shall apply those amendments for annual periods beginning on or after 1 January 2016. Earlier application is permitted. If an entity applies those amendments for an earlier period it shall disclose that fact.

Transition

C2 An entity shall apply this IFRS retrospectively, in accordance with IAS 8 *Accounting Policies, Changes in Accounting Estimates and Errors*, except as specified in paragraphs C2A–C6.

C2A Notwithstanding the requirements of paragraph 28 of IAS 8, when this IFRS is first applied, and, if later, when the *Investment Entities* and *Investment Entities: Applying the Consolidation Exception* amendments to this IFRS are first applied, an entity need only present the quantitative information required by paragraph 28(f) of IAS 8 for the annual period immediately preceding the date of initial application of this IFRS (the 'immediately preceding period'). An entity may also present this information for the current period or for earlier comparative periods, but is not required to do so.

C2B   For the purposes of this IFRS, the date of initial application is the beginning of the annual reporting period for which this IFRS is applied for the first time.

C3   At the date of initial application, an entity is not required to make adjustments to the previous accounting for its involvement with either:

(a)   entities that would be consolidated at that date in accordance with IAS 27 *Consolidated and Separate Financial Statements* and SIC-12 *Consolidation — Special Purpose Entities* and are still consolidated in accordance with this IFRS; or

(b)   entities that would not be consolidated at that date in accordance with IAS 27 and SIC-12 and are not consolidated in accordance with this IFRS.

C3A   At the date of initial application, an entity shall assess whether it is an investment entity on the basis of the facts and circumstances that exist at that date. If, at the date of initial application, an entity concludes that it is an investment entity, it shall apply the requirements of paragraphs C3B–C3F instead of paragraphs C5–C5A.

C3B   Except for any subsidiary that is consolidated in accordance with paragraph 32 (to which paragraphs C3 and C6 or paragraphs C4–C4C, whichever is relevant, apply), an investment entity shall measure its investment in each subsidiary at fair value through profit or loss as if the requirements of this IFRS had always been effective. The investment entity shall retrospectively adjust both the annual period that immediately precedes the date of initial application and equity at the beginning of the immediately preceding period for any difference between:

(a)   the previous carrying amount of the subsidiary; and

(b)   the fair value of the investment entity's investment in the subsidiary.

The cumulative amount of any fair value adjustments previously recognised in other comprehensive income shall be transferred to retained earnings at the beginning of the annual period immediately preceding the date of initial application.

C3C   Before the date that IFRS 13 *Fair Value Measurement* is adopted, an investment entity shall use the fair value amounts that were previously reported to investors or to management, if those amounts represent the amount for which the investment could have been exchanged between knowledgeable, willing parties in an arm's length transaction at the date of the valuation.

C3D   If measuring an investment in a subsidiary in accordance with paragraphs C3B–C3C is impracticable (as defined in IAS 8), an investment entity shall apply the requirements of this IFRS at the beginning of the earliest period for which application of paragraphs C3B–C3C is practicable, which may be the current period. The investor shall retrospectively adjust the annual period that immediately precedes the date of initial application, unless the beginning of the earliest period for which application of this paragraph is practicable is the current period. If this is the case, the adjustment to equity shall be recognised at the beginning of the current period.

C3E   If an investment entity has disposed of, or has lost control of, an investment in a subsidiary before the date of initial application of this IFRS, the investment entity is not required to make adjustments to the previous accounting for that subsidiary.

C3F   If an entity applies the *Investment Entities* amendments for a period later than when it applies IFRS 10 for the first time, references to 'the date of initial application' in paragraphs C3A–C3E shall be read as 'the beginning of the annual reporting period for which the amendments in *Investment Entities* (Amendments to IFRS 10, IFRS 12 and IAS 27), issued in October 2012, are applied for the first time.'

C4   If, at the date of initial application, an investor concludes that it shall consolidate an investee that was not consolidated in accordance with IAS 27 and SIC-12, the investor shall:

(a)   if the investee is a business (as defined in IFRS 3 *Business Combinations*), measure the assets, liabilities and non-controlling interests in that previously unconsolidated investee as if that investee had been consolidated (and thus had applied acquisition accounting in accordance with IFRS 3) from the date when the investor obtained control of that investee on the basis of the requirements of this IFRS. The investor shall adjust retrospectively the annual period immediately preceding the date of initial application. When the date that control was obtained is earlier than the beginning of the immediately preceding period, the investor shall recognise, as an adjustment to equity at the beginning of the immediately preceding period, any difference between:

(i)   the amount of assets, liabilities and non-controlling interests recognised; and

(ii)   the previous carrying amount of the investor's involvement with the investee.

(b)   if the investee is not a business (as defined in IFRS 3), measure the assets, liabilities and non-controlling interests in that previously unconsolidated investee as if that investee had been consolidated (applying the acquisition method as described in IFRS 3 but without recognising any goodwill for the investee) from the date when the investor obtained control of that investee on the basis of the requirements of this IFRS. The investor shall adjust retrospectively the annual period immediately preceding the date of initial application. When the date that control was obtained is earlier than the beginning of the immediately preceding period, the investor shall recognise, as an adjustment to equity at the beginning of the immediately preceding period, any difference between:

(i)   the amount of assets, liabilities and non-controlling interests recognised; and

(ii)   the previous carrying amount of the investor's involvement with the investee.

C4A   If measuring an investee's assets, liabilities and non-controlling interests in accordance with paragraph C4(a) or (b) is impracticable (as defined in IAS 8), an investor shall:

(a)   if the investee is a business, apply the requirements of IFRS 3 as of the deemed acquisition date. The deemed acquisition date shall be the beginning of the earliest period for which application of paragraph C4(a) is practicable, which may be the current period.

(b)   if the investee is not a business, apply the acquisition method as described in IFRS 3 but without recognising any goodwill for the investee as of the deemed acquisition date. The deemed acquisition date shall be the beginning of the earliest period for which the application of paragraph C4(b) is practicable, which may be the current period.

The investor shall adjust retrospectively the annual period immediately preceding the date of initial application, unless the beginning of the earliest period for which application of this paragraph is practicable is the current period. When the deemed acquisition date is earlier than the beginning of the immediately preceding period, the investor shall recognise, as an adjustment to equity at the beginning of the immediately preceding period, any difference between:

(c)   the amount of assets, liabilities and non-controlling interests recognised; and

(d)   the previous carrying amount of the investor's involvement with the investee.

If the earliest period for which application of this paragraph is practicable is the current period, the adjustment to equity shall be recognised at the beginning of the current period.

C4B   When an investor applies paragraphs C4–C4A and the date that control was obtained in accordance with this IFRS is later than the effective date of IFRS 3 as revised in 2008 (IFRS 3 (2008)), the reference to IFRS 3 in paragraphs C4 and C4A shall be to IFRS 3 (2008). If control was obtained before the effective date of IFRS 3 (2008), an investor shall apply either IFRS 3 (2008) or IFRS 3 (issued in 2004).

C4C   When an investor applies paragraphs C4–C4A and the date that control was obtained in accordance with this IFRS is later than the effective date of IAS 27 as revised in 2008 (IAS 27 (2008)), an investor shall apply the requirements of this IFRS for all periods that the investee is retrospectively consolidated in accordance with paragraphs C4–C4A. If control was obtained before the effective date of IAS 27 (2008), an investor shall apply either:

(a)   the requirements of this IFRS for all periods that the investee is retrospectively consolidated in accordance with paragraphs C4–C4A; or

(b)   the requirements of the version of IAS 27 issued in 2003 (IAS 27 (2003)) for those periods prior to the effective date of IAS 27 (2008) and thereafter the requirements of this IFRS for subsequent periods.

C5   If, at the date of initial application, an investor concludes that it will no longer consolidate an investee that was consolidated in accordance with IAS 27 and SIC-12, the investor shall measure its interest in the investee at the amount at which it would have been measured if the requirements of this IFRS had been effective when the investor became involved with (but did not obtain control in accordance with this IFRS), or lost control of, the investee. The investor shall adjust retrospectively the annual period immediately preceding the date of initial application. When the date that the investor became involved with (but did not obtain control in accordance with this IFRS), or lost control of, the investee is earlier than the beginning of the immediately preceding period, the investor shall recognise, as an adjustment to equity at the beginning of the immediately preceding period, any difference between:

(a)   the previous carrying amount of the assets, liabilities and non-controlling interests; and

(b)   the recognised amount of the investor's interest in the investee.

C5A   If measuring the interest in the investee in accordance with paragraph C5 is impracticable (as defined in IAS 8), an investor shall apply the requirements of this IFRS at the beginning of the earliest period for which application of paragraph C5 is practicable, which may be the current period. The investor shall adjust retrospectively the annual period immediately preceding the date of initial application, unless the beginning of the earliest period for which application of this paragraph is practicable is the current period. When the date that the investor became involved with (but did not obtain control in accordance with this IFRS), or lost control of, the investee is earlier than the beginning of the immediately preceding period, the investor shall recognise, as an adjustment to equity at the beginning of the immediately preceding period, any difference between:

(a)   the previous carrying amount of the assets, liabilities and non-controlling interests; and

(b)   the recognised amount of the investor's interest in the investee.

If the earliest period for which application of this paragraph is practicable is the current period, the adjustment to equity shall be recognised at the beginning of the current period.

C6   Paragraphs 23, 25, B94 and B96–B99 were amendments to IAS 27 made in 2008 that were carried forward into IFRS 10. Except when an entity applies paragraph C3, or is required to apply paragraphs C4–C5A, the entity shall apply the requirements in those paragraphs as follows:

(a) An entity shall not restate any profit or loss attribution for reporting periods before it applied the amendment in paragraph B94 for the first time.

(b) The requirements in paragraphs 23 and B96 for accounting for changes in ownership interests in a subsidiary after control is obtained do not apply to changes that occurred before an entity applied these amendments for the first time.

(c) An entity shall not restate the carrying amount of an investment in a former subsidiary if control was lost before it applied the amendments in paragraphs 25 and B97–B99 for the first time. In addition, an entity shall not recalculate any gain or loss on the loss of control of a subsidiary that occurred before the amendments in paragraphs 25 and B97–B99 were applied for the first time.

References to the 'immediately preceding period'

C6A Notwithstanding the references to the annual period immediately preceding the date of initial application (the 'immediately preceding period') in paragraphs C3B–C5A, an entity may also present adjusted comparative information for any earlier periods presented, but is not required to do so. If an entity does present adjusted comparative information for any earlier periods, all references to the 'immediately preceding period' in paragraphs C3B–C5A shall be read as the 'earliest adjusted comparative period presented'.

C6B If an entity presents unadjusted comparative information for any earlier periods, it shall clearly identify the information that has not been adjusted, state that it has been prepared on a different basis, and explain that basis.

References to IFRS 9

C7 If an entity applies this IFRS but does not yet apply IFRS 9, any reference in this IFRS to IFRS 9 shall be read as a reference to IAS 39 *Financial Instruments: Recognition and Measurement*.

Withdrawal of other IFRSs

C8 This IFRS supersedes the requirements relating to consolidated financial statements in IAS 27 (as amended in 2008).

C9 This IFRS also supersedes SIC-12 *Consolidation – Special Purpose Entities*.

Appendix D
Amendments to other IFRSs

This appendix sets out the amendments to other IFRSs that are a consequence of the Board issuing this IFRS. An entity shall apply the amendments for annual periods beginning on or after 1 January 2013. If an entity applies this IFRS for an earlier period, it shall apply these amendments for that earlier period. Amended paragraphs are shown with new text underlined and deleted text struck through.

* * * * *

The amendments contained in this appendix when this IFRS was issued in 2011 have been incorporated into the relevant IFRSs published in this volume.

© IFRS Foundation

Approval by the Board of IFRS 10 issued in May 2011

International Financial Reporting Standard 10 *Consolidated Financial Statements* was approved for issue by the fifteen members of the International Accounting Standards Board.

Sir David Tweedie	Chairman
Stephen Cooper	
Philippe Danjou	
Jan Engström	
Patrick Finnegan	
Amaro Luiz de Oliveira Gomes	
Prabhakar Kalavacherla	
Elke König	
Patricia McConnell	
Warren J McGregor	
Paul Pacter	
Darrel Scott	
John T Smith	
Tatsumi Yamada	
Wei-Guo Zhang	

Approval by the Board of *Consolidated Financial Statements, Joint Arrangements and Disclosure of Interests in Other Entities: Transition Guidance* (Amendments to IFRS 10, IFRS 11 and IFRS 12) issued in June 2012

Consolidated Financial Statements, Joint Arrangements and Disclosure of Interests in Other Entities: Transition Guidance (Amendments to IFRS 10, IFRS 11 and IFRS 12) was approved for issue by the fourteen members of the International Accounting Standards Board.

Hans Hoogervorst	Chairman
Ian Mackintosh	Vice-Chairman
Stephen Cooper	
Philippe Danjou	
Jan Engström	
Patrick Finnegan	
Amaro Luiz de Oliveira Gomes	
Prabhakar Kalavacherla	
Patricia McConnell	
Takatsugu Ochi	
Paul Pacter	
Darrel Scott	
John T Smith	
Wei-Guo Zhang	

Approval by the Board of *Investment Entities* (Amendments to IFRS 10, IFRS 12 and IAS 27) issued in October 2012

Investment Entities (Amendments to IFRS 10, IFRS 12 and IAS 27) was approved for issue by the fifteen members of the International Accounting Standards Board.

Hans Hoogervorst	Chairman
Ian Mackintosh	Vice-Chairman
Stephen Cooper	
Philippe Danjou	
Martin Edelmann	
Jan Engström	
Patrick Finnegan	
Amaro Luiz de Oliveira Gomes	
Prabhakar Kalavacherla	
Patricia McConnell	
Takatsugu Ochi	
Paul Pacter	
Darrel Scott	
Chungwoo Suh	
Zhang Wei-Guo	

Approval by the Board of *Investment Entities: Applying the Consolidation Exception* (Amendments to IFRS 10, IFRS 12 and IAS 28) issued in December 2014

Investment Entities: Applying the Consolidation Exception was approved for issue by the fourteen members of the International Accounting Standards Board.

Hans Hoogervorst	Chairman
Ian Mackintosh	Vice-Chairman
Stephen Cooper	
Philippe Danjou	
Amaro Luiz De Oliveira Gomes	
Martin Edelmann	
Patrick Finnegan	
Gary Kabureck	
Suzanne Lloyd	
Takatsugu Ochi	
Darrel Scott	
Chungwoo Suh	
Mary Tokar	
Wei-Guo Zhang	

IFRS 11

Joint Arrangements

In April 2001 the International Accounting Standards Board (Board) adopted IAS 31 *Financial Reporting of Interests in Joint Ventures*, which had originally been issued by the International Accounting Standards Committee in December 1990.

In December 2003 the Board amended and renamed IAS 31 with a new title—*Interests in Joint Ventures*. This amendment was done in conjunction with amendments to IAS 27 *Consolidated Financial Statements and Accounting for Investments in Subsidiaries* and IAS 28 *Accounting for Investments in Associates*.

In May 2011 the Board issued IFRS 11 *Joint Arrangements* to replace IAS 31. IFRS 12 *Disclosure of Interests in Other Entities*, also issued in May 2011, replaced the disclosure requirements in IAS 31. IFRS 11 incorporated the guidance contained in a related Interpretation (SIC-13 *Jointly Controlled Entities-Non-Monetary Contributions by Venturers*).

In June 2012 IFRS 11 was amended by *Consolidated Financial Statements, Joint Arrangements and Disclosure of Interests in Other Entities: Transition Guidance* (Amendments to IFRS 10, IFRS 11 and IFRS 12). These amendments provided additional transition relief to IFRS 11, limiting the requirement to present adjusted comparative information to only the annual period immediately preceding the first annual period for which IFRS 11 is applied.

In May 2014 the Board amended IFRS 11 to provide guidance on the accounting for acquisitions of interests in joint operations in which the activity constitutes a business.

Other Standards have made minor amendments to IFRS 11, including *Annual Improvements to IFRS Standards 2015–2017 Cycle* (issued December 2017).

Contents

FOR THE ACCOMPANYING GUIDANCE LISTED BELOW, SEE PART B OF THIS EDITION

FOR THE BASIS FOR CONCLUSIONS, SEE PART C OF THIS EDITION

International Financial Reporting Standard 11 *Joint Arrangements* (IFRS 11) is set out in paragraphs 1–27 and Appendices A–D. All the paragraphs have equal authority. Paragraphs in **bold type** state the main principles. Terms defined in Appendix A are in *italics* the first time they appear in the Standard. Definitions of other terms are given in the Glossary for International Financial Reporting Standards. IFRS 11 should be read in the context of its objective and the Basis for Conclusions, the *Preface to IFRS Standards* and the *Conceptual Framework for Financial Reporting*. IAS 8 *Accounting Policies, Changes in Accounting Estimates and Errors* provides a basis for selecting and applying accounting policies in the absence of explicit guidance.

International Financial Reporting Standard 11
Joint Arrangements

Objective

1 The objective of this IFRS is to establish principles for financial reporting by entities that have an interest in arrangements that are controlled jointly (ie *joint arrangements*).

Meeting the objective

2 To meet the objective in paragraph 1, this IFRS defines *joint control* and requires an entity that is a *party to a joint arrangement* to determine the type of joint arrangement in which it is involved by assessing its rights and obligations and to account for those rights and obligations in accordance with that type of joint arrangement.

Scope

3 This IFRS shall be applied by all entities that are a party to a joint arrangement.

Joint arrangements

4 A joint arrangement is an arrangement of which two or more parties have joint control.

5 A joint arrangement has the following characteristics:

(a) The parties are bound by a contractual arrangement (see paragraphs B2–B4).

(b) The contractual arrangement gives two or more of those parties joint control of the arrangement (see paragraphs 7–13).

6 A joint arrangement is either a *joint operation* or a *joint venture*.

Joint control

7 Joint control is the contractually agreed sharing of control of an arrangement, which exists only when decisions about the relevant activities require the unanimous consent of the parties sharing control.

8 An entity that is a party to an arrangement shall assess whether the contractual arrangement gives all the parties, or a group of the parties, control of the arrangement collectively. All the parties, or a group of the parties, control the arrangement collectively when they must act together to direct the activities that significantly affect the returns of the arrangement (ie the relevant activities).

9   Once it has been determined that all the parties, or a group of the parties, control the arrangement collectively, joint control exists only when decisions about the relevant activities require the unanimous consent of the parties that control the arrangement collectively.

10   In a joint arrangement, no single party controls the arrangement on its own. A party with joint control of an arrangement can prevent any of the other parties, or a group of the parties, from controlling the arrangement.

11   An arrangement can be a joint arrangement even though not all of its parties have joint control of the arrangement. This IFRS distinguishes between parties that have joint control of a joint arrangement (*joint operators* or *joint venturers*) and parties that participate in, but do not have joint control of, a joint arrangement.

12   An entity will need to apply judgement when assessing whether all the parties, or a group of the parties, have joint control of an arrangement. An entity shall make this assessment by considering all facts and circumstances (see paragraphs B5–B11).

13   If facts and circumstances change, an entity shall reassess whether it still has joint control of the arrangement.

Types of joint arrangement

14   An entity shall determine the type of joint arrangement in which it is involved. The classification of a joint arrangement as a joint operation or a joint venture depends upon the rights and obligations of the parties to the arrangement.

15   A joint operation is a joint arrangement whereby the parties that have joint control of the arrangement have rights to the assets, and obligations for the liabilities, relating to the arrangement. Those parties are called joint operators.

16   A joint venture is a joint arrangement whereby the parties that have joint control of the arrangement have rights to the net assets of the arrangement. Those parties are called joint venturers.

17   An entity applies judgement when assessing whether a joint arrangement is a joint operation or a joint venture. An entity shall determine the type of joint arrangement in which it is involved by considering its rights and obligations arising from the arrangement. An entity assesses its rights and obligations by considering the structure and legal form of the arrangement, the terms agreed by the parties in the contractual arrangement and, when relevant, other facts and circumstances (see paragraphs B12–B33).

18   Sometimes the parties are bound by a framework agreement that sets up the general contractual terms for undertaking one or more activities. The framework agreement might set out that the parties establish different joint arrangements to deal with specific activities that form part of the agreement. Even though those joint arrangements are related to the same framework agreement, their type might be different if the parties' rights and obligations

differ when undertaking the different activities dealt with in the framework agreement. Consequently, joint operations and joint ventures can coexist when the parties undertake different activities that form part of the same framework agreement.

19 If facts and circumstances change, an entity shall reassess whether the type of joint arrangement in which it is involved has changed.

Financial statements of parties to a joint arrangement

Joint operations

20 A joint operator shall recognise in relation to its interest in a joint operation:

(a) its assets, including its share of any assets held jointly;

(b) its liabilities, including its share of any liabilities incurred jointly;

(c) its revenue from the sale of its share of the output arising from the joint operation;

(d) its share of the revenue from the sale of the output by the joint operation; and

(e) its expenses, including its share of any expenses incurred jointly.

21 A joint operator shall account for the assets, liabilities, revenues and expenses relating to its interest in a joint operation in accordance with the IFRSs applicable to the particular assets, liabilities, revenues and expenses.

21A When an entity acquires an interest in a joint operation in which the activity of the joint operation constitutes a business, as defined in IFRS 3 *Business Combinations*, it shall apply, to the extent of its share in accordance with paragraph 20, all of the principles on business combinations accounting in IFRS 3, and other IFRSs, that do not conflict with the guidance in this IFRS and disclose the information that is required in those IFRSs in relation to business combinations. This applies to the acquisition of both the initial interest and additional interests in a joint operation in which the activity of the joint operation constitutes a business. The accounting for the acquisition of an interest in such a joint operation is specified in paragraphs B33A–B33D.

22 The accounting for transactions such as the sale, contribution or purchase of assets between an entity and a joint operation in which it is a joint operator is specified in paragraphs B34–B37.

23 A party that participates in, but does not have joint control of, a joint operation shall also account for its interest in the arrangement in accordance with paragraphs 20–22 if that party has rights to the assets, and obligations for the liabilities, relating to the joint operation. If a party that participates in, but does not have joint control of, a joint operation does not have rights to the assets, and obligations for the liabilities, relating to that joint operation, it shall account for its interest in the joint operation in accordance with the IFRSs applicable to that interest.

Joint ventures

24 A joint venturer shall recognise its interest in a joint venture as an investment and shall account for that investment using the equity method in accordance with IAS 28 *Investments in Associates and Joint Ventures* unless the entity is exempted from applying the equity method as specified in that standard.

25 A party that participates in, but does not have joint control of, a joint venture shall account for its interest in the arrangement in accordance with IFRS 9 *Financial Instruments*, unless it has significant influence over the joint venture, in which case it shall account for it in accordance with IAS 28 (as amended in 2011).

Separate financial statements

26 In its separate financial statements, a joint operator or joint venturer shall account for its interest in:

(a) a joint operation in accordance with paragraphs 20–22;

(b) a joint venture in accordance with paragraph 10 of IAS 27 *Separate Financial Statements*.

27 In its separate financial statements, a party that participates in, but does not have joint control of, a joint arrangement shall account for its interest in:

(a) a joint operation in accordance with paragraph 23;

(b) a joint venture in accordance with IFRS 9, unless the entity has significant influence over the joint venture, in which case it shall apply paragraph 10 of IAS 27 (as amended in 2011).

Appendix A
Defined terms

This appendix is an integral part of the IFRS.

joint arrangement	An arrangement of which two or more parties have **joint control**.
joint control	The contractually agreed sharing of control of an arrangement, which exists only when decisions about the relevant activities require the unanimous consent of the parties sharing control.
joint operation	A **joint arrangement** whereby the parties that have **joint control** of the arrangement have rights to the assets, and obligations for the liabilities, relating to the arrangement.
joint operator	A party to a **joint operation** that has **joint control** of that joint operation.
joint venture	A **joint arrangement** whereby the parties that have **joint control** of the arrangement have rights to the net assets of the arrangement.
joint venturer	A party to a **joint venture** that has **joint control** of that joint venture.
party to a joint arrangement	An entity that participates in a **joint arrangement**, regardless of whether that entity has **joint control** of the arrangement.
separate vehicle	A separately identifiable financial structure, including separate legal entities or entities recognised by statute, regardless of whether those entities have a legal personality.

The following terms are defined in IAS 27 (as amended in 2011), IAS 28 (as amended in 2011) or IFRS 10 *Consolidated Financial Statements* and are used in this IFRS with the meanings specified in those IFRSs:

* control of an investee

* equity method

* power

* protective rights

* relevant activities

* separate financial statements

* significant influence.

Appendix B
Application guidance

This appendix is an integral part of the IFRS. It describes the application of paragraphs 1–27 and has the same authority as the other parts of the IFRS.

B1   The examples in this appendix portray hypothetical situations. Although some aspects of the examples may be present in actual fact patterns, all relevant facts and circumstances of a particular fact pattern would need to be evaluated when applying IFRS 11.

Joint arrangements

Contractual arrangement (paragraph 5)

B2   Contractual arrangements can be evidenced in several ways. An enforceable contractual arrangement is often, but not always, in writing, usually in the form of a contract or documented discussions between the parties. Statutory mechanisms can also create enforceable arrangements, either on their own or in conjunction with contracts between the parties.

B3   When joint arrangements are structured through a *separate vehicle* (see paragraphs B19–B33), the contractual arrangement, or some aspects of the contractual arrangement, will in some cases be incorporated in the articles, charter or by-laws of the separate vehicle.

B4   The contractual arrangement sets out the terms upon which the parties participate in the activity that is the subject of the arrangement. The contractual arrangement generally deals with such matters as:

  (a)   the purpose, activity and duration of the joint arrangement.

  (b)   how the members of the board of directors, or equivalent governing body, of the joint arrangement, are appointed.

  (c)   the decision-making process: the matters requiring decisions from the parties, the voting rights of the parties and the required level of support for those matters. The decision-making process reflected in the contractual arrangement establishes joint control of the arrangement (see paragraphs B5–B11).

  (d)   the capital or other contributions required of the parties.

  (e)   how the parties share assets, liabilities, revenues, expenses or profit or loss relating to the joint arrangement.

Joint control (paragraphs 7–13)

B5   In assessing whether an entity has joint control of an arrangement, an entity shall assess first whether all the parties, or a group of the parties, control the arrangement. IFRS 10 defines control and shall be used to determine whether all the parties, or a group of the parties, are exposed, or have rights, to variable returns from their involvement with the arrangement and have the ability to affect those returns through their power over the arrangement. When all the parties, or a group of the parties, considered collectively, are able to direct the activities that significantly affect the returns of the arrangement (ie the relevant activities), the parties control the arrangement collectively.

B6 After concluding that all the parties, or a group of the parties, control the arrangement collectively, an entity shall assess whether it has joint control of the arrangement. Joint control exists only when decisions about the relevant activities require the unanimous consent of the parties that collectively control the arrangement. Assessing whether the arrangement is jointly controlled by all of its parties or by a group of the parties, or controlled by one of its parties alone, can require judgement.

B7 Sometimes the decision-making process that is agreed upon by the parties in their contractual arrangement implicitly leads to joint control. For example, assume two parties establish an arrangement in which each has 50 per cent of the voting rights and the contractual arrangement between them specifies that at least 51 per cent of the voting rights are required to make decisions about the relevant activities. In this case, the parties have implicitly agreed that they have joint control of the arrangement because decisions about the relevant activities cannot be made without both parties agreeing.

B8 In other circumstances, the contractual arrangement requires a minimum proportion of the voting rights to make decisions about the relevant activities. When that minimum required proportion of the voting rights can be achieved by more than one combination of the parties agreeing together, that arrangement is not a joint arrangement unless the contractual arrangement specifies which parties (or combination of parties) are required to agree unanimously to decisions about the relevant activities of the arrangement.

Application examples

Example 1

Assume that three parties establish an arrangement: A has 50 per cent of the voting rights in the arrangement, B has 30 per cent and C has 20 per cent. The contractual arrangement between A, B and C specifies that at least 75 per cent of the voting rights are required to make decisions about the relevant activities of the arrangement. Even though A can block any decision, it does not control the arrangement because it needs the agreement of B. The terms of their contractual arrangement requiring at least 75 per cent of the voting rights to make decisions about the relevant activities imply that A and B have joint control of the arrangement because decisions about the relevant activities of the arrangement cannot be made without both A and B agreeing.

continued...

...*continued*

Application examples
Example 2
Assume an arrangement has three parties: A has 50 per cent of the voting rights in the arrangement and B and C each have 25 per cent. The contractual arrangement between A, B and C specifies that at least 75 per cent of the voting rights are required to make decisions about the relevant activities of the arrangement. Even though A can block any decision, it does not control the arrangement because it needs the agreement of either B or C. In this example, A, B and C collectively control the arrangement. However, there is more than one combination of parties that can agree to reach 75 per cent of the voting rights (ie either A and B or A and C). In such a situation, to be a joint arrangement the contractual arrangement between the parties would need to specify which combination of the parties is required to agree unanimously to decisions about the relevant activities of the arrangement.
Example 3
Assume an arrangement in which A and B each have 35 per cent of the voting rights in the arrangement with the remaining 30 per cent being widely dispersed. Decisions about the relevant activities require approval by a majority of the voting rights. A and B have joint control of the arrangement only if the contractual arrangement specifies that decisions about the relevant activities of the arrangement require both A and B agreeing.

B9 The requirement for unanimous consent means that any party with joint control of the arrangement can prevent any of the other parties, or a group of the parties, from making unilateral decisions (about the relevant activities) without its consent. If the requirement for unanimous consent relates only to decisions that give a party protective rights and not to decisions about the relevant activities of an arrangement, that party is not a party with joint control of the arrangement.

B10 A contractual arrangement might include clauses on the resolution of disputes, such as arbitration. These provisions may allow for decisions to be made in the absence of unanimous consent among the parties that have joint control. The existence of such provisions does not prevent the arrangement from being jointly controlled and, consequently, from being a joint arrangement.

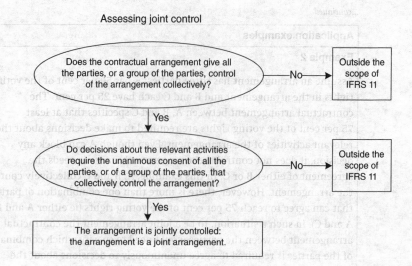

Assessing joint control

B11   When an arrangement is outside the scope of IFRS 11, an entity accounts for its interest in the arrangement in accordance with relevant IFRSs, such as IFRS 10, IAS 28 (as amended in 2011) or IFRS 9.

Types of joint arrangement (paragraphs 14–19)

B12   Joint arrangements are established for a variety of purposes (eg as a way for parties to share costs and risks, or as a way to provide the parties with access to new technology or new markets), and can be established using different structures and legal forms.

B13   Some arrangements do not require the activity that is the subject of the arrangement to be undertaken in a separate vehicle. However, other arrangements involve the establishment of a separate vehicle.

B14   The classification of joint arrangements required by this IFRS depends upon the parties' rights and obligations arising from the arrangement in the normal course of business. This IFRS classifies joint arrangements as either joint operations or joint ventures. When an entity has rights to the assets, and obligations for the liabilities, relating to the arrangement, the arrangement is a joint operation. When an entity has rights to the net assets of the arrangement, the arrangement is a joint venture. Paragraphs B16–B33 set out the assessment an entity carries out to determine whether it has an interest in a joint operation or an interest in a joint venture.

Classification of a joint arrangement

B15   As stated in paragraph B14, the classification of joint arrangements requires the parties to assess their rights and obligations arising from the arrangement. When making that assessment, an entity shall consider the following:

(a)   the structure of the joint arrangement (see paragraphs B16–B21).

(b)   when the joint arrangement is structured through a separate vehicle:

(i)   the legal form of the separate vehicle (see paragraphs B22–B24);

(ii)   the terms of the contractual arrangement (see paragraphs B25–B28); and

(iii) when relevant, other facts and circumstances (see paragraphs B29–B33).

Structure of the joint arrangement

Joint arrangements not structured through a separate vehicle

B16   A joint arrangement that is not structured through a separate vehicle is a joint operation. In such cases, the contractual arrangement establishes the parties' rights to the assets, and obligations for the liabilities, relating to the arrangement, and the parties' rights to the corresponding revenues and obligations for the corresponding expenses.

B17   The contractual arrangement often describes the nature of the activities that are the subject of the arrangement and how the parties intend to undertake those activities together. For example, the parties to a joint arrangement could agree to manufacture a product together, with each party being responsible for a specific task and each using its own assets and incurring its own liabilities. The contractual arrangement could also specify how the revenues and expenses that are common to the parties are to be shared among them. In such a case, each joint operator recognises in its financial statements the assets and liabilities used for the specific task, and recognises its share of the revenues and expenses in accordance with the contractual arrangement.

B18   In other cases, the parties to a joint arrangement might agree, for example, to share and operate an asset together. In such a case, the contractual arrangement establishes the parties' rights to the asset that is operated jointly, and how output or revenue from the asset and operating costs are shared among the parties. Each joint operator accounts for its share of the joint asset and its agreed share of any liabilities, and recognises its share of the output, revenues and expenses in accordance with the contractual arrangement.

Joint arrangements structured through a separate vehicle

B19   A joint arrangement in which the assets and liabilities relating to the arrangement are held in a separate vehicle can be either a joint venture or a joint operation.

B20   Whether a party is a joint operator or a joint venturer depends on the party's rights to the assets, and obligations for the liabilities, relating to the arrangement that are held in the separate vehicle.

B21   As stated in paragraph B15, when the parties have structured a joint arrangement in a separate vehicle, the parties need to assess whether the legal form of the separate vehicle, the terms of the contractual arrangement and, when relevant, any other facts and circumstances give them:

(a) rights to the assets, and obligations for the liabilities, relating to the arrangement (ie the arrangement is a joint operation); or

(b) rights to the net assets of the arrangement (ie the arrangement is a joint venture).

Classification of a joint arrangement: assessment of the parties' rights and obligations arising from the arrangement

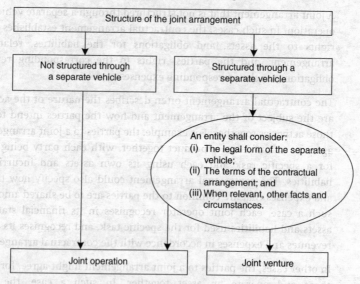

Classification of a joint arrangement: assessment of the parties' rights and obligations arising from the arrangement

The legal form of the separate vehicle

B22 The legal form of the separate vehicle is relevant when assessing the type of joint arrangement. The legal form assists in the initial assessment of the parties' rights to the assets and obligations for the liabilities held in the separate vehicle, such as whether the parties have interests in the assets held in the separate vehicle and whether they are liable for the liabilities held in the separate vehicle.

B23 For example, the parties might conduct the joint arrangement through a separate vehicle, whose legal form causes the separate vehicle to be considered in its own right (ie the assets and liabilities held in the separate vehicle are the assets and liabilities of the separate vehicle and not the assets and liabilities of the parties). In such a case, the assessment of the rights and obligations conferred upon the parties by the legal form of the separate vehicle indicates that the arrangement is a joint venture. However, the terms agreed by the parties in their contractual arrangement (see paragraphs B25–B28) and, when relevant, other facts and circumstances (see paragraphs B29–B33) can override the assessment of the rights and obligations conferred upon the parties by the legal form of the separate vehicle.

B24   The assessment of the rights and obligations conferred upon the parties by the legal form of the separate vehicle is sufficient to conclude that the arrangement is a joint operation only if the parties conduct the joint arrangement in a separate vehicle whose legal form does not confer separation between the parties and the separate vehicle (ie the assets and liabilities held in the separate vehicle are the parties' assets and liabilities).

Assessing the terms of the contractual arrangement

B25   In many cases, the rights and obligations agreed to by the parties in their contractual arrangements are consistent, or do not conflict, with the rights and obligations conferred on the parties by the legal form of the separate vehicle in which the arrangement has been structured.

B26   In other cases, the parties use the contractual arrangement to reverse or modify the rights and obligations conferred by the legal form of the separate vehicle in which the arrangement has been structured.

Application example
Example 4
Assume that two parties structure a joint arrangement in an incorporated entity. Each party has a 50 per cent ownership interest in the incorporated entity. The incorporation enables the separation of the entity from its owners and as a consequence the assets and liabilities held in the entity are the assets and liabilities of the incorporated entity. In such a case, the assessment of the rights and obligations conferred upon the parties by the legal form of the separate vehicle indicates that the parties have rights to the net assets of the arrangement.
However, the parties modify the features of the corporation through their contractual arrangement so that each has an interest in the assets of the incorporated entity and each is liable for the liabilities of the incorporated entity in a specified proportion. Such contractual modifications to the features of a corporation can cause an arrangement to be a joint operation.

B27   The following table compares common terms in contractual arrangements of parties to a joint operation and common terms in contractual arrangements of parties to a joint venture. The examples of the contractual terms provided in the following table are not exhaustive.

Assessing the terms of the contractual arrangement		
	Joint operation	**Joint venture**
The terms of the contractual arrangement	The contractual arrangement provides the parties to the joint arrangement with rights to the assets, and obligations for the liabilities, relating to the arrangement.	The contractual arrangement provides the parties to the joint arrangement with rights to the net assets of the arrangement (ie it is the separate vehicle, not the parties, that has rights to the assets, and obligations for the liabilities, relating to the arrangement).
Rights to assets	The contractual arrangement establishes that the parties to the joint arrangement share all interests (eg rights, title or ownership) in the assets relating to the arrangement in a specified proportion (eg in proportion to the parties' ownership interest in the arrangement or in proportion to the activity carried out through the arrangement that is directly attributed to them).	The contractual arrangement establishes that the assets brought into the arrangement or subsequently acquired by the joint arrangement are the arrangement's assets. The parties have no interests (ie no rights, title or ownership) in the assets of the arrangement.

continued...

...continued

Assessing the terms of the contractual arrangement		
	Joint operation	**Joint venture**
Obligations for liabilities	The contractual arrangement establishes that the parties to the joint arrangement share all liabilities, obligations, costs and expenses in a specified proportion (eg in proportion to the parties' ownership interest in the arrangement or in proportion to the activity carried out through the arrangement that is directly attributed to them).	The contractual arrangement establishes that the joint arrangement is liable for the debts and obligations of the arrangement.
		The contractual arrangement establishes that the parties to the joint arrangement are liable to the arrangement only to the extent of their respective investments in the arrangement or to their respective obligations to contribute any unpaid or additional capital to the arrangement, or both.
	The contractual arrangement establishes that the parties to the joint arrangement are liable for claims raised by third parties.	The contractual arrangement states that creditors of the joint arrangement do not have rights of recourse against any party with respect to debts or obligations of the arrangement.

continued...

...continued

Assessing the terms of the contractual arrangement		
	Joint operation	**Joint venture**
Revenues, expenses, profit or loss	The contractual arrangement establishes the allocation of revenues and expenses on the basis of the relative performance of each party to the joint arrangement. For example, the contractual arrangement might establish that revenues and expenses are allocated on the basis of the capacity that each party uses in a plant operated jointly, which could differ from their ownership interest in the joint arrangement. In other instances, the parties might have agreed to share the profit or loss relating to the arrangement on the basis of a specified proportion such as the parties' ownership interest in the arrangement. This would not prevent the arrangement from being a joint operation if the parties have rights to the assets, and obligations for the liabilities, relating to the arrangement.	The contractual arrangement establishes each party's share in the profit or loss relating to the activities of the arrangement.

continued...

...continued

Assessing the terms of the contractual arrangement		
	Joint operation	**Joint venture**
Guarantees	The parties to joint arrangements are often required to provide guarantees to third parties that, for example, receive a service from, or provide financing to, the joint arrangement. The provision of such guarantees, or the commitment by the parties to provide them, does not, by itself, determine that the joint arrangement is a joint operation. The feature that determines whether the joint arrangement is a joint operation or a joint venture is whether the parties have obligations for the liabilities relating to the arrangement (for some of which the parties might or might not have provided a guarantee).	

B28   When the contractual arrangement specifies that the parties have rights to the assets, and obligations for the liabilities, relating to the arrangement, they are parties to a joint operation and do not need to consider other facts and circumstances (paragraphs B29–B33) for the purposes of classifying the joint arrangement.

Assessing other facts and circumstances

B29   When the terms of the contractual arrangement do not specify that the parties have rights to the assets, and obligations for the liabilities, relating to the arrangement, the parties shall consider other facts and circumstances to assess whether the arrangement is a joint operation or a joint venture.

B30   A joint arrangement might be structured in a separate vehicle whose legal form confers separation between the parties and the separate vehicle. The contractual terms agreed among the parties might not specify the parties' rights to the assets and obligations for the liabilities, yet consideration of other facts and circumstances can lead to such an arrangement being classified as a joint operation. This will be the case when other facts and circumstances give the parties rights to the assets, and obligations for the liabilities, relating to the arrangement.

B31   When the activities of an arrangement are primarily designed for the provision of output to the parties, this indicates that the parties have rights to substantially all the economic benefits of the assets of the arrangement. The parties to such arrangements often ensure their access to the outputs provided by the arrangement by preventing the arrangement from selling output to third parties.

B32   The effect of an arrangement with such a design and purpose is that the liabilities incurred by the arrangement are, in substance, satisfied by the cash flows received from the parties through their purchases of the output. When the parties are substantially the only source of cash flows contributing to the continuity of the operations of the arrangement, this indicates that the parties have an obligation for the liabilities relating to the arrangement.

Application example

Example 5

Assume that two parties structure a joint arrangement in an incorporated entity (entity C) in which each party has a 50 per cent ownership interest. The purpose of the arrangement is to manufacture materials required by the parties for their own, individual manufacturing processes. The arrangement ensures that the parties operate the facility that produces the materials to the quantity and quality specifications of the parties.

The legal form of entity C (an incorporated entity) through which the activities are conducted initially indicates that the assets and liabilities held in entity C are the assets and liabilities of entity C. The contractual arrangement between the parties does not specify that the parties have rights to the assets or obligations for the liabilities of entity C. Accordingly, the legal form of entity C and the terms of the contractual arrangement indicate that the arrangement is a joint venture.

However, the parties also consider the following aspects of the arrangement:

- The parties agreed to purchase all the output produced by entity C in a ratio of 50:50. Entity C cannot sell any of the output to third parties, unless this is approved by the two parties to the arrangement. Because the purpose of the arrangement is to provide the parties with output they require, such sales to third parties are expected to be uncommon and not material.

- The price of the output sold to the parties is set by both parties at a level that is designed to cover the costs of production and administrative expenses incurred by entity C. On the basis of this operating model, the arrangement is intended to operate at a break-even level.

continued...

...*continued*

> **Application example**
>
> From the fact pattern above, the following facts and circumstances are relevant:
>
> - The obligation of the parties to purchase all the output produced by entity C reflects the exclusive dependence of entity C upon the parties for the generation of cash flows and, thus, the parties have an obligation to fund the settlement of the liabilities of entity C.
>
> - The fact that the parties have rights to all the output produced by entity C means that the parties are consuming, and therefore have rights to, all the economic benefits of the assets of entity C.
>
> These facts and circumstances indicate that the arrangement is a joint operation. The conclusion about the classification of the joint arrangement in these circumstances would not change if, instead of the parties using their share of the output themselves in a subsequent manufacturing process, the parties sold their share of the output to third parties.
>
> If the parties changed the terms of the contractual arrangement so that the arrangement was able to sell output to third parties, this would result in entity C assuming demand, inventory and credit risks. In that scenario, such a change in the facts and circumstances would require reassessment of the classification of the joint arrangement. Such facts and circumstances would indicate that the arrangement is a joint venture.

B33   The following flow chart reflects the assessment an entity follows to classify
         an arrangement when the joint arrangement is structured through a separate
         vehicle:

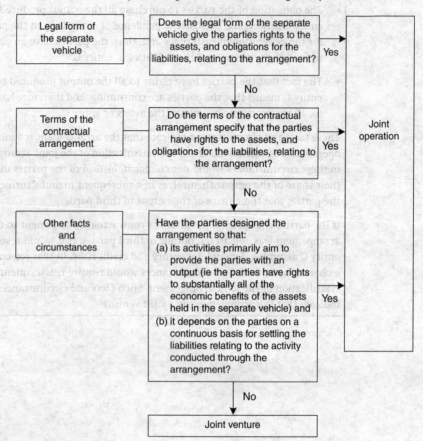

Classification of a joint arrangement structured through a separate vehicle

Financial statements of parties to a joint arrangement (paragraphs 21A–22)

Accounting for acquisitions of interests in joint operations

B33A   When an entity acquires an interest in a joint operation in which the activity
         of the joint operation constitutes a business, as defined in IFRS 3, it shall
         apply, to the extent of its share in accordance with paragraph 20, all of the
         principles on business combinations accounting in IFRS 3, and other IFRSs,
         that do not conflict with the guidance in this IFRS and disclose the
         information required by those IFRSs in relation to business combinations. The
         principles on business combinations accounting that do not conflict with the
         guidance in this IFRS include but are not limited to:

(a) measuring identifiable assets and liabilities at fair value, other than items for which exceptions are given in IFRS 3 and other IFRSs;

(b) recognising acquisition-related costs as expenses in the periods in which the costs are incurred and the services are received, with the exception that the costs to issue debt or equity securities are recognised in accordance with IAS 32 *Financial Instruments: Presentation* and IFRS 9;[1]

(c) recognising deferred tax assets and deferred tax liabilities that arise from the initial recognition of assets or liabilities, except for deferred tax liabilities that arise from the initial recognition of goodwill, as required by IFRS 3 and IAS 12 *Income Taxes* for business combinations;

(d) recognising the excess of the consideration transferred over the net of the acquisition-date amounts of the identifiable assets acquired and the liabilities assumed, if any, as goodwill; and

(e) testing for impairment a cash-generating unit to which goodwill has been allocated at least annually, and whenever there is an indication that the unit may be impaired, as required by IAS 36 *Impairment of Assets* for goodwill acquired in a business combination.

B33B   Paragraphs 21A and B33A also apply to the formation of a joint operation if, and only if, an existing business, as defined in IFRS 3, is contributed to the joint operation on its formation by one of the parties that participate in the joint operation. However, those paragraphs do not apply to the formation of a joint operation if all of the parties that participate in the joint operation only contribute assets or groups of assets that do not constitute businesses to the joint operation on its formation.

B33C   A joint operator might increase its interest in a joint operation in which the activity of the joint operation constitutes a business, as defined in IFRS 3, by acquiring an additional interest in the joint operation. In such cases, previously held interests in the joint operation are not remeasured if the joint operator retains joint control.

B33CA   A party that participates in, but does not have joint control of, a joint operation might obtain joint control of the joint operation in which the activity of the joint operation constitutes a business as defined in IFRS 3. In such cases, previously held interests in the joint operation are not remeasured.

B33D   Paragraphs 21A and B33A–B33C do not apply on the acquisition of an interest in a joint operation when the parties sharing joint control, including the entity acquiring the interest in the joint operation, are under the common control of the same ultimate controlling party or parties both before and after the acquisition, and that control is not transitory.

---

1   If an entity applies these amendments but does not yet apply IFRS 9, the reference in these amendments to IFRS 9 shall be read as a reference to IAS 39 *Financial Instruments: Recognition and Measurement*.

Accounting for sales or contributions of assets to a joint operation

B34   When an entity enters into a transaction with a joint operation in which it is a joint operator, such as a sale or contribution of assets, it is conducting the transaction with the other parties to the joint operation and, as such, the joint operator shall recognise gains and losses resulting from such a transaction only to the extent of the other parties' interests in the joint operation.

B35   When such transactions provide evidence of a reduction in the net realisable value of the assets to be sold or contributed to the joint operation, or of an impairment loss of those assets, those losses shall be recognised fully by the joint operator.

Accounting for purchases of assets from a joint operation

B36   When an entity enters into a transaction with a joint operation in which it is a joint operator, such as a purchase of assets, it shall not recognise its share of the gains and losses until it resells those assets to a third party.

B37   When such transactions provide evidence of a reduction in the net realisable value of the assets to be purchased or of an impairment loss of those assets, a joint operator shall recognise its share of those losses.

Appendix C
Effective date, transition and withdrawal of other IFRSs

This appendix is an integral part of the IFRS and has the same authority as the other parts of the IFRS.

Effective date

C1 An entity shall apply this IFRS for annual periods beginning on or after 1 January 2013. Earlier application is permitted. If an entity applies this IFRS earlier, it shall disclose that fact and apply IFRS 10, IFRS 12 *Disclosure of Interests in Other Entities*, IAS 27 (as amended in 2011) and IAS 28 (as amended in 2011) at the same time.

C1A *Consolidated Financial Statements, Joint Arrangements and Disclosure of Interests in Other Entities: Transition Guidance* (Amendments to IFRS 10, IFRS 11 and IFRS 12), issued in June 2012, amended paragraphs C2–C5, C7–C10 and C12 and added paragraphs C1B and C12A–C12B. An entity shall apply those amendments for annual periods beginning on or after 1 January 2013. If an entity applies IFRS 11 for an earlier period, it shall apply those amendments for that earlier period.

C1AA *Accounting for Acquisitions of Interests in Joint Operations* (Amendments to IFRS 11), issued in May 2014, amended the heading after paragraph B33 and added paragraphs 21A, B33A–B33D and C14A and their related headings. An entity shall apply those amendments prospectively in annual periods beginning on or after 1 January 2016. Earlier application is permitted. If an entity applies those amendments in an earlier period it shall disclose that fact.

C1AB *Annual Improvements to IFRS Standards 2015–2017 Cycle*, issued in December 2017, added paragraph B33CA. An entity shall apply those amendments to transactions in which it obtains joint control on or after the beginning of the first annual reporting period beginning on or after 1 January 2019. Earlier application is permitted. If an entity applies those amendments earlier, it shall disclose that fact.

Transition

C1B Notwithstanding the requirements of paragraph 28 of IAS 8 *Accounting Policies, Changes in Accounting Estimates and Errors*, when this IFRS is first applied, an entity need only present the quantitative information required by paragraph 28(f) of IAS 8 for the annual period immediately preceding the first annual period for which IFRS 11 is applied (the 'immediately preceding period'). An entity may also present this information for the current period or for earlier comparative periods, but is not required to do so.

Joint ventures—transition from proportionate consolidation to the equity method

C2   When changing from proportionate consolidation to the equity method, an entity shall recognise its investment in the joint venture as at the beginning of the immediately preceding period. That initial investment shall be measured as the aggregate of the carrying amounts of the assets and liabilities that the entity had previously proportionately consolidated, including any goodwill arising from acquisition. If the goodwill previously belonged to a larger cash-generating unit, or to a group of cash-generating units, the entity shall allocate goodwill to the joint venture on the basis of the relative carrying amounts of the joint venture and the cash-generating unit or group of cash-generating units to which it belonged.

C3   The opening balance of the investment determined in accordance with paragraph C2 is regarded as the deemed cost of the investment at initial recognition. An entity shall apply paragraphs 40–43 of IAS 28 (as amended in 2011) to the opening balance of the investment to assess whether the investment is impaired and shall recognise any impairment loss as an adjustment to retained earnings at the beginning of the immediately preceding period. The initial recognition exception in paragraphs 15 and 24 of IAS 12 *Income Taxes* does not apply when the entity recognises an investment in a joint venture resulting from applying the transition requirements for joint ventures that had previously been proportionately consolidated.

C4   If aggregating all previously proportionately consolidated assets and liabilities results in negative net assets, an entity shall assess whether it has legal or constructive obligations in relation to the negative net assets and, if so, the entity shall recognise the corresponding liability. If the entity concludes that it does not have legal or constructive obligations in relation to the negative net assets, it shall not recognise the corresponding liability but it shall adjust retained earnings at the beginning of the immediately preceding period. The entity shall disclose this fact, along with its cumulative unrecognised share of losses of its joint ventures as at the beginning of the immediately preceding period and at the date at which this IFRS is first applied.

C5   An entity shall disclose a breakdown of the assets and liabilities that have been aggregated into the single line investment balance as at the beginning of the immediately preceding period. That disclosure shall be prepared in an aggregated manner for all joint ventures for which an entity applies the transition requirements referred to in paragraphs C2–C6.

C6   After initial recognition, an entity shall account for its investment in the joint venture using the equity method in accordance with IAS 28 (as amended in 2011).

Approval by the Board of IFRS 11 issued in May 2011

International Financial Reporting Standard 11 *Joint Arrangements* was approved for issue by the fifteen members of the International Accounting Standards Board.

Sir David Tweedie   Chairman

Stephen Cooper

Philippe Danjou

Jan Engström

Patrick Finnegan

Amaro Luiz de Oliveira Gomes

Prabhakar Kalavacherla

Elke König

Patricia McConnell

Warren J McGregor

Paul Pacter

Darrel Scott

John T Smith

Tatsumi Yamada

Wei-Guo Zhang

Approval by the Board of *Consolidated Financial Statements, Joint Arrangements and Disclosure of Interests in Other Entities: Transition Guidance* (Amendments to IFRS 10, IFRS 11 and IFRS 12) issued in June 2012

Consolidated Financial Statements, Joint Arrangements and Disclosure of Interests in Other Entities: Transition Guidance (Amendments to IFRS 10, IFRS 11 and IFRS 12) was approved for issue by the fourteen members of the International Accounting Standards Board.

Hans Hoogervorst	Chairman
Ian Mackintosh	Vice-Chairman
Stephen Cooper	
Philippe Danjou	
Jan Engström	
Patrick Finnegan	
Amaro Luiz de Oliveira Gomes	
Prabhakar Kalavacherla	
Patricia McConnell	
Takatsugu Ochi	
Paul Pacter	
Darrel Scott	
John T Smith	
Wei-Guo Zhang	

Approval by the Board of *Accounting for Acquisitions of Interests in Joint Operations* (Amendments to IFRS 11) issued in May 2014

Accounting for Acquisitions of Interests in Joint Operations was approved for issue by the sixteen members of the International Accounting Standards Board.

Hans Hoogervorst	Chairman
Ian Mackintosh	Vice-Chairman
Stephen Cooper	
Philippe Danjou	
Martin Edelmann	
Jan Engström	
Patrick Finnegan	
Amaro Luiz de Oliveira Gomes	
Gary Kabureck	
Suzanne Lloyd	
Patricia McConnell	
Takatsugu Ochi	
Darrel Scott	
Chungwoo Suh	
Mary Tokar	
Wei-Guo Zhang	

IFRS 12

Disclosure of Interests in Other Entities

In May 2011 the International Accounting Standards Board issued IFRS 12 *Disclosure of Interests in Other Entities*. IFRS 12 replaced the disclosure requirements in IAS 27 *Consolidated and Separate Financial Statements*, IAS 28 *Investments in Associates* and IAS 31 *Interests in Joint Ventures*.

In June 2012 IFRS 12 was amended by *Consolidated Financial Statements, Joint Arrangements and Disclosure of Interests in Other Entities: Transition Guidance* (Amendments to IFRS 10, IFRS 11 and IFRS 12). These amendments provided additional transition relief in IFRS 12, limiting the requirement to present adjusted comparative information to only the annual period immediately preceding the first annual period for which IFRS 12 is applied. Furthermore, for disclosures related to unconsolidated structured entities, the amendments removed the requirement to present comparative information for periods before IFRS 12 is first applied.

In October 2012 *Investment Entities* (Amendments to IFRS 10, IFRS 12 and IAS 27) introduced new disclosure requirements for investment entities that, in accordance with IFRS 10 *Consolidated Financial Statements*, measure their subsidiaries at fair value through profit or loss instead of consolidating them.

Other Standards have made minor amendments to IFRS 12, including *Investment Entities: Applying the Consolidation Exception* (Amendments to IFRS 10, IFRS 12 and IAS 28) (issued December 2014), *Annual Improvements to IFRS® Standards 2014–2016 Cycle* (issued December 2016) and *Amendments to References to the Conceptual Framework in IFRS Standards* (issued March 2018).

CONTENTS

continued...

...*continued*

FOR THE BASIS FOR CONCLUSIONS, SEE PART C OF THIS EDITION

BASIS FOR CONCLUSIONS

International Financial Reporting Standard 12 *Disclosure of Interests in Other Entities* (IFRS 12) is set out in paragraphs 1–31 and Appendices A–D. All the paragraphs have equal authority. Paragraphs in **bold type** state the main principles. Terms defined in Appendix A are in *italics* the first time they appear in the IFRS. Definitions of other terms are given in the Glossary for International Financial Reporting Standards. IFRS 12 should be read in the context of its objective and the Basis for Conclusions, the *Preface to IFRS Standards* and the *Conceptual Framework for Financial Reporting*. IAS 8 *Accounting Policies, Changes in Accounting Estimates and Errors* provides a basis for selecting and applying accounting policies in the absence of explicit guidance.

International Financial Reporting Standard 12
Disclosure of Interests in Other Entities

Objective

1   The objective of this IFRS is to require an entity to disclose information that enables users of its financial statements to evaluate:

    (a)   the nature of, and risks associated with, its *interests in other entities*; and

    (b)   the effects of those interests on its financial position, financial performance and cash flows.

Meeting the objective

2   To meet the objective in paragraph 1, an entity shall disclose:

    (a)   the significant judgements and assumptions it has made in determining:

        (i)   the nature of its interest in another entity or arrangement;

        (ii)   the type of joint arrangement in which it has an interest (paragraphs 7–9);

        (iii)   that it meets the definition of an investment entity, if applicable (paragraph 9A); and

    (b)   information about its interests in:

        (i)   subsidiaries (paragraphs 10–19);

        (ii)   joint arrangements and associates (paragraphs 20–23); and

        (iii)   *structured entities* that are not controlled by the entity (unconsolidated structured entities) (paragraphs 24–31).

3   If the disclosures required by this IFRS, together with disclosures required by other IFRSs, do not meet the objective in paragraph 1, an entity shall disclose whatever additional information is necessary to meet that objective.

4   An entity shall consider the level of detail necessary to satisfy the disclosure objective and how much emphasis to place on each of the requirements in this IFRS. It shall aggregate or disaggregate disclosures so that useful information is not obscured by either the inclusion of a large amount of insignificant detail or the aggregation of items that have different characteristics (see paragraphs B2–B6).

Scope

5   This IFRS shall be applied by an entity that has an interest in any of the following:

    (a)   subsidiaries

(b)   joint arrangements (ie joint operations or joint ventures)

(c)   associates

(d)   unconsolidated structured entities.

5A   Except as described in paragraph B17, the requirements in this IFRS apply to an entity's interests listed in paragraph 5 that are classified (or included in a disposal group that is classified) as held for sale or discontinued operations in accordance with IFRS 5 *Non-current Assets Held for Sale and Discontinued Operations*.

6   This IFRS does not apply to:

(a)   post-employment benefit plans or other long-term employee benefit plans to which IAS 19 *Employee Benefits* applies.

(b)   an entity's separate financial statements to which IAS 27 *Separate Financial Statements* applies. However:

(i)   if an entity has interests in unconsolidated structured entities and prepares separate financial statements as its only financial statements, it shall apply the requirements in paragraphs 24–31 when preparing those separate financial statements.

(ii)   an investment entity that prepares financial statements in which all of its subsidiaries are measured at fair value through profit or loss in accordance with paragraph 31 of IFRS 10 shall present the disclosures relating to investment entities required by this IFRS.

(c)   an interest held by an entity that participates in, but does not have joint control of, a joint arrangement unless that interest results in significant influence over the arrangement or is an interest in a structured entity.

(d)   an interest in another entity that is accounted for in accordance with IFRS 9 *Financial Instruments*. However, an entity shall apply this IFRS:

(i)   when that interest is an interest in an associate or a joint venture that, in accordance with IAS 28 *Investments in Associates and Joint Ventures*, is measured at fair value through profit or loss; or

(ii)   when that interest is an interest in an unconsolidated structured entity.

Significant judgements and assumptions

7   An entity shall disclose information about significant judgements and assumptions it has made (and changes to those judgements and assumptions) in determining:

(a)   that it has control of another entity, ie an investee as described in paragraphs 5 and 6 of IFRS 10 *Consolidated Financial Statements*;

(b)   that it has joint control of an arrangement or significant influence over another entity; and

(c)   the type of joint arrangement (ie joint operation or joint venture) when the arrangement has been structured through a separate vehicle.

8   The significant judgements and assumptions disclosed in accordance with paragraph 7 include those made by the entity when changes in facts and circumstances are such that the conclusion about whether it has control, joint control or significant influence changes during the reporting period.

9   To comply with paragraph 7, an entity shall disclose, for example, significant judgements and assumptions made in determining that:

(a)   it does not control another entity even though it holds more than half of the voting rights of the other entity.

(b)   it controls another entity even though it holds less than half of the voting rights of the other entity.

(c)   it is an agent or a principal (see paragraphs B58–B72 of IFRS 10).

(d)   it does not have significant influence even though it holds 20 per cent or more of the voting rights of another entity.

(e)   it has significant influence even though it holds less than 20 per cent of the voting rights of another entity.

Investment entity status

9A   **When a parent determines that it is an investment entity in accordance with paragraph 27 of IFRS 10, the investment entity shall disclose information about significant judgements and assumptions it has made in determining that it is an investment entity. If the investment entity does not have one or more of the typical characteristics of an investment entity (see paragraph 28 of IFRS 10), it shall disclose its reasons for concluding that it is nevertheless an investment entity.**

9B   When an entity becomes, or ceases to be, an investment entity, it shall disclose the change of investment entity status and the reasons for the change. In addition, an entity that becomes an investment entity shall disclose the effect of the change of status on the financial statements for the period presented, including:

(a)   the total fair value, as of the date of change of status, of the subsidiaries that cease to be consolidated;

(b)   the total gain or loss, if any, calculated in accordance with paragraph B101 of IFRS 10; and

(c)   the line item(s) in profit or loss in which the gain or loss is recognised (if not presented separately).

Interests in subsidiaries

10 An entity shall disclose information that enables users of its consolidated financial statements

    (a) to understand:

        (i) the composition of the group; and

        (ii) the interest that non-controlling interests have in the group's activities and cash flows (paragraph 12); and

    (b) to evaluate:

        (i) the nature and extent of significant restrictions on its ability to access or use assets, and settle liabilities, of the group (paragraph 13);

        (ii) the nature of, and changes in, the risks associated with its interests in consolidated structured entities (paragraphs 14–17);

        (iii) the consequences of changes in its ownership interest in a subsidiary that do not result in a loss of control (paragraph 18); and

        (iv) the consequences of losing control of a subsidiary during the reporting period (paragraph 19).

11 When the financial statements of a subsidiary used in the preparation of consolidated financial statements are as of a date or for a period that is different from that of the consolidated financial statements (see paragraphs B92 and B93 of IFRS 10), an entity shall disclose:

    (a) the date of the end of the reporting period of the financial statements of that subsidiary; and

    (b) the reason for using a different date or period.

The interest that non-controlling interests have in the group's activities and cash flows

12 An entity shall disclose for each of its subsidiaries that have non-controlling interests that are material to the reporting entity:

    (a) the name of the subsidiary.

    (b) the principal place of business (and country of incorporation if different from the principal place of business) of the subsidiary.

    (c) the proportion of ownership interests held by non-controlling interests.

    (d) the proportion of voting rights held by non-controlling interests, if different from the proportion of ownership interests held.

(e) the profit or loss allocated to non-controlling interests of the subsidiary during the reporting period.

(f) accumulated non-controlling interests of the subsidiary at the end of the reporting period.

(g) summarised financial information about the subsidiary (see paragraph B10).

The nature and extent of significant restrictions

13 An entity shall disclose:

(a) significant restrictions (eg statutory, contractual and regulatory restrictions) on its ability to access or use the assets and settle the liabilities of the group, such as:

 (i) those that restrict the ability of a parent or its subsidiaries to transfer cash or other assets to (or from) other entities within the group.

 (ii) guarantees or other requirements that may restrict dividends and other capital distributions being paid, or loans and advances being made or repaid, to (or from) other entities within the group.

(b) the nature and extent to which protective rights of non-controlling interests can significantly restrict the entity's ability to access or use the assets and settle the liabilities of the group (such as when a parent is obliged to settle liabilities of a subsidiary before settling its own liabilities, or approval of non-controlling interests is required either to access the assets or to settle the liabilities of a subsidiary).

(c) the carrying amounts in the consolidated financial statements of the assets and liabilities to which those restrictions apply.

Nature of the risks associated with an entity's interests in consolidated structured entities

14 An entity shall disclose the terms of any contractual arrangements that could require the parent or its subsidiaries to provide financial support to a consolidated structured entity, including events or circumstances that could expose the reporting entity to a loss (eg liquidity arrangements or credit rating triggers associated with obligations to purchase assets of the structured entity or provide financial support).

15 If during the reporting period a parent or any of its subsidiaries has, without having a contractual obligation to do so, provided financial or other support to a consolidated structured entity (eg purchasing assets of or instruments issued by the structured entity), the entity shall disclose:

(a) the type and amount of support provided, including situations in which the parent or its subsidiaries assisted the structured entity in obtaining financial support; and

(b)   the reasons for providing the support.

16   If during the reporting period a parent or any of its subsidiaries has, without having a contractual obligation to do so, provided financial or other support to a previously unconsolidated structured entity and that provision of support resulted in the entity controlling the structured entity, the entity shall disclose an explanation of the relevant factors in reaching that decision.

17   An entity shall disclose any current intentions to provide financial or other support to a consolidated structured entity, including intentions to assist the structured entity in obtaining financial support.

Consequences of changes in a parent's ownership interest in a subsidiary that do not result in a loss of control

18   An entity shall present a schedule that shows the effects on the equity attributable to owners of the parent of any changes in its ownership interest in a subsidiary that do not result in a loss of control.

Consequences of losing control of a subsidiary during the reporting period

19   An entity shall disclose the gain or loss, if any, calculated in accordance with paragraph 25 of IFRS 10, and:

(a)   the portion of that gain or loss attributable to measuring any investment retained in the former subsidiary at its fair value at the date when control is lost; and

(b)   the line item(s) in profit or loss in which the gain or loss is recognised (if not presented separately).

Interests in unconsolidated subsidiaries (investment entities)

19A   An investment entity that, in accordance with IFRS 10, is required to apply the exception to consolidation and instead account for its investment in a subsidiary at fair value through profit or loss shall disclose that fact.

19B   For each unconsolidated subsidiary, an investment entity shall disclose:

(a)   the subsidiary's name;

(b)   the principal place of business (and country of incorporation if different from the principal place of business) of the subsidiary; and

(c)   the proportion of ownership interest held by the investment entity and, if different, the proportion of voting rights held.

19C   If an investment entity is the parent of another investment entity, the parent shall also provide the disclosures in 19B(a)–(c) for investments that are controlled by its investment entity subsidiary. The disclosure may be provided by including, in the financial statements of the parent, the financial statements of the subsidiary (or subsidiaries) that contain the above information.

19D   An investment entity shall disclose:

(a)   the nature and extent of any significant restrictions (eg resulting from borrowing arrangements, regulatory requirements or contractual arrangements) on the ability of an unconsolidated subsidiary to transfer funds to the investment entity in the form of cash dividends or to repay loans or advances made to the unconsolidated subsidiary by the investment entity; and

(b)   any current commitments or intentions to provide financial or other support to an unconsolidated subsidiary, including commitments or intentions to assist the subsidiary in obtaining financial support.

19E   If, during the reporting period, an investment entity or any of its subsidiaries has, without having a contractual obligation to do so, provided financial or other support to an unconsolidated subsidiary (eg purchasing assets of, or instruments issued by, the subsidiary or assisting the subsidiary in obtaining financial support), the entity shall disclose:

(a)   the type and amount of support provided to each unconsolidated subsidiary; and

(b)   the reasons for providing the support.

19F   An investment entity shall disclose the terms of any contractual arrangements that could require the entity or its unconsolidated subsidiaries to provide financial support to an unconsolidated, controlled, structured entity, including events or circumstances that could expose the reporting entity to a loss (eg liquidity arrangements or credit rating triggers associated with obligations to purchase assets of the structured entity or to provide financial support).

19G   If during the reporting period an investment entity or any of its unconsolidated subsidiaries has, without having a contractual obligation to do so, provided financial or other support to an unconsolidated, structured entity that the investment entity did not control, and if that provision of support resulted in the investment entity controlling the structured entity, the investment entity shall disclose an explanation of the relevant factors in reaching the decision to provide that support.

Interests in joint arrangements and associates

20   An entity shall disclose information that enables users of its financial statements to evaluate:

(a)   the nature, extent and financial effects of its interests in joint arrangements and associates, including the nature and effects of its contractual relationship with the other investors with joint control of, or significant influence over, joint arrangements and associates (paragraphs 21 and 22); and

(b)   the nature of, and changes in, the risks associated with its interests in joint ventures and associates (paragraph 23).

Nature, extent and financial effects of an entity's interests in joint arrangements and associates

21   An entity shall disclose:

(a)   for each joint arrangement and associate that is material to the reporting entity:

(i)   the name of the joint arrangement or associate.

(ii)   the nature of the entity's relationship with the joint arrangement or associate (by, for example, describing the nature of the activities of the joint arrangement or associate and whether they are strategic to the entity's activities).

(iii)   the principal place of business (and country of incorporation, if applicable and different from the principal place of business) of the joint arrangement or associate.

(iv)   the proportion of ownership interest or participating share held by the entity and, if different, the proportion of voting rights held (if applicable).

(b)   for each joint venture and associate that is material to the reporting entity:

(i)   whether the investment in the joint venture or associate is measured using the equity method or at fair value.

(ii)   summarised financial information about the joint venture or associate as specified in paragraphs B12 and B13.

(iii)   if the joint venture or associate is accounted for using the equity method, the fair value of its investment in the joint venture or associate, if there is a quoted market price for the investment.

(c)   financial information as specified in paragraph B16 about the entity's investments in joint ventures and associates that are not individually material:

(i)   in aggregate for all individually immaterial joint ventures and, separately,

(ii)   in aggregate for all individually immaterial associates.

21A   An investment entity need not provide the disclosures required by paragraphs 21(b)–21(c).

    (d)   a comparison of the carrying amounts of the assets and liabilities of the entity that relate to its interests in unconsolidated structured entities and the entity's maximum exposure to loss from those entities.

30   If during the reporting period an entity has, without having a contractual obligation to do so, provided financial or other support to an unconsolidated structured entity in which it previously had or currently has an interest (for example, purchasing assets of or instruments issued by the structured entity), the entity shall disclose:

    (a)   the type and amount of support provided, including situations in which the entity assisted the structured entity in obtaining financial support; and

    (b)   the reasons for providing the support.

31   An entity shall disclose any current intentions to provide financial or other support to an unconsolidated structured entity, including intentions to assist the structured entity in obtaining financial support.

Appendix A
Defined terms

This appendix is an integral part of the IFRS.

income from a structured entity	For the purpose of this IFRS, income from a **structured entity** includes, but is not limited to, recurring and non-recurring fees, interest, dividends, gains or losses on the remeasurement or derecognition of interests in structured entities and gains or losses from the transfer of assets and liabilities to the structured entity.
interest in another entity	For the purpose of this IFRS, an interest in another entity refers to contractual and non-contractual involvement that exposes an entity to variability of returns from the performance of the other entity. An interest in another entity can be evidenced by, but is not limited to, the holding of equity or debt instruments as well as other forms of involvement such as the provision of funding, liquidity support, credit enhancement and guarantees. It includes the means by which an entity has control or joint control of, or significant influence over, another entity. An entity does not necessarily have an interest in another entity solely because of a typical customer supplier relationship.
	Paragraphs B7–B9 provide further information about interests in other entities.
	Paragraphs B55–B57 of IFRS 10 explain variability of returns.
structured entity	An entity that has been designed so that voting or similar rights are not the dominant factor in deciding who controls the entity, such as when any voting rights relate to administrative tasks only and the relevant activities are directed by means of contractual arrangements.
	Paragraphs B22–B24 provide further information about structured entities.

The following terms are defined in IAS 27 (as amended in 2011), IAS 28 (as amended in 2011), IFRS 10 and IFRS 11 *Joint Arrangements* and are used in this IFRS with the meanings specified in those IFRSs:

- associate
- consolidated financial statements
- control of an entity
- equity method
- group
- investment entity
- joint arrangement

- joint control

- joint operation

- joint venture

- non-controlling interest

- parent

- protective rights

- relevant activities

- separate financial statements

- separate vehicle

- significant influence

- subsidiary.

Appendix B
Application guidance

This appendix is an integral part of the IFRS. It describes the application of paragraphs 1–31 and has the same authority as the other parts of the IFRS.

B1   The examples in this appendix portray hypothetical situations. Although some aspects of the examples may be present in actual fact patterns, all relevant facts and circumstances of a particular fact pattern would need to be evaluated when applying IFRS 12.

Aggregation (paragraph 4)

B2   An entity shall decide, in the light of its circumstances, how much detail it provides to satisfy the information needs of users, how much emphasis it places on different aspects of the requirements and how it aggregates the information. It is necessary to strike a balance between burdening financial statements with excessive detail that may not assist users of financial statements and obscuring information as a result of too much aggregation.

B3   An entity may aggregate the disclosures required by this IFRS for interests in similar entities if aggregation is consistent with the disclosure objective and the requirement in paragraph B4, and does not obscure the information provided. An entity shall disclose how it has aggregated its interests in similar entities.

B4   An entity shall present information separately for interests in:

(a)   subsidiaries;

(b)   joint ventures;

(c)   joint operations;

(d)   associates; and

(e)   unconsolidated structured entities.

B5   In determining whether to aggregate information, an entity shall consider quantitative and qualitative information about the different risk and return characteristics of each entity it is considering for aggregation and the significance of each such entity to the reporting entity. The entity shall present the disclosures in a manner that clearly explains to users of financial statements the nature and extent of its interests in those other entities.

B6   Examples of aggregation levels within the classes of entities set out in paragraph B4 that might be appropriate are:

(a)   nature of activities (eg a research and development entity, a revolving credit card securitisation entity).

(b)   industry classification.

(c)   geography (eg country or region).

© IFRS Foundation

Interests in other entities

B7   An interest in another entity refers to contractual and non-contractual involvement that exposes the reporting entity to variability of returns from the performance of the other entity. Consideration of the purpose and design of the other entity may help the reporting entity when assessing whether it has an interest in that entity and, therefore, whether it is required to provide the disclosures in this IFRS. That assessment shall include consideration of the risks that the other entity was designed to create and the risks the other entity was designed to pass on to the reporting entity and other parties.

B8   A reporting entity is typically exposed to variability of returns from the performance of another entity by holding instruments (such as equity or debt instruments issued by the other entity) or having another involvement that absorbs variability. For example, assume a structured entity holds a loan portfolio. The structured entity obtains a credit default swap from another entity (the reporting entity) to protect itself from the default of interest and principal payments on the loans. The reporting entity has involvement that exposes it to variability of returns from the performance of the structured entity because the credit default swap absorbs variability of returns of the structured entity.

B9   Some instruments are designed to transfer risk from a reporting entity to another entity. Such instruments create variability of returns for the other entity but do not typically expose the reporting entity to variability of returns from the performance of the other entity. For example, assume a structured entity is established to provide investment opportunities for investors who wish to have exposure to entity Z's credit risk (entity Z is unrelated to any party involved in the arrangement). The structured entity obtains funding by issuing to those investors notes that are linked to entity Z's credit risk (credit-linked notes) and uses the proceeds to invest in a portfolio of risk-free financial assets. The structured entity obtains exposure to entity Z's credit risk by entering into a credit default swap (CDS) with a swap counterparty. The CDS passes entity Z's credit risk to the structured entity in return for a fee paid by the swap counterparty. The investors in the structured entity receive a higher return that reflects both the structured entity's return from its asset portfolio and the CDS fee. The swap counterparty does not have involvement with the structured entity that exposes it to variability of returns from the performance of the structured entity because the CDS transfers variability to the structured entity, rather than absorbing variability of returns of the structured entity.

Summarised financial information for subsidiaries, joint ventures and associates (paragraphs 12 and 21)

B10   For each subsidiary that has non-controlling interests that are material to the reporting entity, an entity shall disclose:

(a)   dividends paid to non-controlling interests.

(b)   summarised financial information about the assets, liabilities, profit or loss and cash flows of the subsidiary that enables users to understand the interest that non-controlling interests have in the group's activities and cash flows. That information might include but is not limited to, for example, current assets, non-current assets, current liabilities, non-current liabilities, revenue, profit or loss and total comprehensive income.

B11   The summarised financial information required by paragraph B10(b) shall be the amounts before inter-company eliminations.

B12   For each joint venture and associate that is material to the reporting entity, an entity shall disclose:

(a)   dividends received from the joint venture or associate.

(b)   summarised financial information for the joint venture or associate (see paragraphs B14 and B15) including, but not necessarily limited to:

     (i)   current assets.

     (ii)   non-current assets.

     (iii)   current liabilities.

     (iv)   non-current liabilities.

     (v)   revenue.

     (vi)   profit or loss from continuing operations.

     (vii)   post-tax profit or loss from discontinued operations.

     (viii)   other comprehensive income.

     (ix)   total comprehensive income.

B13   In addition to the summarised financial information required by paragraph B12, an entity shall disclose for each joint venture that is material to the reporting entity the amount of:

(a)   cash and cash equivalents included in paragraph B12(b)(i).

(b)   current financial liabilities (excluding trade and other payables and provisions) included in paragraph B12(b)(iii).

(c)   non-current financial liabilities (excluding trade and other payables and provisions) included in paragraph B12(b)(iv).

(d)   depreciation and amortisation.

(e)   interest income.

(f)   interest expense.

(g)   income tax expense or income.

B14   The summarised financial information presented in accordance with paragraphs B12 and B13 shall be the amounts included in the IFRS financial statements of the joint venture or associate (and not the entity's share of those amounts). If the entity accounts for its interest in the joint venture or associate using the equity method:

       (a)   the amounts included in the IFRS financial statements of the joint venture or associate shall be adjusted to reflect adjustments made by the entity when using the equity method, such as fair value adjustments made at the time of acquisition and adjustments for differences in accounting policies.

       (b)   the entity shall provide a reconciliation of the summarised financial information presented to the carrying amount of its interest in the joint venture or associate.

B15   An entity may present the summarised financial information required by paragraphs B12 and B13 on the basis of the joint venture's or associate's financial statements if:

       (a)   the entity measures its interest in the joint venture or associate at fair value in accordance with IAS 28 (as amended in 2011); and

       (b)   the joint venture or associate does not prepare IFRS financial statements and preparation on that basis would be impracticable or cause undue cost.

    In that case, the entity shall disclose the basis on which the summarised financial information has been prepared.

B16   An entity shall disclose, in aggregate, the carrying amount of its interests in all individually immaterial joint ventures or associates that are accounted for using the equity method. An entity shall also disclose separately the aggregate amount of its share of those joint ventures' or associates':

       (a)   profit or loss from continuing operations.

       (b)   post-tax profit or loss from discontinued operations.

       (c)   other comprehensive income.

       (d)   total comprehensive income.

    An entity provides the disclosures separately for joint ventures and associates.

B17   When an entity's interest in a subsidiary, a joint venture or an associate (or a portion of its interest in a joint venture or an associate) is classified (or included in a disposal group that is classified) as held for sale in accordance with IFRS 5, the entity is not required to disclose summarised financial information for that subsidiary, joint venture or associate in accordance with paragraphs B10–B16.

Commitments for joint ventures (paragraph 23(a))

B18   An entity shall disclose total commitments it has made but not recognised at the reporting date (including its share of commitments made jointly with other investors with joint control of a joint venture) relating to its interests in joint ventures. Commitments are those that may give rise to a future outflow of cash or other resources.

B19   Unrecognised commitments that may give rise to a future outflow of cash or other resources include:

    (a)   unrecognised commitments to contribute funding or resources as a result of, for example:

        (i)   the constitution or acquisition agreements of a joint venture (that, for example, require an entity to contribute funds over a specific period).

        (ii)   capital-intensive projects undertaken by a joint venture.

        (iii)   unconditional purchase obligations, comprising procurement of equipment, inventory or services that an entity is committed to purchasing from, or on behalf of, a joint venture.

        (iv)   unrecognised commitments to provide loans or other financial support to a joint venture.

        (v)   unrecognised commitments to contribute resources to a joint venture, such as assets or services.

        (vi)   other non-cancellable unrecognised commitments relating to a joint venture.

    (b)   unrecognised commitments to acquire another party's ownership interest (or a portion of that ownership interest) in a joint venture if a particular event occurs or does not occur in the future.

B20   The requirements and examples in paragraphs B18 and B19 illustrate some of the types of disclosure required by paragraph 18 of IAS 24 *Related Party Disclosures*.

Interests in unconsolidated structured entities (paragraphs 24–31)

Structured entities

B21   A structured entity is an entity that has been designed so that voting or similar rights are not the dominant factor in deciding who controls the entity, such as when any voting rights relate to administrative tasks only and the relevant activities are directed by means of contractual arrangements.

B22   A structured entity often has some or all of the following features or attributes:

    (a)   restricted activities.

(b)   a narrow and well-defined objective, such as to effect a tax-efficient lease, carry out research and development activities, provide a source of capital or funding to an entity or provide investment opportunities for investors by passing on risks and rewards associated with the assets of the structured entity to investors.

(c)   insufficient equity to permit the structured entity to finance its activities without subordinated financial support.

(d)   financing in the form of multiple contractually linked instruments to investors that create concentrations of credit or other risks (tranches).

B23   Examples of entities that are regarded as structured entities include, but are not limited to:

(a)   securitisation vehicles.

(b)   asset-backed financings.

(c)   some investment funds.

B24   An entity that is controlled by voting rights is not a structured entity simply because, for example, it receives funding from third parties following a restructuring.

Nature of risks from interests in unconsolidated structured entities (paragraphs 29–31)

B25   In addition to the information required by paragraphs 29–31, an entity shall disclose additional information that is necessary to meet the disclosure objective in paragraph 24(b).

B26   Examples of additional information that, depending on the circumstances, might be relevant to an assessment of the risks to which an entity is exposed when it has an interest in an unconsolidated structured entity are:

(a)   the terms of an arrangement that could require the entity to provide financial support to an unconsolidated structured entity (eg liquidity arrangements or credit rating triggers associated with obligations to purchase assets of the structured entity or provide financial support), including:

(i)   a description of events or circumstances that could expose the reporting entity to a loss.

(ii)   whether there are any terms that would limit the obligation.

(iii)   whether there are any other parties that provide financial support and, if so, how the reporting entity's obligation ranks with those of other parties.

(b)   losses incurred by the entity during the reporting period relating to its interests in unconsolidated structured entities.

(c)   the types of income the entity received during the reporting period from its interests in unconsolidated structured entities.

(d)   whether the entity is required to absorb losses of an unconsolidated structured entity before other parties, the maximum limit of such losses for the entity, and (if relevant) the ranking and amounts of potential losses borne by parties whose interests rank lower than the entity's interest in the unconsolidated structured entity.

(e)   information about any liquidity arrangements, guarantees or other commitments with third parties that may affect the fair value or risk of the entity's interests in unconsolidated structured entities.

(f)   any difficulties an unconsolidated structured entity has experienced in financing its activities during the reporting period.

(g)   in relation to the funding of an unconsolidated structured entity, the forms of funding (eg commercial paper or medium-term notes) and their weighted-average life. That information might include maturity analyses of the assets and funding of an unconsolidated structured entity if the structured entity has longer-term assets funded by shorter-term funding.

Appendix C
Effective date and transition

This appendix is an integral part of the IFRS and has the same authority as the other parts of the IFRS.

Effective date and transition

C1   An entity shall apply this IFRS for annual periods beginning on or after 1 January 2013. Earlier application is permitted.

C1A   *Consolidated Financial Statements, Joint Arrangements and Disclosure of Interests in Other Entities: Transition Guidance* (Amendments to IFRS 10, IFRS 11 and IFRS 12), issued in June 2012, added paragraphs C2A–C2B. An entity shall apply those amendments for annual periods beginning on or after 1 January 2013. If an entity applies IFRS 12 for an earlier period, it shall apply those amendments for that earlier period.

C1B   *Investment Entities* (Amendments to IFRS 10, IFRS 12 and IAS 27), issued in October 2012, amended paragraph 2 and Appendix A, and added paragraphs 9A–9B, 19A–19G, 21A and 25A. An entity shall apply those amendments for annual periods beginning on or after 1 January 2014. Early adoption is permitted. If an entity applies those amendments earlier, it shall disclose that fact and apply all amendments included in *Investment Entities* at the same time.

C1C   *Investment Entities: Applying the Consolidation Exception* (Amendments to IFRS 10, IFRS 12 and IAS 28), issued in December 2014, amended paragraph 6. An entity shall apply that amendment for annual periods beginning on or after 1 January 2016. Earlier application is permitted. If an entity applies that amendment for an earlier period it shall disclose that fact.

C1D   *Annual Improvements to IFRS Standards 2014–2016 Cycle*, issued in December 2016, added paragraph 5A and amended paragraph B17. An entity shall apply those amendments retrospectively in accordance with IAS 8 *Accounting Policies, Changes in Accounting Estimates and Errors* for annual periods beginning on or after 1 January 2017.

C2   An entity is encouraged to provide information required by this IFRS earlier than annual periods beginning on or after 1 January 2013. Providing some of the disclosures required by this IFRS does not compel the entity to comply with all the requirements of this IFRS or to apply IFRS 10, IFRS 11, IAS 27 (as amended in 2011) and IAS 28 (as amended in 2011) early.

C2A   The disclosure requirements of this IFRS need not be applied for any period presented that begins before the annual period immediately preceding the first annual period for which IFRS 12 is applied.

C2B   The disclosure requirements of paragraphs 24–31 and the corresponding guidance in paragraphs B21–B26 of this IFRS need not be applied for any period presented that begins before the first annual period for which IFRS 12 is applied.

References to IFRS 9

C3   If an entity applies this IFRS but does not yet apply IFRS 9, any reference to IFRS 9 shall be read as a reference to IAS 39 *Financial Instruments: Recognition and Measurement*.

Appendix D
Amendments to other IFRSs

This appendix sets out amendments to other IFRSs that are a consequence of the Board issuing IFRS 12. An entity shall apply the amendments for annual periods beginning on or after 1 January 2013. If an entity applies IFRS 12 for an earlier period, it shall apply the amendments for that earlier period. Amended paragraphs are shown with new text underlined and deleted text struck through.

* * * * *

The amendments contained in this appendix when this IFRS was issued in 2011 have been incorporated into the relevant IFRSs published in this volume.

Approval by the Board of IFRS 12 issued in May 2011

International Financial Reporting Standard 12 *Disclosure of Interests in Other Entities* was approved for issue by the fifteen members of the International Accounting Standards Board.

Sir David Tweedie	Chairman

Stephen Cooper

Philippe Danjou

Jan Engström

Patrick Finnegan

Amaro Luiz de Oliveira Gomes

Prabhakar Kalavacherla

Elke König

Patricia McConnell

Warren J McGregor

Paul Pacter

Darrel Scott

John T Smith

Tatsumi Yamada

Wei-Guo Zhang

Approval by the Board of *Consolidated Financial Statements, Joint Arrangements and Disclosure of Interests in Other Entities: Transition Guidance* (Amendments to IFRS 10, IFRS 11 and IFRS 12) issued in June 2012

Consolidated Financial Statements, Joint Arrangements and Disclosure of Interests in Other Entities: Transition Guidance (Amendments to IFRS 10, IFRS 11 and IFRS 12) was approved for issue by the fourteen members of the International Accounting Standards Board.

Hans Hoogervorst	Chairman
Ian Mackintosh	Vice-Chairman
Stephen Cooper	
Philippe Danjou	
Jan Engström	
Patrick Finnegan	
Amaro Luiz de Oliveira Gomes	
Prabhakar Kalavacherla	
Patricia McConnell	
Takatsugu Ochi	
Paul Pacter	
Darrel Scott	
John T Smith	
Wei-Guo Zhang	

Approval by the Board of *Investment Entities* (Amendments to IFRS 10, IFRS 12 and IAS 27) issued in October 2012

Investment Entities (Amendments to IFRS 10, IFRS 12 and IAS 27) was approved for issue by the fifteen members of the International Accounting Standards Board.

Hans Hoogervorst	Chairman
Ian Mackintosh	Vice-Chairman
Stephen Cooper	
Philippe Danjou	
Martin Edelmann	
Jan Engström	
Patrick Finnegan	
Amaro Luiz de Oliveira Gomes	
Prabhakar Kalavacherla	
Patricia McConnell	
Takatsugu Ochi	
Paul Pacter	
Darrel Scott	
Chungwoo Suh	
Zhang Wei-Guo	

Approval by the Board of *Investment Entities: Applying the Consolidation Exception* (Amendments to IFRS 10, IFRS 12 and IAS 28) issued in December 2014

Investment Entities: Applying the Consolidation Exception was approved for issue by the fourteen members of the International Accounting Standards Board.

Hans Hoogervorst	Chairman
Ian Mackintosh	Vice-Chairman
Stephen Cooper	
Philippe Danjou	
Amaro Luiz De Oliveira Gomes	
Martin Edelmann	
Patrick Finnegan	
Gary Kabureck	
Suzanne Lloyd	
Takatsugu Ochi	
Darrel Scott	
Chungwoo Suh	
Mary Tokar	
Wei-Guo Zhang	

Approval by the Board of Investment Entities: Applying the Consolidation Exception (Amendments to IFRS 10, IFRS 12 and IAS 28) issued in December 2014

Investment Entities: Applying the Consolidation Exception was approved for issue by the fourteen members of the International Accounting Standards Board.

Hans Hoogervorst	Chairman
Ian Mackintosh	Vice-Chairman
Stephen Cooper	
Philippe Danjou	
Amaro Luiz De Oliveira Gomes	
Martin Edelmann	
Patrick Finnegan	
Gary Kabureck	
Suzanne Lloyd	
Takatsugu Ochi	
Darrel Scott	
Chungwoo Suh	
Mary Tokar	
Wei-Guo Zhang	

IFRS 13

Fair Value Measurement

In May 2011 the International Accounting Standards Board issued IFRS 13 *Fair Value Measurement*. IFRS 13 defines fair value and replaces the requirement contained in individual Standards.

Other Standards have made minor consequential amendments to IFRS 13. They include IAS 19 *Employee Benefits* (issued June 2011), *Annual Improvements to IFRSs 2011–2013 Cycle* (issued December 2013), IFRS 9 *Financial Instruments* (issued July 2014) and IFRS 16 *Leases* (issued January 2016).

CONTENTS

FOR THE ACCOMPANYING GUIDANCE LISTED BELOW, SEE PART B OF THIS EDITION

FOR THE BASIS FOR CONCLUSIONS, SEE PART C OF THIS EDITION

International Financial Reporting Standard 13 *Fair Value Measurement* (IFRS 13) is set out in paragraphs 1–99 and Appendices A–D. All the paragraphs have equal authority. Paragraphs in **bold type** state the main principles. Terms defined in Appendix A are in *italics* the first time they appear in the IFRS. Definitions of other terms are given in the Glossary for International Financial Reporting Standards. IFRS 13 should be read in the context of its objective and the Basis for Conclusions, the *Preface to IFRS Standards* and the *Conceptual Framework for Financial Reporting*. IAS 8 *Accounting Policies, Changes in Accounting Estimates and Errors* provides a basis for selecting and applying accounting policies in the absence of explicit guidance.

International Financial Reporting Standard 13
Fair Value Measurement

Objective

1   This IFRS:

    (a)   defines *fair value*;

    (b)   sets out in a single IFRS a framework for measuring fair value; and

    (c)   requires disclosures about fair value measurements.

2   Fair value is a market-based measurement, not an entity-specific measurement. For some assets and liabilities, observable market transactions or market information might be available. For other assets and liabilities, observable market transactions and market information might not be available. However, the objective of a fair value measurement in both cases is the same—to estimate the price at which an *orderly transaction* to sell the asset or to transfer the liability would take place between *market participants* at the measurement date under current market conditions (ie an *exit price* at the measurement date from the perspective of a market participant that holds the asset or owes the liability).

3   When a price for an identical asset or liability is not observable, an entity measures fair value using another valuation technique that maximises the use of relevant *observable inputs* and minimises the use of *unobservable inputs*. Because fair value is a market-based measurement, it is measured using the assumptions that market participants would use when pricing the asset or liability, including assumptions about risk. As a result, an entity's intention to hold an asset or to settle or otherwise fulfil a liability is not relevant when measuring fair value.

4   The definition of fair value focuses on assets and liabilities because they are a primary subject of accounting measurement. In addition, this IFRS shall be applied to an entity's own equity instruments measured at fair value.

Scope

5   This IFRS applies when another IFRS requires or permits fair value measurements or disclosures about fair value measurements (and measurements, such as fair value less costs to sell, based on fair value or disclosures about those measurements), except as specified in paragraphs 6 and 7.

6   The measurement and disclosure requirements of this IFRS do not apply to the following:

    (a)   share-based payment transactions within the scope of IFRS 2 *Share-based Payment*;

    (b)   leasing transactions accounted for in accordance with IFRS 16 *Leases*; and

(c)   measurements that have some similarities to fair value but are not fair value, such as net realisable value in IAS 2 *Inventories* or value in use in IAS 36 *Impairment of Assets*.

7   The disclosures required by this IFRS are not required for the following:

(a)   plan assets measured at fair value in accordance with IAS 19 *Employee Benefits*;

(b)   retirement benefit plan investments measured at fair value in accordance with IAS 26 *Accounting and Reporting by Retirement Benefit Plans*; and

(c)   assets for which recoverable amount is fair value less costs of disposal in accordance with IAS 36.

8   The fair value measurement framework described in this IFRS applies to both initial and subsequent measurement if fair value is required or permitted by other IFRSs.

Measurement

Definition of fair value

9   This IFRS defines fair value as the price that would be received to sell an asset or paid to transfer a liability in an orderly transaction between market participants at the measurement date.

10   Paragraph B2 describes the overall fair value measurement approach.

The asset or liability

11   A fair value measurement is for a particular asset or liability. Therefore, when measuring fair value an entity shall take into account the characteristics of the asset or liability if market participants would take those characteristics into account when pricing the asset or liability at the measurement date. Such characteristics include, for example, the following:

(a)   the condition and location of the asset; and

(b)   restrictions, if any, on the sale or use of the asset.

12   The effect on the measurement arising from a particular characteristic will differ depending on how that characteristic would be taken into account by market participants.

13   The asset or liability measured at fair value might be either of the following:

(a)   a stand-alone asset or liability (eg a financial instrument or a non-financial asset); or

(b)   a group of assets, a group of liabilities or a group of assets and liabilities (eg a cash-generating unit or a business).

14   Whether the asset or liability is a stand-alone asset or liability, a group of assets, a group of liabilities or a group of assets and liabilities for recognition or disclosure purposes depends on its *unit of account*. The unit of account for the asset or liability shall be determined in accordance with the IFRS that requires or permits the fair value measurement, except as provided in this IFRS.

The transaction

15   A fair value measurement assumes that the asset or liability is exchanged in an orderly transaction between market participants to sell the asset or transfer the liability at the measurement date under current market conditions.

16   A fair value measurement assumes that the transaction to sell the asset or transfer the liability takes place either:

(a)   in the *principal market* for the asset or liability; or

(b)   in the absence of a principal market, in the *most advantageous market* for the asset or liability.

17   An entity need not undertake an exhaustive search of all possible markets to identify the principal market or, in the absence of a principal market, the most advantageous market, but it shall take into account all information that is reasonably available. In the absence of evidence to the contrary, the market in which the entity would normally enter into a transaction to sell the asset or to transfer the liability is presumed to be the principal market or, in the absence of a principal market, the most advantageous market.

18   If there is a principal market for the asset or liability, the fair value measurement shall represent the price in that market (whether that price is directly observable or estimated using another valuation technique), even if the price in a different market is potentially more advantageous at the measurement date.

19   The entity must have access to the principal (or most advantageous) market at the measurement date. Because different entities (and businesses within those entities) with different activities may have access to different markets, the principal (or most advantageous) market for the same asset or liability might be different for different entities (and businesses within those entities). Therefore, the principal (or most advantageous) market (and thus, market participants) shall be considered from the perspective of the entity, thereby allowing for differences between and among entities with different activities.

20   Although an entity must be able to access the market, the entity does not need to be able to sell the particular asset or transfer the particular liability on the measurement date to be able to measure fair value on the basis of the price in that market.

21   Even when there is no observable market to provide pricing information about the sale of an asset or the transfer of a liability at the measurement date, a fair value measurement shall assume that a transaction takes place at that date, considered from the perspective of a market participant that holds the asset or owes the liability. That assumed transaction establishes a basis for estimating the price to sell the asset or to transfer the liability.

Market participants

22   **An entity shall measure the fair value of an asset or a liability using the assumptions that market participants would use when pricing the asset or liability, assuming that market participants act in their economic best interest.**

23   In developing those assumptions, an entity need not identify specific market participants. Rather, the entity shall identify characteristics that distinguish market participants generally, considering factors specific to all the following:

(a)   the asset or liability;

(b)   the principal (or most advantageous) market for the asset or liability; and

(c)   market participants with whom the entity would enter into a transaction in that market.

The price

24   **Fair value is the price that would be received to sell an asset or paid to transfer a liability in an orderly transaction in the principal (or most advantageous) market at the measurement date under current market conditions (ie an exit price) regardless of whether that price is directly observable or estimated using another valuation technique.**

25   The price in the principal (or most advantageous) market used to measure the fair value of the asset or liability shall not be adjusted for *transaction costs*. Transaction costs shall be accounted for in accordance with other IFRSs. Transaction costs are not a characteristic of an asset or a liability; rather, they are specific to a transaction and will differ depending on how an entity enters into a transaction for the asset or liability.

26   Transaction costs do not include *transport costs*. If location is a characteristic of the asset (as might be the case, for example, for a commodity), the price in the principal (or most advantageous) market shall be adjusted for the costs, if any, that would be incurred to transport the asset from its current location to that market.

Application to non-financial assets

Highest and best use for non-financial assets

27   A fair value measurement of a non-financial asset takes into account a market participant's ability to generate economic benefits by using the asset in its *highest and best use* or by selling it to another market participant that would use the asset in its highest and best use.

28   The highest and best use of a non-financial asset takes into account the use of the asset that is physically possible, legally permissible and financially feasible, as follows:

(a)   A use that is physically possible takes into account the physical characteristics of the asset that market participants would take into account when pricing the asset (eg the location or size of a property).

(b)   A use that is legally permissible takes into account any legal restrictions on the use of the asset that market participants would take into account when pricing the asset (eg the zoning regulations applicable to a property).

(c)   A use that is financially feasible takes into account whether a use of the asset that is physically possible and legally permissible generates adequate income or cash flows (taking into account the costs of converting the asset to that use) to produce an investment return that market participants would require from an investment in that asset put to that use.

29   Highest and best use is determined from the perspective of market participants, even if the entity intends a different use. However, an entity's current use of a non-financial asset is presumed to be its highest and best use unless market or other factors suggest that a different use by market participants would maximise the value of the asset.

30   To protect its competitive position, or for other reasons, an entity may intend not to use an acquired non-financial asset actively or it may intend not to use the asset according to its highest and best use. For example, that might be the case for an acquired intangible asset that the entity plans to use defensively by preventing others from using it. Nevertheless, the entity shall measure the fair value of a non-financial asset assuming its highest and best use by market participants.

Valuation premise for non-financial assets

31   The highest and best use of a non-financial asset establishes the valuation premise used to measure the fair value of the asset, as follows:

(a)   The highest and best use of a non-financial asset might provide maximum value to market participants through its use in combination with other assets as a group (as installed or otherwise configured for use) or in combination with other assets and liabilities (eg a business).

(i) If the highest and best use of the asset is to use the asset in combination with other assets or with other assets and liabilities, the fair value of the asset is the price that would be received in a current transaction to sell the asset assuming that the asset would be used with other assets or with other assets and liabilities and that those assets and liabilities (ie its complementary assets and the associated liabilities) would be available to market participants.

(ii) Liabilities associated with the asset and with the complementary assets include liabilities that fund working capital, but do not include liabilities used to fund assets other than those within the group of assets.

(iii) Assumptions about the highest and best use of a non-financial asset shall be consistent for all the assets (for which highest and best use is relevant) of the group of assets or the group of assets and liabilities within which the asset would be used.

(b) The highest and best use of a non-financial asset might provide maximum value to market participants on a stand-alone basis. If the highest and best use of the asset is to use it on a stand-alone basis, the fair value of the asset is the price that would be received in a current transaction to sell the asset to market participants that would use the asset on a stand-alone basis.

32 The fair value measurement of a non-financial asset assumes that the asset is sold consistently with the unit of account specified in other IFRSs (which may be an individual asset). That is the case even when that fair value measurement assumes that the highest and best use of the asset is to use it in combination with other assets or with other assets and liabilities because a fair value measurement assumes that the market participant already holds the complementary assets and the associated liabilities.

33 Paragraph B3 describes the application of the valuation premise concept for non-financial assets.

Application to liabilities and an entity's own equity instruments

General principles

34 A fair value measurement assumes that a financial or non-financial liability or an entity's own equity instrument (eg equity interests issued as consideration in a business combination) is transferred to a market participant at the measurement date. The transfer of a liability or an entity's own equity instrument assumes the following:

(a) A liability would remain outstanding and the market participant transferee would be required to fulfil the obligation. The liability would not be settled with the counterparty or otherwise extinguished on the measurement date.

(b) An entity's own equity instrument would remain outstanding and the market participant transferee would take on the rights and responsibilities associated with the instrument. The instrument would not be cancelled or otherwise extinguished on the measurement date.

35 Even when there is no observable market to provide pricing information about the transfer of a liability or an entity's own equity instrument (eg because contractual or other legal restrictions prevent the transfer of such items), there might be an observable market for such items if they are held by other parties as assets (eg a corporate bond or a call option on an entity's shares).

36 In all cases, an entity shall maximise the use of relevant observable inputs and minimise the use of unobservable inputs to meet the objective of a fair value measurement, which is to estimate the price at which an orderly transaction to transfer the liability or equity instrument would take place between market participants at the measurement date under current market conditions.

Liabilities and equity instruments held by other parties as assets

37 When a quoted price for the transfer of an identical or a similar liability or entity's own equity instrument is not available and the identical item is held by another party as an asset, an entity shall measure the fair value of the liability or equity instrument from the perspective of a market participant that holds the identical item as an asset at the measurement date.

38 In such cases, an entity shall measure the fair value of the liability or equity instrument as follows:

(a) using the quoted price in an *active market* for the identical item held by another party as an asset, if that price is available.

(b) if that price is not available, using other observable inputs, such as the quoted price in a market that is not active for the identical item held by another party as an asset.

(c) if the observable prices in (a) and (b) are not available, using another valuation technique, such as:

(i) an *income approach* (eg a present value technique that takes into account the future cash flows that a market participant would expect to receive from holding the liability or equity instrument as an asset; see paragraphs B10 and B11).

(ii) a *market approach* (eg using quoted prices for similar liabilities or equity instruments held by other parties as assets; see paragraphs B5–B7).

39 An entity shall adjust the quoted price of a liability or an entity's own equity instrument held by another party as an asset only if there are factors specific to the asset that are not applicable to the fair value measurement of the liability or equity instrument. An entity shall ensure that the price of the asset does not reflect the effect of a restriction preventing the sale of that asset.

Some factors that may indicate that the quoted price of the asset should be adjusted include the following:

(a) The quoted price for the asset relates to a similar (but not identical) liability or equity instrument held by another party as an asset. For example, the liability or equity instrument may have a particular characteristic (eg the credit quality of the issuer) that is different from that reflected in the fair value of the similar liability or equity instrument held as an asset.

(b) The unit of account for the asset is not the same as for the liability or equity instrument. For example, for liabilities, in some cases the price for an asset reflects a combined price for a package comprising both the amounts due from the issuer and a third-party credit enhancement. If the unit of account for the liability is not for the combined package, the objective is to measure the fair value of the issuer's liability, not the fair value of the combined package. Thus, in such cases, the entity would adjust the observed price for the asset to exclude the effect of the third-party credit enhancement.

Liabilities and equity instruments not held by other parties as assets

40 **When a quoted price for the transfer of an identical or a similar liability or entity's own equity instrument is not available and the identical item is not held by another party as an asset, an entity shall measure the fair value of the liability or equity instrument using a valuation technique from the perspective of a market participant that owes the liability or has issued the claim on equity.**

41 For example, when applying a present value technique an entity might take into account either of the following:

(a) the future cash outflows that a market participant would expect to incur in fulfilling the obligation, including the compensation that a market participant would require for taking on the obligation (see paragraphs B31–B33).

(b) the amount that a market participant would receive to enter into or issue an identical liability or equity instrument, using the assumptions that market participants would use when pricing the identical item (eg having the same credit characteristics) in the principal (or most advantageous) market for issuing a liability or an equity instrument with the same contractual terms.

Non-performance risk

42 The fair value of a liability reflects the effect of *non-performance risk*. Non-performance risk includes, but may not be limited to, an entity's own credit risk (as defined in IFRS 7 *Financial Instruments: Disclosures*). Non-performance risk is assumed to be the same before and after the transfer of the liability.

43   When measuring the fair value of a liability, an entity shall take into account the effect of its credit risk (credit standing) and any other factors that might influence the likelihood that the obligation will or will not be fulfilled. That effect may differ depending on the liability, for example:

(a)   whether the liability is an obligation to deliver cash (a financial liability) or an obligation to deliver goods or services (a non-financial liability).

(b)   the terms of credit enhancements related to the liability, if any.

44   The fair value of a liability reflects the effect of non-performance risk on the basis of its unit of account. The issuer of a liability issued with an inseparable third-party credit enhancement that is accounted for separately from the liability shall not include the effect of the credit enhancement (eg a third-party guarantee of debt) in the fair value measurement of the liability. If the credit enhancement is accounted for separately from the liability, the issuer would take into account its own credit standing and not that of the third party guarantor when measuring the fair value of the liability.

Restriction preventing the transfer of a liability or an entity's own equity instrument

45   When measuring the fair value of a liability or an entity's own equity instrument, an entity shall not include a separate input or an adjustment to other *inputs* relating to the existence of a restriction that prevents the transfer of the item. The effect of a restriction that prevents the transfer of a liability or an entity's own equity instrument is either implicitly or explicitly included in the other inputs to the fair value measurement.

46   For example, at the transaction date, both the creditor and the obligor accepted the transaction price for the liability with full knowledge that the obligation includes a restriction that prevents its transfer. As a result of the restriction being included in the transaction price, a separate input or an adjustment to an existing input is not required at the transaction date to reflect the effect of the restriction on transfer. Similarly, a separate input or an adjustment to an existing input is not required at subsequent measurement dates to reflect the effect of the restriction on transfer.

Financial liability with a demand feature

47   The fair value of a financial liability with a demand feature (eg a demand deposit) is not less than the amount payable on demand, discounted from the first date that the amount could be required to be paid.

Application to financial assets and financial liabilities with offsetting positions in market risks or counterparty credit risk

48   An entity that holds a group of financial assets and financial liabilities is exposed to market risks (as defined in IFRS 7) and to the credit risk (as defined in IFRS 7) of each of the counterparties. If the entity manages that group of financial assets and financial liabilities on the basis of its net exposure to

either market risks or credit risk, the entity is permitted to apply an exception to this IFRS for measuring fair value. That exception permits an entity to measure the fair value of a group of financial assets and financial liabilities on the basis of the price that would be received to sell a net long position (ie an asset) for a particular risk exposure or paid to transfer a net short position (ie a liability) for a particular risk exposure in an orderly transaction between market participants at the measurement date under current market conditions. Accordingly, an entity shall measure the fair value of the group of financial assets and financial liabilities consistently with how market participants would price the net risk exposure at the measurement date.

49   An entity is permitted to use the exception in paragraph 48 only if the entity does all the following:

(a)   manages the group of financial assets and financial liabilities on the basis of the entity's net exposure to a particular market risk (or risks) or to the credit risk of a particular counterparty in accordance with the entity's documented risk management or investment strategy;

(b)   provides information on that basis about the group of financial assets and financial liabilities to the entity's key management personnel, as defined in IAS 24 *Related Party Disclosures*; and

(c)   is required or has elected to measure those financial assets and financial liabilities at fair value in the statement of financial position at the end of each reporting period.

50   The exception in paragraph 48 does not pertain to financial statement presentation. In some cases the basis for the presentation of financial instruments in the statement of financial position differs from the basis for the measurement of financial instruments, for example, if an IFRS does not require or permit financial instruments to be presented on a net basis. In such cases an entity may need to allocate the portfolio-level adjustments (see paragraphs 53–56) to the individual assets or liabilities that make up the group of financial assets and financial liabilities managed on the basis of the entity's net risk exposure. An entity shall perform such allocations on a reasonable and consistent basis using a methodology appropriate in the circumstances.

51   An entity shall make an accounting policy decision in accordance with IAS 8 *Accounting Policies, Changes in Accounting Estimates and Errors* to use the exception in paragraph 48. An entity that uses the exception shall apply that accounting policy, including its policy for allocating bid-ask adjustments (see paragraphs 53–55) and credit adjustments (see paragraph 56), if applicable, consistently from period to period for a particular portfolio.

52   The exception in paragraph 48 applies only to financial assets, financial liabilities and other contracts within the scope of IFRS 9 *Financial Instruments* (or IAS 39 *Financial Instruments: Recognition and Measurement*, if IFRS 9 has not yet been adopted). The references to financial assets and financial liabilities in paragraphs 48–51 and 53–56 should be read as applying to all contracts within the scope of, and accounted for in accordance with, IFRS 9 (or

IAS 39, if IFRS 9 has not yet been adopted), regardless of whether they meet the definitions of financial assets or financial liabilities in IAS 32 *Financial Instruments: Presentation*.

Exposure to market risks

53   When using the exception in paragraph 48 to measure the fair value of a group of financial assets and financial liabilities managed on the basis of the entity's net exposure to a particular market risk (or risks), the entity shall apply the price within the bid-ask spread that is most representative of fair value in the circumstances to the entity's net exposure to those market risks (see paragraphs 70 and 71).

54   When using the exception in paragraph 48, an entity shall ensure that the market risk (or risks) to which the entity is exposed within that group of financial assets and financial liabilities is substantially the same. For example, an entity would not combine the interest rate risk associated with a financial asset with the commodity price risk associated with a financial liability because doing so would not mitigate the entity's exposure to interest rate risk or commodity price risk. When using the exception in paragraph 48, any basis risk resulting from the market risk parameters not being identical shall be taken into account in the fair value measurement of the financial assets and financial liabilities within the group.

55   Similarly, the duration of the entity's exposure to a particular market risk (or risks) arising from the financial assets and financial liabilities shall be substantially the same. For example, an entity that uses a 12-month futures contract against the cash flows associated with 12 months' worth of interest rate risk exposure on a five-year financial instrument within a group made up of only those financial assets and financial liabilities measures the fair value of the exposure to 12-month interest rate risk on a net basis and the remaining interest rate risk exposure (ie years 2–5) on a gross basis.

Exposure to the credit risk of a particular counterparty

56   When using the exception in paragraph 48 to measure the fair value of a group of financial assets and financial liabilities entered into with a particular counterparty, the entity shall include the effect of the entity's net exposure to the credit risk of that counterparty or the counterparty's net exposure to the credit risk of the entity in the fair value measurement when market participants would take into account any existing arrangements that mitigate credit risk exposure in the event of default (eg a master netting agreement with the counterparty or an agreement that requires the exchange of collateral on the basis of each party's net exposure to the credit risk of the other party). The fair value measurement shall reflect market participants' expectations about the likelihood that such an arrangement would be legally enforceable in the event of default.

Fair value at initial recognition

57   When an asset is acquired or a liability is assumed in an exchange transaction for that asset or liability, the transaction price is the price paid to acquire the asset or received to assume the liability (an *entry price*). In contrast, the fair value of the asset or liability is the price that would be received to sell the asset or paid to transfer the liability (an exit price). Entities do not necessarily sell assets at the prices paid to acquire them. Similarly, entities do not necessarily transfer liabilities at the prices received to assume them.

58   In many cases the transaction price will equal the fair value (eg that might be the case when on the transaction date the transaction to buy an asset takes place in the market in which the asset would be sold).

59   When determining whether fair value at initial recognition equals the transaction price, an entity shall take into account factors specific to the transaction and to the asset or liability. Paragraph B4 describes situations in which the transaction price might not represent the fair value of an asset or a liability at initial recognition.

60   If another IFRS requires or permits an entity to measure an asset or a liability initially at fair value and the transaction price differs from fair value, the entity shall recognise the resulting gain or loss in profit or loss unless that IFRS specifies otherwise.

Valuation techniques

61   **An entity shall use valuation techniques that are appropriate in the circumstances and for which sufficient data are available to measure fair value, maximising the use of relevant observable inputs and minimising the use of unobservable inputs.**

62   The objective of using a valuation technique is to estimate the price at which an orderly transaction to sell the asset or to transfer the liability would take place between market participants at the measurement date under current market conditions. Three widely used valuation techniques are the market approach, the *cost approach* and the income approach. The main aspects of those approaches are summarised in paragraphs B5–B11. An entity shall use valuation techniques consistent with one or more of those approaches to measure fair value.

63   In some cases a single valuation technique will be appropriate (eg when valuing an asset or a liability using quoted prices in an active market for identical assets or liabilities). In other cases, multiple valuation techniques will be appropriate (eg that might be the case when valuing a cash-generating unit). If multiple valuation techniques are used to measure fair value, the results (ie respective indications of fair value) shall be evaluated considering the reasonableness of the range of values indicated by those results. A fair value measurement is the point within that range that is most representative of fair value in the circumstances.

64   If the transaction price is fair value at initial recognition and a valuation technique that uses unobservable inputs will be used to measure fair value in subsequent periods, the valuation technique shall be calibrated so that at initial recognition the result of the valuation technique equals the transaction price. Calibration ensures that the valuation technique reflects current market conditions, and it helps an entity to determine whether an adjustment to the valuation technique is necessary (eg there might be a characteristic of the asset or liability that is not captured by the valuation technique). After initial recognition, when measuring fair value using a valuation technique or techniques that use unobservable inputs, an entity shall ensure that those valuation techniques reflect observable market data (eg the price for a similar asset or liability) at the measurement date.

65   Valuation techniques used to measure fair value shall be applied consistently. However, a change in a valuation technique or its application (eg a change in its weighting when multiple valuation techniques are used or a change in an adjustment applied to a valuation technique) is appropriate if the change results in a measurement that is equally or more representative of fair value in the circumstances. That might be the case if, for example, any of the following events take place:

(a)   new markets develop;

(b)   new information becomes available;

(c)   information previously used is no longer available;

(d)   valuation techniques improve; or

(e)   market conditions change.

66   Revisions resulting from a change in the valuation technique or its application shall be accounted for as a change in accounting estimate in accordance with IAS 8. However, the disclosures in IAS 8 for a change in accounting estimate are not required for revisions resulting from a change in a valuation technique or its application.

Inputs to valuation techniques

General principles

67   **Valuation techniques used to measure fair value shall maximise the use of relevant observable inputs and minimise the use of unobservable inputs.**

68   Examples of markets in which inputs might be observable for some assets and liabilities (eg financial instruments) include exchange markets, dealer markets, brokered markets and principal-to-principal markets (see paragraph B34).

69   An entity shall select inputs that are consistent with the characteristics of the asset or liability that market participants would take into account in a transaction for the asset or liability (see paragraphs 11 and 12). In some cases those characteristics result in the application of an adjustment, such as a premium or discount (eg a control premium or non-controlling interest

discount). However, a fair value measurement shall not incorporate a premium or discount that is inconsistent with the unit of account in the IFRS that requires or permits the fair value measurement (see paragraphs 13 and 14). Premiums or discounts that reflect size as a characteristic of the entity's holding (specifically, a blockage factor that adjusts the quoted price of an asset or a liability because the market's normal daily trading volume is not sufficient to absorb the quantity held by the entity, as described in paragraph 80) rather than as a characteristic of the asset or liability (eg a control premium when measuring the fair value of a controlling interest) are not permitted in a fair value measurement. In all cases, if there is a quoted price in an active market (ie a *Level 1 input*) for an asset or a liability, an entity shall use that price without adjustment when measuring fair value, except as specified in paragraph 79.

Inputs based on bid and ask prices

70   If an asset or a liability measured at fair value has a bid price and an ask price (eg an input from a dealer market), the price within the bid-ask spread that is most representative of fair value in the circumstances shall be used to measure fair value regardless of where the input is categorised within the fair value hierarchy (ie Level 1, 2 or 3; see paragraphs 72–90). The use of bid prices for asset positions and ask prices for liability positions is permitted, but is not required.

71   This IFRS does not preclude the use of mid-market pricing or other pricing conventions that are used by market participants as a practical expedient for fair value measurements within a bid-ask spread.

Fair value hierarchy

72   To increase consistency and comparability in fair value measurements and related disclosures, this IFRS establishes a fair value hierarchy that categorises into three levels (see paragraphs 76–90) the inputs to valuation techniques used to measure fair value. The fair value hierarchy gives the highest priority to quoted prices (unadjusted) in active markets for identical assets or liabilities (Level 1 inputs) and the lowest priority to unobservable inputs (*Level 3 inputs*).

73   In some cases, the inputs used to measure the fair value of an asset or a liability might be categorised within different levels of the fair value hierarchy. In those cases, the fair value measurement is categorised in its entirety in the same level of the fair value hierarchy as the lowest level input that is significant to the entire measurement. Assessing the significance of a particular input to the entire measurement requires judgement, taking into account factors specific to the asset or liability. Adjustments to arrive at measurements based on fair value, such as costs to sell when measuring fair value less costs to sell, shall not be taken into account when determining the level of the fair value hierarchy within which a fair value measurement is categorised.

74   The availability of relevant inputs and their relative subjectivity might affect the selection of appropriate valuation techniques (see paragraph 61). However, the fair value hierarchy prioritises the inputs to valuation techniques, not the valuation techniques used to measure fair value. For example, a fair value measurement developed using a present value technique might be categorised within Level 2 or Level 3, depending on the inputs that are significant to the entire measurement and the level of the fair value hierarchy within which those inputs are categorised.

75   If an observable input requires an adjustment using an unobservable input and that adjustment results in a significantly higher or lower fair value measurement, the resulting measurement would be categorised within Level 3 of the fair value hierarchy. For example, if a market participant would take into account the effect of a restriction on the sale of an asset when estimating the price for the asset, an entity would adjust the quoted price to reflect the effect of that restriction. If that quoted price is a *Level 2 input* and the adjustment is an unobservable input that is significant to the entire measurement, the measurement would be categorised within Level 3 of the fair value hierarchy.

Level 1 inputs

76   Level 1 inputs are quoted prices (unadjusted) in active markets for identical assets or liabilities that the entity can access at the measurement date.

77   A quoted price in an active market provides the most reliable evidence of fair value and shall be used without adjustment to measure fair value whenever available, except as specified in paragraph 79.

78   A Level 1 input will be available for many financial assets and financial liabilities, some of which might be exchanged in multiple active markets (eg on different exchanges). Therefore, the emphasis within Level 1 is on determining both of the following:

(a)   the principal market for the asset or liability or, in the absence of a principal market, the most advantageous market for the asset or liability; and

(b)   whether the entity can enter into a transaction for the asset or liability at the price in that market at the measurement date.

79   An entity shall not make an adjustment to a Level 1 input except in the following circumstances:

(a)   when an entity holds a large number of similar (but not identical) assets or liabilities (eg debt securities) that are measured at fair value and a quoted price in an active market is available but not readily accessible for each of those assets or liabilities individually (ie given the large number of similar assets or liabilities held by the entity, it would be difficult to obtain pricing information for each individual asset or liability at the measurement date). In that case, as a practical expedient, an entity may measure fair value using an alternative pricing method that does not rely exclusively on quoted prices (eg matrix pricing). However, the use of an alternative pricing method results in a fair value measurement categorised within a lower level of the fair value hierarchy.

(b)   when a quoted price in an active market does not represent fair value at the measurement date. That might be the case if, for example, significant events (such as transactions in a principal-to-principal market, trades in a brokered market or announcements) take place after the close of a market but before the measurement date. An entity shall establish and consistently apply a policy for identifying those events that might affect fair value measurements. However, if the quoted price is adjusted for new information, the adjustment results in a fair value measurement categorised within a lower level of the fair value hierarchy.

(c)   when measuring the fair value of a liability or an entity's own equity instrument using the quoted price for the identical item traded as an asset in an active market and that price needs to be adjusted for factors specific to the item or the asset (see paragraph 39). If no adjustment to the quoted price of the asset is required, the result is a fair value measurement categorised within Level 1 of the fair value hierarchy. However, any adjustment to the quoted price of the asset results in a fair value measurement categorised within a lower level of the fair value hierarchy.

80   If an entity holds a position in a single asset or liability (including a position comprising a large number of identical assets or liabilities, such as a holding of financial instruments) and the asset or liability is traded in an active market, the fair value of the asset or liability shall be measured within Level 1 as the product of the quoted price for the individual asset or liability and the quantity held by the entity. That is the case even if a market's normal daily trading volume is not sufficient to absorb the quantity held and placing orders to sell the position in a single transaction might affect the quoted price.

Level 2 inputs

81   Level 2 inputs are inputs other than quoted prices included within Level 1 that are observable for the asset or liability, either directly or indirectly.

82   If the asset or liability has a specified (contractual) term, a Level 2 input must be observable for substantially the full term of the asset or liability. Level 2 inputs include the following:

(a)   quoted prices for similar assets or liabilities in active markets.

(b)   quoted prices for identical or similar assets or liabilities in markets that are not active.

(c)   inputs other than quoted prices that are observable for the asset or liability, for example:

(i)   interest rates and yield curves observable at commonly quoted intervals;

(ii)   implied volatilities; and

(iii)   credit spreads.

(d)   *market-corroborated inputs.*

83   Adjustments to Level 2 inputs will vary depending on factors specific to the asset or liability. Those factors include the following:

(a)   the condition or location of the asset;

(b)   the extent to which inputs relate to items that are comparable to the asset or liability (including those factors described in paragraph 39); and

(c)   the volume or level of activity in the markets within which the inputs are observed.

84   An adjustment to a Level 2 input that is significant to the entire measurement might result in a fair value measurement categorised within Level 3 of the fair value hierarchy if the adjustment uses significant unobservable inputs.

85   Paragraph B35 describes the use of Level 2 inputs for particular assets and liabilities.

Level 3 inputs

86   Level 3 inputs are unobservable inputs for the asset or liability.

87   Unobservable inputs shall be used to measure fair value to the extent that relevant observable inputs are not available, thereby allowing for situations in which there is little, if any, market activity for the asset or liability at the measurement date. However, the fair value measurement objective remains the same, ie an exit price at the measurement date from the perspective of a market participant that holds the asset or owes the liability. Therefore, unobservable inputs shall reflect the assumptions that market participants would use when pricing the asset or liability, including assumptions about risk.

88   Assumptions about risk include the risk inherent in a particular valuation technique used to measure fair value (such as a pricing model) and the risk inherent in the inputs to the valuation technique. A measurement that does not include an adjustment for risk would not represent a fair value measurement if market participants would include one when pricing the asset or liability. For example, it might be necessary to include a risk adjustment when there is significant measurement uncertainty (eg when there has been a significant decrease in the volume or level of activity when compared with normal market activity for the asset or liability, or similar assets or liabilities, and the entity has determined that the transaction price or quoted price does not represent fair value, as described in paragraphs B37–B47).

89   An entity shall develop unobservable inputs using the best information available in the circumstances, which might include the entity's own data. In developing unobservable inputs, an entity may begin with its own data, but it shall adjust those data if reasonably available information indicates that other

market participants would use different data or there is something particular to the entity that is not available to other market participants (eg an entity-specific synergy). An entity need not undertake exhaustive efforts to obtain information about market participant assumptions. However, an entity shall take into account all information about market participant assumptions that is reasonably available. Unobservable inputs developed in the manner described above are considered market participant assumptions and meet the objective of a fair value measurement.

90   Paragraph B36 describes the use of Level 3 inputs for particular assets and liabilities.

Disclosure

91   An entity shall disclose information that helps users of its financial statements assess both of the following:

(a)   for assets and liabilities that are measured at fair value on a recurring or non-recurring basis in the statement of financial position after initial recognition, the valuation techniques and inputs used to develop those measurements.

(b)   for recurring fair value measurements using significant unobservable inputs (Level 3), the effect of the measurements on profit or loss or other comprehensive income for the period.

92   To meet the objectives in paragraph 91, an entity shall consider all the following:

(a)   the level of detail necessary to satisfy the disclosure requirements;

(b)   how much emphasis to place on each of the various requirements;

(c)   how much aggregation or disaggregation to undertake; and

(d)   whether users of financial statements need additional information to evaluate the quantitative information disclosed.

If the disclosures provided in accordance with this IFRS and other IFRSs are insufficient to meet the objectives in paragraph 91, an entity shall disclose additional information necessary to meet those objectives.

93   To meet the objectives in paragraph 91, an entity shall disclose, at a minimum, the following information for each class of assets and liabilities (see paragraph 94 for information on determining appropriate classes of assets and liabilities) measured at fair value (including measurements based on fair value within the scope of this IFRS) in the statement of financial position after initial recognition:

(a)   for recurring and non-recurring fair value measurements, the fair value measurement at the end of the reporting period, and for non-recurring fair value measurements, the reasons for the measurement. Recurring fair value measurements of assets or liabilities are those that other IFRSs require or permit in the statement of financial position at the end of each reporting period. Non-recurring fair value measurements of assets or liabilities are those that other IFRSs require or permit in the statement of financial position in particular circumstances (eg when an entity measures an asset held for sale at fair value less costs to sell in accordance with IFRS 5 *Non-current Assets Held for Sale and Discontinued Operations* because the asset's fair value less costs to sell is lower than its carrying amount).

(b)   for recurring and non-recurring fair value measurements, the level of the fair value hierarchy within which the fair value measurements are categorised in their entirety (Level 1, 2 or 3).

(c)   for assets and liabilities held at the end of the reporting period that are measured at fair value on a recurring basis, the amounts of any transfers between Level 1 and Level 2 of the fair value hierarchy, the reasons for those transfers and the entity's policy for determining when transfers between levels are deemed to have occurred (see paragraph 95). Transfers into each level shall be disclosed and discussed separately from transfers out of each level.

(d)   for recurring and non-recurring fair value measurements categorised within Level 2 and Level 3 of the fair value hierarchy, a description of the valuation technique(s) and the inputs used in the fair value measurement. If there has been a change in valuation technique (eg changing from a market approach to an income approach or the use of an additional valuation technique), the entity shall disclose that change and the reason(s) for making it. For fair value measurements categorised within Level 3 of the fair value hierarchy, an entity shall provide quantitative information about the significant unobservable inputs used in the fair value measurement. An entity is not required to create quantitative information to comply with this disclosure requirement if quantitative unobservable inputs are not developed by the entity when measuring fair value (eg when an entity uses prices from prior transactions or third-party pricing information without adjustment). However, when providing this disclosure an entity cannot ignore quantitative unobservable inputs that are significant to the fair value measurement and are reasonably available to the entity.

(e)   for recurring fair value measurements categorised within Level 3 of the fair value hierarchy, a reconciliation from the opening balances to the closing balances, disclosing separately changes during the period attributable to the following:

(i)   total gains or losses for the period recognised in profit or loss, and the line item(s) in profit or loss in which those gains or losses are recognised.

(ii)   total gains or losses for the period recognised in other comprehensive income, and the line item(s) in other comprehensive income in which those gains or losses are recognised.

(iii)   purchases, sales, issues and settlements (each of those types of changes disclosed separately).

(iv)   the amounts of any transfers into or out of Level 3 of the fair value hierarchy, the reasons for those transfers and the entity's policy for determining when transfers between levels are deemed to have occurred (see paragraph 95). Transfers into Level 3 shall be disclosed and discussed separately from transfers out of Level 3.

(f)   for recurring fair value measurements categorised within Level 3 of the fair value hierarchy, the amount of the total gains or losses for the period in (e)(i) included in profit or loss that is attributable to the change in unrealised gains or losses relating to those assets and liabilities held at the end of the reporting period, and the line item(s) in profit or loss in which those unrealised gains or losses are recognised.

(g)   for recurring and non-recurring fair value measurements categorised within Level 3 of the fair value hierarchy, a description of the valuation processes used by the entity (including, for example, how an entity decides its valuation policies and procedures and analyses changes in fair value measurements from period to period).

(h)   for recurring fair value measurements categorised within Level 3 of the fair value hierarchy:

(i)   for all such measurements, a narrative description of the sensitivity of the fair value measurement to changes in unobservable inputs if a change in those inputs to a different amount might result in a significantly higher or lower fair value measurement. If there are interrelationships between those inputs and other unobservable inputs used in the fair value measurement, an entity shall also provide a description of those interrelationships and of how they might magnify or mitigate the effect of changes in the unobservable inputs on the fair value measurement. To comply with that disclosure requirement, the narrative description of the sensitivity to changes in unobservable inputs shall include, at a minimum, the unobservable inputs disclosed when complying with (d).

(ii)   for financial assets and financial liabilities, if changing one or more of the unobservable inputs to reflect reasonably possible alternative assumptions would change fair value significantly, an entity shall state that fact and disclose the effect of those changes. The entity shall disclose how the effect of a change to reflect a reasonably possible alternative assumption was calculated. For that purpose, significance shall be judged with respect to profit or loss, and total assets or total liabilities, or, when changes in fair value are recognised in other comprehensive income, total equity.

(i)   for recurring and non-recurring fair value measurements, if the highest and best use of a non-financial asset differs from its current use, an entity shall disclose that fact and why the non-financial asset is being used in a manner that differs from its highest and best use.

94   An entity shall determine appropriate classes of assets and liabilities on the basis of the following:

(a)   the nature, characteristics and risks of the asset or liability; and

(b)   the level of the fair value hierarchy within which the fair value measurement is categorised.

The number of classes may need to be greater for fair value measurements categorised within Level 3 of the fair value hierarchy because those measurements have a greater degree of uncertainty and subjectivity. Determining appropriate classes of assets and liabilities for which disclosures about fair value measurements should be provided requires judgement. A class of assets and liabilities will often require greater disaggregation than the line items presented in the statement of financial position. However, an entity shall provide information sufficient to permit reconciliation to the line items presented in the statement of financial position. If another IFRS specifies the class for an asset or a liability, an entity may use that class in providing the disclosures required in this IFRS if that class meets the requirements in this paragraph.

95   An entity shall disclose and consistently follow its policy for determining when transfers between levels of the fair value hierarchy are deemed to have occurred in accordance with paragraph 93(c) and (e)(iv). The policy about the timing of recognising transfers shall be the same for transfers into the levels as for transfers out of the levels. Examples of policies for determining the timing of transfers include the following:

(a)   the date of the event or change in circumstances that caused the transfer.

(b)   the beginning of the reporting period.

(c)   the end of the reporting period.

96   If an entity makes an accounting policy decision to use the exception in paragraph 48, it shall disclose that fact.

97   For each class of assets and liabilities not measured at fair value in the statement of financial position but for which the fair value is disclosed, an entity shall disclose the information required by paragraph 93(b), (d) and (i). However, an entity is not required to provide the quantitative disclosures about significant unobservable inputs used in fair value measurements categorised within Level 3 of the fair value hierarchy required by paragraph 93(d). For such assets and liabilities, an entity does not need to provide the other disclosures required by this IFRS.

98   For a liability measured at fair value and issued with an inseparable third-party credit enhancement, an issuer shall disclose the existence of that credit enhancement and whether it is reflected in the fair value measurement of the liability.

99   An entity shall present the quantitative disclosures required by this IFRS in a tabular format unless another format is more appropriate.

Appendix A
Defined terms

This appendix is an integral part of the IFRS.

active market	A market in which transactions for the asset or liability take place with sufficient frequency and volume to provide pricing information on an ongoing basis.
cost approach	A valuation technique that reflects the amount that would be required currently to replace the service capacity of an asset (often referred to as current replacement cost).
entry price	The price paid to acquire an asset or received to assume a liability in an exchange transaction.
exit price	The price that would be received to sell an asset or paid to transfer a liability.
expected cash flow	The probability-weighted average (ie mean of the distribution) of possible future cash flows.
fair value	The price that would be received to sell an asset or paid to transfer a liability in an orderly transaction between market participants at the measurement date.
highest and best use	The use of a non-financial asset by market participants that would maximise the value of the asset or the group of assets and liabilities (eg a business) within which the asset would be used.
income approach	Valuation techniques that convert future amounts (eg cash flows or income and expenses) to a single current (ie discounted) amount. The fair value measurement is determined on the basis of the value indicated by current market expectations about those future amounts.
inputs	The assumptions that market participants would use when pricing the asset or liability, including assumptions about risk, such as the following:

(a) the risk inherent in a particular valuation technique used to measure fair value (such as a pricing model); and

(b) the risk inherent in the inputs to the valuation technique.

Inputs may be observable or unobservable.

Level 1 inputs	Quoted prices (unadjusted) in active markets for identical assets or liabilities that the entity can access at the measurement date.

Level 2 inputs	Inputs other than quoted prices included within Level 1 that are observable for the asset or liability, either directly or indirectly.
Level 3 inputs	Unobservable inputs for the asset or liability.
market approach	A valuation technique that uses prices and other relevant information generated by market transactions involving identical or comparable (ie similar) assets, liabilities or a group of assets and liabilities, such as a business.
market-corroborated inputs	Inputs that are derived principally from or corroborated by observable market data by correlation or other means.
market participant	Buyers and sellers in the principal (or most advantageous) market for the asset or liability that have all of the following characteristics:

<blockquote>

(a)   They are independent of each other, ie they are not related parties as defined in IAS 24, although the price in a related party transaction may be used as an input to a fair value measurement if the entity has evidence that the transaction was entered into at market terms.

(b)   They are knowledgeable, having a reasonable understanding about the asset or liability and the transaction using all available information, including information that might be obtained through due diligence efforts that are usual and customary.

(c)   They are able to enter into a transaction for the asset or liability.

(d)   They are willing to enter into a transaction for the asset or liability, ie they are motivated but not forced or otherwise compelled to do so.

</blockquote>

most advantageous market	The market that maximises the amount that would be received to sell the asset or minimises the amount that would be paid to transfer the liability, after taking into account transaction costs and transport costs.
non-performance risk	The risk that an entity will not fulfil an obligation. Non-performance risk includes, but may not be limited to, the entity's own credit risk.
observable inputs	Inputs that are developed using market data, such as publicly available information about actual events or transactions, and that reflect the assumptions that market participants would use when pricing the asset or liability.

orderly transaction	A transaction that assumes exposure to the market for a period before the measurement date to allow for marketing activities that are usual and customary for transactions involving such assets or liabilities; it is not a forced transaction (eg a forced liquidation or distress sale).
principal market	The market with the greatest volume and level of activity for the asset or liability.
risk premium	Compensation sought by risk-averse market participants for bearing the uncertainty inherent in the cash flows of an asset or a liability. Also referred to as a 'risk adjustment'.
transaction costs	The costs to sell an asset or transfer a liability in the principal (or most advantageous) market for the asset or liability that are directly attributable to the disposal of the asset or the transfer of the liability and meet both of the following criteria:

(a) They result directly from and are essential to that transaction.

(b) They would not have been incurred by the entity had the decision to sell the asset or transfer the liability not been made (similar to costs to sell, as defined in IFRS 5).

transport costs	The costs that would be incurred to transport an asset from its current location to its principal (or most advantageous) market.
unit of account	The level at which an asset or a liability is aggregated or disaggregated in an IFRS for recognition purposes.
unobservable inputs	Inputs for which market data are not available and that are developed using the best information available about the assumptions that market participants would use when pricing the asset or liability.

Appendix B
Application guidance

This appendix is an integral part of the IFRS. It describes the application of paragraphs 1–99 and has the same authority as the other parts of the IFRS.

B1 The judgements applied in different valuation situations may be different. This appendix describes the judgements that might apply when an entity measures fair value in different valuation situations.

The fair value measurement approach

B2 The objective of a fair value measurement is to estimate the price at which an orderly transaction to sell the asset or to transfer the liability would take place between market participants at the measurement date under current market conditions. A fair value measurement requires an entity to determine all the following:

    (a) the particular asset or liability that is the subject of the measurement (consistently with its unit of account).

    (b) for a non-financial asset, the valuation premise that is appropriate for the measurement (consistently with its highest and best use).

    (c) the principal (or most advantageous) market for the asset or liability.

    (d) the valuation technique(s) appropriate for the measurement, considering the availability of data with which to develop inputs that represent the assumptions that market participants would use when pricing the asset or liability and the level of the fair value hierarchy within which the inputs are categorised.

Valuation premise for non-financial assets (paragraphs 31–33)

B3 When measuring the fair value of a non-financial asset used in combination with other assets as a group (as installed or otherwise configured for use) or in combination with other assets and liabilities (eg a business), the effect of the valuation premise depends on the circumstances. For example:

    (a) the fair value of the asset might be the same whether the asset is used on a stand-alone basis or in combination with other assets or with other assets and liabilities. That might be the case if the asset is a business that market participants would continue to operate. In that case, the transaction would involve valuing the business in its entirety. The use of the assets as a group in an ongoing business would generate synergies that would be available to market participants (ie market participant synergies that, therefore, should affect the fair value of the asset on either a stand-alone basis or in combination with other assets or with other assets and liabilities).

(b)   an asset's use in combination with other assets or with other assets and liabilities might be incorporated into the fair value measurement through adjustments to the value of the asset used on a stand-alone basis. That might be the case if the asset is a machine and the fair value measurement is determined using an observed price for a similar machine (not installed or otherwise configured for use), adjusted for transport and installation costs so that the fair value measurement reflects the current condition and location of the machine (installed and configured for use).

(c)   an asset's use in combination with other assets or with other assets and liabilities might be incorporated into the fair value measurement through the market participant assumptions used to measure the fair value of the asset. For example, if the asset is work in progress inventory that is unique and market participants would convert the inventory into finished goods, the fair value of the inventory would assume that market participants have acquired or would acquire any specialised machinery necessary to convert the inventory into finished goods.

(d)   an asset's use in combination with other assets or with other assets and liabilities might be incorporated into the valuation technique used to measure the fair value of the asset. That might be the case when using the multi-period excess earnings method to measure the fair value of an intangible asset because that valuation technique specifically takes into account the contribution of any complementary assets and the associated liabilities in the group in which such an intangible asset would be used.

(e)   in more limited situations, when an entity uses an asset within a group of assets, the entity might measure the asset at an amount that approximates its fair value when allocating the fair value of the asset group to the individual assets of the group. That might be the case if the valuation involves real property and the fair value of improved property (ie an asset group) is allocated to its component assets (such as land and improvements).

Fair value at initial recognition (paragraphs 57–60)

B4   When determining whether fair value at initial recognition equals the transaction price, an entity shall take into account factors specific to the transaction and to the asset or liability. For example, the transaction price might not represent the fair value of an asset or a liability at initial recognition if any of the following conditions exist:

(a)   The transaction is between related parties, although the price in a related party transaction may be used as an input into a fair value measurement if the entity has evidence that the transaction was entered into at market terms.

(b)   The transaction takes place under duress or the seller is forced to accept the price in the transaction. For example, that might be the case if the seller is experiencing financial difficulty.

(c)   The unit of account represented by the transaction price is different from the unit of account for the asset or liability measured at fair value. For example, that might be the case if the asset or liability measured at fair value is only one of the elements in the transaction (eg in a business combination), the transaction includes unstated rights and privileges that are measured separately in accordance with another IFRS, or the transaction price includes transaction costs.

(d)   The market in which the transaction takes place is different from the principal market (or most advantageous market). For example, those markets might be different if the entity is a dealer that enters into transactions with customers in the retail market, but the principal (or most advantageous) market for the exit transaction is with other dealers in the dealer market.

Valuation techniques (paragraphs 61–66)

Market approach

B5   The market approach uses prices and other relevant information generated by market transactions involving identical or comparable (ie similar) assets, liabilities or a group of assets and liabilities, such as a business.

B6   For example, valuation techniques consistent with the market approach often use market multiples derived from a set of comparables. Multiples might be in ranges with a different multiple for each comparable. The selection of the appropriate multiple within the range requires judgement, considering qualitative and quantitative factors specific to the measurement.

B7   Valuation techniques consistent with the market approach include matrix pricing. Matrix pricing is a mathematical technique used principally to value some types of financial instruments, such as debt securities, without relying exclusively on quoted prices for the specific securities, but rather relying on the securities' relationship to other benchmark quoted securities.

Cost approach

B8   The cost approach reflects the amount that would be required currently to replace the service capacity of an asset (often referred to as current replacement cost).

B9   From the perspective of a market participant seller, the price that would be received for the asset is based on the cost to a market participant buyer to acquire or construct a substitute asset of comparable utility, adjusted for obsolescence. That is because a market participant buyer would not pay more for an asset than the amount for which it could replace the service capacity of that asset. Obsolescence encompasses physical deterioration, functional (technological) obsolescence and economic (external) obsolescence and is broader than depreciation for financial reporting purposes (an allocation of historical cost) or tax purposes (using specified service lives). In many cases the current replacement cost method is used to measure the fair value of tangible assets that are used in combination with other assets or with other assets and liabilities.

Income approach

B10 The income approach converts future amounts (eg cash flows or income and expenses) to a single current (ie discounted) amount. When the income approach is used, the fair value measurement reflects current market expectations about those future amounts.

B11 Those valuation techniques include, for example, the following:

(a) present value techniques (see paragraphs B12–B30);

(b) option pricing models, such as the Black-Scholes-Merton formula or a binomial model (ie a lattice model), that incorporate present value techniques and reflect both the time value and the intrinsic value of an option; and

(c) the multi-period excess earnings method, which is used to measure the fair value of some intangible assets.

Present value techniques

B12 Paragraphs B13–B30 describe the use of present value techniques to measure fair value. Those paragraphs focus on a discount rate adjustment technique and an *expected cash flow* (expected present value) technique. Those paragraphs neither prescribe the use of a single specific present value technique nor limit the use of present value techniques to measure fair value to the techniques discussed. The present value technique used to measure fair value will depend on facts and circumstances specific to the asset or liability being measured (eg whether prices for comparable assets or liabilities can be observed in the market) and the availability of sufficient data.

The components of a present value measurement

B13 Present value (ie an application of the income approach) is a tool used to link future amounts (eg cash flows or values) to a present amount using a discount rate. A fair value measurement of an asset or a liability using a present value technique captures all the following elements from the perspective of market participants at the measurement date:

(a) an estimate of future cash flows for the asset or liability being measured.

(b) expectations about possible variations in the amount and timing of the cash flows representing the uncertainty inherent in the cash flows.

(c) the time value of money, represented by the rate on risk-free monetary assets that have maturity dates or durations that coincide with the period covered by the cash flows and pose neither uncertainty in timing nor risk of default to the holder (ie a risk-free interest rate).

(d) the price for bearing the uncertainty inherent in the cash flows (ie a *risk premium*).

(e) other factors that market participants would take into account in the circumstances.

(f) for a liability, the non-performance risk relating to that liability, including the entity's (ie the obligor's) own credit risk.

General principles

B14 Present value techniques differ in how they capture the elements in paragraph B13. However, all the following general principles govern the application of any present value technique used to measure fair value:

(a) Cash flows and discount rates should reflect assumptions that market participants would use when pricing the asset or liability.

(b) Cash flows and discount rates should take into account only the factors attributable to the asset or liability being measured.

(c) To avoid double-counting or omitting the effects of risk factors, discount rates should reflect assumptions that are consistent with those inherent in the cash flows. For example, a discount rate that reflects the uncertainty in expectations about future defaults is appropriate if using contractual cash flows of a loan (ie a discount rate adjustment technique). That same rate should not be used if using expected (ie probability-weighted) cash flows (ie an expected present value technique) because the expected cash flows already reflect assumptions about the uncertainty in future defaults; instead, a discount rate that is commensurate with the risk inherent in the expected cash flows should be used.

(d) Assumptions about cash flows and discount rates should be internally consistent. For example, nominal cash flows, which include the effect of inflation, should be discounted at a rate that includes the effect of inflation. The nominal risk-free interest rate includes the effect of inflation. Real cash flows, which exclude the effect of inflation, should be discounted at a rate that excludes the effect of inflation. Similarly, after-tax cash flows should be discounted using an after-tax discount rate. Pre-tax cash flows should be discounted at a rate consistent with those cash flows.

(e) Discount rates should be consistent with the underlying economic factors of the currency in which the cash flows are denominated.

Risk and uncertainty

B15 A fair value measurement using present value techniques is made under conditions of uncertainty because the cash flows used are estimates rather than known amounts. In many cases both the amount and timing of the cash flows are uncertain. Even contractually fixed amounts, such as the payments on a loan, are uncertain if there is risk of default.

B16 Market participants generally seek compensation (ie a risk premium) for bearing the uncertainty inherent in the cash flows of an asset or a liability. A fair value measurement should include a risk premium reflecting the amount that market participants would demand as compensation for the uncertainty inherent in the cash flows. Otherwise, the measurement would not faithfully represent fair value. In some cases determining the appropriate risk premium might be difficult. However, the degree of difficulty alone is not a sufficient reason to exclude a risk premium.

B17 Present value techniques differ in how they adjust for risk and in the type of cash flows they use. For example:

(a) The discount rate adjustment technique (see paragraphs B18–B22) uses a risk-adjusted discount rate and contractual, promised or most likely cash flows.

(b) Method 1 of the expected present value technique (see paragraph B25) uses risk-adjusted expected cash flows and a risk-free rate.

(c) Method 2 of the expected present value technique (see paragraph B26) uses expected cash flows that are not risk-adjusted and a discount rate adjusted to include the risk premium that market participants require. That rate is different from the rate used in the discount rate adjustment technique.

Discount rate adjustment technique

B18 The discount rate adjustment technique uses a single set of cash flows from the range of possible estimated amounts, whether contractual or promised (as is the case for a bond) or most likely cash flows. In all cases, those cash flows are conditional upon the occurrence of specified events (eg contractual or promised cash flows for a bond are conditional on the event of no default by the debtor). The discount rate used in the discount rate adjustment technique is derived from observed rates of return for comparable assets or liabilities that are traded in the market. Accordingly, the contractual, promised or most likely cash flows are discounted at an observed or estimated market rate for such conditional cash flows (ie a market rate of return).

B19 The discount rate adjustment technique requires an analysis of market data for comparable assets or liabilities. Comparability is established by considering the nature of the cash flows (eg whether the cash flows are contractual or non-contractual and are likely to respond similarly to changes in economic conditions), as well as other factors (eg credit standing, collateral, duration, restrictive covenants and liquidity). Alternatively, if a single comparable asset or liability does not fairly reflect the risk inherent in the cash flows of the asset or liability being measured, it may be possible to derive a discount rate using data for several comparable assets or liabilities in conjunction with the risk-free yield curve (ie using a 'build-up' approach).

B20   To illustrate a build-up approach, assume that Asset A is a contractual right to receive CU800[1] in one year (ie there is no timing uncertainty). There is an established market for comparable assets, and information about those assets, including price information, is available. Of those comparable assets:

(a)   Asset B is a contractual right to receive CU1,200 in one year and has a market price of CU1,083. Thus, the implied annual rate of return (ie a one-year market rate of return) is 10.8 per cent [(CU1,200/CU1,083) – 1].

(b)   Asset C is a contractual right to receive CU700 in two years and has a market price of CU566. Thus, the implied annual rate of return (ie a two-year market rate of return) is 11.2 per cent [(CU700/CU566)^0.5 – 1].

(c)   All three assets are comparable with respect to risk (ie dispersion of possible pay-offs and credit).

B21   On the basis of the timing of the contractual payments to be received for Asset A relative to the timing for Asset B and Asset C (ie one year for Asset B versus two years for Asset C), Asset B is deemed more comparable to Asset A. Using the contractual payment to be received for Asset A (CU800) and the one-year market rate derived from Asset B (10.8 per cent), the fair value of Asset A is CU722 (CU800/1.108). Alternatively, in the absence of available market information for Asset B, the one-year market rate could be derived from Asset C using the build-up approach. In that case the two-year market rate indicated by Asset C (11.2 per cent) would be adjusted to a one-year market rate using the term structure of the risk-free yield curve. Additional information and analysis might be required to determine whether the risk premiums for one-year and two-year assets are the same. If it is determined that the risk premiums for one-year and two-year assets are not the same, the two-year market rate of return would be further adjusted for that effect.

B22   When the discount rate adjustment technique is applied to fixed receipts or payments, the adjustment for risk inherent in the cash flows of the asset or liability being measured is included in the discount rate. In some applications of the discount rate adjustment technique to cash flows that are not fixed receipts or payments, an adjustment to the cash flows may be necessary to achieve comparability with the observed asset or liability from which the discount rate is derived.

Expected present value technique

B23   The expected present value technique uses as a starting point a set of cash flows that represents the probability-weighted average of all possible future cash flows (ie the expected cash flows). The resulting estimate is identical to expected value, which, in statistical terms, is the weighted average of a discrete random variable's possible values with the respective probabilities as

---

1   In this IFRS monetary amounts are denominated in 'currency units (CU)'.

the weights. Because all possible cash flows are probability-weighted, the resulting expected cash flow is not conditional upon the occurrence of any specified event (unlike the cash flows used in the discount rate adjustment technique).

B24 In making an investment decision, risk-averse market participants would take into account the risk that the actual cash flows may differ from the expected cash flows. Portfolio theory distinguishes between two types of risk:

(a) unsystematic (diversifiable) risk, which is the risk specific to a particular asset or liability.

(b) systematic (non-diversifiable) risk, which is the common risk shared by an asset or a liability with the other items in a diversified portfolio.

Portfolio theory holds that in a market in equilibrium, market participants will be compensated only for bearing the systematic risk inherent in the cash flows. (In markets that are inefficient or out of equilibrium, other forms of return or compensation might be available.)

B25 Method 1 of the expected present value technique adjusts the expected cash flows of an asset for systematic (ie market) risk by subtracting a cash risk premium (ie risk-adjusted expected cash flows). Those risk-adjusted expected cash flows represent a certainty-equivalent cash flow, which is discounted at a risk-free interest rate. A certainty-equivalent cash flow refers to an expected cash flow (as defined), adjusted for risk so that a market participant is indifferent to trading a certain cash flow for an expected cash flow. For example, if a market participant was willing to trade an expected cash flow of CU1,200 for a certain cash flow of CU1,000, the CU1,000 is the certainty equivalent of the CU1,200 (ie the CU200 would represent the cash risk premium). In that case the market participant would be indifferent as to the asset held.

B26 In contrast, Method 2 of the expected present value technique adjusts for systematic (ie market) risk by applying a risk premium to the risk-free interest rate. Accordingly, the expected cash flows are discounted at a rate that corresponds to an expected rate associated with probability-weighted cash flows (ie an expected rate of return). Models used for pricing risky assets, such as the capital asset pricing model, can be used to estimate the expected rate of return. Because the discount rate used in the discount rate adjustment technique is a rate of return relating to conditional cash flows, it is likely to be higher than the discount rate used in Method 2 of the expected present value technique, which is an expected rate of return relating to expected or probability-weighted cash flows.

B27 To illustrate Methods 1 and 2, assume that an asset has expected cash flows of CU780 in one year determined on the basis of the possible cash flows and probabilities shown below. The applicable risk-free interest rate for cash flows with a one-year horizon is 5 per cent, and the systematic risk premium for an asset with the same risk profile is 3 per cent.

Possible cash flows	Probability	Probability-weighted cash flows
CU500	15%	CU75
CU800	60%	CU480
CU900	25%	CU225
Expected cash flows		CU780

B28 In this simple illustration, the expected cash flows (CU780) represent the probability-weighted average of the three possible outcomes. In more realistic situations, there could be many possible outcomes. However, to apply the expected present value technique, it is not always necessary to take into account distributions of all possible cash flows using complex models and techniques. Rather, it might be possible to develop a limited number of discrete scenarios and probabilities that capture the array of possible cash flows. For example, an entity might use realised cash flows for some relevant past period, adjusted for changes in circumstances occurring subsequently (eg changes in external factors, including economic or market conditions, industry trends and competition as well as changes in internal factors affecting the entity more specifically), taking into account the assumptions of market participants.

B29 In theory, the present value (ie the fair value) of the asset's cash flows is the same whether determined using Method 1 or Method 2, as follows:

(a) Using Method 1, the expected cash flows are adjusted for systematic (ie market) risk. In the absence of market data directly indicating the amount of the risk adjustment, such adjustment could be derived from an asset pricing model using the concept of certainty equivalents. For example, the risk adjustment (ie the cash risk premium of CU22) could be determined using the systematic risk premium of 3 per cent (CU780 − [CU780 × (1.05/1.08)]), which results in risk-adjusted expected cash flows of CU758 (CU780 − CU22). The CU758 is the certainty equivalent of CU780 and is discounted at the risk-free interest rate (5 per cent). The present value (ie the fair value) of the asset is CU722 (CU758/1.05).

(b) Using Method 2, the expected cash flows are not adjusted for systematic (ie market) risk. Rather, the adjustment for that risk is included in the discount rate. Thus, the expected cash flows are discounted at an expected rate of return of 8 per cent (ie the 5 per cent risk-free interest rate plus the 3 per cent systematic risk premium). The present value (ie the fair value) of the asset is CU722 (CU780/1.08).

B30 When using an expected present value technique to measure fair value, either Method 1 or Method 2 could be used. The selection of Method 1 or Method 2 will depend on facts and circumstances specific to the asset or liability being measured, the extent to which sufficient data are available and the judgements applied.

Applying present value techniques to liabilities and an entity's own equity instruments not held by other parties as assets (paragraphs 40 and 41)

B31   When using a present value technique to measure the fair value of a liability that is not held by another party as an asset (eg a decommissioning liability), an entity shall, among other things, estimate the future cash outflows that market participants would expect to incur in fulfilling the obligation. Those future cash outflows shall include market participants' expectations about the costs of fulfilling the obligation and the compensation that a market participant would require for taking on the obligation. Such compensation includes the return that a market participant would require for the following:

    (a)   undertaking the activity (ie the value of fulfilling the obligation; eg by using resources that could be used for other activities); and

    (b)   assuming the risk associated with the obligation (ie a risk premium that reflects the risk that the actual cash outflows might differ from the expected cash outflows; see paragraph B33).

B32   For example, a non-financial liability does not contain a contractual rate of return and there is no observable market yield for that liability. In some cases the components of the return that market participants would require will be indistinguishable from one another (eg when using the price a third party contractor would charge on a fixed fee basis). In other cases an entity needs to estimate those components separately (eg when using the price a third party contractor would charge on a cost plus basis because the contractor in that case would not bear the risk of future changes in costs).

B33   An entity can include a risk premium in the fair value measurement of a liability or an entity's own equity instrument that is not held by another party as an asset in one of the following ways:

    (a)   by adjusting the cash flows (ie as an increase in the amount of cash outflows); or

    (b)   by adjusting the rate used to discount the future cash flows to their present values (ie as a reduction in the discount rate).

An entity shall ensure that it does not double-count or omit adjustments for risk. For example, if the estimated cash flows are increased to take into account the compensation for assuming the risk associated with the obligation, the discount rate should not be adjusted to reflect that risk.

Inputs to valuation techniques (paragraphs 67–71)

B34   Examples of markets in which inputs might be observable for some assets and liabilities (eg financial instruments) include the following:

    (a)   *Exchange markets.* In an exchange market, closing prices are both readily available and generally representative of fair value. An example of such a market is the London Stock Exchange.

(b)   *Dealer markets.* In a dealer market, dealers stand ready to trade (either buy or sell for their own account), thereby providing liquidity by using their capital to hold an inventory of the items for which they make a market. Typically bid and ask prices (representing the price at which the dealer is willing to buy and the price at which the dealer is willing to sell, respectively) are more readily available than closing prices. Over-the-counter markets (for which prices are publicly reported) are dealer markets. Dealer markets also exist for some other assets and liabilities, including some financial instruments, commodities and physical assets (eg used equipment).

(c)   *Brokered markets.* In a brokered market, brokers attempt to match buyers with sellers but do not stand ready to trade for their own account. In other words, brokers do not use their own capital to hold an inventory of the items for which they make a market. The broker knows the prices bid and asked by the respective parties, but each party is typically unaware of another party's price requirements. Prices of completed transactions are sometimes available. Brokered markets include electronic communication networks, in which buy and sell orders are matched, and commercial and residential real estate markets.

(d)   *Principal-to-principal markets.* In a principal-to-principal market, transactions, both originations and resales, are negotiated independently with no intermediary. Little information about those transactions may be made available publicly.

Fair value hierarchy (paragraphs 72–90)

Level 2 inputs (paragraphs 81–85)

B35   Examples of Level 2 inputs for particular assets and liabilities include the following:

(a)   *Receive-fixed, pay-variable interest rate swap based on the London Interbank Offered Rate (LIBOR) swap rate.* A Level 2 input would be the LIBOR swap rate if that rate is observable at commonly quoted intervals for substantially the full term of the swap.

(b)   *Receive-fixed, pay-variable interest rate swap based on a yield curve denominated in a foreign currency.* A Level 2 input would be the swap rate based on a yield curve denominated in a foreign currency that is observable at commonly quoted intervals for substantially the full term of the swap. That would be the case if the term of the swap is 10 years and that rate is observable at commonly quoted intervals for 9 years, provided that any reasonable extrapolation of the yield curve for year 10 would not be significant to the fair value measurement of the swap in its entirety.

(c) *Receive-fixed, pay-variable interest rate swap based on a specific bank's prime rate.* A Level 2 input would be the bank's prime rate derived through extrapolation if the extrapolated values are corroborated by observable market data, for example, by correlation with an interest rate that is observable over substantially the full term of the swap.

(d) *Three-year option on exchange-traded shares.* A Level 2 input would be the implied volatility for the shares derived through extrapolation to year 3 if both of the following conditions exist:

    (i) Prices for one-year and two-year options on the shares are observable.

    (ii) The extrapolated implied volatility of a three-year option is corroborated by observable market data for substantially the full term of the option.

In that case the implied volatility could be derived by extrapolating from the implied volatility of the one-year and two-year options on the shares and corroborated by the implied volatility for three-year options on comparable entities' shares, provided that correlation with the one-year and two-year implied volatilities is established.

(e) *Licensing arrangement.* For a licensing arrangement that is acquired in a business combination and was recently negotiated with an unrelated party by the acquired entity (the party to the licensing arrangement), a Level 2 input would be the royalty rate in the contract with the unrelated party at inception of the arrangement.

(f) *Finished goods inventory at a retail outlet.* For finished goods inventory that is acquired in a business combination, a Level 2 input would be either a price to customers in a retail market or a price to retailers in a wholesale market, adjusted for differences between the condition and location of the inventory item and the comparable (ie similar) inventory items so that the fair value measurement reflects the price that would be received in a transaction to sell the inventory to another retailer that would complete the requisite selling efforts. Conceptually, the fair value measurement will be the same, whether adjustments are made to a retail price (downward) or to a wholesale price (upward). Generally, the price that requires the least amount of subjective adjustments should be used for the fair value measurement.

(g) *Building held and used.* A Level 2 input would be the price per square metre for the building (a valuation multiple) derived from observable market data, eg multiples derived from prices in observed transactions involving comparable (ie similar) buildings in similar locations.

(h) *Cash-generating unit.* A Level 2 input would be a valuation multiple (eg a multiple of earnings or revenue or a similar performance measure) derived from observable market data, eg multiples derived from prices in observed transactions involving comparable (ie similar) businesses, taking into account operational, market, financial and non-financial factors.

compared with other indications of fair value that reflect the results of transactions) on quotes that do not reflect the result of transactions.

B47 Furthermore, the nature of a quote (eg whether the quote is an indicative price or a binding offer) shall be taken into account when weighting the available evidence, with more weight given to quotes provided by third parties that represent binding offers.

Appendix C
Effective date and transition

This appendix is an integral part of the IFRS and has the same authority as the other parts of the IFRS.

C1   An entity shall apply this IFRS for annual periods beginning on or after 1 January 2013. Earlier application is permitted. If an entity applies this IFRS for an earlier period, it shall disclose that fact.

C2   This IFRS shall be applied prospectively as of the beginning of the annual period in which it is initially applied.

C3   The disclosure requirements of this IFRS need not be applied in comparative information provided for periods before initial application of this IFRS.

C4   *Annual Improvements Cycle 2011–2013* issued in December 2013 amended paragraph 52. An entity shall apply that amendment for annual periods beginning on or after 1 July 2014. An entity shall apply that amendment prospectively from the beginning of the annual period in which IFRS 13 was initially applied. Earlier application is permitted. If an entity applies that amendment for an earlier period it shall disclose that fact.

C5   IFRS 9, as issued in July 2014, amended paragraph 52. An entity shall apply that amendment when it applies IFRS 9.

C6   IFRS 16 *Leases*, issued in January 2016, amended paragraph 6. An entity shall apply that amendment when it applies IFRS 16.

Appendix D
Amendments to other IFRSs

This appendix sets out amendments to other IFRSs that are a consequence of the Board issuing IFRS 13. An entity shall apply the amendments for annual periods beginning on or after 1 January 2013. If an entity applies IFRS 13 for an earlier period, it shall apply the amendments for that earlier period. Amended paragraphs are shown with new text underlined and deleted text struck through.

* * * * *

The amendments contained in this appendix when this IFRS was issued in 2011 have been incorporated into the relevant IFRSs published in this volume.

Approval by the Board of IFRS 13 issued in May 2011

International Financial Reporting Standard 13 *Fair Value Measurement* was approved for issue by the fifteen members of the International Accounting Standards Board.

Sir David Tweedie   Chairman

Stephen Cooper

Philippe Danjou

Jan Engström

Patrick Finnegan

Amaro Luiz de Oliveira Gomes

Prabhakar Kalavacherla

Elke König

Patricia McConnell

Warren J McGregor

Paul Pacter

Darrel Scott

John T Smith

Tatsumi Yamada

Wei-Guo Zhang

Appendix A
Defined terms

This appendix is an integral part of the Standard.

first IFRS financial statements	The first annual financial statements in which an entity adopts International Financial Reporting Standards (IFRS), by an explicit and unreserved statement of compliance with IFRS.
first-time adopter	An entity that presents its **first IFRS financial statements**.
previous GAAP	The basis of accounting that a **first-time adopter** used immediately before adopting IFRS.
rate-regulated activities	An entity's activities that are subject to **rate regulation**.
rate regulation	A framework for establishing the prices that can be charged to customers for goods or services and that framework is subject to oversight and/or approval by a **rate regulator**.
rate regulator	An authorised body that is empowered by statute or regulation to establish the rate or a range of rates that bind an entity. The **rate regulator** may be a third-party body or a related party of the entity, including the entity's own governing board, if that body is required by statute or regulation to set rates both in the interest of the customers and to ensure the overall financial viability of the entity.
regulatory deferral account balance	The balance of any expense (or income) account that would not be recognised as an asset or a liability in accordance with other Standards, but that qualifies for deferral because it is included, or is expected to be included, by the **rate regulator** in establishing the rate(s) that can be charged to customers.

Appendix B
Application Guidance

This appendix is an integral part of the Standard.

Rate-regulated activities

B1 Historically, rate regulation applied to all activities of an entity. However, with acquisitions, diversification and deregulation, rate regulation may now apply to only a portion of an entity's activities, resulting in it having both regulated and non-regulated activities. This Standard applies only to the rate-regulated activities that are subject to statutory or regulatory restrictions through the actions of a rate regulator, regardless of the type of entity or the industry to which it belongs.

B2 An entity shall not apply this Standard to activities that are self-regulated, ie activities that are not subject to a pricing framework that is overseen and/or approved by a rate regulator. This does not prevent the entity from being eligible to apply this Standard when:

(a) the entity's own governing body or a related party establishes rates both in the interest of the customers and to ensure the overall financial viability of the entity within a specified pricing framework; and

(b) the framework is subject to oversight and/or approval by an authorised body that is empowered by statute or regulation.

Continuation of existing accounting policies

B3 For the purposes of this Standard, a regulatory deferral account balance is defined as the balance of any expense (or income) account that would not be recognised as an asset or a liability in accordance with other Standards, but that qualifies for deferral because it is included, or is expected to be included, by the rate regulator in establishing the rate(s) that can be charged to customers. Some items of expense (income) may be outside the regulated rate(s) because, for example, the amounts are not expected to be accepted by the rate regulator or because they are not within the scope of the rate regulation. Consequently, such an item is recognised as income or expense as incurred, unless another Standard permits or requires it to be included in the carrying amount of an asset or liability.

B4 In some cases, other Standards explicitly prohibit an entity from recognising, in the statement of financial position, regulatory deferral account balances that might be recognised, either separately or included within other line items such as property, plant and equipment in accordance with previous GAAP accounting policies. However, in accordance with paragraph 11 of this Standard, an entity that elects to apply this Standard in its first IFRS financial statements applies the exemption from paragraph 11 of IAS 8 in order to continue to apply its previous GAAP accounting policies for the recognition, measurement, impairment, and derecognition of regulatory deferral account balances. Such accounting policies may include, for example, the following practices:

(a) recognising a regulatory deferral account debit balance when the entity has the right, as a result of the actual or expected actions of the rate regulator, to increase rates in future periods in order to recover its allowable costs (ie the costs for which the regulated rate(s) is intended to provide recovery);

(b) recognising, as a regulatory deferral account debit or credit balance, an amount that is equivalent to any loss or gain on the disposal or retirement of both items of property, plant and equipment and of intangible assets, which is expected to be recovered or reversed through future rates;

(c) recognising a regulatory deferral account credit balance when the entity is required, as a result of the actual or expected actions of the rate regulator, to decrease rates in future periods in order to reverse over-recoveries of allowable costs (ie amounts in excess of the recoverable amount specified by the rate regulator); and

(d) measuring regulatory deferral account balances on an undiscounted basis or on a discounted basis that uses an interest or discount rate specified by the rate regulator.

B5   The following are examples of the types of costs that rate regulators might allow in rate-setting decisions and that an entity might, therefore, recognise in regulatory deferral account balances:

(i) volume or purchase price variances;

(ii) costs of approved 'green energy' initiatives (in excess of amounts that are capitalised as part of the cost of property, plant and equipment in accordance with IAS 16 *Property, Plant and Equipment*);

(iii) non-directly-attributable overhead costs that are treated as capital costs for rate regulation purposes (but are not permitted, in accordance with IAS 16, to be included in the cost of an item of property, plant and equipment);

(iv) project cancellation costs;

(v) storm damage costs; and

(vi) deemed interest (including amounts allowed for funds that are used during construction that provide the entity with a return on the owner's equity capital as well as borrowings).

B6   Regulatory deferral account balances usually represent timing differences between the recognition of items of income or expenses for regulatory purposes and the recognition of those items for financial reporting purposes. When an entity changes an accounting policy on the first-time adoption of IFRS or on the initial application of a new or revised Standard, new or revised timing differences may arise that create new or revised regulatory deferral account balances. The prohibition in paragraph 13 that prevents an entity from changing its accounting policy in order to start to recognise regulatory deferral account balances does not prohibit the recognition of the new or revised regulatory deferral account balances that are created because of other changes in accounting policies required by IFRS. This is because the recognition of regulatory deferral account balances for such timing differences would be consistent with the existing recognition policy applied in accordance with paragraph 11 and would not represent the introduction of a new accounting policy. Similarly, paragraph 13 does not prohibit the recognition of regulatory deferral account balances arising from timing differences that did not exist immediately prior to the date of transition to IFRS but are consistent with the entity's accounting policies established in accordance with paragraph 11 (for example, storm damage costs).

Applicability of other Standards

B7   An entity that is within the scope of, and that elects to apply, the requirements of this Standard shall continue to apply its previous GAAP accounting policies for the recognition, measurement, impairment and derecognition of regulatory deferral account balances. However, paragraphs 16–17 state that, in some situations, other Standards might also need to be applied to regulatory deferral account balances in order to reflect them appropriately in the financial statements. The following paragraphs outline how some other Standards interact with the requirements of this Standard. In particular, the following paragraphs clarify specific exceptions to, and exemptions from, other Standards and additional presentation and disclosure requirements that are expected to be applicable.

Application of IAS 10 *Events after the Reporting Period*

B8   An entity may need to use estimates and assumptions in the recognition and measurement of its regulatory deferral account balances. For events that occur between the end of the reporting period and the date when the financial statements are authorised for issue, the entity shall apply IAS 10 to identify whether those estimates and assumptions should be adjusted to reflect those events.

Application of IAS 12 *Income Taxes*

B9   IAS 12 requires, with certain limited exceptions, an entity to recognise a deferred tax liability and (subject to certain conditions) a deferred tax asset for all temporary differences. A rate-regulated entity shall apply IAS 12 to all of its activities, including its rate-regulated activities, to identify the amount of income tax that is to be recognised.

B10   In some rate-regulatory schemes, the rate regulator permits or requires an entity to increase its future rates in order to recover some or all of the entity's income tax expense. In such circumstances, this might result in the entity recognising a regulatory deferral account balance in the statement of financial position related to income tax, in accordance with its accounting policies established in accordance with paragraphs 11–12. The recognition of this regulatory deferral account balance that relates to income tax might itself create an additional temporary difference for which a further deferred tax amount would be recognised.

B11 Notwithstanding the presentation and disclosure requirements of IAS 12, when an entity recognises a deferred tax asset or a deferred tax liability as a result of recognising regulatory deferral account balances, the entity shall not include that deferred tax amount within the total deferred tax asset (liability) balances. Instead, the entity shall present the deferred tax asset (liability) that arises as a result of recognising regulatory deferral account balances either:

(a) with the line items that are presented for the regulatory deferral account debit balances and credit balances; or

(b) as a separate line item alongside the related regulatory deferral account debit balances and credit balances.

B12 Similarly, when an entity recognises the movement in a deferred tax asset (liability) that arises as a result of recognising regulatory deferral account balances, the entity shall not include the movement in that deferred tax amount within the tax expense (income) line item that is presented in the statement(s) of profit or loss and other comprehensive income in accordance with IAS 12. Instead, the entity shall present the movement in the deferred tax asset (liability) that arises as a result of recognising regulatory deferral account balances either:

(a) with the line items that are presented in the statement(s) of profit or loss and other comprehensive income for the movements in regulatory deferral account balances; or

(b) as a separate line item alongside the related line items that are presented in the statement(s) of profit or loss and other comprehensive income for the movements in regulatory deferral account balances.

Application of IAS 33 *Earnings per Share*

B13 Paragraph 66 of IAS 33 requires some entities to present, in the statement of profit or loss and other comprehensive income, basic and diluted earnings per share both for profit or loss from continuing operations and profit or loss that is attributable to the ordinary equity holders of the parent entity. In addition, paragraph 68 of IAS 33 requires an entity that reports a discontinued operation to disclose the basic and diluted amounts per share for the discontinued operation, either in the statement of profit or loss and other comprehensive income or in the notes.

B14 For each earnings per share amount presented in accordance with IAS 33, an entity applying this Standard shall present additional basic and diluted earnings per share amounts that are calculated in the same way, except that those amounts shall exclude the net movement in the regulatory deferral account balances. Consistent with the requirement in paragraph 73 of IAS 33, an entity shall present the earnings per share required by paragraph 26 of this

Standard with equal prominence to the earnings per share required by IAS 33 for all periods presented.

Application of IAS 36 *Impairment of Assets*

B15   Paragraphs 11–12 require an entity to continue to apply its previous GAAP accounting policies for the identification, recognition, measurement and reversal of any impairment of its recognised regulatory deferral account balances. Consequently, IAS 36 does not apply to the separate regulatory deferral account balances recognised.

B16   However, IAS 36 might require an entity to perform an impairment test on a cash-generating unit (CGU) that includes regulatory deferral account balances. This test might be required because the CGU contains goodwill, or because one or more of the impairment indicators described in IAS 36 have been identified relating to the CGU. In such situations, paragraphs 74–79 of IAS 36 contain requirements for identifying the recoverable amount and the carrying amount of a CGU. An entity shall apply those requirements to decide whether any of the regulatory deferral account balances recognised are included in the carrying amount of the CGU for the purpose of the impairment test. The remaining requirements of IAS 36 shall then be applied to any impairment loss that is recognised as a result of this test.

Application of IFRS 3 *Business Combinations*

B17   The core principle of IFRS 3 is that an acquirer of a business recognises the assets acquired and the liabilities assumed at their acquisition-date fair values. IFRS 3 provides limited exceptions to its recognition and measurement principles. Paragraph B18 of this Standard provides an additional exception.

B18   Paragraphs 11–12 require an entity to continue to apply its previous GAAP accounting policies for the recognition, measurement, impairment and derecognition of regulatory deferral account balances. Consequently, if an entity acquires a business, it shall apply, in its consolidated financial statements, its accounting policies established in accordance with paragraphs 11–12 for the recognition and measurement of the acquiree's regulatory deferral account balances at the date of acquisition. The acquiree's regulatory deferral account balances shall be recognised in the consolidated financial statements of the acquirer in accordance with the acquirer's policies, irrespective of whether the acquiree recognises those balances in its own financial statements.

Application of IFRS 5 *Non-current Assets Held for Sale and Discontinued Operations*

B19   Paragraphs 11–12 require an entity to continue to apply its previous accounting policies for the recognition, measurement, impairment and derecognition of regulatory deferral account balances. Consequently, the measurement requirements of IFRS 5 shall not apply to the regulatory deferral account balances recognised.

IFRS 15

Revenue from Contracts with Customers

In April 2001 the International Accounting Standards Board (Board) adopted IAS 11 *Construction Contracts* and IAS 18 *Revenue*, both of which had originally been issued by the International Accounting Standards Committee (IASC) in December 1993. IAS 18 replaced a previous version: *Revenue Recognition* (issued in December 1982). IAS 11 replaced parts of IAS 11 *Accounting for Construction Contracts* (issued in March 1979).

In December 2001 the Board issued SIC-31 *Revenue—Barter Transactions Involving Advertising Services*. The Interpretation was originally developed by the Standards Interpretations Committee of the IASC to determine the circumstances in which a seller of advertising services can reliably measure revenue at the fair value of advertising services provided in a barter transaction.

In June 2007 the Board issued IFRIC 13 *Customer Loyalty Programmes*. The Interpretation was developed by the IFRS Interpretations Committee (the 'Interpretations Committee') to address the accounting by the entity that grants award credits to its customers.

In July 2008 the Board issued IFRIC 15 *Agreements for the Construction of Real Estate*. The Interpretation was developed by the Interpretations Committee to apply to the accounting for revenue and associated expenses by entities that undertake the construction of real estate directly or through subcontractors.

In January 2009 the Board issued IFRIC 18 *Transfers of Assets from Customers*. The Interpretation was developed by the Interpretations Committee to apply to the accounting for transfers of items of property, plant and equipment by entities that receive such transfers from their customers.

In May 2014 the Board issued IFRS 15 *Revenue from Contracts with Customers*, together with the introduction of Topic 606 into the Financial Accounting Standards Board's *Accounting Standards Codification*®. IFRS 15 replaces IAS 11, IAS 18, IFRIC 13, IFRIC 15, IFRIC 18 and SIC-31. IFRS 15 provides a comprehensive framework for recognising revenue from contracts with customers.

In September 2015 the Board issued *Effective Date of IFRS 15* which deferred the mandatory effective date of IFRS 15 to 1 January 2018.

In April 2016 the Board issued *Clarifications to IFRS 15* Revenue from Contracts with Customers clarifying the Board's intentions when developing some of the requirements in IFRS 15. These amendments do not change the underlying principles of IFRS 15 but clarify how those principles should be applied and provide additional transitional relief.

Other Standards have made minor consequential amendments to IFRS 15, including IFRS 16 *Leases* (issued January 2016) and *Amendments to References to the Conceptual Framework in IFRS Standards* (issued March 2018).

Contents

continued...

...continued

FOR THE ACCOMPANYING GUIDANCE LISTED BELOW, SEE PART B OF THIS EDITION

ILLUSTRATIVE EXAMPLES

APPENDIX

Amendments to the guidance on other Standards

FOR THE BASIS FOR CONCLUSIONS, SEE PART C OF THIS EDITION

BASIS FOR CONCLUSIONS

DISSENTING OPINION

APPENDICES TO THE BASIS FOR CONCLUSIONS

A Comparison of IFRS 15 and Topic 606

B Amendments to the Basis for Conclusions on other Standards

International Financial Reporting Standard 15 *Revenue from Contracts with Customers* (IFRS 15) is set out in paragraphs 1–129 and Appendices A–D. All the paragraphs have equal authority. Paragraphs in **bold type** state the main principles. Terms defined in Appendix A are in *italics* the first time that they appear in the Standard. Definitions of other terms are given in the Glossary for International Financial Reporting Standards. The Standard should be read in the context of its objective and the Basis for Conclusions, the *Preface to IFRS Standards* and the *Conceptual Framework for Financial Reporting*. IAS 8 *Accounting Policies, Changes in Accounting Estimates and Errors* provides a basis for selecting and applying accounting policies in the absence of explicit guidance.

International Financial Reporting Standard 15
Revenue from Contracts with Customers

Objective

1   The objective of this Standard is to establish the principles that an entity shall apply to report useful information to users of financial statements about the nature, amount, timing and uncertainty of *revenue* and cash flows arising from a *contract* with a *customer*.

Meeting the objective

2   To meet the objective in paragraph 1, the core principle of this Standard is that an entity shall recognise revenue to depict the transfer of promised goods or services to customers in an amount that reflects the consideration to which the entity expects to be entitled in exchange for those goods or services.

3   An entity shall consider the terms of the contract and all relevant facts and circumstances when applying this Standard. An entity shall apply this Standard, including the use of any practical expedients, consistently to contracts with similar characteristics and in similar circumstances.

4   This Standard specifies the accounting for an individual contract with a customer. However, as a practical expedient, an entity may apply this Standard to a portfolio of contracts (or *performance obligations*) with similar characteristics if the entity reasonably expects that the effects on the financial statements of applying this Standard to the portfolio would not differ materially from applying this Standard to the individual contracts (or performance obligations) within that portfolio. When accounting for a portfolio, an entity shall use estimates and assumptions that reflect the size and composition of the portfolio.

Scope

5   An entity shall apply this Standard to all contracts with customers, except the following:

    (a)   lease contracts within the scope of IFRS 16 *Leases*;

    (b)   insurance contracts within the scope of IFRS 4 *Insurance Contracts*;

    (c)   financial instruments and other contractual rights or obligations within the scope of IFRS 9 *Financial Instruments*, IFRS 10 *Consolidated Financial Statements*, IFRS 11 *Joint Arrangements*, IAS 27 *Separate Financial Statements* and IAS 28 *Investments in Associates and Joint Ventures*; and

    (d)   non-monetary exchanges between entities in the same line of business to facilitate sales to customers or potential customers. For example, this Standard would not apply to a contract between two oil companies that agree to an exchange of oil to fulfil demand from their customers in different specified locations on a timely basis.

6   An entity shall apply this Standard to a contract (other than a contract listed in paragraph 5) only if the counterparty to the contract is a customer. A customer is a party that has contracted with an entity to obtain goods or services that are an output of the entity's ordinary activities in exchange for consideration. A counterparty to the contract would not be a customer if, for example, the counterparty has contracted with the entity to participate in an activity or process in which the parties to the contract share in the risks and benefits that result from the activity or process (such as developing an asset in a collaboration arrangement) rather than to obtain the output of the entity's ordinary activities.

7   A contract with a customer may be partially within the scope of this Standard and partially within the scope of other Standards listed in paragraph 5.

(a)   If the other Standards specify how to separate and/or initially measure one or more parts of the contract, then an entity shall first apply the separation and/or measurement requirements in those Standards. An entity shall exclude from the *transaction price* the amount of the part (or parts) of the contract that are initially measured in accordance with other Standards and shall apply paragraphs 73–86 to allocate the amount of the transaction price that remains (if any) to each performance obligation within the scope of this Standard and to any other parts of the contract identified by paragraph 7(b).

(b)   If the other Standards do not specify how to separate and/or initially measure one or more parts of the contract, then the entity shall apply this Standard to separate and/or initially measure the part (or parts) of the contract.

8   This Standard specifies the accounting for the incremental costs of obtaining a contract with a customer and for the costs incurred to fulfil a contract with a customer if those costs are not within the scope of another Standard (see paragraphs 91–104). An entity shall apply those paragraphs only to the costs incurred that relate to a contract with a customer (or part of that contract) that is within the scope of this Standard.

Recognition

Identifying the contract

9   An entity shall account for a contract with a customer that is within the scope of this Standard only when all of the following criteria are met:

(a)   the parties to the contract have approved the contract (in writing, orally or in accordance with other customary business practices) and are committed to perform their respective obligations;

(b)   the entity can identify each party's rights regarding the goods or services to be transferred;

(c)   the entity can identify the payment terms for the goods or services to be transferred;

    (d)   the contract has commercial substance (ie the risk, timing or amount of the entity's future cash flows is expected to change as a result of the contract); and

    (e)   it is probable that the entity will collect the consideration to which it will be entitled in exchange for the goods or services that will be transferred to the customer. In evaluating whether collectability of an amount of consideration is probable, an entity shall consider only the customer's ability and intention to pay that amount of consideration when it is due. The amount of consideration to which the entity will be entitled may be less than the price stated in the contract if the consideration is variable because the entity may offer the customer a price concession (see paragraph 52).

10   A contract is an agreement between two or more parties that creates enforceable rights and obligations. Enforceability of the rights and obligations in a contract is a matter of law. Contracts can be written, oral or implied by an entity's customary business practices. The practices and processes for establishing contracts with customers vary across legal jurisdictions, industries and entities. In addition, they may vary within an entity (for example, they may depend on the class of customer or the nature of the promised goods or services). An entity shall consider those practices and processes in determining whether and when an agreement with a customer creates enforceable rights and obligations.

11   Some contracts with customers may have no fixed duration and can be terminated or modified by either party at any time. Other contracts may automatically renew on a periodic basis that is specified in the contract. An entity shall apply this Standard to the duration of the contract (ie the contractual period) in which the parties to the contract have present enforceable rights and obligations.

12   For the purpose of applying this Standard, a contract does not exist if each party to the contract has the unilateral enforceable right to terminate a wholly unperformed contract without compensating the other party (or parties). A contract is wholly unperformed if both of the following criteria are met:

    (a)   the entity has not yet transferred any promised goods or services to the customer; and

    (b)   the entity has not yet received, and is not yet entitled to receive, any consideration in exchange for promised goods or services.

13   If a contract with a customer meets the criteria in paragraph 9 at contract inception, an entity shall not reassess those criteria unless there is an indication of a significant change in facts and circumstances. For example, if a customer's ability to pay the consideration deteriorates significantly, an entity would reassess whether it is probable that the entity will collect the consideration to which the entity will be entitled in exchange for the remaining goods or services that will be transferred to the customer.

14   If a contract with a customer does not meet the criteria in paragraph 9, an entity shall continue to assess the contract to determine whether the criteria in paragraph 9 are subsequently met.

15   When a contract with a customer does not meet the criteria in paragraph 9 and an entity receives consideration from the customer, the entity shall recognise the consideration received as revenue only when either of the following events has occurred:

(a)   the entity has no remaining obligations to transfer goods or services to the customer and all, or substantially all, of the consideration promised by the customer has been received by the entity and is non-refundable; or

(b)   the contract has been terminated and the consideration received from the customer is non-refundable.

16   An entity shall recognise the consideration received from a customer as a liability until one of the events in paragraph 15 occurs or until the criteria in paragraph 9 are subsequently met (see paragraph 14). Depending on the facts and circumstances relating to the contract, the liability recognised represents the entity's obligation to either transfer goods or services in the future or refund the consideration received. In either case, the liability shall be measured at the amount of consideration received from the customer.

Combination of contracts

17   An entity shall combine two or more contracts entered into at or near the same time with the same customer (or related parties of the customer) and account for the contracts as a single contract if one or more of the following criteria are met:

(a)   the contracts are negotiated as a package with a single commercial objective;

(b)   the amount of consideration to be paid in one contract depends on the price or performance of the other contract; or

(c)   the goods or services promised in the contracts (or some goods or services promised in each of the contracts) are a single performance obligation in accordance with paragraphs 22–30.

Contract modifications

18   A contract modification is a change in the scope or price (or both) of a contract that is approved by the parties to the contract. In some industries and jurisdictions, a contract modification may be described as a change order, a variation or an amendment. A contract modification exists when the parties to a contract approve a modification that either creates new or changes existing enforceable rights and obligations of the parties to the contract. A contract modification could be approved in writing, by oral agreement or implied by customary business practices. If the parties to the contract have

not approved a contract modification, an entity shall continue to apply this Standard to the existing contract until the contract modification is approved.

19   A contract modification may exist even though the parties to the contract have a dispute about the scope or price (or both) of the modification or the parties have approved a change in the scope of the contract but have not yet determined the corresponding change in price. In determining whether the rights and obligations that are created or changed by a modification are enforceable, an entity shall consider all relevant facts and circumstances including the terms of the contract and other evidence. If the parties to a contract have approved a change in the scope of the contract but have not yet determined the corresponding change in price, an entity shall estimate the change to the transaction price arising from the modification in accordance with paragraphs 50–54 on estimating variable consideration and paragraphs 56–58 on constraining estimates of variable consideration.

20   An entity shall account for a contract modification as a separate contract if both of the following conditions are present:

(a)   the scope of the contract increases because of the addition of promised goods or services that are distinct (in accordance with paragraphs 26–30); and

(b)   the price of the contract increases by an amount of consideration that reflects the entity's *stand-alone selling prices* of the additional promised goods or services and any appropriate adjustments to that price to reflect the circumstances of the particular contract. For example, an entity may adjust the stand-alone selling price of an additional good or service for a discount that the customer receives, because it is not necessary for the entity to incur the selling-related costs that it would incur when selling a similar good or service to a new customer.

21   If a contract modification is not accounted for as a separate contract in accordance with paragraph 20, an entity shall account for the promised goods or services not yet transferred at the date of the contract modification (ie the remaining promised goods or services) in whichever of the following ways is applicable:

(a)   An entity shall account for the contract modification as if it were a termination of the existing contract and the creation of a new contract, if the remaining goods or services are distinct from the goods or services transferred on or before the date of the contract modification. The amount of consideration to be allocated to the remaining performance obligations (or to the remaining distinct goods or services in a single performance obligation identified in accordance with paragraph 22(b)) is the sum of:

(i)   the consideration promised by the customer (including amounts already received from the customer) that was included in the estimate of the transaction price and that had not been recognised as revenue; and

(ii) the consideration promised as part of the contract modification.

(b) An entity shall account for the contract modification as if it were a part of the existing contract if the remaining goods or services are not distinct and, therefore, form part of a single performance obligation that is partially satisfied at the date of the contract modification. The effect that the contract modification has on the transaction price, and on the entity's measure of progress towards complete satisfaction of the performance obligation, is recognised as an adjustment to revenue (either as an increase in or a reduction of revenue) at the date of the contract modification (ie the adjustment to revenue is made on a cumulative catch-up basis).

(c) If the remaining goods or services are a combination of items (a) and (b), then the entity shall account for the effects of the modification on the unsatisfied (including partially unsatisfied) performance obligations in the modified contract in a manner that is consistent with the objectives of this paragraph.

Identifying performance obligations

22 At contract inception, an entity shall assess the goods or services promised in a contract with a customer and shall identify as a performance obligation each promise to transfer to the customer either:

(a) a good or service (or a bundle of goods or services) that is distinct; or

(b) a series of distinct goods or services that are substantially the same and that have the same pattern of transfer to the customer (see paragraph 23).

23 A series of distinct goods or services has the same pattern of transfer to the customer if both of the following criteria are met:

(a) each distinct good or service in the series that the entity promises to transfer to the customer would meet the criteria in paragraph 35 to be a performance obligation satisfied over time; and

(b) in accordance with paragraphs 39–40, the same method would be used to measure the entity's progress towards complete satisfaction of the performance obligation to transfer each distinct good or service in the series to the customer.

Promises in contracts with customers

24 A contract with a customer generally explicitly states the goods or services that an entity promises to transfer to a customer. However, the performance obligations identified in a contract with a customer may not be limited to the goods or services that are explicitly stated in that contract. This is because a contract with a customer may also include promises that are implied by an entity's customary business practices, published policies or specific statements if, at the time of entering into the contract, those promises create a valid

expectation of the customer that the entity will transfer a good or service to the customer.

25   Performance obligations do not include activities that an entity must undertake to fulfil a contract unless those activities transfer a good or service to a customer. For example, a services provider may need to perform various administrative tasks to set up a contract. The performance of those tasks does not transfer a service to the customer as the tasks are performed. Therefore, those setup activities are not a performance obligation.

Distinct goods or services

26   Depending on the contract, promised goods or services may include, but are not limited to, the following:

(a)   sale of goods produced by an entity (for example, inventory of a manufacturer);

(b)   resale of goods purchased by an entity (for example, merchandise of a retailer);

(c)   resale of rights to goods or services purchased by an entity (for example, a ticket resold by an entity acting as a principal, as described in paragraphs B34–B38);

(d)   performing a contractually agreed-upon task (or tasks) for a customer;

(e)   providing a service of standing ready to provide goods or services (for example, unspecified updates to software that are provided on a when-and-if-available basis) or of making goods or services available for a customer to use as and when the customer decides;

(f)   providing a service of arranging for another party to transfer goods or services to a customer (for example, acting as an agent of another party, as described in paragraphs B34–B38);

(g)   granting rights to goods or services to be provided in the future that a customer can resell or provide to its customer (for example, an entity selling a product to a retailer promises to transfer an additional good or service to an individual who purchases the product from the retailer);

(h)   constructing, manufacturing or developing an asset on behalf of a customer;

(i)   granting licences (see paragraphs B52–B63B); and

(j)   granting options to purchase additional goods or services (when those options provide a customer with a material right, as described in paragraphs B39–B43).

27   A good or service that is promised to a customer is distinct if both of the following criteria are met:

    (a)   the customer can benefit from the good or service either on its own or together with other resources that are readily available to the customer (ie the good or service is capable of being distinct); and

    (b)   the entity's promise to transfer the good or service to the customer is separately identifiable from other promises in the contract (ie the promise to transfer the good or service is distinct within the context of the contract).

28   A customer can benefit from a good or service in accordance with paragraph 27(a) if the good or service could be used, consumed, sold for an amount that is greater than scrap value or otherwise held in a way that generates economic benefits. For some goods or services, a customer may be able to benefit from a good or service on its own. For other goods or services, a customer may be able to benefit from the good or service only in conjunction with other readily available resources. A readily available resource is a good or service that is sold separately (by the entity or another entity) or a resource that the customer has already obtained from the entity (including goods or services that the entity will have already transferred to the customer under the contract) or from other transactions or events. Various factors may provide evidence that the customer can benefit from a good or service either on its own or in conjunction with other readily available resources. For example, the fact that the entity regularly sells a good or service separately would indicate that a customer can benefit from the good or service on its own or with other readily available resources.

29   In assessing whether an entity's promises to transfer goods or services to the customer are separately identifiable in accordance with paragraph 27(b), the objective is to determine whether the nature of the promise, within the context of the contract, is to transfer each of those goods or services individually or, instead, to transfer a combined item or items to which the promised goods or services are inputs. Factors that indicate that two or more promises to transfer goods or services to a customer are not separately identifiable include, but are not limited to, the following:

    (a)   the entity provides a significant service of integrating the goods or services with other goods or services promised in the contract into a bundle of goods or services that represent the combined output or outputs for which the customer has contracted. In other words, the entity is using the goods or services as inputs to produce or deliver the combined output or outputs specified by the customer. A combined output or outputs might include more than one phase, element or unit.

    (b)   one or more of the goods or services significantly modifies or customises, or are significantly modified or customised by, one or more of the other goods or services promised in the contract.

(c)   the goods or services are highly interdependent or highly interrelated. In other words, each of the goods or services is significantly affected by one or more of the other goods or services in the contract. For example, in some cases, two or more goods or services are significantly affected by each other because the entity would not be able to fulfil its promise by transferring each of the goods or services independently.

30   If a promised good or service is not distinct, an entity shall combine that good or service with other promised goods or services until it identifies a bundle of goods or services that is distinct. In some cases, that would result in the entity accounting for all the goods or services promised in a contract as a single performance obligation.

Satisfaction of performance obligations

31   **An entity shall recognise revenue when (or as) the entity satisfies a performance obligation by transferring a promised good or service (ie an asset) to a customer. An asset is transferred when (or as) the customer obtains control of that asset.**

32   For each performance obligation identified in accordance with paragraphs 22–30, an entity shall determine at contract inception whether it satisfies the performance obligation over time (in accordance with paragraphs 35–37) or satisfies the performance obligation at a point in time (in accordance with paragraph 38). If an entity does not satisfy a performance obligation over time, the performance obligation is satisfied at a point in time.

33   Goods and services are assets, even if only momentarily, when they are received and used (as in the case of many services). Control of an asset refers to the ability to direct the use of, and obtain substantially all of the remaining benefits from, the asset. Control includes the ability to prevent other entities from directing the use of, and obtaining the benefits from, an asset. The benefits of an asset are the potential cash flows (inflows or savings in outflows) that can be obtained directly or indirectly in many ways, such as by:

(a)   using the asset to produce goods or provide services (including public services);

(b)   using the asset to enhance the value of other assets;

(c)   using the asset to settle liabilities or reduce expenses;

(d)   selling or exchanging the asset;

(e)   pledging the asset to secure a loan; and

(f)   holding the asset.

34   When evaluating whether a customer obtains control of an asset, an entity shall consider any agreement to repurchase the asset (see paragraphs B64–B76).

Performance obligations satisfied over time

35   An entity transfers control of a good or service over time and, therefore, satisfies a performance obligation and recognises revenue over time, if one of the following criteria is met:

(a)   the customer simultaneously receives and consumes the benefits provided by the entity's performance as the entity performs (see paragraphs B3–B4);

(b)   the entity's performance creates or enhances an asset (for example, work in progress) that the customer controls as the asset is created or enhanced (see paragraph B5); or

(c)   the entity's performance does not create an asset with an alternative use to the entity (see paragraph 36) and the entity has an enforceable right to payment for performance completed to date (see paragraph 37).

36   An asset created by an entity's performance does not have an alternative use to an entity if the entity is either restricted contractually from readily directing the asset for another use during the creation or enhancement of that asset or limited practically from readily directing the asset in its completed state for another use. The assessment of whether an asset has an alternative use to the entity is made at contract inception. After contract inception, an entity shall not update the assessment of the alternative use of an asset unless the parties to the contract approve a contract modification that substantively changes the performance obligation. Paragraphs B6–B8 provide guidance for assessing whether an asset has an alternative use to an entity.

37   An entity shall consider the terms of the contract, as well as any laws that apply to the contract, when evaluating whether it has an enforceable right to payment for performance completed to date in accordance with paragraph 35(c). The right to payment for performance completed to date does not need to be for a fixed amount. However, at all times throughout the duration of the contract, the entity must be entitled to an amount that at least compensates the entity for performance completed to date if the contract is terminated by the customer or another party for reasons other than the entity's failure to perform as promised. Paragraphs B9–B13 provide guidance for assessing the existence and enforceability of a right to payment and whether an entity's right to payment would entitle the entity to be paid for its performance completed to date.

Performance obligations satisfied at a point in time

38   If a performance obligation is not satisfied over time in accordance with paragraphs 35–37, an entity satisfies the performance obligation at a point in time. To determine the point in time at which a customer obtains control of a promised asset and the entity satisfies a performance obligation, the entity shall consider the requirements for control in paragraphs 31–34. In addition, an entity shall consider indicators of the transfer of control, which include, but are not limited to, the following:

(a)   The entity has a present right to payment for the asset—if a customer is presently obliged to pay for an asset, then that may indicate that the customer has obtained the ability to direct the use of, and obtain substantially all of the remaining benefits from, the asset in exchange.

(b)   The customer has legal title to the asset—legal title may indicate which party to a contract has the ability to direct the use of, and obtain substantially all of the remaining benefits from, an asset or to restrict the access of other entities to those benefits. Therefore, the transfer of legal title of an asset may indicate that the customer has obtained control of the asset. If an entity retains legal title solely as protection against the customer's failure to pay, those rights of the entity would not preclude the customer from obtaining control of an asset.

(c)   The entity has transferred physical possession of the asset—the customer's physical possession of an asset may indicate that the customer has the ability to direct the use of, and obtain substantially all of the remaining benefits from, the asset or to restrict the access of other entities to those benefits. However, physical possession may not coincide with control of an asset. For example, in some repurchase agreements and in some consignment arrangements, a customer or consignee may have physical possession of an asset that the entity controls. Conversely, in some bill-and-hold arrangements, the entity may have physical possession of an asset that the customer controls. Paragraphs B64–B76, B77–B78 and B79–B82 provide guidance on accounting for repurchase agreements, consignment arrangements and bill-and-hold arrangements, respectively.

(d)   The customer has the significant risks and rewards of ownership of the asset—the transfer of the significant risks and rewards of ownership of an asset to the customer may indicate that the customer has obtained the ability to direct the use of, and obtain substantially all of the remaining benefits from, the asset. However, when evaluating the risks and rewards of ownership of a promised asset, an entity shall exclude any risks that give rise to a separate performance obligation in addition to the performance obligation to transfer the asset. For example, an entity may have transferred control of an asset to a customer but not yet satisfied an additional performance obligation to provide maintenance services related to the transferred asset.

(e)   The customer has accepted the asset—the customer's acceptance of an asset may indicate that it has obtained the ability to direct the use of, and obtain substantially all of the remaining benefits from, the asset. To evaluate the effect of a contractual customer acceptance clause on when control of an asset is transferred, an entity shall consider the guidance in paragraphs B83–B86.

Measuring progress towards complete satisfaction of a performance obligation

39 For each performance obligation satisfied over time in accordance with paragraphs 35–37, an entity shall recognise revenue over time by measuring the progress towards complete satisfaction of that performance obligation. The objective when measuring progress is to depict an entity's performance in transferring control of goods or services promised to a customer (ie the satisfaction of an entity's performance obligation).

40 An entity shall apply a single method of measuring progress for each performance obligation satisfied over time and the entity shall apply that method consistently to similar performance obligations and in similar circumstances. At the end of each reporting period, an entity shall remeasure its progress towards complete satisfaction of a performance obligation satisfied over time.

Methods for measuring progress

41 Appropriate methods of measuring progress include output methods and input methods. Paragraphs B14–B19 provide guidance for using output methods and input methods to measure an entity's progress towards complete satisfaction of a performance obligation. In determining the appropriate method for measuring progress, an entity shall consider the nature of the good or service that the entity promised to transfer to the customer.

42 When applying a method for measuring progress, an entity shall exclude from the measure of progress any goods or services for which the entity does not transfer control to a customer. Conversely, an entity shall include in the measure of progress any goods or services for which the entity does transfer control to a customer when satisfying that performance obligation.

43 As circumstances change over time, an entity shall update its measure of progress to reflect any changes in the outcome of the performance obligation. Such changes to an entity's measure of progress shall be accounted for as a change in accounting estimate in accordance with IAS 8 *Accounting Policies, Changes in Accounting Estimates and Errors.*

Reasonable measures of progress

44 An entity shall recognise revenue for a performance obligation satisfied over time only if the entity can reasonably measure its progress towards complete satisfaction of the performance obligation. An entity would not be able to reasonably measure its progress towards complete satisfaction of a performance obligation if it lacks reliable information that would be required to apply an appropriate method of measuring progress.

45 In some circumstances (for example, in the early stages of a contract), an entity may not be able to reasonably measure the outcome of a performance obligation, but the entity expects to recover the costs incurred in satisfying the performance obligation. In those circumstances, the entity shall recognise revenue only to the extent of the costs incurred until such time that it can reasonably measure the outcome of the performance obligation.

circumstances. To account for a refund liability relating to a sale with a right of return, an entity shall apply the guidance in paragraphs B20–B27.

Constraining estimates of variable consideration

56   An entity shall include in the transaction price some or all of an amount of variable consideration estimated in accordance with paragraph 53 only to the extent that it is highly probable that a significant reversal in the amount of cumulative revenue recognised will not occur when the uncertainty associated with the variable consideration is subsequently resolved.

57   In assessing whether it is highly probable that a significant reversal in the amount of cumulative revenue recognised will not occur once the uncertainty related to the variable consideration is subsequently resolved, an entity shall consider both the likelihood and the magnitude of the revenue reversal. Factors that could increase the likelihood or the magnitude of a revenue reversal include, but are not limited to, any of the following:

   (a)   the amount of consideration is highly susceptible to factors outside the entity's influence. Those factors may include volatility in a market, the judgement or actions of third parties, weather conditions and a high risk of obsolescence of the promised good or service.

   (b)   the uncertainty about the amount of consideration is not expected to be resolved for a long period of time.

   (c)   the entity's experience (or other evidence) with similar types of contracts is limited, or that experience (or other evidence) has limited predictive value.

   (d)   the entity has a practice of either offering a broad range of price concessions or changing the payment terms and conditions of similar contracts in similar circumstances.

   (e)   the contract has a large number and broad range of possible consideration amounts.

58   An entity shall apply paragraph B63 to account for consideration in the form of a sales-based or usage-based royalty that is promised in exchange for a licence of intellectual property.

Reassessment of variable consideration

59   At the end of each reporting period, an entity shall update the estimated transaction price (including updating its assessment of whether an estimate of variable consideration is constrained) to represent faithfully the circumstances present at the end of the reporting period and the changes in circumstances during the reporting period. The entity shall account for changes in the transaction price in accordance with paragraphs 87–90.

The existence of a significant financing component in the contract

60   In determining the transaction price, an entity shall adjust the promised amount of consideration for the effects of the time value of money if the timing of payments agreed to by the parties to the contract (either explicitly or implicitly) provides the customer or the entity with a significant benefit of financing the transfer of goods or services to the customer. In those circumstances, the contract contains a significant financing component. A significant financing component may exist regardless of whether the promise of financing is explicitly stated in the contract or implied by the payment terms agreed to by the parties to the contract.

61   The objective when adjusting the promised amount of consideration for a significant financing component is for an entity to recognise revenue at an amount that reflects the price that a customer would have paid for the promised goods or services if the customer had paid cash for those goods or services when (or as) they transfer to the customer (ie the cash selling price). An entity shall consider all relevant facts and circumstances in assessing whether a contract contains a financing component and whether that financing component is significant to the contract, including both of the following:

(a)   the difference, if any, between the amount of promised consideration and the cash selling price of the promised goods or services; and

(b)   the combined effect of both of the following:

(i)   the expected length of time between when the entity transfers the promised goods or services to the customer and when the customer pays for those goods or services; and

(ii)   the prevailing interest rates in the relevant market.

62   Notwithstanding the assessment in paragraph 61, a contract with a customer would not have a significant financing component if any of the following factors exist:

(a)   the customer paid for the goods or services in advance and the timing of the transfer of those goods or services is at the discretion of the customer.

(b)   a substantial amount of the consideration promised by the customer is variable and the amount or timing of that consideration varies on the basis of the occurrence or non-occurrence of a future event that is not substantially within the control of the customer or the entity (for example, if the consideration is a sales-based royalty).

(c)   the difference between the promised consideration and the cash selling price of the good or service (as described in paragraph 61) arises for reasons other than the provision of finance to either the customer or the entity, and the difference between those amounts is proportional to the reason for the difference. For example, the payment terms might provide the entity or the customer with protection from the other party failing to adequately complete some or all of its obligations under the contract.

63   As a practical expedient, an entity need not adjust the promised amount of consideration for the effects of a significant financing component if the entity expects, at contract inception, that the period between when the entity transfers a promised good or service to a customer and when the customer pays for that good or service will be one year or less.

64   To meet the objective in paragraph 61 when adjusting the promised amount of consideration for a significant financing component, an entity shall use the discount rate that would be reflected in a separate financing transaction between the entity and its customer at contract inception. That rate would reflect the credit characteristics of the party receiving financing in the contract, as well as any collateral or security provided by the customer or the entity, including assets transferred in the contract. An entity may be able to determine that rate by identifying the rate that discounts the nominal amount of the promised consideration to the price that the customer would pay in cash for the goods or services when (or as) they transfer to the customer. After contract inception, an entity shall not update the discount rate for changes in interest rates or other circumstances (such as a change in the assessment of the customer's credit risk).

65   An entity shall present the effects of financing (interest revenue or interest expense) separately from revenue from contracts with customers in the statement of comprehensive income. Interest revenue or interest expense is recognised only to the extent that a *contract asset* (or receivable) or a contract liability is recognised in accounting for a contract with a customer.

Non-cash consideration

66   To determine the transaction price for contracts in which a customer promises consideration in a form other than cash, an entity shall measure the non-cash consideration (or promise of non-cash consideration) at fair value.

67   If an entity cannot reasonably estimate the fair value of the non-cash consideration, the entity shall measure the consideration indirectly by reference to the stand-alone selling price of the goods or services promised to the customer (or class of customer) in exchange for the consideration.

68   The fair value of the non-cash consideration may vary because of the form of the consideration (for example, a change in the price of a share to which an entity is entitled to receive from a customer). If the fair value of the non-cash consideration promised by a customer varies for reasons other than only the form of the consideration (for example, the fair value could vary because of the entity's performance), an entity shall apply the requirements in paragraphs 56–58.

69   If a customer contributes goods or services (for example, materials, equipment or labour) to facilitate an entity's fulfilment of the contract, the entity shall assess whether it obtains control of those contributed goods or services. If so, the entity shall account for the contributed goods or services as non-cash consideration received from the customer.

Consideration payable to a customer

70   Consideration payable to a customer includes cash amounts that an entity pays, or expects to pay, to the customer (or to other parties that purchase the entity's goods or services from the customer). Consideration payable to a customer also includes credit or other items (for example, a coupon or voucher) that can be applied against amounts owed to the entity (or to other parties that purchase the entity's goods or services from the customer). An entity shall account for consideration payable to a customer as a reduction of the transaction price and, therefore, of revenue unless the payment to the customer is in exchange for a distinct good or service (as described in paragraphs 26–30) that the customer transfers to the entity. If the consideration payable to a customer includes a variable amount, an entity shall estimate the transaction price (including assessing whether the estimate of variable consideration is constrained) in accordance with paragraphs 50–58.

71   If consideration payable to a customer is a payment for a distinct good or service from the customer, then an entity shall account for the purchase of the good or service in the same way that it accounts for other purchases from suppliers. If the amount of consideration payable to the customer exceeds the fair value of the distinct good or service that the entity receives from the customer, then the entity shall account for such an excess as a reduction of the transaction price. If the entity cannot reasonably estimate the fair value of the good or service received from the customer, it shall account for all of the consideration payable to the customer as a reduction of the transaction price.

72   Accordingly, if consideration payable to a customer is accounted for as a reduction of the transaction price, an entity shall recognise the reduction of revenue when (or as) the later of either of the following events occurs:

(a)   the entity recognises revenue for the transfer of the related goods or services to the customer; and

(b)   the entity pays or promises to pay the consideration (even if the payment is conditional on a future event). That promise might be implied by the entity's customary business practices.

Allocating the transaction price to performance obligations

73   The objective when allocating the transaction price is for an entity to allocate the transaction price to each performance obligation (or distinct good or service) in an amount that depicts the amount of consideration to which the entity expects to be entitled in exchange for transferring the promised goods or services to the customer.

74   To meet the allocation objective, an entity shall allocate the transaction price to each performance obligation identified in the contract on a relative stand-alone selling price basis in accordance with paragraphs 76–80, except as specified in paragraphs 81–83 (for allocating discounts) and paragraphs 84–86 (for allocating consideration that includes variable amounts).

75   Paragraphs 76–86 do not apply if a contract has only one performance obligation. However, paragraphs 84–86 may apply if an entity promises to transfer a series of distinct goods or services identified as a single performance obligation in accordance with paragraph 22(b) and the promised consideration includes variable amounts.

Allocation based on stand-alone selling prices

76   To allocate the transaction price to each performance obligation on a relative stand-alone selling price basis, an entity shall determine the stand-alone selling price at contract inception of the distinct good or service underlying each performance obligation in the contract and allocate the transaction price in proportion to those stand-alone selling prices.

77   The stand-alone selling price is the price at which an entity would sell a promised good or service separately to a customer. The best evidence of a stand-alone selling price is the observable price of a good or service when the entity sells that good or service separately in similar circumstances and to similar customers. A contractually stated price or a list price for a good or service may be (but shall not be presumed to be) the stand-alone selling price of that good or service.

78   If a stand-alone selling price is not directly observable, an entity shall estimate the stand-alone selling price at an amount that would result in the allocation of the transaction price meeting the allocation objective in paragraph 73. When estimating a stand-alone selling price, an entity shall consider all information (including market conditions, entity-specific factors and information about the customer or class of customer) that is reasonably available to the entity. In doing so, an entity shall maximise the use of observable inputs and apply estimation methods consistently in similar circumstances.

79   Suitable methods for estimating the stand-alone selling price of a good or service include, but are not limited to, the following:

(a)   Adjusted market assessment approach—an entity could evaluate the market in which it sells goods or services and estimate the price that a customer in that market would be willing to pay for those goods or services. That approach might also include referring to prices from the entity's competitors for similar goods or services and adjusting those prices as necessary to reflect the entity's costs and margins.

(b)   Expected cost plus a margin approach—an entity could forecast its expected costs of satisfying a performance obligation and then add an appropriate margin for that good or service.

(c)   Residual approach—an entity may estimate the stand-alone selling price by reference to the total transaction price less the sum of the observable stand-alone selling prices of other goods or services promised in the contract. However, an entity may use a residual approach to estimate, in accordance with paragraph 78, the stand-alone selling price of a good or service only if one of the following criteria is met:

(i)   the entity sells the same good or service to different customers (at or near the same time) for a broad range of amounts (ie the selling price is highly variable because a representative stand-alone selling price is not discernible from past transactions or other observable evidence); or

(ii)   the entity has not yet established a price for that good or service and the good or service has not previously been sold on a stand-alone basis (ie the selling price is uncertain).

80   A combination of methods may need to be used to estimate the stand-alone selling prices of the goods or services promised in the contract if two or more of those goods or services have highly variable or uncertain stand-alone selling prices. For example, an entity may use a residual approach to estimate the aggregate stand-alone selling price for those promised goods or services with highly variable or uncertain stand-alone selling prices and then use another method to estimate the stand-alone selling prices of the individual goods or services relative to that estimated aggregate stand-alone selling price determined by the residual approach. When an entity uses a combination of methods to estimate the stand-alone selling price of each promised good or service in the contract, the entity shall evaluate whether allocating the transaction price at those estimated stand-alone selling prices would be consistent with the allocation objective in paragraph 73 and the requirements for estimating stand-alone selling prices in paragraph 78.

Allocation of a discount

81   A customer receives a discount for purchasing a bundle of goods or services if the sum of the stand-alone selling prices of those promised goods or services in the contract exceeds the promised consideration in a contract. Except when an entity has observable evidence in accordance with paragraph 82 that the entire discount relates to only one or more, but not all, performance obligations in a contract, the entity shall allocate a discount proportionately to all performance obligations in the contract. The proportionate allocation of the discount in those circumstances is a consequence of the entity allocating the transaction price to each performance obligation on the basis of the relative stand-alone selling prices of the underlying distinct goods or services.

82   An entity shall allocate a discount entirely to one or more, but not all, performance obligations in the contract if all of the following criteria are met:

(a)   the entity regularly sells each distinct good or service (or each bundle of distinct goods or services) in the contract on a stand-alone basis;

(b)   the entity also regularly sells on a stand-alone basis a bundle (or bundles) of some of those distinct goods or services at a discount to the stand-alone selling prices of the goods or services in each bundle; and

(c)   the discount attributable to each bundle of goods or services described in paragraph 82(b) is substantially the same as the discount in the contract and an analysis of the goods or services in each bundle provides observable evidence of the performance obligation (or performance obligations) to which the entire discount in the contract belongs.

83   If a discount is allocated entirely to one or more performance obligations in the contract in accordance with paragraph 82, an entity shall allocate the discount before using the residual approach to estimate the stand-alone selling price of a good or service in accordance with paragraph 79(c).

Allocation of variable consideration

84   Variable consideration that is promised in a contract may be attributable to the entire contract or to a specific part of the contract, such as either of the following:

(a)   one or more, but not all, performance obligations in the contract (for example, a bonus may be contingent on an entity transferring a promised good or service within a specified period of time); or

(b)   one or more, but not all, distinct goods or services promised in a series of distinct goods or services that forms part of a single performance obligation in accordance with paragraph 22(b) (for example, the consideration promised for the second year of a two-year cleaning service contract will increase on the basis of movements in a specified inflation index).

85   An entity shall allocate a variable amount (and subsequent changes to that amount) entirely to a performance obligation or to a distinct good or service that forms part of a single performance obligation in accordance with paragraph 22(b) if both of the following criteria are met:

(a)   the terms of a variable payment relate specifically to the entity's efforts to satisfy the performance obligation or transfer the distinct good or service (or to a specific outcome from satisfying the performance obligation or transferring the distinct good or service); and

(b)   allocating the variable amount of consideration entirely to the performance obligation or the distinct good or service is consistent with the allocation objective in paragraph 73 when considering all of the performance obligations and payment terms in the contract.

86   The allocation requirements in paragraphs 73–83 shall be applied to allocate the remaining amount of the transaction price that does not meet the criteria in paragraph 85.

Changes in the transaction price

87   After contract inception, the transaction price can change for various reasons, including the resolution of uncertain events or other changes in circumstances that change the amount of consideration to which an entity expects to be entitled in exchange for the promised goods or services.

88 An entity shall allocate to the performance obligations in the contract any subsequent changes in the transaction price on the same basis as at contract inception. Consequently, an entity shall not reallocate the transaction price to reflect changes in stand-alone selling prices after contract inception. Amounts allocated to a satisfied performance obligation shall be recognised as revenue, or as a reduction of revenue, in the period in which the transaction price changes.

89 An entity shall allocate a change in the transaction price entirely to one or more, but not all, performance obligations or distinct goods or services promised in a series that forms part of a single performance obligation in accordance with paragraph 22(b) only if the criteria in paragraph 85 on allocating variable consideration are met.

90 An entity shall account for a change in the transaction price that arises as a result of a contract modification in accordance with paragraphs 18–21. However, for a change in the transaction price that occurs after a contract modification, an entity shall apply paragraphs 87–89 to allocate the change in the transaction price in whichever of the following ways is applicable:

(a) An entity shall allocate the change in the transaction price to the performance obligations identified in the contract before the modification if, and to the extent that, the change in the transaction price is attributable to an amount of variable consideration promised before the modification and the modification is accounted for in accordance with paragraph 21(a).

(b) In all other cases in which the modification was not accounted for as a separate contract in accordance with paragraph 20, an entity shall allocate the change in the transaction price to the performance obligations in the modified contract (ie the performance obligations that were unsatisfied or partially unsatisfied immediately after the modification).

Contract costs

Incremental costs of obtaining a contract

91 An entity shall recognise as an asset the incremental costs of obtaining a contract with a customer if the entity expects to recover those costs.

92 The incremental costs of obtaining a contract are those costs that an entity incurs to obtain a contract with a customer that it would not have incurred if the contract had not been obtained (for example, a sales commission).

93 Costs to obtain a contract that would have been incurred regardless of whether the contract was obtained shall be recognised as an expense when incurred, unless those costs are explicitly chargeable to the customer regardless of whether the contract is obtained.

94   As a practical expedient, an entity may recognise the incremental costs of obtaining a contract as an expense when incurred if the amortisation period of the asset that the entity otherwise would have recognised is one year or less.

Costs to fulfil a contract

95   If the costs incurred in fulfilling a contract with a customer are not within the scope of another Standard (for example, IAS 2 *Inventories*, IAS 16 *Property, Plant and Equipment* or IAS 38 *Intangible Assets*), an entity shall recognise an asset from the costs incurred to fulfil a contract only if those costs meet all of the following criteria:

(a)   the costs relate directly to a contract or to an anticipated contract that the entity can specifically identify (for example, costs relating to services to be provided under renewal of an existing contract or costs of designing an asset to be transferred under a specific contract that has not yet been approved);

(b)   the costs generate or enhance resources of the entity that will be used in satisfying (or in continuing to satisfy) performance obligations in the future; and

(c)   the costs are expected to be recovered.

96   For costs incurred in fulfilling a contract with a customer that are within the scope of another Standard, an entity shall account for those costs in accordance with those other Standards.

97   Costs that relate directly to a contract (or a specific anticipated contract) include any of the following:

(a)   direct labour (for example, salaries and wages of employees who provide the promised services directly to the customer);

(b)   direct materials (for example, supplies used in providing the promised services to a customer);

(c)   allocations of costs that relate directly to the contract or to contract activities (for example, costs of contract management and supervision, insurance and depreciation of tools, equipment and right-of-use assets used in fulfilling the contract);

(d)   costs that are explicitly chargeable to the customer under the contract; and

(e)   other costs that are incurred only because an entity entered into the contract (for example, payments to subcontractors).

98   An entity shall recognise the following costs as expenses when incurred:

(a)   general and administrative costs (unless those costs are explicitly chargeable to the customer under the contract, in which case an entity shall evaluate those costs in accordance with paragraph 97);

(b)   costs of wasted materials, labour or other resources to fulfil the contract that were not reflected in the price of the contract;

(c)   costs that relate to satisfied performance obligations (or partially satisfied performance obligations) in the contract (ie costs that relate to past performance); and

(d)   costs for which an entity cannot distinguish whether the costs relate to unsatisfied performance obligations or to satisfied performance obligations (or partially satisfied performance obligations).

Amortisation and impairment

99   An asset recognised in accordance with paragraph 91 or 95 shall be amortised on a systematic basis that is consistent with the transfer to the customer of the goods or services to which the asset relates. The asset may relate to goods or services to be transferred under a specific anticipated contract (as described in paragraph 95(a)).

100   An entity shall update the amortisation to reflect a significant change in the entity's expected timing of transfer to the customer of the goods or services to which the asset relates. Such a change shall be accounted for as a change in accounting estimate in accordance with IAS 8.

101   An entity shall recognise an impairment loss in profit or loss to the extent that the carrying amount of an asset recognised in accordance with paragraph 91 or 95 exceeds:

(a)   the remaining amount of consideration that the entity expects to receive in exchange for the goods or services to which the asset relates; less

(b)   the costs that relate directly to providing those goods or services and that have not been recognised as expenses (see paragraph 97).

102   For the purposes of applying paragraph 101 to determine the amount of consideration that an entity expects to receive, an entity shall use the principles for determining the transaction price (except for the requirements in paragraphs 56–58 on constraining estimates of variable consideration) and adjust that amount to reflect the effects of the customer's credit risk.

103   Before an entity recognises an impairment loss for an asset recognised in accordance with paragraph 91 or 95, the entity shall recognise any impairment loss for assets related to the contract that are recognised in accordance with another Standard (for example, IAS 2, IAS 16 and IAS 38). After applying the impairment test in paragraph 101, an entity shall include the resulting carrying amount of the asset recognised in accordance with paragraph 91 or 95 in the carrying amount of the cash-generating unit to which it belongs for the purpose of applying IAS 36 *Impairment of Assets* to that cash-generating unit.

104   An entity shall recognise in profit or loss a reversal of some or all of an impairment loss previously recognised in accordance with paragraph 101 when the impairment conditions no longer exist or have improved. The increased carrying amount of the asset shall not exceed the amount that would have been determined (net of amortisation) if no impairment loss had been recognised previously.

Presentation

105   When either party to a contract has performed, an entity shall present the contract in the statement of financial position as a contract asset or a contract liability, depending on the relationship between the entity's performance and the customer's payment. An entity shall present any unconditional rights to consideration separately as a receivable.

106   If a customer pays consideration, or an entity has a right to an amount of consideration that is unconditional (ie a receivable), before the entity transfers a good or service to the customer, the entity shall present the contract as a contract liability when the payment is made or the payment is due (whichever is earlier). A contract liability is an entity's obligation to transfer goods or services to a customer for which the entity has received consideration (or an amount of consideration is due) from the customer.

107   If an entity performs by transferring goods or services to a customer before the customer pays consideration or before payment is due, the entity shall present the contract as a contract asset, excluding any amounts presented as a receivable. A contract asset is an entity's right to consideration in exchange for goods or services that the entity has transferred to a customer. An entity shall assess a contract asset for impairment in accordance with IFRS 9. An impairment of a contract asset shall be measured, presented and disclosed on the same basis as a financial asset that is within the scope of IFRS 9 (see also paragraph 113(b)).

108   A receivable is an entity's right to consideration that is unconditional. A right to consideration is unconditional if only the passage of time is required before payment of that consideration is due. For example, an entity would recognise a receivable if it has a present right to payment even though that amount may be subject to refund in the future. An entity shall account for a receivable in accordance with IFRS 9. Upon initial recognition of a receivable from a contract with a customer, any difference between the measurement of the receivable in accordance with IFRS 9 and the corresponding amount of revenue recognised shall be presented as an expense (for example, as an impairment loss).

109   This Standard uses the terms 'contract asset' and 'contract liability' but does not prohibit an entity from using alternative descriptions in the statement of financial position for those items. If an entity uses an alternative description for a contract asset, the entity shall provide sufficient information for a user of the financial statements to distinguish between receivables and contract assets.

Disclosure

110   The objective of the disclosure requirements is for an entity to disclose sufficient information to enable users of financial statements to understand the nature, amount, timing and uncertainty of revenue and cash flows arising from contracts with customers. To achieve that objective, an entity shall disclose qualitative and quantitative information about all of the following:

   (a)   its contracts with customers (see paragraphs 113–122);

   (b)   the significant judgements, and changes in the judgements, made in applying this Standard to those contracts (see paragraphs 123–126); and

   (c)   any assets recognised from the costs to obtain or fulfil a contract with a customer in accordance with paragraph 91 or 95 (see paragraphs 127–128).

111   An entity shall consider the level of detail necessary to satisfy the disclosure objective and how much emphasis to place on each of the various requirements. An entity shall aggregate or disaggregate disclosures so that useful information is not obscured by either the inclusion of a large amount of insignificant detail or the aggregation of items that have substantially different characteristics.

112   An entity need not disclose information in accordance with this Standard if it has provided the information in accordance with another Standard.

Contracts with customers

113   An entity shall disclose all of the following amounts for the reporting period unless those amounts are presented separately in the statement of comprehensive income in accordance with other Standards:

   (a)   revenue recognised from contracts with customers, which the entity shall disclose separately from its other sources of revenue; and

   (b)   any impairment losses recognised (in accordance with IFRS 9) on any receivables or contract assets arising from an entity's contracts with customers, which the entity shall disclose separately from impairment losses from other contracts.

Disaggregation of revenue

114   An entity shall disaggregate revenue recognised from contracts with customers into categories that depict how the nature, amount, timing and uncertainty of revenue and cash flows are affected by economic factors. An entity shall apply the guidance in paragraphs B87–B89 when selecting the categories to use to disaggregate revenue.

115   In addition, an entity shall disclose sufficient information to enable users of financial statements to understand the relationship between the disclosure of disaggregated revenue (in accordance with paragraph 114) and revenue information that is disclosed for each reportable segment, if the entity applies IFRS 8 *Operating Segments*.

Contract balances

116   An entity shall disclose all of the following:

(a)   the opening and closing balances of receivables, contract assets and contract liabilities from contracts with customers, if not otherwise separately presented or disclosed;

(b)   revenue recognised in the reporting period that was included in the contract liability balance at the beginning of the period; and

(c)   revenue recognised in the reporting period from performance obligations satisfied (or partially satisfied) in previous periods (for example, changes in transaction price).

117   An entity shall explain how the timing of satisfaction of its performance obligations (see paragraph 119(a)) relates to the typical timing of payment (see paragraph 119(b)) and the effect that those factors have on the contract asset and the contract liability balances. The explanation provided may use qualitative information.

118   An entity shall provide an explanation of the significant changes in the contract asset and the contract liability balances during the reporting period. The explanation shall include qualitative and quantitative information. Examples of changes in the entity's balances of contract assets and contract liabilities include any of the following:

(a)   changes due to business combinations;

(b)   cumulative catch-up adjustments to revenue that affect the corresponding contract asset or contract liability, including adjustments arising from a change in the measure of progress, a change in an estimate of the transaction price (including any changes in the assessment of whether an estimate of variable consideration is constrained) or a contract modification;

(c)   impairment of a contract asset;

(d)   a change in the time frame for a right to consideration to become unconditional (ie for a contract asset to be reclassified to a receivable); and

(e)   a change in the time frame for a performance obligation to be satisfied (ie for the recognition of revenue arising from a contract liability).

Performance obligations

119 An entity shall disclose information about its performance obligations in contracts with customers, including a description of all of the following:

(a) when the entity typically satisfies its performance obligations (for example, upon shipment, upon delivery, as services are rendered or upon completion of service), including when performance obligations are satisfied in a bill-and-hold arrangement;

(b) the significant payment terms (for example, when payment is typically due, whether the contract has a significant financing component, whether the consideration amount is variable and whether the estimate of variable consideration is typically constrained in accordance with paragraphs 56–58);

(c) the nature of the goods or services that the entity has promised to transfer, highlighting any performance obligations to arrange for another party to transfer goods or services (ie if the entity is acting as an agent);

(d) obligations for returns, refunds and other similar obligations; and

(e) types of warranties and related obligations.

Transaction price allocated to the remaining performance obligations

120 An entity shall disclose the following information about its remaining performance obligations:

(a) the aggregate amount of the transaction price allocated to the performance obligations that are unsatisfied (or partially unsatisfied) as of the end of the reporting period; and

(b) an explanation of when the entity expects to recognise as revenue the amount disclosed in accordance with paragraph 120(a), which the entity shall disclose in either of the following ways:

(i) on a quantitative basis using the time bands that would be most appropriate for the duration of the remaining performance obligations; or

(ii) by using qualitative information.

121 As a practical expedient, an entity need not disclose the information in paragraph 120 for a performance obligation if either of the following conditions is met:

(a) the performance obligation is part of a contract that has an original expected duration of one year or less; or

(b) the entity recognises revenue from the satisfaction of the performance obligation in accordance with paragraph B16.

122   An entity shall explain qualitatively whether it is applying the practical expedient in paragraph 121 and whether any consideration from contracts with customers is not included in the transaction price and, therefore, not included in the information disclosed in accordance with paragraph 120. For example, an estimate of the transaction price would not include any estimated amounts of variable consideration that are constrained (see paragraphs 56–58).

Significant judgements in the application of this Standard

123   An entity shall disclose the judgements, and changes in the judgements, made in applying this Standard that significantly affect the determination of the amount and timing of revenue from contracts with customers. In particular, an entity shall explain the judgements, and changes in the judgements, used in determining both of the following:

(a)   the timing of satisfaction of performance obligations (see paragraphs 124–125); and

(b)   the transaction price and the amounts allocated to performance obligations (see paragraph 126).

Determining the timing of satisfaction of performance obligations

124   For performance obligations that an entity satisfies over time, an entity shall disclose both of the following:

(a)   the methods used to recognise revenue (for example, a description of the output methods or input methods used and how those methods are applied); and

(b)   an explanation of why the methods used provide a faithful depiction of the transfer of goods or services.

125   For performance obligations satisfied at a point in time, an entity shall disclose the significant judgements made in evaluating when a customer obtains control of promised goods or services.

Determining the transaction price and the amounts allocated to performance obligations

126   An entity shall disclose information about the methods, inputs and assumptions used for all of the following:

(a)   determining the transaction price, which includes, but is not limited to, estimating variable consideration, adjusting the consideration for the effects of the time value of money and measuring non-cash consideration;

(b)   assessing whether an estimate of variable consideration is constrained;

(c)   allocating the transaction price, including estimating stand-alone selling prices of promised goods or services and allocating discounts and variable consideration to a specific part of the contract (if applicable); and

(d) measuring obligations for returns, refunds and other similar obligations.

Assets recognised from the costs to obtain or fulfil a contract with a customer

127 An entity shall describe both of the following:

(a) the judgements made in determining the amount of the costs incurred to obtain or fulfil a contract with a customer (in accordance with paragraph 91 or 95); and

(b) the method it uses to determine the amortisation for each reporting period.

128 An entity shall disclose all of the following:

(a) the closing balances of assets recognised from the costs incurred to obtain or fulfil a contract with a customer (in accordance with paragraph 91 or 95), by main category of asset (for example, costs to obtain contracts with customers, pre-contract costs and setup costs); and

(b) the amount of amortisation and any impairment losses recognised in the reporting period.

Practical expedients

129 If an entity elects to use the practical expedient in either paragraph 63 (about the existence of a significant financing component) or paragraph 94 (about the incremental costs of obtaining a contract), the entity shall disclose that fact.

Appendix A
Defined terms

This appendix is an integral part of the Standard.

contract	An agreement between two or more parties that creates enforceable rights and obligations.
contract asset	An entity's right to consideration in exchange for goods or services that the entity has transferred to a **customer** when that right is conditioned on something other than the passage of time (for example, the entity's future performance).
contract liability	An entity's obligation to transfer goods or services to a **customer** for which the entity has received consideration (or the amount is due) from the customer.
customer	A party that has contracted with an entity to obtain goods or services that are an output of the entity's ordinary activities in exchange for consideration.
income	Increases in economic benefits during the accounting period in the form of inflows or enhancements of assets or decreases of liabilities that result in an increase in equity, other than those relating to contributions from equity participants.
performance obligation	A promise in a **contract** with a **customer** to transfer to the customer either:
	(a) a good or service (or a bundle of goods or services) that is distinct; or
	(b) a series of distinct goods or services that are substantially the same and that have the same pattern of transfer to the customer.
revenue	**Income** arising in the course of an entity's ordinary activities.
stand-alone selling price (of a good or service)	The price at which an entity would sell a promised good or service separately to a **customer**.
transaction price (for a contract with a customer)	The amount of consideration to which an entity expects to be entitled in exchange for transferring promised goods or services to a **customer**, excluding amounts collected on behalf of third parties.

Appendix B
Application Guidance

This appendix is an integral part of the Standard. It describes the application of paragraphs 1–129 and has the same authority as the other parts of the Standard.

B1   This application guidance is organised into the following categories:

(a)   performance obligations satisfied over time (paragraphs B2–B13);

(b)   methods for measuring progress towards complete satisfaction of a performance obligation (paragraphs B14–B19);

(c)   sale with a right of return (paragraphs B20–B27);

(d)   warranties (paragraphs B28–B33);

(e)   principal versus agent considerations (paragraphs B34–B38);

(f)   customer options for additional goods or services (paragraphs B39–B43);

(g)   customers' unexercised rights (paragraphs B44–B47);

(h)   non-refundable upfront fees (and some related costs) (paragraphs B48–B51);

(i)   licensing (paragraphs B52–B63B);

(j)   repurchase agreements (paragraphs B64–B76);

(k)   consignment arrangements (paragraphs B77–B78);

(l)   bill-and-hold arrangements (paragraphs B79–B82);

(m)   customer acceptance (paragraphs B83–B86); and

(n)   disclosure of disaggregated revenue (paragraphs B87–B89).

Performance obligations satisfied over time

B2   In accordance with paragraph 35, a performance obligation is satisfied over time if one of the following criteria is met:

(a)   the customer simultaneously receives and consumes the benefits provided by the entity's performance as the entity performs (see paragraphs B3–B4);

(b)   the entity's performance creates or enhances an asset (for example, work in progress) that the customer controls as the asset is created or enhanced (see paragraph B5); or

(c)   the entity's performance does not create an asset with an alternative use to the entity (see paragraphs B6–B8) and the entity has an enforceable right to payment for performance completed to date (see paragraphs B9–B13).

Simultaneous receipt and consumption of the benefits of the entity's performance (paragraph 35(a))

B3   For some types of performance obligations, the assessment of whether a customer receives the benefits of an entity's performance as the entity performs and simultaneously consumes those benefits as they are received will be straightforward. Examples include routine or recurring services (such as a cleaning service) in which the receipt and simultaneous consumption by the customer of the benefits of the entity's performance can be readily identified.

B4   For other types of performance obligations, an entity may not be able to readily identify whether a customer simultaneously receives and consumes the benefits from the entity's performance as the entity performs. In those circumstances, a performance obligation is satisfied over time if an entity determines that another entity would not need to substantially re-perform the work that the entity has completed to date if that other entity were to fulfil the remaining performance obligation to the customer. In determining whether another entity would not need to substantially re-perform the work the entity has completed to date, an entity shall make both of the following assumptions:

    (a)   disregard potential contractual restrictions or practical limitations that otherwise would prevent the entity from transferring the remaining performance obligation to another entity; and

    (b)   presume that another entity fulfilling the remainder of the performance obligation would not have the benefit of any asset that is presently controlled by the entity and that would remain controlled by the entity if the performance obligation were to transfer to another entity.

Customer controls the asset as it is created or enhanced (paragraph 35(b))

B5   In determining whether a customer controls an asset as it is created or enhanced in accordance with paragraph 35(b), an entity shall apply the requirements for control in paragraphs 31–34 and 38. The asset that is being created or enhanced (for example, a work-in-progress asset) could be either tangible or intangible.

Entity's performance does not create an asset with an alternative use (paragraph 35(c))

B6   In assessing whether an asset has an alternative use to an entity in accordance with paragraph 36, an entity shall consider the effects of contractual restrictions and practical limitations on the entity's ability to readily direct that asset for another use, such as selling it to a different customer. The possibility of the contract with the customer being terminated is not a relevant consideration in assessing whether the entity would be able to readily direct the asset for another use.

B7   A contractual restriction on an entity's ability to direct an asset for another use must be substantive for the asset not to have an alternative use to the entity. A contractual restriction is substantive if a customer could enforce its rights to the promised asset if the entity sought to direct the asset for another use. In contrast, a contractual restriction is not substantive if, for example, an asset is largely interchangeable with other assets that the entity could transfer to another customer without breaching the contract and without incurring significant costs that otherwise would not have been incurred in relation to that contract.

B8   A practical limitation on an entity's ability to direct an asset for another use exists if an entity would incur significant economic losses to direct the asset for another use. A significant economic loss could arise because the entity either would incur significant costs to rework the asset or would only be able to sell the asset at a significant loss. For example, an entity may be practically limited from redirecting assets that either have design specifications that are unique to a customer or are located in remote areas.

Right to payment for performance completed to date (paragraph 35(c))

B9   In accordance with paragraph 37, an entity has a right to payment for performance completed to date if the entity would be entitled to an amount that at least compensates the entity for its performance completed to date in the event that the customer or another party terminates the contract for reasons other than the entity's failure to perform as promised. An amount that would compensate an entity for performance completed to date would be an amount that approximates the selling price of the goods or services transferred to date (for example, recovery of the costs incurred by an entity in satisfying the performance obligation plus a reasonable profit margin) rather than compensation for only the entity's potential loss of profit if the contract were to be terminated. Compensation for a reasonable profit margin need not equal the profit margin expected if the contract was fulfilled as promised, but an entity should be entitled to compensation for either of the following amounts:

(a)   a proportion of the expected profit margin in the contract that reasonably reflects the extent of the entity's performance under the contract before termination by the customer (or another party); or

(b)   a reasonable return on the entity's cost of capital for similar contracts (or the entity's typical operating margin for similar contracts) if the contract-specific margin is higher than the return the entity usually generates from similar contracts.

B10   An entity's right to payment for performance completed to date need not be a present unconditional right to payment. In many cases, an entity will have an unconditional right to payment only at an agreed-upon milestone or upon complete satisfaction of the performance obligation. In assessing whether it has a right to payment for performance completed to date, an entity shall consider whether it would have an enforceable right to demand or retain payment for performance completed to date if the contract were to be terminated before completion for reasons other than the entity's failure to perform as promised.

B11   In some contracts, a customer may have a right to terminate the contract only at specified times during the life of the contract or the customer might not have any right to terminate the contract. If a customer acts to terminate a contract without having the right to terminate the contract at that time (including when a customer fails to perform its obligations as promised), the contract (or other laws) might entitle the entity to continue to transfer to the customer the goods or services promised in the contract and require the customer to pay the consideration promised in exchange for those goods or services. In those circumstances, an entity has a right to payment for performance completed to date because the entity has a right to continue to perform its obligations in accordance with the contract and to require the customer to perform its obligations (which include paying the promised consideration).

B12   In assessing the existence and enforceability of a right to payment for performance completed to date, an entity shall consider the contractual terms as well as any legislation or legal precedent that could supplement or override those contractual terms. This would include an assessment of whether:

(a)   legislation, administrative practice or legal precedent confers upon the entity a right to payment for performance to date even though that right is not specified in the contract with the customer;

(b)   relevant legal precedent indicates that similar rights to payment for performance completed to date in similar contracts have no binding legal effect; or

(c)   an entity's customary business practices of choosing not to enforce a right to payment has resulted in the right being rendered unenforceable in that legal environment. However, notwithstanding that an entity may choose to waive its right to payment in similar contracts, an entity would continue to have a right to payment to date if, in the contract with the customer, its right to payment for performance to date remains enforceable.

B13   The payment schedule specified in a contract does not necessarily indicate whether an entity has an enforceable right to payment for performance completed to date. Although the payment schedule in a contract specifies the timing and amount of consideration that is payable by a customer, the payment schedule might not necessarily provide evidence of the entity's right to payment for performance completed to date. This is because, for example, the contract could specify that the consideration received from the customer is refundable for reasons other than the entity failing to perform as promised in the contract.

Methods for measuring progress towards complete satisfaction of a performance obligation

B14   Methods that can be used to measure an entity's progress towards complete satisfaction of a performance obligation satisfied over time in accordance with paragraphs 35–37 include the following:

   (a)   output methods (see paragraphs B15–B17); and

   (b)   input methods (see paragraphs B18–B19).

Output methods

B15   Output methods recognise revenue on the basis of direct measurements of the value to the customer of the goods or services transferred to date relative to the remaining goods or services promised under the contract. Output methods include methods such as surveys of performance completed to date, appraisals of results achieved, milestones reached, time elapsed and units produced or units delivered. When an entity evaluates whether to apply an output method to measure its progress, the entity shall consider whether the output selected would faithfully depict the entity's performance towards complete satisfaction of the performance obligation. An output method would not provide a faithful depiction of the entity's performance if the output selected would fail to measure some of the goods or services for which control has transferred to the customer. For example, output methods based on units produced or units delivered would not faithfully depict entity's performance in satisfying a performance obligation if, at the end of the reporting period, the entity's performance has produced work in progress or finished goods controlled by the customer that are not included in the measurement of the output.

B16   As a practical expedient, if an entity has a right to consideration from a customer in an amount that corresponds directly with the value to the customer of the entity's performance completed to date (for example, a service contract in which an entity bills a fixed amount for each hour of service provided), the entity may recognise revenue in the amount to which the entity has a right to invoice.

B17   The disadvantages of output methods are that the outputs used to measure progress may not be directly observable and the information required to apply them may not be available to an entity without undue cost. Therefore, an input method may be necessary.

Input methods

B18   Input methods recognise revenue on the basis of the entity's efforts or inputs to the satisfaction of a performance obligation (for example, resources consumed, labour hours expended, costs incurred, time elapsed or machine hours used) relative to the total expected inputs to the satisfaction of that performance obligation. If the entity's efforts or inputs are expended evenly throughout the performance period, it may be appropriate for the entity to recognise revenue on a straight-line basis.

B19   A shortcoming of input methods is that there may not be a direct relationship between an entity's inputs and the transfer of control of goods or services to a customer. Therefore, an entity shall exclude from an input method the effects of any inputs that, in accordance with the objective of measuring progress in paragraph 39, do not depict the entity's performance in transferring control of goods or services to the customer. For instance, when using a cost-based input method, an adjustment to the measure of progress may be required in the following circumstances:

(a)   When a cost incurred does not contribute to an entity's progress in satisfying the performance obligation. For example, an entity would not recognise revenue on the basis of costs incurred that are attributable to significant inefficiencies in the entity's performance that were not reflected in the price of the contract (for example, the costs of unexpected amounts of wasted materials, labour or other resources that were incurred to satisfy the performance obligation).

(b)   When a cost incurred is not proportionate to the entity's progress in satisfying the performance obligation. In those circumstances, the best depiction of the entity's performance may be to adjust the input method to recognise revenue only to the extent of that cost incurred. For example, a faithful depiction of an entity's performance might be to recognise revenue at an amount equal to the cost of a good used to satisfy a performance obligation if the entity expects at contract inception that all of the following conditions would be met:

(i)   the good is not distinct;

(ii)   the customer is expected to obtain control of the good significantly before receiving services related to the good;

(iii) the cost of the transferred good is significant relative to the total expected costs to completely satisfy the performance obligation; and

(iv)   the entity procures the good from a third party and is not significantly involved in designing and manufacturing the good (but the entity is acting as a principal in accordance with paragraphs B34–B38).

Sale with a right of return

B20   In some contracts, an entity transfers control of a product to a customer and also grants the customer the right to return the product for various reasons (such as dissatisfaction with the product) and receive any combination of the following:

(a)   a full or partial refund of any consideration paid;

(b)   a credit that can be applied against amounts owed, or that will be owed, to the entity; and

(c)   another product in exchange.

B21   To account for the transfer of products with a right of return (and for some services that are provided subject to a refund), an entity shall recognise all of the following:

(a)   revenue for the transferred products in the amount of consideration to which the entity expects to be entitled (therefore, revenue would not be recognised for the products expected to be returned);

(b)   a refund liability; and

(c)   an asset (and corresponding adjustment to cost of sales) for its right to recover products from customers on settling the refund liability.

B22   An entity's promise to stand ready to accept a returned product during the return period shall not be accounted for as a performance obligation in addition to the obligation to provide a refund.

B23   An entity shall apply the requirements in paragraphs 47–72 (including the requirements for constraining estimates of variable consideration in paragraphs 56–58) to determine the amount of consideration to which the entity expects to be entitled (ie excluding the products expected to be returned). For any amounts received (or receivable) for which an entity does not expect to be entitled, the entity shall not recognise revenue when it transfers products to customers but shall recognise those amounts received (or receivable) as a refund liability. Subsequently, at the end of each reporting period, the entity shall update its assessment of amounts for which it expects to be entitled in exchange for the transferred products and make a corresponding change to the transaction price and, therefore, in the amount of revenue recognised.

B24   An entity shall update the measurement of the refund liability at the end of each reporting period for changes in expectations about the amount of refunds. An entity shall recognise corresponding adjustments as revenue (or reductions of revenue).

B25   An asset recognised for an entity's right to recover products from a customer on settling a refund liability shall initially be measured by reference to the former carrying amount of the product (for example, inventory) less any expected costs to recover those products (including potential decreases in the value to the entity of returned products). At the end of each reporting period, an entity shall update the measurement of the asset arising from changes in expectations about products to be returned. An entity shall present the asset separately from the refund liability.

B26   Exchanges by customers of one product for another of the same type, quality, condition and price (for example, one colour or size for another) are not considered returns for the purposes of applying this Standard.

B27   Contracts in which a customer may return a defective product in exchange for a functioning product shall be evaluated in accordance with the guidance on warranties in paragraphs B28–B33.

Warranties

B28   It is common for an entity to provide (in accordance with the contract, the law or the entity's customary business practices) a warranty in connection with the sale of a product (whether a good or service). The nature of a warranty can vary significantly across industries and contracts. Some warranties provide a customer with assurance that the related product will function as the parties intended because it complies with agreed-upon specifications. Other warranties provide the customer with a service in addition to the assurance that the product complies with agreed-upon specifications.

B29   If a customer has the option to purchase a warranty separately (for example, because the warranty is priced or negotiated separately), the warranty is a distinct service because the entity promises to provide the service to the customer in addition to the product that has the functionality described in the contract. In those circumstances, an entity shall account for the promised warranty as a performance obligation in accordance with paragraphs 22–30 and allocate a portion of the transaction price to that performance obligation in accordance with paragraphs 73–86.

B30   If a customer does not have the option to purchase a warranty separately, an entity shall account for the warranty in accordance with IAS 37 *Provisions, Contingent Liabilities and Contingent Assets* unless the promised warranty, or a part of the promised warranty, provides the customer with a service in addition to the assurance that the product complies with agreed-upon specifications.

B31   In assessing whether a warranty provides a customer with a service in addition to the assurance that the product complies with agreed-upon specifications, an entity shall consider factors such as:

   (a) Whether the warranty is required by law—if the entity is required by law to provide a warranty, the existence of that law indicates that the promised warranty is not a performance obligation because such requirements typically exist to protect customers from the risk of purchasing defective products.

   (b) The length of the warranty coverage period—the longer the coverage period, the more likely it is that the promised warranty is a performance obligation because it is more likely to provide a service in addition to the assurance that the product complies with agreed-upon specifications.

   (c) The nature of the tasks that the entity promises to perform—if it is necessary for an entity to perform specified tasks to provide the assurance that a product complies with agreed-upon specifications (for example, a return shipping service for a defective product), then those tasks likely do not give rise to a performance obligation.

B32   If a warranty, or a part of a warranty, provides a customer with a service in addition to the assurance that the product complies with agreed-upon specifications, the promised service is a performance obligation. Therefore, an entity shall allocate the transaction price to the product and the service. If an entity promises both an assurance-type warranty and a service-type warranty but cannot reasonably account for them separately, the entity shall account for both of the warranties together as a single performance obligation.

B33   A law that requires an entity to pay compensation if its products cause harm or damage does not give rise to a performance obligation. For example, a manufacturer might sell products in a jurisdiction in which the law holds the manufacturer liable for any damages (for example, to personal property) that might be caused by a consumer using a product for its intended purpose. Similarly, an entity's promise to indemnify the customer for liabilities and damages arising from claims of patent, copyright, trademark or other infringement by the entity's products does not give rise to a performance obligation. The entity shall account for such obligations in accordance with IAS 37.

Principal versus agent considerations

B34   When another party is involved in providing goods or services to a customer, the entity shall determine whether the nature of its promise is a performance obligation to provide the specified goods or services itself (ie the entity is a principal) or to arrange for those goods or services to be provided by the other party (ie the entity is an agent). An entity determines whether it is a principal or an agent for each specified good or service promised to the customer. A specified good or service is a distinct good or service (or a distinct bundle of goods or services) to be provided to the customer (see paragraphs 27–30). If a contract with a customer includes more than one specified good or service, an entity could be a principal for some specified goods or services and an agent for others.

B34A   To determine the nature of its promise (as described in paragraph B34), the entity shall:

(a)   identify the specified goods or services to be provided to the customer (which, for example, could be a right to a good or service to be provided by another party (see paragraph 26)); and

(b)   assess whether it controls (as described in paragraph 33) each specified good or service before that good or service is transferred to the customer.

B35   An entity is a principal if it controls the specified good or service before that good or service is transferred to a customer. However, an entity does not necessarily control a specified good if the entity obtains legal title to that good only momentarily before legal title is transferred to a customer. An entity that is a principal may satisfy its performance obligation to provide the specified good or service itself or it may engage another party (for example, a subcontractor) to satisfy some or all of the performance obligation on its behalf.

B35A When another party is involved in providing goods or services to a customer, an entity that is a principal obtains control of any one of the following:

(a) a good or another asset from the other party that it then transfers to the customer.

(b) a right to a service to be performed by the other party, which gives the entity the ability to direct that party to provide the service to the customer on the entity's behalf.

(c) a good or service from the other party that it then combines with other goods or services in providing the specified good or service to the customer. For example, if an entity provides a significant service of integrating goods or services (see paragraph 29(a)) provided by another party into the specified good or service for which the customer has contracted, the entity controls the specified good or service before that good or service is transferred to the customer. This is because the entity first obtains control of the inputs to the specified good or service (which includes goods or services from other parties) and directs their use to create the combined output that is the specified good or service.

B35B When (or as) an entity that is a principal satisfies a performance obligation, the entity recognises revenue in the gross amount of consideration to which it expects to be entitled in exchange for the specified good or service transferred.

B36 An entity is an agent if the entity's performance obligation is to arrange for the provision of the specified good or service by another party. An entity that is an agent does not control the specified good or service provided by another party before that good or service is transferred to the customer. When (or as) an entity that is an agent satisfies a performance obligation, the entity recognises revenue in the amount of any fee or commission to which it expects to be entitled in exchange for arranging for the specified goods or services to be provided by the other party. An entity's fee or commission might be the net amount of consideration that the entity retains after paying the other party the consideration received in exchange for the goods or services to be provided by that party.

B37 Indicators that an entity controls the specified good or service before it is transferred to the customer (and is therefore a principal (see paragraph B35)) include, but are not limited to, the following:

(a) the entity is primarily responsible for fulfilling the promise to provide the specified good or service. This typically includes responsibility for the acceptability of the specified good or service (for example, primary responsibility for the good or service meeting customer specifications). If the entity is primarily responsible for fulfilling the promise to provide the specified good or service, this may indicate that the other party involved in providing the specified good or service is acting on the entity's behalf.

(b)   the entity has inventory risk before the specified good or service has been transferred to a customer or after transfer of control to the customer (for example, if the customer has a right of return). For example, if the entity obtains, or commits itself to obtain, the specified good or service before obtaining a contract with a customer, that may indicate that the entity has the ability to direct the use of, and obtain substantially all of the remaining benefits from, the good or service before it is transferred to the customer.

(c)   the entity has discretion in establishing the price for the specified good or service. Establishing the price that the customer pays for the specified good or service may indicate that the entity has the ability to direct the use of that good or service and obtain substantially all of the remaining benefits. However, an agent can have discretion in establishing prices in some cases. For example, an agent may have some flexibility in setting prices in order to generate additional revenue from its service of arranging for goods or services to be provided by other parties to customers.

B37A   The indicators in paragraph B37 may be more or less relevant to the assessment of control depending on the nature of the specified good or service and the terms and conditions of the contract. In addition, different indicators may provide more persuasive evidence in different contracts.

B38   If another entity assumes the entity's performance obligations and contractual rights in the contract so that the entity is no longer obliged to satisfy the performance obligation to transfer the specified good or service to the customer (ie the entity is no longer acting as the principal), the entity shall not recognise revenue for that performance obligation. Instead, the entity shall evaluate whether to recognise revenue for satisfying a performance obligation to obtain a contract for the other party (ie whether the entity is acting as an agent).

Customer options for additional goods or services

B39   Customer options to acquire additional goods or services for free or at a discount come in many forms, including sales incentives, customer award credits (or points), contract renewal options or other discounts on future goods or services.

B40   If, in a contract, an entity grants a customer the option to acquire additional goods or services, that option gives rise to a performance obligation in the contract only if the option provides a material right to the customer that it would not receive without entering into that contract (for example, a discount that is incremental to the range of discounts typically given for those goods or services to that class of customer in that geographical area or market). If the option provides a material right to the customer, the customer in effect pays the entity in advance for future goods or services and the entity recognises revenue when those future goods or services are transferred or when the option expires.

B41   If a customer has the option to acquire an additional good or service at a price that would reflect the stand-alone selling price for that good or service, that option does not provide the customer with a material right even if the option can be exercised only by entering into a previous contract. In those cases, the entity has made a marketing offer that it shall account for in accordance with this Standard only when the customer exercises the option to purchase the additional goods or services.

B42   Paragraph 74 requires an entity to allocate the transaction price to performance obligations on a relative stand-alone selling price basis. If the stand-alone selling price for a customer's option to acquire additional goods or services is not directly observable, an entity shall estimate it. That estimate shall reflect the discount that the customer would obtain when exercising the option, adjusted for both of the following:

(a)   any discount that the customer could receive without exercising the option; and

(b)   the likelihood that the option will be exercised.

B43   If a customer has a material right to acquire future goods or services and those goods or services are similar to the original goods or services in the contract and are provided in accordance with the terms of the original contract, then an entity may, as a practical alternative to estimating the stand-alone selling price of the option, allocate the transaction price to the optional goods or services by reference to the goods or services expected to be provided and the corresponding expected consideration. Typically, those types of options are for contract renewals.

Customers' unexercised rights

B44   In accordance with paragraph 106, upon receipt of a prepayment from a customer, an entity shall recognise a contract liability in the amount of the prepayment for its performance obligation to transfer, or to stand ready to transfer, goods or services in the future. An entity shall derecognise that contract liability (and recognise revenue) when it transfers those goods or services and, therefore, satisfies its performance obligation.

B45   A customer's non-refundable prepayment to an entity gives the customer a right to receive a good or service in the future (and obliges the entity to stand ready to transfer a good or service). However, customers may not exercise all of their contractual rights. Those unexercised rights are often referred to as breakage.

B46   If an entity expects to be entitled to a breakage amount in a contract liability, the entity shall recognise the expected breakage amount as revenue in proportion to the pattern of rights exercised by the customer. If an entity does not expect to be entitled to a breakage amount, the entity shall recognise the expected breakage amount as revenue when the likelihood of the customer exercising its remaining rights becomes remote. To determine whether an entity expects to be entitled to a breakage amount, the entity shall consider the requirements in paragraphs 56–58 on constraining estimates of variable consideration.

B47 An entity shall recognise a liability (and not revenue) for any consideration received that is attributable to a customer's unexercised rights for which the entity is required to remit to another party, for example, a government entity in accordance with applicable unclaimed property laws.

Non-refundable upfront fees (and some related costs)

B48 In some contracts, an entity charges a customer a non-refundable upfront fee at or near contract inception. Examples include joining fees in health club membership contracts, activation fees in telecommunication contracts, setup fees in some services contracts and initial fees in some supply contracts.

B49 To identify performance obligations in such contracts, an entity shall assess whether the fee relates to the transfer of a promised good or service. In many cases, even though a non-refundable upfront fee relates to an activity that the entity is required to undertake at or near contract inception to fulfil the contract, that activity does not result in the transfer of a promised good or service to the customer (see paragraph 25). Instead, the upfront fee is an advance payment for future goods or services and, therefore, would be recognised as revenue when those future goods or services are provided. The revenue recognition period would extend beyond the initial contractual period if the entity grants the customer the option to renew the contract and that option provides the customer with a material right as described in paragraph B40.

B50 If the non-refundable upfront fee relates to a good or service, the entity shall evaluate whether to account for the good or service as a separate performance obligation in accordance with paragraphs 22–30.

B51 An entity may charge a non-refundable fee in part as compensation for costs incurred in setting up a contract (or other administrative tasks as described in paragraph 25). If those setup activities do not satisfy a performance obligation, the entity shall disregard those activities (and related costs) when measuring progress in accordance with paragraph B19. That is because the costs of setup activities do not depict the transfer of services to the customer. The entity shall assess whether costs incurred in setting up a contract have resulted in an asset that shall be recognised in accordance with paragraph 95.

Licensing

B52 A licence establishes a customer's rights to the intellectual property of an entity. Licences of intellectual property may include, but are not limited to, licences of any of the following:

(a) software and technology;

(b) motion pictures, music and other forms of media and entertainment;

(c) franchises; and

(d) patents, trademarks and copyrights.

from, the licence at the point in time at which the licence transfers. An entity shall account for the promise to provide a right to use the entity's intellectual property as a performance obligation satisfied at a point in time. An entity shall apply paragraph 38 to determine the point in time at which the licence transfers to the customer. However, revenue cannot be recognised for a licence that provides a right to use the entity's intellectual property before the beginning of the period during which the customer is able to use and benefit from the licence. For example, if a software licence period begins before an entity provides (or otherwise makes available) to the customer a code that enables the customer to immediately use the software, the entity would not recognise revenue before that code has been provided (or otherwise made available).

B62   An entity shall disregard the following factors when determining whether a licence provides a right to access the entity's intellectual property or a right to use the entity's intellectual property:

(a)   Restrictions of time, geographical region or use—those restrictions define the attributes of the promised licence, rather than define whether the entity satisfies its performance obligation at a point in time or over time.

(b)   Guarantees provided by the entity that it has a valid patent to intellectual property and that it will defend that patent from unauthorised use—a promise to defend a patent right is not a performance obligation because the act of defending a patent protects the value of the entity's intellectual property assets and provides assurance to the customer that the licence transferred meets the specifications of the licence promised in the contract.

Sales-based or usage-based royalties

B63   Notwithstanding the requirements in paragraphs 56–59, an entity shall recognise revenue for a sales-based or usage-based royalty promised in exchange for a licence of intellectual property only when (or as) the later of the following events occurs:

(a)   the subsequent sale or usage occurs; and

(b)   the performance obligation to which some or all of the sales-based or usage-based royalty has been allocated has been satisfied (or partially satisfied).

B63A   The requirement for a sales-based or usage-based royalty in paragraph B63 applies when the royalty relates only to a licence of intellectual property or when a licence of intellectual property is the predominant item to which the royalty relates (for example, the licence of intellectual property may be the predominant item to which the royalty relates when the entity has a reasonable expectation that the customer would ascribe significantly more value to the licence than to the other goods or services to which the royalty relates).

B63B   When the requirement in paragraph B63A is met, revenue from a sales-based or usage-based royalty shall be recognised wholly in accordance with paragraph B63. When the requirement in paragraph B63A is not met, the requirements on variable consideration in paragraphs 50–59 apply to the sales-based or usage-based royalty.

Repurchase agreements

B64   A repurchase agreement is a contract in which an entity sells an asset and also promises or has the option (either in the same contract or in another contract) to repurchase the asset. The repurchased asset may be the asset that was originally sold to the customer, an asset that is substantially the same as that asset, or another asset of which the asset that was originally sold is a component.

B65   Repurchase agreements generally come in three forms:

(a)   an entity's obligation to repurchase the asset (a forward);

(b)   an entity's right to repurchase the asset (a call option); and

(c)   an entity's obligation to repurchase the asset at the customer's request (a put option).

A forward or a call option

B66   If an entity has an obligation or a right to repurchase the asset (a forward or a call option), a customer does not obtain control of the asset because the customer is limited in its ability to direct the use of, and obtain substantially all of the remaining benefits from, the asset even though the customer may have physical possession of the asset. Consequently, the entity shall account for the contract as either of the following:

(a)   a lease in accordance with IFRS 16 *Leases* if the entity can or must repurchase the asset for an amount that is less than the original selling price of the asset, unless the contract is part of a sale and leaseback transaction. If the contract is part of a sale and leaseback transaction, the entity shall continue to recognise the asset and shall recognise a financial liability for any consideration received from the customer. The entity shall account for the financial liability in accordance with IFRS 9; or

(b)   a financing arrangement in accordance with paragraph B68 if the entity can or must repurchase the asset for an amount that is equal to or more than the original selling price of the asset.

B67   When comparing the repurchase price with the selling price, an entity shall consider the time value of money.

B68   If the repurchase agreement is a financing arrangement, the entity shall continue to recognise the asset and also recognise a financial liability for any consideration received from the customer. The entity shall recognise the difference between the amount of consideration received from the customer

(b) the product must be identified separately as belonging to the customer;

(c) the product currently must be ready for physical transfer to the customer; and

(d) the entity cannot have the ability to use the product or to direct it to another customer.

B82 If an entity recognises revenue for the sale of a product on a bill-and-hold basis, the entity shall consider whether it has remaining performance obligations (for example, for custodial services) in accordance with paragraphs 22–30 to which the entity shall allocate a portion of the transaction price in accordance with paragraphs 73–86.

Customer acceptance

B83 In accordance with paragraph 38(e), a customer's acceptance of an asset may indicate that the customer has obtained control of the asset. Customer acceptance clauses allow a customer to cancel a contract or require an entity to take remedial action if a good or service does not meet agreed-upon specifications. An entity shall consider such clauses when evaluating when a customer obtains control of a good or service.

B84 If an entity can objectively determine that control of a good or service has been transferred to the customer in accordance with the agreed-upon specifications in the contract, then customer acceptance is a formality that would not affect the entity's determination of when the customer has obtained control of the good or service. For example, if the customer acceptance clause is based on meeting specified size and weight characteristics, an entity would be able to determine whether those criteria have been met before receiving confirmation of the customer's acceptance. The entity's experience with contracts for similar goods or services may provide evidence that a good or service provided to the customer is in accordance with the agreed-upon specifications in the contract. If revenue is recognised before customer acceptance, the entity still must consider whether there are any remaining performance obligations (for example, installation of equipment) and evaluate whether to account for them separately.

B85 However, if an entity cannot objectively determine that the good or service provided to the customer is in accordance with the agreed-upon specifications in the contract, then the entity would not be able to conclude that the customer has obtained control until the entity receives the customer's acceptance. That is because in that circumstance the entity cannot determine that the customer has the ability to direct the use of, and obtain substantially all of the remaining benefits from, the good or service.

B86 If an entity delivers products to a customer for trial or evaluation purposes and the customer is not committed to pay any consideration until the trial period lapses, control of the product is not transferred to the customer until either the customer accepts the product or the trial period lapses.

Disclosure of disaggregated revenue

B87   Paragraph 114 requires an entity to disaggregate revenue from contracts with customers into categories that depict how the nature, amount, timing and uncertainty of revenue and cash flows are affected by economic factors. Consequently, the extent to which an entity's revenue is disaggregated for the purposes of this disclosure depends on the facts and circumstances that pertain to the entity's contracts with customers. Some entities may need to use more than one type of category to meet the objective in paragraph 114 for disaggregating revenue. Other entities may meet the objective by using only one type of category to disaggregate revenue.

B88   When selecting the type of category (or categories) to use to disaggregate revenue, an entity shall consider how information about the entity's revenue has been presented for other purposes, including all of the following:

    (a)   disclosures presented outside the financial statements (for example, in earnings releases, annual reports or investor presentations);

    (b)   information regularly reviewed by the chief operating decision maker for evaluating the financial performance of operating segments; and

    (c)   other information that is similar to the types of information identified in paragraph B88(a) and (b) and that is used by the entity or users of the entity's financial statements to evaluate the entity's financial performance or make resource allocation decisions.

B89   Examples of categories that might be appropriate include, but are not limited to, all of the following:

    (a)   type of good or service (for example, major product lines);

    (b)   geographical region (for example, country or region);

    (c)   market or type of customer (for example, government and non-government customers);

    (d)   type of contract (for example, fixed-price and time-and-materials contracts);

    (e)   contract duration (for example, short-term and long-term contracts);

    (f)   timing of transfer of goods or services (for example, revenue from goods or services transferred to customers at a point in time and revenue from goods or services transferred over time); and

    (g)   sales channels (for example, goods sold directly to consumers and goods sold through intermediaries).

Appendix C
Effective date and transition

This appendix is an integral part of the Standard and has the same authority as the other parts of the Standard.

Effective date

C1 An entity shall apply this Standard for annual reporting periods beginning on or after 1 January 2018. Earlier application is permitted. If an entity applies this Standard earlier, it shall disclose that fact.

C1A IFRS 16 *Leases*, issued in January 2016, amended paragraphs 5, 97, B66 and B70. An entity shall apply those amendments when it applies IFRS 16.

C1B *Clarifications to IFRS 15* Revenue from Contracts with Customers, issued in April 2016, amended paragraphs 26, 27, 29, B1, B34–B38, B52–B53, B58, C2, C5 and C7, deleted paragraph B57 and added paragraphs B34A, B35A, B35B, B37A, B59A, B63A, B63B, C7A and C8A. An entity shall apply those amendments for annual reporting periods beginning on or after 1 January 2018. Earlier application is permitted. If an entity applies those amendments for an earlier period, it shall disclose that fact.

C1C *[This paragraph refers to amendments that are not yet effective, and is therefore not included in this edition.]*

Transition

C2 For the purposes of the transition requirements in paragraphs C3–C8A:

    (a) the date of initial application is the start of the reporting period in which an entity first applies this Standard; and

    (b) a completed contract is a contract for which the entity has transferred all of the goods or services identified in accordance with IAS 11 *Construction Contracts*, IAS 18 *Revenue* and related Interpretations.

C3 An entity shall apply this Standard using one of the following two methods:

    (a) retrospectively to each prior reporting period presented in accordance with IAS 8 *Accounting Policies, Changes in Accounting Estimates and Errors*, subject to the expedients in paragraph C5; or

    (b) retrospectively with the cumulative effect of initially applying this Standard recognised at the date of initial application in accordance with paragraphs C7–C8.

C4 Notwithstanding the requirements of paragraph 28 of IAS 8, when this Standard is first applied, an entity need only present the quantitative information required by paragraph 28(f) of IAS 8 for the annual period immediately preceding the first annual period for which this Standard is applied (the 'immediately preceding period') and only if the entity applies this Standard retrospectively in accordance with paragraph C3(a). An entity may also present this information for the current period or for earlier comparative periods, but is not required to do so.

C5   An entity may use one or more of the following practical expedients when applying this Standard retrospectively in accordance with paragraph C3(a):

(a)   for completed contracts, an entity need not restate contracts that:

(i)   begin and end within the same annual reporting period; or

(ii)   are completed contracts at the beginning of the earliest period presented.

(b)   for completed contracts that have variable consideration, an entity may use the transaction price at the date the contract was completed rather than estimating variable consideration amounts in the comparative reporting periods.

(c)   for contracts that were modified before the beginning of the earliest period presented, an entity need not retrospectively restate the contract for those contract modifications in accordance with paragraphs 20–21. Instead, an entity shall reflect the aggregate effect of all of the modifications that occur before the beginning of the earliest period presented when:

(i)   identifying the satisfied and unsatisfied performance obligations;

(ii)   determining the transaction price; and

(iii)   allocating the transaction price to the satisfied and unsatisfied performance obligations.

(d)   for all reporting periods presented before the date of initial application, an entity need not disclose the amount of the transaction price allocated to the remaining performance obligations and an explanation of when the entity expects to recognise that amount as revenue (see paragraph 120).

C6   For any of the practical expedients in paragraph C5 that an entity uses, the entity shall apply that expedient consistently to all contracts within all reporting periods presented. In addition, the entity shall disclose all of the following information:

(a)   the expedients that have been used; and

(b)   to the extent reasonably possible, a qualitative assessment of the estimated effect of applying each of those expedients.

C7   If an entity elects to apply this Standard retrospectively in accordance with paragraph C3(b), the entity shall recognise the cumulative effect of initially applying this Standard as an adjustment to the opening balance of retained earnings (or other component of equity, as appropriate) of the annual reporting period that includes the date of initial application. Under this transition method, an entity may elect to apply this Standard retrospectively only to contracts that are not completed contracts at the date of initial application (for example, 1 January 2018 for an entity with a 31 December year-end).

C7A   An entity applying this Standard retrospectively in accordance with paragraph C3(b) may also use the practical expedient described in paragraph C5(c), either:

(a)   for all contract modifications that occur before the beginning of the earliest period presented; or

(b)   for all contract modifications that occur before the date of initial application.

If an entity uses this practical expedient, the entity shall apply the expedient consistently to all contracts and disclose the information required by paragraph C6.

C8   For reporting periods that include the date of initial application, an entity shall provide both of the following additional disclosures if this Standard is applied retrospectively in accordance with paragraph C3(b):

(a)   the amount by which each financial statement line item is affected in the current reporting period by the application of this Standard as compared to IAS 11, IAS 18 and related Interpretations that were in effect before the change; and

(b)   an explanation of the reasons for significant changes identified in C8(a).

C8A   An entity shall apply *Clarifications to IFRS 15* (see paragraph C1B) retrospectively in accordance with IAS 8. In applying the amendments retrospectively, an entity shall apply the amendments as if they had been included in IFRS 15 at the date of initial application. Consequently, an entity does not apply the amendments to reporting periods or to contracts to which the requirements of IFRS 15 are not applied in accordance with paragraphs C2–C8. For example, if an entity applies IFRS 15 in accordance with paragraph C3(b) only to contracts that are not completed contracts at the date of initial application, the entity does not restate the completed contracts at the date of initial application of IFRS 15 for the effects of these amendments.

References to IFRS 9

C9   If an entity applies this Standard but does not yet apply IFRS 9 *Financial Instruments*, any reference in this Standard to IFRS 9 shall be read as a reference to IAS 39 *Financial Instruments: Recognition and Measurement*.

Withdrawal of other Standards

C10   This Standard supersedes the following Standards:

(a)   IAS 11 *Construction Contracts*;

(b)   IAS 18 *Revenue*;

(c)   IFRIC 13 *Customer Loyalty Programmes*;

(d)   IFRIC 15 *Agreements for the Construction of Real Estate*;

(e)   IFRIC 18 *Transfers of Assets from Customers*; and

(f)   SIC-31 *Revenue — Barter Transactions Involving Advertising Services*.

Appendix D
Amendments to other Standards

This Appendix describes the amendments to other Standards that the IASB made when it finalised IFRS 15. An entity shall apply the amendments for annual periods beginning on or after 1 January 2018. If an entity applies IFRS 15 for an earlier period, these amendments shall be applied for that earlier period.

* * * * *

The amendments contained in this appendix when this Standard was issued in 2014 have been incorporated into the text of the relevant Standards included in this volume.

Approval by the Board of IFRS 15 *Revenue from Contracts with Customers* issued in May 2014

IFRS 15 *Revenue from Contracts with Customers* was approved for issue by all sixteen members of the International Accounting Standards Board.[1]

Hans Hoogervorst	Chairman
Ian Mackintosh	Vice-Chairman
Stephen Cooper	
Philippe Danjou	
Martin Edelmann	
Jan Engström	
Patrick Finnegan	
Gary Kabureck	
Suzanne Lloyd	
Amaro Luiz de Oliveira Gomes	
Patricia McConnell	
Takatsugu Ochi	
Darrel Scott	
Chungwoo Suh	
Mary Tokar	
Wei-Guo Zhang	

---

1 Prabhakar Kalavacherla was a member of the IASB when it voted in November 2013 to begin the balloting process for IFRS 15. However, IFRS 15 was finalised and ready for approval by members of the IASB only after Mr Kalavacherla had retired from the IASB at the completion of his term on 31 December 2013.

Approval by the Board of *Effective Date of IFRS 15* issued in September 2015

Effective Date of IFRS 15 was approved for publication by the fourteen members of the International Accounting Standards Board.

Hans Hoogervorst	Chairman
Ian Mackintosh	Vice-Chairman
Stephen Cooper	
Philippe Danjou	
Amaro Luiz De Oliveira Gomes	
Martin Edelmann	
Patrick Finnegan	
Gary Kabureck	
Suzanne Lloyd	
Takatsugu Ochi	
Darrel Scott	
Chungwoo Suh	
Mary Tokar	
Wei-Guo Zhang	

Approval by the Board of *Clarifications to IFRS 15* Revenue from Contracts with Customers issued in April 2016

Clarifications to IFRS 15 Revenue from Contracts with Customers was approved for issue by thirteen of the fourteen members of the International Accounting Standards Board. Mr Ochi dissented. His dissenting opinion is set out after the Basis for Conclusions.

Hans Hoogervorst	Chairman
Ian Mackintosh	Vice-Chairman
Stephen Cooper	
Philippe Danjou	
Martin Edelmann	
Patrick Finnegan	
Amaro Gomes	
Gary Kabureck	
Suzanne Lloyd	
Takatsugu Ochi	
Darrel Scott	
Chungwoo Suh	
Mary Tokar	
Wei-Guo Zhang	

IFRS 16

Leases

Other Standards have made consequential amendments to IFRS 16 including Amendments to References to the Conceptual Framework in IFRS Standards (issued March 2018).

In April 2001 the International Accounting Standards Board (Board) adopted IAS 17 *Leases*, which had originally been issued by the International Accounting Standards Committee (IASC) in December 1997. IAS 17 *Leases* replaced IAS 17 *Accounting for Leases* that was issued in September 1982.

In April 2001 the Board adopted SIC-15 *Operating Leases—Incentives*, which had originally been issued by the Standing Interpretations Committee of the IASC in December 1998.

In December 2001 the Board issued SIC-27 *Evaluating the Substance of Transactions Involving the Legal Form of a Lease*. SIC-27 had originally been developed by the Standing Interpretations Committee of the IASC to provide guidance on determining, amongst other things, whether an arrangement that involves the legal form of a lease meets the definition of a lease under IAS 17.

In December 2003 the Board issued a revised IAS 17 as part of its initial agenda of technical projects.

In December 2004 the Board issued IFRIC 4 *Determining whether an Arrangement contains a Lease*. The Interpretation was developed by the Interpretations Committee to provide guidance on determining whether transactions that do not take the legal form of a lease but convey the right to use an asset in return for a payment or series of payments are, or contain, leases that should be accounted for in accordance with IAS 17.

In January 2016 the Board issued IFRS 16 *Leases*. IFRS 16 replaces IAS 17, IFRIC 4, SIC-15 and SIC-27. IFRS 16 sets out the principles for the recognition, measurement, presentation and disclosure of leases.

In May 2020 the Board issued *Covid-19-Related Rent Concessions*, which amended IFRS 16. The amendment permits lessees, as a practical expedient, not to assess whether rent concessions that occur as a direct consequence of the covid-19 pandemic and meet specified conditions are lease modifications. Instead, the lessee accounts for those rent concessions as if they were not lease modifications.

In August 2020 the Board issued *Interest Rate Benchmark Reform—Phase 2* which amended requirements in IFRS 9, IAS 39, IFRS 7, IFRS 4 and IFRS 16 relating to:

- changes in the basis for determining contractual cash flows of financial assets, financial liabilities and lease liabilities;

- hedge accounting; and

- disclosures.

The Phase 2 amendments apply only to changes required by the interest rate benchmark reform to financial instruments and hedging relationships.

In March 2021 the Board issued *Covid-19-Related Rent Concessions beyond 30 June 2021*, which extended by one year the application period of the practical expedient in paragraph 46A to help lessees accounting for covid-19-related rent concessions.

Other Standards have made minor consequential amendments to IFRS 16, including *Amendments to References to the Conceptual Framework in IFRS Standards* (issued March 2018).

Contents

continued...

...continued

Amendments to guidance on other Standards

FOR THE BASIS FOR CONCLUSIONS, SEE PART C OF THIS EDITION

BASIS FOR CONCLUSIONS

DISSENTING OPINION

APPENDIX TO THE BASIS FOR CONCLUSIONS

Amendments to the Basis for Conclusions on other Standards

International Financial Reporting Standard 16 *Leases* (IFRS 16) is set out in paragraphs 1–106 and Appendices A–D. All the paragraphs have equal authority. Paragraphs in **bold type** state the main principles. Terms defined in Appendix A are in *italics* the first time that they appear in the Standard. Definitions of other terms are given in the Glossary for International Financial Reporting Standards. The Standard should be read in the context of its objective and the Basis for Conclusions, the *Preface to IFRS Standards* and the *Conceptual Framework for Financial Reporting*. IAS 8 *Accounting Policies, Changes in Accounting Estimates and Errors* provides a basis for selecting and applying accounting policies in the absence of explicit guidance.

International Financial Reporting Standard 16
Leases

Objective

1   This Standard sets out the principles for the recognition, measurement, presentation and disclosure of *leases*. The objective is to ensure that *lessees* and *lessors* provide relevant information in a manner that faithfully represents those transactions. This information gives a basis for users of financial statements to assess the effect that leases have on the financial position, financial performance and cash flows of an entity.

2   An entity shall consider the terms and conditions of *contracts* and all relevant facts and circumstances when applying this Standard. An entity shall apply this Standard consistently to contracts with similar characteristics and in similar circumstances.

Scope

3   An entity shall apply this Standard to all leases, including leases of *right-of-use assets* in a *sublease*, except for:

(a)   leases to explore for or use minerals, oil, natural gas and similar non-regenerative resources;

(b)   leases of biological assets within the scope of IAS 41 *Agriculture* held by a lessee;

(c)   service concession arrangements within the scope of IFRIC 12 *Service Concession Arrangements*;

(d)   licences of intellectual property granted by a lessor within the scope of IFRS 15 *Revenue from Contracts with Customers*; and

(e)   rights held by a lessee under licensing agreements within the scope of IAS 38 *Intangible Assets* for such items as motion picture films, video recordings, plays, manuscripts, patents and copyrights.

4   A lessee may, but is not required to, apply this Standard to leases of intangible assets other than those described in paragraph 3(e).

Recognition exemptions (paragraphs B3–B8)

5   A lessee may elect not to apply the requirements in paragraphs 22–49 to:

(a)   *short-term leases*; and

(b)   leases for which the *underlying asset* is of low value (as described in paragraphs B3–B8).

6   If a lessee elects not to apply the requirements in paragraphs 22–49 to either short-term leases or leases for which the underlying asset is of low value, the lessee shall recognise the *lease payments* associated with those leases as an expense on either a straight-line basis over the *lease term* or another systematic basis. The lessee shall apply another systematic basis if that basis is more representative of the pattern of the lessee's benefit.

7   If a lessee accounts for short-term leases applying paragraph 6, the lessee shall consider the lease to be a new lease for the purposes of this Standard if:

(a)   there is a *lease modification*; or

(b)   there is any change in the lease term (for example, the lessee exercises an option not previously included in its determination of the lease term).

8   The election for short-term leases shall be made by class of underlying asset to which the right of use relates. A class of underlying asset is a grouping of underlying assets of a similar nature and use in an entity's operations. The election for leases for which the underlying asset is of low value can be made on a lease-by-lease basis.

Identifying a lease (paragraphs B9–B33)

9   At inception of a contract, an entity shall assess whether the contract is, or contains, a lease. A contract is, or contains, a lease if the contract conveys the right to control the use of an identified asset for a period of time in exchange for consideration. Paragraphs B9–B31 set out guidance on the assessment of whether a contract is, or contains, a lease.

10   A period of time may be described in terms of the amount of use of an identified asset (for example, the number of production units that an item of equipment will be used to produce).

11   An entity shall reassess whether a contract is, or contains, a lease only if the terms and conditions of the contract are changed.

Separating components of a contract

12   For a contract that is, or contains, a lease, an entity shall account for each lease component within the contract as a lease separately from non-lease components of the contract, unless the entity applies the practical expedient in paragraph 15. Paragraphs B32–B33 set out guidance on separating components of a contract.

Lessee

13   For a contract that contains a lease component and one or more additional lease or non-lease components, a lessee shall allocate the consideration in the contract to each lease component on the basis of the relative stand-alone price of the lease component and the aggregate stand-alone price of the non-lease components.

14   The relative stand-alone price of lease and non-lease components shall be determined on the basis of the price the lessor, or a similar supplier, would charge an entity for that component, or a similar component, separately. If an observable stand-alone price is not readily available, the lessee shall estimate the stand-alone price, maximising the use of observable information.

15   As a practical expedient, a lessee may elect, by class of underlying asset, not to separate non-lease components from lease components, and instead account for each lease component and any associated non-lease components as a single lease component. A lessee shall not apply this practical expedient to embedded derivatives that meet the criteria in paragraph 4.3.3 of IFRS 9 *Financial Instruments*.

16   Unless the practical expedient in paragraph 15 is applied, a lessee shall account for non-lease components applying other applicable Standards.

Lessor

17   For a contract that contains a lease component and one or more additional lease or non-lease components, a lessor shall allocate the consideration in the contract applying paragraphs 73–90 of IFRS 15.

Lease term (paragraphs B34–B41)

18   An entity shall determine the lease term as the non-cancellable period of a lease, together with both:

(a)   periods covered by an option to extend the lease if the lessee is reasonably certain to exercise that option; and

(b)   periods covered by an option to terminate the lease if the lessee is reasonably certain not to exercise that option.

19   In assessing whether a lessee is reasonably certain to exercise an option to extend a lease, or not to exercise an option to terminate a lease, an entity shall consider all relevant facts and circumstances that create an economic incentive for the lessee to exercise the option to extend the lease, or not to exercise the option to terminate the lease, as described in paragraphs B37–B40.

20   A lessee shall reassess whether it is reasonably certain to exercise an extension option, or not to exercise a termination option, upon the occurrence of either a significant event or a significant change in circumstances that:

(a)   is within the control of the lessee; and

(b)   affects whether the lessee is reasonably certain to exercise an option not previously included in its determination of the lease term, or not to exercise an option previously included in its determination of the lease term (as described in paragraph B41).

21   An entity shall revise the lease term if there is a change in the non-cancellable period of a lease. For example, the non-cancellable period of a lease will change if:

(a) the lessee exercises an option not previously included in the entity's determination of the lease term;

(b) the lessee does not exercise an option previously included in the entity's determination of the lease term;

(c) an event occurs that contractually obliges the lessee to exercise an option not previously included in the entity's determination of the lease term; or

(d) an event occurs that contractually prohibits the lessee from exercising an option previously included in the entity's determination of the lease term.

Lessee

Recognition

22   At the *commencement date*, a lessee shall recognise a right-of-use asset and a lease liability.

Measurement

Initial measurement

Initial measurement of the right-of-use asset

23   At the commencement date, a lessee shall measure the right-of-use asset at cost.

24   The cost of the right-of-use asset shall comprise:

(a) the amount of the initial measurement of the lease liability, as described in paragraph 26;

(b) any lease payments made at or before the commencement date, less any *lease incentives* received;

(c) any *initial direct costs* incurred by the lessee; and

(d) an estimate of costs to be incurred by the lessee in dismantling and removing the underlying asset, restoring the site on which it is located or restoring the underlying asset to the condition required by the terms and conditions of the lease, unless those costs are incurred to produce inventories. The lessee incurs the obligation for those costs either at the commencement date or as a consequence of having used the underlying asset during a particular period.

25   A lessee shall recognise the costs described in paragraph 24(d) as part of the cost of the right-of-use asset when it incurs an obligation for those costs. A lessee applies IAS 2 *Inventories* to costs that are incurred during a particular period as a consequence of having used the right-of-use asset to produce inventories during that period. The obligations for such costs accounted for applying this Standard or IAS 2 are recognised and measured applying IAS 37 *Provisions, Contingent Liabilities and Contingent Assets*.

Initial measurement of the lease liability

26   At the commencement date, a lessee shall measure the lease liability at the present value of the lease payments that are not paid at that date. The lease payments shall be discounted using the *interest rate implicit in the lease*, if that rate can be readily determined. If that rate cannot be readily determined, the lessee shall use the *lessee's incremental borrowing rate*.

27   At the commencement date, the lease payments included in the measurement of the lease liability comprise the following payments for the right to use the underlying asset during the lease term that are not paid at the commencement date:

    (a)   *fixed payments* (including in-substance fixed payments as described in paragraph B42), less any lease incentives receivable;

    (b)   *variable lease payments* that depend on an index or a rate, initially measured using the index or rate as at the commencement date (as described in paragraph 28);

    (c)   amounts expected to be payable by the lessee under *residual value guarantees*;

    (d)   the exercise price of a purchase option if the lessee is reasonably certain to exercise that option (assessed considering the factors described in paragraphs B37–B40); and

    (e)   payments of penalties for terminating the lease, if the lease term reflects the lessee exercising an option to terminate the lease.

28   Variable lease payments that depend on an index or a rate described in paragraph 27(b) include, for example, payments linked to a consumer price index, payments linked to a benchmark interest rate (such as LIBOR) or payments that vary to reflect changes in market rental rates.

Subsequent measurement

Subsequent measurement of the right-of-use asset

29   After the commencement date, a lessee shall measure the right-of-use asset applying a cost model, unless it applies either of the measurement models described in paragraphs 34 and 35.

Cost model

30   To apply a cost model, a lessee shall measure the right-of-use asset at cost:

    (a)   less any accumulated depreciation and any accumulated impairment losses; and

    (b)   adjusted for any remeasurement of the lease liability specified in paragraph 36(c).

31   A lessee shall apply the depreciation requirements in IAS 16 *Property, Plant and Equipment* in depreciating the right-of-use asset, subject to the requirements in paragraph 32.

32   If the lease transfers ownership of the underlying asset to the lessee by the end of the lease term or if the cost of the right-of-use asset reflects that the lessee will exercise a purchase option, the lessee shall depreciate the right-of-use asset from the commencement date to the end of the *useful life* of the underlying asset. Otherwise, the lessee shall depreciate the right-of-use asset from the commencement date to the earlier of the end of the *useful life* of the right-of-use asset or the end of the lease term.

33   A lessee shall apply IAS 36 *Impairment of Assets* to determine whether the right-of-use asset is impaired and to account for any impairment loss identified.

Other measurement models

34   If a lessee applies the fair value model in IAS 40 *Investment Property* to its investment property, the lessee shall also apply that fair value model to right-of-use assets that meet the definition of investment property in IAS 40.

35   If right-of-use assets relate to a class of property, plant and equipment to which the lessee applies the revaluation model in IAS 16, a lessee may elect to apply that revaluation model to all of the right-of-use assets that relate to that class of property, plant and equipment.

Subsequent measurement of the lease liability

36   After the commencement date, a lessee shall measure the lease liability by:

    (a)   increasing the carrying amount to reflect interest on the lease liability;

    (b)   reducing the carrying amount to reflect the lease payments made; and

    (c)   remeasuring the carrying amount to reflect any reassessment or lease modifications specified in paragraphs 39–46, or to reflect revised in-substance fixed lease payments (see paragraph B42).

37   Interest on the lease liability in each period during the lease term shall be the amount that produces a constant periodic rate of interest on the remaining balance of the lease liability. The periodic rate of interest is the discount rate described in paragraph 26, or if applicable the revised discount rate described in paragraph 41, paragraph 43 or paragraph 45(c).

38   After the commencement date, a lessee shall recognise in profit or loss, unless the costs are included in the carrying amount of another asset applying other applicable Standards, both:

    (a)   interest on the lease liability; and

    (b)   variable lease payments not included in the measurement of the lease liability in the period in which the event or condition that triggers those payments occurs.

Reassessment of the lease liability

39   After the commencement date, a lessee shall apply paragraphs 40–43 to remeasure the lease liability to reflect changes to the lease payments. A lessee shall recognise the amount of the remeasurement of the lease liability as an adjustment to the right-of-use asset. However, if the carrying amount of the right-of-use asset is reduced to zero and there is a further reduction in the measurement of the lease liability, a lessee shall recognise any remaining amount of the remeasurement in profit or loss.

40   A lessee shall remeasure the lease liability by discounting the revised lease payments using a revised discount rate, if either:

    (a)   there is a change in the lease term, as described in paragraphs 20–21. A lessee shall determine the revised lease payments on the basis of the revised lease term; or

    (b)   there is a change in the assessment of an option to purchase the underlying asset, assessed considering the events and circumstances described in paragraphs 20–21 in the context of a purchase option. A lessee shall determine the revised lease payments to reflect the change in amounts payable under the purchase option.

41   In applying paragraph 40, a lessee shall determine the revised discount rate as the interest rate implicit in the lease for the remainder of the lease term, if that rate can be readily determined, or the lessee's incremental borrowing rate at the date of reassessment, if the interest rate implicit in the lease cannot be readily determined.

42   A lessee shall remeasure the lease liability by discounting the revised lease payments, if either:

    (a)   there is a change in the amounts expected to be payable under a residual value guarantee. A lessee shall determine the revised lease payments to reflect the change in amounts expected to be payable under the residual value guarantee.

    (b)   there is a change in future lease payments resulting from a change in an index or a rate used to determine those payments, including for example a change to reflect changes in market rental rates following a market rent review. The lessee shall remeasure the lease liability to reflect those revised lease payments only when there is a change in the cash flows (ie when the adjustment to the lease payments takes effect). A lessee shall determine the revised lease payments for the remainder of the lease term based on the revised contractual payments.

43   In applying paragraph 42, a lessee shall use an unchanged discount rate, unless the change in lease payments results from a change in floating interest rates. In that case, the lessee shall use a revised discount rate that reflects changes in the interest rate.

Lease modifications

44 A lessee shall account for a lease modification as a separate lease if both:

    (a) the modification increases the scope of the lease by adding the right to use one or more underlying assets; and

    (b) the consideration for the lease increases by an amount commensurate with the stand-alone price for the increase in scope and any appropriate adjustments to that stand-alone price to reflect the circumstances of the particular contract.

45 For a lease modification that is not accounted for as a separate lease, at the *effective date of the lease modification* a lessee shall:

    (a) allocate the consideration in the modified contract applying paragraphs 13–16;

    (b) determine the lease term of the modified lease applying paragraphs 18–19; and

    (c) remeasure the lease liability by discounting the revised lease payments using a revised discount rate. The revised discount rate is determined as the interest rate implicit in the lease for the remainder of the lease term, if that rate can be readily determined, or the lessee's incremental borrowing rate at the effective date of the modification, if the interest rate implicit in the lease cannot be readily determined.

46 For a lease modification that is not accounted for as a separate lease, the lessee shall account for the remeasurement of the lease liability by:

    (a) decreasing the carrying amount of the right-of-use asset to reflect the partial or full termination of the lease for lease modifications that decrease the scope of the lease. The lessee shall recognise in profit or loss any gain or loss relating to the partial or full termination of the lease.

    (b) making a corresponding adjustment to the right-of-use asset for all other lease modifications.

46A As a practical expedient, a lessee may elect not to assess whether a rent concession that meets the conditions in paragraph 46B is a lease modification. A lessee that makes this election shall account for any change in lease payments resulting from the rent concession the same way it would account for the change applying this Standard if the change were not a lease modification.

46B The practical expedient in paragraph 46A applies only to rent concessions occurring as a direct consequence of the covid-19 pandemic and only if all of the following conditions are met:

    (a) the change in lease payments results in revised consideration for the lease that is substantially the same as, or less than, the consideration for the lease immediately preceding the change;

(b) any reduction in lease payments affects only payments originally due on or before 30 June 2022 (for example, a rent concession would meet this condition if it results in reduced lease payments on or before 30 June 2022 and increased lease payments that extend beyond 30 June 2022); and

(c) there is no substantive change to other terms and conditions of the lease.

Presentation

47 A lessee shall either present in the statement of financial position, or disclose in the notes:

(a) right-of-use assets separately from other assets. If a lessee does not present right-of-use assets separately in the statement of financial position, the lessee shall:

(i) include right-of-use assets within the same line item as that within which the corresponding underlying assets would be presented if they were owned; and

(ii) disclose which line items in the statement of financial position include those right-of-use assets.

(b) lease liabilities separately from other liabilities. If the lessee does not present lease liabilities separately in the statement of financial position, the lessee shall disclose which line items in the statement of financial position include those liabilities.

48 The requirement in paragraph 47(a) does not apply to right-of-use assets that meet the definition of investment property, which shall be presented in the statement of financial position as investment property.

49 In the statement of profit or loss and other comprehensive income, a lessee shall present interest expense on the lease liability separately from the depreciation charge for the right-of-use asset. Interest expense on the lease liability is a component of finance costs, which paragraph 82(b) of IAS 1 *Presentation of Financial Statements* requires to be presented separately in the statement of profit or loss and other comprehensive income.

50 In the statement of cash flows, a lessee shall classify:

(a) cash payments for the principal portion of the lease liability within financing activities;

(b) cash payments for the interest portion of the lease liability applying the requirements in IAS 7 *Statement of Cash Flows* for interest paid; and

(c) short-term lease payments, payments for leases of low-value assets and variable lease payments not included in the measurement of the lease liability within operating activities.

Disclosure

51   The objective of the disclosures is for lessees to disclose information in the notes that, together with the information provided in the statement of financial position, statement of profit or loss and statement of cash flows, gives a basis for users of financial statements to assess the effect that leases have on the financial position, financial performance and cash flows of the lessee. Paragraphs 52–60 specify requirements on how to meet this objective.

52   A lessee shall disclose information about its leases for which it is a lessee in a single note or separate section in its financial statements. However, a lessee need not duplicate information that is already presented elsewhere in the financial statements, provided that the information is incorporated by cross-reference in the single note or separate section about leases.

53   A lessee shall disclose the following amounts for the reporting period:

    (a)   depreciation charge for right-of-use assets by class of underlying asset;

    (b)   interest expense on lease liabilities;

    (c)   the expense relating to short-term leases accounted for applying paragraph 6. This expense need not include the expense relating to leases with a lease term of one month or less;

    (d)   the expense relating to leases of low-value assets accounted for applying paragraph 6. This expense shall not include the expense relating to short-term leases of low-value assets included in paragraph 53(c);

    (e)   the expense relating to variable lease payments not included in the measurement of lease liabilities;

    (f)   income from subleasing right-of-use assets;

    (g)   total cash outflow for leases;

    (h)   additions to right-of-use assets;

    (i)   gains or losses arising from sale and leaseback transactions; and

    (j)   the carrying amount of right-of-use assets at the end of the reporting period by class of underlying asset.

54   A lessee shall provide the disclosures specified in paragraph 53 in a tabular format, unless another format is more appropriate. The amounts disclosed shall include costs that a lessee has included in the carrying amount of another asset during the reporting period.

55   A lessee shall disclose the amount of its lease commitments for short-term leases accounted for applying paragraph 6 if the portfolio of short-term leases to which it is committed at the end of the reporting period is dissimilar to the portfolio of short-term leases to which the short-term lease expense disclosed applying paragraph 53(c) relates.

56   If right-of-use assets meet the definition of investment property, a lessee shall apply the disclosure requirements in IAS 40. In that case, a lessee is not required to provide the disclosures in paragraph 53(a), (f), (h) or (j) for those right-of-use assets.

57   If a lessee measures right-of-use assets at revalued amounts applying IAS 16, the lessee shall disclose the information required by paragraph 77 of IAS 16 for those right-of-use assets.

58   A lessee shall disclose a maturity analysis of lease liabilities applying paragraphs 39 and B11 of IFRS 7 *Financial Instruments: Disclosures* separately from the maturity analyses of other financial liabilities.

59   In addition to the disclosures required in paragraphs 53–58, a lessee shall disclose additional qualitative and quantitative information about its leasing activities necessary to meet the disclosure objective in paragraph 51 (as described in paragraph B48). This additional information may include, but is not limited to, information that helps users of financial statements to assess:

    (a)   the nature of the lessee's leasing activities;

    (b)   future cash outflows to which the lessee is potentially exposed that are not reflected in the measurement of lease liabilities. This includes exposure arising from:

        (i)   variable lease payments (as described in paragraph B49);

        (ii)   extension options and termination options (as described in paragraph B50);

        (iii)   residual value guarantees (as described in paragraph B51); and

        (iv)   leases not yet commenced to which the lessee is committed.

    (c)   restrictions or covenants imposed by leases; and

    (d)   sale and leaseback transactions (as described in paragraph B52).

60   A lessee that accounts for short-term leases or leases of low-value assets applying paragraph 6 shall disclose that fact.

60A   If a lessee applies the practical expedient in paragraph 46A, the lessee shall disclose:

    (a)   that it has applied the practical expedient to all rent concessions that meet the conditions in paragraph 46B or, if not applied to all such rent concessions, information about the nature of the contracts to which it has applied the practical expedient (see paragraph 2); and

    (b)   the amount recognised in profit or loss for the reporting period to reflect changes in lease payments that arise from rent concessions to which the lessee has applied the practical expedient in paragraph 46A.

Lessor

Classification of leases (paragraphs B53–B58)

61   A lessor shall classify each of its leases as either an *operating lease or a finance lease*.

62   A lease is classified as a finance lease if it transfers substantially all the risks and rewards incidental to ownership of an underlying asset. A lease is classified as an operating lease if it does not transfer substantially all the risks and rewards incidental to ownership of an underlying asset.

63   Whether a lease is a finance lease or an operating lease depends on the substance of the transaction rather than the form of the contract. Examples of situations that individually or in combination would normally lead to a lease being classified as a finance lease are:

    (a)   the lease transfers ownership of the underlying asset to the lessee by the end of the lease term;

    (b)   the lessee has the option to purchase the underlying asset at a price that is expected to be sufficiently lower than the *fair value* at the date the option becomes exercisable for it to be reasonably certain, at the *inception date*, that the option will be exercised;

    (c)   the lease term is for the major part of the *economic life* of the underlying asset even if title is not transferred;

    (d)   at the inception date, the present value of the lease payments amounts to at least substantially all of the fair value of the underlying asset; and

    (e)   the underlying asset is of such a specialised nature that only the lessee can use it without major modifications.

64   Indicators of situations that individually or in combination could also lead to a lease being classified as a finance lease are:

    (a)   if the lessee can cancel the lease, the lessor's losses associated with the cancellation are borne by the lessee;

    (b)   gains or losses from the fluctuation in the fair value of the residual accrue to the lessee (for example, in the form of a rent rebate equaling most of the sales proceeds at the end of the lease); and

    (c)   the lessee has the ability to continue the lease for a secondary period at a rent that is substantially lower than market rent.

65   The examples and indicators in paragraphs 63–64 are not always conclusive. If it is clear from other features that the lease does not transfer substantially all the risks and rewards incidental to ownership of an underlying asset, the lease is classified as an operating lease. For example, this may be the case if ownership of the underlying asset transfers at the end of the lease for a variable payment equal to its then fair value, or if there are variable lease payments, as a result of which the lessor does not transfer substantially all such risks and rewards.

66   Lease classification is made at the inception date and is reassessed only if there is a lease modification. Changes in estimates (for example, changes in estimates of the economic life or of the residual value of the underlying asset), or changes in circumstances (for example, default by the lessee), do not give rise to a new classification of a lease for accounting purposes.

Finance leases

Recognition and measurement

67   **At the commencement date, a lessor shall recognise assets held under a finance lease in its statement of financial position and present them as a receivable at an amount equal to the *net investment in the lease*.**

Initial measurement

68   The lessor shall use the interest rate implicit in the lease to measure the net investment in the lease. In the case of a sublease, if the interest rate implicit in the sublease cannot be readily determined, an intermediate lessor may use the discount rate used for the head lease (adjusted for any initial direct costs associated with the sublease) to measure the net investment in the sublease.

69   Initial direct costs, other than those incurred by manufacturer or dealer lessors, are included in the initial measurement of the net investment in the lease and reduce the amount of income recognised over the lease term. The interest rate implicit in the lease is defined in such a way that the initial direct costs are included automatically in the net investment in the lease; there is no need to add them separately.

Initial measurement of the lease payments included in the net investment in the lease

70   At the commencement date, the lease payments included in the measurement of the net investment in the lease comprise the following payments for the right to use the underlying asset during the lease term that are not received at the commencement date:

(a)   fixed payments (including in-substance fixed payments as described in paragraph B42), less any lease incentives payable;

(b)   variable lease payments that depend on an index or a rate, initially measured using the index or rate as at the commencement date;

(c)   any residual value guarantees provided to the lessor by the lessee, a party related to the lessee or a third party unrelated to the lessor that is financially capable of discharging the obligations under the guarantee;

(d)   the exercise price of a purchase option if the lessee is reasonably certain to exercise that option (assessed considering the factors described in paragraph B37); and

(e)   payments of penalties for terminating the lease, if the lease term reflects the lessee exercising an option to terminate the lease.

Manufacturer or dealer lessors

71   At the commencement date, a manufacturer or dealer lessor shall recognise the following for each of its finance leases:

(a)   revenue being the fair value of the underlying asset, or, if lower, the present value of the lease payments accruing to the lessor, discounted using a market rate of interest;

(b)   the cost of sale being the cost, or carrying amount if different, of the underlying asset less the present value of the *unguaranteed residual value*; and

(c)   selling profit or loss (being the difference between revenue and the cost of sale) in accordance with its policy for outright sales to which IFRS 15 applies. A manufacturer or dealer lessor shall recognise selling profit or loss on a finance lease at the commencement date, regardless of whether the lessor transfers the underlying asset as described in IFRS 15.

72   Manufacturers or dealers often offer to customers the choice of either buying or leasing an asset. A finance lease of an asset by a manufacturer or dealer lessor gives rise to profit or loss equivalent to the profit or loss resulting from an outright sale of the underlying asset, at normal selling prices, reflecting any applicable volume or trade discounts.

73   Manufacturer or dealer lessors sometimes quote artificially low rates of interest in order to attract customers. The use of such a rate would result in a lessor recognising an excessive portion of the total income from the transaction at the commencement date. If artificially low rates of interest are quoted, a manufacturer or dealer lessor shall restrict selling profit to that which would apply if a market rate of interest were charged.

74   A manufacturer or dealer lessor shall recognise as an expense costs incurred in connection with obtaining a finance lease at the commencement date because they are mainly related to earning the manufacturer or dealer's selling profit. Costs incurred by manufacturer or dealer lessors in connection with obtaining a finance lease are excluded from the definition of initial direct costs and, thus, are excluded from the net investment in the lease.

Subsequent measurement

75   A lessor shall recognise finance income over the lease term, based on a pattern reflecting a constant periodic rate of return on the lessor's net investment in the lease.

76   A lessor aims to allocate finance income over the lease term on a systematic and rational basis. A lessor shall apply the lease payments relating to the period against the *gross investment in the lease* to reduce both the principal and the *unearned finance income*.

77 A lessor shall apply the derecognition and impairment requirements in IFRS 9 to the net investment in the lease. A lessor shall review regularly estimated unguaranteed residual values used in computing the gross investment in the lease. If there has been a reduction in the estimated unguaranteed residual value, the lessor shall revise the income allocation over the lease term and recognise immediately any reduction in respect of amounts accrued.

78 A lessor that classifies an asset under a finance lease as held for sale (or includes it in a disposal group that is classified as held for sale) applying IFRS 5 *Non-current Assets Held for Sale and Discontinued Operations* shall account for the asset in accordance with that Standard.

Lease modifications

79 A lessor shall account for a modification to a finance lease as a separate lease if both:

(a) the modification increases the scope of the lease by adding the right to use one or more underlying assets; and

(b) the consideration for the lease increases by an amount commensurate with the stand-alone price for the increase in scope and any appropriate adjustments to that stand-alone price to reflect the circumstances of the particular contract.

80 For a modification to a finance lease that is not accounted for as a separate lease, a lessor shall account for the modification as follows:

(a) if the lease would have been classified as an operating lease had the modification been in effect at the inception date, the lessor shall:

(i) account for the lease modification as a new lease from the effective date of the modification; and

(ii) measure the carrying amount of the underlying asset as the net investment in the lease immediately before the effective date of the lease modification.

(b) otherwise, the lessor shall apply the requirements of IFRS 9.

Operating leases

Recognition and measurement

81 A lessor shall recognise lease payments from operating leases as income on either a straight-line basis or another systematic basis. The lessor shall apply another systematic basis if that basis is more representative of the pattern in which benefit from the use of the underlying asset is diminished.

82 A lessor shall recognise costs, including depreciation, incurred in earning the lease income as an expense.

83 A lessor shall add initial direct costs incurred in obtaining an operating lease to the carrying amount of the underlying asset and recognise those costs as an expense over the lease term on the same basis as the lease income.

84 The depreciation policy for depreciable underlying assets subject to operating leases shall be consistent with the lessor's normal depreciation policy for similar assets. A lessor shall calculate depreciation in accordance with IAS 16 and IAS 38.

85 A lessor shall apply IAS 36 to determine whether an underlying asset subject to an operating lease is impaired and to account for any impairment loss identified.

86 A manufacturer or dealer lessor does not recognise any selling profit on entering into an operating lease because it is not the equivalent of a sale.

Lease modifications

87 A lessor shall account for a modification to an operating lease as a new lease from the effective date of the modification, considering any prepaid or accrued lease payments relating to the original lease as part of the lease payments for the new lease.

Presentation

88 A lessor shall present underlying assets subject to operating leases in its statement of financial position according to the nature of the underlying asset.

Disclosure

89 The objective of the disclosures is for lessors to disclose information in the notes that, together with the information provided in the statement of financial position, statement of profit or loss and statement of cash flows, gives a basis for users of financial statements to assess the effect that leases have on the financial position, financial performance and cash flows of the lessor. Paragraphs 90–97 specify requirements on how to meet this objective.

90 A lessor shall disclose the following amounts for the reporting period:

(a) for finance leases:

(i) selling profit or loss;

(ii) finance income on the net investment in the lease; and

(iii) income relating to variable lease payments not included in the measurement of the net investment in the lease.

(b) for operating leases, lease income, separately disclosing income relating to variable lease payments that do not depend on an index or a rate.

91 A lessor shall provide the disclosures specified in paragraph 90 in a tabular format, unless another format is more appropriate.

92   A lessor shall disclose additional qualitative and quantitative information about its leasing activities necessary to meet the disclosure objective in paragraph 89. This additional information includes, but is not limited to, information that helps users of financial statements to assess:

(a)   the nature of the lessor's leasing activities; and

(b)   how the lessor manages the risk associated with any rights it retains in underlying assets. In particular, a lessor shall disclose its risk management strategy for the rights it retains in underlying assets, including any means by which the lessor reduces that risk. Such means may include, for example, buy-back agreements, residual value guarantees or variable lease payments for use in excess of specified limits.

Finance leases

93   A lessor shall provide a qualitative and quantitative explanation of the significant changes in the carrying amount of the net investment in finance leases.

94   A lessor shall disclose a maturity analysis of the lease payments receivable, showing the undiscounted lease payments to be received on an annual basis for a minimum of each of the first five years and a total of the amounts for the remaining years. A lessor shall reconcile the undiscounted lease payments to the net investment in the lease. The reconciliation shall identify the unearned finance income relating to the lease payments receivable and any discounted unguaranteed residual value.

Operating leases

95   For items of property, plant and equipment subject to an operating lease, a lessor shall apply the disclosure requirements of IAS 16. In applying the disclosure requirements in IAS 16, a lessor shall disaggregate each class of property, plant and equipment into assets subject to operating leases and assets not subject to operating leases. Accordingly, a lessor shall provide the disclosures required by IAS 16 for assets subject to an operating lease (by class of underlying asset) separately from owned assets held and used by the lessor.

96   A lessor shall apply the disclosure requirements in IAS 36, IAS 38, IAS 40 and IAS 41 for assets subject to operating leases.

97   A lessor shall disclose a maturity analysis of lease payments, showing the undiscounted lease payments to be received on an annual basis for a minimum of each of the first five years and a total of the amounts for the remaining years.

Sale and leaseback transactions

98   If an entity (the seller-lessee) transfers an asset to another entity (the buyer-lessor) and leases that asset back from the buyer-lessor, both the seller-lessee and the buyer-lessor shall account for the transfer contract and the lease applying paragraphs 99–103.

Assessing whether the transfer of the asset is a sale

99   An entity shall apply the requirements for determining when a performance obligation is satisfied in IFRS 15 to determine whether the transfer of an asset is accounted for as a sale of that asset.

Transfer of the asset is a sale

100   If the transfer of an asset by the seller-lessee satisfies the requirements of IFRS 15 to be accounted for as a sale of the asset:

(a)   the seller-lessee shall measure the right-of-use asset arising from the leaseback at the proportion of the previous carrying amount of the asset that relates to the right of use retained by the seller-lessee. Accordingly, the seller-lessee shall recognise only the amount of any gain or loss that relates to the rights transferred to the buyer-lessor.

(b)   the buyer-lessor shall account for the purchase of the asset applying applicable Standards, and for the lease applying the lessor accounting requirements in this Standard.

101   If the fair value of the consideration for the sale of an asset does not equal the fair value of the asset, or if the payments for the lease are not at market rates, an entity shall make the following adjustments to measure the sale proceeds at fair value:

(a)   any below-market terms shall be accounted for as a prepayment of lease payments; and

(b)   any above-market terms shall be accounted for as additional financing provided by the buyer-lessor to the seller-lessee.

102   The entity shall measure any potential adjustment required by paragraph 101 on the basis of the more readily determinable of:

(a)   the difference between the fair value of the consideration for the sale and the fair value of the asset; and

(b)   the difference between the present value of the contractual payments for the lease and the present value of payments for the lease at market rates.

Transfer of the asset is not a sale

103   If the transfer of an asset by the seller-lessee does not satisfy the requirements of IFRS 15 to be accounted for as a sale of the asset:

(a)   the seller-lessee shall continue to recognise the transferred asset and shall recognise a financial liability equal to the transfer proceeds. It shall account for the financial liability applying IFRS 9.

(b)   the buyer-lessor shall not recognise the transferred asset and shall recognise a financial asset equal to the transfer proceeds. It shall account for the financial asset applying IFRS 9.

Temporary exception arising from interest rate benchmark reform

104   A lessee shall apply paragraphs 105–106 to all lease modifications that change the basis for determining future lease payments as a result of interest rate benchmark reform (see paragraphs 5.4.6 and 5.4.8 of IFRS 9). These paragraphs apply only to such lease modifications. For this purpose, the term 'interest rate benchmark reform' refers to the market-wide reform of an interest rate benchmark as described in paragraph 6.8.2 of IFRS 9.

105   As a practical expedient, a lessee shall apply paragraph 42 to account for a lease modification required by interest rate benchmark reform. This practical expedient applies only to such modifications. For this purpose, a lease modification is required by interest rate benchmark reform if, and only if, both of these conditions are met:

      (a)   the modification is necessary as a direct consequence of interest rate benchmark reform; and

      (b)   the new basis for determining the lease payments is economically equivalent to the previous basis (ie the basis immediately preceding the modification).

106   However, if lease modifications are made in addition to those lease modifications required by interest rate benchmark reform, a lessee shall apply the applicable requirements in this Standard to account for all lease modifications made at the same time, including those required by interest rate benchmark reform.

Appendix A
Defined terms

This appendix is an integral part of the Standard.

commencement date of the lease (commencement date)	The date on which a **lessor** makes an **underlying asset** available for use by a **lessee**.
economic life	Either the period over which an asset is expected to be economically usable by one or more users or the number of production or similar units expected to be obtained from an asset by one or more users.
effective date of the modification	The date when both parties agree to a **lease modification**.
fair value	For the purpose of applying the **lessor** accounting requirements in this Standard, the amount for which an asset could be exchanged, or a liability settled, between knowledgeable, willing parties in an arm's length transaction.
finance lease	A **lease** that transfers substantially all the risks and rewards incidental to ownership of an **underlying asset**.
fixed payments	Payments made by a **lessee** to a **lessor** for the right to use an **underlying asset** during the **lease term**, excluding **variable lease payments**.
gross investment in the lease	The sum of:
	(a) the **lease payments** receivable by a **lessor** under a **finance lease**; and
	(b) any **unguaranteed residual value** accruing to the lessor.
inception date of the lease (inception date)	The earlier of the date of a **lease** agreement and the date of commitment by the parties to the principal terms and conditions of the lease.
initial direct costs	Incremental costs of obtaining a **lease** that would not have been incurred if the lease had not been obtained, except for such costs incurred by a manufacturer or dealer **lessor** in connection with a **finance lease**.
interest rate implicit in the lease	The rate of interest that causes the present value of (a) the **lease payments** and (b) the **unguaranteed residual value** to equal the sum of (i) the **fair value** of the **underlying asset** and (ii) any **initial direct costs** of the lessor.
lease	A contract, or part of a contract, that conveys the right to use an asset (the **underlying asset**) for a period of time in exchange for consideration.
lease incentives	Payments made by a **lessor** to a **lessee** associated with a **lease**, or the reimbursement or assumption by a lessor of costs of a lessee.

lease modification	A change in the scope of a **lease**, or the consideration for a lease, that was not part of the original terms and conditions of the lease (for example, adding or terminating the right to use one or more **underlying assets**, or extending or shortening the contractual **lease term**).
lease payments	Payments made by a **lessee** to a **lessor** relating to the right to use an **underlying asset** during the **lease term**, comprising the following:

(a)   **fixed payments** (including in-substance fixed payments), less any **lease incentives**;

(b)   **variable lease payments** that depend on an index or a rate;

(c)   the exercise price of a purchase option if the lessee is reasonably certain to exercise that option; and

(d)   payments of penalties for terminating the **lease**, if the lease term reflects the lessee exercising an option to terminate the lease.

For the lessee, lease payments also include amounts expected to be payable by the lessee under **residual value guarantees**. Lease payments do not include payments allocated to non-lease components of a contract, unless the lessee elects to combine non-lease components with a lease component and to account for them as a single lease component.

For the lessor, lease payments also include any residual value guarantees provided to the lessor by the lessee, a party related to the lessee or a third party unrelated to the lessor that is financially capable of discharging the obligations under the guarantee. Lease payments do not include payments allocated to non-lease components.

lease term	The non-cancellable period for which a **lessee** has the right to use an **underlying asset**, together with both:

(a)   periods covered by an option to extend the **lease** if the lessee is reasonably certain to exercise that option; and

(b)   periods covered by an option to terminate the lease if the lessee is reasonably certain not to exercise that option.

lessee	An entity that obtains the right to use an **underlying asset** for a period of time in exchange for consideration.
lessee's incremental borrowing rate	The rate of interest that a **lessee** would have to pay to borrow over a similar term, and with a similar security, the funds necessary to obtain an asset of a similar value to the **right-of-use asset** in a similar economic environment.

lessor	An entity that provides the right to use an **underlying asset** for a period of time in exchange for consideration.
net investment in the lease	The **gross investment in the lease** discounted at the **interest rate implicit in the lease**.
operating lease	A **lease** that does not transfer substantially all the risks and rewards incidental to ownership of an **underlying asset**.
optional lease payments	Payments to be made by a **lessee** to a **lessor** for the right to use an **underlying asset** during periods covered by an option to extend or terminate a **lease** that are not included in the **lease term**.
period of use	The total period of time that an asset is used to fulfil a contract with a customer (including any non-consecutive periods of time).
residual value guarantee	A guarantee made to a **lessor** by a party unrelated to the lessor that the value (or part of the value) of an **underlying asset** at the end of a **lease** will be at least a specified amount.
right-of-use asset	An asset that represents a **lessee's** right to use an **underlying asset** for the **lease term**.
short-term lease	A **lease** that, at the **commencement date**, has a **lease term** of 12 months or less. A lease that contains a purchase option is not a short-term lease.
sublease	A transaction for which an **underlying asset** is re-leased by a **lessee** ('intermediate lessor') to a third party, and the **lease** ('head lease') between the head lessor and lessee remains in effect.
underlying asset	An asset that is the subject of a **lease**, for which the right to use that asset has been provided by a **lessor** to a **lessee**.
unearned finance income	The difference between: (a) the **gross investment in the lease**; and (b) the **net investment in the lease**.
unguaranteed residual value	That portion of the residual value of the **underlying asset**, the realisation of which by a **lessor** is not assured or is guaranteed solely by a party related to the lessor.
variable lease payments	The portion of payments made by a **lessee** to a **lessor** for the right to use an **underlying asset** during the **lease term** that varies because of changes in facts or circumstances occurring after the **commencement date**, other than the passage of time.

Terms defined in other Standards and used in this Standard with the same meaning

contract	An agreement between two or more parties that creates enforceable rights and obligations.

useful life   The period over which an asset is expected to be available for use by an entity; or the number of production or similar units expected to be obtained from an asset by an entity.

Appendix B
Application guidance

*This appendix is an integral part of the Standard. It describes the application of paragraphs 1–103
and has the same authority as the other parts of the Standard.*

Portfolio application

B1   This Standard specifies the accounting for an individual lease. However, as a
practical expedient, an entity may apply this Standard to a portfolio of leases
with similar characteristics if the entity reasonably expects that the effects on
the financial statements of applying this Standard to the portfolio would not
differ materially from applying this Standard to the individual leases within
that portfolio. If accounting for a portfolio, an entity shall use estimates and
assumptions that reflect the size and composition of the portfolio.

Combination of contracts

B2   In applying this Standard, an entity shall combine two or more contracts
entered into at or near the same time with the same counterparty (or related
parties of the counterparty), and account for the contracts as a single contract
if one or more of the following criteria are met:

     (a)   the contracts are negotiated as a package with an overall commercial
objective that cannot be understood without considering the contracts
together;

     (b)   the amount of consideration to be paid in one contract depends on the
price or performance of the other contract; or

     (c)   the rights to use underlying assets conveyed in the contracts (or some
rights to use underlying assets conveyed in each of the contracts) form
a single lease component as described in paragraph B32.

Recognition exemption: leases for which the underlying asset is of low value (paragraphs 5–8)

B3   Except as specified in paragraph B7, this Standard permits a lessee to apply
paragraph 6 to account for leases for which the underlying asset is of low
value. A lessee shall assess the value of an underlying asset based on the value
of the asset when it is new, regardless of the age of the asset being leased.

B4   The assessment of whether an underlying asset is of low value is performed on
an absolute basis. Leases of low-value assets qualify for the accounting
treatment in paragraph 6 regardless of whether those leases are material to
the lessee. The assessment is not affected by the size, nature or circumstances
of the lessee. Accordingly, different lessees are expected to reach the same
conclusions about whether a particular underlying asset is of low value.

B5   An underlying asset can be of low value only if:

    (a)   the lessee can benefit from use of the underlying asset on its own or together with other resources that are readily available to the lessee; and

    (b)   the underlying asset is not highly dependent on, or highly interrelated with, other assets.

B6   A lease of an underlying asset does not qualify as a lease of a low-value asset if the nature of the asset is such that, when new, the asset is typically not of low value. For example, leases of cars would not qualify as leases of low-value assets because a new car would typically not be of low value.

B7   If a lessee subleases an asset, or expects to sublease an asset, the head lease does not qualify as a lease of a low-value asset.

B8   Examples of low-value underlying assets can include tablet and personal computers, small items of office furniture and telephones.

Identifying a lease (paragraphs 9–11)

B9   To assess whether a contract conveys the right to control the use of an identified asset (see paragraphs B13–B20) for a period of time, an entity shall assess whether, throughout the *period of use*, the customer has both of the following:

    (a)   the right to obtain substantially all of the economic benefits from use of the identified asset (as described in paragraphs B21–B23); and

    (b)   the right to direct the use of the identified asset (as described in paragraphs B24–B30).

B10   If the customer has the right to control the use of an identified asset for only a portion of the term of the contract, the contract contains a lease for that portion of the term.

B11   A contract to receive goods or services may be entered into by a joint arrangement, or on behalf of a joint arrangement, as defined in IFRS 11 *Joint Arrangements*. In this case, the joint arrangement is considered to be the customer in the contract. Accordingly, in assessing whether such a contract contains a lease, an entity shall assess whether the joint arrangement has the right to control the use of an identified asset throughout the period of use.

B12   An entity shall assess whether a contract contains a lease for each potential separate lease component. Refer to paragraph B32 for guidance on separate lease components.

Identified asset

B13   An asset is typically identified by being explicitly specified in a contract. However, an asset can also be identified by being implicitly specified at the time that the asset is made available for use by the customer.

B31　　The following flowchart may assist entities in making the assessment of whether a contract is, or contains, a lease.

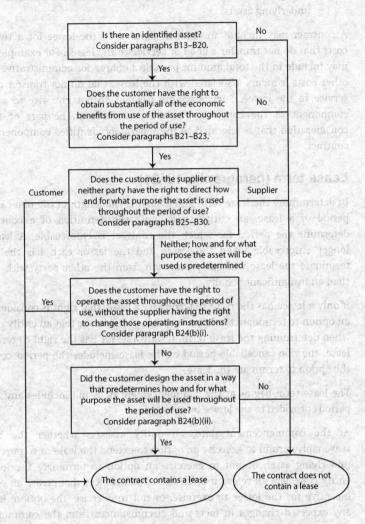

Separating components of a contract (paragraphs 12–17)

B32　　The right to use an underlying asset is a separate lease component if both:

(a)　　the lessee can benefit from use of the underlying asset either on its own or together with other resources that are readily available to the lessee. Readily available resources are goods or services that are sold or leased separately (by the lessor or other suppliers) or resources that the lessee has already obtained (from the lessor or from other transactions or events); and

(b)　　the underlying asset is neither highly dependent on, nor highly interrelated with, the other underlying assets in the contract. For example, the fact that a lessee could decide not to lease the underlying asset without significantly affecting its rights to use other underlying assets in the contract might indicate that the underlying asset is not highly dependent on, or highly interrelated with, those other underlying assets.

B33 A contract may include an amount payable by the lessee for activities and costs that do not transfer a good or service to the lessee. For example, a lessor may include in the total amount payable a charge for administrative tasks, or other costs it incurs associated with the lease, that do not transfer a good or service to the lessee. Such amounts payable do not give rise to a separate component of the contract, but are considered to be part of the total consideration that is allocated to the separately identified components of the contract.

Lease term (paragraphs 18–21)

B34 In determining the lease term and assessing the length of the non-cancellable period of a lease, an entity shall apply the definition of a contract and determine the period for which the contract is enforceable. A lease is no longer enforceable when the lessee and the lessor each has the right to terminate the lease without permission from the other party with no more than an insignificant penalty.

B35 If only a lessee has the right to terminate a lease, that right is considered to be an option to terminate the lease available to the lessee that an entity considers when determining the lease term. If only a lessor has the right to terminate a lease, the non-cancellable period of the lease includes the period covered by the option to terminate the lease.

B36 The lease term begins at the commencement date and includes any rent-free periods provided to the lessee by the lessor.

B37 At the commencement date, an entity assesses whether the lessee is reasonably certain to exercise an option to extend the lease or to purchase the underlying asset, or not to exercise an option to terminate the lease. The entity considers all relevant facts and circumstances that create an economic incentive for the lessee to exercise, or not to exercise, the option, including any expected changes in facts and circumstances from the commencement date until the exercise date of the option. Examples of factors to consider include, but are not limited to:

(a) contractual terms and conditions for the optional periods compared with market rates, such as:

(i) the amount of payments for the lease in any optional period;

(ii) the amount of any variable payments for the lease or other contingent payments, such as payments resulting from termination penalties and residual value guarantees; and

(iii) the terms and conditions of any options that are exercisable after initial optional periods (for example, a purchase option that is exercisable at the end of an extension period at a rate that is currently below market rates).

(b)   significant leasehold improvements undertaken (or expected to be undertaken) over the term of the contract that are expected to have significant economic benefit for the lessee when the option to extend or terminate the lease, or to purchase the underlying asset, becomes exercisable;

(c)   costs relating to the termination of the lease, such as negotiation costs, relocation costs, costs of identifying another underlying asset suitable for the lessee's needs, costs of integrating a new asset into the lessee's operations, or termination penalties and similar costs, including costs associated with returning the underlying asset in a contractually specified condition or to a contractually specified location;

(d)   the importance of that underlying asset to the lessee's operations, considering, for example, whether the underlying asset is a specialised asset, the location of the underlying asset and the availability of suitable alternatives; and

(e)   conditionality associated with exercising the option (ie when the option can be exercised only if one or more conditions are met), and the likelihood that those conditions will exist.

B38   An option to extend or terminate a lease may be combined with one or more other contractual features (for example, a residual value guarantee) such that the lessee guarantees the lessor a minimum or fixed cash return that is substantially the same regardless of whether the option is exercised. In such cases, and notwithstanding the guidance on in-substance fixed payments in paragraph B42, an entity shall assume that the lessee is reasonably certain to exercise the option to extend the lease, or not to exercise the option to terminate the lease.

B39   The shorter the non-cancellable period of a lease, the more likely a lessee is to exercise an option to extend the lease or not to exercise an option to terminate the lease. This is because the costs associated with obtaining a replacement asset are likely to be proportionately higher the shorter the non-cancellable period.

B40   A lessee's past practice regarding the period over which it has typically used particular types of assets (whether leased or owned), and its economic reasons for doing so, may provide information that is helpful in assessing whether the lessee is reasonably certain to exercise, or not to exercise, an option. For example, if a lessee has typically used particular types of assets for a particular period of time or if the lessee has a practice of frequently exercising options on leases of particular types of underlying assets, the lessee shall consider the economic reasons for that past practice in assessing whether it is reasonably certain to exercise an option on leases of those assets.

B41   Paragraph 20 specifies that, after the commencement date, a lessee reassesses the lease term upon the occurrence of a significant event or a significant change in circumstances that is within the control of the lessee and affects whether the lessee is reasonably certain to exercise an option not previously included in its determination of the lease term, or not to exercise an option previously included in its determination of the lease term. Examples of significant events or changes in circumstances include:

(a)   significant leasehold improvements not anticipated at the commencement date that are expected to have significant economic benefit for the lessee when the option to extend or terminate the lease, or to purchase the underlying asset, becomes exercisable;

(b)   a significant modification to, or customisation of, the underlying asset that was not anticipated at the commencement date;

(c)   the inception of a sublease of the underlying asset for a period beyond the end of the previously determined lease term; and

(d)   a business decision of the lessee that is directly relevant to exercising, or not exercising, an option (for example, a decision to extend the lease of a complementary asset, to dispose of an alternative asset or to dispose of a business unit within which the right-of-use asset is employed).

In-substance fixed lease payments (paragraphs 27(a), 36(c) and 70(a))

B42   Lease payments include any in-substance fixed lease payments. In-substance fixed lease payments are payments that may, in form, contain variability but that, in substance, are unavoidable. In-substance fixed lease payments exist, for example, if:

(a)   payments are structured as variable lease payments, but there is no genuine variability in those payments. Those payments contain variable clauses that do not have real economic substance. Examples of those types of payments include:

(i)   payments that must be made only if an asset is proven to be capable of operating during the lease, or only if an event occurs that has no genuine possibility of not occurring; or

(ii)   payments that are initially structured as variable lease payments linked to the use of the underlying asset but for which the variability will be resolved at some point after the commencement date so that the payments become fixed for the remainder of the lease term. Those payments become in-substance fixed payments when the variability is resolved.

(b)   there is more than one set of payments that a lessee could make, but only one of those sets of payments is realistic. In this case, an entity shall consider the realistic set of payments to be lease payments.

(c)   there is more than one realistic set of payments that a lessee could make, but it must make at least one of those sets of payments. In this case, an entity shall consider the set of payments that aggregates to the lowest amount (on a discounted basis) to be lease payments.

Lessee involvement with the underlying asset before the commencement date

Costs of the lessee relating to the construction or design of the underlying asset

B43 An entity may negotiate a lease before the underlying asset is available for use by the lessee. For some leases, the underlying asset may need to be constructed or redesigned for use by the lessee. Depending on the terms and conditions of the contract, a lessee may be required to make payments relating to the construction or design of the asset.

B44 If a lessee incurs costs relating to the construction or design of an underlying asset, the lessee shall account for those costs applying other applicable Standards, such as IAS 16. Costs relating to the construction or design of an underlying asset do not include payments made by the lessee for the right to use the underlying asset. Payments for the right to use an underlying asset are payments for a lease, regardless of the timing of those payments.

Legal title to the underlying asset

B45 A lessee may obtain legal title to an underlying asset before that legal title is transferred to the lessor and the asset is leased to the lessee. Obtaining legal title does not in itself determine how to account for the transaction.

B46 If the lessee controls (or obtains control of) the underlying asset before that asset is transferred to the lessor, the transaction is a sale and leaseback transaction that is accounted for applying paragraphs 98–103.

B47 However, if the lessee does not obtain control of the underlying asset before the asset is transferred to the lessor, the transaction is not a sale and leaseback transaction. For example, this may be the case if a manufacturer, a lessor and a lessee negotiate a transaction for the purchase of an asset from the manufacturer by the lessor, which is in turn leased to the lessee. The lessee may obtain legal title to the underlying asset before legal title transfers to the lessor. In this case, if the lessee obtains legal title to the underlying asset but does not obtain control of the asset before it is transferred to the lessor, the transaction is not accounted for as a sale and leaseback transaction, but as a lease.

Lessee disclosures (paragraph 59)

B48 In determining whether additional information about leasing activities is necessary to meet the disclosure objective in paragraph 51, a lessee shall consider:

(a) whether that information is relevant to users of financial statements. A lessee shall provide additional information specified in paragraph 59 only if that information is expected to be relevant to users of financial statements. In this context, this is likely to be the case if it helps those users to understand:

(i)   the flexibility provided by leases. Leases may provide flexibility if, for example, a lessee can reduce its exposure by exercising termination options or renewing leases with favourable terms and conditions.

(ii)   restrictions imposed by leases. Leases may impose restrictions, for example, by requiring the lessee to maintain particular financial ratios.

(iii)   sensitivity of reported information to key variables. Reported information may be sensitive to, for example, future variable lease payments.

(iv)   exposure to other risks arising from leases.

(v)   deviations from industry practice. Such deviations may include, for example, unusual or unique lease terms and conditions that affect a lessee's lease portfolio.

(b)   whether that information is apparent from information either presented in the primary financial statements or disclosed in the notes. A lessee need not duplicate information that is already presented elsewhere in the financial statements.

B49   Additional information relating to variable lease payments that, depending on the circumstances, may be needed to satisfy the disclosure objective in paragraph 51 could include information that helps users of financial statements to assess, for example:

(a)   the lessee's reasons for using variable lease payments and the prevalence of those payments;

(b)   the relative magnitude of variable lease payments to fixed payments;

(c)   key variables upon which variable lease payments depend and how payments are expected to vary in response to changes in those key variables; and

(d)   other operational and financial effects of variable lease payments.

B50   Additional information relating to extension options or termination options that, depending on the circumstances, may be needed to satisfy the disclosure objective in paragraph 51 could include information that helps users of financial statements to assess, for example:

(a)   the lessee's reasons for using extension options or termination options and the prevalence of those options;

(b)   the relative magnitude of *optional lease payments* to lease payments;

(c)   the prevalence of the exercise of options that were not included in the measurement of lease liabilities; and

(d)   other operational and financial effects of those options.

B51   Additional information relating to residual value guarantees that, depending on the circumstances, may be needed to satisfy the disclosure objective in paragraph 51 could include information that helps users of financial statements to assess, for example:

      (a)   the lessee's reasons for providing residual value guarantees and the prevalence of those guarantees;

      (b)   the magnitude of a lessee's exposure to residual value risk;

      (c)   the nature of underlying assets for which those guarantees are provided; and

      (d)   other operational and financial effects of those guarantees.

B52   Additional information relating to sale and leaseback transactions that, depending on the circumstances, may be needed to satisfy the disclosure objective in paragraph 51 could include information that helps users of financial statements to assess, for example:

      (a)   the lessee's reasons for sale and leaseback transactions and the prevalence of those transactions;

      (b)   key terms and conditions of individual sale and leaseback transactions;

      (c)   payments not included in the measurement of lease liabilities; and

      (d)   the cash flow effect of sale and leaseback transactions in the reporting period.

Lessor lease classification (paragraphs 61–66)

B53   The classification of leases for lessors in this Standard is based on the extent to which the lease transfers the risks and rewards incidental to ownership of an underlying asset. Risks include the possibilities of losses from idle capacity or technological obsolescence and of variations in return because of changing economic conditions. Rewards may be represented by the expectation of profitable operation over the underlying asset's economic life and of gain from appreciation in value or realisation of a residual value.

B54   A lease contract may include terms and conditions to adjust the lease payments for particular changes that occur between the inception date and the commencement date (such as a change in the lessor's cost of the underlying asset or a change in the lessor's cost of financing the lease). In that case, for the purposes of classifying the lease, the effect of any such changes shall be deemed to have taken place at the inception date.

B55   When a lease includes both land and buildings elements, a lessor shall assess the classification of each element as a finance lease or an operating lease separately applying paragraphs 62–66 and B53–B54. In determining whether the land element is an operating lease or a finance lease, an important consideration is that land normally has an indefinite economic life.

B56   Whenever necessary in order to classify and account for a lease of land and buildings, a lessor shall allocate lease payments (including any lump-sum upfront payments) between the land and the buildings elements in proportion to the relative fair values of the leasehold interests in the land element and buildings element of the lease at the inception date. If the lease payments cannot be allocated reliably between these two elements, the entire lease is classified as a finance lease, unless it is clear that both elements are operating leases, in which case the entire lease is classified as an operating lease.

B57   For a lease of land and buildings in which the amount for the land element is immaterial to the lease, a lessor may treat the land and buildings as a single unit for the purpose of lease classification and classify it as a finance lease or an operating lease applying paragraphs 62–66 and B53–B54. In such a case, a lessor shall regard the economic life of the buildings as the economic life of the entire underlying asset.

Sublease classification

B58   In classifying a sublease, an intermediate lessor shall classify the sublease as a finance lease or an operating lease as follows:

(a)   if the head lease is a short-term lease that the entity, as a lessee, has accounted for applying paragraph 6, the sublease shall be classified as an operating lease.

(b)   otherwise, the sublease shall be classified by reference to the right-of-use asset arising from the head lease, rather than by reference to the underlying asset (for example, the item of property, plant or equipment that is the subject of the lease).

Appendix C
Effective date and transition

This appendix is an integral part of the Standard and has the same authority as the other parts of the Standard.

Effective date

C1   An entity shall apply this Standard for annual reporting periods beginning on or after 1 January 2019. Earlier application is permitted for entities that apply IFRS 15 *Revenue from Contracts with Customers* at or before the date of initial application of this Standard. If an entity applies this Standard earlier, it shall disclose that fact.

C1A   *Covid-19-Related Rent Concessions*, issued in May 2020, added paragraphs 46A, 46B, 60A, C20A and C20B. A lessee shall apply that amendment for annual reporting periods beginning on or after 1 June 2020. Earlier application is permitted, including in financial statements not authorised for issue at 28 May 2020.

C1B   *Interest Rate Benchmark Reform—Phase 2*, which amended IFRS 9, IAS 39, IFRS 7, IFRS 4 and IFRS 16, issued in August 2020, added paragraphs 104–106 and C20C–C20D. An entity shall apply these amendments for annual reporting periods beginning on or after 1 January 2021. Earlier application is permitted. If an entity applies these amendments for an earlier period, it shall disclose that fact.

C1C   *Covid-19-Related Rent Concessions beyond 30 June 2021*, issued in March 2021, amended paragraph 46B and added paragraphs C20BA–C20BC. A lessee shall apply that amendment for annual reporting periods beginning on or after 1 April 2021. Earlier application is permitted, including in financial statements not authorised for issue at 31 March 2021.

Transition

C2   For the purposes of the requirements in paragraphs C1–C19, the date of initial application is the beginning of the annual reporting period in which an entity first applies this Standard.

Definition of a lease

C3   As a practical expedient, an entity is not required to reassess whether a contract is, or contains, a lease at the date of initial application. Instead, the entity is permitted:

(a)   to apply this Standard to contracts that were previously identified as leases applying IAS 17 *Leases* and IFRIC 4 *Determining whether an Arrangement contains a Lease*. The entity shall apply the transition requirements in paragraphs C5–C18 to those leases.

(b)   not to apply this Standard to contracts that were not previously identified as containing a lease applying IAS 17 and IFRIC 4.

C4   If an entity chooses the practical expedient in paragraph C3, it shall disclose that fact and apply the practical expedient to all of its contracts. As a result, the entity shall apply the requirements in paragraphs 9–11 only to contracts entered into (or changed) on or after the date of initial application.

Lessees

C5   A lessee shall apply this Standard to its leases either:

(a)   retrospectively to each prior reporting period presented applying IAS 8 *Accounting Policies, Changes in Accounting Estimates and Errors*; or

(b)   retrospectively with the cumulative effect of initially applying the Standard recognised at the date of initial application in accordance with paragraphs C7–C13.

C6   A lessee shall apply the election described in paragraph C5 consistently to all of its leases in which it is a lessee.

C7   If a lessee elects to apply this Standard in accordance with paragraph C5(b), the lessee shall not restate comparative information. Instead, the lessee shall recognise the cumulative effect of initially applying this Standard as an adjustment to the opening balance of retained earnings (or other component of equity, as appropriate) at the date of initial application.

Leases previously classified as operating leases

C8   If a lessee elects to apply this Standard in accordance with paragraph C5(b), the lessee shall:

(a)   recognise a lease liability at the date of initial application for leases previously classified as an operating lease applying IAS 17. The lessee shall measure that lease liability at the present value of the remaining lease payments, discounted using the lessee's incremental borrowing rate at the date of initial application.

(b)   recognise a right-of-use asset at the date of initial application for leases previously classified as an operating lease applying IAS 17. The lessee shall choose, on a lease-by-lease basis, to measure that right-of-use asset at either:

(i)   its carrying amount as if the Standard had been applied since the commencement date, but discounted using the lessee's incremental borrowing rate at the date of initial application; or

(ii)   an amount equal to the lease liability, adjusted by the amount of any prepaid or accrued lease payments relating to that lease recognised in the statement of financial position immediately before the date of initial application.

(c)   apply IAS 36 *Impairment of Assets* to right-of-use assets at the date of initial application, unless the lessee applies the practical expedient in paragraph C10(b).

C9   Notwithstanding the requirements in paragraph C8, for leases previously classified as operating leases applying IAS 17, a lessee:

(a)   is not required to make any adjustments on transition for leases for which the underlying asset is of low value (as described in paragraphs B3–B8) that will be accounted for applying paragraph 6. The lessee shall account for those leases applying this Standard from the date of initial application.

(b)   is not required to make any adjustments on transition for leases previously accounted for as investment property using the fair value model in IAS 40 *Investment Property*. The lessee shall account for the right-of-use asset and the lease liability arising from those leases applying IAS 40 and this Standard from the date of initial application.

(c)   shall measure the right-of-use asset at fair value at the date of initial application for leases previously accounted for as operating leases applying IAS 17 and that will be accounted for as investment property using the fair value model in IAS 40 from the date of initial application. The lessee shall account for the right-of-use asset and the lease liability arising from those leases applying IAS 40 and this Standard from the date of initial application.

C10   A lessee may use one or more of the following practical expedients when applying this Standard retrospectively in accordance with paragraph C5(b) to leases previously classified as operating leases applying IAS 17. A lessee is permitted to apply these practical expedients on a lease-by-lease basis:

(a)   a lessee may apply a single discount rate to a portfolio of leases with reasonably similar characteristics (such as leases with a similar remaining lease term for a similar class of underlying asset in a similar economic environment).

(b)   a lessee may rely on its assessment of whether leases are onerous applying IAS 37 *Provisions, Contingent Liabilities and Contingent Assets* immediately before the date of initial application as an alternative to performing an impairment review. If a lessee chooses this practical expedient, the lessee shall adjust the right-of-use asset at the date of initial application by the amount of any provision for onerous leases recognised in the statement of financial position immediately before the date of initial application.

(c)   a lessee may elect not to apply the requirements in paragraph C8 to leases for which the lease term ends within 12 months of the date of initial application. In this case, a lessee shall:

(i)   account for those leases in the same way as short-term leases as described in paragraph 6; and

     (ii)   include the cost associated with those leases within the disclosure of short-term lease expense in the annual reporting period that includes the date of initial application.

(d)   a lessee may exclude initial direct costs from the measurement of the right-of-use asset at the date of initial application.

(e)   a lessee may use hindsight, such as in determining the lease term if the contract contains options to extend or terminate the lease.

Leases previously classified as finance leases

C11   If a lessee elects to apply this Standard in accordance with paragraph C5(b), for leases that were classified as finance leases applying IAS 17, the carrying amount of the right-of-use asset and the lease liability at the date of initial application shall be the carrying amount of the lease asset and lease liability immediately before that date measured applying IAS 17. For those leases, a lessee shall account for the right-of-use asset and the lease liability applying this Standard from the date of initial application.

Disclosure

C12   If a lessee elects to apply this Standard in accordance with paragraph C5(b), the lessee shall disclose information about initial application required by paragraph 28 of IAS 8, except for the information specified in paragraph 28(f) of IAS 8. Instead of the information specified in paragraph 28(f) of IAS 8, the lessee shall disclose:

(a)   the weighted average lessee's incremental borrowing rate applied to lease liabilities recognised in the statement of financial position at the date of initial application; and

(b)   an explanation of any difference between:

    (i)   operating lease commitments disclosed applying IAS 17 at the end of the annual reporting period immediately preceding the date of initial application, discounted using the incremental borrowing rate at the date of initial application as described in paragraph C8(a); and

    (ii)   lease liabilities recognised in the statement of financial position at the date of initial application.

C13   If a lessee uses one or more of the specified practical expedients in paragraph C10, it shall disclose that fact.

Lessors

C14   Except as described in paragraph C15, a lessor is not required to make any adjustments on transition for leases in which it is a lessor and shall account for those leases applying this Standard from the date of initial application.

C15   An intermediate lessor shall:

(a)   reassess subleases that were classified as operating leases applying IAS 17 and are ongoing at the date of initial application, to determine whether each sublease should be classified as an operating lease or a finance lease applying this Standard. The intermediate lessor shall perform this assessment at the date of initial application on the basis of the remaining contractual terms and conditions of the head lease and sublease at that date.

(b)   for subleases that were classified as operating leases applying IAS 17 but finance leases applying this Standard, account for the sublease as a new finance lease entered into at the date of initial application.

Sale and leaseback transactions before the date of initial application

C16   An entity shall not reassess sale and leaseback transactions entered into before the date of initial application to determine whether the transfer of the underlying asset satisfies the requirements in IFRS 15 to be accounted for as a sale.

C17   If a sale and leaseback transaction was accounted for as a sale and a finance lease applying IAS 17, the seller-lessee shall:

(a)   account for the leaseback in the same way as it accounts for any other finance lease that exists at the date of initial application; and

(b)   continue to amortise any gain on sale over the lease term.

C18   If a sale and leaseback transaction was accounted for as a sale and operating lease applying IAS 17, the seller-lessee shall:

(a)   account for the leaseback in the same way as it accounts for any other operating lease that exists at the date of initial application; and

(b)   adjust the leaseback right-of-use asset for any deferred gains or losses that relate to off-market terms recognised in the statement of financial position immediately before the date of initial application.

Amounts previously recognised in respect of business combinations

C19   If a lessee previously recognised an asset or a liability applying IFRS 3 *Business Combinations* relating to favourable or unfavourable terms of an operating lease acquired as part of a business combination, the lessee shall derecognise that asset or liability and adjust the carrying amount of the right-of-use asset by a corresponding amount at the date of initial application.

References to IFRS 9

C20   If an entity applies this Standard but does not yet apply IFRS 9 *Financial Instruments*, any reference in this Standard to IFRS 9 shall be read as a reference to IAS 39 *Financial Instruments: Recognition and Measurement*.

Covid-19-related rent concessions for lessees

C20A   A lessee shall apply *Covid-19-Related Rent Concessions* (see paragraph C1A) retrospectively, recognising the cumulative effect of initially applying that amendment as an adjustment to the opening balance of retained earnings (or other component of equity, as appropriate) at the beginning of the annual reporting period in which the lessee first applies the amendment.

C20B   In the reporting period in which a lessee first applies *Covid-19-Related Rent Concessions*, a lessee is not required to disclose the information required by paragraph 28(f) of IAS 8.

C20BA   A lessee shall apply *Covid-19-Related Rent Concessions beyond 30 June 2021* (see paragraph C1C) retrospectively, recognising the cumulative effect of initially applying that amendment as an adjustment to the opening balance of retained earnings (or other component of equity, as appropriate) at the beginning of the annual reporting period in which the lessee first applies the amendment.

C20BB   In the reporting period in which a lessee first applies *Covid-19-Related Rent Concessions beyond 30 June 2021*, a lessee is not required to disclose the information required by paragraph 28(f) of IAS 8.

C20BC   Applying paragraph 2 of this Standard, a lessee shall apply the practical expedient in paragraph 46A consistently to eligible contracts with similar characteristics and in similar circumstances, irrespective of whether the contract became eligible for the practical expedient as a result of the lessee applying *Covid-19-Related Rent Concessions* (see paragraph C1A) or *Covid-19-Related Rent Concessions beyond 30 June 2021* (see paragraph C1C).

Interest Rate Benchmark Reform—Phase 2

C20C   An entity shall apply these amendments retrospectively in accordance with IAS 8, except as specified in paragraph C20D.

C20D   An entity is not required to restate prior periods to reflect the application of these amendments. The entity may restate prior periods if, and only if, it is possible without the use of hindsight. If an entity does not restate prior periods, the entity shall recognise any difference between the previous carrying amount and the carrying amount at the beginning of the annual reporting period that includes the date of initial application of these amendments in the opening retained earnings (or other component of equity, as appropriate) of the annual reporting period that includes the date of initial application of these amendments.

Withdrawal of other Standards

C21   This Standard supersedes the following Standards and Interpretations:

(a)   IAS 17 *Leases*;

(b)   IFRIC 4 *Determining whether an Arrangement contains a Lease*;

(c)   SIC-15 *Operating Leases — Incentives*; and

(d)   SIC-27 *Evaluating the Substance of Transactions Involving the Legal Form of a Lease.*

Appendix D
Amendments to other Standards

This appendix sets out the amendments to other Standards that are a consequence of the IASB issuing this Standard. An entity shall apply the amendments for annual periods beginning on or after 1 January 2019. If an entity applies this Standard for an earlier period, it shall also apply these amendments for that earlier period.

An entity is not permitted to apply IFRS 16 before applying IFRS 15 Revenue from Contracts with Customers *(see paragraph C1).*

Consequently, for Standards that were effective on 1 January 2016, the amendments in this appendix are presented based on the text of those Standards that was effective on 1 January 2016, as amended by IFRS 15. The text of those Standards in this appendix does not include any other amendments that were not effective at 1 January 2016.

For Standards that were not effective on 1 January 2016, the amendments in this appendix are presented based on the text of the initial publication of that Standard, as amended by IFRS 15. The text of those Standards in this appendix does not include any other amendments that were not effective at 1 January 2016.

* * * * *

The amendments contained in this appendix when this Standard was issued in 2016 have been incorporated into the text of the relevant Standards included in this volume.

Approval by the Board of IFRS 16 *Leases* issued in January 2016

IFRS 16 *Leases* was approved for issue by thirteen of the fourteen members of the International Accounting Standards Board. Mr Zhang dissented. His dissenting opinion is set out after the Basis for Conclusions.

Hans Hoogervorst	Chairman
Ian Mackintosh	Vice-Chairman
Stephen Cooper	
Philippe Danjou	
Martin Edelmann	
Patrick Finnegan	
Gary Kabureck	
Suzanne Lloyd	
Amaro Luiz de Oliveira Gomes	
Takatsugu Ochi	
Darrel Scott	
Chungwoo Suh	
Mary Tokar	
Wei-Guo Zhang	

Approval by the Board of *Covid-19-Related Rent Concessions* issued in May 2020

Covid-19-Related Rent Concessions, which amended IFRS 16, was approved for issue by all 14 members of the International Accounting Standards Board.

Hans Hoogervorst	Chairman
Suzanne Lloyd	Vice-Chair
Nick Anderson	
Tadeu Cendon	
Martin Edelmann	
Françoise Flores	
Gary Kabureck	
Jianqiao Lu	
Darrel Scott	
Thomas Scott	
Chungwoo Suh	
Rika Suzuki	
Ann Tarca	
Mary Tokar	

Approval by the Board of *Interest Rate Benchmark Reform—Phase 2* issued in August 2020

Interest Rate Benchmark Reform—Phase 2, which amended IFRS 9, IAS 39, IFRS 7, IFRS 4 and IFRS 16, was approved for issue by 12 of 13 members of the International Accounting Standards Board (Board). Mr Gast abstained in view of his recent appointment to the Board.

Hans Hoogervorst	Chairman
Suzanne Lloyd	Vice-Chair
Nick Anderson	
Tadeu Cendon	
Martin Edelmann	
Françoise Flores	
Zach Gast	
Jianqiao Lu	
Darrel Scott	
Thomas Scott	
Rika Suzuki	
Ann Tarca	
Mary Tokar	

Approval by the Board of Covid-19-Related Rent Concessions beyond 30 June 2021 issued in March 2021

Approval by the Board of Covid-19-Related Rent Concessions beyond 30 June 2021, which amended IFRS 16, was approved for issue by 11 of 13 members of the International Accounting Standards Board. Messrs Anderson and Gast dissented. Their dissenting opinion is set out after the Basis for Conclusions.

Hans Hoogervorst	Chairman
Suzanne Lloyd	Vice-Chair
Nick Anderson	
Tadeu Cendon	
Martin Edelmann	
Françoise Flores	
Zachary Gast	
Jianqiao Lu	
Bruce Mackenzie	
Thomas Scott	
Rika Suzuki	
Ann Tarca	
Mary Tokar	

IAS 1

Presentation of Financial Statements

In April 2001 the International Accounting Standards Board (Board) adopted IAS 1 *Presentation of Financial Statements*, which had originally been issued by the International Accounting Standards Committee in September 1997. IAS 1 *Presentation of Financial Statements* replaced IAS 1 *Disclosure of Accounting Policies* (issued in 1975), IAS 5 *Information to be Disclosed in Financial Statements* (originally approved in 1977) and IAS 13 *Presentation of Current Assets and Current Liabilities* (approved in 1979).

In December 2003 the Board issued a revised IAS 1 as part of its initial agenda of technical projects. The Board issued an amended IAS 1 in September 2007, which included an amendment to the presentation of owner changes in equity and comprehensive income and a change in terminology in the titles of financial statements. In June 2011 the Board amended IAS 1 to improve how items of other income comprehensive income should be presented.

In December 2014 IAS 1 was amended by *Disclosure Initiative* (Amendments to IAS 1), which addressed concerns expressed about some of the existing presentation and disclosure requirements in IAS 1 and ensured that entities are able to use judgement when applying those requirements. In addition, the amendments clarified the requirements in paragraph 82A of IAS 1.

In October 2018 the Board issued *Definition of Material* (Amendments to IAS 1 and IAS 8). This amendment clarified the definition of material and how it should be applied by (a) including in the definition guidance that until now has featured elsewhere in IFRS Standards; (b) improving the explanations accompanying the definition; and (c) ensuring that the definition of material is consistent across all IFRS Standards.

Other Standards have made minor consequential amendments to IAS 1. They include *Improvement to IFRSs* (issued April 2009), *Improvement to IFRSs* (issued May 2010), IFRS 10 *Consolidated Financial Statements* (issued May 2011), IFRS 12 *Disclosures of Interests in Other Entities* (issued May 2011), IFRS 13 *Fair Value Measurement* (issued May 2011), IAS 19 *Employee Benefits* (issued June 2011), *Annual Improvements to IFRSs 2009–2011 Cycle* (issued May 2012), IFRS 9 *Financial Instruments* (Hedge Accounting and amendments to IFRS 9, IFRS 7 and IAS 39) (issued November 2013), IFRS 15 *Revenue from Contracts with Customers* (issued May 2014), *Agriculture: Bearer Plants* (Amendments to IAS 16 and IAS 41) (issued June 2014), IFRS 9 *Financial Instruments* (issued July 2014), IFRS 16 *Leases* (issued January 2016), *Disclosure Initiative* (Amendments to IAS 7) (issued January 2016) and *Amendments to References to the Conceptual Framework in IFRS Standards* (issued March 2018).

Contents

FOR THE ACCOMPANYING GUIDANCE LISTED BELOW, SEE PART B OF THIS EDITION

FOR THE BASIS FOR CONCLUSIONS, SEE PART C OF THIS EDITION

continued...

International Accounting Standard 1 *Presentation of Financial Statements* (IAS 1) is set out in paragraphs 1–140 and the Appendix. All the paragraphs have equal authority. IAS 1 should be read in the context of its objective and the Basis for Conclusions, the *Preface to IFRS Standards* and the *Conceptual Framework for Financial Reporting*. IAS 8 *Accounting Policies, Changes in Accounting Estimates and Errors* provides a basis for selecting and applying accounting policies in the absence of explicit guidance.

International Accounting Standard 1
Presentation of Financial Statements

Objective

1   This Standard prescribes the basis for presentation of general purpose financial statements to ensure comparability both with the entity's financial statements of previous periods and with the financial statements of other entities. It sets out overall requirements for the presentation of financial statements, guidelines for their structure and minimum requirements for their content.

Scope

2   An entity shall apply this Standard in preparing and presenting general purpose financial statements in accordance with International Financial Reporting Standards (IFRSs).

3   Other IFRSs set out the recognition, measurement and disclosure requirements for specific transactions and other events.

4   This Standard does not apply to the structure and content of condensed interim financial statements prepared in accordance with IAS 34 *Interim Financial Reporting*. However, paragraphs 15–35 apply to such financial statements. This Standard applies equally to all entities, including those that present consolidated financial statements in accordance with IFRS 10 *Consolidated Financial Statements* and those that present separate financial statements in accordance with IAS 27 *Separate Financial Statements*.

5   This Standard uses terminology that is suitable for profit-oriented entities, including public sector business entities. If entities with not-for-profit activities in the private sector or the public sector apply this Standard, they may need to amend the descriptions used for particular line items in the financial statements and for the financial statements themselves.

6   Similarly, entities that do not have equity as defined in IAS 32 *Financial Instruments: Presentation* (eg some mutual funds) and entities whose share capital is not equity (eg some co-operative entities) may need to adapt the financial statement presentation of members' or unitholders' interests.

Definitions

7   The following terms are used in this Standard with the meanings specified:

General purpose financial statements (referred to as 'financial statements') are those intended to meet the needs of users who are not in a position to require an entity to prepare reports tailored to their particular information needs.

Impracticable Applying a requirement is impracticable when the entity cannot apply it after making every reasonable effort to do so.

International Financial Reporting Standards (IFRSs) are Standards and Interpretations issued by the International Accounting Standards Board (IASB). They comprise:

(a)   International Financial Reporting Standards;

(b)   International Accounting Standards;

(c)   IFRIC Interpretations; and

(d)   SIC Interpretations.[1]

Material:

Information is material if omitting, misstating or obscuring it could reasonably be expected to influence decisions that the primary users of general purpose financial statements make on the basis of those financial statements, which provide financial information about a specific reporting entity.

Materiality depends on the nature or magnitude of information, or both. An entity assesses whether information, either individually or in combination with other information, is material in the context of its financial statements taken as a whole.

Information is obscured if it is communicated in a way that would have a similar effect for primary users of financial statements to omitting or misstating that information. The following are examples of circumstances that may result in material information being obscured:

(a)   information regarding a material item, transaction or other event is disclosed in the financial statements but the language used is vague or unclear;

(b)   information regarding a material item, transaction or other event is scattered throughout the financial statements;

(c)   dissimilar items, transactions or other events are inappropriately aggregated;

(d)   similar items, transactions or other events are inappropriately disaggregated; and

(e)   the understandability of the financial statements is reduced as a result of material information being hidden by immaterial information to the extent that a primary user is unable to determine what information is material.

Assessing whether information could reasonably be expected to influence decisions made by the primary users of a specific reporting entity's general purpose financial statements requires an entity to consider the characteristics of those users while also considering the entity's own circumstances.

---

1   Definition of IFRSs amended after the name changes introduced by the revised Constitution of the IFRS Foundation in 2010.

Many existing and potential investors, lenders and other creditors cannot require reporting entities to provide information directly to them and must rely on general purpose financial statements for much of the financial information they need. Consequently, they are the primary users to whom general purpose financial statements are directed. Financial statements are prepared for users who have a reasonable knowledge of business and economic activities and who review and analyse the information diligently. At times, even well-informed and diligent users may need to seek the aid of an adviser to understand information about complex economic phenomena.

Notes contain information in addition to that presented in the statement of financial position, statement(s) of profit or loss and other comprehensive income, statement of changes in equity and statement of cash flows. Notes provide narrative descriptions or disaggregations of items presented in those statements and information about items that do not qualify for recognition in those statements.

Other comprehensive income comprises items of income and expense (including reclassification adjustments) that are not recognised in profit or loss as required or permitted by other IFRSs.

The components of other comprehensive income include:

(a)   changes in revaluation surplus (see IAS 16 *Property, Plant and Equipment* and IAS 38 *Intangible Assets*);

(b)   remeasurements of defined benefit plans (see IAS 19 *Employee Benefits*);

(c)   gains and losses arising from translating the financial statements of a foreign operation (see IAS 21 *The Effects of Changes in Foreign Exchange Rates*);

(d)   gains and losses from investments in equity instruments designated at fair value through other comprehensive income in accordance with paragraph 5.7.5 of IFRS 9 *Financial Instruments*;

(da) gains and losses on financial assets measured at fair value through other comprehensive income in accordance with paragraph 4.1.2A of IFRS 9.

(e)   the effective portion of gains and losses on hedging instruments in a cash flow hedge and the gains and losses on hedging instruments that hedge investments in equity instruments measured at fair value through other comprehensive income in accordance with paragraph 5.7.5 of IFRS 9 (see Chapter 6 of IFRS 9);

(f)   for particular liabilities designated as at fair value through profit or loss, the amount of the change in fair value that is attributable to changes in the liability's credit risk (see paragraph 5.7.7 of IFRS 9);

(g)   changes in the value of the time value of options when separating the intrinsic value and time value of an option contract and designating as the hedging instrument only the changes in the intrinsic value (see Chapter 6 of IFRS 9); and

(h)   changes in the value of the forward elements of forward contracts when separating the forward element and spot element of a forward contract and designating as the hedging instrument only the changes in the spot element, and changes in the value of the foreign currency basis spread of a financial instrument when excluding it from the designation of that financial instrument as the hedging instrument (see Chapter 6 of IFRS 9).

Owners are holders of instruments classified as equity.

Profit or loss is the total of income less expenses, excluding the components of other comprehensive income.

Reclassification adjustments are amounts reclassified to profit or loss in the current period that were recognised in other comprehensive income in the current or previous periods.

Total comprehensive income is the change in equity during a period resulting from transactions and other events, other than those changes resulting from transactions with owners in their capacity as owners.

Total comprehensive income comprises all components of 'profit or loss' and of 'other comprehensive income'.

8   Although this Standard uses the terms 'other comprehensive income', 'profit or loss' and 'total comprehensive income', an entity may use other terms to describe the totals as long as the meaning is clear. For example, an entity may use the term 'net income' to describe profit or loss.

8A   The following terms are described in IAS 32 *Financial Instruments: Presentation* and are used in this Standard with the meaning specified in IAS 32:

(a)   puttable financial instrument classified as an equity instrument (described in paragraphs 16A and 16B of IAS 32)

(b)   an instrument that imposes on the entity an obligation to deliver to another party a pro rata share of the net assets of the entity only on liquidation and is classified as an equity instrument (described in paragraphs 16C and 16D of IAS 32).

Financial statements

Purpose of financial statements

9   Financial statements are a structured representation of the financial position and financial performance of an entity. The objective of financial statements is to provide information about the financial position, financial performance and cash flows of an entity that is useful to a wide range of users in making economic decisions. Financial statements also show the results of the management's stewardship of the resources entrusted to it. To meet this objective, financial statements provide information about an entity's:

(a)   assets;

26   In assessing whether the going concern assumption is appropriate, management takes into account all available information about the future, which is at least, but is not limited to, twelve months from the end of the reporting period. The degree of consideration depends on the facts in each case. When an entity has a history of profitable operations and ready access to financial resources, the entity may reach a conclusion that the going concern basis of accounting is appropriate without detailed analysis. In other cases, management may need to consider a wide range of factors relating to current and expected profitability, debt repayment schedules and potential sources of replacement financing before it can satisfy itself that the going concern basis is appropriate.

Accrual basis of accounting

27   **An entity shall prepare its financial statements, except for cash flow information, using the accrual basis of accounting.**

28   When the accrual basis of accounting is used, an entity recognises items as assets, liabilities, equity, income and expenses (the elements of financial statements) when they satisfy the definitions and recognition criteria for those elements in the *Conceptual Framework*.

Materiality and aggregation

29   **An entity shall present separately each material class of similar items. An entity shall present separately items of a dissimilar nature or function unless they are immaterial.**

30   Financial statements result from processing large numbers of transactions or other events that are aggregated into classes according to their nature or function. The final stage in the process of aggregation and classification is the presentation of condensed and classified data, which form line items in the financial statements. If a line item is not individually material, it is aggregated with other items either in those statements or in the notes. An item that is not sufficiently material to warrant separate presentation in those statements may warrant separate presentation in the notes.

30A   When applying this and other IFRSs an entity shall decide, taking into consideration all relevant facts and circumstances, how it aggregates information in the financial statements, which include the notes. An entity shall not reduce the understandability of its financial statements by obscuring material information with immaterial information or by aggregating material items that have different natures or functions.

31   Some IFRSs specify information that is required to be included in the financial statements, which include the notes. An entity need not provide a specific disclosure required by an IFRS if the information resulting from that disclosure is not material. This is the case even if the IFRS contains a list of specific requirements or describes them as minimum requirements. An entity shall also consider whether to provide additional disclosures when compliance with the specific requirements in IFRS is insufficient to enable users of financial statements to understand the impact of particular transactions,

other events and conditions on the entity's financial position and financial performance.

Offsetting

32　An entity shall not offset assets and liabilities or income and expenses, unless required or permitted by an IFRS.

33　An entity reports separately both assets and liabilities, and income and expenses. Offsetting in the statement(s) of profit or loss and other comprehensive income or financial position, except when offsetting reflects the substance of the transaction or other event, detracts from the ability of users both to understand the transactions, other events and conditions that have occurred and to assess the entity's future cash flows. Measuring assets net of valuation allowances—for example, obsolescence allowances on inventories and doubtful debts allowances on receivables—is not offsetting.

34　IFRS 15 *Revenue from Contracts with Customers* requires an entity to measure revenue from contracts with customers at the amount of consideration to which the entity expects to be entitled in exchange for transferring promised goods or services. For example, the amount of revenue recognised reflects any trade discounts and volume rebates the entity allows. An entity undertakes, in the course of its ordinary activities, other transactions that do not generate revenue but are incidental to the main revenue-generating activities. An entity presents the results of such transactions, when this presentation reflects the substance of the transaction or other event, by netting any income with related expenses arising on the same transaction. For example:

(a)　an entity presents gains and losses on the disposal of non-current assets, including investments and operating assets, by deducting from the amount of consideration on disposal the carrying amount of the asset and related selling expenses; and

(b)　an entity may net expenditure related to a provision that is recognised in accordance with IAS 37 *Provisions, Contingent Liabilities and Contingent Assets* and reimbursed under a contractual arrangement with a third party (for example, a supplier's warranty agreement) against the related reimbursement.

35　In addition, an entity presents on a net basis gains and losses arising from a group of similar transactions, for example, foreign exchange gains and losses or gains and losses arising on financial instruments held for trading. However, an entity presents such gains and losses separately if they are material.

Frequency of reporting

36　An entity shall present a complete set of financial statements (including comparative information) at least annually. When an entity changes the end of its reporting period and presents financial statements for a period longer or shorter than one year, an entity shall disclose, in addition to the period covered by the financial statements:

(a)　the reason for using a longer or shorter period, and

(b) the fact that amounts presented in the financial statements are not entirely comparable.

37 Normally, an entity consistently prepares financial statements for a one-year period. However, for practical reasons, some entities prefer to report, for example, for a 52-week period. This Standard does not preclude this practice.

Comparative information

Minimum comparative information

38 Except when IFRSs permit or require otherwise, an entity shall present comparative information in respect of the preceding period for all amounts reported in the current period's financial statements. An entity shall include comparative information for narrative and descriptive information if it is relevant to understanding the current period's financial statements.

38A An entity shall present, as a minimum, two statements of financial position, two statements of profit or loss and other comprehensive income, two separate statements of profit or loss (if presented), two statements of cash flows and two statements of changes in equity, and related notes.

38B In some cases, narrative information provided in the financial statements for the preceding period(s) continues to be relevant in the current period. For example, an entity discloses in the current period details of a legal dispute, the outcome of which was uncertain at the end of the preceding period and is yet to be resolved. Users may benefit from the disclosure of information that the uncertainty existed at the end of the preceding period and from the disclosure of information about the steps that have been taken during the period to resolve the uncertainty.

Additional comparative information

38C An entity may present comparative information in addition to the minimum comparative financial statements required by IFRSs, as long as that information is prepared in accordance with IFRSs. This comparative information may consist of one or more statements referred to in paragraph 10, but need not comprise a complete set of financial statements. When this is the case, the entity shall present related note information for those additional statements.

38D For example, an entity may present a third statement of profit or loss and other comprehensive income (thereby presenting the current period, the preceding period and one additional comparative period). However, the entity is not required to present a third statement of financial position, a third statement of cash flows or a third statement of changes in equity (ie an additional financial statement comparative). The entity is required to present, in the notes to the financial statements, the comparative information related to that additional statement of profit or loss and other comprehensive income.

39–40 [Deleted]

Change in accounting policy, retrospective restatement or reclassification

40A An entity shall present a third statement of financial position as at the beginning of the preceding period in addition to the minimum comparative financial statements required in paragraph 38A if:

(a) it applies an accounting policy retrospectively, makes a retrospective restatement of items in its financial statements or reclassifies items in its financial statements; and

(b) the retrospective application, retrospective restatement or the reclassification has a material effect on the information in the statement of financial position at the beginning of the preceding period.

40B In the circumstances described in paragraph 40A, an entity shall present three statements of financial position as at:

(a) the end of the current period;

(b) the end of the preceding period; and

(c) the beginning of the preceding period.

40C When an entity is required to present an additional statement of financial position in accordance with paragraph 40A, it must disclose the information required by paragraphs 41–44 and IAS 8. However, it need not present the related notes to the opening statement of financial position as at the beginning of the preceding period.

40D The date of that opening statement of financial position shall be as at the beginning of the preceding period regardless of whether an entity's financial statements present comparative information for earlier periods (as permitted in paragraph 38C).

41 If an entity changes the presentation or classification of items in its financial statements, it shall reclassify comparative amounts unless reclassification is impracticable. When an entity reclassifies comparative amounts, it shall disclose (including as at the beginning of the preceding period):

(a) the nature of the reclassification;

(b) the amount of each item or class of items that is reclassified; and

(c) the reason for the reclassification.

42 When it is impracticable to reclassify comparative amounts, an entity shall disclose:

(a) the reason for not reclassifying the amounts, and

(b) the nature of the adjustments that would have been made if the amounts had been reclassified.

43   Enhancing the inter-period comparability of information assists users in making economic decisions, especially by allowing the assessment of trends in financial information for predictive purposes. In some circumstances, it is impracticable to reclassify comparative information for a particular prior period to achieve comparability with the current period. For example, an entity may not have collected data in the prior period(s) in a way that allows reclassification, and it may be impracticable to recreate the information.

44   IAS 8 sets out the adjustments to comparative information required when an entity changes an accounting policy or corrects an error.

Consistency of presentation

45   An entity shall retain the presentation and classification of items in the financial statements from one period to the next unless:

   (a)   it is apparent, following a significant change in the nature of the entity's operations or a review of its financial statements, that another presentation or classification would be more appropriate having regard to the criteria for the selection and application of accounting policies in IAS 8; or

   (b)   an IFRS requires a change in presentation.

46   For example, a significant acquisition or disposal, or a review of the presentation of the financial statements, might suggest that the financial statements need to be presented differently. An entity changes the presentation of its financial statements only if the changed presentation provides information that is reliable and more relevant to users of the financial statements and the revised structure is likely to continue, so that comparability is not impaired. When making such changes in presentation, an entity reclassifies its comparative information in accordance with paragraphs 41 and 42.

Structure and content

Introduction

47   This Standard requires particular disclosures in the statement of financial position or the statement(s) of profit or loss and other comprehensive income, or in the statement of changes in equity and requires disclosure of other line items either in those statements or in the notes. IAS 7 *Statement of Cash Flows* sets out requirements for the presentation of cash flow information.

48   This Standard sometimes uses the term 'disclosure' in a broad sense, encompassing items presented in the financial statements. Disclosures are also required by other IFRSs. Unless specified to the contrary elsewhere in this Standard or in another IFRS, such disclosures may be made in the financial statements.

Identification of the financial statements

49 An entity shall clearly identify the financial statements and distinguish them from other information in the same published document.

50 IFRSs apply only to financial statements, and not necessarily to other information presented in an annual report, a regulatory filing, or another document. Therefore, it is important that users can distinguish information that is prepared using IFRSs from other information that may be useful to users but is not the subject of those requirements.

51 An entity shall clearly identify each financial statement and the notes. In addition, an entity shall display the following information prominently, and repeat it when necessary for the information presented to be understandable:

 (a) the name of the reporting entity or other means of identification, and any change in that information from the end of the preceding reporting period;

 (b) whether the financial statements are of an individual entity or a group of entities;

 (c) the date of the end of the reporting period or the period covered by the set of financial statements or notes;

 (d) the presentation currency, as defined in IAS 21; and

 (e) the level of rounding used in presenting amounts in the financial statements.

52 An entity meets the requirements in paragraph 51 by presenting appropriate headings for pages, statements, notes, columns and the like. Judgement is required in determining the best way of presenting such information. For example, when an entity presents the financial statements electronically, separate pages are not always used; an entity then presents the above items to ensure that the information included in the financial statements can be understood.

53 An entity often makes financial statements more understandable by presenting information in thousands or millions of units of the presentation currency. This is acceptable as long as the entity discloses the level of rounding and does not omit material information.

Statement of financial position

Information to be presented in the statement of financial position

54 The statement of financial position shall include line items that present the following amounts:

 (a) property, plant and equipment;

 (b) investment property;

 (c) intangible assets;

  © IFRS Foundation

(d)   financial assets (excluding amounts shown under (e), (h) and (i));

(e)   investments accounted for using the equity method;

(f)   biological assets within the scope of IAS 41 *Agriculture*;

(g)   inventories;

(h)   trade and other receivables;

(i)   cash and cash equivalents;

(j)   the total of assets classified as held for sale and assets included in disposal groups classified as held for sale in accordance with IFRS 5 *Non-current Assets Held for Sale and Discontinued Operations*;

(k)   trade and other payables;

(l)   provisions;

(m)   financial liabilities (excluding amounts shown under (k) and (l));

(n)   liabilities and assets for current tax, as defined in IAS 12 *Income Taxes*;

(o)   deferred tax liabilities and deferred tax assets, as defined in IAS 12;

(p)   liabilities included in disposal groups classified as held for sale in accordance with IFRS 5;

(q)   non-controlling interests, presented within equity; and

(r)   issued capital and reserves attributable to owners of the parent.

55   An entity shall present additional line items (including by disaggregating the line items listed in paragraph 54), headings and subtotals in the statement of financial position when such presentation is relevant to an understanding of the entity's financial position.

55A   When an entity presents subtotals in accordance with paragraph 55, those subtotals shall:

(a)   be comprised of line items made up of amounts recognised and measured in accordance with IFRS;

(b)   be presented and labelled in a manner that makes the line items that constitute the subtotal clear and understandable;

(c)   be consistent from period to period, in accordance with paragraph 45; and

(d)   not be displayed with more prominence than the subtotals and totals required in IFRS for the statement of financial position.

56   When an entity presents current and non-current assets, and current and non-current liabilities, as separate classifications in its statement of financial position, it shall not classify deferred tax assets (liabilities) as current assets (liabilities).

57   This Standard does not prescribe the order or format in which an entity presents items. Paragraph 54 simply lists items that are sufficiently different in nature or function to warrant separate presentation in the statement of financial position. In addition:

    (a)   line items are included when the size, nature or function of an item or aggregation of similar items is such that separate presentation is relevant to an understanding of the entity's financial position; and

    (b)   the descriptions used and the ordering of items or aggregation of similar items may be amended according to the nature of the entity and its transactions, to provide information that is relevant to an understanding of the entity's financial position. For example, a financial institution may amend the above descriptions to provide information that is relevant to the operations of a financial institution.

58   An entity makes the judgement about whether to present additional items separately on the basis of an assessment of:

    (a)   the nature and liquidity of assets;

    (b)   the function of assets within the entity; and

    (c)   the amounts, nature and timing of liabilities.

59   The use of different measurement bases for different classes of assets suggests that their nature or function differs and, therefore, that an entity presents them as separate line items. For example, different classes of property, plant and equipment can be carried at cost or at revalued amounts in accordance with IAS 16.

Current/non-current distinction

60   **An entity shall present current and non-current assets, and current and non-current liabilities, as separate classifications in its statement of financial position in accordance with paragraphs 66–76 except when a presentation based on liquidity provides information that is reliable and more relevant. When that exception applies, an entity shall present all assets and liabilities in order of liquidity.**

61   **Whichever method of presentation is adopted, an entity shall disclose the amount expected to be recovered or settled after more than twelve months for each asset and liability line item that combines amounts expected to be recovered or settled:**

    (a)   **no more than twelve months after the reporting period, and**

    (b)   **more than twelve months after the reporting period.**

62   When an entity supplies goods or services within a clearly identifiable operating cycle, separate classification of current and non-current assets and liabilities in the statement of financial position provides useful information by distinguishing the net assets that are continuously circulating as working capital from those used in the entity's long-term operations. It also highlights

assets that are expected to be realised within the current operating cycle, and liabilities that are due for settlement within the same period.

63　For some entities, such as financial institutions, a presentation of assets and liabilities in increasing or decreasing order of liquidity provides information that is reliable and more relevant than a current/non-current presentation because the entity does not supply goods or services within a clearly identifiable operating cycle.

64　In applying paragraph 60, an entity is permitted to present some of its assets and liabilities using a current/non-current classification and others in order of liquidity when this provides information that is reliable and more relevant. The need for a mixed basis of presentation might arise when an entity has diverse operations.

65　Information about expected dates of realisation of assets and liabilities is useful in assessing the liquidity and solvency of an entity. IFRS 7 *Financial Instruments: Disclosures* requires disclosure of the maturity dates of financial assets and financial liabilities. Financial assets include trade and other receivables, and financial liabilities include trade and other payables. Information on the expected date of recovery of non-monetary assets such as inventories and expected date of settlement for liabilities such as provisions is also useful, whether assets and liabilities are classified as current or as non-current. For example, an entity discloses the amount of inventories that are expected to be recovered more than twelve months after the reporting period.

Current assets

66　An entity shall classify an asset as current when:

(a)　it expects to realise the asset, or intends to sell or consume it, in its normal operating cycle;

(b)　it holds the asset primarily for the purpose of trading;

(c)　it expects to realise the asset within twelve months after the reporting period; or

(d)　the asset is cash or a cash equivalent (as defined in IAS 7) unless the asset is restricted from being exchanged or used to settle a liability for at least twelve months after the reporting period.

An entity shall classify all other assets as non-current.

67　This Standard uses the term 'non-current' to include tangible, intangible and financial assets of a long-term nature. It does not prohibit the use of alternative descriptions as long as the meaning is clear.

68　The operating cycle of an entity is the time between the acquisition of assets for processing and their realisation in cash or cash equivalents. When the entity's normal operating cycle is not clearly identifiable, it is assumed to be twelve months. Current assets include assets (such as inventories and trade receivables) that are sold, consumed or realised as part of the normal operating cycle even when they are not expected to be realised within twelve months after the reporting period. Current assets also include assets held primarily for the purpose of trading (examples include some financial assets that meet the definition of held for trading in IFRS 9) and the current portion of non-current financial assets.

Current liabilities

69   An entity shall classify a liability as current when:

(a)   it expects to settle the liability in its normal operating cycle;

(b)   it holds the liability primarily for the purpose of trading;

(c)   the liability is due to be settled within twelve months after the reporting period; or

(d)   it does not have an unconditional right to defer settlement of the liability for at least twelve months after the reporting period (see paragraph 73). Terms of a liability that could, at the option of the counterparty, result in its settlement by the issue of equity instruments do not affect its classification.

An entity shall classify all other liabilities as non-current.

70   Some current liabilities, such as trade payables and some accruals for employee and other operating costs, are part of the working capital used in the entity's normal operating cycle. An entity classifies such operating items as current liabilities even if they are due to be settled more than twelve months after the reporting period. The same normal operating cycle applies to the classification of an entity's assets and liabilities. When the entity's normal operating cycle is not clearly identifiable, it is assumed to be twelve months.

71   Other current liabilities are not settled as part of the normal operating cycle, but are due for settlement within twelve months after the reporting period or held primarily for the purpose of trading. Examples are some financial liabilities that meet the definition of held for trading in IFRS 9, bank overdrafts, and the current portion of non-current financial liabilities, dividends payable, income taxes and other non-trade payables. Financial liabilities that provide financing on a long-term basis (ie are not part of the working capital used in the entity's normal operating cycle) and are not due for settlement within twelve months after the reporting period are non-current liabilities, subject to paragraphs 74 and 75.

72   An entity classifies its financial liabilities as current when they are due to be settled within twelve months after the reporting period, even if:

(a)   the original term was for a period longer than twelve months, and

(b)   an agreement to refinance, or to reschedule payments, on a long-term basis is completed after the reporting period and before the financial statements are authorised for issue.

72A   *[This paragraph refers to amendments that are not yet effective, and is therefore not included in this edition.]*

73   If an entity expects, and has the discretion, to refinance or roll over an obligation for at least twelve months after the reporting period under an existing loan facility, it classifies the obligation as non-current, even if it would otherwise be due within a shorter period. However, when refinancing or rolling over the obligation is not at the discretion of the entity (for example, there is no arrangement for refinancing), the entity does not consider the potential to refinance the obligation and classifies the obligation as current.

74   When an entity breaches a provision of a long-term loan arrangement on or before the end of the reporting period with the effect that the liability becomes payable on demand, it classifies the liability as current, even if the lender agreed, after the reporting period and before the authorisation of the financial statements for issue, not to demand payment as a consequence of the breach. An entity classifies the liability as current because, at the end of the reporting period, it does not have an unconditional right to defer its settlement for at least twelve months after that date.

75   However, an entity classifies the liability as non-current if the lender agreed by the end of the reporting period to provide a period of grace ending at least twelve months after the reporting period, within which the entity can rectify the breach and during which the lender cannot demand immediate repayment.

75A   *[This paragraph refers to amendments that are not yet effective, and is therefore not included in this edition.]*

76   In respect of loans classified as current liabilities, if the following events occur between the end of the reporting period and the date the financial statements are authorised for issue, those events are disclosed as non-adjusting events in accordance with IAS 10 *Events after the Reporting Period*:

      (a)   refinancing on a long-term basis;

      (b)   rectification of a breach of a long-term loan arrangement; and

      (c)   the granting by the lender of a period of grace to rectify a breach of a long-term loan arrangement ending at least twelve months after the reporting period.

76A−76B   *[These paragraphs refer to amendments that are not yet effective, and are therefore not included in this edition.]*

Information to be presented either in the statement of financial position or in the notes

77   An entity shall disclose, either in the statement of financial position or in the notes, further subclassifications of the line items presented, classified in a manner appropriate to the entity's operations.

78   The detail provided in subclassifications depends on the requirements of IFRSs and on the size, nature and function of the amounts involved. An entity also uses the factors set out in paragraph 58 to decide the basis of subclassification. The disclosures vary for each item, for example:

(a)   items of property, plant and equipment are disaggregated into classes in accordance with IAS 16;

(b)   receivables are disaggregated into amounts receivable from trade customers, receivables from related parties, prepayments and other amounts;

(c)   inventories are disaggregated, in accordance with IAS 2 *Inventories*, into classifications such as merchandise, production supplies, materials, work in progress and finished goods;

(d)   provisions are disaggregated into provisions for employee benefits and other items; and

(e)   equity capital and reserves are disaggregated into various classes, such as paid-in capital, share premium and reserves.

79   An entity shall disclose the following, either in the statement of financial position or the statement of changes in equity, or in the notes:

    (a)   for each class of share capital:

        (i)   the number of shares authorised;

        (ii)   the number of shares issued and fully paid, and issued but not fully paid;

        (iii)   par value per share, or that the shares have no par value;

        (iv)   a reconciliation of the number of shares outstanding at the beginning and at the end of the period;

        (v)   the rights, preferences and restrictions attaching to that class including restrictions on the distribution of dividends and the repayment of capital;

        (vi)   shares in the entity held by the entity or by its subsidiaries or associates; and

        (vii)   shares reserved for issue under options and contracts for the sale of shares, including terms and amounts; and

    (b)   a description of the nature and purpose of each reserve within equity.

80   An entity without share capital, such as a partnership or trust, shall disclose information equivalent to that required by paragraph 79(a), showing changes during the period in each category of equity interest, and the rights, preferences and restrictions attaching to each category of equity interest.

80A   If an entity has reclassified

    (a)   a puttable financial instrument classified as an equity instrument, or

(c)   following the order of the line items in the statement(s) of profit or loss and other comprehensive income and the statement of financial position, such as:

   (i)   statement of compliance with IFRSs (see paragraph 16);

   (ii)   significant accounting policies applied (see paragraph 117);

   (iii)   supporting information for items presented in the statements of financial position and in the statement(s) of profit or loss and other comprehensive income, and in the statements of changes in equity and of cash flows, in the order in which each statement and each line item is presented; and

   (iv)   other disclosures, including:

      (1)   contingent liabilities (see IAS 37) and unrecognised contractual commitments; and

      (2)   non-financial disclosures, eg the entity's financial risk management objectives and policies (see IFRS 7).

115   [Deleted]

116   An entity may present notes providing information about the basis of preparation of the financial statements and specific accounting policies as a separate section of the financial statements.

Disclosure of accounting policies

117   An entity shall disclose its significant accounting policies comprising:

(a)   the measurement basis (or bases) used in preparing the financial statements; and

(b)   the other accounting policies used that are relevant to an understanding of the financial statements.

117A–
117E   *[These paragraphs refer to amendments that are not yet effective, and are therefore not included in this edition.]*

118   It is important for an entity to inform users of the measurement basis or bases used in the financial statements (for example, historical cost, current cost, net realisable value, fair value or recoverable amount) because the basis on which an entity prepares the financial statements significantly affects users' analysis. When an entity uses more than one measurement basis in the financial statements, for example when particular classes of assets are revalued, it is sufficient to provide an indication of the categories of assets and liabilities to which each measurement basis is applied.

119   In deciding whether a particular accounting policy should be disclosed, management considers whether disclosure would assist users in understanding how transactions, other events and conditions are reflected in reported financial performance and financial position. Each entity considers the nature of its operations and the policies that the users of its financial statements would expect to be disclosed for that type of entity. Disclosure of

particular accounting policies is especially useful to users when those policies are selected from alternatives allowed in IFRSs. An example is disclosure of whether an entity applies the fair value or cost model to its investment property (see IAS 40 *Investment Property*). Some IFRSs specifically require disclosure of particular accounting policies, including choices made by management between different policies they allow. For example, IAS 16 requires disclosure of the measurement bases used for classes of property, plant and equipment.

120   [Deleted]

121   An accounting policy may be significant because of the nature of the entity's operations even if amounts for current and prior periods are not material. It is also appropriate to disclose each significant accounting policy that is not specifically required by IFRSs but the entity selects and applies in accordance with IAS 8.

122   **An entity shall disclose, along with its significant accounting policies or other notes, the judgements, apart from those involving estimations (see paragraph 125), that management has made in the process of applying the entity's accounting policies and that have the most significant effect on the amounts recognised in the financial statements.**

123   In the process of applying the entity's accounting policies, management makes various judgements, apart from those involving estimations, that can significantly affect the amounts it recognises in the financial statements. For example, management makes judgements in determining:

(a)   [deleted]

(b)   when substantially all the significant risks and rewards of ownership of financial assets and, for lessors, assets subject to leases are transferred to other entities;

(c)   whether, in substance, particular sales of goods are financing arrangements and therefore do not give rise to revenue; and

(d)   whether the contractual terms of a financial asset give rise on specified dates to cash flows that are solely payments of principal and interest on the principal amount outstanding.

124   Some of the disclosures made in accordance with paragraph 122 are required by other IFRSs. For example, IFRS 12 *Disclosure of Interests in Other Entities* requires an entity to disclose the judgements it has made in determining whether it controls another entity. IAS 40 *Investment Property* requires disclosure of the criteria developed by the entity to distinguish investment property from owner-occupied property and from property held for sale in the ordinary course of business, when classification of the property is difficult.

Sources of estimation uncertainty

125   An entity shall disclose information about the assumptions it makes about the future, and other major sources of estimation uncertainty at the end of the reporting period, that have a significant risk of resulting in a material adjustment to the carrying amounts of assets and liabilities within the next financial year. In respect of those assets and liabilities, the notes shall include details of:

    (a)   their nature, and

    (b)   their carrying amount as at the end of the reporting period.

126   Determining the carrying amounts of some assets and liabilities requires estimation of the effects of uncertain future events on those assets and liabilities at the end of the reporting period. For example, in the absence of recently observed market prices, future-oriented estimates are necessary to measure the recoverable amount of classes of property, plant and equipment, the effect of technological obsolescence on inventories, provisions subject to the future outcome of litigation in progress, and long-term employee benefit liabilities such as pension obligations. These estimates involve assumptions about such items as the risk adjustment to cash flows or discount rates, future changes in salaries and future changes in prices affecting other costs.

127   The assumptions and other sources of estimation uncertainty disclosed in accordance with paragraph 125 relate to the estimates that require management's most difficult, subjective or complex judgements. As the number of variables and assumptions affecting the possible future resolution of the uncertainties increases, those judgements become more subjective and complex, and the potential for a consequential material adjustment to the carrying amounts of assets and liabilities normally increases accordingly.

128   The disclosures in paragraph 125 are not required for assets and liabilities with a significant risk that their carrying amounts might change materially within the next financial year if, at the end of the reporting period, they are measured at fair value based on a quoted price in an active market for an identical asset or liability. Such fair values might change materially within the next financial year but these changes would not arise from assumptions or other sources of estimation uncertainty at the end of the reporting period.

129   An entity presents the disclosures in paragraph 125 in a manner that helps users of financial statements to understand the judgements that management makes about the future and about other sources of estimation uncertainty. The nature and extent of the information provided vary according to the nature of the assumption and other circumstances. Examples of the types of disclosures an entity makes are:

    (a)   the nature of the assumption or other estimation uncertainty;

    (b)   the sensitivity of carrying amounts to the methods, assumptions and estimates underlying their calculation, including the reasons for the sensitivity;

(c)   the expected resolution of an uncertainty and the range of reasonably possible outcomes within the next financial year in respect of the carrying amounts of the assets and liabilities affected; and

(d)   an explanation of changes made to past assumptions concerning those assets and liabilities, if the uncertainty remains unresolved.

130   This Standard does not require an entity to disclose budget information or forecasts in making the disclosures in paragraph 125.

131   Sometimes it is impracticable to disclose the extent of the possible effects of an assumption or another source of estimation uncertainty at the end of the reporting period. In such cases, the entity discloses that it is reasonably possible, on the basis of existing knowledge, that outcomes within the next financial year that are different from the assumption could require a material adjustment to the carrying amount of the asset or liability affected. In all cases, the entity discloses the nature and carrying amount of the specific asset or liability (or class of assets or liabilities) affected by the assumption.

132   The disclosures in paragraph 122 of particular judgements that management made in the process of applying the entity's accounting policies do not relate to the disclosures of sources of estimation uncertainty in paragraph 125.

133   Other IFRSs require the disclosure of some of the assumptions that would otherwise be required in accordance with paragraph 125. For example, IAS 37 requires disclosure, in specified circumstances, of major assumptions concerning future events affecting classes of provisions. IFRS 13 *Fair Value Measurement* requires disclosure of significant assumptions (including the valuation technique(s) and inputs) the entity uses when measuring the fair values of assets and liabilities that are carried at fair value.

Capital

134   **An entity shall disclose information that enables users of its financial statements to evaluate the entity's objectives, policies and processes for managing capital.**

135   To comply with paragraph 134, the entity discloses the following:

(a)   qualitative information about its objectives, policies and processes for managing capital, including:

(i)   a description of what it manages as capital;

(ii)   when an entity is subject to externally imposed capital requirements, the nature of those requirements and how those requirements are incorporated into the management of capital; and

(iii)   how it is meeting its objectives for managing capital.

IAS 2

Inventories

In April 2001 the International Accounting Standards Board (Board) adopted IAS 2 *Inventories*, which had originally been issued by the International Accounting Standards Committee in December 1993. IAS 2 *Inventories* replaced IAS 2 *Valuation and Presentation of Inventories in the Context of the Historical Cost System* (issued in October 1975).

In December 2003 the Board issued a revised IAS 2 as part of its initial agenda of technical projects. The revised IAS 2 also incorporated the guidance contained in a related Interpretation (SIC-1 *Consistency — Different Cost Formulas for Inventories*).

Other Standards have made minor consequential amendments to IAS 2. They include IFRS 13 *Fair Value Measurement* (issued May 2011), IFRS 9 *Financial Instruments* (Hedge Accounting and amendments to IFRS 9, IFRS 7 and IAS 39) (issued November 2013), IFRS 15 *Revenue from Contracts with Customers* (issued May 2014), IFRS 9 *Financial Instruments* (issued July 2014) and IFRS 16 *Leases* (issued January 2016).

Contents

FOR THE BASIS FOR CONCLUSIONS, SEE PART C OF THIS EDITION

BASIS FOR CONCLUSIONS

are measured at fair value less costs to sell, they are excluded from only the measurement requirements of this Standard.

Definitions

6   The following terms are used in this Standard with the meanings specified:

Inventories are assets:

(a)   held for sale in the ordinary course of business;

(b)   in the process of production for such sale; or

(c)   in the form of materials or supplies to be consumed in the production process or in the rendering of services.

Net realisable value is the estimated selling price in the ordinary course of business less the estimated costs of completion and the estimated costs necessary to make the sale.

Fair value is the price that would be received to sell an asset or paid to transfer a liability in an orderly transaction between market participants at the measurement date. (See IFRS 13 *Fair Value Measurement*.)

7   Net realisable value refers to the net amount that an entity expects to realise from the sale of inventory in the ordinary course of business. Fair value reflects the price at which an orderly transaction to sell the same inventory in the principal (or most advantageous) market for that inventory would take place between market participants at the measurement date. The former is an entity-specific value; the latter is not. Net realisable value for inventories may not equal fair value less costs to sell.

8   Inventories encompass goods purchased and held for resale including, for example, merchandise purchased by a retailer and held for resale, or land and other property held for resale. Inventories also encompass finished goods produced, or work in progress being produced, by the entity and include materials and supplies awaiting use in the production process. Costs incurred to fulfil a contract with a customer that do not give rise to inventories (or assets within the scope of another Standard) are accounted for in accordance with IFRS 15 *Revenue from Contracts with Customers*.

Measurement of inventories

9   Inventories shall be measured at the lower of cost and net realisable value.

Cost of inventories

10   The cost of inventories shall comprise all costs of purchase, costs of conversion and other costs incurred in bringing the inventories to their present location and condition.

Costs of purchase

11 The costs of purchase of inventories comprise the purchase price, import duties and other taxes (other than those subsequently recoverable by the entity from the taxing authorities), and transport, handling and other costs directly attributable to the acquisition of finished goods, materials and services. Trade discounts, rebates and other similar items are deducted in determining the costs of purchase.

Costs of conversion

12 The costs of conversion of inventories include costs directly related to the units of production, such as direct labour. They also include a systematic allocation of fixed and variable production overheads that are incurred in converting materials into finished goods. Fixed production overheads are those indirect costs of production that remain relatively constant regardless of the volume of production, such as depreciation and maintenance of factory buildings, equipment and right-of-use assets used in the production process, and the cost of factory management and administration. Variable production overheads are those indirect costs of production that vary directly, or nearly directly, with the volume of production, such as indirect materials and indirect labour.

13 The allocation of fixed production overheads to the costs of conversion is based on the normal capacity of the production facilities. Normal capacity is the production expected to be achieved on average over a number of periods or seasons under normal circumstances, taking into account the loss of capacity resulting from planned maintenance. The actual level of production may be used if it approximates normal capacity. The amount of fixed overhead allocated to each unit of production is not increased as a consequence of low production or idle plant. Unallocated overheads are recognised as an expense in the period in which they are incurred. In periods of abnormally high production, the amount of fixed overhead allocated to each unit of production is decreased so that inventories are not measured above cost. Variable production overheads are allocated to each unit of production on the basis of the actual use of the production facilities.

14 A production process may result in more than one product being produced simultaneously. This is the case, for example, when joint products are produced or when there is a main product and a by-product. When the costs of conversion of each product are not separately identifiable, they are allocated between the products on a rational and consistent basis. The allocation may be based, for example, on the relative sales value of each product either at the stage in the production process when the products become separately identifiable, or at the completion of production. Most by-products, by their nature, are immaterial. When this is the case, they are often measured at net realisable value and this value is deducted from the cost of the main product. As a result, the carrying amount of the main product is not materially different from its cost.

Other costs

15 Other costs are included in the cost of inventories only to the extent that they are incurred in bringing the inventories to their present location and condition. For example, it may be appropriate to include non-production overheads or the costs of designing products for specific customers in the cost of inventories.

16 Examples of costs excluded from the cost of inventories and recognised as expenses in the period in which they are incurred are:

(a) abnormal amounts of wasted materials, labour or other production costs;

(b) storage costs, unless those costs are necessary in the production process before a further production stage;

(c) administrative overheads that do not contribute to bringing inventories to their present location and condition; and

(d) selling costs.

17 IAS 23 *Borrowing Costs* identifies limited circumstances where borrowing costs are included in the cost of inventories.

18 An entity may purchase inventories on deferred settlement terms. When the arrangement effectively contains a financing element, that element, for example a difference between the purchase price for normal credit terms and the amount paid, is recognised as interest expense over the period of the financing.

19 [Deleted]

Cost of agricultural produce harvested from biological assets

20 In accordance with IAS 41 *Agriculture* inventories comprising agricultural produce that an entity has harvested from its biological assets are measured on initial recognition at their fair value less costs to sell at the point of harvest. This is the cost of the inventories at that date for application of this Standard.

Techniques for the measurement of cost

21 Techniques for the measurement of the cost of inventories, such as the standard cost method or the retail method, may be used for convenience if the results approximate cost. Standard costs take into account normal levels of materials and supplies, labour, efficiency and capacity utilisation. They are regularly reviewed and, if necessary, revised in the light of current conditions.

22 The retail method is often used in the retail industry for measuring inventories of large numbers of rapidly changing items with similar margins for which it is impracticable to use other costing methods. The cost of the inventory is determined by reducing the sales value of the inventory by the appropriate percentage gross margin. The percentage used takes into

consideration inventory that has been marked down to below its original selling price. An average percentage for each retail department is often used.

Cost formulas

23   **The cost of inventories of items that are not ordinarily interchangeable and goods or services produced and segregated for specific projects shall be assigned by using specific identification of their individual costs.**

24   Specific identification of cost means that specific costs are attributed to identified items of inventory. This is the appropriate treatment for items that are segregated for a specific project, regardless of whether they have been bought or produced. However, specific identification of costs is inappropriate when there are large numbers of items of inventory that are ordinarily interchangeable. In such circumstances, the method of selecting those items that remain in inventories could be used to obtain predetermined effects on profit or loss.

25   **The cost of inventories, other than those dealt with in paragraph 23, shall be assigned by using the first-in, first-out (FIFO) or weighted average cost formula. An entity shall use the same cost formula for all inventories having a similar nature and use to the entity. For inventories with a different nature or use, different cost formulas may be justified.**

26   For example, inventories used in one operating segment may have a use to the entity different from the same type of inventories used in another operating segment. However, a difference in geographical location of inventories (or in the respective tax rules), by itself, is not sufficient to justify the use of different cost formulas.

27   The FIFO formula assumes that the items of inventory that were purchased or produced first are sold first, and consequently the items remaining in inventory at the end of the period are those most recently purchased or produced. Under the weighted average cost formula, the cost of each item is determined from the weighted average of the cost of similar items at the beginning of a period and the cost of similar items purchased or produced during the period. The average may be calculated on a periodic basis, or as each additional shipment is received, depending upon the circumstances of the entity.

Net realisable value

28   The cost of inventories may not be recoverable if those inventories are damaged, if they have become wholly or partially obsolete, or if their selling prices have declined. The cost of inventories may also not be recoverable if the estimated costs of completion or the estimated costs to be incurred to make the sale have increased. The practice of writing inventories down below cost to net realisable value is consistent with the view that assets should not be carried in excess of amounts expected to be realised from their sale or use.

29   Inventories are usually written down to net realisable value item by item. In some circumstances, however, it may be appropriate to group similar or related items. This may be the case with items of inventory relating to the same product line that have similar purposes or end uses, are produced and marketed in the same geographical area, and cannot be practicably evaluated separately from other items in that product line. It is not appropriate to write inventories down on the basis of a classification of inventory, for example, finished goods, or all the inventories in a particular operating segment.

30   Estimates of net realisable value are based on the most reliable evidence available at the time the estimates are made, of the amount the inventories are expected to realise. These estimates take into consideration fluctuations of price or cost directly relating to events occurring after the end of the period to the extent that such events confirm conditions existing at the end of the period.

31   Estimates of net realisable value also take into consideration the purpose for which the inventory is held. For example, the net realisable value of the quantity of inventory held to satisfy firm sales or service contracts is based on the contract price. If the sales contracts are for less than the inventory quantities held, the net realisable value of the excess is based on general selling prices. Provisions may arise from firm sales contracts in excess of inventory quantities held or from firm purchase contracts. Such provisions are dealt with under IAS 37 *Provisions, Contingent Liabilities and Contingent Assets*.

32   Materials and other supplies held for use in the production of inventories are not written down below cost if the finished products in which they will be incorporated are expected to be sold at or above cost. However, when a decline in the price of materials indicates that the cost of the finished products exceeds net realisable value, the materials are written down to net realisable value. In such circumstances, the replacement cost of the materials may be the best available measure of their net realisable value.

33   A new assessment is made of net realisable value in each subsequent period. When the circumstances that previously caused inventories to be written down below cost no longer exist or when there is clear evidence of an increase in net realisable value because of changed economic circumstances, the amount of the write-down is reversed (ie the reversal is limited to the amount of the original write-down) so that the new carrying amount is the lower of the cost and the revised net realisable value. This occurs, for example, when an item of inventory that is carried at net realisable value, because its selling price has declined, is still on hand in a subsequent period and its selling price has increased.

Recognition as an expense

34   When inventories are sold, the carrying amount of those inventories shall be recognised as an expense in the period in which the related revenue is recognised. The amount of any write-down of inventories to net realisable value and all losses of inventories shall be recognised as an expense in the period the write-down or loss occurs. The amount of any reversal of any

write-down of inventories, arising from an increase in net realisable value, shall be recognised as a reduction in the amount of inventories recognised as an expense in the period in which the reversal occurs.

35   Some inventories may be allocated to other asset accounts, for example, inventory used as a component of self-constructed property, plant or equipment. Inventories allocated to another asset in this way are recognised as an expense during the useful life of that asset.

Disclosure

36   The financial statements shall disclose:

(a)   the accounting policies adopted in measuring inventories, including the cost formula used;

(b)   the total carrying amount of inventories and the carrying amount in classifications appropriate to the entity;

(c)   the carrying amount of inventories carried at fair value less costs to sell;

(d)   the amount of inventories recognised as an expense during the period;

(e)   the amount of any write-down of inventories recognised as an expense in the period in accordance with paragraph 34;

(f)   the amount of any reversal of any write-down that is recognised as a reduction in the amount of inventories recognised as expense in the period in accordance with paragraph 34;

(g)   the circumstances or events that led to the reversal of a write-down of inventories in accordance with paragraph 34; and

(h)   the carrying amount of inventories pledged as security for liabilities.

37   Information about the carrying amounts held in different classifications of inventories and the extent of the changes in these assets is useful to financial statement users. Common classifications of inventories are merchandise, production supplies, materials, work in progress and finished goods.

38   The amount of inventories recognised as an expense during the period, which is often referred to as cost of sales, consists of those costs previously included in the measurement of inventory that has now been sold and unallocated production overheads and abnormal amounts of production costs of inventories. The circumstances of the entity may also warrant the inclusion of other amounts, such as distribution costs.

39   Some entities adopt a format for profit or loss that results in amounts being disclosed other than the cost of inventories recognised as an expense during the period. Under this format, an entity presents an analysis of expenses using a classification based on the nature of expenses. In this case, the entity discloses the costs recognised as an expense for raw materials and

consumables, labour costs and other costs together with the amount of the net change in inventories for the period.

Effective date

40 An entity shall apply this Standard for annual periods beginning on or after 1 January 2005. Earlier application is encouraged. If an entity applies this Standard for a period beginning before 1 January 2005, it shall disclose that fact.

40A [Deleted]

40B [Deleted]

40C IFRS 13, issued in May 2011, amended the definition of fair value in paragraph 6 and amended paragraph 7. An entity shall apply those amendments when it applies IFRS 13.

40D [Deleted]

40E IFRS 15 *Revenue from Contracts with Customers*, issued in May 2014, amended paragraphs 2, 8, 29 and 37 and deleted paragraph 19. An entity shall apply those amendments when it applies IFRS 15.

40F IFRS 9, as issued in July 2014, amended paragraphs 2 and deleted paragraphs 40A, 40B and 40D. An entity shall apply those amendments when it applies IFRS 9.

40G IFRS 16 *Leases*, issued in January 2016, amended paragraph 12. An entity shall apply that amendment when it applies IFRS 16.

Withdrawal of other pronouncements

41 This Standard supersedes IAS 2 *Inventories* (revised in 1993).

42 This Standard supersedes SIC-1 *Consistency — Different Cost Formulas for Inventories*.

Appendix
Amendments to other pronouncements

The amendments in this appendix shall be applied for annual periods beginning on or after 1 January 2005. If an entity applies this Standard for an earlier period, these amendments shall be applied for that earlier period.

* * * * *

The amendments contained in this appendix when this Standard was revised in 2003 have been incorporated into the relevant pronouncements published in this volume.

Approval by the Board of IAS 2 issued in December 2003

International Accounting Standard 2 *Inventories* (as revised in 2003) was approved for issue by the fourteen members of the International Accounting Standards Board.

Sir David Tweedie	Chairman
Thomas E Jones	Vice-Chairman
Mary E Barth	
Hans-Georg Bruns	
Anthony T Cope	
Robert P Garnett	
Gilbert Gélard	
James J Leisenring	
Warren J McGregor	
Patricia L O'Malley	
Harry K Schmid	
John T Smith	
Geoffrey Whittington	
Tatsumi Yamada	

IAS 7

Statement of Cash Flows

In April 2001 the International Accounting Standards Board adopted IAS 7 *Cash Flow Statements*, which had originally been issued by the International Accounting Standards Committee in December 1992. IAS 7 *Cash Flow Statements* replaced IAS 7 *Statement of Changes in Financial Position* (issued in October 1977).

As a result of the changes in terminology used throughout the IFRS Standards arising from requirements in IAS 1 *Presentation of Financial Statements* (issued in 2007), the title of IAS 7 was changed to *Statement of Cash Flows*.

In January 2016 IAS 7 was amended by *Disclosure Initiative* (Amendments to IAS 7). These amendments require entities to provide disclosures about changes in liabilities arising from financing activities.

Other Standards have made minor consequential amendments to IAS 7. They include IFRS 10 *Consolidated Financial Statements* (issued May 2011), IFRS 11 *Joint Arrangements* (issued May 2011), *Investment Entities* (Amendments to IFRS 10, IFRS 12 and IAS 27) (issued October 2012) and IFRS 16 *Leases* (issued January 2016).

Contents

FOR THE ACCOMPANYING GUIDANCE LISTED BELOW, SEE PART B OF THIS EDITION

ILLUSTRATIVE EXAMPLES

FOR THE BASIS FOR CONCLUSIONS, SEE PART C OF THIS EDITION

BASIS FOR CONCLUSIONS

DISSENTING OPINION

International Accounting Standard 7 *Statement of Cash Flows* (IAS 7) is set out in paragraphs 1–60. All the paragraphs have equal authority but retain the IASC format of the Standard when it was adopted by the IASB. IAS 7 should be read in the context of its objective and the Basis for Conclusions, the *Preface to IFRS Standards* and the *Conceptual Framework for Financial Reporting*. IAS 8 *Accounting Policies, Changes in Accounting Estimates and Errors* provides a basis for selecting and applying accounting policies in the absence of explicit guidance.

International Accounting Standard 7
Statement of Cash Flows[1]

Objective

Information about the cash flows of an entity is useful in providing users of financial statements with a basis to assess the ability of the entity to generate cash and cash equivalents and the needs of the entity to utilise those cash flows. The economic decisions that are taken by users require an evaluation of the ability of an entity to generate cash and cash equivalents and the timing and certainty of their generation.

The objective of this Standard is to require the provision of information about the historical changes in cash and cash equivalents of an entity by means of a statement of cash flows which classifies cash flows during the period from operating, investing and financing activities.

Scope

1   An entity shall prepare a statement of cash flows in accordance with the requirements of this Standard and shall present it as an integral part of its financial statements for each period for which financial statements are presented.

2   This Standard supersedes IAS 7 *Statement of Changes in Financial Position*, approved in July 1977.

3   Users of an entity's financial statements are interested in how the entity generates and uses cash and cash equivalents. This is the case regardless of the nature of the entity's activities and irrespective of whether cash can be viewed as the product of the entity, as may be the case with a financial institution. Entities need cash for essentially the same reasons however different their principal revenue-producing activities might be. They need cash to conduct their operations, to pay their obligations, and to provide returns to their investors. Accordingly, this Standard requires all entities to present a statement of cash flows.

Benefits of cash flow information

4   A statement of cash flows, when used in conjunction with the rest of the financial statements, provides information that enables users to evaluate the changes in net assets of an entity, its financial structure (including its liquidity and solvency) and its ability to affect the amounts and timing of cash flows in order to adapt to changing circumstances and opportunities. Cash flow information is useful in assessing the ability of the entity to generate cash and cash equivalents and enables users to develop models to assess and compare the present value of the future cash flows of different entities. It also enhances the comparability of the reporting of operating

---

1   In September 2007 the IASB amended the title of IAS 7 from *Cash Flow Statements* to *Statement of Cash Flows* as a consequence of the revision of IAS 1 *Presentation of Financial Statements* in 2007.

performance by different entities because it eliminates the effects of using different accounting treatments for the same transactions and events.

5   Historical cash flow information is often used as an indicator of the amount, timing and certainty of future cash flows. It is also useful in checking the accuracy of past assessments of future cash flows and in examining the relationship between profitability and net cash flow and the impact of changing prices.

Definitions

6   The following terms are used in this Standard with the meanings specified:

Cash comprises cash on hand and demand deposits.

Cash equivalents are short-term, highly liquid investments that are readily convertible to known amounts of cash and which are subject to an insignificant risk of changes in value.

Cash flows are inflows and outflows of cash and cash equivalents.

Operating activities are the principal revenue-producing activities of the entity and other activities that are not investing or financing activities.

Investing activities are the acquisition and disposal of long-term assets and other investments not included in cash equivalents.

Financing activities are activities that result in changes in the size and composition of the contributed equity and borrowings of the entity.

Cash and cash equivalents

7   Cash equivalents are held for the purpose of meeting short-term cash commitments rather than for investment or other purposes. For an investment to qualify as a cash equivalent it must be readily convertible to a known amount of cash and be subject to an insignificant risk of changes in value. Therefore, an investment normally qualifies as a cash equivalent only when it has a short maturity of, say, three months or less from the date of acquisition. Equity investments are excluded from cash equivalents unless they are, in substance, cash equivalents, for example in the case of preferred shares acquired within a short period of their maturity and with a specified redemption date.

8   Bank borrowings are generally considered to be financing activities. However, in some countries, bank overdrafts which are repayable on demand form an integral part of an entity's cash management. In these circumstances, bank overdrafts are included as a component of cash and cash equivalents. A characteristic of such banking arrangements is that the bank balance often fluctuates from being positive to overdrawn.

9   Cash flows exclude movements between items that constitute cash or cash equivalents because these components are part of the cash management of an entity rather than part of its operating, investing and financing activities. Cash management includes the investment of excess cash in cash equivalents.

Presentation of a statement of cash flows

10   The statement of cash flows shall report cash flows during the period classified by operating, investing and financing activities.

11   An entity presents its cash flows from operating, investing and financing activities in a manner which is most appropriate to its business. Classification by activity provides information that allows users to assess the impact of those activities on the financial position of the entity and the amount of its cash and cash equivalents. This information may also be used to evaluate the relationships among those activities.

12   A single transaction may include cash flows that are classified differently. For example, when the cash repayment of a loan includes both interest and capital, the interest element may be classified as an operating activity and the capital element is classified as a financing activity.

Operating activities

13   The amount of cash flows arising from operating activities is a key indicator of the extent to which the operations of the entity have generated sufficient cash flows to repay loans, maintain the operating capability of the entity, pay dividends and make new investments without recourse to external sources of financing. Information about the specific components of historical operating cash flows is useful, in conjunction with other information, in forecasting future operating cash flows.

14   Cash flows from operating activities are primarily derived from the principal revenue-producing activities of the entity. Therefore, they generally result from the transactions and other events that enter into the determination of profit or loss. Examples of cash flows from operating activities are:

(a)   cash receipts from the sale of goods and the rendering of services;

(b)   cash receipts from royalties, fees, commissions and other revenue;

(c)   cash payments to suppliers for goods and services;

(d)   cash payments to and on behalf of employees;

(e)   cash receipts and cash payments of an insurance entity for premiums and claims, annuities and other policy benefits;

(f)   cash payments or refunds of income taxes unless they can be specifically identified with financing and investing activities; and

(g)   cash receipts and payments from contracts held for dealing or trading purposes.

Some transactions, such as the sale of an item of plant, may give rise to a gain or loss that is included in recognised profit or loss. The cash flows relating to such transactions are cash flows from investing activities. However, cash payments to manufacture or acquire assets held for rental to others and subsequently held for sale as described in paragraph 68A of IAS 16 *Property, Plant and Equipment* are cash flows from operating activities. The cash receipts from rents and subsequent sales of such assets are also cash flows from operating activities.

15   An entity may hold securities and loans for dealing or trading purposes, in which case they are similar to inventory acquired specifically for resale. Therefore, cash flows arising from the purchase and sale of dealing or trading securities are classified as operating activities. Similarly, cash advances and loans made by financial institutions are usually classified as operating activities since they relate to the main revenue-producing activity of that entity.

Investing activities

16   The separate disclosure of cash flows arising from investing activities is important because the cash flows represent the extent to which expenditures have been made for resources intended to generate future income and cash flows. Only expenditures that result in a recognised asset in the statement of financial position are eligible for classification as investing activities. Examples of cash flows arising from investing activities are:

(a)   cash payments to acquire property, plant and equipment, intangibles and other long-term assets. These payments include those relating to capitalised development costs and self-constructed property, plant and equipment;

(b)   cash receipts from sales of property, plant and equipment, intangibles and other long-term assets;

(c)   cash payments to acquire equity or debt instruments of other entities and interests in joint ventures (other than payments for those instruments considered to be cash equivalents or those held for dealing or trading purposes);

(d)   cash receipts from sales of equity or debt instruments of other entities and interests in joint ventures (other than receipts for those instruments considered to be cash equivalents and those held for dealing or trading purposes);

(e)   cash advances and loans made to other parties (other than advances and loans made by a financial institution);

(f)   cash receipts from the repayment of advances and loans made to other parties (other than advances and loans of a financial institution);

(g)   cash payments for futures contracts, forward contracts, option contracts and swap contracts except when the contracts are held for dealing or trading purposes, or the payments are classified as financing activities; and

(h)   cash receipts from futures contracts, forward contracts, option contracts and swap contracts except when the contracts are held for dealing or trading purposes, or the receipts are classified as financing activities.

When a contract is accounted for as a hedge of an identifiable position the cash flows of the contract are classified in the same manner as the cash flows of the position being hedged.

Financing activities

17   The separate disclosure of cash flows arising from financing activities is important because it is useful in predicting claims on future cash flows by providers of capital to the entity. Examples of cash flows arising from financing activities are:

(a)   cash proceeds from issuing shares or other equity instruments;

(b)   cash payments to owners to acquire or redeem the entity's shares;

(c)   cash proceeds from issuing debentures, loans, notes, bonds, mortgages and other short-term or long-term borrowings;

(d)   cash repayments of amounts borrowed; and

(e)   cash payments by a lessee for the reduction of the outstanding liability relating to a lease.

Reporting cash flows from operating activities

18   An entity shall report cash flows from operating activities using either:

(a)   the direct method, whereby major classes of gross cash receipts and gross cash payments are disclosed; or

(b)   the indirect method, whereby profit or loss is adjusted for the effects of transactions of a non-cash nature, any deferrals or accruals of past or future operating cash receipts or payments, and items of income or expense associated with investing or financing cash flows.

19   Entities are encouraged to report cash flows from operating activities using the direct method. The direct method provides information which may be useful in estimating future cash flows and which is not available under the indirect method. Under the direct method, information about major classes of gross cash receipts and gross cash payments may be obtained either:

(a)   from the accounting records of the entity; or

(b)   by adjusting sales, cost of sales (interest and similar income and interest expense and similar charges for a financial institution) and other items in the statement of comprehensive income for:

(i)   changes during the period in inventories and operating receivables and payables;

(ii)   other non-cash items; and

(iii)   other items for which the cash effects are investing or financing cash flows.

20   Under the indirect method, the net cash flow from operating activities is determined by adjusting profit or loss for the effects of:

(a)   changes during the period in inventories and operating receivables and payables;

(b)   non-cash items such as depreciation, provisions, deferred taxes, unrealised foreign currency gains and losses, and undistributed profits of associates; and

(c)   all other items for which the cash effects are investing or financing cash flows.

Alternatively, the net cash flow from operating activities may be presented under the indirect method by showing the revenues and expenses disclosed in the statement of comprehensive income and the changes during the period in inventories and operating receivables and payables.

Reporting cash flows from investing and financing activities

21   An entity shall report separately major classes of gross cash receipts and gross cash payments arising from investing and financing activities, except to the extent that cash flows described in paragraphs 22 and 24 are reported on a net basis.

Reporting cash flows on a net basis

22   Cash flows arising from the following operating, investing or financing activities may be reported on a net basis:

(a)   cash receipts and payments on behalf of customers when the cash flows reflect the activities of the customer rather than those of the entity; and

(b)   cash receipts and payments for items in which the turnover is quick, the amounts are large, and the maturities are short.

23   Examples of cash receipts and payments referred to in paragraph 22(a) are:

(a)   the acceptance and repayment of demand deposits of a bank;

(b)   funds held for customers by an investment entity; and

(c)   rents collected on behalf of, and paid over to, the owners of properties.

23A   Examples of cash receipts and payments referred to in paragraph 22(b) are advances made for, and the repayment of:

(a)   principal amounts relating to credit card customers;

(b)   the purchase and sale of investments; and

(c)   other short-term borrowings, for example, those which have a maturity period of three months or less.

24   Cash flows arising from each of the following activities of a financial institution may be reported on a net basis:

(a)   cash receipts and payments for the acceptance and repayment of deposits with a fixed maturity date;

(b)   the placement of deposits with and withdrawal of deposits from other financial institutions; and

(c)   cash advances and loans made to customers and the repayment of those advances and loans.

Foreign currency cash flows

25   Cash flows arising from transactions in a foreign currency shall be recorded in an entity's functional currency by applying to the foreign currency amount the exchange rate between the functional currency and the foreign currency at the date of the cash flow.

26   The cash flows of a foreign subsidiary shall be translated at the exchange rates between the functional currency and the foreign currency at the dates of the cash flows.

27   Cash flows denominated in a foreign currency are reported in a manner consistent with IAS 21 *The Effects of Changes in Foreign Exchange Rates*. This permits the use of an exchange rate that approximates the actual rate. For example, a weighted average exchange rate for a period may be used for recording foreign currency transactions or the translation of the cash flows of a foreign subsidiary. However, IAS 21 does not permit use of the exchange rate at the end of the reporting period when translating the cash flows of a foreign subsidiary.

28   Unrealised gains and losses arising from changes in foreign currency exchange rates are not cash flows. However, the effect of exchange rate changes on cash and cash equivalents held or due in a foreign currency is reported in the statement of cash flows in order to reconcile cash and cash equivalents at the beginning and the end of the period. This amount is presented separately from cash flows from operating, investing and financing activities and includes the differences, if any, had those cash flows been reported at end of period exchange rates.

29   [Deleted]

30   [Deleted]

Interest and dividends

31   Cash flows from interest and dividends received and paid shall each be disclosed separately. Each shall be classified in a consistent manner from period to period as either operating, investing or financing activities.

32   The total amount of interest paid during a period is disclosed in the statement of cash flows whether it has been recognised as an expense in profit or loss or capitalised in accordance with IAS 23 *Borrowing Costs*.

33   Interest paid and interest and dividends received are usually classified as operating cash flows for a financial institution. However, there is no consensus on the classification of these cash flows for other entities. Interest paid and interest and dividends received may be classified as operating cash flows because they enter into the determination of profit or loss. Alternatively, interest paid and interest and dividends received may be classified as financing cash flows and investing cash flows respectively, because they are costs of obtaining financial resources or returns on investments.

34   Dividends paid may be classified as a financing cash flow because they are a cost of obtaining financial resources. Alternatively, dividends paid may be classified as a component of cash flows from operating activities in order to assist users to determine the ability of an entity to pay dividends out of operating cash flows.

Taxes on income

35   **Cash flows arising from taxes on income shall be separately disclosed and shall be classified as cash flows from operating activities unless they can be specifically identified with financing and investing activities.**

36   Taxes on income arise on transactions that give rise to cash flows that are classified as operating, investing or financing activities in a statement of cash flows. While tax expense may be readily identifiable with investing or financing activities, the related tax cash flows are often impracticable to identify and may arise in a different period from the cash flows of the underlying transaction. Therefore, taxes paid are usually classified as cash flows from operating activities. However, when it is practicable to identify the tax cash flow with an individual transaction that gives rise to cash flows that are classified as investing or financing activities the tax cash flow is classified as an investing or financing activity as appropriate. When tax cash flows are allocated over more than one class of activity, the total amount of taxes paid is disclosed.

Investments in subsidiaries, associates and joint ventures

37   When accounting for an investment in an associate, a joint venture or a subsidiary accounted for by use of the equity or cost method, an investor restricts its reporting in the statement of cash flows to the cash flows between itself and the investee, for example, to dividends and advances.

38   An entity that reports its interest in an associate or a joint venture using the equity method includes in its statement of cash flows the cash flows in respect of its investments in the associate or joint venture, and distributions and other payments or receipts between it and the associate or joint venture.

Changes in ownership interests in subsidiaries and other businesses

39   The aggregate cash flows arising from obtaining or losing control of subsidiaries or other businesses shall be presented separately and classified as investing activities.

40   An entity shall disclose, in aggregate, in respect of both obtaining and losing control of subsidiaries or other businesses during the period each of the following:

(a)   the total consideration paid or received;

(b)   the portion of the consideration consisting of cash and cash equivalents;

(c)   the amount of cash and cash equivalents in the subsidiaries or other businesses over which control is obtained or lost; and

(d)   the amount of the assets and liabilities other than cash or cash equivalents in the subsidiaries or other businesses over which control is obtained or lost, summarised by each major category.

40A   An investment entity, as defined in IFRS 10 *Consolidated Financial Statements*, need not apply paragraphs 40(c) or 40(d) to an investment in a subsidiary that is required to be measured at fair value through profit or loss.

41   The separate presentation of the cash flow effects of obtaining or losing control of subsidiaries or other businesses as single line items, together with the separate disclosure of the amounts of assets and liabilities acquired or disposed of, helps to distinguish those cash flows from the cash flows arising from the other operating, investing and financing activities. The cash flow effects of losing control are not deducted from those of obtaining control.

42   The aggregate amount of the cash paid or received as consideration for obtaining or losing control of subsidiaries or other businesses is reported in the statement of cash flows net of cash and cash equivalents acquired or disposed of as part of such transactions, events or changes in circumstances.

42A   Cash flows arising from changes in ownership interests in a subsidiary that do not result in a loss of control shall be classified as cash flows from financing activities, unless the subsidiary is held by an investment entity, as defined in IFRS 10, and is required to be measured at fair value through profit or loss.

42B   Changes in ownership interests in a subsidiary that do not result in a loss of control, such as the subsequent purchase or sale by a parent of a subsidiary's equity instruments, are accounted for as equity transactions (see IFRS 10), unless the subsidiary is held by an investment entity and is required to be measured at fair value through profit or loss. Accordingly, the resulting cash flows are classified in the same way as other transactions with owners described in paragraph 17.

Non-cash transactions

43   Investing and financing transactions that do not require the use of cash or cash equivalents shall be excluded from a statement of cash flows. Such transactions shall be disclosed elsewhere in the financial statements in a way that provides all the relevant information about these investing and financing activities.

44   Many investing and financing activities do not have a direct impact on current cash flows although they do affect the capital and asset structure of an entity. The exclusion of non-cash transactions from the statement of cash flows is consistent with the objective of a statement of cash flows as these items do not involve cash flows in the current period. Examples of non-cash transactions are:

(a)   the acquisition of assets either by assuming directly related liabilities or by means of a lease;

(b)   the acquisition of an entity by means of an equity issue; and

(c)   the conversion of debt to equity.

Changes in liabilities arising from financing activities

44A   An entity shall provide disclosures that enable users of financial statements to evaluate changes in liabilities arising from financing activities, including both changes arising from cash flows and non-cash changes.

44B   To the extent necessary to satisfy the requirement in paragraph 44A, an entity shall disclose the following changes in liabilities arising from financing activities:

(a)   changes from financing cash flows;

(b)   changes arising from obtaining or losing control of subsidiaries or other businesses;

(c)   the effect of changes in foreign exchange rates;

(d)   changes in fair values; and

(e)   other changes.

44C   Liabilities arising from financing activities are liabilities for which cash flows were, or future cash flows will be, classified in the statement of cash flows as cash flows from financing activities. In addition, the disclosure requirement in paragraph 44A also applies to changes in financial assets (for example, assets that hedge liabilities arising from financing activities) if cash flows from those financial assets were, or future cash flows will be, included in cash flows from financing activities.

44D One way to fulfil the disclosure requirement in paragraph 44A is by providing a reconciliation between the opening and closing balances in the statement of financial position for liabilities arising from financing activities, including the changes identified in paragraph 44B. Where an entity discloses such a reconciliation, it shall provide sufficient information to enable users of the financial statements to link items included in the reconciliation to the statement of financial position and the statement of cash flows.

44E If an entity provides the disclosure required by paragraph 44A in combination with disclosures of changes in other assets and liabilities, it shall disclose the changes in liabilities arising from financing activities separately from changes in those other assets and liabilities.

Components of cash and cash equivalents

45 **An entity shall disclose the components of cash and cash equivalents and shall present a reconciliation of the amounts in its statement of cash flows with the equivalent items reported in the statement of financial position.**

46 In view of the variety of cash management practices and banking arrangements around the world and in order to comply with IAS 1 *Presentation of Financial Statements*, an entity discloses the policy which it adopts in determining the composition of cash and cash equivalents.

47 The effect of any change in the policy for determining components of cash and cash equivalents, for example, a change in the classification of financial instruments previously considered to be part of an entity's investment portfolio, is reported in accordance with IAS 8 *Accounting Policies, Changes in Accounting Estimates and Errors.*

Other disclosures

48 **An entity shall disclose, together with a commentary by management, the amount of significant cash and cash equivalent balances held by the entity that are not available for use by the group.**

49 There are various circumstances in which cash and cash equivalent balances held by an entity are not available for use by the group. Examples include cash and cash equivalent balances held by a subsidiary that operates in a country where exchange controls or other legal restrictions apply when the balances are not available for general use by the parent or other subsidiaries.

50 Additional information may be relevant to users in understanding the financial position and liquidity of an entity. Disclosure of this information, together with a commentary by management, is encouraged and may include:

(a) the amount of undrawn borrowing facilities that may be available for future operating activities and to settle capital commitments, indicating any restrictions on the use of these facilities;

(b) [deleted]

(c)   the aggregate amount of cash flows that represent increases in operating capacity separately from those cash flows that are required to maintain operating capacity; and

(d)   the amount of the cash flows arising from the operating, investing and financing activities of each reportable segment (see IFRS 8 *Operating Segments*).

51   The separate disclosure of cash flows that represent increases in operating capacity and cash flows that are required to maintain operating capacity is useful in enabling the user to determine whether the entity is investing adequately in the maintenance of its operating capacity. An entity that does not invest adequately in the maintenance of its operating capacity may be prejudicing future profitability for the sake of current liquidity and distributions to owners.

52   The disclosure of segmental cash flows enables users to obtain a better understanding of the relationship between the cash flows of the business as a whole and those of its component parts and the availability and variability of segmental cash flows.

Effective date

53   This Standard becomes operative for financial statements covering periods beginning on or after 1 January 1994.

54   IAS 27 (as amended in 2008) amended paragraphs 39–42 and added paragraphs 42A and 42B. An entity shall apply those amendments for annual periods beginning on or after 1 July 2009. If an entity applies IAS 27 (amended 2008) for an earlier period, the amendments shall be applied for that earlier period. The amendments shall be applied retrospectively.

55   Paragraph 14 was amended by *Improvements to IFRSs* issued in May 2008. An entity shall apply that amendment for annual periods beginning on or after 1 January 2009. Earlier application is permitted. If an entity applies the amendment for an earlier period it shall disclose that fact and apply paragraph 68A of IAS 16.

56   Paragraph 16 was amended by *Improvements to IFRSs* issued in April 2009. An entity shall apply that amendment for annual periods beginning on or after 1 January 2010. Earlier application is permitted. If an entity applies the amendment for an earlier period it shall disclose that fact.

57   IFRS 10 and IFRS 11 *Joint Arrangements*, issued in May 2011, amended paragraphs 37, 38 and 42B and deleted paragraph 50(b). An entity shall apply those amendments when it applies IFRS 10 and IFRS 11.

58   *Investment Entities* (Amendments to IFRS 10, IFRS 12 and IAS 27), issued in October 2012, amended paragraphs 42A and 42B and added paragraph 40A. An entity shall apply those amendments for annual periods beginning on or after 1 January 2014. Earlier application of *Investment Entities* is permitted. If an entity applies those amendments earlier it shall also apply all amendments included in *Investment Entities* at the same time.

59   IFRS 16 *Leases*, issued in January 2016, amended paragraphs 17 and 44. An entity shall apply those amendments when it applies IFRS 16.

60   *Disclosure Initiative* (Amendments to IAS 7), issued in January 2016, added paragraphs 44A–44E. An entity shall apply those amendments for annual periods beginning on or after 1 January 2017. Earlier application is permitted. When the entity first applies those amendments, it is not required to provide comparative information for preceding periods.

61   *[This paragraph refers to amendments that are not yet effective, and is therefore not included in this edition.]*

Approval by the Board of *Disclosure Initiative* (Amendments to IAS 7) issued in January 2016

Disclosure Initiative (Amendments to IAS 7) was approved for issue by thirteen of the fourteen members of the International Accounting Standards Board. Mr Ochi dissented. His dissenting opinion is set out after the Basis for Conclusions.

Hans Hoogervorst	Chairman
Ian Mackintosh	Vice-Chairman
Stephen Cooper	
Philippe Danjou	
Martin Edelmann	
Patrick Finnegan	
Amaro Gomes	
Gary Kabureck	
Suzanne Lloyd	
Takatsugu Ochi	
Darrel Scott	
Chungwoo Suh	
Mary Tokar	
Wei-Guo Zhang	

IAS 8

Accounting Policies, Changes in Accounting Estimates and Errors

In April 2001 the International Accounting Standards Board (Board) adopted IAS 8 *Net Profit or Loss for the Period, Fundamental Errors and Changes in Accounting Policies*, which had originally been issued by the International Accounting Standards Committee in December 1993. IAS 8 *Net Profit or Loss for the Period, Fundamental Errors and Changes in Accounting Policies* replaced IAS 8 *Unusual and Prior Period Items and Changes in Accounting Policies* (issued in February 1978).

In December 2003 the Board issued a revised IAS 8 with a new title—*Accounting Policies, Changes in Accounting Estimates and Errors*. This revised IAS 8 was part of the Board's initial agenda of technical projects. The revised IAS 8 also incorporated the guidance contained in two related Interpretations (SIC-2 *Consistency—Capitalisation of Borrowing Costs* and SIC-18 *Consistency—Alternative Methods*).

In October 2018 the Board issued *Definition of Material* (Amendments to IAS 1 and IAS 8). This amendment clarified the definition of material and how it should be applied by (a) including in the definition guidance that until now has featured elsewhere in IFRS Standards; (b) improving the explanations accompanying the definition; and (c) ensuring that the definition of material is consistent across all IFRS Standards.

Other Standards have made minor consequential amendments to IAS 8. They include IFRS 13 *Fair Value Measurement* (issued May 2011), IFRS 9 *Financial Instruments* (Hedge Accounting and amendments to IFRS 9, IFRS 7 and IAS 39) (issued November 2013), IFRS 9 *Financial Instruments* (issued July 2014) and *Amendments to References to the Conceptual Framework in IFRS Standards* (issued March 2018).

Contents

International Accounting Standard 8 *Accounting Policies, Changes in Accounting Estimates and Errors* (IAS 8) is set out in paragraphs 1–56 and the Appendix. All the paragraphs have equal authority but retain the IASC format of the Standard when it was adopted by the IASB. IAS 8 should be read in the context of its objective and the Basis for Conclusions, the *Preface to IFRS Standards* and the *Conceptual Framework for Financial Reporting*.

International Accounting Standard 8
Accounting Policies, Changes in Accounting Estimates and Errors

Objective

1   The objective of this Standard is to prescribe the criteria for selecting and changing accounting policies, together with the accounting treatment and disclosure of changes in accounting policies, changes in accounting estimates and corrections of errors. The Standard is intended to enhance the relevance and reliability of an entity's financial statements, and the comparability of those financial statements over time and with the financial statements of other entities.

2   Disclosure requirements for accounting policies, except those for changes in accounting policies, are set out in IAS 1 *Presentation of Financial Statements*.

Scope

3   This Standard shall be applied in selecting and applying accounting policies, and accounting for changes in accounting policies, changes in accounting estimates and corrections of prior period errors.

4   The tax effects of corrections of prior period errors and of retrospective adjustments made to apply changes in accounting policies are accounted for and disclosed in accordance with IAS 12 *Income Taxes*.

Definitions

5   The following terms are used in this Standard with the meanings specified:

Accounting policies are the specific principles, bases, conventions, rules and practices applied by an entity in preparing and presenting financial statements.

A *change in accounting estimate* is an adjustment of the carrying amount of an asset or a liability, or the amount of the periodic consumption of an asset, that results from the assessment of the present status of, and expected future benefits and obligations associated with, assets and liabilities. Changes in accounting estimates result from new information or new developments and, accordingly, are not corrections of errors.

International Financial Reporting Standards (IFRSs) are Standards and Interpretations issued by the International Accounting Standards Board (IASB). They comprise:

(a)   International Financial Reporting Standards;

(b)   International Accounting Standards;

(c)   IFRIC Interpretations; and

(d)   SIC Interpretations.[1]

Material is defined in paragraph 7 of IAS 1 and is used in this Standard with the same meaning.

Prior period errors are omissions from, and misstatements in, the entity's financial statements for one or more prior periods arising from a failure to use, or misuse of, reliable information that:

(a)   was available when financial statements for those periods were authorised for issue; and

(b)   could reasonably be expected to have been obtained and taken into account in the preparation and presentation of those financial statements.

Such errors include the effects of mathematical mistakes, mistakes in applying accounting policies, oversights or misinterpretations of facts, and fraud.

Retrospective application is applying a new accounting policy to transactions, other events and conditions as if that policy had always been applied.

Retrospective restatement is correcting the recognition, measurement and disclosure of amounts of elements of financial statements as if a prior period error had never occurred.

Impracticable Applying a requirement is impracticable when the entity cannot apply it after making every reasonable effort to do so. For a particular prior period, it is impracticable to apply a change in an accounting policy retrospectively or to make a retrospective restatement to correct an error if:

(a)   the effects of the retrospective application or retrospective restatement are not determinable;

(b)   the retrospective application or retrospective restatement requires assumptions about what management's intent would have been in that period; or

(c)   the retrospective application or retrospective restatement requires significant estimates of amounts and it is impossible to distinguish objectively information about those estimates that:

(i)   provides evidence of circumstances that existed on the date(s) as at which those amounts are to be recognised, measured or disclosed; and

(ii)   would have been available when the financial statements for that prior period were authorised for issue from other information.

---

1   Definition of IFRSs amended after the name changes introduced by the revised *Constitution of the IFRS Foundation* in 2010.

Prospective application of a change in accounting policy and of recognising the effect of a change in an accounting estimate, respectively, are:

(a)   applying the new accounting policy to transactions, other events and conditions occurring after the date as at which the policy is changed; and

(b)   recognising the effect of the change in the accounting estimate in the current and future periods affected by the change.

6   [Deleted]

Accounting policies

Selection and application of accounting policies

7   When an IFRS specifically applies to a transaction, other event or condition, the accounting policy or policies applied to that item shall be determined by applying the IFRS.

8   IFRSs set out accounting policies that the IASB has concluded result in financial statements containing relevant and reliable information about the transactions, other events and conditions to which they apply. Those policies need not be applied when the effect of applying them is immaterial. However, it is inappropriate to make, or leave uncorrected, immaterial departures from IFRSs to achieve a particular presentation of an entity's financial position, financial performance or cash flows.

9   IFRSs are accompanied by guidance to assist entities in applying their requirements. All such guidance states whether it is an integral part of IFRSs. Guidance that is an integral part of the IFRSs is mandatory. Guidance that is not an integral part of the IFRSs does not contain requirements for financial statements.

10 In the absence of an IFRS that specifically applies to a transaction, other event or condition, management shall use its judgement in developing and applying an accounting policy that results in information that is:

(a)   relevant to the economic decision-making needs of users; and

(b)   reliable, in that the financial statements:

(i)   represent faithfully the financial position, financial performance and cash flows of the entity;

(ii)   reflect the economic substance of transactions, other events and conditions, and not merely the legal form;

(iii) are neutral, ie free from bias;

(iv) are prudent; and

(v)   are complete in all material respects.

11   In making the judgement described in paragraph 10, management shall refer to, and consider the applicability of, the following sources in descending order:

(a)   the requirements in IFRSs dealing with similar and related issues; and

(b)   the definitions, recognition criteria and measurement concepts for assets, liabilities, income and expenses in the *Conceptual Framework for Financial Reporting (Conceptual Framework).*[2]

12   In making the judgement described in paragraph 10, management may also consider the most recent pronouncements of other standard-setting bodies that use a similar conceptual framework to develop accounting standards, other accounting literature and accepted industry practices, to the extent that these do not conflict with the sources in paragraph 11.

Consistency of accounting policies

13   An entity shall select and apply its accounting policies consistently for similar transactions, other events and conditions, unless an IFRS specifically requires or permits categorisation of items for which different policies may be appropriate. If an IFRS requires or permits such categorisation, an appropriate accounting policy shall be selected and applied consistently to each category.

Changes in accounting policies

14   An entity shall change an accounting policy only if the change:

(a)   is required by an IFRS; or

(b)   results in the financial statements providing reliable and more relevant information about the effects of transactions, other events or conditions on the entity's financial position, financial performance or cash flows.

15   Users of financial statements need to be able to compare the financial statements of an entity over time to identify trends in its financial position, financial performance and cash flows. Therefore, the same accounting policies are applied within each period and from one period to the next unless a change in accounting policy meets one of the criteria in paragraph 14.

16   The following are not changes in accounting policies:

(a)   the application of an accounting policy for transactions, other events or conditions that differ in substance from those previously occurring; and

(b)   the application of a new accounting policy for transactions, other events or conditions that did not occur previously or were immaterial.

---

2   Paragraph 54G explains how this requirement is amended for regulatory account balances.

17   The initial application of a policy to revalue assets in accordance with IAS 16 *Property, Plant and Equipment* or IAS 38 *Intangible Assets* is a change in an accounting policy to be dealt with as a revaluation in accordance with IAS 16 or IAS 38, rather than in accordance with this Standard.

18   Paragraphs 19–31 do not apply to the change in accounting policy described in paragraph 17.

Applying changes in accounting policies

19   Subject to paragraph 23:

(a)   an entity shall account for a change in accounting policy resulting from the initial application of an IFRS in accordance with the specific transitional provisions, if any, in that IFRS; and

(b)   when an entity changes an accounting policy upon initial application of an IFRS that does not include specific transitional provisions applying to that change, or changes an accounting policy voluntarily, it shall apply the change retrospectively.

20   For the purpose of this Standard, early application of an IFRS is not a voluntary change in accounting policy.

21   In the absence of an IFRS that specifically applies to a transaction, other event or condition, management may, in accordance with paragraph 12, apply an accounting policy from the most recent pronouncements of other standard-setting bodies that use a similar conceptual framework to develop accounting standards. If, following an amendment of such a pronouncement, the entity chooses to change an accounting policy, that change is accounted for and disclosed as a voluntary change in accounting policy.

Retrospective application

22   Subject to paragraph 23, when a change in accounting policy is applied retrospectively in accordance with paragraph 19(a) or (b), the entity shall adjust the opening balance of each affected component of equity for the earliest prior period presented and the other comparative amounts disclosed for each prior period presented as if the new accounting policy had always been applied.

Limitations on retrospective application

23   When retrospective application is required by paragraph 19(a) or (b), a change in accounting policy shall be applied retrospectively except to the extent that it is impracticable to determine either the period-specific effects or the cumulative effect of the change.

24   When it is impracticable to determine the period-specific effects of changing an accounting policy on comparative information for one or more prior periods presented, the entity shall apply the new accounting policy to the carrying amounts of assets and liabilities as at the beginning of the earliest period for which retrospective application is practicable, which may be the current period, and shall make a corresponding

adjustment to the opening balance of each affected component of equity for that period.

25   When it is impracticable to determine the cumulative effect, at the beginning of the current period, of applying a new accounting policy to all prior periods, the entity shall adjust the comparative information to apply the new accounting policy prospectively from the earliest date practicable.

26   When an entity applies a new accounting policy retrospectively, it applies the new accounting policy to comparative information for prior periods as far back as is practicable. Retrospective application to a prior period is not practicable unless it is practicable to determine the cumulative effect on the amounts in both the opening and closing statements of financial position for that period. The amount of the resulting adjustment relating to periods before those presented in the financial statements is made to the opening balance of each affected component of equity of the earliest prior period presented. Usually the adjustment is made to retained earnings. However, the adjustment may be made to another component of equity (for example, to comply with an IFRS). Any other information about prior periods, such as historical summaries of financial data, is also adjusted as far back as is practicable.

27   When it is impracticable for an entity to apply a new accounting policy retrospectively, because it cannot determine the cumulative effect of applying the policy to all prior periods, the entity, in accordance with paragraph 25, applies the new policy prospectively from the start of the earliest period practicable. It therefore disregards the portion of the cumulative adjustment to assets, liabilities and equity arising before that date. Changing an accounting policy is permitted even if it is impracticable to apply the policy prospectively for any prior period. Paragraphs 50–53 provide guidance on when it is impracticable to apply a new accounting policy to one or more prior periods.

Disclosure

28   When initial application of an IFRS has an effect on the current period or any prior period, would have such an effect except that it is impracticable to determine the amount of the adjustment, or might have an effect on future periods, an entity shall disclose:

    (a)   the title of the IFRS;

    (b)   when applicable, that the change in accounting policy is made in accordance with its transitional provisions;

    (c)   the nature of the change in accounting policy;

    (d)   when applicable, a description of the transitional provisions;

    (e)   when applicable, the transitional provisions that might have an effect on future periods;

    (f)   for the current period and each prior period presented, to the extent practicable, the amount of the adjustment:

> (i) for each financial statement line item affected; and
>
> (ii) if IAS 33 *Earnings per Share* applies to the entity, for basic and diluted earnings per share;

(g) the amount of the adjustment relating to periods before those presented, to the extent practicable; and

(h) if retrospective application required by paragraph 19(a) or (b) is impracticable for a particular prior period, or for periods before those presented, the circumstances that led to the existence of that condition and a description of how and from when the change in accounting policy has been applied.

Financial statements of subsequent periods need not repeat these disclosures.

29 When a voluntary change in accounting policy has an effect on the current period or any prior period, would have an effect on that period except that it is impracticable to determine the amount of the adjustment, or might have an effect on future periods, an entity shall disclose:

(a) the nature of the change in accounting policy;

(b) the reasons why applying the new accounting policy provides reliable and more relevant information;

(c) for the current period and each prior period presented, to the extent practicable, the amount of the adjustment:

> (i) for each financial statement line item affected; and
>
> (ii) if IAS 33 applies to the entity, for basic and diluted earnings per share;

(d) the amount of the adjustment relating to periods before those presented, to the extent practicable; and

(e) if retrospective application is impracticable for a particular prior period, or for periods before those presented, the circumstances that led to the existence of that condition and a description of how and from when the change in accounting policy has been applied.

Financial statements of subsequent periods need not repeat these disclosures.

30 When an entity has not applied a new IFRS that has been issued but is not yet effective, the entity shall disclose:

(a) this fact; and

(b) known or reasonably estimable information relevant to assessing the possible impact that application of the new IFRS will have on the entity's financial statements in the period of initial application.

31 In complying with paragraph 30, an entity considers disclosing:

(a) the title of the new IFRS;

(b)   the nature of the impending change or changes in accounting policy;

(c)   the date by which application of the IFRS is required;

(d)   the date as at which it plans to apply the IFRS initially; and

(e)   either:

(i)   a discussion of the impact that initial application of the IFRS is expected to have on the entity's financial statements; or

(ii)   if that impact is not known or reasonably estimable, a statement to that effect.

Changes in accounting estimates

32   As a result of the uncertainties inherent in business activities, many items in financial statements cannot be measured with precision but can only be estimated. Estimation involves judgements based on the latest available, reliable information. For example, estimates may be required of:

(a)   bad debts;

(b)   inventory obsolescence;

(c)   the fair value of financial assets or financial liabilities;

(d)   the useful lives of, or expected pattern of consumption of the future economic benefits embodied in, depreciable assets; and

(e)   warranty obligations.

32A–32B [These paragraphs refer to amendments that are not yet effective, and are therefore not included in this edition.]

33   The use of reasonable estimates is an essential part of the preparation of financial statements and does not undermine their reliability.

34   An estimate may need revision if changes occur in the circumstances on which the estimate was based or as a result of new information or more experience. By its nature, the revision of an estimate does not relate to prior periods and is not the correction of an error.

34A   [This paragraph refers to amendments that are not yet effective, and is therefore not included in this edition.]

35   A change in the measurement basis applied is a change in an accounting policy, and is not a change in an accounting estimate. When it is difficult to distinguish a change in an accounting policy from a change in an accounting estimate, the change is treated as a change in an accounting estimate.

36   **The effect of a change in an accounting estimate, other than a change to which paragraph 37 applies, shall be recognised prospectively by including it in profit or loss in:**

(a)   the period of the change, if the change affects that period only; or

(b)   the period of the change and future periods, if the change affects both.

37   To the extent that a change in an accounting estimate gives rise to changes in assets and liabilities, or relates to an item of equity, it shall be recognised by adjusting the carrying amount of the related asset, liability or equity item in the period of the change.

38   Prospective recognition of the effect of a change in an accounting estimate means that the change is applied to transactions, other events and conditions from the date of the change in estimate. A change in an accounting estimate may affect only the current period's profit or loss, or the profit or loss of both the current period and future periods. For example, a change in the estimate of the amount of bad debts affects only the current period's profit or loss and therefore is recognised in the current period. However, a change in the estimated useful life of, or the expected pattern of consumption of the future economic benefits embodied in, a depreciable asset affects depreciation expense for the current period and for each future period during the asset's remaining useful life. In both cases, the effect of the change relating to the current period is recognised as income or expense in the current period. The effect, if any, on future periods is recognised as income or expense in those future periods.

Disclosure

39   An entity shall disclose the nature and amount of a change in an accounting estimate that has an effect in the current period or is expected to have an effect in future periods, except for the disclosure of the effect on future periods when it is impracticable to estimate that effect.

40   If the amount of the effect in future periods is not disclosed because estimating it is impracticable, an entity shall disclose that fact.

Errors

41   Errors can arise in respect of the recognition, measurement, presentation or disclosure of elements of financial statements. Financial statements do not comply with IFRSs if they contain either material errors or immaterial errors made intentionally to achieve a particular presentation of an entity's financial position, financial performance or cash flows. Potential current period errors discovered in that period are corrected before the financial statements are authorised for issue. However, material errors are sometimes not discovered until a subsequent period, and these prior period errors are corrected in the comparative information presented in the financial statements for that subsequent period (see paragraphs 42–47).

42   Subject to paragraph 43, an entity shall correct material prior period errors retrospectively in the first set of financial statements authorised for issue after their discovery by:

(a)   restating the comparative amounts for the prior period(s) presented in which the error occurred; or

(b)   if the error occurred before the earliest prior period presented, restating the opening balances of assets, liabilities and equity for the earliest prior period presented.

Limitations on retrospective restatement

43   A prior period error shall be corrected by retrospective restatement except to the extent that it is impracticable to determine either the period-specific effects or the cumulative effect of the error.

44   When it is impracticable to determine the period-specific effects of an error on comparative information for one or more prior periods presented, the entity shall restate the opening balances of assets, liabilities and equity for the earliest period for which retrospective restatement is practicable (which may be the current period).

45   When it is impracticable to determine the cumulative effect, at the beginning of the current period, of an error on all prior periods, the entity shall restate the comparative information to correct the error prospectively from the earliest date practicable.

46   The correction of a prior period error is excluded from profit or loss for the period in which the error is discovered. Any information presented about prior periods, including any historical summaries of financial data, is restated as far back as is practicable.

47   When it is impracticable to determine the amount of an error (eg a mistake in applying an accounting policy) for all prior periods, the entity, in accordance with paragraph 45, restates the comparative information prospectively from the earliest date practicable. It therefore disregards the portion of the cumulative restatement of assets, liabilities and equity arising before that date. Paragraphs 50–53 provide guidance on when it is impracticable to correct an error for one or more prior periods.

48   Corrections of errors are distinguished from changes in accounting estimates. Accounting estimates by their nature are approximations that may need revision as additional information becomes known. For example, the gain or loss recognised on the outcome of a contingency is not the correction of an error.

Disclosure of prior period errors

49   In applying paragraph 42, an entity shall disclose the following:

(a)   the nature of the prior period error;

(b)   for each prior period presented, to the extent practicable, the amount of the correction:

   (i)   for each financial statement line item affected; and

   (ii)   if IAS 33 applies to the entity, for basic and diluted earnings per share;

    (c)   **the amount of the correction at the beginning of the earliest prior period presented; and**

    (d)   **if retrospective restatement is impracticable for a particular prior period, the circumstances that led to the existence of that condition and a description of how and from when the error has been corrected.**

Financial statements of subsequent periods need not repeat these disclosures.

Impracticability in respect of retrospective application and retrospective restatement

50   In some circumstances, it is impracticable to adjust comparative information for one or more prior periods to achieve comparability with the current period. For example, data may not have been collected in the prior period(s) in a way that allows either retrospective application of a new accounting policy (including, for the purpose of paragraphs 51–53, its prospective application to prior periods) or retrospective restatement to correct a prior period error, and it may be impracticable to recreate the information.

51   It is frequently necessary to make estimates in applying an accounting policy to elements of financial statements recognised or disclosed in respect of transactions, other events or conditions. Estimation is inherently subjective, and estimates may be developed after the reporting period. Developing estimates is potentially more difficult when retrospectively applying an accounting policy or making a retrospective restatement to correct a prior period error, because of the longer period of time that might have passed since the affected transaction, other event or condition occurred. However, the objective of estimates related to prior periods remains the same as for estimates made in the current period, namely, for the estimate to reflect the circumstances that existed when the transaction, other event or condition occurred.

52   Therefore, retrospectively applying a new accounting policy or correcting a prior period error requires distinguishing information that

    (a)   provides evidence of circumstances that existed on the date(s) as at which the transaction, other event or condition occurred, and

    (b)   would have been available when the financial statements for that prior period were authorised for issue

from other information. For some types of estimates (eg a fair value measurement that uses significant unobservable inputs), it is impracticable to distinguish these types of information. When retrospective application or retrospective restatement would require making a significant estimate for which it is impossible to distinguish these two types of information, it is impracticable to apply the new accounting policy or correct the prior period error retrospectively.

53   Hindsight should not be used when applying a new accounting policy to, or correcting amounts for, a prior period, either in making assumptions about what management's intentions would have been in a prior period or estimating the amounts recognised, measured or disclosed in a prior period. For example, when an entity corrects a prior period error in calculating its liability for employees' accumulated sick leave in accordance with IAS 19 *Employee Benefits*, it disregards information about an unusually severe influenza season during the next period that became available after the financial statements for the prior period were authorised for issue. The fact that significant estimates are frequently required when amending comparative information presented for prior periods does not prevent reliable adjustment or correction of the comparative information.

Effective date and transition

54   An entity shall apply this Standard for annual periods beginning on or after 1 January 2005. Earlier application is encouraged. If an entity applies this Standard for a period beginning before 1 January 2005, it shall disclose that fact.

54A   [Deleted]

54B   [Deleted]

54C   IFRS 13 *Fair Value Measurement*, issued in May 2011, amended paragraph 52. An entity shall apply that amendment when it applies IFRS 13.

54D   [Deleted]

54E   IFRS 9 *Financial Instruments*, as issued in July 2014, amended paragraph 53 and deleted paragraphs 54A, 54B and 54D. An entity shall apply those amendments when it applies IFRS 9.

54F   *Amendments to References to the Conceptual Framework in IFRS Standards*, issued in 2018, amended paragraphs 6 and 11(b). An entity shall apply those amendments for annual periods beginning on or after 1 January 2020. Earlier application is permitted if at the same time an entity also applies all other amendments made by *Amendments to References to the Conceptual Framework in IFRS Standards*. An entity shall apply the amendments to paragraphs 6 and 11(b) retrospectively in accordance with this Standard. However, if an entity determines that retrospective application would be impracticable or would involve undue cost or effort, it shall apply the amendments to paragraphs 6 and 11(b) by reference to paragraphs 23–28 of this Standard. If retrospective application of any amendment in *Amendments to References to the Conceptual Framework in IFRS Standards* would involve undue cost or effort, an entity shall, in applying paragraphs 23–28 of this Standard, read any reference except in the last sentence of paragraph 27 to 'is impracticable' as 'involves undue cost or effort' and any reference to 'practicable' as 'possible without undue cost or effort'.

54G   If an entity does not apply IFRS 14 *Regulatory Deferral Accounts*, the entity shall, in applying paragraph 11(b) to regulatory account balances, continue to refer to, and consider the applicability of, the definitions, recognition criteria, and measurement concepts in the *Framework for the Preparation and Presentation of Financial Statements*[3] instead of those in the *Conceptual Framework*. A regulatory account balance is the balance of any expense (or income) account that is not recognised as an asset or a liability in accordance with other applicable IFRS Standards but is included, or is expected to be included, by the rate regulator in establishing the rate(s) that can be charged to customers. A rate regulator is an authorised body that is empowered by statute or regulation to establish the rate or a range of rates that bind an entity. The rate regulator may be a third-party body or a related party of the entity, including the entity's own governing board, if that body is required by statute or regulation to set rates both in the interest of the customers and to ensure the overall financial viability of the entity.

54H   *Definition of Material* (Amendments to IAS 1 and IAS 8), issued in October 2018, amended paragraph 7 of IAS 1 and paragraph 5 of IAS 8, and deleted paragraph 6 of IAS 8. An entity shall apply those amendments prospectively for annual periods beginning on or after 1 January 2020. Earlier application is permitted. If an entity applies those amendments for an earlier period, it shall disclose that fact.

54I   *[This paragraph refers to amendments that are not yet effective, and is therefore not included in this edition.]*

Withdrawal of other pronouncements

55   This Standard supersedes IAS 8 *Net Profit or Loss for the Period, Fundamental Errors and Changes in Accounting Policies*, revised in 1993.

56   This Standard supersedes the following Interpretations:

        (a)   SIC-2 *Consistency — Capitalisation of Borrowing Costs*; and

        (b)   SIC-18 *Consistency — Alternative Methods*.

---

3   The reference is to the IASC's *Framework for the Preparation and Presentation of Financial Statements* adopted by the Board in 2001.

    [Editor's note: An extract from the IASC's *Framework for the Preparation and Presentation of Financial Statements*, adopted by the Board in 2001, is available on the IAS 8 page of the 'Supporting Implementation' area of the Foundation's website, under 'Supporting Implementation by IFRS Standard'.]

Appendix
Amendments to other pronouncements

The amendments in this appendix shall be applied for annual periods beginning on or after 1 January 2005. If an entity applies this Standard for an earlier period, these amendments shall be applied for that earlier period.

* * * * *

The amendments contained in this appendix when this Standard was revised in 2003 have been incorporated into the relevant pronouncements published in this volume.

Approval by the Board of IAS 8 issued in December 2003

International Accounting Standard 8 *Accounting Policies, Changes in Accounting Estimates and Errors* (as revised in 2003) was approved for issue by the fourteen members of the International Accounting Standards Board.

Sir David Tweedie	Chairman
Thomas E Jones	Vice-Chairman
Mary E Barth	
Hans-Georg Bruns	
Anthony T Cope	
Robert P Garnett	
Gilbert Gélard	
James J Leisenring	
Warren J McGregor	
Patricia L O'Malley	
Harry K Schmid	
John T Smith	
Geoffrey Whittington	
Tatsumi Yamada	

Approval by the Board of *Definition of Material* (Amendments to IAS 1 and IAS 8) issued in October 2018

Definition of Material (Amendments to IAS 1 and IAS 8) was approved for issue by the fourteen members of the International Accounting Standards Board.

Hans Hoogervorst	Chairman
Suzanne Lloyd	Vice-Chair
Nick Anderson	
Martin Edelmann	
Françoise Flores	
Amaro Luiz de Oliveira Gomes	
Gary Kabureck	
Jianqiao Lu	
Takatsugu Ochi	
Darrel Scott	
Thomas Scott	
Chungwoo Suh	
Ann Tarca	
Mary Tokar	

Events after the Reporting Period

In April 2001 the International Accounting Standards Board (Board) adopted IAS 10 *Events After the Balance Sheet Date*, which had originally been issued by the International Accounting Standards Committee in May 1999. IAS 10 *Events After the Balance Sheet Date* replaced parts of IAS 10 *Contingencies and Events Occurring After the Balance Sheet Date* (issued in June 1978) that were not replaced by IAS 37 *Provisions and Contingent Assets and Contingent Liabilities* (issued in 1998).

In December 2003 the Board issued a revised IAS 10 with a modified title—*Events after the Balance Sheet Date*. This revised IAS 10 was part of the Board's initial agenda of technical projects. As a result of the changes in terminology made by IAS 1 *Presentation of Financial Statements* in 2007, the title of IAS 10 was changed to *Events after the Reporting Period*.

Other Standards have made minor consequential amendments to IAS 10. They include IFRS 13 *Fair Value Measurement* (issued May 2011), IFRS 9 *Financial Instruments* (issued July 2014) and *Definition of Material* (Amendments to IAS 1 and IAS 8) (issued October 2018).

CONTENTS

FOR THE BASIS FOR CONCLUSIONS, SEE PART C OF THIS EDITION

BASIS FOR CONCLUSIONS

International Accounting Standard 10 *Events after the Reporting Period* (IAS 10) is set out in paragraphs 1–24 and the Appendix. All the paragraphs have equal authority but retain the IASC format of the Standard when it was adopted by the IASB. IAS 10 should be read in the context of its objective and the Basis for Conclusions, the *Preface to IFRS Standards* and the *Conceptual Framework for Financial Reporting*. IAS 8 *Accounting Policies, Changes in Accounting Estimates and Errors* provides a basis for selecting and applying accounting policies in the absence of explicit guidance.

International Accounting Standard 10
Events after the Reporting Period

Objective

1   The objective of this Standard is to prescribe:

(a)   when an entity should adjust its financial statements for events after the reporting period; and

(b)   the disclosures that an entity should give about the date when the financial statements were authorised for issue and about events after the reporting period.

The Standard also requires that an entity should not prepare its financial statements on a going concern basis if events after the reporting period indicate that the going concern assumption is not appropriate.

Scope

2   This Standard shall be applied in the accounting for, and disclosure of, events after the reporting period.

Definitions

3   The following terms are used in this Standard with the meanings specified:

Events after the reporting period are those events, favourable and unfavourable, that occur between the end of the reporting period and the date when the financial statements are authorised for issue. Two types of events can be identified:

(a)   those that provide evidence of conditions that existed at the end of the reporting period (*adjusting events after the reporting period*); and

(b)   those that are indicative of conditions that arose after the reporting period (*non-adjusting events after the reporting period*).

4   The process involved in authorising the financial statements for issue will vary depending upon the management structure, statutory requirements and procedures followed in preparing and finalising the financial statements.

5   In some cases, an entity is required to submit its financial statements to its shareholders for approval after the financial statements have been issued. In such cases, the financial statements are authorised for issue on the date of issue, not the date when shareholders approve the financial statements.

> **Example**
>
> The management of an entity completes draft financial statements for the year to 31 December 20X1 on 28 February 20X2. On 18 March 20X2, the board of directors reviews the financial statements and authorises them for issue. The entity announces its profit and selected other financial information on 19 March 20X2. The financial statements are made available to shareholders and others on 1 April 20X2. The shareholders approve the financial statements at their annual meeting on 15 May 20X2 and the approved financial statements are then filed with a regulatory body on 17 May 20X2.
>
> *The financial statements are authorised for issue on 18 March 20X2 (date of board authorisation for issue).*

6 In some cases, the management of an entity is required to issue its financial statements to a supervisory board (made up solely of non-executives) for approval. In such cases, the financial statements are authorised for issue when the management authorises them for issue to the supervisory board.

> **Example**
>
> On 18 March 20X2, the management of an entity authorises financial statements for issue to its supervisory board. The supervisory board is made up solely of non-executives and may include representatives of employees and other outside interests. The supervisory board approves the financial statements on 26 March 20X2. The financial statements are made available to shareholders and others on 1 April 20X2. The shareholders approve the financial statements at their annual meeting on 15 May 20X2 and the financial statements are then filed with a regulatory body on 17 May 20X2.
>
> *The financial statements are authorised for issue on 18 March 20X2 (date of management authorisation for issue to the supervisory board).*

7 Events after the reporting period include all events up to the date when the financial statements are authorised for issue, even if those events occur after the public announcement of profit or of other selected financial information.

Recognition and measurement

Adjusting events after the reporting period

8 An entity shall adjust the amounts recognised in its financial statements to reflect adjusting events after the reporting period.

9 The following are examples of adjusting events after the reporting period that require an entity to adjust the amounts recognised in its financial statements, or to recognise items that were not previously recognised:

(a)   the settlement after the reporting period of a court case that confirms that the entity had a present obligation at the end of the reporting period. The entity adjusts any previously recognised provision related to this court case in accordance with IAS 37 *Provisions, Contingent Liabilities and Contingent Assets* or recognises a new provision. The entity does not merely disclose a contingent liability because the settlement provides additional evidence that would be considered in accordance with paragraph 16 of IAS 37.

(b)   the receipt of information after the reporting period indicating that an asset was impaired at the end of the reporting period, or that the amount of a previously recognised impairment loss for that asset needs to be adjusted. For example:

　　(i)   the bankruptcy of a customer that occurs after the reporting period usually confirms that the customer was credit-impaired at the end of the reporting period; and

　　(ii)   the sale of inventories after the reporting period may give evidence about their net realisable value at the end of the reporting period.

(c)   the determination after the reporting period of the cost of assets purchased, or the proceeds from assets sold, before the end of the reporting period.

(d)   the determination after the reporting period of the amount of profit-sharing or bonus payments, if the entity had a present legal or constructive obligation at the end of the reporting period to make such payments as a result of events before that date (see IAS 19 *Employee Benefits*).

(e)   the discovery of fraud or errors that show that the financial statements are incorrect.

Non-adjusting events after the reporting period

10   An entity shall not adjust the amounts recognised in its financial statements to reflect non-adjusting events after the reporting period.

11   An example of a non-adjusting event after the reporting period is a decline in fair value of investments between the end of the reporting period and the date when the financial statements are authorised for issue. The decline in fair value does not normally relate to the condition of the investments at the end of the reporting period, but reflects circumstances that have arisen subsequently. Therefore, an entity does not adjust the amounts recognised in its financial statements for the investments. Similarly, the entity does not update the amounts disclosed for the investments as at the end of the reporting period, although it may need to give additional disclosure under paragraph 21.

Dividends

12   If an entity declares dividends to holders of equity instruments (as defined in IAS 32 *Financial Instruments: Presentation*) after the reporting period, the entity shall not recognise those dividends as a liability at the end of the reporting period.

13   If dividends are declared after the reporting period but before the financial statements are authorised for issue, the dividends are not recognised as a liability at the end of the reporting period because no obligation exists at that time. Such dividends are disclosed in the notes in accordance with IAS 1 *Presentation of Financial Statements*.

Going concern

14   An entity shall not prepare its financial statements on a going concern basis if management determines after the reporting period either that it intends to liquidate the entity or to cease trading, or that it has no realistic alternative but to do so.

15   Deterioration in operating results and financial position after the reporting period may indicate a need to consider whether the going concern assumption is still appropriate. If the going concern assumption is no longer appropriate, the effect is so pervasive that this Standard requires a fundamental change in the basis of accounting, rather than an adjustment to the amounts recognised within the original basis of accounting.

16   IAS 1 specifies required disclosures if:

(a)   the financial statements are not prepared on a going concern basis; or

(b)   management is aware of material uncertainties related to events or conditions that may cast significant doubt upon the entity's ability to continue as a going concern. The events or conditions requiring disclosure may arise after the reporting period.

Disclosure

Date of authorisation for issue

17   An entity shall disclose the date when the financial statements were authorised for issue and who gave that authorisation. If the entity's owners or others have the power to amend the financial statements after issue, the entity shall disclose that fact.

18   It is important for users to know when the financial statements were authorised for issue, because the financial statements do not reflect events after this date.

Updating disclosure about conditions at the end of the reporting period

19   If an entity receives information after the reporting period about conditions that existed at the end of the reporting period, it shall update disclosures that relate to those conditions, in the light of the new information.

20   In some cases, an entity needs to update the disclosures in its financial statements to reflect information received after the reporting period, even when the information does not affect the amounts that it recognises in its financial statements. One example of the need to update disclosures is when evidence becomes available after the reporting period about a contingent liability that existed at the end of the reporting period. In addition to considering whether it should recognise or change a provision under IAS 37, an entity updates its disclosures about the contingent liability in the light of that evidence.

Non-adjusting events after the reporting period

21   If non-adjusting events after the reporting period are material, non-disclosure could reasonably be expected to influence decisions that the primary users of general purpose financial statements make on the basis of those financial statements, which provide financial information about a specific reporting entity. Accordingly, an entity shall disclose the following for each material category of non-adjusting event after the reporting period:

(a)   the nature of the event; and

(b)   an estimate of its financial effect, or a statement that such an estimate cannot be made.

22   The following are examples of non-adjusting events after the reporting period that would generally result in disclosure:

(a)   a major business combination after the reporting period (IFRS 3 *Business Combinations* requires specific disclosures in such cases) or disposing of a major subsidiary;

(b)   announcing a plan to discontinue an operation;

(c)   major purchases of assets, classification of assets as held for sale in accordance with IFRS 5 *Non-current Assets Held for Sale and Discontinued Operations*, other disposals of assets, or expropriation of major assets by government;

(d)   the destruction of a major production plant by a fire after the reporting period;

(e)   announcing, or commencing the implementation of, a major restructuring (see IAS 37);

(f)   major ordinary share transactions and potential ordinary share transactions after the reporting period (IAS 33 *Earnings per Share* requires an entity to disclose a description of such transactions, other than when such transactions involve capitalisation or bonus issues, share splits or reverse share splits all of which are required to be adjusted under IAS 33);

(g)   abnormally large changes after the reporting period in asset prices or foreign exchange rates;

(h)   changes in tax rates or tax laws enacted or announced after the reporting period that have a significant effect on current and deferred tax assets and liabilities (see IAS 12 *Income Taxes*);

(i)   entering into significant commitments or contingent liabilities, for example, by issuing significant guarantees; and

(j)   commencing major litigation arising solely out of events that occurred after the reporting period.

Effective date

23   An entity shall apply this Standard for annual periods beginning on or after 1 January 2005. Earlier application is encouraged. If an entity applies this Standard for a period beginning before 1 January 2005, it shall disclose that fact.

23A   IFRS 13 *Fair Value Measurement*, issued in May 2011, amended paragraph 11. An entity shall apply that amendment when it applies IFRS 13.

23B   IFRS 9 *Financial Instruments*, as issued in July 2014, amended paragraph 9. An entity shall apply that amendment when it applies IFRS 9.

23C   *Definition of Material* (Amendments to IAS 1 and IAS 8), issued in October 2018, amended paragraph 21. An entity shall apply those amendments prospectively for annual periods beginning on or after 1 January 2020. Earlier application is permitted. If an entity applies those amendments for an earlier period, it shall disclose that fact. An entity shall apply those amendments when it applies the amendments to the definition of material in paragraph 7 of IAS 1 and paragraphs 5 and 6 of IAS 8.

Withdrawal of IAS 10 (revised 1999)

24   This Standard supersedes IAS 10 *Events After the Balance Sheet Date* (revised in 1999).

Appendix
Amendments to other pronouncements

The amendments in this appendix shall be applied for annual periods beginning on or after 1 January 2005. If an entity applies this Standard for an earlier period, these amendments shall be applied for that earlier period.

* * * * *

The amendments contained in this appendix when this Standard was revised in 2003 have been incorporated into the relevant IFRSs published in this volume.

Approval by the Board of IAS 10 issued in December 2003

International Accounting Standard 10 *Events after the Balance Sheet Date* (as revised in 2003) was approved for issue by the fourteen members of the International Accounting Standards Board.

Sir David Tweedie	Chairman
Thomas E Jones	Vice-Chairman
Mary E Barth	
Hans-Georg Bruns	
Anthony T Cope	
Robert P Garnett	
Gilbert Gélard	
James J Leisenring	
Warren J McGregor	
Patricia L O'Malley	
Harry K Schmid	
John T Smith	
Geoffrey Whittington	
Tatsumi Yamada	

Approval by the Board of IAS 10 issued in December 2003

IAS 12

Income Taxes

In April 2001 the International Accounting Standards Board (Board) adopted IAS 12 *Income Taxes*, which had originally been issued by the International Accounting Standards Committee in October 1996. IAS 12 *Income Taxes* replaced parts of IAS 12 *Accounting for Income Taxes* (issued in July 1979).

In December 2010 the Board amended IAS 12 to address an issue that arises when entities apply the measurement principle in IAS 12 to temporary differences relating to investment properties that are measured at fair value. That amendment also incorporated some guidance from a related Interpretation (SIC-21 *Income Taxes – Recovery of Revalued Non-Depreciable Assets*).

In January 2016 the Board issued *Recognition of Deferred Tax Assets for Unrealised Losses* (Amendments to IAS 12) to clarify the requirements on recognition of deferred tax assets related to debt instruments measured at fair value.

Other Standards have made minor consequential amendments to IAS 12. They include IFRS 11 *Joint Arrangements* (issued May 2011), *Presentation of Items of Other Comprehensive Income* (Amendments to IAS 1) (issued June 2011), *Investment Entities* (Amendments to IFRS 10, IFRS 12 and IAS 27) (issued October 2012), IFRS 9 *Financial Instruments* (Hedge Accounting and amendments to IFRS 9, IFRS 7 and IAS 39) (issued November 2013), IFRS 15 *Revenue from Contracts with Customers* (issued May 2014), IFRS 9 *Financial Instruments* (issued July 2014), IFRS 16 *Leases* (issued January 2016), *Annual Improvements to IFRS Standards 2015–2017 Cycle* (issued December 2017) and *Amendments to References to the Conceptual Framework in IFRS Standards* (issued March 2018).

CONTENTS

FOR THE ACCOMPANYING GUIDANCE LISTED BELOW, SEE PART B OF THIS EDITION

ILLUSTRATIVE EXAMPLES

FOR THE BASIS FOR CONCLUSIONS, SEE PART C OF THIS EDITION

BASIS FOR CONCLUSIONS

International Accounting Standard 12 *Income Taxes* (IAS 12) is set out in paragraphs 1–99. All the paragraphs have equal authority but retain the IASC format of the Standard when it was adopted by the IASB. IAS 12 should be read in the context of its objective and the Basis for Conclusions, the *Preface to IFRS Standards* and the *Conceptual Framework for Financial Reporting*. IAS 8 *Accounting Policies, Changes in Accounting Estimates and Errors* provides a basis for selecting and applying accounting policies in the absence of explicit guidance.

International Accounting Standard 12
Income Taxes

Objective

The objective of this Standard is to prescribe the accounting treatment for income taxes. The principal issue in accounting for income taxes is how to account for the current and future tax consequences of:

(a)   the future recovery (settlement) of the carrying amount of assets (liabilities) that are recognised in an entity's statement of financial position; and

(b)   transactions and other events of the current period that are recognised in an entity's financial statements.

It is inherent in the recognition of an asset or liability that the reporting entity expects to recover or settle the carrying amount of that asset or liability. If it is probable that recovery or settlement of that carrying amount will make future tax payments larger (smaller) than they would be if such recovery or settlement were to have no tax consequences, this Standard requires an entity to recognise a deferred tax liability (deferred tax asset), with certain limited exceptions.

This Standard requires an entity to account for the tax consequences of transactions and other events in the same way that it accounts for the transactions and other events themselves. Thus, for transactions and other events recognised in profit or loss, any related tax effects are also recognised in profit or loss. For transactions and other events recognised outside profit or loss (either in other comprehensive income or directly in equity), any related tax effects are also recognised outside profit or loss (either in other comprehensive income or directly in equity, respectively). Similarly, the recognition of deferred tax assets and liabilities in a business combination affects the amount of goodwill arising in that business combination or the amount of the bargain purchase gain recognised.

This Standard also deals with the recognition of deferred tax assets arising from unused tax losses or unused tax credits, the presentation of income taxes in the financial statements and the disclosure of information relating to income taxes.

Scope

1   This Standard shall be applied in accounting for income taxes.

2   For the purposes of this Standard, income taxes include all domestic and foreign taxes which are based on taxable profits. Income taxes also include taxes, such as withholding taxes, which are payable by a subsidiary, associate or joint arrangement on distributions to the reporting entity.

3   [Deleted]

4   This Standard does not deal with the methods of accounting for government grants (see IAS 20 *Accounting for Government Grants and Disclosure of Government Assistance*) or investment tax credits. However, this Standard does deal with the accounting for temporary differences that may arise from such grants or investment tax credits.

Definitions

5   The following terms are used in this Standard with the meanings specified:

Accounting profit is profit or loss for a period before deducting tax expense.

Taxable profit (*tax loss*) is the profit (loss) for a period, determined in accordance with the rules established by the taxation authorities, upon which income taxes are payable (recoverable).

Tax expense (*tax income*) is the aggregate amount included in the determination of profit or loss for the period in respect of current tax and deferred tax.

Current tax is the amount of income taxes payable (recoverable) in respect of the taxable profit (tax loss) for a period.

Deferred tax liabilities are the amounts of income taxes payable in future periods in respect of taxable temporary differences.

Deferred tax assets are the amounts of income taxes recoverable in future periods in respect of:

(a)   deductible temporary differences;

(b)   the carryforward of unused tax losses; and

(c)   the carryforward of unused tax credits.

Temporary differences are differences between the carrying amount of an asset or liability in the statement of financial position and its tax base. Temporary differences may be either:

(a)   *taxable temporary differences*, which are temporary differences that will result in taxable amounts in determining taxable profit (tax loss) of future periods when the carrying amount of the asset or liability is recovered or settled; or

(b)   *deductible temporary differences*, which are temporary differences that will result in amounts that are deductible in determining taxable profit (tax loss) of future periods when the carrying amount of the asset or liability is recovered or settled.

The *tax base* of an asset or liability is the amount attributed to that asset or liability for tax purposes.

6   Tax expense (tax income) comprises current tax expense (current tax income) and deferred tax expense (deferred tax income).

Tax base

7   The tax base of an asset is the amount that will be deductible for tax purposes against any taxable economic benefits that will flow to an entity when it recovers the carrying amount of the asset. If those economic benefits will not be taxable, the tax base of the asset is equal to its carrying amount.

Examples
1   A machine cost 100. For tax purposes, depreciation of 30 has already been deducted in the current and prior periods and the remaining cost will be deductible in future periods, either as depreciation or through a deduction on disposal. Revenue generated by using the machine is taxable, any gain on disposal of the machine will be taxable and any loss on disposal will be deductible for tax purposes. *The tax base of the machine is 70.*
2   Interest receivable has a carrying amount of 100. The related interest revenue will be taxed on a cash basis. *The tax base of the interest receivable is nil.*
3   Trade receivables have a carrying amount of 100. The related revenue has already been included in taxable profit (tax loss). *The tax base of the trade receivables is 100.*
4   Dividends receivable from a subsidiary have a carrying amount of 100. The dividends are not taxable. *In substance, the entire carrying amount of the asset is deductible against the economic benefits. Consequently, the tax base of the dividends receivable is 100.*[a]
5   A loan receivable has a carrying amount of 100. The repayment of the loan will have no tax consequences. *The tax base of the loan is 100.*
(a) Under this analysis, there is no taxable temporary difference. An alternative analysis is that the accrued dividends receivable have a tax base of nil and that a tax rate of nil is applied to the resulting taxable temporary difference of 100. Under both analyses, there is no deferred tax liability.

8   The tax base of a liability is its carrying amount, less any amount that will be deductible for tax purposes in respect of that liability in future periods. In the case of revenue which is received in advance, the tax base of the resulting liability is its carrying amount, less any amount of the revenue that will not be taxable in future periods.

Examples
1   Current liabilities include accrued expenses with a carrying amount of 100. The related expense will be deducted for tax purposes on a cash basis. *The tax base of the accrued expenses is nil.*
2   Current liabilities include interest revenue received in advance, with a carrying amount of 100. The related interest revenue was taxed on a cash basis. *The tax base of the interest received in advance is nil.*

continued...

...continued

Examples

3   Current liabilities include accrued expenses with a carrying amount of 100. The related expense has already been deducted for tax purposes. *The tax base of the accrued expenses is 100.*

4   Current liabilities include accrued fines and penalties with a carrying amount of 100. Fines and penalties are not deductible for tax purposes. *The tax base of the accrued fines and penalties is 100.*[a]

5   A loan payable has a carrying amount of 100. The repayment of the loan will have no tax consequences. *The tax base of the loan is 100.*

(a)   Under this analysis, there is no deductible temporary difference. An alternative analysis is that the accrued fines and penalties payable have a tax base of nil and that a tax rate of nil is applied to the resulting deductible temporary difference of 100. Under both analyses, there is no deferred tax asset.

---

9   Some items have a tax base but are not recognised as assets and liabilities in the statement of financial position. For example, research costs are recognised as an expense in determining accounting profit in the period in which they are incurred but may not be permitted as a deduction in determining taxable profit (tax loss) until a later period. The difference between the tax base of the research costs, being the amount the taxation authorities will permit as a deduction in future periods, and the carrying amount of nil is a deductible temporary difference that results in a deferred tax asset.

10   Where the tax base of an asset or liability is not immediately apparent, it is helpful to consider the fundamental principle upon which this Standard is based: that an entity shall, with certain limited exceptions, recognise a deferred tax liability (asset) whenever recovery or settlement of the carrying amount of an asset or liability would make future tax payments larger (smaller) than they would be if such recovery or settlement were to have no tax consequences. Example C following paragraph 51A illustrates circumstances when it may be helpful to consider this fundamental principle, for example, when the tax base of an asset or liability depends on the expected manner of recovery or settlement.

11   In consolidated financial statements, temporary differences are determined by comparing the carrying amounts of assets and liabilities in the consolidated financial statements with the appropriate tax base. The tax base is determined by reference to a consolidated tax return in those jurisdictions in which such a return is filed. In other jurisdictions, the tax base is determined by reference to the tax returns of each entity in the group.

Recognition of current tax liabilities and current tax assets

12   Current tax for current and prior periods shall, to the extent unpaid, be recognised as a liability. If the amount already paid in respect of current and prior periods exceeds the amount due for those periods, the excess shall be recognised as an asset.

13   The benefit relating to a tax loss that can be carried back to recover current tax of a previous period shall be recognised as an asset.

14   When a tax loss is used to recover current tax of a previous period, an entity recognises the benefit as an asset in the period in which the tax loss occurs because it is probable that the benefit will flow to the entity and the benefit can be reliably measured.

Recognition of deferred tax liabilities and deferred tax assets

Taxable temporary differences

15   A deferred tax liability shall be recognised for all taxable temporary differences, except to the extent that the deferred tax liability arises from:

     (a)   the initial recognition of goodwill; or

     (b)   the initial recognition of an asset or liability in a transaction which:

         (i)   is not a business combination; and

         (ii)   at the time of the transaction, affects neither accounting profit nor taxable profit (tax loss).

     However, for taxable temporary differences associated with investments in subsidiaries, branches and associates, and interests in joint arrangements, a deferred tax liability shall be recognised in accordance with paragraph 39.

16   It is inherent in the recognition of an asset that its carrying amount will be recovered in the form of economic benefits that flow to the entity in future periods. When the carrying amount of the asset exceeds its tax base, the amount of taxable economic benefits will exceed the amount that will be allowed as a deduction for tax purposes. This difference is a taxable temporary difference and the obligation to pay the resulting income taxes in future periods is a deferred tax liability. As the entity recovers the carrying amount of the asset, the taxable temporary difference will reverse and the entity will have taxable profit. This makes it probable that economic benefits will flow from the entity in the form of tax payments. Therefore, this Standard requires the recognition of all deferred tax liabilities, except in certain circumstances described in paragraphs 15 and 39.

> **Example**
>
> An asset which cost 150 has a carrying amount of 100. Cumulative depreciation for tax purposes is 90 and the tax rate is 25%.
>
> *The tax base of the asset is 60 (cost of 150 less cumulative tax depreciation of 90). To recover the carrying amount of 100, the entity must earn taxable income of 100, but will only be able to deduct tax depreciation of 60. Consequently, the entity will pay income taxes of 10 (40 at 25%) when it recovers the carrying amount of the asset. The difference between the carrying amount of 100 and the tax base of 60 is a taxable temporary difference of 40. Therefore, the entity recognises a deferred tax liability of 10 (40 at 25%) representing the income taxes that it will pay when it recovers the carrying amount of the asset.*

17   Some temporary differences arise when income or expense is included in accounting profit in one period but is included in taxable profit in a different period. Such temporary differences are often described as timing differences. The following are examples of temporary differences of this kind which are taxable temporary differences and which therefore result in deferred tax liabilities:

(a)   interest revenue is included in accounting profit on a time proportion basis but may, in some jurisdictions, be included in taxable profit when cash is collected. The tax base of any receivable recognised in the statement of financial position with respect to such revenues is nil because the revenues do not affect taxable profit until cash is collected;

(b)   depreciation used in determining taxable profit (tax loss) may differ from that used in determining accounting profit. The temporary difference is the difference between the carrying amount of the asset and its tax base which is the original cost of the asset less all deductions in respect of that asset permitted by the taxation authorities in determining taxable profit of the current and prior periods. A taxable temporary difference arises, and results in a deferred tax liability, when tax depreciation is accelerated (if tax depreciation is less rapid than accounting depreciation, a deductible temporary difference arises, and results in a deferred tax asset); and

(c)   development costs may be capitalised and amortised over future periods in determining accounting profit but deducted in determining taxable profit in the period in which they are incurred. Such development costs have a tax base of nil as they have already been deducted from taxable profit. The temporary difference is the difference between the carrying amount of the development costs and their tax base of nil.

18   Temporary differences also arise when:

(a)   the identifiable assets acquired and liabilities assumed in a business combination are recognised at their fair values in accordance with IFRS 3 *Business Combinations*, but no equivalent adjustment is made for tax purposes (see paragraph 19);

(b)   assets are revalued and no equivalent adjustment is made for tax purposes (see paragraph 20);

(c)   goodwill arises in a business combination (see paragraph 21);

(d)   the tax base of an asset or liability on initial recognition differs from its initial carrying amount, for example when an entity benefits from non-taxable government grants related to assets (see paragraphs 22 and 33); or

(e)   the carrying amount of investments in subsidiaries, branches and associates or interests in joint arrangements becomes different from the tax base of the investment or interest (see paragraphs 38–45).

Business combinations

19   With limited exceptions, the identifiable assets acquired and liabilities assumed in a business combination are recognised at their fair values at the acquisition date. Temporary differences arise when the tax bases of the identifiable assets acquired and liabilities assumed are not affected by the business combination or are affected differently. For example, when the carrying amount of an asset is increased to fair value but the tax base of the asset remains at cost to the previous owner, a taxable temporary difference arises which results in a deferred tax liability. The resulting deferred tax liability affects goodwill (see paragraph 66).

Assets carried at fair value

20   IFRSs permit or require certain assets to be carried at fair value or to be revalued (see, for example, IAS 16 *Property, Plant and Equipment*, IAS 38 *Intangible Assets*, IAS 40 *Investment Property*, IFRS 9 *Financial Instruments* and IFRS 16 *Leases*). In some jurisdictions, the revaluation or other restatement of an asset to fair value affects taxable profit (tax loss) for the current period. As a result, the tax base of the asset is adjusted and no temporary difference arises. In other jurisdictions, the revaluation or restatement of an asset does not affect taxable profit in the period of the revaluation or restatement and, consequently, the tax base of the asset is not adjusted. Nevertheless, the future recovery of the carrying amount will result in a taxable flow of economic benefits to the entity and the amount that will be deductible for tax purposes will differ from the amount of those economic benefits. The difference between the carrying amount of a revalued asset and its tax base is a temporary difference and gives rise to a deferred tax liability or asset. This is true even if:

(a)   the entity does not intend to dispose of the asset. In such cases, the revalued carrying amount of the asset will be recovered through use and this will generate taxable income which exceeds the depreciation that will be allowable for tax purposes in future periods; or

(b)   tax on capital gains is deferred if the proceeds of the disposal of the asset are invested in similar assets. In such cases, the tax will ultimately become payable on sale or use of the similar assets.

Goodwill

21 Goodwill arising in a business combination is measured as the excess of (a) over (b) below:

(a) the aggregate of:

(i) the consideration transferred measured in accordance with IFRS 3, which generally requires acquisition-date fair value;

(ii) the amount of any non-controlling interest in the acquiree recognised in accordance with IFRS 3; and

(iii) in a business combination achieved in stages, the acquisition-date fair value of the acquirer's previously held equity interest in the acquiree.

(b) the net of the acquisition-date amounts of the identifiable assets acquired and liabilities assumed measured in accordance with IFRS 3.

Many taxation authorities do not allow reductions in the carrying amount of goodwill as a deductible expense in determining taxable profit. Moreover, in such jurisdictions, the cost of goodwill is often not deductible when a subsidiary disposes of its underlying business. In such jurisdictions, goodwill has a tax base of nil. Any difference between the carrying amount of goodwill and its tax base of nil is a taxable temporary difference. However, this Standard does not permit the recognition of the resulting deferred tax liability because goodwill is measured as a residual and the recognition of the deferred tax liability would increase the carrying amount of goodwill.

21A Subsequent reductions in a deferred tax liability that is unrecognised because it arises from the initial recognition of goodwill are also regarded as arising from the initial recognition of goodwill and are therefore not recognised under paragraph 15(a). For example, if in a business combination an entity recognises goodwill of CU100 that has a tax base of nil, paragraph 15(a) prohibits the entity from recognising the resulting deferred tax liability. If the entity subsequently recognises an impairment loss of CU20 for that goodwill, the amount of the taxable temporary difference relating to the goodwill is reduced from CU100 to CU80, with a resulting decrease in the value of the unrecognised deferred tax liability. That decrease in the value of the unrecognised deferred tax liability is also regarded as relating to the initial recognition of the goodwill and is therefore prohibited from being recognised under paragraph 15(a).

21B Deferred tax liabilities for taxable temporary differences relating to goodwill are, however, recognised to the extent they do not arise from the initial recognition of goodwill. For example, if in a business combination an entity recognises goodwill of CU100 that is deductible for tax purposes at a rate of 20 per cent per year starting in the year of acquisition, the tax base of the goodwill is CU100 on initial recognition and CU80 at the end of the year of acquisition. If the carrying amount of goodwill at the end of the year of acquisition remains unchanged at CU100, a taxable temporary difference of CU20 arises at the end of that year. Because that taxable temporary difference does not relate to the initial recognition of the goodwill, the resulting deferred tax liability is recognised.

Initial recognition of an asset or liability

22   A temporary difference may arise on initial recognition of an asset or liability, for example if part or all of the cost of an asset will not be deductible for tax purposes. The method of accounting for such a temporary difference depends on the nature of the transaction that led to the initial recognition of the asset or liability:

(a)   in a business combination, an entity recognises any deferred tax liability or asset and this affects the amount of goodwill or bargain purchase gain it recognises (see paragraph 19);

(b)   if the transaction affects either accounting profit or taxable profit, an entity recognises any deferred tax liability or asset and recognises the resulting deferred tax expense or income in profit or loss (see paragraph 59);

(c)   if the transaction is not a business combination, and affects neither accounting profit nor taxable profit, an entity would, in the absence of the exemption provided by paragraphs 15 and 24, recognise the resulting deferred tax liability or asset and adjust the carrying amount of the asset or liability by the same amount. Such adjustments would make the financial statements less transparent. Therefore, this Standard does not permit an entity to recognise the resulting deferred tax liability or asset, either on initial recognition or subsequently (see example below). Furthermore, an entity does not recognise subsequent changes in the unrecognised deferred tax liability or asset as the asset is depreciated.

Example illustrating paragraph 22(c)

An entity intends to use an asset which cost 1,000 throughout its useful life of five years and then dispose of it for a residual value of nil. The tax rate is 40%. Depreciation of the asset is not deductible for tax purposes. On disposal, any capital gain would not be taxable and any capital loss would not be deductible.

As it recovers the carrying amount of the asset, the entity will earn taxable income of 1,000 and pay tax of 400. The entity does not recognise the resulting deferred tax liability of 400 because it results from the initial recognition of the asset.

In the following year, the carrying amount of the asset is 800. In earning taxable income of 800, the entity will pay tax of 320. The entity does not recognise the deferred tax liability of 320 because it results from the initial recognition of the asset.

22A   [This paragraph refers to amendments that are not yet effective, and is therefore not included in this edition.]

23 In accordance with IAS 32 *Financial Instruments: Presentation* the issuer of a compound financial instrument (for example, a convertible bond) classifies the instrument's liability component as a liability and the equity component as equity. In some jurisdictions, the tax base of the liability component on initial recognition is equal to the initial carrying amount of the sum of the liability and equity components. The resulting taxable temporary difference arises from the initial recognition of the equity component separately from the liability component. Therefore, the exception set out in paragraph 15(b) does not apply. Consequently, an entity recognises the resulting deferred tax liability. In accordance with paragraph 61A, the deferred tax is charged directly to the carrying amount of the equity component. In accordance with paragraph 58, subsequent changes in the deferred tax liability are recognised in profit or loss as deferred tax expense (income).

Deductible temporary differences

24 A deferred tax asset shall be recognised for all deductible temporary differences to the extent that it is probable that taxable profit will be available against which the deductible temporary difference can be utilised, unless the deferred tax asset arises from the initial recognition of an asset or liability in a transaction that:

(a) is not a business combination; and

(b) at the time of the transaction, affects neither accounting profit nor taxable profit (tax loss).

However, for deductible temporary differences associated with investments in subsidiaries, branches and associates, and interests in joint arrangements, a deferred tax asset shall be recognised in accordance with paragraph 44.

25 It is inherent in the recognition of a liability that the carrying amount will be settled in future periods through an outflow from the entity of resources embodying economic benefits. When resources flow from the entity, part or all of their amounts may be deductible in determining taxable profit of a period later than the period in which the liability is recognised. In such cases, a temporary difference exists between the carrying amount of the liability and its tax base. Accordingly, a deferred tax asset arises in respect of the income taxes that will be recoverable in the future periods when that part of the liability is allowed as a deduction in determining taxable profit. Similarly, if the carrying amount of an asset is less than its tax base, the difference gives rise to a deferred tax asset in respect of the income taxes that will be recoverable in future periods.

> **Example**
>
> An entity recognises a liability of 100 for accrued product warranty costs. For tax purposes, the product warranty costs will not be deductible until the entity pays claims. The tax rate is 25%.
>
> *The tax base of the liability is nil (carrying amount of 100, less the amount that will be deductible for tax purposes in respect of that liability in future periods). In settling the liability for its carrying amount, the entity will reduce its future taxable profit by an amount of 100 and, consequently, reduce its future tax payments by 25 (100 at 25%). The difference between the carrying amount of 100 and the tax base of nil is a deductible temporary difference of 100. Therefore, the entity recognises a deferred tax asset of 25 (100 at 25%), provided that it is probable that the entity will earn sufficient taxable profit in future periods to benefit from a reduction in tax payments.*

26   The following are examples of deductible temporary differences that result in deferred tax assets:

(a)   retirement benefit costs may be deducted in determining accounting profit as service is provided by the employee, but deducted in determining taxable profit either when contributions are paid to a fund by the entity or when retirement benefits are paid by the entity. A temporary difference exists between the carrying amount of the liability and its tax base; the tax base of the liability is usually nil. Such a deductible temporary difference results in a deferred tax asset as economic benefits will flow to the entity in the form of a deduction from taxable profits when contributions or retirement benefits are paid;

(b)   research costs are recognised as an expense in determining accounting profit in the period in which they are incurred but may not be permitted as a deduction in determining taxable profit (tax loss) until a later period. The difference between the tax base of the research costs, being the amount the taxation authorities will permit as a deduction in future periods, and the carrying amount of nil is a deductible temporary difference that results in a deferred tax asset;

(c)   with limited exceptions, an entity recognises the identifiable assets acquired and liabilities assumed in a business combination at their fair values at the acquisition date. When a liability assumed is recognised at the acquisition date but the related costs are not deducted in determining taxable profits until a later period, a deductible temporary difference arises which results in a deferred tax asset. A deferred tax asset also arises when the fair value of an identifiable asset acquired is less than its tax base. In both cases, the resulting deferred tax asset affects goodwill (see paragraph 66); and

(d)   certain assets may be carried at fair value, or may be revalued, without an equivalent adjustment being made for tax purposes (see paragraph 20). A deductible temporary difference arises if the tax base of the asset exceeds its carrying amount.

Example illustrating paragraph 26(d)

Identification of a deductible temporary difference at the end of Year 2:

Entity A purchases for CU1,000, at the beginning of Year 1, a debt instrument with a nominal value of CU1,000 payable on maturity in 5 years with an interest rate of 2% payable at the end of each year. The effective interest rate is 2%. The debt instrument is measured at fair value.

At the end of Year 2, the fair value of the debt instrument has decreased to CU918 as a result of an increase in market interest rates to 5%. It is probable that Entity A will collect all the contractual cash flows if it continues to hold the debt instrument.

Any gains (losses) on the debt instrument are taxable (deductible) only when realised. The gains (losses) arising on the sale or maturity of the debt instrument are calculated for tax purposes as the difference between the amount collected and the original cost of the debt instrument.

Accordingly, the tax base of the debt instrument is its original cost.

The difference between the carrying amount of the debt instrument in Entity A's statement of financial position of CU918 and its tax base of CU1,000 gives rise to a deductible temporary difference of CU82 at the end of Year 2 (see paragraphs 20 and 26(d)), irrespective of whether Entity A expects to recover the carrying amount of the debt instrument by sale or by use, ie by holding it and collecting contractual cash flows, or a combination of both.

This is because deductible temporary differences are differences between the carrying amount of an asset or liability in the statement of financial position and its tax base that will result in amounts that are deductible in determining taxable profit (tax loss) of future periods, when the carrying amount of the asset or liability is recovered or settled (see paragraph 5). Entity A obtains a deduction equivalent to the tax base of the asset of CU1,000 in determining taxable profit (tax loss) either on sale or on maturity.

---

27   The reversal of deductible temporary differences results in deductions in determining taxable profits of future periods. However, economic benefits in the form of reductions in tax payments will flow to the entity only if it earns sufficient taxable profits against which the deductions can be offset. Therefore, an entity recognises deferred tax assets only when it is probable that taxable profits will be available against which the deductible temporary differences can be utilised.

27A   When an entity assesses whether taxable profits will be available against which it can utilise a deductible temporary difference, it considers whether tax law restricts the sources of taxable profits against which it may make deductions on the reversal of that deductible temporary difference. If tax law imposes no such restrictions, an entity assesses a deductible temporary difference in combination with all of its other deductible temporary differences. However, if tax law restricts the utilisation of losses to deduction against income of a specific type, a deductible temporary difference is assessed in combination only with other deductible temporary differences of the appropriate type.

28   It is probable that taxable profit will be available against which a deductible temporary difference can be utilised when there are sufficient taxable temporary differences relating to the same taxation authority and the same taxable entity which are expected to reverse:

(a)   in the same period as the expected reversal of the deductible temporary difference; or

(b)   in periods into which a tax loss arising from the deferred tax asset can be carried back or forward.

In such circumstances, the deferred tax asset is recognised in the period in which the deductible temporary differences arise.

29   When there are insufficient taxable temporary differences relating to the same taxation authority and the same taxable entity, the deferred tax asset is recognised to the extent that:

(a)   it is probable that the entity will have sufficient taxable profit relating to the same taxation authority and the same taxable entity in the same period as the reversal of the deductible temporary difference (or in the periods into which a tax loss arising from the deferred tax asset can be carried back or forward). In evaluating whether it will have sufficient taxable profit in future periods, an entity:

(i)   compares the deductible temporary differences with future taxable profit that excludes tax deductions resulting from the reversal of those deductible temporary differences. This comparison shows the extent to which the future taxable profit is sufficient for the entity to deduct the amounts resulting from the reversal of those deductible temporary differences; and

(ii)   ignores taxable amounts arising from deductible temporary differences that are expected to originate in future periods, because the deferred tax asset arising from these deductible temporary differences will itself require future taxable profit in order to be utilised; or

(b)   tax planning opportunities are available to the entity that will create taxable profit in appropriate periods.

29A   The estimate of probable future taxable profit may include the recovery of some of an entity's assets for more than their carrying amount if there is sufficient evidence that it is probable that the entity will achieve this. For example, when an asset is measured at fair value, the entity shall consider whether there is sufficient evidence to conclude that it is probable that the entity will recover the asset for more than its carrying amount. This may be the case, for example, when an entity expects to hold a fixed-rate debt instrument and collect the contractual cash flows.

30   Tax planning opportunities are actions that the entity would take in order to create or increase taxable income in a particular period before the expiry of a tax loss or tax credit carryforward. For example, in some jurisdictions, taxable profit may be created or increased by:

(a) electing to have interest income taxed on either a received or receivable basis;

(b) deferring the claim for certain deductions from taxable profit;

(c) selling, and perhaps leasing back, assets that have appreciated but for which the tax base has not been adjusted to reflect such appreciation; and

(d) selling an asset that generates non-taxable income (such as, in some jurisdictions, a government bond) in order to purchase another investment that generates taxable income.

Where tax planning opportunities advance taxable profit from a later period to an earlier period, the utilisation of a tax loss or tax credit carryforward still depends on the existence of future taxable profit from sources other than future originating temporary differences.

31   When an entity has a history of recent losses, the entity considers the guidance in paragraphs 35 and 36.

32   [Deleted]

Goodwill

32A   If the carrying amount of goodwill arising in a business combination is less than its tax base, the difference gives rise to a deferred tax asset. The deferred tax asset arising from the initial recognition of goodwill shall be recognised as part of the accounting for a business combination to the extent that it is probable that taxable profit will be available against which the deductible temporary difference could be utilised.

Initial recognition of an asset or liability

33   One case when a deferred tax asset arises on initial recognition of an asset is when a non-taxable government grant related to an asset is deducted in arriving at the carrying amount of the asset but, for tax purposes, is not deducted from the asset's depreciable amount (in other words its tax base); the carrying amount of the asset is less than its tax base and this gives rise to a deductible temporary difference. Government grants may also be set up as deferred income in which case the difference between the deferred income and its tax base of nil is a deductible temporary difference. Whichever method of presentation an entity adopts, the entity does not recognise the resulting deferred tax asset, for the reason given in paragraph 22.

Unused tax losses and unused tax credits

34   A deferred tax asset shall be recognised for the carryforward of unused tax losses and unused tax credits to the extent that it is probable that future taxable profit will be available against which the unused tax losses and unused tax credits can be utilised.

35   The criteria for recognising deferred tax assets arising from the carryforward of unused tax losses and tax credits are the same as the criteria for recognising deferred tax assets arising from deductible temporary differences. However, the existence of unused tax losses is strong evidence that future taxable profit may not be available. Therefore, when an entity has a history of recent losses, the entity recognises a deferred tax asset arising from unused tax losses or tax credits only to the extent that the entity has sufficient taxable temporary differences or there is convincing other evidence that sufficient taxable profit will be available against which the unused tax losses or unused tax credits can be utilised by the entity. In such circumstances, paragraph 82 requires disclosure of the amount of the deferred tax asset and the nature of the evidence supporting its recognition.

36   An entity considers the following criteria in assessing the probability that taxable profit will be available against which the unused tax losses or unused tax credits can be utilised:

(a)   whether the entity has sufficient taxable temporary differences relating to the same taxation authority and the same taxable entity, which will result in taxable amounts against which the unused tax losses or unused tax credits can be utilised before they expire;

(b)   whether it is probable that the entity will have taxable profits before the unused tax losses or unused tax credits expire;

(c)   whether the unused tax losses result from identifiable causes which are unlikely to recur; and

(d)   whether tax planning opportunities (see paragraph 30) are available to the entity that will create taxable profit in the period in which the unused tax losses or unused tax credits can be utilised.

To the extent that it is not probable that taxable profit will be available against which the unused tax losses or unused tax credits can be utilised, the deferred tax asset is not recognised.

Reassessment of unrecognised deferred tax assets

37   At the end of each reporting period, an entity reassesses unrecognised deferred tax assets. The entity recognises a previously unrecognised deferred tax asset to the extent that it has become probable that future taxable profit will allow the deferred tax asset to be recovered. For example, an improvement in trading conditions may make it more probable that the entity will be able to generate sufficient taxable profit in the future for the deferred tax asset to meet the recognition criteria set out in paragraph 24 or 34. Another example is when an entity reassesses deferred tax assets at the date of a business combination or subsequently (see paragraphs 67 and 68).

Investments in subsidiaries, branches and associates and interests in joint arrangements

38   Temporary differences arise when the carrying amount of investments in subsidiaries, branches and associates or interests in joint arrangements (namely the parent or investor's share of the net assets of the subsidiary, branch, associate or investee, including the carrying amount of goodwill) becomes different from the tax base (which is often cost) of the investment or interest. Such differences may arise in a number of different circumstances, for example:

(a)   the existence of undistributed profits of subsidiaries, branches, associates and joint arrangements;

(b)   changes in foreign exchange rates when a parent and its subsidiary are based in different countries; and

(c)   a reduction in the carrying amount of an investment in an associate to its recoverable amount.

In consolidated financial statements, the temporary difference may be different from the temporary difference associated with that investment in the parent's separate financial statements if the parent carries the investment in its separate financial statements at cost or revalued amount.

39   **An entity shall recognise a deferred tax liability for all taxable temporary differences associated with investments in subsidiaries, branches and associates, and interests in joint arrangements, except to the extent that both of the following conditions are satisfied:**

(a)   **the parent, investor, joint venturer or joint operator is able to control the timing of the reversal of the temporary difference; and**

(b)   **it is probable that the temporary difference will not reverse in the foreseeable future.**

40   As a parent controls the dividend policy of its subsidiary, it is able to control the timing of the reversal of temporary differences associated with that investment (including the temporary differences arising not only from undistributed profits but also from any foreign exchange translation differences). Furthermore, it would often be impracticable to determine the amount of income taxes that would be payable when the temporary difference reverses. Therefore, when the parent has determined that those profits will not be distributed in the foreseeable future the parent does not recognise a deferred tax liability. The same considerations apply to investments in branches.

41   The non-monetary assets and liabilities of an entity are measured in its functional currency (see IAS 21 *The Effects of Changes in Foreign Exchange Rates*). If the entity's taxable profit or tax loss (and, hence, the tax base of its non-monetary assets and liabilities) is determined in a different currency, changes in the exchange rate give rise to temporary differences that result in a recognised deferred tax liability or (subject to paragraph 24) asset. The

resulting deferred tax is charged or credited to profit or loss (see paragraph 58).

42 An investor in an associate does not control that entity and is usually not in a position to determine its dividend policy. Therefore, in the absence of an agreement requiring that the profits of the associate will not be distributed in the foreseeable future, an investor recognises a deferred tax liability arising from taxable temporary differences associated with its investment in the associate. In some cases, an investor may not be able to determine the amount of tax that would be payable if it recovers the cost of its investment in an associate, but can determine that it will equal or exceed a minimum amount. In such cases, the deferred tax liability is measured at this amount.

43 The arrangement between the parties to a joint arrangement usually deals with the distribution of the profits and identifies whether decisions on such matters require the consent of all the parties or a group of the parties. When the joint venturer or joint operator can control the timing of the distribution of its share of the profits of the joint arrangement and it is probable that its share of the profits will not be distributed in the foreseeable future, a deferred tax liability is not recognised.

44 **An entity shall recognise a deferred tax asset for all deductible temporary differences arising from investments in subsidiaries, branches and associates, and interests in joint arrangements, to the extent that, and only to the extent that, it is probable that:**

   (a) **the temporary difference will reverse in the foreseeable future; and**

   (b) **taxable profit will be available against which the temporary difference can be utilised.**

45 In deciding whether a deferred tax asset is recognised for deductible temporary differences associated with its investments in subsidiaries, branches and associates, and its interests in joint arrangements, an entity considers the guidance set out in paragraphs 28 to 31.

Measurement

46 **Current tax liabilities (assets) for the current and prior periods shall be measured at the amount expected to be paid to (recovered from) the taxation authorities, using the tax rates (and tax laws) that have been enacted or substantively enacted by the end of the reporting period.**

47 **Deferred tax assets and liabilities shall be measured at the tax rates that are expected to apply to the period when the asset is realised or the liability is settled, based on tax rates (and tax laws) that have been enacted or substantively enacted by the end of the reporting period.**

48 Current and deferred tax assets and liabilities are usually measured using the tax rates (and tax laws) that have been enacted. However, in some jurisdictions, announcements of tax rates (and tax laws) by the government have the substantive effect of actual enactment, which may follow the announcement by a period of several months. In these circumstances, tax

assets and liabilities are measured using the announced tax rate (and tax laws).

49   When different tax rates apply to different levels of taxable income, deferred tax assets and liabilities are measured using the average rates that are expected to apply to the taxable profit (tax loss) of the periods in which the temporary differences are expected to reverse.

50   [Deleted]

51   **The measurement of deferred tax liabilities and deferred tax assets shall reflect the tax consequences that would follow from the manner in which the entity expects, at the end of the reporting period, to recover or settle the carrying amount of its assets and liabilities.**

51A   In some jurisdictions, the manner in which an entity recovers (settles) the carrying amount of an asset (liability) may affect either or both of:

(a)   the tax rate applicable when the entity recovers (settles) the carrying amount of the asset (liability); and

(b)   the tax base of the asset (liability).

In such cases, an entity measures deferred tax liabilities and deferred tax assets using the tax rate and the tax base that are consistent with the expected manner of recovery or settlement.

Example A

An item of property, plant and equipment has a carrying amount of 100 and a tax base of 60. A tax rate of 20% would apply if the item were sold and a tax rate of 30% would apply to other income.

The entity recognises a deferred tax liability of 8 (40 at 20%) if it expects to sell the item without further use and a deferred tax liability of 12 (40 at 30%) if it expects to retain the item and recover its carrying amount through use.

Example B

An item or property, plant and equipment with a cost of 100 and a carrying amount of 80 is revalued to 150. No equivalent adjustment is made for tax purposes. Cumulative depreciation for tax purposes is 30 and the tax rate is 30%. If the item is sold for more than cost, the cumulative tax depreciation of 30 will be included in taxable income but sale proceeds in excess of cost will not be taxable.

The tax base of the item is 70 and there is a taxable temporary difference of 80. If the entity expects to recover the carrying amount by using the item, it must generate taxable income of 150, but will only be able to deduct depreciation of 70. On this basis, there is a deferred tax liability of 24 (80 at 30%). If the entity expects to recover the carrying amount by selling the item immediately for proceeds of 150, the deferred tax liability is computed as follows:

---

continued...

...continued

Example B			
	Taxable Temporary Difference	Tax Rate	Deferred Tax Liability
Cumulative tax depreciation	30	30%	9
Proceeds in excess of cost	50	nil	–
Total	80		9

(note: in accordance with paragraph 61A, the additional deferred tax that arises on the revaluation is recognised in other comprehensive income)

Example C

The facts are as in example B, except that if the item is sold for more than cost, the cumulative tax depreciation will be included in taxable income (taxed at 30%) and the sale proceeds will be taxed at 40%, after deducting an inflation-adjusted cost of 110.

If the entity expects to recover the carrying amount by using the item, it must generate taxable income of 150, but will only be able to deduct depreciation of 70. On this basis, the tax base is 70, there is a taxable temporary difference of 80 and there is a deferred tax liability of 24 (80 at 30%), as in example B.

If the entity expects to recover the carrying amount by selling the item immediately for proceeds of 150, the entity will be able to deduct the indexed cost of 110. The net proceeds of 40 will be taxed at 40%. In addition, the cumulative tax depreciation of 30 will be included in taxable income and taxed at 30%. On this basis, the tax base is 80 (110 less 30), there is a taxable temporary difference of 70 and there is a deferred tax liability of 25 (40 at 40% plus 30 at 30%). If the tax base is not immediately apparent in this example, it may be helpful to consider the fundamental principle set out in paragraph 10.

(note: in accordance with paragraph 61A, the additional deferred tax that arises on the revaluation is recognised in other comprehensive income)

51B   If a deferred tax liability or deferred tax asset arises from a non-depreciable asset measured using the revaluation model in IAS 16, the measurement of the deferred tax liability or deferred tax asset shall reflect the tax consequences of recovering the carrying amount of the non-depreciable asset through sale, regardless of the basis of measuring the carrying amount of that asset. Accordingly, if the tax law specifies a tax rate applicable to the taxable amount derived from the sale of an asset that differs from the tax rate applicable to the taxable amount derived from using an asset, the former rate is applied in measuring the deferred tax liability or asset related to a non-depreciable asset.

51C If a deferred tax liability or asset arises from investment property that is measured using the fair value model in IAS 40, there is a rebuttable presumption that the carrying amount of the investment property will be recovered through sale. Accordingly, unless the presumption is rebutted, the measurement of the deferred tax liability or deferred tax asset shall reflect the tax consequences of recovering the carrying amount of the investment property entirely through sale. This presumption is rebutted if the investment property is depreciable and is held within a business model whose objective is to consume substantially all of the economic benefits embodied in the investment property over time, rather than through sale. If the presumption is rebutted, the requirements of paragraphs 51 and 51A shall be followed.

Example illustrating paragraph 51C

An investment property has a cost of 100 and fair value of 150. It is measured using the fair value model in IAS 40. It comprises land with a cost of 40 and fair value of 60 and a building with a cost of 60 and fair value of 90. The land has an unlimited useful life.

Cumulative depreciation of the building for tax purposes is 30. Unrealised changes in the fair value of the investment property do not affect taxable profit. If the investment property is sold for more than cost, the reversal of the cumulative tax depreciation of 30 will be included in taxable profit and taxed at an ordinary tax rate of 30%. For sales proceeds in excess of cost, tax law specifies tax rates of 25% for assets held for less than two years and 20% for assets held for two years or more.

Because the investment property is measured using the fair value model in IAS 40, there is a rebuttable presumption that the entity will recover the carrying amount of the investment property entirely through sale. If that presumption is not rebutted, the deferred tax reflects the tax consequences of recovering the carrying amount entirely through sale, even if the entity expects to earn rental income from the property before sale.

The tax base of the land if it is sold is 40 and there is a taxable temporary difference of 20 (60 − 40). The tax base of the building if it is sold is 30 (60 − 30) and there is a taxable temporary difference of 60 (90 − 30). As a result, the total taxable temporary difference relating to the investment property is 80 (20 + 60).

In accordance with paragraph 47, the tax rate is the rate expected to apply to the period when the investment property is realised. Thus, the resulting deferred tax liability is computed as follows, if the entity expects to sell the property after holding it for more than two years:

	Taxable Temporary Difference	Tax Rate	Deferred Tax Liability
Cumulative tax depreciation	30	30%	9
Proceeds in excess of cost	50	20%	10
Total	80		19

continued...

...continued

Example illustrating paragraph 51C

If the entity expects to sell the property after holding it for less than two years, the above computation would be amended to apply a tax rate of 25%, rather than 20%, to the proceeds in excess of cost.

If, instead, the entity holds the building within a business model whose objective is to consume substantially all of the economic benefits embodied in the building over time, rather than through sale, this presumption would be rebutted for the building. However, the land is not depreciable. Therefore the presumption of recovery through sale would not be rebutted for the land. It follows that the deferred tax liability would reflect the tax consequences of recovering the carrying amount of the building through use and the carrying amount of the land through sale.

The tax base of the building if it is used is 30 (60 − 30) and there is a taxable temporary difference of 60 (90 − 30), resulting in a deferred tax liability of 18 (60 at 30%).

The tax base of the land if it is sold is 40 and there is a taxable temporary difference of 20 (60 − 40), resulting in a deferred tax liability of 4 (20 at 20%).

As a result, if the presumption of recovery through sale is rebutted for the building, the deferred tax liability relating to the investment property is 22 (18 + 4).

51D   The rebuttable presumption in paragraph 51C also applies when a deferred tax liability or a deferred tax asset arises from measuring investment property in a business combination if the entity will use the fair value model when subsequently measuring that investment property.

51E   Paragraphs 51B–51D do not change the requirements to apply the principles in paragraphs 24–33 (deductible temporary differences) and paragraphs 34–36 (unused tax losses and unused tax credits) of this Standard when recognising and measuring deferred tax assets.

52   [moved and renumbered 51A]

52A   In some jurisdictions, income taxes are payable at a higher or lower rate if part or all of the net profit or retained earnings is paid out as a dividend to shareholders of the entity. In some other jurisdictions, income taxes may be refundable or payable if part or all of the net profit or retained earnings is paid out as a dividend to shareholders of the entity. In these circumstances, current and deferred tax assets and liabilities are measured at the tax rate applicable to undistributed profits.

52B   [Deleted]

Example illustrating paragraphs 52A and 57A

The following example deals with the measurement of current and deferred tax assets and liabilities for an entity in a jurisdiction where income taxes are payable at a higher rate on undistributed profits (50%) with an amount being refundable when profits are distributed. The tax rate on distributed profits is 35%. At the end of the reporting period, 31 December 20X1, the entity does not recognise a liability for dividends proposed or declared after the reporting period. As a result, no dividends are recognised in the year 20X1. Taxable income for 20X1 is 100,000. The net taxable temporary difference for the year 20X1 is 40,000.

The entity recognises a current tax liability and a current income tax expense of 50,000. No asset is recognised for the amount potentially recoverable as a result of future dividends. The entity also recognises a deferred tax liability and deferred tax expense of 20,000 (40,000 at 50%) representing the income taxes that the entity will pay when it recovers or settles the carrying amounts of its assets and liabilities based on the tax rate applicable to undistributed profits.

Subsequently, on 15 March 20X2 the entity recognises dividends of 10,000 from previous operating profits as a liability.

On 15 March 20X2, the entity recognises the recovery of income taxes of 1,500 (15% of the dividends recognised as a liability) as a current tax asset and as a reduction of current income tax expense for 20X2.

---

53 **Deferred tax assets and liabilities shall not be discounted.**

54 The reliable determination of deferred tax assets and liabilities on a discounted basis requires detailed scheduling of the timing of the reversal of each temporary difference. In many cases such scheduling is impracticable or highly complex. Therefore, it is inappropriate to require discounting of deferred tax assets and liabilities. To permit, but not to require, discounting would result in deferred tax assets and liabilities which would not be comparable between entities. Therefore, this Standard does not require or permit the discounting of deferred tax assets and liabilities.

55 Temporary differences are determined by reference to the carrying amount of an asset or liability. This applies even where that carrying amount is itself determined on a discounted basis, for example in the case of retirement benefit obligations (see IAS 19 *Employee Benefits*).

56 **The carrying amount of a deferred tax asset shall be reviewed at the end of each reporting period. An entity shall reduce the carrying amount of a deferred tax asset to the extent that it is no longer probable that sufficient taxable profit will be available to allow the benefit of part or all of that deferred tax asset to be utilised. Any such reduction shall be reversed to the extent that it becomes probable that sufficient taxable profit will be available.**

Recognition of current and deferred tax

57　　Accounting for the current and deferred tax effects of a transaction or other event is consistent with the accounting for the transaction or event itself. Paragraphs 58 to 68C implement this principle.

57A　　An entity shall recognise the income tax consequences of dividends as defined in IFRS 9 when it recognises a liability to pay a dividend. The income tax consequences of dividends are linked more directly to past transactions or events that generated distributable profits than to distributions to owners. Therefore, an entity shall recognise the income tax consequences of dividends in profit or loss, other comprehensive income or equity according to where the entity originally recognised those past transactions or events.

Items recognised in profit or loss

58　　**Current and deferred tax shall be recognised as income or an expense and included in profit or loss for the period, except to the extent that the tax arises from:**

　　(a)　**a transaction or event which is recognised, in the same or a different period, outside profit or loss, either in other comprehensive income or directly in equity (see paragraphs 61A–65); or**

　　(b)　**a business combination (other than the acquisition by an investment entity, as defined in IFRS 10 *Consolidated Financial Statements*, of a subsidiary that is required to be measured at fair value through profit or loss) (see paragraphs 66–68).**

59　　Most deferred tax liabilities and deferred tax assets arise where income or expense is included in accounting profit in one period, but is included in taxable profit (tax loss) in a different period. The resulting deferred tax is recognised in profit or loss. Examples are when:

　　(a)　interest, royalty or dividend revenue is received in arrears and is included in accounting profit in accordance with IFRS 15 *Revenue from Contracts with Customers*, IAS 39 *Financial Instruments: Recognition and Measurement* or IFRS 9 *Financial Instruments*, as relevant, but is included in taxable profit (tax loss) on a cash basis; and

　　(b)　costs of intangible assets have been capitalised in accordance with IAS 38 and are being amortised in profit or loss, but were deducted for tax purposes when they were incurred.

60　　The carrying amount of deferred tax assets and liabilities may change even though there is no change in the amount of the related temporary differences. This can result, for example, from:

　　(a)　a change in tax rates or tax laws;

　　(b)　a reassessment of the recoverability of deferred tax assets; or

　　(c)　a change in the expected manner of recovery of an asset.

The resulting deferred tax is recognised in profit or loss, except to the extent that it relates to items previously recognised outside profit or loss (see paragraph 63).

Items recognised outside profit or loss

61   [Deleted]

61A   Current tax and deferred tax shall be recognised outside profit or loss if the tax relates to items that are recognised, in the same or a different period, outside profit or loss. Therefore, current tax and deferred tax that relates to items that are recognised, in the same or a different period:

    (a)   in other comprehensive income, shall be recognised in other comprehensive income (see paragraph 62).

    (b)   directly in equity, shall be recognised directly in equity (see paragraph 62A).

62   International Financial Reporting Standards require or permit particular items to be recognised in other comprehensive income. Examples of such items are:

    (a)   a change in carrying amount arising from the revaluation of property, plant and equipment (see IAS 16); and

    (b)   [deleted]

    (c)   exchange differences arising on the translation of the financial statements of a foreign operation (see IAS 21).

    (d)   [deleted]

62A   International Financial Reporting Standards require or permit particular items to be credited or charged directly to equity. Examples of such items are:

    (a)   an adjustment to the opening balance of retained earnings resulting from either a change in accounting policy that is applied retrospectively or the correction of an error (see IAS 8 *Accounting Policies, Changes in Accounting Estimates and Errors*); and

    (b)   amounts arising on initial recognition of the equity component of a compound financial instrument (see paragraph 23).

63   In exceptional circumstances it may be difficult to determine the amount of current and deferred tax that relates to items recognised outside profit or loss (either in other comprehensive income or directly in equity). This may be the case, for example, when:

    (a)   there are graduated rates of income tax and it is impossible to determine the rate at which a specific component of taxable profit (tax loss) has been taxed;

    (b)   a change in the tax rate or other tax rules affects a deferred tax asset or liability relating (in whole or in part) to an item that was previously recognised outside profit or loss; or

(c)   an entity determines that a deferred tax asset should be recognised, or should no longer be recognised in full, and the deferred tax asset relates (in whole or in part) to an item that was previously recognised outside profit or loss.

In such cases, the current and deferred tax related to items that are recognised outside profit or loss are based on a reasonable pro rata allocation of the current and deferred tax of the entity in the tax jurisdiction concerned, or other method that achieves a more appropriate allocation in the circumstances.

64   IAS 16 does not specify whether an entity should transfer each year from revaluation surplus to retained earnings an amount equal to the difference between the depreciation or amortisation on a revalued asset and the depreciation or amortisation based on the cost of that asset. If an entity makes such a transfer, the amount transferred is net of any related deferred tax. Similar considerations apply to transfers made on disposal of an item of property, plant or equipment.

65   When an asset is revalued for tax purposes and that revaluation is related to an accounting revaluation of an earlier period, or to one that is expected to be carried out in a future period, the tax effects of both the asset revaluation and the adjustment of the tax base are recognised in other comprehensive income in the periods in which they occur. However, if the revaluation for tax purposes is not related to an accounting revaluation of an earlier period, or to one that is expected to be carried out in a future period, the tax effects of the adjustment of the tax base are recognised in profit or loss.

65A   When an entity pays dividends to its shareholders, it may be required to pay a portion of the dividends to taxation authorities on behalf of shareholders. In many jurisdictions, this amount is referred to as a withholding tax. Such an amount paid or payable to taxation authorities is charged to equity as a part of the dividends.

Deferred tax arising from a business combination

66   As explained in paragraphs 19 and 26(c), temporary differences may arise in a business combination. In accordance with IFRS 3, an entity recognises any resulting deferred tax assets (to the extent that they meet the recognition criteria in paragraph 24) or deferred tax liabilities as identifiable assets and liabilities at the acquisition date. Consequently, those deferred tax assets and deferred tax liabilities affect the amount of goodwill or the bargain purchase gain the entity recognises. However, in accordance with paragraph 15(a), an entity does not recognise deferred tax liabilities arising from the initial recognition of goodwill.

67   As a result of a business combination, the probability of realising a pre-acquisition deferred tax asset of the acquirer could change. An acquirer may consider it probable that it will recover its own deferred tax asset that was not recognised before the business combination. For example, the acquirer may be able to utilise the benefit of its unused tax losses against the future taxable profit of the acquiree. Alternatively, as a result of the business

combination it might no longer be probable that future taxable profit will allow the deferred tax asset to be recovered. In such cases, the acquirer recognises a change in the deferred tax asset in the period of the business combination, but does not include it as part of the accounting for the business combination. Therefore, the acquirer does not take it into account in measuring the goodwill or bargain purchase gain it recognises in the business combination.

68   The potential benefit of the acquiree's income tax loss carryforwards or other deferred tax assets might not satisfy the criteria for separate recognition when a business combination is initially accounted for but might be realised subsequently. An entity shall recognise acquired deferred tax benefits that it realises after the business combination as follows:

(a)   Acquired deferred tax benefits recognised within the measurement period that result from new information about facts and circumstances that existed at the acquisition date shall be applied to reduce the carrying amount of any goodwill related to that acquisition. If the carrying amount of that goodwill is zero, any remaining deferred tax benefits shall be recognised in profit or loss.

(b)   All other acquired deferred tax benefits realised shall be recognised in profit or loss (or, if this Standard so requires, outside profit or loss).

Current and deferred tax arising from share-based payment transactions

68A   In some tax jurisdictions, an entity receives a tax deduction (ie an amount that is deductible in determining taxable profit) that relates to remuneration paid in shares, share options or other equity instruments of the entity. The amount of that tax deduction may differ from the related cumulative remuneration expense, and may arise in a later accounting period. For example, in some jurisdictions, an entity may recognise an expense for the consumption of employee services received as consideration for share options granted, in accordance with IFRS 2 *Share-based Payment*, and not receive a tax deduction until the share options are exercised, with the measurement of the tax deduction based on the entity's share price at the date of exercise.

68B   As with the research costs discussed in paragraphs 9 and 26(b) of this Standard, the difference between the tax base of the employee services received to date (being the amount the taxation authorities will permit as a deduction in future periods), and the carrying amount of nil, is a deductible temporary difference that results in a deferred tax asset. If the amount the taxation authorities will permit as a deduction in future periods is not known at the end of the period, it shall be estimated, based on information available at the end of the period. For example, if the amount that the taxation authorities will permit as a deduction in future periods is dependent upon the entity's share price at a future date, the measurement of the deductible temporary difference should be based on the entity's share price at the end of the period.

68C As noted in paragraph 68A, the amount of the tax deduction (or estimated future tax deduction, measured in accordance with paragraph 68B) may differ from the related cumulative remuneration expense. Paragraph 58 of the Standard requires that current and deferred tax should be recognised as income or an expense and included in profit or loss for the period, except to the extent that the tax arises from (a) a transaction or event that is recognised, in the same or a different period, outside profit or loss, or (b) a business combination (other than the acquisition by an investment entity of a subsidiary that is required to be measured at fair value through profit or loss). If the amount of the tax deduction (or estimated future tax deduction) exceeds the amount of the related cumulative remuneration expense, this indicates that the tax deduction relates not only to remuneration expense but also to an equity item. In this situation, the excess of the associated current or deferred tax should be recognised directly in equity.

Presentation

Tax assets and tax liabilities

69–70 [Deleted]

Offset

71 An entity shall offset current tax assets and current tax liabilities if, and only if, the entity:

(a) has a legally enforceable right to set off the recognised amounts; and

(b) intends either to settle on a net basis, or to realise the asset and settle the liability simultaneously.

72 Although current tax assets and liabilities are separately recognised and measured they are offset in the statement of financial position subject to criteria similar to those established for financial instruments in IAS 32. An entity will normally have a legally enforceable right to set off a current tax asset against a current tax liability when they relate to income taxes levied by the same taxation authority and the taxation authority permits the entity to make or receive a single net payment.

73 In consolidated financial statements, a current tax asset of one entity in a group is offset against a current tax liability of another entity in the group if, and only if, the entities concerned have a legally enforceable right to make or receive a single net payment and the entities intend to make or receive such a net payment or to recover the asset and settle the liability simultaneously.

74 An entity shall offset deferred tax assets and deferred tax liabilities if, and only if:

(a) the entity has a legally enforceable right to set off current tax assets against current tax liabilities; and

(b)   the deferred tax assets and the deferred tax liabilities relate to income taxes levied by the same taxation authority on either:

  (i)   the same taxable entity; or

  (ii)   different taxable entities which intend either to settle current tax liabilities and assets on a net basis, or to realise the assets and settle the liabilities simultaneously, in each future period in which significant amounts of deferred tax liabilities or assets are expected to be settled or recovered.

75   To avoid the need for detailed scheduling of the timing of the reversal of each temporary difference, this Standard requires an entity to set off a deferred tax asset against a deferred tax liability of the same taxable entity if, and only if, they relate to income taxes levied by the same taxation authority and the entity has a legally enforceable right to set off current tax assets against current tax liabilities.

76   In rare circumstances, an entity may have a legally enforceable right of set-off, and an intention to settle net, for some periods but not for others. In such rare circumstances, detailed scheduling may be required to establish reliably whether the deferred tax liability of one taxable entity will result in increased tax payments in the same period in which a deferred tax asset of another taxable entity will result in decreased payments by that second taxable entity.

Tax expense

Tax expense (income) related to profit or loss from ordinary activities

77   The tax expense (income) related to profit or loss from ordinary activities shall be presented as part of profit or loss in the statement(s) of profit or loss and other comprehensive income.

77A   [Deleted]

Exchange differences on deferred foreign tax liabilities or assets

78   IAS 21 requires certain exchange differences to be recognised as income or expense but does not specify where such differences should be presented in the statement of comprehensive income. Accordingly, where exchange differences on deferred foreign tax liabilities or assets are recognised in the statement of comprehensive income, such differences may be classified as deferred tax expense (income) if that presentation is considered to be the most useful to financial statement users.

Disclosure

79   The major components of tax expense (income) shall be disclosed separately.

80   Components of tax expense (income) may include:

  (a)   current tax expense (income);

(b) any adjustments recognised in the period for current tax of prior periods;

(c) the amount of deferred tax expense (income) relating to the origination and reversal of temporary differences;

(d) the amount of deferred tax expense (income) relating to changes in tax rates or the imposition of new taxes;

(e) the amount of the benefit arising from a previously unrecognised tax loss, tax credit or temporary difference of a prior period that is used to reduce current tax expense;

(f) the amount of the benefit from a previously unrecognised tax loss, tax credit or temporary difference of a prior period that is used to reduce deferred tax expense;

(g) deferred tax expense arising from the write-down, or reversal of a previous write-down, of a deferred tax asset in accordance with paragraph 56; and

(h) the amount of tax expense (income) relating to those changes in accounting policies and errors that are included in profit or loss in accordance with IAS 8, because they cannot be accounted for retrospectively.

81 The following shall also be disclosed separately:

(a) the aggregate current and deferred tax relating to items that are charged or credited directly to equity (see paragraph 62A);

(ab) the amount of income tax relating to each component of other comprehensive income (see paragraph 62 and IAS 1 (as revised in 2007));

(b) [deleted]

(c) an explanation of the relationship between tax expense (income) and accounting profit in either or both of the following forms:

(i) a numerical reconciliation between tax expense (income) and the product of accounting profit multiplied by the applicable tax rate(s), disclosing also the basis on which the applicable tax rate(s) is (are) computed; or

(ii) a numerical reconciliation between the average effective tax rate and the applicable tax rate, disclosing also the basis on which the applicable tax rate is computed;

(d) an explanation of changes in the applicable tax rate(s) compared to the previous accounting period;

(e) the amount (and expiry date, if any) of deductible temporary differences, unused tax losses, and unused tax credits for which no deferred tax asset is recognised in the statement of financial position;

(f)   the aggregate amount of temporary differences associated with investments in subsidiaries, branches and associates and interests in joint arrangements, for which deferred tax liabilities have not been recognised (see paragraph 39);

(g)   in respect of each type of temporary difference, and in respect of each type of unused tax losses and unused tax credits:

         (i)   the amount of the deferred tax assets and liabilities recognised in the statement of financial position for each period presented;

         (ii)   the amount of the deferred tax income or expense recognised in profit or loss, if this is not apparent from the changes in the amounts recognised in the statement of financial position;

(h)   in respect of discontinued operations, the tax expense relating to:

         (i)   the gain or loss on discontinuance; and

         (ii)   the profit or loss from the ordinary activities of the discontinued operation for the period, together with the corresponding amounts for each prior period presented;

(i)   the amount of income tax consequences of dividends to shareholders of the entity that were proposed or declared before the financial statements were authorised for issue, but are not recognised as a liability in the financial statements;

(j)   if a business combination in which the entity is the acquirer causes a change in the amount recognised for its pre-acquisition deferred tax asset (see paragraph 67), the amount of that change; and

(k)   if the deferred tax benefits acquired in a business combination are not recognised at the acquisition date but are recognised after the acquisition date (see paragraph 68), a description of the event or change in circumstances that caused the deferred tax benefits to be recognised.

82   An entity shall disclose the amount of a deferred tax asset and the nature of the evidence supporting its recognition, when:

(a)   the utilisation of the deferred tax asset is dependent on future taxable profits in excess of the profits arising from the reversal of existing taxable temporary differences; and

(b)   the entity has suffered a loss in either the current or preceding period in the tax jurisdiction to which the deferred tax asset relates.

82A   In the circumstances described in paragraph 52A, an entity shall disclose the nature of the potential income tax consequences that would result from the payment of dividends to its shareholders. In addition, the entity shall disclose the amounts of the potential income tax consequences practically determinable and whether there are any potential income tax consequences not practically determinable.

83   [Deleted]

84   The disclosures required by paragraph 81(c) enable users of financial statements to understand whether the relationship between tax expense (income) and accounting profit is unusual and to understand the significant factors that could affect that relationship in the future. The relationship between tax expense (income) and accounting profit may be affected by such factors as revenue that is exempt from taxation, expenses that are not deductible in determining taxable profit (tax loss), the effect of tax losses and the effect of foreign tax rates.

85   In explaining the relationship between tax expense (income) and accounting profit, an entity uses an applicable tax rate that provides the most meaningful information to the users of its financial statements. Often, the most meaningful rate is the domestic rate of tax in the country in which the entity is domiciled, aggregating the tax rate applied for national taxes with the rates applied for any local taxes which are computed on a substantially similar level of taxable profit (tax loss). However, for an entity operating in several jurisdictions, it may be more meaningful to aggregate separate reconciliations prepared using the domestic rate in each individual jurisdiction. The following example illustrates how the selection of the applicable tax rate affects the presentation of the numerical reconciliation.

Example illustrating paragraph 85

In 19X2, an entity has accounting profit in its own jurisdiction (country A) of 1,500 (19X1: 2,000) and in country B of 1,500 (19X1: 500). The tax rate is 30% in country A and 20% in country B. In country A, expenses of 100 (19X1: 200) are not deductible for tax purposes.

The following is an example of a reconciliation to the domestic tax rate.

	19X1	19X2
Accounting profit	2,500	3,000
Tax at the domestic rate of 30%	750	900
Tax effect of expenses that are not deductible for tax purposes	60	30
Effect of lower tax rates in country B	(50)	(150)
Tax expense	760	780

continued...

...continued

Example illustrating paragraph 85

The following is an example of a reconciliation prepared by aggregating separate reconciliations for each national jurisdiction. Under this method, the effect of differences between the reporting entity's own domestic tax rate and the domestic tax rate in other jurisdictions does not appear as a separate item in the reconciliation. An entity may need to discuss the effect of significant changes in either tax rates, or the mix of profits earned in different jurisdictions, in order to explain changes in the applicable tax rate(s), as required by paragraph 81(d).

Accounting profit	2,500	3,000
Tax at the domestic rates applicable to profits in the country concerned	700	750
Tax effect of expenses that are not deductible for tax purposes	60	30
Tax expense	760	780

---

86   The average effective tax rate is the tax expense (income) divided by the accounting profit.

87   It would often be impracticable to compute the amount of unrecognised deferred tax liabilities arising from investments in subsidiaries, branches and associates and interests in joint arrangements (see paragraph 39). Therefore, this Standard requires an entity to disclose the aggregate amount of the underlying temporary differences but does not require disclosure of the deferred tax liabilities. Nevertheless, where practicable, entities are encouraged to disclose the amounts of the unrecognised deferred tax liabilities because financial statement users may find such information useful.

87A   Paragraph 82A requires an entity to disclose the nature of the potential income tax consequences that would result from the payment of dividends to its shareholders. An entity discloses the important features of the income tax systems and the factors that will affect the amount of the potential income tax consequences of dividends.

87B   It would sometimes not be practicable to compute the total amount of the potential income tax consequences that would result from the payment of dividends to shareholders. This may be the case, for example, where an entity has a large number of foreign subsidiaries. However, even in such circumstances, some portions of the total amount may be easily determinable. For example, in a consolidated group, a parent and some of its subsidiaries may have paid income taxes at a higher rate on undistributed profits and be aware of the amount that would be refunded on the payment of future dividends to shareholders from consolidated retained earnings. In this case, that refundable amount is disclosed. If applicable, the entity also discloses that there are additional potential income tax consequences not practicably determinable. In the parent's separate financial statements, if any, the disclosure of the potential income tax consequences relates to the parent's retained earnings.

87C   An entity required to provide the disclosures in paragraph 82A may also be required to provide disclosures related to temporary differences associated with investments in subsidiaries, branches and associates or interests in joint arrangements. In such cases, an entity considers this in determining the information to be disclosed under paragraph 82A. For example, an entity may be required to disclose the aggregate amount of temporary differences associated with investments in subsidiaries for which no deferred tax liabilities have been recognised (see paragraph 81(f)). If it is impracticable to compute the amounts of unrecognised deferred tax liabilities (see paragraph 87) there may be amounts of potential income tax consequences of dividends not practicably determinable related to these subsidiaries.

88   An entity discloses any tax-related contingent liabilities and contingent assets in accordance with IAS 37 *Provisions, Contingent Liabilities and Contingent Assets*. Contingent liabilities and contingent assets may arise, for example, from unresolved disputes with the taxation authorities. Similarly, where changes in tax rates or tax laws are enacted or announced after the reporting period, an entity discloses any significant effect of those changes on its current and deferred tax assets and liabilities (see IAS 10 *Events after the Reporting Period*).

Effective date

89   This Standard becomes operative for financial statements covering periods beginning on or after 1 January 1998, except as specified in paragraph 91. If an entity applies this Standard for financial statements covering periods beginning before 1 January 1998, the entity shall disclose the fact it has applied this Standard instead of IAS 12 *Accounting for Taxes on Income*, approved in 1979.

90   This Standard supersedes IAS 12 *Accounting for Taxes on Income*, approved in 1979.

91   Paragraphs 52A, 52B, 65A, 81(i), 82A, 87A, 87B, 87C and the deletion of paragraphs 3 and 50 become operative for annual financial statements[1] covering periods beginning on or after 1 January 2001. Earlier adoption is encouraged. If earlier adoption affects the financial statements, an entity shall disclose that fact.

92   IAS 1 (as revised in 2007) amended the terminology used throughout IFRSs. In addition it amended paragraphs 23, 52, 58, 60, 62, 63, 65, 68C, 77 and 81, deleted paragraph 61 and added paragraphs 61A, 62A and 77A. An entity shall apply those amendments for annual periods beginning on or after 1 January 2009. If an entity applies IAS 1 (revised 2007) for an earlier period, the amendments shall be applied for that earlier period.

---

1   Paragraph 91 refers to 'annual financial statements' in line with more explicit language for writing effective dates adopted in 1998. Paragraph 89 refers to 'financial statements'.

93   Paragraph 68 shall be applied prospectively from the effective date of IFRS 3 (as revised in 2008) to the recognition of deferred tax assets acquired in business combinations.

94   Therefore, entities shall not adjust the accounting for prior business combinations if tax benefits failed to satisfy the criteria for separate recognition as of the acquisition date and are recognised after the acquisition date, unless the benefits are recognised within the measurement period and result from new information about facts and circumstances that existed at the acquisition date. Other tax benefits recognised shall be recognised in profit or loss (or, if this Standard so requires, outside profit or loss).

95   IFRS 3 (as revised in 2008) amended paragraphs 21 and 67 and added paragraphs 32A and 81(j) and (k). An entity shall apply those amendments for annual periods beginning on or after 1 July 2009. If an entity applies IFRS 3 (revised 2008) for an earlier period, the amendments shall also be applied for that earlier period.

96   [Deleted]

97   [Deleted]

98   Paragraph 52 was renumbered as 51A, paragraph 10 and the examples following paragraph 51A were amended, and paragraphs 51B and 51C and the following example and paragraphs 51D, 51E and 99 were added by *Deferred Tax: Recovery of Underlying Assets*, issued in December 2010. An entity shall apply those amendments for annual periods beginning on or after 1 January 2012. Earlier application is permitted. If an entity applies the amendments for an earlier period, it shall disclose that fact.

98A   IFRS 11 *Joint Arrangements*, issued in May 2011, amended paragraphs 2, 15, 18(e), 24, 38, 39, 43–45, 81(f), 87 and 87C. An entity shall apply those amendments when it applies IFRS 11.

98B   *Presentation of Items of Other Comprehensive Income* (Amendments to IAS 1), issued in June 2011, amended paragraph 77 and deleted paragraph 77A. An entity shall apply those amendments when it applies IAS 1 as amended in June 2011.

98C   *Investment Entities* (Amendments to IFRS 10, IFRS 12 and IAS 27), issued in October 2012, amended paragraphs 58 and 68C. An entity shall apply those amendments for annual periods beginning on or after 1 January 2014. Earlier application of *Investment Entities* is permitted. If an entity applies those amendments earlier it shall also apply all amendments included in *Investment Entities* at the same time.

98D   [Deleted]

98E   IFRS 15 *Revenue from Contracts with Customers*, issued in May 2014, amended paragraph 59. An entity shall apply that amendment when it applies IFRS 15.

98F   IFRS 9, as issued in July 2014, amended paragraph 20 and deleted paragraphs 96, 97 and 98D. An entity shall apply those amendments when it applies IFRS 9.

98G   IFRS 16, issued in January 2016, amended paragraph 20. An entity shall apply that amendment when it applies IFRS 16.

98H   *Recognition of Deferred Tax Assets for Unrealised Losses* (Amendments to IAS 12), issued in January 2016, amended paragraph 29 and added paragraphs 27A, 29A and the example following paragraph 26. An entity shall apply those amendments for annual periods beginning on or after 1 January 2017. Earlier application is permitted. If an entity applies those amendments for an earlier period, it shall disclose that fact. An entity shall apply those amendments retrospectively in accordance with IAS 8 *Accounting Policies, Changes in Accounting Estimates and Errors.* However, on initial application of the amendment, the change in the opening equity of the earliest comparative period may be recognised in opening retained earnings (or in another component of equity, as appropriate), without allocating the change between opening retained earnings and other components of equity. If an entity applies this relief, it shall disclose that fact.

98I   *Annual Improvements to IFRS Standards 2015–2017 Cycle,* issued in December 2017, added paragraph 57A and deleted paragraph 52B. An entity shall apply those amendments for annual reporting periods beginning on or after 1 January 2019. Earlier application is permitted. If an entity applies those amendments earlier, it shall disclose that fact. When an entity first applies those amendments, it shall apply them to the income tax consequences of dividends recognised on or after the beginning of the earliest comparative period.

98J–98L   *[These paragraphs refer to amendments that are not yet effective, and are therefore not included in this edition.]*

Withdrawal of SIC-21

99   The amendments made by *Deferred Tax: Recovery of Underlying Assets,* issued in December 2010, supersede SIC Interpretation 21 *Income Taxes—Recovery of Revalued Non-Depreciable Assets.*

Approval by the Board of *Deferred Tax: Recovery of Underlying Assets* (Amendments to IAS 12) issued in December 2010

Deferred Tax: Recovery of Underlying Assets (Amendments to IAS 12) was approved for publication by the fifteen members of the International Accounting Standards Board.

Sir David Tweedie	Chairman

Stephen Cooper

Philippe Danjou

Jan Engström

Patrick Finnegan

Amaro Luiz de Oliveira Gomes

Prabhakar Kalavacherla

Elke König

Patricia McConnell

Warren J McGregor

Paul Pacter

Darrel Scott

John T Smith

Tatsumi Yamada

Wei-Guo Zhang

Approval by the Board of *Recognition of Deferred Tax Assets for Unrealised Losses* (Amendments to IAS 12) issued in January 2016

Recognition of Deferred Tax Assets for Unrealised Losses was approved for issue by the fourteen members of the International Accounting Standards Board.

Hans Hoogervorst	Chairman
Ian Mackintosh	Vice-Chairman
Stephen Cooper	
Philippe Danjou	
Martin Edelmann	
Patrick Finnegan	
Amaro Gomes	
Gary Kabureck	
Suzanne Lloyd	
Takatsugu Ochi	
Darrel Scott	
Chungwoo Suh	
Mary Tokar	
Wei-Guo Zhang	

© IFRS Foundation

IAS 16

Property, Plant and Equipment

In April 2001 the International Accounting Standards Board (Board) adopted IAS 16 *Property, Plant and Equipment*, which had originally been issued by the International Accounting Standards Committee in December 1993. IAS 16 *Property, Plant and Equipment* replaced IAS 16 *Accounting for Property, Plant and Equipment* (issued in March 1982). IAS 16 that was issued in March 1982 also replaced some parts in IAS 4 *Depreciation Accounting* that was approved in November 1975.

In December 2003 the Board issued a revised IAS 16 as part of its initial agenda of technical projects. The revised Standard also replaced the guidance in three Interpretations (SIC-6 *Costs of Modifying Existing Software*, SIC-14 *Property, Plant and Equipment — Compensation for the Impairment or Loss of Items* and SIC-23 *Property, Plant and Equipment — Major Inspection or Overhaul Costs*).

In May 2014 the Board amended IAS 16 to prohibit the use of a revenue-based depreciation method.

In June 2014 the Board amended the scope of IAS 16 to include bearer plants related to agricultural activity.

In May 2020, the Board issued *Property, Plant and Equipment: Proceeds before Intended Use* (Amendments to IAS 16) which prohibit a company from deducting from the cost of property, plant and equipment amounts received from selling items produced while the company is preparing the asset for its intended use. Instead, a company will recognise such sales proceeds and related cost in profit or loss.

Other Standards have made minor consequential amendments to IAS 16. They include IFRS 13 *Fair Value Measurement* (issued May 2011), *Annual Improvements to IFRSs 2009–2011 Cycle* (issued May 2012), *Annual Improvements to IFRSs 2010–2012 Cycle* (issued December 2013), IFRS 15 *Revenue from Contracts with Customers* (issued May 2014), IFRS 16 *Leases* (issued January 2016) and *Amendments to References to the Conceptual Framework in IFRS Standards* (issued March 2018).

Contents

APPROVAL BY THE BOARD OF IAS 16 ISSUED IN DECEMBER 2003

APPROVAL BY THE BOARD OF AMENDMENTS TO IAS 16:

Clarification of Acceptable Methods of Depreciation and Amortisation
(Amendments to IAS 16 and IAS 38) issued in May 2014

Agriculture: Bearer Plants (Amendments to IAS 16 and IAS 41) issued in
June 2014

Property, Plant and Equipment— Proceeds before Intended Use
(Amendments to IAS 16) issued in May 2020

FOR THE BASIS FOR CONCLUSIONS, SEE PART C OF THIS EDITION

BASIS FOR CONCLUSIONS

DISSENTING OPINIONS

International Accounting Standard 16 *Property, Plant and Equipment* (IAS 16) is set out in paragraphs 1–83 and the Appendix. All the paragraphs have equal authority but retain the IASC format of the Standard when it was adopted by the IASB. IAS 16 should be read in the context of its objective and the Basis for Conclusions, the *Preface to IFRS Standards* and the *Conceptual Framework for Financial Reporting*. IAS 8 *Accounting Policies, Changes in Accounting Estimates and Errors* provides a basis for selecting and applying accounting policies in the absence of explicit guidance.

International Accounting Standard 16
Property, Plant and Equipment

Objective

1   The objective of this Standard is to prescribe the accounting treatment for property, plant and equipment so that users of the financial statements can discern information about an entity's investment in its property, plant and equipment and the changes in such investment. The principal issues in accounting for property, plant and equipment are the recognition of the assets, the determination of their carrying amounts and the depreciation charges and impairment losses to be recognised in relation to them.

Scope

2   This Standard shall be applied in accounting for property, plant and equipment except when another Standard requires or permits a different accounting treatment.

3   This Standard does not apply to:

(a)   property, plant and equipment classified as held for sale in accordance with IFRS 5 *Non-current Assets Held for Sale and Discontinued Operations*.

(b)   biological assets related to agricultural activity other than bearer plants (see IAS 41 *Agriculture*). This Standard applies to bearer plants but it does not apply to the produce on bearer plants.

(c)   the recognition and measurement of exploration and evaluation assets (see IFRS 6 *Exploration for and Evaluation of Mineral Resources*).

(d)   mineral rights and mineral reserves such as oil, natural gas and similar non-regenerative resources.

However, this Standard applies to property, plant and equipment used to develop or maintain the assets described in (b)–(d).

4   [Deleted]

5   An entity using the cost model for investment property in accordance with IAS 40 *Investment Property* shall use the cost model in this Standard for owned investment property.

Definitions

6   The following terms are used in this Standard with the meanings specified:

A *bearer plant* is a living plant that:

(a)   is used in the production or supply of agricultural produce;

(b)   is expected to bear produce for more than one period; and

(c) has a remote likelihood of being sold as agricultural produce, except for incidental scrap sales.

(Paragraphs 5A–5B of IAS 41 elaborate on this definition of a bearer plant.)

Carrying amount is the amount at which an asset is recognised after deducting any accumulated depreciation and accumulated impairment losses.

Cost is the amount of cash or cash equivalents paid or the fair value of the other consideration given to acquire an asset at the time of its acquisition or construction or, where applicable, the amount attributed to that asset when initially recognised in accordance with the specific requirements of other IFRSs, eg IFRS 2 *Share-based Payment*.

Depreciable amount is the cost of an asset, or other amount substituted for cost, less its residual value.

Depreciation is the systematic allocation of the depreciable amount of an asset over its useful life.

Entity-specific value is the present value of the cash flows an entity expects to arise from the continuing use of an asset and from its disposal at the end of its useful life or expects to incur when settling a liability.

Fair value is the price that would be received to sell an asset or paid to transfer a liability in an orderly transaction between market participants at the measurement date. (See IFRS 13 *Fair Value Measurement*.)

An *impairment loss* is the amount by which the carrying amount of an asset exceeds its recoverable amount.

Property, plant and equipment are tangible items that:

(a) are held for use in the production or supply of goods or services, for rental to others, or for administrative purposes; and

(b) are expected to be used during more than one period.

Recoverable amount is the higher of an asset's fair value less costs of disposal and its value in use.

The *residual value* of an asset is the estimated amount that an entity would currently obtain from disposal of the asset, after deducting the estimated costs of disposal, if the asset were already of the age and in the condition expected at the end of its useful life.

Useful life is:

(a) the period over which an asset is expected to be available for use by an entity; or

(b) the number of production or similar units expected to be obtained from the asset by an entity.

Recognition

7　　The cost of an item of property, plant and equipment shall be recognised as an asset if, and only if:

　　　(a)　　it is probable that future economic benefits associated with the item will flow to the entity; and

　　　(b)　　the cost of the item can be measured reliably.

8　　Items such as spare parts, stand-by equipment and servicing equipment are recognised in accordance with this IFRS when they meet the definition of property, plant and equipment. Otherwise, such items are classified as inventory.

9　　This Standard does not prescribe the unit of measure for recognition, ie what constitutes an item of property, plant and equipment. Thus, judgement is required in applying the recognition criteria to an entity's specific circumstances. It may be appropriate to aggregate individually insignificant items, such as moulds, tools and dies, and to apply the criteria to the aggregate value.

10　　An entity evaluates under this recognition principle all its property, plant and equipment costs at the time they are incurred. These costs include costs incurred initially to acquire or construct an item of property, plant and equipment and costs incurred subsequently to add to, replace part of, or service it. The cost of an item of property, plant and equipment may include costs incurred relating to leases of assets that are used to construct, add to, replace part of or service an item of property, plant and equipment, such as depreciation of right-of-use assets.

Initial costs

11　　Items of property, plant and equipment may be acquired for safety or environmental reasons. The acquisition of such property, plant and equipment, although not directly increasing the future economic benefits of any particular existing item of property, plant and equipment, may be necessary for an entity to obtain the future economic benefits from its other assets. Such items of property, plant and equipment qualify for recognition as assets because they enable an entity to derive future economic benefits from related assets in excess of what could be derived had those items not been acquired. For example, a chemical manufacturer may install new chemical handling processes to comply with environmental requirements for the production and storage of dangerous chemicals; related plant enhancements are recognised as an asset because without them the entity is unable to manufacture and sell chemicals. However, the resulting carrying amount of such an asset and related assets is reviewed for impairment in accordance with IAS 36 Impairment of Assets.

Subsequent costs

12   Under the recognition principle in paragraph 7, an entity does not recognise in the carrying amount of an item of property, plant and equipment the costs of the day-to-day servicing of the item. Rather, these costs are recognised in profit or loss as incurred. Costs of day-to-day servicing are primarily the costs of labour and consumables, and may include the cost of small parts. The purpose of these expenditures is often described as for the 'repairs and maintenance' of the item of property, plant and equipment.

13   Parts of some items of property, plant and equipment may require replacement at regular intervals. For example, a furnace may require relining after a specified number of hours of use, or aircraft interiors such as seats and galleys may require replacement several times during the life of the airframe. Items of property, plant and equipment may also be acquired to make a less frequently recurring replacement, such as replacing the interior walls of a building, or to make a nonrecurring replacement. Under the recognition principle in paragraph 7, an entity recognises in the carrying amount of an item of property, plant and equipment the cost of replacing part of such an item when that cost is incurred if the recognition criteria are met. The carrying amount of those parts that are replaced is derecognised in accordance with the derecognition provisions of this Standard (see paragraphs 67–72).

14   A condition of continuing to operate an item of property, plant and equipment (for example, an aircraft) may be performing regular major inspections for faults regardless of whether parts of the item are replaced. When each major inspection is performed, its cost is recognised in the carrying amount of the item of property, plant and equipment as a replacement if the recognition criteria are satisfied. Any remaining carrying amount of the cost of the previous inspection (as distinct from physical parts) is derecognised. This occurs regardless of whether the cost of the previous inspection was identified in the transaction in which the item was acquired or constructed. If necessary, the estimated cost of a future similar inspection may be used as an indication of what the cost of the existing inspection component was when the item was acquired or constructed.

Measurement at recognition

15   An item of property, plant and equipment that qualifies for recognition as an asset shall be measured at its cost.

Elements of cost

16   The cost of an item of property, plant and equipment comprises:

   (a)   its purchase price, including import duties and non-refundable purchase taxes, after deducting trade discounts and rebates.

   (b)   any costs directly attributable to bringing the asset to the location and condition necessary for it to be capable of operating in the manner intended by management.

(c)   the initial estimate of the costs of dismantling and removing the item and restoring the site on which it is located, the obligation for which an entity incurs either when the item is acquired or as a consequence of having used the item during a particular period for purposes other than to produce inventories during that period.

17   Examples of directly attributable costs are:

(a)   costs of employee benefits (as defined in IAS 19 *Employee Benefits*) arising directly from the construction or acquisition of the item of property, plant and equipment;

(b)   costs of site preparation;

(c)   initial delivery and handling costs;

(d)   installation and assembly costs;

(e)   costs of testing whether the asset is functioning properly (ie assessing whether the technical and physical performance of the asset is such that it is capable of being used in the production or supply of goods or services, for rental to others, or for administrative purposes); and

(f)   professional fees.

18   An entity applies IAS 2 *Inventories* to the costs of obligations for dismantling, removing and restoring the site on which an item is located that are incurred during a particular period as a consequence of having used the item to produce inventories during that period. The obligations for costs accounted for in accordance with IAS 2 or IAS 16 are recognised and measured in accordance with IAS 37 *Provisions, Contingent Liabilities and Contingent Assets*.

19   Examples of costs that are not costs of an item of property, plant and equipment are:

(a)   costs of opening a new facility;

(b)   costs of introducing a new product or service (including costs of advertising and promotional activities);

(c)   costs of conducting business in a new location or with a new class of customer (including costs of staff training); and

(d)   administration and other general overhead costs.

20   Recognition of costs in the carrying amount of an item of property, plant and equipment ceases when the item is in the location and condition necessary for it to be capable of operating in the manner intended by management. Therefore, costs incurred in using or redeploying an item are not included in the carrying amount of that item. For example, the following costs are not included in the carrying amount of an item of property, plant and equipment:

(a)   costs incurred while an item capable of operating in the manner intended by management has yet to be brought into use or is operated at less than full capacity;

(b)   initial operating losses, such as those incurred while demand for the item's output builds up; and

(c)   costs of relocating or reorganising part or all of an entity's operations.

20A   Items may be produced while bringing an item of property, plant and equipment to the location and condition necessary for it to be capable of operating in the manner intended by management (such as samples produced when testing whether the asset is functioning properly). An entity recognises the proceeds from selling any such items, and the cost of those items, in profit or loss in accordance with applicable Standards. The entity measures the cost of those items applying the measurement requirements of IAS 2.

21   Some operations occur in connection with the construction or development of an item of property, plant and equipment, but are not necessary to bring the item to the location and condition necessary for it to be capable of operating in the manner intended by management. These incidental operations may occur before or during the construction or development activities. For example, income may be earned through using a building site as a car park until construction starts. Because incidental operations are not necessary to bring an item to the location and condition necessary for it to be capable of operating in the manner intended by management, the income and related expenses of incidental operations are recognised in profit or loss and included in their respective classifications of income and expense.

22   The cost of a self-constructed asset is determined using the same principles as for an acquired asset. If an entity makes similar assets for sale in the normal course of business, the cost of the asset is usually the same as the cost of constructing an asset for sale (see IAS 2). Therefore, any internal profits are eliminated in arriving at such costs. Similarly, the cost of abnormal amounts of wasted material, labour, or other resources incurred in self-constructing an asset is not included in the cost of the asset. IAS 23 *Borrowing Costs* establishes criteria for the recognition of interest as a component of the carrying amount of a self-constructed item of property, plant and equipment.

22A   Bearer plants are accounted for in the same way as self-constructed items of property, plant and equipment before they are in the location and condition necessary to be capable of operating in the manner intended by management. Consequently, references to 'construction' in this Standard should be read as covering activities that are necessary to cultivate the bearer plants before they are in the location and condition necessary to be capable of operating in the manner intended by management.

Measurement of cost

23   The cost of an item of property, plant and equipment is the cash price equivalent at the recognition date. If payment is deferred beyond normal credit terms, the difference between the cash price equivalent and the total payment is recognised as interest over the period of credit unless such interest is capitalised in accordance with IAS 23.

24   One or more items of property, plant and equipment may be acquired in exchange for a non-monetary asset or assets, or a combination of monetary and non-monetary assets. The following discussion refers simply to an exchange of one non-monetary asset for another, but it also applies to all exchanges described in the preceding sentence. The cost of such an item of property, plant and equipment is measured at fair value unless (a) the exchange transaction lacks commercial substance or (b) the fair value of neither the asset received nor the asset given up is reliably measurable. The acquired item is measured in this way even if an entity cannot immediately derecognise the asset given up. If the acquired item is not measured at fair value, its cost is measured at the carrying amount of the asset given up.

25   An entity determines whether an exchange transaction has commercial substance by considering the extent to which its future cash flows are expected to change as a result of the transaction. An exchange transaction has commercial substance if:

   (a)   the configuration (risk, timing and amount) of the cash flows of the asset received differs from the configuration of the cash flows of the asset transferred; or

   (b)   the entity-specific value of the portion of the entity's operations affected by the transaction changes as a result of the exchange; and

   (c)   the difference in (a) or (b) is significant relative to the fair value of the assets exchanged.

   For the purpose of determining whether an exchange transaction has commercial substance, the entity-specific value of the portion of the entity's operations affected by the transaction shall reflect post-tax cash flows. The result of these analyses may be clear without an entity having to perform detailed calculations.

26   The fair value of an asset is reliably measurable if (a) the variability in the range of reasonable fair value measurements is not significant for that asset or (b) the probabilities of the various estimates within the range can be reasonably assessed and used when measuring fair value. If an entity is able to measure reliably the fair value of either the asset received or the asset given up, then the fair value of the asset given up is used to measure the cost of the asset received unless the fair value of the asset received is more clearly evident.

27   [Deleted]

28   The carrying amount of an item of property, plant and equipment may be reduced by government grants in accordance with IAS 20 *Accounting for Government Grants and Disclosure of Government Assistance*.

Measurement after recognition

29   An entity shall choose either the cost model in paragraph 30 or the revaluation model in paragraph 31 as its accounting policy and shall apply that policy to an entire class of property, plant and equipment.

29A–29B   *[These paragraphs refer to amendments that are not yet effective, and are therefore not included in this edition.]*

Cost model

30   After recognition as an asset, an item of property, plant and equipment shall be carried at its cost less any accumulated depreciation and any accumulated impairment losses.

Revaluation model

31   After recognition as an asset, an item of property, plant and equipment whose fair value can be measured reliably shall be carried at a revalued amount, being its fair value at the date of the revaluation less any subsequent accumulated depreciation and subsequent accumulated impairment losses. Revaluations shall be made with sufficient regularity to ensure that the carrying amount does not differ materially from that which would be determined using fair value at the end of the reporting period.

32–33   [Deleted]

34   The frequency of revaluations depends upon the changes in fair values of the items of property, plant and equipment being revalued. When the fair value of a revalued asset differs materially from its carrying amount, a further revaluation is required. Some items of property, plant and equipment experience significant and volatile changes in fair value, thus necessitating annual revaluation. Such frequent revaluations are unnecessary for items of property, plant and equipment with only insignificant changes in fair value. Instead, it may be necessary to revalue the item only every three or five years.

35   When an item of property, plant and equipment is revalued, the carrying amount of that asset is adjusted to the revalued amount. At the date of the revaluation, the asset is treated in one of the following ways:

(a)   the gross carrying amount is adjusted in a manner that is consistent with the revaluation of the carrying amount of the asset. For example, the gross carrying amount may be restated by reference to observable market data or it may be restated proportionately to the change in the carrying amount. The accumulated depreciation at the date of the revaluation is adjusted to equal the difference between the gross carrying amount and the carrying amount of the asset after taking into account accumulated impairment losses; or

(b)   the accumulated depreciation is eliminated against the gross carrying amount of the asset.

The amount of the adjustment of accumulated depreciation forms part of the increase or decrease in carrying amount that is accounted for in accordance with paragraphs 39 and 40.

36   **If an item of property, plant and equipment is revalued, the entire class of property, plant and equipment to which that asset belongs shall be revalued.**

37   A class of property, plant and equipment is a grouping of assets of a similar nature and use in an entity's operations. The following are examples of separate classes:

     (a)   land;

     (b)   land and buildings;

     (c)   machinery;

     (d)   ships;

     (e)   aircraft;

     (f)   motor vehicles;

     (g)   furniture and fixtures;

     (h)   office equipment; and

     (i)   bearer plants.

38   The items within a class of property, plant and equipment are revalued simultaneously to avoid selective revaluation of assets and the reporting of amounts in the financial statements that are a mixture of costs and values as at different dates. However, a class of assets may be revalued on a rolling basis provided revaluation of the class of assets is completed within a short period and provided the revaluations are kept up to date.

39   **If an asset's carrying amount is increased as a result of a revaluation, the increase shall be recognised in other comprehensive income and accumulated in equity under the heading of revaluation surplus. However, the increase shall be recognised in profit or loss to the extent that it reverses a revaluation decrease of the same asset previously recognised in profit or loss.**

40   **If an asset's carrying amount is decreased as a result of a revaluation, the decrease shall be recognised in profit or loss. However, the decrease shall be recognised in other comprehensive income to the extent of any credit balance existing in the revaluation surplus in respect of that asset. The decrease recognised in other comprehensive income reduces the amount accumulated in equity under the heading of revaluation surplus.**

41   The revaluation surplus included in equity in respect of an item of property, plant and equipment may be transferred directly to retained earnings when the asset is derecognised. This may involve transferring the whole of the surplus when the asset is retired or disposed of. However, some of the surplus may be transferred as the asset is used by an entity. In such a case, the amount of the surplus transferred would be the difference between depreciation based on the revalued carrying amount of the asset and depreciation based on the asset's original cost. Transfers from revaluation surplus to retained earnings are not made through profit or loss.

42   The effects of taxes on income, if any, resulting from the revaluation of property, plant and equipment are recognised and disclosed in accordance with IAS 12 *Income Taxes*.

Depreciation

43   **Each part of an item of property, plant and equipment with a cost that is significant in relation to the total cost of the item shall be depreciated separately.**

44   An entity allocates the amount initially recognised in respect of an item of property, plant and equipment to its significant parts and depreciates separately each such part. For example, it may be appropriate to depreciate separately the airframe and engines of an aircraft. Similarly, if an entity acquires property, plant and equipment subject to an operating lease in which it is the lessor, it may be appropriate to depreciate separately amounts reflected in the cost of that item that are attributable to favourable or unfavourable lease terms relative to market terms.

45   A significant part of an item of property, plant and equipment may have a useful life and a depreciation method that are the same as the useful life and the depreciation method of another significant part of that same item. Such parts may be grouped in determining the depreciation charge.

46   To the extent that an entity depreciates separately some parts of an item of property, plant and equipment, it also depreciates separately the remainder of the item. The remainder consists of the parts of the item that are individually not significant. If an entity has varying expectations for these parts, approximation techniques may be necessary to depreciate the remainder in a manner that faithfully represents the consumption pattern and/or useful life of its parts.

47   An entity may choose to depreciate separately the parts of an item that do not have a cost that is significant in relation to the total cost of the item.

48   **The depreciation charge for each period shall be recognised in profit or loss unless it is included in the carrying amount of another asset.**

49   The depreciation charge for a period is usually recognised in profit or loss. However, sometimes, the future economic benefits embodied in an asset are absorbed in producing other assets. In this case, the depreciation charge constitutes part of the cost of the other asset and is included in its carrying amount. For example, the depreciation of manufacturing plant and equipment is included in the costs of conversion of inventories (see IAS 2). Similarly, depreciation of property, plant and equipment used for development activities may be included in the cost of an intangible asset recognised in accordance with IAS 38 *Intangible Assets*.

Depreciable amount and depreciation period

50   **The depreciable amount of an asset shall be allocated on a systematic basis over its useful life.**

51   The residual value and the useful life of an asset shall be reviewed at least at each financial year-end and, if expectations differ from previous estimates, the change(s) shall be accounted for as a change in an accounting estimate in accordance with IAS 8 *Accounting Policies, Changes in Accounting Estimates and Errors.*

52   Depreciation is recognised even if the fair value of the asset exceeds its carrying amount, as long as the asset's residual value does not exceed its carrying amount. Repair and maintenance of an asset do not negate the need to depreciate it.

53   The depreciable amount of an asset is determined after deducting its residual value. In practice, the residual value of an asset is often insignificant and therefore immaterial in the calculation of the depreciable amount.

54   The residual value of an asset may increase to an amount equal to or greater than the asset's carrying amount. If it does, the asset's depreciation charge is zero unless and until its residual value subsequently decreases to an amount below the asset's carrying amount.

55   Depreciation of an asset begins when it is available for use, ie when it is in the location and condition necessary for it to be capable of operating in the manner intended by management. Depreciation of an asset ceases at the earlier of the date that the asset is classified as held for sale (or included in a disposal group that is classified as held for sale) in accordance with IFRS 5 and the date that the asset is derecognised. Therefore, depreciation does not cease when the asset becomes idle or is retired from active use unless the asset is fully depreciated. However, under usage methods of depreciation the depreciation charge can be zero while there is no production.

56   The future economic benefits embodied in an asset are consumed by an entity principally through its use. However, other factors, such as technical or commercial obsolescence and wear and tear while an asset remains idle, often result in the diminution of the economic benefits that might have been obtained from the asset. Consequently, all the following factors are considered in determining the useful life of an asset:

(a)   expected usage of the asset. Usage is assessed by reference to the asset's expected capacity or physical output.

(b)   expected physical wear and tear, which depends on operational factors such as the number of shifts for which the asset is to be used and the repair and maintenance programme, and the care and maintenance of the asset while idle.

(c)   technical or commercial obsolescence arising from changes or improvements in production, or from a change in the market demand for the product or service output of the asset. Expected future reductions in the selling price of an item that was produced using an asset could indicate the expectation of technical or commercial obsolescence of the asset, which, in turn, might reflect a reduction of the future economic benefits embodied in the asset.

(d)   legal or similar limits on the use of the asset, such as the expiry dates of related leases.

57   The useful life of an asset is defined in terms of the asset's expected utility to the entity. The asset management policy of the entity may involve the disposal of assets after a specified time or after consumption of a specified proportion of the future economic benefits embodied in the asset. Therefore, the useful life of an asset may be shorter than its economic life. The estimation of the useful life of the asset is a matter of judgement based on the experience of the entity with similar assets.

58   Land and buildings are separable assets and are accounted for separately, even when they are acquired together. With some exceptions, such as quarries and sites used for landfill, land has an unlimited useful life and therefore is not depreciated. Buildings have a limited useful life and therefore are depreciable assets. An increase in the value of the land on which a building stands does not affect the determination of the depreciable amount of the building.

59   If the cost of land includes the costs of site dismantlement, removal and restoration, that portion of the land asset is depreciated over the period of benefits obtained by incurring those costs. In some cases, the land itself may have a limited useful life, in which case it is depreciated in a manner that reflects the benefits to be derived from it.

Depreciation method

60   **The depreciation method used shall reflect the pattern in which the asset's future economic benefits are expected to be consumed by the entity.**

61   **The depreciation method applied to an asset shall be reviewed at least at each financial year-end and, if there has been a significant change in the expected pattern of consumption of the future economic benefits embodied in the asset, the method shall be changed to reflect the changed pattern. Such a change shall be accounted for as a change in an accounting estimate in accordance with IAS 8.**

62   A variety of depreciation methods can be used to allocate the depreciable amount of an asset on a systematic basis over its useful life. These methods include the straight-line method, the diminishing balance method and the units of production method. Straight-line depreciation results in a constant charge over the useful life if the asset's residual value does not change. The diminishing balance method results in a decreasing charge over the useful life. The units of production method results in a charge based on the expected use or output. The entity selects the method that most closely reflects the expected pattern of consumption of the future economic benefits embodied in the asset. That method is applied consistently from period to period unless there is a change in the expected pattern of consumption of those future economic benefits.

62A   A depreciation method that is based on revenue that is generated by an activity that includes the use of an asset is not appropriate. The revenue generated by an activity that includes the use of an asset generally reflects factors other than the consumption of the economic benefits of the asset. For example, revenue is affected by other inputs and processes, selling activities and changes in sales volumes and prices. The price component of revenue may be affected by inflation, which has no bearing upon the way in which an asset is consumed.

Impairment

63 To determine whether an item of property, plant and equipment is impaired, an entity applies IAS 36 *Impairment of Assets*. That Standard explains how an entity reviews the carrying amount of its assets, how it determines the recoverable amount of an asset, and when it recognises, or reverses the recognition of, an impairment loss.

64 [Deleted]

Compensation for impairment

65 **Compensation from third parties for items of property, plant and equipment that were impaired, lost or given up shall be included in profit or loss when the compensation becomes receivable.**

66 Impairments or losses of items of property, plant and equipment, related claims for or payments of compensation from third parties and any subsequent purchase or construction of replacement assets are separate economic events and are accounted for separately as follows:

(a) impairments of items of property, plant and equipment are recognised in accordance with IAS 36;

(b) derecognition of items of property, plant and equipment retired or disposed of is determined in accordance with this Standard;

(c) compensation from third parties for items of property, plant and equipment that were impaired, lost or given up is included in determining profit or loss when it becomes receivable; and

(d) the cost of items of property, plant and equipment restored, purchased or constructed as replacements is determined in accordance with this Standard.

Derecognition

67 **The carrying amount of an item of property, plant and equipment shall be derecognised:**

(a) **on disposal; or**

(b) **when no future economic benefits are expected from its use or disposal.**

68 **The gain or loss arising from the derecognition of an item of property, plant and equipment shall be included in profit or loss when the item is derecognised** (unless IFRS 16 *Leases* requires otherwise on a sale and leaseback). **Gains shall not be classified as revenue.**

68A However, an entity that, in the course of its ordinary activities, routinely sells items of property, plant and equipment that it has held for rental to others shall transfer such assets to inventories at their carrying amount when they cease to be rented and become held for sale. The proceeds from the sale of such assets shall be recognised as revenue in accordance with IFRS 15 *Revenue from Contracts with Customers*. IFRS 5 does not apply when assets that are held for sale in the ordinary course of business are transferred to inventories.

69 The disposal of an item of property, plant and equipment may occur in a variety of ways (eg by sale, by entering into a finance lease or by donation). The date of disposal of an item of property, plant and equipment is the date the recipient obtains control of that item in accordance with the requirements for determining when a performance obligation is satisfied in IFRS 15. IFRS 16 applies to disposal by a sale and leaseback.

70 If, under the recognition principle in paragraph 7, an entity recognises in the carrying amount of an item of property, plant and equipment the cost of a replacement for part of the item, then it derecognises the carrying amount of the replaced part regardless of whether the replaced part had been depreciated separately. If it is not practicable for an entity to determine the carrying amount of the replaced part, it may use the cost of the replacement as an indication of what the cost of the replaced part was at the time it was acquired or constructed.

71 **The gain or loss arising from the derecognition of an item of property, plant and equipment shall be determined as the difference between the net disposal proceeds, if any, and the carrying amount of the item.**

72 The amount of consideration to be included in the gain or loss arising from the derecognition of an item of property, plant and equipment is determined in accordance with the requirements for determining the transaction price in paragraphs 47–72 of IFRS 15. Subsequent changes to the estimated amount of the consideration included in the gain or loss shall be accounted for in accordance with the requirements for changes in the transaction price in IFRS 15.

Disclosure

73 The financial statements shall disclose, for each class of property, plant and equipment:

    (a)   the measurement bases used for determining the gross carrying amount;

    (b)   the depreciation methods used;

    (c)   the useful lives or the depreciation rates used;

    (d)   the gross carrying amount and the accumulated depreciation (aggregated with accumulated impairment losses) at the beginning and end of the period; and

(e)   a reconciliation of the carrying amount at the beginning and end of the period showing:

    (i)   additions;

    (ii)   assets classified as held for sale or included in a disposal group classified as held for sale in accordance with IFRS 5 and other disposals;

    (iii)   acquisitions through business combinations;

    (iv)   increases or decreases resulting from revaluations under paragraphs 31, 39 and 40 and from impairment losses recognised or reversed in other comprehensive income in accordance with IAS 36;

    (v)   impairment losses recognised in profit or loss in accordance with IAS 36;

    (vi)   impairment losses reversed in profit or loss in accordance with IAS 36;

    (vii)   depreciation;

    (viii)   the net exchange differences arising on the translation of the financial statements from the functional currency into a different presentation currency, including the translation of a foreign operation into the presentation currency of the reporting entity; and

    (ix)   other changes.

74   The financial statements shall also disclose:

    (a)   the existence and amounts of restrictions on title, and property, plant and equipment pledged as security for liabilities;

    (b)   the amount of expenditures recognised in the carrying amount of an item of property, plant and equipment in the course of its construction; and

    (c)   the amount of contractual commitments for the acquisition of property, plant and equipment.

74A   If not presented separately in the statement of comprehensive income, the financial statements shall also disclose:

    (a)   the amount of compensation from third parties for items of property, plant and equipment that were impaired, lost or given up that is included in profit or loss; and

    (b)   the amounts of proceeds and cost included in profit or loss in accordance with paragraph 20A that relate to items produced that are not an output of the entity's ordinary activities, and which line item(s) in the statement of comprehensive income include(s) such proceeds and cost.

75   Selection of the depreciation method and estimation of the useful life of assets are matters of judgement. Therefore, disclosure of the methods adopted and the estimated useful lives or depreciation rates provides users of financial statements with information that allows them to review the policies selected by management and enables comparisons to be made with other entities. For similar reasons, it is necessary to disclose:

(a)   depreciation, whether recognised in profit or loss or as a part of the cost of other assets, during a period; and

(b)   accumulated depreciation at the end of the period.

76   In accordance with IAS 8 an entity discloses the nature and effect of a change in an accounting estimate that has an effect in the current period or is expected to have an effect in subsequent periods. For property, plant and equipment, such disclosure may arise from changes in estimates with respect to:

(a)   residual values;

(b)   the estimated costs of dismantling, removing or restoring items of property, plant and equipment;

(c)   useful lives; and

(d)   depreciation methods.

77   **If items of property, plant and equipment are stated at revalued amounts, the following shall be disclosed in addition to the disclosures required by IFRS 13:**

(a)   **the effective date of the revaluation;**

(b)   **whether an independent valuer was involved;**

(c)–(d)   [deleted]

(e)   **for each revalued class of property, plant and equipment, the carrying amount that would have been recognised had the assets been carried under the cost model; and**

(f)   **the revaluation surplus, indicating the change for the period and any restrictions on the distribution of the balance to shareholders.**

78   In accordance with IAS 36 an entity discloses information on impaired property, plant and equipment in addition to the information required by paragraph 73(e)(iv)–(vi).

79   Users of financial statements may also find the following information relevant to their needs:

(a)   the carrying amount of temporarily idle property, plant and equipment;

(b)   the gross carrying amount of any fully depreciated property, plant and equipment that is still in use;

(c)   the carrying amount of property, plant and equipment retired from active use and not classified as held for sale in accordance with IFRS 5; and

(d)   when the cost model is used, the fair value of property, plant and equipment when this is materially different from the carrying amount.

Therefore, entities are encouraged to disclose these amounts.

Transitional provisions

80   **The requirements of paragraphs 24–26 regarding the initial measurement of an item of property, plant and equipment acquired in an exchange of assets transaction shall be applied prospectively only to future transactions.**

80A   Paragraph 35 was amended by *Annual Improvements to IFRSs 2010–2012 Cycle*. An entity shall apply that amendment to all revaluations recognised in annual periods beginning on or after the date of initial application of that amendment and in the immediately preceding annual period. An entity may also present adjusted comparative information for any earlier periods presented, but it is not required to do so. If an entity presents unadjusted comparative information for any earlier periods, it shall clearly identify the information that has not been adjusted, state that it has been presented on a different basis and explain that basis.

80B   In the reporting period when *Agriculture: Bearer Plants* (Amendments to IAS 16 and IAS 41) is first applied an entity need not disclose the quantitative information required by paragraph 28(f) of IAS 8 for the current period. However, an entity shall present the quantitative information required by paragraph 28(f) of IAS 8 for each prior period presented.

80C   An entity may elect to measure an item of bearer plants at its fair value at the beginning of the earliest period presented in the financial statements for the reporting period in which the entity first applies *Agriculture: Bearer Plants* (Amendments to IAS 16 and IAS 41) and use that fair value as its deemed cost at that date. Any difference between the previous carrying amount and fair value shall be recognised in opening retained earnings at the beginning of the earliest period presented.

80D   *Property, Plant and Equipment—Proceeds before Intended Use*, issued in May 2020, amended paragraphs 17 and 74 and added paragraphs 20A and 74A. An entity shall apply those amendments retrospectively, but only to items of property, plant and equipment that are brought to the location and condition necessary for them to be capable of operating in the manner intended by management on or after the beginning of the earliest period presented in the financial statements in which the entity first applies the amendments. The entity shall recognise the cumulative effect of initially applying the amendments as an adjustment to the opening balance of retained earnings (or other component of equity, as appropriate) at the beginning of that earliest period presented.

Effective date

81   An entity shall apply this Standard for annual periods beginning on or after 1 January 2005. Earlier application is encouraged. If an entity applies this Standard for a period beginning before 1 January 2005, it shall disclose that fact.

81A An entity shall apply the amendments in paragraph 3 for annual periods beginning on or after 1 January 2006. If an entity applies IFRS 6 for an earlier period, those amendments shall be applied for that earlier period.

81B IAS 1 *Presentation of Financial Statements* (as revised in 2007) amended the terminology used throughout IFRSs. In addition it amended paragraphs 39, 40 and 73(e)(iv). An entity shall apply those amendments for annual periods beginning on or after 1 January 2009. If an entity applies IAS 1 (revised 2007) for an earlier period, the amendments shall be applied for that earlier period.

81C IFRS 3 *Business Combinations* (as revised in 2008) amended paragraph 44. An entity shall apply that amendment for annual periods beginning on or after 1 July 2009. If an entity applies IFRS 3 (revised 2008) for an earlier period, the amendment shall also be applied for that earlier period.

81D Paragraphs 6 and 69 were amended and paragraph 68A was added by *Improvements to IFRSs* issued in May 2008. An entity shall apply those amendments for annual periods beginning on or after 1 January 2009. Earlier application is permitted. If an entity applies the amendments for an earlier period it shall disclose that fact and at the same time apply the related amendments to IAS 7 *Statement of Cash Flows*.

81E Paragraph 5 was amended by *Improvements to IFRSs* issued in May 2008. An entity shall apply that amendment prospectively for annual periods beginning on or after 1 January 2009. Earlier application is permitted if an entity also applies the amendments to paragraphs 8, 9, 22, 48, 53, 53A, 53B, 54, 57 and 85B of IAS 40 at the same time. If an entity applies the amendment for an earlier period it shall disclose that fact.

81F IFRS 13, issued in May 2011, amended the definition of fair value and the definition of recoverable amount in paragraph 6, amended paragraphs 26, 35 and 77 and deleted paragraphs 32 and 33. An entity shall apply those amendments when it applies IFRS 13.

81G *Annual Improvements 2009–2011 Cycle*, issued in May 2012, amended paragraph 8. An entity shall apply that amendment retrospectively in accordance with IAS 8 *Accounting Policies, Changes in Accounting Estimates and Errors* for annual periods beginning on or after 1 January 2013. Earlier application is permitted. If an entity applies that amendment for an earlier period it shall disclose that fact.

81H *Annual Improvements to IFRSs 2010–2012 Cycle*, issued in December 2013, amended paragraph 35 and added paragraph 80A. An entity shall apply that amendment for annual periods beginning on or after 1 July 2014. Earlier application is permitted. If an entity applies that amendment for an earlier period it shall disclose that fact.

81I *Clarification of Acceptable Methods of Depreciation and Amortisation* (Amendments to IAS 16 and IAS 38), issued in May 2014, amended paragraph 56 and added paragraph 62A. An entity shall apply those amendments prospectively for annual periods beginning on or after 1 January 2016. Earlier application is permitted. If an entity applies those amendments for an earlier period it shall disclose that fact.

81J IFRS 15 *Revenue from Contracts with Customers*, issued in May 2014, amended paragraphs 68A, 69 and 72. An entity shall apply those amendments when it applies IFRS 15.

81K *Agriculture: Bearer Plants* (Amendments to IAS 16 and IAS 41), issued in June 2014, amended paragraphs 3, 6 and 37 and added paragraphs 22A and 80B–80C. An entity shall apply those amendments for annual periods beginning on or after 1 January 2016. Earlier application is permitted. If an entity applies those amendments for an earlier period, it shall disclose that fact. An entity shall apply those amendments retrospectively, in accordance with IAS 8, except as specified in paragraph 80C.

81L IFRS 16, issued in January 2016, deleted paragraphs 4 and 27 and amended paragraphs 5, 10, 44 and 68–69. An entity shall apply those amendments when it applies IFRS 16.

81M *[This paragraph refers to amendments that are not yet effective, and is therefore not included in this edition.]*

81N *Property, Plant and Equipment—Proceeds before Intended Use*, issued in May 2020, amended paragraphs 17 and 74, and added paragraphs 20A, 74A and 80D. An entity shall apply those amendments for annual reporting periods beginning on or after 1 January 2022. Earlier application is permitted. If an entity applies those amendments for an earlier period, it shall disclose that fact.

Withdrawal of other pronouncements

82 This Standard supersedes IAS 16 *Property, Plant and Equipment* (revised in 1998).

83 This Standard supersedes the following Interpretations:

   (a) SIC-6 *Costs of Modifying Existing Software*;

   (b) SIC-14 *Property, Plant and Equipment—Compensation for the Impairment or Loss of Items*; and

   (c) SIC-23 *Property, Plant and Equipment—Major Inspection or Overhaul Costs*.

Appendix
Amendments to other pronouncements

The amendments in this appendix shall be applied for annual periods beginning on or after 1 January 2005. If an entity applies this Standard for an earlier period, these amendments shall be applied for that earlier period.

* * * * *

The amendments contained in this appendix when this Standard was issued in 2003 have been incorporated into the relevant pronouncements published in this volume.

Approval by the Board of IAS 16 issued in December 2003

International Accounting Standard 16 *Property, Plant and Equipment* (as revised in 2003) was approved for issue by the fourteen members of the International Accounting Standards Board.

Sir David Tweedie	Chairman
Thomas E Jones	Vice-Chairman
Mary E Barth	
Hans-Georg Bruns	
Anthony T Cope	
Robert P Garnett	
Gilbert Gélard	
James J Leisenring	
Warren J McGregor	
Patricia L O'Malley	
Harry K Schmid	
John T Smith	
Geoffrey Whittington	
Tatsumi Yamada	

Approval by the Board of *Clarification of Acceptable Methods of Depreciation and Amortisation* (Amendments to IAS 16 and IAS 38) issued in May 2014

Clarification of Acceptable Methods of Depreciation and Amortisation was approved for issue by fifteen of the sixteen members of the International Accounting Standards Board. Ms Tokar dissented. Her dissenting opinion is set out after the Basis for Conclusions.

Hans Hoogervorst	Chairman
Ian Mackintosh	Vice-Chairman
Stephen Cooper	
Philippe Danjou	
Martin Edelmann	
Jan Engström	
Patrick Finnegan	
Amaro Luiz de Oliveira Gomes	
Gary Kabureck	
Suzanne Lloyd	
Patricia McConnell	
Takatsugu Ochi	
Darrel Scott	
Chungwoo Suh	
Mary Tokar	
Wei-Guo Zhang	

Approval by the Board of *Agriculture: Bearer Plants* (Amendments to IAS 16 and IAS 41) issued in June 2014

Agriculture: Bearer Plants was approved for issue by fourteen of the sixteen members of the International Accounting Standards Board. Mr Finnegan and Ms McConnell voted against its publication. Their dissenting opinions are set out after the Basis for Conclusions.

Hans Hoogervorst	Chairman
Ian Mackintosh	Vice-Chairman
Stephen Cooper	
Philippe Danjou	
Martin Edelmann	
Jan Engström	
Patrick Finnegan	
Amaro Luiz de Oliveira Gomes	
Gary Kabureck	
Suzanne Lloyd	
Patricia McConnell	
Takatsugu Ochi	
Darrel Scott	
Chungwoo Suh	
Mary Tokar	
Wei-Guo Zhang	

Approval by the Board of *Property, Plant and Equipment—Proceeds before Intended Use* issued in May 2020

Property, Plant and Equipment—Proceeds before Intended Use, which amended IAS 16, was approved for issue by all 14 members of the International Accounting Standards Board.

Hans Hoogervorst	Chairman
Suzanne Lloyd	Vice-Chair
Nick Anderson	
Tadeu Cendon	
Martin Edelmann	
Françoise Flores	
Gary Kabureck	
Jianqiao Lu	
Darrel Scott	
Thomas Scott	
Chungwoo Suh	
Rika Suzuki	
Ann Tarca	
Mary Tokar	

IAS 19

Employee Benefits

In April 2001 the International Accounting Standards Board (Board) adopted IAS 19 *Employee Benefits*, which had originally been issued by the International Accounting Standards Committee in February 1998. IAS 19 *Employee Benefits* replaced IAS 19 *Accounting for Retirement Benefits in the Financial Statements of Employers* (issued in January 1983). IAS 19 was further amended in 1993 and renamed as IAS 19 *Retirement Benefit Costs*.

The Board amended the accounting for multi-employer plans and group plans in December 2004. In June 2011 the Board revised IAS 19; this included eliminating an option that allowed an entity to defer the recognition of changes in net defined benefit liability and amending some of the disclosure requirements for defined benefit plans and multi-employer plans.

In November 2013 IAS 19 was amended by *Defined Benefit Plans: Employee Contributions* (Amendments to IAS 19). The amendments simplified the requirements for contributions from employees or third parties to a defined benefit plan, when those contributions are applied to a simple contributory plan that is linked to service.

Other Standards have made minor consequential amendments to IAS 19, including *Annual Improvements to IFRSs 2012–2014 Cycle* (issued September 2014), *Annual Improvements to IFRS Standards 2014–2016 Cycle* (issued December 2016), *Plan Amendment, Curtailment or Settlement* (Amendments to IAS 19) (issued February 2018) and *Amendments to References to the Conceptual Framework in IFRS Standards* (issued March 2018).

CONTENTS

continued...

...continued

APPENDICES

A Application Guidance

B Amendments to other IFRS

APPROVAL BY THE BOARD OF *ACTUARIAL GAINS AND LOSSES, GROUP PLANS AND DISCLOSURES* **(AMENDMENT TO IAS 19) ISSUED IN DECEMBER 2004**

APPROVAL BY THE BOARD OF IAS 19 ISSUED IN JUNE 2011

APPROVAL BY THE BOARD OF *DEFINED BENEFIT PLANS: EMPLOYEE CONTRIBUTIONS* **(AMENDMENTS TO IAS 19) ISSUED IN NOVEMBER 2013**

APPROVAL BY THE BOARD OF *PLAN AMENDMENT, CURTAILMENT OR SETTLEMENT* **(AMENDMENTS TO IAS 19) ISSUED IN FEBRUARY 2018**

FOR THE ACCOMPANYING GUIDANCE LISTED BELOW, SEE PART B OF THIS EDITION

TABLE OF CONCORDANCE

AMENDMENTS TO GUIDANCE ON OTHER IFRSS

FOR THE BASIS FOR CONCLUSIONS, SEE PART C OF THIS EDITION

BASIS FOR CONCLUSIONS

APPENDIX TO THE BASIS FOR CONCLUSIONS

Amendments to the Basis for Conclusions on other IFRSs

DISSENTING OPINIONS

International Accounting Standard 19 *Employee Benefits* (IAS 19) is set out in paragraphs 1–179 and Appendices A–B. All the paragraphs have equal authority but retain the IASC format of the Standard when it was adopted by the IASB. IAS 19 should be read in the context of its objective and the Basis for Conclusions, the *Preface to IFRS Standards* and the *Conceptual Framework for Financial Reporting*. IAS 8 *Accounting Policies, Changes in Accounting Estimates and Errors* provides a basis for selecting and applying accounting policies in the absence of explicit guidance.

International Accounting Standard 19
Employee Benefits

Objective

1   The objective of this Standard is to prescribe the accounting and disclosure for employee benefits. The Standard requires an entity to recognise:

    (a)   a liability when an employee has provided service in exchange for employee benefits to be paid in the future; and

    (b)   an expense when the entity consumes the economic benefit arising from service provided by an employee in exchange for employee benefits.

Scope

2   **This Standard shall be applied by an employer in accounting for all employee benefits, except those to which IFRS 2 *Share-based Payment* applies.**

3   This Standard does not deal with reporting by employee benefit plans (see IAS 26 *Accounting and Reporting by Retirement Benefit Plans*).

4   The employee benefits to which this Standard applies include those provided:

    (a)   under formal plans or other formal agreements between an entity and individual employees, groups of employees or their representatives;

    (b)   under legislative requirements, or through industry arrangements, whereby entities are required to contribute to national, state, industry or other multi-employer plans; or

    (c)   by those informal practices that give rise to a constructive obligation. Informal practices give rise to a constructive obligation where the entity has no realistic alternative but to pay employee benefits. An example of a constructive obligation is where a change in the entity's informal practices would cause unacceptable damage to its relationship with employees.

5   Employee benefits include:

    (a)   short-term employee benefits, such as the following, if expected to be settled wholly before twelve months after the end of the annual reporting period in which the employees render the related services:

        (i)   wages, salaries and social security contributions;

        (ii)   paid annual leave and paid sick leave;

        (iii)   profit-sharing and bonuses; and

        (iv)   non-monetary benefits (such as medical care, housing, cars and free or subsidised goods or services) for current employees;

    (b)   post-employment benefits, such as the following:

        (i)   retirement benefits (eg pensions and lump sum payments on retirement); and

        (ii)   other post-employment benefits, such as post-employment life insurance and post-employment medical care;

    (c)   other long-term employee benefits, such as the following:

        (i)   long-term paid absences such as long-service leave or sabbatical leave;

        (ii)   jubilee or other long-service benefits; and

        (iii)   long-term disability benefits; and

    (d)   termination benefits.

6   Employee benefits include benefits provided either to employees or to their dependants or beneficiaries and may be settled by payments (or the provision of goods or services) made either directly to the employees, to their spouses, children or other dependants or to others, such as insurance companies.

7   An employee may provide services to an entity on a full-time, part-time, permanent, casual or temporary basis. For the purpose of this Standard, employees include directors and other management personnel.

Definitions

8   The following terms are used in this Standard with the meanings specified:

Definitions of employee benefits

Employee benefits are all forms of consideration given by an entity in exchange for service rendered by employees or for the termination of employment.

Short-term employee benefits are employee benefits (other than termination benefits) that are expected to be settled wholly before twelve months after the end of the annual reporting period in which the employees render the related service.

Post-employment benefits are employee benefits (other than termination benefits and short-term employee benefits) that are payable after the completion of employment.

Other long-term employee benefits are all employee benefits other than short-term employee benefits, post-employment benefits and termination benefits.

Termination benefits are employee benefits provided in exchange for the termination of an employee's employment as a result of either:

    (a)   an entity's decision to terminate an employee's employment before the normal retirement date; or

(b)   an employee's decision to accept an offer of benefits in exchange for the termination of employment.

Definitions relating to classification of plans

Post-employment benefit plans are formal or informal arrangements under which an entity provides post-employment benefits for one or more employees.

Defined contribution plans are post-employment benefit plans under which an entity pays fixed contributions into a separate entity (a fund) and will have no legal or constructive obligation to pay further contributions if the fund does not hold sufficient assets to pay all employee benefits relating to employee service in the current and prior periods.

Defined benefit plans are post-employment benefit plans other than defined contribution plans.

Multi-employer plans are defined contribution plans (other than state plans) or defined benefit plans (other than state plans) that:

(a)   pool the assets contributed by various entities that are not under common control; and

(b)   use those assets to provide benefits to employees of more than one entity, on the basis that contribution and benefit levels are determined without regard to the identity of the entity that employs the employees.

Definitions relating to the net defined benefit liability (asset)

The *net defined benefit liability* (asset) is the deficit or surplus, adjusted for any effect of limiting a net defined benefit asset to the asset ceiling.

The *deficit or surplus* is:

(a)   the present value of the defined benefit obligation less

(b)   the fair value of plan assets (if any).

The *asset ceiling* is the present value of any economic benefits available in the form of refunds from the plan or reductions in future contributions to the plan.

The *present value of a defined benefit obligation* is the present value, without deducting any plan assets, of expected future payments required to settle the obligation resulting from employee service in the current and prior periods.

Plan assets comprise:

(a)   assets held by a long-term employee benefit fund; and

(b)   qualifying insurance policies.

Assets held by a long-term employee benefit fund are assets (other than non-transferable financial instruments issued by the reporting entity) that:

(a) are held by an entity (a fund) that is legally separate from the reporting entity and exists solely to pay or fund employee benefits; and

(b) are available to be used only to pay or fund employee benefits, are not available to the reporting entity's own creditors (even in bankruptcy), and cannot be returned to the reporting entity, unless either:

    (i) the remaining assets of the fund are sufficient to meet all the related employee benefit obligations of the plan or the reporting entity; or

    (ii) the assets are returned to the reporting entity to reimburse it for employee benefits already paid.

A *qualifying insurance policy* is an insurance policy[1] issued by an insurer that is not a related party (as defined in IAS 24 *Related Party Disclosures*) of the reporting entity, if the proceeds of the policy:

(a) can be used only to pay or fund employee benefits under a defined benefit plan; and

(b) are not available to the reporting entity's own creditors (even in bankruptcy) and cannot be paid to the reporting entity, unless either:

    (i) the proceeds represent surplus assets that are not needed for the policy to meet all the related employee benefit obligations; or

    (ii) the proceeds are returned to the reporting entity to reimburse it for employee benefits already paid.

Fair value is the price that would be received to sell an asset or paid to transfer a liability in an orderly transaction between market participants at the measurement date. (See IFRS 13 *Fair Value Measurement*.)

Definitions relating to defined benefit cost

Service cost comprises:

(a) *current service cost*, which is the increase in the present value of the defined benefit obligation resulting from employee service in the current period;

(b) *past service cost*, which is the change in the present value of the defined benefit obligation for employee service in prior periods, resulting from a plan amendment (the introduction or withdrawal of, or changes to, a defined benefit plan) or a curtailment (a

---

1   A qualifying insurance policy is not necessarily an insurance contract, as defined in IFRS 4 *Insurance Contracts*.

significant reduction by the entity in the number of employees covered by a plan); and

(c)   any gain or loss on settlement.

Net interest on the net defined benefit liability (asset) is the change during the period in the net defined benefit liability (asset) that arises from the passage of time.

Remeasurements of the net defined benefit liability (asset) comprise:

(a)   actuarial gains and losses;

(b)   the return on plan assets, excluding amounts included in net interest on the net defined benefit liability (asset); and

(c)   any change in the effect of the asset ceiling, excluding amounts included in net interest on the net defined benefit liability (asset).

Actuarial gains and losses are changes in the present value of the defined benefit obligation resulting from:

(a)   experience adjustments (the effects of differences between the previous actuarial assumptions and what has actually occurred); and

(b)   the effects of changes in actuarial assumptions.

The *return on plan assets* is interest, dividends and other income derived from the plan assets, together with realised and unrealised gains or losses on the plan assets, less:

(a)   any costs of managing plan assets; and

(b)   any tax payable by the plan itself, other than tax included in the actuarial assumptions used to measure the present value of the defined benefit obligation.

A *settlement* is a transaction that eliminates all further legal or constructive obligations for part or all of the benefits provided under a defined benefit plan, other than a payment of benefits to, or on behalf of, employees that is set out in the terms of the plan and included in the actuarial assumptions.

Short-term employee benefits

9   Short-term employee benefits include items such as the following, if expected to be settled wholly before twelve months after the end of the annual reporting period in which the employees render the related services:

(a)   wages, salaries and social security contributions;

(b)   paid annual leave and paid sick leave;

(c)   profit-sharing and bonuses; and

(d)   non-monetary benefits (such as medical care, housing, cars and free or subsidised goods or services) for current employees.

10   An entity need not reclassify a short-term employee benefit if the entity's expectations of the timing of settlement change temporarily. However, if the characteristics of the benefit change (such as a change from a non-accumulating benefit to an accumulating benefit) or if a change in expectations of the timing of settlement is not temporary, then the entity considers whether the benefit still meets the definition of short-term employee benefits.

Recognition and measurement

All short-term employee benefits

11   When an employee has rendered service to an entity during an accounting period, the entity shall recognise the undiscounted amount of short-term employee benefits expected to be paid in exchange for that service:

(a)   as a liability (accrued expense), after deducting any amount already paid. If the amount already paid exceeds the undiscounted amount of the benefits, an entity shall recognise that excess as an asset (prepaid expense) to the extent that the prepayment will lead to, for example, a reduction in future payments or a cash refund.

(b)   as an expense, unless another IFRS requires or permits the inclusion of the benefits in the cost of an asset (see, for example, IAS 2 *Inventories* and IAS 16 *Property, Plant and Equipment*).

12   Paragraphs 13, 16 and 19 explain how an entity shall apply paragraph 11 to short-term employee benefits in the form of paid absences and profit-sharing and bonus plans.

Short-term paid absences

13   An entity shall recognise the expected cost of short-term employee benefits in the form of paid absences under paragraph 11 as follows:

(a)   in the case of accumulating paid absences, when the employees render service that increases their entitlement to future paid absences.

(b)   in the case of non-accumulating paid absences, when the absences occur.

14   An entity may pay employees for absence for various reasons including holidays, sickness and short-term disability, maternity or paternity, jury service and military service. Entitlement to paid absences falls into two categories:

(a)   accumulating; and

(b)   non-accumulating.

15   Accumulating paid absences are those that are carried forward and can be used in future periods if the current period's entitlement is not used in full. Accumulating paid absences may be either vesting (in other words, employees are entitled to a cash payment for unused entitlement on leaving the entity) or

non-vesting (when employees are not entitled to a cash payment for unused entitlement on leaving). An obligation arises as employees render service that increases their entitlement to future paid absences. The obligation exists, and is recognised, even if the paid absences are non-vesting, although the possibility that employees may leave before they use an accumulated non-vesting entitlement affects the measurement of that obligation.

16   **An entity shall measure the expected cost of accumulating paid absences as the additional amount that the entity expects to pay as a result of the unused entitlement that has accumulated at the end of the reporting period.**

17   The method specified in the previous paragraph measures the obligation at the amount of the additional payments that are expected to arise solely from the fact that the benefit accumulates. In many cases, an entity may not need to make detailed computations to estimate that there is no material obligation for unused paid absences. For example, a sick leave obligation is likely to be material only if there is a formal or informal understanding that unused paid sick leave may be taken as paid annual leave.

Example illustrating paragraphs 16 and 17

An entity has 100 employees, who are each entitled to five working days of paid sick leave for each year. Unused sick leave may be carried forward for one calendar year. Sick leave is taken first out of the current year's entitlement and then out of any balance brought forward from the previous year (a LIFO basis). At 31 December 20X1 the average unused entitlement is two days per employee. The entity expects, on the basis of experience that is expected to continue, that 92 employees will take no more than five days of paid sick leave in 20X2 and that the remaining eight employees will take an average of six and a half days each.

The entity expects that it will pay an additional twelve days of sick pay as a result of the unused entitlement that has accumulated at 31 December 20X1 (one and a half days each, for eight employees). Therefore, the entity recognises a liability equal to twelve days of sick pay.

---

18   Non-accumulating paid absences do not carry forward: they lapse if the current period's entitlement is not used in full and do not entitle employees to a cash payment for unused entitlement on leaving the entity. This is commonly the case for sick pay (to the extent that unused past entitlement does not increase future entitlement), maternity or paternity leave and paid absences for jury service or military service. An entity recognises no liability or expense until the time of the absence, because employee service does not increase the amount of the benefit.

Profit-sharing and bonus plans

19   **An entity shall recognise the expected cost of profit-sharing and bonus payments under paragraph 11 when, and only when:**

(a)   **the entity has a present legal or constructive obligation to make such payments as a result of past events; and**

(b)   a reliable estimate of the obligation can be made.

A present obligation exists when, and only when, the entity has no realistic alternative but to make the payments.

20   Under some profit-sharing plans, employees receive a share of the profit only if they remain with the entity for a specified period. Such plans create a constructive obligation as employees render service that increases the amount to be paid if they remain in service until the end of the specified period. The measurement of such constructive obligations reflects the possibility that some employees may leave without receiving profit-sharing payments.

Example illustrating paragraph 20

A profit-sharing plan requires an entity to pay a specified proportion of its profit for the year to employees who serve throughout the year. If no employees leave during the year, the total profit-sharing payments for the year will be 3 per cent of profit. The entity estimates that staff turnover will reduce the payments to 2.5 per cent of profit.

The entity recognises a liability and an expense of 2.5 per cent of profit.

---

21   An entity may have no legal obligation to pay a bonus. Nevertheless, in some cases, an entity has a practice of paying bonuses. In such cases, the entity has a constructive obligation because the entity has no realistic alternative but to pay the bonus. The measurement of the constructive obligation reflects the possibility that some employees may leave without receiving a bonus.

22   An entity can make a reliable estimate of its legal or constructive obligation under a profit-sharing or bonus plan when, and only when:

(a)   the formal terms of the plan contain a formula for determining the amount of the benefit;

(b)   the entity determines the amounts to be paid before the financial statements are authorised for issue; or

(c)   past practice gives clear evidence of the amount of the entity's constructive obligation.

23   An obligation under profit-sharing and bonus plans results from employee service and not from a transaction with the entity's owners. Therefore, an entity recognises the cost of profit-sharing and bonus plans not as a distribution of profit but as an expense.

24   If profit-sharing and bonus payments are not expected to be settled wholly before twelve months after the end of the annual reporting period in which the employees render the related service, those payments are other long-term employee benefits (see paragraphs 153–158).

Disclosure

25   Although this Standard does not require specific disclosures about short-term employee benefits, other IFRSs may require disclosures. For example, IAS 24 requires disclosures about employee benefits for key management personnel. IAS 1 *Presentation of Financial Statements* requires disclosure of employee benefits expense.

Post-employment benefits: distinction between defined contribution plans and defined benefit plans

26   Post-employment benefits include items such as the following:

     (a)   retirement benefits (eg pensions and lump sum payments on retirement); and

     (b)   other post-employment benefits, such as post-employment life insurance and post-employment medical care.

     Arrangements whereby an entity provides post-employment benefits are post-employment benefit plans. An entity applies this Standard to all such arrangements whether or not they involve the establishment of a separate entity to receive contributions and to pay benefits.

27   Post-employment benefit plans are classified as either defined contribution plans or defined benefit plans, depending on the economic substance of the plan as derived from its principal terms and conditions.

28   Under defined contribution plans the entity's legal or constructive obligation is limited to the amount that it agrees to contribute to the fund. Thus, the amount of the post-employment benefits received by the employee is determined by the amount of contributions paid by an entity (and perhaps also the employee) to a post-employment benefit plan or to an insurance company, together with investment returns arising from the contributions. In consequence, actuarial risk (that benefits will be less than expected) and investment risk (that assets invested will be insufficient to meet expected benefits) fall, in substance, on the employee.

29   Examples of cases where an entity's obligation is not limited to the amount that it agrees to contribute to the fund are when the entity has a legal or constructive obligation through:

     (a)   a plan benefit formula that is not linked solely to the amount of contributions and requires the entity to provide further contributions if assets are insufficient to meet the benefits in the plan benefit formula;

     (b)   a guarantee, either indirectly through a plan or directly, of a specified return on contributions; or

     (c)   those informal practices that give rise to a constructive obligation. For example, a constructive obligation may arise where an entity has a history of increasing benefits for former employees to keep pace with inflation even where there is no legal obligation to do so.

30   Under defined benefit plans:

       (a)   the entity's obligation is to provide the agreed benefits to current and former employees; and

       (b)   actuarial risk (that benefits will cost more than expected) and investment risk fall, in substance, on the entity. If actuarial or investment experience are worse than expected, the entity's obligation may be increased.

31   Paragraphs 32–49 explain the distinction between defined contribution plans and defined benefit plans in the context of multi-employer plans, defined benefit plans that share risks between entities under common control, state plans and insured benefits.

Multi-employer plans

32   An entity shall classify a multi-employer plan as a defined contribution plan or a defined benefit plan under the terms of the plan (including any constructive obligation that goes beyond the formal terms).

33   If an entity participates in a multi-employer defined benefit plan, unless paragraph 34 applies, it shall:

       (a)   account for its proportionate share of the defined benefit obligation, plan assets and cost associated with the plan in the same way as for any other defined benefit plan; and

       (b)   disclose the information required by paragraphs 135–148 (excluding paragraph 148(d)).

34   When sufficient information is not available to use defined benefit accounting for a multi-employer defined benefit plan, an entity shall:

       (a)   account for the plan in accordance with paragraphs 51 and 52 as if it were a defined contribution plan; and

       (b)   disclose the information required by paragraph 148.

35   One example of a multi-employer defined benefit plan is one where:

       (a)   the plan is financed on a pay-as-you-go basis: contributions are set at a level that is expected to be sufficient to pay the benefits falling due in the same period; and future benefits earned during the current period will be paid out of future contributions; and

       (b)   employees' benefits are determined by the length of their service and the participating entities have no realistic means of withdrawing from the plan without paying a contribution for the benefits earned by employees up to the date of withdrawal. Such a plan creates actuarial risk for the entity: if the ultimate cost of benefits already earned at the end of the reporting period is more than expected, the entity will have either to increase its contributions or to persuade employees to accept a reduction in benefits. Therefore, such a plan is a defined benefit plan.

36   Where sufficient information is available about a multi-employer defined benefit plan, an entity accounts for its proportionate share of the defined benefit obligation, plan assets and post-employment cost associated with the plan in the same way as for any other defined benefit plan. However, an entity may not be able to identify its share of the underlying financial position and performance of the plan with sufficient reliability for accounting purposes. This may occur if:

(a)   the plan exposes the participating entities to actuarial risks associated with the current and former employees of other entities, with the result that there is no consistent and reliable basis for allocating the obligation, plan assets and cost to individual entities participating in the plan; or

(b)   the entity does not have access to sufficient information about the plan to satisfy the requirements of this Standard.

In those cases, an entity accounts for the plan as if it were a defined contribution plan and discloses the information required by paragraph 148.

37   There may be a contractual agreement between the multi-employer plan and its participants that determines how the surplus in the plan will be distributed to the participants (or the deficit funded). A participant in a multi-employer plan with such an agreement that accounts for the plan as a defined contribution plan in accordance with paragraph 34 shall recognise the asset or liability that arises from the contractual agreement and the resulting income or expense in profit or loss.

Example illustrating paragraph 37

An entity participates in a multi-employer defined benefit plan that does not prepare plan valuations on an IAS 19 basis. It therefore accounts for the plan as if it were a defined contribution plan. A non-IAS 19 funding valuation shows a deficit of CU100 million[a] in the plan. The plan has agreed under contract a schedule of contributions with the participating employers in the plan that will eliminate the deficit over the next five years. The entity's total contributions under the contract are CU8 million.

The entity recognises a liability for the contributions adjusted for the time value of money and an equal expense in profit or loss.

(a) In this Standard monetary amounts are denominated in 'currency units (CU)'.

---

38   Multi-employer plans are distinct from group administration plans. A group administration plan is merely an aggregation of single employer plans combined to allow participating employers to pool their assets for investment purposes and reduce investment management and administration costs, but the claims of different employers are segregated for the sole benefit of their own employees. Group administration plans pose no particular accounting problems because information is readily available to treat them in the same way as any other single employer plan and because such plans do not expose the participating entities to actuarial risks associated with the current and former employees of other entities. The definitions in this Standard require an

entity to classify a group administration plan as a defined contribution plan or a defined benefit plan in accordance with the terms of the plan (including any constructive obligation that goes beyond the formal terms).

39 **In determining when to recognise, and how to measure, a liability relating to the wind-up of a multi-employer defined benefit plan, or the entity's withdrawal from a multi-employer defined benefit plan, an entity shall apply IAS 37** *Provisions, Contingent Liabilities and Contingent Assets.*

Defined benefit plans that share risks between entities under common control

40 Defined benefit plans that share risks between entities under common control, for example, a parent and its subsidiaries, are not multi-employer plans.

41 An entity participating in such a plan shall obtain information about the plan as a whole measured in accordance with this Standard on the basis of assumptions that apply to the plan as a whole. If there is a contractual agreement or stated policy for charging to individual group entities the net defined benefit cost for the plan as a whole measured in accordance with this Standard, the entity shall, in its separate or individual financial statements, recognise the net defined benefit cost so charged. If there is no such agreement or policy, the net defined benefit cost shall be recognised in the separate or individual financial statements of the group entity that is legally the sponsoring employer for the plan. The other group entities shall, in their separate or individual financial statements, recognise a cost equal to their contribution payable for the period.

42 Participation in such a plan is a related party transaction for each individual group entity. An entity shall therefore, in its separate or individual financial statements, disclose the information required by paragraph 149.

State plans

43 **An entity shall account for a state plan in the same way as for a multi-employer plan (see paragraphs 32–39).**

44 State plans are established by legislation to cover all entities (or all entities in a particular category, for example, a specific industry) and are operated by national or local government or by another body (for example, an autonomous agency created specifically for this purpose) that is not subject to control or influence by the reporting entity. Some plans established by an entity provide both compulsory benefits, as a substitute for benefits that would otherwise be covered under a state plan, and additional voluntary benefits. Such plans are not state plans.

45 State plans are characterised as defined benefit or defined contribution, depending on the entity's obligation under the plan. Many state plans are funded on a pay-as-you-go basis: contributions are set at a level that is expected to be sufficient to pay the required benefits falling due in the same period; future benefits earned during the current period will be paid out of

future contributions. Nevertheless, in most state plans the entity has no legal or constructive obligation to pay those future benefits: its only obligation is to pay the contributions as they fall due and if the entity ceases to employ members of the state plan, it will have no obligation to pay the benefits earned by its own employees in previous years. For this reason, state plans are normally defined contribution plans. However, when a state plan is a defined benefit plan an entity applies paragraphs 32–39.

Insured benefits

46   An entity may pay insurance premiums to fund a post-employment benefit plan. The entity shall treat such a plan as a defined contribution plan unless the entity will have (either directly, or indirectly through the plan) a legal or constructive obligation either:

    (a)   to pay the employee benefits directly when they fall due; or

    (b)   to pay further amounts if the insurer does not pay all future employee benefits relating to employee service in the current and prior periods.

    If the entity retains such a legal or constructive obligation, the entity shall treat the plan as a defined benefit plan.

47   The benefits insured by an insurance policy need not have a direct or automatic relationship with the entity's obligation for employee benefits. Post-employment benefit plans involving insurance policies are subject to the same distinction between accounting and funding as other funded plans.

48   Where an entity funds a post-employment benefit obligation by contributing to an insurance policy under which the entity (either directly, indirectly through the plan, through the mechanism for setting future premiums or through a related party relationship with the insurer) retains a legal or constructive obligation, the payment of the premiums does not amount to a defined contribution arrangement. It follows that the entity:

    (a)   accounts for a qualifying insurance policy as a plan asset (see paragraph 8); and

    (b)   recognises other insurance policies as reimbursement rights (if the policies satisfy the criterion in paragraph 116).

49   Where an insurance policy is in the name of a specified plan participant or a group of plan participants and the entity does not have any legal or constructive obligation to cover any loss on the policy, the entity has no obligation to pay benefits to the employees and the insurer has sole responsibility for paying the benefits. The payment of fixed premiums under such contracts is, in substance, the settlement of the employee benefit obligation, rather than an investment to meet the obligation. Consequently, the entity no longer has an asset or a liability. Therefore, an entity treats such payments as contributions to a defined contribution plan.

Post-employment benefits: defined contribution plans

50   Accounting for defined contribution plans is straightforward because the reporting entity's obligation for each period is determined by the amounts to be contributed for that period. Consequently, no actuarial assumptions are required to measure the obligation or the expense and there is no possibility of any actuarial gain or loss. Moreover, the obligations are measured on an undiscounted basis, except where they are not expected to be settled wholly before twelve months after the end of the annual reporting period in which the employees render the related service.

Recognition and measurement

51   When an employee has rendered service to an entity during a period, the entity shall recognise the contribution payable to a defined contribution plan in exchange for that service:

    (a)   as a liability (accrued expense), after deducting any contribution already paid. If the contribution already paid exceeds the contribution due for service before the end of the reporting period, an entity shall recognise that excess as an asset (prepaid expense) to the extent that the prepayment will lead to, for example, a reduction in future payments or a cash refund.

    (b)   as an expense, unless another IFRS requires or permits the inclusion of the contribution in the cost of an asset (see, for example, IAS 2 and IAS 16).

52   When contributions to a defined contribution plan are not expected to be settled wholly before twelve months after the end of the annual reporting period in which the employees render the related service, they shall be discounted using the discount rate specified in paragraph 83.

Disclosure

53   An entity shall disclose the amount recognised as an expense for defined contribution plans.

54   Where required by IAS 24 an entity discloses information about contributions to defined contribution plans for key management personnel.

Post-employment benefits: defined benefit plans

55   Accounting for defined benefit plans is complex because actuarial assumptions are required to measure the obligation and the expense and there is a possibility of actuarial gains and losses. Moreover, the obligations are measured on a discounted basis because they may be settled many years after the employees render the related service.

Recognition and measurement

56 Defined benefit plans may be unfunded, or they may be wholly or partly funded by contributions by an entity, and sometimes its employees, into an entity, or fund, that is legally separate from the reporting entity and from which the employee benefits are paid. The payment of funded benefits when they fall due depends not only on the financial position and the investment performance of the fund but also on an entity's ability, and willingness, to make good any shortfall in the fund's assets. Therefore, the entity is, in substance, underwriting the actuarial and investment risks associated with the plan. Consequently, the expense recognised for a defined benefit plan is not necessarily the amount of the contribution due for the period.

57 Accounting by an entity for defined benefit plans involves the following steps:

  (a) determining the deficit or surplus. This involves:

     (i) using an actuarial technique, the projected unit credit method, to make a reliable estimate of the ultimate cost to the entity of the benefit that employees have earned in return for their service in the current and prior periods (see paragraphs 67–69). This requires an entity to determine how much benefit is attributable to the current and prior periods (see paragraphs 70–74) and to make estimates (actuarial assumptions) about demographic variables (such as employee turnover and mortality) and financial variables (such as future increases in salaries and medical costs) that will affect the cost of the benefit (see paragraphs 75–98).

     (ii) discounting that benefit in order to determine the present value of the defined benefit obligation and the current service cost (see paragraphs 67–69 and 83–86).

     (iii) deducting the fair value of any plan assets (see paragraphs 113–115) from the present value of the defined benefit obligation.

  (b) determining the amount of the net defined benefit liability (asset) as the amount of the deficit or surplus determined in (a), adjusted for any effect of limiting a net defined benefit asset to the asset ceiling (see paragraph 64).

  (c) determining amounts to be recognised in profit or loss:

     (i) current service cost (see paragraphs 70–74 and paragraph 122A).

     (ii) any past service cost and gain or loss on settlement (see paragraphs 99–112).

     (iii) net interest on the net defined benefit liability (asset) (see paragraphs 123–126).

  (d) determining the remeasurements of the net defined benefit liability (asset), to be recognised in other comprehensive income, comprising:

      (i)   actuarial gains and losses (see paragraphs 128 and 129);

      (ii)   return on plan assets, excluding amounts included in net interest on the net defined benefit liability (asset) (see paragraph 130); and

      (iii)   any change in the effect of the asset ceiling (see paragraph 64), excluding amounts included in net interest on the net defined benefit liability (asset).

Where an entity has more than one defined benefit plan, the entity applies these procedures for each material plan separately.

58   **An entity shall determine the net defined benefit liability (asset) with sufficient regularity that the amounts recognised in the financial statements do not differ materially from the amounts that would be determined at the end of the reporting period.**

59   This Standard encourages, but does not require, an entity to involve a qualified actuary in the measurement of all material post-employment benefit obligations. For practical reasons, an entity may request a qualified actuary to carry out a detailed valuation of the obligation before the end of the reporting period. Nevertheless, the results of that valuation are updated for any material transactions and other material changes in circumstances (including changes in market prices and interest rates) up to the end of the reporting period.

60   In some cases, estimates, averages and computational short cuts may provide a reliable approximation of the detailed computations illustrated in this Standard.

Accounting for the constructive obligation

61   **An entity shall account not only for its legal obligation under the formal terms of a defined benefit plan, but also for any constructive obligation that arises from the entity's informal practices. Informal practices give rise to a constructive obligation where the entity has no realistic alternative but to pay employee benefits. An example of a constructive obligation is where a change in the entity's informal practices would cause unacceptable damage to its relationship with employees.**

62   The formal terms of a defined benefit plan may permit an entity to terminate its obligation under the plan. Nevertheless, it is usually difficult for an entity to terminate its obligation under a plan (without payment) if employees are to be retained. Therefore, in the absence of evidence to the contrary, accounting for post-employment benefits assumes that an entity that is currently promising such benefits will continue to do so over the remaining working lives of employees.

Statement of financial position

63   **An entity shall recognise the net defined benefit liability (asset) in the statement of financial position.**

                                      © IFRS Foundation

64   When an entity has a surplus in a defined benefit plan, it shall measure the net defined benefit asset at the lower of:

(a)   the surplus in the defined benefit plan; and

(b)   the asset ceiling, determined using the discount rate specified in paragraph 83.

65   A net defined benefit asset may arise where a defined benefit plan has been overfunded or where actuarial gains have arisen. An entity recognises a net defined benefit asset in such cases because:

(a)   the entity controls a resource, which is the ability to use the surplus to generate future benefits;

(b)   that control is a result of past events (contributions paid by the entity and service rendered by the employee); and

(c)   future economic benefits are available to the entity in the form of a reduction in future contributions or a cash refund, either directly to the entity or indirectly to another plan in deficit. The asset ceiling is the present value of those future benefits.

Recognition and measurement: present value of defined benefit obligations and current service cost

66   The ultimate cost of a defined benefit plan may be influenced by many variables, such as final salaries, employee turnover and mortality, employee contributions and medical cost trends. The ultimate cost of the plan is uncertain and this uncertainty is likely to persist over a long period of time. In order to measure the present value of the post-employment benefit obligations and the related current service cost, it is necessary:

(a)   to apply an actuarial valuation method (see paragraphs 67–69);

(b)   to attribute benefit to periods of service (see paragraphs 70–74); and

(c)   to make actuarial assumptions (see paragraphs 75–98).

Actuarial valuation method

67   An entity shall use the projected unit credit method to determine the present value of its defined benefit obligations and the related current service cost and, where applicable, past service cost.

68   The projected unit credit method (sometimes known as the accrued benefit method pro-rated on service or as the benefit/years of service method) sees each period of service as giving rise to an additional unit of benefit entitlement (see paragraphs 70–74) and measures each unit separately to build up the final obligation (see paragraphs 75–98).

Example illustrating paragraph 68

A lump sum benefit is payable on termination of service and equal to
1 per cent of final salary for each year of service. The salary in year 1 is
CU10,000 and is assumed to increase at 7 per cent (compound) each year.
The discount rate used is 10 per cent per year. The following table shows
how the obligation builds up for an employee who is expected to leave at the
end of year 5, assuming that there are no changes in actuarial assumptions.
For simplicity, this example ignores the additional adjustment needed to
reflect the probability that the employee may leave the entity at an earlier or
later date.

Year	1	2	3	4	5
	CU	CU	CU	CU	CU
Benefit attributed to:					
– prior years	0	131	262	393	524
– current year (1% of final salary)	131	131	131	131	131
– current and prior years	131	262	393	524	655
Opening obligation	–	89	196	324	476
Interest at 10%	–	9	20	33	48
Current service cost	89	98	108	119	131
Closing obligation	89	196	324	476	655

Note:

1   *The opening obligation is the present value of the benefit attributed to prior years.*

2   *The current service cost is the present value of the benefit attributed to the current year.*

3   *The closing obligation is the present value of the benefit attributed to current and prior years.*

---

69   An entity discounts the whole of a post-employment benefit obligation, even if
part of the obligation is expected to be settled before twelve months after the
reporting period.

Attributing benefit to periods of service

70   In determining the present value of its defined benefit obligations and the
related current service cost and, where applicable, past service cost, an
entity shall attribute benefit to periods of service under the plan's benefit
formula. However, if an employee's service in later years will lead to a

materially higher level of benefit than in earlier years, an entity shall attribute benefit on a straight-line basis from:

(a)   the date when service by the employee first leads to benefits under the plan (whether or not the benefits are conditional on further service) until

(b)   the date when further service by the employee will lead to no material amount of further benefits under the plan, other than from further salary increases.

71   The projected unit credit method requires an entity to attribute benefit to the current period (in order to determine current service cost) and the current and prior periods (in order to determine the present value of defined benefit obligations). An entity attributes benefit to periods in which the obligation to provide post-employment benefits arises. That obligation arises as employees render services in return for post-employment benefits that an entity expects to pay in future reporting periods. Actuarial techniques allow an entity to measure that obligation with sufficient reliability to justify recognition of a liability.

Examples illustrating paragraph 71
1   A defined benefit plan provides a lump sum benefit of CU100 payable on retirement for each year of service.
A benefit of CU100 is attributed to each year. The current service cost is the present value of CU100. The present value of the defined benefit obligation is the present value of CU100, multiplied by the number of years of service up to the end of the reporting period.
If the benefit is payable immediately when the employee leaves the entity, the current service cost and the present value of the defined benefit obligation reflect the date at which the employee is expected to leave. Thus, because of the effect of discounting, they are less than the amounts that would be determined if the employee left at the end of the reporting period.
2   A plan provides a monthly pension of 0.2 per cent of final salary for each year of service. The pension is payable from the age of 65.
Benefit equal to the present value, at the expected retirement date, of a monthly pension of 0.2 per cent of the estimated final salary payable from the expected retirement date until the expected date of death is attributed to each year of service. The current service cost is the present value of that benefit. The present value of the defined benefit obligation is the present value of monthly pension payments of 0.2 per cent of final salary, multiplied by the number of years of service up to the end of the reporting period. The current service cost and the present value of the defined benefit obligation are discounted because pension payments begin at the age of 65.

72   Employee service gives rise to an obligation under a defined benefit plan even if the benefits are conditional on future employment (in other words they are not vested). Employee service before the vesting date gives rise to a constructive obligation because, at the end of each successive reporting

period, the amount of future service that an employee will have to render before becoming entitled to the benefit is reduced. In measuring its defined benefit obligation, an entity considers the probability that some employees may not satisfy any vesting requirements. Similarly, although some post-employment benefits, for example, post-employment medical benefits, become payable only if a specified event occurs when an employee is no longer employed, an obligation is created when the employee renders service that will provide entitlement to the benefit if the specified event occurs. The probability that the specified event will occur affects the measurement of the obligation, but does not determine whether the obligation exists.

Examples illustrating paragraph 72

1   A plan pays a benefit of CU100 for each year of service. The benefits vest after ten years of service.

A benefit of CU100 is attributed to each year. In each of the first ten years, the current service cost and the present value of the obligation reflect the probability that the employee may not complete ten years of service.

2   A plan pays a benefit of CU100 for each year of service, excluding service before the age of 25. The benefits vest immediately.

No benefit is attributed to service before the age of 25 because service before that date does not lead to benefits (conditional or unconditional). A benefit of CU100 is attributed to each subsequent year.

---

73   The obligation increases until the date when further service by the employee will lead to no material amount of further benefits. Therefore, all benefit is attributed to periods ending on or before that date. Benefit is attributed to individual accounting periods under the plan's benefit formula. However, if an employee's service in later years will lead to a materially higher level of benefit than in earlier years, an entity attributes benefit on a straight-line basis until the date when further service by the employee will lead to no material amount of further benefits. That is because the employee's service throughout the entire period will ultimately lead to benefit at that higher level.

Examples illustrating paragraph 73

1   A plan pays a lump sum benefit of CU1,000 that vests after ten years of service. The plan provides no further benefit for subsequent service.

A benefit of CU100 (CU1,000 divided by ten) is attributed to each of the first ten years.

The current service cost in each of the first ten years reflects the probability that the employee may not complete ten years of service. No benefit is attributed to subsequent years.

continued...

...continued

Examples illustrating paragraph 73

2   A plan pays a lump sum retirement benefit of CU2,000 to all employees who are still employed at the age of 55 after twenty years of service, or who are still employed at the age of 65, regardless of their length of service.

For employees who join before the age of 35, service first leads to benefits under the plan at the age of 35 (an employee could leave at the age of 30 and return at the age of 33, with no effect on the amount or timing of benefits). Those benefits are conditional on further service. Also, service beyond the age of 55 will lead to no material amount of further benefits. For these employees, the entity attributes benefit of CU100 (CU2,000 divided by twenty) to each year from the age of 35 to the age of 55.

For employees who join between the ages of 35 and 45, service beyond twenty years will lead to no material amount of further benefits. For these employees, the entity attributes benefit of 100 (2,000 divided by twenty) to each of the first twenty years.

For an employee who joins at the age of 55, service beyond ten years will lead to no material amount of further benefits. For this employee, the entity attributes benefit of CU200 (CU2,000 divided by ten) to each of the first ten years.

For all employees, the current service cost and the present value of the obligation reflect the probability that the employee may not complete the necessary period of service.

3   A post-employment medical plan reimburses 40 per cent of an employee's post-employment medical costs if the employee leaves after more than ten and less than twenty years of service and 50 per cent of those costs if the employee leaves after twenty or more years of service.

Under the plan's benefit formula, the entity attributes 4 per cent of the present value of the expected medical costs (40 per cent divided by ten) to each of the first ten years and 1 per cent (10 per cent divided by ten) to each of the second ten years. The current service cost in each year reflects the probability that the employee may not complete the necessary period of service to earn part or all of the benefits. For employees expected to leave within ten years, no benefit is attributed.

continued...

...continued

Examples illustrating paragraph 73

4   A post-employment medical plan reimburses 10 per cent of an employee's post-employment medical costs if the employee leaves after more than ten and less than twenty years of service and 50 per cent of those costs if the employee leaves after twenty or more years of service.

Service in later years will lead to a materially higher level of benefit than in earlier years. Therefore, for employees expected to leave after twenty or more years, the entity attributes benefit on a straight-line basis under paragraph 71. Service beyond twenty years will lead to no material amount of further benefits. Therefore, the benefit attributed to each of the first twenty years is 2.5 per cent of the present value of the expected medical costs (50 per cent divided by twenty).

For employees expected to leave between ten and twenty years, the benefit attributed to each of the first ten years is 1 per cent of the present value of the expected medical costs.

For these employees, no benefit is attributed to service between the end of the tenth year and the estimated date of leaving.

For employees expected to leave within ten years, no benefit is attributed.

---

74   Where the amount of a benefit is a constant proportion of final salary for each year of service, future salary increases will affect the amount required to settle the obligation that exists for service before the end of the reporting period, but do not create an additional obligation. Therefore:

(a)   for the purpose of paragraph 70(b), salary increases do not lead to further benefits, even though the amount of the benefits is dependent on final salary; and

(b)   the amount of benefit attributed to each period is a constant proportion of the salary to which the benefit is linked.

Example illustrating paragraph 74

Employees are entitled to a benefit of 3 per cent of final salary for each year of service before the age of 55.

Benefit of 3 per cent of estimated final salary is attributed to each year up to the age of 55. This is the date when further service by the employee will lead to no material amount of further benefits under the plan. No benefit is attributed to service after that age.

Actuarial assumptions

75   **Actuarial assumptions shall be unbiased and mutually compatible.**

76   Actuarial assumptions are an entity's best estimates of the variables that will determine the ultimate cost of providing post-employment benefits. Actuarial assumptions comprise:

(a) demographic assumptions about the future characteristics of current and former employees (and their dependants) who are eligible for benefits. Demographic assumptions deal with matters such as:

    (i) mortality (see paragraphs 81 and 82);

    (ii) rates of employee turnover, disability and early retirement;

    (iii) the proportion of plan members with dependants who will be eligible for benefits;

    (iv) the proportion of plan members who will select each form of payment option available under the plan terms; and

    (v) claim rates under medical plans.

(b) financial assumptions, dealing with items such as:

    (i) the discount rate (see paragraphs 83–86);

    (ii) benefit levels, excluding any cost of the benefits to be met by employees, and future salary (see paragraphs 87–95);

    (iii) in the case of medical benefits, future medical costs, including claim handling costs (ie the costs that will be incurred in processing and resolving claims, including legal and adjuster's fees) (see paragraphs 96–98); and

    (iv) taxes payable by the plan on contributions relating to service before the reporting date or on benefits resulting from that service.

77 Actuarial assumptions are unbiased if they are neither imprudent nor excessively conservative.

78 Actuarial assumptions are mutually compatible if they reflect the economic relationships between factors such as inflation, rates of salary increase and discount rates. For example, all assumptions that depend on a particular inflation level (such as assumptions about interest rates and salary and benefit increases) in any given future period assume the same inflation level in that period.

79 An entity determines the discount rate and other financial assumptions in nominal (stated) terms, unless estimates in real (inflation-adjusted) terms are more reliable, for example, in a hyperinflationary economy (see IAS 29 *Financial Reporting in Hyperinflationary Economies*), or where the benefit is index-linked and there is a deep market in index-linked bonds of the same currency and term.

80 **Financial assumptions shall be based on market expectations, at the end of the reporting period, for the period over which the obligations are to be settled.**

Actuarial assumptions: mortality

81   An entity shall determine its mortality assumptions by reference to its best estimate of the mortality of plan members both during and after employment.

82   In order to estimate the ultimate cost of the benefit an entity takes into consideration expected changes in mortality, for example by modifying standard mortality tables with estimates of mortality improvements.

Actuarial assumptions: discount rate

83   The rate used to discount post-employment benefit obligations (both funded and unfunded) shall be determined by reference to market yields at the end of the reporting period on high quality corporate bonds. For currencies for which there is no deep market in such high quality corporate bonds, the market yields (at the end of the reporting period) on government bonds denominated in that currency shall be used. The currency and term of the corporate bonds or government bonds shall be consistent with the currency and estimated term of the post-employment benefit obligations.

84   One actuarial assumption that has a material effect is the discount rate. The discount rate reflects the time value of money but not the actuarial or investment risk. Furthermore, the discount rate does not reflect the entity-specific credit risk borne by the entity's creditors, nor does it reflect the risk that future experience may differ from actuarial assumptions.

85   The discount rate reflects the estimated timing of benefit payments. In practice, an entity often achieves this by applying a single weighted average discount rate that reflects the estimated timing and amount of benefit payments and the currency in which the benefits are to be paid.

86   In some cases, there may be no deep market in bonds with a sufficiently long maturity to match the estimated maturity of all the benefit payments. In such cases, an entity uses current market rates of the appropriate term to discount shorter-term payments, and estimates the discount rate for longer maturities by extrapolating current market rates along the yield curve. The total present value of a defined benefit obligation is unlikely to be particularly sensitive to the discount rate applied to the portion of benefits that is payable beyond the final maturity of the available corporate or government bonds.

Actuarial assumptions: salaries, benefits and medical costs

87   An entity shall measure its defined benefit obligations on a basis that reflects:

    (a)   the benefits set out in the terms of the plan (or resulting from any constructive obligation that goes beyond those terms) at the end of the reporting period;

    (b)   any estimated future salary increases that affect the benefits payable;

(c)   the effect of any limit on the employer's share of the cost of the future benefits;

(d)   contributions from employees or third parties that reduce the ultimate cost to the entity of those benefits; and

(e)   estimated future changes in the level of any state benefits that affect the benefits payable under a defined benefit plan, if, and only if, either:

(i)   those changes were enacted before the end of the reporting period; or

(ii)   historical data, or other reliable evidence, indicate that those state benefits will change in some predictable manner, for example, in line with future changes in general price levels or general salary levels.

88   Actuarial assumptions reflect future benefit changes that are set out in the formal terms of a plan (or a constructive obligation that goes beyond those terms) at the end of the reporting period. This is the case if, for example:

(a)   the entity has a history of increasing benefits, for example, to mitigate the effects of inflation, and there is no indication that this practice will change in the future;

(b)   the entity is obliged, by either the formal terms of a plan (or a constructive obligation that goes beyond those terms) or legislation, to use any surplus in the plan for the benefit of plan participants (see paragraph 108(c)); or

(c)   benefits vary in response to a performance target or other criteria. For example, the terms of the plan may state that it will pay reduced benefits or require additional contributions from employees if the plan assets are insufficient. The measurement of the obligation reflects the best estimate of the effect of the performance target or other criteria.

89   Actuarial assumptions do not reflect future benefit changes that are not set out in the formal terms of the plan (or a constructive obligation) at the end of the reporting period. Such changes will result in:

(a)   past service cost, to the extent that they change benefits for service before the change; and

(b)   current service cost for periods after the change, to the extent that they change benefits for service after the change.

90   Estimates of future salary increases take account of inflation, seniority, promotion and other relevant factors, such as supply and demand in the employment market.

91   Some defined benefit plans limit the contributions that an entity is required to pay. The ultimate cost of the benefits takes account of the effect of a limit on contributions. The effect of a limit on contributions is determined over the shorter of:

(a)   the estimated life of the entity; and

(b)   the estimated life of the plan.

92   Some defined benefit plans require employees or third parties to contribute to the cost of the plan. Contributions by employees reduce the cost of the benefits to the entity. An entity considers whether third-party contributions reduce the cost of the benefits to the entity, or are a reimbursement right as described in paragraph 116. Contributions by employees or third parties are either set out in the formal terms of the plan (or arise from a constructive obligation that goes beyond those terms), or are discretionary. Discretionary contributions by employees or third parties reduce service cost upon payment of these contributions to the plan.

93   Contributions from employees or third parties set out in the formal terms of the plan either reduce service cost (if they are linked to service), or affect remeasurements of the net defined benefit liability (asset) (if they are not linked to service). An example of contributions that are not linked to service is when the contributions are required to reduce a deficit arising from losses on plan assets or from actuarial losses. If contributions from employees or third parties are linked to service, those contributions reduce the service cost as follows:

(a)   if the amount of the contributions is dependent on the number of years of service, an entity shall attribute the contributions to periods of service using the same attribution method required by paragraph 70 for the gross benefit (ie either using the plan's contribution formula or on a straight-line basis); or

(b)   if the amount of the contributions is independent of the number of years of service, the entity is permitted to recognise such contributions as a reduction of the service cost in the period in which the related service is rendered. Examples of contributions that are independent of the number of years of service include those that are a fixed percentage of the employee's salary, a fixed amount throughout the service period or dependent on the employee's age.

Paragraph A1 provides related application guidance.

94   For contributions from employees or third parties that are attributed to periods of service in accordance with paragraph 93(a), changes in the contributions result in:

(a)   current and past service cost (if those changes are not set out in the formal terms of a plan and do not arise from a constructive obligation); or

(b)   actuarial gains and losses (if those changes are set out in the formal terms of a plan, or arise from a constructive obligation).

95   Some post-employment benefits are linked to variables such as the level of state retirement benefits or state medical care. The measurement of such benefits reflects the best estimate of such variables, based on historical data and other reliable evidence.

96   Assumptions about medical costs shall take account of estimated future changes in the cost of medical services, resulting from both inflation and specific changes in medical costs.

97   Measurement of post-employment medical benefits requires assumptions about the level and frequency of future claims and the cost of meeting those claims. An entity estimates future medical costs on the basis of historical data about the entity's own experience, supplemented where necessary by historical data from other entities, insurance companies, medical providers or other sources. Estimates of future medical costs consider the effect of technological advances, changes in health care utilisation or delivery patterns and changes in the health status of plan participants.

98   The level and frequency of claims is particularly sensitive to the age, health status and sex of employees (and their dependants) and may be sensitive to other factors such as geographical location. Therefore, historical data are adjusted to the extent that the demographic mix of the population differs from that of the population used as a basis for the data. They are also adjusted where there is reliable evidence that historical trends will not continue.

Past service cost and gains and losses on settlement

99   When determining past service cost, or a gain or loss on settlement, an entity shall remeasure the net defined benefit liability (asset) using the current fair value of plan assets and current actuarial assumptions, including current market interest rates and other current market prices, reflecting:

(a)   the benefits offered under the plan and the plan assets before the plan amendment, curtailment or settlement; and

(b)   the benefits offered under the plan and the plan assets after the plan amendment, curtailment or settlement.

100   An entity need not distinguish between past service cost resulting from a plan amendment, past service cost resulting from a curtailment and a gain or loss on settlement if these transactions occur together. In some cases, a plan amendment occurs before a settlement, such as when an entity changes the benefits under the plan and settles the amended benefits later. In those cases an entity recognises past service cost before any gain or loss on settlement.

101   A settlement occurs together with a plan amendment and curtailment if a plan is terminated with the result that the obligation is settled and the plan ceases to exist. However, the termination of a plan is not a settlement if the plan is replaced by a new plan that offers benefits that are, in substance, the same.

101A   When a plan amendment, curtailment or settlement occurs, an entity shall recognise and measure any past service cost, or a gain or loss on settlement, in accordance with paragraphs 99–101 and paragraphs 102–112. In doing so, an entity shall not consider the effect of the asset ceiling. An entity shall then determine the effect of the asset ceiling after the plan amendment, curtailment or settlement and shall recognise any change in that effect in accordance with paragraph 57(d).

Past service cost

102 Past service cost is the change in the present value of the defined benefit obligation resulting from a plan amendment or curtailment.

103 **An entity shall recognise past service cost as an expense at the earlier of the following dates:**

   (a)   **when the plan amendment or curtailment occurs; and**

   (b)   **when the entity recognises related restructuring costs (see IAS 37) or termination benefits (see paragraph 165).**

104 A plan amendment occurs when an entity introduces, or withdraws, a defined benefit plan or changes the benefits payable under an existing defined benefit plan.

105 A curtailment occurs when an entity significantly reduces the number of employees covered by a plan. A curtailment may arise from an isolated event, such as the closing of a plant, discontinuance of an operation or termination or suspension of a plan.

106 Past service cost may be either positive (when benefits are introduced or changed so that the present value of the defined benefit obligation increases) or negative (when benefits are withdrawn or changed so that the present value of the defined benefit obligation decreases).

107 Where an entity reduces benefits payable under an existing defined benefit plan and, at the same time, increases other benefits payable under the plan for the same employees, the entity treats the change as a single net change.

108 Past service cost excludes:

   (a)   the effect of differences between actual and previously assumed salary increases on the obligation to pay benefits for service in prior years (there is no past service cost because actuarial assumptions allow for projected salaries);

   (b)   underestimates and overestimates of discretionary pension increases when an entity has a constructive obligation to grant such increases (there is no past service cost because actuarial assumptions allow for such increases);

   (c)   estimates of benefit improvements that result from actuarial gains or from the return on plan assets that have been recognised in the financial statements if the entity is obliged, by either the formal terms of a plan (or a constructive obligation that goes beyond those terms) or legislation, to use any surplus in the plan for the benefit of plan participants, even if the benefit increase has not yet been formally awarded (there is no past service cost because the resulting increase in the obligation is an actuarial loss, see paragraph 88); and

(d)   the increase in vested benefits (ie benefits that are not conditional on future employment, see paragraph 72) when, in the absence of new or improved benefits, employees complete vesting requirements (there is no past service cost because the entity recognised the estimated cost of benefits as current service cost as the service was rendered).

Gains and losses on settlement

109   The gain or loss on a settlement is the difference between:

(a)   the present value of the defined benefit obligation being settled, as determined on the date of settlement; and

(b)   the settlement price, including any plan assets transferred and any payments made directly by the entity in connection with the settlement.

110   **An entity shall recognise a gain or loss on the settlement of a defined benefit plan when the settlement occurs.**

111   A settlement occurs when an entity enters into a transaction that eliminates all further legal or constructive obligation for part or all of the benefits provided under a defined benefit plan (other than a payment of benefits to, or on behalf of, employees in accordance with the terms of the plan and included in the actuarial assumptions). For example, a one-off transfer of significant employer obligations under the plan to an insurance company through the purchase of an insurance policy is a settlement; a lump sum cash payment, under the terms of the plan, to plan participants in exchange for their rights to receive specified post-employment benefits is not.

112   In some cases, an entity acquires an insurance policy to fund some or all of the employee benefits relating to employee service in the current and prior periods. The acquisition of such a policy is not a settlement if the entity retains a legal or constructive obligation (see paragraph 46) to pay further amounts if the insurer does not pay the employee benefits specified in the insurance policy. Paragraphs 116–119 deal with the recognition and measurement of reimbursement rights under insurance policies that are not plan assets.

Recognition and measurement: plan assets

Fair value of plan assets

113   The fair value of any plan assets is deducted from the present value of the defined benefit obligation in determining the deficit or surplus.

114   Plan assets exclude unpaid contributions due from the reporting entity to the fund, as well as any non-transferable financial instruments issued by the entity and held by the fund. Plan assets are reduced by any liabilities of the fund that do not relate to employee benefits, for example, trade and other payables and liabilities resulting from derivative financial instruments.

115   Where plan assets include qualifying insurance policies that exactly match the amount and timing of some or all of the benefits payable under the plan, the fair value of those insurance policies is deemed to be the present value of the related obligations (subject to any reduction required if the amounts receivable under the insurance policies are not recoverable in full).

Reimbursements

116   When, and only when, it is virtually certain that another party will reimburse some or all of the expenditure required to settle a defined benefit obligation, an entity shall:

(a)   recognise its right to reimbursement as a separate asset. The entity shall measure the asset at fair value.

(b)   disaggregate and recognise changes in the fair value of its right to reimbursement in the same way as for changes in the fair value of plan assets (see paragraphs 124 and 125). The components of defined benefit cost recognised in accordance with paragraph 120 may be recognised net of amounts relating to changes in the carrying amount of the right to reimbursement.

117   Sometimes, an entity is able to look to another party, such as an insurer, to pay part or all of the expenditure required to settle a defined benefit obligation. Qualifying insurance policies, as defined in paragraph 8, are plan assets. An entity accounts for qualifying insurance policies in the same way as for all other plan assets and paragraph 116 is not relevant (see paragraphs 46–49 and 115).

118   When an insurance policy held by an entity is not a qualifying insurance policy, that insurance policy is not a plan asset. Paragraph 116 is relevant to such cases: the entity recognises its right to reimbursement under the insurance policy as a separate asset, rather than as a deduction in determining the defined benefit deficit or surplus. Paragraph 140(b) requires the entity to disclose a brief description of the link between the reimbursement right and the related obligation.

119   If the right to reimbursement arises under an insurance policy that exactly matches the amount and timing of some or all of the benefits payable under a defined benefit plan, the fair value of the reimbursement right is deemed to be the present value of the related obligation (subject to any reduction required if the reimbursement is not recoverable in full).

Components of defined benefit cost

120   An entity shall recognise the components of defined benefit cost, except to the extent that another IFRS requires or permits their inclusion in the cost of an asset, as follows:

(a)   service cost (see paragraphs 66–112 and paragraph 122A) in profit or loss;

(b)   net interest on the net defined benefit liability (asset) (see paragraphs 123–126) in profit or loss; and

(c)   remeasurements of the net defined benefit liability (asset) (see paragraphs 127–130) in other comprehensive income.

121   Other IFRSs require the inclusion of some employee benefit costs within the cost of assets, such as inventories and property, plant and equipment (see IAS 2 and IAS 16). Any post-employment benefit costs included in the cost of such assets include the appropriate proportion of the components listed in paragraph 120.

122   Remeasurements of the net defined benefit liability (asset) recognised in other comprehensive income shall not be reclassified to profit or loss in a subsequent period. However, the entity may transfer those amounts recognised in other comprehensive income within equity.

Current service cost

122A   An entity shall determine current service cost using actuarial assumptions determined at the start of the annual reporting period. However, if an entity remeasures the net defined benefit liability (asset) in accordance with paragraph 99, it shall determine current service cost for the remainder of the annual reporting period after the plan amendment, curtailment or settlement using the actuarial assumptions used to remeasure the net defined benefit liability (asset) in accordance with paragraph 99(b).

Net interest on the net defined benefit liability (asset)

123   An entity shall determine net interest on the net defined benefit liability (asset) by multiplying the net defined benefit liability (asset) by the discount rate specified in paragraph 83.

123A   To determine net interest in accordance with paragraph 123, an entity shall use the net defined benefit liability (asset) and the discount rate determined at the start of the annual reporting period. However, if an entity remeasures the net defined benefit liability (asset) in accordance with paragraph 99, the entity shall determine net interest for the remainder of the annual reporting period after the plan amendment, curtailment or settlement using:

(a)   the net defined benefit liability (asset) determined in accordance with paragraph 99(b); and

(b)   the discount rate used to remeasure the net defined benefit liability (asset) in accordance with paragraph 99(b).

In applying paragraph 123A, the entity shall also take into account any changes in the net defined benefit liability (asset) during the period resulting from contributions or benefit payments.

124   Net interest on the net defined benefit liability (asset) can be viewed as comprising interest income on plan assets, interest cost on the defined benefit obligation and interest on the effect of the asset ceiling mentioned in paragraph 64.

125   Interest income on plan assets is a component of the return on plan assets, and is determined by multiplying the fair value of the plan assets by the discount rate specified in paragraph 123A. An entity shall determine the fair value of the plan assets at the start of the annual reporting period. However, if an entity remeasures the net defined benefit liability (asset) in accordance with paragraph 99, the entity shall determine interest income for the remainder of the annual reporting period after the plan amendment, curtailment or settlement using the plan assets used to remeasure the net defined benefit liability (asset) in accordance with paragraph 99(b). In applying paragraph 125, the entity shall also take into account any changes in the plan assets held during the period resulting from contributions or benefit payments. The difference between the interest income on plan assets and the return on plan assets is included in the remeasurement of the net defined benefit liability (asset).

126   Interest on the effect of the asset ceiling is part of the total change in the effect of the asset ceiling, and is determined by multiplying the effect of the asset ceiling by the discount rate specified in paragraph 123A. An entity shall determine the effect of the asset ceiling at the start of the annual reporting period. However, if an entity remeasures the net defined benefit liability (asset) in accordance with paragraph 99, the entity shall determine interest on the effect of the asset ceiling for the remainder of the annual reporting period after the plan amendment, curtailment or settlement taking into account any change in the effect of the asset ceiling determined in accordance with paragraph 101A. The difference between interest on the effect of the asset ceiling and the total change in the effect of the asset ceiling is included in the remeasurement of the net defined benefit liability (asset).

Remeasurements of the net defined benefit liability (asset)

127   Remeasurements of the net defined benefit liability (asset) comprise:

(a)   actuarial gains and losses (see paragraphs 128 and 129);

(b)   the return on plan assets (see paragraph 130), excluding amounts included in net interest on the net defined benefit liability (asset) (see paragraph 125); and

(c)   any change in the effect of the asset ceiling, excluding amounts included in net interest on the net defined benefit liability (asset) (see paragraph 126).

128   Actuarial gains and losses result from increases or decreases in the present value of the defined benefit obligation because of changes in actuarial assumptions and experience adjustments. Causes of actuarial gains and losses include, for example:

(a)   unexpectedly high or low rates of employee turnover, early retirement or mortality or of increases in salaries, benefits (if the formal or constructive terms of a plan provide for inflationary benefit increases) or medical costs;

(b)   the effect of changes to assumptions concerning benefit payment options;

(c)   the effect of changes in estimates of future employee turnover, early retirement or mortality or of increases in salaries, benefits (if the formal or constructive terms of a plan provide for inflationary benefit increases) or medical costs; and

(d)   the effect of changes in the discount rate.

129   Actuarial gains and losses do not include changes in the present value of the defined benefit obligation because of the introduction, amendment, curtailment or settlement of the defined benefit plan, or changes to the benefits payable under the defined benefit plan. Such changes result in past service cost or gains or losses on settlement.

130   In determining the return on plan assets, an entity deducts the costs of managing the plan assets and any tax payable by the plan itself, other than tax included in the actuarial assumptions used to measure the defined benefit obligation (paragraph 76). Other administration costs are not deducted from the return on plan assets.

Presentation

Offset

131   An entity shall offset an asset relating to one plan against a liability relating to another plan when, and only when, the entity:

(a)   has a legally enforceable right to use a surplus in one plan to settle obligations under the other plan; and

(b)   intends either to settle the obligations on a net basis, or to realise the surplus in one plan and settle its obligation under the other plan simultaneously.

132   The offsetting criteria are similar to those established for financial instruments in IAS 32 *Financial Instruments: Presentation*.

Current/non-current distinction

133   Some entities distinguish current assets and liabilities from non-current assets and liabilities. This Standard does not specify whether an entity should distinguish current and non-current portions of assets and liabilities arising from post-employment benefits.

Components of defined benefit cost

134   Paragraph 120 requires an entity to recognise service cost and net interest on the net defined benefit liability (asset) in profit or loss. This Standard does not specify how an entity should present service cost and net interest on the net defined benefit liability (asset). An entity presents those components in accordance with IAS 1.

Disclosure

135   An entity shall disclose information that:

(a)   explains the characteristics of its defined benefit plans and risks associated with them (see paragraph 139);

(b)   identifies and explains the amounts in its financial statements arising from its defined benefit plans (see paragraphs 140–144); and

(c)   describes how its defined benefit plans may affect the amount, timing and uncertainty of the entity's future cash flows (see paragraphs 145–147).

136   To meet the objectives in paragraph 135, an entity shall consider all the following:

(a)   the level of detail necessary to satisfy the disclosure requirements;

(b)   how much emphasis to place on each of the various requirements;

(c)   how much aggregation or disaggregation to undertake; and

(d)   whether users of financial statements need additional information to evaluate the quantitative information disclosed.

137   If the disclosures provided in accordance with the requirements in this Standard and other IFRSs are insufficient to meet the objectives in paragraph 135, an entity shall disclose additional information necessary to meet those objectives. For example, an entity may present an analysis of the present value of the defined benefit obligation that distinguishes the nature, characteristics and risks of the obligation. Such a disclosure could distinguish:

(a)   between amounts owing to active members, deferred members, and pensioners.

(b)   between vested benefits and accrued but not vested benefits.

(c)   between conditional benefits, amounts attributable to future salary increases and other benefits.

138   An entity shall assess whether all or some disclosures should be disaggregated to distinguish plans or groups of plans with materially different risks. For example, an entity may disaggregate disclosure about plans showing one or more of the following features:

(a)   different geographical locations.

(b)   different characteristics such as flat salary pension plans, final salary pension plans or post-employment medical plans.

(c)   different regulatory environments.

(d)   different reporting segments.

(e)   different funding arrangements (eg wholly unfunded, wholly or partly funded).

Characteristics of defined benefit plans and risks associated with them

139   An entity shall disclose:

(a)   information about the characteristics of its defined benefit plans, including:

(i)   the nature of the benefits provided by the plan (eg final salary defined benefit plan or contribution-based plan with guarantee).

(ii)   a description of the regulatory framework in which the plan operates, for example the level of any minimum funding requirements, and any effect of the regulatory framework on the plan, such as the asset ceiling (see paragraph 64).

(iii)   a description of any other entity's responsibilities for the governance of the plan, for example responsibilities of trustees or of board members of the plan.

(b)   a description of the risks to which the plan exposes the entity, focused on any unusual, entity-specific or plan-specific risks, and of any significant concentrations of risk. For example, if plan assets are invested primarily in one class of investments, eg property, the plan may expose the entity to a concentration of property market risk.

(c)   a description of any plan amendments, curtailments and settlements.

Explanation of amounts in the financial statements

140   An entity shall provide a reconciliation from the opening balance to the closing balance for each of the following, if applicable:

(a)   the net defined benefit liability (asset), showing separate reconciliations for:

(i)   plan assets.

(ii)   the present value of the defined benefit obligation.

(iii)   the effect of the asset ceiling.

(b)   any reimbursement rights. An entity shall also describe the relationship between any reimbursement right and the related obligation.

141   Each reconciliation listed in paragraph 140 shall show each of the following, if applicable:

(a)   current service cost.

(b)   interest income or expense.

(c)   remeasurements of the net defined benefit liability (asset), showing separately:

(i)   the return on plan assets, excluding amounts included in interest in (b).

(ii)   actuarial gains and losses arising from changes in demographic assumptions (see paragraph 76(a)).

(iii)   actuarial gains and losses arising from changes in financial assumptions (see paragraph 76(b)).

(iv)   changes in the effect of limiting a net defined benefit asset to the asset ceiling, excluding amounts included in interest in (b). An entity shall also disclose how it determined the maximum economic benefit available, ie whether those benefits would be in the form of refunds, reductions in future contributions or a combination of both.

(d)   past service cost and gains and losses arising from settlements. As permitted by paragraph 100, past service cost and gains and losses arising from settlements need not be distinguished if they occur together.

(e)   the effect of changes in foreign exchange rates.

(f)   contributions to the plan, showing separately those by the employer and by plan participants.

(g)   payments from the plan, showing separately the amount paid in respect of any settlements.

(h)   the effects of business combinations and disposals.

142   An entity shall disaggregate the fair value of the plan assets into classes that distinguish the nature and risks of those assets, subdividing each class of plan asset into those that have a quoted market price in an active market (as defined in IFRS 13 *Fair Value Measurement*) and those that do not. For example, and considering the level of disclosure discussed in paragraph 136, an entity could distinguish between:

(a)   cash and cash equivalents;

(b)   equity instruments (segregated by industry type, company size, geography etc);

(c)   debt instruments (segregated by type of issuer, credit quality, geography etc);

(d)   real estate (segregated by geography etc);

(e)   derivatives (segregated by type of underlying risk in the contract, for example, interest rate contracts, foreign exchange contracts, equity contracts, credit contracts, longevity swaps etc);

(f)   investment funds (segregated by type of fund);

(g)   asset-backed securities; and

(h)   structured debt.

143   An entity shall disclose the fair value of the entity's own transferable financial instruments held as plan assets, and the fair value of plan assets that are property occupied by, or other assets used by, the entity.

144   An entity shall disclose the significant actuarial assumptions used to determine the present value of the defined benefit obligation (see paragraph 76). Such disclosure shall be in absolute terms (eg as an absolute percentage, and not just as a margin between different percentages and other variables). When an entity provides disclosures in total for a grouping of plans, it shall provide such disclosures in the form of weighted averages or relatively narrow ranges.

Amount, timing and uncertainty of future cash flows

145   An entity shall disclose:

   (a)   a sensitivity analysis for each significant actuarial assumption (as disclosed under paragraph 144) as of the end of the reporting period, showing how the defined benefit obligation would have been affected by changes in the relevant actuarial assumption that were reasonably possible at that date.

   (b)   the methods and assumptions used in preparing the sensitivity analyses required by (a) and the limitations of those methods.

   (c)   changes from the previous period in the methods and assumptions used in preparing the sensitivity analyses, and the reasons for such changes.

146   An entity shall disclose a description of any asset-liability matching strategies used by the plan or the entity, including the use of annuities and other techniques, such as longevity swaps, to manage risk.

147   To provide an indication of the effect of the defined benefit plan on the entity's future cash flows, an entity shall disclose:

   (a)   a description of any funding arrangements and funding policy that affect future contributions.

   (b)   the expected contributions to the plan for the next annual reporting period.

   (c)   information about the maturity profile of the defined benefit obligation. This will include the weighted average duration of the defined benefit obligation and may include other information about the distribution of the timing of benefit payments, such as a maturity analysis of the benefit payments.

Multi-employer plans

148   If an entity participates in a multi-employer defined benefit plan, it shall disclose:

(a)   a description of the funding arrangements, including the method used to determine the entity's rate of contributions and any minimum funding requirements.

(b)   a description of the extent to which the entity can be liable to the plan for other entities' obligations under the terms and conditions of the multi-employer plan.

(c)   a description of any agreed allocation of a deficit or surplus on:

     (i)   wind-up of the plan; or

     (ii)   the entity's withdrawal from the plan.

(d)   if the entity accounts for that plan as if it were a defined contribution plan in accordance with paragraph 34, it shall disclose the following, in addition to the information required by (a)–(c) and instead of the information required by paragraphs 139–147:

     (i)   the fact that the plan is a defined benefit plan.

     (ii)   the reason why sufficient information is not available to enable the entity to account for the plan as a defined benefit plan.

     (iii)   the expected contributions to the plan for the next annual reporting period.

     (iv)   information about any deficit or surplus in the plan that may affect the amount of future contributions, including the basis used to determine that deficit or surplus and the implications, if any, for the entity.

     (v)   an indication of the level of participation of the entity in the plan compared with other participating entities. Examples of measures that might provide such an indication include the entity's proportion of the total contributions to the plan or the entity's proportion of the total number of active members, retired members, and former members entitled to benefits, if that information is available.

Defined benefit plans that share risks between entities under common control

149   If an entity participates in a defined benefit plan that shares risks between entities under common control, it shall disclose:

(a)   the contractual agreement or stated policy for charging the net defined benefit cost or the fact that there is no such policy.

(b)   the policy for determining the contribution to be paid by the entity.

(c)   if the entity accounts for an allocation of the net defined benefit cost as noted in paragraph 41, all the information about the plan as a whole required by paragraphs 135–147.

(d)   if the entity accounts for the contribution payable for the period as noted in paragraph 41, the information about the plan as a whole required by paragraphs 135–137, 139, 142–144 and 147(a) and (b).

150   The information required by paragraph 149(c) and (d) can be disclosed by cross-reference to disclosures in another group entity's financial statements if:

(a)   that group entity's financial statements separately identify and disclose the information required about the plan; and

(b)   that group entity's financial statements are available to users of the financial statements on the same terms as the financial statements of the entity and at the same time as, or earlier than, the financial statements of the entity.

Disclosure requirements in other IFRSs

151   Where required by IAS 24 an entity discloses information about:

(a)   related party transactions with post-employment benefit plans; and

(b)   post-employment benefits for key management personnel.

152   Where required by IAS 37 an entity discloses information about contingent liabilities arising from post-employment benefit obligations.

Other long-term employee benefits

153   Other long-term employee benefits include items such as the following, if not expected to be settled wholly before twelve months after the end of the annual reporting period in which the employees render the related service:

(a)   long-term paid absences such as long-service or sabbatical leave;

(b)   jubilee or other long-service benefits;

(c)   long-term disability benefits;

(d)   profit-sharing and bonuses; and

(e)   deferred remuneration.

154   The measurement of other long-term employee benefits is not usually subject to the same degree of uncertainty as the measurement of post-employment benefits. For this reason, this Standard requires a simplified method of accounting for other long-term employee benefits. Unlike the accounting required for post-employment benefits, this method does not recognise remeasurements in other comprehensive income.

Recognition and measurement

155   **In recognising and measuring the surplus or deficit in an other long-term employee benefit plan, an entity shall apply paragraphs 56–98 and 113–115. An entity shall apply paragraphs 116–119 in recognising and measuring any reimbursement right.**

156   For other long-term employee benefits, an entity shall recognise the net total of the following amounts in profit or loss, except to the extent that another IFRS requires or permits their inclusion in the cost of an asset:

(a)   service cost (see paragraphs 66–112 and paragraph 122A);

(b)   net interest on the net defined benefit liability (asset) (see paragraphs 123–126); and

(c)   remeasurements of the net defined benefit liability (asset) (see paragraphs 127–130).

157   One form of other long-term employee benefit is long-term disability benefit. If the level of benefit depends on the length of service, an obligation arises when the service is rendered. Measurement of that obligation reflects the probability that payment will be required and the length of time for which payment is expected to be made. If the level of benefit is the same for any disabled employee regardless of years of service, the expected cost of those benefits is recognised when an event occurs that causes a long-term disability.

Disclosure

158   Although this Standard does not require specific disclosures about other long-term employee benefits, other IFRSs may require disclosures. For example, IAS 24 requires disclosures about employee benefits for key management personnel. IAS 1 requires disclosure of employee benefits expense.

Termination benefits

159   This Standard deals with termination benefits separately from other employee benefits because the event that gives rise to an obligation is the termination of employment rather than employee service. Termination benefits result from either an entity's decision to terminate the employment or an employee's decision to accept an entity's offer of benefits in exchange for termination of employment.

160   Termination benefits do not include employee benefits resulting from termination of employment at the request of the employee without an entity's offer, or as a result of mandatory retirement requirements, because those benefits are post-employment benefits. Some entities provide a lower level of benefit for termination of employment at the request of the employee (in substance, a post-employment benefit) than for termination of employment at the request of the entity. The difference between the benefit provided for termination of employment at the request of the employee and a higher benefit provided at the request of the entity is a termination benefit.

161   The form of the employee benefit does not determine whether it is provided in exchange for service or in exchange for termination of the employee's employment. Termination benefits are typically lump sum payments, but sometimes also include:

(a) enhancement of post-employment benefits, either indirectly through an employee benefit plan or directly.

(b) salary until the end of a specified notice period if the employee renders no further service that provides economic benefits to the entity.

162 Indicators that an employee benefit is provided in exchange for services include the following:

(a) the benefit is conditional on future service being provided (including benefits that increase if further service is provided).

(b) the benefit is provided in accordance with the terms of an employee benefit plan.

163 Some termination benefits are provided in accordance with the terms of an existing employee benefit plan. For example, they may be specified by statute, employment contract or union agreement, or may be implied as a result of the employer's past practice of providing similar benefits. As another example, if an entity makes an offer of benefits available for more than a short period, or there is more than a short period between the offer and the expected date of actual termination, the entity considers whether it has established a new employee benefit plan and hence whether the benefits offered under that plan are termination benefits or post-employment benefits. Employee benefits provided in accordance with the terms of an employee benefit plan are termination benefits if they both result from an entity's decision to terminate an employee's employment and are not conditional on future service being provided.

164 Some employee benefits are provided regardless of the reason for the employee's departure. The payment of such benefits is certain (subject to any vesting or minimum service requirements) but the timing of their payment is uncertain. Although such benefits are described in some jurisdictions as termination indemnities or termination gratuities, they are post-employment benefits rather than termination benefits, and an entity accounts for them as post-employment benefits.

Recognition

165 An entity shall recognise a liability and expense for termination benefits at the earlier of the following dates:

(a) when the entity can no longer withdraw the offer of those benefits; and

(b) when the entity recognises costs for a restructuring that is within the scope of IAS 37 and involves the payment of termination benefits.

166 For termination benefits payable as a result of an employee's decision to accept an offer of benefits in exchange for the termination of employment, the time when an entity can no longer withdraw the offer of termination benefits is the earlier of:

(a)   when the employee accepts the offer; and

(b)   when a restriction (eg a legal, regulatory or contractual requirement or other restriction) on the entity's ability to withdraw the offer takes effect. This would be when the offer is made, if the restriction existed at the time of the offer.

167   For termination benefits payable as a result of an entity's decision to terminate an employee's employment, the entity can no longer withdraw the offer when the entity has communicated to the affected employees a plan of termination meeting all of the following criteria:

(a)   Actions required to complete the plan indicate that it is unlikely that significant changes to the plan will be made.

(b)   The plan identifies the number of employees whose employment is to be terminated, their job classifications or functions and their locations (but the plan need not identify each individual employee) and the expected completion date.

(c)   The plan establishes the termination benefits that employees will receive in sufficient detail that employees can determine the type and amount of benefits they will receive when their employment is terminated.

168   When an entity recognises termination benefits, the entity may also have to account for a plan amendment or a curtailment of other employee benefits (see paragraph 103).

Measurement

169   An entity shall measure termination benefits on initial recognition, and shall measure and recognise subsequent changes, in accordance with the nature of the employee benefit, provided that if the termination benefits are an enhancement to post-employment benefits, the entity shall apply the requirements for post-employment benefits. Otherwise:

(a)   if the termination benefits are expected to be settled wholly before twelve months after the end of the annual reporting period in which the termination benefit is recognised, the entity shall apply the requirements for short-term employee benefits.

(b)   if the termination benefits are not expected to be settled wholly before twelve months after the end of the annual reporting period, the entity shall apply the requirements for other long-term employee benefits.

170   Because termination benefits are not provided in exchange for service, paragraphs 70–74 relating to the attribution of the benefit to periods of service are not relevant.

Example illustrating paragraphs 159–170

Background

As a result of a recent acquisition, an entity plans to close a factory in ten months and, at that time, terminate the employment of all of the remaining employees at the factory. Because the entity needs the expertise of the employees at the factory to complete some contracts, it announces a plan of termination as follows.

Each employee who stays and renders service until the closure of the factory will receive on the termination date a cash payment of CU30,000. Employees leaving before closure of the factory will receive CU10,000.

There are 120 employees at the factory. At the time of announcing the plan, the entity expects 20 of them to leave before closure. Therefore, the total expected cash outflows under the plan are CU3,200,000 (ie 20 × CU10,000 + 100 × CU30,000). As required by paragraph 160, the entity accounts for benefits provided in exchange for termination of employment as termination benefits and accounts for benefits provided in exchange for services as short-term employee benefits.

Termination benefits

The benefit provided in exchange for termination of employment is CU10,000. This is the amount that an entity would have to pay for terminating the employment regardless of whether the employees stay and render service until closure of the factory or they leave before closure. Even though the employees can leave before closure, the termination of all employees' employment is a result of the entity's decision to close the factory and terminate their employment (ie all employees will leave employment when the factory closes). Therefore the entity recognises a liability of CU1,200,000 (ie 120 × CU10,000) for the termination benefits provided in accordance with the employee benefit plan at the earlier of when the plan of termination is announced and when the entity recognises the restructuring costs associated with the closure of the factory.

Benefits provided in exchange for service

The incremental benefits that employees will receive if they provide services for the full ten-month period are in exchange for services provided over that period. The entity accounts for them as short-term employee benefits because the entity expects to settle them before twelve months after the end of the annual reporting period. In this example, discounting is not required, so an expense of CU200,000 (ie CU2,000,000 ÷ 10) is recognised in each month during the service period of ten months, with a corresponding increase in the carrying amount of the liability.

Disclosure

171   Although this Standard does not require specific disclosures about termination benefits, other IFRSs may require disclosures. For example, IAS 24 requires disclosures about employee benefits for key management personnel. IAS 1 requires disclosure of employee benefits expense.

Transition and effective date

172   An entity shall apply this Standard for annual periods beginning on or after 1 January 2013. Earlier application is permitted. If an entity applies this Standard for an earlier period, it shall disclose that fact.

173   An entity shall apply this Standard retrospectively, in accordance with IAS 8 *Accounting Policies, Changes in Accounting Estimates and Errors*, except that:

(a)   an entity need not adjust the carrying amount of assets outside the scope of this Standard for changes in employee benefit costs that were included in the carrying amount before the date of initial application. The date of initial application is the beginning of the earliest prior period presented in the first financial statements in which the entity adopts this Standard.

(b)   in financial statements for periods beginning before 1 January 2014, an entity need not present comparative information for the disclosures required by paragraph 145 about the sensitivity of the defined benefit obligation.

174   IFRS 13, issued in May 2011, amended the definition of fair value in paragraph 8 and amended paragraph 113. An entity shall apply those amendments when it applies IFRS 13.

175   *Defined Benefit Plans: Employee Contributions* (Amendments to IAS 19), issued in November 2013, amended paragraphs 93–94. An entity shall apply those amendments for annual periods beginning on or after 1 July 2014 retrospectively in accordance with IAS 8 *Accounting Policies, Changes in Accounting Estimates and Errors*. Earlier application is permitted. If an entity applies those amendments for an earlier period, it shall disclose that fact.

176   *Annual Improvements to IFRSs 2012–2014 Cycle*, issued in September 2014, amended paragraph 83 and added paragraph 177. An entity shall apply that amendment for annual periods beginning on or after 1 January 2016. Earlier application is permitted. If an entity applies that amendment for an earlier period it shall disclose that fact.

177   An entity shall apply the amendment in paragraph 176 from the beginning of the earliest comparative period presented in the first financial statements in which the entity applies the amendment. Any initial adjustment arising from the application of the amendment shall be recognised in retained earnings at the beginning of that period.

178   *[This paragraph refers to amendments that are not yet effective, and is therefore not included in this edition.]*

179   *Plan Amendment, Curtailment or Settlement* (Amendments to IAS 19), issued in February 2018, added paragraphs 101A, 122A and 123A, and amended paragraphs 57, 99, 120, 123, 125, 126 and 156. An entity shall apply these amendments to plan amendments, curtailments or settlements occurring on or after the beginning of the first annual reporting period that begins on or after 1 January 2019. Earlier application is permitted. If an entity applies these amendments earlier, it shall disclose that fact.

Appendix A
Application Guidance

This appendix is an integral part of the IFRS. It describes the application of paragraphs 92–93 and has the same authority as the other parts of the IFRS.

A1   The accounting requirements for contributions from employees or third parties are illustrated in the diagram below.

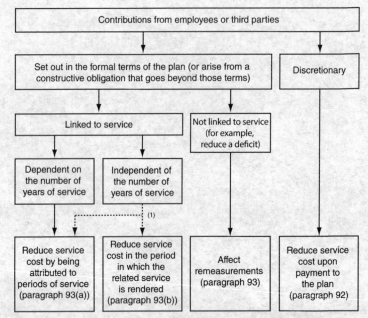

(1) This dotted arrow means that an entity is permitted to choose either accounting.

Appendix B
Amendments to other IFRSs

This appendix sets out amendments to other IFRSs that are a consequence of the Board amending IAS 19 in June 2011. An entity shall apply these amendments when it applies IAS 19 as amended. Amended paragraphs are shown with new text underlined and deleted text struck through.

* * * * *

The amendments contained in this appendix when this Standard was amended in 2011 have been incorporated into the relevant IFRSs published in this volume.

Approval by the Board of *Actuarial Gains and Losses, Group Plans and Disclosures* (Amendment to IAS 19) issued in December 2004

Actuarial Gains and Losses, Group Plans and Disclosures (Amendment to IAS 19) was approved for issue by twelve of the fourteen members of the International Accounting Standards Board. Messrs Leisenring and Yamada dissented. Their dissenting opinions are set out after the Basis for Conclusions.

Sir David Tweedie	Chairman
Thomas E Jones	Vice-Chairman
Mary E Barth	
Hans-Georg Bruns	
Anthony T Cope	
Jan Engström	
Robert P Garnett	
Gilbert Gélard	
James J Leisenring	
Warren J McGregor	
Patricia L O'Malley	
John T Smith	
Geoffrey Whittington	
Tatsumi Yamada	

Approval by the Board of IAS 19 issued in June 2011

International Accounting Standard 19 *Employee Benefits* (as amended in 2011) was approved for issue by thirteen of the fifteen members of the International Accounting Standards Board. Messrs Engström and Yamada dissented. Their dissenting opinions are set out after the Basis for Conclusions.

Sir David Tweedie	Chairman

Stephen Cooper

Philippe Danjou

Jan Engström

Patrick Finnegan

Amaro Luiz de Oliveira Gomes

Prabhakar Kalavacherla

Elke König

Patricia McConnell

Warren J McGregor

Paul Pacter

Darrel Scott

John T Smith

Tatsumi Yamada

Wei-Guo Zhang

Approval by the Board of *Defined Benefit Plans: Employee Contributions* (Amendments to IAS 19) issued in November 2013

Defined Benefit Plans: Employee Contributions was approved for issue by the sixteen members of the International Accounting Standards Board.

Hans Hoogervorst	Chairman
Ian Mackintosh	Vice-Chairman
Stephen Cooper	
Philippe Danjou	
Martin Edelmann	
Jan Engström	
Patrick Finnegan	
Amaro Luiz de Oliveira Gomes	
Gary Kabureck	
Prabhakar Kalavacherla	
Patricia McConnell	
Takatsugu Ochi	
Darrel Scott	
Mary Tokar	
Chungwoo Suh	
Wei-Guo Zhang	

Approval by the Board of *Plan Amendment, Curtailment or Settlement* (Amendments to IAS 19) issued in February 2018

Plan Amendment, Curtailment or Settlement (Amendments to IAS 19) was approved for issue by 13 of 14 members of the International Accounting Standards Board (Board). Ms Tarca abstained in view of her recent appointment to the Board.

Hans Hoogervorst	Chairman
Suzanne Lloyd	Vice-Chair
Nick Anderson	
Martin Edelmann	
Françoise Flores	
Amaro Luiz de Oliveira Gomes	
Gary Kabureck	
Jianqiao Lu	
Takatsugu Ochi	
Darrel Scott	
Thomas Scott	
Chungwoo Suh	
Ann Tarca	
Mary Tokar	

IAS 20

Accounting for Government Grants and Disclosure of Government Assistance

In April 2001 the International Accounting Standards Board adopted IAS 20 *Accounting for Government Grants and Disclosure of Government Assistance*, which had originally been issued by the International Accounting Standards Committee in April 1983.

Other Standards have made minor consequential amendments to IAS 20. They include IFRS 13 *Fair Value Measurement* (issued May 2011), *Presentation of Items of Other Comprehensive Income* (Amendments to IAS 1) (issued June 2011), IFRS 9 *Financial Instruments* (Hedge Accounting and amendments to IFRS 9, IFRS 7 and IAS 39) (issued November 2013) and IFRS 9 *Financial Instruments* (issued July 2014).

Contents

International Accounting Standard 20 *Accounting for Government Grants and Disclosure of Government Assistance* (IAS 20) is set out in paragraphs 1–48. All the paragraphs have equal authority but retain the IASC format of the Standard when it was adopted by the IASB. IAS 20 should be read in the context of the Basis for Conclusions, the *Preface to IFRS Standards* and the *Conceptual Framework for Financial Reporting*. IAS 8 *Accounting Policies, Changes in Accounting Estimates and Errors* provides a basis for selecting and applying accounting policies in the absence of explicit guidance.

International Accounting Standard 20
Accounting for Government Grants and Disclosure of Government Assistance[1]

Scope

1   This Standard shall be applied in accounting for, and in the disclosure of, government grants and in the disclosure of other forms of government assistance.

2   This Standard does not deal with:

(a)   the special problems arising in accounting for government grants in financial statements reflecting the effects of changing prices or in supplementary information of a similar nature.

(b)   government assistance that is provided for an entity in the form of benefits that are available in determining taxable profit or tax loss, or are determined or limited on the basis of income tax liability. Examples of such benefits are income tax holidays, investment tax credits, accelerated depreciation allowances and reduced income tax rates.

(c)   government participation in the ownership of the entity.

(d)   government grants covered by IAS 41 *Agriculture*.

Definitions

3   The following terms are used in this Standard with the meanings specified:

Government refers to government, government agencies and similar bodies whether local, national or international.

Government assistance is action by government designed to provide an economic benefit specific to an entity or range of entities qualifying under certain criteria. Government assistance for the purpose of this Standard does not include benefits provided only indirectly through action affecting general trading conditions, such as the provision of infrastructure in development areas or the imposition of trading constraints on competitors.

Government grants are assistance by government in the form of transfers of resources to an entity in return for past or future compliance with certain conditions relating to the operating activities of the entity. They exclude those forms of government assistance which cannot reasonably have a

---

1   As part of *Improvements to IFRSs* issued in May 2008 the Board amended terminology used in this Standard to be consistent with other IFRSs as follows: (a) 'taxable income' was amended to 'taxable profit or tax loss', (b) 'recognised as income/expense' was amended to 'recognised in profit or loss', (c) 'credited directly to shareholders' interests/equity' was amended to 'recognised outside profit or loss', and (d) 'revision to an accounting estimate' was amended to 'change in accounting estimate'.

value placed upon them and transactions with government which cannot be distinguished from the normal trading transactions of the entity.[2]

Grants related to assets are government grants whose primary condition is that an entity qualifying for them should purchase, construct or otherwise acquire long-term assets. Subsidiary conditions may also be attached restricting the type or location of the assets or the periods during which they are to be acquired or held.

Grants related to income are government grants other than those related to assets.

Forgivable loans are loans which the lender undertakes to waive repayment of under certain prescribed conditions.

Fair value is the price that would be received to sell an asset or paid to transfer a liability in an orderly transaction between market participants at the measurement date. (See IFRS 13 *Fair Value Measurement*.)

4   Government assistance takes many forms varying both in the nature of the assistance given and in the conditions which are usually attached to it. The purpose of the assistance may be to encourage an entity to embark on a course of action which it would not normally have taken if the assistance was not provided.

5   The receipt of government assistance by an entity may be significant for the preparation of the financial statements for two reasons. Firstly, if resources have been transferred, an appropriate method of accounting for the transfer must be found. Secondly, it is desirable to give an indication of the extent to which the entity has benefited from such assistance during the reporting period. This facilitates comparison of an entity's financial statements with those of prior periods and with those of other entities.

6   Government grants are sometimes called by other names such as subsidies, subventions, or premiums.

Government grants

7   Government grants, including non-monetary grants at fair value, shall not be recognised until there is reasonable assurance that:

(a)   the entity will comply with the conditions attaching to them; and

(b)   the grants will be received.

8   A government grant is not recognised until there is reasonable assurance that the entity will comply with the conditions attaching to it, and that the grant will be received. Receipt of a grant does not of itself provide conclusive evidence that the conditions attaching to the grant have been or will be fulfilled.

---

2   See also SIC-10 *Government Assistance—No Specific Relation to Operating Activities*.

9   The manner in which a grant is received does not affect the accounting method to be adopted in regard to the grant. Thus a grant is accounted for in the same manner whether it is received in cash or as a reduction of a liability to the government.

10   A forgivable loan from government is treated as a government grant when there is reasonable assurance that the entity will meet the terms for forgiveness of the loan.

10A The benefit of a government loan at a below-market rate of interest is treated as a government grant. The loan shall be recognised and measured in accordance with IFRS 9 *Financial Instruments*. The benefit of the below-market rate of interest shall be measured as the difference between the initial carrying value of the loan determined in accordance with IFRS 9 and the proceeds received. The benefit is accounted for in accordance with this Standard. The entity shall consider the conditions and obligations that have been, or must be, met when identifying the costs for which the benefit of the loan is intended to compensate.

11   Once a government grant is recognised, any related contingent liability or contingent asset is treated in accordance with IAS 37 *Provisions, Contingent Liabilities and Contingent Assets*.

12   **Government grants shall be recognised in profit or loss on a systematic basis over the periods in which the entity recognises as expenses the related costs for which the grants are intended to compensate.**

13   There are two broad approaches to the accounting for government grants: the capital approach, under which a grant is recognised outside profit or loss, and the income approach, under which a grant is recognised in profit or loss over one or more periods.

14   Those in support of the capital approach argue as follows:

(a)   government grants are a financing device and should be dealt with as such in the statement of financial position rather than be recognised in profit or loss to offset the items of expense that they finance. Because no repayment is expected, such grants should be recognised outside profit or loss.

(b)   it is inappropriate to recognise government grants in profit or loss, because they are not earned but represent an incentive provided by government without related costs.

15   Arguments in support of the income approach are as follows:

(a)   because government grants are receipts from a source other than shareholders, they should not be recognised directly in equity but should be recognised in profit or loss in appropriate periods.

(b)   government grants are rarely gratuitous. The entity earns them through compliance with their conditions and meeting the envisaged obligations. They should therefore be recognised in profit or loss over the periods in which the entity recognises as expenses the related costs for which the grant is intended to compensate.

(c)   because income and other taxes are expenses, it is logical to deal also with government grants, which are an extension of fiscal policies, in profit or loss.

16   It is fundamental to the income approach that government grants should be recognised in profit or loss on a systematic basis over the periods in which the entity recognises as expenses the related costs for which the grant is intended to compensate. Recognition of government grants in profit or loss on a receipts basis is not in accordance with the accrual accounting assumption (see IAS 1 *Presentation of Financial Statements*) and would be acceptable only if no basis existed for allocating a grant to periods other than the one in which it was received.

17   In most cases the periods over which an entity recognises the costs or expenses related to a government grant are readily ascertainable. Thus grants in recognition of specific expenses are recognised in profit or loss in the same period as the relevant expenses. Similarly, grants related to depreciable assets are usually recognised in profit or loss over the periods and in the proportions in which depreciation expense on those assets is recognised.

18   Grants related to non-depreciable assets may also require the fulfilment of certain obligations and would then be recognised in profit or loss over the periods that bear the cost of meeting the obligations. As an example, a grant of land may be conditional upon the erection of a building on the site and it may be appropriate to recognise the grant in profit or loss over the life of the building.

19   Grants are sometimes received as part of a package of financial or fiscal aids to which a number of conditions are attached. In such cases, care is needed in identifying the conditions giving rise to costs and expenses which determine the periods over which the grant will be earned. It may be appropriate to allocate part of a grant on one basis and part on another.

20   **A government grant that becomes receivable as compensation for expenses or losses already incurred or for the purpose of giving immediate financial support to the entity with no future related costs shall be recognised in profit or loss of the period in which it becomes receivable.**

21   In some circumstances, a government grant may be awarded for the purpose of giving immediate financial support to an entity rather than as an incentive to undertake specific expenditures. Such grants may be confined to a particular entity and may not be available to a whole class of beneficiaries. These circumstances may warrant recognising a grant in profit or loss of the period in which the entity qualifies to receive it, with disclosure to ensure that its effect is clearly understood.

22   A government grant may become receivable by an entity as compensation for expenses or losses incurred in a previous period. Such a grant is recognised in profit or loss of the period in which it becomes receivable, with disclosure to ensure that its effect is clearly understood.

Non-monetary government grants

23   A government grant may take the form of a transfer of a non-monetary asset, such as land or other resources, for the use of the entity. In these circumstances it is usual to assess the fair value of the non-monetary asset and to account for both grant and asset at that fair value. An alternative course that is sometimes followed is to record both asset and grant at a nominal amount.

Presentation of grants related to assets

24   **Government grants related to assets, including non-monetary grants at fair value, shall be presented in the statement of financial position either by setting up the grant as deferred income or by deducting the grant in arriving at the carrying amount of the asset.**

25   Two methods of presentation in financial statements of grants (or the appropriate portions of grants) related to assets are regarded as acceptable alternatives.

26   One method recognises the grant as deferred income that is recognised in profit or loss on a systematic basis over the useful life of the asset.

27   The other method deducts the grant in calculating the carrying amount of the asset. The grant is recognised in profit or loss over the life of a depreciable asset as a reduced depreciation expense.

28   The purchase of assets and the receipt of related grants can cause major movements in the cash flow of an entity. For this reason and in order to show the gross investment in assets, such movements are often disclosed as separate items in the statement of cash flows regardless of whether or not the grant is deducted from the related asset for presentation purposes in the statement of financial position.

Presentation of grants related to income

29   Grants related to income are presented as part of profit or loss, either separately or under a general heading such as 'Other income'; alternatively, they are deducted in reporting the related expense.

29A   [Deleted]

30   Supporters of the first method claim that it is inappropriate to net income and expense items and that separation of the grant from the expense facilitates comparison with other expenses not affected by a grant. For the second method it is argued that the expenses might well not have been incurred by the entity if the grant had not been available and presentation of the expense without offsetting the grant may therefore be misleading.

31   Both methods are regarded as acceptable for the presentation of grants related to income. Disclosure of the grant may be necessary for a proper understanding of the financial statements. Disclosure of the effect of the grants on any item of income or expense which is required to be separately disclosed is usually appropriate.

Repayment of government grants

32   A government grant that becomes repayable shall be accounted for as a change in accounting estimate (see IAS 8 *Accounting Policies, Changes in Accounting Estimates and Errors*). Repayment of a grant related to income shall be applied first against any unamortised deferred credit recognised in respect of the grant. To the extent that the repayment exceeds any such deferred credit, or when no deferred credit exists, the repayment shall be recognised immediately in profit or loss. Repayment of a grant related to an asset shall be recognised by increasing the carrying amount of the asset or reducing the deferred income balance by the amount repayable. The cumulative additional depreciation that would have been recognised in profit or loss to date in the absence of the grant shall be recognised immediately in profit or loss.

33   Circumstances giving rise to repayment of a grant related to an asset may require consideration to be given to the possible impairment of the new carrying amount of the asset.

Government assistance

34   Excluded from the definition of government grants in paragraph 3 are certain forms of government assistance which cannot reasonably have a value placed upon them and transactions with government which cannot be distinguished from the normal trading transactions of the entity.

35   Examples of assistance that cannot reasonably have a value placed upon them are free technical or marketing advice and the provision of guarantees. An example of assistance that cannot be distinguished from the normal trading transactions of the entity is a government procurement policy that is responsible for a portion of the entity's sales. The existence of the benefit might be unquestioned but any attempt to segregate the trading activities from government assistance could well be arbitrary.

36   The significance of the benefit in the above examples may be such that disclosure of the nature, extent and duration of the assistance is necessary in order that the financial statements may not be misleading.

37   [Deleted]

38   In this Standard, government assistance does not include the provision of infrastructure by improvement to the general transport and communication network and the supply of improved facilities such as irrigation or water reticulation which is available on an ongoing indeterminate basis for the benefit of an entire local community.

Disclosure

39   The following matters shall be disclosed:

   (a)   the accounting policy adopted for government grants, including the methods of presentation adopted in the financial statements;

   (b)   the nature and extent of government grants recognised in the financial statements and an indication of other forms of government assistance from which the entity has directly benefited; and

   (c)   unfulfilled conditions and other contingencies attaching to government assistance that has been recognised.

Transitional provisions

40   An entity adopting the Standard for the first time shall:

   (a)   comply with the disclosure requirements, where appropriate; and

   (b)   either:

      (i)   adjust its financial statements for the change in accounting policy in accordance with IAS 8; or

      (ii)   apply the accounting provisions of the Standard only to grants or portions of grants becoming receivable or repayable after the effective date of the Standard.

Effective date

41   This Standard becomes operative for financial statements covering periods beginning on or after 1 January 1984.

42   IAS 1 (as revised in 2007) amended the terminology used throughout IFRSs. In addition it added paragraph 29A. An entity shall apply those amendments for annual periods beginning on or after 1 January 2009. If an entity applies IAS 1 (revised 2007) for an earlier period, the amendments shall be applied for that earlier period.

43   Paragraph 37 was deleted and paragraph 10A added by *Improvements to IFRSs* issued in May 2008. An entity shall apply those amendments prospectively to government loans received in periods beginning on or after 1 January 2009. Earlier application is permitted. If an entity applies the amendments for an earlier period it shall disclose that fact.

44   [Deleted]

45   IFRS 13, issued in May 2011, amended the definition of fair value in paragraph 3. An entity shall apply that amendment when it applies IFRS 13.

46   *Presentation of Items of Other Comprehensive Income* (Amendments to IAS 1), issued in June 2011, amended paragraph 29 and deleted paragraph 29A. An entity shall apply those amendments when it applies IAS 1 as amended in June 2011.

47   [Deleted]

48   IFRS 9, as issued in July 2014, amended paragraph 10A and deleted paragraphs 44 and 47. An entity shall apply those amendments when it applies IFRS 9.

IAS 21

The Effects of Changes in Foreign Exchange Rates

In April 2001 the International Accounting Standards Board (Board) adopted IAS 21 *The Effects of Changes in Foreign Exchange Rates*, which had originally been issued by the International Accounting Standards Committee in December 1983. IAS 21 *The Effects of Changes in Foreign Exchange Rates* replaced IAS 21 *Accounting for the Effects of Changes in Foreign Exchange Rates* (issued in July 1983).

In December 2003 the Board issued a revised IAS 21 as part of its initial agenda of technical projects. The revised IAS 21 also incorporated the guidance contained in three related Interpretations (SIC-11 *Foreign Exchange – Capitalisation of Losses Resulting from Severe Currency Devaluations*, SIC-19 *Reporting Currency – Measurement and Presentation of Financial Statements under IAS 21 and IAS 29* and SIC-30 *Reporting Currency – Translation from Measurement Currency to Presentation Currency*). The Board also amended SIC-7 *Introduction of the Euro*.

The Board amended IAS 21 in December 2005 to require that some types of exchange differences arising from a monetary item should be separately recognised as equity.

Other Standards have made minor consequential amendments to IAS 21. They include *Improvements to IFRSs* (issued May 2010), IFRS 10 *Consolidated Financial Statements* (issued May 2011), IFRS 11 *Joint Arrangements* (issued May 2011), IFRS 13 *Fair Value Measurement* (issued May 2011), *Presentation of Items of Other Comprehensive Income* (Amendments to IAS 1) (issued June 2011), IFRS 9 *Financial Instruments* (Hedge Accounting and amendments to IFRS 9, IFRS 7 and IAS 39) (issued November 2013), IFRS 9 *Financial Instruments* (issued July 2014), IFRS 16 *Leases* (issued January 2016) and *Amendments to References to the Conceptual Framework in IFRS Standards* (issued March 2018).

CONTENTS

FOR THE BASIS FOR CONCLUSIONS, SEE PART C OF THIS EDITION

BASIS FOR CONCLUSIONS

International Accounting Standard 21 *The Effects of Changes in Foreign Exchange Rates* (IAS 21) is set out in paragraphs 1–62 and the Appendix. All the paragraphs have equal authority but retain the IASC format of the Standard when it was adopted by the IASB. IAS 21 should be read in the context of its objective and the Basis for Conclusions, the *Preface to IFRS Standards* and the *Conceptual Framework for Financial Reporting*. IAS 8 *Accounting Policies, Changes in Accounting Estimates and Errors* provides a basis for selecting and applying accounting policies in the absence of explicit guidance.

International Accounting Standard 21
The Effects of Changes in Foreign Exchange Rates

Objective

1   An entity may carry on foreign activities in two ways. It may have transactions in foreign currencies or it may have foreign operations. In addition, an entity may present its financial statements in a foreign currency. The objective of this Standard is to prescribe how to include foreign currency transactions and foreign operations in the financial statements of an entity and how to translate financial statements into a presentation currency.

2   The principal issues are which exchange rate(s) to use and how to report the effects of changes in exchange rates in the financial statements.

Scope

3   This Standard shall be applied:[1]

(a)   in accounting for transactions and balances in foreign currencies, except for those derivative transactions and balances that are within the scope of IFRS 9 *Financial Instruments*;

(b)   in translating the results and financial position of foreign operations that are included in the financial statements of the entity by consolidation or the equity method; and

(c)   in translating an entity's results and financial position into a presentation currency.

4   IFRS 9 applies to many foreign currency derivatives and, accordingly, these are excluded from the scope of this Standard. However, those foreign currency derivatives that are not within the scope of IFRS 9 (eg some foreign currency derivatives that are embedded in other contracts) are within the scope of this Standard. In addition, this Standard applies when an entity translates amounts relating to derivatives from its functional currency to its presentation currency.

5   This Standard does not apply to hedge accounting for foreign currency items, including the hedging of a net investment in a foreign operation. IFRS 9 applies to hedge accounting.

6   This Standard applies to the presentation of an entity's financial statements in a foreign currency and sets out requirements for the resulting financial statements to be described as complying with International Financial Reporting Standards (IFRSs). For translations of financial information into a foreign currency that do not meet these requirements, this Standard specifies information to be disclosed.

---

1   See also SIC-7 *Introduction of the Euro*

7   This Standard does not apply to the presentation in a statement of cash flows of the cash flows arising from transactions in a foreign currency, or to the translation of cash flows of a foreign operation (see IAS 7 *Statement of Cash Flows*).

Definitions

8   The following terms are used in this Standard with the meanings specified:

Closing rate is the spot exchange rate at the end of the reporting period.

Exchange difference is the difference resulting from translating a given number of units of one currency into another currency at different exchange rates.

Exchange rate is the ratio of exchange for two currencies.

Fair value is the price that would be received to sell an asset or paid to transfer a liability in an orderly transaction between market participants at the measurement date. (See IFRS 13 *Fair Value Measurement*.)

Foreign currency is a currency other than the functional currency of the entity.

Foreign operation is an entity that is a subsidiary, associate, joint arrangement or branch of a reporting entity, the activities of which are based or conducted in a country or currency other than those of the reporting entity.

Functional currency is the currency of the primary economic environment in which the entity operates.

A group is a parent and all its subsidiaries.

Monetary items are units of currency held and assets and liabilities to be received or paid in a fixed or determinable number of units of currency.

Net investment in a foreign operation is the amount of the reporting entity's interest in the net assets of that operation.

Presentation currency is the currency in which the financial statements are presented.

Spot exchange rate is the exchange rate for immediate delivery.

Elaboration on the definitions

Functional currency

9   The primary economic environment in which an entity operates is normally the one in which it primarily generates and expends cash. An entity considers the following factors in determining its functional currency:

(a)   the currency:

          (i)   that mainly influences sales prices for goods and services (this will often be the currency in which sales prices for its goods and services are denominated and settled); and

          (ii)   of the country whose competitive forces and regulations mainly determine the sales prices of its goods and services.

    (b)   the currency that mainly influences labour, material and other costs of providing goods or services (this will often be the currency in which such costs are denominated and settled).

10   The following factors may also provide evidence of an entity's functional currency:

    (a)   the currency in which funds from financing activities (ie issuing debt and equity instruments) are generated.

    (b)   the currency in which receipts from operating activities are usually retained.

11   The following additional factors are considered in determining the functional currency of a foreign operation, and whether its functional currency is the same as that of the reporting entity (the reporting entity, in this context, being the entity that has the foreign operation as its subsidiary, branch, associate or joint arrangement):

    (a)   whether the activities of the foreign operation are carried out as an extension of the reporting entity, rather than being carried out with a significant degree of autonomy. An example of the former is when the foreign operation only sells goods imported from the reporting entity and remits the proceeds to it. An example of the latter is when the operation accumulates cash and other monetary items, incurs expenses, generates income and arranges borrowings, all substantially in its local currency.

    (b)   whether transactions with the reporting entity are a high or a low proportion of the foreign operation's activities.

    (c)   whether cash flows from the activities of the foreign operation directly affect the cash flows of the reporting entity and are readily available for remittance to it.

    (d)   whether cash flows from the activities of the foreign operation are sufficient to service existing and normally expected debt obligations without funds being made available by the reporting entity.

12   When the above indicators are mixed and the functional currency is not obvious, management uses its judgement to determine the functional currency that most faithfully represents the economic effects of the underlying transactions, events and conditions. As part of this approach, management gives priority to the primary indicators in paragraph 9 before considering the indicators in paragraphs 10 and 11, which are designed to provide additional supporting evidence to determine an entity's functional currency.

13   An entity's functional currency reflects the underlying transactions, events and conditions that are relevant to it. Accordingly, once determined, the functional currency is not changed unless there is a change in those underlying transactions, events and conditions.

14   If the functional currency is the currency of a hyperinflationary economy, the entity's financial statements are restated in accordance with IAS 29 *Financial Reporting in Hyperinflationary Economies*. An entity cannot avoid restatement in accordance with IAS 29 by, for example, adopting as its functional currency a currency other than the functional currency determined in accordance with this Standard (such as the functional currency of its parent).

Net investment in a foreign operation

15   An entity may have a monetary item that is receivable from or payable to a foreign operation. An item for which settlement is neither planned nor likely to occur in the foreseeable future is, in substance, a part of the entity's net investment in that foreign operation, and is accounted for in accordance with paragraphs 32 and 33. Such monetary items may include long-term receivables or loans. They do not include trade receivables or trade payables.

15A   The entity that has a monetary item receivable from or payable to a foreign operation described in paragraph 15 may be any subsidiary of the group. For example, an entity has two subsidiaries, A and B. Subsidiary B is a foreign operation. Subsidiary A grants a loan to Subsidiary B. Subsidiary A's loan receivable from Subsidiary B would be part of the entity's net investment in Subsidiary B if settlement of the loan is neither planned nor likely to occur in the foreseeable future. This would also be true if Subsidiary A were itself a foreign operation.

Monetary items

16   The essential feature of a monetary item is a right to receive (or an obligation to deliver) a fixed or determinable number of units of currency. Examples include: pensions and other employee benefits to be paid in cash; provisions that are to be settled in cash; lease liabilities; and cash dividends that are recognised as a liability. Similarly, a contract to receive (or deliver) a variable number of the entity's own equity instruments or a variable amount of assets in which the fair value to be received (or delivered) equals a fixed or determinable number of units of currency is a monetary item. Conversely, the essential feature of a non-monetary item is the absence of a right to receive (or an obligation to deliver) a fixed or determinable number of units of currency. Examples include: amounts prepaid for goods and services; goodwill; intangible assets; inventories; property, plant and equipment; right-of-use assets; and provisions that are to be settled by the delivery of a non-monetary asset.

Summary of the approach required by this Standard

17   In preparing financial statements, each entity—whether a stand-alone entity, an entity with foreign operations (such as a parent) or a foreign operation (such as a subsidiary or branch)—determines its functional currency in accordance with paragraphs 9–14. The entity translates foreign currency items into its functional currency and reports the effects of such translation in accordance with paragraphs 20–37 and 50.

18   Many reporting entities comprise a number of individual entities (eg a group is made up of a parent and one or more subsidiaries). Various types of entities, whether members of a group or otherwise, may have investments in associates or joint arrangements. They may also have branches. It is necessary for the results and financial position of each individual entity included in the reporting entity to be translated into the currency in which the reporting entity presents its financial statements. This Standard permits the presentation currency of a reporting entity to be any currency (or currencies). The results and financial position of any individual entity within the reporting entity whose functional currency differs from the presentation currency are translated in accordance with paragraphs 38–50.

19   This Standard also permits a stand-alone entity preparing financial statements or an entity preparing separate financial statements in accordance with IAS 27 *Separate Financial Statements* to present its financial statements in any currency (or currencies). If the entity's presentation currency differs from its functional currency, its results and financial position are also translated into the presentation currency in accordance with paragraphs 38–50.

Reporting foreign currency transactions in the functional currency

Initial recognition

20   A foreign currency transaction is a transaction that is denominated or requires settlement in a foreign currency, including transactions arising when an entity:

(a)   buys or sells goods or services whose price is denominated in a foreign currency;

(b)   borrows or lends funds when the amounts payable or receivable are denominated in a foreign currency; or

(c)   otherwise acquires or disposes of assets, or incurs or settles liabilities, denominated in a foreign currency.

21   **A foreign currency transaction shall be recorded, on initial recognition in the functional currency, by applying to the foreign currency amount the spot exchange rate between the functional currency and the foreign currency at the date of the transaction.**

22 The date of a transaction is the date on which the transaction first qualifies for recognition in accordance with IFRSs. For practical reasons, a rate that approximates the actual rate at the date of the transaction is often used, for example, an average rate for a week or a month might be used for all transactions in each foreign currency occurring during that period. However, if exchange rates fluctuate significantly, the use of the average rate for a period is inappropriate.

Reporting at the ends of subsequent reporting periods

23 At the end of each reporting period:

(a) foreign currency monetary items shall be translated using the closing rate;

(b) non-monetary items that are measured in terms of historical cost in a foreign currency shall be translated using the exchange rate at the date of the transaction; and

(c) non-monetary items that are measured at fair value in a foreign currency shall be translated using the exchange rates at the date when the fair value was measured.

24 The carrying amount of an item is determined in conjunction with other relevant Standards. For example, property, plant and equipment may be measured in terms of fair value or historical cost in accordance with IAS 16 *Property, Plant and Equipment*. Whether the carrying amount is determined on the basis of historical cost or on the basis of fair value, if the amount is determined in a foreign currency it is then translated into the functional currency in accordance with this Standard.

25 The carrying amount of some items is determined by comparing two or more amounts. For example, the carrying amount of inventories is the lower of cost and net realisable value in accordance with IAS 2 *Inventories*. Similarly, in accordance with IAS 36 *Impairment of Assets*, the carrying amount of an asset for which there is an indication of impairment is the lower of its carrying amount before considering possible impairment losses and its recoverable amount. When such an asset is non-monetary and is measured in a foreign currency, the carrying amount is determined by comparing:

(a) the cost or carrying amount, as appropriate, translated at the exchange rate at the date when that amount was determined (ie the rate at the date of the transaction for an item measured in terms of historical cost); and

(b) the net realisable value or recoverable amount, as appropriate, translated at the exchange rate at the date when that value was determined (eg the closing rate at the end of the reporting period).

The effect of this comparison may be that an impairment loss is recognised in the functional currency but would not be recognised in the foreign currency, or vice versa.

26   When several exchange rates are available, the rate used is that at which the future cash flows represented by the transaction or balance could have been settled if those cash flows had occurred at the measurement date. If exchangeability between two currencies is temporarily lacking, the rate used is the first subsequent rate at which exchanges could be made.

Recognition of exchange differences

27   As noted in paragraphs 3(a) and 5, IFRS 9 applies to hedge accounting for foreign currency items. The application of hedge accounting requires an entity to account for some exchange differences differently from the treatment of exchange differences required by this Standard. For example, IFRS 9 requires that exchange differences on monetary items that qualify as hedging instruments in a cash flow hedge are recognised initially in other comprehensive income to the extent that the hedge is effective.

28   **Exchange differences arising on the settlement of monetary items or on translating monetary items at rates different from those at which they were translated on initial recognition during the period or in previous financial statements shall be recognised in profit or loss in the period in which they arise, except as described in paragraph 32.**

29   When monetary items arise from a foreign currency transaction and there is a change in the exchange rate between the transaction date and the date of settlement, an exchange difference results. When the transaction is settled within the same accounting period as that in which it occurred, all the exchange difference is recognised in that period. However, when the transaction is settled in a subsequent accounting period, the exchange difference recognised in each period up to the date of settlement is determined by the change in exchange rates during each period.

30   **When a gain or loss on a non-monetary item is recognised in other comprehensive income, any exchange component of that gain or loss shall be recognised in other comprehensive income. Conversely, when a gain or loss on a non-monetary item is recognised in profit or loss, any exchange component of that gain or loss shall be recognised in profit or loss.**

31   Other IFRSs require some gains and losses to be recognised in other comprehensive income. For example, IAS 16 requires some gains and losses arising on a revaluation of property, plant and equipment to be recognised in other comprehensive income. When such an asset is measured in a foreign currency, paragraph 23(c) of this Standard requires the revalued amount to be translated using the rate at the date the value is determined, resulting in an exchange difference that is also recognised in other comprehensive income.

32   **Exchange differences arising on a monetary item that forms part of a reporting entity's net investment in a foreign operation (see paragraph 15) shall be recognised in profit or loss in the separate financial statements of the reporting entity or the individual financial statements of the foreign operation, as appropriate. In the financial statements that include the foreign operation and the reporting entity (eg consolidated financial statements when the foreign operation is a subsidiary), such exchange**

differences shall be recognised initially in other comprehensive income and reclassified from equity to profit or loss on disposal of the net investment in accordance with paragraph 48.

33   When a monetary item forms part of a reporting entity's net investment in a foreign operation and is denominated in the functional currency of the reporting entity, an exchange difference arises in the foreign operation's individual financial statements in accordance with paragraph 28. If such an item is denominated in the functional currency of the foreign operation, an exchange difference arises in the reporting entity's separate financial statements in accordance with paragraph 28. If such an item is denominated in a currency other than the functional currency of either the reporting entity or the foreign operation, an exchange difference arises in the reporting entity's separate financial statements and in the foreign operation's individual financial statements in accordance with paragraph 28. Such exchange differences are recognised in other comprehensive income in the financial statements that include the foreign operation and the reporting entity (ie financial statements in which the foreign operation is consolidated or accounted for using the equity method).

34   When an entity keeps its books and records in a currency other than its functional currency, at the time the entity prepares its financial statements all amounts are translated into the functional currency in accordance with paragraphs 20–26. This produces the same amounts in the functional currency as would have occurred had the items been recorded initially in the functional currency. For example, monetary items are translated into the functional currency using the closing rate, and non-monetary items that are measured on a historical cost basis are translated using the exchange rate at the date of the transaction that resulted in their recognition.

Change in functional currency

35   **When there is a change in an entity's functional currency, the entity shall apply the translation procedures applicable to the new functional currency prospectively from the date of the change.**

36   As noted in paragraph 13, the functional currency of an entity reflects the underlying transactions, events and conditions that are relevant to the entity. Accordingly, once the functional currency is determined, it can be changed only if there is a change to those underlying transactions, events and conditions. For example, a change in the currency that mainly influences the sales prices of goods and services may lead to a change in an entity's functional currency.

37   The effect of a change in functional currency is accounted for prospectively. In other words, an entity translates all items into the new functional currency using the exchange rate at the date of the change. The resulting translated amounts for non-monetary items are treated as their historical cost. Exchange differences arising from the translation of a foreign operation previously recognised in other comprehensive income in accordance with paragraphs 32

and 39(c) are not reclassified from equity to profit or loss until the disposal of the operation.

Use of a presentation currency other than the functional currency

Translation to the presentation currency

38   An entity may present its financial statements in any currency (or currencies). If the presentation currency differs from the entity's functional currency, it translates its results and financial position into the presentation currency. For example, when a group contains individual entities with different functional currencies, the results and financial position of each entity are expressed in a common currency so that consolidated financial statements may be presented.

39   The results and financial position of an entity whose functional currency is not the currency of a hyperinflationary economy shall be translated into a different presentation currency using the following procedures:

(a)   assets and liabilities for each statement of financial position presented (ie including comparatives) shall be translated at the closing rate at the date of that statement of financial position;

(b)   income and expenses for each statement presenting profit or loss and other comprehensive income (ie including comparatives) shall be translated at exchange rates at the dates of the transactions; and

(c)   all resulting exchange differences shall be recognised in other comprehensive income.

40   For practical reasons, a rate that approximates the exchange rates at the dates of the transactions, for example an average rate for the period, is often used to translate income and expense items. However, if exchange rates fluctuate significantly, the use of the average rate for a period is inappropriate.

41   The exchange differences referred to in paragraph 39(c) result from:

(a)   translating income and expenses at the exchange rates at the dates of the transactions and assets and liabilities at the closing rate.

(b)   translating the opening net assets at a closing rate that differs from the previous closing rate.

These exchange differences are not recognised in profit or loss because the changes in exchange rates have little or no direct effect on the present and future cash flows from operations. The cumulative amount of the exchange differences is presented in a separate component of equity until disposal of the foreign operation. When the exchange differences relate to a foreign operation that is consolidated but not wholly-owned, accumulated exchange differences arising from translation and attributable to non-controlling interests are allocated to, and recognised as part of, non-controlling interests in the consolidated statement of financial position.

42   The results and financial position of an entity whose functional currency is the currency of a hyperinflationary economy shall be translated into a different presentation currency using the following procedures:

(a)   all amounts (ie assets, liabilities, equity items, income and expenses, including comparatives) shall be translated at the closing rate at the date of the most recent statement of financial position, except that

(b)   when amounts are translated into the currency of a non-hyperinflationary economy, comparative amounts shall be those that were presented as current year amounts in the relevant prior year financial statements (ie not adjusted for subsequent changes in the price level or subsequent changes in exchange rates).

43   When an entity's functional currency is the currency of a hyperinflationary economy, the entity shall restate its financial statements in accordance with IAS 29 before applying the translation method set out in paragraph 42, except for comparative amounts that are translated into a currency of a non-hyperinflationary economy (see paragraph 42(b)). When the economy ceases to be hyperinflationary and the entity no longer restates its financial statements in accordance with IAS 29, it shall use as the historical costs for translation into the presentation currency the amounts restated to the price level at the date the entity ceased restating its financial statements.

Translation of a foreign operation

44   Paragraphs 45–47, in addition to paragraphs 38–43, apply when the results and financial position of a foreign operation are translated into a presentation currency so that the foreign operation can be included in the financial statements of the reporting entity by consolidation or the equity method.

45   The incorporation of the results and financial position of a foreign operation with those of the reporting entity follows normal consolidation procedures, such as the elimination of intragroup balances and intragroup transactions of a subsidiary (see IFRS 10 *Consolidated Financial Statements*). However, an intragroup monetary asset (or liability), whether short-term or long-term, cannot be eliminated against the corresponding intragroup liability (or asset) without showing the results of currency fluctuations in the consolidated financial statements. This is because the monetary item represents a commitment to convert one currency into another and exposes the reporting entity to a gain or loss through currency fluctuations. Accordingly, in the consolidated financial statements of the reporting entity, such an exchange difference is recognised in profit or loss or, if it arises from the circumstances described in paragraph 32, it is recognised in other comprehensive income and accumulated in a separate component of equity until the disposal of the foreign operation.

46   When the financial statements of a foreign operation are as of a date different from that of the reporting entity, the foreign operation often prepares additional statements as of the same date as the reporting entity's financial statements. When this is not done, IFRS 10 allows the use of a different date

provided that the difference is no greater than three months and adjustments are made for the effects of any significant transactions or other events that occur between the different dates. In such a case, the assets and liabilities of the foreign operation are translated at the exchange rate at the end of the reporting period of the foreign operation. Adjustments are made for significant changes in exchange rates up to the end of the reporting period of the reporting entity in accordance with IFRS 10. The same approach is used in applying the equity method to associates and joint ventures in accordance with IAS 28 (as amended in 2011).

47   Any goodwill arising on the acquisition of a foreign operation and any fair value adjustments to the carrying amounts of assets and liabilities arising on the acquisition of that foreign operation shall be treated as assets and liabilities of the foreign operation. Thus they shall be expressed in the functional currency of the foreign operation and shall be translated at the closing rate in accordance with paragraphs 39 and 42.

Disposal or partial disposal of a foreign operation

48   On the disposal of a foreign operation, the cumulative amount of the exchange differences relating to that foreign operation, recognised in other comprehensive income and accumulated in the separate component of equity, shall be reclassified from equity to profit or loss (as a reclassification adjustment) when the gain or loss on disposal is recognised (see IAS 1 *Presentation of Financial Statements* (as revised in 2007)).

48A   In addition to the disposal of an entity's entire interest in a foreign operation, the following partial disposals are accounted for as disposals:

(a)   when the partial disposal involves the loss of control of a subsidiary that includes a foreign operation, regardless of whether the entity retains a non-controlling interest in its former subsidiary after the partial disposal; and

(b)   when the retained interest after the partial disposal of an interest in a joint arrangement or a partial disposal of an interest in an associate that includes a foreign operation is a financial asset that includes a foreign operation.

48B   On disposal of a subsidiary that includes a foreign operation, the cumulative amount of the exchange differences relating to that foreign operation that have been attributed to the non-controlling interests shall be derecognised, but shall not be reclassified to profit or loss.

48C   On the partial disposal of a subsidiary that includes a foreign operation, the entity shall re-attribute the proportionate share of the cumulative amount of the exchange differences recognised in other comprehensive income to the non-controlling interests in that foreign operation. In any other partial disposal of a foreign operation the entity shall reclassify to profit or loss only the proportionate share of the cumulative amount of the exchange differences recognised in other comprehensive income.

48D   A partial disposal of an entity's interest in a foreign operation is any reduction in an entity's ownership interest in a foreign operation, except those reductions in paragraph 48A that are accounted for as disposals.

49   An entity may dispose or partially dispose of its interest in a foreign operation through sale, liquidation, repayment of share capital or abandonment of all, or part of, that entity. A write-down of the carrying amount of a foreign operation, either because of its own losses or because of an impairment recognised by the investor, does not constitute a partial disposal. Accordingly, no part of the foreign exchange gain or loss recognised in other comprehensive income is reclassified to profit or loss at the time of a write-down.

Tax effects of all exchange differences

50   Gains and losses on foreign currency transactions and exchange differences arising on translating the results and financial position of an entity (including a foreign operation) into a different currency may have tax effects. IAS 12 *Income Taxes* applies to these tax effects.

Disclosure

51   In paragraphs 53 and 55–57 references to 'functional currency' apply, in the case of a group, to the functional currency of the parent.

52   An entity shall disclose:

    (a)   the amount of exchange differences recognised in profit or loss except for those arising on financial instruments measured at fair value through profit or loss in accordance with IFRS 9; and

    (b)   net exchange differences recognised in other comprehensive income and accumulated in a separate component of equity, and a reconciliation of the amount of such exchange differences at the beginning and end of the period.

53   When the presentation currency is different from the functional currency, that fact shall be stated, together with disclosure of the functional currency and the reason for using a different presentation currency.

54   When there is a change in the functional currency of either the reporting entity or a significant foreign operation, that fact and the reason for the change in functional currency shall be disclosed.

55   When an entity presents its financial statements in a currency that is different from its functional currency, it shall describe the financial statements as complying with IFRSs only if they comply with all the requirements of IFRSs including the translation method set out in paragraphs 39 and 42.

56   An entity sometimes presents its financial statements or other financial information in a currency that is not its functional currency without meeting the requirements of paragraph 55. For example, an entity may convert into another currency only selected items from its financial statements. Or, an entity whose functional currency is not the currency of a hyperinflationary economy may convert the financial statements into another currency by translating all items at the most recent closing rate. Such conversions are not in accordance with IFRSs and the disclosures set out in paragraph 57 are required.

57   **When an entity displays its financial statements or other financial information in a currency that is different from either its functional currency or its presentation currency and the requirements of paragraph 55 are not met, it shall:**

      (a)   **clearly identify the information as supplementary information to distinguish it from the information that complies with IFRSs;**

      (b)   **disclose the currency in which the supplementary information is displayed; and**

      (c)   **disclose the entity's functional currency and the method of translation used to determine the supplementary information.**

Effective date and transition

58   An entity shall apply this Standard for annual periods beginning on or after 1 January 2005. Earlier application is encouraged. If an entity applies this Standard for a period beginning before 1 January 2005, it shall disclose that fact.

58A   *Net Investment in a Foreign Operation* (Amendment to IAS 21), issued in December 2005, added paragraph 15A and amended paragraph 33. An entity shall apply those amendments for annual periods beginning on or after 1 January 2006. Earlier application is encouraged.

59   An entity shall apply paragraph 47 prospectively to all acquisitions occurring after the beginning of the financial reporting period in which this Standard is first applied. Retrospective application of paragraph 47 to earlier acquisitions is permitted. For an acquisition of a foreign operation treated prospectively but which occurred before the date on which this Standard is first applied, the entity shall not restate prior years and accordingly may, when appropriate, treat goodwill and fair value adjustments arising on that acquisition as assets and liabilities of the entity rather than as assets and liabilities of the foreign operation. Therefore, those goodwill and fair value adjustments either are already expressed in the entity's functional currency or are non-monetary foreign currency items, which are reported using the exchange rate at the date of the acquisition.

60   All other changes resulting from the application of this Standard shall be accounted for in accordance with the requirements of IAS 8 *Accounting Policies, Changes in Accounting Estimates and Errors*.

60A   IAS 1 (as revised in 2007) amended the terminology used throughout IFRSs. In addition it amended paragraphs 27, 30–33, 37, 39, 41, 45, 48 and 52. An entity shall apply those amendments for annual periods beginning on or after 1 January 2009. If an entity applies IAS 1 (revised 2007) for an earlier period, the amendments shall be applied for that earlier period.

60B   IAS 27 (as amended in 2008) added paragraphs 48A–48D and amended paragraph 49. An entity shall apply those amendments prospectively for annual periods beginning on or after 1 July 2009. If an entity applies IAS 27 (amended 2008) for an earlier period, the amendments shall be applied for that earlier period.

60C   [Deleted]

60D   Paragraph 60B was amended by *Improvements to IFRSs* issued in May 2010. An entity shall apply that amendment for annual periods beginning on or after 1 July 2010. Earlier application is permitted.

60E   [Deleted]

60F   IFRS 10 and IFRS 11 *Joint Arrangements*, issued in May 2011, amended paragraphs 3(b), 8, 11, 18, 19, 33, 44–46 and 48A. An entity shall apply those amendments when it applies IFRS 10 and IFRS 11.

60G   IFRS 13, issued in May 2011, amended the definition of fair value in paragraph 8 and amended paragraph 23. An entity shall apply those amendments when it applies IFRS 13.

60H   *Presentation of Items of Other Comprehensive Income* (Amendments to IAS 1), issued in June 2011, amended paragraph 39. An entity shall apply that amendment when it applies IAS 1 as amended in June 2011.

60I   [Deleted]

60J   IFRS 9, as issued in July 2014, amended paragraphs 3, 4, 5, 27 and 52 and deleted paragraphs 60C, 60E and 60I. An entity shall apply those amendments when it applies IFRS 9.

60K   IFRS 16 *Leases*, issued in January 2016, amended paragraph 16. An entity shall apply that amendment when it applies IFRS 16.

Withdrawal of other pronouncements

61   This Standard supersedes IAS 21 *The Effects of Changes in Foreign Exchange Rates* (revised in 1993).

62   This Standard supersedes the following Interpretations:

   (a)   SIC-11 *Foreign Exchange—Capitalisation of Losses Resulting from Severe Currency Devaluations*;

   (b)   SIC-19 *Reporting Currency—Measurement and Presentation of Financial Statements under IAS 21 and IAS 29*; and

   (c)   SIC-30 *Reporting Currency—Translation from Measurement Currency to Presentation Currency*.

Appendix
Amendments to other pronouncements

The amendments in this appendix shall be applied for annual periods beginning on or after 1 January 2005. If an entity applies this Standard for an earlier period, these amendments shall be applied for that earlier period.

*****

The amendments contained in this appendix when this Standard was issued in 2003 have been incorporated into the relevant pronouncements published in this volume.

© IFRS Foundation

Approval by the Board of IAS 21 issued in December 2003

International Accounting Standard 21 *The Effects of Changes in Foreign Exchange Rates* (as revised in 2003) was approved for issue by the fourteen members of the International Accounting Standards Board.

Sir David Tweedie	Chairman
Thomas E Jones	Vice-Chairman
Mary E Barth	
Hans-Georg Bruns	
Anthony T Cope	
Robert P Garnett	
Gilbert Gélard	
James J Leisenring	
Warren J McGregor	
Patricia L O'Malley	
Harry K Schmid	
John T Smith	
Geoffrey Whittington	
Tatsumi Yamada	

Approval by the Board of *Net Investment in a Foreign Operation* (Amendment to IAS 21) issued in December 2005

Net Investment in a Foreign Operation (Amendment to IAS 21) was approved for issue by the fourteen members of the International Accounting Standards Board.

Sir David Tweedie	Chairman
Thomas E Jones	Vice-Chairman
Mary E Barth	
Hans-Georg Bruns	
Anthony T Cope	
Jan Engström	
Robert P Garnett	
Gilbert Gélard	
James J Leisenring	
Warren J McGregor	
Patricia L O'Malley	
John T Smith	
Geoffrey Whittington	
Tatsumi Yamada	

IAS 23

Borrowing Costs

In April 2001 the International Accounting Standards Board (Board) adopted IAS 23 *Borrowing Costs*, which had originally been issued by the International Accounting Standards Committee in December 1993. IAS 23 *Borrowing Costs* replaced IAS 23 *Capitalisation of Borrowing Costs* (issued in March 1984).

In March 2007 the Board issued a revised IAS 23 that eliminated the option of immediate recognition of borrowing costs as an expense.

Other Standards have made minor consequential amendments to IAS 23. They include *Agriculture: Bearer Plants* (Amendments to IAS 16 and IAS 41) (issued June 2014), IFRS 9 *Financial Instruments* (issued July 2014), IFRS 16 *Leases* (issued January 2016) and *Annual Improvements to IFRS Standards 2015–2017 Cycle* (issued December 2017).

Contents

FOR THE ACCOMPANYING GUIDANCE LISTED BELOW, SEE PART B OF THIS EDITION

FOR THE BASIS FOR CONCLUSIONS, SEE PART C OF THIS EDITION

International Accounting Standard 23 *Borrowing Costs* (IAS 23) is set out in paragraphs 1–30 and the Appendix. All of the paragraphs have equal authority but retain the IASC format of the Standard when it was adopted by the IASB. IAS 23 should be read in the context of its core principle and the Basis for Conclusions, the *Preface to IFRS Standards* and the *Conceptual Framework for Financial Reporting*. IAS 8 *Accounting Policies, Changes in Accounting Estimates and Errors* provides a basis for selecting and applying accounting policies in the absence of explicit guidance.

International Accounting Standard 23
Borrowing Costs

Core principle

1   Borrowing costs that are directly attributable to the acquisition,
         construction or production of a qualifying asset form part of the cost of
         that asset. Other borrowing costs are recognised as an expense.

Scope

2   An entity shall apply this Standard in accounting for borrowing costs.

3   The Standard does not deal with the actual or imputed cost of equity,
         including preferred capital not classified as a liability.

4   An entity is not required to apply the Standard to borrowing costs directly
         attributable to the acquisition, construction or production of:

         (a)   a qualifying asset measured at fair value, for example a biological asset
                  within the scope of IAS 41 *Agriculture*; or

         (b)   inventories that are manufactured, or otherwise produced, in large
                  quantities on a repetitive basis.

Definitions

5   This Standard uses the following terms with the meanings specified:

         Borrowing costs are interest and other costs that an entity incurs in
         connection with the borrowing of funds.

         A *qualifying asset* is an asset that necessarily takes a substantial period of
         time to get ready for its intended use or sale.

6   Borrowing costs may include:

         (a)   interest expense calculated using the effective interest method as
                  described in IFRS 9;

         (b)   [deleted]

         (c)   [deleted]

         (d)   interest in respect of lease liabilities recognised in accordance with
                  IFRS 16 *Leases*; and

         (e)   exchange differences arising from foreign currency borrowings to the
                  extent that they are regarded as an adjustment to interest costs.

7   Depending on the circumstances, any of the following may be qualifying
         assets:

         (a)   inventories

         (b)   manufacturing plants

(c)   power generation facilities

(d)   intangible assets

(e)   investment properties

(f)   bearer plants.

Financial assets, and inventories that are manufactured, or otherwise produced, over a short period of time, are not qualifying assets. Assets that are ready for their intended use or sale when acquired are not qualifying assets.

Recognition

8   **An entity shall capitalise borrowing costs that are directly attributable to the acquisition, construction or production of a qualifying asset as part of the cost of that asset. An entity shall recognise other borrowing costs as an expense in the period in which it incurs them.**

9   Borrowing costs that are directly attributable to the acquisition, construction or production of a qualifying asset are included in the cost of that asset. Such borrowing costs are capitalised as part of the cost of the asset when it is probable that they will result in future economic benefits to the entity and the costs can be measured reliably. When an entity applies IAS 29 *Financial Reporting in Hyperinflationary Economies*, it recognises as an expense the part of borrowing costs that compensates for inflation during the same period in accordance with paragraph 21 of that Standard.

Borrowing costs eligible for capitalisation

10   The borrowing costs that are directly attributable to the acquisition, construction or production of a qualifying asset are those borrowing costs that would have been avoided if the expenditure on the qualifying asset had not been made. When an entity borrows funds specifically for the purpose of obtaining a particular qualifying asset, the borrowing costs that directly relate to that qualifying asset can be readily identified.

11   It may be difficult to identify a direct relationship between particular borrowings and a qualifying asset and to determine the borrowings that could otherwise have been avoided. Such a difficulty occurs, for example, when the financing activity of an entity is co-ordinated centrally. Difficulties also arise when a group uses a range of debt instruments to borrow funds at varying rates of interest, and lends those funds on various bases to other entities in the group. Other complications arise through the use of loans denominated in or linked to foreign currencies, when the group operates in highly inflationary economies, and from fluctuations in exchange rates. As a result, the determination of the amount of borrowing costs that are directly attributable to the acquisition of a qualifying asset is difficult and the exercise of judgement is required.

12   To the extent that an entity borrows funds specifically for the purpose of obtaining a qualifying asset, the entity shall determine the amount of borrowing costs eligible for capitalisation as the actual borrowing costs incurred on that borrowing during the period less any investment income on the temporary investment of those borrowings.

13   The financing arrangements for a qualifying asset may result in an entity obtaining borrowed funds and incurring associated borrowing costs before some or all of the funds are used for expenditures on the qualifying asset. In such circumstances, the funds are often temporarily invested pending their expenditure on the qualifying asset. In determining the amount of borrowing costs eligible for capitalisation during a period, any investment income earned on such funds is deducted from the borrowing costs incurred.

14   To the extent that an entity borrows funds generally and uses them for the purpose of obtaining a qualifying asset, the entity shall determine the amount of borrowing costs eligible for capitalisation by applying a capitalisation rate to the expenditures on that asset. The capitalisation rate shall be the weighted average of the borrowing costs applicable to all borrowings of the entity that are outstanding during the period. However, an entity shall exclude from this calculation borrowing costs applicable to borrowings made specifically for the purpose of obtaining a qualifying asset until substantially all the activities necessary to prepare that asset for its intended use or sale are complete. The amount of borrowing costs that an entity capitalises during a period shall not exceed the amount of borrowing costs it incurred during that period.

15   In some circumstances, it is appropriate to include all borrowings of the parent and its subsidiaries when computing a weighted average of the borrowing costs; in other circumstances, it is appropriate for each subsidiary to use a weighted average of the borrowing costs applicable to its own borrowings.

Excess of the carrying amount of the qualifying asset over recoverable amount

16   When the carrying amount or the expected ultimate cost of the qualifying asset exceeds its recoverable amount or net realisable value, the carrying amount is written down or written off in accordance with the requirements of other Standards. In certain circumstances, the amount of the write-down or write-off is written back in accordance with those other Standards.

Commencement of capitalisation

17   An entity shall begin capitalising borrowing costs as part of the cost of a qualifying asset on the commencement date. The commencement date for capitalisation is the date when the entity first meets all of the following conditions:

(a)   it incurs expenditures for the asset;

(b)   it incurs borrowing costs; and

        © IFRS Foundation

(c)   it undertakes activities that are necessary to prepare the asset for its intended use or sale.

18   Expenditures on a qualifying asset include only those expenditures that have resulted in payments of cash, transfers of other assets or the assumption of interest-bearing liabilities. Expenditures are reduced by any progress payments received and grants received in connection with the asset (see IAS 20 *Accounting for Government Grants and Disclosure of Government Assistance*). The average carrying amount of the asset during a period, including borrowing costs previously capitalised, is normally a reasonable approximation of the expenditures to which the capitalisation rate is applied in that period.

19   The activities necessary to prepare the asset for its intended use or sale encompass more than the physical construction of the asset. They include technical and administrative work prior to the commencement of physical construction, such as the activities associated with obtaining permits prior to the commencement of the physical construction. However, such activities exclude the holding of an asset when no production or development that changes the asset's condition is taking place. For example, borrowing costs incurred while land is under development are capitalised during the period in which activities related to the development are being undertaken. However, borrowing costs incurred while land acquired for building purposes is held without any associated development activity do not qualify for capitalisation.

Suspension of capitalisation

20   An entity shall suspend capitalisation of borrowing costs during extended periods in which it suspends active development of a qualifying asset.

21   An entity may incur borrowing costs during an extended period in which it suspends the activities necessary to prepare an asset for its intended use or sale. Such costs are costs of holding partially completed assets and do not qualify for capitalisation. However, an entity does not normally suspend capitalising borrowing costs during a period when it carries out substantial technical and administrative work. An entity also does not suspend capitalising borrowing costs when a temporary delay is a necessary part of the process of getting an asset ready for its intended use or sale. For example, capitalisation continues during the extended period that high water levels delay construction of a bridge, if such high water levels are common during the construction period in the geographical region involved.

Cessation of capitalisation

22   An entity shall cease capitalising borrowing costs when substantially all the activities necessary to prepare the qualifying asset for its intended use or sale are complete.

23   An asset is normally ready for its intended use or sale when the physical construction of the asset is complete even though routine administrative work might still continue. If minor modifications, such as the decoration of a property to the purchaser's or user's specification, are all that are outstanding, this indicates that substantially all the activities are complete.

24   When an entity completes the construction of a qualifying asset in parts and each part is capable of being used while construction continues on other parts, the entity shall cease capitalising borrowing costs when it completes substantially all the activities necessary to prepare that part for its intended use or sale.

25   A business park comprising several buildings, each of which can be used individually, is an example of a qualifying asset for which each part is capable of being usable while construction continues on other parts. An example of a qualifying asset that needs to be complete before any part can be used is an industrial plant involving several processes which are carried out in sequence at different parts of the plant within the same site, such as a steel mill.

Disclosure

26   An entity shall disclose:

(a)   the amount of borrowing costs capitalised during the period; and

(b)   the capitalisation rate used to determine the amount of borrowing costs eligible for capitalisation.

Transitional provisions

27   When application of this Standard constitutes a change in accounting policy, an entity shall apply the Standard to borrowing costs relating to qualifying assets for which the commencement date for capitalisation is on or after the effective date.

28   However, an entity may designate any date before the effective date and apply the Standard to borrowing costs relating to all qualifying assets for which the commencement date for capitalisation is on or after that date.

28A   *Annual Improvements to IFRS Standards 2015–2017 Cycle*, issued in December 2017, amended paragraph 14. An entity shall apply those amendments to borrowing costs incurred on or after the beginning of the annual reporting period in which the entity first applies those amendments.

Effective date

29   An entity shall apply the Standard for annual periods beginning on or after 1 January 2009. Earlier application is permitted. If an entity applies the Standard from a date before 1 January 2009, it shall disclose that fact.

29A   Paragraph 6 was amended by *Improvements to IFRSs* issued in May 2008. An entity shall apply that amendment for annual periods beginning on or after 1 January 2009. Earlier application is permitted. If an entity applies the amendment for an earlier period it shall disclose that fact.

29B   IFRS 9, as issued in July 2014, amended paragraph 6. An entity shall apply that amendment when it applies IFRS 9.

29C IFRS 16, issued in January 2016, amended paragraph 6. An entity shall apply that amendment when it applies IFRS 16.

29D *Annual Improvements to IFRS Standards 2015–2017 Cycle*, issued in December 2017, amended paragraph 14 and added paragraph 28A. An entity shall apply those amendments for annual reporting periods beginning on or after 1 January 2019. Earlier application is permitted. If an entity applies those amendments earlier, it shall disclose that fact.

Withdrawal of IAS 23 (revised 1993)

30 This Standard supersedes IAS 23 *Borrowing Costs* revised in 1993.

Appendix
Amendments to other pronouncements

The amendments in this appendix shall be applied for annual periods beginning on or after 1 January 2009. If an entity applies this Standard for an earlier period, the amendments in this appendix shall be applied for that earlier period. In the amended paragraphs, new text is underlined and deleted text is struck through.

The amendments contained in this appendix when this IFRS was issued in 2007 have been incorporated into the relevant IFRSs published in this volume.

Approval by the Board of IAS 23 issued in March 2007

International Accounting Standard 23 *Borrowing Costs* (as revised in 2007) was approved for issue by eleven of the fourteen members of the International Accounting Standards Board. Messrs Cope, Danjou and Garnett dissented. Their dissenting opinions are set out after the Basis for Conclusions.

Sir David Tweedie	Chairman
Thomas E Jones	Vice-Chairman
Mary E Barth	
Hans-Georg Bruns	
Anthony T Cope	
Philippe Danjou	
Jan Engström	
Robert P Garnett	
Gilbert Gélard	
James J Leisenring	
Warren J McGregor	
Patricia L O'Malley	
John T Smith	
Tatsumi Yamada	

IAS 24

Related Party Disclosures

In April 2001 the International Accounting Standards Board (Board) adopted IAS 24 *Related Party Disclosures*, which had originally been issued by the International Accounting Standards Committee in July 1984.

In December 2003 the Board issued a revised IAS 24 as part of its initial agenda of technical projects that included amending disclosures on management compensation and related party disclosures in separate financial statements. The Board revised IAS 24 again to address the disclosures in government-related entities.

In November 2009 the Board issued a revised IAS 24 to simplify the definition of 'related party' and to provide an exemption from the disclosure requirements for some government-related entities.

Other Standards have made minor consequential amendments to IAS 24. They include IFRS 10 *Consolidated Financial Statements* (issued May 2011), IFRS 11 *Joint Arrangements* (issued May 2011), IFRS 12 *Disclosure of Interests in Other Entities* (issued May 2011), IAS 19 *Employee Benefits* (issued June 2011), *Investment Entities* (Amendments to IFRS 10, IFRS 12 and IAS 27) (issued October 2012) and *Annual Improvements to IFRSs 2010–2012 Cycle* (issued December 2013).

CONTENTS

FOR THE ACCOMPANYING GUIDANCE LISTED BELOW, SEE PART B OF THIS EDITION

FOR THE BASIS FOR CONCLUSIONS, SEE PART C OF THIS EDITION

International Accounting Standard 24 *Related Party Disclosures* (IAS 24) is set out in paragraphs 1–29 and the Appendix. All of the paragraphs have equal authority but retain the IASC format of the Standard when it was adopted by the IASB. IAS 24 should be read in the context of its objective and the Basis for Conclusions, the *Preface to IFRS Standards* and the *Conceptual Framework for Financial Reporting*. IAS 8 *Accounting Policies, Changes in Accounting Estimates and Errors* provides a basis for selecting and applying accounting policies in the absence of explicit guidance.

International Accounting Standard 24
Related Party Disclosures

Objective

1   The objective of this Standard is to ensure that an entity's financial statements contain the disclosures necessary to draw attention to the possibility that its financial position and profit or loss may have been affected by the existence of related parties and by transactions and outstanding balances, including commitments, with such parties.

Scope

2   This Standard shall be applied in:

     (a)   identifying related party relationships and transactions;

     (b)   identifying outstanding balances, including commitments, between an entity and its related parties;

     (c)   identifying the circumstances in which disclosure of the items in (a) and (b) is required; and

     (d)   determining the disclosures to be made about those items.

3   This Standard requires disclosure of related party relationships, transactions and outstanding balances, including commitments, in the consolidated and separate financial statements of a parent or investors with joint control of, or significant influence over, an investee presented in accordance with IFRS 10 *Consolidated Financial Statements* or IAS 27 *Separate Financial Statements*. This Standard also applies to individual financial statements.

4   Related party transactions and outstanding balances with other entities in a group are disclosed in an entity's financial statements. Intragroup related party transactions and outstanding balances are eliminated, except for those between an investment entity and its subsidiaries measured at fair value through profit or loss, in the preparation of consolidated financial statements of the group.

Purpose of related party disclosures

5   Related party relationships are a normal feature of commerce and business. For example, entities frequently carry on parts of their activities through subsidiaries, joint ventures and associates. In those circumstances, the entity has the ability to affect the financial and operating policies of the investee through the presence of control, joint control or significant influence.

6   A related party relationship could have an effect on the profit or loss and financial position of an entity. Related parties may enter into transactions that unrelated parties would not. For example, an entity that sells goods to its parent at cost might not sell on those terms to another customer. Also,

transactions between related parties may not be made at the same amounts as between unrelated parties.

7   The profit or loss and financial position of an entity may be affected by a related party relationship even if related party transactions do not occur. The mere existence of the relationship may be sufficient to affect the transactions of the entity with other parties. For example, a subsidiary may terminate relations with a trading partner on acquisition by the parent of a fellow subsidiary engaged in the same activity as the former trading partner. Alternatively, one party may refrain from acting because of the significant influence of another—for example, a subsidiary may be instructed by its parent not to engage in research and development.

8   For these reasons, knowledge of an entity's transactions, outstanding balances, including commitments, and relationships with related parties may affect assessments of its operations by users of financial statements, including assessments of the risks and opportunities facing the entity.

Definitions

9   The following terms are used in this Standard with the meanings specified:

A *related party* is a person or entity that is related to the entity that is preparing its financial statements (in this Standard referred to as the 'reporting entity').

(a)   A person or a close member of that person's family is related to a reporting entity if that person:

    (i)   has control or joint control of the reporting entity;

    (ii)   has significant influence over the reporting entity; or

    (iii)   is a member of the key management personnel of the reporting entity or of a parent of the reporting entity.

(b)   An entity is related to a reporting entity if any of the following conditions applies:

    (i)   The entity and the reporting entity are members of the same group (which means that each parent, subsidiary and fellow subsidiary is related to the others).

    (ii)   One entity is an associate or joint venture of the other entity (or an associate or joint venture of a member of a group of which the other entity is a member).

    (iii)   Both entities are joint ventures of the same third party.

    (iv)   One entity is a joint venture of a third entity and the other entity is an associate of the third entity.

(v)   The entity is a post-employment benefit plan for the benefit of employees of either the reporting entity or an entity related to the reporting entity. If the reporting entity is itself such a plan, the sponsoring employers are also related to the reporting entity.

(vi)   The entity is controlled or jointly controlled by a person identified in (a).

(vii)   A person identified in (a)(i) has significant influence over the entity or is a member of the key management personnel of the entity (or of a parent of the entity).

(viii)   The entity, or any member of a group of which it is a part, provides key management personnel services to the reporting entity or to the parent of the reporting entity.

A *related party transaction* is a transfer of resources, services or obligations between a reporting entity and a related party, regardless of whether a price is charged.

Close members of the family of a person are those family members who may be expected to influence, or be influenced by, that person in their dealings with the entity and include:

(a)   that person's children and spouse or domestic partner;

(b)   children of that person's spouse or domestic partner; and

(c)   dependants of that person or that person's spouse or domestic partner.

Compensation includes all employee benefits (as defined in IAS 19 *Employee Benefits*) including employee benefits to which IFRS 2 *Share-based Payment* applies. Employee benefits are all forms of consideration paid, payable or provided by the entity, or on behalf of the entity, in exchange for services rendered to the entity. It also includes such consideration paid on behalf of a parent of the entity in respect of the entity. Compensation includes:

(a)   short-term employee benefits, such as wages, salaries and social security contributions, paid annual leave and paid sick leave, profit-sharing and bonuses (if payable within twelve months of the end of the period) and non-monetary benefits (such as medical care, housing, cars and free or subsidised goods or services) for current employees;

(b)   post-employment benefits such as pensions, other retirement benefits, post-employment life insurance and post-employment medical care;

(c) other long-term employee benefits, including long-service leave or sabbatical leave, jubilee or other long-service benefits, long-term disability benefits and, if they are not payable wholly within twelve months after the end of the period, profit-sharing, bonuses and deferred compensation;

(d) termination benefits; and

(e) share-based payment.

Key management personnel are those persons having authority and responsibility for planning, directing and controlling the activities of the entity, directly or indirectly, including any director (whether executive or otherwise) of that entity.

Government refers to government, government agencies and similar bodies whether local, national or international.

A *government-related entity* is an entity that is controlled, jointly controlled or significantly influenced by a government.

The terms 'control' and 'investment entity', 'joint control' and 'significant influence' are defined in IFRS 10, IFRS 11 *Joint Arrangements* and IAS 28 *Investments in Associates and Joint Ventures* respectively and are used in this Standard with the meanings specified in those IFRSs.

10 In considering each possible related party relationship, attention is directed to the substance of the relationship and not merely the legal form.

11 In the context of this Standard, the following are not related parties:

(a) two entities simply because they have a director or other member of key management personnel in common or because a member of key management personnel of one entity has significant influence over the other entity.

(b) two joint venturers simply because they share joint control of a joint venture.

(c) (i) providers of finance,

(ii) trade unions,

(iii) public utilities, and

(iv) departments and agencies of a government that does not control, jointly control or significant influence the reporting entity,

simply by virtue of their normal dealings with an entity (even though they may affect the freedom of action of an entity or participate in its decision-making process).

(d) a customer, supplier, franchisor, distributor or general agent with whom an entity transacts a significant volume of business, simply by virtue of the resulting economic dependence.

12   In the definition of a related party, an associate includes subsidiaries of the associate and a joint venture includes subsidiaries of the joint venture. Therefore, for example, an associate's subsidiary and the investor that has significant influence over the associate are related to each other.

Disclosures

All entities

13   Relationships between a parent and its subsidiaries shall be disclosed irrespective of whether there have been transactions between them. An entity shall disclose the name of its parent and, if different, the ultimate controlling party. If neither the entity's parent nor the ultimate controlling party produces consolidated financial statements available for public use, the name of the next most senior parent that does so shall also be disclosed.

14   To enable users of financial statements to form a view about the effects of related party relationships on an entity, it is appropriate to disclose the related party relationship when control exists, irrespective of whether there have been transactions between the related parties.

15   The requirement to disclose related party relationships between a parent and its subsidiaries is in addition to the disclosure requirements in IAS 27 and IFRS 12 *Disclosure of Interests in Other Entities*.

16   Paragraph 13 refers to the next most senior parent. This is the first parent in the group above the immediate parent that produces consolidated financial statements available for public use.

17   An entity shall disclose key management personnel compensation in total and for each of the following categories:

(a)   short-term employee benefits;

(b)   post-employment benefits;

(c)   other long-term benefits;

(d)   termination benefits; and

(e)   share-based payment.

17A   If an entity obtains key management personnel services from another entity (the 'management entity'), the entity is not required to apply the requirements in paragraph 17 to the compensation paid or payable by the management entity to the management entity's employees or directors.

18   If an entity has had related party transactions during the periods covered by the financial statements, it shall disclose the nature of the related party relationship as well as information about those transactions and outstanding balances, including commitments, necessary for users to understand the potential effect of the relationship on the financial

statements. These disclosure requirements are in addition to those in paragraph 17. At a minimum, disclosures shall include:

(a) the amount of the transactions;

(b) the amount of outstanding balances, including commitments, and:

   (i) their terms and conditions, including whether they are secured, and the nature of the consideration to be provided in settlement; and

   (ii) details of any guarantees given or received;

(c) provisions for doubtful debts related to the amount of outstanding balances; and

(d) the expense recognised during the period in respect of bad or doubtful debts due from related parties.

18A   Amounts incurred by the entity for the provision of key management personnel services that are provided by a separate management entity shall be disclosed.

19   The disclosures required by paragraph 18 shall be made separately for each of the following categories:

(a) the parent;

(b) entities with joint control of, or significant influence over, the entity;

(c) subsidiaries;

(d) associates;

(e) joint ventures in which the entity is a joint venturer;

(f) key management personnel of the entity or its parent; and

(g) other related parties.

20   The classification of amounts payable to, and receivable from, related parties in the different categories as required in paragraph 19 is an extension of the disclosure requirement in IAS 1 *Presentation of Financial Statements* for information to be presented either in the statement of financial position or in the notes. The categories are extended to provide a more comprehensive analysis of related party balances and apply to related party transactions.

21   The following are examples of transactions that are disclosed if they are with a related party:

(a) purchases or sales of goods (finished or unfinished);

(b) purchases or sales of property and other assets;

(c) rendering or receiving of services;

(d) leases;

(e) transfers of research and development;

(f)   transfers under licence agreements;

(g)   transfers under finance arrangements (including loans and equity contributions in cash or in kind);

(h)   provision of guarantees or collateral;

(i)   commitments to do something if a particular event occurs or does not occur in the future, including executory contracts[1] (recognised and unrecognised); and

(j)   settlement of liabilities on behalf of the entity or by the entity on behalf of that related party.

22   Participation by a parent or subsidiary in a defined benefit plan that shares risks between group entities is a transaction between related parties (see paragraph 42 of IAS 19 (as amended in 2011)).

23   Disclosures that related party transactions were made on terms equivalent to those that prevail in arm's length transactions are made only if such terms can be substantiated.

24   Items of a similar nature may be disclosed in aggregate except when separate disclosure is necessary for an understanding of the effects of related party transactions on the financial statements of the entity.

Government-related entities

25   A reporting entity is exempt from the disclosure requirements of paragraph 18 in relation to related party transactions and outstanding balances, including commitments, with:

(a)   a government that has control or joint control of, or significant influence over, the reporting entity; and

(b)   another entity that is a related party because the same government has control or joint control of, or significant influence over, both the reporting entity and the other entity.

26   If a reporting entity applies the exemption in paragraph 25, it shall disclose the following about the transactions and related outstanding balances referred to in paragraph 25:

(a)   the name of the government and the nature of its relationship with the reporting entity (ie control, joint control or significant influence);

(b)   the following information in sufficient detail to enable users of the entity's financial statements to understand the effect of related party transactions on its financial statements:

---

1   IAS 37 *Provisions, Contingent Liabilities and Contingent Assets* defines executory contracts as contracts under which neither party has performed any of its obligations or both parties have partially performed their obligations to an equal extent.

      (i)   the nature and amount of each individually significant transaction; and

      (ii)   for other transactions that are collectively, but not individually, significant, a qualitative or quantitative indication of their extent. Types of transactions include those listed in paragraph 21.

27   In using its judgement to determine the level of detail to be disclosed in accordance with the requirements in paragraph 26(b), the reporting entity shall consider the closeness of the related party relationship and other factors relevant in establishing the level of significance of the transaction such as whether it is:

      (a)   significant in terms of size;

      (b)   carried out on non-market terms;

      (c)   outside normal day-to-day business operations, such as the purchase and sale of businesses;

      (d)   disclosed to regulatory or supervisory authorities;

      (e)   reported to senior management;

      (f)   subject to shareholder approval.

Effective date and transition

28   An entity shall apply this Standard retrospectively for annual periods beginning on or after 1 January 2011. Earlier application is permitted, either of the whole Standard or of the partial exemption in paragraphs 25–27 for government-related entities. If an entity applies either the whole Standard or that partial exemption for a period beginning before 1 January 2011, it shall disclose that fact.

28A   IFRS 10, IFRS 11 *Joint Arrangements* and IFRS 12, issued in May 2011, amended paragraphs 3, 9, 11(b), 15, 19(b) and (e) and 25. An entity shall apply those amendments when it applies IFRS 10, IFRS 11 and IFRS 12.

28B   *Investment Entities* (Amendments to IFRS 10, IFRS 12 and IAS 27), issued in October 2012, amended paragraphs 4 and 9. An entity shall apply those amendments for annual periods beginning on or after 1 January 2014. Earlier application of *Investment Entities* is permitted. If an entity applies those amendments earlier it shall also apply all amendments included in *Investment Entities* at the same time.

28C   *Annual Improvements to IFRSs 2010–2012 Cycle*, issued in December 2013, amended paragraph 9 and added paragraphs 17A and 18A. An entity shall apply that amendment for annual periods beginning on or after 1 July 2014. Earlier application is permitted. If an entity applies that amendment for an earlier period it shall disclose that fact.

Withdrawal of IAS 24 (2003)

29   This Standard supersedes IAS 24 *Related Party Disclosures* (as revised in 2003).

© IFRS Foundation

Appendix
Amendment to IFRS 8 *Operating Segments*

This amendment contained in this appendix when this Standard was issued in 2009 has been incorporated into IFRS 8 as published in this volume.

Approval by the Board of IAS 24 issued in November 2009

International Accounting Standard 24 *Related Party Disclosures* (as revised in 2009) was approved for issue by thirteen of the fifteen members of the International Accounting Standards Board. Mr Garnett dissented. His dissenting opinion is set out after the Basis for Conclusions. Ms McConnell abstained from voting in view of her recent appointment to the Board.

Sir David Tweedie	Chairman
Stephen Cooper	
Philippe Danjou	
Jan Engström	
Patrick Finnegan	
Robert P Garnett	
Gilbert Gélard	
Amaro Luiz de Oliveira Gomes	
Prabhakar Kalavacherla	
James J Leisenring	
Patricia McConnell	
Warren J McGregor	
John T Smith	
Tatsumi Yamada	
Wei-Guo Zhang	

Accounting and Reporting by Retirement Benefit Plans

In April 2001 the International Accounting Standards Board adopted IAS 26 *Accounting and Reporting by Retirement Benefit Plans*, which had originally been issued by the International Accounting Standards Committee in January 1987.

Contents

International Accounting Standard 26 *Accounting and Reporting by Retirement Benefit Plans* (IAS 26) is set out in paragraphs 1–37. All the paragraphs have equal authority but retain the IASC format of the Standard when it was adopted by the IASB. IAS 26 should be read in the context of the *Preface to IFRS Standards* and the *Conceptual Framework for Financial Reporting*. IAS 8 *Accounting Policies, Changes in Accounting Estimates and Errors* provides a basis for selecting and applying accounting policies in the absence of explicit guidance.

International Accounting Standard 26
Accounting and Reporting by Retirement Benefit Plans

Scope

1   This Standard shall be applied in the financial statements of retirement benefit plans where such financial statements are prepared.

2   Retirement benefit plans are sometimes referred to by various other names, such as 'pension schemes', 'superannuation schemes' or 'retirement benefit schemes'. This Standard regards a retirement benefit plan as a reporting entity separate from the employers of the participants in the plan. All other Standards apply to the financial statements of retirement benefit plans to the extent that they are not superseded by this Standard.

3   This Standard deals with accounting and reporting by the plan to all participants as a group. It does not deal with reports to individual participants about their retirement benefit rights.

4   IAS 19 *Employee Benefits* is concerned with the determination of the cost of retirement benefits in the financial statements of employers having plans. Hence this Standard complements IAS 19.

5   Retirement benefit plans may be defined contribution plans or defined benefit plans. Many require the creation of separate funds, which may or may not have separate legal identity and may or may not have trustees, to which contributions are made and from which retirement benefits are paid. This Standard applies regardless of whether such a fund is created and regardless of whether there are trustees.

6   Retirement benefit plans with assets invested with insurance companies are subject to the same accounting and funding requirements as privately invested arrangements. Accordingly, they are within the scope of this Standard unless the contract with the insurance company is in the name of a specified participant or a group of participants and the retirement benefit obligation is solely the responsibility of the insurance company.

7   This Standard does not deal with other forms of employment benefits such as employment termination indemnities, deferred compensation arrangements, long-service leave benefits, special early retirement or redundancy plans, health and welfare plans or bonus plans. Government social security type arrangements are also excluded from the scope of this Standard.

Definitions

8   The following terms are used in this Standard with the meanings specified:

Retirement benefit plans are arrangements whereby an entity provides benefits for employees on or after termination of service (either in the form of an annual income or as a lump sum) when such benefits, or the contributions towards them, can be determined or estimated in advance of retirement from the provisions of a document or from the entity's practices.

Defined contribution plans are retirement benefit plans under which amounts to be paid as retirement benefits are determined by contributions to a fund together with investment earnings thereon.

Defined benefit plans are retirement benefit plans under which amounts to be paid as retirement benefits are determined by reference to a formula usually based on employees' earnings and/or years of service.

Funding is the transfer of assets to an entity (the *fund*) separate from the employer's entity to meet future obligations for the payment of retirement benefits.

For the purposes of this Standard the following terms are also used:

Participants are the members of a retirement benefit plan and others who are entitled to benefits under the plan.

Net assets available for benefits are the assets of a plan less liabilities other than the actuarial present value of promised retirement benefits.

Actuarial present value of promised retirement benefits is the present value of the expected payments by a retirement benefit plan to existing and past employees, attributable to the service already rendered.

Vested benefits are benefits, the rights to which, under the conditions of a retirement benefit plan, are not conditional on continued employment.

9   Some retirement benefit plans have sponsors other than employers; this Standard also applies to the financial statements of such plans.

10   Most retirement benefit plans are based on formal agreements. Some plans are informal but have acquired a degree of obligation as a result of employers' established practices. While some plans permit employers to limit their obligations under the plans, it is usually difficult for an employer to cancel a plan if employees are to be retained. The same basis of accounting and reporting applies to an informal plan as to a formal plan.

11   Many retirement benefit plans provide for the establishment of separate funds into which contributions are made and out of which benefits are paid. Such funds may be administered by parties who act independently in managing fund assets. Those parties are called trustees in some countries. The term trustee is used in this Standard to describe such parties regardless of whether a trust has been formed.

12   Retirement benefit plans are normally described as either defined contribution plans or defined benefit plans, each having their own distinctive characteristics. Occasionally plans exist that contain characteristics of both. Such hybrid plans are considered to be defined benefit plans for the purposes of this Standard.

Defined contribution plans

13   The financial statements of a defined contribution plan shall contain a statement of net assets available for benefits and a description of the funding policy.

14   Under a defined contribution plan, the amount of a participant's future benefits is determined by the contributions paid by the employer, the participant, or both, and the operating efficiency and investment earnings of the fund. An employer's obligation is usually discharged by contributions to the fund. An actuary's advice is not normally required although such advice is sometimes used to estimate future benefits that may be achievable based on present contributions and varying levels of future contributions and investment earnings.

15   The participants are interested in the activities of the plan because they directly affect the level of their future benefits. Participants are interested in knowing whether contributions have been received and proper control has been exercised to protect the rights of beneficiaries. An employer is interested in the efficient and fair operation of the plan.

16   The objective of reporting by a defined contribution plan is periodically to provide information about the plan and the performance of its investments. That objective is usually achieved by providing financial statements including the following:

   (a)   a description of significant activities for the period and the effect of any changes relating to the plan, and its membership and terms and conditions;

   (b)   statements reporting on the transactions and investment performance for the period and the financial position of the plan at the end of the period; and

   (c)   a description of the investment policies.

Defined benefit plans

17   The financial statements of a defined benefit plan shall contain either:

   (a)   a statement that shows:

       (i)   the net assets available for benefits;

       (ii)   the actuarial present value of promised retirement benefits, distinguishing between vested benefits and non-vested benefits; and

       (iii)   the resulting excess or deficit; or

   (b)   a statement of net assets available for benefits including either:

       (i)   a note disclosing the actuarial present value of promised retirement benefits, distinguishing between vested benefits and non-vested benefits; or

(ii)   a reference to this information in an accompanying actuarial report.

If an actuarial valuation has not been prepared at the date of the financial statements, the most recent valuation shall be used as a base and the date of the valuation disclosed.

18   For the purposes of paragraph 17, the actuarial present value of promised retirement benefits shall be based on the benefits promised under the terms of the plan on service rendered to date using either current salary levels or projected salary levels with disclosure of the basis used. The effect of any changes in actuarial assumptions that have had a significant effect on the actuarial present value of promised retirement benefits shall also be disclosed.

19   The financial statements shall explain the relationship between the actuarial present value of promised retirement benefits and the net assets available for benefits, and the policy for the funding of promised benefits.

20   Under a defined benefit plan, the payment of promised retirement benefits depends on the financial position of the plan and the ability of contributors to make future contributions to the plan as well as the investment performance and operating efficiency of the plan.

21   A defined benefit plan needs the periodic advice of an actuary to assess the financial condition of the plan, review the assumptions and recommend future contribution levels.

22   The objective of reporting by a defined benefit plan is periodically to provide information about the financial resources and activities of the plan that is useful in assessing the relationships between the accumulation of resources and plan benefits over time. This objective is usually achieved by providing financial statements including the following:

(a)   a description of significant activities for the period and the effect of any changes relating to the plan, and its membership and terms and conditions;

(b)   statements reporting on the transactions and investment performance for the period and the financial position of the plan at the end of the period;

(c)   actuarial information either as part of the statements or by way of a separate report; and

(d)   a description of the investment policies.

Actuarial present value of promised retirement benefits

23   The present value of the expected payments by a retirement benefit plan may be calculated and reported using current salary levels or projected salary levels up to the time of retirement of participants.

24   The reasons given for adopting a current salary approach include:

(a)   the actuarial present value of promised retirement benefits, being the sum of the amounts presently attributable to each participant in the plan, can be calculated more objectively than with projected salary levels because it involves fewer assumptions;

(b)   increases in benefits attributable to a salary increase become an obligation of the plan at the time of the salary increase; and

(c)   the amount of the actuarial present value of promised retirement benefits using current salary levels is generally more closely related to the amount payable in the event of termination or discontinuance of the plan.

25   Reasons given for adopting a projected salary approach include:

(a)   financial information should be prepared on a going concern basis, irrespective of the assumptions and estimates that must be made;

(b)   under final pay plans, benefits are determined by reference to salaries at or near retirement date; hence salaries, contribution levels and rates of return must be projected; and

(c)   failure to incorporate salary projections, when most funding is based on salary projections, may result in the reporting of an apparent overfunding when the plan is not overfunded, or in reporting adequate funding when the plan is underfunded.

26   The actuarial present value of promised retirement benefits based on current salaries is disclosed in the financial statements of a plan to indicate the obligation for benefits earned to the date of the financial statements. The actuarial present value of promised retirement benefits based on projected salaries is disclosed to indicate the magnitude of the potential obligation on a going concern basis which is generally the basis for funding. In addition to disclosure of the actuarial present value of promised retirement benefits, sufficient explanation may need to be given so as to indicate clearly the context in which the actuarial present value of promised retirement benefits should be read. Such explanation may be in the form of information about the adequacy of the planned future funding and of the funding policy based on salary projections. This may be included in the financial statements or in the actuary's report.

Frequency of actuarial valuations

27   In many countries, actuarial valuations are not obtained more frequently than every three years. If an actuarial valuation has not been prepared at the date of the financial statements, the most recent valuation is used as a base and the date of the valuation disclosed.

Financial statement content

28   For defined benefit plans, information is presented in one of the following formats which reflect different practices in the disclosure and presentation of actuarial information:

(a)   a statement is included in the financial statements that shows the net assets available for benefits, the actuarial present value of promised retirement benefits, and the resulting excess or deficit. The financial statements of the plan also contain statements of changes in net assets available for benefits and changes in the actuarial present value of promised retirement benefits. The financial statements may be accompanied by a separate actuary's report supporting the actuarial present value of promised retirement benefits;

(b)   financial statements that include a statement of net assets available for benefits and a statement of changes in net assets available for benefits. The actuarial present value of promised retirement benefits is disclosed in a note to the statements. The financial statements may also be accompanied by a report from an actuary supporting the actuarial present value of promised retirement benefits; and

(c)   financial statements that include a statement of net assets available for benefits and a statement of changes in net assets available for benefits with the actuarial present value of promised retirement benefits contained in a separate actuarial report.

In each format a trustees' report in the nature of a management or directors' report and an investment report may also accompany the financial statements.

29   Those in favour of the formats described in paragraph 28(a) and (b) believe that the quantification of promised retirement benefits and other information provided under those approaches help users to assess the current status of the plan and the likelihood of the plan's obligations being met. They also believe that financial statements should be complete in themselves and not rely on accompanying statements. However, some believe that the format described in paragraph 28(a) could give the impression that a liability exists, whereas the actuarial present value of promised retirement benefits does not in their opinion have all the characteristics of a liability.

30   Those who favour the format described in paragraph 28(c) believe that the actuarial present value of promised retirement benefits should not be included in a statement of net assets available for benefits as in the format described in paragraph 28(a) or even be disclosed in a note as in paragraph 28(b), because it will be compared directly with plan assets and such a comparison may not be valid. They contend that actuaries do not necessarily compare actuarial present value of promised retirement benefits with market values of investments but may instead assess the present value of cash flows expected from the investments. Therefore, those in favour of this format believe that such a comparison is unlikely to reflect the actuary's overall assessment of the plan and that it may be misunderstood. Also, some

believe that, regardless of whether quantified, the information about promised retirement benefits should be contained solely in the separate actuarial report where a proper explanation can be provided.

31   This Standard accepts the views in favour of permitting disclosure of the information concerning promised retirement benefits in a separate actuarial report. It rejects arguments against the quantification of the actuarial present value of promised retirement benefits. Accordingly, the formats described in paragraph 28(a) and (b) are considered acceptable under this Standard, as is the format described in paragraph 28(c) so long as the financial statements contain a reference to, and are accompanied by, an actuarial report that includes the actuarial present value of promised retirement benefits.

All plans

Valuation of plan assets

32   Retirement benefit plan investments shall be carried at fair value. In the case of marketable securities fair value is market value. Where plan investments are held for which an estimate of fair value is not possible disclosure shall be made of the reason why fair value is not used.

33   In the case of marketable securities fair value is usually market value because this is considered the most useful measure of the securities at the report date and of the investment performance for the period. Those securities that have a fixed redemption value and that have been acquired to match the obligations of the plan, or specific parts thereof, may be carried at amounts based on their ultimate redemption value assuming a constant rate of return to maturity. Where plan investments are held for which an estimate of fair value is not possible, such as total ownership of an entity, disclosure is made of the reason why fair value is not used. To the extent that investments are carried at amounts other than market value or fair value, fair value is generally also disclosed. Assets used in the operations of the fund are accounted for in accordance with the applicable Standards.

Disclosure

34   The financial statements of a retirement benefit plan, whether defined benefit or defined contribution, shall also contain the following information:

(a)   a statement of changes in net assets available for benefits;

(b)   a summary of significant accounting policies; and

(c)   a description of the plan and the effect of any changes in the plan during the period.

35   Financial statements provided by retirement benefit plans include the following, if applicable:

(a)   a statement of net assets available for benefits disclosing:

(i)   assets at the end of the period suitably classified;

(ii)   the basis of valuation of assets;

(iii)   details of any single investment exceeding either 5% of the net assets available for benefits or 5% of any class or type of security;

(iv)   details of any investment in the employer; and

(v)   liabilities other than the actuarial present value of promised retirement benefits;

(b)   a statement of changes in net assets available for benefits showing the following:

(i)   employer contributions;

(ii)   employee contributions;

(iii)   investment income such as interest and dividends;

(iv)   other income;

(v)   benefits paid or payable (analysed, for example, as retirement, death and disability benefits, and lump sum payments);

(vi)   administrative expenses;

(vii) other expenses;

(viii) taxes on income;

(ix)   profits and losses on disposal of investments and changes in value of investments; and

(x)   transfers from and to other plans;

(c)   a description of the funding policy;

(d)   for defined benefit plans, the actuarial present value of promised retirement benefits (which may distinguish between vested benefits and non-vested benefits) based on the benefits promised under the terms of the plan, on service rendered to date and using either current salary levels or projected salary levels; this information may be included in an accompanying actuarial report to be read in conjunction with the related financial statements; and

(e)   for defined benefit plans, a description of the significant actuarial assumptions made and the method used to calculate the actuarial present value of promised retirement benefits.

36   The report of a retirement benefit plan contains a description of the plan, either as part of the financial statements or in a separate report. It may contain the following:

(a)   the names of the employers and the employee groups covered;

(b)   the number of participants receiving benefits and the number of other participants, classified as appropriate;

(c)   the type of plan – defined contribution or defined benefit;

(d)   a note as to whether participants contribute to the plan;

(e)   a description of the retirement benefits promised to participants;

(f)   a description of any plan termination terms; and

(g)   changes in items (a) to (f) during the period covered by the report.

It is not uncommon to refer to other documents that are readily available to users and in which the plan is described, and to include only information on subsequent changes.

Effective date

37   This Standard becomes operative for financial statements of retirement benefit plans covering periods beginning on or after 1 January 1988.

38   *[This paragraph refers to amendments that are not yet effective, and is therefore not included in this edition.]*

IAS 27

Separate Financial Statements

In April 2001 the International Accounting Standards Board (Board) adopted IAS 27 *Consolidated Financial Statements and Accounting for Investments in Subsidiaries*, which had originally been issued by the International Accounting Standards Committee in April 1989. That standard replaced IAS 3 *Consolidated Financial Statements* (issued in June 1976), except for those parts that dealt with accounting for investment in associates.

In December 2003 the Board issued a revised IAS 27 with a new title—*Consolidated and Separate Financial Statements*. This revised IAS 27 was part of the IASB's initial agenda of technical projects. The revised IAS 27 also incorporated the guidance from two related Interpretations (SIC-12 *Consolidation—Special Purpose Entities* and SIC-33 *Consolidation and Equity Method—Potential Voting Rights and Allocation of Ownership Interests*).

The Board amended IAS 27 in January 2008 to address the accounting for non-controlling interests and loss of control of a subsidiary as part of its business combinations project.

In May 2011 the Board issued a revised IAS 27 with a modified title—*Separate Financial Statements*. IFRS 10 *Consolidated Financial Statements* addresses the principle of control and the requirements relating to the preparation of consolidated financial statements.

In October 2012 IAS 27 was amended by *Investment Entities* (Amendments to IFRS 10, IFRS 12 and IAS 27). These amendments introduced new disclosure requirements for investment entities.

In August 2014 IAS 27 was amended by *Equity Method in Separate Financial Statements* (Amendments to IAS 27). These amendments allowed entities to use the equity method to account for investments in subsidiaries, joint ventures and associates in their separate financial statements.

Contents

FOR THE ACCOMPANYING GUIDANCE LISTED BELOW, SEE PART B OF THIS EDITION

TABLE OF CONCORDANCE

FOR THE BASIS FOR CONCLUSIONS, SEE PART C OF THIS EDITION

BASIS FOR CONCLUSIONS

DISSENTING OPINIONS

International Accounting Standard 27 *Separate Financial Statements* (IAS 27) is set out in paragraphs 1–20. All the paragraphs have equal authority but retain the IASC format of the Standard when it was adopted by the IASB. IAS 27 should be read in the context of its objective and the Basis for Conclusions, the *Preface to IFRS Standards* and the *Conceptual Framework for Financial Reporting*. IAS 8 *Accounting Policies, Changes in Accounting Estimates and Errors* provides a basis for selecting and applying accounting policies in the absence of explicit guidance.

International Accounting Standard 27
Separate Financial Statements

Objective

1   The objective of this Standard is to prescribe the accounting and disclosure requirements for investments in subsidiaries, joint ventures and associates when an entity prepares separate financial statements.

Scope

2   This Standard shall be applied in accounting for investments in subsidiaries, joint ventures and associates when an entity elects, or is required by local regulations, to present separate financial statements.

3   This Standard does not mandate which entities produce separate financial statements. It applies when an entity prepares separate financial statements that comply with International Financial Reporting Standards.

Definitions

4   The following terms are used in this Standard with the meanings specified:

Consolidated financial statements are the financial statements of a group in which the assets, liabilities, equity, income, expenses and cash flows of the parent and its subsidiaries are presented as those of a single economic entity.

Separate financial statements are those presented by an entity in which the entity could elect, subject to the requirements in this Standard, to account for its investments in subsidiaries, joint ventures and associates either at cost, in accordance with IFRS 9 *Financial Instruments*, or using the equity method as described in IAS 28 *Investments in Associates and Joint Ventures*.

5   The following terms are defined in Appendix A of IFRS 10 *Consolidated Financial Statements*, Appendix A of IFRS 11 *Joint Arrangements* and paragraph 3 of IAS 28:

- associate

- control of an investee

- equity method

- group

- investment entity

- joint control

- joint venture

- joint venturer

- parent

- significant influence
- subsidiary.

6   Separate financial statements are those presented in addition to consolidated financial statements or in addition to the financial statements of an investor that does not have investments in subsidiaries but has investments in associates or joint ventures in which the investments in associates or joint ventures are required by IAS 28 to be accounted for using the equity method, other than in the circumstances set out in paragraphs 8–8A.

7   The financial statements of an entity that does not have a subsidiary, associate or joint venturer's interest in a joint venture are not separate financial statements.

8   An entity that is exempted in accordance with paragraph 4(a) of IFRS 10 from consolidation or paragraph 17 of IAS 28 (as amended in 2011) from applying the equity method may present separate financial statements as its only financial statements.

8A   An investment entity that is required, throughout the current period and all comparative periods presented, to apply the exception to consolidation for all of its subsidiaries in accordance with paragraph 31 of IFRS 10 presents separate financial statements as its only financial statements.

Preparation of separate financial statements

9   Separate financial statements shall be prepared in accordance with all applicable IFRSs, except as provided in paragraph 10.

10   When an entity prepares separate financial statements, it shall account for investments in subsidiaries, joint ventures and associates either:

(a)   at cost;

(b)   in accordance with IFRS 9; or

(c)   using the equity method as described in IAS 28.

The entity shall apply the same accounting for each category of investments. Investments accounted for at cost or using the equity method shall be accounted for in accordance with IFRS 5 *Non-current Assets Held for Sale and Discontinued Operations* when they are classified as held for sale or for distribution (or included in a disposal group that is classified as held for sale or for distribution). The measurement of investments accounted for in accordance with IFRS 9 is not changed in such circumstances.

11   If an entity elects, in accordance with paragraph 18 of IAS 28 (as amended in 2011), to measure its investments in associates or joint ventures at fair value through profit or loss in accordance with IFRS 9, it shall also account for those investments in the same way in its separate financial statements.

11A   If a parent is required, in accordance with paragraph 31 of IFRS 10, to measure its investment in a subsidiary at fair value through profit or loss in accordance with IFRS 9, it shall also account for its investment in a subsidiary in the same way in its separate financial statements.

11B   When a parent ceases to be an investment entity, or becomes an investment entity, it shall account for the change from the date when the change in status occurred, as follows:

    (a)   when an entity ceases to be an investment entity, the entity shall account for an investment in a subsidiary in accordance with paragraph 10. The date of the change of status shall be the deemed acquisition date. The fair value of the subsidiary at the deemed acquisition date shall represent the transferred deemed consideration when accounting for the investment in accordance with paragraph 10.

        (i)   [deleted]

        (ii)   [deleted]

    (b)   when an entity becomes an investment entity, it shall account for an investment in a subsidiary at fair value through profit or loss in accordance with IFRS 9. The difference between the previous carrying amount of the subsidiary and its fair value at the date of the change of status of the investor shall be recognised as a gain or loss in profit or loss. The cumulative amount of any gain or loss previously recognised in other comprehensive income in respect of those subsidiaries shall be treated as if the investment entity had disposed of those subsidiaries at the date of change in status.

12   **Dividends from a subsidiary, a joint venture or an associate are recognised in the separate financial statements of an entity when the entity's right to receive the dividend is established. The dividend is recognised in profit or loss unless the entity elects to use the equity method, in which case the dividend is recognised as a reduction from the carrying amount of the investment.**

13   When a parent reorganises the structure of its group by establishing a new entity as its parent in a manner that satisfies the following criteria:

    (a)   the new parent obtains control of the original parent by issuing equity instruments in exchange for existing equity instruments of the original parent;

    (b)   the assets and liabilities of the new group and the original group are the same immediately before and after the reorganisation; and

    (c)   the owners of the original parent before the reorganisation have the same absolute and relative interests in the net assets of the original group and the new group immediately before and after the reorganisation, and the new parent accounts for its investment in the original parent in accordance with paragraph 10(a) in its separate financial statements, the new parent shall measure cost at the carrying amount of its share of the equity items shown in the separate financial statements of the original parent at the date of the reorganisation.

14   Similarly, an entity that is not a parent might establish a new entity as its parent in a manner that satisfies the criteria in paragraph 13. The requirements in paragraph 13 apply equally to such reorganisations. In such cases, references to 'original parent' and 'original group' are to the 'original entity'.

Disclosure

15   **An entity shall apply all applicable IFRSs when providing disclosures in its separate financial statements, including the requirements in paragraphs 16–17.**

16   **When a parent, in accordance with paragraph 4(a) of IFRS 10, elects not to prepare consolidated financial statements and instead prepares separate financial statements, it shall disclose in those separate financial statements:**

   (a)   **the fact that the financial statements are separate financial statements; that the exemption from consolidation has been used; the name and principal place of business (and country of incorporation, if different) of the entity whose consolidated financial statements that comply with International Financial Reporting Standards have been produced for public use; and the address where those consolidated financial statements are obtainable.**

   (b)   **a list of significant investments in subsidiaries, joint ventures and associates, including:**

      (i)   **the name of those investees.**

      (ii)   **the principal place of business (and country of incorporation, if different) of those investees.**

      (iii) **its proportion of the ownership interest (and its proportion of the voting rights, if different) held in those investees.**

   (c)   **a description of the method used to account for the investments listed under (b).**

16A   **When an investment entity that is a parent (other than a parent covered by paragraph 16) prepares, in accordance with paragraph 8A, separate financial statements as its only financial statements, it shall disclose that fact. The investment entity shall also present the disclosures relating to investment entities required by IFRS 12** *Disclosure of Interests in Other Entities.*

17 When a parent (other than a parent covered by paragraphs 16–16A) or an investor with joint control of, or significant influence over, an investee prepares separate financial statements, the parent or investor shall identify the financial statements prepared in accordance with IFRS 10, IFRS 11 or IAS 28 (as amended in 2011) to which they relate. The parent or investor shall also disclose in its separate financial statements:

 (a) the fact that the statements are separate financial statements and the reasons why those statements are prepared if not required by law.

 (b) a list of significant investments in subsidiaries, joint ventures and associates, including:

  (i) the name of those investees.

  (ii) the principal place of business (and country of incorporation, if different) of those investees.

  (iii) its proportion of the ownership interest (and its proportion of the voting rights, if different) held in those investees.

 (c) a description of the method used to account for the investments listed under (b).

Effective date and transition

18 An entity shall apply this Standard for annual periods beginning on or after 1 January 2013. Earlier application is permitted. If an entity applies this Standard earlier, it shall disclose that fact and apply IFRS 10, IFRS 11, IFRS 12 and IAS 28 (as amended in 2011) at the same time.

18A *Investment Entities* (Amendments to IFRS 10, IFRS 12 and IAS 27), issued in October 2012, amended paragraphs 5, 6, 17 and 18, and added paragraphs 8A, 11A–11B, 16A and 18B–18I. An entity shall apply those amendments for annual periods beginning on or after 1 January 2014. Early adoption is permitted. If an entity applies those amendments earlier, it shall disclose that fact and apply all amendments included in *Investment Entities* at the same time.

18B If, at the date of initial application of the *Investment Entities* amendments (which, for the purposes of this IFRS, is the beginning of the annual reporting period for which those amendments are applied for the first time), a parent concludes that it is an investment entity, it shall apply paragraphs 18C–18I to its investment in a subsidiary.

18C At the date of initial application, an investment entity that previously measured its investment in a subsidiary at cost shall instead measure that investment at fair value through profit or loss as if the requirements of this IFRS had always been effective. The investment entity shall adjust retrospectively the annual period immediately preceding the date of initial application and shall adjust retained earnings at the beginning of the immediately preceding period for any difference between:

 (a) the previous carrying amount of the investment; and

(b)   the fair value of the investor's investment in the subsidiary.

18D   At the date of initial application, an investment entity that previously measured its investment in a subsidiary at fair value through other comprehensive income shall continue to measure that investment at fair value. The cumulative amount of any fair value adjustment previously recognised in other comprehensive income shall be transferred to retained earnings at the beginning of the annual period immediately preceding the date of initial application.

18E   At the date of initial application, an investment entity shall not make adjustments to the previous accounting for an interest in a subsidiary that it had previously elected to measure at fair value through profit or loss in accordance with IFRS 9, as permitted in paragraph 10.

18F   Before the date that IFRS 13 *Fair Value Measurement* is adopted, an investment entity shall use the fair value amounts previously reported to investors or to management, if those amounts represent the amount for which the investment could have been exchanged between knowledgeable, willing parties in an arm's length transaction at the date of the valuation.

18G   If measuring the investment in the subsidiary in accordance with paragraphs 18C–18F is impracticable (as defined in IAS 8 *Accounting Policies, Changes in Accounting Estimates and Errors*), an investment entity shall apply the requirements of this IFRS at the beginning of the earliest period for which application of paragraphs 18C–18F is practicable, which may be the current period. The investor shall adjust retrospectively the annual period immediately preceding the date of initial application, unless the beginning of the earliest period for which application of this paragraph is practicable is the current period. When the date that it is practicable for the investment entity to measure the fair value of the subsidiary is earlier than the beginning of the immediately preceding period, the investor shall adjust equity at the beginning of the immediately preceding period for any difference between:

(a)   the previous carrying amount of the investment; and

(b)   the fair value of the investor's investment in the subsidiary.

If the earliest period for which application of this paragraph is practicable is the current period, the adjustment to equity shall be recognised at the beginning of the current period.

18H   If an investment entity has disposed of, or lost control of, an investment in a subsidiary before the date of initial application of the *Investment Entities* amendments, the investment entity is not required to make adjustments to the previous accounting for that investment.

18I   Notwithstanding the references to the annual period immediately preceding the date of initial application (the 'immediately preceding period') in paragraphs 18C–18G, an entity may also present adjusted comparative information for any earlier periods presented, but is not required to do so. If an entity does present adjusted comparative information for any earlier periods, all references to the 'immediately preceding period' in paragraphs

18C–18G shall be read as the 'earliest adjusted comparative period presented'. If an entity presents unadjusted comparative information for any earlier periods, it shall clearly identify the information that has not been adjusted, state that it has been prepared on a different basis, and explain that basis.

18J   *Equity Method in Separate Financial Statements* (Amendments to IAS 27), issued in August 2014, amended paragraphs 4–7, 10, 11B and 12. An entity shall apply those amendments for annual periods beginning on or after 1 January 2016 retrospectively in accordance with IAS 8 *Accounting Policies, Changes in Accounting Estimates and Errors*. Earlier application is permitted. If an entity applies those amendments for an earlier period, it shall disclose that fact.

References to IFRS 9

19   If an entity applies this Standard but does not yet apply IFRS 9, any reference to IFRS 9 shall be read as a reference to IAS 39 *Financial Instruments: Recognition and Measurement*.

Withdrawal of IAS 27 (2008)

20   This Standard is issued concurrently with IFRS 10. Together, the two IFRSs supersede IAS 27 *Consolidated and Separate Financial Statements* (as amended in 2008).

Approval by the Board of IAS 27 issued in December 2003

International Accounting Standard 27 *Consolidated and Separate Financial Statements* (as revised in 2003) was approved for issue by thirteen of the fourteen members of the International Accounting Standards Board. Mr Yamada dissented. His dissenting opinion related to consolidated financial statements and is set out after the Basis for Conclusions on IFRS 10 *Consolidated Financial Statements*.

Sir David Tweedie	Chairman
Thomas E Jones	Vice-Chairman
Mary E Barth	
Hans-Georg Bruns	
Anthony T Cope	
Robert P Garnett	
Gilbert Gélard	
James J Leisenring	
Warren J McGregor	
Patricia L O'Malley	
Harry K Schmid	
John T Smith	
Geoffrey Whittington	
Tatsumi Yamada	

Approval by the Board of *Cost of an Investment in a Subsidiary, Jointly Controlled Entity or Associate* (Amendments to IFRS 1 and IAS 27) issued in May 2008

Cost of an Investment in a Subsidiary, Jointly Controlled Entity or Associate (Amendments to IFRS 1 *First-time Adoption of International Financial Reporting Standards* and IAS 27) was approved for issue by eleven of the thirteen members of the International Accounting Standards Board. Professor Barth and Mr Danjou dissented. Their dissenting opinions are set out after the Basis for Conclusions.

Sir David Tweedie	Chairman
Thomas E Jones	Vice-Chairman
Mary E Barth	
Stephen Cooper	
Philippe Danjou	
Jan Engström	
Robert P Garnett	
Gilbert Gélard	
James J Leisenring	
Warren J McGregor	
John T Smith	
Tatsumi Yamada	
Wei-Guo Zhang	

Approval by the Board of *Investment Entities* (Amendments to IFRS 10, IFRS 12 and IAS 27) issued in October 2012

Investment Entities (Amendments to IFRS 10, IFRS 12 and IAS 27) was approved for issue by the fifteen members of the International Accounting Standards Board.

Hans Hoogervorst	Chairman
Ian Mackintosh	Vice-Chairman
Stephen Cooper	
Philippe Danjou	
Martin Edelmann	
Jan Engström	
Patrick Finnegan	
Amaro Luiz de Oliveira Gomes	
Prabhakar Kalavacherla	
Patricia McConnell	
Takatsugu Ochi	
Paul Pacter	
Darrel Scott	
Chungwoo Suh	
Zhang Wei-Guo	

Approval by the Board of *Equity Method in Separate Financial Statements* (Amendments to IAS 27) issued in August 2014

Equity Method in Separate Financial Statements was approved for issue by the fourteen members of the International Accounting Standards Board.

Hans Hoogervorst	Chairman
Ian Mackintosh	Vice-Chairman
Stephen Cooper	
Philippe Danjou	
Martin Edelmann	
Patrick Finnegan	
Amaro Luiz de Oliveira Gomes	
Gary Kabureck	
Suzanne Lloyd	
Takatsugu Ochi	
Darrel Scott	
Chungwoo Suh	
Mary Tokar	
Wei-Guo Zhang	

IAS 28

Investments in Associates and Joint Ventures

In April 2001 the International Accounting Standards Board (Board) adopted IAS 28 *Accounting for Investments in Associates*, which had originally been issued by the International Accounting Standards Committee in April 1989. IAS 28 *Accounting for Investments in Associates* replaced those parts of IAS 3 *Consolidated Financial Statements* (issued in June 1976) that dealt with accounting for investment in associates.

In December 2003 the Board issued a revised IAS 28 with a new title—*Investments in Associates*. This revised IAS 28 was part of the Board's initial agenda of technical projects and also incorporated the guidance contained in three related Interpretations (SIC-3 *Elimination of Unrealised Profits and Losses on Transactions with Associates*, SIC-20 *Equity Accounting Method—Recognition of Losses* and SIC-33 *Consolidation and Equity Method—Potential Voting Rights and Allocation of Ownership Interests*).

In May 2011 the Board issued a revised IAS 28 with a new title—*Investments in Associates and Joint Ventures*.

In December 2014 IAS 28 was amended by *Investment Entities: Applying the Consolidation Exception* (Amendments to IFRS 10, IFRS 12 and IAS 28). These amendments provided relief whereby a non-investment entity investor can, when applying the equity method, choose to retain the fair value through profit or loss measurement applied by its investment entity associates and joint ventures to their subsidiaries.

In October 2017, IAS 28 was amended by *Long-term Interests in Associates and Joint Ventures* (Amendments to IAS 28). These amendments clarify that entities apply IFRS 9 *Financial Instruments* to long-term interests in an associate or joint venture to which the equity method is not applied.

Other Standards have made minor consequential amendments to IAS 28. They include IFRS 9 *Financial Instruments* (issued July 2014), *Equity Method in Separate Financial Statements* (Amendments to IAS 27) (issued August 2014), *Annual Improvements to IFRS Standards 2014–2016 Cycle* (issued December 2016) and *Amendments to References to the Conceptual Framework in IFRS Standards* (issued March 2018).

Contents

FOR THE ACCOMPANYING GUIDANCE AND SUPPORTING MATERIAL LISTED BELOW,
SEE PART B OF THIS EDITION

FOR THE BASIS FOR CONCLUSIONS, SEE PART C OF THIS EDITION

International Accounting Standard 28 *Investments in Associates and Joint Ventures* (IAS 28) is set out in paragraphs 1–47. All the paragraphs have equal authority but retain the IASC format of the Standard when it was adopted by the IASB. IAS 28 should be read in the context of its objective and the Basis for Conclusions, the *Preface to IFRS Standards* and the *Conceptual Framework for Financial Reporting*. IAS 8 *Accounting Policies, Changes in Accounting Estimates and Errors* provides a basis for selecting and applying accounting policies in the absence of explicit guidance.

International Accounting Standard 28
Investments in Associates and Joint Ventures

Objective

1   The objective of this Standard is to prescribe the accounting for investments in associates and to set out the requirements for the application of the equity method when accounting for investments in associates and joint ventures.

Scope

2   This Standard shall be applied by all entities that are investors with joint control of, or significant influence over, an investee.

Definitions

3   The following terms are used in this Standard with the meanings specified:

An *associate* is an entity over which the investor has significant influence.

Consolidated financial statements are the financial statements of a group in which assets, liabilities, equity, income, expenses and cash flows of the parent and its subsidiaries are presented as those of a single economic entity.

The *equity method* is a method of accounting whereby the investment is initially recognised at cost and adjusted thereafter for the post-acquisition change in the investor's share of the investee's net assets. The investor's profit or loss includes its share of the investee's profit or loss and the investor's other comprehensive income includes its share of the investee's other comprehensive income.

A *joint arrangement* is an arrangement of which two or more parties have joint control.

Joint control is the contractually agreed sharing of control of an arrangement, which exists only when decisions about the relevant activities require the unanimous consent of the parties sharing control.

A *joint venture* is a joint arrangement whereby the parties that have joint control of the arrangement have rights to the net assets of the arrangement.

A *joint venturer* is a party to a joint venture that has joint control of that joint venture.

Significant influence is the power to participate in the financial and operating policy decisions of the investee but is not control or joint control of those policies.

4   The following terms are defined in paragraph 4 of IAS 27 *Separate Financial Statements* and in Appendix A of IFRS 10 *Consolidated Financial Statements* and are used in this Standard with the meanings specified in the IFRSs in which they are defined:

- control of an investee

- group

- parent

- separate financial statements

- subsidiary.

Significant influence

5   If an entity holds, directly or indirectly (eg through subsidiaries), 20 per cent or more of the voting power of the investee, it is presumed that the entity has significant influence, unless it can be clearly demonstrated that this is not the case. Conversely, if the entity holds, directly or indirectly (eg through subsidiaries), less than 20 per cent of the voting power of the investee, it is presumed that the entity does not have significant influence, unless such influence can be clearly demonstrated. A substantial or majority ownership by another investor does not necessarily preclude an entity from having significant influence.

6   The existence of significant influence by an entity is usually evidenced in one or more of the following ways:

(a)   representation on the board of directors or equivalent governing body of the investee;

(b)   participation in policy-making processes, including participation in decisions about dividends or other distributions;

(c)   material transactions between the entity and its investee;

(d)   interchange of managerial personnel; or

(e)   provision of essential technical information.

7   An entity may own share warrants, share call options, debt or equity instruments that are convertible into ordinary shares, or other similar instruments that have the potential, if exercised or converted, to give the entity additional voting power or to reduce another party's voting power over the financial and operating policies of another entity (ie potential voting rights). The existence and effect of potential voting rights that are currently exercisable or convertible, including potential voting rights held by other entities, are considered when assessing whether an entity has significant influence. Potential voting rights are not currently exercisable or convertible when, for example, they cannot be exercised or converted until a future date or until the occurrence of a future event.

8   In assessing whether potential voting rights contribute to significant
         influence, the entity examines all facts and circumstances (including the
         terms of exercise of the potential voting rights and any other contractual
         arrangements whether considered individually or in combination) that affect
         potential rights, except the intentions of management and the financial ability
         to exercise or convert those potential rights.

9   An entity loses significant influence over an investee when it loses the power
         to participate in the financial and operating policy decisions of that investee.
         The loss of significant influence can occur with or without a change in
         absolute or relative ownership levels. It could occur, for example, when an
         associate becomes subject to the control of a government, court, administrator
         or regulator. It could also occur as a result of a contractual arrangement.

Equity method

10   Under the equity method, on initial recognition the investment in an associate
         or a joint venture is recognised at cost, and the carrying amount is increased
         or decreased to recognise the investor's share of the profit or loss of the
         investee after the date of acquisition. The investor's share of the investee's
         profit or loss is recognised in the investor's profit or loss. Distributions
         received from an investee reduce the carrying amount of the investment.
         Adjustments to the carrying amount may also be necessary for changes in the
         investor's proportionate interest in the investee arising from changes in the
         investee's other comprehensive income. Such changes include those arising
         from the revaluation of property, plant and equipment and from foreign
         exchange translation differences. The investor's share of those changes is
         recognised in the investor's other comprehensive income (see IAS 1
         Presentation of Financial Statements).

11   The recognition of income on the basis of distributions received may not be an
         adequate measure of the income earned by an investor on an investment in an
         associate or a joint venture because the distributions received may bear little
         relation to the performance of the associate or joint venture. Because the
         investor has joint control of, or significant influence over, the investee, the
         investor has an interest in the associate's or joint venture's performance and,
         as a result, the return on its investment. The investor accounts for this
         interest by extending the scope of its financial statements to include its share
         of the profit or loss of such an investee. As a result, application of the equity
         method provides more informative reporting of the investor's net assets and
         profit or loss.

12   When potential voting rights or other derivatives containing potential voting
         rights exist, an entity's interest in an associate or a joint venture is
         determined solely on the basis of existing ownership interests and does not
         reflect the possible exercise or conversion of potential voting rights and other
         derivative instruments, unless paragraph 13 applies.

13   In some circumstances, an entity has, in substance, an existing ownership as a result of a transaction that currently gives it access to the returns associated with an ownership interest. In such circumstances, the proportion allocated to the entity is determined by taking into account the eventual exercise of those potential voting rights and other derivative instruments that currently give the entity access to the returns.

14   IFRS 9 *Financial Instruments* does not apply to interests in associates and joint ventures that are accounted for using the equity method. When instruments containing potential voting rights in substance currently give access to the returns associated with an ownership interest in an associate or a joint venture, the instruments are not subject to IFRS 9. In all other cases, instruments containing potential voting rights in an associate or a joint venture are accounted for in accordance with IFRS 9.

14A   An entity also applies IFRS 9 to other financial instruments in an associate or joint venture to which the equity method is not applied. These include long-term interests that, in substance, form part of the entity's net investment in an associate or joint venture (see paragraph 38). An entity applies IFRS 9 to such long-term interests before it applies paragraph 38 and paragraphs 40–43 of this Standard. In applying IFRS 9, the entity does not take account of any adjustments to the carrying amount of long-term interests that arise from applying this Standard.

15   Unless an investment, or a portion of an investment, in an associate or a joint venture is classified as held for sale in accordance with IFRS 5 *Non-current Assets Held for Sale and Discontinued Operations*, the investment, or any retained interest in the investment not classified as held for sale, shall be classified as a non-current asset.

Application of the equity method

16   An entity with joint control of, or significant influence over, an investee shall account for its investment in an associate or a joint venture using the equity method except when that investment qualifies for exemption in accordance with paragraphs 17–19.

Exemptions from applying the equity method

17   An entity need not apply the equity method to its investment in an associate or a joint venture if the entity is a parent that is exempt from preparing consolidated financial statements by the scope exception in paragraph 4(a) of IFRS 10 or if all the following apply:

   (a)   The entity is a wholly-owned subsidiary, or is a partially-owned subsidiary of another entity and its other owners, including those not otherwise entitled to vote, have been informed about, and do not object to, the entity not applying the equity method.

   (b)   The entity's debt or equity instruments are not traded in a public market (a domestic or foreign stock exchange or an over-the-counter market, including local and regional markets).

(c)   The entity did not file, nor is it in the process of filing, its financial statements with a securities commission or other regulatory organisation, for the purpose of issuing any class of instruments in a public market.

(d)   The ultimate or any intermediate parent of the entity produces financial statements available for public use that comply with IFRSs, in which subsidiaries are consolidated or are measured at fair value through profit or loss in accordance with IFRS 10.

18   When an investment in an associate or a joint venture is held by, or is held indirectly through, an entity that is a venture capital organisation, or a mutual fund, unit trust and similar entities including investment-linked insurance funds, the entity may elect to measure that investment at fair value through profit or loss in accordance with IFRS 9. An entity shall make this election separately for each associate or joint venture, at initial recognition of the associate or joint venture.

19   When an entity has an investment in an associate, a portion of which is held indirectly through a venture capital organisation, or a mutual fund, unit trust and similar entities including investment-linked insurance funds, the entity may elect to measure that portion of the investment in the associate at fair value through profit or loss in accordance with IFRS 9 regardless of whether the venture capital organisation, or the mutual fund, unit trust and similar entities including investment-linked insurance funds, has significant influence over that portion of the investment. If the entity makes that election, the entity shall apply the equity method to any remaining portion of its investment in an associate that is not held through a venture capital organisation, or a mutual fund, unit trust and similar entities including investment-linked insurance funds.

Classification as held for sale

20   An entity shall apply IFRS 5 to an investment, or a portion of an investment, in an associate or a joint venture that meets the criteria to be classified as held for sale. Any retained portion of an investment in an associate or a joint venture that has not been classified as held for sale shall be accounted for using the equity method until disposal of the portion that is classified as held for sale takes place. After the disposal takes place, an entity shall account for any retained interest in the associate or joint venture in accordance with IFRS 9 unless the retained interest continues to be an associate or a joint venture, in which case the entity uses the equity method.

21   When an investment, or a portion of an investment, in an associate or a joint venture previously classified as held for sale no longer meets the criteria to be so classified, it shall be accounted for using the equity method retrospectively as from the date of its classification as held for sale. Financial statements for the periods since classification as held for sale shall be amended accordingly.

Discontinuing the use of the equity method

22   An entity shall discontinue the use of the equity method from the date when its investment ceases to be an associate or a joint venture as follows:

    (a)   If the investment becomes a subsidiary, the entity shall account for its investment in accordance with IFRS 3 *Business Combinations* and IFRS 10.

    (b)   If the retained interest in the former associate or joint venture is a financial asset, the entity shall measure the retained interest at fair value. The fair value of the retained interest shall be regarded as its fair value on initial recognition as a financial asset in accordance with IFRS 9. The entity shall recognise in profit or loss any difference between:

        (i)   the fair value of any retained interest and any proceeds from disposing of a part interest in the associate or joint venture; and

        (ii)   the carrying amount of the investment at the date the equity method was discontinued.

    (c)   When an entity discontinues the use of the equity method, the entity shall account for all amounts previously recognised in other comprehensive income in relation to that investment on the same basis as would have been required if the investee had directly disposed of the related assets or liabilities.

23   Therefore, if a gain or loss previously recognised in other comprehensive income by the investee would be reclassified to profit or loss on the disposal of the related assets or liabilities, the entity reclassifies the gain or loss from equity to profit or loss (as a reclassification adjustment) when the equity method is discontinued. For example, if an associate or a joint venture has cumulative exchange differences relating to a foreign operation and the entity discontinues the use of the equity method, the entity shall reclassify to profit or loss the gain or loss that had previously been recognised in other comprehensive income in relation to the foreign operation.

24   If an investment in an associate becomes an investment in a joint venture or an investment in a joint venture becomes an investment in an associate, the entity continues to apply the equity method and does not remeasure the retained interest.

Changes in ownership interest

25   If an entity's ownership interest in an associate or a joint venture is reduced, but the investment continues to be classified either as an associate or a joint venture respectively, the entity shall reclassify to profit or loss the proportion of the gain or loss that had previously been recognised in other comprehensive income relating to that reduction in ownership interest if that gain or loss would be required to be reclassified to profit or loss on the disposal of the related assets or liabilities.

Equity method procedures

26   Many of the procedures that are appropriate for the application of the equity method are similar to the consolidation procedures described in IFRS 10. Furthermore, the concepts underlying the procedures used in accounting for the acquisition of a subsidiary are also adopted in accounting for the acquisition of an investment in an associate or a joint venture.

27   A group's share in an associate or a joint venture is the aggregate of the holdings in that associate or joint venture by the parent and its subsidiaries. The holdings of the group's other associates or joint ventures are ignored for this purpose. When an associate or a joint venture has subsidiaries, associates or joint ventures, the profit or loss, other comprehensive income and net assets taken into account in applying the equity method are those recognised in the associate's or joint venture's financial statements (including the associate's or joint venture's share of the profit or loss, other comprehensive income and net assets of its associates and joint ventures), after any adjustments necessary to give effect to uniform accounting policies (see paragraphs 35–36A).

28   Gains and losses resulting from 'upstream' and 'downstream' transactions between an entity (including its consolidated subsidiaries) and its associate or joint venture are recognised in the entity's financial statements only to the extent of unrelated investors' interests in the associate or joint venture. 'Upstream' transactions are, for example, sales of assets from an associate or a joint venture to the investor. 'Downstream' transactions are, for example, sales or contributions of assets from the investor to its associate or its joint venture. The investor's share in the associate's or joint venture's gains or losses resulting from these transactions is eliminated.

29   When downstream transactions provide evidence of a reduction in the net realisable value of the assets to be sold or contributed, or of an impairment loss of those assets, those losses shall be recognised in full by the investor. When upstream transactions provide evidence of a reduction in the net realisable value of the assets to be purchased or of an impairment loss of those assets, the investor shall recognise its share in those losses.

30   The contribution of a non-monetary asset to an associate or a joint venture in exchange for an equity interest in the associate or joint venture shall be accounted for in accordance with paragraph 28, except when the contribution lacks commercial substance, as that term is described in IAS 16 *Property, Plant and Equipment*. If such a contribution lacks commercial substance, the gain or loss is regarded as unrealised and is not recognised unless paragraph 31 also applies. Such unrealised gains and losses shall be eliminated against the investment accounted for using the equity method and shall not be presented as deferred gains or losses in the entity's consolidated statement of financial position or in the entity's statement of financial position in which investments are accounted for using the equity method.

31   If, in addition to receiving an equity interest in an associate or a joint venture, an entity receives monetary or non-monetary assets, the entity recognises in full in profit or loss the portion of the gain or loss on the non-monetary contribution relating to the monetary or non-monetary assets received.

31A–31B   *[These paragraphs refer to amendments that are not yet effective, and are therefore not included in this edition.]*

32   An investment is accounted for using the equity method from the date on which it becomes an associate or a joint venture. On acquisition of the investment, any difference between the cost of the investment and the entity's share of the net fair value of the investee's identifiable assets and liabilities is accounted for as follows:

    (a)   Goodwill relating to an associate or a joint venture is included in the carrying amount of the investment. Amortisation of that goodwill is not permitted.

    (b)   Any excess of the entity's share of the net fair value of the investee's identifiable assets and liabilities over the cost of the investment is included as income in the determination of the entity's share of the associate or joint venture's profit or loss in the period in which the investment is acquired.

    Appropriate adjustments to the entity's share of the associate's or joint venture's profit or loss after acquisition are made in order to account, for example, for depreciation of the depreciable assets based on their fair values at the acquisition date. Similarly, appropriate adjustments to the entity's share of the associate's or joint venture's profit or loss after acquisition are made for impairment losses such as for goodwill or property, plant and equipment.

33   The most recent available financial statements of the associate or joint venture are used by the entity in applying the equity method. When the end of the reporting period of the entity is different from that of the associate or joint venture, the associate or joint venture prepares, for the use of the entity, financial statements as of the same date as the financial statements of the entity unless it is impracticable to do so.

34   When, in accordance with paragraph 33, the financial statements of an associate or a joint venture used in applying the equity method are prepared as of a date different from that used by the entity, adjustments shall be made for the effects of significant transactions or events that occur between that date and the date of the entity's financial statements. In any case, the difference between the end of the reporting period of the associate or joint venture and that of the entity shall be no more than three months. The length of the reporting periods and any difference between the ends of the reporting periods shall be the same from period to period.

35   The entity's financial statements shall be prepared using uniform accounting policies for like transactions and events in similar circumstances.

36   Except as described in paragraph 36A, if an associate or a joint venture uses accounting policies other than those of the entity for like transactions and events in similar circumstances, adjustments shall be made to make the associate's or joint venture's accounting policies conform to those of the entity when the associate's or joint venture's financial statements are used by the entity in applying the equity method.

36A   Notwithstanding the requirement in paragraph 36, if an entity that is not itself an investment entity has an interest in an associate or joint venture that is an investment entity, the entity may, when applying the equity method, elect to retain the fair value measurement applied by that investment entity associate or joint venture to the investment entity associate's or joint venture's interests in subsidiaries. This election is made separately for each investment entity associate or joint venture, at the later of the date on which (a) the investment entity associate or joint venture is initially recognised; (b) the associate or joint venture becomes an investment entity; and (c) the investment entity associate or joint venture first becomes a parent.

37   If an associate or a joint venture has outstanding cumulative preference shares that are held by parties other than the entity and are classified as equity, the entity computes its share of profit or loss after adjusting for the dividends on such shares, whether or not the dividends have been declared.

38   If an entity's share of losses of an associate or a joint venture equals or exceeds its interest in the associate or joint venture, the entity discontinues recognising its share of further losses. The interest in an associate or a joint venture is the carrying amount of the investment in the associate or joint venture determined using the equity method together with any long-term interests that, in substance, form part of the entity's net investment in the associate or joint venture. For example, an item for which settlement is neither planned nor likely to occur in the foreseeable future is, in substance, an extension of the entity's investment in that associate or joint venture. Such items may include preference shares and long-term receivables or loans, but do not include trade receivables, trade payables or any long-term receivables for which adequate collateral exists, such as secured loans. Losses recognised using the equity method in excess of the entity's investment in ordinary shares are applied to the other components of the entity's interest in an associate or a joint venture in the reverse order of their seniority (ie priority in liquidation).

39   After the entity's interest is reduced to zero, additional losses are provided for, and a liability is recognised, only to the extent that the entity has incurred legal or constructive obligations or made payments on behalf of the associate or joint venture. If the associate or joint venture subsequently reports profits, the entity resumes recognising its share of those profits only after its share of the profits equals the share of losses not recognised.

Impairment losses

40   After application of the equity method, including recognising the associate's or joint venture's losses in accordance with paragraph 38, the entity applies paragraphs 41A–41C to determine whether there is any objective evidence that its net investment in the associate or joint venture is impaired.

41   [Deleted]

41A   The net investment in an associate or joint venture is impaired and impairment losses are incurred if, and only if, there is objective evidence of impairment as a result of one or more events that occurred after the initial recognition of the net investment (a 'loss event') and that loss event (or events) has an impact on the estimated future cash flows from the net investment that can be reliably estimated. It may not be possible to identify a single, discrete event that caused the impairment. Rather the combined effect of several events may have caused the impairment. Losses expected as a result of future events, no matter how likely, are not recognised. Objective evidence that the net investment is impaired includes observable data that comes to the attention of the entity about the following loss events:

(a)   significant financial difficulty of the associate or joint venture;

(b)   a breach of contract, such as a default or delinquency in payments by the associate or joint venture;

(c)   the entity, for economic or legal reasons relating to its associate's or joint venture's financial difficulty, granting to the associate or joint venture a concession that the entity would not otherwise consider;

(d)   it becoming probable that the associate or joint venture will enter bankruptcy or other financial reorganisation; or

(e)   the disappearance of an active market for the net investment because of financial difficulties of the associate or joint venture.

41B   The disappearance of an active market because the associate's or joint venture's equity or financial instruments are no longer publicly traded is not evidence of impairment. A downgrade of an associate's or joint venture's credit rating or a decline in the fair value of the associate or joint venture, is not of itself, evidence of impairment, although it may be evidence of impairment when considered with other available information.

41C   In addition to the types of events in paragraph 41A, objective evidence of impairment for the net investment in the equity instruments of the associate or joint venture includes information about significant changes with an adverse effect that have taken place in the technological, market, economic or legal environment in which the associate or joint venture operates, and indicates that the cost of the investment in the equity instrument may not be recovered. A significant or prolonged decline in the fair value of an investment in an equity instrument below its cost is also objective evidence of impairment.

42   Because goodwill that forms part of the carrying amount of the net investment in an associate or a joint venture is not separately recognised, it is not tested for impairment separately by applying the requirements for impairment testing goodwill in IAS 36 *Impairment of Assets*. Instead, the entire carrying amount of the investment is tested for impairment in accordance with IAS 36 as a single asset, by comparing its recoverable amount (higher of value in use and fair value less costs of disposal) with its carrying amount whenever application of paragraphs 41A–41C indicates that the net investment may be impaired. An impairment loss recognised in those circumstances is not allocated to any asset, including goodwill, that forms part of the carrying amount of the net investment in the associate or joint venture. Accordingly, any reversal of that impairment loss is recognised in accordance with IAS 36 to the extent that the recoverable amount of the net investment subsequently increases. In determining the value in use of the net investment, an entity estimates:

(a)   its share of the present value of the estimated future cash flows expected to be generated by the associate or joint venture, including the cash flows from the operations of the associate or joint venture and the proceeds from the ultimate disposal of the investment; or

(b)   the present value of the estimated future cash flows expected to arise from dividends to be received from the investment and from its ultimate disposal.

Using appropriate assumptions, both methods give the same result.

43   The recoverable amount of an investment in an associate or a joint venture shall be assessed for each associate or joint venture, unless the associate or joint venture does not generate cash inflows from continuing use that are largely independent of those from other assets of the entity.

Separate financial statements

44   An investment in an associate or a joint venture shall be accounted for in the entity's separate financial statements in accordance with paragraph 10 of IAS 27 (as amended in 2011).

Effective date and transition

45   An entity shall apply this Standard for annual periods beginning on or after 1 January 2013. Earlier application is permitted. If an entity applies this Standard earlier, it shall disclose that fact and apply IFRS 10, IFRS 11 *Joint Arrangements*, IFRS 12 *Disclosure of Interests in Other Entities* and IAS 27 (as amended in 2011) at the same time.

45A   IFRS 9, as issued in July 2014, amended paragraphs 40–42 and added paragraphs 41A–41C. An entity shall apply those amendments when it applies IFRS 9.

45B　　*Equity Method in Separate Financial Statements* (Amendments to IAS 27), issued in August 2014, amended paragraph 25. An entity shall apply that amendment for annual periods beginning on or after 1 January 2016 retrospectively in accordance with IAS 8 *Accounting Policies, Changes in Accounting Estimates and Errors*. Earlier application is permitted. If an entity applies that amendment for an earlier period, it shall disclose that fact.

45C　　*[This paragraph refers to amendments that are not yet effective, and is therefore not included in this edition.]*

45D　　*Investment Entities: Applying the Consolidation Exception* (Amendments to IFRS 10, IFRS 12 and IAS 28), issued in December 2014, amended paragraphs 17, 27 and 36 and added paragraph 36A. An entity shall apply those amendments for annual periods beginning on or after 1 January 2016. Earlier application is permitted. If an entity applies those amendments for an earlier period, it shall disclose that fact.

45E　　*Annual Improvements to IFRS Standards 2014–2016 Cycle*, issued in December 2016, amended paragraphs 18 and 36A. An entity shall apply those amendments retrospectively in accordance with IAS 8 for annual periods beginning on or after 1 January 2018. Earlier application is permitted. If an entity applies those amendments for an earlier period, it shall disclose that fact.

45F　　*[This paragraph refers to amendments that are not yet effective, and is therefore not included in this edition.]*

45G　　*Long-term Interests in Associates and Joint Ventures*, issued in October 2017, added paragraph 14A and deleted paragraph 41. An entity shall apply those amendments retrospectively in accordance with IAS 8 for annual reporting periods beginning on or after 1 January 2019, except as specified in paragraphs 45H–45K. Earlier application is permitted. If an entity applies those amendments earlier, it shall disclose that fact.

45H　　An entity that first applies the amendments in paragraph 45G at the same time it first applies IFRS 9 shall apply the transition requirements in IFRS 9 to the long-term interests described in paragraph 14A.

45I　　An entity that first applies the amendments in paragraph 45G after it first applies IFRS 9 shall apply the transition requirements in IFRS 9 necessary for applying the requirements set out in paragraph 14A to long-term interests. For that purpose, references to the date of initial application in IFRS 9 shall be read as referring to the beginning of the annual reporting period in which the entity first applies the amendments (the date of initial application of the amendments). The entity is not required to restate prior periods to reflect the application of the amendments. The entity may restate prior periods only if it is possible without the use of hindsight.

45J　　When first applying the amendments in paragraph 45G, an entity that applies the temporary exemption from IFRS 9 in accordance with IFRS 4 *Insurance Contracts* is not required to restate prior periods to reflect the application of the amendments. The entity may restate prior periods only if it is possible without the use of hindsight.

45K   If an entity does not restate prior periods applying paragraph 45I or paragraph 45J, at the date of initial application of the amendments it shall recognise in the opening retained earnings (or other component of equity, as appropriate) any difference between:

(a)   the previous carrying amount of long-term interests described in paragraph 14A at that date; and

(b)   the carrying amount of those long-term interests at that date.

References to IFRS 9

46   If an entity applies this Standard but does not yet apply IFRS 9, any reference to IFRS 9 shall be read as a reference to IAS 39.

Withdrawal of IAS 28 (2003)

47   This Standard supersedes IAS 28 *Investments in Associates* (as revised in 2003).

Approval by the Board of IAS 28 issued in December 2003

International Accounting Standard 28 *Investments in Associates* (as revised in 2003) was approved for issue by the fourteen members of the International Accounting Standards Board.

Sir David Tweedie	Chairman
Thomas E Jones	Vice-Chairman
Mary E Barth	
Hans-Georg Bruns	
Anthony T Cope	
Robert P Garnett	
Gilbert Gélard	
James J Leisenring	
Warren J McGregor	
Patricia L O'Malley	
Harry K Schmid	
John T Smith	
Geoffrey Whittington	
Tatsumi Yamada	

Approval by the Board of *Investment Entities: Applying the Consolidation Exception* (Amendments to IFRS 10, IFRS 12 and IAS 28) issued in December 2014

Investment Entities: Applying the Consolidation Exception was approved for issue by the fourteen members of the International Accounting Standards Board.

Hans Hoogervorst	Chairman
Ian Mackintosh	Vice-Chairman
Stephen Cooper	
Philippe Danjou	
Amaro Luiz De Oliveira Gomes	
Martin Edelmann	
Patrick Finnegan	
Gary Kabureck	
Suzanne Lloyd	
Takatsugu Ochi	
Darrel Scott	
Chungwoo Suh	
Mary Tokar	
Wei-Guo Zhang	

Approval by the Board of *Long-term Interests in Associates and Joint Ventures* (Amendments to IAS 28) issued in October 2017

Long-term Interests in Associates and Joint Ventures (Amendments to IAS 28) was approved for issue by 10 of 14 members of the International Accounting Standards Board (Board). Mr Ochi dissented. His dissenting opinion is set out after the Basis for Conclusions. Messrs Anderson and Lu and Ms Tarca abstained in view of their recent appointments to the Board.

Hans Hoogervorst	Chairman
Suzanne Lloyd	Vice-Chair
Nick Anderson	
Martin Edelmann	
Françoise Flores	
Amaro Luiz de Oliveira Gomes	
Gary Kabureck	
Jianqiao Lu	
Takatsugu Ochi	
Darrel Scott	
Thomas Scott	
Chungwoo Suh	
Ann Tarca	
Mary Tokar	

Approval by the Board of Long-term Interests in Associates and Joint Ventures (Amendments to IAS 28) issued in October 2017

Long-term Interests in Associates and Joint Ventures (Amendments to IAS 28) was approved for issue by 13 of 14 members of the International Accounting Standards Board (Board). Mr Ochi dissented. His dissenting opinion is set out after the Basis for Conclusions. Messrs Anderson and Uhl and Ms Tarca abstained in view of their recent appointment to the Board.

Hans Hoogervorst	Chairman
Suzanne Lloyd	Vice-Chair
Nick Anderson	
Martin Edelmann	
Françoise Flores	
Amaro Luiz de Oliveira Gomes	
Gary Kabureck	
Jianqiao Lu	
Takatsugu Ochi	
Darrel Scott	
Thomas Scott	
Chungwoo Suh	
Ann Tarca	
Mary Tokar	

IAS 29

Financial Reporting in Hyperinflationary Economies

In April 2001 the International Accounting Standards Board adopted IAS 29 *Financial Reporting in Hyperinflationary Economies*, which had originally been issued by the International Accounting Standards Committee in July 1989.

Contents

FOR THE BASIS FOR CONCLUSIONS, SEE PART C OF THIS EDITION

BASIS FOR CONCLUSIONS

International Accounting Standard 29 *Financial Reporting in Hyperinflationary Economies* (IAS 29) is set out in paragraphs 1–41. All the paragraphs have equal authority but retain the IASC format of the Standard when it was adopted by the IASB. IAS 29 should be read in the context of the Basis for Conclusions, the *Preface to IFRS Standards* and the *Conceptual Framework for Financial Reporting*. IAS 8 *Accounting Policies, Changes in Accounting Estimates and Errors* provides a basis for selecting and applying accounting policies in the absence of explicit guidance.

International Accounting Standard 29
Financial Reporting in Hyperinflationary Economies[1]

Scope

1   This Standard shall be applied to the financial statements, including the consolidated financial statements, of any entity whose functional currency is the currency of a hyperinflationary economy.

2   In a hyperinflationary economy, reporting of operating results and financial position in the local currency without restatement is not useful. Money loses purchasing power at such a rate that comparison of amounts from transactions and other events that have occurred at different times, even within the same accounting period, is misleading.

3   This Standard does not establish an absolute rate at which hyperinflation is deemed to arise. It is a matter of judgement when restatement of financial statements in accordance with this Standard becomes necessary. Hyperinflation is indicated by characteristics of the economic environment of a country which include, but are not limited to, the following:

(a)   the general population prefers to keep its wealth in non-monetary assets or in a relatively stable foreign currency. Amounts of local currency held are immediately invested to maintain purchasing power;

(b)   the general population regards monetary amounts not in terms of the local currency but in terms of a relatively stable foreign currency. Prices may be quoted in that currency;

(c)   sales and purchases on credit take place at prices that compensate for the expected loss of purchasing power during the credit period, even if the period is short;

(d)   interest rates, wages and prices are linked to a price index; and

(e)   the cumulative inflation rate over three years is approaching, or exceeds, 100%.

4   It is preferable that all entities that report in the currency of the same hyperinflationary economy apply this Standard from the same date. Nevertheless, this Standard applies to the financial statements of any entity from the beginning of the reporting period in which it identifies the existence of hyperinflation in the country in whose currency it reports.

---

1   As part of *Improvements to IFRSs* issued in May 2008, the Board changed terms used in IAS 29 to be consistent with other IFRSs as follows: (a) 'market value' was amended to 'fair value', and (b) 'results of operations' and 'net income' were amended to 'profit or loss'.

The restatement of financial statements

5   Prices change over time as the result of various specific or general political, economic and social forces. Specific forces such as changes in supply and demand and technological changes may cause individual prices to increase or decrease significantly and independently of each other. In addition, general forces may result in changes in the general level of prices and therefore in the general purchasing power of money.

6   Entities that prepare financial statements on the historical cost basis of accounting do so without regard either to changes in the general level of prices or to increases in specific prices of recognised assets or liabilities. The exceptions to this are those assets and liabilities that the entity is required, or chooses, to measure at fair value. For example, property, plant and equipment may be revalued to fair value and biological assets are generally required to be measured at fair value. Some entities, however, present financial statements that are based on a current cost approach that reflects the effects of changes in the specific prices of assets held.

7   In a hyperinflationary economy, financial statements, whether they are based on a historical cost approach or a current cost approach, are useful only if they are expressed in terms of the measuring unit current at the end of the reporting period. As a result, this Standard applies to the financial statements of entities reporting in the currency of a hyperinflationary economy. Presentation of the information required by this Standard as a supplement to unrestated financial statements is not permitted. Furthermore, separate presentation of the financial statements before restatement is discouraged.

8   **The financial statements of an entity whose functional currency is the currency of a hyperinflationary economy, whether they are based on a historical cost approach or a current cost approach, shall be stated in terms of the measuring unit current at the end of the reporting period. The corresponding figures for the previous period required by IAS 1** *Presentation of Financial Statements* **(as revised in 2007) and any information in respect of earlier periods shall also be stated in terms of the measuring unit current at the end of the reporting period. For the purpose of presenting comparative amounts in a different presentation currency, paragraphs 42(b) and 43 of IAS 21** *The Effects of Changes in Foreign Exchange Rates* **apply.**

9   **The gain or loss on the net monetary position shall be included in profit or loss and separately disclosed.**

10   The restatement of financial statements in accordance with this Standard requires the application of certain procedures as well as judgement. The consistent application of these procedures and judgements from period to period is more important than the precise accuracy of the resulting amounts included in the restated financial statements.

Historical cost financial statements

Statement of financial position

11   Statement of financial position amounts not already expressed in terms of the measuring unit current at the end of the reporting period are restated by applying a general price index.

12   Monetary items are not restated because they are already expressed in terms of the monetary unit current at the end of the reporting period. Monetary items are money held and items to be received or paid in money.

13   Assets and liabilities linked by agreement to changes in prices, such as index linked bonds and loans, are adjusted in accordance with the agreement in order to ascertain the amount outstanding at the end of the reporting period. These items are carried at this adjusted amount in the restated statement of financial position.

14   All other assets and liabilities are non-monetary. Some non-monetary items are carried at amounts current at the end of the reporting period, such as net realisable value and fair value, so they are not restated. All other non-monetary assets and liabilities are restated.

15   Most non-monetary items are carried at cost or cost less depreciation; hence they are expressed at amounts current at their date of acquisition. The restated cost, or cost less depreciation, of each item is determined by applying to its historical cost and accumulated depreciation the change in a general price index from the date of acquisition to the end of the reporting period. For example, property, plant and equipment, inventories of raw materials and merchandise, goodwill, patents, trademarks and similar assets are restated from the dates of their purchase. Inventories of partly-finished and finished goods are restated from the dates on which the costs of purchase and of conversion were incurred.

16   Detailed records of the acquisition dates of items of property, plant and equipment may not be available or capable of estimation. In these rare circumstances, it may be necessary, in the first period of application of this Standard, to use an independent professional assessment of the value of the items as the basis for their restatement.

17   A general price index may not be available for the periods for which the restatement of property, plant and equipment is required by this Standard. In these circumstances, it may be necessary to use an estimate based, for example, on the movements in the exchange rate between the functional currency and a relatively stable foreign currency.

18   Some non-monetary items are carried at amounts current at dates other than that of acquisition or that of the statement of financial position, for example property, plant and equipment that has been revalued at some earlier date. In these cases, the carrying amounts are restated from the date of the revaluation.

19 The restated amount of a non-monetary item is reduced, in accordance with appropriate IFRSs, when it exceeds its recoverable amount. For example, restated amounts of property, plant and equipment, goodwill, patents and trademarks are reduced to recoverable amount and restated amounts of inventories are reduced to net realisable value.

20 An investee that is accounted for under the equity method may report in the currency of a hyperinflationary economy. The statement of financial position and statement of comprehensive income of such an investee are restated in accordance with this Standard in order to calculate the investor's share of its net assets and profit or loss. When the restated financial statements of the investee are expressed in a foreign currency they are translated at closing rates.

21 The impact of inflation is usually recognised in borrowing costs. It is not appropriate both to restate the capital expenditure financed by borrowing and to capitalise that part of the borrowing costs that compensates for the inflation during the same period. This part of the borrowing costs is recognised as an expense in the period in which the costs are incurred.

22 An entity may acquire assets under an arrangement that permits it to defer payment without incurring an explicit interest charge. Where it is impracticable to impute the amount of interest, such assets are restated from the payment date and not the date of purchase.

23 [Deleted]

24 At the beginning of the first period of application of this Standard, the components of owners' equity, except retained earnings and any revaluation surplus, are restated by applying a general price index from the dates the components were contributed or otherwise arose. Any revaluation surplus that arose in previous periods is eliminated. Restated retained earnings are derived from all the other amounts in the restated statement of financial position.

25 At the end of the first period and in subsequent periods, all components of owners' equity are restated by applying a general price index from the beginning of the period or the date of contribution, if later. The movements for the period in owners' equity are disclosed in accordance with IAS 1.

Statement of comprehensive income

26 This Standard requires that all items in the statement of comprehensive income are expressed in terms of the measuring unit current at the end of the reporting period. Therefore all amounts need to be restated by applying the change in the general price index from the dates when the items of income and expenses were initially recorded in the financial statements.

Gain or loss on net monetary position

27 In a period of inflation, an entity holding an excess of monetary assets over monetary liabilities loses purchasing power and an entity with an excess of monetary liabilities over monetary assets gains purchasing power to the extent the assets and liabilities are not linked to a price level. This gain or loss on the net monetary position may be derived as the difference resulting from the restatement of non-monetary assets, owners' equity and items in the statement of comprehensive income and the adjustment of index linked assets and liabilities. The gain or loss may be estimated by applying the change in a general price index to the weighted average for the period of the difference between monetary assets and monetary liabilities.

28 The gain or loss on the net monetary position is included in profit or loss. The adjustment to those assets and liabilities linked by agreement to changes in prices made in accordance with paragraph 13 is offset against the gain or loss on net monetary position. Other income and expense items, such as interest income and expense, and foreign exchange differences related to invested or borrowed funds, are also associated with the net monetary position. Although such items are separately disclosed, it may be helpful if they are presented together with the gain or loss on net monetary position in the statement of comprehensive income.

Current cost financial statements

Statement of financial position

29 Items stated at current cost are not restated because they are already expressed in terms of the measuring unit current at the end of the reporting period. Other items in the statement of financial position are restated in accordance with paragraphs 11 to 25.

Statement of comprehensive income

30 The current cost statement of comprehensive income, before restatement, generally reports costs current at the time at which the underlying transactions or events occurred. Cost of sales and depreciation are recorded at current costs at the time of consumption; sales and other expenses are recorded at their money amounts when they occurred. Therefore all amounts need to be restated into the measuring unit current at the end of the reporting period by applying a general price index.

Gain or loss on net monetary position

31 The gain or loss on the net monetary position is accounted for in accordance with paragraphs 27 and 28.

Taxes

32 The restatement of financial statements in accordance with this Standard may give rise to differences between the carrying amount of individual assets and liabilities in the statement of financial position and their tax bases. These differences are accounted for in accordance with IAS 12 *Income Taxes*.

Statement of cash flows

33   This Standard requires that all items in the statement of cash flows are expressed in terms of the measuring unit current at the end of the reporting period.

Corresponding figures

34   Corresponding figures for the previous reporting period, whether they were based on a historical cost approach or a current cost approach, are restated by applying a general price index so that the comparative financial statements are presented in terms of the measuring unit current at the end of the reporting period. Information that is disclosed in respect of earlier periods is also expressed in terms of the measuring unit current at the end of the reporting period. For the purpose of presenting comparative amounts in a different presentation currency, paragraphs 42(b) and 43 of IAS 21 apply.

Consolidated financial statements

35   A parent that reports in the currency of a hyperinflationary economy may have subsidiaries that also report in the currencies of hyperinflationary economies. The financial statements of any such subsidiary need to be restated by applying a general price index of the country in whose currency it reports before they are included in the consolidated financial statements issued by its parent. Where such a subsidiary is a foreign subsidiary, its restated financial statements are translated at closing rates. The financial statements of subsidiaries that do not report in the currencies of hyperinflationary economies are dealt with in accordance with IAS 21.

36   If financial statements with different ends of the reporting periods are consolidated, all items, whether non-monetary or monetary, need to be restated into the measuring unit current at the date of the consolidated financial statements.

Selection and use of the general price index

37   The restatement of financial statements in accordance with this Standard requires the use of a general price index that reflects changes in general purchasing power. It is preferable that all entities that report in the currency of the same economy use the same index.

Economies ceasing to be hyperinflationary

38   When an economy ceases to be hyperinflationary and an entity discontinues the preparation and presentation of financial statements prepared in accordance with this Standard, it shall treat the amounts expressed in the measuring unit current at the end of the previous reporting period as the basis for the carrying amounts in its subsequent financial statements.

Disclosures

39   The following disclosures shall be made:

    (a)   the fact that the financial statements and the corresponding figures for previous periods have been restated for the changes in the general purchasing power of the functional currency and, as a result, are stated in terms of the measuring unit current at the end of the reporting period;

    (b)   whether the financial statements are based on a historical cost approach or a current cost approach; and

    (c)   the identity and level of the price index at the end of the reporting period and the movement in the index during the current and the previous reporting period.

40   The disclosures required by this Standard are needed to make clear the basis of dealing with the effects of inflation in the financial statements. They are also intended to provide other information necessary to understand that basis and the resulting amounts.

Effective date

41   This Standard becomes operative for financial statements covering periods beginning on or after 1 January 1990.

IAS 32

Financial Instruments: Presentation

In April 2001 the International Accounting Standards Board (Board) adopted IAS 32 *Financial Instruments: Disclosure and Presentation*, which had been issued by the International Accounting Standards Committee in 2000. IAS 32 *Financial Instruments: Disclosure and Presentation* had originally been issued in June 1995 and had been subsequently amended in 1998 and 2000.

The Board issued a revised IAS 32 in December 2003 as part of its initial agenda of technical projects. This revised IAS 32 also incorporated the guidance contained in related Interpretations (SIC-5 *Classification of Financial Instruments-Contingent Settlement Provisions*, SIC-16 *Share Capital-Reacquired Own Equity Instruments (Treasury Shares)* and SIC-17 *Equity—Costs of an Equity Transaction*). It also incorporated guidance previously proposed in draft SIC Interpretation D34 *Financial Instruments—Instruments or Rights Redeemable by the Holder*.

In December 2005 the Board amended IAS 32 by relocating all disclosures relating to financial instruments to IFRS 7 *Financial Instruments: Disclosures*. Consequently, the title of IAS 32 changed to *Financial Instruments: Presentation*.

In February 2008 IAS 32 was changed to require some puttable financial instruments and obligations arising on liquidation to be classified as equity. In October 2009 the Board amended IAS 32 to require some rights that are denominated in a foreign currency to be classified as equity. The application guidance in IAS 32 was amended in December 2011 to address some inconsistencies relating to the offsetting financial assets and financial liabilities criteria.

Other Standards have made minor consequential amendments to IAS 32. They include *Improvements to IFRSs* (issued May 2010), IFRS 10 *Consolidated Financial Statements* (issued May 2011), IFRS 11 *Joint Arrangements* (issued May 2011), IFRS 13 *Fair Value Measurement* (issued May 2011), *Presentation of Items of Other Comprehensive Income* (Amendments to IAS 1) (issued June 2011), *Disclosures—Offsetting Financial Assets and Financial Liabilities* (Amendments to IFRS 7) (issued December 2011), *Annual Improvements to IFRSs 2009–2011 Cycle* (issued May 2012), *Investment Entities* (Amendments to IFRS 10, IFRS 12 and IAS 27) (issued October 2012), IFRS 9 *Financial Instruments* (Hedge Accounting and amendments to IFRS 9, IFRS 7 and IAS 39) (issued November 2013), IFRS 15 *Revenue from Contracts with Customers* (issued May 2014), IFRS 9 *Financial Instruments* (issued July 2014), IFRS 16 *Leases* (issued January 2016), *Annual Improvements to IFRS Standards 2015–2017 Cycle* (issued December 2017) and *Amendments to References to the Conceptual Framework in IFRS Standards* (issued March 2018).

Contents

FOR THE ACCOMPANYING GUIDANCE LISTED BELOW, SEE PART B OF THIS EDITION

ILLUSTRATIVE EXAMPLES

FOR THE BASIS FOR CONCLUSIONS, SEE PART C OF THIS EDITION

BASIS FOR CONCLUSIONS

DISSENTING OPINIONS

International Accounting Standard 32 *Financial Instruments: Presentation* (IAS 32) is set out in paragraphs 2–100 and the Appendix. All the paragraphs have equal authority but retain the IASC format of the Standard when it was adopted by the IASB. IAS 32 should be read in the context of its objective and the Basis for Conclusions, the *Preface to IFRS Standards* and the *Conceptual Framework for Financial Reporting*. IAS 8 *Accounting Policies, Changes in Accounting Estimates and Errors* provides a basis for selecting and applying accounting policies in the absence of explicit guidance.

International Accounting Standard 32
Financial Instruments: Presentation

Objective

1   [Deleted]

2   The objective of this Standard is to establish principles for presenting financial instruments as liabilities or equity and for offsetting financial assets and financial liabilities. It applies to the classification of financial instruments, from the perspective of the issuer, into financial assets, financial liabilities and equity instruments; the classification of related interest, dividends, losses and gains; and the circumstances in which financial assets and financial liabilities should be offset.

3   The principles in this Standard complement the principles for recognising and measuring financial assets and financial liabilities in IFRS 9 *Financial Instruments*, and for disclosing information about them in IFRS 7 *Financial Instruments: Disclosures*.

Scope

4   This Standard shall be applied by all entities to all types of financial instruments except:

(a)   those interests in subsidiaries, associates or joint ventures that are accounted for in accordance with IFRS 10 *Consolidated Financial Statements*, IAS 27 *Separate Financial Statements* or IAS 28 *Investments in Associates and Joint Ventures*. However, in some cases, IFRS 10, IAS 27 or IAS 28 require or permit an entity to account for an interest in a subsidiary, associate or joint venture using IFRS 9; in those cases, entities shall apply the requirements of this Standard. Entities shall also apply this Standard to all derivatives linked to interests in subsidiaries, associates or joint ventures.

(b)   employers' rights and obligations under employee benefit plans, to which IAS 19 *Employee Benefits* applies.

(c)   [deleted]

(d)   insurance contracts as defined in IFRS 4 *Insurance Contracts*. However, this Standard applies to derivatives that are embedded in insurance contracts if IFRS 9 requires the entity to account for them separately. Moreover, an issuer shall apply this Standard to financial guarantee contracts if the issuer applies IFRS 9 in recognising and measuring the contracts, but shall apply IFRS 4 if the issuer elects, in accordance with paragraph 4(d) of IFRS 4, to apply IFRS 4 in recognising and measuring them.

(e) financial instruments that are within the scope of IFRS 4 because they contain a discretionary participation feature. The issuer of these instruments is exempt from applying to these features paragraphs 15–32 and AG25–AG35 of this Standard regarding the distinction between financial liabilities and equity instruments. However, these instruments are subject to all other requirements of this Standard. Furthermore, this Standard applies to derivatives that are embedded in these instruments (see IFRS 9).

(f) financial instruments, contracts and obligations under share-based payment transactions to which IFRS 2 *Share-based Payment* applies, except for

(i) contracts within the scope of paragraphs 8–10 of this Standard, to which this Standard applies,

(ii) paragraphs 33 and 34 of this Standard, which shall be applied to treasury shares purchased, sold, issued or cancelled in connection with employee share option plans, employee share purchase plans, and all other share-based payment arrangements.

5–7 [Deleted]

8 This Standard shall be applied to those contracts to buy or sell a non-financial item that can be settled net in cash or another financial instrument, or by exchanging financial instruments, as if the contracts were financial instruments, with the exception of contracts that were entered into and continue to be held for the purpose of the receipt or delivery of a non-financial item in accordance with the entity's expected purchase, sale or usage requirements. However, this Standard shall be applied to those contracts that an entity designates as measured at fair value through profit or loss in accordance with paragraph 2.5 of IFRS 9 *Financial Instruments*.

9 There are various ways in which a contract to buy or sell a non-financial item can be settled net in cash or another financial instrument or by exchanging financial instruments. These include:

(a) when the terms of the contract permit either party to settle it net in cash or another financial instrument or by exchanging financial instruments;

(b) when the ability to settle net in cash or another financial instrument, or by exchanging financial instruments, is not explicit in the terms of the contract, but the entity has a practice of settling similar contracts net in cash or another financial instrument, or by exchanging financial instruments (whether with the counterparty, by entering into offsetting contracts or by selling the contract before its exercise or lapse);

(c) when, for similar contracts, the entity has a practice of taking delivery of the underlying and selling it within a short period after delivery for the purpose of generating a profit from short-term fluctuations in price or dealer's margin; and

(d) when the non-financial item that is the subject of the contract is readily convertible to cash.

A contract to which (b) or (c) applies is not entered into for the purpose of the receipt or delivery of the non-financial item in accordance with the entity's expected purchase, sale or usage requirements, and, accordingly, is within the scope of this Standard. Other contracts to which paragraph 8 applies are evaluated to determine whether they were entered into and continue to be held for the purpose of the receipt or delivery of the non-financial item in accordance with the entity's expected purchase, sale or usage requirement, and accordingly, whether they are within the scope of this Standard.

10 A written option to buy or sell a non-financial item that can be settled net in cash or another financial instrument, or by exchanging financial instruments, in accordance with paragraph 9(a) or (d) is within the scope of this Standard. Such a contract cannot be entered into for the purpose of the receipt or delivery of the non-financial item in accordance with the entity's expected purchase, sale or usage requirements.

Definitions (see also paragraphs AG3–AG23)

11 The following terms are used in this Standard with the meanings specified:

A *financial instrument* is any contract that gives rise to a financial asset of one entity and a financial liability or equity instrument of another entity.

A *financial asset* is any asset that is:

(a) cash;

(b) an equity instrument of another entity;

(c) a contractual right:

(i) to receive cash or another financial asset from another entity; or

(ii) to exchange financial assets or financial liabilities with another entity under conditions that are potentially favourable to the entity; or

(d) a contract that will or may be settled in the entity's own equity instruments and is:

(i) a non-derivative for which the entity is or may be obliged to receive a variable number of the entity's own equity instruments; or

(ii) a derivative that will or may be settled other than by the exchange of a fixed amount of cash or another financial asset for a fixed number of the entity's own equity instruments. For this purpose the entity's own equity instruments do not include puttable financial instruments classified as equity instruments in accordance with paragraphs 16A and 16B, instruments that impose on the entity an obligation to deliver to another party a pro rata share of the net assets of the entity only on liquidation and are classified as equity instruments in accordance with paragraphs 16C and 16D, or instruments that are contracts for the future receipt or delivery of the entity's own equity instruments.

A *financial liability* is any liability that is:

(a) a contractual obligation:

    (i) to deliver cash or another financial asset to another entity; or

    (ii) to exchange financial assets or financial liabilities with another entity under conditions that are potentially unfavourable to the entity; or

(b) a contract that will or may be settled in the entity's own equity instruments and is:

    (i) a non-derivative for which the entity is or may be obliged to deliver a variable number of the entity's own equity instruments; or

    (ii) a derivative that will or may be settled other than by the exchange of a fixed amount of cash or another financial asset for a fixed number of the entity's own equity instruments. For this purpose, rights, options or warrants to acquire a fixed number of the entity's own equity instruments for a fixed amount of any currency are equity instruments if the entity offers the rights, options or warrants pro rata to all of its existing owners of the same class of its own non-derivative equity instruments. Also, for these purposes the entity's own equity instruments do not include puttable financial instruments that are classified as equity instruments in accordance with paragraphs 16A and 16B, instruments that impose on the entity an obligation to deliver to another party a pro rata share of the net assets of the entity only on liquidation and are classified as equity instruments in accordance with paragraphs 16C and 16D, or instruments that are contracts for the future receipt or delivery of the entity's own equity instruments.

As an exception, an instrument that meets the definition of a financial liability is classified as an equity instrument if it has all the features and meets the conditions in paragraphs 16A and 16B or paragraphs 16C and 16D.

An *equity instrument* is any contract that evidences a residual interest in the assets of an entity after deducting all of its liabilities.

Fair value is the price that would be received to sell an asset or paid to transfer a liability in an orderly transaction between market participants at the measurement date. (See IFRS 13 *Fair Value Measurement*.)

A *puttable instrument* is a financial instrument that gives the holder the right to put the instrument back to the issuer for cash or another financial asset or is automatically put back to the issuer on the occurrence of an uncertain future event or the death or retirement of the instrument holder.

12   The following terms are defined in Appendix A of IFRS 9 or paragraph 9 of IAS 39 *Financial Instruments: Recognition and Measurement* and are used in this Standard with the meaning specified in IAS 39 and IFRS 9.

- amortised cost of a financial asset or financial liability
- derecognition
- derivative
- effective interest method
- financial guarantee contract
- financial liability at fair value through profit or loss
- firm commitment
- forecast transaction
- hedge effectiveness
- hedged item
- hedging instrument
- held for trading
- regular way purchase or sale
- transaction costs

13   In this Standard, 'contract' and 'contractual' refer to an agreement between two or more parties that has clear economic consequences that the parties have little, if any, discretion to avoid, usually because the agreement is enforceable by law. Contracts, and thus financial instruments, may take a variety of forms and need not be in writing.

14   In this Standard, 'entity' includes individuals, partnerships, incorporated bodies, trusts and government agencies.

Presentation

Liabilities and equity (see also paragraphs AG13–AG14J and AG25–AG29A)

15 The issuer of a financial instrument shall classify the instrument, or its component parts, on initial recognition as a financial liability, a financial asset or an equity instrument in accordance with the substance of the contractual arrangement and the definitions of a financial liability, a financial asset and an equity instrument.

16 When an issuer applies the definitions in paragraph 11 to determine whether a financial instrument is an equity instrument rather than a financial liability, the instrument is an equity instrument if, and only if, both conditions (a) and (b) below are met.

   (a)   The instrument includes no contractual obligation:

      (i)   to deliver cash or another financial asset to another entity; or

      (ii)   to exchange financial assets or financial liabilities with another entity under conditions that are potentially unfavourable to the issuer.

   (b)   If the instrument will or may be settled in the issuer's own equity instruments, it is:

      (i)   a non-derivative that includes no contractual obligation for the issuer to deliver a variable number of its own equity instruments; or

      (ii)   a derivative that will be settled only by the issuer exchanging a fixed amount of cash or another financial asset for a fixed number of its own equity instruments. For this purpose, rights, options or warrants to acquire a fixed number of the entity's own equity instruments for a fixed amount of any currency are equity instruments if the entity offers the rights, options or warrants pro rata to all of its existing owners of the same class of its own non-derivative equity instruments. Also, for these purposes the issuer's own equity instruments do not include instruments that have all the features and meet the conditions described in paragraphs 16A and 16B or paragraphs 16C and 16D, or instruments that are contracts for the future receipt or delivery of the issuer's own equity instruments.

A contractual obligation, including one arising from a derivative financial instrument, that will or may result in the future receipt or delivery of the issuer's own equity instruments, but does not meet conditions (a) and (b) above, is not an equity instrument. As an exception, an instrument that meets the definition of a financial liability is classified as an equity instrument if it has all the features and meets the conditions in paragraphs 16A and 16B or paragraphs 16C and 16D.

Puttable instruments

16A   A puttable financial instrument includes a contractual obligation for the issuer to repurchase or redeem that instrument for cash or another financial asset on exercise of the put. As an exception to the definition of a financial liability, an instrument that includes such an obligation is classified as an equity instrument if it has all the following features:

(a)   It entitles the holder to a pro rata share of the entity's net assets in the event of the entity's liquidation. The entity's net assets are those assets that remain after deducting all other claims on its assets. A pro rata share is determined by:

(i)   dividing the entity's net assets on liquidation into units of equal amount; and

(ii)   multiplying that amount by the number of the units held by the financial instrument holder.

(b)   The instrument is in the class of instruments that is subordinate to all other classes of instruments. To be in such a class the instrument:

(i)   has no priority over other claims to the assets of the entity on liquidation, and

(ii)   does not need to be converted into another instrument before it is in the class of instruments that is subordinate to all other classes of instruments.

(c)   All financial instruments in the class of instruments that is subordinate to all other classes of instruments have identical features. For example, they must all be puttable, and the formula or other method used to calculate the repurchase or redemption price is the same for all instruments in that class.

(d)   Apart from the contractual obligation for the issuer to repurchase or redeem the instrument for cash or another financial asset, the instrument does not include any contractual obligation to deliver cash or another financial asset to another entity, or to exchange financial assets or financial liabilities with another entity under conditions that are potentially unfavourable to the entity, and it is not a contract that will or may be settled in the entity's own equity instruments as set out in subparagraph (b) of the definition of a financial liability.

(e)   The total expected cash flows attributable to the instrument over the life of the instrument are based substantially on the profit or loss, the change in the recognised net assets or the change in the fair value of the recognised and unrecognised net assets of the entity over the life of the instrument (excluding any effects of the instrument).

16B   For an instrument to be classified as an equity instrument, in addition to the instrument having all the above features, the issuer must have no other financial instrument or contract that has:

(a) total cash flows based substantially on the profit or loss, the change in the recognised net assets or the change in the fair value of the recognised and unrecognised net assets of the entity (excluding any effects of such instrument or contract) and

(b) the effect of substantially restricting or fixing the residual return to the puttable instrument holders.

For the purposes of applying this condition, the entity shall not consider non-financial contracts with a holder of an instrument described in paragraph 16A that have contractual terms and conditions that are similar to the contractual terms and conditions of an equivalent contract that might occur between a non-instrument holder and the issuing entity. If the entity cannot determine that this condition is met, it shall not classify the puttable instrument as an equity instrument.

Instruments, or components of instruments, that impose on the entity an obligation to deliver to another party a pro rata share of the net assets of the entity only on liquidation

16C   Some financial instruments include a contractual obligation for the issuing entity to deliver to another entity a pro rata share of its net assets only on liquidation. The obligation arises because liquidation either is certain to occur and outside the control of the entity (for example, a limited life entity) or is uncertain to occur but is at the option of the instrument holder. As an exception to the definition of a financial liability, an instrument that includes such an obligation is classified as an equity instrument if it has all the following features:

(a) It entitles the holder to a pro rata share of the entity's net assets in the event of the entity's liquidation. The entity's net assets are those assets that remain after deducting all other claims on its assets. A pro rata share is determined by:

(i) dividing the net assets of the entity on liquidation into units of equal amount; and

(ii) multiplying that amount by the number of the units held by the financial instrument holder.

(b) The instrument is in the class of instruments that is subordinate to all other classes of instruments. To be in such a class the instrument:

(i) has no priority over other claims to the assets of the entity on liquidation, and

(ii) does not need to be converted into another instrument before it is in the class of instruments that is subordinate to all other classes of instruments.

(c) All financial instruments in the class of instruments that is subordinate to all other classes of instruments must have an identical contractual obligation for the issuing entity to deliver a pro rata share of its net assets on liquidation.

16D   For an instrument to be classified as an equity instrument, in addition to the instrument having all the above features, the issuer must have no other financial instrument or contract that has:

(a)   total cash flows based substantially on the profit or loss, the change in the recognised net assets or the change in the fair value of the recognised and unrecognised net assets of the entity (excluding any effects of such instrument or contract) and

(b)   the effect of substantially restricting or fixing the residual return to the instrument holders.

For the purposes of applying this condition, the entity shall not consider non-financial contracts with a holder of an instrument described in paragraph 16C that have contractual terms and conditions that are similar to the contractual terms and conditions of an equivalent contract that might occur between a non-instrument holder and the issuing entity. If the entity cannot determine that this condition is met, it shall not classify the instrument as an equity instrument.

Reclassification of puttable instruments and instruments that impose on the entity an obligation to deliver to another party a pro rata share of the net assets of the entity only on liquidation

16E   An entity shall classify a financial instrument as an equity instrument in accordance with paragraphs 16A and 16B or paragraphs 16C and 16D from the date when the instrument has all the features and meets the conditions set out in those paragraphs. An entity shall reclassify a financial instrument from the date when the instrument ceases to have all the features or meet all the conditions set out in those paragraphs. For example, if an entity redeems all its issued non-puttable instruments and any puttable instrument that remain outstanding have all the features and meet all the conditions in paragraphs 16A and 16B, the entity shall reclassify the puttable instruments as equity instruments from the date when it redeems the non-puttable instruments.

16F   An entity shall account as follows for the reclassification of an instrument in accordance with paragraph 16E:

(a)   It shall reclassify an equity instrument as a financial liability from the date when the instrument ceases to have all the features or meet the conditions in paragraphs 16A and 16B or paragraphs 16C and 16D. The financial liability shall be measured at the instrument's fair value at the date of reclassification. The entity shall recognise in equity any difference between the carrying value of the equity instrument and the fair value of the financial liability at the date of reclassification.

(b)   It shall reclassify a financial liability as equity from the date when the instrument has all the features and meets the conditions set out in paragraphs 16A and 16B or paragraphs 16C and 16D. An equity instrument shall be measured at the carrying value of the financial liability at the date of reclassification.

No contractual obligation to deliver cash or another financial asset (paragraph 16(a))

17 With the exception of the circumstances described in paragraphs 16A and 16B or paragraphs 16C and 16D, a critical feature in differentiating a financial liability from an equity instrument is the existence of a contractual obligation of one party to the financial instrument (the issuer) either to deliver cash or another financial asset to the other party (the holder) or to exchange financial assets or financial liabilities with the holder under conditions that are potentially unfavourable to the issuer. Although the holder of an equity instrument may be entitled to receive a pro rata share of any dividends or other distributions of equity, the issuer does not have a contractual obligation to make such distributions because it cannot be required to deliver cash or another financial asset to another party.

18 The substance of a financial instrument, rather than its legal form, governs its classification in the entity's statement of financial position. Substance and legal form are commonly consistent, but not always. Some financial instruments take the legal form of equity but are liabilities in substance and others may combine features associated with equity instruments and features associated with financial liabilities. For example:

(a) a preference share that provides for mandatory redemption by the issuer for a fixed or determinable amount at a fixed or determinable future date, or gives the holder the right to require the issuer to redeem the instrument at or after a particular date for a fixed or determinable amount, is a financial liability.

(b) a financial instrument that gives the holder the right to put it back to the issuer for cash or another financial asset (a 'puttable instrument') is a financial liability, except for those instruments classified as equity instruments in accordance with paragraphs 16A and 16B or paragraphs 16C and 16D. The financial instrument is a financial liability even when the amount of cash or other financial assets is determined on the basis of an index or other item that has the potential to increase or decrease. The existence of an option for the holder to put the instrument back to the issuer for cash or another financial asset means that the puttable instrument meets the definition of a financial liability, except for those instruments classified as equity instruments in accordance with paragraphs 16A and 16B or paragraphs 16C and 16D. For example, open-ended mutual funds, unit trusts, partnerships and some co-operative entities may provide their unitholders or members with a right to redeem their interests in the issuer at any time for cash, which results in the unitholders' or members' interests being classified as financial liabilities, except for those instruments classified as equity instruments in accordance with paragraphs 16A and 16B or paragraphs 16C and 16D. However, classification as a financial liability does not preclude the use of descriptors such as 'net asset value attributable to unitholders' and 'change in net asset value attributable to unitholders' in the financial statements of an entity that has no contributed equity (such as some mutual funds and unit trusts, see Illustrative Example 7) or the use of additional disclosure to show that total members' interests comprise items such as reserves that meet the definition of equity and puttable instruments that do not (see Illustrative Example 8).

19   If an entity does not have an unconditional right to avoid delivering cash or another financial asset to settle a contractual obligation, the obligation meets the definition of a financial liability, except for those instruments classified as equity instruments in accordance with paragraphs 16A and 16B or paragraphs 16C and 16D. For example:

(a)   a restriction on the ability of an entity to satisfy a contractual obligation, such as lack of access to foreign currency or the need to obtain approval for payment from a regulatory authority, does not negate the entity's contractual obligation or the holder's contractual right under the instrument.

(b)   a contractual obligation that is conditional on a counterparty exercising its right to redeem is a financial liability because the entity does not have the unconditional right to avoid delivering cash or another financial asset.

20   A financial instrument that does not explicitly establish a contractual obligation to deliver cash or another financial asset may establish an obligation indirectly through its terms and conditions. For example:

(a)   a financial instrument may contain a non-financial obligation that must be settled if, and only if, the entity fails to make distributions or to redeem the instrument. If the entity can avoid a transfer of cash or another financial asset only by settling the non-financial obligation, the financial instrument is a financial liability.

(b)   a financial instrument is a financial liability if it provides that on settlement the entity will deliver either:

(i)   cash or another financial asset; or

(ii)   its own shares whose value is determined to exceed substantially the value of the cash or other financial asset.

Although the entity does not have an explicit contractual obligation to deliver cash or another financial asset, the value of the share settlement alternative is such that the entity will settle in cash. In any event, the holder has in substance been guaranteed receipt of an amount that is at least equal to the cash settlement option (see paragraph 21).

Settlement in the entity's own equity instruments (paragraph 16(b))

21   A contract is not an equity instrument solely because it may result in the receipt or delivery of the entity's own equity instruments. An entity may have a contractual right or obligation to receive or deliver a number of its own shares or other equity instruments that varies so that the fair value of the entity's own equity instruments to be received or delivered equals the amount

of the contractual right or obligation. Such a contractual right or obligation may be for a fixed amount or an amount that fluctuates in part or in full in response to changes in a variable other than the market price of the entity's own equity instruments (eg an interest rate, a commodity price or a financial instrument price). Two examples are (a) a contract to deliver as many of the entity's own equity instruments as are equal in value to CU100,[1] and (b) a contract to deliver as many of the entity's own equity instruments as are equal in value to the value of 100 ounces of gold. Such a contract is a financial liability of the entity even though the entity must or can settle it by delivering its own equity instruments. It is not an equity instrument because the entity uses a variable number of its own equity instruments as a means to settle the contract. Accordingly, the contract does not evidence a residual interest in the entity's assets after deducting all of its liabilities.

22   Except as stated in paragraph 22A, a contract that will be settled by the entity (receiving or) delivering a fixed number of its own equity instruments in exchange for a fixed amount of cash or another financial asset is an equity instrument. For example, an issued share option that gives the counterparty a right to buy a fixed number of the entity's shares for a fixed price or for a fixed stated principal amount of a bond is an equity instrument. Changes in the fair value of a contract arising from variations in market interest rates that do not affect the amount of cash or other financial assets to be paid or received, or the number of equity instruments to be received or delivered, on settlement of the contract do not preclude the contract from being an equity instrument. Any consideration received (such as the premium received for a written option or warrant on the entity's own shares) is added directly to equity. Any consideration paid (such as the premium paid for a purchased option) is deducted directly from equity. Changes in the fair value of an equity instrument are not recognised in the financial statements.

22A   If the entity's own equity instruments to be received, or delivered, by the entity upon settlement of a contract are puttable financial instruments with all the features and meeting the conditions described in paragraphs 16A and 16B, or instruments that impose on the entity an obligation to deliver to another party a pro rata share of the net assets of the entity only on liquidation with all the features and meeting the conditions described in paragraphs 16C and 16D, the contract is a financial asset or a financial liability. This includes a contract that will be settled by the entity receiving or delivering a fixed number of such instruments in exchange for a fixed amount of cash or another financial asset.

23   With the exception of the circumstances described in paragraphs 16A and 16B or paragraphs 16C and 16D, a contract that contains an obligation for an entity to purchase its own equity instruments for cash or another financial asset gives rise to a financial liability for the present value of the redemption amount (for example, for the present value of the forward repurchase price, option exercise price or other redemption amount). This is the case even if the contract itself is an equity instrument. One example is an entity's obligation

---

1   In this Standard, monetary amounts are denominated in 'currency units (CU)'.

under a forward contract to purchase its own equity instruments for cash. The financial liability is recognised initially at the present value of the redemption amount, and is reclassified from equity. Subsequently, the financial liability is measured in accordance with IFRS 9. If the contract expires without delivery, the carrying amount of the financial liability is reclassified to equity. An entity's contractual obligation to purchase its own equity instruments gives rise to a financial liability for the present value of the redemption amount even if the obligation to purchase is conditional on the counterparty exercising a right to redeem (eg a written put option that gives the counterparty the right to sell an entity's own equity instruments to the entity for a fixed price).

24   A contract that will be settled by the entity delivering or receiving a fixed number of its own equity instruments in exchange for a variable amount of cash or another financial asset is a financial asset or financial liability. An example is a contract for the entity to deliver 100 of its own equity instruments in return for an amount of cash calculated to equal the value of 100 ounces of gold.

Contingent settlement provisions

25   A financial instrument may require the entity to deliver cash or another financial asset, or otherwise to settle it in such a way that it would be a financial liability, in the event of the occurrence or non-occurrence of uncertain future events (or on the outcome of uncertain circumstances) that are beyond the control of both the issuer and the holder of the instrument, such as a change in a stock market index, consumer price index, interest rate or taxation requirements, or the issuer's future revenues, net income or debt-to-equity ratio. The issuer of such an instrument does not have the unconditional right to avoid delivering cash or another financial asset (or otherwise to settle it in such a way that it would be a financial liability). Therefore, it is a financial liability of the issuer unless:

(a)   the part of the contingent settlement provision that could require settlement in cash or another financial asset (or otherwise in such a way that it would be a financial liability) is not genuine;

(b)   the issuer can be required to settle the obligation in cash or another financial asset (or otherwise to settle it in such a way that it would be a financial liability) only in the event of liquidation of the issuer; or

(c)   the instrument has all the features and meets the conditions in paragraphs 16A and 16B.

Settlement options

26   When a derivative financial instrument gives one party a choice over how it is settled (eg the issuer or the holder can choose settlement net in cash or by exchanging shares for cash), it is a financial asset or a financial liability unless all of the settlement alternatives would result in it being an equity instrument.

27   An example of a derivative financial instrument with a settlement option that is a financial liability is a share option that the issuer can decide to settle net in cash or by exchanging its own shares for cash. Similarly, some contracts to buy or sell a non-financial item in exchange for the entity's own equity instruments are within the scope of this Standard because they can be settled either by delivery of the non-financial item or net in cash or another financial instrument (see paragraphs 8–10). Such contracts are financial assets or financial liabilities and not equity instruments.

Compound financial instruments (see also paragraphs AG30–AG35 and Illustrative Examples 9–12)

28   **The issuer of a non-derivative financial instrument shall evaluate the terms of the financial instrument to determine whether it contains both a liability and an equity component. Such components shall be classified separately as financial liabilities, financial assets or equity instruments in accordance with paragraph 15.**

29   An entity recognises separately the components of a financial instrument that (a) creates a financial liability of the entity and (b) grants an option to the holder of the instrument to convert it into an equity instrument of the entity. For example, a bond or similar instrument convertible by the holder into a fixed number of ordinary shares of the entity is a compound financial instrument. From the perspective of the entity, such an instrument comprises two components: a financial liability (a contractual arrangement to deliver cash or another financial asset) and an equity instrument (a call option granting the holder the right, for a specified period of time, to convert it into a fixed number of ordinary shares of the entity). The economic effect of issuing such an instrument is substantially the same as issuing simultaneously a debt instrument with an early settlement provision and warrants to purchase ordinary shares, or issuing a debt instrument with detachable share purchase warrants. Accordingly, in all cases, the entity presents the liability and equity components separately in its statement of financial position.

30   Classification of the liability and equity components of a convertible instrument is not revised as a result of a change in the likelihood that a conversion option will be exercised, even when exercise of the option may appear to have become economically advantageous to some holders. Holders may not always act in the way that might be expected because, for example, the tax consequences resulting from conversion may differ among holders. Furthermore, the likelihood of conversion will change from time to time. The entity's contractual obligation to make future payments remains outstanding until it is extinguished through conversion, maturity of the instrument or some other transaction.

31   IFRS 9 deals with the measurement of financial assets and financial liabilities. Equity instruments are instruments that evidence a residual interest in the assets of an entity after deducting all of its liabilities. Therefore, when the initial carrying amount of a compound financial instrument is allocated to its equity and liability components, the equity component is assigned the

residual amount after deducting from the fair value of the instrument as a whole the amount separately determined for the liability component. The value of any derivative features (such as a call option) embedded in the compound financial instrument other than the equity component (such as an equity conversion option) is included in the liability component. The sum of the carrying amounts assigned to the liability and equity components on initial recognition is always equal to the fair value that would be ascribed to the instrument as a whole. No gain or loss arises from initially recognising the components of the instrument separately.

32 Under the approach described in paragraph 31, the issuer of a bond convertible into ordinary shares first determines the carrying amount of the liability component by measuring the fair value of a similar liability (including any embedded non-equity derivative features) that does not have an associated equity component. The carrying amount of the equity instrument represented by the option to convert the instrument into ordinary shares is then determined by deducting the fair value of the financial liability from the fair value of the compound financial instrument as a whole.

Treasury shares (see also paragraph AG36)

33 If an entity reacquires its own equity instruments, those instruments ('treasury shares') shall be deducted from equity. No gain or loss shall be recognised in profit or loss on the purchase, sale, issue or cancellation of an entity's own equity instruments. Such treasury shares may be acquired and held by the entity or by other members of the consolidated group. Consideration paid or received shall be recognised directly in equity.

33A *[This paragraph refers to amendments that are not yet effective, and is therefore not included in this edition.]*

34 The amount of treasury shares held is disclosed separately either in the statement of financial position or in the notes, in accordance with IAS 1 *Presentation of Financial Statements*. An entity provides disclosure in accordance with IAS 24 *Related Party Disclosures* if the entity reacquires its own equity instruments from related parties.

Interest, dividends, losses and gains (see also paragraph AG37)

35 Interest, dividends, losses and gains relating to a financial instrument or a component that is a financial liability shall be recognised as income or expense in profit or loss. Distributions to holders of an equity instrument shall be recognised by the entity directly in equity. Transaction costs of an equity transaction shall be accounted for as a deduction from equity.

35A Income tax relating to distributions to holders of an equity instrument and to transaction costs of an equity transaction shall be accounted for in accordance with IAS 12 *Income Taxes*.

36   The classification of a financial instrument as a financial liability or an equity instrument determines whether interest, dividends, losses and gains relating to that instrument are recognised as income or expense in profit or loss. Thus, dividend payments on shares wholly recognised as liabilities are recognised as expenses in the same way as interest on a bond. Similarly, gains and losses associated with redemptions or refinancings of financial liabilities are recognised in profit or loss, whereas redemptions or refinancings of equity instruments are recognised as changes in equity. Changes in the fair value of an equity instrument are not recognised in the financial statements.

37   An entity typically incurs various costs in issuing or acquiring its own equity instruments. Those costs might include registration and other regulatory fees, amounts paid to legal, accounting and other professional advisers, printing costs and stamp duties. The transaction costs of an equity transaction are accounted for as a deduction from equity to the extent they are incremental costs directly attributable to the equity transaction that otherwise would have been avoided. The costs of an equity transaction that is abandoned are recognised as an expense.

38   Transaction costs that relate to the issue of a compound financial instrument are allocated to the liability and equity components of the instrument in proportion to the allocation of proceeds. Transaction costs that relate jointly to more than one transaction (for example, costs of a concurrent offering of some shares and a stock exchange listing of other shares) are allocated to those transactions using a basis of allocation that is rational and consistent with similar transactions.

39   The amount of transaction costs accounted for as a deduction from equity in the period is disclosed separately in accordance with IAS 1.

40   Dividends classified as an expense may be presented in the statement(s) of profit or loss and other comprehensive income either with interest on other liabilities or as a separate item. In addition to the requirements of this Standard, disclosure of interest and dividends is subject to the requirements of IAS 1 and IFRS 7. In some circumstances, because of the differences between interest and dividends with respect to matters such as tax deductibility, it is desirable to disclose them separately in the statement(s) of profit or loss and other comprehensive income. Disclosures of the tax effects are made in accordance with IAS 12.

41   Gains and losses related to changes in the carrying amount of a financial liability are recognised as income or expense in profit or loss even when they relate to an instrument that includes a right to the residual interest in the assets of the entity in exchange for cash or another financial asset (see paragraph 18(b)). Under IAS 1 the entity presents any gain or loss arising from remeasurement of such an instrument separately in the statement of comprehensive income when it is relevant in explaining the entity's performance.

Offsetting a financial asset and a financial liability (see also paragraphs AG38A–AG38F and AG39)

42   A financial asset and a financial liability shall be offset and the net amount presented in the statement of financial position when, and only when, an entity:

(a)   currently has a legally enforceable right to set off the recognised amounts; and

(b)   intends either to settle on a net basis, or to realise the asset and settle the liability simultaneously.

In accounting for a transfer of a financial asset that does not qualify for derecognition, the entity shall not offset the transferred asset and the associated liability (see IFRS 9, paragraph 3.2.22).

43   This Standard requires the presentation of financial assets and financial liabilities on a net basis when doing so reflects an entity's expected future cash flows from settling two or more separate financial instruments. When an entity has the right to receive or pay a single net amount and intends to do so, it has, in effect, only a single financial asset or financial liability. In other circumstances, financial assets and financial liabilities are presented separately from each other consistently with their characteristics as resources or obligations of the entity. An entity shall disclose the information required in paragraphs 13B–13E of IFRS 7 for recognised financial instruments that are within the scope of paragraph 13A of IFRS 7.

44   Offsetting a recognised financial asset and a recognised financial liability and presenting the net amount differs from the derecognition of a financial asset or a financial liability. Although offsetting does not give rise to recognition of a gain or loss, the derecognition of a financial instrument not only results in the removal of the previously recognised item from the statement of financial position but also may result in recognition of a gain or loss.

45   A right of set-off is a debtor's legal right, by contract or otherwise, to settle or otherwise eliminate all or a portion of an amount due to a creditor by applying against that amount an amount due from the creditor. In unusual circumstances, a debtor may have a legal right to apply an amount due from a third party against the amount due to a creditor provided that there is an agreement between the three parties that clearly establishes the debtor's right of set-off. Because the right of set-off is a legal right, the conditions supporting the right may vary from one legal jurisdiction to another and the laws applicable to the relationships between the parties need to be considered.

46   The existence of an enforceable right to set off a financial asset and a financial liability affects the rights and obligations associated with a financial asset and a financial liability and may affect an entity's exposure to credit and liquidity risk. However, the existence of the right, by itself, is not a sufficient basis for offsetting. In the absence of an intention to exercise the right or to settle simultaneously, the amount and timing of an entity's future cash flows are not affected. When an entity intends to exercise the right or to settle simultaneously, presentation of the asset and liability on a net basis reflects

more appropriately the amounts and timing of the expected future cash flows, as well as the risks to which those cash flows are exposed. An intention by one or both parties to settle on a net basis without the legal right to do so is not sufficient to justify offsetting because the rights and obligations associated with the individual financial asset and financial liability remain unaltered.

47   An entity's intentions with respect to settlement of particular assets and liabilities may be influenced by its normal business practices, the requirements of the financial markets and other circumstances that may limit the ability to settle net or to settle simultaneously. When an entity has a right of set-off, but does not intend to settle net or to realise the asset and settle the liability simultaneously, the effect of the right on the entity's credit risk exposure is disclosed in accordance with paragraph 36 of IFRS 7.

48   Simultaneous settlement of two financial instruments may occur through, for example, the operation of a clearing house in an organised financial market or a face-to-face exchange. In these circumstances the cash flows are, in effect, equivalent to a single net amount and there is no exposure to credit or liquidity risk. In other circumstances, an entity may settle two instruments by receiving and paying separate amounts, becoming exposed to credit risk for the full amount of the asset or liquidity risk for the full amount of the liability. Such risk exposures may be significant even though relatively brief. Accordingly, realisation of a financial asset and settlement of a financial liability are treated as simultaneous only when the transactions occur at the same moment.

49   The conditions set out in paragraph 42 are generally not satisfied and offsetting is usually inappropriate when:

(a)   several different financial instruments are used to emulate the features of a single financial instrument (a 'synthetic instrument');

(b)   financial assets and financial liabilities arise from financial instruments having the same primary risk exposure (for example, assets and liabilities within a portfolio of forward contracts or other derivative instruments) but involve different counterparties;

(c)   financial or other assets are pledged as collateral for non-recourse financial liabilities;

(d)   financial assets are set aside in trust by a debtor for the purpose of discharging an obligation without those assets having been accepted by the creditor in settlement of the obligation (for example, a sinking fund arrangement); or

(e)   obligations incurred as a result of events giving rise to losses are expected to be recovered from a third party by virtue of a claim made under an insurance contract.

50   An entity that undertakes a number of financial instrument transactions with a single counterparty may enter into a 'master netting arrangement' with that counterparty. Such an agreement provides for a single net settlement of all financial instruments covered by the agreement in the event of default on, or

termination of, any one contract. These arrangements are commonly used by financial institutions to provide protection against loss in the event of bankruptcy or other circumstances that result in a counterparty being unable to meet its obligations. A master netting arrangement commonly creates a right of set-off that becomes enforceable and affects the realisation or settlement of individual financial assets and financial liabilities only following a specified event of default or in other circumstances not expected to arise in the normal course of business. A master netting arrangement does not provide a basis for offsetting unless both of the criteria in paragraph 42 are satisfied. When financial assets and financial liabilities subject to a master netting arrangement are not offset, the effect of the arrangement on an entity's exposure to credit risk is disclosed in accordance with paragraph 36 of IFRS 7.

51–95   [Deleted]

Effective date and transition

96   An entity shall apply this Standard for annual periods beginning on or after 1 January 2005. Earlier application is permitted. An entity shall not apply this Standard for annual periods beginning before 1 January 2005 unless it also applies IAS 39 (issued December 2003), including the amendments issued in March 2004. If an entity applies this Standard for a period beginning before 1 January 2005, it shall disclose that fact.

96A   *Puttable Financial Instruments and Obligations Arising on Liquidation* (Amendments to IAS 32 and IAS 1), issued in February 2008, required financial instruments that contain all the features and meet the conditions in paragraphs 16A and 16B or paragraphs 16C and 16D to be classified as an equity instrument, amended paragraphs 11, 16, 17–19, 22, 23, 25, AG13, AG14 and AG27, and inserted paragraphs 16A–16F, 22A, 96B, 96C, 97C, AG14A–AG14J and AG29A. An entity shall apply those amendments for annual periods beginning on or after 1 January 2009. Earlier application is permitted. If an entity applies the changes for an earlier period, it shall disclose that fact and apply the related amendments to IAS 1, IAS 39, IFRS 7 and IFRIC 2 at the same time.

96B   *Puttable Financial Instruments and Obligations Arising on Liquidation* introduced a limited scope exception; therefore, an entity shall not apply the exception by analogy.

96C   The classification of instruments under this exception shall be restricted to the accounting for such an instrument under IAS 1, IAS 32, IAS 39, IFRS 7 and IFRS 9. The instrument shall not be considered an equity instrument under other guidance, for example IFRS 2.

97   This Standard shall be applied retrospectively.

97A   IAS 1 (as revised in 2007) amended the terminology used throughout IFRSs. In addition it amended paragraph 40. An entity shall apply those amendments for annual periods beginning on or after 1 January 2009. If an entity applies IAS 1 (revised 2007) for an earlier period, the amendments shall be applied for that earlier period.

97B   IFRS 3 *Business Combinations* (as revised in 2008) deleted paragraph 4(c). An entity shall apply that amendment for annual periods beginning on or after 1 July 2009. If an entity applies IFRS 3 (revised 2008) for an earlier period, the amendment shall also be applied for that earlier period. However, the amendment does not apply to contingent consideration that arose from a business combination for which the acquisition date preceded the application of IFRS 3 (revised 2008). Instead, an entity shall account for such consideration in accordance with paragraphs 65A–65E of IFRS 3 (as amended in 2010).

97C   When applying the amendments described in paragraph 96A, an entity is required to split a compound financial instrument with an obligation to deliver to another party a pro rata share of the net assets of the entity only on liquidation into separate liability and equity components. If the liability component is no longer outstanding, a retrospective application of those amendments to IAS 32 would involve separating two components of equity. The first component would be in retained earnings and represent the cumulative interest accreted on the liability component. The other component would represent the original equity component. Therefore, an entity need not separate these two components if the liability component is no longer outstanding at the date of application of the amendments.

97D   Paragraph 4 was amended by *Improvements to IFRSs* issued in May 2008. An entity shall apply that amendment for annual periods beginning on or after 1 January 2009. Earlier application is permitted. If an entity applies the amendment for an earlier period it shall disclose that fact and apply for that earlier period the amendments to paragraph 3 of IFRS 7, paragraph 1 of IAS 28 and paragraph 1 of IAS 31 issued in May 2008. An entity is permitted to apply the amendment prospectively.

97E   Paragraphs 11 and 16 were amended by *Classification of Rights Issues* issued in October 2009. An entity shall apply that amendment for annual periods beginning on or after 1 February 2010. Earlier application is permitted. If an entity applies the amendment for an earlier period, it shall disclose that fact.

97F   [Deleted]

97G   Paragraph 97B was amended by *Improvements to IFRSs* issued in May 2010. An entity shall apply that amendment for annual periods beginning on or after 1 July 2010. Earlier application is permitted.

97H   [Deleted]

97I   IFRS 10 and IFRS 11 *Joint Arrangements*, issued in May 2011, amended paragraphs 4(a) and AG29. An entity shall apply those amendments when it applies IFRS 10 and IFRS 11.

97J   IFRS 13, issued in May 2011, amended the definition of fair value in paragraph 11 and amended paragraphs 23 and AG31. An entity shall apply those amendments when it applies IFRS 13.

97K   *Presentation of Items of Other Comprehensive Income* (Amendments to IAS 1), issued in June 2011, amended paragraph 40. An entity shall apply that amendment when it applies IAS 1 as amended in June 2011.

97L   *Offsetting Financial Assets and Financial Liabilities* (Amendments to IAS 32), issued in December 2011, deleted paragraph AG38 and added paragraphs AG38A–AG38F. An entity shall apply those amendments for annual periods beginning on or after 1 January 2014. An entity shall apply those amendments retrospectively. Earlier application is permitted. If an entity applies those amendments from an earlier date, it shall disclose that fact and shall also make the disclosures required by *Disclosures—Offsetting Financial Assets and Financial Liabilities* (Amendments to IFRS 7) issued in December 2011.

97M   *Disclosures—Offsetting Financial Assets and Financial Liabilities* (Amendments to IFRS 7), issued in December 2011, amended paragraph 43 by requiring an entity to disclose the information required in paragraphs 13B–13E of IFRS 7 for recognised financial assets that are within the scope of paragraph 13A of IFRS 7. An entity shall apply that amendment for annual periods beginning on or after 1 January 2013 and interim periods within those annual periods. An entity shall provide the disclosures required by this amendment retrospectively.

97N   *Annual Improvements 2009–2011 Cycle*, issued in May 2012, amended paragraphs 35, 37 and 39 and added paragraph 35A. An entity shall apply that amendment retrospectively in accordance with IAS 8 *Accounting Policies, Changes in Accounting Estimates and Errors* for annual periods beginning on or after 1 January 2013. Earlier application is permitted. If an entity applies that amendment for an earlier period it shall disclose that fact.

97O   *Investment Entities* (Amendments to IFRS 10, IFRS 12 and IAS 27), issued in October 2012, amended paragraph 4. An entity shall apply that amendment for annual periods beginning on or after 1 January 2014. Earlier application of *Investment Entities* is permitted. If an entity applies that amendment earlier it shall also apply all amendments included in *Investment Entities* at the same time.

97P   [Deleted]

97Q   IFRS 15 *Revenue from Contracts with Customers*, issued in May 2014, amended paragraph AG21. An entity shall apply that amendment when it applies IFRS 15.

97R   IFRS 9, as issued in July 2014, amended paragraphs 3, 4, 8, 12, 23, 31, 42, 96C, AG2 and AG30 and deleted paragraphs 97F, 97H and 97P. An entity shall apply those amendments when it applies IFRS 9.

97S   IFRS 16 *Leases*, issued in January 2016, amended paragraphs AG9 and AG10. An entity shall apply those amendments when it applies IFRS 16.

97T   *[This paragraph refers to amendments that are not yet effective, and is therefore not included in this edition.]*

Withdrawal of other pronouncements

98   This Standard supersedes IAS 32 *Financial Instruments: Disclosure and Presentation* revised in 2000.[2]

99   This Standard supersedes the following Interpretations:

(a)   SIC-5 *Classification of Financial Instruments — Contingent Settlement Provisions*;

(b)   SIC-16 *Share Capital — Reacquired Own Equity Instruments (Treasury Shares)*; and

(c)   SIC-17 *Equity — Costs of an Equity Transaction*.

100   This Standard withdraws draft SIC Interpretation D34 *Financial Instruments — Instruments or Rights Redeemable by the Holder*.

---

2   In August 2005 the IASB relocated all disclosures relating to financial instruments to IFRS 7 *Financial Instruments: Disclosures*.

Appendix
Application Guidance
IAS 32 *Financial Instruments: Presentation*

This appendix is an integral part of the Standard.

AG1   This Application Guidance explains the application of particular aspects of the Standard.

AG2   The Standard does not deal with the recognition or measurement of financial instruments. Requirements about the recognition and measurement of financial assets and financial liabilities are set out in IFRS 9.

Definitions (paragraphs 11–14)

Financial assets and financial liabilities

AG3   Currency (cash) is a financial asset because it represents the medium of exchange and is therefore the basis on which all transactions are measured and recognised in financial statements. A deposit of cash with a bank or similar financial institution is a financial asset because it represents the contractual right of the depositor to obtain cash from the institution or to draw a cheque or similar instrument against the balance in favour of a creditor in payment of a financial liability.

AG4   Common examples of financial assets representing a contractual right to receive cash in the future and corresponding financial liabilities representing a contractual obligation to deliver cash in the future are:

(a)   trade accounts receivable and payable;

(b)   notes receivable and payable;

(c)   loans receivable and payable; and

(d)   bonds receivable and payable.

In each case, one party's contractual right to receive (or obligation to pay) cash is matched by the other party's corresponding obligation to pay (or right to receive).

AG5   Another type of financial instrument is one for which the economic benefit to be received or given up is a financial asset other than cash. For example, a note payable in government bonds gives the holder the contractual right to receive and the issuer the contractual obligation to deliver government bonds, not cash. The bonds are financial assets because they represent obligations of the issuing government to pay cash. The note is, therefore, a financial asset of the note holder and a financial liability of the note issuer.

AG6   'Perpetual' debt instruments (such as 'perpetual' bonds, debentures and capital notes) normally provide the holder with the contractual right to receive payments on account of interest at fixed dates extending into the indefinite future, either with no right to receive a return of principal or a right to a return of principal under terms that make it very unlikely or very far in the future. For example, an entity may issue a financial instrument requiring it to make annual payments in perpetuity equal to a stated interest rate of 8 per cent applied to a stated par or principal amount of CU1,000.[3] Assuming 8 per cent to be the market rate of interest for the instrument when issued, the issuer assumes a contractual obligation to make a stream of future interest payments having a fair value (present value) of CU1,000 on initial recognition. The holder and issuer of the instrument have a financial asset and a financial liability, respectively.

AG7   A contractual right or contractual obligation to receive, deliver or exchange financial instruments is itself a financial instrument. A chain of contractual rights or contractual obligations meets the definition of a financial instrument if it will ultimately lead to the receipt or payment of cash or to the acquisition or issue of an equity instrument.

AG8   The ability to exercise a contractual right or the requirement to satisfy a contractual obligation may be absolute, or it may be contingent on the occurrence of a future event. For example, a financial guarantee is a contractual right of the lender to receive cash from the guarantor, and a corresponding contractual obligation of the guarantor to pay the lender, if the borrower defaults. The contractual right and obligation exist because of a past transaction or event (assumption of the guarantee), even though the lender's ability to exercise its right and the requirement for the guarantor to perform under its obligation are both contingent on a future act of default by the borrower. A contingent right and obligation meet the definition of a financial asset and a financial liability, even though such assets and liabilities are not always recognised in the financial statements. Some of these contingent rights and obligations may be insurance contracts within the scope of IFRS 4.

AG9   A lease typically creates an entitlement of the lessor to receive, and an obligation of the lessee to pay, a stream of payments that are substantially the same as blended payments of principal and interest under a loan agreement. The lessor accounts for its investment in the amount receivable under a finance lease rather than the underlying asset itself that is subject to the finance lease. Accordingly, a lessor regards a finance lease as a financial instrument. Under IFRS 16, a lessor does not recognise its entitlement to receive lease payments under an operating lease. The lessor continues to account for the underlying asset itself rather than any amount receivable in the future under the contract. Accordingly, a lessor does not regard an operating lease as a financial instrument, except as regards individual payments currently due and payable by the lessee.

AG10   Physical assets (such as inventories, property, plant and equipment), right-of-use assets and intangible assets (such as patents and trademarks) are not financial assets. Control of such physical assets, right-of-use assets and intangible assets creates an opportunity to generate an inflow of cash or another financial asset, but it does not give rise to a present right to receive cash or another financial asset.

---

3   In this guidance, monetary amounts are denominated in 'currency units (CU)'.

AG11 Assets (such as prepaid expenses) for which the future economic benefit is the receipt of goods or services, rather than the right to receive cash or another financial asset, are not financial assets. Similarly, items such as deferred revenue and most warranty obligations are not financial liabilities because the outflow of economic benefits associated with them is the delivery of goods and services rather than a contractual obligation to pay cash or another financial asset.

AG12 Liabilities or assets that are not contractual (such as income taxes that are created as a result of statutory requirements imposed by governments) are not financial liabilities or financial assets. Accounting for income taxes is dealt with in IAS 12. Similarly, constructive obligations, as defined in IAS 37 *Provisions, Contingent Liabilities and Contingent Assets*, do not arise from contracts and are not financial liabilities.

Equity instruments

AG13 Examples of equity instruments include non-puttable ordinary shares, some puttable instruments (see paragraphs 16A and 16B), some instruments that impose on the entity an obligation to deliver to another party a pro rata share of the net assets of the entity only on liquidation (see paragraphs 16C and 16D), some types of preference shares (see paragraphs AG25 and AG26), and warrants or written call options that allow the holder to subscribe for or purchase a fixed number of non-puttable ordinary shares in the issuing entity in exchange for a fixed amount of cash or another financial asset. An entity's obligation to issue or purchase a fixed number of its own equity instruments in exchange for a fixed amount of cash or another financial asset is an equity instrument of the entity (except as stated in paragraph 22A). However, if such a contract contains an obligation for the entity to pay cash or another financial asset (other than a contract classified as equity in accordance with paragraphs 16A and 16B or paragraphs 16C and 16D), it also gives rise to a liability for the present value of the redemption amount (see paragraph AG27(a)). An issuer of non-puttable ordinary shares assumes a liability when it formally acts to make a distribution and becomes legally obliged to the shareholders to do so. This may be the case following the declaration of a dividend or when the entity is being wound up and any assets remaining after the satisfaction of liabilities become distributable to shareholders.

AG14 A purchased call option or other similar contract acquired by an entity that gives it the right to reacquire a fixed number of its own equity instruments in exchange for delivering a fixed amount of cash or another financial asset is not a financial asset of the entity (except as stated in paragraph 22A). Instead, any consideration paid for such a contract is deducted from equity.

The class of instruments that is subordinate to all other classes (paragraphs 16A(b) and 16C(b))

AG14A One of the features of paragraphs 16A and 16C is that the financial instrument is in the class of instruments that is subordinate to all other classes.

AG14B   When determining whether an instrument is in the subordinate class, an entity evaluates the instrument's claim on liquidation as if it were to liquidate on the date when it classifies the instrument. An entity shall reassess the classification if there is a change in relevant circumstances. For example, if the entity issues or redeems another financial instrument, this may affect whether the instrument in question is in the class of instruments that is subordinate to all other classes.

AG14C   An instrument that has a preferential right on liquidation of the entity is not an instrument with an entitlement to a pro rata share of the net assets of the entity. For example, an instrument has a preferential right on liquidation if it entitles the holder to a fixed dividend on liquidation, in addition to a share of the entity's net assets, when other instruments in the subordinate class with a right to a pro rata share of the net assets of the entity do not have the same right on liquidation.

AG14D   If an entity has only one class of financial instruments, that class shall be treated as if it were subordinate to all other classes.

Total expected cash flows attributable to the instrument over the life of the instrument (paragraph 16A(e))

AG14E   The total expected cash flows of the instrument over the life of the instrument must be substantially based on the profit or loss, change in the recognised net assets or fair value of the recognised and unrecognised net assets of the entity over the life of the instrument. Profit or loss and the change in the recognised net assets shall be measured in accordance with relevant IFRSs.

Transactions entered into by an instrument holder other than as owner of the entity (paragraphs 16A and 16C)

AG14F   The holder of a puttable financial instrument or an instrument that imposes on the entity an obligation to deliver to another party a pro rata share of the net assets of the entity only on liquidation may enter into transactions with the entity in a role other than that of an owner. For example, an instrument holder may also be an employee of the entity. Only the cash flows and the contractual terms and conditions of the instrument that relate to the instrument holder as an owner of the entity shall be considered when assessing whether the instrument should be classified as equity under paragraph 16A or paragraph 16C.

AG14G   An example is a limited partnership that has limited and general partners. Some general partners may provide a guarantee to the entity and may be remunerated for providing that guarantee. In such situations, the guarantee and the associated cash flows relate to the instrument holders in their role as guarantors and not in their roles as owners of the entity. Therefore, such a guarantee and the associated cash flows would not result in the general partners being considered subordinate to the limited partners, and would be disregarded when assessing whether the contractual terms of the limited partnership instruments and the general partnership instruments are identical.

AG14H   Another example is a profit or loss sharing arrangement that allocates profit or loss to the instrument holders on the basis of services rendered or business generated during the current and previous years. Such arrangements are transactions with instrument holders in their role as non-owners and should not be considered when assessing the features listed in paragraph 16A or paragraph 16C. However, profit or loss sharing arrangements that allocate profit or loss to instrument holders based on the nominal amount of their instruments relative to others in the class represent transactions with the instrument holders in their roles as owners and should be considered when assessing the features listed in paragraph 16A or paragraph 16C.

AG14I   The cash flows and contractual terms and conditions of a transaction between the instrument holder (in the role as a non-owner) and the issuing entity must be similar to an equivalent transaction that might occur between a non-instrument holder and the issuing entity.

No other financial instrument or contract with total cash flows that substantially fixes or restricts the residual return to the instrument holder (paragraphs 16B and 16D)

AG14J   A condition for classifying as equity a financial instrument that otherwise meets the criteria in paragraph 16A or paragraph 16C is that the entity has no other financial instrument or contract that has (a) total cash flows based substantially on the profit or loss, the change in the recognised net assets or the change in the fair value of the recognised and unrecognised net assets of the entity and (b) the effect of substantially restricting or fixing the residual return. The following instruments, when entered into on normal commercial terms with unrelated parties, are unlikely to prevent instruments that otherwise meet the criteria in paragraph 16A or paragraph 16C from being classified as equity:

(a)   instruments with total cash flows substantially based on specific assets of the entity.

(b)   instruments with total cash flows based on a percentage of revenue.

(c)   contracts designed to reward individual employees for services rendered to the entity.

(d)   contracts requiring the payment of an insignificant percentage of profit for services rendered or goods provided.

Derivative financial instruments

AG15   Financial instruments include primary instruments (such as receivables, payables and equity instruments) and derivative financial instruments (such as financial options, futures and forwards, interest rate swaps and currency swaps). Derivative financial instruments meet the definition of a financial instrument and, accordingly, are within the scope of this Standard.

AG16   Derivative financial instruments create rights and obligations that have the effect of transferring between the parties to the instrument one or more of the financial risks inherent in an underlying primary financial instrument. On inception, derivative financial instruments give one party a contractual right to exchange financial assets or financial liabilities with another party under conditions that are potentially favourable, or a contractual obligation to exchange financial assets or financial liabilities with another party under conditions that are potentially unfavourable. However, they generally[4] do not result in a transfer of the underlying primary financial instrument on inception of the contract, nor does such a transfer necessarily take place on maturity of the contract. Some instruments embody both a right and an obligation to make an exchange. Because the terms of the exchange are determined on inception of the derivative instrument, as prices in financial markets change those terms may become either favourable or unfavourable.

AG17   A put or call option to exchange financial assets or financial liabilities (ie financial instruments other than an entity's own equity instruments) gives the holder a right to obtain potential future economic benefits associated with changes in the fair value of the financial instrument underlying the contract. Conversely, the writer of an option assumes an obligation to forgo potential future economic benefits or bear potential losses of economic benefits associated with changes in the fair value of the underlying financial instrument. The contractual right of the holder and obligation of the writer meet the definition of a financial asset and a financial liability, respectively. The financial instrument underlying an option contract may be any financial asset, including shares in other entities and interest-bearing instruments. An option may require the writer to issue a debt instrument, rather than transfer a financial asset, but the instrument underlying the option would constitute a financial asset of the holder if the option were exercised. The option-holder's right to exchange the financial asset under potentially favourable conditions and the writer's obligation to exchange the financial asset under potentially unfavourable conditions are distinct from the underlying financial asset to be exchanged upon exercise of the option. The nature of the holder's right and of the writer's obligation are not affected by the likelihood that the option will be exercised.

AG18   Another example of a derivative financial instrument is a forward contract to be settled in six months' time in which one party (the purchaser) promises to deliver CU1,000,000 cash in exchange for CU1,000,000 face amount of fixed rate government bonds, and the other party (the seller) promises to deliver CU1,000,000 face amount of fixed rate government bonds in exchange for CU1,000,000 cash. During the six months, both parties have a contractual right and a contractual obligation to exchange financial instruments. If the market price of the government bonds rises above CU1,000,000, the conditions will be favourable to the purchaser and unfavourable to the seller; if the market price falls below CU1,000,000, the effect will be the opposite. The purchaser has a contractual right (a financial asset) similar to the right under

---

4   This is true of most, but not all derivatives, eg in some cross-currency interest rate swaps principal is exchanged on inception (and re-exchanged on maturity).

a call option held and a contractual obligation (a financial liability) similar to the obligation under a put option written; the seller has a contractual right (a financial asset) similar to the right under a put option held and a contractual obligation (a financial liability) similar to the obligation under a call option written. As with options, these contractual rights and obligations constitute financial assets and financial liabilities separate and distinct from the underlying financial instruments (the bonds and cash to be exchanged). Both parties to a forward contract have an obligation to perform at the agreed time, whereas performance under an option contract occurs only if and when the holder of the option chooses to exercise it.

AG19 Many other types of derivative instruments embody a right or obligation to make a future exchange, including interest rate and currency swaps, interest rate caps, collars and floors, loan commitments, note issuance facilities and letters of credit. An interest rate swap contract may be viewed as a variation of a forward contract in which the parties agree to make a series of future exchanges of cash amounts, one amount calculated with reference to a floating interest rate and the other with reference to a fixed interest rate. Futures contracts are another variation of forward contracts, differing primarily in that the contracts are standardised and traded on an exchange.

Contracts to buy or sell non-financial items (paragraphs 8–10)

AG20 Contracts to buy or sell non-financial items do not meet the definition of a financial instrument because the contractual right of one party to receive a non-financial asset or service and the corresponding obligation of the other party do not establish a present right or obligation of either party to receive, deliver or exchange a financial asset. For example, contracts that provide for settlement only by the receipt or delivery of a non-financial item (eg an option, futures or forward contract on silver) are not financial instruments. Many commodity contracts are of this type. Some are standardised in form and traded on organised markets in much the same fashion as some derivative financial instruments. For example, a commodity futures contract may be bought and sold readily for cash because it is listed for trading on an exchange and may change hands many times. However, the parties buying and selling the contract are, in effect, trading the underlying commodity. The ability to buy or sell a commodity contract for cash, the ease with which it may be bought or sold and the possibility of negotiating a cash settlement of the obligation to receive or deliver the commodity do not alter the fundamental character of the contract in a way that creates a financial instrument. Nevertheless, some contracts to buy or sell non-financial items that can be settled net or by exchanging financial instruments, or in which the non-financial item is readily convertible to cash, are within the scope of the Standard as if they were financial instruments (see paragraph 8).

AG21 Except as required by IFRS 15 *Revenue from Contracts with Customers*, a contract that involves the receipt or delivery of physical assets does not give rise to a financial asset of one party and a financial liability of the other party unless any corresponding payment is deferred past the date on which the physical assets are transferred. Such is the case with the purchase or sale of goods on trade credit.

AG22 Some contracts are commodity-linked, but do not involve settlement through the physical receipt or delivery of a commodity. They specify settlement through cash payments that are determined according to a formula in the contract, rather than through payment of fixed amounts. For example, the principal amount of a bond may be calculated by applying the market price of oil prevailing at the maturity of the bond to a fixed quantity of oil. The principal is indexed by reference to a commodity price, but is settled only in cash. Such a contract constitutes a financial instrument.

AG23 The definition of a financial instrument also encompasses a contract that gives rise to a non-financial asset or non-financial liability in addition to a financial asset or financial liability. Such financial instruments often give one party an option to exchange a financial asset for a non-financial asset. For example, an oil-linked bond may give the holder the right to receive a stream of fixed periodic interest payments and a fixed amount of cash on maturity, with the option to exchange the principal amount for a fixed quantity of oil. The desirability of exercising this option will vary from time to time depending on the fair value of oil relative to the exchange ratio of cash for oil (the exchange price) inherent in the bond. The intentions of the bondholder concerning the exercise of the option do not affect the substance of the component assets. The financial asset of the holder and the financial liability of the issuer make the bond a financial instrument, regardless of the other types of assets and liabilities also created.

AG24 [Deleted]

Presentation

Liabilities and equity (paragraphs 15–27)

No contractual obligation to deliver cash or another financial asset (paragraphs 17–20)

AG25 Preference shares may be issued with various rights. In determining whether a preference share is a financial liability or an equity instrument, an issuer assesses the particular rights attaching to the share to determine whether it exhibits the fundamental characteristic of a financial liability. For example, a preference share that provides for redemption on a specific date or at the option of the holder contains a financial liability because the issuer has an obligation to transfer financial assets to the holder of the share. The potential inability of an issuer to satisfy an obligation to redeem a preference share when contractually required to do so, whether because of a lack of funds, a statutory restriction or insufficient profits or reserves, does not negate the obligation. An option of the issuer to redeem the shares for cash does not satisfy the definition of a financial liability because the issuer does not have a present obligation to transfer financial assets to the shareholders. In this case, redemption of the shares is solely at the discretion of the issuer. An obligation may arise, however, when the issuer of the shares exercises its option, usually by formally notifying the shareholders of an intention to redeem the shares.

AG26   When preference shares are non-redeemable, the appropriate classification is determined by the other rights that attach to them. Classification is based on an assessment of the substance of the contractual arrangements and the definitions of a financial liability and an equity instrument. When distributions to holders of the preference shares, whether cumulative or non-cumulative, are at the discretion of the issuer, the shares are equity instruments. The classification of a preference share as an equity instrument or a financial liability is not affected by, for example:

(a)   a history of making distributions;

(b)   an intention to make distributions in the future;

(c)   a possible negative impact on the price of ordinary shares of the issuer if distributions are not made (because of restrictions on paying dividends on the ordinary shares if dividends are not paid on the preference shares);

(d)   the amount of the issuer's reserves;

(e)   an issuer's expectation of a profit or loss for a period; or

(f)   an ability or inability of the issuer to influence the amount of its profit or loss for the period.

Settlement in the entity's own equity instruments (paragraphs 21–24)

AG27   The following examples illustrate how to classify different types of contracts on an entity's own equity instruments:

(a)   A contract that will be settled by the entity receiving or delivering a fixed number of its own shares for no future consideration, or exchanging a fixed number of its own shares for a fixed amount of cash or another financial asset, is an equity instrument (except as stated in paragraph 22A). Accordingly, any consideration received or paid for such a contract is added directly to or deducted directly from equity. One example is an issued share option that gives the counterparty a right to buy a fixed number of the entity's shares for a fixed amount of cash. However, if the contract requires the entity to purchase (redeem) its own shares for cash or another financial asset at a fixed or determinable date or on demand, the entity also recognises a financial liability for the present value of the redemption amount (with the exception of instruments that have all the features and meet the conditions in paragraphs 16A and 16B or paragraphs 16C and 16D). One example is an entity's obligation under a forward contract to repurchase a fixed number of its own shares for a fixed amount of cash.

(b)   An entity's obligation to purchase its own shares for cash gives rise to a financial liability for the present value of the redemption amount even if the number of shares that the entity is obliged to repurchase is not fixed or if the obligation is conditional on the counterparty exercising a right to redeem (except as stated in paragraphs 16A and 16B or paragraphs 16C and 16D). One example of a conditional obligation is an issued option that requires the entity to repurchase its own shares for cash if the counterparty exercises the option.

(c)   A contract that will be settled in cash or another financial asset is a financial asset or financial liability even if the amount of cash or another financial asset that will be received or delivered is based on changes in the market price of the entity's own equity (except as stated in paragraphs 16A and 16B or paragraphs 16C and 16D). One example is a net cash-settled share option.

(d)   A contract that will be settled in a variable number of the entity's own shares whose value equals a fixed amount or an amount based on changes in an underlying variable (eg a commodity price) is a financial asset or a financial liability. An example is a written option to buy gold that, if exercised, is settled net in the entity's own instruments by the entity delivering as many of those instruments as are equal to the value of the option contract. Such a contract is a financial asset or financial liability even if the underlying variable is the entity's own share price rather than gold. Similarly, a contract that will be settled in a fixed number of the entity's own shares, but the rights attaching to those shares will be varied so that the settlement value equals a fixed amount or an amount based on changes in an underlying variable, is a financial asset or a financial liability.

Contingent settlement provisions (paragraph 25)

AG28   Paragraph 25 requires that if a part of a contingent settlement provision that could require settlement in cash or another financial asset (or in another way that would result in the instrument being a financial liability) is not genuine, the settlement provision does not affect the classification of a financial instrument. Thus, a contract that requires settlement in cash or a variable number of the entity's own shares only on the occurrence of an event that is extremely rare, highly abnormal and very unlikely to occur is an equity instrument. Similarly, settlement in a fixed number of an entity's own shares may be contractually precluded in circumstances that are outside the control of the entity, but if these circumstances have no genuine possibility of occurring, classification as an equity instrument is appropriate.

Treatment in consolidated financial statements

AG29   In consolidated financial statements, an entity presents non-controlling interests—ie the interests of other parties in the equity and income of its subsidiaries—in accordance with IAS 1 and IFRS 10. When classifying a financial instrument (or a component of it) in consolidated financial statements, an entity considers all terms and conditions agreed between members of the group and the holders of the instrument in determining whether the group as a whole has an obligation to deliver cash or another financial asset in respect of the instrument or to settle it in a manner that results in liability classification. When a subsidiary in a group issues a financial instrument and a parent or other group entity agrees additional terms directly with the holders of the instrument (eg a guarantee), the group may not have discretion over distributions or redemption. Although the subsidiary may appropriately classify the instrument without regard to these additional terms in its individual financial statements, the effect of other agreements between members of the group and the holders of the instrument is considered in order to ensure that consolidated financial statements reflect the contracts and transactions entered into by the group as a whole. To the extent that there is such an obligation or settlement provision, the instrument (or the component of it that is subject to the obligation) is classified as a financial liability in consolidated financial statements.

AG29A   Some types of instruments that impose a contractual obligation on the entity are classified as equity instruments in accordance with paragraphs 16A and 16B or paragraphs 16C and 16D. Classification in accordance with those paragraphs is an exception to the principles otherwise applied in this Standard to the classification of an instrument. This exception is not extended to the classification of non-controlling interests in the consolidated financial statements. Therefore, instruments classified as equity instruments in accordance with either paragraphs 16A and 16B or paragraphs 16C and 16D in the separate or individual financial statements that are non-controlling interests are classified as liabilities in the consolidated financial statements of the group.

Compound financial instruments (paragraphs 28–32)

AG30   Paragraph 28 applies only to issuers of non-derivative compound financial instruments. Paragraph 28 does not deal with compound financial instruments from the perspective of holders. IFRS 9 deals with the classification and measurement of financial assets that are compound financial instruments from the holder's perspective.

AG31   A common form of compound financial instrument is a debt instrument with an embedded conversion option, such as a bond convertible into ordinary shares of the issuer, and without any other embedded derivative features. Paragraph 28 requires the issuer of such a financial instrument to present the liability component and the equity component separately in the statement of financial position, as follows:

(a)   The issuer's obligation to make scheduled payments of interest and principal is a financial liability that exists as long as the instrument is not converted. On initial recognition, the fair value of the liability component is the present value of the contractually determined stream of future cash flows discounted at the rate of interest applied at that time by the market to instruments of comparable credit status and providing substantially the same cash flows, on the same terms, but without the conversion option.

(b)   The equity instrument is an embedded option to convert the liability into equity of the issuer. This option has value on initial recognition even when it is out of the money.

AG32   On conversion of a convertible instrument at maturity, the entity derecognises the liability component and recognises it as equity. The original equity component remains as equity (although it may be transferred from one line item within equity to another). There is no gain or loss on conversion at maturity.

AG33   When an entity extinguishes a convertible instrument before maturity through an early redemption or repurchase in which the original conversion privileges are unchanged, the entity allocates the consideration paid and any transaction costs for the repurchase or redemption to the liability and equity components of the instrument at the date of the transaction. The method used in allocating the consideration paid and transaction costs to the separate components is consistent with that used in the original allocation to the separate components of the proceeds received by the entity when the convertible instrument was issued, in accordance with paragraphs 28–32.

AG34   Once the allocation of the consideration is made, any resulting gain or loss is treated in accordance with accounting principles applicable to the related component, as follows:

(a)   the amount of gain or loss relating to the liability component is recognised in profit or loss; and

(b)   the amount of consideration relating to the equity component is recognised in equity.

AG35   An entity may amend the terms of a convertible instrument to induce early conversion, for example by offering a more favourable conversion ratio or paying other additional consideration in the event of conversion before a specified date. The difference, at the date the terms are amended, between the fair value of the consideration the holder receives on conversion of the instrument under the revised terms and the fair value of the consideration the holder would have received under the original terms is recognised as a loss in profit or loss.

Treasury shares (paragraphs 33 and 34)

AG36   An entity's own equity instruments are not recognised as a financial asset regardless of the reason for which they are reacquired. Paragraph 33 requires an entity that reacquires its own equity instruments to deduct those equity instruments from equity. However, when an entity holds its own equity on behalf of others, eg a financial institution holding its own equity on behalf of a client, there is an agency relationship and as a result those holdings are not included in the entity's statement of financial position.

Interest, dividends, losses and gains (paragraphs 35–41)

AG37   The following example illustrates the application of paragraph 35 to a compound financial instrument. Assume that a non-cumulative preference share is mandatorily redeemable for cash in five years, but that dividends are payable at the discretion of the entity before the redemption date. Such an instrument is a compound financial instrument, with the liability component being the present value of the redemption amount. The unwinding of the discount on this component is recognised in profit or loss and classified as interest expense. Any dividends paid relate to the equity component and, accordingly, are recognised as a distribution of profit or loss. A similar treatment would apply if the redemption was not mandatory but at the option of the holder, or if the share was mandatorily convertible into a variable number of ordinary shares calculated to equal a fixed amount or an amount based on changes in an underlying variable (eg commodity). However, if any unpaid dividends are added to the redemption amount, the entire instrument is a liability. In such a case, any dividends are classified as interest expense.

Offsetting a financial asset and a financial liability (paragraphs 42–50)

AG38   [Deleted]

Criterion that an entity 'currently has a legally enforceable right to set off the recognised amounts' (paragraph 42(a))

AG38A   A right of set-off may be currently available or it may be contingent on a future event (for example, the right may be triggered or exercisable only on the occurrence of some future event, such as the default, insolvency or bankruptcy of one of the counterparties). Even if the right of set-off is not contingent on a future event, it may only be legally enforceable in the normal course of business, or in the event of default, or in the event of insolvency or bankruptcy, of one or all of the counterparties.

AG38B   To meet the criterion in paragraph 42(a), an entity must currently have a legally enforceable right of set-off. This means that the right of set-off:

    (a)   must not be contingent on a future event; and

    (b)   must be legally enforceable in all of the following circumstances:

        (i)   the normal course of business;

        (ii)   the event of default; and

        (iii)   the event of insolvency or bankruptcy

     of the entity and all of the counterparties.

AG38C   The nature and extent of the right of set-off, including any conditions attached to its exercise and whether it would remain in the event of default or insolvency or bankruptcy, may vary from one legal jurisdiction to another. Consequently, it cannot be assumed that the right of set-off is automatically available outside of the normal course of business. For example, the bankruptcy or insolvency laws of a jurisdiction may prohibit, or restrict, the right of set-off in the event of bankruptcy or insolvency in some circumstances.

AG38D   The laws applicable to the relationships between the parties (for example, contractual provisions, the laws governing the contract, or the default, insolvency or bankruptcy laws applicable to the parties) need to be considered to ascertain whether the right of set-off is enforceable in the normal course of business, in an event of default, and in the event of insolvency or bankruptcy, of the entity and all of the counterparties (as specified in paragraph AG38B(b)).

Criterion that an entity 'intends either to settle on a net basis, or to realise the asset and settle the liability simultaneously' (paragraph 42(b))

AG38E   To meet the criterion in paragraph 42(b) an entity must intend either to settle on a net basis or to realise the asset and settle the liability simultaneously. Although the entity may have a right to settle net, it may still realise the asset and settle the liability separately.

AG38F   If an entity can settle amounts in a manner such that the outcome is, in effect, equivalent to net settlement, the entity will meet the net settlement criterion in paragraph 42(b). This will occur if, and only if, the gross settlement mechanism has features that eliminate or result in insignificant credit and liquidity risk, and that will process receivables and payables in a single settlement process or cycle. For example, a gross settlement system that has all of the following characteristics would meet the net settlement criterion in paragraph 42(b):

(a)   financial assets and financial liabilities eligible for set-off are submitted at the same point in time for processing;

(b)   once the financial assets and financial liabilities are submitted for processing, the parties are committed to fulfil the settlement obligation;

(c)   there is no potential for the cash flows arising from the assets and liabilities to change once they have been submitted for processing (unless the processing fails — see (d) below);

(d)   assets and liabilities that are collateralised with securities will be settled on a securities transfer or similar system (for example, delivery versus payment), so that if the transfer of securities fails, the processing of the related receivable or payable for which the securities are collateral will also fail (and vice versa);

(e)   any transactions that fail, as outlined in (d), will be re-entered for processing until they are settled;

(f)   settlement is carried out through the same settlement institution (for example, a settlement bank, a central bank or a central securities depository); and

(g)   an intraday credit facility is in place that will provide sufficient overdraft amounts to enable the processing of payments at the settlement date for each of the parties, and it is virtually certain that the intraday credit facility will be honoured if called upon.

AG39   The Standard does not provide special treatment for so-called 'synthetic instruments', which are groups of separate financial instruments acquired and held to emulate the characteristics of another instrument. For example, a floating rate long-term debt combined with an interest rate swap that involves receiving floating payments and making fixed payments synthesises a fixed rate long-term debt. Each of the individual financial instruments that together constitute a 'synthetic instrument' represents a contractual right or obligation with its own terms and conditions and each may be transferred or settled separately. Each financial instrument is exposed to risks that may differ from the risks to which other financial instruments are exposed. Accordingly, when one financial instrument in a 'synthetic instrument' is an asset and another is a liability, they are not offset and presented in an entity's statement of financial position on a net basis unless they meet the criteria for offsetting in paragraph 42.

AG40   [Deleted]

Approval by the Board of IAS 32 issued in December 2003

International Accounting Standard 32 *Financial Instruments: Disclosure and Presentation* (as revised in 2003) was approved for issue by thirteen of the fourteen members of the International Accounting Standards Board. Mr Leisenring dissented. His dissenting opinion is set out after the Basis for Conclusions.

Sir David Tweedie	Chairman
Thomas E Jones	Vice-Chairman
Mary E Barth	
Hans-Georg Bruns	
Anthony T Cope	
Robert P Garnett	
Gilbert Gélard	
James J Leisenring	
Warren J McGregor	
Patricia L O'Malley	
Harry K Schmid	
John T Smith	
Geoffrey Whittington	
Tatsumi Yamada	

Approval by the Board of *Puttable Financial Instruments and Obligations Arising on Liquidation* (Amendments to IAS 32 and IAS 1) issued in February 2008

Puttable Financial Instruments and Obligations Arising on Liquidation (Amendments to IAS 32 and IAS 1 *Presentation of Financial Statements*) was approved for issue by eleven of the thirteen members of the International Accounting Standards Board. Professor Barth and Mr Garnett dissented. Their dissenting opinions are set out after the Basis for Conclusions.

Sir David Tweedie	Chairman
Thomas E Jones	Vice-Chairman
Mary E Barth	
Stephen Cooper	
Philippe Danjou	
Jan Engström	
Robert P Garnett	
Gilbert Gélard	
James J Leisenring	
Warren J McGregor	
John T Smith	
Tatsumi Yamada	
Wei-Guo Zhang	

Approval by the Board of *Classification of Rights Issues* (Amendment to IAS 32) issued in October 2009

Classification of Rights Issues (Amendment to IAS 32) was approved for issue by thirteen of the fifteen members of the International Accounting Standards Board. Messrs Leisenring and Smith dissented from the issue of the amendment. Their dissenting opinions are set out after the Basis for Conclusions.

Sir David Tweedie   Chairman

Stephen Cooper

Philippe Danjou

Jan Engström

Patrick Finnegan

Robert P Garnett

Gilbert Gélard

Amaro Luiz de Oliveira Gomes

Prabhakar Kalavacherla

James J Leisenring

Patricia McConnell

Warren J McGregor

John T Smith

Tatsumi Yamada

Wei-Guo Zhang

Approval by the Board of *Offsetting Financial Assets and Financial Liabilities* (Amendments to IAS 32) issued in December 2011

Offsetting Financial Assets and Financial Liabilities (Amendments to IAS 32) was approved for issue by the fifteen members of the International Accounting Standards Board.

Hans Hoogervorst	Chairman
Ian Mackintosh	Vice-Chairman
Stephen Cooper	
Philippe Danjou	
Jan Engström	
Patrick Finnegan	
Amaro Luiz de Oliveira Gomes	
Prabhakar Kalavacherla	
Elke König	
Patricia McConnell	
Takatsugu Ochi	
Paul Pacter	
Darrel Scott	
John T Smith	
Wei-Guo Zhang	

IAS 33

Earnings per Share

In April 2001 the International Accounting Standards Board (Board) adopted IAS 33 *Earnings per Share*, which had been issued by the International Accounting Standards Committee in February 1997.

In December 2003 the Board revised IAS 33 and changed the title to *Earnings per Share*. This IAS 33 also incorporated the guidance contained in a related Interpretation (SIC-24 *Earnings Per Share—Financial Instruments and Other Contracts that May be Settled in Shares*).

Other Standards have made minor consequential amendments to IAS 33. They include IFRS 10 *Consolidated Financial Statements* (issued May 2011), IFRS 11 *Joint Arrangements* (issued May 2011), IFRS 13 *Fair Value Measurement* (issued May 2011), *Presentation of Items of Other Comprehensive Income* (Amendments to IAS 1) (issued June 2011) and IFRS 9 *Financial Instruments* (issued July 2014).

CONTENTS

FOR THE ACCOMPANYING GUIDANCE LISTED BELOW, SEE PART B OF THIS EDITION

ILLUSTRATIVE EXAMPLES

FOR THE BASIS FOR CONCLUSIONS, SEE PART C OF THIS EDITION

BASIS FOR CONCLUSIONS

International Accounting Standard 33 *Earnings per Share* (IAS 33) is set out in paragraphs 1–76 and Appendices A and B. All the paragraphs have equal authority but retain the IASC format of the Standard when it was adopted by the IASB. IAS 33 should be read in the context of its objective and the Basis for Conclusions, the *Preface to IFRS Standards* and the *Conceptual Framework for Financial Reporting*. IAS 8 *Accounting Policies, Changes in Accounting Estimates and Errors* provides a basis for selecting and applying accounting policies in the absence of explicit guidance.

International Accounting Standard 33
Earnings per Share

Objective

1   The objective of this Standard is to prescribe principles for the determination and presentation of earnings per share, so as to improve performance comparisons between different entities in the same reporting period and between different reporting periods for the same entity. Even though earnings per share data have limitations because of the different accounting policies that may be used for determining 'earnings', a consistently determined denominator enhances financial reporting. The focus of this Standard is on the denominator of the earnings per share calculation.

Scope

2   This Standard shall apply to

   (a)   the separate or individual financial statements of an entity:

      (i)   whose ordinary shares or potential ordinary shares are traded in a public market (a domestic or foreign stock exchange or an over-the-counter market, including local and regional markets) or

      (ii)   that files, or is in the process of filing, its financial statements with a securities commission or other regulatory organisation for the purpose of issuing ordinary shares in a public market; and

   (b)   the consolidated financial statements of a group with a parent:

      (i)   whose ordinary shares or potential ordinary shares are traded in a public market (a domestic or foreign stock exchange or an over-the-counter market, including local and regional markets) or

      (ii)   that files, or is in the process of filing, its financial statements with a securities commission or other regulatory organisation for the purpose of issuing ordinary shares in a public market.

3   An entity that discloses earnings per share shall calculate and disclose earnings per share in accordance with this Standard.

4   When an entity presents both consolidated financial statements and separate financial statements prepared in accordance with IFRS 10 *Consolidated Financial Statements* and IAS 27 *Separate Financial Statements* respectively, the disclosures required by this Standard need be presented only on the basis of the consolidated information. An entity that chooses to disclose earnings per share based on its separate financial statements shall present such earnings per share information only in its statement of

comprehensive income. An entity shall not present such earnings per share information in the consolidated financial statements.

4A   If an entity presents items of profit or loss in a separate statement as described in paragraph 10A of IAS 1 *Presentation of Financial Statements* (as amended in 2011), it presents earnings per share only in that separate statement.

Definitions

5   The following terms are used in this Standard with the meanings specified:

Antidilution is an increase in earnings per share or a reduction in loss per share resulting from the assumption that convertible instruments are converted, that options or warrants are exercised, or that ordinary shares are issued upon the satisfaction of specified conditions.

A *contingent share agreement* is an agreement to issue shares that is dependent on the satisfaction of specified conditions.

Contingently issuable ordinary shares are ordinary shares issuable for little or no cash or other consideration upon the satisfaction of specified conditions in a contingent share agreement.

Dilution is a reduction in earnings per share or an increase in loss per share resulting from the assumption that convertible instruments are converted, that options or warrants are exercised, or that ordinary shares are issued upon the satisfaction of specified conditions.

Options, warrants and their equivalents are financial instruments that give the holder the right to purchase ordinary shares.

An *ordinary share* is an equity instrument that is subordinate to all other classes of equity instruments.

A *potential ordinary share* is a financial instrument or other contract that may entitle its holder to ordinary shares.

Put options on ordinary shares are contracts that give the holder the right to sell ordinary shares at a specified price for a given period.

6   Ordinary shares participate in profit for the period only after other types of shares such as preference shares have participated. An entity may have more than one class of ordinary shares. Ordinary shares of the same class have the same rights to receive dividends.

7   Examples of potential ordinary shares are:

(a)   financial liabilities or equity instruments, including preference shares, that are convertible into ordinary shares;

(b)   options and warrants;

(c)   shares that would be issued upon the satisfaction of conditions resulting from contractual arrangements, such as the purchase of a business or other assets.

8   Terms defined in IAS 32 *Financial Instruments: Presentation* are used in this Standard with the meanings specified in paragraph 11 of IAS 32, unless otherwise noted. IAS 32 defines financial instrument, financial asset, financial liability and equity instrument, and provides guidance on applying those definitions. IFRS 13 *Fair Value Measurement* defines fair value and sets out requirements for applying that definition.

Measurement

Basic earnings per share

9   An entity shall calculate basic earnings per share amounts for profit or loss attributable to ordinary equity holders of the parent entity and, if presented, profit or loss from continuing operations attributable to those equity holders.

10   Basic earnings per share shall be calculated by dividing profit or loss attributable to ordinary equity holders of the parent entity (the numerator) by the weighted average number of ordinary shares outstanding (the denominator) during the period.

11   The objective of basic earnings per share information is to provide a measure of the interests of each ordinary share of a parent entity in the performance of the entity over the reporting period.

Earnings

12   For the purpose of calculating basic earnings per share, the amounts attributable to ordinary equity holders of the parent entity in respect of:

(a)   profit or loss from continuing operations attributable to the parent entity; and

(b)   profit or loss attributable to the parent entity

shall be the amounts in (a) and (b) adjusted for the after-tax amounts of preference dividends, differences arising on the settlement of preference shares, and other similar effects of preference shares classified as equity.

13   All items of income and expense attributable to ordinary equity holders of the parent entity that are recognised in a period, including tax expense and dividends on preference shares classified as liabilities are included in the determination of profit or loss for the period attributable to ordinary equity holders of the parent entity (see IAS 1).

14   The after-tax amount of preference dividends that is deducted from profit or loss is:

(a)   the after-tax amount of any preference dividends on non-cumulative preference shares declared in respect of the period; and

(b)   the after-tax amount of the preference dividends for cumulative preference shares required for the period, whether or not the dividends have been declared. The amount of preference dividends for the period does not include the amount of any preference dividends for cumulative preference shares paid or declared during the current period in respect of previous periods.

15   Preference shares that provide for a low initial dividend to compensate an entity for selling the preference shares at a discount, or an above-market dividend in later periods to compensate investors for purchasing preference shares at a premium, are sometimes referred to as increasing rate preference shares. Any original issue discount or premium on increasing rate preference shares is amortised to retained earnings using the effective interest method and treated as a preference dividend for the purposes of calculating earnings per share.

16   Preference shares may be repurchased under an entity's tender offer to the holders. The excess of the fair value of the consideration paid to the preference shareholders over the carrying amount of the preference shares represents a return to the holders of the preference shares and a charge to retained earnings for the entity. This amount is deducted in calculating profit or loss attributable to ordinary equity holders of the parent entity.

17   Early conversion of convertible preference shares may be induced by an entity through favourable changes to the original conversion terms or the payment of additional consideration. The excess of the fair value of the ordinary shares or other consideration paid over the fair value of the ordinary shares issuable under the original conversion terms is a return to the preference shareholders, and is deducted in calculating profit or loss attributable to ordinary equity holders of the parent entity.

18   Any excess of the carrying amount of preference shares over the fair value of the consideration paid to settle them is added in calculating profit or loss attributable to ordinary equity holders of the parent entity.

Shares

19   **For the purpose of calculating basic earnings per share, the number of ordinary shares shall be the weighted average number of ordinary shares outstanding during the period.**

20   Using the weighted average number of ordinary shares outstanding during the period reflects the possibility that the amount of shareholders' capital varied during the period as a result of a larger or smaller number of shares being outstanding at any time. The weighted average number of ordinary shares outstanding during the period is the number of ordinary shares outstanding at the beginning of the period, adjusted by the number of ordinary shares bought back or issued during the period multiplied by a time-weighting factor. The time-weighting factor is the number of days that the shares are outstanding as a proportion of the total number of days in the period; a reasonable approximation of the weighted average is adequate in many circumstances.

21 Shares are usually included in the weighted average number of shares from the date consideration is receivable (which is generally the date of their issue), for example:

(a) ordinary shares issued in exchange for cash are included when cash is receivable;

(b) ordinary shares issued on the voluntary reinvestment of dividends on ordinary or preference shares are included when dividends are reinvested;

(c) ordinary shares issued as a result of the conversion of a debt instrument to ordinary shares are included from the date that interest ceases to accrue;

(d) ordinary shares issued in place of interest or principal on other financial instruments are included from the date that interest ceases to accrue;

(e) ordinary shares issued in exchange for the settlement of a liability of the entity are included from the settlement date;

(f) ordinary shares issued as consideration for the acquisition of an asset other than cash are included as of the date on which the acquisition is recognised; and

(g) ordinary shares issued for the rendering of services to the entity are included as the services are rendered.

The timing of the inclusion of ordinary shares is determined by the terms and conditions attaching to their issue. Due consideration is given to the substance of any contract associated with the issue.

22 Ordinary shares issued as part of the consideration transferred in a business combination are included in the weighted average number of shares from the acquisition date. This is because the acquirer incorporates into its statement of comprehensive income the acquiree's profits and losses from that date.

23 Ordinary shares that will be issued upon the conversion of a mandatorily convertible instrument are included in the calculation of basic earnings per share from the date the contract is entered into.

24 Contingently issuable shares are treated as outstanding and are included in the calculation of basic earnings per share only from the date when all necessary conditions are satisfied (ie the events have occurred). Shares that are issuable solely after the passage of time are not contingently issuable shares, because the passage of time is a certainty. Outstanding ordinary shares that are contingently returnable (ie subject to recall) are not treated as outstanding and are excluded from the calculation of basic earnings per share until the date the shares are no longer subject to recall.

25 [Deleted]

26   The weighted average number of ordinary shares outstanding during the period and for all periods presented shall be adjusted for events, other than the conversion of potential ordinary shares, that have changed the number of ordinary shares outstanding without a corresponding change in resources.

27   Ordinary shares may be issued, or the number of ordinary shares outstanding may be reduced, without a corresponding change in resources. Examples include:

    (a)   a capitalisation or bonus issue (sometimes referred to as a stock dividend);

    (b)   a bonus element in any other issue, for example a bonus element in a rights issue to existing shareholders;

    (c)   a share split; and

    (d)   a reverse share split (consolidation of shares).

28   In a capitalisation or bonus issue or a share split, ordinary shares are issued to existing shareholders for no additional consideration. Therefore, the number of ordinary shares outstanding is increased without an increase in resources. The number of ordinary shares outstanding before the event is adjusted for the proportionate change in the number of ordinary shares outstanding as if the event had occurred at the beginning of the earliest period presented. For example, on a two-for-one bonus issue, the number of ordinary shares outstanding before the issue is multiplied by three to obtain the new total number of ordinary shares, or by two to obtain the number of additional ordinary shares.

29   A consolidation of ordinary shares generally reduces the number of ordinary shares outstanding without a corresponding reduction in resources. However, when the overall effect is a share repurchase at fair value, the reduction in the number of ordinary shares outstanding is the result of a corresponding reduction in resources. An example is a share consolidation combined with a special dividend. The weighted average number of ordinary shares outstanding for the period in which the combined transaction takes place is adjusted for the reduction in the number of ordinary shares from the date the special dividend is recognised.

Diluted earnings per share

30   An entity shall calculate diluted earnings per share amounts for profit or loss attributable to ordinary equity holders of the parent entity and, if presented, profit or loss from continuing operations attributable to those equity holders.

31   For the purpose of calculating diluted earnings per share, an entity shall adjust profit or loss attributable to ordinary equity holders of the parent entity, and the weighted average number of shares outstanding, for the effects of all dilutive potential ordinary shares.

32   The objective of diluted earnings per share is consistent with that of basic earnings per share—to provide a measure of the interest of each ordinary share in the performance of an entity—while giving effect to all dilutive potential ordinary shares outstanding during the period. As a result:

(a)   profit or loss attributable to ordinary equity holders of the parent entity is increased by the after-tax amount of dividends and interest recognised in the period in respect of the dilutive potential ordinary shares and is adjusted for any other changes in income or expense that would result from the conversion of the dilutive potential ordinary shares; and

(b)   the weighted average number of ordinary shares outstanding is increased by the weighted average number of additional ordinary shares that would have been outstanding assuming the conversion of all dilutive potential ordinary shares.

Earnings

33   For the purpose of calculating diluted earnings per share, an entity shall adjust profit or loss attributable to ordinary equity holders of the parent entity, as calculated in accordance with paragraph 12, by the after-tax effect of:

(a)   any dividends or other items related to dilutive potential ordinary shares deducted in arriving at profit or loss attributable to ordinary equity holders of the parent entity as calculated in accordance with paragraph 12;

(b)   any interest recognised in the period related to dilutive potential ordinary shares; and

(c)   any other changes in income or expense that would result from the conversion of the dilutive potential ordinary shares.

34   After the potential ordinary shares are converted into ordinary shares, the items identified in paragraph 33(a)–(c) no longer arise. Instead, the new ordinary shares are entitled to participate in profit or loss attributable to ordinary equity holders of the parent entity. Therefore, profit or loss attributable to ordinary equity holders of the parent entity calculated in accordance with paragraph 12 is adjusted for the items identified in paragraph 33(a)–(c) and any related taxes. The expenses associated with potential ordinary shares include transaction costs and discounts accounted for in accordance with the effective interest method (see IFRS 9).

35   The conversion of potential ordinary shares may lead to consequential changes in income or expenses. For example, the reduction of interest expense related to potential ordinary shares and the resulting increase in profit or reduction in loss may lead to an increase in the expense related to a non-discretionary employee profit-sharing plan. For the purpose of calculating diluted earnings per share, profit or loss attributable to ordinary equity holders of the parent entity is adjusted for any such consequential changes in income or expense.

Shares

36   For the purpose of calculating diluted earnings per share, the number of ordinary shares shall be the weighted average number of ordinary shares calculated in accordance with paragraphs 19 and 26, plus the weighted average number of ordinary shares that would be issued on the conversion of all the dilutive potential ordinary shares into ordinary shares. Dilutive potential ordinary shares shall be deemed to have been converted into ordinary shares at the beginning of the period or, if later, the date of the issue of the potential ordinary shares.

37   Dilutive potential ordinary shares shall be determined independently for each period presented. The number of dilutive potential ordinary shares included in the year-to-date period is not a weighted average of the dilutive potential ordinary shares included in each interim computation.

38   Potential ordinary shares are weighted for the period they are outstanding. Potential ordinary shares that are cancelled or allowed to lapse during the period are included in the calculation of diluted earnings per share only for the portion of the period during which they are outstanding. Potential ordinary shares that are converted into ordinary shares during the period are included in the calculation of diluted earnings per share from the beginning of the period to the date of conversion; from the date of conversion, the resulting ordinary shares are included in both basic and diluted earnings per share.

39   The number of ordinary shares that would be issued on conversion of dilutive potential ordinary shares is determined from the terms of the potential ordinary shares. When more than one basis of conversion exists, the calculation assumes the most advantageous conversion rate or exercise price from the standpoint of the holder of the potential ordinary shares.

40   A subsidiary, joint venture or associate may issue to parties other than the parent or investors with joint control of, or significant influence over, the investee potential ordinary shares that are convertible into either ordinary shares of the subsidiary, joint venture or associate, or ordinary shares of the parent or investors with joint control of, or significant influence (the reporting entity) over, the investee. If these potential ordinary shares of the subsidiary, joint venture or associate have a dilutive effect on the basic earnings per share of the reporting entity, they are included in the calculation of diluted earnings per share.

Dilutive potential ordinary shares

41   Potential ordinary shares shall be treated as dilutive when, and only when, their conversion to ordinary shares would decrease earnings per share or increase loss per share from continuing operations.

42   An entity uses profit or loss from continuing operations attributable to the parent entity as the control number to establish whether potential ordinary shares are dilutive or antidilutive. Profit or loss from continuing operations attributable to the parent entity is adjusted in accordance with paragraph 12 and excludes items relating to discontinued operations.

43   Potential ordinary shares are antidilutive when their conversion to ordinary shares would increase earnings per share or decrease loss per share from continuing operations. The calculation of diluted earnings per share does not assume conversion, exercise, or other issue of potential ordinary shares that would have an antidilutive effect on earnings per share.

44   In determining whether potential ordinary shares are dilutive or antidilutive, each issue or series of potential ordinary shares is considered separately rather than in aggregate. The sequence in which potential ordinary shares are considered may affect whether they are dilutive. Therefore, to maximise the dilution of basic earnings per share, each issue or series of potential ordinary shares is considered in sequence from the most dilutive to the least dilutive, ie dilutive potential ordinary shares with the lowest 'earnings per incremental share' are included in the diluted earnings per share calculation before those with a higher earnings per incremental share. Options and warrants are generally included first because they do not affect the numerator of the calculation.

Options, warrants and their equivalents

45   **For the purpose of calculating diluted earnings per share, an entity shall assume the exercise of dilutive options and warrants of the entity. The assumed proceeds from these instruments shall be regarded as having been received from the issue of ordinary shares at the average market price of ordinary shares during the period. The difference between the number of ordinary shares issued and the number of ordinary shares that would have been issued at the average market price of ordinary shares during the period shall be treated as an issue of ordinary shares for no consideration.**

46   Options and warrants are dilutive when they would result in the issue of ordinary shares for less than the average market price of ordinary shares during the period. The amount of the dilution is the average market price of ordinary shares during the period minus the issue price. Therefore, to calculate diluted earnings per share, potential ordinary shares are treated as consisting of both the following:

(a)   a contract to issue a certain number of the ordinary shares at their average market price during the period. Such ordinary shares are assumed to be fairly priced and to be neither dilutive nor antidilutive. They are ignored in the calculation of diluted earnings per share.

(b)   a contract to issue the remaining ordinary shares for no consideration. Such ordinary shares generate no proceeds and have no effect on profit or loss attributable to ordinary shares outstanding. Therefore, such shares are dilutive and are added to the number of ordinary shares outstanding in the calculation of diluted earnings per share.

47   Options and warrants have a dilutive effect only when the average market price of ordinary shares during the period exceeds the exercise price of the options or warrants (ie they are 'in the money'). Previously reported earnings per share are not retroactively adjusted to reflect changes in prices of ordinary shares.

47A   For share options and other share-based payment arrangements to which IFRS 2 *Share-based Payment* applies, the issue price referred to in paragraph 46 and the exercise price referred to in paragraph 47 shall include the fair value (measured in accordance with IFRS 2) of any goods or services to be supplied to the entity in the future under the share option or other share-based payment arrangement.

48   Employee share options with fixed or determinable terms and non-vested ordinary shares are treated as options in the calculation of diluted earnings per share, even though they may be contingent on vesting. They are treated as outstanding on the grant date. Performance-based employee share options are treated as contingently issuable shares because their issue is contingent upon satisfying specified conditions in addition to the passage of time.

Convertible instruments

49   The dilutive effect of convertible instruments shall be reflected in diluted earnings per share in accordance with paragraphs 33 and 36.

50   Convertible preference shares are antidilutive whenever the amount of the dividend on such shares declared in or accumulated for the current period per ordinary share obtainable on conversion exceeds basic earnings per share. Similarly, convertible debt is antidilutive whenever its interest (net of tax and other changes in income or expense) per ordinary share obtainable on conversion exceeds basic earnings per share.

51   The redemption or induced conversion of convertible preference shares may affect only a portion of the previously outstanding convertible preference shares. In such cases, any excess consideration referred to in paragraph 17 is attributed to those shares that are redeemed or converted for the purpose of determining whether the remaining outstanding preference shares are dilutive. The shares redeemed or converted are considered separately from those shares that are not redeemed or converted.

Contingently issuable shares

52   As in the calculation of basic earnings per share, contingently issuable ordinary shares are treated as outstanding and included in the calculation of diluted earnings per share if the conditions are satisfied (ie the events have occurred). Contingently issuable shares are included from the beginning of the period (or from the date of the contingent share agreement, if later). If the conditions are not satisfied, the number of contingently issuable shares included in the diluted earnings per share calculation is based on the number of shares that would be issuable if the end of the period were the end of the contingency period. Restatement is not permitted if the conditions are not met when the contingency period expires.

53   If attainment or maintenance of a specified amount of earnings for a period is the condition for contingent issue and if that amount has been attained at the end of the reporting period but must be maintained beyond the end of the reporting period for an additional period, then the additional ordinary shares are treated as outstanding, if the effect is dilutive, when calculating diluted earnings per share. In that case, the calculation of diluted earnings per share

is based on the number of ordinary shares that would be issued if the amount of earnings at the end of the reporting period were the amount of earnings at the end of the contingency period. Because earnings may change in a future period, the calculation of basic earnings per share does not include such contingently issuable ordinary shares until the end of the contingency period because not all necessary conditions have been satisfied.

54 The number of ordinary shares contingently issuable may depend on the future market price of the ordinary shares. In that case, if the effect is dilutive, the calculation of diluted earnings per share is based on the number of ordinary shares that would be issued if the market price at the end of the reporting period were the market price at the end of the contingency period. If the condition is based on an average of market prices over a period of time that extends beyond the end of the reporting period, the average for the period of time that has lapsed is used. Because the market price may change in a future period, the calculation of basic earnings per share does not include such contingently issuable ordinary shares until the end of the contingency period because not all necessary conditions have been satisfied.

55 The number of ordinary shares contingently issuable may depend on future earnings and future prices of the ordinary shares. In such cases, the number of ordinary shares included in the diluted earnings per share calculation is based on both conditions (ie earnings to date and the current market price at the end of the reporting period). Contingently issuable ordinary shares are not included in the diluted earnings per share calculation unless both conditions are met.

56 In other cases, the number of ordinary shares contingently issuable depends on a condition other than earnings or market price (for example, the opening of a specific number of retail stores). In such cases, assuming that the present status of the condition remains unchanged until the end of the contingency period, the contingently issuable ordinary shares are included in the calculation of diluted earnings per share according to the status at the end of the reporting period.

57 Contingently issuable potential ordinary shares (other than those covered by a contingent share agreement, such as contingently issuable convertible instruments) are included in the diluted earnings per share calculation as follows:

(a) an entity determines whether the potential ordinary shares may be assumed to be issuable on the basis of the conditions specified for their issue in accordance with the contingent ordinary share provisions in paragraphs 52–56; and

(b) if those potential ordinary shares should be reflected in diluted earnings per share, an entity determines their impact on the calculation of diluted earnings per share by following the provisions for options and warrants in paragraphs 45–48, the provisions for convertible instruments in paragraphs 49–51, the provisions for contracts that may be settled in ordinary shares or cash in paragraphs 58–61, or other provisions, as appropriate.

However, exercise or conversion is not assumed for the purpose of calculating diluted earnings per share unless exercise or conversion of similar outstanding potential ordinary shares that are not contingently issuable is assumed.

Contracts that may be settled in ordinary shares or cash

58   When an entity has issued a contract that may be settled in ordinary shares or cash at the entity's option, the entity shall presume that the contract will be settled in ordinary shares, and the resulting potential ordinary shares shall be included in diluted earnings per share if the effect is dilutive.

59   When such a contract is presented for accounting purposes as an asset or a liability, or has an equity component and a liability component, the entity shall adjust the numerator for any changes in profit or loss that would have resulted during the period if the contract had been classified wholly as an equity instrument. That adjustment is similar to the adjustments required in paragraph 33.

60   For contracts that may be settled in ordinary shares or cash at the holder's option, the more dilutive of cash settlement and share settlement shall be used in calculating diluted earnings per share.

61   An example of a contract that may be settled in ordinary shares or cash is a debt instrument that, on maturity, gives the entity the unrestricted right to settle the principal amount in cash or in its own ordinary shares. Another example is a written put option that gives the holder a choice of settling in ordinary shares or cash.

Purchased options

62   Contracts such as purchased put options and purchased call options (ie options held by the entity on its own ordinary shares) are not included in the calculation of diluted earnings per share because including them would be antidilutive. The put option would be exercised only if the exercise price were higher than the market price and the call option would be exercised only if the exercise price were lower than the market price.

Written put options

63   Contracts that require the entity to repurchase its own shares, such as written put options and forward purchase contracts, are reflected in the calculation of diluted earnings per share if the effect is dilutive. If these contracts are 'in the money' during the period (ie the exercise or settlement price is above the average market price for that period), the potential dilutive effect on earnings per share shall be calculated as follows:

(a)   it shall be assumed that at the beginning of the period sufficient ordinary shares will be issued (at the average market price during the period) to raise proceeds to satisfy the contract;

(b)   it shall be assumed that the proceeds from the issue are used to satisfy the contract (ie to buy back ordinary shares); and

(c)   the incremental ordinary shares (the difference between the number of ordinary shares assumed issued and the number of ordinary shares received from satisfying the contract) shall be included in the calculation of diluted earnings per share.

Retrospective adjustments

64   If the number of ordinary or potential ordinary shares outstanding increases as a result of a capitalisation, bonus issue or share split, or decreases as a result of a reverse share split, the calculation of basic and diluted earnings per share for all periods presented shall be adjusted retrospectively. If these changes occur after the reporting period but before the financial statements are authorised for issue, the per share calculations for those and any prior period financial statements presented shall be based on the new number of shares. The fact that per share calculations reflect such changes in the number of shares shall be disclosed. In addition, basic and diluted earnings per share of all periods presented shall be adjusted for the effects of errors and adjustments resulting from changes in accounting policies accounted for retrospectively.

65   An entity does not restate diluted earnings per share of any prior period presented for changes in the assumptions used in earnings per share calculations or for the conversion of potential ordinary shares into ordinary shares.

Presentation

66   An entity shall present in the statement of comprehensive income basic and diluted earnings per share for profit or loss from continuing operations attributable to the ordinary equity holders of the parent entity and for profit or loss attributable to the ordinary equity holders of the parent entity for the period for each class of ordinary shares that has a different right to share in profit for the period. An entity shall present basic and diluted earnings per share with equal prominence for all periods presented.

67   Earnings per share is presented for every period for which a statement of comprehensive income is presented. If diluted earnings per share is reported for at least one period, it shall be reported for all periods presented, even if it equals basic earnings per share. If basic and diluted earnings per share are equal, dual presentation can be accomplished in one line in the statement of comprehensive income.

67A   If an entity presents items of profit or loss in a separate statement as described in paragraph 10A of IAS 1 (as amended in 2011), it presents basic and diluted earnings per share, as required in paragraphs 66 and 67, in that separate statement.

68   An entity that reports a discontinued operation shall disclose the basic and diluted amounts per share for the discontinued operation either in the statement of comprehensive income or in the notes.

68A   If an entity presents items of profit or loss in a separate statement as described in paragraph 10A of IAS 1 (as amended in 2011), it presents basic and diluted earnings per share for the discontinued operation, as required in paragraph 68, in that separate statement or in the notes.

69   An entity shall present basic and diluted earnings per share, even if the amounts are negative (ie a loss per share).

Disclosure

70   An entity shall disclose the following:

(a)   the amounts used as the numerators in calculating basic and diluted earnings per share, and a reconciliation of those amounts to profit or loss attributable to the parent entity for the period. The reconciliation shall include the individual effect of each class of instruments that affects earnings per share.

(b)   the weighted average number of ordinary shares used as the denominator in calculating basic and diluted earnings per share, and a reconciliation of these denominators to each other. The reconciliation shall include the individual effect of each class of instruments that affects earnings per share.

(c)   instruments (including contingently issuable shares) that could potentially dilute basic earnings per share in the future, but were not included in the calculation of diluted earnings per share because they are antidilutive for the period(s) presented.

(d)   a description of ordinary share transactions or potential ordinary share transactions, other than those accounted for in accordance with paragraph 64, that occur after the reporting period and that would have changed significantly the number of ordinary shares or potential ordinary shares outstanding at the end of the period if those transactions had occurred before the end of the reporting period.

71   Examples of transactions in paragraph 70(d) include:

(a)   an issue of shares for cash;

(b)   an issue of shares when the proceeds are used to repay debt or preference shares outstanding at the end of the reporting period;

(c)   the redemption of ordinary shares outstanding;

(d)   the conversion or exercise of potential ordinary shares outstanding at the end of the reporting period into ordinary shares;

(e)   an issue of options, warrants, or convertible instruments; and

(f)   the achievement of conditions that would result in the issue of contingently issuable shares.

Earnings per share amounts are not adjusted for such transactions occurring after the reporting period because such transactions do not affect the amount of capital used to produce profit or loss for the period.

72   Financial instruments and other contracts generating potential ordinary shares may incorporate terms and conditions that affect the measurement of basic and diluted earnings per share. These terms and conditions may determine whether any potential ordinary shares are dilutive and, if so, the effect on the weighted average number of shares outstanding and any consequent adjustments to profit or loss attributable to ordinary equity holders. The disclosure of the terms and conditions of such financial instruments and other contracts is encouraged, if not otherwise required (see IFRS 7 *Financial Instruments: Disclosures*).

73   If an entity discloses, in addition to basic and diluted earnings per share, amounts per share using a reported component of the statement of comprehensive income other than one required by this Standard, such amounts shall be calculated using the weighted average number of ordinary shares determined in accordance with this Standard. Basic and diluted amounts per share relating to such a component shall be disclosed with equal prominence and presented in the notes. An entity shall indicate the basis on which the numerator(s) is (are) determined, including whether amounts per share are before tax or after tax. If a component of the statement of comprehensive income is used that is not reported as a line item in the statement of comprehensive income, a reconciliation shall be provided between the component used and a line item that is reported in the statement of comprehensive income.

73A   Paragraph 73 applies also to an entity that discloses, in addition to basic and diluted earnings per share, amounts per share using a reported item of profit or loss, other than one required by this Standard.

Effective date

74   An entity shall apply this Standard for annual periods beginning on or after 1 January 2005. Earlier application is encouraged. If an entity applies the Standard for a period beginning before 1 January 2005, it shall disclose that fact.

74A   IAS 1 (as revised in 2007) amended the terminology used throughout IFRSs. In addition it added paragraphs 4A, 67A, 68A and 73A. An entity shall apply those amendments for annual periods beginning on or after 1 January 2009. If an entity applies IAS 1 (revised 2007) for an earlier period, the amendments shall be applied for that earlier period.

74B   IFRS 10 and IFRS 11 *Joint Arrangements*, issued in May 2011, amended paragraphs 4, 40 and A11. An entity shall apply those amendments when it applies IFRS 10 and IFRS 11.

74C   IFRS 13, issued in May 2011, amended paragraphs 8, 47A and A2. An entity shall apply those amendments when it applies IFRS 13.

74D   *Presentation of Items of Other Comprehensive Income* (Amendments to IAS 1), issued in June 2011, amended paragraphs 4A, 67A, 68A and 73A. An entity shall apply those amendments when it applies IAS 1 as amended in June 2011.

74E   IFRS 9 *Financial Instruments*, as issued in July 2014, amended paragraph 34. An entity shall apply that amendment when it applies IFRS 9.

Withdrawal of other pronouncements

75   This Standard supersedes IAS 33 *Earnings Per Share* (issued in 1997).

76   This Standard supersedes SIC-24 *Earnings Per Share—Financial Instruments and Other Contracts that May Be Settled in Shares*.

Appendix A
Application guidance

This appendix is an integral part of the Standard.

Profit or loss attributable to the parent entity

A1   For the purpose of calculating earnings per share based on the consolidated financial statements, profit or loss attributable to the parent entity refers to profit or loss of the consolidated entity after adjusting for non-controlling interests.

Rights issues

A2   The issue of ordinary shares at the time of exercise or conversion of potential ordinary shares does not usually give rise to a bonus element. This is because the potential ordinary shares are usually issued for fair value, resulting in a proportionate change in the resources available to the entity. In a rights issue, however, the exercise price is often less than the fair value of the shares. Therefore, as noted in paragraph 27(b), such a rights issue includes a bonus element. If a rights issue is offered to all existing shareholders, the number of ordinary shares to be used in calculating basic and diluted earnings per share for all periods before the rights issue is the number of ordinary shares outstanding before the issue, multiplied by the following factor:

$$\frac{\text{Fair value per share immediately before the exercise of rights}}{\text{Theoretical ex-rights fair value per share}}$$

The theoretical ex-rights fair value per share is calculated by adding the aggregate fair value of the shares immediately before the exercise of the rights to the proceeds from the exercise of the rights, and dividing by the number of shares outstanding after the exercise of the rights. Where the rights are to be publicly traded separately from the shares before the exercise date, fair value is measured at the close of the last day on which the shares are traded together with the rights.

Control number

A3   To illustrate the application of the control number notion described in paragraphs 42 and 43, assume that an entity has profit from continuing operations attributable to the parent entity of CU4,800,[1] a loss from discontinued operations attributable to the parent entity of (CU7,200), a loss attributable to the parent entity of (CU2,400), and 2,000 ordinary shares and 400 potential ordinary shares outstanding. The entity's basic earnings per share is CU2.40 for continuing operations, (CU3.60) for discontinued operations and (CU1.20) for the loss. The 400 potential ordinary shares are included in the diluted earnings per share calculation because the resulting

---

1   In this guidance, monetary amounts are denominated in 'currency units (CU)'.

CU2.00 earnings per share for continuing operations is dilutive, assuming no profit or loss impact of those 400 potential ordinary shares. Because profit from continuing operations attributable to the parent entity is the control number, the entity also includes those 400 potential ordinary shares in the calculation of the other earnings per share amounts, even though the resulting earnings per share amounts are antidilutive to their comparable basic earnings per share amounts, ie the loss per share is less [(CU3.00) per share for the loss from discontinued operations and (CU1.00) per share for the loss].

Average market price of ordinary shares

A4　For the purpose of calculating diluted earnings per share, the average market price of ordinary shares assumed to be issued is calculated on the basis of the average market price of the ordinary shares during the period. Theoretically, every market transaction for an entity's ordinary shares could be included in the determination of the average market price. As a practical matter, however, a simple average of weekly or monthly prices is usually adequate.

A5　Generally, closing market prices are adequate for calculating the average market price. When prices fluctuate widely, however, an average of the high and low prices usually produces a more representative price. The method used to calculate the average market price is used consistently unless it is no longer representative because of changed conditions. For example, an entity that uses closing market prices to calculate the average market price for several years of relatively stable prices might change to an average of high and low prices if prices start fluctuating greatly and the closing market prices no longer produce a representative average price.

Options, warrants and their equivalents

A6　Options or warrants to purchase convertible instruments are assumed to be exercised to purchase the convertible instrument whenever the average prices of both the convertible instrument and the ordinary shares obtainable upon conversion are above the exercise price of the options or warrants. However, exercise is not assumed unless conversion of similar outstanding convertible instruments, if any, is also assumed.

A7　Options or warrants may permit or require the tendering of debt or other instruments of the entity (or its parent or a subsidiary) in payment of all or a portion of the exercise price. In the calculation of diluted earnings per share, those options or warrants have a dilutive effect if (a) the average market price of the related ordinary shares for the period exceeds the exercise price or (b) the selling price of the instrument to be tendered is below that at which the instrument may be tendered under the option or warrant agreement and the resulting discount establishes an effective exercise price below the market price of the ordinary shares obtainable upon exercise. In the calculation of diluted earnings per share, those options or warrants are assumed to be exercised and the debt or other instruments are assumed to be tendered. If tendering cash is more advantageous to the option or warrant holder and the contract permits tendering cash, tendering of cash is assumed. Interest (net of tax) on any debt assumed to be tendered is added back as an adjustment to the numerator.

A8   Similar treatment is given to preference shares that have similar provisions or to other instruments that have conversion options that permit the investor to pay cash for a more favourable conversion rate.

A9   The underlying terms of certain options or warrants may require the proceeds received from the exercise of those instruments to be applied to redeem debt or other instruments of the entity (or its parent or a subsidiary). In the calculation of diluted earnings per share, those options or warrants are assumed to be exercised and the proceeds applied to purchase the debt at its average market price rather than to purchase ordinary shares. However, the excess proceeds received from the assumed exercise over the amount used for the assumed purchase of debt are considered (ie assumed to be used to buy back ordinary shares) in the diluted earnings per share calculation. Interest (net of tax) on any debt assumed to be purchased is added back as an adjustment to the numerator.

Written put options

A10   To illustrate the application of paragraph 63, assume that an entity has outstanding 120 written put options on its ordinary shares with an exercise price of CU35. The average market price of its ordinary shares for the period is CU28. In calculating diluted earnings per share, the entity assumes that it issued 150 shares at CU28 per share at the beginning of the period to satisfy its put obligation of CU4,200. The difference between the 150 ordinary shares issued and the 120 ordinary shares received from satisfying the put option (30 incremental ordinary shares) is added to the denominator in calculating diluted earnings per share.

Instruments of subsidiaries, joint ventures or associates

A11   Potential ordinary shares of a subsidiary, joint venture or associate convertible into either ordinary shares of the subsidiary, joint venture or associate, or ordinary shares of the parent or investors with joint control of, or significant influence (the reporting entity) over, the investee are included in the calculation of diluted earnings per share as follows:

(a)   instruments issued by a subsidiary, joint venture or associate that enable their holders to obtain ordinary shares of the subsidiary, joint venture or associate are included in calculating the diluted earnings per share data of the subsidiary, joint venture or associate. Those earnings per share are then included in the reporting entity's earnings per share calculations based on the reporting entity's holding of the instruments of the subsidiary, joint venture or associate.

(b)   instruments of a subsidiary, joint venture or associate that are convertible into the reporting entity's ordinary shares are considered among the potential ordinary shares of the reporting entity for the purpose of calculating diluted earnings per share. Likewise, options or warrants issued by a subsidiary, joint venture or associate to purchase ordinary shares of the reporting entity are considered among the potential ordinary shares of the reporting entity in the calculation of consolidated diluted earnings per share.

A12 For the purpose of determining the earnings per share effect of instruments issued by a reporting entity that are convertible into ordinary shares of a subsidiary, joint venture or associate, the instruments are assumed to be converted and the numerator (profit or loss attributable to ordinary equity holders of the parent entity) adjusted as necessary in accordance with paragraph 33. In addition to those adjustments, the numerator is adjusted for any change in the profit or loss recorded by the reporting entity (such as dividend income or equity method income) that is attributable to the increase in the number of ordinary shares of the subsidiary, joint venture or associate outstanding as a result of the assumed conversion. The denominator of the diluted earnings per share calculation is not affected because the number of ordinary shares of the reporting entity outstanding would not change upon assumed conversion.

Participating equity instruments and two-class ordinary shares

A13 The equity of some entities includes:

(a) instruments that participate in dividends with ordinary shares according to a predetermined formula (for example, two for one) with, at times, an upper limit on the extent of participation (for example, up to, but not beyond, a specified amount per share).

(b) a class of ordinary shares with a different dividend rate from that of another class of ordinary shares but without prior or senior rights.

A14 For the purpose of calculating diluted earnings per share, conversion is assumed for those instruments described in paragraph A13 that are convertible into ordinary shares if the effect is dilutive. For those instruments that are not convertible into a class of ordinary shares, profit or loss for the period is allocated to the different classes of shares and participating equity instruments in accordance with their dividend rights or other rights to participate in undistributed earnings. To calculate basic and diluted earnings per share:

(a) profit or loss attributable to ordinary equity holders of the parent entity is adjusted (a profit reduced and a loss increased) by the amount of dividends declared in the period for each class of shares and by the contractual amount of dividends (or interest on participating bonds) that must be paid for the period (for example, unpaid cumulative dividends).

(b) the remaining profit or loss is allocated to ordinary shares and participating equity instruments to the extent that each instrument shares in earnings as if all of the profit or loss for the period had been distributed. The total profit or loss allocated to each class of equity instrument is determined by adding together the amount allocated for dividends and the amount allocated for a participation feature.

(c) the total amount of profit or loss allocated to each class of equity instrument is divided by the number of outstanding instruments to which the earnings are allocated to determine the earnings per share for the instrument.

For the calculation of diluted earnings per share, all potential ordinary shares assumed to have been issued are included in outstanding ordinary shares.

Partly paid shares

A15 Where ordinary shares are issued but not fully paid, they are treated in the calculation of basic earnings per share as a fraction of an ordinary share to the extent that they were entitled to participate in dividends during the period relative to a fully paid ordinary share.

A16 To the extent that partly paid shares are not entitled to participate in dividends during the period they are treated as the equivalent of warrants or options in the calculation of diluted earnings per share. The unpaid balance is assumed to represent proceeds used to purchase ordinary shares. The number of shares included in diluted earnings per share is the difference between the number of shares subscribed and the number of shares assumed to be purchased.

Appendix B
Amendments to other pronouncements

The amendments in this appendix shall be applied for annual periods beginning on or after 1 January 2005. If an entity applies this Standard for an earlier period, these amendments shall be applied for that earlier period.

* * * * *

The amendments contained in this appendix when this Standard was revised in 2003 have been incorporated into the relevant pronouncements published in this volume.

Approval by the Board of IAS 33 issued in December 2003

International Accounting Standard 33 *Earnings per Share* (as revised in 2003) was approved for issue by the fourteen members of the International Accounting Standards Board.

Sir David Tweedie	Chairman
Thomas E Jones	Vice-Chairman
Mary E Barth	
Hans-Georg Bruns	
Anthony T Cope	
Robert P Garnett	
Gilbert Gélard	
James J Leisenring	
Warren J McGregor	
Patricia L O'Malley	
Harry K Schmid	
John T Smith	
Geoffrey Whittington	
Tatsumi Yamada	

IAS 34

Interim Financial Reporting

In April 2001 the International Accounting Standards Board adopted IAS 34 *Interim Financial Reporting*, which had originally been issued by the International Accounting Standards Committee in 2000. IAS 34 that was issued in 2000 replaced the original version that was published in February 1998.

Other Standards have made minor consequential amendments to IAS 34. They include *Improvements to IFRSs* (issued May 2010), IFRS 13 *Fair Value Measurement* (issued May 2011), *Presentation of Items of Other Comprehensive Income* (Amendments to IAS 1) (issued June 2011), *Annual Improvements to IFRSs 2009–2011 Cycle* (issued May 2012), *Investment Entities* (Amendments to IFRS 10, IFRS 12 and IAS 27) (issued October 2012), IFRS 15 *Revenue from Contracts with Customers* (issued May 2014), *Annual Improvements to IFRSs 2012–2014 Cycle* (issued September 2014), *Disclosure Initiative* (Amendments to IAS 1) (issued December 2014), IFRS 16 *Leases* (issued January 2016), *Amendments to References to the Conceptual Framework in IFRS Standards* (issued March 2018) and Definition of Material (Amendments to IAS 1 and IAS 8) (issued October 2018).

CONTENTS

FOR THE ACCOMPANYING GUIDANCE LISTED BELOW, SEE PART B OF THIS EDITION

ILLUSTRATIVE EXAMPLES

FOR THE BASIS FOR CONCLUSIONS, SEE PART C OF THIS EDITION

BASIS FOR CONCLUSIONS

International Accounting Standard 34 *Interim Financial Reporting* (IAS 34) is set out in paragraphs 1–59. All the paragraphs have equal authority but retain the IASC format of the Standard when it was adopted by the IASB. IAS 34 should be read in the context of its objective and the Basis for Conclusions, the *Preface to IFRS Standards* and the *Conceptual Framework for Financial Reporting*. IAS 8 *Accounting Policies, Changes in Accounting Estimates and Errors* provides a basis for selecting and applying accounting policies in the absence of explicit guidance.

International Accounting Standard 34
Interim Financial Reporting

Objective

The objective of this Standard is to prescribe the minimum content of an interim financial report and to prescribe the principles for recognition and measurement in complete or condensed financial statements for an interim period. Timely and reliable interim financial reporting improves the ability of investors, creditors, and others to understand an entity's capacity to generate earnings and cash flows and its financial condition and liquidity.

Scope

1   This Standard does not mandate which entities should be required to publish interim financial reports, how frequently, or how soon after the end of an interim period. However, governments, securities regulators, stock exchanges, and accountancy bodies often require entities whose debt or equity securities are publicly traded to publish interim financial reports. This Standard applies if an entity is required or elects to publish an interim financial report in accordance with International Financial Reporting Standards (IFRSs). The International Accounting Standards Committee[1] encourages publicly traded entities to provide interim financial reports that conform to the recognition, measurement, and disclosure principles set out in this Standard. Specifically, publicly traded entities are encouraged:

   (a)   to provide interim financial reports at least as of the end of the first half of their financial year; and

   (b)   to make their interim financial reports available not later than 60 days after the end of the interim period.

2   Each financial report, annual or interim, is evaluated on its own for conformity to IFRSs. The fact that an entity may not have provided interim financial reports during a particular financial year or may have provided interim financial reports that do not comply with this Standard does not prevent the entity's annual financial statements from conforming to IFRSs if they otherwise do so.

3   If an entity's interim financial report is described as complying with IFRSs, it must comply with all of the requirements of this Standard. Paragraph 19 requires certain disclosures in that regard.

---

1   The International Accounting Standards Committee was succeeded by the International Accounting Standards Board, which began operations in 2001.

Definitions

4   The following terms are used in this Standard with the meanings specified:

Interim period is a financial reporting period shorter than a full financial year.

Interim financial report means a financial report containing either a complete set of financial statements (as described in IAS 1 *Presentation of Financial Statements* (as revised in 2007)) or a set of condensed financial statements (as described in this Standard) for an interim period.

Content of an interim financial report

5   IAS 1 defines a complete set of financial statements as including the following components:

(a)   a statement of financial position as at the end of the period;

(b)   a statement of profit or loss and other comprehensive income for the period;

(c)   a statement of changes in equity for the period;

(d)   a statement of cash flows for the period;

(e)   notes, comprising significant accounting policies and other explanatory information;

(ea)   comparative information in respect of the preceding period as specified in paragraphs 38 and 38A of IAS 1; and

(f)   a statement of financial position as at the beginning of the preceding period when an entity applies an accounting policy retrospectively or makes a retrospective restatement of items in its financial statements, or when it reclassifies items in its financial statements in accordance with paragraphs 40A–40D of IAS 1.

An entity may use titles for the statements other than those used in this Standard. For example, an entity may use the title 'statement of comprehensive income' instead of 'statement of profit or loss and other comprehensive income'.

6   In the interest of timeliness and cost considerations and to avoid repetition of information previously reported, an entity may be required to or may elect to provide less information at interim dates as compared with its annual financial statements. This Standard defines the minimum content of an interim financial report as including condensed financial statements and selected explanatory notes. The interim financial report is intended to provide an update on the latest complete set of annual financial statements. Accordingly, it focuses on new activities, events, and circumstances and does not duplicate information previously reported.

7   Nothing in this Standard is intended to prohibit or discourage an entity from publishing a complete set of financial statements (as described in IAS 1) in its interim financial report, rather than condensed financial statements and selected explanatory notes. Nor does this Standard prohibit or discourage an entity from including in condensed interim financial statements more than the minimum line items or selected explanatory notes as set out in this Standard. The recognition and measurement guidance in this Standard applies also to complete financial statements for an interim period, and such statements would include all of the disclosures required by this Standard (particularly the selected note disclosures in paragraph 16A) as well as those required by other IFRSs.

Minimum components of an interim financial report

8   An interim financial report shall include, at a minimum, the following components:

(a)   a condensed statement of financial position;

(b)   a condensed statement or condensed statements of profit or loss and other comprehensive income;

(c)   a condensed statement of changes in equity;

(d)   a condensed statement of cash flows; and

(e)   selected explanatory notes.

8A   If an entity presents items of profit or loss in a separate statement as described in paragraph 10A of IAS 1 (as amended in 2011), it presents interim condensed information from that statement.

Form and content of interim financial statements

9   If an entity publishes a complete set of financial statements in its interim financial report, the form and content of those statements shall conform to the requirements of IAS 1 for a complete set of financial statements.

10   If an entity publishes a set of condensed financial statements in its interim financial report, those condensed statements shall include, at a minimum, each of the headings and subtotals that were included in its most recent annual financial statements and the selected explanatory notes as required by this Standard. Additional line items or notes shall be included if their omission would make the condensed interim financial statements misleading.

11   In the statement that presents the components of profit or loss for an interim period, an entity shall present basic and diluted earnings per share for that period when the entity is within the scope of IAS 33 *Earnings per Share*.[2]

---

2   This paragraph was amended by *Improvements to IFRSs* issued in May 2008 to clarify the scope of IAS 34.

11A   If an entity presents items of profit or loss in a separate statement as described in paragraph 10A of IAS 1 (as amended in 2011), it presents basic and diluted earnings per share in that statement.

12   IAS 1 (as revised in 2007) provides guidance on the structure of financial statements. The Implementation Guidance for IAS 1 illustrates ways in which the statement of financial position, statement of comprehensive income and statement of changes in equity may be presented.

13   [Deleted]

14   An interim financial report is prepared on a consolidated basis if the entity's most recent annual financial statements were consolidated statements. The parent's separate financial statements are not consistent or comparable with the consolidated statements in the most recent annual financial report. If an entity's annual financial report included the parent's separate financial statements in addition to consolidated financial statements, this Standard neither requires nor prohibits the inclusion of the parent's separate statements in the entity's interim financial report.

Significant events and transactions

15   An entity shall include in its interim financial report an explanation of events and transactions that are significant to an understanding of the changes in financial position and performance of the entity since the end of the last annual reporting period. Information disclosed in relation to those events and transactions shall update the relevant information presented in the most recent annual financial report.

15A   A user of an entity's interim financial report will have access to the most recent annual financial report of that entity. Therefore, it is unnecessary for the notes to an interim financial report to provide relatively insignificant updates to the information that was reported in the notes in the most recent annual financial report.

15B   The following is a list of events and transactions for which disclosures would be required if they are significant: the list is not exhaustive.

(a)   the write-down of inventories to net realisable value and the reversal of such a write-down;

(b)   recognition of a loss from the impairment of financial assets, property, plant and equipment, intangible assets, assets arising from contracts with customers, or other assets, and the reversal of such an impairment loss;

(c)   the reversal of any provisions for the costs of restructuring;

(d)   acquisitions and disposals of items of property, plant and equipment;

(e)   commitments for the purchase of property, plant and equipment;

(f)   litigation settlements;

(g)   corrections of prior period errors;

(h) changes in the business or economic circumstances that affect the fair value of the entity's financial assets and financial liabilities, whether those assets or liabilities are recognised at fair value or amortised cost;

(i) any loan default or breach of a loan agreement that has not been remedied on or before the end of the reporting period;

(j) related party transactions;

(k) transfers between levels of the fair value hierarchy used in measuring the fair value of financial instruments;

(l) changes in the classification of financial assets as a result of a change in the purpose or use of those assets; and

(m) changes in contingent liabilities or contingent assets.

15C Individual IFRSs provide guidance regarding disclosure requirements for many of the items listed in paragraph 15B. When an event or transaction is significant to an understanding of the changes in an entity's financial position or performance since the last annual reporting period, its interim financial report should provide an explanation of and an update to the relevant information included in the financial statements of the last annual reporting period.

16 [Deleted]

Other disclosures

16A In addition to disclosing significant events and transactions in accordance with paragraphs 15–15C, an entity shall include the following information, in the notes to its interim financial statements or elsewhere in the interim financial report. The following disclosures shall be given either in the interim financial statements or incorporated by cross-reference from the interim financial statements to some other statement (such as management commentary or risk report) that is available to users of the financial statements on the same terms as the interim financial statements and at the same time. If users of the financial statements do not have access to the information incorporated by cross-reference on the same terms and at the same time, the interim financial report is incomplete. The information shall normally be reported on a financial year-to-date basis.

(a) a statement that the same accounting policies and methods of computation are followed in the interim financial statements as compared with the most recent annual financial statements or, if those policies or methods have been changed, a description of the nature and effect of the change.

(b) explanatory comments about the seasonality or cyclicality of interim operations.

(c) the nature and amount of items affecting assets, liabilities, equity, net income or cash flows that are unusual because of their nature, size or incidence.

(d) the nature and amount of changes in estimates of amounts reported in prior interim periods of the current financial year or changes in estimates of amounts reported in prior financial years.

(e) issues, repurchases and repayments of debt and equity securities.

(f) dividends paid (aggregate or per share) separately for ordinary shares and other shares.

(g) the following segment information (disclosure of segment information is required in an entity's interim financial report only if IFRS 8 *Operating Segments* requires that entity to disclose segment information in its annual financial statements):

   (i) revenues from external customers, if included in the measure of segment profit or loss reviewed by the chief operating decision maker or otherwise regularly provided to the chief operating decision maker.

   (ii) intersegment revenues, if included in the measure of segment profit or loss reviewed by the chief operating decision maker or otherwise regularly provided to the chief operating decision maker.

   (iii) a measure of segment profit or loss.

   (iv) a measure of total assets and liabilities for a particular reportable segment if such amounts are regularly provided to the chief operating decision maker and if there has been a material change from the amount disclosed in the last annual financial statements for that reportable segment.

   (v) a description of differences from the last annual financial statements in the basis of segmentation or in the basis of measurement of segment profit or loss.

   (vi) a reconciliation of the total of the reportable segments' measures of profit or loss to the entity's profit or loss before tax expense (tax income) and discontinued operations. However, if an entity allocates to reportable segments items such as tax expense (tax income), the entity may reconcile the total of the segments' measures of profit or loss to profit or loss after those items. Material reconciling items shall be separately identified and described in that reconciliation.

(h) events after the interim period that have not been reflected in the financial statements for the interim period.

(i) the effect of changes in the composition of the entity during the interim period, including business combinations, obtaining or losing control of subsidiaries and long-term investments, restructurings, and discontinued operations. In the case of business combinations, the entity shall disclose the information required by IFRS 3 *Business Combinations*.

(j)   for financial instruments, the disclosures about fair value required by paragraphs 91–93(h), 94–96, 98 and 99 of IFRS 13 *Fair Value Measurement* and paragraphs 25, 26 and 28–30 of IFRS 7 *Financial Instruments: Disclosures*.

(k)   for entities becoming, or ceasing to be, investment entities, as defined in IFRS 10 *Consolidated Financial Statements*, the disclosures in IFRS 12 *Disclosure of Interests in Other Entities* paragraph 9B.

(l)   the disaggregation of revenue from contracts with customers required by paragraphs 114–115 of IFRS 15 *Revenue from Contracts with Customers*.

17–18   [Deleted]

Disclosure of compliance with IFRSs

19   If an entity's interim financial report is in compliance with this Standard, that fact shall be disclosed. An interim financial report shall not be described as complying with IFRSs unless it complies with all the requirements of IFRSs.

Periods for which interim financial statements are required to be presented

20   Interim reports shall include interim financial statements (condensed or complete) for periods as follows:

(a)   statement of financial position as of the end of the current interim period and a comparative statement of financial position as of the end of the immediately preceding financial year.

(b)   statements of profit or loss and other comprehensive income for the current interim period and cumulatively for the current financial year to date, with comparative statements of profit or loss and other comprehensive income for the comparable interim periods (current and year-to-date) of the immediately preceding financial year. As permitted by IAS 1 (as amended in 2011), an interim report may present for each period a statement or statements of profit or loss and other comprehensive income.

(c)   statement of changes in equity cumulatively for the current financial year to date, with a comparative statement for the comparable year-to-date period of the immediately preceding financial year.

(d)   statement of cash flows cumulatively for the current financial year to date, with a comparative statement for the comparable year-to-date period of the immediately preceding financial year.

21   For an entity whose business is highly seasonal, financial information for the twelve months up to the end of the interim period and comparative information for the prior twelve-month period may be useful. Accordingly, entities whose business is highly seasonal are encouraged to consider

reporting such information in addition to the information called for in the preceding paragraph.

22   Part A of the illustrative examples accompanying this Standard illustrates the periods required to be presented by an entity that reports half-yearly and an entity that reports quarterly.

Materiality

23   **In deciding how to recognise, measure, classify, or disclose an item for interim financial reporting purposes, materiality shall be assessed in relation to the interim period financial data. In making assessments of materiality, it shall be recognised that interim measurements may rely on estimates to a greater extent than measurements of annual financial data.**

24   IAS 1 defines material information and requires separate disclosure of material items, including (for example) discontinued operations, and IAS 8 *Accounting Policies, Changes in Accounting Estimates and Errors* requires disclosure of changes in accounting estimates, errors, and changes in accounting policies. The two Standards do not contain quantified guidance as to materiality.

25   While judgement is always required in assessing materiality, this Standard bases the recognition and disclosure decision on data for the interim period by itself for reasons of understandability of the interim figures. Thus, for example, unusual items, changes in accounting policies or estimates, and errors are recognised and disclosed on the basis of materiality in relation to interim period data to avoid misleading inferences that might result from non-disclosure. The overriding goal is to ensure that an interim financial report includes all information that is relevant to understanding an entity's financial position and performance during the interim period.

Disclosure in annual financial statements

26   **If an estimate of an amount reported in an interim period is changed significantly during the final interim period of the financial year but a separate financial report is not published for that final interim period, the nature and amount of that change in estimate shall be disclosed in a note to the annual financial statements for that financial year.**

27   IAS 8 requires disclosure of the nature and (if practicable) the amount of a change in estimate that either has a material effect in the current period or is expected to have a material effect in subsequent periods. Paragraph 16A(d) of this Standard requires similar disclosure in an interim financial report. Examples include changes in estimate in the final interim period relating to inventory write-downs, restructurings, or impairment losses that were reported in an earlier interim period of the financial year. The disclosure required by the preceding paragraph is consistent with the IAS 8 requirement and is intended to be narrow in scope—relating only to the change in estimate. An entity is not required to include additional interim period financial information in its annual financial statements.

Recognition and measurement

Same accounting policies as annual

28   An entity shall apply the same accounting policies in its interim financial statements as are applied in its annual financial statements, except for accounting policy changes made after the date of the most recent annual financial statements that are to be reflected in the next annual financial statements. However, the frequency of an entity's reporting (annual, half-yearly, or quarterly) shall not affect the measurement of its annual results. To achieve that objective, measurements for interim reporting purposes shall be made on a year-to-date basis.

29   Requiring that an entity apply the same accounting policies in its interim financial statements as in its annual statements may seem to suggest that interim period measurements are made as if each interim period stands alone as an independent reporting period. However, by providing that the frequency of an entity's reporting shall not affect the measurement of its annual results, paragraph 28 acknowledges that an interim period is a part of a larger financial year. Year-to-date measurements may involve changes in estimates of amounts reported in prior interim periods of the current financial year. But the principles for recognising assets, liabilities, income, and expenses for interim periods are the same as in annual financial statements.

30   To illustrate:

    (a)   the principles for recognising and measuring losses from inventory write-downs, restructurings, or impairments in an interim period are the same as those that an entity would follow if it prepared only annual financial statements. However, if such items are recognised and measured in one interim period and the estimate changes in a subsequent interim period of that financial year, the original estimate is changed in the subsequent interim period either by accrual of an additional amount of loss or by reversal of the previously recognised amount;

    (b)   a cost that does not meet the definition of an asset at the end of an interim period is not deferred in the statement of financial position either to await future information as to whether it has met the definition of an asset or to smooth earnings over interim periods within a financial year; and

    (c)   income tax expense is recognised in each interim period based on the best estimate of the weighted average annual income tax rate expected for the full financial year. Amounts accrued for income tax expense in one interim period may have to be adjusted in a subsequent interim period of that financial year if the estimate of the annual income tax rate changes.

31   Under the *Conceptual Framework for Financial Reporting (Conceptual Framework)*, recognition is the process of capturing, for inclusion in the statement of financial position or the statement(s) of financial performance, an item that meets the definition of one of the elements of the financial statements. The definitions of assets, liabilities, income, and expenses are fundamental to recognition, at the end of both annual and interim financial reporting periods.

32   For assets, the same tests of future economic benefits apply at interim dates and at the end of an entity's financial year. Costs that, by their nature, would not qualify as assets at financial year-end would not qualify at interim dates either. Similarly, a liability at the end of an interim reporting period must represent an existing obligation at that date, just as it must at the end of an annual reporting period.

33   An essential characteristic of income (revenue) and expenses is that the related inflows and outflows of assets and liabilities have already taken place. If those inflows or outflows have taken place, the related revenue and expense are recognised; otherwise they are not recognised. The *Conceptual Framework* does not allow the recognition of items in the statement of financial position which do not meet the definition of assets or liabilities.

34   In measuring the assets, liabilities, income, expenses, and cash flows reported in its financial statements, an entity that reports only annually is able to take into account information that becomes available throughout the financial year. Its measurements are, in effect, on a year-to-date basis.

35   An entity that reports half-yearly uses information available by mid-year or shortly thereafter in making the measurements in its financial statements for the first six-month period and information available by year-end or shortly thereafter for the twelve-month period. The twelve-month measurements will reflect possible changes in estimates of amounts reported for the first six-month period. The amounts reported in the interim financial report for the first six-month period are not retrospectively adjusted. Paragraphs 16A(d) and 26 require, however, that the nature and amount of any significant changes in estimates be disclosed.

36   An entity that reports more frequently than half-yearly measures income and expenses on a year-to-date basis for each interim period using information available when each set of financial statements is being prepared. Amounts of income and expenses reported in the current interim period will reflect any changes in estimates of amounts reported in prior interim periods of the financial year. The amounts reported in prior interim periods are not retrospectively adjusted. Paragraphs 16A(d) and 26 require, however, that the nature and amount of any significant changes in estimates be disclosed.

Revenues received seasonally, cyclically, or occasionally

37   Revenues that are received seasonally, cyclically, or occasionally within a financial year shall not be anticipated or deferred as of an interim date if anticipation or deferral would not be appropriate at the end of the entity's financial year.

38   Examples include dividend revenue, royalties, and government grants. Additionally, some entities consistently earn more revenues in certain interim periods of a financial year than in other interim periods, for example, seasonal revenues of retailers. Such revenues are recognised when they occur.

Costs incurred unevenly during the financial year

39   Costs that are incurred unevenly during an entity's financial year shall be anticipated or deferred for interim reporting purposes if, and only if, it is also appropriate to anticipate or defer that type of cost at the end of the financial year.

Applying the recognition and measurement principles

40   Part B of the illustrative examples accompanying this Standard provides examples of applying the general recognition and measurement principles set out in paragraphs 28–39.

Use of estimates

41   The measurement procedures to be followed in an interim financial report shall be designed to ensure that the resulting information is reliable and that all material financial information that is relevant to an understanding of the financial position or performance of the entity is appropriately disclosed. While measurements in both annual and interim financial reports are often based on reasonable estimates, the preparation of interim financial reports generally will require a greater use of estimation methods than annual financial reports.

42   Part C of the illustrative examples accompanying this Standard provides examples of the use of estimates in interim periods.

Restatement of previously reported interim periods

43   A change in accounting policy, other than one for which the transition is specified by a new IFRS, shall be reflected by:

(a)   restating the financial statements of prior interim periods of the current financial year and the comparable interim periods of any prior financial years that will be restated in the annual financial statements in accordance with IAS 8; or

(b)   when it is impracticable to determine the cumulative effect at the beginning of the financial year of applying a new accounting policy to all prior periods, adjusting the financial statements of prior interim periods of the current financial year, and comparable interim periods of prior financial years to apply the new accounting policy prospectively from the earliest date practicable.

44   One objective of the preceding principle is to ensure that a single accounting policy is applied to a particular class of transactions throughout an entire financial year. Under IAS 8, a change in accounting policy is reflected by retrospective application, with restatement of prior period financial data as far back as is practicable. However, if the cumulative amount of the adjustment relating to prior financial years is impracticable to determine, then under IAS 8 the new policy is applied prospectively from the earliest date practicable. The effect of the principle in paragraph 43 is to require that within the current financial year any change in accounting policy is applied either retrospectively or, if that is not practicable, prospectively, from no later than the beginning of the financial year.

45   To allow accounting changes to be reflected as of an interim date within the financial year would allow two differing accounting policies to be applied to a particular class of transactions within a single financial year. The result would be interim allocation difficulties, obscured operating results, and complicated analysis and understandability of interim period information.

Effective date

46   This Standard becomes operative for financial statements covering periods beginning on or after 1 January 1999. Earlier application is encouraged.

47   IAS 1 (as revised in 2007) amended the terminology used throughout IFRSs. In addition it amended paragraphs 4, 5, 8, 11, 12 and 20, deleted paragraph 13 and added paragraphs 8A and 11A. An entity shall apply those amendments for annual periods beginning on or after 1 January 2009. If an entity applies IAS 1 (revised 2007) for an earlier period, the amendments shall be applied for that earlier period.

48   IFRS 3 (as revised in 2008) amended paragraph 16(i). An entity shall apply that amendment for annual periods beginning on or after 1 July 2009. If an entity applies IFRS 3 (revised 2008) for an earlier period, the amendment shall also be applied for that earlier period.

49   Paragraphs 15, 27, 35 and 36 were amended, paragraphs 15A–15C and 16A were added and paragraphs 16–18 were deleted by *Improvements to IFRSs* in May 2010. An entity shall apply those amendments for annual periods beginning on or after 1 January 2011. Earlier application is permitted. If an entity applies the amendments for an earlier period it shall disclose that fact.

50   IFRS 13, issued in May 2011, added paragraph 16A(j). An entity shall apply that amendment when it applies IFRS 13.

51   *Presentation of Items of Other Comprehensive Income* (Amendments to IAS 1), issued in June 2011, amended paragraphs 8, 8A, 11A and 20. An entity shall apply those amendments when it applies IAS 1 as amended in June 2011.

52   *Annual Improvements 2009–2011 Cycle*, issued in May 2012, amended paragraph 5 as a consequential amendment derived from the amendment to IAS 1 *Presentation of Financial Statements*. An entity shall apply that amendment retrospectively in accordance with IAS 8 *Accounting Policies, Changes in*

Accounting Estimates and Errors for annual periods beginning on or after 1 January 2013. Earlier application is permitted. If an entity applies that amendment for an earlier period it shall disclose that fact.

53   *Annual Improvements 2009–2011 Cycle*, issued in May 2012, amended paragraph 16A. An entity shall apply that amendment retrospectively in accordance with IAS 8 *Accounting Policies, Changes in Accounting Estimates and Errors* for annual periods beginning on or after 1 January 2013. Earlier application is permitted. If an entity applies that amendment for an earlier period it shall disclose that fact.

54   *Investment Entities* (Amendments to IFRS 10, IFRS 12 and IAS 27), issued in October 2012, amended paragraph 16A. An entity shall apply that amendment for annual periods beginning on or after 1 January 2014. Earlier application of *Investment Entities* is permitted. If an entity applies that amendment earlier it shall also apply all amendments included in *Investment Entities* at the same time.

55   IFRS 15 *Revenue from Contracts with Customers*, issued in May 2014, amended paragraphs 15B and 16A. An entity shall apply those amendments when it applies IFRS 15.

56   *Annual Improvements to IFRSs 2012–2014 Cycle*, issued in September 2014, amended paragraph 16A. An entity shall apply that amendment retrospectively in accordance with IAS 8 *Accounting Policies, Changes in Accounting Estimates and Errors* for annual periods beginning on or after 1 January 2016. Earlier application is permitted. If an entity applies the amendment for an earlier period it shall disclose that fact.

57   *Disclosure Initiative* (Amendments to IAS 1), issued in December 2014, amended paragraph 5. An entity shall apply that amendment for annual periods beginning on or after 1 January 2016. Earlier application of that amendment is permitted.

58   *Amendments to References to the Conceptual Framework in IFRS Standards*, issued in 2018, amended paragraphs 31 and 33. An entity shall apply those amendments for annual periods beginning on or after 1 January 2020. Earlier application is permitted if at the same time an entity also applies all other amendments made by *Amendments to References to the Conceptual Framework in IFRS Standards*. An entity shall apply the amendments to IAS 34 retrospectively in accordance with IAS 8 *Accounting Policies, Changes in Accounting Estimates and Errors*. However, if an entity determines that retrospective application would be impracticable or would involve undue cost or effort, it shall apply the amendments to IAS 34 by reference to paragraphs 43–45 of this Standard and paragraphs 23–28, 50–53 and 54F of IAS 8.

59   *Definition of Material* (Amendments to IAS 1 and IAS 8), issued in October 2018, amended paragraph 24. An entity shall apply those amendments prospectively for annual periods beginning on or after 1 January 2020. Earlier application is permitted. If an entity applies those amendments for an earlier period, it shall disclose that fact. An entity shall apply those amendments when it applies the

amendments to the definition of material in paragraph 7 of IAS 1 and paragraphs 5 and 6 of IAS 8.

60   *[This paragraph refers to amendments that are not yet effective, and is therefore not included in this edition.]*

IAS 36

Impairment of Assets

In April 2001 the International Accounting Standards Board (Board) adopted IAS 36 *Impairment of Assets*, which had originally been issued by the International Accounting Standards Committee in June 1998. That standard consolidated all the requirements on how to assess for recoverability of an asset. These requirements were contained in IAS 16 *Property, Plant and Equipment*, IAS 22 *Business Combinations*, IAS 28 *Accounting for Associates* and IAS 31 *Financial Reporting of Interests in Joint Ventures*.

The Board revised IAS 36 in March 2004 as part of the first phase of its business combinations project. In January 2008 the Board amended IAS 36 again as part of the second phase of its business combinations project.

In May 2013 IAS 36 was amended by *Recoverable Amount Disclosures for Non-Financial Assets* (Amendments to IAS 36). The amendments required the disclosure of information about the recoverable amount of impaired assets, if that amount is based on fair value less costs of disposal and the disclosure of additional information about that fair value measurement.

Other Standards have made minor consequential amendments to IAS 36. They include IFRS 10 *Consolidated Financial Statements* (issued May 2011), IFRS 11 *Joint Arrangements* (issued May 2011), IFRS 13 *Fair Value Measurement* (issued May 2011), IFRS 9 *Financial Instruments* (Hedge Accounting and amendments to IFRS 9, IFRS 7 and IAS 39) (issued November 2013), IFRS 15 *Revenue from Contracts with Customers* (issued May 2014), *Agriculture: Bearer Plants* (Amendments to IAS 16 and IAS 41) (issued June 2014), IFRS 9 *Financial Instruments* (issued July 2014) and *Amendments to References to the Conceptual Framework in IFRS Standards* (issued March 2018).

CONTENTS

FOR THE ACCOMPANYING GUIDANCE LISTED BELOW, SEE PART B OF THIS EDITION

ILLUSTRATIVE EXAMPLES

continued...

...continued

FOR THE BASIS FOR CONCLUSIONS, SEE PART C OF THIS EDITION

BASIS FOR CONCLUSIONS

DISSENTING OPINIONS

International Accounting Standard 36 *Impairment of Assets* (IAS 36) is set out in paragraphs 1–141 and Appendices A–C. All the paragraphs have equal authority but retain the IASC format of the Standard when it was adopted by the IASB. IAS 36 should be read in the context of its objective and the Basis for Conclusions, the *Preface to IFRS Standards* and the *Conceptual Framework for Financial Reporting*. IAS 8 *Accounting Policies, Changes in Accounting Estimates and Errors* provides a basis for selecting and applying accounting policies in the absence of explicit guidance.

International Accounting Standard 36
Impairment of Assets

Objective

1   The objective of this Standard is to prescribe the procedures that an entity applies to ensure that its assets are carried at no more than their recoverable amount. An asset is carried at more than its recoverable amount if its carrying amount exceeds the amount to be recovered through use or sale of the asset. If this is the case, the asset is described as impaired and the Standard requires the entity to recognise an impairment loss. The Standard also specifies when an entity should reverse an impairment loss and prescribes disclosures.

Scope

2   This Standard shall be applied in accounting for the impairment of all assets, other than:

   (a)   inventories (see IAS 2 *Inventories*);

   (b)   contract assets and assets arising from costs to obtain or fulfil a contract that are recognised in accordance with IFRS 15 *Revenue from Contracts with Customers*;

   (c)   deferred tax assets (see IAS 12 *Income Taxes*);

   (d)   assets arising from employee benefits (see IAS 19 *Employee Benefits*);

   (e)   financial assets that are within the scope of IFRS 9 *Financial Instruments*;

   (f)   investment property that is measured at fair value (see IAS 40 *Investment Property*);

   (g)   biological assets related to agricultural activity within the scope of IAS 41 *Agriculture* that are measured at fair value less costs to sell;

   (h)   deferred acquisition costs, and intangible assets, arising from an insurer's contractual rights under insurance contracts within the scope of IFRS 4 *Insurance Contracts*; and

   (i)   non-current assets (or disposal groups) classified as held for sale in accordance with IFRS 5 *Non-current Assets Held for Sale and Discontinued Operations*.

3   This Standard does not apply to inventories, assets arising from construction contracts, deferred tax assets, assets arising from employee benefits, or assets classified as held for sale (or included in a disposal group that is classified as held for sale) because existing IFRSs applicable to these assets contain requirements for recognising and measuring these assets.

4   This Standard applies to financial assets classified as:

   (a)   subsidiaries, as defined in IFRS 10 *Consolidated Financial Statements*;

(b)   associates, as defined in IAS 28 *Investments in Associates and Joint Ventures*; and

(c)   joint ventures, as defined in IFRS 11 *Joint Arrangements*.

For impairment of other financial assets, refer to IFRS 9.

5   This Standard does not apply to financial assets within the scope of IFRS 9, investment property measured at fair value within the scope of IAS 40, or biological assets related to agricultural activity measured at fair value less costs to sell within the scope of IAS 41. However, this Standard applies to assets that are carried at revalued amount (ie fair value at the date of the revaluation less any subsequent accumulated depreciation and subsequent accumulated impairment losses) in accordance with other IFRSs, such as the revaluation model in IAS 16 *Property, Plant and Equipment* and IAS 38 *Intangible Assets*. The only difference between an asset's fair value and its fair value less costs of disposal is the direct incremental costs attributable to the disposal of the asset.

(a)   If the disposal costs are negligible, the recoverable amount of the revalued asset is necessarily close to, or greater than, its revalued amount. In this case, after the revaluation requirements have been applied, it is unlikely that the revalued asset is impaired and recoverable amount need not be estimated.

(b)   [deleted]

(c)   If the disposal costs are not negligible, the fair value less costs of disposal of the revalued asset is necessarily less than its fair value. Therefore, the revalued asset will be impaired if its value in use is less than its revalued amount. In this case, after the revaluation requirements have been applied, an entity applies this Standard to determine whether the asset may be impaired.

Definitions

6   The following terms are used in this Standard with the meanings specified:

Carrying amount is the amount at which an asset is recognised after deducting any accumulated depreciation (amortisation) and accumulated impairment losses thereon.

A *cash-generating unit* is the smallest identifiable group of assets that generates cash inflows that are largely independent of the cash inflows from other assets or groups of assets.

Corporate assets are assets other than goodwill that contribute to the future cash flows of both the cash-generating unit under review and other cash-generating units.

Costs of disposal are incremental costs directly attributable to the disposal of an asset or cash-generating unit, excluding finance costs and income tax expense.

Depreciable amount is the cost of an asset, or other amount substituted for cost in the financial statements, less its residual value.

Depreciation (Amortisation) is the systematic allocation of the depreciable amount of an asset over its useful life.[1]

Fair value is the price that would be received to sell an asset or paid to transfer a liability in an orderly transaction between market participants at the measurement date. (See IFRS 13 *Fair Value Measurement*.)

An *impairment loss* is the amount by which the carrying amount of an asset or a cash-generating unit exceeds its recoverable amount.

The *recoverable amount* of an asset or a cash-generating unit is the higher of its fair value less costs of disposal and its value in use.

Useful life is either:

(a)   the period of time over which an asset is expected to be used by the entity; or

(b)   the number of production or similar units expected to be obtained from the asset by the entity.

Value in use is the present value of the future cash flows expected to be derived from an asset or cash-generating unit.

Identifying an asset that may be impaired

7   Paragraphs 8–17 specify when recoverable amount shall be determined. These requirements use the term 'an asset' but apply equally to an individual asset or a cash-generating unit. The remainder of this Standard is structured as follows:

(a)   paragraphs 18–57 set out the requirements for measuring recoverable amount. These requirements also use the term 'an asset' but apply equally to an individual asset and a cash-generating unit.

(b)   paragraphs 58–108 set out the requirements for recognising and measuring impairment losses. Recognition and measurement of impairment losses for individual assets other than goodwill are dealt with in paragraphs 58–64. Paragraphs 65–108 deal with the recognition and measurement of impairment losses for cash-generating units and goodwill.

(c)   paragraphs 109–116 set out the requirements for reversing an impairment loss recognised in prior periods for an asset or a cash-generating unit. Again, these requirements use the term 'an asset' but apply equally to an individual asset or a cash-generating unit. Additional requirements for an individual asset are set out in paragraphs 117–121, for a cash-generating unit in paragraphs 122 and 123, and for goodwill in paragraphs 124 and 125.

---

1   In the case of an intangible asset, the term 'amortisation' is generally used instead of 'depreciation'. The two terms have the same meaning.

(d)   paragraphs 126–133 specify the information to be disclosed about impairment losses and reversals of impairment losses for assets and cash-generating units. Paragraphs 134–137 specify additional disclosure requirements for cash-generating units to which goodwill or intangible assets with indefinite useful lives have been allocated for impairment testing purposes.

8   An asset is impaired when its carrying amount exceeds its recoverable amount. Paragraphs 12–14 describe some indications that an impairment loss may have occurred. If any of those indications is present, an entity is required to make a formal estimate of recoverable amount. Except as described in paragraph 10, this Standard does not require an entity to make a formal estimate of recoverable amount if no indication of an impairment loss is present.

9   **An entity shall assess at the end of each reporting period whether there is any indication that an asset may be impaired. If any such indication exists, the entity shall estimate the recoverable amount of the asset.**

10   **Irrespective of whether there is any indication of impairment, an entity shall also:**

     (a)   **test an intangible asset with an indefinite useful life or an intangible asset not yet available for use for impairment annually by comparing its carrying amount with its recoverable amount. This impairment test may be performed at any time during an annual period, provided it is performed at the same time every year. Different intangible assets may be tested for impairment at different times. However, if such an intangible asset was initially recognised during the current annual period, that intangible asset shall be tested for impairment before the end of the current annual period.**

     (b)   **test goodwill acquired in a business combination for impairment annually in accordance with paragraphs 80–99.**

11   The ability of an intangible asset to generate sufficient future economic benefits to recover its carrying amount is usually subject to greater uncertainty before the asset is available for use than after it is available for use. Therefore, this Standard requires an entity to test for impairment, at least annually, the carrying amount of an intangible asset that is not yet available for use.

12   **In assessing whether there is any indication that an asset may be impaired, an entity shall consider, as a minimum, the following indications:**

External sources of information

     (a)   **there are observable indications that the asset's value has declined during the period significantly more than would be expected as a result of the passage of time or normal use.**

(b) significant changes with an adverse effect on the entity have taken place during the period, or will take place in the near future, in the technological, market, economic or legal environment in which the entity operates or in the market to which an asset is dedicated.

(c) market interest rates or other market rates of return on investments have increased during the period, and those increases are likely to affect the discount rate used in calculating an asset's value in use and decrease the asset's recoverable amount materially.

(d) the carrying amount of the net assets of the entity is more than its market capitalisation.

Internal sources of information

(e) evidence is available of obsolescence or physical damage of an asset.

(f) significant changes with an adverse effect on the entity have taken place during the period, or are expected to take place in the near future, in the extent to which, or manner in which, an asset is used or is expected to be used. These changes include the asset becoming idle, plans to discontinue or restructure the operation to which an asset belongs, plans to dispose of an asset before the previously expected date, and reassessing the useful life of an asset as finite rather than indefinite.[2]

(g) evidence is available from internal reporting that indicates that the economic performance of an asset is, or will be, worse than expected.

Dividend from a subsidiary, joint venture or associate

(h) for an investment in a subsidiary, joint venture or associate, the investor recognises a dividend from the investment and evidence is available that:

  (i) the carrying amount of the investment in the separate financial statements exceeds the carrying amounts in the consolidated financial statements of the investee's net assets, including associated goodwill; or

  (ii) the dividend exceeds the total comprehensive income of the subsidiary, joint venture or associate in the period the dividend is declared.

13 The list in paragraph 12 is not exhaustive. An entity may identify other indications that an asset may be impaired and these would also require the entity to determine the asset's recoverable amount or, in the case of goodwill, perform an impairment test in accordance with paragraphs 80–99.

---

2 Once an asset meets the criteria to be classified as held for sale (or is included in a disposal group that is classified as held for sale), it is excluded from the scope of this Standard and is accounted for in accordance with IFRS 5 *Non-current Assets Held for Sale and Discontinued Operations.*

14   Evidence from internal reporting that indicates that an asset may be impaired includes the existence of:

    (a)   cash flows for acquiring the asset, or subsequent cash needs for operating or maintaining it, that are significantly higher than those originally budgeted;

    (b)   actual net cash flows or operating profit or loss flowing from the asset that are significantly worse than those budgeted;

    (c)   a significant decline in budgeted net cash flows or operating profit, or a significant increase in budgeted loss, flowing from the asset; or

    (d)   operating losses or net cash outflows for the asset, when current period amounts are aggregated with budgeted amounts for the future.

15   As indicated in paragraph 10, this Standard requires an intangible asset with an indefinite useful life or not yet available for use and goodwill to be tested for impairment, at least annually. Apart from when the requirements in paragraph 10 apply, the concept of materiality applies in identifying whether the recoverable amount of an asset needs to be estimated. For example, if previous calculations show that an asset's recoverable amount is significantly greater than its carrying amount, the entity need not re-estimate the asset's recoverable amount if no events have occurred that would eliminate that difference. Similarly, previous analysis may show that an asset's recoverable amount is not sensitive to one (or more) of the indications listed in paragraph 12.

16   As an illustration of paragraph 15, if market interest rates or other market rates of return on investments have increased during the period, an entity is not required to make a formal estimate of an asset's recoverable amount in the following cases:

    (a)   if the discount rate used in calculating the asset's value in use is unlikely to be affected by the increase in these market rates. For example, increases in short-term interest rates may not have a material effect on the discount rate used for an asset that has a long remaining useful life.

    (b)   if the discount rate used in calculating the asset's value in use is likely to be affected by the increase in these market rates but previous sensitivity analysis of recoverable amount shows that:

        (i)   it is unlikely that there will be a material decrease in recoverable amount because future cash flows are also likely to increase (eg in some cases, an entity may be able to demonstrate that it adjusts its revenues to compensate for any increase in market rates); or

        (ii)   the decrease in recoverable amount is unlikely to result in a material impairment loss.

17   If there is an indication that an asset may be impaired, this may indicate that the remaining useful life, the depreciation (amortisation) method or the residual value for the asset needs to be reviewed and adjusted in accordance with the Standard applicable to the asset, even if no impairment loss is recognised for the asset.

Measuring recoverable amount

18   This Standard defines recoverable amount as the higher of an asset's or cash-generating unit's fair value less costs of disposal and its value in use. Paragraphs 19–57 set out the requirements for measuring recoverable amount. These requirements use the term 'an asset' but apply equally to an individual asset or a cash-generating unit.

19   It is not always necessary to determine both an asset's fair value less costs of disposal and its value in use. If either of these amounts exceeds the asset's carrying amount, the asset is not impaired and it is not necessary to estimate the other amount.

20   It may be possible to measure fair value less costs of disposal, even if there is not a quoted price in an active market for an identical asset. However, sometimes it will not be possible to measure fair value less costs of disposal because there is no basis for making a reliable estimate of the price at which an orderly transaction to sell the asset would take place between market participants at the measurement date under current market conditions. In this case, the entity may use the asset's value in use as its recoverable amount.

21   If there is no reason to believe that an asset's value in use materially exceeds its fair value less costs of disposal, the asset's fair value less costs of disposal may be used as its recoverable amount. This will often be the case for an asset that is held for disposal. This is because the value in use of an asset held for disposal will consist mainly of the net disposal proceeds, as the future cash flows from continuing use of the asset until its disposal are likely to be negligible.

22   Recoverable amount is determined for an individual asset, unless the asset does not generate cash inflows that are largely independent of those from other assets or groups of assets. If this is the case, recoverable amount is determined for the cash-generating unit to which the asset belongs (see paragraphs 65–103), unless either:

      (a)   the asset's fair value less costs of disposal is higher than its carrying amount; or

      (b)   the asset's value in use can be estimated to be close to its fair value less costs of disposal and fair value less costs of disposal can be measured.

23   In some cases, estimates, averages and computational short cuts may provide reasonable approximations of the detailed computations illustrated in this Standard for determining fair value less costs of disposal or value in use.

Measuring the recoverable amount of an intangible asset with an indefinite useful life

24   Paragraph 10 requires an intangible asset with an indefinite useful life to be tested for impairment annually by comparing its carrying amount with its recoverable amount, irrespective of whether there is any indication that it may be impaired. However, the most recent detailed calculation of such an asset's recoverable amount made in a preceding period may be used in the impairment test for that asset in the current period, provided all of the following criteria are met:

    (a)   if the intangible asset does not generate cash inflows from continuing use that are largely independent of those from other assets or groups of assets and is therefore tested for impairment as part of the cash-generating unit to which it belongs, the assets and liabilities making up that unit have not changed significantly since the most recent recoverable amount calculation;

    (b)   the most recent recoverable amount calculation resulted in an amount that exceeded the asset's carrying amount by a substantial margin; and

    (c)   based on an analysis of events that have occurred and circumstances that have changed since the most recent recoverable amount calculation, the likelihood that a current recoverable amount determination would be less than the asset's carrying amount is remote.

Fair value less costs of disposal

25–27   [Deleted]

28   Costs of disposal, other than those that have been recognised as liabilities, are deducted in measuring fair value less costs of disposal. Examples of such costs are legal costs, stamp duty and similar transaction taxes, costs of removing the asset, and direct incremental costs to bring an asset into condition for its sale. However, termination benefits (as defined in IAS 19) and costs associated with reducing or reorganising a business following the disposal of an asset are not direct incremental costs to dispose of the asset.

29   Sometimes, the disposal of an asset would require the buyer to assume a liability and only a single fair value less costs of disposal is available for both the asset and the liability. Paragraph 78 explains how to deal with such cases.

Value in use

30   The following elements shall be reflected in the calculation of an asset's value in use:

    (a)   an estimate of the future cash flows the entity expects to derive from the asset;

    (b)   expectations about possible variations in the amount or timing of those future cash flows;

(c)   the time value of money, represented by the current market risk-free rate of interest;

(d)   the price for bearing the uncertainty inherent in the asset; and

(e)   other factors, such as illiquidity, that market participants would reflect in pricing the future cash flows the entity expects to derive from the asset.

31   Estimating the value in use of an asset involves the following steps:

(a)   estimating the future cash inflows and outflows to be derived from continuing use of the asset and from its ultimate disposal; and

(b)   applying the appropriate discount rate to those future cash flows.

32   The elements identified in paragraph 30(b), (d) and (e) can be reflected either as adjustments to the future cash flows or as adjustments to the discount rate. Whichever approach an entity adopts to reflect expectations about possible variations in the amount or timing of future cash flows, the result shall be to reflect the expected present value of the future cash flows, ie the weighted average of all possible outcomes. Appendix A provides additional guidance on the use of present value techniques in measuring an asset's value in use.

Basis for estimates of future cash flows

33   In measuring value in use an entity shall:

(a)   base cash flow projections on reasonable and supportable assumptions that represent management's best estimate of the range of economic conditions that will exist over the remaining useful life of the asset. Greater weight shall be given to external evidence.

(b)   base cash flow projections on the most recent financial budgets/forecasts approved by management, but shall exclude any estimated future cash inflows or outflows expected to arise from future restructurings or from improving or enhancing the asset's performance. Projections based on these budgets/forecasts shall cover a maximum period of five years, unless a longer period can be justified.

(c)   estimate cash flow projections beyond the period covered by the most recent budgets/forecasts by extrapolating the projections based on the budgets/forecasts using a steady or declining growth rate for subsequent years, unless an increasing rate can be justified. This growth rate shall not exceed the long-term average growth rate for the products, industries, or country or countries in which the entity operates, or for the market in which the asset is used, unless a higher rate can be justified.

34   Management assesses the reasonableness of the assumptions on which its current cash flow projections are based by examining the causes of differences between past cash flow projections and actual cash flows. Management shall ensure that the assumptions on which its current cash flow projections are

based are consistent with past actual outcomes, provided the effects of subsequent events or circumstances that did not exist when those actual cash flows were generated make this appropriate.

35   Detailed, explicit and reliable financial budgets/forecasts of future cash flows for periods longer than five years are generally not available. For this reason, management's estimates of future cash flows are based on the most recent budgets/forecasts for a maximum of five years. Management may use cash flow projections based on financial budgets/forecasts over a period longer than five years if it is confident that these projections are reliable and it can demonstrate its ability, based on past experience, to forecast cash flows accurately over that longer period.

36   Cash flow projections until the end of an asset's useful life are estimated by extrapolating the cash flow projections based on the financial budgets/forecasts using a growth rate for subsequent years. This rate is steady or declining, unless an increase in the rate matches objective information about patterns over a product or industry lifecycle. If appropriate, the growth rate is zero or negative.

37   When conditions are favourable, competitors are likely to enter the market and restrict growth. Therefore, entities will have difficulty in exceeding the average historical growth rate over the long term (say, twenty years) for the products, industries, or country or countries in which the entity operates, or for the market in which the asset is used.

38   In using information from financial budgets/forecasts, an entity considers whether the information reflects reasonable and supportable assumptions and represents management's best estimate of the set of economic conditions that will exist over the remaining useful life of the asset.

Composition of estimates of future cash flows

39   Estimates of future cash flows shall include:

    (a)   projections of cash inflows from the continuing use of the asset;

    (b)   projections of cash outflows that are necessarily incurred to generate the cash inflows from continuing use of the asset (including cash outflows to prepare the asset for use) and can be directly attributed, or allocated on a reasonable and consistent basis, to the asset; and

    (c)   net cash flows, if any, to be received (or paid) for the disposal of the asset at the end of its useful life.

40   Estimates of future cash flows and the discount rate reflect consistent assumptions about price increases attributable to general inflation. Therefore, if the discount rate includes the effect of price increases attributable to general inflation, future cash flows are estimated in nominal terms. If the discount rate excludes the effect of price increases attributable to general inflation, future cash flows are estimated in real terms (but include future specific price increases or decreases).

41   Projections of cash outflows include those for the day-to-day servicing of the asset as well as future overheads that can be attributed directly, or allocated on a reasonable and consistent basis, to the use of the asset.

42   When the carrying amount of an asset does not yet include all the cash outflows to be incurred before it is ready for use or sale, the estimate of future cash outflows includes an estimate of any further cash outflow that is expected to be incurred before the asset is ready for use or sale. For example, this is the case for a building under construction or for a development project that is not yet completed.

43   To avoid double-counting, estimates of future cash flows do not include:

(a)   cash inflows from assets that generate cash inflows that are largely independent of the cash inflows from the asset under review (for example, financial assets such as receivables); and

(b)   cash outflows that relate to obligations that have been recognised as liabilities (for example, payables, pensions or provisions).

44   **Future cash flows shall be estimated for the asset in its current condition. Estimates of future cash flows shall not include estimated future cash inflows or outflows that are expected to arise from:**

(a)   **a future restructuring to which an entity is not yet committed; or**

(b)   **improving or enhancing the asset's performance.**

45   Because future cash flows are estimated for the asset in its current condition, value in use does not reflect:

(a)   future cash outflows or related cost savings (for example reductions in staff costs) or benefits that are expected to arise from a future restructuring to which an entity is not yet committed; or

(b)   future cash outflows that will improve or enhance the asset's performance or the related cash inflows that are expected to arise from such outflows.

46   A restructuring is a programme that is planned and controlled by management and materially changes either the scope of the business undertaken by an entity or the manner in which the business is conducted. IAS 37 *Provisions, Contingent Liabilities and Contingent Assets* contains guidance clarifying when an entity is committed to a restructuring.

47   When an entity becomes committed to a restructuring, some assets are likely to be affected by this restructuring. Once the entity is committed to the restructuring:

(a)   its estimates of future cash inflows and cash outflows for the purpose of determining value in use reflect the cost savings and other benefits from the restructuring (based on the most recent financial budgets/ forecasts approved by management); and

(b)   its estimates of future cash outflows for the restructuring are included in a restructuring provision in accordance with IAS 37.

Illustrative Example 5 illustrates the effect of a future restructuring on a value in use calculation.

48   Until an entity incurs cash outflows that improve or enhance the asset's performance, estimates of future cash flows do not include the estimated future cash inflows that are expected to arise from the increase in economic benefits associated with the cash outflow (see Illustrative Example 6).

49   Estimates of future cash flows include future cash outflows necessary to maintain the level of economic benefits expected to arise from the asset in its current condition. When a cash-generating unit consists of assets with different estimated useful lives, all of which are essential to the ongoing operation of the unit, the replacement of assets with shorter lives is considered to be part of the day-to-day servicing of the unit when estimating the future cash flows associated with the unit. Similarly, when a single asset consists of components with different estimated useful lives, the replacement of components with shorter lives is considered to be part of the day-to-day servicing of the asset when estimating the future cash flows generated by the asset.

50   **Estimates of future cash flows shall not include:**

    (a)   **cash inflows or outflows from financing activities; or**

    (b)   **income tax receipts or payments.**

51   Estimated future cash flows reflect assumptions that are consistent with the way the discount rate is determined. Otherwise, the effect of some assumptions will be counted twice or ignored. Because the time value of money is considered by discounting the estimated future cash flows, these cash flows exclude cash inflows or outflows from financing activities. Similarly, because the discount rate is determined on a pre-tax basis, future cash flows are also estimated on a pre-tax basis.

52   **The estimate of net cash flows to be received (or paid) for the disposal of an asset at the end of its useful life shall be the amount that an entity expects to obtain from the disposal of the asset in an arm's length transaction between knowledgeable, willing parties, after deducting the estimated costs of disposal.**

53   The estimate of net cash flows to be received (or paid) for the disposal of an asset at the end of its useful life is determined in a similar way to an asset's fair value less costs of disposal, except that, in estimating those net cash flows:

    (a)   an entity uses prices prevailing at the date of the estimate for similar assets that have reached the end of their useful life and have operated under conditions similar to those in which the asset will be used.

    (b)   the entity adjusts those prices for the effect of both future price increases due to general inflation and specific future price increases or decreases. However, if estimates of future cash flows from the asset's continuing use and the discount rate exclude the effect of general inflation, the entity also excludes this effect from the estimate of net cash flows on disposal.

53A   Fair value differs from value in use. Fair value reflects the assumptions market participants would use when pricing the asset. In contrast, value in use reflects the effects of factors that may be specific to the entity and not applicable to entities in general. For example, fair value does not reflect any of the following factors to the extent that they would not be generally available to market participants:

    (a)   additional value derived from the grouping of assets (such as the creation of a portfolio of investment properties in different locations);

    (b)   synergies between the asset being measured and other assets;

    (c)   legal rights or legal restrictions that are specific only to the current owner of the asset; and

    (d)   tax benefits or tax burdens that are specific to the current owner of the asset.

Foreign currency future cash flows

54   Future cash flows are estimated in the currency in which they will be generated and then discounted using a discount rate appropriate for that currency. An entity translates the present value using the spot exchange rate at the date of the value in use calculation.

Discount rate

55   The discount rate (rates) shall be a pre-tax rate (rates) that reflect(s) current market assessments of:

    (a)   the time value of money; and

    (b)   the risks specific to the asset for which the future cash flow estimates have not been adjusted.

56   A rate that reflects current market assessments of the time value of money and the risks specific to the asset is the return that investors would require if they were to choose an investment that would generate cash flows of amounts, timing and risk profile equivalent to those that the entity expects to derive from the asset. This rate is estimated from the rate implicit in current market transactions for similar assets or from the weighted average cost of capital of a listed entity that has a single asset (or a portfolio of assets) similar in terms of service potential and risks to the asset under review. However, the discount rate(s) used to measure an asset's value in use shall not reflect risks for which the future cash flow estimates have been adjusted. Otherwise, the effect of some assumptions will be double-counted.

57   When an asset-specific rate is not directly available from the market, an entity uses surrogates to estimate the discount rate. Appendix A provides additional guidance on estimating the discount rate in such circumstances.

Recognising and measuring an impairment loss

58   Paragraphs 59–64 set out the requirements for recognising and measuring impairment losses for an individual asset other than goodwill. Recognising and measuring impairment losses for cash-generating units and goodwill are dealt with in paragraphs 65–108.

59   **If, and only if, the recoverable amount of an asset is less than its carrying amount, the carrying amount of the asset shall be reduced to its recoverable amount. That reduction is an impairment loss.**

60   **An impairment loss shall be recognised immediately in profit or loss, unless the asset is carried at revalued amount in accordance with another Standard (for example, in accordance with the revaluation model in IAS 16). Any impairment loss of a revalued asset shall be treated as a revaluation decrease in accordance with that other Standard.**

61   An impairment loss on a non-revalued asset is recognised in profit or loss. However, an impairment loss on a revalued asset is recognised in other comprehensive income to the extent that the impairment loss does not exceed the amount in the revaluation surplus for that same asset. Such an impairment loss on a revalued asset reduces the revaluation surplus for that asset.

62   **When the amount estimated for an impairment loss is greater than the carrying amount of the asset to which it relates, an entity shall recognise a liability if, and only if, that is required by another Standard.**

63   **After the recognition of an impairment loss, the depreciation (amortisation) charge for the asset shall be adjusted in future periods to allocate the asset's revised carrying amount, less its residual value (if any), on a systematic basis over its remaining useful life.**

64   If an impairment loss is recognised, any related deferred tax assets or liabilities are determined in accordance with IAS 12 by comparing the revised carrying amount of the asset with its tax base (see Illustrative Example 3).

Cash-generating units and goodwill

65   Paragraphs 66–108 and Appendix C set out the requirements for identifying the cash-generating unit to which an asset belongs and determining the carrying amount of, and recognising impairment losses for, cash-generating units and goodwill.

Identifying the cash-generating unit to which an asset belongs

66   **If there is any indication that an asset may be impaired, recoverable amount shall be estimated for the individual asset. If it is not possible to estimate the recoverable amount of the individual asset, an entity shall determine the recoverable amount of the cash-generating unit to which the asset belongs (the asset's cash-generating unit).**

67   The recoverable amount of an individual asset cannot be determined if:

(a)   the asset's value in use cannot be estimated to be close to its fair value less costs of disposal (for example, when the future cash flows from continuing use of the asset cannot be estimated to be negligible); and

(b)   the asset does not generate cash inflows that are largely independent of those from other assets.

In such cases, value in use and, therefore, recoverable amount, can be determined only for the asset's cash-generating unit.

Example
A mining entity owns a private railway to support its mining activities. The private railway could be sold only for scrap value and it does not generate cash inflows that are largely independent of the cash inflows from the other assets of the mine.
It is not possible to estimate the recoverable amount of the private railway because its value in use cannot be determined and is probably different from scrap value. Therefore, the entity estimates the recoverable amount of the cash-generating unit to which the private railway belongs, ie the mine as a whole.

68   As defined in paragraph 6, an asset's cash-generating unit is the smallest group of assets that includes the asset and generates cash inflows that are largely independent of the cash inflows from other assets or groups of assets. Identification of an asset's cash-generating unit involves judgement. If recoverable amount cannot be determined for an individual asset, an entity identifies the lowest aggregation of assets that generate largely independent cash inflows.

Example
A bus company provides services under contract with a municipality that requires minimum service on each of five separate routes. Assets devoted to each route and the cash flows from each route can be identified separately. One of the routes operates at a significant loss.
Because the entity does not have the option to curtail any one bus route, the lowest level of identifiable cash inflows that are largely independent of the cash inflows from other assets or groups of assets is the cash inflows generated by the five routes together. The cash-generating unit for each route is the bus company as a whole.

69   Cash inflows are inflows of cash and cash equivalents received from parties external to the entity. In identifying whether cash inflows from an asset (or group of assets) are largely independent of the cash inflows from other assets (or groups of assets), an entity considers various factors including how management monitors the entity's operations (such as by product lines, businesses, individual locations, districts or regional areas) or how management makes decisions about continuing or disposing of the entity's assets and operations. Illustrative Example 1 gives examples of identification of a cash-generating unit.

70   If an active market exists for the output produced by an asset or group of assets, that asset or group of assets shall be identified as a cash-generating unit, even if some or all of the output is used internally. If the cash inflows generated by any asset or cash-generating unit are affected by internal transfer pricing, an entity shall use management's best estimate of future price(s) that could be achieved in arm's length transactions in estimating:

    (a)   the future cash inflows used to determine the asset's or cash-generating unit's value in use; and

    (b)   the future cash outflows used to determine the value in use of any other assets or cash-generating units that are affected by the internal transfer pricing.

71   Even if part or all of the output produced by an asset or a group of assets is used by other units of the entity (for example, products at an intermediate stage of a production process), this asset or group of assets forms a separate cash-generating unit if the entity could sell the output on an active market. This is because the asset or group of assets could generate cash inflows that would be largely independent of the cash inflows from other assets or groups of assets. In using information based on financial budgets/forecasts that relates to such a cash-generating unit, or to any other asset or cash-generating unit affected by internal transfer pricing, an entity adjusts this information if internal transfer prices do not reflect management's best estimate of future prices that could be achieved in arm's length transactions.

72   **Cash-generating units shall be identified consistently from period to period for the same asset or types of assets, unless a change is justified.**

73   If an entity determines that an asset belongs to a cash-generating unit different from that in previous periods, or that the types of assets aggregated for the asset's cash-generating unit have changed, paragraph 130 requires disclosures about the cash-generating unit, if an impairment loss is recognised or reversed for the cash-generating unit.

Recoverable amount and carrying amount of a cash-generating unit

74   The recoverable amount of a cash-generating unit is the higher of the cash-generating unit's fair value less costs of disposal and its value in use. For the purpose of determining the recoverable amount of a cash-generating unit, any reference in paragraphs 19–57 to 'an asset' is read as a reference to 'a cash-generating unit'.

75   **The carrying amount of a cash-generating unit shall be determined on a basis consistent with the way the recoverable amount of the cash-generating unit is determined.**

76   The carrying amount of a cash-generating unit:

(a)   includes the carrying amount of only those assets that can be attributed directly, or allocated on a reasonable and consistent basis, to the cash-generating unit and will generate the future cash inflows used in determining the cash-generating unit's value in use; and

(b)   does not include the carrying amount of any recognised liability, unless the recoverable amount of the cash-generating unit cannot be determined without consideration of this liability.

This is because fair value less costs of disposal and value in use of a cash-generating unit are determined excluding cash flows that relate to assets that are not part of the cash-generating unit and liabilities that have been recognised (see paragraphs 28 and 43).

77   When assets are grouped for recoverability assessments, it is important to include in the cash-generating unit all assets that generate or are used to generate the relevant stream of cash inflows. Otherwise, the cash-generating unit may appear to be fully recoverable when in fact an impairment loss has occurred. In some cases, although some assets contribute to the estimated future cash flows of a cash-generating unit, they cannot be allocated to the cash-generating unit on a reasonable and consistent basis. This might be the case for goodwill or corporate assets such as head office assets. Paragraphs 80–103 explain how to deal with these assets in testing a cash-generating unit for impairment.

78   It may be necessary to consider some recognised liabilities to determine the recoverable amount of a cash-generating unit. This may occur if the disposal of a cash-generating unit would require the buyer to assume the liability. In this case, the fair value less costs of disposal (or the estimated cash flow from ultimate disposal) of the cash-generating unit is the price to sell the assets of the cash-generating unit and the liability together, less the costs of disposal. To perform a meaningful comparison between the carrying amount of the cash-generating unit and its recoverable amount, the carrying amount of the liability is deducted in determining both the cash-generating unit's value in use and its carrying amount.

Example

A company operates a mine in a country where legislation requires that the owner must restore the site on completion of its mining operations. The cost of restoration includes the replacement of the overburden, which must be removed before mining operations commence. A provision for the costs to replace the overburden was recognised as soon as the overburden was removed. The amount provided was recognised as part of the cost of the mine and is being depreciated over the mine's useful life. The carrying amount of the provision for restoration costs is CU500,[a] which is equal to the present value of the restoration costs.

continued...

...continued

Example

The entity is testing the mine for impairment. The cash-generating unit for the mine is the mine as a whole. The entity has received various offers to buy the mine at a price of around CU800. This price reflects the fact that the buyer will assume the obligation to restore the overburden. Disposal costs for the mine are negligible. The value in use of the mine is approximately CU1,200, excluding restoration costs. The carrying amount of the mine is CU1,000.

The cash-generating unit's fair value less costs of disposal is CU800. This amount considers restoration costs that have already been provided for. As a consequence, the value in use for the cash-generating unit is determined after consideration of the restoration costs and is estimated to be CU700 (CU1,200 less CU500). The carrying amount of the cash-generating unit is CU500, which is the carrying amount of the mine (CU1,000) less the carrying amount of the provision for restoration costs (CU500). Therefore, the recoverable amount of the cash-generating unit exceeds its carrying amount.

(a) In this Standard, monetary amounts are denominated in 'currency units (CU)'.

---

79   For practical reasons, the recoverable amount of a cash-generating unit is sometimes determined after consideration of assets that are not part of the cash-generating unit (for example, receivables or other financial assets) or liabilities that have been recognised (for example, payables, pensions and other provisions). In such cases, the carrying amount of the cash-generating unit is increased by the carrying amount of those assets and decreased by the carrying amount of those liabilities.

Goodwill

Allocating goodwill to cash-generating units

80   For the purpose of impairment testing, goodwill acquired in a business combination shall, from the acquisition date, be allocated to each of the acquirer's cash-generating units, or groups of cash-generating units, that is expected to benefit from the synergies of the combination, irrespective of whether other assets or liabilities of the acquiree are assigned to those units or groups of units. Each unit or group of units to which the goodwill is so allocated shall:

(a)   represent the lowest level within the entity at which the goodwill is monitored for internal management purposes; and

(b)   not be larger than an operating segment as defined by paragraph 5 of IFRS 8 *Operating Segments* before aggregation.

81   Goodwill recognised in a business combination is an asset representing the future economic benefits arising from other assets acquired in a business combination that are not individually identified and separately recognised. Goodwill does not generate cash flows independently of other assets or groups

of assets, and often contributes to the cash flows of multiple cash-generating units. Goodwill sometimes cannot be allocated on a non-arbitrary basis to individual cash-generating units, but only to groups of cash-generating units. As a result, the lowest level within the entity at which the goodwill is monitored for internal management purposes sometimes comprises a number of cash-generating units to which the goodwill relates, but to which it cannot be allocated. References in paragraphs 83–99 and Appendix C to a cash-generating unit to which goodwill is allocated should be read as references also to a group of cash-generating units to which goodwill is allocated.

82   Applying the requirements in paragraph 80 results in goodwill being tested for impairment at a level that reflects the way an entity manages its operations and with which the goodwill would naturally be associated. Therefore, the development of additional reporting systems is typically not necessary.

83   A cash-generating unit to which goodwill is allocated for the purpose of impairment testing may not coincide with the level at which goodwill is allocated in accordance with IAS 21 *The Effects of Changes in Foreign Exchange Rates* for the purpose of measuring foreign currency gains and losses. For example, if an entity is required by IAS 21 to allocate goodwill to relatively low levels for the purpose of measuring foreign currency gains and losses, it is not required to test the goodwill for impairment at that same level unless it also monitors the goodwill at that level for internal management purposes.

84   **If the initial allocation of goodwill acquired in a business combination cannot be completed before the end of the annual period in which the business combination is effected, that initial allocation shall be completed before the end of the first annual period beginning after the acquisition date.**

85   In accordance with IFRS 3 *Business Combinations*, if the initial accounting for a business combination can be determined only provisionally by the end of the period in which the combination is effected, the acquirer:

(a)   accounts for the combination using those provisional values; and

(b)   recognises any adjustments to those provisional values as a result of completing the initial accounting within the measurement period, which will not exceed twelve months from the acquisition date.

In such circumstances, it might also not be possible to complete the initial allocation of the goodwill recognised in the combination before the end of the annual period in which the combination is effected. When this is the case, the entity discloses the information required by paragraph 133.

86   **If goodwill has been allocated to a cash-generating unit and the entity disposes of an operation within that unit, the goodwill associated with the operation disposed of shall be:**

(a)   **included in the carrying amount of the operation when determining the gain or loss on disposal; and**

(b)   measured on the basis of the relative values of the operation disposed of and the portion of the cash-generating unit retained, unless the entity can demonstrate that some other method better reflects the goodwill associated with the operation disposed of.

Example

An entity sells for CU100 an operation that was part of a cash-generating unit to which goodwill has been allocated. The goodwill allocated to the unit cannot be identified or associated with an asset group at a level lower than that unit, except arbitrarily. The recoverable amount of the portion of the cash-generating unit retained is CU300.

Because the goodwill allocated to the cash-generating unit cannot be non-arbitrarily identified or associated with an asset group at a level lower than that unit, the goodwill associated with the operation disposed of is measured on the basis of the relative values of the operation disposed of and the portion of the unit retained. Therefore, 25 per cent of the goodwill allocated to the cash-generating unit is included in the carrying amount of the operation that is sold.

---

87   If an entity reorganises its reporting structure in a way that changes the composition of one or more cash-generating units to which goodwill has been allocated, the goodwill shall be reallocated to the units affected. This reallocation shall be performed using a relative value approach similar to that used when an entity disposes of an operation within a cash-generating unit, unless the entity can demonstrate that some other method better reflects the goodwill associated with the reorganised units.

Example

Goodwill had previously been allocated to cash-generating unit A. The goodwill allocated to A cannot be identified or associated with an asset group at a level lower than A, except arbitrarily. A is to be divided and integrated into three other cash-generating units, B, C and D.

Because the goodwill allocated to A cannot be non-arbitrarily identified or associated with an asset group at a level lower than A, it is reallocated to units B, C and D on the basis of the relative values of the three portions of A before those portions are integrated with B, C and D.

Testing cash-generating units with goodwill for impairment

88   When, as described in paragraph 81, goodwill relates to a cash-generating unit but has not been allocated to that unit, the unit shall be tested for impairment, whenever there is an indication that the unit may be impaired, by comparing the unit's carrying amount, excluding any goodwill, with its recoverable amount. Any impairment loss shall be recognised in accordance with paragraph 104.

89   If a cash-generating unit described in paragraph 88 includes in its carrying amount an intangible asset that has an indefinite useful life or is not yet available for use and that asset can be tested for impairment only as part of the cash-generating unit, paragraph 10 requires the unit also to be tested for impairment annually.

90   **A cash-generating unit to which goodwill has been allocated shall be tested for impairment annually, and whenever there is an indication that the unit may be impaired, by comparing the carrying amount of the unit, including the goodwill, with the recoverable amount of the unit. If the recoverable amount of the unit exceeds the carrying amount of the unit, the unit and the goodwill allocated to that unit shall be regarded as not impaired. If the carrying amount of the unit exceeds the recoverable amount of the unit, the entity shall recognise the impairment loss in accordance with paragraph 104.**

91–95   [Deleted]

Timing of impairment tests

96   The annual impairment test for a cash-generating unit to which goodwill has been allocated may be performed at any time during an annual period, provided the test is performed at the same time every year. Different cash-generating units may be tested for impairment at different times. However, if some or all of the goodwill allocated to a cash-generating unit was acquired in a business combination during the current annual period, that unit shall be tested for impairment before the end of the current annual period.

97   If the assets constituting the cash-generating unit to which goodwill has been allocated are tested for impairment at the same time as the unit containing the goodwill, they shall be tested for impairment before the unit containing the goodwill. Similarly, if the cash-generating units constituting a group of cash-generating units to which goodwill has been allocated are tested for impairment at the same time as the group of units containing the goodwill, the individual units shall be tested for impairment before the group of units containing the goodwill.

98   At the time of impairment testing a cash-generating unit to which goodwill has been allocated, there may be an indication of an impairment of an asset within the unit containing the goodwill. In such circumstances, the entity tests the asset for impairment first, and recognises any impairment loss for that asset before testing for impairment the cash-generating unit containing the goodwill. Similarly, there may be an indication of an impairment of a cash-generating unit within a group of units containing the goodwill. In such circumstances, the entity tests the cash-generating unit for impairment first, and recognises any impairment loss for that unit, before testing for impairment the group of units to which the goodwill is allocated.

99 The most recent detailed calculation made in a preceding period of the recoverable amount of a cash-generating unit to which goodwill has been allocated may be used in the impairment test of that unit in the current period provided all of the following criteria are met:

(a) the assets and liabilities making up the unit have not changed significantly since the most recent recoverable amount calculation;

(b) the most recent recoverable amount calculation resulted in an amount that exceeded the carrying amount of the unit by a substantial margin; and

(c) based on an analysis of events that have occurred and circumstances that have changed since the most recent recoverable amount calculation, the likelihood that a current recoverable amount determination would be less than the current carrying amount of the unit is remote.

Corporate assets

100 Corporate assets include group or divisional assets such as the building of a headquarters or a division of the entity, EDP equipment or a research centre. The structure of an entity determines whether an asset meets this Standard's definition of corporate assets for a particular cash-generating unit. The distinctive characteristics of corporate assets are that they do not generate cash inflows independently of other assets or groups of assets and their carrying amount cannot be fully attributed to the cash-generating unit under review.

101 Because corporate assets do not generate separate cash inflows, the recoverable amount of an individual corporate asset cannot be determined unless management has decided to dispose of the asset. As a consequence, if there is an indication that a corporate asset may be impaired, recoverable amount is determined for the cash-generating unit or group of cash-generating units to which the corporate asset belongs, and is compared with the carrying amount of this cash-generating unit or group of cash-generating units. Any impairment loss is recognised in accordance with paragraph 104.

102 In testing a cash-generating unit for impairment, an entity shall identify all the corporate assets that relate to the cash-generating unit under review. If a portion of the carrying amount of a corporate asset:

(a) can be allocated on a reasonable and consistent basis to that unit, the entity shall compare the carrying amount of the unit, including the portion of the carrying amount of the corporate asset allocated to the unit, with its recoverable amount. Any impairment loss shall be recognised in accordance with paragraph 104.

(b) cannot be allocated on a reasonable and consistent basis to that unit, the entity shall:

(i)   compare the carrying amount of the unit, excluding the corporate asset, with its recoverable amount and recognise any impairment loss in accordance with paragraph 104;

(ii)   identify the smallest group of cash-generating units that includes the cash-generating unit under review and to which a portion of the carrying amount of the corporate asset can be allocated on a reasonable and consistent basis; and

(iii)   compare the carrying amount of that group of cash-generating units, including the portion of the carrying amount of the corporate asset allocated to that group of units, with the recoverable amount of the group of units. Any impairment loss shall be recognised in accordance with paragraph 104.

103   Illustrative Example 8 illustrates the application of these requirements to corporate assets.

Impairment loss for a cash-generating unit

104   An impairment loss shall be recognised for a cash-generating unit (the smallest group of cash-generating units to which goodwill or a corporate asset has been allocated) if, and only if, the recoverable amount of the unit (group of units) is less than the carrying amount of the unit (group of units). The impairment loss shall be allocated to reduce the carrying amount of the assets of the unit (group of units) in the following order:

(a)   first, to reduce the carrying amount of any goodwill allocated to the cash-generating unit (group of units); and

(b)   then, to the other assets of the unit (group of units) pro rata on the basis of the carrying amount of each asset in the unit (group of units).

These reductions in carrying amounts shall be treated as impairment losses on individual assets and recognised in accordance with paragraph 60.

105   In allocating an impairment loss in accordance with paragraph 104, an entity shall not reduce the carrying amount of an asset below the highest of:

(a)   its fair value less costs of disposal (if measurable);

(b)   its value in use (if determinable); and

(c)   zero.

The amount of the impairment loss that would otherwise have been allocated to the asset shall be allocated pro rata to the other assets of the unit (group of units).

106   If it is not practicable to estimate the recoverable amount of each individual asset of a cash-generating unit, this Standard requires an arbitrary allocation of an impairment loss between the assets of that unit, other than goodwill, because all assets of a cash-generating unit work together.

107   If the recoverable amount of an individual asset cannot be determined (see paragraph 67):

(a)   an impairment loss is recognised for the asset if its carrying amount is greater than the higher of its fair value less costs of disposal and the results of the allocation procedures described in paragraphs 104 and 105; and

(b)   no impairment loss is recognised for the asset if the related cash-generating unit is not impaired. This applies even if the asset's fair value less costs of disposal is less than its carrying amount.

Example

A machine has suffered physical damage but is still working, although not as well as before it was damaged. The machine's fair value less costs of disposal is less than its carrying amount. The machine does not generate independent cash inflows. The smallest identifiable group of assets that includes the machine and generates cash inflows that are largely independent of the cash inflows from other assets is the production line to which the machine belongs. The recoverable amount of the production line shows that the production line taken as a whole is not impaired.

Assumption 1: budgets/forecasts approved by management reflect no commitment of management to replace the machine.

The recoverable amount of the machine alone cannot be estimated because the machine's value in use:

(a)   may differ from its fair value less costs of disposal; and

(b)   can be determined only for the cash-generating unit to which the machine belongs (the production line).

The production line is not impaired. Therefore, no impairment loss is recognised for the machine. Nevertheless, the entity may need to reassess the depreciation period or the depreciation method for the machine. Perhaps a shorter depreciation period or a faster depreciation method is required to reflect the expected remaining useful life of the machine or the pattern in which economic benefits are expected to be consumed by the entity.

continued...

...continued

Example
Assumption 2: budgets/forecasts approved by management reflect a commitment of management to replace the machine and sell it in the near future. Cash flows from continuing use of the machine until its disposal are estimated to be negligible. *The machine's value in use can be estimated to be close to its fair value less costs of disposal. Therefore, the recoverable amount of the machine can be determined and no consideration is given to the cash-generating unit to which the machine belongs (ie the production line). Because the machine's fair value less costs of disposal is less than its carrying amount, an impairment loss is recognised for the machine.*

108   After the requirements in paragraphs 104 and 105 have been applied, a liability shall be recognised for any remaining amount of an impairment loss for a cash-generating unit if, and only if, that is required by another IFRS.

Reversing an impairment loss

109   Paragraphs 110–116 set out the requirements for reversing an impairment loss recognised for an asset or a cash-generating unit in prior periods. These requirements use the term 'an asset' but apply equally to an individual asset or a cash-generating unit. Additional requirements for an individual asset are set out in paragraphs 117–121, for a cash-generating unit in paragraphs 122 and 123 and for goodwill in paragraphs 124 and 125.

110   An entity shall assess at the end of each reporting period whether there is any indication that an impairment loss recognised in prior periods for an asset other than goodwill may no longer exist or may have decreased. If any such indication exists, the entity shall estimate the recoverable amount of that asset.

111   In assessing whether there is any indication that an impairment loss recognised in prior periods for an asset other than goodwill may no longer exist or may have decreased, an entity shall consider, as a minimum, the following indications:

External sources of information

(a)   there are observable indications that the asset's value has increased significantly during the period.

(b)   significant changes with a favourable effect on the entity have taken place during the period, or will take place in the near future, in the technological, market, economic or legal environment in which the entity operates or in the market to which the asset is dedicated.

    (c)   market interest rates or other market rates of return on investments have decreased during the period, and those decreases are likely to affect the discount rate used in calculating the asset's value in use and increase the asset's recoverable amount materially.

Internal sources of information

    (d)   significant changes with a favourable effect on the entity have taken place during the period, or are expected to take place in the near future, in the extent to which, or manner in which, the asset is used or is expected to be used. These changes include costs incurred during the period to improve or enhance the asset's performance or restructure the operation to which the asset belongs.

    (e)   evidence is available from internal reporting that indicates that the economic performance of the asset is, or will be, better than expected.

112   Indications of a potential decrease in an impairment loss in paragraph 111 mainly mirror the indications of a potential impairment loss in paragraph 12.

113   If there is an indication that an impairment loss recognised for an asset other than goodwill may no longer exist or may have decreased, this may indicate that the remaining useful life, the depreciation (amortisation) method or the residual value may need to be reviewed and adjusted in accordance with the IFRS applicable to the asset, even if no impairment loss is reversed for the asset.

114   An impairment loss recognised in prior periods for an asset other than goodwill shall be reversed if, and only if, there has been a change in the estimates used to determine the asset's recoverable amount since the last impairment loss was recognised. If this is the case, the carrying amount of the asset shall, except as described in paragraph 117, be increased to its recoverable amount. That increase is a reversal of an impairment loss.

115   A reversal of an impairment loss reflects an increase in the estimated service potential of an asset, either from use or from sale, since the date when an entity last recognised an impairment loss for that asset. Paragraph 130 requires an entity to identify the change in estimates that causes the increase in estimated service potential. Examples of changes in estimates include:

    (a)   a change in the basis for recoverable amount (ie whether recoverable amount is based on fair value less costs of disposal or value in use);

    (b)   if recoverable amount was based on value in use, a change in the amount or timing of estimated future cash flows or in the discount rate; or

    (c)   if recoverable amount was based on fair value less costs of disposal, a change in estimate of the components of fair value less costs of disposal.

116 An asset's value in use may become greater than the asset's carrying amount simply because the present value of future cash inflows increases as they become closer. However, the service potential of the asset has not increased. Therefore, an impairment loss is not reversed just because of the passage of time (sometimes called the 'unwinding' of the discount), even if the recoverable amount of the asset becomes higher than its carrying amount.

Reversing an impairment loss for an individual asset

117 The increased carrying amount of an asset other than goodwill attributable to a reversal of an impairment loss shall not exceed the carrying amount that would have been determined (net of amortisation or depreciation) had no impairment loss been recognised for the asset in prior years.

118 Any increase in the carrying amount of an asset other than goodwill above the carrying amount that would have been determined (net of amortisation or depreciation) had no impairment loss been recognised for the asset in prior years is a revaluation. In accounting for such a revaluation, an entity applies the IFRS applicable to the asset.

119 A reversal of an impairment loss for an asset other than goodwill shall be recognised immediately in profit or loss, unless the asset is carried at revalued amount in accordance with another IFRS (for example, the revaluation model in IAS 16). Any reversal of an impairment loss of a revalued asset shall be treated as a revaluation increase in accordance with that other IFRS.

120 A reversal of an impairment loss on a revalued asset is recognised in other comprehensive income and increases the revaluation surplus for that asset. However, to the extent that an impairment loss on the same revalued asset was previously recognised in profit or loss, a reversal of that impairment loss is also recognised in profit or loss.

121 After a reversal of an impairment loss is recognised, the depreciation (amortisation) charge for the asset shall be adjusted in future periods to allocate the asset's revised carrying amount, less its residual value (if any), on a systematic basis over its remaining useful life.

Reversing an impairment loss for a cash-generating unit

122 A reversal of an impairment loss for a cash-generating unit shall be allocated to the assets of the unit, except for goodwill, pro rata with the carrying amounts of those assets. These increases in carrying amounts shall be treated as reversals of impairment losses for individual assets and recognised in accordance with paragraph 119.

123 In allocating a reversal of an impairment loss for a cash-generating unit in accordance with paragraph 122, the carrying amount of an asset shall not be increased above the lower of:

(a) its recoverable amount (if determinable); and

(b)   the carrying amount that would have been determined (net of amortisation or depreciation) had no impairment loss been recognised for the asset in prior periods.

The amount of the reversal of the impairment loss that would otherwise have been allocated to the asset shall be allocated pro rata to the other assets of the unit, except for goodwill.

Reversing an impairment loss for goodwill

124   An impairment loss recognised for goodwill shall not be reversed in a subsequent period.

125   IAS 38 *Intangible Assets* prohibits the recognition of internally generated goodwill. Any increase in the recoverable amount of goodwill in the periods following the recognition of an impairment loss for that goodwill is likely to be an increase in internally generated goodwill, rather than a reversal of the impairment loss recognised for the acquired goodwill.

Disclosure

126   An entity shall disclose the following for each class of assets:

(a)   the amount of impairment losses recognised in profit or loss during the period and the line item(s) of the statement of comprehensive income in which those impairment losses are included.

(b)   the amount of reversals of impairment losses recognised in profit or loss during the period and the line item(s) of the statement of comprehensive income in which those impairment losses are reversed.

(c)   the amount of impairment losses on revalued assets recognised in other comprehensive income during the period.

(d)   the amount of reversals of impairment losses on revalued assets recognised in other comprehensive income during the period.

127   A class of assets is a grouping of assets of similar nature and use in an entity's operations.

128   The information required in paragraph 126 may be presented with other information disclosed for the class of assets. For example, this information may be included in a reconciliation of the carrying amount of property, plant and equipment, at the beginning and end of the period, as required by IAS 16.

129   An entity that reports segment information in accordance with IFRS 8 shall disclose the following for each reportable segment:

(a)   the amount of impairment losses recognised in profit or loss and in other comprehensive income during the period.

(b)   the amount of reversals of impairment losses recognised in profit or loss and in other comprehensive income during the period.

130   An entity shall disclose the following for an individual asset (including goodwill) or a cash-generating unit, for which an impairment loss has been recognised or reversed during the period:

(a)   the events and circumstances that led to the recognition or reversal of the impairment loss.

(b)   the amount of the impairment loss recognised or reversed.

(c)   for an individual asset:

   (i)   the nature of the asset; and

   (ii)   if the entity reports segment information in accordance with IFRS 8, the reportable segment to which the asset belongs.

(d)   for a cash-generating unit:

   (i)   a description of the cash-generating unit (such as whether it is a product line, a plant, a business operation, a geographical area, or a reportable segment as defined in IFRS 8);

   (ii)   the amount of the impairment loss recognised or reversed by class of assets and, if the entity reports segment information in accordance with IFRS 8, by reportable segment; and

   (iii) if the aggregation of assets for identifying the cash-generating unit has changed since the previous estimate of the cash-generating unit's recoverable amount (if any), a description of the current and former way of aggregating assets and the reasons for changing the way the cash-generating unit is identified.

(e)   the recoverable amount of the asset (cash-generating unit) and whether the recoverable amount of the asset (cash-generating unit) is its fair value less costs of disposal or its value in use.

(f)   if the recoverable amount is fair value less costs of disposal, the entity shall disclose the following information:

   (i)   the level of the fair value hierarchy (see IFRS 13) within which the fair value measurement of the asset (cash-generating unit) is categorised in its entirety (without taking into account whether the 'costs of disposal' are observable);

   (ii)   for fair value measurements categorised within Level 2 and Level 3 of the fair value hierarchy, a description of the valuation technique(s) used to measure fair value less costs of disposal. If there has been a change in valuation technique, the entity shall disclose that change and the reason(s) for making it; and

(iii)   for fair value measurements categorised within Level 2 and Level 3 of the fair value hierarchy, each key assumption on which management has based its determination of fair value less costs of disposal. Key assumptions are those to which the asset's (cash-generating unit's) recoverable amount is most sensitive. The entity shall also disclose the discount rate(s) used in the current measurement and previous measurement if fair value less costs of disposal is measured using a present value technique.

(g)   if recoverable amount is value in use, the discount rate(s) used in the current estimate and previous estimate (if any) of value in use.

131   An entity shall disclose the following information for the aggregate impairment losses and the aggregate reversals of impairment losses recognised during the period for which no information is disclosed in accordance with paragraph 130:

(a)   the main classes of assets affected by impairment losses and the main classes of assets affected by reversals of impairment losses.

(b)   the main events and circumstances that led to the recognition of these impairment losses and reversals of impairment losses.

132   An entity is encouraged to disclose assumptions used to determine the recoverable amount of assets (cash-generating units) during the period. However, paragraph 134 requires an entity to disclose information about the estimates used to measure the recoverable amount of a cash-generating unit when goodwill or an intangible asset with an indefinite useful life is included in the carrying amount of that unit.

133   If, in accordance with paragraph 84, any portion of the goodwill acquired in a business combination during the period has not been allocated to a cash-generating unit (group of units) at the end of the reporting period, the amount of the unallocated goodwill shall be disclosed together with the reasons why that amount remains unallocated.

Estimates used to measure recoverable amounts of cash-generating units containing goodwill or intangible assets with indefinite useful lives

134   An entity shall disclose the information required by (a)–(f) for each cash-generating unit (group of units) for which the carrying amount of goodwill or intangible assets with indefinite useful lives allocated to that unit (group of units) is significant in comparison with the entity's total carrying amount of goodwill or intangible assets with indefinite useful lives:

(a)   the carrying amount of goodwill allocated to the unit (group of units).

(b)   the carrying amount of intangible assets with indefinite useful lives allocated to the unit (group of units).

    (c)   the basis on which the unit's (group of units') recoverable amount has been determined (ie value in use or fair value less costs of disposal).

    (d)   if the unit's (group of units') recoverable amount is based on value in use:

        (i)   each key assumption on which management has based its cash flow projections for the period covered by the most recent budgets/forecasts. Key assumptions are those to which the unit's (group of units') recoverable amount is most sensitive.

        (ii)   a description of management's approach to determining the value(s) assigned to each key assumption, whether those value(s) reflect past experience or, if appropriate, are consistent with external sources of information, and, if not, how and why they differ from past experience or external sources of information.

        (iii)   the period over which management has projected cash flows based on financial budgets/forecasts approved by management and, when a period greater than five years is used for a cash-generating unit (group of units), an explanation of why that longer period is justified.

        (iv)   the growth rate used to extrapolate cash flow projections beyond the period covered by the most recent budgets/forecasts, and the justification for using any growth rate that exceeds the long-term average growth rate for the products, industries, or country or countries in which the entity operates, or for the market to which the unit (group of units) is dedicated.

        (v)   the discount rate(s) applied to the cash flow projections.

    (e)   if the unit's (group of units') recoverable amount is based on fair value less costs of disposal, the valuation technique(s) used to measure fair value less costs of disposal. An entity is not required to provide the disclosures required by IFRS 13. If fair value less costs of disposal is not measured using a quoted price for an identical unit (group of units), an entity shall disclose the following information:

        (i)   each key assumption on which management has based its determination of fair value less costs of disposal. Key assumptions are those to which the unit's (group of units') recoverable amount is most sensitive.

        (ii)   a description of management's approach to determining the value (or values) assigned to each key assumption, whether those values reflect past experience or, if appropriate, are consistent with external sources of information, and, if not, how and why they differ from past experience or external sources of information.

(iiA)   the level of the fair value hierarchy (see IFRS 13) within which the fair value measurement is categorised in its entirety (without giving regard to the observability of 'costs of disposal').

(iiB)   if there has been a change in valuation technique, the change and the reason(s) for making it.

If fair value less costs of disposal is measured using discounted cash flow projections, an entity shall disclose the following information:

(iii)   the period over which management has projected cash flows.

(iv)   the growth rate used to extrapolate cash flow projections.

(v)   the discount rate(s) applied to the cash flow projections.

(f)   if a reasonably possible change in a key assumption on which management has based its determination of the unit's (group of units') recoverable amount would cause the unit's (group of units') carrying amount to exceed its recoverable amount:

(i)   the amount by which the unit's (group of units') recoverable amount exceeds its carrying amount.

(ii)   the value assigned to the key assumption.

(iii)   the amount by which the value assigned to the key assumption must change, after incorporating any consequential effects of that change on the other variables used to measure recoverable amount, in order for the unit's (group of units') recoverable amount to be equal to its carrying amount.

135   If some or all of the carrying amount of goodwill or intangible assets with indefinite useful lives is allocated across multiple cash-generating units (groups of units), and the amount so allocated to each unit (group of units) is not significant in comparison with the entity's total carrying amount of goodwill or intangible assets with indefinite useful lives, that fact shall be disclosed, together with the aggregate carrying amount of goodwill or intangible assets with indefinite useful lives allocated to those units (groups of units). In addition, if the recoverable amounts of any of those units (groups of units) are based on the same key assumption(s) and the aggregate carrying amount of goodwill or intangible assets with indefinite useful lives allocated to them is significant in comparison with the entity's total carrying amount of goodwill or intangible assets with indefinite useful lives, an entity shall disclose that fact, together with:

(a)   the aggregate carrying amount of goodwill allocated to those units (groups of units).

(b)   the aggregate carrying amount of intangible assets with indefinite useful lives allocated to those units (groups of units).

(c)   a description of the key assumption(s).

(d)   a description of management's approach to determining the value(s) assigned to the key assumption(s), whether those value(s) reflect past experience or, if appropriate, are consistent with external sources of information, and, if not, how and why they differ from past experience or external sources of information.

(e)   if a reasonably possible change in the key assumption(s) would cause the aggregate of the units' (groups of units') carrying amounts to exceed the aggregate of their recoverable amounts:

    (i)   the amount by which the aggregate of the units' (groups of units') recoverable amounts exceeds the aggregate of their carrying amounts.

    (ii)   the value(s) assigned to the key assumption(s).

    (iii)   the amount by which the value(s) assigned to the key assumption(s) must change, after incorporating any consequential effects of the change on the other variables used to measure recoverable amount, in order for the aggregate of the units' (groups of units') recoverable amounts to be equal to the aggregate of their carrying amounts.

136   The most recent detailed calculation made in a preceding period of the recoverable amount of a cash-generating unit (group of units) may, in accordance with paragraph 24 or 99, be carried forward and used in the impairment test for that unit (group of units) in the current period provided specified criteria are met. When this is the case, the information for that unit (group of units) that is incorporated into the disclosures required by paragraphs 134 and 135 relate to the carried forward calculation of recoverable amount.

137   Illustrative Example 9 illustrates the disclosures required by paragraphs 134 and 135.

Transition provisions and effective date

138   [Deleted]

139   An entity shall apply this Standard:

(a)   to goodwill and intangible assets acquired in business combinations for which the agreement date is on or after 31 March 2004; and

(b)   to all other assets prospectively from the beginning of the first annual period beginning on or after 31 March 2004.

140   Entities to which paragraph 139 applies are encouraged to apply the requirements of this Standard before the effective dates specified in paragraph 139. However, if an entity applies this Standard before those effective dates, it also shall apply IFRS 3 and IAS 38 (as revised in 2004) at the same time.

140A   IAS 1 *Presentation of Financial Statements* (as revised in 2007) amended the terminology used throughout IFRSs. In addition it amended paragraphs 61, 120, 126 and 129. An entity shall apply those amendments for annual periods beginning on or after 1 January 2009. If an entity applies IAS 1 (revised 2007) for an earlier period, the amendments shall be applied for that earlier period.

140B   IFRS 3 (as revised in 2008) amended paragraphs 65, 81, 85 and 139, deleted paragraphs 91–95 and 138 and added Appendix C. An entity shall apply those amendments for annual periods beginning on or after 1 July 2009. If an entity applies IFRS 3 (revised 2008) for an earlier period, the amendments shall also be applied for that earlier period.

140C   Paragraph 134(e) was amended by *Improvements to IFRSs* issued in May 2008. An entity shall apply that amendment for annual periods beginning on or after 1 January 2009. Earlier application is permitted. If an entity applies the amendment for an earlier period it shall disclose that fact.

140D   *Cost of an Investment in a Subsidiary, Jointly Controlled Entity or Associate* (Amendments to IFRS 1 *First-time Adoption of International Financial Reporting Standards* and IAS 27), issued in May 2008, added paragraph 12(h). An entity shall apply that amendment prospectively for annual periods beginning on or after 1 January 2009. Earlier application is permitted. If an entity applies the related amendments in paragraphs 4 and 38A of IAS 27 for an earlier period, it shall apply the amendment in paragraph 12(h) at the same time.

140E   *Improvements to IFRSs* issued in April 2009 amended paragraph 80(b). An entity shall apply that amendment prospectively for annual periods beginning on or after 1 January 2010. Earlier application is permitted. If an entity applies the amendment for an earlier period it shall disclose that fact.

140F   [Deleted]

140G   [Deleted]

140H   IFRS 10 and IFRS 11, issued in May 2011, amended paragraph 4, the heading above paragraph 12(h) and paragraph 12(h). An entity shall apply those amendments when it applies IFRS 10 and IFRS 11.

140I   IFRS 13, issued in May 2011, amended paragraphs 5, 6, 12, 20, 22, 28, 78, 105, 111, 130 and 134, deleted paragraphs 25–27 and added paragraph 53A. An entity shall apply those amendments when it applies IFRS 13.

140J   In May 2013 paragraphs 130 and 134 and the heading above paragraph 138 were amended. An entity shall apply those amendments retrospectively for annual periods beginning on or after 1 January 2014. Earlier application is permitted. An entity shall not apply those amendments in periods (including comparative periods) in which it does not also apply IFRS 13.

140K   [Deleted]

140L   IFRS 15 *Revenue from Contracts with Customers*, issued in May 2014, amended paragraph 2. An entity shall apply that amendment when it applies IFRS 15.

140M   IFRS 9, as issued in July 2014, amended paragraphs 2, 4 and 5 and deleted paragraphs 140F, 140G and 140K. An entity shall apply those amendments when it applies IFRS 9.

140N   *[This paragraph refers to amendments that are not yet effective, and is therefore not included in this edition.]*

Withdrawal of IAS 36 (issued 1998)

141   This Standard supersedes IAS 36 *Impairment of Assets* (issued in 1998).

Appendix A
Using present value techniques to measure value in use

This appendix is an integral part of the Standard. It provides guidance on the use of present value techniques in measuring value in use. Although the guidance uses the term 'asset', it equally applies to a group of assets forming a cash-generating unit.

The components of a present value measurement

A1   The following elements together capture the economic differences between assets:

   (a)   an estimate of the future cash flow, or in more complex cases, series of future cash flows the entity expects to derive from the asset;

   (b)   expectations about possible variations in the amount or timing of those cash flows;

   (c)   the time value of money, represented by the current market risk-free rate of interest;

   (d)   the price for bearing the uncertainty inherent in the asset; and

   (e)   other, sometimes unidentifiable, factors (such as illiquidity) that market participants would reflect in pricing the future cash flows the entity expects to derive from the asset.

A2   This appendix contrasts two approaches to computing present value, either of which may be used to estimate the value in use of an asset, depending on the circumstances. Under the 'traditional' approach, adjustments for factors (b)–(e) described in paragraph A1 are embedded in the discount rate. Under the 'expected cash flow' approach, factors (b), (d) and (e) cause adjustments in arriving at risk-adjusted expected cash flows. Whichever approach an entity adopts to reflect expectations about possible variations in the amount or timing of future cash flows, the result should be to reflect the expected present value of the future cash flows, ie the weighted average of all possible outcomes.

General principles

A3   The techniques used to estimate future cash flows and interest rates will vary from one situation to another depending on the circumstances surrounding the asset in question. However, the following general principles govern any application of present value techniques in measuring assets:

   (a)   interest rates used to discount cash flows should reflect assumptions that are consistent with those inherent in the estimated cash flows. Otherwise, the effect of some assumptions will be double-counted or ignored. For example, a discount rate of 12 per cent might be applied to contractual cash flows of a loan receivable. That rate reflects expectations about future defaults from loans with particular characteristics. That same 12 per cent rate should not be used to discount expected cash flows because those cash flows already reflect assumptions about future defaults.

(b)   estimated cash flows and discount rates should be free from both bias and factors unrelated to the asset in question. For example, deliberately understating estimated net cash flows to enhance the apparent future profitability of an asset introduces a bias into the measurement.

(c)   estimated cash flows or discount rates should reflect the range of possible outcomes rather than a single most likely, minimum or maximum possible amount.

Traditional and expected cash flow approaches to present value

Traditional approach

A4   Accounting applications of present value have traditionally used a single set of estimated cash flows and a single discount rate, often described as 'the rate commensurate with the risk'. In effect, the traditional approach assumes that a single discount rate convention can incorporate all the expectations about the future cash flows and the appropriate risk premium. Therefore, the traditional approach places most of the emphasis on selection of the discount rate.

A5   In some circumstances, such as those in which comparable assets can be observed in the marketplace, a traditional approach is relatively easy to apply. For assets with contractual cash flows, it is consistent with the manner in which marketplace participants describe assets, as in 'a 12 per cent bond'.

A6   However, the traditional approach may not appropriately address some complex measurement problems, such as the measurement of non-financial assets for which no market for the item or a comparable item exists. A proper search for 'the rate commensurate with the risk' requires analysis of at least two items—an asset that exists in the marketplace and has an observed interest rate and the asset being measured. The appropriate discount rate for the cash flows being measured must be inferred from the observable rate of interest in that other asset. To draw that inference, the characteristics of the other asset's cash flows must be similar to those of the asset being measured. Therefore, the measurer must do the following:

(a)   identify the set of cash flows that will be discounted;

(b)   identify another asset in the marketplace that appears to have similar cash flow characteristics;

(c)   compare the cash flow sets from the two items to ensure that they are similar (for example, are both sets contractual cash flows, or is one contractual and the other an estimated cash flow?);

(d)   evaluate whether there is an element in one item that is not present in the other (for example, is one less liquid than the other?); and

(e)   evaluate whether both sets of cash flows are likely to behave (ie vary) in a similar fashion in changing economic conditions.

Expected cash flow approach

A7   The expected cash flow approach is, in some situations, a more effective measurement tool than the traditional approach. In developing a measurement, the expected cash flow approach uses all expectations about possible cash flows instead of the single most likely cash flow. For example, a cash flow might be CU100, CU200 or CU300 with probabilities of 10 per cent, 60 per cent and 30 per cent, respectively. The expected cash flow is CU220. The expected cash flow approach thus differs from the traditional approach by focusing on direct analysis of the cash flows in question and on more explicit statements of the assumptions used in the measurement.

A8   The expected cash flow approach also allows use of present value techniques when the timing of cash flows is uncertain. For example, a cash flow of CU1,000 may be received in one year, two years or three years with probabilities of 10 per cent, 60 per cent and 30 per cent, respectively. The example below shows the computation of expected present value in that situation.

Present value of CU1,000 in 1 year at 5%	CU952.38	
Probability	10.00%	CU95.24
Present value of CU1,000 in 2 years at 5.25%	CU902.73	
Probability	60.00%	CU541.64
Present value of CU1,000 in 3 years at 5.50%	CU851.61	
Probability	30.00%	CU255.48
Expected present value		CU892.36

A9   The expected present value of CU892.36 differs from the traditional notion of a best estimate of CU902.73 (the 60 per cent probability). A traditional present value computation applied to this example requires a decision about which of the possible timings of cash flows to use and, accordingly, would not reflect the probabilities of other timings. This is because the discount rate in a traditional present value computation cannot reflect uncertainties in timing.

A10   The use of probabilities is an essential element of the expected cash flow approach. Some question whether assigning probabilities to highly subjective estimates suggests greater precision than, in fact, exists. However, the proper application of the traditional approach (as described in paragraph A6) requires the same estimates and subjectivity without providing the computational transparency of the expected cash flow approach.

A11   Many estimates developed in current practice already incorporate the elements of expected cash flows informally. In addition, accountants often face the need to measure an asset using limited information about the probabilities of possible cash flows. For example, an accountant might be confronted with the following situations:

(a)   the estimated amount falls somewhere between CU50 and CU250, but no amount in the range is more likely than any other amount. Based on that limited information, the estimated expected cash flow is CU150 [(50 + 250)/2].

(b)   the estimated amount falls somewhere between CU50 and CU250, and the most likely amount is CU100. However, the probabilities attached to each amount are unknown. Based on that limited information, the estimated expected cash flow is CU133.33 [(50 + 100 + 250)/3].

(c)   the estimated amount will be CU50 (10 per cent probability), CU250 (30 per cent probability), or CU100 (60 per cent probability). Based on that limited information, the estimated expected cash flow is CU140 [(50 × 0.10) + (250 × 0.30) + (100 × 0.60)].

In each case, the estimated expected cash flow is likely to provide a better estimate of value in use than the minimum, most likely or maximum amount taken alone.

A12   The application of an expected cash flow approach is subject to a cost-benefit constraint. In some cases, an entity may have access to extensive data and may be able to develop many cash flow scenarios. In other cases, an entity may not be able to develop more than general statements about the variability of cash flows without incurring substantial cost. The entity needs to balance the cost of obtaining additional information against the additional reliability that information will bring to the measurement.

A13   Some maintain that expected cash flow techniques are inappropriate for measuring a single item or an item with a limited number of possible outcomes. They offer an example of an asset with two possible outcomes: a 90 per cent probability that the cash flow will be CU10 and a 10 per cent probability that the cash flow will be CU1,000. They observe that the expected cash flow in that example is CU109 and criticise that result as not representing either of the amounts that may ultimately be paid.

A14   Assertions like the one just outlined reflect underlying disagreement with the measurement objective. If the objective is accumulation of costs to be incurred, expected cash flows may not produce a representationally faithful estimate of the expected cost. However, this Standard is concerned with measuring the recoverable amount of an asset. The recoverable amount of the asset in this example is not likely to be CU10, even though that is the most likely cash flow. This is because a measurement of CU10 does not incorporate the uncertainty of the cash flow in the measurement of the asset. Instead, the uncertain cash flow is presented as if it were a certain cash flow. No rational entity would sell an asset with these characteristics for CU10.

Discount rate

A15   Whichever approach an entity adopts for measuring the value in use of an asset, interest rates used to discount cash flows should not reflect risks for which the estimated cash flows have been adjusted. Otherwise, the effect of some assumptions will be double-counted.

A16   When an asset-specific rate is not directly available from the market, an entity uses surrogates to estimate the discount rate. The purpose is to estimate, as far as possible, a market assessment of:

    (a)   the time value of money for the periods until the end of the asset's useful life; and

    (b)   factors (b), (d) and (e) described in paragraph A1, to the extent those factors have not caused adjustments in arriving at estimated cash flows.

A17   As a starting point in making such an estimate, the entity might take into account the following rates:

    (a)   the entity's weighted average cost of capital determined using techniques such as the Capital Asset Pricing Model;

    (b)   the entity's incremental borrowing rate; and

    (c)   other market borrowing rates.

A18   However, these rates must be adjusted:

    (a)   to reflect the way that the market would assess the specific risks associated with the asset's estimated cash flows; and

    (b)   to exclude risks that are not relevant to the asset's estimated cash flows or for which the estimated cash flows have been adjusted.

Consideration should be given to risks such as country risk, currency risk and price risk.

A19   The discount rate is independent of the entity's capital structure and the way the entity financed the purchase of the asset, because the future cash flows expected to arise from an asset do not depend on the way in which the entity financed the purchase of the asset.

A20   Paragraph 55 requires the discount rate used to be a pre-tax rate. Therefore, when the basis used to estimate the discount rate is post-tax, that basis is adjusted to reflect a pre-tax rate.

A21   An entity normally uses a single discount rate for the estimate of an asset's value in use. However, an entity uses separate discount rates for different future periods where value in use is sensitive to a difference in risks for different periods or to the term structure of interest rates.

Appendix B
Amendment to IAS 16

The amendment in this appendix shall be applied when an entity applies IAS 16 Property, Plant and Equipment (as revised in 2003). It is superseded when IAS 36 Impairment of Assets (as revised in 2004) becomes effective. This appendix replaces the consequential amendments made by IAS 16 (as revised in 2003) to IAS 36 Impairment of Assets (issued in 1998). IAS 36 (as revised in 2004) incorporates the requirements of the paragraphs in this appendix. Consequently, the amendments from IAS 16 (as revised in 2003) are not necessary once an entity is subject to IAS 36 (as revised in 2004). Accordingly, this appendix is applicable only to entities that elect to apply IAS 16 (as revised in 2003) before its effective date.

* * * * *

The text of this appendix has been omitted from this volume.

Appendix C
Impairment testing cash-generating units with goodwill and non-controlling interests

This appendix is an integral part of the Standard.

C1   In accordance with IFRS 3 (as revised in 2008), the acquirer measures and recognises goodwill as of the acquisition date as the excess of (a) over (b) below:

(a)   the aggregate of:

(i)   the consideration transferred measured in accordance with IFRS 3, which generally requires acquisition-date fair value;

(ii)   the amount of any non-controlling interest in the acquiree measured in accordance with IFRS 3; and

(iii)   in a business combination achieved in stages, the acquisition-date fair value of the acquirer's previously held equity interest in the acquiree.

(b)   the net of the acquisition-date amounts of the identifiable assets acquired and liabilities assumed measured in accordance with IFRS 3.

Allocation of goodwill

C2   Paragraph 80 of this Standard requires goodwill acquired in a business combination to be allocated to each of the acquirer's cash-generating units, or groups of cash-generating units, expected to benefit from the synergies of the combination, irrespective of whether other assets or liabilities of the acquiree are assigned to those units, or groups of units. It is possible that some of the synergies resulting from a business combination will be allocated to a cash-generating unit in which the non-controlling interest does not have an interest.

Testing for impairment

C3   Testing for impairment involves comparing the recoverable amount of a cash-generating unit with the carrying amount of the cash-generating unit.

C4   If an entity measures non-controlling interests as its proportionate interest in the net identifiable assets of a subsidiary at the acquisition date, rather than at fair value, goodwill attributable to non-controlling interests is included in the recoverable amount of the related cash-generating unit but is not recognised in the parent's consolidated financial statements. As a consequence, an entity shall gross up the carrying amount of goodwill allocated to the unit to include the goodwill attributable to the non-controlling interest. This adjusted carrying amount is then compared with the recoverable amount of the unit to determine whether the cash-generating unit is impaired.

Allocating an impairment loss

C5   Paragraph 104 requires any identified impairment loss to be allocated first to reduce the carrying amount of goodwill allocated to the unit and then to the other assets of the unit pro rata on the basis of the carrying amount of each asset in the unit.

C6   If a subsidiary, or part of a subsidiary, with a non-controlling interest is itself a cash-generating unit, the impairment loss is allocated between the parent and the non-controlling interest on the same basis as that on which profit or loss is allocated.

C7   If a subsidiary, or part of a subsidiary, with a non-controlling interest is part of a larger cash-generating unit, goodwill impairment losses are allocated to the parts of the cash-generating unit that have a non-controlling interest and the parts that do not. The impairment losses should be allocated to the parts of the cash-generating unit on the basis of:

(a)   to the extent that the impairment relates to goodwill in the cash-generating unit, the relative carrying values of the goodwill of the parts before the impairment; and

(b)   to the extent that the impairment relates to identifiable assets in the cash-generating unit, the relative carrying values of the net identifiable assets of the parts before the impairment. Any such impairment is allocated to the assets of the parts of each unit pro rata on the basis of the carrying amount of each asset in the part.

In those parts that have a non-controlling interest, the impairment loss is allocated between the parent and the non-controlling interest on the same basis as that on which profit or loss is allocated.

C8   If an impairment loss attributable to a non-controlling interest relates to goodwill that is not recognised in the parent's consolidated financial statements (see paragraph C4), that impairment is not recognised as a goodwill impairment loss. In such cases, only the impairment loss relating to the goodwill that is allocated to the parent is recognised as a goodwill impairment loss.

C9   Illustrative Example 7 illustrates the impairment testing of a non-wholly-owned cash-generating unit with goodwill.

Approval by the Board of IAS 36 issued in March 2004

International Accounting Standard 36 *Impairment of Assets* (as revised in 2004) was approved for issue by eleven of the fourteen members of the International Accounting Standards Board. Messrs Cope and Leisenring and Professor Whittington dissented. Their dissenting opinions are set out after the Basis for Conclusions.

Sir David Tweedie	Chairman
Thomas E Jones	Vice-Chairman
Mary E Barth	
Hans-Georg Bruns	
Anthony T Cope	
Robert P Garnett	
Gilbert Gélard	
James J Leisenring	
Warren J McGregor	
Patricia L O'Malley	
Harry K Schmid	
John T Smith	
Geoffrey Whittington	
Tatsumi Yamada	

Approval by the Board of *Recoverable Amount Disclosures for Non-Financial Assets* (Amendments to IAS 36) issued in May 2013

Recoverable Amount Disclosures for Non-Financial Assets was approved for issue by fifteen members of the International Accounting Standards Board (IASB). Mr Kabureck abstained from voting in view of his recent appointment to the IASB.

Hans Hoogervorst	Chairman
Ian Mackintosh	Vice-Chairman
Stephen Cooper	
Philippe Danjou	
Martin Edelmann	
Jan Engström	
Patrick Finnegan	
Amaro Luiz de Oliveira Gomes	
Gary Kabureck	
Prabhakar Kalavacherla	
Patricia McConnell	
Takatsugu Ochi	
Darrel Scott	
Chungwoo Suh	
Mary Tokar	
Wei-Guo Zhang	

IAS 37

Provisions, Contingent Liabilities and Contingent Assets

In April 2001 the International Accounting Standards Board adopted IAS 37 *Provisions, Contingent Liabilities and Contingent Assets*, which had originally been issued by the International Accounting Standards Committee in September 1998. That standard replaced parts of IAS 10 *Contingencies and Events Occurring after the Balance Sheet Date* that was issued in 1978 and that dealt with contingencies.

In May 2020 the Board issued *Onerous Contracts—Cost of Fulfilling a Contract*. This amended IAS 37 to clarify that for the purpose of assessing whether a contract is onerous, the cost of fulfilling the contract includes both the incremental costs of fulfilling that contract and an allocation of other costs that relate directly to fulfilling contracts.

Other Standards have made minor consequential amendments to IAS 37. They include IFRS 9 *Financial Instruments* (Hedge Accounting and amendments to IFRS 9, IFRS 7 and IAS 39) (issued November 2013), *Annual Improvements to IFRSs 2010–2012 Cycle* (issued December 2013), IFRS 15 *Revenue from Contracts with Customers* (issued May 2014), IFRS 9 *Financial Instruments* (issued July 2014), IFRS 16 *Leases* (issued January 2016), *Amendments to References to the Conceptual Framework in IFRS Standards* (issued March 2018) and *Definition of Material* (Amendments to IAS 1 and IAS 8) (issued October 2018).

Contents

FOR THE ACCOMPANYING GUIDANCE LISTED BELOW, SEE PART B OF THIS EDITION

IMPLEMENTATION GUIDANCE

FOR THE BASIS FOR CONCLUSIONS, SEE PART C OF THIS EDITION

BASIS FOR CONCLUSIONS

International Accounting Standard 37 *Provisions, Contingent Liabilities and Contingent Assets* (IAS 37) is set out in paragraphs 1–105. All the paragraphs have equal authority but retain the IASC format of the Standard when it was adopted by the IASB. IAS 37 should be read in the context of its objective, the *Preface to IFRS Standards* and the *Conceptual Framework for Financial Reporting*. IAS 8 *Accounting Policies, Changes in Accounting Estimates and Errors* provides a basis for selecting and applying accounting policies in the absence of explicit guidance.

International Accounting Standard 37
Provisions, Contingent Liabilities and Contingent Assets

Objective

The objective of this Standard is to ensure that appropriate recognition criteria and measurement bases are applied to provisions, contingent liabilities and contingent assets and that sufficient information is disclosed in the notes to enable users to understand their nature, timing and amount.

Scope

1   **This Standard shall be applied by all entities in accounting for provisions, contingent liabilities and contingent assets, except:**

   (a)   **those resulting from executory contracts, except where the contract is onerous; and**

   (b)   **[deleted]**

   (c)   **those covered by another Standard.**

2   This Standard does not apply to financial instruments (including guarantees) that are within the scope of IFRS 9 *Financial Instruments*.

3   Executory contracts are contracts under which neither party has performed any of its obligations or both parties have partially performed their obligations to an equal extent. This Standard does not apply to executory contracts unless they are onerous.

4   [Deleted]

5   When another Standard deals with a specific type of provision, contingent liability or contingent asset, an entity applies that Standard instead of this Standard. For example, some types of provisions are addressed in Standards on:

   (a)   [deleted]

   (b)   income taxes (see IAS 12 *Income Taxes*);

   (c)   leases (see IFRS 16 *Leases*). However, this Standard applies to any lease that becomes onerous before the commencement date of the lease as defined in IFRS 16. This Standard also applies to short-term leases and leases for which the underlying asset is of low value accounted for in accordance with paragraph 6 of IFRS 16 and that have become onerous;

   (d)   employee benefits (see IAS 19 *Employee Benefits*);

   (e)   insurance contracts (see IFRS 4 *Insurance Contracts*). However, this Standard applies to provisions, contingent liabilities and contingent assets of an insurer, other than those arising from its contractual obligations and rights under insurance contracts within the scope of IFRS 4;

(f)   contingent consideration of an acquirer in a business combination (see IFRS 3 *Business Combinations*); and

(g)   revenue from contracts with customers (see IFRS 15 *Revenue from Contracts with Customers*). However, as IFRS 15 contains no specific requirements to address contracts with customers that are, or have become, onerous, this Standard applies to such cases.

6   [Deleted]

7   This Standard defines provisions as liabilities of uncertain timing or amount. In some countries the term 'provision' is also used in the context of items such as depreciation, impairment of assets and doubtful debts: these are adjustments to the carrying amounts of assets and are not addressed in this Standard.

8   Other Standards specify whether expenditures are treated as assets or as expenses. These issues are not addressed in this Standard. Accordingly, this Standard neither prohibits nor requires capitalisation of the costs recognised when a provision is made.

9   This Standard applies to provisions for restructurings (including discontinued operations). When a restructuring meets the definition of a discontinued operation, additional disclosures may be required by IFRS 5 *Non-current Assets Held for Sale and Discontinued Operations*.

Definitions

10   The following terms are used in this Standard with the meanings specified:

A *provision* is a liability of uncertain timing or amount.

A *liability* is a present obligation of the entity arising from past events, the settlement of which is expected to result in an outflow from the entity of resources embodying economic benefits.[1]

An *obligating event* is an event that creates a legal or constructive obligation that results in an entity having no realistic alternative to settling that obligation.

A *legal obligation* is an obligation that derives from:

(a)   a contract (through its explicit or implicit terms);

(b)   legislation; or

(c)   other operation of law.

---

1   The definition of a liability in this Standard was not revised following the revision of the definition of a liability in the *Conceptual Framework for Financial Reporting* issued in 2018.

A *constructive obligation* is an obligation that derives from an entity's actions where:

(a)   by an established pattern of past practice, published policies or a sufficiently specific current statement, the entity has indicated to other parties that it will accept certain responsibilities; and

(b)   as a result, the entity has created a valid expectation on the part of those other parties that it will discharge those responsibilities.

A *contingent liability* is:

(a)   a possible obligation that arises from past events and whose existence will be confirmed only by the occurrence or non-occurrence of one or more uncertain future events not wholly within the control of the entity; or

(b)   a present obligation that arises from past events but is not recognised because:

(i)   it is not probable that an outflow of resources embodying economic benefits will be required to settle the obligation; or

(ii)   the amount of the obligation cannot be measured with sufficient reliability.

A *contingent asset* is a possible asset that arises from past events and whose existence will be confirmed only by the occurrence or non-occurrence of one or more uncertain future events not wholly within the control of the entity.

An *onerous contract* is a contract in which the unavoidable costs of meeting the obligations under the contract exceed the economic benefits expected to be received under it.

A *restructuring* is a programme that is planned and controlled by management, and materially changes either:

(a)   the scope of a business undertaken by an entity; or

(b)   the manner in which that business is conducted.

Provisions and other liabilities

11   Provisions can be distinguished from other liabilities such as trade payables and accruals because there is uncertainty about the timing or amount of the future expenditure required in settlement. By contrast:

(a)   trade payables are liabilities to pay for goods or services that have been received or supplied and have been invoiced or formally agreed with the supplier; and

(b)   accruals are liabilities to pay for goods or services that have been received or supplied but have not been paid, invoiced or formally agreed with the supplier, including amounts due to employees (for example, amounts relating to accrued vacation pay). Although it is sometimes necessary to estimate the amount or timing of accruals, the uncertainty is generally much less than for provisions.

Accruals are often reported as part of trade and other payables, whereas provisions are reported separately.

Relationship between provisions and contingent liabilities

12   In a general sense, all provisions are contingent because they are uncertain in timing or amount. However, within this Standard the term 'contingent' is used for liabilities and assets that are not recognised because their existence will be confirmed only by the occurrence or non-occurrence of one or more uncertain future events not wholly within the control of the entity. In addition, the term 'contingent liability' is used for liabilities that do not meet the recognition criteria.

13   This Standard distinguishes between:

    (a)   provisions – which are recognised as liabilities (assuming that a reliable estimate can be made) because they are present obligations and it is probable that an outflow of resources embodying economic benefits will be required to settle the obligations; and

    (b)   contingent liabilities – which are not recognised as liabilities because they are either:

        (i)   possible obligations, as it has yet to be confirmed whether the entity has a present obligation that could lead to an outflow of resources embodying economic benefits; or

        (ii)   present obligations that do not meet the recognition criteria in this Standard (because either it is not probable that an outflow of resources embodying economic benefits will be required to settle the obligation, or a sufficiently reliable estimate of the amount of the obligation cannot be made).

Recognition

Provisions

14   A *provision* shall be recognised when:

    (a)   an entity has a present obligation (legal or constructive) as a result of a past event;

    (b)   it is probable that an outflow of resources embodying economic benefits will be required to settle the obligation; and

    (c)   a reliable estimate can be made of the amount of the obligation.

If these conditions are not met, no provision shall be recognised.

Present obligation

15   In rare cases it is not clear whether there is a present obligation. In these cases, a past event is deemed to give rise to a present obligation if, taking account of all available evidence, it is more likely than not that a present obligation exists at the end of the reporting period.

16   In almost all cases it will be clear whether a past event has given rise to a present obligation. In rare cases, for example in a lawsuit, it may be disputed either whether certain events have occurred or whether those events result in a present obligation. In such a case, an entity determines whether a present obligation exists at the end of the reporting period by taking account of all available evidence, including, for example, the opinion of experts. The evidence considered includes any additional evidence provided by events after the reporting period. On the basis of such evidence:

(a)   where it is more likely than not that a present obligation exists at the end of the reporting period, the entity recognises a provision (if the recognition criteria are met); and

(b)   where it is more likely that no present obligation exists at the end of the reporting period, the entity discloses a contingent liability, unless the possibility of an outflow of resources embodying economic benefits is remote (see paragraph 86).

Past event

17   A past event that leads to a present obligation is called an obligating event. For an event to be an obligating event, it is necessary that the entity has no realistic alternative to settling the obligation created by the event. This is the case only:

(a)   where the settlement of the obligation can be enforced by law; or

(b)   in the case of a constructive obligation, where the event (which may be an action of the entity) creates valid expectations in other parties that the entity will discharge the obligation.

18   Financial statements deal with the financial position of an entity at the end of its reporting period and not its possible position in the future. Therefore, no provision is recognised for costs that need to be incurred to operate in the future. The only liabilities recognised in an entity's statement of financial position are those that exist at the end of the reporting period.

19   It is only those obligations arising from past events existing independently of an entity's future actions (ie the future conduct of its business) that are recognised as provisions. Examples of such obligations are penalties or clean-up costs for unlawful environmental damage, both of which would lead to an outflow of resources embodying economic benefits in settlement regardless of the future actions of the entity. Similarly, an entity recognises a provision for the decommissioning costs of an oil installation or a nuclear power station to the extent that the entity is obliged to rectify damage already caused. In contrast, because of commercial pressures or legal requirements, an entity may intend or need to carry out expenditure to operate in a particular

way in the future (for example, by fitting smoke filters in a certain type of factory). Because the entity can avoid the future expenditure by its future actions, for example by changing its method of operation, it has no present obligation for that future expenditure and no provision is recognised.

20 An obligation always involves another party to whom the obligation is owed. It is not necessary, however, to know the identity of the party to whom the obligation is owed—indeed the obligation may be to the public at large. Because an obligation always involves a commitment to another party, it follows that a management or board decision does not give rise to a constructive obligation at the end of the reporting period unless the decision has been communicated before the end of the reporting period to those affected by it in a sufficiently specific manner to raise a valid expectation in them that the entity will discharge its responsibilities.

21 An event that does not give rise to an obligation immediately may do so at a later date, because of changes in the law or because an act (for example, a sufficiently specific public statement) by the entity gives rise to a constructive obligation. For example, when environmental damage is caused there may be no obligation to remedy the consequences. However, the causing of the damage will become an obligating event when a new law requires the existing damage to be rectified or when the entity publicly accepts responsibility for rectification in a way that creates a constructive obligation.

22 Where details of a proposed new law have yet to be finalised, an obligation arises only when the legislation is virtually certain to be enacted as drafted. For the purpose of this Standard, such an obligation is treated as a legal obligation. Differences in circumstances surrounding enactment make it impossible to specify a single event that would make the enactment of a law virtually certain. In many cases it will be impossible to be virtually certain of the enactment of a law until it is enacted.

Probable outflow of resources embodying economic benefits

23 For a liability to qualify for recognition there must be not only a present obligation but also the probability of an outflow of resources embodying economic benefits to settle that obligation. For the purpose of this Standard,[2] an outflow of resources or other event is regarded as probable if the event is more likely than not to occur, ie the probability that the event will occur is greater than the probability that it will not. Where it is not probable that a present obligation exists, an entity discloses a contingent liability, unless the possibility of an outflow of resources embodying economic benefits is remote (see paragraph 86).

24 Where there are a number of similar obligations (eg product warranties or similar contracts) the probability that an outflow will be required in settlement is determined by considering the class of obligations as a whole. Although the likelihood of outflow for any one item may be small, it may well be probable that some outflow of resources will be needed to settle the class of

---

2 The interpretation of 'probable' in this Standard as 'more likely than not' does not necessarily apply in other Standards.

obligations as a whole. If that is the case, a provision is recognised (if the other recognition criteria are met).

Reliable estimate of the obligation

25 The use of estimates is an essential part of the preparation of financial statements and does not undermine their reliability. This is especially true in the case of provisions, which by their nature are more uncertain than most other items in the statement of financial position. Except in extremely rare cases, an entity will be able to determine a range of possible outcomes and can therefore make an estimate of the obligation that is sufficiently reliable to use in recognising a provision.

26 In the extremely rare case where no reliable estimate can be made, a liability exists that cannot be recognised. That liability is disclosed as a contingent liability (see paragraph 86).

Contingent liabilities

27 **An entity shall not recognise a contingent liability.**

28 A contingent liability is disclosed, as required by paragraph 86, unless the possibility of an outflow of resources embodying economic benefits is remote.

29 Where an entity is jointly and severally liable for an obligation, the part of the obligation that is expected to be met by other parties is treated as a contingent liability. The entity recognises a provision for the part of the obligation for which an outflow of resources embodying economic benefits is probable, except in the extremely rare circumstances where no reliable estimate can be made.

30 Contingent liabilities may develop in a way not initially expected. Therefore, they are assessed continually to determine whether an outflow of resources embodying economic benefits has become probable. If it becomes probable that an outflow of future economic benefits will be required for an item previously dealt with as a contingent liability, a provision is recognised in the financial statements of the period in which the change in probability occurs (except in the extremely rare circumstances where no reliable estimate can be made).

Contingent assets

31 **An entity shall not recognise a contingent asset.**

32 Contingent assets usually arise from unplanned or other unexpected events that give rise to the possibility of an inflow of economic benefits to the entity. An example is a claim that an entity is pursuing through legal processes, where the outcome is uncertain.

33 Contingent assets are not recognised in financial statements since this may result in the recognition of income that may never be realised. However, when the realisation of income is virtually certain, then the related asset is not a contingent asset and its recognition is appropriate.

34   A contingent asset is disclosed, as required by paragraph 89, where an inflow of economic benefits is probable.

35   Contingent assets are assessed continually to ensure that developments are appropriately reflected in the financial statements. If it has become virtually certain that an inflow of economic benefits will arise, the asset and the related income are recognised in the financial statements of the period in which the change occurs. If an inflow of economic benefits has become probable, an entity discloses the contingent asset (see paragraph 89).

Measurement

Best estimate

36   **The amount recognised as a provision shall be the best estimate of the expenditure required to settle the present obligation at the end of the reporting period.**

37   The best estimate of the expenditure required to settle the present obligation is the amount that an entity would rationally pay to settle the obligation at the end of the reporting period or to transfer it to a third party at that time. It will often be impossible or prohibitively expensive to settle or transfer an obligation at the end of the reporting period. However, the estimate of the amount that an entity would rationally pay to settle or transfer the obligation gives the best estimate of the expenditure required to settle the present obligation at the end of the reporting period.

38   The estimates of outcome and financial effect are determined by the judgement of the management of the entity, supplemented by experience of similar transactions and, in some cases, reports from independent experts. The evidence considered includes any additional evidence provided by events after the reporting period.

39   Uncertainties surrounding the amount to be recognised as a provision are dealt with by various means according to the circumstances. Where the provision being measured involves a large population of items, the obligation is estimated by weighting all possible outcomes by their associated probabilities. The name for this statistical method of estimation is 'expected value'. The provision will therefore be different depending on whether the probability of a loss of a given amount is, for example, 60 per cent or 90 per cent. Where there is a continuous range of possible outcomes, and each point in that range is as likely as any other, the mid-point of the range is used.

> **Example**
>
> An entity sells goods with a warranty under which customers are covered for the cost of repairs of any manufacturing defects that become apparent within the first six months after purchase. If minor defects were detected in all products sold, repair costs of 1 million would result. If major defects were detected in all products sold, repair costs of 4 million would result. The entity's past experience and future expectations indicate that, for the coming year, 75 per cent of the goods sold will have no defects, 20 per cent of the goods sold will have minor defects and 5 per cent of the goods sold will have major defects. In accordance with paragraph 24, an entity assesses the probability of an outflow for the warranty obligations as a whole.
>
> The expected value of the cost of repairs is:
>
> (75% of nil) + (20% of 1m) + (5% of 4m) = 400,000

40   Where a single obligation is being measured, the individual most likely outcome may be the best estimate of the liability. However, even in such a case, the entity considers other possible outcomes. Where other possible outcomes are either mostly higher or mostly lower than the most likely outcome, the best estimate will be a higher or lower amount. For example, if an entity has to rectify a serious fault in a major plant that it has constructed for a customer, the individual most likely outcome may be for the repair to succeed at the first attempt at a cost of 1,000, but a provision for a larger amount is made if there is a significant chance that further attempts will be necessary.

41   The provision is measured before tax, as the tax consequences of the provision, and changes in it, are dealt with under IAS 12.

Risks and uncertainties

42   **The risks and uncertainties that inevitably surround many events and circumstances shall be taken into account in reaching the best estimate of a provision.**

43   Risk describes variability of outcome. A risk adjustment may increase the amount at which a liability is measured. Caution is needed in making judgements under conditions of uncertainty, so that income or assets are not overstated and expenses or liabilities are not understated. However, uncertainty does not justify the creation of excessive provisions or a deliberate overstatement of liabilities. For example, if the projected costs of a particularly adverse outcome are estimated on a prudent basis, that outcome is not then deliberately treated as more probable than is realistically the case. Care is needed to avoid duplicating adjustments for risk and uncertainty with consequent overstatement of a provision.

44   Disclosure of the uncertainties surrounding the amount of the expenditure is made under paragraph 85(b).

Present value

45　Where the effect of the time value of money is material, the amount of a provision shall be the present value of the expenditures expected to be required to settle the obligation.

46　Because of the time value of money, provisions relating to cash outflows that arise soon after the reporting period are more onerous than those where cash outflows of the same amount arise later. Provisions are therefore discounted, where the effect is material.

47　The discount rate (or rates) shall be a pre-tax rate (or rates) that reflect(s) current market assessments of the time value of money and the risks specific to the liability. The discount rate(s) shall not reflect risks for which future cash flow estimates have been adjusted.

Future events

48　Future events that may affect the amount required to settle an obligation shall be reflected in the amount of a provision where there is sufficient objective evidence that they will occur.

49　Expected future events may be particularly important in measuring provisions. For example, an entity may believe that the cost of cleaning up a site at the end of its life will be reduced by future changes in technology. The amount recognised reflects a reasonable expectation of technically qualified, objective observers, taking account of all available evidence as to the technology that will be available at the time of the clean-up. Thus it is appropriate to include, for example, expected cost reductions associated with increased experience in applying existing technology or the expected cost of applying existing technology to a larger or more complex clean-up operation than has previously been carried out. However, an entity does not anticipate the development of a completely new technology for cleaning up unless it is supported by sufficient objective evidence.

50　The effect of possible new legislation is taken into consideration in measuring an existing obligation when sufficient objective evidence exists that the legislation is virtually certain to be enacted. The variety of circumstances that arise in practice makes it impossible to specify a single event that will provide sufficient, objective evidence in every case. Evidence is required both of what legislation will demand and of whether it is virtually certain to be enacted and implemented in due course. In many cases sufficient objective evidence will not exist until the new legislation is enacted.

Expected disposal of assets

51　Gains from the expected disposal of assets shall not be taken into account in measuring a provision.

52   Gains on the expected disposal of assets are not taken into account in measuring a provision, even if the expected disposal is closely linked to the event giving rise to the provision. Instead, an entity recognises gains on expected disposals of assets at the time specified by the Standard dealing with the assets concerned.

Reimbursements

53   **Where some or all of the expenditure required to settle a provision is expected to be reimbursed by another party, the reimbursement shall be recognised when, and only when, it is virtually certain that reimbursement will be received if the entity settles the obligation. The reimbursement shall be treated as a separate asset. The amount recognised for the reimbursement shall not exceed the amount of the provision.**

54   **In the statement of comprehensive income, the expense relating to a provision may be presented net of the amount recognised for a reimbursement.**

55   Sometimes, an entity is able to look to another party to pay part or all of the expenditure required to settle a provision (for example, through insurance contracts, indemnity clauses or suppliers' warranties). The other party may either reimburse amounts paid by the entity or pay the amounts directly.

56   In most cases the entity will remain liable for the whole of the amount in question so that the entity would have to settle the full amount if the third party failed to pay for any reason. In this situation, a provision is recognised for the full amount of the liability, and a separate asset for the expected reimbursement is recognised when it is virtually certain that reimbursement will be received if the entity settles the liability.

57   In some cases, the entity will not be liable for the costs in question if the third party fails to pay. In such a case the entity has no liability for those costs and they are not included in the provision.

58   As noted in paragraph 29, an obligation for which an entity is jointly and severally liable is a contingent liability to the extent that it is expected that the obligation will be settled by the other parties.

Changes in provisions

59   **Provisions shall be reviewed at the end of each reporting period and adjusted to reflect the current best estimate. If it is no longer probable that an outflow of resources embodying economic benefits will be required to settle the obligation, the provision shall be reversed.**

60   Where discounting is used, the carrying amount of a provision increases in each period to reflect the passage of time. This increase is recognised as borrowing cost.

Use of provisions

61   A provision shall be used only for expenditures for which the provision was originally recognised.

62   Only expenditures that relate to the original provision are set against it. Setting expenditures against a provision that was originally recognised for another purpose would conceal the impact of two different events.

Application of the recognition and measurement rules

Future operating losses

63   Provisions shall not be recognised for future operating losses.

64   Future operating losses do not meet the definition of a liability in paragraph 10 and the general recognition criteria set out for provisions in paragraph 14.

65   An expectation of future operating losses is an indication that certain assets of the operation may be impaired. An entity tests these assets for impairment under IAS 36 *Impairment of Assets*.

Onerous contracts

66   If an entity has a contract that is onerous, the present obligation under the contract shall be recognised and measured as a provision.

67   Many contracts (for example, some routine purchase orders) can be cancelled without paying compensation to the other party, and therefore there is no obligation. Other contracts establish both rights and obligations for each of the contracting parties. Where events make such a contract onerous, the contract falls within the scope of this Standard and a liability exists which is recognised. Executory contracts that are not onerous fall outside the scope of this Standard.

68   This Standard defines an onerous contract as a contract in which the unavoidable costs of meeting the obligations under the contract exceed the economic benefits expected to be received under it. The unavoidable costs under a contract reflect the least net cost of exiting from the contract, which is the lower of the cost of fulfilling it and any compensation or penalties arising from failure to fulfil it.

68A   The cost of fulfilling a contract comprises the costs that relate directly to the contract. Costs that relate directly to a contract consist of both:

(a)   the incremental costs of fulfilling that contract – for example, direct labour and materials; and

(b)   an allocation of other costs that relate directly to fulfilling contracts – for example, an allocation of the depreciation charge for an item of property, plant and equipment used in fulfilling that contract among others.

69   Before a separate provision for an onerous contract is established, an entity recognises any impairment loss that has occurred on assets used in fulfilling the contract (see IAS 36).

Restructuring

70   The following are examples of events that may fall under the definition of restructuring:

(a)   sale or termination of a line of business;

(b)   the closure of business locations in a country or region or the relocation of business activities from one country or region to another;

(c)   changes in management structure, for example, eliminating a layer of management; and

(d)   fundamental reorganisations that have a material effect on the nature and focus of the entity's operations.

71   A provision for restructuring costs is recognised only when the general recognition criteria for provisions set out in paragraph 14 are met. Paragraphs 72–83 set out how the general recognition criteria apply to restructurings.

72   **A constructive obligation to restructure arises only when an entity:**

(a)   **has a detailed formal plan for the restructuring identifying at least:**

(i)   **the business or part of a business concerned;**

(ii)   **the principal locations affected;**

(iii)   **the location, function, and approximate number of employees who will be compensated for terminating their services;**

(iv)   **the expenditures that will be undertaken; and**

(v)   **when the plan will be implemented; and**

(b)   **has raised a valid expectation in those affected that it will carry out the restructuring by starting to implement that plan or announcing its main features to those affected by it.**

73   Evidence that an entity has started to implement a restructuring plan would be provided, for example, by dismantling plant or selling assets or by the public announcement of the main features of the plan. A public announcement of a detailed plan to restructure constitutes a constructive obligation to restructure only if it is made in such a way and in sufficient detail (ie setting out the main features of the plan) that it gives rise to valid expectations in other parties such as customers, suppliers and employees (or their representatives) that the entity will carry out the restructuring.

74   For a plan to be sufficient to give rise to a constructive obligation when communicated to those affected by it, its implementation needs to be planned to begin as soon as possible and to be completed in a timeframe that makes significant changes to the plan unlikely. If it is expected that there will be a long delay before the restructuring begins or that the restructuring will take an unreasonably long time, it is unlikely that the plan will raise a valid expectation on the part of others that the entity is at present committed to restructuring, because the timeframe allows opportunities for the entity to change its plans.

75   A management or board decision to restructure taken before the end of the reporting period does not give rise to a constructive obligation at the end of the reporting period unless the entity has, before the end of the reporting period:

(a)   started to implement the restructuring plan; or

(b)   announced the main features of the restructuring plan to those affected by it in a sufficiently specific manner to raise a valid expectation in them that the entity will carry out the restructuring.

If an entity starts to implement a restructuring plan, or announces its main features to those affected, only after the reporting period, disclosure is required under IAS 10 *Events after the Reporting Period*, if the restructuring is material and non-disclosure could reasonably be expected to influence decisions that the primary users of general purpose financial statements make on the basis of those financial statements, which provide financial information about a specific reporting entity.

76   Although a constructive obligation is not created solely by a management decision, an obligation may result from other earlier events together with such a decision. For example, negotiations with employee representatives for termination payments, or with purchasers for the sale of an operation, may have been concluded subject only to board approval. Once that approval has been obtained and communicated to the other parties, the entity has a constructive obligation to restructure, if the conditions of paragraph 72 are met.

77   In some countries, the ultimate authority is vested in a board whose membership includes representatives of interests other than those of management (eg employees) or notification to such representatives may be necessary before the board decision is taken. Because a decision by such a board involves communication to these representatives, it may result in a constructive obligation to restructure.

78   **No obligation arises for the sale of an operation until the entity is committed to the sale, ie there is a binding sale agreement.**

79   Even when an entity has taken a decision to sell an operation and announced that decision publicly, it cannot be committed to the sale until a purchaser has been identified and there is a binding sale agreement. Until there is a binding sale agreement, the entity will be able to change its mind and indeed will have to take another course of action if a purchaser cannot be found on

acceptable terms. When the sale of an operation is envisaged as part of a restructuring, the assets of the operation are reviewed for impairment, under IAS 36. When a sale is only part of a restructuring, a constructive obligation can arise for the other parts of the restructuring before a binding sale agreement exists.

80   A restructuring provision shall include only the direct expenditures arising from the restructuring, which are those that are both:

    (a)   necessarily entailed by the restructuring; and

    (b)   not associated with the ongoing activities of the entity.

81   A restructuring provision does not include such costs as:

    (a)   retraining or relocating continuing staff;

    (b)   marketing; or

    (c)   investment in new systems and distribution networks.

These expenditures relate to the future conduct of the business and are not liabilities for restructuring at the end of the reporting period. Such expenditures are recognised on the same basis as if they arose independently of a restructuring.

82   Identifiable future operating losses up to the date of a restructuring are not included in a provision, unless they relate to an onerous contract as defined in paragraph 10.

83   As required by paragraph 51, gains on the expected disposal of assets are not taken into account in measuring a restructuring provision, even if the sale of assets is envisaged as part of the restructuring.

Disclosure

84   For each class of provision, an entity shall disclose:

    (a)   the carrying amount at the beginning and end of the period;

    (b)   additional provisions made in the period, including increases to existing provisions;

    (c)   amounts used (ie incurred and charged against the provision) during the period;

    (d)   unused amounts reversed during the period; and

    (e)   the increase during the period in the discounted amount arising from the passage of time and the effect of any change in the discount rate.

Comparative information is not required.

85   An entity shall disclose the following for each class of provision:

    (a)   a brief description of the nature of the obligation and the expected timing of any resulting outflows of economic benefits;

(b) an indication of the uncertainties about the amount or timing of those outflows. Where necessary to provide adequate information, an entity shall disclose the major assumptions made concerning future events, as addressed in paragraph 48; and

(c) the amount of any expected reimbursement, stating the amount of any asset that has been recognised for that expected reimbursement.

86 Unless the possibility of any outflow in settlement is remote, an entity shall disclose for each class of contingent liability at the end of the reporting period a brief description of the nature of the contingent liability and, where practicable:

(a) an estimate of its financial effect, measured under paragraphs 36–52;

(b) an indication of the uncertainties relating to the amount or timing of any outflow; and

(c) the possibility of any reimbursement.

87 In determining which provisions or contingent liabilities may be aggregated to form a class, it is necessary to consider whether the nature of the items is sufficiently similar for a single statement about them to fulfil the requirements of paragraphs 85(a) and (b) and 86(a) and (b). Thus, it may be appropriate to treat as a single class of provision amounts relating to warranties of different products, but it would not be appropriate to treat as a single class amounts relating to normal warranties and amounts that are subject to legal proceedings.

88 Where a provision and a contingent liability arise from the same set of circumstances, an entity makes the disclosures required by paragraphs 84–86 in a way that shows the link between the provision and the contingent liability.

89 Where an inflow of economic benefits is probable, an entity shall disclose a brief description of the nature of the contingent assets at the end of the reporting period, and, where practicable, an estimate of their financial effect, measured using the principles set out for provisions in paragraphs 36–52.

90 It is important that disclosures for contingent assets avoid giving misleading indications of the likelihood of income arising.

91 Where any of the information required by paragraphs 86 and 89 is not disclosed because it is not practicable to do so, that fact shall be stated.

92 In extremely rare cases, disclosure of some or all of the information required by paragraphs 84–89 can be expected to prejudice seriously the position of the entity in a dispute with other parties on the subject matter of the provision, contingent liability or contingent asset. In such cases, an entity need not disclose the information, but shall disclose the general

nature of the dispute, together with the fact that, and reason why, the information has not been disclosed.

Transitional provisions

93   The effect of adopting this Standard on its effective date (or earlier) shall be reported as an adjustment to the opening balance of retained earnings for the period in which the Standard is first adopted. Entities are encouraged, but not required, to adjust the opening balance of retained earnings for the earliest period presented and to restate comparative information. If comparative information is not restated, this fact shall be disclosed.

94   [Deleted]

94A   *Onerous Contracts—Cost of Fulfilling a Contract*, issued in May 2020, added paragraph 68A and amended paragraph 69. An entity shall apply those amendments to contracts for which it has not yet fulfilled all its obligations at the beginning of the annual reporting period in which it first applies the amendments (the date of initial application). The entity shall not restate comparative information. Instead, the entity shall recognise the cumulative effect of initially applying the amendments as an adjustment to the opening balance of retained earnings or other component of equity, as appropriate, at the date of initial application.

Effective date

95   This Standard becomes operative for annual financial statements covering periods beginning on or after 1 July 1999. Earlier application is encouraged. If an entity applies this Standard for periods beginning before 1 July 1999, it shall disclose that fact.

96   [Deleted]

97   [Deleted]

98   [Deleted]

99   *Annual Improvements to IFRSs 2010–2012 Cycle*, issued in December 2013, amended paragraph 5 as a consequential amendment derived from the amendment to IFRS 3. An entity shall apply that amendment prospectively to business combinations to which the amendment to IFRS 3 applies.

100   IFRS 15 *Revenue from Contracts with Customers*, issued in May 2014, amended paragraph 5 and deleted paragraph 6. An entity shall apply those amendments when it applies IFRS 15.

101   IFRS 9, as issued in July 2014, amended paragraph 2 and deleted paragraphs 97 and 98. An entity shall apply those amendments when it applies IFRS 9.

102   IFRS 16, issued in January 2016, amended paragraph 5. An entity shall apply that amendment when it applies IFRS 16.

103   *[This paragraph refers to amendments that are not yet effective, and is therefore not included in this edition.]*

104   *Definition of Material* (Amendments to IAS 1 and IAS 8), issued in October 2018, amended paragraph 75. An entity shall apply those amendments prospectively for annual periods beginning on or after 1 January 2020. Earlier application is permitted. If an entity applies those amendments for an earlier period, it shall disclose that fact. An entity shall apply those amendments when it applies the amendments to the definition of material in paragraph 7 of IAS 1 and paragraphs 5 and 6 of IAS 8.

105   *Onerous Contracts—Cost of Fulfilling a Contract,* issued in May 2020, added paragraphs 68A and 94A and amended paragraph 69. An entity shall apply those amendments for annual reporting periods beginning on or after 1 January 2022. Earlier application is permitted. If an entity applies those amendments for an earlier period, it shall disclose that fact.

Approval by the Board of *Onerous Contracts—Cost of Fulfilling a Contract* issued in May 2020

Onerous Contracts—Cost of Fulfilling a Contract, which amended IAS 37, was approved for issue by all 14 members of the International Accounting Standards Board.

Hans Hoogervorst	Chairman
Suzanne Lloyd	Vice-Chair
Nick Anderson	
Tadeu Cendon	
Martin Edelmann	
Françoise Flores	
Gary Kabureck	
Jianqiao Lu	
Darrel Scott	
Thomas Scott	
Chungwoo Suh	
Rika Suzuki	
Ann Tarca	
Mary Tokar	

IAS 38

Intangible Assets

In April 2001 the International Accounting Standards Board (Board) adopted IAS 38 *Intangible Assets*, which had originally been issued by the International Accounting Standards Committee in September 1998. That Standard had replaced IAS 9 *Research and Development Costs*, which had been issued in 1993, which itself replaced an earlier version called *Accounting for Research and Development Activities* that had been issued in July 1978.

The Board revised IAS 38 in March 2004 as part of the first phase of its Business Combinations project. In January 2008 the Board amended IAS 38 again as part of the second phase of its Business Combinations project.

In May 2014 the Board amended IAS 38 to clarify when the use of a revenue-based amortisation method is appropriate.

Other Standards have made minor consequential amendments to IAS 38. They include IFRS 10 *Consolidated Financial Statements* (issued May 2011), IFRS 11 *Joint Arrangements* (issued May 2011), IFRS 13 *Fair Value Measurement* (issued May 2011), *Annual Improvements to IFRSs 2010–2012 Cycle* (issued December 2013), IFRS 15 *Revenue from Contracts with Customers* (issued May 2014), IFRS 16 *Leases* (issued January 2016) and *Amendments to References to the Conceptual Framework in IFRS Standards* (issued March 2018).

CONTENTS

continued...

...continued

APPROVAL BY THE BOARD OF IAS 38 ISSUED IN MARCH 2004

APPROVAL BY THE BOARD OF *CLARIFICATION OF ACCEPTABLE METHODS OF DEPRECIATION AND AMORTISATION* (AMENDMENTS TO IAS 16 AND IAS 38) ISSUED IN MAY 2014

FOR THE ACCOMPANYING GUIDANCE LISTED BELOW, SEE PART B OF THIS EDITION

ILLUSTRATIVE EXAMPLES

Assessing the useful lives of intangible assets

FOR THE BASIS FOR CONCLUSIONS, SEE PART C OF THIS EDITION

BASIS FOR CONCLUSIONS

DISSENTING OPINIONS

International Accounting Standard 38 *Intangible Assets* (IAS 38) is set out in paragraphs 1–133. All the paragraphs have equal authority but retain the IASC format of the Standard when it was adopted by the IASB. IAS 38 should be read in the context of its objective and the Basis for Conclusions, the *Preface to IFRS Standards* and the *Conceptual Framework for Financial Reporting*. IAS 8 *Accounting Policies, Changes in Accounting Estimates and Errors* provides a basis for selecting and applying accounting policies in the absence of explicit guidance.

International Accounting Standard 38
Intangible Assets

Objective

1   The objective of this Standard is to prescribe the accounting treatment for intangible assets that are not dealt with specifically in another Standard. This Standard requires an entity to recognise an intangible asset if, and only if, specified criteria are met. The Standard also specifies how to measure the carrying amount of intangible assets and requires specified disclosures about intangible assets.

Scope

2   This Standard shall be applied in accounting for intangible assets, except:

   (a)   intangible assets that are within the scope of another Standard;

   (b)   financial assets, as defined in IAS 32 *Financial Instruments: Presentation*;

   (c)   the recognition and measurement of exploration and evaluation assets (see IFRS 6 *Exploration for and Evaluation of Mineral Resources*); and

   (d)   expenditure on the development and extraction of minerals, oil, natural gas and similar non-regenerative resources.

3   If another Standard prescribes the accounting for a specific type of intangible asset, an entity applies that Standard instead of this Standard. For example, this Standard does not apply to:

   (a)   intangible assets held by an entity for sale in the ordinary course of business (see IAS 2 *Inventories*).

   (b)   deferred tax assets (see IAS 12 *Income Taxes*).

   (c)   leases of intangible assets accounted for in accordance with IFRS 16 *Leases*.

   (d)   assets arising from employee benefits (see IAS 19 *Employee Benefits*).

   (e)   financial assets as defined in IAS 32. The recognition and measurement of some financial assets are covered by IFRS 10 *Consolidated Financial Statements*, IAS 27 *Separate Financial Statements* and IAS 28 *Investments in Associates and Joint Ventures*.

   (f)   goodwill acquired in a business combination (see IFRS 3 *Business Combinations*).

   (g)   deferred acquisition costs, and intangible assets, arising from an insurer's contractual rights under insurance contracts within the scope of IFRS 4 *Insurance Contracts*. IFRS 4 sets out specific disclosure requirements for those deferred acquisition costs but not for those intangible assets. Therefore, the disclosure requirements in this Standard apply to those intangible assets.

(h) non-current intangible assets classified as held for sale (or included in a disposal group that is classified as held for sale) in accordance with IFRS 5 *Non-current Assets Held for Sale and Discontinued Operations*.

(i) assets arising from contracts with customers that are recognised in accordance with IFRS 15 *Revenue from Contracts with Customers*.

4 Some intangible assets may be contained in or on a physical substance such as a compact disc (in the case of computer software), legal documentation (in the case of a licence or patent) or film. In determining whether an asset that incorporates both intangible and tangible elements should be treated under IAS 16 *Property, Plant and Equipment* or as an intangible asset under this Standard, an entity uses judgement to assess which element is more significant. For example, computer software for a computer-controlled machine tool that cannot operate without that specific software is an integral part of the related hardware and it is treated as property, plant and equipment. The same applies to the operating system of a computer. When the software is not an integral part of the related hardware, computer software is treated as an intangible asset.

5 This Standard applies to, among other things, expenditure on advertising, training, start-up, research and development activities. Research and development activities are directed to the development of knowledge. Therefore, although these activities may result in an asset with physical substance (eg a prototype), the physical element of the asset is secondary to its intangible component, ie the knowledge embodied in it.

6 Rights held by a lessee under licensing agreements for items such as motion picture films, video recordings, plays, manuscripts, patents and copyrights are within the scope of this Standard and are excluded from the scope of IFRS 16.

7 Exclusions from the scope of a Standard may occur if activities or transactions are so specialised that they give rise to accounting issues that may need to be dealt with in a different way. Such issues arise in the accounting for expenditure on the exploration for, or development and extraction of, oil, gas and mineral deposits in extractive industries and in the case of insurance contracts. Therefore, this Standard does not apply to expenditure on such activities and contracts. However, this Standard applies to other intangible assets used (such as computer software), and other expenditure incurred (such as start-up costs), in extractive industries or by insurers.

Definitions

8 The following terms are used in this Standard with the meanings specified:

Amortisation is the systematic allocation of the depreciable amount of an intangible asset over its useful life.

An *asset* is a resource:

(a)   controlled by an entity as a result of past events; and

(b)   from which future economic benefits are expected to flow to the entity.[1]

Carrying amount is the amount at which an asset is recognised in the statement of financial position after deducting any accumulated amortisation and accumulated impairment losses thereon.

Cost is the amount of cash or cash equivalents paid or the fair value of other consideration given to acquire an asset at the time of its acquisition or construction, or, when applicable, the amount attributed to that asset when initially recognised in accordance with the specific requirements of other IFRSs, eg IFRS 2 *Share-based Payment*.

Depreciable amount is the cost of an asset, or other amount substituted for cost, less its residual value.

Development is the application of research findings or other knowledge to a plan or design for the production of new or substantially improved materials, devices, products, processes, systems or services before the start of commercial production or use.

Entity-specific value is the present value of the cash flows an entity expects to arise from the continuing use of an asset and from its disposal at the end of its useful life or expects to incur when settling a liability.

Fair value is the price that would be received to sell an asset or paid to transfer a liability in an orderly transaction between market participants at the measurement date. (See IFRS 13 *Fair Value Measurement*.)

An *impairment loss* is the amount by which the carrying amount of an asset exceeds its recoverable amount.

An *intangible asset* is an identifiable non-monetary asset without physical substance.

Monetary assets are money held and assets to be received in fixed or determinable amounts of money.

Research is original and planned investigation undertaken with the prospect of gaining new scientific or technical knowledge and understanding.

The *residual value* of an intangible asset is the estimated amount that an entity would currently obtain from disposal of the asset, after deducting the estimated costs of disposal, if the asset were already of the age and in the condition expected at the end of its useful life.

---

1   The definition of an asset in this Standard was not revised following the revision of the definition of an asset in the *Conceptual Framework for Financial Reporting* issued in 2018.

Useful life is:

(a) the period over which an asset is expected to be available for use by an entity; or

(b) the number of production or similar units expected to be obtained from the asset by an entity.

Intangible assets

9 Entities frequently expend resources, or incur liabilities, on the acquisition, development, maintenance or enhancement of intangible resources such as scientific or technical knowledge, design and implementation of new processes or systems, licences, intellectual property, market knowledge and trademarks (including brand names and publishing titles). Common examples of items encompassed by these broad headings are computer software, patents, copyrights, motion picture films, customer lists, mortgage servicing rights, fishing licences, import quotas, franchises, customer or supplier relationships, customer loyalty, market share and marketing rights.

10 Not all the items described in paragraph 9 meet the definition of an intangible asset, ie identifiability, control over a resource and existence of future economic benefits. If an item within the scope of this Standard does not meet the definition of an intangible asset, expenditure to acquire it or generate it internally is recognised as an expense when it is incurred. However, if the item is acquired in a business combination, it forms part of the goodwill recognised at the acquisition date (see paragraph 68).

Identifiability

11 The definition of an intangible asset requires an intangible asset to be identifiable to distinguish it from goodwill. Goodwill recognised in a business combination is an asset representing the future economic benefits arising from other assets acquired in a business combination that are not individually identified and separately recognised. The future economic benefits may result from synergy between the identifiable assets acquired or from assets that, individually, do not qualify for recognition in the financial statements.

12 An asset is identifiable if it either:

(a) is separable, ie is capable of being separated or divided from the entity and sold, transferred, licensed, rented or exchanged, either individually or together with a related contract, identifiable asset or liability, regardless of whether the entity intends to do so; or

(b) arises from contractual or other legal rights, regardless of whether those rights are transferable or separable from the entity or from other rights and obligations.

Control

13   An entity controls an asset if the entity has the power to obtain the future economic benefits flowing from the underlying resource and to restrict the access of others to those benefits. The capacity of an entity to control the future economic benefits from an intangible asset would normally stem from legal rights that are enforceable in a court of law. In the absence of legal rights, it is more difficult to demonstrate control. However, legal enforceability of a right is not a necessary condition for control because an entity may be able to control the future economic benefits in some other way.

14   Market and technical knowledge may give rise to future economic benefits. An entity controls those benefits if, for example, the knowledge is protected by legal rights such as copyrights, a restraint of trade agreement (where permitted) or by a legal duty on employees to maintain confidentiality.

15   An entity may have a team of skilled staff and may be able to identify incremental staff skills leading to future economic benefits from training. The entity may also expect that the staff will continue to make their skills available to the entity. However, an entity usually has insufficient control over the expected future economic benefits arising from a team of skilled staff and from training for these items to meet the definition of an intangible asset. For a similar reason, specific management or technical talent is unlikely to meet the definition of an intangible asset, unless it is protected by legal rights to use it and to obtain the future economic benefits expected from it, and it also meets the other parts of the definition.

16   An entity may have a portfolio of customers or a market share and expect that, because of its efforts in building customer relationships and loyalty, the customers will continue to trade with the entity. However, in the absence of legal rights to protect, or other ways to control, the relationships with customers or the loyalty of the customers to the entity, the entity usually has insufficient control over the expected economic benefits from customer relationships and loyalty for such items (eg portfolio of customers, market shares, customer relationships and customer loyalty) to meet the definition of intangible assets. In the absence of legal rights to protect customer relationships, exchange transactions for the same or similar non-contractual customer relationships (other than as part of a business combination) provide evidence that the entity is nonetheless able to control the expected future economic benefits flowing from the customer relationships. Because such exchange transactions also provide evidence that the customer relationships are separable, those customer relationships meet the definition of an intangible asset.

Future economic benefits

17   The future economic benefits flowing from an intangible asset may include revenue from the sale of products or services, cost savings, or other benefits resulting from the use of the asset by the entity. For example, the use of intellectual property in a production process may reduce future production costs rather than increase future revenues.

Recognition and measurement

18   The recognition of an item as an intangible asset requires an entity to demonstrate that the item meets:

   (a)   the definition of an intangible asset (see paragraphs 8–17); and

   (b)   the recognition criteria (see paragraphs 21–23).

   This requirement applies to costs incurred initially to acquire or internally generate an intangible asset and those incurred subsequently to add to, replace part of, or service it.

19   Paragraphs 25–32 deal with the application of the recognition criteria to separately acquired intangible assets, and paragraphs 33–43 deal with their application to intangible assets acquired in a business combination. Paragraph 44 deals with the initial measurement of intangible assets acquired by way of a government grant, paragraphs 45–47 with exchanges of intangible assets, and paragraphs 48–50 with the treatment of internally generated goodwill. Paragraphs 51–67 deal with the initial recognition and measurement of internally generated intangible assets.

20   The nature of intangible assets is such that, in many cases, there are no additions to such an asset or replacements of part of it. Accordingly, most subsequent expenditures are likely to maintain the expected future economic benefits embodied in an existing intangible asset rather than meet the definition of an intangible asset and the recognition criteria in this Standard. In addition, it is often difficult to attribute subsequent expenditure directly to a particular intangible asset rather than to the business as a whole. Therefore, only rarely will subsequent expenditure—expenditure incurred after the initial recognition of an acquired intangible asset or after completion of an internally generated intangible asset—be recognised in the carrying amount of an asset. Consistently with paragraph 63, subsequent expenditure on brands, mastheads, publishing titles, customer lists and items similar in substance (whether externally acquired or internally generated) is always recognised in profit or loss as incurred. This is because such expenditure cannot be distinguished from expenditure to develop the business as a whole.

21   An intangible asset shall be recognised if, and only if:

   (a)   it is probable that the expected future economic benefits that are attributable to the asset will flow to the entity; and

   (b)   the cost of the asset can be measured reliably.

22   An entity shall assess the probability of expected future economic benefits using reasonable and supportable assumptions that represent management's best estimate of the set of economic conditions that will exist over the useful life of the asset.

23   An entity uses judgement to assess the degree of certainty attached to the flow of future economic benefits that are attributable to the use of the asset on the basis of the evidence available at the time of initial recognition, giving greater weight to external evidence.

24   An intangible asset shall be measured initially at cost.

Separate acquisition

25   Normally, the price an entity pays to acquire separately an intangible asset will reflect expectations about the probability that the expected future economic benefits embodied in the asset will flow to the entity. In other words, the entity expects there to be an inflow of economic benefits, even if there is uncertainty about the timing or the amount of the inflow. Therefore, the probability recognition criterion in paragraph 21(a) is always considered to be satisfied for separately acquired intangible assets.

26   In addition, the cost of a separately acquired intangible asset can usually be measured reliably. This is particularly so when the purchase consideration is in the form of cash or other monetary assets.

27   The cost of a separately acquired intangible asset comprises:

      (a)   its purchase price, including import duties and non-refundable purchase taxes, after deducting trade discounts and rebates; and

      (b)   any directly attributable cost of preparing the asset for its intended use.

28   Examples of directly attributable costs are:

      (a)   costs of employee benefits (as defined in IAS 19) arising directly from bringing the asset to its working condition;

      (b)   professional fees arising directly from bringing the asset to its working condition; and

      (c)   costs of testing whether the asset is functioning properly.

29   Examples of expenditures that are not part of the cost of an intangible asset are:

      (a)   costs of introducing a new product or service (including costs of advertising and promotional activities);

      (b)   costs of conducting business in a new location or with a new class of customer (including costs of staff training); and

      (c)   administration and other general overhead costs.

30   Recognition of costs in the carrying amount of an intangible asset ceases when the asset is in the condition necessary for it to be capable of operating in the manner intended by management. Therefore, costs incurred in using or redeploying an intangible asset are not included in the carrying amount of that asset. For example, the following costs are not included in the carrying amount of an intangible asset:

      (a)   costs incurred while an asset capable of operating in the manner intended by management has yet to be brought into use; and

      (b)   initial operating losses, such as those incurred while demand for the asset's output builds up.

31   Some operations occur in connection with the development of an intangible asset, but are not necessary to bring the asset to the condition necessary for it to be capable of operating in the manner intended by management. These incidental operations may occur before or during the development activities. Because incidental operations are not necessary to bring an asset to the condition necessary for it to be capable of operating in the manner intended by management, the income and related expenses of incidental operations are recognised immediately in profit or loss, and included in their respective classifications of income and expense.

32   If payment for an intangible asset is deferred beyond normal credit terms, its cost is the cash price equivalent. The difference between this amount and the total payments is recognised as interest expense over the period of credit unless it is capitalised in accordance with IAS 23 *Borrowing Costs*.

Acquisition as part of a business combination

33   In accordance with IFRS 3 *Business Combinations*, if an intangible asset is acquired in a business combination, the cost of that intangible asset is its fair value at the acquisition date. The fair value of an intangible asset will reflect market participants' expectations at the acquisition date about the probability that the expected future economic benefits embodied in the asset will flow to the entity. In other words, the entity expects there to be an inflow of economic benefits, even if there is uncertainty about the timing or the amount of the inflow. Therefore, the probability recognition criterion in paragraph 21(a) is always considered to be satisfied for intangible assets acquired in business combinations. If an asset acquired in a business combination is separable or arises from contractual or other legal rights, sufficient information exists to measure reliably the fair value of the asset. Thus, the reliable measurement criterion in paragraph 21(b) is always considered to be satisfied for intangible assets acquired in business combinations.

34   In accordance with this Standard and IFRS 3 (as revised in 2008), an acquirer recognises at the acquisition date, separately from goodwill, an intangible asset of the acquiree, irrespective of whether the asset had been recognised by the acquiree before the business combination. This means that the acquirer recognises as an asset separately from goodwill an in-process research and development project of the acquiree if the project meets the definition of an intangible asset. An acquiree's in-process research and development project meets the definition of an intangible asset when it:

(a)   meets the definition of an asset; and

(b)   is identifiable, ie is separable or arises from contractual or other legal rights.

Intangible asset acquired in a business combination

35   If an intangible asset acquired in a business combination is separable or arises from contractual or other legal rights, sufficient information exists to measure reliably the fair value of the asset. When, for the estimates used to measure an intangible asset's fair value, there is a range of possible outcomes with different probabilities, that uncertainty enters into the measurement of the asset's fair value.

36   An intangible asset acquired in a business combination might be separable, but only together with a related contract, identifiable asset or liability. In such cases, the acquirer recognises the intangible asset separately from goodwill, but together with the related item.

37   The acquirer may recognise a group of complementary intangible assets as a single asset provided the individual assets have similar useful lives. For example, the terms 'brand' and 'brand name' are often used as synonyms for trademarks and other marks. However, the former are general marketing terms that are typically used to refer to a group of complementary assets such as a trademark (or service mark) and its related trade name, formulas, recipes and technological expertise.

38–41   [Deleted]

Subsequent expenditure on an acquired in-process research and development project

42   Research or development expenditure that:

(a)   relates to an in-process research or development project acquired separately or in a business combination and recognised as an intangible asset; and

(b)   is incurred after the acquisition of that project

shall be accounted for in accordance with paragraphs 54–62.

43   Applying the requirements in paragraphs 54–62 means that subsequent expenditure on an in-process research or development project acquired separately or in a business combination and recognised as an intangible asset is:

(a)   recognised as an expense when incurred if it is research expenditure;

(b)   recognised as an expense when incurred if it is development expenditure that does not satisfy the criteria for recognition as an intangible asset in paragraph 57; and

(c)   added to the carrying amount of the acquired in-process research or development project if it is development expenditure that satisfies the recognition criteria in paragraph 57.

Acquisition by way of a government grant

44   In some cases, an intangible asset may be acquired free of charge, or for nominal consideration, by way of a government grant. This may happen when a government transfers or allocates to an entity intangible assets such as airport landing rights, licences to operate radio or television stations, import licences or quotas or rights to access other restricted resources. In accordance with IAS 20 *Accounting for Government Grants and Disclosure of Government Assistance*, an entity may choose to recognise both the intangible asset and the grant initially at fair value. If an entity chooses not to recognise the asset initially at fair value, the entity recognises the asset initially at a nominal amount (the other treatment permitted by IAS 20) plus any expenditure that is directly attributable to preparing the asset for its intended use.

Exchanges of assets

45   One or more intangible assets may be acquired in exchange for a non-monetary asset or assets, or a combination of monetary and non-monetary assets. The following discussion refers simply to an exchange of one non-monetary asset for another, but it also applies to all exchanges described in the preceding sentence. The cost of such an intangible asset is measured at fair value unless (a) the exchange transaction lacks commercial substance or (b) the fair value of neither the asset received nor the asset given up is reliably measurable. The acquired asset is measured in this way even if an entity cannot immediately derecognise the asset given up. If the acquired asset is not measured at fair value, its cost is measured at the carrying amount of the asset given up.

46   An entity determines whether an exchange transaction has commercial substance by considering the extent to which its future cash flows are expected to change as a result of the transaction. An exchange transaction has commercial substance if:

(a)   the configuration (ie risk, timing and amount) of the cash flows of the asset received differs from the configuration of the cash flows of the asset transferred; or

(b)   the entity-specific value of the portion of the entity's operations affected by the transaction changes as a result of the exchange; and

(c)   the difference in (a) or (b) is significant relative to the fair value of the assets exchanged.

For the purpose of determining whether an exchange transaction has commercial substance, the entity-specific value of the portion of the entity's operations affected by the transaction shall reflect post-tax cash flows. The result of these analyses may be clear without an entity having to perform detailed calculations.

47   Paragraph 21(b) specifies that a condition for the recognition of an intangible asset is that the cost of the asset can be measured reliably. The fair value of an intangible asset is reliably measurable if (a) the variability in the range of reasonable fair value measurements is not significant for that asset or (b) the

probabilities of the various estimates within the range can be reasonably assessed and used when measuring fair value. If an entity is able to measure reliably the fair value of either the asset received or the asset given up, then the fair value of the asset given up is used to measure cost unless the fair value of the asset received is more clearly evident.

Internally generated goodwill

48   **Internally generated goodwill shall not be recognised as an asset.**

49   In some cases, expenditure is incurred to generate future economic benefits, but it does not result in the creation of an intangible asset that meets the recognition criteria in this Standard. Such expenditure is often described as contributing to internally generated goodwill. Internally generated goodwill is not recognised as an asset because it is not an identifiable resource (ie it is not separable nor does it arise from contractual or other legal rights) controlled by the entity that can be measured reliably at cost.

50   Differences between the fair value of an entity and the carrying amount of its identifiable net assets at any time may capture a range of factors that affect the fair value of the entity. However, such differences do not represent the cost of intangible assets controlled by the entity.

Internally generated intangible assets

51   It is sometimes difficult to assess whether an internally generated intangible asset qualifies for recognition because of problems in:

(a)   identifying whether and when there is an identifiable asset that will generate expected future economic benefits; and

(b)   determining the cost of the asset reliably. In some cases, the cost of generating an intangible asset internally cannot be distinguished from the cost of maintaining or enhancing the entity's internally generated goodwill or of running day-to-day operations.

Therefore, in addition to complying with the general requirements for the recognition and initial measurement of an intangible asset, an entity applies the requirements and guidance in paragraphs 52–67 to all internally generated intangible assets.

52   To assess whether an internally generated intangible asset meets the criteria for recognition, an entity classifies the generation of the asset into:

(a)   a research phase; and

(b)   a development phase.

Although the terms 'research' and 'development' are defined, the terms 'research phase' and 'development phase' have a broader meaning for the purpose of this Standard.

53   If an entity cannot distinguish the research phase from the development phase of an internal project to create an intangible asset, the entity treats the expenditure on that project as if it were incurred in the research phase only.

Research phase

54   **No intangible asset arising from research (or from the research phase of an internal project) shall be recognised. Expenditure on research (or on the research phase of an internal project) shall be recognised as an expense when it is incurred.**

55   In the research phase of an internal project, an entity cannot demonstrate that an intangible asset exists that will generate probable future economic benefits. Therefore, this expenditure is recognised as an expense when it is incurred.

56   Examples of research activities are:

       (a)   activities aimed at obtaining new knowledge;

       (b)   the search for, evaluation and final selection of, applications of research findings or other knowledge;

       (c)   the search for alternatives for materials, devices, products, processes, systems or services; and

       (d)   the formulation, design, evaluation and final selection of possible alternatives for new or improved materials, devices, products, processes, systems or services.

Development phase

57   **An intangible asset arising from development (or from the development phase of an internal project) shall be recognised if, and only if, an entity can demonstrate all of the following:**

       (a)   **the technical feasibility of completing the intangible asset so that it will be available for use or sale.**

       (b)   **its intention to complete the intangible asset and use or sell it.**

       (c)   **its ability to use or sell the intangible asset.**

       (d)   **how the intangible asset will generate probable future economic benefits. Among other things, the entity can demonstrate the existence of a market for the output of the intangible asset or the intangible asset itself or, if it is to be used internally, the usefulness of the intangible asset.**

       (e)   **the availability of adequate technical, financial and other resources to complete the development and to use or sell the intangible asset.**

       (f)   **its ability to measure reliably the expenditure attributable to the intangible asset during its development.**

58   In the development phase of an internal project, an entity can, in some instances, identify an intangible asset and demonstrate that the asset will generate probable future economic benefits. This is because the development phase of a project is further advanced than the research phase.

           © IFRS Foundation

59   Examples of development activities are:

(a)   the design, construction and testing of pre-production or pre-use prototypes and models;

(b)   the design of tools, jigs, moulds and dies involving new technology;

(c)   the design, construction and operation of a pilot plant that is not of a scale economically feasible for commercial production; and

(d)   the design, construction and testing of a chosen alternative for new or improved materials, devices, products, processes, systems or services.

60   To demonstrate how an intangible asset will generate probable future economic benefits, an entity assesses the future economic benefits to be received from the asset using the principles in IAS 36 *Impairment of Assets*. If the asset will generate economic benefits only in combination with other assets, the entity applies the concept of cash-generating units in IAS 36.

61   Availability of resources to complete, use and obtain the benefits from an intangible asset can be demonstrated by, for example, a business plan showing the technical, financial and other resources needed and the entity's ability to secure those resources. In some cases, an entity demonstrates the availability of external finance by obtaining a lender's indication of its willingness to fund the plan.

62   An entity's costing systems can often measure reliably the cost of generating an intangible asset internally, such as salary and other expenditure incurred in securing copyrights or licences or developing computer software.

63   **Internally generated brands, mastheads, publishing titles, customer lists and items similar in substance shall not be recognised as intangible assets.**

64   Expenditure on internally generated brands, mastheads, publishing titles, customer lists and items similar in substance cannot be distinguished from the cost of developing the business as a whole. Therefore, such items are not recognised as intangible assets.

Cost of an internally generated intangible asset

65   The cost of an internally generated intangible asset for the purpose of paragraph 24 is the sum of expenditure incurred from the date when the intangible asset first meets the recognition criteria in paragraphs 21, 22 and 57. Paragraph 71 prohibits reinstatement of expenditure previously recognised as an expense.

66   The cost of an internally generated intangible asset comprises all directly attributable costs necessary to create, produce, and prepare the asset to be capable of operating in the manner intended by management. Examples of directly attributable costs are:

(a)   costs of materials and services used or consumed in generating the intangible asset;

(b)   costs of employee benefits (as defined in IAS 19) arising from the generation of the intangible asset;

(c)   fees to register a legal right; and

(d)   amortisation of patents and licences that are used to generate the intangible asset.

IAS 23 specifies criteria for the recognition of interest as an element of the cost of an internally generated intangible asset.

67   The following are not components of the cost of an internally generated intangible asset:

(a)   selling, administrative and other general overhead expenditure unless this expenditure can be directly attributed to preparing the asset for use;

(b)   identified inefficiencies and initial operating losses incurred before the asset achieves planned performance; and

(c)   expenditure on training staff to operate the asset.

Example illustrating paragraph 65

An entity is developing a new production process. During 20X5, expenditure incurred was CU1,000,[a] of which CU900 was incurred before 1 December 20X5 and CU100 was incurred between 1 December 20X5 and 31 December 20X5. The entity is able to demonstrate that, at 1 December 20X5, the production process met the criteria for recognition as an intangible asset. The recoverable amount of the know-how embodied in the process (including future cash outflows to complete the process before it is available for use) is estimated to be CU500.

At the end of 20X5, the production process is recognised as an intangible asset at a cost of CU100 (expenditure incurred since the date when the recognition criteria were met, ie 1 December 20X5). The CU900 expenditure incurred before 1 December 20X5 is recognised as an expense because the recognition criteria were not met until 1 December 20X5. This expenditure does not form part of the cost of the production process recognised in the statement of financial position.

During 20X6, expenditure incurred is CU2,000. At the end of 20X6, the recoverable amount of the know-how embodied in the process (including future cash outflows to complete the process before it is available for use) is estimated to be CU1,900.

At the end of 20X6, the cost of the production process is CU2,100 (CU100 expenditure recognised at the end of 20X5 plus CU2,000 expenditure recognised in 20X6). The entity recognises an impairment loss of CU200 to adjust the carrying amount of the process before impairment loss (CU2,100) to its recoverable amount (CU1,900). This impairment loss will be reversed in a subsequent period if the requirements for the reversal of an impairment loss in IAS 36 are met.

(a)   In this Standard, monetary amounts are denominated in 'currency units (CU)'.

Recognition of an expense

68   Expenditure on an intangible item shall be recognised as an expense when it is incurred unless:

     (a)   it forms part of the cost of an intangible asset that meets the recognition criteria (see paragraphs 18–67); or

     (b)   the item is acquired in a business combination and cannot be recognised as an intangible asset. If this is the case, it forms part of the amount recognised as goodwill at the acquisition date (see IFRS 3).

69   In some cases, expenditure is incurred to provide future economic benefits to an entity, but no intangible asset or other asset is acquired or created that can be recognised. In the case of the supply of goods, the entity recognises such expenditure as an expense when it has a right to access those goods. In the case of the supply of services, the entity recognises the expenditure as an expense when it receives the services. For example, expenditure on research is recognised as an expense when it is incurred (see paragraph 54), except when it is acquired as part of a business combination. Other examples of expenditure that is recognised as an expense when it is incurred include:

     (a)   expenditure on start-up activities (ie start-up costs), unless this expenditure is included in the cost of an item of property, plant and equipment in accordance with IAS 16. Start-up costs may consist of establishment costs such as legal and secretarial costs incurred in establishing a legal entity, expenditure to open a new facility or business (ie pre-opening costs) or expenditures for starting new operations or launching new products or processes (ie pre-operating costs).

     (b)   expenditure on training activities.

     (c)   expenditure on advertising and promotional activities (including mail order catalogues).

     (d)   expenditure on relocating or reorganising part or all of an entity.

69A   An entity has a right to access goods when it owns them. Similarly, it has a right to access goods when they have been constructed by a supplier in accordance with the terms of a supply contract and the entity could demand delivery of them in return for payment. Services are received when they are performed by a supplier in accordance with a contract to deliver them to the entity and not when the entity uses them to deliver another service, for example, to deliver an advertisement to customers.

70   Paragraph 68 does not preclude an entity from recognising a prepayment as an asset when payment for goods has been made in advance of the entity obtaining a right to access those goods. Similarly, paragraph 68 does not preclude an entity from recognising a prepayment as an asset when payment for services has been made in advance of the entity receiving those services.

Past expenses not to be recognised as an asset

71   Expenditure on an intangible item that was initially recognised as an expense shall not be recognised as part of the cost of an intangible asset at a later date.

Measurement after recognition

72   An entity shall choose either the cost model in paragraph 74 or the revaluation model in paragraph 75 as its accounting policy. If an intangible asset is accounted for using the revaluation model, all the other assets in its class shall also be accounted for using the same model, unless there is no active market for those assets.

73   A class of intangible assets is a grouping of assets of a similar nature and use in an entity's operations. The items within a class of intangible assets are revalued simultaneously to avoid selective revaluation of assets and the reporting of amounts in the financial statements representing a mixture of costs and values as at different dates.

Cost model

74   After initial recognition, an intangible asset shall be carried at its cost less any accumulated amortisation and any accumulated impairment losses.

Revaluation model

75   After initial recognition, an intangible asset shall be carried at a revalued amount, being its fair value at the date of the revaluation less any subsequent accumulated amortisation and any subsequent accumulated impairment losses. For the purpose of revaluations under this Standard, fair value shall be measured by reference to an active market. Revaluations shall be made with such regularity that at the end of the reporting period the carrying amount of the asset does not differ materially from its fair value.

76   The revaluation model does not allow:

        (a)   the revaluation of intangible assets that have not previously been recognised as assets; or

        (b)   the initial recognition of intangible assets at amounts other than cost.

77   The revaluation model is applied after an asset has been initially recognised at cost. However, if only part of the cost of an intangible asset is recognised as an asset because the asset did not meet the criteria for recognition until part of the way through the process (see paragraph 65), the revaluation model may be applied to the whole of that asset. Also, the revaluation model may be applied to an intangible asset that was received by way of a government grant and recognised at a nominal amount (see paragraph 44).

78   It is uncommon for an active market to exist for an intangible asset, although this may happen. For example, in some jurisdictions, an active market may exist for freely transferable taxi licences, fishing licences or production quotas. However, an active market cannot exist for brands, newspaper mastheads, music and film publishing rights, patents or trademarks, because each such asset is unique. Also, although intangible assets are bought and sold, contracts are negotiated between individual buyers and sellers, and transactions are relatively infrequent. For these reasons, the price paid for one asset may not provide sufficient evidence of the fair value of another. Moreover, prices are often not available to the public.

79   The frequency of revaluations depends on the volatility of the fair values of the intangible assets being revalued. If the fair value of a revalued asset differs materially from its carrying amount, a further revaluation is necessary. Some intangible assets may experience significant and volatile movements in fair value, thus necessitating annual revaluation. Such frequent revaluations are unnecessary for intangible assets with only insignificant movements in fair value.

80   When an intangible asset is revalued, the carrying amount of that asset is adjusted to the revalued amount. At the date of the revaluation, the asset is treated in one of the following ways:

(a)   the gross carrying amount is adjusted in a manner that is consistent with the revaluation of the carrying amount of the asset. For example, the gross carrying amount may be restated by reference to observable market data or it may be restated proportionately to the change in the carrying amount. The accumulated amortisation at the date of the revaluation is adjusted to equal the difference between the gross carrying amount and the carrying amount of the asset after taking into account accumulated impairment losses; or

(b)   the accumulated amortisation is eliminated against the gross carrying amount of the asset.

The amount of the adjustment of accumulated amortisation forms part of the increase or decrease in the carrying amount that is accounted for in accordance with paragraphs 85 and 86.

81   **If an intangible asset in a class of revalued intangible assets cannot be revalued because there is no active market for this asset, the asset shall be carried at its cost less any accumulated amortisation and impairment losses.**

82   **If the fair value of a revalued intangible asset can no longer be measured by reference to an active market, the carrying amount of the asset shall be its revalued amount at the date of the last revaluation by reference to the active market less any subsequent accumulated amortisation and any subsequent accumulated impairment losses.**

83   The fact that an active market no longer exists for a revalued intangible asset may indicate that the asset may be impaired and that it needs to be tested in accordance with IAS 36.

84   If the fair value of the asset can be measured by reference to an active market at a subsequent measurement date, the revaluation model is applied from that date.

85   **If an intangible asset's carrying amount is increased as a result of a revaluation, the increase shall be recognised in other comprehensive income and accumulated in equity under the heading of revaluation surplus. However, the increase shall be recognised in profit or loss to the extent that it reverses a revaluation decrease of the same asset previously recognised in profit or loss.**

86   **If an intangible asset's carrying amount is decreased as a result of a revaluation, the decrease shall be recognised in profit or loss. However, the decrease shall be recognised in other comprehensive income to the extent of any credit balance in the revaluation surplus in respect of that asset. The decrease recognised in other comprehensive income reduces the amount accumulated in equity under the heading of revaluation surplus.**

87   The cumulative revaluation surplus included in equity may be transferred directly to retained earnings when the surplus is realised. The whole surplus may be realised on the retirement or disposal of the asset. However, some of the surplus may be realised as the asset is used by the entity; in such a case, the amount of the surplus realised is the difference between amortisation based on the revalued carrying amount of the asset and amortisation that would have been recognised based on the asset's historical cost. The transfer from revaluation surplus to retained earnings is not made through profit or loss.

Useful life

88   **An entity shall assess whether the useful life of an intangible asset is finite or indefinite and, if finite, the length of, or number of production or similar units constituting, that useful life. An intangible asset shall be regarded by the entity as having an indefinite useful life when, based on an analysis of all of the relevant factors, there is no foreseeable limit to the period over which the asset is expected to generate net cash inflows for the entity.**

89   The accounting for an intangible asset is based on its useful life. An intangible asset with a finite useful life is amortised (see paragraphs 97–106), and an intangible asset with an indefinite useful life is not (see paragraphs 107–110). The Illustrative Examples accompanying this Standard illustrate the determination of useful life for different intangible assets, and the subsequent accounting for those assets based on the useful life determinations.

90   Many factors are considered in determining the useful life of an intangible asset, including:

      (a)   the expected usage of the asset by the entity and whether the asset could be managed efficiently by another management team;

(b)   typical product life cycles for the asset and public information on estimates of useful lives of similar assets that are used in a similar way;

(c)   technical, technological, commercial or other types of obsolescence;

(d)   the stability of the industry in which the asset operates and changes in the market demand for the products or services output from the asset;

(e)   expected actions by competitors or potential competitors;

(f)   the level of maintenance expenditure required to obtain the expected future economic benefits from the asset and the entity's ability and intention to reach such a level;

(g)   the period of control over the asset and legal or similar limits on the use of the asset, such as the expiry dates of related leases; and

(h)   whether the useful life of the asset is dependent on the useful life of other assets of the entity.

91   The term 'indefinite' does not mean 'infinite'. The useful life of an intangible asset reflects only that level of future maintenance expenditure required to maintain the asset at its standard of performance assessed at the time of estimating the asset's useful life, and the entity's ability and intention to reach such a level. A conclusion that the useful life of an intangible asset is indefinite should not depend on planned future expenditure in excess of that required to maintain the asset at that standard of performance.

92   Given the history of rapid changes in technology, computer software and many other intangible assets are susceptible to technological obsolescence. Therefore, it will often be the case that their useful life is short. Expected future reductions in the selling price of an item that was produced using an intangible asset could indicate the expectation of technological or commercial obsolescence of the asset, which, in turn, might reflect a reduction of the future economic benefits embodied in the asset.

93   The useful life of an intangible asset may be very long or even indefinite. Uncertainty justifies estimating the useful life of an intangible asset on a prudent basis, but it does not justify choosing a life that is unrealistically short.

94   **The useful life of an intangible asset that arises from contractual or other legal rights shall not exceed the period of the contractual or other legal rights, but may be shorter depending on the period over which the entity expects to use the asset. If the contractual or other legal rights are conveyed for a limited term that can be renewed, the useful life of the intangible asset shall include the renewal period(s) only if there is evidence to support renewal by the entity without significant cost. The useful life of a reacquired right recognised as an intangible asset in a business combination is the remaining contractual period of the contract in which the right was granted and shall not include renewal periods.**

95   There may be both economic and legal factors influencing the useful life of an intangible asset. Economic factors determine the period over which future economic benefits will be received by the entity. Legal factors may restrict the period over which the entity controls access to these benefits. The useful life is the shorter of the periods determined by these factors.

96   Existence of the following factors, among others, indicates that an entity would be able to renew the contractual or other legal rights without significant cost:

(a)   there is evidence, possibly based on experience, that the contractual or other legal rights will be renewed. If renewal is contingent upon the consent of a third party, this includes evidence that the third party will give its consent;

(b)   there is evidence that any conditions necessary to obtain renewal will be satisfied; and

(c)   the cost to the entity of renewal is not significant when compared with the future economic benefits expected to flow to the entity from renewal.

If the cost of renewal is significant when compared with the future economic benefits expected to flow to the entity from renewal, the 'renewal' cost represents, in substance, the cost to acquire a new intangible asset at the renewal date.

Intangible assets with finite useful lives

Amortisation period and amortisation method

97   The depreciable amount of an intangible asset with a finite useful life shall be allocated on a systematic basis over its useful life. Amortisation shall begin when the asset is available for use, ie when it is in the location and condition necessary for it to be capable of operating in the manner intended by management. Amortisation shall cease at the earlier of the date that the asset is classified as held for sale (or included in a disposal group that is classified as held for sale) in accordance with IFRS 5 and the date that the asset is derecognised. The amortisation method used shall reflect the pattern in which the asset's future economic benefits are expected to be consumed by the entity. If that pattern cannot be determined reliably, the straight-line method shall be used. The amortisation charge for each period shall be recognised in profit or loss unless this or another Standard permits or requires it to be included in the carrying amount of another asset.

98   A variety of amortisation methods can be used to allocate the depreciable amount of an asset on a systematic basis over its useful life. These methods include the straight-line method, the diminishing balance method and the units of production method. The method used is selected on the basis of the expected pattern of consumption of the expected future economic benefits embodied in the asset and is applied consistently from period to period, unless

there is a change in the expected pattern of consumption of those future economic benefits.

98A   There is a rebuttable presumption that an amortisation method that is based on the revenue generated by an activity that includes the use of an intangible asset is inappropriate. The revenue generated by an activity that includes the use of an intangible asset typically reflects factors that are not directly linked to the consumption of the economic benefits embodied in the intangible asset. For example, revenue is affected by other inputs and processes, selling activities and changes in sales volumes and prices. The price component of revenue may be affected by inflation, which has no bearing upon the way in which an asset is consumed. This presumption can be overcome only in the limited circumstances:

   (a)   in which the intangible asset is expressed as a measure of revenue, as described in paragraph 98C; or

   (b)   when it can be demonstrated that revenue and the consumption of the economic benefits of the intangible asset are highly correlated.

98B   In choosing an appropriate amortisation method in accordance with paragraph 98, an entity could determine the predominant limiting factor that is inherent in the intangible asset. For example, the contract that sets out the entity's rights over its use of an intangible asset might specify the entity's use of the intangible asset as a predetermined number of years (ie time), as a number of units produced or as a fixed total amount of revenue to be generated. Identification of such a predominant limiting factor could serve as the starting point for the identification of the appropriate basis of amortisation, but another basis may be applied if it more closely reflects the expected pattern of consumption of economic benefits.

98C   In the circumstance in which the predominant limiting factor that is inherent in an intangible asset is the achievement of a revenue threshold, the revenue to be generated can be an appropriate basis for amortisation. For example, an entity could acquire a concession to explore and extract gold from a gold mine. The expiry of the contract might be based on a fixed amount of total revenue to be generated from the extraction (for example, a contract may allow the extraction of gold from the mine until total cumulative revenue from the sale of gold reaches CU2 billion) and not be based on time or on the amount of gold extracted. In another example, the right to operate a toll road could be based on a fixed total amount of revenue to be generated from cumulative tolls charged (for example, a contract could allow operation of the toll road until the cumulative amount of tolls generated from operating the road reaches CU100 million). In the case in which revenue has been established as the predominant limiting factor in the contract for the use of the intangible asset, the revenue that is to be generated might be an appropriate basis for amortising the intangible asset, provided that the contract specifies a fixed total amount of revenue to be generated on which amortisation is to be determined.

99   Amortisation is usually recognised in profit or loss. However, sometimes the
        future economic benefits embodied in an asset are absorbed in producing
        other assets. In this case, the amortisation charge constitutes part of the cost
        of the other asset and is included in its carrying amount. For example, the
        amortisation of intangible assets used in a production process is included in
        the carrying amount of inventories (see IAS 2 *Inventories*).

Residual value

100   The residual value of an intangible asset with a finite useful life shall be
        assumed to be zero unless:

        (a)   there is a commitment by a third party to purchase the asset at the
                 end of its useful life; or

        (b)   there is an active market (as defined in IFRS 13) for the asset and:

                 (i)   residual value can be determined by reference to that
                          market; and

                 (ii)   it is probable that such a market will exist at the end of the
                          asset's useful life.

101   The depreciable amount of an asset with a finite useful life is determined after
        deducting its residual value. A residual value other than zero implies that an
        entity expects to dispose of the intangible asset before the end of its economic
        life.

102   An estimate of an asset's residual value is based on the amount recoverable
        from disposal using prices prevailing at the date of the estimate for the sale of
        a similar asset that has reached the end of its useful life and has operated
        under conditions similar to those in which the asset will be used. The residual
        value is reviewed at least at each financial year-end. A change in the asset's
        residual value is accounted for as a change in an accounting estimate in
        accordance with IAS 8 *Accounting Policies, Changes in Accounting Estimates and
        Errors*.

103   The residual value of an intangible asset may increase to an amount equal to
        or greater than the asset's carrying amount. If it does, the asset's amortisation
        charge is zero unless and until its residual value subsequently decreases to an
        amount below the asset's carrying amount.

Review of amortisation period and amortisation method

104   The amortisation period and the amortisation method for an intangible
        asset with a finite useful life shall be reviewed at least at each financial
        year-end. If the expected useful life of the asset is different from previous
        estimates, the amortisation period shall be changed accordingly. If there
        has been a change in the expected pattern of consumption of the future
        economic benefits embodied in the asset, the amortisation method shall be
        changed to reflect the changed pattern. Such changes shall be accounted
        for as changes in accounting estimates in accordance with IAS 8.

105   During the life of an intangible asset, it may become apparent that the estimate of its useful life is inappropriate. For example, the recognition of an impairment loss may indicate that the amortisation period needs to be changed.

106   Over time, the pattern of future economic benefits expected to flow to an entity from an intangible asset may change. For example, it may become apparent that a diminishing balance method of amortisation is appropriate rather than a straight-line method. Another example is if use of the rights represented by a licence is deferred pending action on other components of the business plan. In this case, economic benefits that flow from the asset may not be received until later periods.

Intangible assets with indefinite useful lives

107   An intangible asset with an indefinite useful life shall not be amortised.

108   In accordance with IAS 36, an entity is required to test an intangible asset with an indefinite useful life for impairment by comparing its recoverable amount with its carrying amount

    (a)   annually, and

    (b)   whenever there is an indication that the intangible asset may be impaired.

Review of useful life assessment

109   The useful life of an intangible asset that is not being amortised shall be reviewed each period to determine whether events and circumstances continue to support an indefinite useful life assessment for that asset. If they do not, the change in the useful life assessment from indefinite to finite shall be accounted for as a change in an accounting estimate in accordance with IAS 8.

110   In accordance with IAS 36, reassessing the useful life of an intangible asset as finite rather than indefinite is an indicator that the asset may be impaired. As a result, the entity tests the asset for impairment by comparing its recoverable amount, determined in accordance with IAS 36, with its carrying amount, and recognising any excess of the carrying amount over the recoverable amount as an impairment loss.

Recoverability of the carrying amount—impairment losses

111   To determine whether an intangible asset is impaired, an entity applies IAS 36. That Standard explains when and how an entity reviews the carrying amount of its assets, how it determines the recoverable amount of an asset and when it recognises or reverses an impairment loss.

Retirements and disposals

112   An intangible asset shall be derecognised:

    (a)   on disposal; or

    (b)   when no future economic benefits are expected from its use or disposal.

113   The gain or loss arising from the derecognition of an intangible asset shall be determined as the difference between the net disposal proceeds, if any, and the carrying amount of the asset. It shall be recognised in profit or loss when the asset is derecognised (unless IFRS 16 requires otherwise on a sale and leaseback.) Gains shall not be classified as revenue.

114   The disposal of an intangible asset may occur in a variety of ways (eg by sale, by entering into a finance lease, or by donation). The date of disposal of an intangible asset is the date that the recipient obtains control of that asset in accordance with the requirements for determining when a performance obligation is satisfied in IFRS 15. IFRS 16 applies to disposal by a sale and leaseback.

115   If in accordance with the recognition principle in paragraph 21 an entity recognises in the carrying amount of an asset the cost of a replacement for part of an intangible asset, then it derecognises the carrying amount of the replaced part. If it is not practicable for an entity to determine the carrying amount of the replaced part, it may use the cost of the replacement as an indication of what the cost of the replaced part was at the time it was acquired or internally generated.

115A   In the case of a reacquired right in a business combination, if the right is subsequently reissued (sold) to a third party, the related carrying amount, if any, shall be used in determining the gain or loss on reissue.

116   The amount of consideration to be included in the gain or loss arising from the derecognition of an intangible asset is determined in accordance with the requirements for determining the transaction price in paragraphs 47–72 of IFRS 15. Subsequent changes to the estimated amount of the consideration included in the gain or loss shall be accounted for in accordance with the requirements for changes in the transaction price in IFRS 15.

117   Amortisation of an intangible asset with a finite useful life does not cease when the intangible asset is no longer used, unless the asset has been fully depreciated or is classified as held for sale (or included in a disposal group that is classified as held for sale) in accordance with IFRS 5.

Disclosure

General

118   An entity shall disclose the following for each class of intangible assets, distinguishing between internally generated intangible assets and other intangible assets:

(a)   whether the useful lives are indefinite or finite and, if finite, the useful lives or the amortisation rates used;

(b)   the amortisation methods used for intangible assets with finite useful lives;

(c)   the gross carrying amount and any accumulated amortisation (aggregated with accumulated impairment losses) at the beginning and end of the period;

(d)   the line item(s) of the statement of comprehensive income in which any amortisation of intangible assets is included;

(e)   a reconciliation of the carrying amount at the beginning and end of the period showing:

    (i)   additions, indicating separately those from internal development, those acquired separately, and those acquired through business combinations;

    (ii)   assets classified as held for sale or included in a disposal group classified as held for sale in accordance with IFRS 5 and other disposals;

    (iii)   increases or decreases during the period resulting from revaluations under paragraphs 75, 85 and 86 and from impairment losses recognised or reversed in other comprehensive income in accordance with IAS 36 (if any);

    (iv)   impairment losses recognised in profit or loss during the period in accordance with IAS 36 (if any);

    (v)   impairment losses reversed in profit or loss during the period in accordance with IAS 36 (if any);

    (vi)   any amortisation recognised during the period;

    (vii)   net exchange differences arising on the translation of the financial statements into the presentation currency, and on the translation of a foreign operation into the presentation currency of the entity; and

    (viii)   other changes in the carrying amount during the period.

119   A class of intangible assets is a grouping of assets of a similar nature and use in an entity's operations. Examples of separate classes may include:

(a)   brand names;

(b)   mastheads and publishing titles;

(c)   computer software;

(d)   licences and franchises;

(e)   copyrights, patents and other industrial property rights, service and operating rights;

(f)   recipes, formulae, models, designs and prototypes; and

(g)   intangible assets under development.

The classes mentioned above are disaggregated (aggregated) into smaller (larger) classes if this results in more relevant information for the users of the financial statements.

120   An entity discloses information on impaired intangible assets in accordance with IAS 36 in addition to the information required by paragraph 118(e)(iii)–(v).

121   IAS 8 requires an entity to disclose the nature and amount of a change in an accounting estimate that has a material effect in the current period or is expected to have a material effect in subsequent periods. Such disclosure may arise from changes in:

(a)   the assessment of an intangible asset's useful life;

(b)   the amortisation method; or

(c)   residual values.

122   An entity shall also disclose:

(a)   for an intangible asset assessed as having an indefinite useful life, the carrying amount of that asset and the reasons supporting the assessment of an indefinite useful life. In giving these reasons, the entity shall describe the factor(s) that played a significant role in determining that the asset has an indefinite useful life.

(b)   a description, the carrying amount and remaining amortisation period of any individual intangible asset that is material to the entity's financial statements.

(c)   for intangible assets acquired by way of a government grant and initially recognised at fair value (see paragraph 44):

(i)   the fair value initially recognised for these assets;

(ii)   their carrying amount; and

(iii)   whether they are measured after recognition under the cost model or the revaluation model.

(d)   the existence and carrying amounts of intangible assets whose title is restricted and the carrying amounts of intangible assets pledged as security for liabilities.

(e)   the amount of contractual commitments for the acquisition of intangible assets.

123   When an entity describes the factor(s) that played a significant role in determining that the useful life of an intangible asset is indefinite, the entity considers the list of factors in paragraph 90.

Intangible assets measured after recognition using the revaluation model

124   If intangible assets are accounted for at revalued amounts, an entity shall disclose the following:

    (a)   by class of intangible assets:

        (i)   the effective date of the revaluation;

        (ii)   the carrying amount of revalued intangible assets; and

        (iii)   the carrying amount that would have been recognised had the revalued class of intangible assets been measured after recognition using the cost model in paragraph 74; and

    (b)   the amount of the revaluation surplus that relates to intangible assets at the beginning and end of the period, indicating the changes during the period and any restrictions on the distribution of the balance to shareholders.

    (c)   [deleted]

125   It may be necessary to aggregate the classes of revalued assets into larger classes for disclosure purposes. However, classes are not aggregated if this would result in the combination of a class of intangible assets that includes amounts measured under both the cost and revaluation models.

Research and development expenditure

126   An entity shall disclose the aggregate amount of research and development expenditure recognised as an expense during the period.

127   Research and development expenditure comprises all expenditure that is directly attributable to research or development activities (see paragraphs 66 and 67 for guidance on the type of expenditure to be included for the purpose of the disclosure requirement in paragraph 126).

Other information

128   An entity is encouraged, but not required, to disclose the following information:

    (a)   a description of any fully amortised intangible asset that is still in use; and

    (b)   a brief description of significant intangible assets controlled by the entity but not recognised as assets because they did not meet the recognition criteria in this Standard or because they were acquired or generated before the version of IAS 38 *Intangible Assets* issued in 1998 was effective.

Transitional provisions and effective date

129   [Deleted]

130   An entity shall apply this Standard:

   (a)   to the accounting for intangible assets acquired in business combinations for which the agreement date is on or after 31 March 2004; and

   (b)   to the accounting for all other intangible assets prospectively from the beginning of the first annual period beginning on or after 31 March 2004. Thus, the entity shall not adjust the carrying amount of intangible assets recognised at that date. However, the entity shall, at that date, apply this Standard to reassess the useful lives of such intangible assets. If, as a result of that reassessment, the entity changes its assessment of the useful life of an asset, that change shall be accounted for as a change in an accounting estimate in accordance with IAS 8.

130A   An entity shall apply the amendments in paragraph 2 for annual periods beginning on or after 1 January 2006. If an entity applies IFRS 6 for an earlier period, those amendments shall be applied for that earlier period.

130B   IAS 1 *Presentation of Financial Statements* (as revised in 2007) amended the terminology used throughout IFRSs. In addition it amended paragraphs 85, 86 and 118(e)(iii). An entity shall apply those amendments for annual periods beginning on or after 1 January 2009. If an entity applies IAS 1 (revised 2007) for an earlier period, the amendments shall be applied for that earlier period.

130C   IFRS 3 (as revised in 2008) amended paragraphs 12, 33–35, 68, 69, 94 and 130, deleted paragraphs 38 and 129 and added paragraph 115A. *Improvements to IFRSs* issued in April 2009 amended paragraphs 36 and 37. An entity shall apply those amendments prospectively for annual periods beginning on or after 1 July 2009. Therefore, amounts recognised for intangible assets and goodwill in prior business combinations shall not be adjusted. If an entity applies IFRS 3 (revised 2008) for an earlier period, it shall apply the amendments for that earlier period and disclose that fact.

130D   Paragraphs 69, 70 and 98 were amended and paragraph 69A was added by *Improvements to IFRSs* issued in May 2008. An entity shall apply those amendments for annual periods beginning on or after 1 January 2009. Earlier application is permitted. If an entity applies the amendments for an earlier period it shall disclose that fact.

130E   [Deleted]

130F   IFRS 10 and IFRS 11 *Joint Arrangements*, issued in May 2011, amended paragraph 3(e). An entity shall apply that amendment when it applies IFRS 10 and IFRS 11.

130G   IFRS 13, issued in May 2011, amended paragraphs 8, 33, 47, 50, 75, 78, 82, 84, 100 and 124 and deleted paragraphs 39–41 and 130E. An entity shall apply those amendments when it applies IFRS 13.

130H   *Annual Improvements to IFRSs 2010–2012 Cycle*, issued in December 2013, amended paragraph 80. An entity shall apply that amendment for annual periods beginning on or after 1 July 2014. Earlier application is permitted. If an entity applies that amendment for an earlier period it shall disclose that fact.

130I   An entity shall apply the amendment made by *Annual Improvements to IFRSs 2010–2012 Cycle* to all revaluations recognised in annual periods beginning on or after the date of initial application of that amendment and in the immediately preceding annual period. An entity may also present adjusted comparative information for any earlier periods presented, but it is not required to do so. If an entity presents unadjusted comparative information for any earlier periods, it shall clearly identify the information that has not been adjusted, state that it has been presented on a different basis and explain that basis.

130J   *Clarification of Acceptable Methods of Depreciation and Amortisation* (Amendments to IAS 16 and IAS 38), issued in May 2014, amended paragraphs 92 and 98 and added paragraphs 98A–98C. An entity shall apply those amendments prospectively for annual periods beginning on or after 1 January 2016. Earlier application is permitted. If an entity applies those amendments for an earlier period it shall disclose that fact.

130K   IFRS 15 *Revenue from Contracts with Customers*, issued in May 2014, amended paragraphs 3, 114 and 116. An entity shall apply those amendments when it applies IFRS 15.

130L   IFRS 16, issued in January 2016, amended paragraphs 3, 6, 113 and 114. An entity shall apply those amendments when it applies IFRS 16.

130M   *[This paragraph refers to amendments that are not yet effective, and is therefore not included in this edition.]*

Exchanges of similar assets

131   The requirement in paragraphs 129 and 130(b) to apply this Standard prospectively means that if an exchange of assets was measured before the effective date of this Standard on the basis of the carrying amount of the asset given up, the entity does not restate the carrying amount of the asset acquired to reflect its fair value at the acquisition date.

Early application

132   Entities to which paragraph 130 applies are encouraged to apply the requirements of this Standard before the effective dates specified in paragraph 130. However, if an entity applies this Standard before those effective dates, it also shall apply IFRS 3 and IAS 36 (as revised in 2004) at the same time.

Withdrawal of IAS 38 (issued 1998)

133   This Standard supersedes IAS 38 *Intangible Assets* (issued in 1998).

Approval by the Board of IAS 38 issued in March 2004

International Accounting Standard 38 *Intangible Assets* (as revised in 2004) was approved for issue by thirteen of the fourteen members of the International Accounting Standards Board. Professor Whittington dissented. His dissenting opinion is set out after the Basis for Conclusions.

Sir David Tweedie	Chairman
Thomas E Jones	Vice-Chairman
Mary E Barth	
Hans-Georg Bruns	
Anthony T Cope	
Robert P Garnett	
Gilbert Gélard	
James J Leisenring	
Warren J McGregor	
Patricia L O'Malley	
Harry K Schmid	
John T Smith	
Geoffrey Whittington	
Tatsumi Yamada	

Approval by the Board of *Clarification of Acceptable Methods of Depreciation and Amortisation* (Amendments to IAS 16 and IAS 38) issued in May 2014

Clarification of Acceptable Methods of Depreciation and Amortisation was approved for issue by fifteen of the sixteen members of the International Accounting Standards Board. Ms Tokar dissented. Her dissenting opinion is set out after the Basis for Conclusions.

Hans Hoogervorst	Chairman
Ian Mackintosh	Vice-Chairman
Stephen Cooper	
Philippe Danjou	
Martin Edelmann	
Jan Engström	
Patrick Finnegan	
Amaro Luiz de Oliveira Gomes	
Gary Kabureck	
Suzanne Lloyd	
Patricia McConnell	
Takatsugu Ochi	
Darrel Scott	
Chungwoo Suh	
Mary Tokar	
Wei-Guo Zhang	

Financial Instruments: Recognition and Measurement

In April 2001 the International Accounting Standards Board (Board) adopted IAS 39 *Financial Instruments: Recognition and Measurement*, which had originally been issued by the International Accounting Standards Committee (IASC) in March 1999. That Standard had replaced the original IAS 39 *Financial Instruments: Recognition and Measurement*, which had been issued in December 1998. That original IAS 39 had replaced some parts of IAS 25 *Accounting for Investments*, which had been issued in March 1986.

In December 2003 the Board issued a revised IAS 39 as part of its initial agenda of technical projects. The revised IAS 39 also incorporated an Implementation Guidance section, which replaced a series of Questions & Answers that had been developed by the IAS 39 Implementation Guidance Committee.

Following that, the Board made further amendments to IAS 39:

(a)   in March 2004, to enable fair value hedge accounting to be used for a portfolio hedge of interest rate risk;

(b)   in June 2005, relating to when the fair value option could be applied;

(c)   in July 2008, to provide application guidance to illustrate how the principles underlying hedge accounting should be applied;

(d)   in October 2008, to allow some types of financial assets to be reclassified; and

(e)   in March 2009, to address how some embedded derivatives should be measured if they were previously reclassified.

In August 2005 the Board issued IFRS 7 *Financial Instruments: Disclosures*. Consequently, the disclosure requirements that were in IAS 39 were moved to IFRS 7.

In September 2019 the Board amended IFRS 9 and IAS 39 by issuing *Interest Rate Benchmark Reform* to provide specific exceptions to hedge accounting requirements in IFRS 9 and IAS 39 for (a) highly probable requirement; (b) prospective assessments; (c) retrospective assessment (IAS 39 only); and (d) separately identifiable risk components. *Interest Rate Benchmark Reform* also amended IFRS 7 to add specific disclosure requirements for hedging relationships to which an entity applies the exceptions in IFRS 9 or IAS 39.

In August 2020 the Board issued *Interest Rate Benchmark Reform—Phase 2* which amended requirements in IFRS 9, IAS 39, IFRS 7, IFRS 4 and IFRS 16 relating to:

• changes in the basis for determining contractual cash flows of financial assets, financial liabilities and lease liabilities;

• hedge accounting; and

• disclosures.

The Phase 2 amendments apply only to changes required by the interest rate benchmark reform to financial instruments and hedging relationships.

Other Standards have made minor consequential amendments to IAS 39. They include IAS 1 *Presentation of Financial Statements* (issued September 2007), IAS 27 *Consolidated and Separate Financial Statements* (issued January 2008), *Improvements to IFRSs* (issued May 2008), *Eligible Hedged Items* (Amendment to IAS 39 *Financial Instruments: Recognition and Measurement*) (issued July 2008), *Improvements to IFRSs* (issued April 2009), IFRS 13 *Fair Value Measurement* (issued May 2011), *Investment Entities* (Amendments to IFRS 10, IFRS 12 and IAS 27) (issued October 2012), *Novation of Derivatives and Continuation of Hedge Accounting* (Amendments to IAS 39) (issued June 2013), IFRS 9 *Financial Instruments* (Hedge Accounting and amendments to IFRS 9, IFRS 7 and IAS 39) (issued November 2013), IFRS 15 *Revenue from Contracts with Customers* (issued May 2014) and IFRS 9 *Financial Instruments* (issued July 2014).

In response to requests from interested parties that the accounting for financial instruments should be improved quickly, the Board divided its project to replace IAS 39 into three main phases. As the Board completed each phase, it issued chapters in IFRS 9 that replaced the corresponding requirements in IAS 39. The Board had always intended that IFRS 9 *Financial Instruments* would replace IAS 39 in its entirety. However, IFRS 9 permits an entity to choose as its accounting policy either to apply the hedge accounting requirements of IFRS 9 or to continue to apply the hedge accounting requirements in IAS 39. Consequently, although IFRS 9 is effective (with limited exceptions for entities that issue insurance contracts and entities applying the *IFRS for SMEs* Standard), IAS 39, which now contains only its requirements for hedge accounting, also remains effective.

CONTENTS

continued...

---

1   IFRIC 9 was superseded by IFRS 9 *Financial Instruments*, issued in October 2010.

...continued

FOR THE ACCOMPANYING GUIDANCE LISTED BELOW, SEE PART B OF THIS EDITION

ILLUSTRATIVE EXAMPLE

IMPLEMENTATION GUIDANCE

FOR THE BASIS FOR CONCLUSIONS, SEE PART C OF THIS EDITION

BASIS FOR CONCLUSIONS

DISSENTING OPINIONS

International Accounting Standard 39 *Financial Instruments: Recognition and Measurement* (IAS 39) is set out in paragraphs 2–110 and Appendices A and B. All the paragraphs have equal authority but retain the IASC format of the Standard when it was adopted by the IASB. IAS 39 should be read in the context of its objective and the Basis for Conclusions, the *Preface to IFRS Standards* and the *Conceptual Framework for Financial Reporting*. IAS 8 *Accounting Policies, Changes in Accounting Estimates and Errors* provides a basis for selecting and applying accounting policies in the absence of explicit guidance.

International Accounting Standard 39
Financial Instruments: Recognition and Measurement

1   [Deleted]

Scope

2   This Standard shall be applied by all entities to all financial instruments within the scope of IFRS 9 *Financial Instruments* if, and to the extent that:

    (a)   IFRS 9 permits the hedge accounting requirements of this Standard to be applied; and

    (b)   the financial instrument is part of a hedging relationship that qualifies for hedge accounting in accordance with this Standard.

2A–7   [Deleted]

Definitions

8   The terms defined in IFRS 13, IFRS 9 and IAS 32 are used in this Standard with the meanings specified in Appendix A of IFRS 13, Appendix A of IFRS 9 and paragraph 11 of IAS 32. IFRS 13, IFRS 9 and IAS 32 define the following terms:

- amortised cost of a financial asset or financial liability

- derecognition

- derivative

- effective interest method

- effective interest rate

- equity instrument

- fair value

- financial asset

- financial instrument

- financial liability

and provide guidance on applying those definitions.

9   The following terms are used in this Standard with the meanings specified:

Definitions relating to hedge accounting

A *firm commitment* is a binding agreement for the exchange of a specified quantity of resources at a specified price on a specified future date or dates.

A *forecast transaction* is an uncommitted but anticipated future transaction.

A *hedging instrument* is a designated derivative or (for a hedge of the risk of changes in foreign currency exchange rates only) a designated non-derivative financial asset or non-derivative financial liability whose fair value or cash flows are expected to offset changes in the fair value or cash flows of a designated hedged item (paragraphs 72–77 and Appendix A paragraphs AG94–AG97 elaborate on the definition of a hedging instrument).

A *hedged item* is an asset, liability, firm commitment, highly probable forecast transaction or net investment in a foreign operation that (a) exposes the entity to risk of changes in fair value or future cash flows and (b) is designated as being hedged (paragraphs 78–84 and Appendix A paragraphs AG98–AG101 elaborate on the definition of hedged items).

Hedge effectiveness is the degree to which changes in the fair value or cash flows of the hedged item that are attributable to a hedged risk are offset by changes in the fair value or cash flows of the hedging instrument (see Appendix A paragraphs AG105–AG113A).

10–70   [Deleted]

Hedging

71   If an entity applies IFRS 9 and has not chosen as its accounting policy to continue to apply the hedge accounting requirements of this Standard (see paragraph 7.2.21 of IFRS 9), it shall apply the hedge accounting requirements in Chapter 6 of IFRS 9. However, for a fair value hedge of the interest rate exposure of a portion of a portfolio of financial assets or financial liabilities, an entity may, in accordance with paragraph 6.1.3 of IFRS 9, apply the hedge accounting requirements in this Standard instead of those in IFRS 9. In that case the entity must also apply the specific requirements for fair value hedge accounting for a portfolio hedge of interest rate risk (see paragraphs 81A, 89A and AG114–AG132).

Hedging instruments

Qualifying instruments

72   This Standard does not restrict the circumstances in which a derivative may be designated as a hedging instrument provided the conditions in paragraph 88 are met, except for some written options (see Appendix A paragraph AG94). However, a non-derivative financial asset or non-derivative financial liability may be designated as a hedging instrument only for a hedge of a foreign currency risk.

73   For hedge accounting purposes, only instruments that involve a party external to the reporting entity (ie external to the group or individual entity that is being reported on) can be designated as hedging instruments. Although individual entities within a consolidated group or divisions within an entity may enter into hedging transactions with other entities within the group or divisions within the entity, any such intragroup transactions are eliminated on consolidation. Therefore, such hedging transactions do not qualify for

hedge accounting in the consolidated financial statements of the group. However, they may qualify for hedge accounting in the individual or separate financial statements of individual entities within the group provided that they are external to the individual entity that is being reported on.

Designation of hedging instruments

74 There is normally a single fair value measure for a hedging instrument in its entirety, and the factors that cause changes in fair value are co-dependent. Thus, a hedging relationship is designated by an entity for a hedging instrument in its entirety. The only exceptions permitted are:

(a) separating the intrinsic value and time value of an option contract and designating as the hedging instrument only the change in intrinsic value of an option and excluding change in its time value; and

(b) separating the interest element and the spot price of a forward contract.

These exceptions are permitted because the intrinsic value of the option and the premium on the forward can generally be measured separately. A dynamic hedging strategy that assesses both the intrinsic value and time value of an option contract can qualify for hedge accounting.

75 A proportion of the entire hedging instrument, such as 50 per cent of the notional amount, may be designated as the hedging instrument in a hedging relationship. However, a hedging relationship may not be designated for only a portion of the time period during which a hedging instrument remains outstanding.

76 A single hedging instrument may be designated as a hedge of more than one type of risk provided that (a) the risks hedged can be identified clearly; (b) the effectiveness of the hedge can be demonstrated; and (c) it is possible to ensure that there is specific designation of the hedging instrument and different risk positions.

77 Two or more derivatives, or proportions of them (or, in the case of a hedge of currency risk, two or more non-derivatives or proportions of them, or a combination of derivatives and non-derivatives or proportions of them), may be viewed in combination and jointly designated as the hedging instrument, including when the risk(s) arising from some derivatives offset(s) those arising from others. However, an interest rate collar or other derivative instrument that combines a written option and a purchased option does not qualify as a hedging instrument if it is, in effect, a net written option (for which a net premium is received). Similarly, two or more instruments (or proportions of them) may be designated as the hedging instrument only if none of them is a written option or a net written option.

Hedged items

Qualifying items

78   A hedged item can be a recognised asset or liability, an unrecognised firm commitment, a highly probable forecast transaction or a net investment in a foreign operation. The hedged item can be (a) a single asset, liability, firm commitment, highly probable forecast transaction or net investment in a foreign operation, (b) a group of assets, liabilities, firm commitments, highly probable forecast transactions or net investments in foreign operations with similar risk characteristics or (c) in a portfolio hedge of interest rate risk only, a portion of the portfolio of financial assets or financial liabilities that share the risk being hedged.

79   [Deleted]

80   For hedge accounting purposes, only assets, liabilities, firm commitments or highly probable forecast transactions that involve a party external to the entity can be designated as hedged items. It follows that hedge accounting can be applied to transactions between entities in the same group only in the individual or separate financial statements of those entities and not in the consolidated financial statements of the group, except for the consolidated financial statements of an investment entity, as defined in IFRS 10, where transactions between an investment entity and its subsidiaries measured at fair value through profit or loss will not be eliminated in the consolidated financial statements. As an exception, the foreign currency risk of an intragroup monetary item (eg a payable/receivable between two subsidiaries) may qualify as a hedged item in the consolidated financial statements if it results in an exposure to foreign exchange rate gains or losses that are not fully eliminated on consolidation in accordance with IAS 21 *The Effects of Changes in Foreign Exchange Rates.* In accordance with IAS 21, foreign exchange rate gains and losses on intragroup monetary items are not fully eliminated on consolidation when the intragroup monetary item is transacted between two group entities that have different functional currencies. In addition, the foreign currency risk of a highly probable forecast intragroup transaction may qualify as a hedged item in consolidated financial statements provided that the transaction is denominated in a currency other than the functional currency of the entity entering into that transaction and the foreign currency risk will affect consolidated profit or loss.

Designation of financial items as hedged items

81   If the hedged item is a financial asset or financial liability, it may be a hedged item with respect to the risks associated with only a portion of its cash flows or fair value (such as one or more selected contractual cash flows or portions of them or a percentage of the fair value) provided that effectiveness can be measured. For example, an identifiable and separately measurable portion of the interest rate exposure of an interest-bearing asset or interest-bearing liability may be designated as the hedged risk (such as a risk-free interest rate or benchmark interest rate component of the total interest rate exposure of a hedged financial instrument).

81A   In a fair value hedge of the interest rate exposure of a portfolio of financial assets or financial liabilities (and only in such a hedge), the portion hedged may be designated in terms of an amount of a currency (eg an amount of dollars, euro, pounds or rand) rather than as individual assets (or liabilities). Although the portfolio may, for risk management purposes, include assets and liabilities, the amount designated is an amount of assets or an amount of liabilities. Designation of a net amount including assets and liabilities is not permitted. The entity may hedge a portion of the interest rate risk associated with this designated amount. For example, in the case of a hedge of a portfolio containing prepayable assets, the entity may hedge the change in fair value that is attributable to a change in the hedged interest rate on the basis of expected, rather than contractual, repricing dates. When the portion hedged is based on expected repricing dates, the effect that changes in the hedged interest rate have on those expected repricing dates shall be included when determining the change in the fair value of the hedged item. Consequently, if a portfolio that contains prepayable items is hedged with a non-prepayable derivative, ineffectiveness arises if the dates on which items in the hedged portfolio are expected to prepay are revised, or actual prepayment dates differ from those expected.

Designation of non-financial items as hedged items

82   If the hedged item is a non-financial asset or non-financial liability, it shall be designated as a hedged item (a) for foreign currency risks, or (b) in its entirety for all risks, because of the difficulty of isolating and measuring the appropriate portion of the cash flows or fair value changes attributable to specific risks other than foreign currency risks.

Designation of groups of items as hedged items

83   Similar assets or similar liabilities shall be aggregated and hedged as a group only if the individual assets or individual liabilities in the group share the risk exposure that is designated as being hedged. Furthermore, the change in fair value attributable to the hedged risk for each individual item in the group shall be expected to be approximately proportional to the overall change in fair value attributable to the hedged risk of the group of items.

84   Because an entity assesses hedge effectiveness by comparing the change in the fair value or cash flow of a hedging instrument (or group of similar hedging instruments) and a hedged item (or group of similar hedged items), comparing a hedging instrument with an overall net position (eg the net of all fixed rate assets and fixed rate liabilities with similar maturities), rather than with a specific hedged item, does not qualify for hedge accounting.

Hedge accounting

85   Hedge accounting recognises the offsetting effects on profit or loss of changes in the fair values of the hedging instrument and the hedged item.

86   Hedging relationships are of three types:

    (a)   *fair value hedge*: a hedge of the exposure to changes in fair value of a recognised asset or liability or an unrecognised firm commitment, or an identified portion of such an asset, liability or firm commitment, that is attributable to a particular risk and could affect profit or loss.

    (b)   *cash flow hedge*: a hedge of the exposure to variability in cash flows that (i) is attributable to a particular risk associated with a recognised asset or liability (such as all or some future interest payments on variable rate debt) or a highly probable forecast transaction and (ii) could affect profit or loss.

    (c)   *hedge of a net investment in a foreign operation* as defined in IAS 21.

87   A hedge of the foreign currency risk of a firm commitment may be accounted for as a fair value hedge or as a cash flow hedge.

88   A hedging relationship qualifies for hedge accounting under paragraphs 89–102 if, and only if, all of the following conditions are met.

    (a)   At the inception of the hedge there is formal designation and documentation of the hedging relationship and the entity's risk management objective and strategy for undertaking the hedge. That documentation shall include identification of the hedging instrument, the hedged item or transaction, the nature of the risk being hedged and how the entity will assess the hedging instrument's effectiveness in offsetting the exposure to changes in the hedged item's fair value or cash flows attributable to the hedged risk.

    (b)   The hedge is expected to be highly effective (see Appendix A paragraphs AG105–AG113A) in achieving offsetting changes in fair value or cash flows attributable to the hedged risk, consistently with the originally documented risk management strategy for that particular hedging relationship.

    (c)   For cash flow hedges, a forecast transaction that is the subject of the hedge must be highly probable and must present an exposure to variations in cash flows that could ultimately affect profit or loss.

    (d)   The effectiveness of the hedge can be reliably measured, ie the fair value or cash flows of the hedged item that are attributable to the hedged risk and the fair value of the hedging instrument can be reliably measured.

    (e)   The hedge is assessed on an ongoing basis and determined actually to have been highly effective throughout the financial reporting periods for which the hedge was designated.

Fair value hedges

89   If a fair value hedge meets the conditions in paragraph 88 during the period, it shall be accounted for as follows:

(a)   the gain or loss from remeasuring the hedging instrument at fair value (for a derivative hedging instrument) or the foreign currency component of its carrying amount measured in accordance with IAS 21 (for a non-derivative hedging instrument) shall be recognised in profit or loss; and

(b)   the gain or loss on the hedged item attributable to the hedged risk shall adjust the carrying amount of the hedged item and be recognised in profit or loss. This applies if the hedged item is otherwise measured at cost. Recognition of the gain or loss attributable to the hedged risk in profit or loss applies if the hedged item is a financial asset measured at fair value through other comprehensive income in accordance with paragraph 4.1.2A of IFRS 9.

89A   For a fair value hedge of the interest rate exposure of a portion of a portfolio of financial assets or financial liabilities (and only in such a hedge), the requirement in paragraph 89(b) may be met by presenting the gain or loss attributable to the hedged item either:

(a)   in a single separate line item within assets, for those repricing time periods for which the hedged item is an asset; or

(b)   in a single separate line item within liabilities, for those repricing time periods for which the hedged item is a liability.

The separate line items referred to in (a) and (b) above shall be presented next to financial assets or financial liabilities. Amounts included in these line items shall be removed from the statement of financial position when the assets or liabilities to which they relate are derecognised.

90   If only particular risks attributable to a hedged item are hedged, recognised changes in the fair value of the hedged item unrelated to the hedged risk are recognised as set out in paragraph 5.7.1 of IFRS 9.

91   An entity shall discontinue prospectively the hedge accounting specified in paragraph 89 if:

(a)   the hedging instrument expires or is sold, terminated or exercised. For this purpose, the replacement or rollover of a hedging instrument into another hedging instrument is not an expiration or termination if such replacement or rollover is part of the entity's documented hedging strategy. Additionally, for this purpose there is not an expiration or termination of the hedging instrument if:

(i)   as a consequence of laws or regulations or the introduction of laws or regulations, the parties to the hedging instrument agree that one or more clearing counterparties replace their original counterparty to become the new counterparty to each of the parties. For this purpose, a clearing counterparty is a central counterparty (sometimes called a 'clearing organisation' or 'clearing agency') or an entity or entities, for example, a clearing member of a clearing organisation or a client of a clearing member of a clearing organisation, that are acting as counterparty in order to effect clearing by a central counterparty. However, when the parties to the hedging instrument replace their original counterparties with different counterparties this paragraph shall apply only if each of those parties effects clearing with the same central counterparty.

(ii)   other changes, if any, to the hedging instrument are limited to those that are necessary to effect such a replacement of the counterparty. Such changes are limited to those that are consistent with the terms that would be expected if the hedging instrument were originally cleared with the clearing counterparty. These changes include changes in the collateral requirements, rights to offset receivables and payables balances, and charges levied.

(b)   the hedge no longer meets the criteria for hedge accounting in paragraph 88; or

(c)   the entity revokes the designation.

92   Any adjustment arising from paragraph 89(b) to the carrying amount of a hedged financial instrument for which the effective interest method is used (or, in the case of a portfolio hedge of interest rate risk, to the separate line item in the statement of financial position described in paragraph 89A) shall be amortised to profit or loss. Amortisation may begin as soon as an adjustment exists and shall begin no later than when the hedged item ceases to be adjusted for changes in its fair value attributable to the risk being hedged. The adjustment is based on a recalculated effective interest rate at the date amortisation begins. However, if, in the case of a fair value hedge of the interest rate exposure of a portfolio of financial assets or financial liabilities (and only in such a hedge), amortising using a recalculated effective interest rate is not practicable, the adjustment shall be amortised using a straight-line method. The adjustment shall be amortised fully by maturity of the financial instrument or, in the case of a portfolio hedge of interest rate risk, by expiry of the relevant repricing time period.

93   When an unrecognised firm commitment is designated as a hedged item, the subsequent cumulative change in the fair value of the firm commitment attributable to the hedged risk is recognised as an asset or liability with a corresponding gain or loss recognised in profit or loss (see paragraph 89(b)). The changes in the fair value of the hedging instrument are also recognised in profit or loss.

94   When an entity enters into a firm commitment to acquire an asset or assume a liability that is a hedged item in a fair value hedge, the initial carrying amount of the asset or liability that results from the entity meeting the firm commitment is adjusted to include the cumulative change in the fair value of the firm commitment attributable to the hedged risk that was recognised in the statement of financial position.

Cash flow hedges

95   If a cash flow hedge meets the conditions in paragraph 88 during the period, it shall be accounted for as follows:

(a)   the portion of the gain or loss on the hedging instrument that is determined to be an effective hedge (see paragraph 88) shall be recognised in other comprehensive income; and

(b)   the ineffective portion of the gain or loss on the hedging instrument shall be recognised in profit or loss.

96   More specifically, a cash flow hedge is accounted for as follows:

(a)   the separate component of equity associated with the hedged item is adjusted to the lesser of the following (in absolute amounts):

(i)   the cumulative gain or loss on the hedging instrument from inception of the hedge; and

(ii)   the cumulative change in fair value (present value) of the expected future cash flows on the hedged item from inception of the hedge;

(b)   any remaining gain or loss on the hedging instrument or designated component of it (that is not an effective hedge) is recognised in profit or loss; and

(c)   if an entity's documented risk management strategy for a particular hedging relationship excludes from the assessment of hedge effectiveness a specific component of the gain or loss or related cash flows on the hedging instrument (see paragraphs 74, 75 and 88(a)), that excluded component of gain or loss is recognised in accordance with paragraph 5.7.1 of IFRS 9.

97   If a hedge of a forecast transaction subsequently results in the recognition of a financial asset or a financial liability, the associated gains or losses that were recognised in other comprehensive income in accordance with paragraph 95 shall be reclassified from equity to profit or loss as a reclassification adjustment (see IAS 1 (as revised in 2007)) in the same period or periods during which the hedged forecast cash flows affect profit or loss (such as in the periods that interest income or interest expense is recognised). However, if an entity expects that all or a portion of a loss recognised in other comprehensive income will not be recovered in one or more future periods, it shall reclassify into profit or loss as a reclassification adjustment the amount that is not expected to be recovered.

98   If a hedge of a forecast transaction subsequently results in the recognition of a non-financial asset or a non-financial liability, or a forecast transaction for a non-financial asset or non-financial liability becomes a firm commitment for which fair value hedge accounting is applied, then the entity shall adopt (a) or (b) below:

      (a)   It reclassifies the associated gains and losses that were recognised in other comprehensive income in accordance with paragraph 95 to profit or loss as a reclassification adjustment (see IAS 1 (revised 2007)) in the same period or periods during which the asset acquired or liability assumed affects profit or loss (such as in the periods that depreciation expense or cost of sales is recognised). However, if an entity expects that all or a portion of a loss recognised in other comprehensive income will not be recovered in one or more future periods, it shall reclassify from equity to profit or loss as a reclassification adjustment the amount that is not expected to be recovered.

      (b)   It removes the associated gains and losses that were recognised in other comprehensive income in accordance with paragraph 95, and includes them in the initial cost or other carrying amount of the asset or liability.

99   An entity shall adopt either (a) or (b) in paragraph 98 as its accounting policy and shall apply it consistently to all hedges to which paragraph 98 relates.

100   For cash flow hedges other than those covered by paragraphs 97 and 98, amounts that had been recognised in other comprehensive income shall be reclassified from equity to profit or loss as a reclassification adjustment (see IAS 1 (revised 2007)) in the same period or periods during which the hedged forecast cash flows affect profit or loss (for example, when a forecast sale occurs).

101   In any of the following circumstances an entity shall discontinue prospectively the hedge accounting specified in paragraphs 95–100:

      (a)   The hedging instrument expires or is sold, terminated or exercised. In this case, the cumulative gain or loss on the hedging instrument that has been recognised in other comprehensive income from the period when the hedge was effective (see paragraph 95(a)) shall remain separately in equity until the forecast transaction occurs. When the transaction occurs, paragraph 97, 98 or 100 applies. For the purpose of this subparagraph, the replacement or rollover of a hedging instrument into another hedging instrument is not an expiration or termination if such replacement or rollover is part of the entity's documented hedging strategy. Additionally, for the purpose of this subparagraph there is not an expiration or termination of the hedging instrument if:

(i) as a consequence of laws or regulations or the introduction of laws or regulations, the parties to the hedging instrument agree that one or more clearing counterparties replace their original counterparty to become the new counterparty to each of the parties. For this purpose, a clearing counterparty is a central counterparty (sometimes called a 'clearing organisation' or 'clearing agency') or an entity or entities, for example, a clearing member of a clearing organisation or a client of a clearing member of a clearing organisation, that are acting as counterparty in order to effect clearing by a central counterparty. However, when the parties to the hedging instrument replace their original counterparties with different counterparties this paragraph shall apply only if each of those parties effects clearing with the same central counterparty.

(ii) other changes, if any, to the hedging instrument are limited to those that are necessary to effect such a replacement of the counterparty. Such changes are limited to those that are consistent with the terms that would be expected if the hedging instrument were originally cleared with the clearing counterparty. These changes include changes in the collateral requirements, rights to offset receivables and payables balances, and charges levied.

(b) The hedge no longer meets the criteria for hedge accounting in paragraph 88. In this case, the cumulative gain or loss on the hedging instrument that has been recognised in other comprehensive income from the period when the hedge was effective (see paragraph 95(a)) shall remain separately in equity until the forecast transaction occurs. When the transaction occurs, paragraph 97, 98 or 100 applies.

(c) The forecast transaction is no longer expected to occur, in which case any related cumulative gain or loss on the hedging instrument that has been recognised in other comprehensive income from the period when the hedge was effective (see paragraph 95(a)) shall be reclassified from equity to profit or loss as a reclassification adjustment. A forecast transaction that is no longer highly probable (see paragraph 88(c)) may still be expected to occur.

(d) The entity revokes the designation. For hedges of a forecast transaction, the cumulative gain or loss on the hedging instrument that has been recognised in other comprehensive income from the period when the hedge was effective (see paragraph 95(a)) shall remain separately in equity until the forecast transaction occurs or is no longer expected to occur. When the transaction occurs, paragraph 97, 98 or 100 applies. If the transaction is no longer expected to occur, the cumulative gain or loss that had been recognised in other comprehensive income shall be reclassified from equity to profit or loss as a reclassification adjustment.

Hedges of a net investment

102   Hedges of a net investment in a foreign operation, including a hedge of a monetary item that is accounted for as part of the net investment (see IAS 21), shall be accounted for similarly to cash flow hedges:

(a)   the portion of the gain or loss on the hedging instrument that is determined to be an effective hedge (see paragraph 88) shall be recognised in other comprehensive income; and

(b)   the ineffective portion shall be recognised in profit or loss.

The gain or loss on the hedging instrument relating to the effective portion of the hedge that has been recognised in other comprehensive income shall be reclassified from equity to profit or loss as a reclassification adjustment (see IAS 1 (revised 2007)) in accordance with paragraphs 48–49 of IAS 21 on the disposal or partial disposal of the foreign operation.

Temporary exceptions from applying specific hedge accounting requirements

102A   An entity shall apply paragraphs 102D–102N and 108G to all hedging relationships directly affected by interest rate benchmark reform. These paragraphs apply only to such hedging relationships. A hedging relationship is directly affected by interest rate benchmark reform only if the reform gives rise to uncertainties about:

(a)   the interest rate benchmark (contractually or non-contractually specified) designated as a hedged risk; and/or

(b)   the timing or the amount of interest rate benchmark-based cash flows of the hedged item or of the hedging instrument.

102B   For the purpose of applying paragraphs 102D–102N, the term 'interest rate benchmark reform' refers to the market-wide reform of an interest rate benchmark, including the replacement of an interest rate benchmark with an alternative benchmark rate such as that resulting from the recommendations set out in the Financial Stability Board's July 2014 report 'Reforming Major Interest Rate Benchmarks'.[2]

102C   Paragraphs 102D–102N provide exceptions only to the requirements specified in these paragraphs. An entity shall continue to apply all other hedge accounting requirements to hedging relationships directly affected by interest rate benchmark reform.

Highly probable requirement for cash flow hedges

102D   For the purpose of applying the requirement in paragraph 88(c) that a forecast transaction must be highly probable, an entity shall assume that the interest rate benchmark on which the hedged cash flows (contractually or non-contractually specified) are based is not altered as a result of interest rate benchmark reform.

---

2   The report, 'Reforming Major Interest Rate Benchmarks', is available at http://www.fsb.org/wp-content/uploads/r_140722.pdf.

Reclassifying the cumulative gain or loss recognised in other comprehensive income

102E   For the purpose of applying the requirement in paragraph 101(c) in order to determine whether the forecast transaction is no longer expected to occur, an entity shall assume that the interest rate benchmark on which the hedged cash flows (contractually or non-contractually specified) are based is not altered as a result of interest rate benchmark reform.

Effectiveness assessment

102F   For the purpose of applying the requirements in paragraphs 88(b) and AG105(a), an entity shall assume that the interest rate benchmark on which the hedged cash flows and/or the hedged risk (contractually or non-contractually specified) are based, or the interest rate benchmark on which the cash flows of the hedging instrument are based, is not altered as a result of interest rate benchmark reform.

102G   For the purpose of applying the requirement in paragraph 88(e), an entity is not required to discontinue a hedging relationship because the actual results of the hedge do not meet the requirements in paragraph AG105(b). For the avoidance of doubt, an entity shall apply the other conditions in paragraph 88, including the prospective assessment in paragraph 88(b), to assess whether the hedging relationship must be discontinued.

Designating financial items as hedged items

102H   Unless paragraph 102I applies, for a hedge of a non-contractually specified benchmark portion of interest rate risk, an entity shall apply the requirement in paragraphs 81 and AG99F—that the designated portion shall be separately identifiable—only at the inception of the hedging relationship.

102I   When an entity, consistent with its hedge documentation, frequently resets (ie discontinues and restarts) a hedging relationship because both the hedging instrument and the hedged item frequently change (ie the entity uses a dynamic process in which both the hedged items and the hedging instruments used to manage that exposure do not remain the same for long), the entity shall apply the requirement in paragraphs 81 and AG99F—that the designated portion is separately identifiable—only when it initially designates a hedged item in that hedging relationship. A hedged item that has been assessed at the time of its initial designation in the hedging relationship, whether it was at the time of the hedge inception or subsequently, is not reassessed at any subsequent redesignation in the same hedging relationship.

End of application

102J   An entity shall prospectively cease applying paragraph 102D to a hedged item at the earlier of:

(a)   when the uncertainty arising from interest rate benchmark reform is no longer present with respect to the timing and the amount of the interest rate benchmark-based cash flows of the hedged item; and

(b) when the hedging relationship that the hedged item is part of is discontinued.

102K An entity shall prospectively cease applying paragraph 102E at the earlier of:

(a) when the uncertainty arising from interest rate benchmark reform is no longer present with respect to the timing and the amount of the interest rate benchmark-based future cash flows of the hedged item; and

(b) when the entire cumulative gain or loss recognised in other comprehensive income with respect to that discontinued hedging relationship has been reclassified to profit or loss.

102L An entity shall prospectively cease applying paragraph 102F:

(a) to a hedged item, when the uncertainty arising from interest rate benchmark reform is no longer present with respect to the hedged risk or the timing and the amount of the interest rate benchmark-based cash flows of the hedged item; and

(b) to a hedging instrument, when the uncertainty arising from interest rate benchmark reform is no longer present with respect to the timing and the amount of the interest rate benchmark-based cash flows of the hedging instrument.

If the hedging relationship that the hedged item and the hedging instrument are part of is discontinued earlier than the date specified in paragraph 102L(a) or the date specified in paragraph 102L(b), the entity shall prospectively cease applying paragraph 102F to that hedging relationship at the date of discontinuation.

102M An entity shall prospectively cease applying paragraph 102G to a hedging relationship at the earlier of:

(a) when the uncertainty arising from interest rate benchmark reform is no longer present with respect to the hedged risk and the timing and the amount of the interest rate benchmark-based cash flows of the hedged item and of the hedging instrument; and

(b) when the hedging relationship to which the exception is applied is discontinued.

102N When designating a group of items as the hedged item, or a combination of financial instruments as the hedging instrument, an entity shall prospectively cease applying paragraphs 102D–102G to an individual item or financial instrument in accordance with paragraphs 102J, 102K, 102L, or 102M, as relevant, when the uncertainty arising from interest rate benchmark reform is no longer present with respect to the hedged risk and/or the timing and the amount of the interest rate benchmark-based cash flows of that item or financial instrument.

102O   An entity shall prospectively cease applying paragraphs 102H and 102I at the earlier of:

(a)   when changes required by interest rate benchmark reform are made to the non-contractually specified risk portion applying paragraph 102P; or

(b)   when the hedging relationship in which the non-contractually specified risk portion is designated is discontinued.

Additional temporary exceptions arising from interest rate benchmark reform

Hedge accounting

102P   As and when the requirements in paragraphs 102D–102I cease to apply to a hedging relationship (see paragraphs 102J–102O), an entity shall amend the formal designation of that hedging relationship as previously documented to reflect the changes required by interest rate benchmark reform, ie the changes are consistent with the requirements in paragraphs 5.4.6–5.4.8 of IFRS 9. In this context, the hedge designation shall be amended only to make one or more of these changes:

(a)   designating an alternative benchmark rate (contractually or non-contractually specified) as a hedged risk;

(b)   amending the description of the hedged item, including the description of the designated portion of the cash flows or fair value being hedged;

(c)   amending the description of the hedging instrument; or

(d)   amending the description of how the entity will assess hedge effectiveness.

102Q   An entity also shall apply the requirement in paragraph 102P(c) if these three conditions are met:

(a)   the entity makes a change required by interest rate benchmark reform using an approach other than changing the basis for determining the contractual cash flows of the hedging instrument (as described in paragraph 5.4.6 of IFRS 9);

(b)   the original hedging instrument is not derecognised; and

(c)   the chosen approach is economically equivalent to changing the basis for determining the contractual cash flows of the original hedging instrument (as described in paragraphs 5.4.7 and 5.4.8 of IFRS 9).

102R   The requirements in paragraphs 102D–102I may cease to apply at different times. Therefore, applying paragraph 102P, an entity may be required to amend the formal designation of its hedging relationships at different times, or may be required to amend the formal designation of a hedging relationship more than once. When, and only when, such a change is made to the hedge designation, an entity shall apply paragraphs 102V–102Z2 as applicable. An entity also shall apply paragraph 89 (for a fair value hedge) or paragraph 96 (for a cash flow hedge) to account for any changes in the fair value of the hedged item or the hedging instrument.

102S An entity shall amend a hedging relationship as required in paragraph 102P by the end of the reporting period during which a change required by interest rate benchmark reform is made to the hedged risk, hedged item or hedging instrument. For the avoidance of doubt, such an amendment to the formal designation of a hedging relationship constitutes neither the discontinuation of the hedging relationship nor the designation of a new hedging relationship.

102T If changes are made in addition to those changes required by interest rate benchmark reform to the financial asset or financial liability designated in a hedging relationship (as described in paragraphs 5.4.6–5.4.8 of IFRS 9) or to the designation of the hedging relationship (as required by paragraph 102P), an entity shall first apply the applicable requirements in this Standard to determine if those additional changes result in the discontinuation of hedge accounting. If the additional changes do not result in the discontinuation of hedge accounting, an entity shall amend the formal designation of the hedging relationship as specified in paragraph 102P.

102U Paragraphs 102V–102Z3 provide exceptions to the requirements specified in those paragraphs only. An entity shall apply all other hedge accounting requirements in this Standard, including the qualifying criteria in paragraph 88, to hedging relationships that were directly affected by interest rate benchmark reform.

Accounting for qualifying hedging relationships

Retrospective effectiveness assessment

102V For the purpose of assessing the retrospective effectiveness of a hedging relationship on a cumulative basis applying paragraph 88(e) and only for this purpose, an entity may elect to reset to zero the cumulative fair value changes of the hedged item and hedging instrument when ceasing to apply paragraph 102G as required by paragraph 102M. This election is made separately for each hedging relationship (ie on an individual hedging relationship basis).

Cash flow hedges

102W For the purpose of applying paragraph 97, at the point when an entity amends the description of a hedged item as required in paragraph 102P(b), the cumulative gain or loss in other comprehensive income shall be deemed to be based on the alternative benchmark rate on which the hedged future cash flows are determined.

102X For a discontinued hedging relationship, when the interest rate benchmark on which the hedged future cash flows had been based is changed as required by interest rate benchmark reform, for the purpose of applying paragraph 101(c) in order to determine whether the hedged future cash flows are expected to occur, the amount accumulated in other comprehensive income for that hedging relationship shall be deemed to be based on the alternative benchmark rate on which the hedged future cash flows will be based.

Groups of items

102Y   When an entity applies paragraph 102P to groups of items designated as hedged items in a fair value or cash flow hedge, the entity shall allocate the hedged items to subgroups based on the benchmark rate being hedged and designate the benchmark rate as the hedged risk for each subgroup. For example, in a hedging relationship in which a group of items is hedged for changes in an interest rate benchmark subject to interest rate benchmark reform, the hedged cash flows or fair value of some items in the group could be changed to reference an alternative benchmark rate before other items in the group are changed. In this example, in applying paragraph 102P, the entity would designate the alternative benchmark rate as the hedged risk for that relevant subgroup of hedged items. The entity would continue to designate the existing interest rate benchmark as the hedged risk for the other subgroup of hedged items until the hedged cash flows or fair value of those items are changed to reference the alternative benchmark rate or the items expire and are replaced with hedged items that reference the alternative benchmark rate.

102Z   An entity shall assess separately whether each subgroup meets the requirements in paragraphs 78 and 83 to be an eligible hedged item. If any subgroup fails to meet the requirements in paragraphs 78 and 83, the entity shall discontinue hedge accounting prospectively for the hedging relationship in its entirety. An entity also shall apply the requirements in paragraphs 89 or 96 to account for ineffectiveness related to the hedging relationship in its entirety.

Designating financial items as hedged items

102Z1   An alternative benchmark rate designated as a non-contractually specified risk portion that is not separately identifiable (see paragraphs 81 and AG99F) at the date it is designated shall be deemed to have met that requirement at that date, if, and only if, the entity reasonably expects the alternative benchmark rate will be separately identifiable within 24 months. The 24-month period applies to each alternative benchmark rate separately and starts from the date the entity designates the alternative benchmark rate as a non-contractually specified risk portion for the first time (ie the 24-month period applies on a rate-by-rate basis).

102Z2   If subsequently an entity reasonably expects that the alternative benchmark rate will not be separately identifiable within 24 months from the date the entity designated it as a non-contractually specified risk portion for the first time, the entity shall cease applying the requirement in paragraph 102Z1 to that alternative benchmark rate and discontinue hedge accounting prospectively from the date of that reassessment for all hedging relationships in which the alternative benchmark rate was designated as a non-contractually specified risk portion.

102Z3   In addition to those hedging relationships specified in paragraph 102P, an entity shall apply the requirements in paragraphs 102Z1 and 102Z2 to new hedging relationships in which an alternative benchmark rate is designated as a non-contractually specified risk portion (see paragraphs 81 and AG99F) when, because of interest rate benchmark reform, that risk portion is not separately identifiable at the date it is designated.

Effective date and transition

103   An entity shall apply this Standard (including the amendments issued in March 2004) for annual periods beginning on or after 1 January 2005. Earlier application is permitted. An entity shall not apply this Standard (including the amendments issued in March 2004) for annual periods beginning before 1 January 2005 unless it also applies IAS 32 (issued December 2003). If an entity applies this Standard for a period beginning before 1 January 2005, it shall disclose that fact.

103A   [Deleted]

103B   [Deleted]

103C   IAS 1 (as revised in 2007) amended the terminology used throughout IFRSs. In addition it amended paragraphs 95(a), 97, 98, 100, 102, 108 and AG99B. An entity shall apply those amendments for annual periods beginning on or after 1 January 2009. If an entity applies IAS 1 (revised 2007) for an earlier period, the amendments shall be applied for that earlier period.

103D   [Deleted]

103E   IAS 27 (as amended in 2008) amended paragraph 102. An entity shall apply that amendment for annual periods beginning on or after 1 July 2009. If an entity applies IAS 27 (amended 2008) for an earlier period, the amendment shall be applied for that earlier period.

103F   [Deleted]

103G   An entity shall apply paragraphs AG99BA, AG99E, AG99F, AG110A and AG110B retrospectively for annual periods beginning on or after 1 July 2009, in accordance with IAS 8 *Accounting Policies, Changes in Accounting Estimates and Errors*. Earlier application is permitted. If an entity applies *Eligible Hedged Items* (Amendment to IAS 39) for periods beginning before 1 July 2009, it shall disclose that fact.

103H–   [Deleted]
103J

103K   *Improvements to IFRSs* issued in April 2009 amended paragraphs 2(g), 97 and 100. An entity shall apply the amendments to those paragraphs prospectively to all unexpired contracts for annual periods beginning on or after 1 January 2010. Earlier application is permitted. If an entity applies the amendments for an earlier period it shall disclose that fact.

103L–   [Deleted]
103P

103Q   IFRS 13, issued in May 2011, amended paragraphs 9, 13, 28, 47, 88, AG46, AG52, AG64, AG76, AG76A, AG80, AG81 and AG96, added paragraph 43A and deleted paragraphs 48–49, AG69–AG75, AG77–AG79 and AG82. An entity shall apply those amendments when it applies IFRS 13.

103R   *Investment Entities* (Amendments to IFRS 10, IFRS 12 and IAS 27), issued in October 2012, amended paragraphs 2 and 80. An entity shall apply those amendments for annual periods beginning on or after 1 January 2014. Earlier application of *Investment Entities* is permitted. If an entity applies those amendments earlier it shall also apply all amendments included in *Investment Entities* at the same time.

103S   [Deleted]

103T   IFRS 15 *Revenue from Contracts with Customers*, issued in May 2014, amended paragraphs 2, 9, 43, 47, 55, AG2, AG4 and AG48 and added paragraphs 2A, 44A, 55A and AG8A–AG8C. An entity shall apply those amendments when it applies IFRS 15.

103U   IFRS 9, as issued in July 2014, amended paragraphs 2, 8, 9, 71, 88–90, 96, AG95, AG114, AG118 and the headings above AG133 and deleted paragraphs 1, 4–7, 10–70, 79, 103B, 103D, 103F, 103H–103J, 103L–103P, 103S, 105–107A, 108E–108F, AG1–AG93 and AG96. An entity shall apply those amendments when it applies IFRS 9.

103V   *[This paragraph was added for an entity that had not adopted IFRS 9.]*

104   This Standard shall be applied retrospectively except as specified in paragraph 108. The opening balance of retained earnings for the earliest prior period presented and all other comparative amounts shall be adjusted as if this Standard had always been in use unless restating the information would be impracticable. If restatement is impracticable, the entity shall disclose that fact and indicate the extent to which the information was restated.

105–107A [Deleted]

108   An entity shall not adjust the carrying amount of non-financial assets and non-financial liabilities to exclude gains and losses related to cash flow hedges that were included in the carrying amount before the beginning of the financial year in which this Standard is first applied. At the beginning of the financial period in which this Standard is first applied, any amount recognised outside profit or loss (in other comprehensive income or directly in equity) for a hedge of a firm commitment that under this Standard is accounted for as a fair value hedge shall be reclassified as an asset or liability, except for a hedge of foreign currency risk that continues to be treated as a cash flow hedge.

108A   An entity shall apply the last sentence of paragraph 80, and paragraphs AG99A and AG99B, for annual periods beginning on or after 1 January 2006. Earlier application is encouraged. If an entity has designated as the hedged item an external forecast transaction that

(a)   is denominated in the functional currency of the entity entering into the transaction,

(b)   gives rise to an exposure that will have an effect on consolidated profit or loss (ie is denominated in a currency other than the group's presentation currency), and

(c)   would have qualified for hedge accounting had it not been denominated in the functional currency of the entity entering into it,

it may apply hedge accounting in the consolidated financial statements in the period(s) before the date of application of the last sentence of paragraph 80, and paragraphs AG99A and AG99B.

108B   An entity need not apply paragraph AG99B to comparative information relating to periods before the date of application of the last sentence of paragraph 80 and paragraph AG99A.

108C   Paragraphs 73 and AG8 were amended by *Improvements to IFRSs*, issued in May 2008. Paragraph 80 was amended by *Improvements to IFRSs*, issued in April 2009. An entity shall apply those amendments for annual periods beginning on or after 1 January 2009. Earlier application of all the amendments is permitted. If an entity applies the amendments for an earlier period it shall disclose that fact.

108D   *Novation of Derivatives and Continuation of Hedge Accounting* (Amendments to IAS 39), issued in June 2013, amended paragraphs 91 and 101 and added paragraph AG113A. An entity shall apply those paragraphs for annual periods beginning on or after 1 January 2014. An entity shall apply those amendments retrospectively in accordance with IAS 8 *Accounting Policies, Changes in Accounting Estimates and Errors*. Earlier application is permitted. If an entity applies those amendments for an earlier period it shall disclose that fact.

108E–
108F   [Deleted]

108G   *Interest Rate Benchmark Reform*, which amended IFRS 9, IAS 39 and IFRS 7, issued in September 2019, added paragraphs 102A–102N. An entity shall apply these amendments for annual periods beginning on or after 1 January 2020. Earlier application is permitted. If an entity applies these amendments for an earlier period, it shall disclose that fact. An entity shall apply these amendments retrospectively to those hedging relationships that existed at the beginning of the reporting period in which an entity first applies these amendments or were designated thereafter, and to the gain or loss recognised in other comprehensive income that existed at the beginning of the reporting period in which an entity first applies these amendments.

108H   *Interest Rate Benchmark Reform—Phase 2*, which amended IFRS 9, IAS 39, IFRS 7, IFRS 4 and IFRS 16, issued in August 2020, added paragraphs 102O–102Z3 and 108I–108K, and amended paragraph 102M. An entity shall apply these amendments for annual periods beginning on or after 1 January 2021. Earlier application is permitted. If an entity applies these amendments for an earlier period, it shall disclose that fact. An entity shall apply these amendments retrospectively in accordance with IAS 8, except as specified in paragraphs 108I–108K.

108I   An entity shall designate a new hedging relationship (for example, as described in paragraph 102Z3) only prospectively (ie an entity is prohibited from designating a new hedge accounting relationship in prior periods). However, an entity shall reinstate a discontinued hedging relationship if, and only if, these conditions are met:

(a)   the entity had discontinued that hedging relationship solely due to changes required by interest rate benchmark reform and the entity would not have been required to discontinue that hedging relationship if these amendments had been applied at that time; and

(b)   at the beginning of the reporting period in which an entity first applies these amendments (date of initial application of these amendments), that discontinued hedging relationship meets the qualifying criteria for hedge accounting (after taking into account these amendments).

108J   If, in applying paragraph 108I, an entity reinstates a discontinued hedging relationship, the entity shall read references in paragraphs 102Z1 and 102Z2 to the date the alternative benchmark rate is designated as a non-contractually specified risk portion for the first time as referring to the date of initial application of these amendments (ie the 24-month period for that alternative benchmark rate designated as a non-contractually specified risk portion begins from the date of initial application of these amendments).

108K   An entity is not required to restate prior periods to reflect the application of these amendments. The entity may restate prior periods if, and only if, it is possible without the use of hindsight. If an entity does not restate prior periods, the entity shall recognise any difference between the previous carrying amount and the carrying amount at the beginning of the annual reporting period that includes the date of initial application of these amendments in the opening retained earnings (or other component of equity, as appropriate) of the annual reporting period that includes the date of initial application of these amendments.

Withdrawal of other pronouncements

109   This Standard supersedes IAS 39 *Financial Instruments: Recognition and Measurement* revised in October 2000.

110   This Standard and the accompanying Implementation Guidance supersede the Implementation Guidance issued by the IAS 39 Implementation Guidance Committee, established by the former IASC.

Appendix A
Application guidance

This appendix is an integral part of the Standard.

AG1–   [Deleted]
AG93

Hedging (paragraphs 71–102)

Hedging instruments (paragraphs 72–77)

Qualifying instruments (paragraphs 72 and 73)

AG94   The potential loss on an option that an entity writes could be significantly greater than the potential gain in value of a related hedged item. In other words, a written option is not effective in reducing the profit or loss exposure of a hedged item. Therefore, a written option does not qualify as a hedging instrument unless it is designated as an offset to a purchased option, including one that is embedded in another financial instrument (for example, a written call option used to hedge a callable liability). In contrast, a purchased option has potential gains equal to or greater than losses and therefore has the potential to reduce profit or loss exposure from changes in fair values or cash flows. Accordingly, it can qualify as a hedging instrument.

AG95   A financial asset measured at amortised cost may be designated as a hedging instrument in a hedge of foreign currency risk.

AG96   [Deleted]

AG97   An entity's own equity instruments are not financial assets or financial liabilities of the entity and therefore cannot be designated as hedging instruments.

Hedged items (paragraphs 78–84)

Qualifying items (paragraphs 78–80)

AG98   A firm commitment to acquire a business in a business combination cannot be a hedged item, except for foreign exchange risk, because the other risks being hedged cannot be specifically identified and measured. These other risks are general business risks.

AG99   An equity method investment cannot be a hedged item in a fair value hedge because the equity method recognises in profit or loss the investor's share of the associate's profit or loss, rather than changes in the investment's fair value. For a similar reason, an investment in a consolidated subsidiary cannot be a hedged item in a fair value hedge because consolidation recognises in profit or loss the subsidiary's profit or loss, rather than changes in the investment's fair value. A hedge of a net investment in a foreign operation is different because it is a hedge of the foreign currency exposure, not a fair value hedge of the change in the value of the investment.

AG99A   Paragraph 80 states that in consolidated financial statements the foreign currency risk of a highly probable forecast intragroup transaction may qualify as a hedged item in a cash flow hedge, provided the transaction is denominated in a currency other than the functional currency of the entity entering into that transaction and the foreign currency risk will affect consolidated profit or loss. For this purpose an entity can be a parent, subsidiary, associate, joint venture or branch. If the foreign currency risk of a forecast intragroup transaction does not affect consolidated profit or loss, the intragroup transaction cannot qualify as a hedged item. This is usually the case for royalty payments, interest payments or management charges between members of the same group unless there is a related external transaction. However, when the foreign currency risk of a forecast intragroup transaction will affect consolidated profit or loss, the intragroup transaction can qualify as a hedged item. An example is forecast sales or purchases of inventories between members of the same group if there is an onward sale of the inventory to a party external to the group. Similarly, a forecast intragroup sale of plant and equipment from the group entity that manufactured it to a group entity that will use the plant and equipment in its operations may affect consolidated profit or loss. This could occur, for example, because the plant and equipment will be depreciated by the purchasing entity and the amount initially recognised for the plant and equipment may change if the forecast intragroup transaction is denominated in a currency other than the functional currency of the purchasing entity.

AG99B   If a hedge of a forecast intragroup transaction qualifies for hedge accounting, any gain or loss that is recognised in other comprehensive income in accordance with paragraph 95(a) shall be reclassified from equity to profit or loss as a reclassification adjustment in the same period or periods during which the foreign currency risk of the hedged transaction affects consolidated profit or loss.

AG99BA   An entity can designate all changes in the cash flows or fair value of a hedged item in a hedging relationship. An entity can also designate only changes in the cash flows or fair value of a hedged item above or below a specified price or other variable (a one-sided risk). The intrinsic value of a purchased option hedging instrument (assuming that it has the same principal terms as the designated risk), but not its time value, reflects a one-sided risk in a hedged item. For example, an entity can designate the variability of future cash flow outcomes resulting from a price increase of a forecast commodity purchase. In such a situation, only cash flow losses that result from an increase in the price above the specified level are designated. The hedged risk does not include the time value of a purchased option because the time value is not a component of the forecast transaction that affects profit or loss (paragraph 86(b)).

Designation of financial items as hedged items (paragraphs 81 and 81A)

AG99C   If a portion of the cash flows of a financial asset or financial liability is designated as the hedged item, that designated portion must be less than the total cash flows of the asset or liability. For example, in the case of a liability whose effective interest rate is below LIBOR, an entity cannot designate (a) a portion of the liability equal to the principal amount plus interest at LIBOR and (b) a negative residual portion. However, the entity may designate all of the cash flows of the entire financial asset or financial liability as the hedged item and hedge them for only one particular risk (eg only for changes that are attributable to changes in LIBOR). For example, in the case of a financial liability whose effective interest rate is 100 basis points below LIBOR, an entity can designate as the hedged item the entire liability (ie principal plus interest at LIBOR minus 100 basis points) and hedge the change in the fair value or cash flows of that entire liability that is attributable to changes in LIBOR. The entity may also choose a hedge ratio of other than one to one in order to improve the effectiveness of the hedge as described in paragraph AG100.

AG99D   In addition, if a fixed rate financial instrument is hedged some time after its origination and interest rates have changed in the meantime, the entity can designate a portion equal to a benchmark rate that is higher than the contractual rate paid on the item. The entity can do so provided that the benchmark rate is less than the effective interest rate calculated on the assumption that the entity had purchased the instrument on the day it first designates the hedged item. For example, assume an entity originates a fixed rate financial asset of CU100 that has an effective interest rate of 6 per cent at a time when LIBOR is 4 per cent. It begins to hedge that asset some time later when LIBOR has increased to 8 per cent and the fair value of the asset has decreased to CU90. The entity calculates that if it had purchased the asset on the date it first designates it as the hedged item for its then fair value of CU90, the effective yield would have been 9.5 per cent. Because LIBOR is less than this effective yield, the entity can designate a LIBOR portion of 8 per cent that consists partly of the contractual interest cash flows and partly of the difference between the current fair value (ie CU90) and the amount repayable on maturity (ie CU100).

AG99E   Paragraph 81 permits an entity to designate something other than the entire fair value change or cash flow variability of a financial instrument. For example:

(a)   all of the cash flows of a financial instrument may be designated for cash flow or fair value changes attributable to some (but not all) risks; or

(b)   some (but not all) of the cash flows of a financial instrument may be designated for cash flow or fair value changes attributable to all or only some risks (ie a 'portion' of the cash flows of the financial instrument may be designated for changes attributable to all or only some risks).

AG99F   To be eligible for hedge accounting, the designated risks and portions must be separately identifiable components of the financial instrument, and changes in the cash flows or fair value of the entire financial instrument arising from changes in the designated risks and portions must be reliably measurable. For example:

(a)   for a fixed rate financial instrument hedged for changes in fair value attributable to changes in a risk-free or benchmark interest rate, the risk-free or benchmark rate is normally regarded as both a separately identifiable component of the financial instrument and reliably measurable.

(b)   inflation is not separately identifiable and reliably measurable and cannot be designated as a risk or a portion of a financial instrument unless the requirements in (c) are met.

(c)   a contractually specified inflation portion of the cash flows of a recognised inflation-linked bond (assuming there is no requirement to account for an embedded derivative separately) is separately identifiable and reliably measurable as long as other cash flows of the instrument are not affected by the inflation portion.

Designation of non-financial items as hedged items (paragraph 82)

AG100   Changes in the price of an ingredient or component of a non-financial asset or non-financial liability generally do not have a predictable, separately measurable effect on the price of the item that is comparable to the effect of, say, a change in market interest rates on the price of a bond. Thus, a non-financial asset or non-financial liability is a hedged item only in its entirety or for foreign exchange risk. If there is a difference between the terms of the hedging instrument and the hedged item (such as for a hedge of the forecast purchase of Brazilian coffee using a forward contract to purchase Colombian coffee on otherwise similar terms), the hedging relationship nonetheless can qualify as a hedge relationship provided all the conditions in paragraph 88 are met, including that the hedge is expected to be highly effective. For this purpose, the amount of the hedging instrument may be greater or less than that of the hedged item if this improves the effectiveness of the hedging relationship. For example, a regression analysis could be performed to establish a statistical relationship between the hedged item (eg a transaction in Brazilian coffee) and the hedging instrument (eg a transaction in Colombian coffee). If there is a valid statistical relationship between the two variables (ie between the unit prices of Brazilian coffee and Colombian coffee), the slope of the regression line can be used to establish the hedge ratio that will maximise expected effectiveness. For example, if the slope of the regression line is 1.02, a hedge ratio based on 0.98 quantities of hedged items to 1.00 quantities of the hedging instrument maximises expected effectiveness. However, the hedging relationship may result in ineffectiveness that is recognised in profit or loss during the term of the hedging relationship.

Designation of groups of items as hedged items (paragraphs 83 and 84)

AG101   A hedge of an overall net position (eg the net of all fixed rate assets and fixed rate liabilities with similar maturities), rather than of a specific hedged item, does not qualify for hedge accounting. However, almost the same effect on profit or loss of hedge accounting for this type of hedging relationship can be achieved by designating as the hedged item part of the underlying items. For example, if a bank has CU100 of assets and CU90 of liabilities with risks and terms of a similar nature and hedges the net CU10 exposure, it can designate as the hedged item CU10 of those assets. This designation can be used if such assets and liabilities are fixed rate instruments, in which case it is a fair value hedge, or if they are variable rate instruments, in which case it is a cash flow hedge. Similarly, if an entity has a firm commitment to make a purchase in a foreign currency of CU100 and a firm commitment to make a sale in the foreign currency of CU90, it can hedge the net amount of CU10 by acquiring a derivative and designating it as a hedging instrument associated with CU10 of the firm purchase commitment of CU100.

Hedge accounting (paragraphs 85–102)

AG102   An example of a fair value hedge is a hedge of exposure to changes in the fair value of a fixed rate debt instrument as a result of changes in interest rates. Such a hedge could be entered into by the issuer or by the holder.

AG103   An example of a cash flow hedge is the use of a swap to change floating rate debt to fixed rate debt (ie a hedge of a future transaction where the future cash flows being hedged are the future interest payments).

AG104   A hedge of a firm commitment (eg a hedge of the change in fuel price relating to an unrecognised contractual commitment by an electric utility to purchase fuel at a fixed price) is a hedge of an exposure to a change in fair value. Accordingly, such a hedge is a fair value hedge. However, under paragraph 87 a hedge of the foreign currency risk of a firm commitment could alternatively be accounted for as a cash flow hedge.

Assessing hedge effectiveness

AG105   A hedge is regarded as highly effective only if both of the following conditions are met:

(a)   At the inception of the hedge and in subsequent periods, the hedge is expected to be highly effective in achieving offsetting changes in fair value or cash flows attributable to the hedged risk during the period for which the hedge is designated. Such an expectation can be demonstrated in various ways, including a comparison of past changes in the fair value or cash flows of the hedged item that are attributable to the hedged risk with past changes in the fair value or cash flows of the hedging instrument, or by demonstrating a high statistical correlation between the fair value or cash flows of the hedged item and those of the hedging instrument. The entity may choose a hedge ratio of other than one to one in order to improve the effectiveness of the hedge as described in paragraph AG100.

(b)   The actual results of the hedge are within a range of 80–125 per cent. For example, if actual results are such that the loss on the hedging instrument is CU120 and the gain on the cash instrument is CU100, offset can be measured by 120/100, which is 120 per cent, or by 100/120, which is 83 per cent. In this example, assuming the hedge meets the condition in (a), the entity would conclude that the hedge has been highly effective.

AG106   Effectiveness is assessed, at a minimum, at the time an entity prepares its annual or interim financial statements.

AG107   This Standard does not specify a single method for assessing hedge effectiveness. The method an entity adopts for assessing hedge effectiveness depends on its risk management strategy. For example, if the entity's risk management strategy is to adjust the amount of the hedging instrument periodically to reflect changes in the hedged position, the entity needs to demonstrate that the hedge is expected to be highly effective only for the period until the amount of the hedging instrument is next adjusted. In some cases, an entity adopts different methods for different types of hedges. An entity's documentation of its hedging strategy includes its procedures for assessing effectiveness. Those procedures state whether the assessment includes all of the gain or loss on a hedging instrument or whether the instrument's time value is excluded.

AG107A   If an entity hedges less than 100 per cent of the exposure on an item, such as 85 per cent, it shall designate the hedged item as being 85 per cent of the exposure and shall measure ineffectiveness based on the change in that designated 85 per cent exposure. However, when hedging the designated 85 per cent exposure, the entity may use a hedge ratio of other than one to one if that improves the expected effectiveness of the hedge, as explained in paragraph AG100.

AG108   If the principal terms of the hedging instrument and of the hedged asset, liability, firm commitment or highly probable forecast transaction are the same, the changes in fair value and cash flows attributable to the risk being hedged may be likely to offset each other fully, both when the hedge is entered into and afterwards. For example, an interest rate swap is likely to be an effective hedge if the notional and principal amounts, term, repricing dates, dates of interest and principal receipts and payments, and basis for measuring interest rates are the same for the hedging instrument and the hedged item. In addition, a hedge of a highly probable forecast purchase of a commodity with a forward contract is likely to be highly effective if:

(a)   the forward contract is for the purchase of the same quantity of the same commodity at the same time and location as the hedged forecast purchase;

(b)   the fair value of the forward contract at inception is zero; and

(c)   either the change in the discount or premium on the forward contract is excluded from the assessment of effectiveness and recognised in profit or loss or the change in expected cash flows on the highly probable forecast transaction is based on the forward price for the commodity.

AG109   Sometimes the hedging instrument offsets only part of the hedged risk. For example, a hedge would not be fully effective if the hedging instrument and hedged item are denominated in different currencies that do not move in tandem. Also, a hedge of interest rate risk using a derivative would not be fully effective if part of the change in the fair value of the derivative is attributable to the counterparty's credit risk.

AG110   To qualify for hedge accounting, the hedge must relate to a specific identified and designated risk, and not merely to the entity's general business risks, and must ultimately affect the entity's profit or loss. A hedge of the risk of obsolescence of a physical asset or the risk of expropriation of property by a government is not eligible for hedge accounting; effectiveness cannot be measured because those risks are not measurable reliably.

AG110A   Paragraph 74(a) permits an entity to separate the intrinsic value and time value of an option contract and designate as the hedging instrument only the change in the intrinsic value of the option contract. Such a designation may result in a hedging relationship that is perfectly effective in achieving offsetting changes in cash flows attributable to a hedged one-sided risk of a forecast transaction, if the principal terms of the forecast transaction and hedging instrument are the same.

AG110B   If an entity designates a purchased option in its entirety as the hedging instrument of a one-sided risk arising from a forecast transaction, the hedging relationship will not be perfectly effective. This is because the premium paid for the option includes time value and, as stated in paragraph AG99BA, a designated one-sided risk does not include the time value of an option. Therefore, in this situation, there will be no offset between the cash flows relating to the time value of the option premium paid and the designated hedged risk.

AG111   In the case of interest rate risk, hedge effectiveness may be assessed by preparing a maturity schedule for financial assets and financial liabilities that shows the net interest rate exposure for each time period, provided that the net exposure is associated with a specific asset or liability (or a specific group of assets or liabilities or a specific portion of them) giving rise to the net exposure, and hedge effectiveness is assessed against that asset or liability.

AG112   In assessing the effectiveness of a hedge, an entity generally considers the time value of money. The fixed interest rate on a hedged item need not exactly match the fixed interest rate on a swap designated as a fair value hedge. Nor does the variable interest rate on an interest-bearing asset or liability need to be the same as the variable interest rate on a swap designated as a cash flow hedge. A swap's fair value derives from its net settlements. The fixed and variable rates on a swap can be changed without affecting the net settlement if both are changed by the same amount.

AG113   If an entity does not meet hedge effectiveness criteria, the entity discontinues hedge accounting from the last date on which compliance with hedge effectiveness was demonstrated. However, if the entity identifies the event or change in circumstances that caused the hedging relationship to fail the effectiveness criteria, and demonstrates that the hedge was effective before the event or change in circumstances occurred, the entity discontinues hedge accounting from the date of the event or change in circumstances.

AG113A   For the avoidance of doubt, the effects of replacing the original counterparty with a clearing counterparty and making the associated changes as described in paragraphs 91(a)(ii) and 101(a)(ii) shall be reflected in the measurement of the hedging instrument and therefore in the assessment of hedge effectiveness and the measurement of hedge effectiveness.

Fair value hedge accounting for a portfolio hedge of interest rate risk

AG114   For a fair value hedge of interest rate risk associated with a portfolio of financial assets or financial liabilities, an entity would meet the requirements of this Standard if it complies with the procedures set out in (a)–(i) and paragraphs AG115–AG132 below.

(a)   As part of its risk management process the entity identifies a portfolio of items whose interest rate risk it wishes to hedge. The portfolio may comprise only assets, only liabilities or both assets and liabilities. The entity may identify two or more portfolios, in which case it applies the guidance below to each portfolio separately.

(b)   The entity analyses the portfolio into repricing time periods based on expected, rather than contractual, repricing dates. The analysis into repricing time periods may be performed in various ways including scheduling cash flows into the periods in which they are expected to occur, or scheduling notional principal amounts into all periods until repricing is expected to occur.

(c)   On the basis of this analysis, the entity decides the amount it wishes to hedge. The entity designates as the hedged item an amount of assets or liabilities (but not a net amount) from the identified portfolio equal to the amount it wishes to designate as being hedged. This amount also determines the percentage measure that is used for testing effectiveness in accordance with paragraph AG126(b).

(d)   The entity designates the interest rate risk it is hedging. This risk could be a portion of the interest rate risk in each of the items in the hedged position, such as a benchmark interest rate (eg LIBOR).

(e)   The entity designates one or more hedging instruments for each repricing time period.

(f)   Using the designations made in (c)–(e) above, the entity assesses at inception and in subsequent periods, whether the hedge is expected to be highly effective during the period for which the hedge is designated.

(g)   Periodically, the entity measures the change in the fair value of the hedged item (as designated in (c)) that is attributable to the hedged risk (as designated in (d)), on the basis of the expected repricing dates determined in (b). Provided that the hedge is determined actually to have been highly effective when assessed using the entity's documented method of assessing effectiveness, the entity recognises the change in fair value of the hedged item as a gain or loss in profit or loss and in one of two line items in the statement of financial position as described in paragraph 89A. The change in fair value need not be allocated to individual assets or liabilities.

(h)   The entity measures the change in fair value of the hedging instrument(s) (as designated in (e)) and recognises it as a gain or loss in profit or loss. The fair value of the hedging instrument(s) is recognised as an asset or liability in the statement of financial position.

(i)   Any ineffectiveness[3] will be recognised in profit or loss as the difference between the change in fair value referred to in (g) and that referred to in (h).

AG115   This approach is described in more detail below. The approach shall be applied only to a fair value hedge of the interest rate risk associated with a portfolio of financial assets or financial liabilities.

AG116   The portfolio identified in paragraph AG114(a) could contain assets and liabilities. Alternatively, it could be a portfolio containing only assets, or only liabilities. The portfolio is used to determine the amount of the assets or liabilities the entity wishes to hedge. However, the portfolio is not itself designated as the hedged item.

AG117   In applying paragraph AG114(b), the entity determines the expected repricing date of an item as the earlier of the dates when that item is expected to mature or to reprice to market rates. The expected repricing dates are estimated at the inception of the hedge and throughout the term of the hedge, based on historical experience and other available information, including information and expectations regarding prepayment rates, interest rates and the interaction between them. Entities that have no entity-specific experience or insufficient experience use peer group experience for comparable financial instruments. These estimates are reviewed periodically and updated in the light of experience. In the case of a fixed rate item that is prepayable, the expected repricing date is the date on which the item is expected to prepay unless it reprices to market rates on an earlier date. For a group of similar items, the analysis into time periods based on expected repricing dates may take the form of allocating a percentage of the group, rather than individual items, to each time period. An entity may apply other methodologies for such allocation purposes. For example, it may use a prepayment rate multiplier for allocating amortising loans to time periods based on expected repricing dates. However, the methodology for such an allocation shall be in accordance with the entity's risk management procedures and objectives.

AG118   As an example of the designation set out in paragraph AG114(c), if in a particular repricing time period an entity estimates that it has fixed rate assets of CU100 and fixed rate liabilities of CU80 and decides to hedge all of the net position of CU20, it designates as the hedged item assets in the

---

3   The same materiality considerations apply in this context as apply throughout IFRSs.

amount of CU20 (a portion of the assets).[4] The designation is expressed as an 'amount of a currency' (eg an amount of dollars, euro, pounds or rand) rather than as individual assets. It follows that all of the assets (or liabilities) from which the hedged amount is drawn—ie all of the CU100 of assets in the above example—must be:

(a)   items whose fair value changes in response to changes in the interest rate being hedged; and

(b)   items that could have qualified for fair value hedge accounting if they had been designated as hedged individually. In particular, because IFRS 13 specifies that the fair value of a financial liability with a demand feature (such as demand deposits and some types of time deposits) is not less than the amount payable on demand, discounted from the first date that the amount could be required to be paid, such an item cannot qualify for fair value hedge accounting for any time period beyond the shortest period in which the holder can demand payment. In the above example, the hedged position is an amount of assets. Hence, such liabilities are not a part of the designated hedged item, but are used by the entity to determine the amount of the asset that is designated as being hedged. If the position the entity wished to hedge was an amount of liabilities, the amount representing the designated hedged item must be drawn from fixed rate liabilities other than liabilities that the entity can be required to repay in an earlier time period, and the percentage measure used for assessing hedge effectiveness in accordance with paragraph AG126(b) would be calculated as a percentage of these other liabilities. For example, assume that an entity estimates that in a particular repricing time period it has fixed rate liabilities of CU100, comprising CU40 of demand deposits and CU60 of liabilities with no demand feature, and CU70 of fixed rate assets. If the entity decides to hedge all of the net position of CU30, it designates as the hedged item liabilities of CU30 or 50 per cent of the liabilities[5] with no demand feature.

AG119   The entity also complies with the other designation and documentation requirements set out in paragraph 88(a). For a portfolio hedge of interest rate risk, this designation and documentation specifies the entity's policy for all of the variables that are used to identify the amount that is hedged and how effectiveness is measured, including the following:

(a)   which assets and liabilities are to be included in the portfolio hedge and the basis to be used for removing them from the portfolio.

(b)   how the entity estimates repricing dates, including what interest rate assumptions underlie estimates of prepayment rates and the basis for changing those estimates. The same method is used for both the initial estimates made at the time an asset or liability is included in the hedged portfolio and for any later revisions to those estimates.

---

4   The Standard permits an entity to designate any amount of the available qualifying assets or liabilities, ie in this example any amount of assets between CU0 and CU100.

5   $CU30 \div (CU100 - CU40) = 50$ per cent

(c)   the number and duration of repricing time periods.

(d)   how often the entity will test effectiveness and which of the two methods in paragraph AG126 it will use.

(e)   the methodology used by the entity to determine the amount of assets or liabilities that are designated as the hedged item and, accordingly, the percentage measure used when the entity tests effectiveness using the method described in paragraph AG126(b).

(f)   when the entity tests effectiveness using the method described in paragraph AG126(b), whether the entity will test effectiveness for each repricing time period individually, for all time periods in aggregate, or by using some combination of the two.

The policies specified in designating and documenting the hedging relationship shall be in accordance with the entity's risk management procedures and objectives. Changes in policies shall not be made arbitrarily. They shall be justified on the basis of changes in market conditions and other factors and be founded on and consistent with the entity's risk management procedures and objectives.

AG120   The hedging instrument referred to in paragraph AG114(e) may be a single derivative or a portfolio of derivatives all of which contain exposure to the hedged interest rate risk designated in paragraph AG114(d) (eg a portfolio of interest rate swaps all of which contain exposure to LIBOR). Such a portfolio of derivatives may contain offsetting risk positions. However, it may not include written options or net written options, because the Standard[6] does not permit such options to be designated as hedging instruments (except when a written option is designated as an offset to a purchased option). If the hedging instrument hedges the amount designated in paragraph AG114(c) for more than one repricing time period, it is allocated to all of the time periods that it hedges. However, the whole of the hedging instrument must be allocated to those repricing time periods because the Standard[7] does not permit a hedging relationship to be designated for only a portion of the time period during which a hedging instrument remains outstanding.

AG121   When the entity measures the change in the fair value of a prepayable item in accordance with paragraph AG114(g), a change in interest rates affects the fair value of the prepayable item in two ways: it affects the fair value of the contractual cash flows and the fair value of the prepayment option that is contained in a prepayable item. Paragraph 81 of the Standard permits an entity to designate a portion of a financial asset or financial liability, sharing a common risk exposure, as the hedged item, provided effectiveness can be measured. For prepayable items, paragraph 81A permits this to be achieved by designating the hedged item in terms of the change in the fair value that is attributable to changes in the designated interest rate on the basis of *expected*, rather than *contractual*, repricing dates. However, the effect that changes in the hedged interest rate have on those expected repricing dates shall be

---

6   see paragraphs 77 and AG94

7   see paragraph 75

included when determining the change in the fair value of the hedged item. Consequently, if the expected repricing dates are revised (eg to reflect a change in expected prepayments), or if actual repricing dates differ from those expected, ineffectiveness will arise as described in paragraph AG126. Conversely, changes in expected repricing dates that (a) clearly arise from factors other than changes in the hedged interest rate, (b) are uncorrelated with changes in the hedged interest rate and (c) can be reliably separated from changes that are attributable to the hedged interest rate (eg changes in prepayment rates clearly arising from a change in demographic factors or tax regulations rather than changes in interest rate) are excluded when determining the change in the fair value of the hedged item, because they are not attributable to the hedged risk. If there is uncertainty about the factor that gave rise to the change in expected repricing dates or the entity is not able to separate reliably the changes that arise from the hedged interest rate from those that arise from other factors, the change is assumed to arise from changes in the hedged interest rate.

AG122　The Standard does not specify the techniques used to determine the amount referred to in paragraph AG114(g), namely the change in the fair value of the hedged item that is attributable to the hedged risk. If statistical or other estimation techniques are used for such measurement, management must expect the result to approximate closely that which would have been obtained from measurement of all the individual assets or liabilities that constitute the hedged item. It is not appropriate to assume that changes in the fair value of the hedged item equal changes in the value of the hedging instrument.

AG123　Paragraph 89A requires that if the hedged item for a particular repricing time period is an asset, the change in its value is presented in a separate line item within assets. Conversely, if the hedged item for a particular repricing time period is a liability, the change in its value is presented in a separate line item within liabilities. These are the separate line items referred to in paragraph AG114(g). Specific allocation to individual assets (or liabilities) is not required.

AG124　Paragraph AG114(i) notes that ineffectiveness arises to the extent that the change in the fair value of the hedged item that is attributable to the hedged risk differs from the change in the fair value of the hedging derivative. Such a difference may arise for a number of reasons, including:

(a)　actual repricing dates being different from those expected, or expected repricing dates being revised;

(b)　items in the hedged portfolio becoming impaired or being derecognised;

(c)　the payment dates of the hedging instrument and the hedged item being different; and

(d)　other causes (eg when a few of the hedged items bear interest at a rate below the benchmark rate for which they are designated as being hedged, and the resulting ineffectiveness is not so great that the portfolio as a whole fails to qualify for hedge accounting).

Such ineffectiveness[8] shall be identified and recognised in profit or loss.

AG125   Generally, the effectiveness of the hedge will be improved:

(a)   if the entity schedules items with different prepayment characteristics in a way that takes account of the differences in prepayment behaviour.

(b)   when the number of items in the portfolio is larger. When only a few items are contained in the portfolio, relatively high ineffectiveness is likely if one of the items prepays earlier or later than expected. Conversely, when the portfolio contains many items, the prepayment behaviour can be predicted more accurately.

(c)   when the repricing time periods used are narrower (eg 1-month as opposed to 3-month repricing time periods). Narrower repricing time periods reduce the effect of any mismatch between the repricing and payment dates (within the repricing time period) of the hedged item and those of the hedging instrument.

(d)   the greater the frequency with which the amount of the hedging instrument is adjusted to reflect changes in the hedged item (eg because of changes in prepayment expectations).

AG126   An entity tests effectiveness periodically. If estimates of repricing dates change between one date on which an entity assesses effectiveness and the next, it shall calculate the amount of effectiveness either:

(a)   as the difference between the change in the fair value of the hedging instrument (see paragraph AG114(h)) and the change in the value of the entire hedged item that is attributable to changes in the hedged interest rate (including the effect that changes in the hedged interest rate have on the fair value of any embedded prepayment option); or

(b)   using the following approximation. The entity:

(i)   calculates the percentage of the assets (or liabilities) in each repricing time period that was hedged, on the basis of the estimated repricing dates at the last date it tested effectiveness.

(ii)   applies this percentage to its revised estimate of the amount in that repricing time period to calculate the amount of the hedged item based on its revised estimate.

(iii)   calculates the change in the fair value of its revised estimate of the hedged item that is attributable to the hedged risk and presents it as set out in paragraph AG114(g).

(iv)   recognises ineffectiveness equal to the difference between the amount determined in (iii) and the change in the fair value of the hedging instrument (see paragraph AG114(h)).

---

8   The same materiality considerations apply in this context as apply throughout IFRSs.

AG127   When measuring effectiveness, the entity distinguishes revisions to the estimated repricing dates of existing assets (or liabilities) from the origination of new assets (or liabilities), with only the former giving rise to ineffectiveness. All revisions to estimated repricing dates (other than those excluded in accordance with paragraph AG121), including any reallocation of existing items between time periods, are included when revising the estimated amount in a time period in accordance with paragraph AG126(b)(ii) and hence when measuring effectiveness. Once ineffectiveness has been recognised as set out above, the entity establishes a new estimate of the total assets (or liabilities) in each repricing time period, including new assets (or liabilities) that have been originated since it last tested effectiveness, and designates a new amount as the hedged item and a new percentage as the hedged percentage. The procedures set out in paragraph AG126(b) are then repeated at the next date it tests effectiveness.

AG128   Items that were originally scheduled into a repricing time period may be derecognised because of earlier than expected prepayment or write-offs caused by impairment or sale. When this occurs, the amount of change in fair value included in the separate line item referred to in paragraph AG114(g) that relates to the derecognised item shall be removed from the statement of financial position, and included in the gain or loss that arises on derecognition of the item. For this purpose, it is necessary to know the repricing time period(s) into which the derecognised item was scheduled, because this determines the repricing time period(s) from which to remove it and hence the amount to remove from the separate line item referred to in paragraph AG114(g). When an item is derecognised, if it can be determined in which time period it was included, it is removed from that time period. If not, it is removed from the earliest time period if the derecognition resulted from higher than expected prepayments, or allocated to all time periods containing the derecognised item on a systematic and rational basis if the item was sold or became impaired.

AG129   In addition, any amount relating to a particular time period that has not been derecognised when the time period expires is recognised in profit or loss at that time (see paragraph 89A). For example, assume an entity schedules items into three repricing time periods. At the previous redesignation, the change in fair value reported in the single line item in the statement of financial position was an asset of CU25. That amount represents amounts attributable to periods 1, 2 and 3 of CU7, CU8 and CU10, respectively. At the next redesignation, the assets attributable to period 1 have been either realised or rescheduled into other periods. Therefore, CU7 is derecognised from the statement of financial position and recognised in profit or loss. CU8 and CU10 are now attributable to periods 1 and 2, respectively. These remaining periods are then adjusted, as necessary, for changes in fair value as described in paragraph AG114(g).

AG130   As an illustration of the requirements of the previous two paragraphs, assume that an entity scheduled assets by allocating a percentage of the portfolio into each repricing time period. Assume also that it scheduled CU100 into each of the first two time periods. When the first repricing time period expires,

CU110 of assets are derecognised because of expected and unexpected repayments. In this case, all of the amount contained in the separate line item referred to in paragraph AG114(g) that relates to the first time period is removed from the statement of financial position, plus 10 per cent of the amount that relates to the second time period.

AG131 If the hedged amount for a repricing time period is reduced without the related assets (or liabilities) being derecognised, the amount included in the separate line item referred to in paragraph AG114(g) that relates to the reduction shall be amortised in accordance with paragraph 92.

AG132 An entity may wish to apply the approach set out in paragraphs AG114–AG131 to a portfolio hedge that had previously been accounted for as a cash flow hedge in accordance with IAS 39. Such an entity would revoke the previous designation of a cash flow hedge in accordance with paragraph 101(d), and apply the requirements set out in that paragraph. It would also redesignate the hedge as a fair value hedge and apply the approach set out in paragraphs AG114–AG131 prospectively to subsequent accounting periods.

Transition (paragraphs 103–108C)

AG133 An entity may have designated a forecast intragroup transaction as a hedged item at the start of an annual period beginning on or after 1 January 2005 (or, for the purpose of restating comparative information, the start of an earlier comparative period) in a hedge that would qualify for hedge accounting in accordance with this Standard (as amended by the last sentence of paragraph 80). Such an entity may use that designation to apply hedge accounting in consolidated financial statements from the start of the annual period beginning on or after 1 January 2005 (or the start of the earlier comparative period). Such an entity shall also apply paragraphs AG99A and AG99B from the start of the annual period beginning on or after 1 January 2005. However, in accordance with paragraph 108B, it need not apply paragraph AG99B to comparative information for earlier periods.

Appendix B
Amendments to other pronouncements

The amendments in this appendix shall be applied for annual periods beginning on or after 1 January 2005. If an entity applies this Standard for an earlier period, these amendments shall be applied for that earlier period.

* * * * *

The amendments contained in this appendix when this Standard was revised in 2003 have been incorporated into the relevant pronouncements.

Approval by the Board of *Fair Value Hedge Accounting for a Portfolio Hedge of Interest Rate Risk* (Amendments to IAS 39) issued in March 2004

Fair Value Hedge Accounting for a Portfolio Hedge of Interest Rate Risk (Amendments to IAS 39) was approved for issue by thirteen of the fourteen members of the International Accounting Standards Board. Mr Smith dissented. His dissenting opinion is set out after the Basis for Conclusions.

Sir David Tweedie   Chairman

Thomas E Jones   Vice-Chairman

Mary E Barth

Hans-Georg Bruns

Anthony T Cope

Robert P Garnett

Gilbert Gélard

James J Leisenring

Warren J McGregor

Patricia L O'Malley

Harry K Schmid

John T Smith

Geoffrey Whittington

Tatsumi Yamada

Approval by the Board of *Transition and Initial Recognition of Financial Assets and Financial Liabilities* (Amendments to IAS 39) issued in December 2004

Transition and Initial Recognition of Financial Assets and Financial Liabilities (Amendments to IAS 39) was approved for issue by the fourteen members of the International Accounting Standards Board.

Sir David Tweedie	Chairman
Thomas E Jones	Vice-Chairman
Mary E Barth	
Hans-Georg Bruns	
Anthony T Cope	
Jan Engström	
Robert P Garnett	
Gilbert Gélard	
James J Leisenring	
Warren J McGregor	
Patricia L O'Malley	
John T Smith	
Geoffrey Whittington	
Tatsumi Yamada	

Approval by the Board of *Cash Flow Hedge Accounting of Forecast Intragroup Transactions* (Amendments to IAS 39) issued in April 2005

Cash Flow Hedge Accounting of Forecast Intragroup Transactions (Amendments to IAS 39) was approved for issue by the fourteen members of the International Accounting Standards Board.

Sir David Tweedie	Chairman
Thomas E Jones	Vice-Chairman
Mary E Barth	
Hans-Georg Bruns	
Anthony T Cope	
Jan Engström	
Robert P Garnett	
Gilbert Gélard	
James J Leisenring	
Warren J McGregor	
Patricia L O'Malley	
John T Smith	
Geoffrey Whittington	
Tatsumi Yamada	

Approval by the Board of *Financial Guarantee Contracts* (Amendments to IAS 39 and IFRS 4) issued in August 2005

Financial Guarantee Contracts (Amendments to IAS 39 and IFRS 4 *Insurance Contracts*) was approved for issue by the fourteen members of the International Accounting Standards Board.

Sir David Tweedie	Chairman
Thomas E Jones	Vice-Chairman
Mary E Barth	
Hans-Georg Bruns	
Anthony T Cope	
Jan Engström	
Robert P Garnett	
Gilbert Gélard	
James J Leisenring	
Warren J McGregor	
Patricia L O'Malley	
John T Smith	
Geoffrey Whittington	
Tatsumi Yamada	

Approval by the Board of *Eligible Hedged Items* (Amendment to IAS 39) issued in July 2008

Eligible Hedged Items (Amendment to IAS 39) was approved for issue by the thirteen members of the International Accounting Standards Board.

Sir David Tweedie	Chairman
Thomas E Jones	Vice-Chairman
Mary E Barth	
Stephen Cooper	
Philippe Danjou	
Jan Engström	
Robert P Garnett	
Gilbert Gélard	
James J Leisenring	
Warren J McGregor	
John T Smith	
Tatsumi Yamada	
Wei-Guo Zhang	

Approval by the Board of *Embedded Derivatives* (Amendments to IFRIC 9 and IAS 39) issued in March 2009

Embedded Derivatives (Amendments to IFRIC 9 and IAS 39) was approved for issue by the fourteen members of the International Accounting Standards Board.

Sir David Tweedie	Chairman
Thomas E Jones	Vice-Chairman
Mary E Barth	
Stephen Cooper	
Philippe Danjou	
Jan Engström	
Robert P Garnett	
Gilbert Gélard	
Prabhakar Kalavacherla	
James J Leisenring	
Warren J McGregor	
John T Smith	
Tatsumi Yamada	
Wei-Guo Zhang	

Approval by the Board of *Novation of Derivatives and Continuation of Hedge Accounting* (Amendments to IAS 39) issued in June 2013

Novation of Derivatives and Continuation of Hedge Accounting was approved for issue by the sixteen members of the International Accounting Standards Board.

Hans Hoogervorst	Chairman
Ian Mackintosh	Vice-Chairman
Stephen Cooper	
Philippe Danjou	
Martin Edelmann	
Jan Engström	
Patrick Finnegan	
Amaro Luiz de Oliveira Gomes	
Gary Kabureck	
Prabhakar Kalavacherla	
Patricia McConnell	
Takatsugu Ochi	
Darrel Scott	
Chungwoo Suh	
Mary Tokar	
Wei-Guo Zhang	

Approval by the Board of IFRS 9 *Financial Instruments* (Hedge Accounting and amendments to IFRS 9, IFRS 7 and IAS 39) issued in November 2013

IFRS 9 *Financial Instruments* (Hedge Accounting and amendments to IFRS 9, IFRS 7 and IAS 39) was approved for issue by fifteen of the sixteen members of the International Accounting Standards Board. Mr Finnegan dissented. His dissenting opinion is set out after the Basis for Conclusions.

Hans Hoogervorst	Chairman
Ian Mackintosh	Vice-Chairman
Stephen Cooper	
Philippe Danjou	
Martin Edelmann	
Jan Engström	
Patrick Finnegan	
Amaro Luiz de Oliveira Gomes	
Gary Kabureck	
Prabhakar Kalavacherla	
Patricia McConnell	
Takatsugu Ochi	
Darrel Scott	
Chungwoo Suh	
Mary Tokar	
Wei-Guo Zhang	

Approval by the Board of *Interest Rate Benchmark Reform* issued in September 2019

Interest Rate Benchmark Reform, which amended IFRS 9, IAS 39 and IFRS 7, was approved for issue by all 14 members of the International Accounting Standards Board (Board).

Hans Hoogervorst	Chairman
Suzanne Lloyd	Vice-Chair
Nick Anderson	
Tadeu Cendon	
Martin Edelmann	
Françoise Flores	
Gary Kabureck	
Jianqiao Lu	
Darrel Scott	
Thomas Scott	
Chungwoo Suh	
Rika Suzuki	
Ann Tarca	
Mary Tokar	

Approval by the Board of *Interest Rate Benchmark Reform—Phase 2* issued in August 2020

Interest Rate Benchmark Reform—Phase 2, which amended IFRS 9, IAS 39, IFRS 7, IFRS 4 and IFRS 16, was approved for issue by 12 of 13 members of the International Accounting Standards Board (Board). Mr Gast abstained in view of his recent appointment to the Board.

Hans Hoogervorst	Chairman
Suzanne Lloyd	Vice-Chair
Nick Anderson	
Tadeu Cendon	
Martin Edelmann	
Françoise Flores	
Zach Gast	
Jianqiao Lu	
Darrel Scott	
Thomas Scott	
Rika Suzuki	
Ann Tarca	
Mary Tokar	

IAS 40

Investment Property

In April 2001 the International Accounting Standards Board (Board) adopted IAS 40 *Investment Property*, which had originally been issued by the International Accounting Standards Committee in April 2000. That Standard had replaced some parts of IAS 25 *Accounting for Investments*, which had been issued in March 1986 and had not already been replaced by IAS 39 *Financial Instruments: Recognition and Measurement*.

In December 2003 the Board issued a revised IAS 40 as part of its initial agenda of technical projects.

In January 2016, IFRS 16 *Leases* made various amendments to IAS 40, including expanding its scope to include both owned investment property and investment property held by a lessee as a right-of-use asset.

In December 2016, the Board issued *Transfers of Investment Property* (Amendments to IAS 40) which clarifies when there is a transfer to, or from, investment property.

Other Standards have made minor consequential amendments to IAS 40. They include IFRS 13 *Fair Value Measurement* (issued May 2011), *Annual Improvements to IFRSs 2011–2013 Cycle* (issued December 2013), IFRS 15 *Revenue from Contracts with Customers* (issued May 2014), *Agriculture: Bearer Plants* (Amendments to IAS 16 and IAS 41) (issued June 2014) and *Amendments to References to the Conceptual Framework in IFRS Standards* (issued March 2018).

CONTENTS

FOR THE BASIS FOR CONCLUSIONS, SEE PART C OF THIS EDITION

© IFRS Foundation

International Accounting Standard 40 *Investment Property* (IAS 40) is set out in paragraphs 1–86. All the paragraphs have equal authority but retain the IASC format of the Standard when it was adopted by the IASB. IAS 40 should be read in the context of its objective and the IASB's Basis for Conclusions, the *Preface to IFRS Standards* and the *Conceptual Framework for Financial Reporting*. IAS 8 *Accounting Policies, Changes in Accounting Estimates and Errors* provides a basis for selecting and applying accounting policies in the absence of explicit guidance.

International Accounting Standard 40
Investment Property

Objective

1   The objective of this Standard is to prescribe the accounting treatment for investment property and related disclosure requirements.

Scope

2   This Standard shall be applied in the recognition, measurement and disclosure of investment property.

3   [Deleted]

4   This Standard does not apply to:

(a)   biological assets related to agricultural activity (see IAS 41 *Agriculture* and IAS 16 *Property, Plant and Equipment*); and

(b)   mineral rights and mineral reserves such as oil, natural gas and similar non-regenerative resources.

Definitions

5   The following terms are used in this Standard with the meanings specified:

Carrying amount is the amount at which an asset is recognised in the statement of financial position.

Cost is the amount of cash or cash equivalents paid or the fair value of other consideration given to acquire an asset at the time of its acquisition or construction or, where applicable, the amount attributed to that asset when initially recognised in accordance with the specific requirements of other IFRSs, eg IFRS 2 *Share-based Payment*.

Fair value is the price that would be received to sell an asset or paid to transfer a liability in an orderly transaction between market participants at the measurement date. (See IFRS 13 *Fair Value Measurement*).

Investment property is property (land or a building — or part of a building — or both) held (by the owner or by the lessee as a right-of-use asset) to earn rentals or for capital appreciation or both, rather than for:

(a)   use in the production or supply of goods or services or for administrative purposes; or

(b)   sale in the ordinary course of business.

Owner-occupied property is property held (by the owner or by the lessee as a right-of-use asset) for use in the production or supply of goods or services or for administrative purposes.

Classification of property as investment property or owner-occupied property

6   [Deleted]

7   Investment property is held to earn rentals or for capital appreciation or both. Therefore, an investment property generates cash flows largely independently of the other assets held by an entity. This distinguishes investment property from owner-occupied property. The production or supply of goods or services (or the use of property for administrative purposes) generates cash flows that are attributable not only to property, but also to other assets used in the production or supply process. IAS 16 applies to owned owner-occupied property and IFRS 16 *Leases* applies to owner-occupied property held by a lessee as a right-of-use asset.

8   The following are examples of investment property:

(a)   land held for long-term capital appreciation rather than for short-term sale in the ordinary course of business.

(b)   land held for a currently undetermined future use. (If an entity has not determined that it will use the land as owner-occupied property or for short-term sale in the ordinary course of business, the land is regarded as held for capital appreciation.)

(c)   a building owned by the entity (or a right-of-use asset relating to a building held by the entity) and leased out under one or more operating leases.

(d)   a building that is vacant but is held to be leased out under one or more operating leases.

(e)   property that is being constructed or developed for future use as investment property.

9   The following are examples of items that are not investment property and are therefore outside the scope of this Standard:

(a)   property intended for sale in the ordinary course of business or in the process of construction or development for such sale (see IAS 2 *Inventories*), for example, property acquired exclusively with a view to subsequent disposal in the near future or for development and resale.

(b)   [deleted]

(c)   owner-occupied property (see IAS 16 and IFRS 16), including (among other things) property held for future use as owner-occupied property, property held for future development and subsequent use as owner-occupied property, property occupied by employees (whether or not the employees pay rent at market rates) and owner-occupied property awaiting disposal.

(d)   [deleted]

(e)   property that is leased to another entity under a finance lease.

10　Some properties comprise a portion that is held to earn rentals or for capital appreciation and another portion that is held for use in the production or supply of goods or services or for administrative purposes. If these portions could be sold separately (or leased out separately under a finance lease), an entity accounts for the portions separately. If the portions could not be sold separately, the property is investment property only if an insignificant portion is held for use in the production or supply of goods or services or for administrative purposes.

11　In some cases, an entity provides ancillary services to the occupants of a property it holds. An entity treats such a property as investment property if the services are insignificant to the arrangement as a whole. An example is when the owner of an office building provides security and maintenance services to the lessees who occupy the building.

12　In other cases, the services provided are significant. For example, if an entity owns and manages a hotel, services provided to guests are significant to the arrangement as a whole. Therefore, an owner-managed hotel is owner-occupied property, rather than investment property.

13　It may be difficult to determine whether ancillary services are so significant that a property does not qualify as investment property. For example, the owner of a hotel sometimes transfers some responsibilities to third parties under a management contract. The terms of such contracts vary widely. At one end of the spectrum, the owner's position may, in substance, be that of a passive investor. At the other end of the spectrum, the owner may simply have outsourced day-to-day functions while retaining significant exposure to variation in the cash flows generated by the operations of the hotel.

14　Judgement is needed to determine whether a property qualifies as investment property. An entity develops criteria so that it can exercise that judgement consistently in accordance with the definition of investment property and with the related guidance in paragraphs 7–13. Paragraph 75(c) requires an entity to disclose these criteria when classification is difficult.

14A　Judgement is also needed to determine whether the acquisition of investment property is the acquisition of an asset or a group of assets or a business combination within the scope of IFRS 3 *Business Combinations*. Reference should be made to IFRS 3 to determine whether it is a business combination. The discussion in paragraphs 7–14 of this Standard relates to whether or not property is owner-occupied property or investment property and not to determining whether or not the acquisition of property is a business combination as defined in IFRS 3. Determining whether a specific transaction meets the definition of a business combination as defined in IFRS 3 and includes an investment property as defined in this Standard requires the separate application of both Standards.

15　In some cases, an entity owns property that is leased to, and occupied by, its parent or another subsidiary. The property does not qualify as investment property in the consolidated financial statements, because the property is owner-occupied from the perspective of the group. However, from the perspective of the entity that owns it, the property is investment property if it meets the definition in paragraph 5. Therefore, the lessor treats the property as investment property in its individual financial statements.

Recognition

16   An owned investment property shall be recognised as an asset when, and only when:

    (a)   it is probable that the future economic benefits that are associated with the investment property will flow to the entity; and

    (b)   the cost of the investment property can be measured reliably.

17   An entity evaluates under this recognition principle all its investment property costs at the time they are incurred. These costs include costs incurred initially to acquire an investment property and costs incurred subsequently to add to, replace part of, or service a property.

18   Under the recognition principle in paragraph 16, an entity does not recognise in the carrying amount of an investment property the costs of the day-to-day servicing of such a property. Rather, these costs are recognised in profit or loss as incurred. Costs of day-to-day servicing are primarily the cost of labour and consumables, and may include the cost of minor parts. The purpose of these expenditures is often described as for the 'repairs and maintenance' of the property.

19   Parts of investment properties may have been acquired through replacement. For example, the interior walls may be replacements of original walls. Under the recognition principle, an entity recognises in the carrying amount of an investment property the cost of replacing part of an existing investment property at the time that cost is incurred if the recognition criteria are met. The carrying amount of those parts that are replaced is derecognised in accordance with the derecognition provisions of this Standard.

19A   An investment property held by a lessee as a right-of-use asset shall be recognised in accordance with IFRS 16.

Measurement at recognition

20   An owned investment property shall be measured initially at its cost. Transaction costs shall be included in the initial measurement.

21   The cost of a purchased investment property comprises its purchase price and any directly attributable expenditure. Directly attributable expenditure includes, for example, professional fees for legal services, property transfer taxes and other transaction costs.

22   [Deleted]

23   The cost of an investment property is not increased by:

    (a)   start-up costs (unless they are necessary to bring the property to the condition necessary for it to be capable of operating in the manner intended by management),

(b)   operating losses incurred before the investment property achieves the planned level of occupancy, or

(c)   abnormal amounts of wasted material, labour or other resources incurred in constructing or developing the property.

24   If payment for an investment property is deferred, its cost is the cash price equivalent. The difference between this amount and the total payments is recognised as interest expense over the period of credit.

25   [Deleted]

26   [Deleted]

27   One or more investment properties may be acquired in exchange for a non-monetary asset or assets, or a combination of monetary and non-monetary assets. The following discussion refers to an exchange of one non-monetary asset for another, but it also applies to all exchanges described in the preceding sentence. The cost of such an investment property is measured at fair value unless (a) the exchange transaction lacks commercial substance or (b) the fair value of neither the asset received nor the asset given up is reliably measurable. The acquired asset is measured in this way even if an entity cannot immediately derecognise the asset given up. If the acquired asset is not measured at fair value, its cost is measured at the carrying amount of the asset given up.

28   An entity determines whether an exchange transaction has commercial substance by considering the extent to which its future cash flows are expected to change as a result of the transaction. An exchange transaction has commercial substance if:

(a)   the configuration (risk, timing and amount) of the cash flows of the asset received differs from the configuration of the cash flows of the asset transferred, or

(b)   the entity-specific value of the portion of the entity's operations affected by the transaction changes as a result of the exchange, and

(c)   the difference in (a) or (b) is significant relative to the fair value of the assets exchanged.

For the purpose of determining whether an exchange transaction has commercial substance, the entity-specific value of the portion of the entity's operations affected by the transaction shall reflect post-tax cash flows. The result of these analyses may be clear without an entity having to perform detailed calculations.

29   The fair value of an asset is reliably measurable if (a) the variability in the range of reasonable fair value measurements is not significant for that asset or (b) the probabilities of the various estimates within the range can be reasonably assessed and used when measuring fair value. If the entity is able to measure reliably the fair value of either the asset received or the asset given up, then the fair value of the asset given up is used to measure cost unless the fair value of the asset received is more clearly evident.

29A An investment property held by a lessee as a right-of-use asset shall be measured initially at its cost in accordance with IFRS 16.

Measurement after recognition

Accounting policy

30 With the exception noted in paragraph 32A, an entity shall choose as its accounting policy either the fair value model in paragraphs 33–55 or the cost model in paragraph 56 and shall apply that policy to all of its investment property.

31 IAS 8 *Accounting Policies, Changes in Accounting Estimates and Errors* states that a voluntary change in accounting policy shall be made only if the change results in the financial statements providing reliable and more relevant information about the effects of transactions, other events or conditions on the entity's financial position, financial performance or cash flows. It is highly unlikely that a change from the fair value model to the cost model will result in a more relevant presentation.

32 This Standard requires all entities to measure the fair value of investment property, for the purpose of either measurement (if the entity uses the fair value model) or disclosure (if it uses the cost model). An entity is encouraged, but not required, to measure the fair value of investment property on the basis of a valuation by an independent valuer who holds a recognised and relevant professional qualification and has recent experience in the location and category of the investment property being valued.

32A An entity may:

(a) choose either the fair value model or the cost model for all investment property backing liabilities that pay a return linked directly to the fair value of, or returns from, specified assets including that investment property; and

(b) choose either the fair value model or the cost model for all other investment property, regardless of the choice made in (a).

32B Some insurers and other entities operate an internal property fund that issues notional units, with some units held by investors in linked contracts and others held by the entity. Paragraph 32A does not permit an entity to measure the property held by the fund partly at cost and partly at fair value.

32C If an entity chooses different models for the two categories described in paragraph 32A, sales of investment property between pools of assets measured using different models shall be recognised at fair value and the cumulative change in fair value shall be recognised in profit or loss. Accordingly, if an investment property is sold from a pool in which the fair value model is used into a pool in which the cost model is used, the property's fair value at the date of the sale becomes its deemed cost.

Fair value model

33   After initial recognition, an entity that chooses the fair value model shall measure all of its investment property at fair value, except in the cases described in paragraph 53.

34   [Deleted]

35   A gain or loss arising from a change in the fair value of investment property shall be recognised in profit or loss for the period in which it arises.

36–39   [Deleted]

40   When measuring the fair value of investment property in accordance with IFRS 13, an entity shall ensure that the fair value reflects, among other things, rental income from current leases and other assumptions that market participants would use when pricing investment property under current market conditions.

40A   When a lessee uses the fair value model to measure an investment property that is held as a right-of-use asset, it shall measure the right-of-use asset, and not the underlying property, at fair value.

41   IFRS 16 specifies the basis for initial recognition of the cost of an investment property held by a lessee as a right-of-use asset. Paragraph 33 requires the investment property held by a lessee as a right-of-use asset to be remeasured, if necessary, to fair value if the entity chooses the fair value model. When lease payments are at market rates, the fair value of an investment property held by a lessee as a right-of-use asset at acquisition, net of all expected lease payments (including those relating to recognised lease liabilities), should be zero. Thus, remeasuring a right-of-use asset from cost in accordance with IFRS 16 to fair value in accordance with paragraph 33 (taking into account the requirements in paragraph 50) should not give rise to any initial gain or loss, unless fair value is measured at different times. This could occur when an election to apply the fair value model is made after initial recognition.

42–47   [Deleted]

48   In exceptional cases, there is clear evidence when an entity first acquires an investment property (or when an existing property first becomes investment property after a change in use) that the variability in the range of reasonable fair value measurements will be so great, and the probabilities of the various outcomes so difficult to assess, that the usefulness of a single measure of fair value is negated. This may indicate that the fair value of the property will not be reliably measurable on a continuing basis (see paragraph 53).

49   [Deleted]

50   In determining the carrying amount of investment property under the fair value model, an entity does not double-count assets or liabilities that are recognised as separate assets or liabilities. For example:

obligation is satisfied in IFRS 15. IFRS 16 applies to a disposal effected by entering into a finance lease and to a sale and leaseback.

68   If, in accordance with the recognition principle in paragraph 16, an entity recognises in the carrying amount of an asset the cost of a replacement for part of an investment property, it derecognises the carrying amount of the replaced part. For investment property accounted for using the cost model, a replaced part may not be a part that was depreciated separately. If it is not practicable for an entity to determine the carrying amount of the replaced part, it may use the cost of the replacement as an indication of what the cost of the replaced part was at the time it was acquired or constructed. Under the fair value model, the fair value of the investment property may already reflect that the part to be replaced has lost its value. In other cases it may be difficult to discern how much fair value should be reduced for the part being replaced. An alternative to reducing fair value for the replaced part, when it is not practical to do so, is to include the cost of the replacement in the carrying amount of the asset and then to reassess the fair value, as would be required for additions not involving replacement.

69   **Gains or losses arising from the retirement or disposal of investment property shall be determined as the difference between the net disposal proceeds and the carrying amount of the asset and shall be recognised in profit or loss (unless IFRS 16 requires otherwise on a sale and leaseback) in the period of the retirement or disposal.**

70   The amount of consideration to be included in the gain or loss arising from the derecognition of an investment property is determined in accordance with the requirements for determining the transaction price in paragraphs 47–72 of IFRS 15. Subsequent changes to the estimated amount of the consideration included in the gain or loss shall be accounted for in accordance with the requirements for changes in the transaction price in IFRS 15.

71   An entity applies IAS 37 or other Standards, as appropriate, to any liabilities that it retains after disposal of an investment property.

72   **Compensation from third parties for investment property that was impaired, lost or given up shall be recognised in profit or loss when the compensation becomes receivable.**

73   Impairments or losses of investment property, related claims for or payments of compensation from third parties and any subsequent purchase or construction of replacement assets are separate economic events and are accounted for separately as follows:

(a)   impairments of investment property are recognised in accordance with IAS 36;

(b)   retirements or disposals of investment property are recognised in accordance with paragraphs 66–71 of this Standard;

(c)   compensation from third parties for investment property that was impaired, lost or given up is recognised in profit or loss when it becomes receivable; and

(d) the cost of assets restored, purchased or constructed as replacements is determined in accordance with paragraphs 20–29 of this Standard.

Disclosure

Fair value model and cost model

74 The disclosures below apply in addition to those in IFRS 16. In accordance with IFRS 16, the owner of an investment property provides lessors' disclosures about leases into which it has entered. A lessee that holds an investment property as a right-of-use asset provides lessees' disclosures as required by IFRS 16 and lessors' disclosures as required by IFRS 16 for any operating leases into which it has entered.

75 An entity shall disclose:

(a) whether it applies the fair value model or the cost model.

(b) [deleted]

(c) when classification is difficult (see paragraph 14), the criteria it uses to distinguish investment property from owner-occupied property and from property held for sale in the ordinary course of business.

(d) [deleted]

(e) the extent to which the fair value of investment property (as measured or disclosed in the financial statements) is based on a valuation by an independent valuer who holds a recognised and relevant professional qualification and has recent experience in the location and category of the investment property being valued. If there has been no such valuation, that fact shall be disclosed.

(f) the amounts recognised in profit or loss for:

(i) rental income from investment property;

(ii) direct operating expenses (including repairs and maintenance) arising from investment property that generated rental income during the period;

(iii) direct operating expenses (including repairs and maintenance) arising from investment property that did not generate rental income during the period; and

(iv) the cumulative change in fair value recognised in profit or loss on a sale of investment property from a pool of assets in which the cost model is used into a pool in which the fair value model is used (see paragraph 32C).

(g) the existence and amounts of restrictions on the realisability of investment property or the remittance of income and proceeds of disposal.

(h) contractual obligations to purchase, construct or develop investment property or for repairs, maintenance or enhancements.

Fair value model

76 In addition to the disclosures required by paragraph 75, an entity that applies the fair value model in paragraphs 33–55 shall disclose a reconciliation between the carrying amounts of investment property at the beginning and end of the period, showing the following:

(a) additions, disclosing separately those additions resulting from acquisitions and those resulting from subsequent expenditure recognised in the carrying amount of an asset;

(b) additions resulting from acquisitions through business combinations;

(c) assets classified as held for sale or included in a disposal group classified as held for sale in accordance with IFRS 5 and other disposals;

(d) net gains or losses from fair value adjustments;

(e) the net exchange differences arising on the translation of the financial statements into a different presentation currency, and on translation of a foreign operation into the presentation currency of the reporting entity;

(f) transfers to and from inventories and owner-occupied property; and

(g) other changes.

77 When a valuation obtained for investment property is adjusted significantly for the purpose of the financial statements, for example to avoid double-counting of assets or liabilities that are recognised as separate assets and liabilities as described in paragraph 50, the entity shall disclose a reconciliation between the valuation obtained and the adjusted valuation included in the financial statements, showing separately the aggregate amount of any recognised lease liabilities that have been added back, and any other significant adjustments.

78 In the exceptional cases referred to in paragraph 53, when an entity measures investment property using the cost model in IAS 16 or in accordance with IFRS 16, the reconciliation required by paragraph 76 shall disclose amounts relating to that investment property separately from amounts relating to other investment property. In addition, an entity shall disclose:

(a) a description of the investment property;

(b) an explanation of why fair value cannot be measured reliably;

(c) if possible, the range of estimates within which fair value is highly likely to lie; and

(d) on disposal of investment property not carried at fair value:

(i)   the fact that the entity has disposed of investment property not carried at fair value;

(ii)   the carrying amount of that investment property at the time of sale; and

(iii)   the amount of gain or loss recognised.

Cost model

79   In addition to the disclosures required by paragraph 75, an entity that applies the cost model in paragraph 56 shall disclose:

(a)   the depreciation methods used;

(b)   the useful lives or the depreciation rates used;

(c)   the gross carrying amount and the accumulated depreciation (aggregated with accumulated impairment losses) at the beginning and end of the period;

(d)   a reconciliation of the carrying amount of investment property at the beginning and end of the period, showing the following:

    (i)   additions, disclosing separately those additions resulting from acquisitions and those resulting from subsequent expenditure recognised as an asset;

    (ii)   additions resulting from acquisitions through business combinations;

    (iii)   assets classified as held for sale or included in a disposal group classified as held for sale in accordance with IFRS 5 and other disposals;

    (iv)   depreciation;

    (v)   the amount of impairment losses recognised, and the amount of impairment losses reversed, during the period in accordance with IAS 36;

    (vi)   the net exchange differences arising on the translation of the financial statements into a different presentation currency, and on translation of a foreign operation into the presentation currency of the reporting entity;

    (vii) transfers to and from inventories and owner-occupied property; and

    (viii) other changes.

(e)   the fair value of investment property. In the exceptional cases described in paragraph 53, when an entity cannot measure the fair value of the investment property reliably, it shall disclose:

    (i)   a description of the investment property;

(ii)   an explanation of why fair value cannot be measured reliably; and

(iii)   if possible, the range of estimates within which fair value is highly likely to lie.

Transitional provisions

Fair value model

80   An entity that has previously applied IAS 40 (2000) and elects for the first time to classify and account for some or all eligible property interests held under operating leases as investment property shall recognise the effect of that election as an adjustment to the opening balance of retained earnings for the period in which the election is first made. In addition:

(a)   if the entity has previously disclosed publicly (in financial statements or otherwise) the fair value of those property interests in earlier periods (measured on a basis that satisfies the definition of fair value in IFRS 13), the entity is encouraged, but not required:

(i)   to adjust the opening balance of retained earnings for the earliest period presented for which such fair value was disclosed publicly; and

(ii)   to restate comparative information for those periods; and

(b)   if the entity has not previously disclosed publicly the information described in (a), it shall not restate comparative information and shall disclose that fact.

81   This Standard requires a treatment different from that required by IAS 8. IAS 8 requires comparative information to be restated unless such restatement is impracticable.

82   When an entity first applies this Standard, the adjustment to the opening balance of retained earnings includes the reclassification of any amount held in revaluation surplus for investment property.

Cost model

83   IAS 8 applies to any change in accounting policies that is made when an entity first applies this Standard and chooses to use the cost model. The effect of the change in accounting policies includes the reclassification of any amount held in revaluation surplus for investment property.

84   The requirements of paragraphs 27–29 regarding the initial measurement of an investment property acquired in an exchange of assets transaction shall be applied prospectively only to future transactions.

Business Combinations

84A   *Annual Improvements Cycle 2011–2013* issued in December 2013 added paragraph 14A and a heading before paragraph 6. An entity shall apply that amendment prospectively for acquisitions of investment property from the beginning of the first period for which it adopts that amendment. Consequently, accounting for acquisitions of investment property in prior periods shall not be adjusted. However, an entity may choose to apply the amendment to individual acquisitions of investment property that occurred prior to the beginning of the first annual period occurring on or after the effective date if, and only if, information needed to apply the amendment to those earlier transactions is available to the entity.

IFRS 16

84B   An entity applying IFRS 16, and its related amendments to this Standard, for the first time shall apply the transition requirements in Appendix C of IFRS 16 to its investment property held as a right-of-use asset.

Transfers of investment property

84C   *Transfers of Investment Property* (Amendments to IAS 40), issued in December 2016, amended paragraphs 57–58. An entity shall apply those amendments to changes in use that occur on or after the beginning of the annual reporting period in which the entity first applies the amendments (the date of initial application). At the date of initial application, an entity shall reassess the classification of property held at that date and, if applicable, reclassify property applying paragraphs 7–14 to reflect the conditions that exist at that date.

84D   Notwithstanding the requirements in paragraph 84C, an entity is permitted to apply the amendments to paragraphs 57–58 retrospectively in accordance with IAS 8 if, and only if, that is possible without the use of hindsight.

84E   If, in accordance with paragraph 84C, an entity reclassifies property at the date of initial application, the entity shall:

(a)   account for the reclassification applying the requirements in paragraphs 59–64. In applying paragraphs 59–64, an entity shall:

(i)   read any reference to the date of change in use as the date of initial application; and

(ii)   recognise any amount that, in accordance with paragraphs 59–64, would have been recognised in profit or loss as an adjustment to the opening balance of retained earnings at the date of initial application.

(b)   disclose the amounts reclassified to, or from, investment property in accordance with paragraph 84C. The entity shall disclose those amounts reclassified as part of the reconciliation of the carrying amount of investment property at the beginning and end of the period as required by paragraphs 76 and 79.

Effective date

85   An entity shall apply this Standard for annual periods beginning on or after 1 January 2005. Earlier application is encouraged. If an entity applies this Standard for a period beginning before 1 January 2005, it shall disclose that fact.

85A   IAS 1 *Presentation of Financial Statements* (as revised in 2007) amended the terminology used throughout IFRSs. In addition it amended paragraph 62. An entity shall apply those amendments for annual periods beginning on or after 1 January 2009. If an entity applies IAS 1 (revised 2007) for an earlier period, the amendments shall be applied for that earlier period.

85B   Paragraphs 8, 9, 48, 53, 54 and 57 were amended, paragraph 22 was deleted and paragraphs 53A and 53B were added by *Improvements to IFRSs* issued in May 2008. An entity shall apply those amendments prospectively for annual periods beginning on or after 1 January 2009. An entity is permitted to apply the amendments to investment property under construction from any date before 1 January 2009 provided that the fair values of investment properties under construction were measured at those dates. Earlier application is permitted. If an entity applies the amendments for an earlier period it shall disclose that fact and at the same time apply the amendments to paragraphs 5 and 81E of IAS 16 *Property, Plant and Equipment*.

85C   IFRS 13, issued in May 2011, amended the definition of fair value in paragraph 5, amended paragraphs 26, 29, 32, 40, 48, 53, 53B, 78–80 and 85B and deleted paragraphs 36–39, 42–47, 49, 51 and 75(d). An entity shall apply those amendments when it applies IFRS 13.

85D   *Annual Improvements Cycle 2011–2013* issued in December 2013 added headings before paragraph 6 and after paragraph 84 and added paragraphs 14A and 84A. An entity shall apply those amendments for annual periods beginning on or after 1 July 2014. Earlier application is permitted. If an entity applies those amendments for an earlier period it shall disclose that fact.

85E   IFRS 15 *Revenue from Contracts with Customers*, issued in May 2014, amended paragraphs 3(b), 9, 67 and 70. An entity shall apply those amendments when it applies IFRS 15.

85F   IFRS 16, issued in January 2016, amended the scope of IAS 40 by defining investment property to include both owned investment property and property held by a lessee as a right-of-use asset. IFRS 16 amended paragraphs 5, 7, 8, 9, 16, 20, 30, 41, 50, 53, 53A, 54, 56, 60, 61, 62, 67, 69, 74, 75, 77 and 78, added paragraphs 19A, 29A, 40A and 84B and its related heading and deleted paragraphs 3, 6, 25, 26 and 34. An entity shall apply those amendments when it applies IFRS 16.

85G   *Transfers of Investment Property* (Amendments to IAS 40), issued in December 2016, amended paragraphs 57–58 and added paragraphs 84C–84E. An entity shall apply those amendments for annual periods beginning on or after 1 January 2018. Earlier application is permitted. If an entity applies those amendments for an earlier period, it shall disclose that fact.

85H   *[This paragraph refers to amendments that are not yet effective, and is therefore not included in this edition.]*

Withdrawal of IAS 40 (2000)

86   This Standard supersedes IAS 40 *Investment Property* (issued in 2000).

Approval by the Board of IAS 40 issued in December 2003

International Accounting Standard 40 *Investment Property* (as revised in 2003) was approved for issue by the fourteen members of the International Accounting Standards Board.

Sir David Tweedie   Chairman

Thomas E Jones   Vice-Chairman

Mary E Barth

Hans-Georg Bruns

Anthony T Cope

Robert P Garnett

Gilbert Gélard

James J Leisenring

Warren J McGregor

Patricia L O'Malley

Harry K Schmid

John T Smith

Geoffrey Whittington

Tatsumi Yamada

Approval by the Board of *Transfers of Investment Property* (Amendments to IAS 40) issued in December 2016

Transfers of Investment Property (Amendments to IAS 40) was approved for issue by all 12 members of the International Accounting Standards Board.

Hans Hoogervorst	Chairman
Suzanne Lloyd	Vice-Chair
Stephen Cooper	
Philippe Danjou	
Martin Edelmann	
Amaro Gomes	
Gary Kabureck	
Takatsugu Ochi	
Darrel Scott	
Chungwoo Suh	
Mary Tokar	
Wei-Guo Zhang	

IAS 41

Agriculture

In April 2001 the International Accounting Standards Board (Board) adopted IAS 41 *Agriculture*, which had originally been issued by the International Accounting Standards Committee in February 2001.

In December 2003 the Board issued a revised IAS 41 as part of its initial agenda of technical projects.

In June 2014 the Board amended the scope of IAS 16 *Property, Plant and Equipment* to include bearer plants related to agricultural activity. Bearer plants related to agricultural activity were previously within the scope of IAS 41. However, IAS 41 applies to the produce growing on those bearer plants.

Other Standards have made minor consequential amendments to IAS 41, including IFRS 13 *Fair Value Measurement* (issued May 2011), IFRS 16 *Leases* (issued January 2016), *Amendments to References to the Conceptual Framework in IFRS Standards* (issued March 2018) and *Annual Improvements to IFRS Standards 2018–2020* (issued May 2020).

Contents

FOR THE ACCOMPANYING GUIDANCE LISTED BELOW, SEE PART B OF THIS EDITION

ILLUSTRATIVE EXAMPLES

FOR THE BASIS FOR CONCLUSIONS, SEE PART C OF THIS EDITION

BASIS FOR CONCLUSIONS

BASIS FOR IASC'S CONCLUSIONS

DISSENTING OPINIONS

International Accounting Standard 41 *Agriculture* (IAS 41) is set out in paragraphs 1–65. All the paragraphs have equal authority but retain the IASC format of the Standard when it was adopted by the IASB. IAS 41 should be read in the context of its objective and the Basis for Conclusions, the *Preface to IFRS Standards* and the *Conceptual Framework for Financial Reporting*. IAS 8 *Accounting Policies, Changes in Accounting Estimates and Errors* provides a basis for selecting and applying accounting policies in the absence of explicit guidance.

International Accounting Standard 41
Agriculture

Objective

The objective of this Standard is to prescribe the accounting treatment and disclosures related to agricultural activity.

Scope

1   This Standard shall be applied to account for the following when they relate to agricultural activity:

(a)   biological assets, except for bearer plants;

(b)   agricultural produce at the point of harvest; and

(c)   government grants covered by paragraphs 34 and 35.

2   This Standard does not apply to:

(a)   land related to agricultural activity (see IAS 16 *Property, Plant and Equipment* and IAS 40 *Investment Property*).

(b)   bearer plants related to agricultural activity (see IAS 16). However, this Standard applies to the produce on those bearer plants.

(c)   government grants related to bearer plants (see IAS 20 *Accounting for Government Grants and Disclosure of Government Assistance*).

(d)   intangible assets related to agricultural activity (see IAS 38 *Intangible Assets*).

(e)   right-of-use assets arising from a lease of land related to agricultural activity (see IFRS 16 *Leases*).

3   This Standard is applied to agricultural produce, which is the harvested produce of the entity's biological assets, at the point of harvest. Thereafter, IAS 2 *Inventories* or another applicable Standard is applied. Accordingly, this Standard does not deal with the processing of agricultural produce after harvest; for example, the processing of grapes into wine by a vintner who has grown the grapes. While such processing may be a logical and natural extension of agricultural activity, and the events taking place may bear some similarity to biological transformation, such processing is not included within the definition of agricultural activity in this Standard.

4   The table below provides examples of biological assets, agricultural produce, and products that are the result of processing after harvest:

Biological assets	Agricultural produce	Products that are the result of processing after harvest
Sheep	Wool	Yarn, carpet
Trees in a timber plantation	Felled trees	Logs, lumber
Dairy cattle	Milk	Cheese
Pigs	Carcass	Sausages, cured hams
Cotton plants	Harvested cotton	Thread, clothing
Sugarcane	Harvested cane	Sugar
Tobacco plants	Picked leaves	Cured tobacco
Tea bushes	Picked leaves	Tea
Grape vines	Picked grapes	Wine
Fruit trees	Picked fruit	Processed fruit
Oil palms	Picked fruit	Palm oil
Rubber trees	Harvested latex	Rubber products

Some plants, for example, tea bushes, grape vines, oil palms and rubber trees, usually meet the definition of a bearer plant and are within the scope of IAS 16. However, the produce growing on bearer plants, for example, tea leaves, grapes, oil palm fruit and latex, is within the scope of IAS 41.

Definitions

Agriculture-related definitions

5   The following terms are used in this Standard with the meanings specified:

Agricultural activity is the management by an entity of the biological transformation and harvest of biological assets for sale or for conversion into agricultural produce or into additional biological assets.

Agricultural produce is the harvested produce of the entity's biological assets.

A *bearer plant* is a living plant that:

(a)   is used in the production or supply of agricultural produce;

(b)   is expected to bear produce for more than one period; and

(c)   has a remote likelihood of being sold as agricultural produce, except for incidental scrap sales.

A *biological asset* is a living animal or plant.

Biological transformation comprises the processes of growth, degeneration, production, and procreation that cause qualitative or quantitative changes in a biological asset.

Costs to sell are the incremental costs directly attributable to the disposal of an asset, excluding finance costs and income taxes.

A group of biological assets is an aggregation of similar living animals or plants.

Harvest is the detachment of produce from a biological asset or the cessation of a biological asset's life processes.

5A   The following are not bearer plants:

(a)   plants cultivated to be harvested as agricultural produce (for example, trees grown for use as lumber);

(b)   plants cultivated to produce agricultural produce when there is more than a remote likelihood that the entity will also harvest and sell the plant as agricultural produce, other than as incidental scrap sales (for example, trees that are cultivated both for their fruit and their lumber); and

(c)   annual crops (for example, maize and wheat).

5B   When bearer plants are no longer used to bear produce they might be cut down and sold as scrap, for example, for use as firewood. Such incidental scrap sales would not prevent the plant from satisfying the definition of a bearer plant.

5C   Produce growing on bearer plants is a biological asset.

6   Agricultural activity covers a diverse range of activities; for example, raising livestock, forestry, annual or perennial cropping, cultivating orchards and plantations, floriculture and aquaculture (including fish farming). Certain common features exist within this diversity:

(a)   Capability to change. Living animals and plants are capable of biological transformation;

(b)   Management of change. Management facilitates biological transformation by enhancing, or at least stabilising, conditions necessary for the process to take place (for example, nutrient levels, moisture, temperature, fertility, and light). Such management distinguishes agricultural activity from other activities. For example, harvesting from unmanaged sources (such as ocean fishing and deforestation) is not agricultural activity; and

(c)   Measurement of change. The change in quality (for example, genetic merit, density, ripeness, fat cover, protein content, and fibre strength) or quantity (for example, progeny, weight, cubic metres, fibre length or diameter, and number of buds) brought about by biological transformation or harvest is measured and monitored as a routine management function.

7   Biological transformation results in the following types of outcomes:

    (a)   asset changes through (i) growth (an increase in quantity or improvement in quality of an animal or plant), (ii) degeneration (a decrease in the quantity or deterioration in quality of an animal or plant), or (iii) procreation (creation of additional living animals or plants); or

    (b)   production of agricultural produce such as latex, tea leaf, wool, and milk.

General definitions

8   The following terms are used in this Standard with the meanings specified:

Carrying amount is the amount at which an asset is recognised in the statement of financial position.

Fair value is the price that would be received to sell an asset or paid to transfer a liability in an orderly transaction between market participants at the measurement date. (See IFRS 13 *Fair Value Measurement*.)

Government grants are as defined in IAS 20.

9   [Deleted]

Recognition and measurement

10   An entity shall recognise a biological asset or agricultural produce when, and only when:

    (a)   the entity controls the asset as a result of past events;

    (b)   it is probable that future economic benefits associated with the asset will flow to the entity; and

    (c)   the fair value or cost of the asset can be measured reliably.

11   In agricultural activity, control may be evidenced by, for example, legal ownership of cattle and the branding or otherwise marking of the cattle on acquisition, birth, or weaning. The future benefits are normally assessed by measuring the significant physical attributes.

12   A biological asset shall be measured on initial recognition and at the end of each reporting period at its fair value less costs to sell, except for the case described in paragraph 30 where the fair value cannot be measured reliably.

13   Agricultural produce harvested from an entity's biological assets shall be measured at its fair value less costs to sell at the point of harvest. Such measurement is the cost at that date when applying IAS 2 *Inventories* or another applicable Standard.

14   [Deleted]

15   The fair value measurement of a biological asset or agricultural produce may be facilitated by grouping biological assets or agricultural produce according to significant attributes; for example, by age or quality. An entity selects the attributes corresponding to the attributes used in the market as a basis for pricing.

16   Entities often enter into contracts to sell their biological assets or agricultural produce at a future date. Contract prices are not necessarily relevant in measuring fair value, because fair value reflects the current market conditions in which market participant buyers and sellers would enter into a transaction. As a result, the fair value of a biological asset or agricultural produce is not adjusted because of the existence of a contract. In some cases, a contract for the sale of a biological asset or agricultural produce may be an onerous contract, as defined in IAS 37 *Provisions, Contingent Liabilities and Contingent Assets*. IAS 37 applies to onerous contracts.

17–21 [Deleted]

22   An entity does not include any cash flows for financing the assets or re-establishing biological assets after harvest (for example, the cost of replanting trees in a plantation forest after harvest).

23   [Deleted]

24   Cost may sometimes approximate fair value, particularly when:

      (a)   little biological transformation has taken place since initial cost incurrence (for example, for seedlings planted immediately prior to the end of a reporting period or newly acquired livestock); or

      (b)   the impact of the biological transformation on price is not expected to be material (for example, for the initial growth in a 30-year pine plantation production cycle).

25   Biological assets are often physically attached to land (for example, trees in a plantation forest). There may be no separate market for biological assets that are attached to the land but an active market may exist for the combined assets, that is, the biological assets, raw land, and land improvements, as a package. An entity may use information regarding the combined assets to measure the fair value of the biological assets. For example, the fair value of raw land and land improvements may be deducted from the fair value of the combined assets to arrive at the fair value of biological assets.

Gains and losses

26   **A gain or loss arising on initial recognition of a biological asset at fair value less costs to sell and from a change in fair value less costs to sell of a biological asset shall be included in profit or loss for the period in which it arises.**

27   A loss may arise on initial recognition of a biological asset, because costs to sell are deducted in determining fair value less costs to sell of a biological asset. A gain may arise on initial recognition of a biological asset, such as when a calf is born.

28　　A gain or loss arising on initial recognition of agricultural produce at fair value less costs to sell shall be included in profit or loss for the period in which it arises.

29　　A gain or loss may arise on initial recognition of agricultural produce as a result of harvesting.

Inability to measure fair value reliably

30　　There is a presumption that fair value can be measured reliably for a biological asset. However, that presumption can be rebutted only on initial recognition for a biological asset for which quoted market prices are not available and for which alternative fair value measurements are determined to be clearly unreliable. In such a case, that biological asset shall be measured at its cost less any accumulated depreciation and any accumulated impairment losses. Once the fair value of such a biological asset becomes reliably measurable, an entity shall measure it at its fair value less costs to sell. Once a non-current biological asset meets the criteria to be classified as held for sale (or is included in a disposal group that is classified as held for sale) in accordance with IFRS 5 *Non-current Assets Held for Sale and Discontinued Operations*, it is presumed that fair value can be measured reliably.

31　　The presumption in paragraph 30 can be rebutted only on initial recognition. An entity that has previously measured a biological asset at its fair value less costs to sell continues to measure the biological asset at its fair value less costs to sell until disposal.

32　　In all cases, an entity measures agricultural produce at the point of harvest at its fair value less costs to sell. This Standard reflects the view that the fair value of agricultural produce at the point of harvest can always be measured reliably.

33　　In determining cost, accumulated depreciation and accumulated impairment losses, an entity considers IAS 2, IAS 16 and IAS 36 *Impairment of Assets*.

Government grants

34　　An unconditional government grant related to a biological asset measured at its fair value less costs to sell shall be recognised in profit or loss when, and only when, the government grant becomes receivable.

35　　If a government grant related to a biological asset measured at its fair value less costs to sell is conditional, including when a government grant requires an entity not to engage in specified agricultural activity, an entity shall recognise the government grant in profit or loss when, and only when, the conditions attaching to the government grant are met.

36　　Terms and conditions of government grants vary. For example, a grant may require an entity to farm in a particular location for five years and require the entity to return all of the grant if it farms for a period shorter than five years. In this case, the grant is not recognised in profit or loss until the five years have passed. However, if the terms of the grant allow part of it to be retained according to the time that has elapsed, the entity recognises that part in profit or loss as time passes.

37   If a government grant relates to a biological asset measured at its cost less any accumulated depreciation and any accumulated impairment losses (see paragraph 30), IAS 20 is applied.

38   This Standard requires a different treatment from IAS 20, if a government grant relates to a biological asset measured at its fair value less costs to sell or a government grant requires an entity not to engage in specified agricultural activity. IAS 20 is applied only to a government grant related to a biological asset measured at its cost less any accumulated depreciation and any accumulated impairment losses.

Disclosure

39   [Deleted]

General

40   **An entity shall disclose the aggregate gain or loss arising during the current period on initial recognition of biological assets and agricultural produce and from the change in fair value less costs to sell of biological assets.**

41   **An entity shall provide a description of each group of biological assets.**

42   The disclosure required by paragraph 41 may take the form of a narrative or quantified description.

43   An entity is encouraged to provide a quantified description of each group of biological assets, distinguishing between consumable and bearer biological assets or between mature and immature biological assets, as appropriate. For example, an entity may disclose the carrying amounts of consumable biological assets and bearer biological assets by group. An entity may further divide those carrying amounts between mature and immature assets. These distinctions provide information that may be helpful in assessing the timing of future cash flows. An entity discloses the basis for making any such distinctions.

44   Consumable biological assets are those that are to be harvested as agricultural produce or sold as biological assets. Examples of consumable biological assets are livestock intended for the production of meat, livestock held for sale, fish in farms, crops such as maize and wheat, produce on a bearer plant and trees being grown for lumber. Bearer biological assets are those other than consumable biological assets; for example, livestock from which milk is produced and fruit trees from which fruit is harvested. Bearer biological assets are not agricultural produce but, rather, are held to bear produce.

45   Biological assets may be classified either as mature biological assets or immature biological assets. Mature biological assets are those that have attained harvestable specifications (for consumable biological assets) or are able to sustain regular harvests (for bearer biological assets).

46   If not disclosed elsewhere in information published with the financial statements, an entity shall describe:

(a)   the nature of its activities involving each group of biological assets; and

(b)   non-financial measures or estimates of the physical quantities of:

(i)   each group of the entity's biological assets at the end of the period; and

(ii)   output of agricultural produce during the period.

47–48   [Deleted]

49   An entity shall disclose:

(a)   the existence and carrying amounts of biological assets whose title is restricted, and the carrying amounts of biological assets pledged as security for liabilities;

(b)   the amount of commitments for the development or acquisition of biological assets; and

(c)   financial risk management strategies related to agricultural activity.

50   An entity shall present a reconciliation of changes in the carrying amount of biological assets between the beginning and the end of the current period. The reconciliation shall include:

(a)   the gain or loss arising from changes in fair value less costs to sell;

(b)   increases due to purchases;

(c)   decreases attributable to sales and biological assets classified as held for sale (or included in a disposal group that is classified as held for sale) in accordance with IFRS 5;

(d)   decreases due to harvest;

(e)   increases resulting from business combinations;

(f)   net exchange differences arising on the translation of financial statements into a different presentation currency, and on the translation of a foreign operation into the presentation currency of the reporting entity; and

(g)   other changes.

51   The fair value less costs to sell of a biological asset can change due to both physical changes and price changes in the market. Separate disclosure of physical and price changes is useful in appraising current period performance and future prospects, particularly when there is a production cycle of more

than one year. In such cases, an entity is encouraged to disclose, by group or otherwise, the amount of change in fair value less costs to sell included in profit or loss due to physical changes and due to price changes. This information is generally less useful when the production cycle is less than one year (for example, when raising chickens or growing cereal crops).

52   Biological transformation results in a number of types of physical change—growth, degeneration, production, and procreation, each of which is observable and measurable. Each of those physical changes has a direct relationship to future economic benefits. A change in fair value of a biological asset due to harvesting is also a physical change.

53   Agricultural activity is often exposed to climatic, disease and other natural risks. If an event occurs that gives rise to a material item of income or expense, the nature and amount of that item are disclosed in accordance with IAS 1 *Presentation of Financial Statements*. Examples of such an event include an outbreak of a virulent disease, a flood, a severe drought or frost, and a plague of insects.

Additional disclosures for biological assets where fair value cannot be measured reliably

54   If an entity measures biological assets at their cost less any accumulated depreciation and any accumulated impairment losses (see paragraph 30) at the end of the period, the entity shall disclose for such biological assets:

(a)   a description of the biological assets;

(b)   an explanation of why fair value cannot be measured reliably;

(c)   if possible, the range of estimates within which fair value is highly likely to lie;

(d)   the depreciation method used;

(e)   the useful lives or the depreciation rates used; and

(f)   the gross carrying amount and the accumulated depreciation (aggregated with accumulated impairment losses) at the beginning and end of the period.

55   If, during the current period, an entity measures biological assets at their cost less any accumulated depreciation and any accumulated impairment losses (see paragraph 30), an entity shall disclose any gain or loss recognised on disposal of such biological assets and the reconciliation required by paragraph 50 shall disclose amounts related to such biological assets separately. In addition, the reconciliation shall include the following amounts included in profit or loss related to those biological assets:

(a)   impairment losses;

(b)   reversals of impairment losses; and

(c)   depreciation.

56   If the fair value of biological assets previously measured at their cost less any accumulated depreciation and any accumulated impairment losses becomes reliably measurable during the current period, an entity shall disclose for those biological assets:

(a)   a description of the biological assets;

(b)   an explanation of why fair value has become reliably measurable; and

(c)   the effect of the change.

Government grants

57   An entity shall disclose the following related to agricultural activity covered by this Standard:

(a)   the nature and extent of government grants recognised in the financial statements;

(b)   unfulfilled conditions and other contingencies attaching to government grants; and

(c)   significant decreases expected in the level of government grants.

Effective date and transition

58   This Standard becomes operative for annual financial statements covering periods beginning on or after 1 January 2003. Earlier application is encouraged. If an entity applies this Standard for periods beginning before 1 January 2003, it shall disclose that fact.

59   This Standard does not establish any specific transitional provisions. The adoption of this Standard is accounted for in accordance with IAS 8 *Accounting Policies, Changes in Accounting Estimates and Errors*.

60   Paragraphs 5, 6, 17, 20 and 21 were amended and paragraph 14 deleted by *Improvements to IFRSs* issued in May 2008. An entity shall apply those amendments prospectively for annual periods beginning on or after 1 January 2009. Earlier application is permitted. If an entity applies the amendments for an earlier period it shall disclose that fact.

61   IFRS 13, issued in May 2011, amended paragraphs 8, 15, 16, 25 and 30 and deleted paragraphs 9, 17–21, 23, 47 and 48. An entity shall apply those amendments when it applies IFRS 13.

62   *Agriculture: Bearer Plants* (Amendments to IAS 16 and IAS 41), issued in June 2014, amended paragraphs 1–5, 8, 24 and 44 and added paragraphs 5A–5C and 63. An entity shall apply those amendments for annual periods beginning on or after 1 January 2016. Earlier application is permitted. If an entity applies those amendments for an earlier period, it shall disclose that fact. An entity shall apply those amendments retrospectively in accordance with IAS 8.

63   In the reporting period when *Agriculture: Bearer Plants* (Amendments to IAS 16 and IAS 41) is first applied an entity need not disclose the quantitative information required by paragraph 28(f) of IAS 8 for the current period. However, an entity shall present the quantitative information required by paragraph 28(f) of IAS 8 for each prior period presented.

64   IFRS 16, issued in January 2016, amended paragraph 2. An entity shall apply that amendment when it applies IFRS 16.

65   *Annual Improvements to IFRS Standards 2018–2020*, issued in May 2020, amended paragraph 22. An entity shall apply that amendment to fair value measurements on or after the beginning of the first annual reporting period beginning on or after 1 January 2022. Earlier application is permitted. If an entity applies the amendment for an earlier period, it shall disclose that fact.

Approval by the Board of *Agriculture: Bearer Plants* (Amendments to IAS 16 and IAS 41) issued in June 2014

Agriculture: Bearer Plants was approved for issue by fourteen of the sixteen members of the International Accounting Standards Board. Mr Finnegan and Ms McConnell voted against its publication. Their dissenting opinions are set out after the Basis for Conclusions.

Hans Hoogervorst	Chairman
Ian Mackintosh	Vice-Chairman
Stephen Cooper	
Philippe Danjou	
Martin Edelmann	
Jan Engström	
Patrick Finnegan	
Amaro Luiz de Oliveira Gomes	
Gary Kabureck	
Suzanne Lloyd	
Patricia McConnell	
Takatsugu Ochi	
Darrel Scott	
Chungwoo Suh	
Mary Tokar	
Wei-Guo Zhang	

IFRIC 1

Changes in Existing Decommissioning, Restoration and Similar Liabilities

In May 2004 the International Accounting Standards Board issued IFRIC 1 *Changes in Existing Decommissioning, Restoration and Similar Liabilities*. It was developed by the Interpretations Committee.

Other Standards have made minor consequential amendments to IFRIC 1, including IFRS 16 *Leases* (issued January 2016).

CONTENTS

FOR THE ACCOMPANYING GUIDANCE LISTED BELOW, SEE PART B OF THIS EDITION

ILLUSTRATIVE EXAMPLES

FOR THE BASIS FOR CONCLUSIONS, SEE PART C OF THIS EDITION

BASIS FOR CONCLUSIONS

IFRIC Interpretation 1 *Changes in Existing Decommissioning, Restoration and Similar Liabilities* (IFRIC 1) is set out in paragraphs 1–10 and the Appendix. IFRIC 1 is accompanied by illustrative examples and a Basis for Conclusions. The scope and authority of Interpretations are set out in the *Preface to IFRS Standards*.

IFRIC Interpretation 1
Changes in Existing Decommissioning, Restoration and Similar Liabilities

References

- IFRS 16 *Leases*

- IAS 1 *Presentation of Financial Statements* (as revised in 2007)

- IAS 8 *Accounting Policies, Changes in Accounting Estimates and Errors*

- IAS 16 *Property, Plant and Equipment* (as revised in 2003)

- IAS 23 *Borrowing Costs*

- IAS 36 *Impairment of Assets* (as revised in 2004)

- IAS 37 *Provisions, Contingent Liabilities and Contingent Assets*

Background

1   Many entities have obligations to dismantle, remove and restore items of property, plant and equipment. In this Interpretation such obligations are referred to as 'decommissioning, restoration and similar liabilities'. Under IAS 16, the cost of an item of property, plant and equipment includes the initial estimate of the costs of dismantling and removing the item and restoring the site on which it is located, the obligation for which an entity incurs either when the item is acquired or as a consequence of having used the item during a particular period for purposes other than to produce inventories during that period. IAS 37 contains requirements on how to measure decommissioning, restoration and similar liabilities. This Interpretation provides guidance on how to account for the effect of changes in the measurement of existing decommissioning, restoration and similar liabilities.

Scope

2   This Interpretation applies to changes in the measurement of any existing decommissioning, restoration or similar liability that is both:

(a)   recognised as part of the cost of an item of property, plant and equipment in accordance with IAS 16 or as part of the cost of a right-of-use asset in accordance with IFRS 16; and

(b)   recognised as a liability in accordance with IAS 37.

For example, a decommissioning, restoration or similar liability may exist for decommissioning a plant, rehabilitating environmental damage in extractive industries, or removing equipment.

Issue

3   This Interpretation addresses how the effect of the following events that change the measurement of an existing decommissioning, restoration or similar liability should be accounted for:

(a)   a change in the estimated outflow of resources embodying economic benefits (eg cash flows) required to settle the obligation;

(b)   a change in the current market-based discount rate as defined in paragraph 47 of IAS 37 (this includes changes in the time value of money and the risks specific to the liability); and

(c)   an increase that reflects the passage of time (also referred to as the unwinding of the discount).

Consensus

4   Changes in the measurement of an existing decommissioning, restoration and similar liability that result from changes in the estimated timing or amount of the outflow of resources embodying economic benefits required to settle the obligation, or a change in the discount rate, shall be accounted for in accordance with paragraphs 5–7 below.

5   If the related asset is measured using the cost model:

(a)   subject to (b), changes in the liability shall be added to, or deducted from, the cost of the related asset in the current period.

(b)   the amount deducted from the cost of the asset shall not exceed its carrying amount. If a decrease in the liability exceeds the carrying amount of the asset, the excess shall be recognised immediately in profit or loss.

(c)   if the adjustment results in an addition to the cost of an asset, the entity shall consider whether this is an indication that the new carrying amount of the asset may not be fully recoverable. If it is such an indication, the entity shall test the asset for impairment by estimating its recoverable amount, and shall account for any impairment loss, in accordance with IAS 36.

6   If the related asset is measured using the revaluation model:

(a)   changes in the liability alter the revaluation surplus or deficit previously recognised on that asset, so that:

(i)   a decrease in the liability shall (subject to (b)) be recognised in other comprehensive income and increase the revaluation surplus within equity, except that it shall be recognised in profit or loss to the extent that it reverses a revaluation deficit on the asset that was previously recognised in profit or loss;

        (ii)   an increase in the liability shall be recognised in profit or loss, except that it shall be recognised in other comprehensive income and reduce the revaluation surplus within equity to the extent of any credit balance existing in the revaluation surplus in respect of that asset.

   (b)   in the event that a decrease in the liability exceeds the carrying amount that would have been recognised had the asset been carried under the cost model, the excess shall be recognised immediately in profit or loss.

   (c)   a change in the liability is an indication that the asset may have to be revalued in order to ensure that the carrying amount does not differ materially from that which would be determined using fair value at the end of the reporting period. Any such revaluation shall be taken into account in determining the amounts to be recognised in profit or loss or in other comprehensive income under (a). If a revaluation is necessary, all assets of that class shall be revalued.

   (d)   IAS 1 requires disclosure in the statement of comprehensive income of each component of other comprehensive income or expense. In complying with this requirement, the change in the revaluation surplus arising from a change in the liability shall be separately identified and disclosed as such.

7   The adjusted depreciable amount of the asset is depreciated over its useful life. Therefore, once the related asset has reached the end of its useful life, all subsequent changes in the liability shall be recognised in profit or loss as they occur. This applies under both the cost model and the revaluation model.

8   The periodic unwinding of the discount shall be recognised in profit or loss as a finance cost as it occurs. Capitalisation under IAS 23 is not permitted.

Effective date

9   An entity shall apply this Interpretation for annual periods beginning on or after 1 September 2004. Earlier application is encouraged. If an entity applies the Interpretation for a period beginning before 1 September 2004, it shall disclose that fact.

9A   IAS 1 (as revised in 2007) amended the terminology used throughout IFRSs. In addition it amended paragraph 6. An entity shall apply those amendments for annual periods beginning on or after 1 January 2009. If an entity applies IAS 1 (revised 2007) for an earlier period, the amendments shall be applied for that earlier period.

9B   IFRS 16, issued in January 2016, amended paragraph 2. An entity shall apply that amendment when it applies IFRS 16.

                  © IFRS Foundation

Transition

10　　Changes in accounting policies shall be accounted for according to the requirements of IAS 8 *Accounting Policies, Changes in Accounting Estimates and Errors*.[1]

1　If an entity applies this Interpretation for a period beginning before 1 January 2005, the entity shall follow the requirements of the previous version of IAS 8, which was entitled *Net Profit or Loss for the Period, Fundamental Errors and Changes in Accounting Policies*, unless the entity is applying the revised version of that Standard for that earlier period.

Appendix
Amendments to IFRS 1 *First-time Adoption of International Financial Reporting Standards*

The amendments in this appendix shall be applied for annual periods beginning on or after 1 September 2004. If an entity applies this Interpretation for an earlier period, these amendments shall be applied for that earlier period.

* * * * *

The amendments contained in this appendix when this Interpretation was issued in 2004 have been incorporated into IFRS 1 as issued on and after 27 May 2004. In November 2008 a revised version of IFRS 1 was issued.

IFRIC 2

Members' Shares in Co-operative Entities and Similar Instruments

In November 2004 the International Accounting Standards Board issued IFRIC 2 *Members' Shares in Co-operative Entities and Similar Instruments*. It was developed by the Interpretations Committee.

Other Standards have made minor consequential amendments to IFRIC 2. They include *Annual Improvements to IFRSs 2009–2011 Cycle* (issued May 2012), IFRS 13 *Fair Value Measurement* (issued May 2011), IFRS 9 *Financial Instruments* (Hedge Accounting and amendments to IFRS 9, IFRS 7 and IAS 39) (issued November 2013) and IFRS 9 *Financial Instruments* (issued July 2014).

Contents

FOR THE BASIS FOR CONCLUSIONS, SEE PART C OF THIS EDITION

BASIS FOR CONCLUSIONS

IFRIC Interpretation 2 *Members' Shares in Co-operative Entities and Similar Instruments* (IFRIC 2) is set out in paragraphs 1–19 and the Appendix. IFRIC 2 is accompanied by a Basis for Conclusions. The scope and authority of Interpretations are set out in the *Preface to IFRS Standards*.

IFRIC Interpretation 2
Members' Shares in Co-operative Entities and Similar Instruments

References

- IFRS 9 *Financial Instruments*

- IFRS 13 *Fair Value Measurement*

- IAS 32 *Financial Instruments: Disclosure and Presentation* (as revised in 2003)[1]

Background

1   Co-operatives and other similar entities are formed by groups of persons to meet common economic or social needs. National laws typically define a co-operative as a society endeavouring to promote its members' economic advancement by way of a joint business operation (the principle of self-help). Members' interests in a co-operative are often characterised as members' shares, units or the like, and are referred to below as 'members' shares'.

2   IAS 32 establishes principles for the classification of financial instruments as financial liabilities or equity. In particular, those principles apply to the classification of puttable instruments that allow the holder to put those instruments to the issuer for cash or another financial instrument. The application of those principles to members' shares in co-operative entities and similar instruments is difficult. Some of the International Accounting Standards Board's constituents have asked for help in understanding how the principles in IAS 32 apply to members' shares and similar instruments that have certain features, and the circumstances in which those features affect the classification as liabilities or equity.

Scope

3   This Interpretation applies to financial instruments within the scope of IAS 32, including financial instruments issued to members of co-operative entities that evidence the members' ownership interest in the entity. This Interpretation does not apply to financial instruments that will or may be settled in the entity's own equity instruments.

Issue

4   Many financial instruments, including members' shares, have characteristics of equity, including voting rights and rights to participate in dividend distributions. Some financial instruments give the holder the right to request redemption for cash or another financial asset, but may include or be subject

---

1   In August 2005, IAS 32 was amended as IAS 32 *Financial Instruments: Presentation*. In February 2008 the IASB amended IAS 32 by requiring instruments to be classified as equity if those instruments have all the features and meet the conditions in paragraphs 16A and 16B or paragraphs 16C and 16D of IAS 32.

to limits on whether the financial instruments will be redeemed. How should those redemption terms be evaluated in determining whether the financial instruments should be classified as liabilities or equity?

Consensus

5   The contractual right of the holder of a financial instrument (including members' shares in co-operative entities) to request redemption does not, in itself, require that financial instrument to be classified as a financial liability. Rather, the entity must consider all of the terms and conditions of the financial instrument in determining its classification as a financial liability or equity. Those terms and conditions include relevant local laws, regulations and the entity's governing charter in effect at the date of classification, but not expected future amendments to those laws, regulations or charter.

6   Members' shares that would be classified as equity if the members did not have a right to request redemption are equity if either of the conditions described in paragraphs 7 and 8 is present or the members' shares have all the features and meet the conditions in paragraphs 16A and 16B or paragraphs 16C and 16D of IAS 32. Demand deposits, including current accounts, deposit accounts and similar contracts that arise when members act as customers are financial liabilities of the entity.

7   Members' shares are equity if the entity has an unconditional right to refuse redemption of the members' shares.

8   Local law, regulation or the entity's governing charter can impose various types of prohibitions on the redemption of members' shares, eg unconditional prohibitions or prohibitions based on liquidity criteria. If redemption is unconditionally prohibited by local law, regulation or the entity's governing charter, members' shares are equity. However, provisions in local law, regulation or the entity's governing charter that prohibit redemption only if conditions — such as liquidity constraints — are met (or are not met) do not result in members' shares being equity.

9   An unconditional prohibition may be absolute, in that all redemptions are prohibited. An unconditional prohibition may be partial, in that it prohibits redemption of members' shares if redemption would cause the number of members' shares or amount of paid-in capital from members' shares to fall below a specified level. Members' shares in excess of the prohibition against redemption are liabilities, unless the entity has the unconditional right to refuse redemption as described in paragraph 7 or the members' shares have all the features and meet the conditions in paragraphs 16A and 16B or paragraphs 16C and 16D of IAS 32. In some cases, the number of shares or the amount of paid-in capital subject to a redemption prohibition may change from time to time. Such a change in the redemption prohibition leads to a transfer between financial liabilities and equity.

10   At initial recognition, the entity shall measure its financial liability for redemption at fair value. In the case of members' shares with a redemption feature, the entity measures the fair value of the financial liability for redemption at no less than the maximum amount payable under the redemption provisions of its governing charter or applicable law discounted from the first date that the amount could be required to be paid (see example 3).

11   As required by paragraph 35 of IAS 32, distributions to holders of equity instruments are recognised directly in equity. Interest, dividends and other returns relating to financial instruments classified as financial liabilities are expenses, regardless of whether those amounts paid are legally characterised as dividends, interest or otherwise.

12   The Appendix, which is an integral part of the consensus, provides examples of the application of this consensus.

Disclosure

13   When a change in the redemption prohibition leads to a transfer between financial liabilities and equity, the entity shall disclose separately the amount, timing and reason for the transfer.

Effective date

14   The effective date and transition requirements of this Interpretation are the same as those for IAS 32 (as revised in 2003). An entity shall apply this Interpretation for annual periods beginning on or after 1 January 2005. If an entity applies this Interpretation for a period beginning before 1 January 2005, it shall disclose that fact. This Interpretation shall be applied retrospectively.

14A   An entity shall apply the amendments in paragraphs 6, 9, A1 and A12 for annual periods beginning on or after 1 January 2009. If an entity applies *Puttable Financial Instruments and Obligations Arising on Liquidation* (Amendments to IAS 32 and IAS 1), issued in February 2008, for an earlier period, the amendments in paragraphs 6, 9, A1 and A12 shall be applied for that earlier period.

15   [Deleted]

16   IFRS 13, issued in May 2011, amended paragraph A8. An entity shall apply that amendment when it applies IFRS 13.

17   *Annual Improvements 2009–2011 Cycle*, issued in May 2012, amended paragraph 11. An entity shall apply that amendment retrospectively in accordance with IAS 8 *Accounting Policies, Changes in Accounting Estimates and Errors* for annual periods beginning on or after 1 January 2013. If an entity applies that amendment to IAS 32 as a part of the *Annual Improvements 2009–2011 Cycle* (issued in May 2012) for an earlier period, the amendment in paragraph 11 shall be applied for that earlier period.

18   [Deleted]

19   IFRS 9, as issued in July 2014, amended paragraphs A8 and A10 and deleted paragraphs 15 and 18. An entity shall apply those amendments when it applies IFRS 9.

Appendix
Examples of application of the consensus

This appendix is an integral part of the Interpretation.

A1   This appendix sets out seven examples of the application of the IFRIC consensus. The examples do not constitute an exhaustive list; other fact patterns are possible. Each example assumes that there are no conditions other than those set out in the facts of the example that would require the financial instrument to be classified as a financial liability and that the financial instrument does not have all the features or does not meet the conditions in paragraphs 16A and 16B or paragraphs 16C and 16D of IAS 32.

Unconditional right to refuse redemption (paragraph 7)

Example 1

Facts

A2   The entity's charter states that redemptions are made at the sole discretion of the entity. The charter does not provide further elaboration or limitation on that discretion. In its history, the entity has never refused to redeem members' shares, although the governing board has the right to do so.

Classification

A3   The entity has the unconditional right to refuse redemption and the members' shares are equity. IAS 32 establishes principles for classification that are based on the terms of the financial instrument and notes that a history of, or intention to make, discretionary payments does not trigger liability classification. Paragraph AG26 of IAS 32 states:

> When preference shares are non-redeemable, the appropriate classification is determined by the other rights that attach to them. Classification is based on an assessment of the substance of the contractual arrangements and the definitions of a financial liability and an equity instrument. When distributions to holders of the preference shares, whether cumulative or non-cumulative, are at the discretion of the issuer, the shares are equity instruments. The classification of a preference share as an equity instrument or a financial liability is not affected by, for example:
>
> (a)   a history of making distributions;
>
> (b)   an intention to make distributions in the future;
>
> (c)   a possible negative impact on the price of ordinary shares of the issuer if distributions are not made (because of restrictions on paying dividends on the ordinary shares if dividends are not paid on the preference shares);
>
> (d)   the amount of the issuer's reserves;
>
> (e)   an issuer's expectation of a profit or loss for a period; or

(f)   an ability or inability of the issuer to influence the amount of its profit or loss for the period.

Example 2

Facts

A4   The entity's charter states that redemptions are made at the sole discretion of the entity. However, the charter further states that approval of a redemption request is automatic unless the entity is unable to make payments without violating local regulations regarding liquidity or reserves.

Classification

A5   The entity does not have the unconditional right to refuse redemption and the members' shares are a financial liability. The restrictions described above are based on the entity's ability to settle its liability. They restrict redemptions only if the liquidity or reserve requirements are not met and then only until such time as they are met. Hence, they do not, under the principles established in IAS 32, result in the classification of the financial instrument as equity. Paragraph AG25 of IAS 32 states:

> Preference shares may be issued with various rights. In determining whether a preference share is a financial liability or an equity instrument, an issuer assesses the particular rights attaching to the share to determine whether it exhibits the fundamental characteristic of a financial liability. For example, a preference share that provides for redemption on a specific date or at the option of the holder contains a financial liability because the issuer has an obligation to transfer financial assets to the holder of the share. *The potential inability of an issuer to satisfy an obligation to redeem a preference share when contractually required to do so, whether because of a lack of funds, a statutory restriction or insufficient profits or reserves, does not negate the obligation.* [Emphasis added]

Prohibitions against redemption (paragraphs 8 and 9)

Example 3

Facts

A6   A co-operative entity has issued shares to its members at different dates and for different amounts in the past as follows:

(a)   1 January 20X1 100,000 shares at CU10 each (CU1,000,000);

(b)   1 January 20X2 100,000 shares at CU20 each (a further CU2,000,000, so that the total for shares issued is CU3,000,000).

Shares are redeemable on demand at the amount for which they were issued.

A7   The entity's charter states that cumulative redemptions cannot exceed 20 per cent of the highest number of its members' shares ever outstanding. At 31 December 20X2 the entity has 200,000 of outstanding shares, which is the highest number of members' shares ever outstanding and no shares have been redeemed in the past. On 1 January 20X3 the entity amends its governing charter and increases the permitted level of cumulative redemptions to 25 per cent of the highest number of its members' shares ever outstanding.

Classification

Before the governing charter is amended

A8   Members' shares in excess of the prohibition against redemption are financial liabilities. The co-operative entity measures this financial liability at fair value at initial recognition. Because these shares are redeemable on demand, the co-operative entity measures the fair value of such financial liabilities in accordance with paragraph 47 of IFRS 13: 'The fair value of a financial liability with a demand feature (eg a demand deposit) is not less than the amount payable on demand ...'. Accordingly, the co-operative entity classifies as financial liabilities the maximum amount payable on demand under the redemption provisions.

A9   On 1 January 20X1 the maximum amount payable under the redemption provisions is 20,000 shares at CU10 each and accordingly the entity classifies CU200,000 as financial liability and CU800,000 as equity. However, on 1 January 20X2 because of the new issue of shares at CU20, the maximum amount payable under the redemption provisions increases to 40,000 shares at CU20 each. The issue of additional shares at CU20 creates a new liability that is measured on initial recognition at fair value. The liability after these shares have been issued is 20 per cent of the total shares in issue (200,000), measured at CU20, or CU800,000. This requires recognition of an additional liability of CU600,000. In this example no gain or loss is recognised. Accordingly the entity now classifies CU800,000 as financial liabilities and CU2,200,000 as equity. This example assumes these amounts are not changed between 1 January 20X1 and 31 December 20X2.

After the governing charter is amended

A10   Following the change in its governing charter the co-operative entity can now be required to redeem a maximum of 25 per cent of its outstanding shares or a maximum of 50,000 shares at CU20 each. Accordingly, on 1 January 20X3 the co-operative entity classifies as financial liabilities an amount of CU1,000,000 being the maximum amount payable on demand under the redemption provisions, as determined in accordance with paragraph 47 of IFRS 13. It therefore transfers on 1 January 20X3 from equity to financial liabilities an amount of CU200,000, leaving CU2,000,000 classified as equity. In this example the entity does not recognise a gain or loss on the transfer.

Example 4

Facts

A11   Local law governing the operations of co-operatives, or the terms of the entity's governing charter, prohibit an entity from redeeming members' shares if, by redeeming them, it would reduce paid-in capital from members' shares below 75 per cent of the highest amount of paid-in capital from members' shares. The highest amount for a particular co-operative is

CU1,000,000. At the end of the reporting period the balance of paid-in capital is CU900,000.

Classification

A12 In this case, CU750,000 would be classified as equity and CU150,000 would be classified as financial liabilities. In addition to the paragraphs already cited, paragraph 18(b) of IAS 32 states in part:

> ... a financial instrument that gives the holder the right to put it back to the issuer for cash or another financial asset (a 'puttable instrument') is a financial liability, except for those instruments classified as equity instruments in accordance with paragraphs 16A and 16B or paragraphs 16C and 16D. The financial instrument is a financial liability even when the amount of cash or other financial assets is determined on the basis of an index or other item that has the potential to increase or decrease. The existence of an option for the holder to put the instrument back to the issuer for cash or another financial asset means that the puttable instrument meets the definition of a financial liability, except for those instruments classified as equity instruments in accordance with paragraphs 16A and 16B or paragraphs 16C and 16D.

A13 The redemption prohibition described in this example is different from the restrictions described in paragraphs 19 and AG25 of IAS 32. Those restrictions are limitations on the ability of the entity to pay the amount due on a financial liability, ie they prevent payment of the liability only if specified conditions are met. In contrast, this example describes an unconditional prohibition on redemptions beyond a specified amount, regardless of the entity's ability to redeem members' shares (eg given its cash resources, profits or distributable reserves). In effect, the prohibition against redemption prevents the entity from incurring any financial liability to redeem more than a specified amount of paid-in capital. Therefore, the portion of shares subject to the redemption prohibition is not a financial liability. While each member's shares may be redeemable individually, a portion of the total shares outstanding is not redeemable in any circumstances other than liquidation of the entity.

Example 5

Facts

A14 The facts of this example are as stated in example 4. In addition, at the end of the reporting period, liquidity requirements imposed in the local jurisdiction prevent the entity from redeeming any members' shares unless its holdings of cash and short-term investments are greater than a specified amount. The effect of these liquidity requirements at the end of the reporting period is that the entity cannot pay more than CU50,000 to redeem the members' shares.

Classification

A15 As in example 4, the entity classifies CU750,000 as equity and CU150,000 as a financial liability. This is because the amount classified as a liability is based on the entity's unconditional right to refuse redemption and not on conditional restrictions that prevent redemption only if liquidity or other conditions are not met and then only until such time as they are met. The provisions of paragraphs 19 and AG25 of IAS 32 apply in this case.

Example 6

Facts

A16 The entity's governing charter prohibits it from redeeming members' shares, except to the extent of proceeds received from the issue of additional members' shares to new or existing members during the preceding three years. Proceeds from issuing members' shares must be applied to redeem shares for which members have requested redemption. During the three preceding years, the proceeds from issuing members' shares have been CU12,000 and no member's shares have been redeemed.

Classification

A17 The entity classifies CU12,000 of the members' shares as financial liabilities. Consistently with the conclusions described in example 4, members' shares subject to an unconditional prohibition against redemption are not financial liabilities. Such an unconditional prohibition applies to an amount equal to the proceeds of shares issued before the preceding three years, and accordingly, this amount is classified as equity. However, an amount equal to the proceeds from any shares issued in the preceding three years is not subject to an unconditional prohibition on redemption. Accordingly, proceeds from the issue of members' shares in the preceding three years give rise to financial liabilities until they are no longer available for redemption of members' shares. As a result the entity has a financial liability equal to the proceeds of shares issued during the three preceding years, net of any redemptions during that period.

Example 7

Facts

A18 The entity is a co-operative bank. Local law governing the operations of co-operative banks state that at least 50 per cent of the entity's total 'outstanding liabilities' (a term defined in the regulations to include members' share accounts) has to be in the form of members' paid-in capital. The effect of the regulation is that if all of a co-operative's outstanding liabilities are in the form of members' shares, it is able to redeem them all. On 31 December 20X1 the entity has total outstanding liabilities of CU200,000, of which CU125,000 represent members' share accounts. The terms of the members' share accounts permit the holder to redeem them on demand and there are no limitations on redemption in the entity's charter.

Classification

A19 In this example members' shares are classified as financial liabilities. The redemption prohibition is similar to the restrictions described in paragraphs 19 and AG25 of IAS 32. The restriction is a conditional limitation on the ability of the entity to pay the amount due on a financial liability, ie they prevent payment of the liability only if specified conditions are met. More specifically, the entity could be required to redeem the entire amount of members' shares (CU125,000) if it repaid all of its other liabilities (CU75,000). Consequently, the prohibition against redemption does not prevent the entity from incurring a financial liability to redeem more than a specified number of members' shares or amount of paid-in capital. It allows the entity only to defer redemption until a condition is met, ie the repayment of other liabilities. Members' shares in this example are not subject to an unconditional prohibition against redemption and are therefore classified as financial liabilities.

IFRIC 5

Rights to Interests arising from Decommissioning, Restoration and Environmental Rehabilitation Funds

In December 2004 the International Accounting Standards Board issued IFRIC 5 *Rights to Interests arising from Decommissioning, Restoration and Environmental Rehabilitation Funds*. It was developed by the Interpretations Committee.

Other Standards have made minor consequential amendments to IFRIC 5. They include IFRS 10 *Consolidated Financial Statements* (issued May 2011), IFRS 11 *Joint Arrangements* (issued May 2011), IFRS 9 *Financial Instruments* (Hedge Accounting and amendments to IFRS 9, IFRS 7 and IAS 39) (issued November 2013), IFRS 9 *Financial Instruments* (issued July 2014) and *Amendments to References to the Conceptual Framework in IFRS Standards* (issued March 2018).

Contents

FOR THE BASIS FOR CONCLUSIONS, SEE PART C OF THIS EDITION

BASIS FOR CONCLUSIONS

IFRIC Interpretation 5 *Rights to Interests arising from Decommissioning, Restoration and Environmental Rehabilitation Funds* (IFRIC 5) is set out in paragraphs 1–15 and the Appendix. IFRIC 5 is accompanied by a Basis for Conclusions. The scope and authority of Interpretations are set out in the *Preface to IFRS Standards*.

IFRIC Interpretation 5
Rights to Interests arising from Decommissioning, Restoration and Environmental Rehabilitation Funds

References

- IFRS 9 *Financial Instruments*

- IFRS 10 *Consolidated Financial Statements*

- IFRS 11 *Joint Arrangements*

- IAS 8 *Accounting Policies, Changes in Accounting Estimates and Errors*

- IAS 28 *Investments in Associates and Joint Ventures*

- IAS 37 *Provisions, Contingent Liabilities and Contingent Assets*

Background

1   The purpose of decommissioning, restoration and environmental rehabilitation funds, hereafter referred to as 'decommissioning funds' or 'funds', is to segregate assets to fund some or all of the costs of decommissioning plant (such as a nuclear plant) or certain equipment (such as cars), or in undertaking environmental rehabilitation (such as rectifying pollution of water or restoring mined land), together referred to as 'decommissioning'.

2   Contributions to these funds may be voluntary or required by regulation or law. The funds may have one of the following structures:

(a)   funds that are established by a single contributor to fund its own decommissioning obligations, whether for a particular site, or for a number of geographically dispersed sites.

(b)   funds that are established with multiple contributors to fund their individual or joint decommissioning obligations, when contributors are entitled to reimbursement for decommissioning expenses to the extent of their contributions plus any actual earnings on those contributions less their share of the costs of administering the fund. Contributors may have an obligation to make additional contributions, for example, in the event of the bankruptcy of another contributor.

(c)   funds that are established with multiple contributors to fund their individual or joint decommissioning obligations when the required level of contributions is based on the current activity of a contributor and the benefit obtained by that contributor is based on its past activity. In such cases there is a potential mismatch in the amount of contributions made by a contributor (based on current activity) and the value realisable from the fund (based on past activity).

3   Such funds generally have the following features:

(a)   the fund is separately administered by independent trustees.

(b)   entities (contributors) make contributions to the fund, which are invested in a range of assets that may include both debt and equity investments, and are available to help pay the contributors' decommissioning costs. The trustees determine how contributions are invested, within the constraints set by the fund's governing documents and any applicable legislation or other regulations.

(c)   the contributors retain the obligation to pay decommissioning costs. However, contributors are able to obtain reimbursement of decommissioning costs from the fund up to the lower of the decommissioning costs incurred and the contributor's share of assets of the fund.

(d)   the contributors may have restricted access or no access to any surplus of assets of the fund over those used to meet eligible decommissioning costs.

Scope

4   This Interpretation applies to accounting in the financial statements of a contributor for interests arising from decommissioning funds that have both of the following features:

(a)   the assets are administered separately (either by being held in a separate legal entity or as segregated assets within another entity); and

(b)   a contributor's right to access the assets is restricted.

5   A residual interest in a fund that extends beyond a right to reimbursement, such as a contractual right to distributions once all the decommissioning has been completed or on winding up the fund, may be an equity instrument within the scope of IFRS 9 and is not within the scope of this Interpretation.

Issues

6   The issues addressed in this Interpretation are:

(a)   how should a contributor account for its interest in a fund?

(b)   when a contributor has an obligation to make additional contributions, for example, in the event of the bankruptcy of another contributor, how should that obligation be accounted for?

Consensus

Accounting for an interest in a fund

7   The contributor shall recognise its obligation to pay decommissioning costs as a liability and recognise its interest in the fund separately unless the contributor is not liable to pay decommissioning costs even if the fund fails to pay.

8   The contributor shall determine whether it has control or joint control of, or significant influence over, the fund by reference to IFRS 10, IFRS 11 and IAS 28. If it does, the contributor shall account for its interest in the fund in accordance with those Standards.

9   If a contributor does not have control or joint control of, or significant influence over, the fund, the contributor shall recognise the right to receive reimbursement from the fund as a reimbursement in accordance with IAS 37. This reimbursement shall be measured at the lower of:

   (a)   the amount of the decommissioning obligation recognised; and

   (b)   the contributor's share of the fair value of the net assets of the fund attributable to contributors.

   Changes in the carrying value of the right to receive reimbursement other than contributions to and payments from the fund shall be recognised in profit or loss in the period in which these changes occur.

Accounting for obligations to make additional contributions

10   When a contributor has an obligation to make potential additional contributions, for example, in the event of the bankruptcy of another contributor or if the value of the investment assets held by the fund decreases to an extent that they are insufficient to fulfil the fund's reimbursement obligations, this obligation is a contingent liability that is within the scope of IAS 37. The contributor shall recognise a liability only if it is probable that additional contributions will be made.

Disclosure

11   A contributor shall disclose the nature of its interest in a fund and any restrictions on access to the assets in the fund.

12   When a contributor has an obligation to make potential additional contributions that is not recognised as a liability (see paragraph 10), it shall make the disclosures required by paragraph 86 of IAS 37.

13   When a contributor accounts for its interest in the fund in accordance with paragraph 9, it shall make the disclosures required by paragraph 85(c) of IAS 37.

Effective date

14   An entity shall apply this Interpretation for annual periods beginning on or after 1 January 2006. Earlier application is encouraged. If an entity applies this Interpretation to a period beginning before 1 January 2006, it shall disclose that fact.

14A   [Deleted]

14B   IFRS 10 and IFRS 11, issued in May 2011, amended paragraphs 8 and 9. An entity shall apply those amendments when it applies IFRS 10 and IFRS 11.

14C   [Deleted]

14D   IFRS 9, as issued in July 2014, amended paragraph 5 and deleted paragraphs 14A and 14C. An entity shall apply those amendments when it applies IFRS 9.

Transition

15   Changes in accounting policies shall be accounted for in accordance with the requirements of IAS 8.

Appendix
Amendment to IAS 39 *Financial Instruments: Recognition and Measurement*

The amendment in this appendix shall be applied for annual periods beginning on or after 1 January 2006. If an entity applies this Interpretation for an earlier period, the amendment shall be applied for that earlier period.

* * * * *

The amendment contained in this appendix when this Interpretation was issued in 2004 was incorporated into IAS 39 as issued on and after 16 December 2004.

IFRIC 6

Liabilities arising from Participating in a Specific Market — Waste Electrical and Electronic Equipment

In September 2005 the International Accounting Standards Board issued IFRIC 6 *Liabilities arising from Participating in a Specific Market — Waste Electrical and Electronic Equipment*. It was developed by the Interpretations Committee.

Contents

FOR THE BASIS FOR CONCLUSIONS, SEE PART C OF THIS EDITION

BASIS FOR CONCLUSIONS

IFRIC Interpretation 6 *Liabilities arising from Participating in a Specific Market—Waste Electrical and Electronic Equipment* (IFRIC 6) is set out in paragraphs 1–11. IFRIC 6 is accompanied by a Basis for Conclusions. The scope and authority of Interpretations are set out in the *Preface to IFRS Standards*.

IFRIC Interpretation 6
Liabilities arising from Participating in a Specific Market—
Waste Electrical and Electronic Equipment

References

- IAS 8 *Accounting Policies, Changes in Accounting Estimates and Errors*
- IAS 37 *Provisions, Contingent Liabilities and Contingent Assets*

Background

1   Paragraph 17 of IAS 37 specifies that an obligating event is a past event that leads to a present obligation that an entity has no realistic alternative to settling.

2   Paragraph 19 of IAS 37 states that provisions are recognised only for 'obligations arising from past events existing independently of an entity's future actions'.

3   The European Union's Directive on Waste Electrical and Electronic Equipment (WE&EE), which regulates the collection, treatment, recovery and environmentally sound disposal of waste equipment, has given rise to questions about when the liability for the decommissioning of WE&EE should be recognised. The Directive distinguishes between 'new' and 'historical' waste and between waste from private households and waste from sources other than private households. New waste relates to products sold after 13 August 2005. All household equipment sold before that date is deemed to give rise to historical waste for the purposes of the Directive.

4   The Directive states that the cost of waste management for historical household equipment should be borne by producers of that type of equipment that are in the market during a period to be specified in the applicable legislation of each Member State (the measurement period). The Directive states that each Member State shall establish a mechanism to have producers contribute to costs proportionately 'e.g. in proportion to their respective share of the market by type of equipment.'

5   Several terms used in the Interpretation such as 'market share' and 'measurement period' may be defined very differently in the applicable legislation of individual Member States. For example, the length of the measurement period might be a year or only one month. Similarly, the measurement of market share and the formulae for computing the obligation may differ in the various national legislations. However, all of these examples affect only the measurement of the liability, which is not within the scope of the Interpretation.

Scope

6   This Interpretation provides guidance on the recognition, in the financial statements of producers, of liabilities for waste management under the EU Directive on WE&EE in respect of sales of historical household equipment.

7   The Interpretation addresses neither new waste nor historical waste from sources other than private households. The liability for such waste management is adequately covered in IAS 37. However, if, in national legislation, new waste from private households is treated in a similar manner to historical waste from private households, the principles of the Interpretation apply by reference to the hierarchy in paragraphs 10–12 of IAS 8. The IAS 8 hierarchy is also relevant for other regulations that impose obligations in a way that is similar to the cost attribution model specified in the EU Directive.

Issue

8   The IFRIC was asked to determine in the context of the decommissioning of WE&EE what constitutes the obligating event in accordance with paragraph 14(a) of IAS 37 for the recognition of a provision for waste management costs:

- the manufacture or sale of the historical household equipment?

- participation in the market during the measurement period?

- the incurrence of costs in the performance of waste management activities?

Consensus

9   Participation in the market during the measurement period is the obligating event in accordance with paragraph 14(a) of IAS 37. As a consequence, a liability for waste management costs for historical household equipment does not arise as the products are manufactured or sold. Because the obligation for historical household equipment is linked to participation in the market during the measurement period, rather than to production or sale of the items to be disposed of, there is no obligation unless and until a market share exists during the measurement period. The timing of the obligating event may also be independent of the particular period in which the activities to perform the waste management are undertaken and the related costs incurred.

Effective date

10   An entity shall apply this Interpretation for annual periods beginning on or after 1 December 2005. Earlier application is encouraged. If an entity applies the Interpretation for a period beginning before 1 December 2005, it shall disclose that fact.

Transition

11   Changes in accounting policies shall be accounted for in accordance with IAS 8.

IFRIC 7

Applying the Restatement Approach under IAS 29 Financial Reporting in Hyperinflationary Economies

In November 2005 the International Accounting Standards Board issued IFRIC 7 *Applying the Restatement Approach under IAS 29 Financial Reporting in Hyperinflationary Economies*. It was developed by the Interpretations Committee.

Contents

FOR THE ACCOMPANYING GUIDANCE LISTED BELOW, SEE PART B OF THIS EDITION

FOR THE BASIS FOR CONCLUSIONS, SEE PART C OF THIS EDITION

IFRIC Interpretation 7 *Applying the Restatement Approach under IAS 29 Financial Reporting in Hyperinflationary Economies* (IFRIC 7) is set out in paragraphs 1–6. IFRIC 7 is accompanied by an illustrative example and a Basis for Conclusions. The scope and authority of Interpretations are set out in the *Preface to IFRS Standards*.

IFRIC Interpretation 7
Applying the Restatement Approach under IAS 29 Financial Reporting in Hyperinflationary Economies

References

- IAS 12 *Income Taxes*

- IAS 29 *Financial Reporting in Hyperinflationary Economies*

Background

1   This Interpretation provides guidance on how to apply the requirements of IAS 29 in a reporting period in which an entity identifies[1] the existence of hyperinflation in the economy of its functional currency, when that economy was not hyperinflationary in the prior period, and the entity therefore restates its financial statements in accordance with IAS 29.

Issues

2   The questions addressed in this Interpretation are:

(a)   how should the requirement '... stated in terms of the measuring unit current at the end of the reporting period' in paragraph 8 of IAS 29 be interpreted when an entity applies the Standard?

(b)   how should an entity account for opening deferred tax items in its restated financial statements?

Consensus

3   In the reporting period in which an entity identifies the existence of hyperinflation in the economy of its functional currency, not having been hyperinflationary in the prior period, the entity shall apply the requirements of IAS 29 as if the economy had always been hyperinflationary. Therefore, in relation to non-monetary items measured at historical cost, the entity's opening statement of financial position at the beginning of the earliest period presented in the financial statements shall be restated to reflect the effect of inflation from the date the assets were acquired and the liabilities were incurred or assumed until the end of the reporting period. For non-monetary items carried in the opening statement of financial position at amounts current at dates other than those of acquisition or incurrence, that restatement shall reflect instead the effect of inflation from the dates those carrying amounts were determined until the end of the reporting period.

---

1   The identification of hyperinflation is based on the entity's judgement of the criteria in paragraph 3 of IAS 29.

4   At the end of the reporting period, deferred tax items are recognised and measured in accordance with IAS 12. However, the deferred tax figures in the opening statement of financial position for the reporting period shall be determined as follows:

(a)   the entity remeasures the deferred tax items in accordance with IAS 12 after it has restated the nominal carrying amounts of its non-monetary items at the date of the opening statement of financial position of the reporting period by applying the measuring unit at that date.

(b)   the deferred tax items remeasured in accordance with (a) are restated for the change in the measuring unit from the date of the opening statement of financial position of the reporting period to the end of that reporting period.

The entity applies the approach in (a) and (b) in restating the deferred tax items in the opening statement of financial position of any comparative periods presented in the restated financial statements for the reporting period in which the entity applies IAS 29.

5   After an entity has restated its financial statements, all corresponding figures in the financial statements for a subsequent reporting period, including deferred tax items, are restated by applying the change in the measuring unit for that subsequent reporting period only to the restated financial statements for the previous reporting period.

Effective date

6   An entity shall apply this Interpretation for annual periods beginning on or after 1 March 2006. Earlier application is encouraged. If an entity applies this Interpretation to financial statements for a period beginning before 1 March 2006, it shall disclose that fact.

Interim Financial Reporting and Impairment

In July 2006 the International Accounting Standards Board issued IFRIC 10 *Interim Financial Reporting and Impairment*. It was developed by the Interpretations Committee.

Other Standards have made minor consequential amendments to IFRIC 10. They include IFRS 9 *Financial Instruments* (Hedge Accounting and amendments to IFRS 9, IFRS 7 and IAS 39) (issued November 2013) and IFRS 9 *Financial Instruments* (issued July 2014).

Contents

FOR THE BASIS FOR CONCLUSIONS, SEE PART C OF THIS EDITION

BASIS FOR CONCLUSIONS

IFRIC Interpretation 10 *Interim Financial Reporting and Impairment* (IFRIC 10) is set out in paragraphs 1–14. IFRIC 10 is accompanied by a Basis for Conclusions. The scope and authority of Interpretations are set out in the *Preface to IFRS Standards*.

IFRIC Interpretation 10
Interim Financial Reporting and Impairment

References

- IFRS 9 *Financial Instruments*
- IAS 34 *Interim Financial Reporting*
- IAS 36 *Impairment of Assets*

Background

1   An entity is required to assess goodwill for impairment at the end of each reporting period, and, if required, to recognise an impairment loss at that date in accordance with IAS 36. However, at the end of a subsequent reporting period, conditions may have so changed that the impairment loss would have been reduced or avoided had the impairment assessment been made only at that date. This Interpretation provides guidance on whether such impairment losses should ever be reversed.

2   The Interpretation addresses the interaction between the requirements of IAS 34 and the recognition of impairment losses on goodwill in IAS 36, and the effect of that interaction on subsequent interim and annual financial statements.

Issue

3   IAS 34 paragraph 28 requires an entity to apply the same accounting policies in its interim financial statements as are applied in its annual financial statements. It also states that 'the frequency of an entity's reporting (annual, half-yearly, or quarterly) shall not affect the measurement of its annual results. To achieve that objective, measurements for interim reporting purposes shall be made on a year-to-date basis.'

4   IAS 36 paragraph 124 states that 'An impairment loss recognised for goodwill shall not be reversed in a subsequent period.'

5–6   [Deleted]

7   The Interpretation addresses the following issue:

Should an entity reverse impairment losses recognised in an interim period on goodwill if a loss would not have been recognised, or a smaller loss would have been recognised, had an impairment assessment been made only at the end of a subsequent reporting period?

Consensus

8   An entity shall not reverse an impairment loss recognised in a previous interim period in respect of goodwill.

9   An entity shall not extend this consensus by analogy to other areas of potential conflict between IAS 34 and other standards.

Effective date and transition

10   An entity shall apply the Interpretation for annual periods beginning on or after 1 November 2006. Earlier application is encouraged. If an entity applies the Interpretation for a period beginning before 1 November 2006, it shall disclose that fact. An entity shall apply the Interpretation to goodwill prospectively from the date at which it first applied IAS 36; it shall apply the Interpretation to investments in equity instruments or in financial assets carried at cost prospectively from the date at which it first applied the measurement criteria of IAS 39.

11–13   [Deleted]

14   IFRS 9, as issued in July 2014, amended paragraphs 1, 2, 7 and 8 and deleted paragraphs 5, 6, 11–13. An entity shall apply those amendments when it applies IFRS 9.

IFRIC 12

Service Concession Arrangements

In November 2006 the International Accounting Standards Board issued IFRIC 12 *Service Concession Arrangements*. It was developed by the Interpretations Committee.

Other Standards have made minor consequential amendments to IFRIC 12. They include IFRS 9 *Financial Instruments* (Hedge Accounting and amendments to IFRS 9, IFRS 7 and IAS 39) (issued November 2013), IFRS 15 *Revenue from Contracts with Customers* (issued May 2014), IFRS 9 *Financial Instruments* (issued July 2014), IFRS 16 *Leases* (issued January 2016) and *Amendments to References to the Conceptual Framework in IFRS Standards* (issued March 2018).

Contents

FOR THE ACCOMPANYING GUIDANCE LISTED BELOW, SEE PART B OF THIS EDITION

INFORMATION NOTES

ILLUSTRATIVE EXAMPLES

FOR THE BASIS FOR CONCLUSIONS, SEE PART C OF THIS EDITION

BASIS FOR CONCLUSIONS

IFRIC Interpretation 12 *Service Concession Arrangements* (IFRIC 12) is set out in paragraphs 1–30 and Appendices A and B. IFRIC 12 is accompanied by information notes, illustrative examples and a Basis for Conclusions. The scope and authority of Interpretations are set out in the *Preface to IFRS Standards*.

IFRIC Interpretation 12
Service Concession Arrangements

References

- *Framework for the Preparation and Presentation of Financial Statements*[1]

- IFRS 1 *First-time Adoption of International Financial Reporting Standards*

- IFRS 7 *Financial Instruments: Disclosures*

- IFRS 9 *Financial Instruments*

- IFRS 15 *Revenue from Contracts with Customers*

- IFRS 16 *Leases*

- IAS 8 *Accounting Policies, Changes in Accounting Estimates and Errors*

- IAS 16 *Property, Plant and Equipment*

- IAS 20 *Accounting for Government Grants and Disclosure of Government Assistance*

- IAS 23 *Borrowing Costs*

- IAS 32 *Financial Instruments: Presentation*

- IAS 36 *Impairment of Assets*

- IAS 37 *Provisions, Contingent Liabilities and Contingent Assets*

- IAS 38 *Intangible Assets*

- SIC-29 *Service Concession Arrangements: Disclosures*[2]

Background

1   In many countries, infrastructure for public services—such as roads, bridges, tunnels, prisons, hospitals, airports, water distribution facilities, energy supply and telecommunication networks—has traditionally been constructed, operated and maintained by the public sector and financed through public budget appropriation.

2   In some countries, governments have introduced contractual service arrangements to attract private sector participation in the development, financing, operation and maintenance of such infrastructure. The infrastructure may already exist, or may be constructed during the period of the service arrangement. An arrangement within the scope of this Interpretation typically involves a private sector entity (an operator) constructing the infrastructure used to provide the public service or upgrading it (for example, by increasing its capacity) and operating and maintaining that infrastructure for a specified period of time. The operator is

---

1   The reference is to the IASC's *Framework for the Preparation and Presentation of Financial Statements*, adopted by the Board in 2001 and in effect when the Interpretation was developed.

2   The title of SIC-29, formerly *Disclosure—Service Concession Arrangements*, was amended by IFRIC 12.

paid for its services over the period of the arrangement. The arrangement is governed by a contract that sets out performance standards, mechanisms for adjusting prices, and arrangements for arbitrating disputes. Such an arrangement is often described as a 'build-operate-transfer', a 'rehabilitate-operate-transfer' or a 'public-to-private' service concession arrangement.

3   A feature of these service arrangements is the public service nature of the obligation undertaken by the operator. Public policy is for the services related to the infrastructure to be provided to the public, irrespective of the identity of the party that operates the services. The service arrangement contractually obliges the operator to provide the services to the public on behalf of the public sector entity. Other common features are:

   (a)   the party that grants the service arrangement (the grantor) is a public sector entity, including a governmental body, or a private sector entity to which the responsibility for the service has been devolved.

   (b)   the operator is responsible for at least some of the management of the infrastructure and related services and does not merely act as an agent on behalf of the grantor.

   (c)   the contract sets the initial prices to be levied by the operator and regulates price revisions over the period of the service arrangement.

   (d)   the operator is obliged to hand over the infrastructure to the grantor in a specified condition at the end of the period of the arrangement, for little or no incremental consideration, irrespective of which party initially financed it.

Scope

4   This Interpretation gives guidance on the accounting by operators for public-to-private service concession arrangements.

5   This Interpretation applies to public-to-private service concession arrangements if:

   (a)   the grantor controls or regulates what services the operator must provide with the infrastructure, to whom it must provide them, and at what price; and

   (b)   the grantor controls — through ownership, beneficial entitlement or otherwise — any significant residual interest in the infrastructure at the end of the term of the arrangement.

6   Infrastructure used in a public-to-private service concession arrangement for its entire useful life (whole of life assets) is within the scope of this Interpretation if the conditions in paragraph 5(a) are met. Paragraphs AG1–AG8 provide guidance on determining whether, and to what extent, public-to-private service concession arrangements are within the scope of this Interpretation.

7   This Interpretation applies to both:

   (a)   infrastructure that the operator constructs or acquires from a third party for the purpose of the service arrangement; and

   (b)   existing infrastructure to which the grantor gives the operator access for the purpose of the service arrangement.

8   This Interpretation does not specify the accounting for infrastructure that was held and recognised as property, plant and equipment by the operator before entering the service arrangement. The derecognition requirements of IFRSs (set out in IAS 16) apply to such infrastructure.

9   This Interpretation does not specify the accounting by grantors.

Issues

10   This Interpretation sets out general principles on recognising and measuring the obligations and related rights in service concession arrangements. Requirements for disclosing information about service concession arrangements are in SIC-29. The issues addressed in this Interpretation are:

   (a)   treatment of the operator's rights over the infrastructure;

   (b)   recognition and measurement of arrangement consideration;

   (c)   construction or upgrade services;

   (d)   operation services;

   (e)   borrowing costs;

   (f)   subsequent accounting treatment of a financial asset and an intangible asset; and

   (g)   items provided to the operator by the grantor.

Consensus

Treatment of the operator's rights over the infrastructure

11   Infrastructure within the scope of this Interpretation shall not be recognised as property, plant and equipment of the operator because the contractual service arrangement does not convey the right to control the use of the public service infrastructure to the operator. The operator has access to operate the infrastructure to provide the public service on behalf of the grantor in accordance with the terms specified in the contract.

Recognition and measurement of arrangement consideration

12   Under the terms of contractual arrangements within the scope of this Interpretation, the operator acts as a service provider. The operator constructs or upgrades infrastructure (construction or upgrade services) used to provide a public service and operates and maintains that infrastructure (operation services) for a specified period of time.

13   The operator shall recognise and measure revenue in accordance with IFRS 15 for the services it performs. The nature of the consideration determines its subsequent accounting treatment. The subsequent accounting for consideration received as a financial asset and as an intangible asset is detailed in paragraphs 23–26 below.

Construction or upgrade services

14   The operator shall account for construction or upgrade services in accordance with IFRS 15.

Consideration given by the grantor to the operator

15   If the operator provides construction or upgrade services the consideration received or receivable by the operator shall be recognised in accordance with IFRS 15. The consideration may be rights to:

(a)   a financial asset, or

(b)   an intangible asset.

16   The operator shall recognise a financial asset to the extent that it has an unconditional contractual right to receive cash or another financial asset from or at the direction of the grantor for the construction services; the grantor has little, if any, discretion to avoid payment, usually because the agreement is enforceable by law. The operator has an unconditional right to receive cash if the grantor contractually guarantees to pay the operator (a) specified or determinable amounts or (b) the shortfall, if any, between amounts received from users of the public service and specified or determinable amounts, even if payment is contingent on the operator ensuring that the infrastructure meets specified quality or efficiency requirements.

17   The operator shall recognise an intangible asset to the extent that it receives a right (a licence) to charge users of the public service. A right to charge users of the public service is not an unconditional right to receive cash because the amounts are contingent on the extent that the public uses the service.

18   If the operator is paid for the construction services partly by a financial asset and partly by an intangible asset it is necessary to account separately for each component of the operator's consideration. The consideration received or receivable for both components shall be recognised initially in accordance with IFRS 15.

19   The nature of the consideration given by the grantor to the operator shall be determined by reference to the contract terms and, when it exists, relevant contract law. The nature of the consideration determines the subsequent accounting as described in paragraphs 23–26. However, both types of consideration are classified as a contract asset during the construction or upgrade period in accordance with IFRS 15.

Operation services

20   The operator shall account for operation services in accordance with IFRS 15.

Contractual obligations to restore the infrastructure to a specified level of serviceability

21   The operator may have contractual obligations it must fulfil as a condition of its licence (a) to maintain the infrastructure to a specified level of serviceability or (b) to restore the infrastructure to a specified condition before it is handed over to the grantor at the end of the service arrangement. These contractual obligations to maintain or restore infrastructure, except for any upgrade element (see paragraph 14), shall be recognised and measured in accordance with IAS 37, ie at the best estimate of the expenditure that would be required to settle the present obligation at the end of the reporting period.

Borrowing costs incurred by the operator

22   In accordance with IAS 23, borrowing costs attributable to the arrangement shall be recognised as an expense in the period in which they are incurred unless the operator has a contractual right to receive an intangible asset (a right to charge users of the public service). In this case borrowing costs attributable to the arrangement shall be capitalised during the construction phase of the arrangement in accordance with that Standard.

Financial asset

23   IAS 32 and IFRSs 7 and 9 apply to the financial asset recognised under paragraphs 16 and 18.

24   The amount due from or at the direction of the grantor is accounted for in accordance with IFRS 9 as measured at:

(a)   amortised cost; or

(b)   fair value through other comprehensive income; or

(c)   fair value through profit or loss.

25   If the amount due from the grantor is measured at amortised cost or fair value through other comprehensive income, IFRS 9 requires interest calculated using the effective interest method to be recognised in profit or loss.

Intangible asset

26   IAS 38 applies to the intangible asset recognised in accordance with paragraphs 17 and 18. Paragraphs 45–47 of IAS 38 provide guidance on measuring intangible assets acquired in exchange for a non-monetary asset or assets or a combination of monetary and non-monetary assets.

Items provided to the operator by the grantor

27   In accordance with paragraph 11, infrastructure items to which the operator is given access by the grantor for the purposes of the service arrangement are not recognised as property, plant and equipment of the operator. The grantor may also provide other items to the operator that the operator can keep or deal with as it wishes. If such assets form part of the consideration payable by the grantor for the services, they are not government grants as defined in IAS 20. Instead, they are accounted for as part of the transaction price as defined in IFRS 15.

Effective date

28   An entity shall apply this Interpretation for annual periods beginning on or after 1 January 2008. Earlier application is permitted. If an entity applies this Interpretation for a period beginning before 1 January 2008, it shall disclose that fact.

28A–28C   [Deleted]

28D   IFRS 15 *Revenue from Contracts with Customers*, issued in May 2014, amended the 'References' section and paragraphs 13–15, 18–20 and 27. An entity shall apply those amendments when it applies IFRS 15.

28E   IFRS 9, as issued in July 2014, amended paragraphs 23–25 and deleted paragraphs 28A–28C. An entity shall apply those amendments when it applies IFRS 9.

28F   IFRS 16, issued in January 2016, amended paragraph AG8. An entity shall apply that amendment when it applies IFRS 16.

Transition

29   Subject to paragraph 30, changes in accounting policies are accounted for in accordance with IAS 8, ie retrospectively.

30   If, for any particular service arrangement, it is impracticable for an operator to apply this Interpretation retrospectively at the start of the earliest period presented, it shall:

    (a)   recognise financial assets and intangible assets that existed at the start of the earliest period presented;

    (b)   use the previous carrying amounts of those financial and intangible assets (however previously classified) as their carrying amounts as at that date; and

(c)   test financial and intangible assets recognised at that date for impairment, unless this is not practicable, in which case the amounts shall be tested for impairment as at the start of the current period.

Appendix A
Application guidance

This appendix is an integral part of the Interpretation.

Scope (paragraph 5)

AG1   Paragraph 5 of this Interpretation specifies that infrastructure is within the scope of the Interpretation when the following conditions apply:

(a)   the grantor controls or regulates what services the operator must provide with the infrastructure, to whom it must provide them, and at what price; and

(b)   the grantor controls—through ownership, beneficial entitlement or otherwise—any significant residual interest in the infrastructure at the end of the term of the arrangement.

AG2   The control or regulation referred to in condition (a) could be by contract or otherwise (such as through a regulator), and includes circumstances in which the grantor buys all of the output as well as those in which some or all of the output is bought by other users. In applying this condition, the grantor and any related parties shall be considered together. If the grantor is a public sector entity, the public sector as a whole, together with any regulators acting in the public interest, shall be regarded as related to the grantor for the purposes of this Interpretation.

AG3   For the purpose of condition (a), the grantor does not need to have complete control of the price: it is sufficient for the price to be regulated by the grantor, contract or regulator, for example by a capping mechanism. However, the condition shall be applied to the substance of the agreement. Non-substantive features, such as a cap that will apply only in remote circumstances, shall be ignored. Conversely, if for example, a contract purports to give the operator freedom to set prices, but any excess profit is returned to the grantor, the operator's return is capped and the price element of the control test is met.

AG4   For the purpose of condition (b), the grantor's control over any significant residual interest should both restrict the operator's practical ability to sell or pledge the infrastructure and give the grantor a continuing right of use throughout the period of the arrangement. The residual interest in the infrastructure is the estimated current value of the infrastructure as if it were already of the age and in the condition expected at the end of the period of the arrangement.

AG5   Control should be distinguished from management. If the grantor retains both the degree of control described in paragraph 5(a) and any significant residual interest in the infrastructure, the operator is only managing the infrastructure on the grantor's behalf—even though, in many cases, it may have wide managerial discretion.

AG6   Conditions (a) and (b) together identify when the infrastructure, including any replacements required (see paragraph 21), is controlled by the grantor for the whole of its economic life. For example, if the operator has to replace part of an item of infrastructure during the period of the arrangement (eg the top layer of a road or the roof of a building), the item of infrastructure shall be considered as a whole. Thus condition (b) is met for the whole of the infrastructure, including the part that is replaced, if the grantor controls any significant residual interest in the final replacement of that part.

AG7   Sometimes the use of infrastructure is partly regulated in the manner described in paragraph 5(a) and partly unregulated. However, these arrangements take a variety of forms:

     (a)   any infrastructure that is physically separable and capable of being operated independently and meets the definition of a cash-generating unit as defined in IAS 36 shall be analysed separately if it is used wholly for unregulated purposes. For example, this might apply to a private wing of a hospital, where the remainder of the hospital is used by the grantor to treat public patients.

     (b)   when purely ancillary activities (such as a hospital shop) are unregulated, the control tests shall be applied as if those services did not exist, because in cases in which the grantor controls the services in the manner described in paragraph 5, the existence of ancillary activities does not detract from the grantor's control of the infrastructure.

AG8   The operator may have a right to use the separable infrastructure described in paragraph AG7(a), or the facilities used to provide ancillary unregulated services described in paragraph AG7(b). In either case, there may in substance be a lease from the grantor to the operator; if so, it shall be accounted for in accordance with IFRS 16.

              © IFRS Foundation

Appendix B
Amendments to IFRS 1 and to other Interpretations

The amendments in this appendix shall be applied for annual periods beginning on or after 1 January 2008. If an entity applies this Interpretation for an earlier period, these amendments shall be applied for that earlier period.

* * * * *

The amendments contained in this appendix when this Interpretation was issued in 2006 have been incorporated into the text of IFRS 1, IFRIC 4 and SIC-29 as issued on or after 30 November 2006. In November 2008 a revised version of IFRS 1 was issued. In January 2016 IFRIC 4 was superseded by IFRS 16 Leases.

IFRIC 14

IAS 19 – The Limit on a Defined Benefit Asset, Minimum Funding Requirements and their Interaction

In July 2007 the International Accounting Standards Board issued IFRIC 14 *IAS 19 – The Limit on a Defined Benefit Asset, Minimum Funding Requirements and their Interaction*. It was developed by the Interpretations Committee.

In November 2009 IFRIC 14 was amended to address prepayments of future minimum funding requirement contributions.

Other Standards have made minor consequential amendments to IFRIC 14. They include IFRS 13 *Fair Value Measurement* (issued May 2011), IAS 19 *Employee Benefits* (issued June 2011) and *Amendments to References to the Conceptual Framework in IFRS Standards* (issued March 2018).

Contents

FOR THE ACCOMPANYING GUIDANCE LISTED BELOW, SEE PART B OF THIS EDITION

ILLUSTRATIVE EXAMPLES

FOR THE BASIS FOR CONCLUSIONS, SEE PART C OF THIS EDITION

BASIS FOR CONCLUSIONS

IFRIC Interpretation 14 *IAS 19 — The Limit on a Defined Benefit Asset, Minimum Funding Requirements and their Interaction* (IFRIC 14) is set out in paragraphs 1–29. IFRIC 14 is accompanied by illustrative examples and a Basis for Conclusions. The scope and authority of Interpretations are set out in the *Preface to IFRS Standards*.

IFRIC Interpretation 14
IAS 19—The Limit on a Defined Benefit Asset, Minimum Funding Requirements and their Interaction

References

- IAS 1 *Presentation of Financial Statements*

- IAS 8 *Accounting Policies, Changes in Accounting Estimates and Errors*

- IAS 19 *Employee Benefits* (as amended in 2011)

- IAS 37 *Provisions, Contingent Liabilities and Contingent Assets*

Background

1   Paragraph 64 of IAS 19 limits the measurement of a net defined benefit asset to the lower of the surplus in the defined benefit plan and the asset ceiling. Paragraph 8 of IAS 19 defines the asset ceiling as 'the present value of any economic benefits available in the form of refunds from the plan or reductions in future contributions to the plan'. Questions have arisen about when refunds or reductions in future contributions should be regarded as available, particularly when a minimum funding requirement exists.

2   Minimum funding requirements exist in many countries to improve the security of the post-employment benefit promise made to members of an employee benefit plan. Such requirements normally stipulate a minimum amount or level of contributions that must be made to a plan over a given period. Therefore, a minimum funding requirement may limit the ability of the entity to reduce future contributions.

3   Further, the limit on the measurement of a defined benefit asset may cause a minimum funding requirement to be onerous. Normally, a requirement to make contributions to a plan would not affect the measurement of the defined benefit asset or liability. This is because the contributions, once paid, will become plan assets and so the additional net liability is nil. However, a minimum funding requirement may give rise to a liability if the required contributions will not be available to the entity once they have been paid.

3A   In November 2009 the International Accounting Standards Board amended IFRIC 14 to remove an unintended consequence arising from the treatment of prepayments of future contributions in some circumstances when there is a minimum funding requirement.

Scope

4   This Interpretation applies to all post-employment defined benefits and other long-term employee defined benefits.

5   For the purpose of this Interpretation, minimum funding requirements are any requirements to fund a post-employment or other long-term defined benefit plan.

Issues

6   The issues addressed in this Interpretation are:

     (a)   when refunds or reductions in future contributions should be regarded as available in accordance with the definition of the asset ceiling in paragraph 8 of IAS 19.

     (b)   how a minimum funding requirement might affect the availability of reductions in future contributions.

     (c)   when a minimum funding requirement might give rise to a liability.

Consensus

Availability of a refund or reduction in future contributions

7   An entity shall determine the availability of a refund or a reduction in future contributions in accordance with the terms and conditions of the plan and any statutory requirements in the jurisdiction of the plan.

8   An economic benefit, in the form of a refund or a reduction in future contributions, is available if the entity can realise it at some point during the life of the plan or when the plan liabilities are settled. In particular, such an economic benefit may be available even if it is not realisable immediately at the end of the reporting period.

9   The economic benefit available does not depend on how the entity intends to use the surplus. An entity shall determine the maximum economic benefit that is available from refunds, reductions in future contributions or a combination of both. An entity shall not recognise economic benefits from a combination of refunds and reductions in future contributions based on assumptions that are mutually exclusive.

10   In accordance with IAS 1, the entity shall disclose information about the key sources of estimation uncertainty at the end of the reporting period that have a significant risk of causing a material adjustment to the carrying amount of the net asset or liability recognised in the statement of financial position. This might include disclosure of any restrictions on the current realisability of the surplus or disclosure of the basis used to determine the amount of the economic benefit available.

The economic benefit available as a refund

The right to a refund

11   A refund is available to an entity only if the entity has an unconditional right to a refund:

     (a)   during the life of the plan, without assuming that the plan liabilities must be settled in order to obtain the refund (eg in some jurisdictions, the entity may have a right to a refund during the life of the plan, irrespective of whether the plan liabilities are settled); or

(b)   assuming the gradual settlement of the plan liabilities over time until all members have left the plan; or

(c)   assuming the full settlement of the plan liabilities in a single event (ie as a plan wind-up).

An unconditional right to a refund can exist whatever the funding level of a plan at the end of the reporting period.

12   If the entity's right to a refund of a surplus depends on the occurrence or non-occurrence of one or more uncertain future events not wholly within its control, the entity does not have an unconditional right and shall not recognise an asset.

Measurement of the economic benefit

13   An entity shall measure the economic benefit available as a refund as the amount of the surplus at the end of the reporting period (being the fair value of the plan assets less the present value of the defined benefit obligation) that the entity has a right to receive as a refund, less any associated costs. For instance, if a refund would be subject to a tax other than income tax, an entity shall measure the amount of the refund net of the tax.

14   In measuring the amount of a refund available when the plan is wound up (paragraph 11(c)), an entity shall include the costs to the plan of settling the plan liabilities and making the refund. For example, an entity shall deduct professional fees if these are paid by the plan rather than the entity, and the costs of any insurance premiums that may be required to secure the liability on wind-up.

15   If the amount of a refund is determined as the full amount or a proportion of the surplus, rather than a fixed amount, an entity shall make no adjustment for the time value of money, even if the refund is realisable only at a future date.

The economic benefit available as a contribution reduction

16   If there is no minimum funding requirement for contributions relating to future service, the economic benefit available as a reduction in future contributions is the future service cost to the entity for each period over the shorter of the expected life of the plan and the expected life of the entity. The future service cost to the entity excludes amounts that will be borne by employees.

17   An entity shall determine the future service costs using assumptions consistent with those used to determine the defined benefit obligation and with the situation that exists at the end of the reporting period as determined by IAS 19. Therefore, an entity shall assume no change to the benefits to be provided by a plan in the future until the plan is amended and shall assume a stable workforce in the future unless the entity makes a reduction in the number of employees covered by the plan. In the latter case, the assumption about the future workforce shall include the reduction.

The effect of a minimum funding requirement on the economic benefit available as a reduction in future contributions

18   An entity shall analyse any minimum funding requirement at a given date into contributions that are required to cover (a) any existing shortfall for past service on the minimum funding basis and (b) future service.

19   Contributions to cover any existing shortfall on the minimum funding basis in respect of services already received do not affect future contributions for future service. They may give rise to a liability in accordance with paragraphs 23–26.

20   If there is a minimum funding requirement for contributions relating to future service, the economic benefit available as a reduction in future contributions is the sum of:

(a)   any amount that reduces future minimum funding requirement contributions for future service because the entity made a prepayment (ie paid the amount before being required to do so); and

(b)   the estimated future service cost in each period in accordance with paragraphs 16 and 17, less the estimated minimum funding requirement contributions that would be required for future service in those periods if there were no prepayment as described in (a).

21   An entity shall estimate the future minimum funding requirement contributions for future service taking into account the effect of any existing surplus determined using the minimum funding basis but excluding the prepayment described in paragraph 20(a). An entity shall use assumptions consistent with the minimum funding basis and, for any factors not specified by that basis, assumptions consistent with those used to determine the defined benefit obligation and with the situation that exists at the end of the reporting period as determined by IAS 19. The estimate shall include any changes expected as a result of the entity paying the minimum contributions when they are due. However, the estimate shall not include the effect of expected changes in the terms and conditions of the minimum funding basis that are not substantively enacted or contractually agreed at the end of the reporting period.

22   When an entity determines the amount described in paragraph 20(b), if the future minimum funding requirement contributions for future service exceed the future IAS 19 service cost in any given period, that excess reduces the amount of the economic benefit available as a reduction in future contributions. However, the amount described in paragraph 20(b) can never be less than zero.

When a minimum funding requirement may give rise to a liability

23   If an entity has an obligation under a minimum funding requirement to pay contributions to cover an existing shortfall on the minimum funding basis in respect of services already received, the entity shall determine whether the contributions payable will be available as a refund or reduction in future contributions after they are paid into the plan.

24   To the extent that the contributions payable will not be available after they are paid into the plan, the entity shall recognise a liability when the obligation arises. The liability shall reduce the net defined benefit asset or increase the net defined benefit liability so that no gain or loss is expected to result from applying paragraph 64 of IAS 19 when the contributions are paid.

25–26 [Deleted]

Effective date

27   An entity shall apply this Interpretation for annual periods beginning on or after 1 January 2008. Earlier application is permitted.

27A   IAS 1 (as revised in 2007) amended the terminology used throughout IFRSs. In addition it amended paragraph 26. An entity shall apply those amendments for annual periods beginning on or after 1 January 2009. If an entity applies IAS 1 (revised 2007) for an earlier period, the amendments shall be applied for that earlier period.

27B   *Prepayments of a Minimum Funding Requirement* added paragraph 3A and amended paragraphs 16–18 and 20–22. An entity shall apply those amendments for annual periods beginning on or after 1 January 2011. Earlier application is permitted. If an entity applies the amendments for an earlier period, it shall disclose that fact.

27C   IAS 19 (as amended in 2011) amended paragraphs 1, 6, 17 and 24 and deleted paragraphs 25 and 26. An entity shall apply those amendments when it applies IAS 19 (as amended in 2011).

Transition

28   An entity shall apply this Interpretation from the beginning of the first period presented in the first financial statements to which the Interpretation applies. An entity shall recognise any initial adjustment arising from the application of this Interpretation in retained earnings at the beginning of that period.

29   An entity shall apply the amendments in paragraphs 3A, 16–18 and 20–22 from the beginning of the earliest comparative period presented in the first financial statements in which the entity applies this Interpretation. If the entity had previously applied this Interpretation before it applies the amendments, it shall recognise the adjustment resulting from the application of the amendments in retained earnings at the beginning of the earliest comparative period presented.

Approval by the Board of *Prepayments of a Minimum Funding Requirement* issued in November 2009

Prepayments of a Minimum Funding Requirement (Amendments to IFRIC 14) was approved for issue by the fifteen members of the International Accounting Standards Board.

Sir David Tweedie   Chairman

Stephen Cooper

Philippe Danjou

Jan Engström

Patrick Finnegan

Robert P Garnett

Gilbert Gélard

Amaro Luiz de Oliveira Gomes

Prabhakar Kalavacherla

James J Leisenring

Patricia McConnell

Warren J McGregor

John T Smith

Tatsumi Yamada

Wei-Guo Zhang

Hedges of a Net Investment in a Foreign Operation

In July 2008 the International Accounting Standards Board issued IFRIC 16 *Hedges of a Net Investment in a Foreign Operation*. It was developed by the Interpretations Committee.

Other Standards have made minor consequential amendments to IFRIC 16. They include IFRS 11 *Joint Arrangements* (issued May 2011), IFRS 9 *Financial Instruments* (Hedge Accounting and amendments to IFRS 9, IFRS 7 and IAS 39) (issued November 2013) and IFRS 9 *Financial Instruments* (issued July 2014).

Contents

IFRIC Interpretation 16 *Hedges of a Net Investment in a Foreign Operation* (IFRIC 16) is set out in paragraphs 1–19 and the Appendix. IFRIC 16 is accompanied by an illustrative example and a Basis for Conclusions. The scope and authority of Interpretations are set out in the *Preface to IFRS Standards*.

IFRIC Interpretation 16
Hedges of a Net Investment in a Foreign Operation

References

- IFRS 9 *Financial Instruments*
- IAS 8 *Accounting Policies, Changes in Accounting Estimates and Errors*
- IAS 21 *The Effects of Changes in Foreign Exchange Rates*

Background

1   Many reporting entities have investments in foreign operations (as defined in IAS 21 paragraph 8). Such foreign operations may be subsidiaries, associates, joint ventures or branches. IAS 21 requires an entity to determine the functional currency of each of its foreign operations as the currency of the primary economic environment of that operation. When translating the results and financial position of a foreign operation into a presentation currency, the entity is required to recognise foreign exchange differences in other comprehensive income until it disposes of the foreign operation.

2   Hedge accounting of the foreign currency risk arising from a net investment in a foreign operation will apply only when the net assets of that foreign operation are included in the financial statements.[1] The item being hedged with respect to the foreign currency risk arising from the net investment in a foreign operation may be an amount of net assets equal to or less than the carrying amount of the net assets of the foreign operation.

3   IFRS 9 requires the designation of an eligible hedged item and eligible hedging instruments in a hedge accounting relationship. If there is a designated hedging relationship, in the case of a net investment hedge, the gain or loss on the hedging instrument that is determined to be an effective hedge of the net investment is recognised in other comprehensive income and is included with the foreign exchange differences arising on translation of the results and financial position of the foreign operation.

4   An entity with many foreign operations may be exposed to a number of foreign currency risks. This Interpretation provides guidance on identifying the foreign currency risks that qualify as a hedged risk in the hedge of a net investment in a foreign operation.

5   IFRS 9 allows an entity to designate either a derivative or a non-derivative financial instrument (or a combination of derivative and non-derivative financial instruments) as hedging instruments for foreign currency risk. This Interpretation provides guidance on where, within a group, hedging

---

1   This will be the case for consolidated financial statements, financial statements in which investments such as associates or joint ventures are accounted for using the equity method and financial statements that include a branch or a joint operation as defined in IFRS 11 *Joint Arrangements*.

instruments that are hedges of a net investment in a foreign operation can be held to qualify for hedge accounting.

6   IAS 21 and IFRS 9 require cumulative amounts recognised in other comprehensive income relating to both the foreign exchange differences arising on translation of the results and financial position of the foreign operation and the gain or loss on the hedging instrument that is determined to be an effective hedge of the net investment to be reclassified from equity to profit or loss as a reclassification adjustment when the parent disposes of the foreign operation. This Interpretation provides guidance on how an entity should determine the amounts to be reclassified from equity to profit or loss for both the hedging instrument and the hedged item.

Scope

7   This Interpretation applies to an entity that hedges the foreign currency risk arising from its net investments in foreign operations and wishes to qualify for hedge accounting in accordance with IFRS 9. For convenience this Interpretation refers to such an entity as a parent entity and to the financial statements in which the net assets of foreign operations are included as consolidated financial statements. All references to a parent entity apply equally to an entity that has a net investment in a foreign operation that is a joint venture, an associate or a branch.

8   This Interpretation applies only to hedges of net investments in foreign operations; it should not be applied by analogy to other types of hedge accounting.

Issues

9   Investments in foreign operations may be held directly by a parent entity or indirectly by its subsidiary or subsidiaries. The issues addressed in this Interpretation are:

   (a)   *the nature of the hedged risk and the amount of the hedged item for which a hedging relationship may be designated:*

      (i)   whether the parent entity may designate as a hedged risk only the foreign exchange differences arising from a difference between the functional currencies of the parent entity and its foreign operation, or whether it may also designate as the hedged risk the foreign exchange differences arising from the difference between the presentation currency of the parent entity's consolidated financial statements and the functional currency of the foreign operation;

      (ii)   if the parent entity holds the foreign operation indirectly, whether the hedged risk may include only the foreign exchange differences arising from differences in functional currencies between the foreign operation and its immediate parent entity, or whether the hedged risk may also include any foreign exchange differences between the functional currency of the foreign operation and any intermediate or ultimate parent entity (ie whether the fact that the net investment in the foreign operation is held through an intermediate parent affects the economic risk to the ultimate parent).

(b) *where in a group the hedging instrument can be held:*

 (i) whether a qualifying hedge accounting relationship can be established only if the entity hedging its net investment is a party to the hedging instrument or whether any entity in the group, regardless of its functional currency, can hold the hedging instrument;

 (ii) whether the nature of the hedging instrument (derivative or non-derivative) or the method of consolidation affects the assessment of hedge effectiveness.

(c) *what amounts should be reclassified from equity to profit or loss as reclassification adjustments on disposal of the foreign operation:*

 (i) when a foreign operation that was hedged is disposed of, what amounts from the parent entity's foreign currency translation reserve in respect of the hedging instrument and in respect of that foreign operation should be reclassified from equity to profit or loss in the parent entity's consolidated financial statements;

 (ii) whether the method of consolidation affects the determination of the amounts to be reclassified from equity to profit or loss.

Consensus

Nature of the hedged risk and amount of the hedged item for which a hedging relationship may be designated

10 Hedge accounting may be applied only to the foreign exchange differences arising between the functional currency of the foreign operation and the parent entity's functional currency.

11 In a hedge of the foreign currency risks arising from a net investment in a foreign operation, the hedged item can be an amount of net assets equal to or less than the carrying amount of the net assets of the foreign operation in the consolidated financial statements of the parent entity. The carrying amount of the net assets of a foreign operation that may be designated as the hedged item in the consolidated financial statements of a parent depends on whether any lower level parent of the foreign operation has applied hedge accounting for all or part of the net assets of that foreign operation and that accounting has been maintained in the parent's consolidated financial statements.

12 The hedged risk may be designated as the foreign currency exposure arising between the functional currency of the foreign operation and the functional currency of any parent entity (the immediate, intermediate or ultimate parent entity) of that foreign operation. The fact that the net investment is held

through an intermediate parent does not affect the nature of the economic risk arising from the foreign currency exposure to the ultimate parent entity.

13 An exposure to foreign currency risk arising from a net investment in a foreign operation may qualify for hedge accounting only once in the consolidated financial statements. Therefore, if the same net assets of a foreign operation are hedged by more than one parent entity within the group (for example, both a direct and an indirect parent entity) for the same risk, only one hedging relationship will qualify for hedge accounting in the consolidated financial statements of the ultimate parent. A hedging relationship designated by one parent entity in its consolidated financial statements need not be maintained by another higher level parent entity. However, if it is not maintained by the higher level parent entity, the hedge accounting applied by the lower level parent must be reversed before the higher level parent's hedge accounting is recognised.

Where the hedging instrument can be held

14 A derivative or a non-derivative instrument (or a combination of derivative and non-derivative instruments) may be designated as a hedging instrument in a hedge of a net investment in a foreign operation. The hedging instrument(s) may be held by any entity or entities within the group, as long as the designation, documentation and effectiveness requirements of IFRS 9 paragraph 6.4.1 that relate to a net investment hedge are satisfied. In particular, the hedging strategy of the group should be clearly documented because of the possibility of different designations at different levels of the group.

15 For the purpose of assessing effectiveness, the change in value of the hedging instrument in respect of foreign exchange risk is computed by reference to the functional currency of the parent entity against whose functional currency the hedged risk is measured, in accordance with the hedge accounting documentation. Depending on where the hedging instrument is held, in the absence of hedge accounting the total change in value might be recognised in profit or loss, in other comprehensive income, or both. However, the assessment of effectiveness is not affected by whether the change in value of the hedging instrument is recognised in profit or loss or in other comprehensive income. As part of the application of hedge accounting, the total effective portion of the change is included in other comprehensive income. The assessment of effectiveness is not affected by whether the hedging instrument is a derivative or a non-derivative instrument or by the method of consolidation.

Disposal of a hedged foreign operation

16 When a foreign operation that was hedged is disposed of, the amount reclassified to profit or loss as a reclassification adjustment from the foreign currency translation reserve in the consolidated financial statements of the parent in respect of the hedging instrument is the amount that IFRS 9 paragraph 6.5.14 requires to be identified. That amount is the cumulative gain

or loss on the hedging instrument that was determined to be an effective hedge.

17 The amount reclassified to profit or loss from the foreign currency translation reserve in the consolidated financial statements of a parent in respect of the net investment in that foreign operation in accordance with IAS 21 paragraph 48 is the amount included in that parent's foreign currency translation reserve in respect of that foreign operation. In the ultimate parent's consolidated financial statements, the aggregate net amount recognised in the foreign currency translation reserve in respect of all foreign operations is not affected by the consolidation method. However, whether the ultimate parent uses the direct or the step-by-step method of consolidation[2] may affect the amount included in its foreign currency translation reserve in respect of an individual foreign operation. The use of the step-by-step method of consolidation may result in the reclassification to profit or loss of an amount different from that used to determine hedge effectiveness. This difference may be eliminated by determining the amount relating to that foreign operation that would have arisen if the direct method of consolidation had been used. Making this adjustment is not required by IAS 21. However, it is an accounting policy choice that should be followed consistently for all net investments.

Effective date

18 An entity shall apply this Interpretation for annual periods beginning on or after 1 October 2008. An entity shall apply the amendment to paragraph 14 made by *Improvements to IFRSs* issued in April 2009 for annual periods beginning on or after 1 July 2009. Earlier application of both is permitted. If an entity applies this Interpretation for a period beginning before 1 October 2008, or the amendment to paragraph 14 before 1 July 2009, it shall disclose that fact.

18A [Deleted]

18B IFRS 9, as issued in July 2014, amended paragraphs 3, 5–7, 14, 16, AG1 and AG8 and deleted paragraph 18A. An entity shall apply those amendments when it applies IFRS 9.

Transition

19 IAS 8 specifies how an entity applies a change in accounting policy resulting from the initial application of an Interpretation. An entity is not required to comply with those requirements when first applying the Interpretation. If an entity had designated a hedging instrument as a hedge of a net investment but the hedge does not meet the conditions for hedge accounting in this

---

2 The direct method is the method of consolidation in which the financial statements of the foreign operation are translated directly into the functional currency of the ultimate parent. The step-by-step method is the method of consolidation in which the financial statements of the foreign operation are first translated into the functional currency of any intermediate parent(s) and then translated into the functional currency of the ultimate parent (or the presentation currency if different).

Interpretation, the entity shall apply IAS 39 to discontinue that hedge accounting prospectively.

Appendix
Application guidance

This appendix is an integral part of the Interpretation.

AG1   This appendix illustrates the application of the Interpretation using the corporate structure illustrated below. In all cases the hedging relationships described would be tested for effectiveness in accordance with IFRS 9, although this testing is not discussed in this appendix. Parent, being the ultimate parent entity, presents its consolidated financial statements in its functional currency of euro (EUR). Each of the subsidiaries is wholly owned. Parent's £500 million net investment in Subsidiary B (functional currency pounds sterling (GBP)) includes the £159 million equivalent of Subsidiary B's US$300 million net investment in Subsidiary C (functional currency US dollars (USD)). In other words, Subsidiary B's net assets other than its investment in Subsidiary C are £341 million.

Nature of hedged risk for which a hedging relationship may be designated (paragraphs 10–13)

AG2   Parent can hedge its net investment in each of Subsidiaries A, B and C for the foreign exchange risk between their respective functional currencies (Japanese yen (JPY), pounds sterling and US dollars) and euro. In addition, Parent can hedge the USD/GBP foreign exchange risk between the functional currencies of Subsidiary B and Subsidiary C. In its consolidated financial statements, Subsidiary B can hedge its net investment in Subsidiary C for the foreign exchange risk between their functional currencies of US dollars and pounds sterling. In the following examples the designated risk is the spot foreign exchange risk because the hedging instruments are not derivatives. If the hedging instruments were forward contracts, Parent could designate the forward foreign exchange risk.

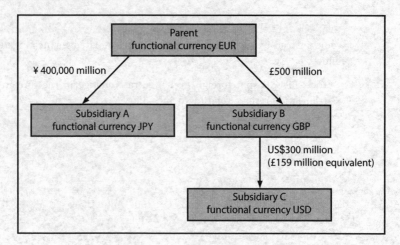

© IFRS Foundation

Amount of hedged item for which a hedging relationship may be designated (paragraphs 10–13)

AG3 Parent wishes to hedge the foreign exchange risk from its net investment in Subsidiary C. Assume that Subsidiary A has an external borrowing of US $300 million. The net assets of Subsidiary A at the start of the reporting period are ¥400,000 million including the proceeds of the external borrowing of US $300 million.

AG4 The hedged item can be an amount of net assets equal to or less than the carrying amount of Parent's net investment in Subsidiary C (US$300 million) in its consolidated financial statements. In its consolidated financial statements Parent can designate the US$300 million external borrowing in Subsidiary A as a hedge of the EUR/USD spot foreign exchange risk associated with its net investment in the US$300 million net assets of Subsidiary C. In this case, both the EUR/USD foreign exchange difference on the US$300 million external borrowing in Subsidiary A and the EUR/USD foreign exchange difference on the US$300 million net investment in Subsidiary C are included in the foreign currency translation reserve in Parent's consolidated financial statements after the application of hedge accounting.

AG5 In the absence of hedge accounting, the total USD/EUR foreign exchange difference on the US$300 million external borrowing in Subsidiary A would be recognised in Parent's consolidated financial statements as follows:

- USD/JPY spot foreign exchange rate change, translated to euro, in profit or loss, and

- JPY/EUR spot foreign exchange rate change in other comprehensive income.

Instead of the designation in paragraph AG4, in its consolidated financial statements Parent can designate the US$300 million external borrowing in Subsidiary A as a hedge of the GBP/USD spot foreign exchange risk between Subsidiary C and Subsidiary B. In this case, the total USD/EUR foreign exchange difference on the US$300 million external borrowing in Subsidiary A would instead be recognised in Parent's consolidated financial statements as follows:

- the GBP/USD spot foreign exchange rate change in the foreign currency translation reserve relating to Subsidiary C,

- GBP/JPY spot foreign exchange rate change, translated to euro, in profit or loss, and

- JPY/EUR spot foreign exchange rate change in other comprehensive income.

AG6 Parent cannot designate the US$300 million external borrowing in Subsidiary A as a hedge of both the EUR/USD spot foreign exchange risk and the GBP/USD spot foreign exchange risk in its consolidated financial statements. A single hedging instrument can hedge the same designated risk only once. Subsidiary B cannot apply hedge accounting in its consolidated financial statements because the hedging instrument is held outside the group comprising Subsidiary B and Subsidiary C.

Where in a group can the hedging instrument be held (paragraphs 14 and 15)?

AG7   As noted in paragraph AG5, the total change in value in respect of foreign exchange risk of the US$300 million external borrowing in Subsidiary A would be recorded in both profit or loss (USD/JPY spot risk) and other comprehensive income (EUR/JPY spot risk) in Parent's consolidated financial statements in the absence of hedge accounting. Both amounts are included for the purpose of assessing the effectiveness of the hedge designated in paragraph AG4 because the change in value of both the hedging instrument and the hedged item are computed by reference to the euro functional currency of Parent against the US dollar functional currency of Subsidiary C, in accordance with the hedge documentation. The method of consolidation (ie direct method or step-by-step method) does not affect the assessment of the effectiveness of the hedge.

Amounts reclassified to profit or loss on disposal of a foreign operation (paragraphs 16 and 17)

AG8   When Subsidiary C is disposed of, the amounts reclassified to profit or loss in Parent's consolidated financial statements from its foreign currency translation reserve (FCTR) are:

(a)   in respect of the US$300 million external borrowing of Subsidiary A, the amount that IFRS 9 requires to be identified, ie the total change in value in respect of foreign exchange risk that was recognised in other comprehensive income as the effective portion of the hedge; and

(b)   in respect of the US$300 million net investment in Subsidiary C, the amount determined by the entity's consolidation method. If Parent uses the direct method, its FCTR in respect of Subsidiary C will be determined directly by the EUR/USD foreign exchange rate. If Parent uses the step-by-step method, its FCTR in respect of Subsidiary C will be determined by the FCTR recognised by Subsidiary B reflecting the GBP/USD foreign exchange rate, translated to Parent's functional currency using the EUR/GBP foreign exchange rate. Parent's use of the step-by-step method of consolidation in prior periods does not require it to or preclude it from determining the amount of FCTR to be reclassified when it disposes of Subsidiary C to be the amount that it would have recognised if it had always used the direct method, depending on its accounting policy.

Hedging more than one foreign operation (paragraphs 11, 13 and 15)

AG9   The following examples illustrate that in the consolidated financial statements of Parent, the risk that can be hedged is always the risk between its functional currency (euro) and the functional currencies of Subsidiaries B and C. No matter how the hedges are designated, the maximum amounts that can be effective hedges to be included in the foreign currency translation reserve in Parent's consolidated financial statements when both foreign operations are hedged are US$300 million for EUR/USD risk and £341 million for EUR/GBP risk. Other changes in value due to changes in foreign exchange rates are included in Parent's consolidated profit or loss. Of course, it would be possible for Parent to designate US$300 million only for changes in the USD/GBP spot foreign exchange rate or £500 million only for changes in the GBP/EUR spot foreign exchange rate.

Parent holds both USD and GBP hedging instruments

AG10   Parent may wish to hedge the foreign exchange risk in relation to its net investment in Subsidiary B as well as that in relation to Subsidiary C. Assume that Parent holds suitable hedging instruments denominated in US dollars and pounds sterling that it could designate as hedges of its net investments in Subsidiary B and Subsidiary C. The designations Parent can make in its consolidated financial statements include, but are not limited to, the following:

(a)   US$300 million hedging instrument designated as a hedge of the US $300 million of net investment in Subsidiary C with the risk being the spot foreign exchange exposure (EUR/USD) between Parent and Subsidiary C and up to £341 million hedging instrument designated as a hedge of £341 million of the net investment in Subsidiary B with the risk being the spot foreign exchange exposure (EUR/GBP) between Parent and Subsidiary B.

(b)   US$300 million hedging instrument designated as a hedge of the US $300 million of net investment in Subsidiary C with the risk being the spot foreign exchange exposure (GBP/USD) between Subsidiary B and Subsidiary C and up to £500 million hedging instrument designated as a hedge of £500 million of the net investment in Subsidiary B with the risk being the spot foreign exchange exposure (EUR/GBP) between Parent and Subsidiary B.

AG11   The EUR/USD risk from Parent's net investment in Subsidiary C is a different risk from the EUR/GBP risk from Parent's net investment in Subsidiary B. However, in the case described in paragraph AG10(a), by its designation of the USD hedging instrument it holds, Parent has already fully hedged the EUR/USD risk from its net investment in Subsidiary C. If Parent also designated a GBP instrument it holds as a hedge of its £500 million net investment in Subsidiary B, £159 million of that net investment, representing the GBP equivalent of its USD net investment in Subsidiary C, would be hedged twice for GBP/EUR risk in Parent's consolidated financial statements.

AG12   In the case described in paragraph AG10(b), if Parent designates the hedged risk as the spot foreign exchange exposure (GBP/USD) between Subsidiary B and Subsidiary C, only the GBP/USD part of the change in the value of its US $300 million hedging instrument is included in Parent's foreign currency translation reserve relating to Subsidiary C. The remainder of the change (equivalent to the GBP/EUR change on £159 million) is included in Parent's consolidated profit or loss, as in paragraph AG5. Because the designation of the USD/GBP risk between Subsidiaries B and C does not include the GBP/EUR risk, Parent is also able to designate up to £500 million of its net investment in Subsidiary B with the risk being the spot foreign exchange exposure (GBP/EUR) between Parent and Subsidiary B.

Subsidiary B holds the USD hedging instrument

AG13   Assume that Subsidiary B holds US$300 million of external debt the proceeds of which were transferred to Parent by an inter-company loan denominated in pounds sterling. Because both its assets and liabilities increased by £159 million, Subsidiary B's net assets are unchanged. Subsidiary B could designate the external debt as a hedge of the GBP/USD risk of its net investment in Subsidiary C in its consolidated financial statements. Parent could maintain Subsidiary B's designation of that hedging instrument as a hedge of its US$300 million net investment in Subsidiary C for the GBP/USD risk (see paragraph 13) and Parent could designate the GBP hedging instrument it holds as a hedge of its entire £500 million net investment in Subsidiary B. The first hedge, designated by Subsidiary B, would be assessed by reference to Subsidiary B's functional currency (pounds sterling) and the second hedge, designated by Parent, would be assessed by reference to Parent's functional currency (euro). In this case, only the GBP/USD risk from Parent's net investment in Subsidiary C has been hedged in Parent's consolidated financial statements by the USD hedging instrument, not the entire EUR/USD risk. Therefore, the entire EUR/GBP risk from Parent's £500 million net investment in Subsidiary B may be hedged in the consolidated financial statements of Parent.

AG14   However, the accounting for Parent's £159 million loan payable to Subsidiary B must also be considered. If Parent's loan payable is not considered part of its net investment in Subsidiary B because it does not satisfy the conditions in IAS 21 paragraph 15, the GBP/EUR foreign exchange difference arising on translating it would be included in Parent's consolidated profit or loss. If the £159 million loan payable to Subsidiary B is considered part of Parent's net investment, that net investment would be only £341 million and the amount Parent could designate as the hedged item for GBP/EUR risk would be reduced from £500 million to £341 million accordingly.

AG15   If Parent reversed the hedging relationship designated by Subsidiary B, Parent could designate the US$300 million external borrowing held by Subsidiary B as a hedge of its US$300 million net investment in Subsidiary C for the EUR/USD risk and designate the GBP hedging instrument it holds itself as a hedge of only up to £341 million of the net investment in Subsidiary B. In this case the effectiveness of both hedges would be computed by reference to Parent's functional currency (euro). Consequently, both the USD/GBP change in value of the external borrowing held by Subsidiary B and the GBP/EUR change in value of Parent's loan payable to Subsidiary B (equivalent to USD/EUR in total) would be included in the foreign currency translation reserve in Parent's consolidated financial statements. Because Parent has already fully hedged the EUR/USD risk from its net investment in Subsidiary C, it can hedge only up to £341 million for the EUR/GBP risk of its net investment in Subsidiary B.

IFRIC 17

Distributions of Non-cash Assets to Owners

In November 2008 the International Accounting Standards Board issued IFRIC 17 *Distributions of Non-cash Assets to Owners*. It was developed by the Interpretations Committee.

The Basis for Conclusions on IFRIC 17 was amended to reflect IFRS 9 *Financial Instruments* (issued July 2014).

Other Standards have made minor consequential amendments to IFRIC 17. They include IFRS 10 *Consolidated Financial Statements* (issued May 2011), IFRS 13 *Fair Value Measurement* (issued May 2011) and *Amendments to References to the Conceptual Framework in IFRS Standards* (issued March 2018).

CONTENTS

FOR THE ACCOMPANYING GUIDANCE LISTED BELOW, SEE PART B OF THIS EDITION

ILLUSTRATIVE EXAMPLES

FOR THE BASIS FOR CONCLUSIONS, SEE PART C OF THIS EDITION

BASIS FOR CONCLUSIONS

IFRIC Interpretation 17 *Distributions of Non-cash Assets to Owners* (IFRIC 17) is set out in paragraphs 1–20 and the Appendix. IFRIC 17 is accompanied by illustrative examples and a Basis for Conclusions. The scope and authority of Interpretations are set out in the *Preface to IFRS Standards*.

IFRIC Interpretation 17
Distributions of Non-cash Assets to Owners

References

- IFRS 3 *Business Combinations* (as revised in 2008)

- IFRS 5 *Non-current Assets Held for Sale and Discontinued Operations*

- IFRS 7 *Financial Instruments: Disclosures*

- IFRS 10 *Consolidated Financial Statements*

- IFRS 13 *Fair Value Measurement*

- IAS 1 *Presentation of Financial Statements* (as revised in 2007)

- IAS 10 *Events after the Reporting Period*

Background

1   Sometimes an entity distributes assets other than cash (non-cash assets) as dividends to its owners[1] acting in their capacity as owners. In those situations, an entity may also give its owners a choice of receiving either non-cash assets or a cash alternative. The IFRIC received requests for guidance on how an entity should account for such distributions.

2   International Financial Reporting Standards (IFRSs) do not provide guidance on how an entity should measure distributions to its owners (commonly referred to as dividends). IAS 1 requires an entity to present details of dividends recognised as distributions to owners either in the statement of changes in equity or in the notes to the financial statements.

Scope

3   This Interpretation applies to the following types of non-reciprocal distributions of assets by an entity to its owners acting in their capacity as owners:

(a)   distributions of non-cash assets (eg items of property, plant and equipment, businesses as defined in IFRS 3, ownership interests in another entity or disposal groups as defined in IFRS 5); and

(b)   distributions that give owners a choice of receiving either non-cash assets or a cash alternative.

4   This Interpretation applies only to distributions in which all owners of the same class of equity instruments are treated equally.

---

1   Paragraph 7 of IAS 1 defines owners as holders of instruments classified as equity.

5   This Interpretation does not apply to a distribution of a non-cash asset that is ultimately controlled by the same party or parties before and after the distribution. This exclusion applies to the separate, individual and consolidated financial statements of an entity that makes the distribution.

6   In accordance with paragraph 5, this Interpretation does not apply when the non-cash asset is ultimately controlled by the same parties both before and after the distribution. Paragraph B2 of IFRS 3 states that 'A group of individuals shall be regarded as controlling an entity when, as a result of contractual arrangements, they collectively have the power to govern its financial and operating policies so as to obtain benefits from its activities.' Therefore, for a distribution to be outside the scope of this Interpretation on the basis that the same parties control the asset both before and after the distribution, a group of individual shareholders receiving the distribution must have, as a result of contractual arrangements, such ultimate collective power over the entity making the distribution.

7   In accordance with paragraph 5, this Interpretation does not apply when an entity distributes some of its ownership interests in a subsidiary but retains control of the subsidiary. The entity making a distribution that results in the entity recognising a non-controlling interest in its subsidiary accounts for the distribution in accordance with IFRS 10.

8   This Interpretation addresses only the accounting by an entity that makes a non-cash asset distribution. It does not address the accounting by shareholders who receive such a distribution.

Issues

9   When an entity declares a distribution and has an obligation to distribute the assets concerned to its owners, it must recognise a liability for the dividend payable. Consequently, this Interpretation addresses the following issues:

   (a)   When should the entity recognise the dividend payable?

   (b)   How should an entity measure the dividend payable?

   (c)   When an entity settles the dividend payable, how should it account for any difference between the carrying amount of the assets distributed and the carrying amount of the dividend payable?

Consensus

When to recognise a dividend payable

10   The liability to pay a dividend shall be recognised when the dividend is appropriately authorised and is no longer at the discretion of the entity, which is the date:

   (a)   when declaration of the dividend, eg by management or the board of directors, is approved by the relevant authority, eg the shareholders, if the jurisdiction requires such approval, or

(b)   when the dividend is declared, eg by management or the board of directors, if the jurisdiction does not require further approval.

Measurement of a dividend payable

11   An entity shall measure a liability to distribute non-cash assets as a dividend to its owners at the fair value of the assets to be distributed.

12   If an entity gives its owners a choice of receiving either a non-cash asset or a cash alternative, the entity shall estimate the dividend payable by considering both the fair value of each alternative and the associated probability of owners selecting each alternative.

13   At the end of each reporting period and at the date of settlement, the entity shall review and adjust the carrying amount of the dividend payable, with any changes in the carrying amount of the dividend payable recognised in equity as adjustments to the amount of the distribution.

Accounting for any difference between the carrying amount of the assets distributed and the carrying amount of the dividend payable when an entity settles the dividend payable

14   When an entity settles the dividend payable, it shall recognise the difference, if any, between the carrying amount of the assets distributed and the carrying amount of the dividend payable in profit or loss.

Presentation and disclosures

15   An entity shall present the difference described in paragraph 14 as a separate line item in profit or loss.

16   An entity shall disclose the following information, if applicable:

(a)   the carrying amount of the dividend payable at the beginning and end of the period; and

(b)   the increase or decrease in the carrying amount recognised in the period in accordance with paragraph 13 as result of a change in the fair value of the assets to be distributed.

17   If, after the end of a reporting period but before the financial statements are authorised for issue, an entity declares a dividend to distribute a non-cash asset, it shall disclose:

(a)   the nature of the asset to be distributed;

(b)   the carrying amount of the asset to be distributed as of the end of the reporting period; and

(c)   the fair value of the asset to be distributed as of the end of the reporting period, if it is different from its carrying amount, and the information about the method(s) used to measure that fair value required by paragraphs 93(b), (d), (g) and (i) and 99 of IFRS 13.

Effective date

18 An entity shall apply this Interpretation prospectively for annual periods beginning on or after 1 July 2009. Retrospective application is not permitted. Earlier application is permitted. If an entity applies this Interpretation for a period beginning before 1 July 2009, it shall disclose that fact and also apply IFRS 3 (as revised in 2008), IAS 27 (as amended in May 2008) and IFRS 5 (as amended by this Interpretation).

19 IFRS 10, issued in May 2011, amended paragraph 7. An entity shall apply that amendment when it applies IFRS 10.

20 IFRS 13, issued in May 2011, amended paragraph 17. An entity shall apply that amendment when it applies IFRS 13.

Appendix
Amendments to IFRS 5 *Non-current Assets Held for Sale and Discontinued Operations* and IAS 10 *Events after the Reporting Period*

The amendments contained in this appendix when this Interpretation was issued in 2008 have been incorporated into IFRS 5 and IAS 10 as published in this volume.

IFRIC 19

Extinguishing Financial Liabilities with Equity Instruments

In November 2009 the International Accounting Standards Board issued IFRIC 19 *Extinguishing Financial Liabilities with Equity Instruments*. It was developed by the Interpretations Committee.

Other Standards have made minor consequential amendments to IFRIC 19. They include IFRS 13 *Fair Value Measurement* (issued May 2011), IFRS 9 *Financial Instruments* (Hedge Accounting and amendments to IFRS 9, IFRS 7 and IAS 39) (issued November 2013), IFRS 9 *Financial Instruments* (issued July 2014) and *Amendments to References to the Conceptual Framework in IFRS Standards* (issued March 2018).

Contents

FOR THE BASIS FOR CONCLUSIONS, SEE PART C OF THIS EDITION

BASIS FOR CONCLUSIONS

IFRIC Interpretation 19 *Extinguishing Financial Liabilities with Equity Instruments* (IFRIC 19) is set out in paragraphs 1–17 and the Appendix. IFRIC 19 is accompanied by a Basis for Conclusions. The scope and authority of Interpretations are set out in the *Preface to IFRS Standards*.

IFRIC Interpretation 19
Extinguishing Financial Liabilities with Equity Instruments

References

- Framework for the Preparation and Presentation of Financial Statements[1]

- IFRS 2 *Share-based Payment*

- IFRS 3 *Business Combinations*

- IFRS 9 *Financial Instruments*

- IFRS 13 *Fair Value Measurement*

- IAS 1 *Presentation of Financial Statements*

- IAS 8 *Accounting Policies, Changes in Accounting Estimates and Errors*

- IAS 32 *Financial Instruments: Presentation*

Background

1   A debtor and creditor might renegotiate the terms of a financial liability with the result that the debtor extinguishes the liability fully or partially by issuing equity instruments to the creditor. These transactions are sometimes referred to as 'debt for equity swaps'. The IFRIC has received requests for guidance on the accounting for such transactions.

Scope

2   This Interpretation addresses the accounting by an entity when the terms of a financial liability are renegotiated and result in the entity issuing equity instruments to a creditor of the entity to extinguish all or part of the financial liability. It does not address the accounting by the creditor.

3   An entity shall not apply this Interpretation to transactions in situations where:

(a)   the creditor is also a direct or indirect shareholder and is acting in its capacity as a direct or indirect existing shareholder.

(b)   the creditor and the entity are controlled by the same party or parties before and after the transaction and the substance of the transaction includes an equity distribution by, or contribution to, the entity.

(c)   extinguishing the financial liability by issuing equity shares is in accordance with the original terms of the financial liability.

---

1   The reference is to the IASC's *Framework for the Preparation and Presentation of Financial Statements*, adopted by the Board in 2001 and in effect when the Interpretation was developed.

Issues

4   This Interpretation addresses the following issues:

    (a)   Are an entity's equity instruments issued to extinguish all or part of a financial liability 'consideration paid' in accordance with paragraph 3.3.3 of IFRS 9?

    (b)   How should an entity initially measure the equity instruments issued to extinguish such a financial liability?

    (c)   How should an entity account for any difference between the carrying amount of the financial liability extinguished and the initial measurement amount of the equity instruments issued?

Consensus

5   The issue of an entity's equity instruments to a creditor to extinguish all or part of a financial liability is consideration paid in accordance with paragraph 3.3.3 of IFRS 9. An entity shall remove a financial liability (or part of a financial liability) from its statement of financial position when, and only when, it is extinguished in accordance with paragraph 3.3.1 of IFRS 9.

6   When equity instruments issued to a creditor to extinguish all or part of a financial liability are recognised initially, an entity shall measure them at the fair value of the equity instruments issued, unless that fair value cannot be reliably measured.

7   If the fair value of the equity instruments issued cannot be reliably measured then the equity instruments shall be measured to reflect the fair value of the financial liability extinguished. In measuring the fair value of a financial liability extinguished that includes a demand feature (eg a demand deposit), paragraph 47 of IFRS 13 is not applied.

8   If only part of the financial liability is extinguished, the entity shall assess whether some of the consideration paid relates to a modification of the terms of the liability that remains outstanding. If part of the consideration paid does relate to a modification of the terms of the remaining part of the liability, the entity shall allocate the consideration paid between the part of the liability extinguished and the part of the liability that remains outstanding. The entity shall consider all relevant facts and circumstances relating to the transaction in making this allocation.

9   The difference between the carrying amount of the financial liability (or part of a financial liability) extinguished, and the consideration paid, shall be recognised in profit or loss, in accordance with paragraph 3.3.3 of IFRS 9. The equity instruments issued shall be recognised initially and measured at the date the financial liability (or part of that liability) is extinguished.

10   When only part of the financial liability is extinguished, consideration shall be allocated in accordance with paragraph 8. The consideration allocated to the remaining liability shall form part of the assessment of whether the terms of that remaining liability have been substantially modified. If the remaining

liability has been substantially modified, the entity shall account for the modification as the extinguishment of the original liability and the recognition of a new liability as required by paragraph 3.3.2 of IFRS 9.

11   An entity shall disclose a gain or loss recognised in accordance with paragraphs 9 and 10 as a separate line item in profit or loss or in the notes.

Effective date and transition

12   An entity shall apply this Interpretation for annual periods beginning on or after 1 July 2010. Earlier application is permitted. If an entity applies this Interpretation for a period beginning before 1 July 2010, it shall disclose that fact.

13   An entity shall apply a change in accounting policy in accordance with IAS 8 from the beginning of the earliest comparative period presented.

14   [Deleted]

15   IFRS 13, issued in May 2011, amended paragraph 7. An entity shall apply that amendment when it applies IFRS 13.

16   [Deleted]

17   IFRS 9, as issued in July 2014, amended paragraphs 4, 5, 7, 9 and 10 and deleted paragraphs 14 and 16. An entity shall apply those amendments when it applies IFRS 9.

Appendix
Amendment to IFRS 1 *First-time Adoption of International Financial Reporting Standards*

The amendment in this appendix shall be applied for annual periods beginning on or after 1 July 2010. If an entity applies this Interpretation for an earlier period, the amendment shall be applied for that earlier period.

* * * * *

The amendment contained in this appendix when this Interpretation was issued in 2009 has been incorporated into the text of IFRS 1 as issued on or after 26 November 2009.

IFRIC 20

Stripping Costs in the Production Phase of a Surface Mine

In October 2011 the International Accounting Standards Board issued IFRIC 20 *Stripping Costs in the Production Phase of a Surface Mine*. It was developed by the Interpretations Committee.

Other Standards have made minor consequential amendments to IFRIC 20, including *Amendments to References to the Conceptual Framework in IFRS Standards* (issued March 2018).

CONTENTS

FOR THE BASIS FOR CONCLUSIONS, SEE PART C OF THIS EDITION

BASIS FOR CONCLUSIONS

IFRIC Interpretation 20 *Stripping Costs in the Production Phase of a Surface Mine* (IFRIC 20) is set out in paragraphs 1–16 and appendices A–B. IFRIC 20 is accompanied by a Basis for Conclusions. The scope and authority of Interpretations are set out in the *Preface to IFRS Standards*.

IFRIC Interpretation 20
Stripping Costs in the Production Phase of a Surface Mine

References

- *Conceptual Framework for Financial Reporting*[1]

- IAS 1 *Presentation of Financial Statements*

- IAS 2 *Inventories*

- IAS 16 *Property, Plant and Equipment*

- IAS 38 *Intangible Assets*

Background

1   In surface mining operations, entities may find it necessary to remove mine waste materials ('overburden') to gain access to mineral ore deposits. This waste removal activity is known as 'stripping'.

2   During the development phase of the mine (before production begins), stripping costs are usually capitalised as part of the depreciable cost of building, developing and constructing the mine. Those capitalised costs are depreciated or amortised on a systematic basis, usually by using the units of production method, once production begins.

3   A mining entity may continue to remove overburden and to incur stripping costs during the production phase of the mine.

4   The material removed when stripping in the production phase will not necessarily be 100 per cent waste; often it will be a combination of ore and waste. The ratio of ore to waste can range from uneconomic low grade to profitable high grade. Removal of material with a low ratio of ore to waste may produce some usable material, which can be used to produce inventory. This removal might also provide access to deeper levels of material that have a higher ratio of ore to waste. There can therefore be two benefits accruing to the entity from the stripping activity: usable ore that can be used to produce inventory and improved access to further quantities of material that will be mined in future periods.

5   This Interpretation considers when and how to account separately for these two benefits arising from the stripping activity, as well as how to measure these benefits both initially and subsequently.

Scope

6   This Interpretation applies to waste removal costs that are incurred in surface mining activity during the production phase of the mine ('production stripping costs').

---

1   The reference is to the *Conceptual Framework for Financial Reporting*, issued in 2010 and in effect when the Interpretation was developed.

Issues

7   This Interpretation addresses the following issues:

(a)   recognition of production stripping costs as an asset;

(b)   initial measurement of the stripping activity asset; and

(c)   subsequent measurement of the stripping activity asset.

Consensus

Recognition of production stripping costs as an asset

8   To the extent that the benefit from the stripping activity is realised in the form of inventory produced, the entity shall account for the costs of that stripping activity in accordance with the principles of IAS 2 *Inventories*. To the extent the benefit is improved access to ore, the entity shall recognise these costs as a non-current asset, if the criteria in paragraph 9 below are met. This Interpretation refers to the non-current asset as the 'stripping activity asset'.

9   An entity shall recognise a stripping activity asset if, and only if, all of the following are met:

(a)   it is probable that the future economic benefit (improved access to the ore body) associated with the stripping activity will flow to the entity;

(b)   the entity can identify the component of the ore body for which access has been improved; and

(c)   the costs relating to the stripping activity associated with that component can be measured reliably.

10   The stripping activity asset shall be accounted for as an addition to, or as an enhancement of, an existing asset. In other words, the stripping activity asset will be accounted for as *part* of an existing asset.

11   The stripping activity asset's classification as a tangible or intangible asset is the same as the existing asset. In other words, the nature of this existing asset will determine whether the entity shall classify the stripping activity asset as tangible or intangible.

Initial measurement of the stripping activity asset

12   The entity shall initially measure the stripping activity asset at cost, this being the accumulation of costs directly incurred to perform the stripping activity that improves access to the identified component of ore, plus an allocation of directly attributable overhead costs. Some incidental operations may take place at the same time as the production stripping activity, but which are not necessary for the production stripping activity to continue as planned. The costs associated with these incidental operations shall not be included in the cost of the stripping activity asset.

13   When the costs of the stripping activity asset and the inventory produced are not separately identifiable, the entity shall allocate the production stripping costs between the inventory produced and the stripping activity asset by using an allocation basis that is based on a relevant production measure. This production measure shall be calculated for the identified component of the ore body, and shall be used as a benchmark to identify the extent to which the additional activity of creating a future benefit has taken place. Examples of such measures include:

(a)   cost of inventory produced compared with expected cost;

(b)   volume of waste extracted compared with expected volume, for a given volume of ore production; and

(c)   mineral content of the ore extracted compared with expected mineral content to be extracted, for a given quantity of ore produced.

Subsequent measurement of the stripping activity asset

14   After initial recognition, the stripping activity asset shall be carried at either its cost or its revalued amount less depreciation or amortisation and less impairment losses, in the same way as the existing asset of which it is a part.

15   The stripping activity asset shall be depreciated or amortised on a systematic basis, over the expected useful life of the identified component of the ore body that becomes more accessible as a result of the stripping activity. The units of production method shall be applied unless another method is more appropriate.

16   The expected useful life of the identified component of the ore body that is used to depreciate or amortise the stripping activity asset will differ from the expected useful life that is used to depreciate or amortise the mine itself and the related life-of-mine assets. The exception to this are those limited circumstances when the stripping activity provides improved access to the whole of the remaining ore body. For example, this might occur towards the end of a mine's useful life when the identified component represents the final part of the ore body to be extracted.

© IFRS Foundation

Appendix A
Effective date and transition

This appendix is an integral part of the Interpretation and has the same authority as the other parts of the Interpretation.

A1   An entity shall apply this Interpretation for annual periods beginning on or after 1 January 2013. Earlier application is permitted. If an entity applies this Interpretation for an earlier period, it shall disclose that fact.

A2   An entity shall apply this Interpretation to production stripping costs incurred on or after the beginning of the earliest period presented.

A3   As at the beginning of the earliest period presented, any previously recognised asset balance that resulted from stripping activity undertaken during the production phase ('predecessor stripping asset') shall be reclassified as a part of an existing asset to which the stripping activity related, to the extent that there remains an identifiable component of the ore body with which the predecessor stripping asset can be associated. Such balances shall be depreciated or amortised over the remaining expected useful life of the identified component of the ore body to which each predecessor stripping asset balance relates.

A4   If there is no identifiable component of the ore body to which that predecessor stripping asset relates, it shall be recognised in opening retained earnings at the beginning of the earliest period presented.

Appendix B
Amendments to IFRS 1 *First-time Adoption of International Financial Reporting Standards*

The amendments in this appendix shall be applied for annual periods beginning on or after 1 January 2013. If an entity applies this Interpretation for an earlier period these amendments shall be applied for that earlier period.

* * * * *

The amendments contained in this appendix when this Interpretation was issued in 2011 have been incorporated into IFRS 1 as issued on and after 27 May 2004. In November 2008 a revised version of IFRS 1 was issued.

© IFRS Foundation

IFRIC 21

Levies

In May 2013 the International Accounting Standards Board issued IFRIC 21 *Levies*. It was developed by the Interpretations Committee.

CONTENTS

> FOR THE ACCOMPANYING GUIDANCE LISTED BELOW, SEE PART B OF THIS EDITION

> FOR THE BASIS FOR CONCLUSIONS, SEE PART C OF THIS EDITION

IFRIC Interpretation 21 *Levies* (IFRIC 21) is set out in paragraphs 1–14 and Appendix A. IFRIC 21 is accompanied by Illustrative Examples and a Basis for Conclusions. The scope and authority of Interpretations are set out in the *Preface of IFRS Standards*.

IFRIC Interpretation 21
Levies

References

- IAS 1 *Presentation of Financial Statements*
- IAS 8 *Accounting Policies, Changes in Accounting Estimates and Errors*
- IAS 12 *Income Taxes*
- IAS 20 *Accounting for Governments Grants and Disclosures of Government Assistance*
- IAS 24 *Related Party Disclosures*
- IAS 34 *Interim Financial Reporting*
- IAS 37 *Provisions, Contingent Liabilities and Contingent Assets*
- IFRIC 6 *Liabilities arising from Participating in a Specific Market — Waste Electrical and Electronic Equipment*

Background

1   A government may impose a levy on an entity. The IFRS Interpretations Committee received requests for guidance on the accounting for levies in the financial statements of the entity that is paying the levy. The question relates to when to recognise a liability to pay a levy that is accounted for in accordance with IAS 37 *Provisions, Contingent Liabilities and Contingent Assets*.

Scope

2   This Interpretation addresses the accounting for a liability to pay a levy if that liability is within the scope of IAS 37. It also addresses the accounting for a liability to pay a levy whose timing and amount is certain.

3   This Interpretation does not address the accounting for the costs that arise from recognising a liability to pay a levy. Entities should apply other Standards to decide whether the recognition of a liability to pay a levy gives rise to an asset or an expense.

4   For the purposes of this Interpretation, a levy is an outflow of resources embodying economic benefits that is imposed by governments on entities in accordance with legislation (ie laws and/or regulations), other than:

     (a)   those outflows of resources that are within the scope of other Standards (such as income taxes that are within the scope of IAS 12 *Income Taxes*); and

     (b)   fines or other penalties that are imposed for breaches of the legislation.

     'Government' refers to government, government agencies and similar bodies whether local, national or international.

5   A payment made by an entity for the acquisition of an asset, or for the rendering of services under a contractual agreement with a government, does not meet the definition of a levy.

6   An entity is not required to apply this Interpretation to liabilities that arise from emissions trading schemes.

Issues

7   To clarify the accounting for a liability to pay a levy, this Interpretation addresses the following issues:

    (a)   what is the obligating event that gives rise to the recognition of a liability to pay a levy?

    (b)   does economic compulsion to continue to operate in a future period create a constructive obligation to pay a levy that will be triggered by operating in that future period?

    (c)   does the going concern assumption imply that an entity has a present obligation to pay a levy that will be triggered by operating in a future period?

    (d)   does the recognition of a liability to pay a levy arise at a point in time or does it, in some circumstances, arise progressively over time?

    (e)   what is the obligating event that gives rise to the recognition of a liability to pay a levy that is triggered if a minimum threshold is reached?

    (f)   are the principles for recognising in the annual financial statements and in the interim financial report a liability to pay a levy the same?

Consensus

8   The obligating event that gives rise to a liability to pay a levy is the activity that triggers the payment of the levy, as identified by the legislation. For example, if the activity that triggers the payment of the levy is the generation of revenue in the current period and the calculation of that levy is based on the revenue that was generated in a previous period, the obligating event for that levy is the generation of revenue in the current period. The generation of revenue in the previous period is necessary, but not sufficient, to create a present obligation.

9   An entity does not have a constructive obligation to pay a levy that will be triggered by operating in a future period as a result of the entity being economically compelled to continue to operate in that future period.

10   The preparation of financial statements under the going concern assumption does not imply that an entity has a present obligation to pay a levy that will be triggered by operating in a future period.

11   The liability to pay a levy is recognised progressively if the obligating event occurs over a period of time (ie if the activity that triggers the payment of the levy, as identified by the legislation, occurs over a period of time). For example, if the obligating event is the generation of revenue over a period of time, the corresponding liability is recognised as the entity generates that revenue.

12   If an obligation to pay a levy is triggered when a minimum threshold is reached, the accounting for the liability that arises from that obligation shall be consistent with the principles established in paragraphs 8–14 of this Interpretation (in particular, paragraphs 8 and 11). For example, if the obligating event is the reaching of a minimum activity threshold (such as a minimum amount of revenue or sales generated or outputs produced), the corresponding liability is recognised when that minimum activity threshold is reached.

13   An entity shall apply the same recognition principles in the interim financial report that it applies in the annual financial statements. As a result, in the interim financial report, a liability to pay a levy:

(a)   shall not be recognised if there is no present obligation to pay the levy at the end of the interim reporting period; and

(b)   shall be recognised if a present obligation to pay the levy exists at the end of the interim reporting period.

14   An entity shall recognise an asset if it has prepaid a levy but does not yet have a present obligation to pay that levy.

Appendix A
Effective date and transition

This appendix is an integral part of the Interpretation and has the same authority as the other parts of the Interpretation.

A1   An entity shall apply this Interpretation for annual periods beginning on or after 1 January 2014. Earlier application is permitted. If an entity applies this Interpretation for an earlier period, it shall disclose that fact.

A2   Changes in accounting policies resulting from the initial application of this Interpretation shall be accounted for retrospectively in accordance with IAS 8 *Accounting Policies, Changes in Accounting Estimates and Errors.*

IFRIC 22

Foreign Currency Transactions and Advance Consideration

In December 2016 the International Accounting Standards Board issued IFRIC 22 *Foreign Currency Transactions and Advance Consideration*. It was developed by the Interpretations Committee.

Other Standards have made minor consequential amendments to IFRIC 22, including *Amendments to References to the Conceptual Framework in IFRS Standards* (issued March 2018).

Contents

FOR THE ACCOMPANYING GUIDANCE LISTED BELOW, SEE PART B OF THIS EDITION

ILLUSTRATIVE EXAMPLES

FOR THE BASIS FOR CONCLUSIONS, SEE PART C OF THIS EDITION

BASIS FOR CONCLUSIONS

IFRIC Interpretation 22 *Foreign Currency Transactions and Advance Consideration* (IFRIC 22) is set out in paragraphs 1–9 and Appendices A and B. IFRIC 22 is accompanied by Illustrative Examples and a Basis for Conclusions. The scope and authority of Interpretations are set out in the *Preface to IFRS Standards*.

IFRIC Interpretation 22
Foreign Currency Transactions and Advance Consideration

References

- *The Conceptual Framework for Financial Reporting*[1]

- IAS 8 *Accounting Policies, Changes in Accounting Estimates and Errors*

- IAS 21 *The Effects of Changes in Foreign Exchange Rates*

Background

1   Paragraph 21 of IAS 21 *The Effects of Changes in Foreign Exchange Rates* requires an entity to record a foreign currency transaction, on initial recognition in its functional currency, by applying to the foreign currency amount the spot exchange rate between the functional currency and the foreign currency (the exchange rate) at the date of the transaction. Paragraph 22 of IAS 21 states that the date of the transaction is the date on which the transaction first qualifies for recognition in accordance with IFRS Standards (Standards).

2   When an entity pays or receives consideration in advance in a foreign currency, it generally recognises a non-monetary asset or non-monetary liability[2] before the recognition of the related asset, expense or income. The related asset, expense or income (or part of it) is the amount recognised applying relevant Standards, which results in the derecognition of the non-monetary asset or non-monetary liability arising from the advance consideration.

3   The IFRS Interpretations Committee (the Interpretations Committee) initially received a question asking how to determine 'the date of the transaction' applying paragraphs 21–22 of IAS 21 when recognising revenue. The question specifically addressed circumstances in which an entity recognises a non-monetary liability arising from the receipt of advance consideration before it recognises the related revenue. In discussing the issue, the Interpretations Committee noted that the receipt or payment of advance consideration in a foreign currency is not restricted to revenue transactions. Accordingly, the Interpretations Committee decided to clarify the date of the transaction for the purpose of determining the exchange rate to use on initial recognition of the related asset, expense or income when an entity has received or paid advance consideration in a foreign currency.

---

1   The reference is to the *Conceptual Framework for Financial Reporting*, issued in 2010 and in effect when the Interpretation was developed.

2   For example, paragraph 106 of IFRS 15 *Revenue from Contracts with Customers* requires that if a customer pays consideration, or an entity has a right to an amount of consideration that is unconditional (ie a receivable), before the entity transfers a good or service to the customer, the entity shall present the contract as a contract liability when the payment is made or the payment is due (whichever is earlier).

Scope

4   This Interpretation applies to a foreign currency transaction (or part of it) when an entity recognises a non-monetary asset or non-monetary liability arising from the payment or receipt of advance consideration before the entity recognises the related asset, expense or income (or part of it).

5   This Interpretation does not apply when an entity measures the related asset, expense or income on initial recognition:

(a)   at fair value; or

(b)   at the fair value of the consideration paid or received at a date other than the date of initial recognition of the non-monetary asset or non-monetary liability arising from advance consideration (for example, the measurement of goodwill applying IFRS 3 *Business Combinations*).

6   An entity is not required to apply this Interpretation to:

(a)   income taxes; or

(b)   insurance contracts (including reinsurance contracts) that it issues or reinsurance contracts that it holds.

Issue

7   This Interpretation addresses how to determine the date of the transaction for the purpose of determining the exchange rate to use on initial recognition of the related asset, expense or income (or part of it) on the derecognition of a non-monetary asset or non-monetary liability arising from the payment or receipt of advance consideration in a foreign currency.

Consensus

8   Applying paragraphs 21–22 of IAS 21, the date of the transaction for the purpose of determining the exchange rate to use on initial recognition of the related asset, expense or income (or part of it) is the date on which an entity initially recognises the non-monetary asset or non-monetary liability arising from the payment or receipt of advance consideration.

9   If there are multiple payments or receipts in advance, the entity shall determine a date of the transaction for each payment or receipt of advance consideration.

Appendix A
Effective date and transition

This Appendix is an integral part of IFRIC 22 and has the same authority as the other parts of IFRIC 22.

Effective date

A1   An entity shall apply this Interpretation for annual reporting periods beginning on or after 1 January 2018. Earlier application is permitted. If an entity applies this Interpretation for an earlier period, it shall disclose that fact.

Transition

A2   On initial application, an entity shall apply this Interpretation either:

(a)   retrospectively applying IAS 8 *Accounting Policies, Changes in Accounting Estimates and Errors*; or

(b)   prospectively to all assets, expenses and income in the scope of the Interpretation initially recognised on or after:

(i)   the beginning of the reporting period in which the entity first applies the Interpretation; or

(ii)   the beginning of a prior reporting period presented as comparative information in the financial statements of the reporting period in which the entity first applies the Interpretation.

A3   An entity that applies paragraph A2(b) shall, on initial application, apply the Interpretation to assets, expenses and income initially recognised on or after the beginning of the reporting period in paragraph A2(b)(i) or (ii) for which the entity has recognised non-monetary assets or non-monetary liabilities arising from advance consideration before that date.

Appendix B

The amendment in this Appendix shall be applied for annual reporting periods beginning on or after 1 January 2018. If an entity applies this Interpretation for an earlier period this amendment shall be applied for that earlier period.

Amendment to IFRS 1 *First-time Adoption of International Financial Reporting Standards*

* * * * *

The amendment contained in this appendix when this Interpretation was issued in 2016 has been incorporated into the text of IFRS 1 published in this volume.

Appendix B

The amendment in this Appendix shall be applied for annual reporting periods beginning on or after 1 January 2018. If an entity applies this Interpretation for an earlier period, this amendment shall be applied for that earlier period.

Amendment to IFRS 1 First-time Adoption of International Financial Reporting Standards

The amendment contained in this appendix when this Interpretation was issued in 2016 has been incorporated into the text of IFRS 1 published in this volume.

IFRIC 23

Uncertainty over Income Tax Treatments

In May 2017, the International Accounting Standards Board (Board) issued IFRIC 23 *Uncertainty over Income Tax Treatments*. It was developed by the IFRS Interpretations Committee.

Contents

FOR THE ACCOMPANYING GUIDANCE LISTED BELOW, SEE PART B OF THIS EDITION

ILLUSTRATIVE EXAMPLES

FOR THE BASIS FOR CONCLUSIONS, SEE PART C OF THIS EDITION

BASIS FOR CONCLUSIONS

IFRIC 23 *Uncertainty over Income Tax Treatments* (IFRIC 23) is set out in paragraphs 1–14 and Appendices A, B and C. IFRIC 23 is accompanied by Illustrative Examples and a Basis for Conclusions. The scope and authority of Interpretations are set out in the *Preface to IFRS Standards*.

IFRIC 23
Uncertainty over Income Tax Treatments

References

- IAS 1 *Presentation of Financial Statements*
- IAS 8 *Accounting Policies, Changes in Accounting Estimates and Errors*
- IAS 10 *Events after the Reporting Period*
- IAS 12 *Income Taxes*

Background

1   IAS 12 *Income Taxes* specifies requirements for current and deferred tax assets and liabilities. An entity applies the requirements in IAS 12 based on applicable tax laws.

2   It may be unclear how tax law applies to a particular transaction or circumstance. The acceptability of a particular tax treatment under tax law may not be known until the relevant taxation authority or a court takes a decision in the future. Consequently, a dispute or examination of a particular tax treatment by the taxation authority may affect an entity's accounting for a current or deferred tax asset or liability.

3   In this Interpretation:

(a)   'tax treatments' refers to the treatments used by an entity or that it plans to use in its income tax filings.

(b)   'taxation authority' refers to the body or bodies that decide whether tax treatments are acceptable under tax law. This might include a court.

(c)   an 'uncertain tax treatment' is a tax treatment for which there is uncertainty over whether the relevant taxation authority will accept the tax treatment under tax law. For example, an entity's decision not to submit any income tax filing in a tax jurisdiction, or not to include particular income in taxable profit, is an uncertain tax treatment if its acceptability is uncertain under tax law.

Scope

4   This Interpretation clarifies how to apply the recognition and measurement requirements in IAS 12 when there is uncertainty over income tax treatments. In such a circumstance, an entity shall recognise and measure its current or deferred tax asset or liability applying the requirements in IAS 12 based on taxable profit (tax loss), tax bases, unused tax losses, unused tax credits and tax rates determined applying this Interpretation.

Issues

5 When there is uncertainty over income tax treatments, this Interpretation addresses:

 (a) whether an entity considers uncertain tax treatments separately;

 (b) the assumptions an entity makes about the examination of tax treatments by taxation authorities;

 (c) how an entity determines taxable profit (tax loss), tax bases, unused tax losses, unused tax credits and tax rates; and

 (d) how an entity considers changes in facts and circumstances.

Consensus

Whether an entity considers uncertain tax treatments separately

6 An entity shall determine whether to consider each uncertain tax treatment separately or together with one or more other uncertain tax treatments based on which approach better predicts the resolution of the uncertainty. In determining the approach that better predicts the resolution of the uncertainty, an entity might consider, for example, (a) how it prepares its income tax filings and supports tax treatments; or (b) how the entity expects the taxation authority to make its examination and resolve issues that might arise from that examination.

7 If, applying paragraph 6, an entity considers more than one uncertain tax treatment together, the entity shall read references to an 'uncertain tax treatment' in this Interpretation as referring to the group of uncertain tax treatments considered together.

Examination by taxation authorities

8 In assessing whether and how an uncertain tax treatment affects the determination of taxable profit (tax loss), tax bases, unused tax losses, unused tax credits and tax rates, an entity shall assume that a taxation authority will examine amounts it has a right to examine and have full knowledge of all related information when making those examinations.

Determination of taxable profit (tax loss), tax bases, unused tax losses, unused tax credits and tax rates

9 An entity shall consider whether it is probable that a taxation authority will accept an uncertain tax treatment.

10 If an entity concludes it is probable that the taxation authority will accept an uncertain tax treatment, the entity shall determine the taxable profit (tax loss), tax bases, unused tax losses, unused tax credits or tax rates consistently with the tax treatment used or planned to be used in its income tax filings.

11   If an entity concludes it is not probable that the taxation authority will accept an uncertain tax treatment, the entity shall reflect the effect of uncertainty in determining the related taxable profit (tax loss), tax bases, unused tax losses, unused tax credits or tax rates. An entity shall reflect the effect of uncertainty for each uncertain tax treatment by using either of the following methods, depending on which method the entity expects to better predict the resolution of the uncertainty:

(a)   the most likely amount—the single most likely amount in a range of possible outcomes. The most likely amount may better predict the resolution of the uncertainty if the possible outcomes are binary or are concentrated on one value.

(b)   the expected value—the sum of the probability-weighted amounts in a range of possible outcomes. The expected value may better predict the resolution of the uncertainty if there is a range of possible outcomes that are neither binary nor concentrated on one value.

12   If an uncertain tax treatment affects current tax and deferred tax (for example, if it affects both taxable profit used to determine current tax and tax bases used to determine deferred tax), an entity shall make consistent judgements and estimates for both current tax and deferred tax.

Changes in facts and circumstances

13   An entity shall reassess a judgement or estimate required by this Interpretation if the facts and circumstances on which the judgement or estimate was based change or as a result of new information that affects the judgement or estimate. For example, a change in facts and circumstances might change an entity's conclusions about the acceptability of a tax treatment or the entity's estimate of the effect of uncertainty, or both. Paragraphs A1–A3 set out guidance on changes in facts and circumstances.

14   An entity shall reflect the effect of a change in facts and circumstances or of new information as a change in accounting estimate applying IAS 8 *Accounting Policies, Changes in Accounting Estimates and Errors*. An entity shall apply IAS 10 *Events after the Reporting Period* to determine whether a change that occurs after the reporting period is an adjusting or non-adjusting event.

Appendix A
Application Guidance

This appendix is an integral part of IFRIC 23 and has the same authority as the other parts of IFRIC 23.

Changes in facts and circumstances (paragraph 13)

A1   In applying paragraph 13 of this Interpretation, an entity shall assess the relevance and effect of a change in facts and circumstances or of new information in the context of applicable tax laws. For example, a particular event might result in the reassessment of a judgement or estimate made for one tax treatment but not another, if those tax treatments are subject to different tax laws.

A2   Examples of changes in facts and circumstances or new information that, depending on the circumstances, can result in the reassessment of a judgement or estimate required by this Interpretation include, but are not limited to, the following:

(a)   examinations or actions by a taxation authority. For example:

(i)   agreement or disagreement by the taxation authority with the tax treatment or a similar tax treatment used by the entity;

(ii)   information that the taxation authority has agreed or disagreed with a similar tax treatment used by another entity; and

(iii)   information about the amount received or paid to settle a similar tax treatment.

(b)   changes in rules established by a taxation authority.

(c)   the expiry of a taxation authority's right to examine or re-examine a tax treatment.

A3   The absence of agreement or disagreement by a taxation authority with a tax treatment, in isolation, is unlikely to constitute a change in facts and circumstances or new information that affects the judgements and estimates required by this Interpretation.

Disclosure

A4   When there is uncertainty over income tax treatments, an entity shall determine whether to disclose:

(a)   judgements made in determining taxable profit (tax loss), tax bases, unused tax losses, unused tax credits and tax rates applying paragraph 122 of IAS 1 *Presentation of Financial Statements*; and

(b)   information about the assumptions and estimates made in determining taxable profit (tax loss), tax bases, unused tax losses, unused tax credits and tax rates applying paragraphs 125–129 of IAS 1.

A5   If an entity concludes it is probable that a taxation authority will accept an uncertain tax treatment, the entity shall determine whether to disclose the potential effect of the uncertainty as a tax-related contingency applying paragraph 88 of IAS 12.

Appendix B
Effective date and transition

This appendix is an integral part of IFRIC 23 and has the same authority as the other parts of IFRIC 23.

Effective date

B1   An entity shall apply this Interpretation for annual reporting periods beginning on or after 1 January 2019. Earlier application is permitted. If an entity applies this Interpretation for an earlier period, it shall disclose that fact.

Transition

B2   On initial application, an entity shall apply this Interpretation either:

   (a)   retrospectively applying IAS 8, if that is possible without the use of hindsight; or

   (b)   retrospectively with the cumulative effect of initially applying the Interpretation recognised at the date of initial application. If an entity selects this transition approach, it shall not restate comparative information. Instead, the entity shall recognise the cumulative effect of initially applying the Interpretation as an adjustment to the opening balance of retained earnings (or other component of equity, as appropriate). The date of initial application is the beginning of the annual reporting period in which an entity first applies this Interpretation.

Appendix C

An entity shall apply the amendment in this Appendix when it applies IFRIC 23.

* * * * *

The amendments contained in this appendix when this Standard was issued in 2017 have been incorporated into the text of the relevant Standards included in this volume.

Introduction of the Euro

In April 2001 the International Accounting Standards Board adopted SIC-7 *Introduction of the Euro*, which had originally been issued by the Standing Interpretations Committee of the International Accounting Standards Committee in May 1998.

Other Standards have made minor consequential amendments to SIC-7, including IFRS 9 *Financial Instruments* (Hedge Accounting and amendments to IFRS 9, IFRS 7 and IAS 39) (issued November 2013).

SIC Interpretation 7 *Introduction of the Euro* (SIC-7) is set out in paragraphs 3 and 4. SIC-7 is accompanied by a Basis for Conclusions. The scope and authority of Interpretations are set out in the *Preface to IFRS Standards*.

FOR THE BASIS FOR CONCLUSIONS, SEE PART C OF THIS EDITION

SIC Interpretation 7
Introduction of the Euro

References

- IAS 1 *Presentation of Financial Statements* (as revised in 2007)
- IAS 8 *Accounting Policies, Changes in Accounting Estimates and Errors*
- IAS 10 *Events after the Reporting Period*
- IAS 21 *The Effects of Changes in Foreign Exchange Rates* (as revised in 2003)
- IAS 27 *Consolidated and Separate Financial Statements* (as amended in 2008)

Issue

1   From 1 January 1999, the effective start of Economic and Monetary Union (EMU), the euro will become a currency in its own right and the conversion rates between the euro and the participating national currencies will be irrevocably fixed, ie the risk of subsequent exchange differences related to these currencies is eliminated from this date on.

2   The issue is the application of IAS 21 to the changeover from the national currencies of participating Member States of the European Union to the euro ('the changeover').

Consensus

3   The requirements of IAS 21 regarding the translation of foreign currency transactions and financial statements of foreign operations should be strictly applied to the changeover. The same rationale applies to the fixing of exchange rates when countries join EMU at later stages.

4   This means that, in particular:

   (a)   foreign currency monetary assets and liabilities resulting from transactions shall continue to be translated into the functional currency at the closing rate. Any resultant exchange differences shall be recognised as income or expense immediately, except that an entity shall continue to apply its existing accounting policy for exchange gains and losses related to hedges of the currency risk of a forecast transaction;

   (b)   cumulative exchange differences relating to the translation of financial statements of foreign operations, recognised in other comprehensive income, shall be accumulated in equity and shall be reclassified from equity to profit or loss only on the disposal or partial disposal of the net investment in the foreign operation; and

   (c)   exchange differences resulting from the translation of liabilities denominated in participating currencies shall not be included in the carrying amount of related assets.

Date of consensus

October 1997

Effective date

This Interpretation becomes effective on 1 June 1998. Changes in accounting policies shall be accounted for according to the requirements of IAS 8.

IAS 1 (as revised in 2007) amended the terminology used throughout IFRSs. In addition it amended paragraph 4. An entity shall apply those amendments for annual periods beginning on or after 1 January 2009. If an entity applies IAS 1 (revised 2007) for an earlier period, the amendments shall be applied for that earlier period.

IAS 27 (as amended in 2008) amended paragraph 4(b). An entity shall apply that amendment for annual periods beginning on or after 1 July 2009. If an entity applies IAS 27 (amended 2008) for an earlier period, the amendment shall be applied for that earlier period.

Government Assistance — No Specific Relation to Operating Activities

In April 2001 the International Accounting Standards Board adopted SIC-10 *Government Assistance — No Specific Relation to Operating Activities*, which had originally been issued by the Standing Interpretations Committee of the International Accounting Standards Committee in July 1998.

SIC Interpretation 10 *Government Assistance—No Specific Relation to Operating Activities* (SIC-10) is set out in paragraph 3. SIC-10 is accompanied by a Basis for Conclusions. The scope and authority of Interpretations are set out in the *Preface to IFRS Standards*.

FOR THE BASIS FOR CONCLUSIONS, SEE PART C OF THIS EDITION

SIC Interpretation 10
Government Assistance—No Specific Relation to Operating Activities

References

- IAS 8 *Accounting Policies, Changes in Accounting Estimates and Errors*

- IAS 20 *Accounting for Government Grants and Disclosure of Government Assistance*

Issue

1   In some countries government assistance to entities may be aimed at encouragement or long-term support of business activities either in certain regions or industry sectors. Conditions to receive such assistance may not be specifically related to the operating activities of the entity. Examples of such assistance are transfers of resources by governments to entities which:

    (a)   operate in a particular industry;

    (b)   continue operating in recently privatised industries; or

    (c)   start or continue to run their business in underdeveloped areas.

2   The issue is whether such government assistance is a 'government grant' within the scope of IAS 20 and, therefore, should be accounted for in accordance with this Standard.

Consensus

3   Government assistance to entities meets the definition of government grants in IAS 20, even if there are no conditions specifically relating to the operating activities of the entity other than the requirement to operate in certain regions or industry sectors. Such grants shall therefore not be credited directly to shareholders' interests.

Date of consensus

January 1998

Effective date

This Interpretation becomes effective on 1 August 1998. Changes in accounting policies shall be accounted for in accordance with IAS 8.

Income Taxes — Changes in the Tax Status of an Entity or its Shareholders

In April 2001 the International Accounting Standards Board adopted SIC-25 *Income Taxes — Changes in the Tax Status of an Entity or its Shareholders*, which had originally been issued by the Standing Interpretations Committee of the International Accounting Standards Committee in July 2000.

SIC Interpretation 25 *Income Taxes—Changes in the Tax Status of an Entity or its Shareholders* (SIC-25) is set out in paragraph 4. SIC-25 is accompanied by a Basis for Conclusions. The scope and authority of Interpretations are set out in the *Preface to IFRS Standards*.

FOR THE BASIS FOR CONCLUSIONS, SEE PART C OF THIS EDITION

SIC Interpretation 25
Income Taxes—Changes in the Tax Status of an Entity or its Shareholders

References

- IAS 1 *Presentation of Financial Statements* (as revised in 2007)
- IAS 8 *Accounting Policies, Changes in Accounting Estimates and Errors*
- IAS 12 *Income Taxes*

Issue

1   A change in the tax status of an entity or of its shareholders may have consequences for an entity by increasing or decreasing its tax liabilities or assets. This may, for example, occur upon the public listing of an entity's equity instruments or upon the restructuring of an entity's equity. It may also occur upon a controlling shareholder's move to a foreign country. As a result of such an event, an entity may be taxed differently; it may for example gain or lose tax incentives or become subject to a different rate of tax in the future.

2   A change in the tax status of an entity or its shareholders may have an immediate effect on the entity's current tax liabilities or assets. The change may also increase or decrease the deferred tax liabilities and assets recognised by the entity, depending on the effect the change in tax status has on the tax consequences that will arise from recovering or settling the carrying amount of the entity's assets and liabilities.

3   The issue is how an entity should account for the tax consequences of a change in its tax status or that of its shareholders.

Consensus

4   A change in the tax status of an entity or its shareholders does not give rise to increases or decreases in amounts recognised outside profit or loss. The current and deferred tax consequences of a change in tax status shall be included in profit or loss for the period, unless those consequences relate to transactions and events that result, in the same or a different period, in a direct credit or charge to the recognised amount of equity or in amounts recognised in other comprehensive income. Those tax consequences that relate to changes in the recognised amount of equity, in the same or a different period (not included in profit or loss), shall be charged or credited directly to equity. Those tax consequences that relate to amounts recognised in other comprehensive income shall be recognised in other comprehensive income.

Date of consensus

August 1999

Effective date

This consensus becomes effective on 15 July 2000. Changes in accounting policies shall be accounted for in accordance with IAS 8.

IAS 1 (as revised in 2007) amended the terminology used throughout IFRSs. In addition it amended paragraph 4. An entity shall apply those amendments for annual periods beginning on or after 1 January 2009. If an entity applies IAS 1 (revised 2007) for an earlier period, the amendments shall be applied for that earlier period.

© IFRS Foundation

Service Concession Arrangements: Disclosures

In December 2001 the International Accounting Standards Board (IASB) issued SIC-29 *Disclosure—Service Concession Arrangements*, which had originally been developed by the Standing Interpretations Committee of the International Accounting Standards Committee.

In November 2006, when the IASB issued IFRIC 12 *Service Concession Arrangements*, SIC-29's title was changed to *Service Concession Arrangements: Disclosures*.

Other Standards have made minor consequential amendments to SIC-29, including IFRS 16 *Leases* (issued January 2016) and *Amendments to References to the Conceptual Framework in IFRS Standards* (issued March 2018).

SIC Interpretation 29 *Service Concession Arrangements: Disclosures* (SIC-29) is set out in paragraphs 6–7. SIC-29 is accompanied by a Basis for Conclusions. The scope and authority of Interpretations are set out in the *Preface to IFRS Standards*.

FOR THE BASIS FOR CONCLUSIONS, SEE PART C OF THIS EDITION

SIC Interpretation 29
Service Concession Arrangements: Disclosures

References

- IFRS 16 *Leases*
- IAS 1 *Presentation of Financial Statements* (as revised in 2007)
- IAS 16 *Property, Plant and Equipment* (as revised in 2003)
- IAS 37 *Provisions, Contingent Liabilities and Contingent Assets*
- IAS 38 *Intangible Assets* (as revised in 2004)
- IFRIC 12 *Service Concession Arrangements*

Issue

1   An entity (the operator) may enter into an arrangement with another entity (the grantor) to provide services that give the public access to major economic and social facilities. The grantor may be a public or private sector entity, including a governmental body. Examples of service concession arrangements involve water treatment and supply facilities, motorways, car parks, tunnels, bridges, airports and telecommunication networks. Examples of arrangements that are not service concession arrangements include an entity outsourcing the operation of its internal services (eg employee cafeteria, building maintenance, and accounting or information technology functions).

2   A service concession arrangement generally involves the grantor conveying for the period of the concession to the operator:

   (a)   the right to provide services that give the public access to major economic and social facilities, and

   (b)   in some cases, the right to use specified tangible assets, intangible assets, or financial assets,

   in exchange for the operator:

   (c)   committing to provide the services according to certain terms and conditions during the concession period, and

   (d)   when applicable, committing to return at the end of the concession period the rights received at the beginning of the concession period and/or acquired during the concession period.

3   The common characteristic of all service concession arrangements is that the operator both receives a right and incurs an obligation to provide public services.

4   The issue is what information should be disclosed in the notes in the financial statements of an operator and a grantor.

5   Certain aspects and disclosures relating to some service concession arrangements are already addressed by existing International Financial Reporting Standards (eg IAS 16 applies to acquisitions of items of property, plant and equipment, IFRS 16 applies to leases of assets, and IAS 38 applies to acquisitions of intangible assets). However, a service concession arrangement may involve executory contracts that are not addressed in International Financial Reporting Standards, unless the contracts are onerous, in which case IAS 37 applies. Therefore, this Interpretation addresses additional disclosures of service concession arrangements.

Consensus

6   All aspects of a service concession arrangement shall be considered in determining the appropriate disclosures in the notes. An operator and a grantor shall disclose the following in each period:

  (a)   a description of the arrangement;

  (b)   significant terms of the arrangement that may affect the amount, timing and certainty of future cash flows (eg the period of the concession, re-pricing dates and the basis upon which re-pricing or re-negotiation is determined);

  (c)   the nature and extent (eg quantity, time period or amount as appropriate) of:

    (i)   rights to use specified assets;

    (ii)   obligations to provide or rights to expect provision of services;

    (iii)   obligations to acquire or build items of property, plant and equipment;

    (iv)   obligations to deliver or rights to receive specified assets at the end of the concession period;

    (v)   renewal and termination options; and

    (vi)   other rights and obligations (eg major overhauls);

  (d)   changes in the arrangement occurring during the period; and

  (e)   how the service arrangement has been classified.

6A   An operator shall disclose the amount of revenue and profits or losses recognised in the period on exchanging construction services for a financial asset or an intangible asset.

7   The disclosures required in accordance with paragraph 6 of this Interpretation shall be provided individually for each service concession arrangement or in aggregate for each class of service concession arrangements. A class is a grouping of service concession arrangements involving services of a similar nature (eg toll collections, telecommunications and water treatment services).

Date of consensus

May 2001

Effective date

This Interpretation becomes effective on 31 December 2001.

An entity shall apply the amendment in paragraphs 6(e) and 6A for annual periods beginning on or after 1 January 2008. If an entity applies IFRIC 12 for an earlier period, the amendment shall be applied for that earlier period.

IFRS 16, issued in January 2016, amended paragraph 5. An entity shall apply that amendment when it applies IFRS 16.

SIC-32

Intangible Assets — Web Site Costs

In March 2002 the International Accounting Standards Board issued SIC-32 *Intangible Assets — Web Site Costs*, which had originally been developed by the Standing Interpretations Committee of the International Accounting Standards Committee.

Other Standards have made minor consequential amendments to SIC-32, including IFRS 15 *Revenue from Contracts with Customers* (issued May 2014), IFRS 16 *Leases* (issued January 2016) and *Amendments to References to the Conceptual Framework in IFRS Standards* (issued March 2018).

SIC Interpretation 32 *Intangible Assets — Web Site Costs* (SIC-32) is set out in paragraphs 7–10. SIC-32 is accompanied by a Basis for Conclusions and an example illustrating the application of the Interpretation. The scope and authority of Interpretations are set out in the *Preface to IFRS Standards*.

FOR THE ACCOMPANYING GUIDANCE LISTED BELOW, SEE PART B OF THIS EDITION

ILLUSTRATIVE EXAMPLE

FOR THE BASIS FOR CONCLUSIONS, SEE PART C OF THIS EDITION

BASIS FOR CONCLUSIONS

SIC Interpretation 32
Intangible Assets—Web Site Costs

References

- IFRS 3 *Business Combinations*
- IFRS 15 *Revenue from Contracts with Customers*
- IFRS 16 *Leases*
- IAS 1 *Presentation of Financial Statements* (as revised in 2007)
- IAS 2 *Inventories* (as revised in 2003)
- IAS 16 *Property, Plant and Equipment* (as revised in 2003)
- IAS 36 *Impairment of Assets* (as revised in 2004)
- IAS 38 *Intangible Assets* (as revised in 2004)

Issue

1   An entity may incur internal expenditure on the development and operation of its own web site for internal or external access. A web site designed for external access may be used for various purposes such as to promote and advertise an entity's own products and services, provide electronic services, and sell products and services. A web site designed for internal access may be used to store company policies and customer details, and search relevant information.

2   The stages of a web site's development can be described as follows:

(a)   Planning—includes undertaking feasibility studies, defining objectives and specifications, evaluating alternatives and selecting preferences.

(b)   Application and Infrastructure Development—includes obtaining a domain name, purchasing and developing hardware and operating software, installing developed applications and stress testing.

(c)   Graphical Design Development—includes designing the appearance of web pages.

(d)   Content Development—includes creating, purchasing, preparing and uploading information, either textual or graphical in nature, on the web site before the completion of the web site's development. This information may either be stored in separate databases that are integrated into (or accessed from) the web site or coded directly into the web pages.

3   Once development of a web site has been completed, the Operating stage begins. During this stage, an entity maintains and enhances the applications, infrastructure, graphical design and content of the web site.

4   When accounting for internal expenditure on the development and operation of an entity's own web site for internal or external access, the issues are:

      (a)   whether the web site is an internally generated intangible asset that is subject to the requirements of IAS 38; and

      (b)   the appropriate accounting treatment of such expenditure.

5   This Interpretation does not apply to expenditure on purchasing, developing, and operating hardware (eg web servers, staging servers, production servers and Internet connections) of a web site. Such expenditure is accounted for under IAS 16. Additionally, when an entity incurs expenditure on an Internet service provider hosting the entity's web site, the expenditure is recognised as an expense under IAS 1.88 and the *Conceptual Framework for Financial Reporting* when the services are received.

6   IAS 38 does not apply to intangible assets held by an entity for sale in the ordinary course of business (see IAS 2 and IFRS 15) or leases of intangible assets accounted for in accordance with IFRS 16. Accordingly, this Interpretation does not apply to expenditure on the development or operation of a web site (or web site software) for sale to another entity or that is accounted for in accordance with IFRS 16.

Consensus

7   An entity's own web site that arises from development and is for internal or external access is an internally generated intangible asset that is subject to the requirements of IAS 38.

8   A web site arising from development shall be recognised as an intangible asset if, and only if, in addition to complying with the general requirements described in IAS 38.21 for recognition and initial measurement, an entity can satisfy the requirements in IAS 38.57. In particular, an entity may be able to satisfy the requirement to demonstrate how its web site will generate probable future economic benefits in accordance with IAS 38.57(d) when, for example, the web site is capable of generating revenues, including direct revenues from enabling orders to be placed. An entity is not able to demonstrate how a web site developed solely or primarily for promoting and advertising its own products and services will generate probable future economic benefits, and consequently all expenditure on developing such a web site shall be recognised as an expense when incurred.

9   Any internal expenditure on the development and operation of an entity's own web site shall be accounted for in accordance with IAS 38. The nature of each activity for which expenditure is incurred (eg training employees and maintaining the web site) and the web site's stage of development or post-development shall be evaluated to determine the appropriate accounting treatment (additional guidance is provided in the illustrative example accompanying this Interpretation). For example:

    (a)   the Planning stage is similar in nature to the research phase in IAS 38.54–.56. Expenditure incurred in this stage shall be recognised as an expense when it is incurred.

    (b)   the Application and Infrastructure Development stage, the Graphical Design stage and the Content Development stage, to the extent that content is developed for purposes other than to advertise and promote an entity's own products and services, are similar in nature to the development phase in IAS 38.57–.64. Expenditure incurred in these stages shall be included in the cost of a web site recognised as an intangible asset in accordance with paragraph 8 of this Interpretation when the expenditure can be directly attributed and is necessary to creating, producing or preparing the web site for it to be capable of operating in the manner intended by management. For example, expenditure on purchasing or creating content (other than content that advertises and promotes an entity's own products and services) specifically for a web site, or expenditure to enable use of the content (eg a fee for acquiring a licence to reproduce) on the web site, shall be included in the cost of development when this condition is met. However, in accordance with IAS 38.71, expenditure on an intangible item that was initially recognised as an expense in previous financial statements shall not be recognised as part of the cost of an intangible asset at a later date (eg if the costs of a copyright have been fully amortised, and the content is subsequently provided on a web site).

    (c)   expenditure incurred in the Content Development stage, to the extent that content is developed to advertise and promote an entity's own products and services (eg digital photographs of products), shall be recognised as an expense when incurred in accordance with IAS 38.69(c). For example, when accounting for expenditure on professional services for taking digital photographs of an entity's own products and for enhancing their display, expenditure shall be recognised as an expense as the professional services are received during the process, not when the digital photographs are displayed on the web site.

    (d)   the Operating stage begins once development of a web site is complete. Expenditure incurred in this stage shall be recognised as an expense when it is incurred unless it meets the recognition criteria in IAS 38.18.

10   A web site that is recognised as an intangible asset under paragraph 8 of this Interpretation shall be measured after initial recognition by applying the requirements of IAS 38.72–.87. The best estimate of a web site's useful life should be short.

Date of consensus

May 2001

Effective date

This Interpretation becomes effective on 25 March 2002. The effects of adopting this Interpretation shall be accounted for using the transition requirements in the version of IAS 38 that was issued in 1998. Therefore, when a web site does not meet the criteria for recognition as an intangible asset, but was previously recognised as an asset, the item shall be derecognised at the date when this Interpretation becomes effective. When a web site exists and the expenditure to develop it meets the criteria for recognition as an intangible asset, but was not previously recognised as an asset, the intangible asset shall not be recognised at the date when this Interpretation becomes effective. When a web site exists and the expenditure to develop it meets the criteria for recognition as an intangible asset, was previously recognised as an asset and initially measured at cost, the amount initially recognised is deemed to have been properly determined.

IAS 1 (as revised in 2007) amended the terminology used throughout IFRSs. In addition it amended paragraph 5. An entity shall apply those amendments for annual periods beginning on or after 1 January 2009. If an entity applies IAS 1 (revised 2007) for an earlier period, the amendments shall be applied for that earlier period.

IFRS 15 *Revenue from Contracts with Customers*, issued in May 2014, amended the 'References' section and paragraph 6. An entity shall apply that amendment when it applies IFRS 15.

IFRS 16, issued in January 2016, amended paragraph 6. An entity shall apply that amendment when it applies IFRS 16.

Amendments to References to the Conceptual Framework in IFRS Standards, issued in 2018, amended paragraph 5. An entity shall apply that amendment for annual periods beginning on or after 1 January 2020. Earlier application is permitted if at the same time an entity also applies all other amendments made by *Amendments to References to the Conceptual Framework in IFRS Standards*. An entity shall apply the amendment to SIC-32 retrospectively in accordance with IAS 8 *Accounting Policies, Changes in Accounting Estimates and Errors*. However, if an entity determines that retrospective application would be impracticable or would involve undue cost or effort, it shall apply the amendment to SIC-32 by reference to paragraphs 23–28, 50–53 and 54F of IAS 8.

Glossary

This glossary is extracted from the International Financial Reporting Standards and International Accounting Standards that are published in this edition. These Standards were issued by the International Accounting Standards Board (Board) or its predecessor, the International Accounting Standards Committee. References are by Standard and paragraph number or Standard and appendix letter.

The glossary also contains extracts from the *Conceptual Framework for Financial Reporting* (the *Conceptual Framework*). References to the *Conceptual Framework* are preceded by CF.

References set out in (brackets) indicate minor variations in wording.

12-month expected credit losses	The portion of lifetime expected credit losses that represent the expected credit losses that result from default events on a financial instrument that are possible within the 12 months after the reporting date.	IFRS 9.A
accounting policies	The specific principles, bases, conventions, rules and practices applied by an entity in preparing and presenting financial statements.	IAS 8.5
accounting profit	Profit or loss for a period before deducting tax expense.	IAS 12.5
acquiree	The business or businesses that the acquirer obtains control of in a business combination.	IFRS 3.A
acquirer	The entity that obtains control of the acquiree.	IFRS 3.A
acquisition date	The date on which the acquirer obtains control of the acquiree.	IFRS 3.A
active market	A market in which transactions for the asset or liability take place with sufficient frequency and volume to provide pricing information on an ongoing basis.	IFRS 13.A
actuarial gains and losses	The changes in the present value of the defined benefit obligation resulting from:	IAS 19.8
	(a) experience adjustments (the effects of differences between the previous actuarial assumptions and what has actually occurred); and	
	(b) the effects of changes in actuarial assumptions.	
actuarial present value of promised retirement benefits	The present value of the expected payments by a retirement benefit plan to existing and past employees, attributable to the service already rendered.	IAS 26.8

aggregation	The adding together of assets, liabilities, equity, income or expenses that have shared characteristics and are included in the same classification.	CF.7.20
agricultural activity	The management by an entity of the biological transformation and harvest of biological assets for sale or for conversion into agricultural produce or into additional biological assets.	IAS 41.5
agricultural produce	The harvested produce of the entity's biological assets.	IAS 41.5
amortisation (depreciation)[1]	The systematic allocation of the depreciable amount of an asset over its useful life.	IAS 36.6, IAS 38.8
amortised cost of a financial asset or financial liability	The amount at which the financial asset or financial liability is measured at initial recognition minus principal repayments, plus or minus the cumulative amortisation using the effective interest method of any difference between that initial amount and the maturity amount and, for financial assets adjusted for any loss allowance.	IFRS 9.A
antidilution	An increase in earnings per share or a reduction in loss per share resulting from the assumption that convertible instruments are converted, that options or warrants are exercised, or that ordinary shares are issued upon the satisfaction of specified conditions.	IAS 33.5
asset	A resource: (a) controlled by an entity as a result of past events; and (b) from which future economic benefits are expected to flow to the entity.	IAS 38.8
asset	A present economic resource controlled by the entity as a result of past events.	CF.4.3
asset ceiling	The present value of any economic benefits available in the form of refunds from the plan or reductions in future contributions to the plan.	IAS 19.8
assets held by a long-term employee benefit fund	Assets (other than non-transferable financial instruments issued by the reporting entity) that:	IAS 19.8

---

1   In the case of an intangible asset, the term 'amortisation' is generally used instead of 'depreciation'. The two terms have the same meaning.

	(a)	are held by an entity (a fund) that is legally separate from the reporting entity and exists solely to pay or fund employee benefits; and	
	(b)	are available to be used only to pay or fund employee benefits, are not available to the reporting entity's own creditors (even in bankruptcy), and cannot be returned to the reporting entity, unless either:	
		(i)	the remaining assets of the fund are sufficient to meet all the related employee benefit obligations of the plan or the reporting entity; or
		(ii)	the assets are returned to the reporting entity to reimburse it for employee benefits already paid.

associate	An entity, over which the investor has significant influence.	IAS 28.3
bearer plant	A living plant that:	IAS 16.6, IAS 41.5
	(a) is used in the production or supply of agricultural produce;	
	(b) is expected to bear produce for more than one period; and	
	(c) has a remote likelihood of being sold as agricultural produce, except for incidental scrap sales.	
biological asset	A living animal or plant.	IAS 41.5
biological transformation	The processes of growth, degeneration, production, and procreation that cause qualitative or quantitative changes in a biological asset.	IAS 41.5
borrowing costs	Interest and other costs that an entity incurs in connection with the borrowing of funds.	IAS 23.5
business	An integrated set of activities and assets that is capable of being conducted and managed for the purpose of providing goods or services to customers, generating investment income (such as dividends or interest) or generating other income from ordinary activities.	IFRS 3.A

business combination	A transaction or other event in which an acquirer obtains control of one or more businesses. Transactions sometimes referred to as 'true mergers' or 'mergers of equals' are also business combinations as that term is used in IFRS 3.	IFRS 3.A
carrying amount	The amount at which an asset is recognised after deducting any accumulated depreciation (amortisation) and accumulated impairment losses thereon.	IAS 16.6, IAS 36.6, IAS 38.8
carrying amount	The amount at which an asset is recognised in the statement of financial position.	IAS 40.5, IAS 41.8
carrying amount	The amount at which an asset, a liability or equity is recognised in the statement of financial position.	CF.5.1
cash	Cash on hand and demand deposits.	IAS 7.6
cash equivalents	Short-term, highly liquid investments that are readily convertible to known amounts of cash and which are subject to an insignificant risk of changes in value.	IAS 7.6
cash flows	Inflows and outflows of cash and cash equivalents.	IAS 7.6
cash-generating unit	The smallest identifiable group of assets that generates cash inflows that are largely independent of the cash inflows from other assets or groups of assets.	IAS 36.6, IFRS 5.A
cash-settled share-based payment transaction	A share-based payment transaction in which the entity acquires goods or services by incurring a liability to transfer cash or other assets to the supplier of those goods or services for amounts that are based on the price (or value) of equity instruments (including shares or share options) of the entity or another group entity.	IFRS 2.A
cedant	The policyholder under a reinsurance contract.	IFRS 4.A
change in accounting estimate	An adjustment of the carrying amount of an asset or a liability, or the amount of the periodic consumption of an asset, that results from the assessment of the present status of, and expected future benefits and obligations associated with, assets and liabilities. Changes in accounting estimates result from new information or new developments and, accordingly, are not corrections of errors.	IAS 8.5

classification	The sorting of assets, liabilities, equity, income or expenses on the basis of shared characteristics for presentation and disclosure purposes.	CF.7.7
close members of the family of a person	Those family members who may be expected to influence, or be influenced by, that person in their dealings with the entity and include:	IAS 24.9

    (a)   that person's children and spouse or domestic partner;

    (b)   children of that person's spouse or domestic partner;

    (c)   dependants of that person or that person's spouse or domestic partner.

closing rate	The spot exchange rate at the end of the reporting period.	IAS 21.8
combined financial statements	Financial statements of a reporting entity that comprises two or more entities that are not all linked by a parent-subsidiary relationship.	CF.3.12
commencement date of the lease (commencement date)	The date on which a lessor makes an underlying asset available for use by a lessee.	IFRS 16.A
compensation	Includes all employee benefits (as defined in IAS 19) including employee benefits to which IFRS 2 applies. Employee benefits are all forms of consideration paid, payable or provided by the entity, or on behalf of the entity, in exchange for services rendered to the entity. It also includes such consideration paid on behalf of a parent of the entity in respect of the entity. Compensation includes:	IAS 24.9

    (a)   short-term employee benefits, such as wages, salaries and social security contributions, paid annual leave and paid sick leave, profit sharing and bonuses (if payable within twelve months of the end of the period) and non-monetary benefits (such as medical care, housing, cars and free or subsidised goods or services) for current employees;

    (b)   post-employment benefits such as pensions, other retirement benefits, post-employment life insurance and post-employment medical care;

	(c) other long-term employee benefits, including long service leave or sabbatical leave, jubilee or other long service benefits, long-term disability benefits and, if they are not payable wholly within twelve months after the end of the period, profit sharing, bonuses and deferred compensation;	
	(d) termination benefits; and	
	(e) share-based payment.	
component of an entity	Operations and cash flows that can be clearly distinguished, operationally and for financial reporting purposes, from the rest of the entity.	IFRS 5.A
consolidated financial statements	The financial statements of a group in which assets, liabilities, equity, income, expenses and cash flow of the parent and its subsidiaries are presented as those of a single economic entity.	IAS 27.4, IAS 28.3, IFRS 10.A
consolidated financial statements	Financial statements of a reporting entity that comprises both the parent and its subsidiaries.	CF.3.11
constructive obligation	An obligation that derives from an entity's actions where:	IAS 37.10
	(a) by an established pattern of past practice, published policies or a sufficiently specific current statement, the entity has indicated to other parties that it will accept certain responsibilities; and	
	(b) as a result, the entity has created a valid expectation on the part of those other parties that it will discharge those responsibilities.	
contingent asset	A possible asset that arises from past events and whose existence will be confirmed only by the occurrence or non-occurrence of one or more uncertain future events not wholly within the control of the entity.	IAS 37.10
contingent consideration	Usually, an obligation of the acquirer to transfer additional assets or equity interests to the former owners of an acquiree as part of the exchange for control of the acquiree if specified future events occur or conditions are met. However, contingent consideration also may give the acquirer the right to the return of	IFRS 3.A

previously transferred consideration if specified conditions are met.

contingent liability	Is:
	
	(a) a possible obligation that arises from past events and whose existence will be confirmed only by the occurrence or non-occurrence of one or more uncertain future events not wholly within the control of the entity; or
	
	(b) a present obligation that arises from past events but is not recognised because:
	
	    (i) it is not probable that an outflow of resources embodying economic benefits will be required to settle the obligation; or
	
	    (ii) the amount of the obligation cannot be measured with sufficient reliability.
		IAS 37.10

contingent share agreement	An agreement to issue shares that is dependent on the satisfaction of specified conditions.	IAS 33.5
contingently issuable ordinary shares	Ordinary shares issuable for little or no cash or other consideration upon the satisfaction of specified conditions in a contingent share agreement.	IAS 33.5
contract	An agreement between two or more parties that creates enforceable rights and obligations.	IFRS 15.A, IFRS 16.A
contract asset	An entity's right to consideration in exchange for goods or services that the entity has transferred to a customer when that right is conditioned on something other than the passage of time (for example, the entity's future performance).	IFRS 15.A, IFRS 9.A
contract liability	An entity's obligation to transfer goods or services to a customer for which the entity has received consideration (or the amount is due) from the customer.	IFRS 15.A
control of an economic resource	The present ability to direct the use of the economic resource and obtain the economic benefits that may flow from it.	CF.4.20

control of an investee	An investor controls an investee when the investor is exposed, or has rights, to variable returns from its involvement with the investee and has the ability to affect those returns through its power over the investee.	IFRS 10.A
corporate assets	Assets other than goodwill that contribute to the future cash flows of both the cash generating unit under review and other cash generating units.	IAS 36.6
cost	The amount of cash or cash equivalents paid or the fair value of the other consideration given to acquire an asset at the time of its acquisition or construction, or, when applicable, the amount attributed to that asset when initially recognised in accordance with the specific requirements of other IFRSs, eg IFRS 2.	IAS 16.6, IAS 38.8, IAS 40.5
cost approach	A valuation technique that reflects the amount that would be required currently to replace the service capacity of an asset (often referred to as current replacement cost).	IFRS 13.A
costs of disposal	Incremental costs directly attributable to the disposal of an asset, excluding finance costs and income tax expense.	IAS 36.6
costs to sell	The incremental costs directly attributable to the disposal of an asset (or disposal group), excluding finance costs and income tax expense.	IFRS 5.A, (IAS 41.5)
credit-adjusted effective interest rate	The rate that exactly discounts the estimated future cash payments or receipts through the expected life of the financial asset to the amortised cost of a financial asset that is a purchased or originated credit-impaired financial asset. When calculating the credit-adjusted effective interest rate, an entity shall estimate the expected cash flows by considering all contractual terms of the financial asset (for example, prepayment, extension, call and similar options) and expected credit losses. The calculation includes all fees and points paid or received between parties to the contract that are an integral part of the effective interest rate (see paragraphs B5.4.1–B5.4.3), transaction costs, and all other premiums or discounts. There is a presumption that the cash flows and the expected life of a group of similar financial instruments can be	IFRS 9.A

estimated reliably. However, in those rare cases when it is not possible to reliably estimate the cash flows or the remaining life of a financial instrument (or group of financial instruments), the entity shall use the contractual cash flows over the full contractual term of the financial instrument (or group of financial instruments).

credit-impaired financial asset	A financial asset is credit-impaired when one or more events that have a detrimental impact on the estimated future cash flows of that financial asset have occurred. Evidence that a financial asset is credit-impaired include observable data about the following events:	IFRS 9.A

(a) significant financial difficulty of the issuer or the borrower;

(b) a breach of contract, such as a default or past due event;

(c) the lender(s) of the borrower, for economic or contractual reasons relating to the borrower's financial difficulty, having granted to the borrower a concession(s) that the lender(s) would not otherwise consider;

(d) it is becoming probable that the borrower will enter bankruptcy or other financial reorganisation;

(e) the disappearance of an active market for that financial asset because of financial difficulties; or

(f) the purchase or origination of a financial asset at a deep discount that reflects the incurred credit losses.

It may not be possible to identify a single discrete event—instead, the combined effect of several events may have caused financial assets to become credit-impaired.

credit loss	The difference between all contractual cash flows that are due to an entity in accordance with the contract and all the cash flows that the entity expects to receive (ie all cash shortfalls), discounted at the original effective interest rate (or credit-adjusted effective interest rate for purchased or originated credit-impaired financial assets). An entity shall	IFRS 9.A

estimate cash flows by considering all contractual terms of the financial instrument (for example, prepayment, extension, call and similar options) through the expected life of that financial instrument. The cash flows that are considered shall include cash flows from the sale of collateral held or other credit enhancements that are integral to the contractual terms. There is a presumption that the expected life of a financial instrument can be estimated reliably. However, in those rare cases when it is not possible to reliably estimate the expected life of a financial instrument, the entity shall use the remaining contractual term of the financial instrument.

credit risk	The risk that one party to a financial instrument will cause a financial loss for the other party by failing to discharge an obligation.	IFRS 7.A
credit risk rating grades	Rating of credit risk based on the risk of a default occurring on the financial instrument.	IFRS 7.A
currency risk	The risk that the fair value or future cash flows of a financial instrument will fluctuate because of changes in foreign exchange rates.	IFRS 7.A
current asset	An entity shall classify an asset as current when:	IAS 1.66, (IFRS 5.A)

(a)   it expects to realise the asset or intends to sell or consume it in its normal operating cycle;

(b)   it holds the asset primarily for the purpose of trading;

(c)   it expects to realise the asset within twelve months after the reporting period; or

(d)   the asset is cash or a cash equivalent (as defined in IAS 7) unless the asset is restricted from being exchanged or used to settle a liability for at least twelve months after the reporting period.

An entity shall classify all other assets as non-current.

current service cost	The increase in the present value of the defined benefit obligation resulting from employee service in the current period.	IAS 19.8

current tax	The amount of income taxes payable (recoverable) in respect of the taxable profit (tax loss) for a period.	IAS 12.5
customer	A party that has contracted with an entity to obtain goods or services that are an output of the entity's ordinary activities in exchange for consideration.	IFRS 15.A
date of transition to IFRSs	The beginning of the earliest period for which an entity presents full comparative information under IFRSs in its first IFRS financial statements.	IFRS 1.A
decision maker	An entity with decision-making rights that is either a principal or an agent for other parties.	IFRS 10.A
deductible temporary differences	Temporary differences between the carrying amount of an asset or liability in the statement of financial position and its tax base that will result in amounts that are deductible in determining taxable profit (tax loss) of future periods when the carrying amount of the asset or liability is recovered or settled.	IAS 12.5
deemed cost	An amount used as a surrogate for cost or depreciated cost at a given date. Subsequent depreciation or amortisation assumes that the entity had initially recognised the asset or liability at the given date and that its cost was equal to the deemed cost.	IFRS 1.A
deferred tax assets	The amounts of income taxes recoverable in future periods in respect of: (a) deductible temporary differences; (b) the carryforward of unused tax losses; and (c) the carryforward of unused tax credits.	IAS 12.5
deferred tax liabilities	The amounts of income taxes payable in future periods in respect of taxable temporary differences.	IAS 12.5
deficit or surplus (of defined benefit liability (asset))	The deficit or surplus is: (a) the present value of the defined benefit obligation less (b) the fair value of the plan assets (if any).	IAS 19.8
defined benefit plans	Post-employment benefit plans other than defined contribution plans.	IAS 19.8

defined benefit plans	Retirement benefit plans under which amounts to be paid as retirement benefits are determined by reference to a formula usually based on employees' earnings and/or years of service.	IAS 26.8
defined contribution plans	Post-employment benefit plans under which an entity pays fixed contributions into a separate entity (a fund) and will have no legal or constructive obligation to pay further contributions if the fund does not hold sufficient assets to pay all employee benefits relating to employee service in the current and prior periods.	IAS 19.8
defined contribution plans	Retirement benefit plans under which amounts to be paid as retirement benefits are determined by contributions to a fund together with investment earnings thereon.	IAS 26.8
deposit component	A contractual component that is not accounted for as a derivative under IFRS 9 and would be within the scope of IFRS 9 if it were a separate instrument.	IFRS 4.A
depreciable amount	The cost of an asset, or other amount substituted for cost (in the financial statements), less its residual value.	IAS 16.6, IAS 36.6, IAS 38.8
depreciation (amortisation)²	The systematic allocation of the depreciable amount of an asset over its useful life.	IAS 16.6, IAS 36.6
derecognition	The removal of a previously recognised financial asset or financial liability from an entity's statement of financial position.	IFRS 9.A
derecognition	The removal of all or part of a recognised asset or liability from an entity's statement of financial position.	CF.5.26
derivative	A financial instrument or other contract within the scope of IFRS 9 (see paragraph 2.1 of IFRS 9) with all three of the following characteristics: (a) its value changes in response to the change in a specified interest rate, financial instrument price, commodity price, foreign exchange rate, index of prices or rates, credit rating or credit index, or other variable, provided in the case of a non-financial variable that the	IFRS 9.A

---

2   In the case of an intangible asset, the term 'amortisation' is generally used instead of 'depreciation'. The two terms have the same meaning.

	variable is not specific to a party to the contract (sometimes called the 'underlying').	
(b)	it requires no initial net investment or an initial net investment that is smaller than would be required for other types of contracts that would be expected to have a similar response to changes in market factors.	
(c)	it is settled at a future date.	

development	The application of research findings or other knowledge to a plan or design for the production of new or substantially improved materials, devices, products, processes, systems or services before the start of commercial production or use.	IAS 38.8
dilution	A reduction in earnings per share or an increase in loss per share resulting from the assumption that convertible instruments are converted, that options or warrants are exercised, or that ordinary shares are issued upon the satisfaction of specified conditions.	IAS 33.5
direct insurance contract	An insurance contract that is not a reinsurance contract.	IFRS 4.A
discontinued operation	A component of an entity that either has been disposed of or is classified as held for sale and:	IFRS 5.A

(a)	represents a separate major line of business or geographical area of operations,
(b)	is part of a single co-ordinated plan to dispose of a separate major line of business or geographical area of operations or
(c)	is a subsidiary acquired exclusively with a view to resale.

discretionary participation feature	A contractual right to receive, as a supplement to guaranteed benefits, additional benefits:	IFRS 4.A

(a)	that are likely to be a significant portion of the total contractual benefits;
(b)	whose amount or timing is contractually at the discretion of the issuer; and

	(c) that are contractually based on:	
	(i) the performance of a specified pool of contracts or a specified type of contract;	
	(ii) realised and/or unrealised investment returns on a specified pool of assets held by the issuer; or	
	(iii) the profit or loss of the company, fund or other entity that issues the contract.	
disposal group	A group of assets to be disposed of, by sale or otherwise, together as a group in a single transaction, and liabilities directly associated with those assets that will be transferred in the transaction. The group includes goodwill acquired in a business combination if the group is a cash-generating unit to which goodwill has been allocated in accordance with the requirements of paragraphs 80–87 of IAS 36 or if it is an operation within such a cash generating unit.	IFRS 5.A
dividends	Distributions of profits to holders of equity instruments in proportion to their holdings of a particular class of capital.	IFRS 9.A
economic life	Either the period over which an asset is expected to be economically usable by one or more users or the number of production or similar units expected to be obtained from an asset by one or more users.	IFRS 16.A
economic resource	A right that has the potential to produce economic benefits.	CF.4.4
effective date of the modification	The date when both parties agree to a lease modification.	IFRS 16.A
effective interest method	The method that is used in the calculation of the amortised cost of a financial asset or a financial liability and in the allocation and recognition of the interest revenue or interest expense in profit or loss over the relevant period.	IFRS 9.A
effective interest rate	The rate that exactly discounts estimated future cash payments or receipts through the expected life of the financial asset or financial liability to the gross carrying amount of the	IFRS 9.A

financial asset or to the amortised cost of a financial liability. When calculating the effective interest rate, an entity shall estimate the expected cash flows by considering all the contractual terms of the financial instrument (for example, prepayment, extension, call and similar options) but shall not consider the expected credit losses. The calculation includes all fees and points paid or received between parties to the contract that are an integral part of the effective interest rate (see paragraphs B5.4.1–B5.4.3 of IFRS 9), transaction costs, and all other premiums or discounts. There is a presumption that the cash flows and the expected life of a group of similar financial instruments can be estimated reliably. However, in those rare cases when it is not possible to reliably estimate (see paragraphs AG8–AG8B or IAS 39) the cash flows or the expected life of a financial instrument (or group of financial instruments), the entity shall use the contractual cash flows over the full contractual term of the financial instrument (or group of financial instruments).

employee benefits	All forms of consideration given by an entity in exchange for service rendered by employees or for the termination of employment.	IAS 19.8
employees and others providing similar services	Individuals who render personal services to the entity and either (a) the individuals are regarded as employees for legal or tax purposes, (b) the individuals work for the entity under its direction in the same way as individuals who are regarded as employees for legal or tax purposes, or (c) the services rendered are similar to those rendered by employees. For example, the term encompasses all management personnel, ie those persons having authority and responsibility for planning, directing and controlling the activities of the entity, including non-executive directors.	IFRS 2.A
enhancing qualitative characteristic	A qualitative characteristic that makes useful information more useful. The enhancing qualitative characteristics are comparability, verifiability, timeliness and understandability.	CF.2.4, CF.2.23

entity-specific value	The present value of the cash flows an entity expects to arise from the continuing use of an asset and from its disposal at the end of its useful life or expects to incur when settling a liability.	IAS 16.6, IAS 38.8
entry price	The price paid to acquire an asset or received to assume a liability in an exchange transaction.	IFRS 13.A
equity	The residual interest in the assets of the entity after deducting all its liabilities.	CF.4.63
equity claim	A claim on the residual interest in the assets of the entity after deducting all its liabilities.	CF.4.64
equity instrument	A contract that evidences a residual interest in the assets of an entity after deducting all of its liabilities.	IAS 32.11, IFRS 2.A
equity instrument granted	The right (conditional or unconditional) to an equity instrument of the entity conferred by the entity on another party, under a share-based payment arrangement.	IFRS 2.A
equity interests	In IFRS 3, is used broadly to mean ownership interests of investor-owned entities and owner, member or participant interests of mutual entities.	IFRS 3.A
equity method	A method of accounting whereby the investment is initially recognised at cost and adjusted thereafter for the post-acquisition change in the investor's share of the investee's net assets. The investor's profit or loss includes its share of the investee's profit or loss and the investor's other comprehensive income includes its share of the investee's other comprehensive income.	IAS 28.3
equity-settled share-based payment transaction	A share-based payment transaction in which the entity (a) receives goods or services as consideration for its own equity instruments (including shares or share options), or (b) receives goods or services but has no obligation to settle the transaction with the supplier.	IFRS 2.A

events after the reporting period	Those events, favourable and unfavourable, that occur between the end of the reporting period and the date when the financial statements are authorised for issue. Two types of events can be identified:	IAS 10.3
	(a) those that provide evidence of conditions that existed at the end of the reporting period (adjusting events after the reporting period); and	
	(b) those that are indicative of conditions that arose after the reporting period (non-adjusting events after the reporting period).	
exchange difference	The difference resulting from translating a given number of units of one currency into another currency at different exchange rates.	IAS 21.8
exchange rate	The ratio of exchange for two currencies.	IAS 21.8
executory contract	A contract, or a portion of a contract, that is equally unperformed — neither party has fulfilled any of its obligations, or both parties have partially fulfilled their obligations to an equal extent.	CF.4.56
existence uncertainty	Uncertainty about whether an asset or liability exists.	CF.4.13, CF.4.35
exit price	The price that would be received to sell an asset or paid to transfer a liability.	IFRS 13.A
expected cash flows	The probability-weighted average (ie mean of the distribution) of possible future cash flows.	IFRS 13.A
expected credit losses	The weighted average of credit losses with the respective risks of a default occurring as the weights.	IFRS 9.A
expenses	Decreases in assets, or increases in liabilities, that result in decreases in equity, other than those relating to distributions to holders of equity claims.	CF.4.69
experience adjustments	The effects of differences between previous actuarial assumptions and what has actually occurred.	IAS 19.8
exploration and evaluation assets	Exploration and evaluation expenditures recognised as assets in accordance with the entity's accounting policy.	IFRS 6.A

exploration and evaluation expenditures	Expenditures incurred by an entity in connection with the exploration for and evaluation of mineral resources before the technical feasibility and commercial viability of extracting a mineral resource are demonstrable.	IFRS 6.A
exploration for and evaluation of mineral resources	The search for mineral resources, including minerals, oil, natural gas and similar non-regenerative resources after the entity has obtained legal rights to explore in a specific area, as well as the determination of the technical feasibility and commercial viability of extracting the mineral resource.	IFRS 6.A
fair value	The price that would be received to sell an asset or paid to transfer a liability in an orderly transaction between market participants at the measurement date.	IAS 2.6, (IAS 16.6), (IAS 19.8), (IAS 20.3), IAS 21.8, IAS 32.11, (IAS 36.6), (IAS 38.8), (IAS 40.5), IAS 41.8, IFRS 1.A, IFRS 3.A, IFRS 4.A, IFRS 5.A, IFRS 9.A, IFRS 13.A
fair value	The amount for which an asset could be exchanged, a liability settled, or an equity instrument granted could be exchanged, between knowledgeable, willing parties in an arm's length transaction.	IFRS 2.A
fair value	For the purpose of applying the lessor accounting requirements in IFRS 16, the amount for which an asset could be exchanged, or a liability settled, between knowledgeable, willing parties in an arm's length transaction.	IFRS 16.A
finance lease	A lease that transfers substantially all the risks and rewards incidental to ownership of an underlying asset.	IFRS 16.A
financial asset	Any asset that is: (a) cash; (b) an equity instrument of another entity;	IAS 32.11

(c)   a contractual right:

    (i)   to receive cash or another financial asset from another entity; or

    (ii)   to exchange financial assets or financial liabilities with another entity under conditions that are potentially favourable to the entity; or

(d)   a contract that will or may be settled in the entity's own equity instruments and is:

    (i)   a non-derivative for which the entity is or may be obliged to receive a variable number of the entity's own equity instruments; or

    (ii)   a derivative that will or may be settled other than by the exchange of a fixed amount of cash or another financial asset for a fixed number of the entity's own equity instruments. For this purpose the entity's own equity instruments do not include puttable financial instruments classified as equity instruments in accordance with paragraphs 16A and 16B of IAS 32, instruments that impose on the entity an obligation to deliver to another party a pro rata share of the net assets of the entity only on liquidation and are classified as equity instruments in accordance with paragraphs 16C and 16D of IAS 32, or instruments that are contracts for the future receipt or delivery of the entity's own equity instruments.

financial guarantee contract	A contract that requires the issuer to make specified payments to reimburse the holder for a loss it incurs because a specified debtor fails to make payment when due in accordance with	IFRS 4.A, IFRS 9.A

the original or modified terms of a debt instrument.

financial instrument   Any contract that gives rise to a financial asset   IAS 32.11
of one entity and a financial liability or equity
instrument of another entity.

financial liability   Any liability that is: IAS 32.11

(a)   a contractual obligation:

(i)   to deliver cash or another financial asset to another entity; or

(ii)   to exchange financial assets or financial liabilities with another entity under conditions that are potentially unfavourable to the entity; or

(b)   a contract that will or may be settled in the entity's own equity instruments and is:

(i)   a non-derivative for which the entity is or may be obliged to deliver a variable number of the entity's own equity instruments; or

(ii)   a derivative that will or may be settled other than by the exchange of a fixed amount of cash or another financial asset for a fixed number of the entity's own equity instruments. For this purpose, rights, options or warrants to acquire a fixed number of the entity's own equity instruments for a fixed amount of any currency are equity instruments if the entity offers the rights, options or warrants pro rata to all of its existing owners of the same class of its own non-derivative equity instruments. Also, for these purposes the entity's own equity instruments do not include puttable financial instruments that are classified as equity instruments in accordance with paragraphs 16A and 16B of IAS 32, instruments that impose on the entity an obligation to deliver to another party a pro rata share of the net assets of the entity only on liquidation and are classified as equity instruments in accordance with paragraphs 16C and 16D of IAS 32, or instruments that are contracts for the future receipt or delivery of the entity's own equity instruments.

As an exception, an instrument that meets the definition of a financial liability is classified as an equity instrument if it has all the features and meets the conditions in paragraphs 16A and 16B or paragraphs 16C and 16D of IAS 32.

financial liability at fair value through profit or loss	A financial liability that meets one of the following conditions:	IFRS 9.A
	(a) it meets the definition of held for trading.	
	(b) upon initial recognition it is designated by the entity as at fair value through profit or loss in accordance with paragraph 4.2.2 or 4.3.5.	
	(c) it is designated either upon initial recognition or subsequently as at fair value through profit or loss in accordance with paragraph 6.7.1.	
financial risk	The risk of a possible future change in one or more of a specified interest rate, financial instrument price, commodity price, foreign exchange rate, index of prices or rates, credit rating or credit index or other variable, provided in the case of a non-financial variable that the variable is not specific to a party to the contract.	IFRS 4.A
financing activities	Activities that result in changes in the size and composition of the contributed equity and borrowings of the entity.	IAS 7.6
firm commitment	A binding agreement for the exchange of a specified quantity of resources at a specified price on a specified future date or dates.	IAS 39.9, IFRS 9.A

firm purchase commitment	An agreement with an unrelated party, binding on both parties and usually legally enforceable, that (a) specifies all significant terms, including the price and timing of the transactions, and (b) includes a disincentive for non-performance that is sufficiently large to make performance highly probable.	IFRS 5.A
first IFRS financial statements	The first annual financial statements in which an entity adopts International Financial Reporting Standards (IFRSs), by an explicit and unreserved statement of compliance with IFRSs.	IFRS 1.A, IFRS 14.A
first IFRS reporting period	The latest reporting period covered by an entity's first IFRS financial statements.	IFRS 1.A
first-time adopter	An entity that presents its first IFRS financial statements.	IFRS 1.A, IFRS 14.A
fixed payments	Payments made by a lessee to a lessor for the right to use an underlying asset during the lease term, excluding variable lease payments.	IFRS 16.A
forecast transaction	An uncommitted but anticipated future transaction.	IFRS 9.A, IAS 39.9
foreign currency	A currency other than the functional currency of the entity.	IAS 21.8
foreign currency transaction	A transaction that is denominated in or requires settlement in a foreign currency.	IAS 21.20
foreign operation	An entity that is a subsidiary, associate, joint venture or branch of the reporting entity, the activities of which are based or conducted in a country or currency other than those of the reporting entity.	IAS 21.8
forgivable loans	Loans which the lender undertakes to waive repayment of under certain prescribed conditions.	IAS 20.3
functional currency	The currency of the primary economic environment in which the entity operates.	IAS 21.8
fundamental qualitative characteristic	A qualitative characteristic that financial information must possess to be useful to the primary users of general purpose financial reports. The fundamental qualitative characteristics are relevance and faithful representation.	CF.2.4, CF.2.5

funding (of retirement benefits)	The transfer of assets to an entity (the fund) separate from the employer's entity to meet future obligations for the payment of retirement benefits.	IAS 26.8
general purpose financial report	A report that provides financial information about the reporting entity's economic resources, claims against the entity and changes in those economic resources and claims that is useful to primary users in making decisions relating to providing resources to the entity.	CF.1.2, CF.1.12
general purpose financial statements	Financial statements that are intended to meet the needs of users who are not in a position to require an entity to prepare reports tailored to their particular information needs.	IAS 1.7
general purpose financial statements	A particular form of general purpose financial reports that provide information about the reporting entity's assets, liabilities, equity, income and expenses.	CF.3.2
goodwill	An asset representing the future economic benefits arising from other assets acquired in a business combination that are not individually identified and separately recognised.	IFRS 3.A
government	Government, government agencies and similar bodies whether local, national or international.	IAS 20.3, IAS 24.9
government assistance	Action by government designed to provide an economic benefit specific to an entity or range of entities qualifying under certain criteria.	IAS 20.3
government grants	Assistance by government in the form of transfers of resources to an entity in return for past or future compliance with certain conditions relating to the operating activities of the entity. They exclude those forms of government assistance which cannot reasonably have a value placed upon them and transactions with government which cannot be distinguished from the normal trading transactions of the entity.	IAS 20.3
government-related entity	An entity that is controlled, jointly controlled or significantly influenced by a government.	IAS 24.9
grant date	The date at which the entity and another party (including an employee) agree to a share-based payment arrangement, being when the entity and the counterparty have a shared	IFRS 2.A

understanding of the terms and conditions of the arrangement. At grant date the entity confers on the counterparty the right to cash, other assets, or equity instruments of the entity, provided the specified vesting conditions, if any, are met. If that agreement is subject to an approval process (for example, by shareholders), grant date is the date when that approval is obtained.

grants related to assets	Government grants whose primary condition is that an entity qualifying for them should purchase, construct or otherwise acquire long-term assets. Subsidiary conditions may also be attached restricting the type or location of the assets or the periods during which they are to be acquired or held.	IAS 20.3
grants related to income	Government grants other than those related to assets.	IAS 20.3
gross carrying amount of a financial asset	The amortised cost of a financial asset, before adjusting for any loss allowance.	IFRS 9.A
gross investment in the lease	The sum of: (a) the lease payments receivable by a lessor under a finance lease; and (b) any unguaranteed residual value accruing to the lessor.	IFRS 16.A
group	A parent and its subsidiaries.	IFRS 10.A, IAS 21.8
group of biological assets	An aggregation of similar living animals or plants.	IAS 41.5
guaranteed benefits	Payments or other benefits to which a particular policyholder or investor has an unconditional right that is not subject to the contractual discretion of the issuer.	IFRS 4.A
guaranteed element	An obligation to pay guaranteed benefits, included in a contract that contains a discretionary participation feature.	IFRS 4.A
harvest	The detachment of produce from a biological asset or the cessation of a biological asset's life processes.	IAS 41.5
hedge effectiveness	The degree to which changes in the fair value or cash flows of the hedged item that are attributable to a hedged risk are offset by changes in the fair value or cash flows of the	IAS 39.9

hedging instrument (see IAS 39 paragraphs AG105–AG113A).

hedge ratio	The relationship between the quantity of the hedging instrument and the quantity of the hedged item in terms of their relative weighting.	IFRS 9.A
hedged item	An asset, liability, firm commitment, highly probable forecast transaction or net investment in a foreign operation that (a) exposes the entity to risk of changes in fair value or future cash flows and (b) is designated as being hedged (IAS 39 paragraphs 78–84 and AG98–AG101 elaborate on the definition of hedged items).	IAS 39.9
hedging instrument	A designated derivative or (for a hedge of the risk of changes in foreign currency exchange rates only) a designated non-derivative financial asset or non-derivative financial liability whose fair value or cash flows are expected to offset changes in the fair value or cash flows of a designated hedged item (IAS 39 paragraphs 72–77 and AG94–AG97 elaborate on the definition of a hedging instrument).	IAS 39.9
held for trading	A financial asset or financial liability that:	IFRS 9.A

(a) is acquired or incurred principally for the purpose of selling or repurchasing it in the near term;

(b) on initial recognition is part of a portfolio of identified financial instruments that are managed together and for which there is evidence of a recent actual pattern of short-term profit-taking; or

(c) is a derivative (except for a derivative that is a financial guarantee contract or a designated and effective hedging instrument).

highest and best use	The use of a non-financial asset by market participants that would maximise the value of the asset or the group of assets and liabilities (eg a business) within which the asset would be used.	IFRS 13.A
highly probable	Significantly more likely than probable.	IFRS 5.A

hyperinflation Loss of purchasing power of money at such a IAS 29.2–3
rate that comparison of amounts from
transactions and other events that have
occurred at different times, even within the
same accounting period, is misleading.

Hyperinflation is indicated by characteristics of
the economic environment of a country which
include, but are not limited to, the following:

(a) the general population prefers to keep
its wealth in non-monetary assets or in
a relatively stable foreign currency.
Amounts of local currency held are
immediately invested to maintain
purchasing power.

(b) the general population regards
monetary amounts not in terms of the
local currency but in terms of a
relatively stable foreign currency. Prices
may be quoted in that currency.

(c) sales and purchases on credit take place
at prices that compensate for the
expected loss of purchasing power
during the credit period, even if the
period is short.

(d) interest rates, wages and prices are
linked to a price index.

(e) the cumulative inflation rate over three
years is approaching, or exceeds, 100%.

identifiable An asset is identifiable if it either: IFRS 3.A

(a) is separable, ie capable of being
separated or divided from the entity and
sold, transferred, licensed, rented or
exchanged, either individually or
together with a related contract,
identifiable asset or liability, regardless
of whether the entity intends to do so;
or

(b) arises from contractual or other legal
rights, regardless of whether those
rights are transferable or separable
from the entity or from other rights and
obligations.

impairment gain or loss	Gains or losses that are recognised in profit or loss in accordance with paragraph 5.5.8 and that arise from applying the impairment requirements in Section 5.5.	IFRS 9.A
impairment loss	The amount by which the carrying amount of an asset exceeds its recoverable amount.	IAS 16.6, (IAS 36.6), IAS 38.8
impracticable	Applying a requirement is impracticable when the entity cannot apply it after making every reasonable effort to do so.	IAS 1.7, (IAS 8.5)
inception date of the lease (inception date)	The earlier of the date of a lease agreement and the date of commitment by the parties to the principal terms and conditions of the lease.	IFRS 16.A
income	Increases in economic benefits during the accounting period in the form of inflows or enhancements of assets or decreases of liabilities that result in an increase in equity, other than those relating to contributions from equity participants.	IFRS 15.A
income	Increases in assets, or decreases in liabilities, that result in increases in equity, other than those relating to contributions from holders of equity claims.	CF.4.68
income approach	Valuation techniques that convert future amounts (eg cash flows or income and expenses) to a single current (eg discounted) amount. The fair value measurement is determined on the basis of the value indicated by current market expectations about those future amounts.	IFRS 13.A
income from a structured entity	For the purpose of IFRS 12, income from a structured entity includes, but is not limited to, recurring and non-recurring fees, interest, dividends, gains or losses on the remeasurement or derecognition of interests in structured entities and gains or losses from the transfer of assets and liabilities to the structured entity.	IFRS 12.A
initial direct costs	Incremental costs of obtaining a lease that would not have been incurred if the lease had not been obtained, except for such costs incurred by a manufacturer or dealer lessor in connection with a finance lease.	IFRS 16.A

inputs	The assumptions that market participants would use when pricing the asset or liability, including assumptions about risk, such as the following:	IFRS 13.A
	(a) the risk inherent in a particular valuation technique used to measure fair value (such as pricing model); and	
	(b) the risk inherent in the inputs to the valuation technique.	
	Inputs may be observable or unobservable.	
insurance asset	An insurer's net contractual rights under an insurance contract.	IFRS 4.A
insurance contract	A contract under which one party (the insurer) accepts significant insurance risk from another party (the policyholder) by agreeing to compensate the policyholder if a specified uncertain future event (the insured event) adversely affects the policyholder. (See IFRS 4 Appendix B for guidance on this definition.)	IFRS 4.A
insurance liability	An insurer's net contractual obligations under an insurance contract.	IFRS 4.A
insurance risk	Risk, other than financial risk, transferred from the holder of a contract to the issuer.	IFRS 4.A
insured event	An uncertain future event that is covered by an insurance contract and creates insurance risk.	IFRS 4.A
insurer	The party that has an obligation under an insurance contract to compensate a policyholder if an insured event occurs.	IFRS 4.A
intangible asset	An identifiable non-monetary asset without physical substance.	IAS 38.8, IFRS 3.A
interest in another entity	For the purpose of IFRS 12, an interest in another entity refers to contractual and non-contractual involvement that exposes an entity to variability of returns from the performance of the other entity. An interest in another entity can be evidenced by, but is not limited to, the holding of equity or debt instruments as well as other forms of involvement such as the provision of funding, liquidity support, credit enhancement and guarantees. It includes the means by which an entity has control or joint control of, or significant influence over, another entity. An	IFRS 12.A

entity does not necessarily have an interest in another entity solely because of a typical customer supplier relationship.

Paragraphs B7–B9 of IFRS 12 provide further information about interests in other entities.

Paragraphs B55–B57 of IFRS 10 explain variability of returns.

interest rate implicit in the lease	The rate of interest that causes the present value of (a) the lease payments and (b) the unguaranteed residual value to equal the sum of (i) the fair value of the underlying asset and (ii) any initial direct costs of the lessor.	IFRS 16.A
interest rate risk	The risk that the fair value or future cash flows of a financial instrument will fluctuate because of changes in market interest rates.	IFRS 7.A
interim financial report	A financial report containing either a complete set of financial statements (as described in IAS 1) or a set of condensed financial statements (as described in IAS 34) for an interim period.	IAS 34.4
interim period	A financial reporting period shorter than a full financial year.	IAS 34.4
International Financial Reporting Standards (IFRSs)	Standards and Interpretations issued by the International Accounting Standards Board. They comprise:	IAS 1.7, IAS 8.5, IFRS 1.A

    (a)   International Financial Reporting Standards;

    (b)   International Accounting Standards;

    (c)   IFRIC Interpretations; and

    (d)   SIC Interpretations.[3]

intrinsic value	The difference between the fair value of the shares to which the counterparty has the (conditional or unconditional) right to subscribe or which it has the right to receive, and the price (if any) the counterparty is (or will be) required to pay for those shares. For example, a share option with an exercise price of CU15,[4] on a share with a fair value of CU20, has an intrinsic value of CU5.	IFRS 2.A

---

3   Definition of IFRSs amended after the name change introduced by the revised Constitution of the IFRS Foundation in 2010.

4   Monetary items are denominated in 'currency units (CU)'.

inventories	Assets:	IAS 2.6, IAS 2.8
	(a) held for sale in the ordinary course of business;	
	(b) in the process of production for such sale; or	
	(c) in the form of materials or supplies to be consumed in the production process or in the rendering of services.	
	Inventories encompass goods purchased and held for resale including, for example, merchandise purchased by a retailer and held for resale, or land and other property held for resale. Inventories also encompass finished goods produced, or work in progress being produced, by the entity and include materials and supplies awaiting use in the production process. Costs incurred to fulfil a contract with a customer that do not give rise to inventories (or assets within the scope of another Standard) are accounted for in accordance with IFRS 15 *Revenue from Contracts with Customers*.	
investing activities	The acquisition and disposal of long-term assets and other investments not included in cash equivalents.	IAS 7.6
investment entity	An entity that:	IFRS 10.A
	(a) obtains funds from one or more investors for the purpose of providing those investor(s) with investment management services;	
	(b) commits to its investor(s) that its business purpose is to invest funds solely for returns from capital appreciation, investment income, or both; and	
	(c) measures and evaluates the performance of substantially all of its investments on a fair value basis.	
investment property	Property (land or a building—or part of a building—or both) held (by the owner or by the lessee as a right-of-use asset) to earn rentals or for capital appreciation or both, rather than for:	IAS 40.5

	(a) use in the production or supply of goods or services or for administrative purposes; or	
	(b) sale in the ordinary course of business.	
joint arrangement	An arrangement of which two or more parties have joint control.	IAS 28.3, IFRS 11.A
joint control	The contractually agreed sharing of control of an arrangement, which exists only when decisions about the relevant activities require the unanimous consent of the parties sharing control.	IAS 28.3, IFRS 11.A
joint operation	A joint arrangement whereby the parties that have joint control of the arrangement have rights to the assets, and obligations for the liabilities, relating to the arrangement.	IFRS 11.A
joint operator	A party to a joint operation that has joint control of that joint operation.	IFRS 11.A
joint venture	A joint arrangement whereby the parties that have joint control of the arrangement have rights to the net assets of the arrangement.	IAS 28.3, IFRS 11.A
joint venturer	A party to a joint venture that has joint control of the joint venture.	IAS 28.3, IFRS 11.A
key management personnel	Those persons having authority and responsibility for planning, directing and controlling the activities of the entity, directly or indirectly, including any director (whether executive or otherwise) of that entity.	IAS 24.9
lease	A contract, or part of a contract, that conveys the right to use an asset (the underlying asset) for a period of time in exchange for consideration.	IFRS 16.A
lease incentives	Payments made by a lessor to a lessee associated with a lease, or the reimbursement or assumption by a lessor of costs of a lessee.	IFRS 16.A
lease modification	A change in the scope of a lease, or the consideration for a lease, that was not part of the original terms and conditions of the lease (for example, adding or terminating the right to use one or more underlying assets, or extending or shortening the contractual lease term).	IFRS 16.A

lease payments Payments made by a lessee to a lessor relating IFRS 16.A
to the right to use an underlying asset during
the lease term, comprising the following:

(a) fixed payments (including in-substance
fixed payments), less any lease
incentives;

(b) variable lease payments that depend on
an index or a rate;

(c) the exercise price of a purchase option
if the lessee is reasonably certain to
exercise that option; and

(d) payments of penalties for terminating
the lease, if the lease term reflects the
lessee exercising an option to terminate
the lease.

For the lessee, lease payments also include
amounts expected to be payable by the lessee
under residual value guarantees. Lease
payments do not include payments allocated to
non-lease components of a contract, unless the
lessee elects to combine non-lease components
with a lease component and to account for
them as a single lease component.

For the lessor, lease payments also include any
residual value guarantees provided to the lessor
by the lessee, a party related to the lessee or a
third party unrelated to the lessor that is
financially capable of discharging the
obligations under the guarantee. Lease
payments do not include payments allocated to
non-lease components.

lease term The non-cancellable period for which a lessee IFRS 16.A
has the right to use an underlying asset,
together with both:

(a) periods covered by an option to extend
the lease if the lessee is reasonably
certain to exercise that option; and

(b) periods covered by an option to
terminate the lease if the lessee is
reasonably certain not to exercise that
option.

legal obligation	An obligation that derives from:	IAS 37.10
	(a) a contract (through its explicit or implicit terms);	
	(b) legislation; or	
	(c) other operation of law.	
lessee	An entity that obtains the right to use an underlying asset for a period of time in exchange for consideration.	IFRS 16.A
lessee's incremental borrowing rate	The rate of interest that a lessee would have to pay to borrow over a similar term, and with a similar security, the funds necessary to obtain an asset of a similar value to the right-of-use asset in a similar economic environment.	IFRS 16.A
lessor	An entity that provides the right to use an underlying asset for a period of time in exchange for consideration.	IFRS 16.A
Level 1 inputs	Quoted prices (unadjusted) in active markets for identical assets or liabilities that the entity can access at the measurement date.	IFRS 13.A
Level 2 inputs	Inputs other than quoted prices included within Level 1 that are observable for the asset or liability, either directly or indirectly.	IFRS 13.A
Level 3 inputs	Unobservable inputs for the asset or liability.	IFRS 13.A
liability	A present obligation of the entity arising from past events, the settlement of which is expected to result in an outflow from the entity of resources embodying economic benefits.	IAS 37.10
liability	A present obligation of the entity to transfer an economic resource as a result of past events.	CF.4.26
liability adequacy test	An assessment of whether the carrying amount of an insurance liability needs to be increased (or the carrying amount of related deferred acquisition costs or related intangible assets decreased), based on a review of future cash flows.	IFRS 4.A
lifetime expected credit losses	The expected credit losses that result from all possible default events over the expected life of a financial instrument.	IFRS 9.A
liquidity risk	The risk that an entity will encounter difficulty in meeting obligations associated with financial liabilities that are settled by delivering cash or another financial asset.	IFRS 7.A

loans payable	Financial liabilities other than short-term trade payables on normal credit terms.	IFRS 7.A
loss allowance	The allowance for expected credit losses on financial assets measured in accordance with paragraph 4.1.2, lease receivables and contract assets, the accumulated impairment amount for financial assets measured in accordance with paragraph 4.1.2A and the provision for expected credit losses on loan commitments and financial guarantee contracts.	IFRS 9.A
market approach	A valuation technique that uses prices and other relevant information generated by market transactions involving identical or comparable (ie similar) assets, liabilities or a group of assets and liabilities, such as a business.	IFRS 13.A
market condition	A performance condition upon which the exercise price, vesting or exercisability of an equity instrument depends that is related to the market price (or value) of the entity's equity instruments (or the equity instruments of another entity in the same group), such as:	IFRS 2.A

    (a)   attaining a specified share price or a specified amount of intrinsic value of a share option; or

    (b)   achieving a specified target that is based on the market price (or value) of the entity's equity instruments (or the equity instruments of another entity in the same group) relative to an index of market prices of equity instruments of other entities.

A market condition requires the counterparty to complete a specified period of service (ie a service condition); the service requirement can be explicit or implicit.

market-corroborated inputs	Inputs that are derived principally from or corroborated by observable market data by correlation or other means.	IFRS 13.A
market participant	Buyers and sellers in the principal (or most advantageous) market for the asset or liability that have all of the following characteristics:	IFRS 13.A

	(a)	They are independent of each other; ie they are not related parties as defined in IAS 24, although the price in a related party transaction may be used as an input to a fair value measurement if the entity has evidence that the transaction was entered into at market terms.	
	(b)	They are knowledgeable, having a reasonable understanding about the asset or liability and the transaction using all available information, including information that might be obtained through due diligence efforts that are usual and customary.	
	(c)	They are able to enter into a transaction for the asset or liability.	
	(d)	They are willing to enter into a transaction for the asset or liability, ie they are motivated but not forced or otherwise compelled to do so.	
market risk		The risk that the fair value or future cash flows of a financial instrument will fluctuate because of changes in market prices. Market risk comprises three types of risk: currency risk, interest rate risk and other price risk.	IFRS 7.A
material		Information is material if omitting, misstating or obscuring it could reasonably be expected to influence decisions that the primary users of general purpose financial statements make on the basis of those financial statements, which provide financial information about a specific reporting entity.	IAS 1.7, (IAS 8.5)
material information		Information is material if omitting, misstating or obscuring it could reasonably be expected to influence decisions that the primary users of general purpose financial reports make on the basis of those reports, which provide financial information about a specific reporting entity.	CF.2.11, (PS 2.5)
measure		The result of applying a measurement basis to an asset or liability and related income and expenses.	CF.6.1
measurement basis		An identified feature—for example, historical cost, fair value or fulfilment value—of an item being measured.	CF.6.1

measurement date	The date at which the fair value of the equity instruments granted is measured for the purposes of this IFRS. For transactions with employees and others providing similar services, the measurement date is grant date. For transactions with parties other than employees (and those providing similar services), the measurement date is the date the entity obtains the goods or the counterparty renders service.	IFRS 2.A
measurement uncertainty	Uncertainty that arises when monetary amounts in financial reports cannot be observed directly and must instead be estimated.	CF.2.19
minority interest	See 'non-controlling interest'.	
modification gain or loss	The amount arising from adjusting the gross carrying amount of a financial asset to reflect the renegotiated or modified contractual cash flows. The entity recalculates the gross carrying amount of a financial asset as the present value of the estimated future cash payments or receipts through the expected life of the renegotiated or modified financial asset that are discounted at the financial asset's original effective interest rate (or the original credit-adjusted effective interest rate for purchased or originated credit-impaired financial assets) or, when applicable, the revised effective interest rate calculated in accordance with paragraph 6.5.10. When estimating the expected cash flows of a financial asset, an entity shall consider all contractual terms of the financial asset (for example, prepayment, call and similar options) but shall not consider the expected credit losses, unless the financial asset is a purchased or originated credit-impaired financial asset, in which case an entity shall also consider the initial expected credit losses that were considered when calculating the original credit-adjusted effective interest rate.	IFRS 9.A
monetary assets	Money held and assets to be received in fixed or determinable amounts of money.	IAS 38.8
monetary items	Units of currency held and assets and liabilities to be received or paid in a fixed or determinable number of units of currency.	IAS 21.8

monetary items	Money held and items to be received or paid in money.	IAS 29.12
most advantageous market	The market that maximises the amount that would be received to sell the asset or minimises the amount that would be paid to transfer the liability, after taking into account transaction costs and transport costs.	IFRS 13.A
multi-employer (benefit) plans	Defined contribution plans (other than state plans) or defined benefit plans (other than state plans) that:	IAS 19.8
	(a) pool the assets contributed by various entities that are not under common control; and	
	(b) use those assets to provide benefits to employees of more than one entity, on the basis that contribution and benefit levels are determined without regard to the identity of the entity that employs the employees concerned.	
mutual entity	An entity, other than an investor-owned entity, that provides dividends, lower costs or other economic benefits directly to its owners, members or participants. For example, a mutual insurance company, a credit union and a co-operative entity are all mutual entities.	IFRS 3.A
net assets available for benefits	The assets of a plan less liabilities other than the actuarial present value of promised retirement benefits.	IAS 26.8
net defined benefit liability (asset)	The deficit or surplus, adjusted for any effects of limiting a net defined benefit asset to the asset ceiling.	IAS 19.8
net interest on the net defined benefit liability (asset)	The change during the period in the net defined benefit liability (asset) that arises from the passage of time.	IAS 19.8
net investment in a foreign operation	The amount of the reporting entity's interest in the net assets of that operation.	IAS 21.8
net investment in the lease	The gross investment in the lease discounted at the interest rate implicit in the lease.	IFRS 16.A
net realisable value	The estimated selling price in the ordinary course of business less the estimated costs of completion and the estimated costs necessary to make the sale.	IAS 2.6–7

	Net realisable value refers to the net amount that an entity expects to realise from the sale of inventory in the ordinary course of business. Fair value reflects the amount for which the same inventory could be exchanged between knowledgeable and willing buyers and sellers in the marketplace. The former is an entity specific value; the latter is not. Net realisable value for inventories may not equal fair value less costs to sell.	
non-adjusting events after the reporting period	See 'events after the reporting period'.	
non-controlling interest	Equity in a subsidiary not attributable, directly or indirectly, to a parent.	IFRS 3.A, IFRS 10.A
non-current asset	An asset that does not meet the definition of a current asset.	IFRS 5.A
non-performance risk	The risk that an entity will not fulfil an obligation. Non-performance risk includes, but may not be limited to, the entity's own credit risk.	IFRS 13.A
notes	Notes contain information in addition to that presented in the statement of financial position, statement of comprehensive income, separate income statement (if presented), statement of changes in equity and statement of cash flows. Notes provide narrative descriptions or disaggregations of items presented in those statements and information about items that do not qualify for recognition in those statements.	IAS 1.7
obligating event	An event that creates a legal or constructive obligation that results in an entity having no realistic alternative to settling that obligation.	IAS 37.10
observable inputs	Inputs that are developed using market data, such as publicly available information about actual events or transactions, and that reflect the assumptions that market participants would use when pricing the asset or liability.	IFRS 13.A
offsetting	Grouping an asset and liability that are recognised and measured as separate units of account into a single net amount in the statement of financial position.	CF.7.10

onerous contract	A contract in which the unavoidable costs of meeting the obligations under the contract exceed the economic benefits expected to be received under it.	IAS 37.10
opening IFRS statement of financial position	An entity's statement of financial position at the date of transition to IFRSs.	IFRS 1.A
operating activities	The principal revenue producing activities of an entity and other activities that are not investing or financing activities.	IAS 7.6
operating lease	A lease that does not transfer substantially all the risks and rewards incidental to ownership of an underlying asset.	IFRS 16.A
optional lease payments	Payments to be made by a lessee to a lessor for the right to use an underlying asset during periods covered by an option to extend or terminate a lease that are not included in the lease term.	IFRS 16.A
operating segment	An operating segment is a component of an entity:	IFRS 8.A

operating segment (continued):

(a) that engages in business activities from which it may earn revenues and incur expenses (including revenues and expenses relating to transactions with other components of the same entity),

(b) whose operating results are regularly reviewed by the entity's chief operating decision maker to make decisions about resources to be allocated to the segment and assess its performance, and

(c) for which discrete financial information is available.

options, warrants and their equivalents	Financial instruments that give the holder the right to purchase ordinary shares.	IAS 33.5
orderly transaction	A transaction that assumes exposure to the market for a period before the measurement date to allow for marketing activities that are usual and customary for transactions involving such assets or liabilities; it is not a forced transaction (eg a forced liquidation or distress sale).	IFRS 13.A
ordinary equity holders	Holders of ordinary shares.	IAS 33.5–7

ordinary share	An equity instrument that is subordinate to all other classes of equity instruments.	IAS 33.5
other comprehensive income	Items of income and expense (including reclassification adjustments) that are not recognised in profit or loss as required or permitted by other IFRSs.	IAS 1.7
other long-term employee benefits	All employee benefits other than short-term employee benefits, post-employment benefits and termination benefits.	IAS 19.8
other price risk	The risk that the fair value or future cash flows of a financial instrument will fluctuate because of changes in market prices (other than those arising from interest rate risk or currency risk), whether those changes are caused by factors specific to the individual financial instrument or its issuer, or factors affecting all similar financial instruments traded in the market.	IFRS 7.A
outcome uncertainty	Uncertainty about the amount or timing of any inflow or outflow of economic benefits that will result from an asset or liability.	CF.6.61
owner-occupied property	Property held (by the owner or by the lessee as a right-of-use asset) for use in the production or supply of goods or services or for administrative purposes.	IAS 40.5
owners	Holders of instruments classified as equity.	IAS 1.7
owners	In IFRS 3 owners is used broadly to include holders of equity interests of investor-owned entities and owners or members of, or participants in, mutual entities.	IFRS 3.A
parent	An entity that controls one or more entities.	IFRS 10.A
participants	The members of a retirement benefit plan and others who are entitled to benefits under the plan.	IAS 26.8
party to a joint arrangement	An entity that participates in a joint arrangement, regardless of whether that entity has joint control of the arrangement.	IFRS 11.A
past due	A financial asset is past due when a counterparty has failed to make a payment when that payment was contractually due.	IFRS 9.A
past service cost	The change in the present value of the defined benefit obligation for employee service in prior periods, resulting from a plan amendment (the introduction or withdrawal of, or change to, a	IAS 19.8

	defined benefit plan) or a curtailment (a significant reduction by the entity in the number of employees covered by a plan).	
performance condition	A vesting condition that requires:	IFRS 2.A

    (a)   the counterparty to complete a specified period of service (ie a service condition); the service requirement can be explicit or implicit; and

    (b)   specified performance target(s) to be met while the counterparty is rendering the service required in (a).

The period of achieving the performance target(s):

    (a)   shall not extend beyond the end of the service period; and

    (b)   may start before the service period on the condition that the commencement date of the performance target is not substantially before the commencement of the service period.

A performance target is defined by reference to:

    (a)   the entity's own operations (or activities) or the operations or activities of another entity in the same group (ie a non-market condition); or

    (b)   the price (or value) of the entity's equity instruments or the equity instruments of another entity in the same group (including shares and share options) (ie a market condition).

A performance target might relate either to the performance of the entity as a whole or to some part of the entity (or part of the group), such as a division or an individual employee.

| **performance obligation** | A promise in a contract with a customer to transfer to the customer either: | IFRS 15.A |

    (a)   a good or service (or a bundle of goods or services) that is distinct; or

	(b) a series of distinct goods or services that are substantially the same and that have the same pattern of transfer to the customer.	
period of use	The total period of time that an asset is used to fulfil a contract with a customer (including any non-consecutive periods of time).	IFRS 16.A
plan assets (of an employee benefit plan)	Comprise: (a) assets held by a long-term employee benefit fund; and (b) qualifying insurance policies.	IAS 19.8
policyholder	A party that has a right to compensation under an insurance contract if an insured event occurs.	IFRS 4.A
post-employment benefits	Employee benefits (other than termination benefits and short-term employee benefits) that are payable after the completion of employment.	IAS 19.8
post-employment benefit plans	Formal or informal arrangements under which an entity provides post-employment benefits for one or more employees.	IAS 19.8
potential ordinary share	A financial instrument or other contract that may entitle its holder to ordinary shares.	IAS 33.5
potential to produce economic benefits	Within an economic resource, a feature that already exists and that, in at least one circumstance, would produce for the entity economic benefits beyond those available to all other parties.	CF.4.14
power	Existing rights that give the current ability to direct the relevant activities.	IFRS 10.A
presentation currency	The currency in which the financial statements are presented.	IAS 21.8
present value of a defined benefit obligation	The present value, without deducting any plan assets, of expected future payments required to settle the obligation resulting from employee service in the current and prior periods.	IAS 19.8
previous GAAP	The basis of accounting that a first-time adopter used immediately before adopting IFRSs.	IFRS 1.A, IFRS 14.A
primary users (of general purpose financial reports)	Existing and potential investors, lenders and other creditors.	CF.1.2

principal market	The market with the greatest volume and level of activity for the asset or liability.	IFRS 13.A
prior period errors	Omissions from, and misstatements in, the entity's financial statements for one or more prior periods arising from a failure to use, or misuse of, reliable information that:	IAS 8.5

(a) was available when financial statements for those periods were authorised for issue; and

(b) could reasonably be expected to have been obtained and taken into account in the preparation and presentation of those financial statements.

Such errors include the effects of mathematical mistakes, mistakes in applying accounting policies, oversights or misinterpretations of facts, and fraud.

probable	More likely than not.	IFRS 5.A, IAS 37.23
profit or loss	The total of income less expenses, excluding the components of other comprehensive income.	IAS 1.7
property, plant and equipment	Tangible items that:	IAS 16.6

(a) are held for use in the production or supply of goods or services, for rental to others, or for administrative purposes; and

(b) are expected to be used during more than one period.

prospective application	Prospective application of a change in accounting policy and of recognising the effect of a change in an accounting estimate, respectively, are:	IAS 8.5

(a) applying the new accounting policy to transactions, other events and conditions occurring after the date as at which the policy is changed; and

(b) recognising the effect of the change in the accounting estimate in the current and future periods affected by the change.

protective rights	Rights designed to protect the interest of the party holding those rights without giving that party power over the entity to which those rights relate.	IFRS 10.A
provision	A liability of uncertain timing or amount.	IAS 37.10
prudence	The exercise of caution when making judgements under conditions of uncertainty. The exercise of prudence means that assets and income are not overstated and liabilities and expenses are not understated. Equally, the exercise of prudence does not allow for the understatement of assets or income or the overstatement of liabilities or expenses.	CF.2.16
purchased or originated credit-impaired financial asset	Purchased or originated financial asset(s) that are credit-impaired on initial recognition.	IFRS 9.A
put options (on ordinary shares)	Contracts that give the holder the right to sell ordinary shares at a specified price for a given period.	IAS 33.5
puttable instrument	A financial instrument that gives the holder the right to put the instrument back to the issuer for cash or another financial asset or is automatically put back to the issuer on the occurrence of an uncertain future event or the death or retirement of the instrument holder.	IAS 32.11
qualifying asset	An asset that necessarily takes a substantial period of time to get ready for its intended use or sale.	IAS 23.5
qualifying insurance policy	An insurance policy issued by an insurer that is not a related party (as defined in IAS 24) of the reporting entity, if the proceeds of the policy:	IAS 19.8

(a)   can be used only to pay or fund employee benefits under a defined benefit plan;

(b)   are not available to the reporting entity's own creditors (even in bankruptcy) and cannot be paid to the reporting entity, unless either:

     (i)   the proceeds represent surplus assets that are not needed for the policy to meet all the related employee benefit obligations; or

		(ii)	the proceeds are returned to the reporting entity to reimburse it for employee benefits already paid.	

rate-regulated activities	An entity's activities that are subject to rate regulation.	IFRS 14.A
rate regulation	A framework for establishing the prices that can be charged to customers for goods or services and that framework is subject to oversight and/or approval by a rate regulator.	IFRS 14.A
rate regulator	An authorised body that is empowered by statute or regulation to establish the rate or a range of rates that bind an entity. The rate regulator may be a third-party body or a related party of the entity, including the entity's own governing board, if that body is required by statute or regulation to set rates both in the interest of the customers and to ensure the overall financial viability of the entity.	IFRS 14.A
reclassification adjustments	Amounts reclassified to profit or loss in the current period that were recognised in other comprehensive income in the current or previous periods.	IAS 1.7
reclassification date	The first day of the first reporting period following the change in business model that results in an entity reclassifying financial assets.	IFRS 9.A
recoverable amount	The higher of an asset's (or cash generating unit's) fair value less costs of disposal and its value in use.	IAS 16.6, IAS 36.6, IFRS 5.A
recognition	The process of capturing for inclusion in the statement of financial position or the statement(s) of financial performance an item that meets the definition of one of the elements of financial statements—an asset, a liability, equity, income or expenses. Recognition involves depicting the item in one of those statements—either alone or in aggregation with other items—in words and by a monetary amount, and including that amount in one or more totals in that statement.	CF.5.1

regular way purchase or sale	A purchase or sale of a financial asset under a contract whose terms require delivery of the asset within the time frame established generally by regulation or convention in the marketplace concerned.	IFRS 9.A
regulatory deferral account balance	The balance of any expense (or income) account that would not be recognised as an asset or a liability in accordance with other Standards, but that qualifies for deferral because it is included, or is expected to be included, by the rate regulator in establishing the rate(s) that can be charged to customers.	IFRS 14.A
reinsurance assets	A cedant's net contractual rights under a reinsurance contract.	IFRS 4.A
reinsurance contract	An insurance contract issued by one insurer (the reinsurer) to compensate another insurer (the cedant) for losses on one or more contracts issued by the cedant.	IFRS 4.A
reinsurer	The party that has an obligation under a reinsurance contract to compensate a cedant if an insured event occurs.	IFRS 4.A
related party	A person or entity that is related to the entity that is preparing its financial statements (in IAS 24 referred to as the 'reporting entity').	IAS 24.9

(a) A person or a close member of that person's family is related to a reporting entity if that person:

    (i) has control or joint control over the reporting entity;

    (ii) has significant influence over the reporting entity; or

    (iii) is a member of the key management personnel of the reporting entity or of a parent of the reporting entity.

(b) An entity is related to a reporting entity if any of the following conditions applies:

    (i) The entity and the reporting entity are members of the same group (which means that each parent, subsidiary and fellow

		subsidiary is related to the others).
	(ii)	One entity is an associate or joint venture of the other entity (or an associate or joint venture of a member of a group of which the other entity is a member).
	(iii)	Both entities are joint ventures of the same third party.
	(iv)	One entity is a joint venture of a third entity and the other entity is an associate of the third entity.
	(v)	The entity is a post-employment benefit plan for the benefit of employees of either the reporting entity or an entity related to the reporting entity. If the reporting entity is itself such a plan, the sponsoring employers are also related to the reporting entity.
	(vi)	The entity is controlled or jointly controlled by a person identified in (a).
	(vii)	A person identified in (a)(i) has significant influence over the entity or is a member of the key management personnel of the entity (or of a parent of the entity).
	(viii)	The entity, or any member of a group of which it is a part, provides key management personnel services to the reporting entity or to the parent of the reporting entity.
related party transaction	A transfer of resources, services or obligations between a reporting entity and a related party, regardless of whether a price is charged.	IAS 24.9
relevant activities	For the purpose of IFRS 10, relevant activities are activities of the investee that significantly affect the investee's returns.	IFRS 10.A

reload feature	A feature that provides for an automatic grant of additional share options whenever the option holder exercises previously granted options using the entity's shares, rather than cash, to satisfy the exercise price.	IFRS 2.A
reload option	A new share option granted when a share is used to satisfy the exercise price of a previous share option.	IFRS 2.A
remeasurement of the net defined benefit liability (asset)	Comprises: (a) actuarial gains and losses; (b) the return on plan assets, excluding amounts included in net interest on the net defined benefit liability (asset); and (c) any change in the effect of the asset ceiling, excluding amounts included in net interest on the net defined benefit liability (asset).	IAS 19.8
removal rights	Rights to deprive the decision maker of its decision-making authority.	IFRS 10.A
reportable segment	An operating segment for which IFRS 8 requires information to be disclosed.	IFRS 8.11
reporting entity	An entity that is required, or chooses, to prepare general purpose financial statements.	CF.3.10
research	Original and planned investigation undertaken with the prospect of gaining new scientific or technical knowledge and understanding.	IAS 38.8
residual value guarantee	A guarantee made to a lessor by a party unrelated to the lessor that the value (or part of the value) of an underlying asset at the end of a lease will be at least a specified amount.	
residual value (of an asset)	The estimated amount that an entity would currently obtain from disposal of an asset, after deducting the estimated costs of disposal, if the asset were already of the age and in the condition expected at the end of its useful life.	IAS 16.6, (IAS 38.8)
restructuring	A programme that is planned and controlled by management, and materially changes either: (a) the scope of a business undertaken by an entity; or (b) the manner in which that business is conducted.	IAS 37.10